Christian Literature

Christian Literature
An Anthology

Edited by
Alister E. McGrath

Copyright © Blackwell Publishers Ltd 2001
Editorial matter and organization copyright © Alister E. McGrath 2001

First published 2001

2 4 6 8 10 9 7 5 3 1

Blackwell Publishers Ltd
108 Cowley Road
Oxford OX4 1JF
UK

Blackwell Publishers Inc.
350 Main Street
Malden, Massachusetts 02148
USA

British Library Cataloguing in Publication Data

A CIP catalogue record for this book is available from the British Library.

Library of Congress Cataloging-in-Publication Data

Christian literature : an anthology / edited by Alister E. McGrath.
        p.   cm.
    Includes bibliographical references and index.
    ISBN 0–631–21605–7 (hardcover : alk. paper) — ISBN 0–631–21606–5
(pbk. :   alk. paper)
    1. Christianity.   2. Christian literature, English.   I. McGrath, Alister E.,
1953–
BR53.C38   2000
230—dc21
                                                                00-023646

Typeset in 10 on 12½ pt Galliard
by Best-set Typesetter Ltd., Hong Kong
Printed in Great Britain by T.J. International, Padstow, Cornwall

This book is printed on acid-free paper.

Contents

Preface   xi
How to Use This Work   xvi
The Structure of the Work   xviii

Part I The Patristic Period, ca. 100–600

Introduction   3
1 Clement of Rome (active around 96)   13
   The First Letter to Corinth   14
2 Ignatius of Antioch (died ca. 107)   17
   The Letter to the Romans   17
3 The Martyrdom of Polycarp (ca. 155)   21
4 Irenaeus of Lyons (ca. 130–ca. 200)   30
   Against all Heresies   31
5 Quintus Septimius Florens Tertullian (ca. 160–ca. 225)   43
   The Apology   44
6 Eusebius of Caesarea (ca. 260–ca. 340)   52
   Ecclesiastical History   52
7 Athanasius of Alexandria (ca. 296–373)   63
   De Incarnatione   64
   The Life of Antony   69
8 Ephraim the Syrian (303–373)   75
   The Pearl   76
9 Cyril of Jerusalem (ca. 315–387)   81
   The Catechetical Lectures   82
10 Gregory of Nyssa (ca. 330–ca. 395)   88
   Funeral Oration on Meletius   89
11 The Peregrination of Egeria (ca. 384)   96
12 Augustine of Hippo (354–430)   105
   Confessions   106

13   Venantius Honorius Clementianus Fortunatus (ca. 530–ca. 610)   115
     Vexilla Regis prodeunt   116

Part II   English and Irish Sources, ca. 600–1050

Introduction   121
14   Caedmon's Hymn (ca. 670)   126
15   Bede (ca. 673–735)   128
     History of the English Church and Nation   129
     Bede's Death Song   133
16   The Deer's Cry (ca. 700)   134
17   The Dream of the Rood (ca. 750)   137
18   The Junius Codex (ca. 870)   142
     Genesis B   143
     Christ and Satan   147
19   The Exeter Book Riddles   151
     Riddle 47   151
     Riddle 26   152
20   The Blickling Homilist (ca. 970)   155
     Homily for Easter Day   155
21   Ælfric (ca. 955–ca. 1020)   161
     The Passion of St Edmund   161
22   Wulfstan (died 1023)   167
     Lupi Sermo ad Anglos   168

Part III   The Middle Ages, 1050–1500

Introduction   175
23   Anselm of Canterbury (1033–1109)   181
     A Prayer to Christ   182
24   Peter Abelard (1079–1142)   186
     The History of Calamities   187
25   Bernard of Clairvaux (1090–1153)   194
     On Loving God   195
26   Francis of Assisi (1182–1226)   198
     The Canticle of the Creatures   199
27   Ancrene Wisse (ca. 1230)   201
28   Thomas Aquinas (1224–1274)   207
     Summa Theologiae   208
29   Hugh of Balma (ca. 1290)   210
     The Roads to Zion   210
30   Dante Alighieri (1265–1321)   212
     Inferno   214
31   Ludolf of Saxony (ca. 1300–1378)   218
     The Life of Christ   219
32   The Cloud of Unknowing (ca. 1350)   221
33   William Langland (ca. 1332–ca. 1400)   229
     Piers Plowman   230

34 Geoffrey Chaucer (ca. 1342–1400)   240
    The Canterbury Tales   241
35 Julian of Norwich (ca. 1342–after 1416)   246
    Revelations of Divine Love   247
36 The York Mystery Plays (ca. 1415)   252
37 Thomas à Kempis (1379–1471)   263
    The Imitation of Christ   264
38 William Dunbar (ca. 1460–ca. 1520)   269
    Rorate coeli desuper   270

Part IV   The Renaissance and Reformation, 1500–1700

Introduction   275
39 Erasmus of Rotterdam (1469?–1536)   287
    Moriae Encomium   289
40 Martin Luther (1483–1546)   299
    Letter on Translating the New Testament   303
    The "Little Instruction Book" or "Lesser Catechism"   313
41 Ignatius Loyola (ca. 1491–1556)   322
    The Spiritual Exercises   323
42 John Calvin (1509–1564)   326
    Institutes of the Christian Religion   328
43 John Foxe (1516–1587)   334
    The Acts and Monuments of Matters Happening in the Church   336
44 Edmund Spenser (1552–1599)   345
    The Hymn of Heavenly Beauty   346
45 The King James Version of the Bible (1611)   356
    The Translators' Preface   358
    Selected Passages   376
46 Sir Walter Ralegh (ca. 1552–1618)   381
    The Passionate Man's Pilgrimage   382
47 Lancelot Andrewes (1555–1626)   384
    Sermon XIV   385
48 William Shakespeare (1564–1616)   396
    Sonnet 146   398
49 John Donne (1571/2–1631)   400
    Sermon 1   401
    Divine Meditations   416
50 George Herbert (1593–1633)   420
    The Temple   421
    A Priest to the Temple   427
51 Sir Thomas Browne (1605–1682)   430
    Religio Medici   431
52 John Milton (1608–1674)   436
    Paradise Lost   437
53 Jeremy Taylor (1613–1667)   442
    The Rules and Exercises of Holy Dying   443

54 Henry Vaughan (1622–1695)   448
    The British Church   448
    Religion   450
55 Andrew Marvell (1621–1678)   453
    Bermudas   454
    The Coronet   456
56 Blaise Pascal (1623–1662)   459
    Pensées   461
57 John Bunyan (1626–1688)   467
58 The Book of Common Prayer (1662)   470
    The "General Confession"   472
    The "General Thanksgiving"   472
    The Solemnization of Matrimony   473
    At the Burial of the Dead   476

Part V   The Modern Period, 1700–2000

Introduction   481
59 Daniel Defoe (1660–1731)   487
60 Joseph Addison (1672–1719)   496
    Ode   497
    Cato   498
61 Isaac Watts (1674–1748)   499
    When I Survey The Wondrous Cross   499
62 Joseph Butler (1692–1752)   501
63 Jonathan Edwards (1703–1758)   507
    Treatise Concerning Religious Affections   508
    The Christian Pilgrim   510
64 John Wesley (1703–1791)   516
    "Preface" to Sermons On Several Occasions   517
    Sermon 2: The Almost Christian   520
65 Charles Wesley (1707–1788)   527
    Love Divine   528
    Free Grace   529
66 John Newton (1725–1807)   532
    The Olney Hymns   533
67 William Paley (1743–1805)   539
    A View of the Evidences of Christianity   540
68 William Blake (1757–1827)   546
    "And did those feet?" from "Milton"   547
69 William Wordsworth (1770–1850)   550
    Tintern Abbey   551
    Intimations of Immortality from Recollections of Early Childhood   557
70 Samuel Taylor Coleridge (1791–1834)   563
    Religious Musings   565
    Confessions of an Enquiring Spirit   567

71 John Keble (1792–1866)   570
    "National Apostasy"   571
72 John Henry Newman (1801–1890)   580
    The Dream of Gerontius   582
73 Ralph Waldo Emerson (1803–1882)   585
    Nature   586
74 Anthony Trollope (1815–1882)   591
    Barchester Towers   593
75 Benjamin Jowett (1817–1893)   598
    The Interpretation of Scripture   599
76 George Eliot (1819–1880)   609
    Scenes of Clerical Life   610
77 Fyodor Mikhailovich Dostoevsky (1821–1881)   620
    The Brothers Karamazov   621
78 Matthew Arnold (1822–1888)   636
    Dover Beach   637
79 George MacDonald (1824–1905)   640
    Lilith: A Romance   641
80 Thomas Hardy (1840–1928)   648
    Jude the Obscure   649
81 Gerald Manley Hopkins (1844–1889)   656
    God's Grandeur   657
82 Oscar Wilde (1854–1900)   659
    The Ballad of Reading Gaol   661
83 Gilbert Keith Chesterton (1874–1936)   679
    Orthodoxy   680
    The Everlasting Man   684
84 T. S. Eliot (1888–1965)   688
    The Waste Land   689
    The Journey of the Magi   692
85 Dorothy L. Sayers (1893–1957)   695
    The Man Born to be King   696
    The Mind of the Maker   702
86 C. S. Lewis (1898–1963)   707
    The Screwtape Letters   709
    Till We Have Faces   713
87 Graham Greene (1904–1991)   718
    The Power and the Glory   719
88 R. S. Thomas (1913–)   728
    Pietà   729
    Via Negativa   730
89 Martin Luther King, Jr. (1929–1968)   733
    I Have a Dream   735
90 David Lodge (1935–)   739
    How Far Can You Go?   739

91 Garrison Keillor (1942–)   747
    Lake Wobegon Days   748

A Glossary of Terms   753
Sources of Extracts   761
For Further Reading   769
Acknowledgments   771
Index   774

Preface

"The church, as a body, has never made up her mind about the Arts." Thus wrote Dorothy L. Sayers, herself no small contributor to the shaping of Christian literature in the twentieth century. There can be no doubt that she is correct in her judgment. Some Christian writers have adopted strongly positive attitudes to literature, seeing it as being a powerful ally in the quest to foster the Christian vision and interact with the world. Others have regarded literature as alien to the Christian faith, with a potential to mislead.

In the early period of the Christian church, a critical and hostile attitude tended to prevail. This attitude can be argued to be rooted in Paul's insistence that Christians should avoid compromising their faith through inappropriate adoption of worldly attitudes and viewpoints. "What do righteousness and wickedness have in common? Or what fellowship can light have with darkness? What harmony is there between Christ and Belial? What does a believer have in common with an unbeliever?" (2 Corinthians 6:14–15). Yet Paul himself shows a clear familiarity with classic literature and poetry. He appeals to the authority of Cleanthes, Aratus, and Epimenides in a speech delivered at the Areopagus in Athens (Acts 17:28). He cites from the native Cretan poet Epimenides when commenting on the moral state of the inhabitants of Crete (Titus 1:12–13). Allusions to Homer, Plato, and Menander can be found elsewhere in his writings.

Yet the classical culture which helped shape early Christian attitudes to literature was itself uncertain as to the precise role of literature. Plato deliberately excluded poets from his ideal republic, an attitude warmly commended by Augustine. For Augustine, the poets "composed fictions with no regard to the truth or set the worst possible examples before wretched people under the pretence that they were divine actions." Yet the rhetorical skills developed by Aristotle and others were recognized as important means of enhancing the effectiveness of communication. There are many points in Paul's speeches, as recorded in the Acts of the Apostles, where a positive influence of Hellenistic rhetoric has been observed. It is therefore no cause for surprise that early Christian attitudes to literature are complex and nuanced, and difficult to characterize. Writers such as Tertullian and Chrysostom were intensely suspicious of Greek and Latin literature, and sought to minimize its importance and influence within the church; Jerome and Augustine were considerably more positive, even though they shared some of the anxieties voiced elsewhere.

At many points, literature was seen by Christian apologists as a means of further enhancing the appeal of their faith to the wider world. Might not the obvious attractions of the gospel be augmented if it were to be presented in words of beauty and power, in which theological precision was supplemented by the lyricism of poetry and the rhetoric of prose? Gravity of form and sublimity of expression in an argument could assist in both the communication and commendation of its substance. The anonymous *Cursor Mundi*, written about 1300, argues along such lines when it suggests that, since people enjoy reading secular literature so much, it makes sense to present religious truth in literary forms. In this way, a work of religious literature will result which will both be a delight to read and nourish the human soul. Yet the tension which this approach generated can be seen from other works of this period. For example, Geoffrey Chaucer concludes his *Canterbury Tales* with a "retraction," in which he asks his readers to forgive him for his "translations and compositions of worldly vanity."

The implication is clear; works of literature are potentially vain, whereas purely religious works, written for the purpose of doctrinal and ethical instruction, are acceptable. Chaucer's obvious concern at this point raises the question of whether the notion of "Christian literature" is inherently indefensible, in that the desire to please and amuse is potentially in tension with the seriousness of Christian doctrine and ethics. This is certainly the view that we find in the noted Puritan writer Richard Baxter, who argued that literature encouraged its readers to waste their time in recreation when they could be doing something more productive, and that it possessed a disquieting potential to be morally corrupting. Baxter's most severe criticism was directed against works of fiction, which he held to actively promote a culture of falsehood which "dangerously bewitcheth and corrupteth the minds of young and empty people."

One manner of reconciling this tension was known throughout Christian history, and became of especial importance during the Romantic period. The language of literature, it was argued, served to elevate its readers, and inspire them to devotion and passion. Was not this sufficient justification for a religious literature? In his "Preface" to the *Lyrical Ballads*, William Wordsworth complained of the "frantic novels, sickly and stupid German Tragedies, and deluges of idle and extravagant stories in verse" by which his age had been seduced, and urged a recovery of the language and concerns of writers such as Shakespeare and Milton. For Wordsworth himself, there was an obvious affinity between religion and poetry; indeed, Wordsworth's literature increasingly adopted the characteristics of religion. This development is of particular importance to the development of seeing the Bible as literature. For Percy Bysshe Shelley, the Bible is revered on account of its literary character, rather than the religious views which it propounded.

Yet it must not be assumed that a Christian interest in literature was a purely pragmatic consequence of a desire for church growth and a consolidation of religious faith. From the outset, Christian writers have found the notion of "God as author" as offering a substantial theological foundation and encouragement for the writing of literature. In the beginning, God created through God's word, spoken over the face of chaos. Did this not point to the critical role of words in the Christian understanding of the world? And was there not the most natural of connections between the verbal origins of the world and a concern with words, revelation, texts, literature, and reading and writing? The production of Christian literature was thus seen by some as resting upon rigorous theological foundations.

The potential importance of literature for Christianity can be appreciated by considering the three main elements which make up this important and dynamic religion.

1   *A set of beliefs.* Although there are differences between Christians on a number of doctrinal matters, it is relatively easy to show that a common core of beliefs lies behind the different versions of Christianity. These are set out in the Creeds of Christianity, which are accepted as statements of faith by all the main Christian churches. These beliefs have a significant impact on the way in which Christians live. Several genres of Christian literature – for example, credal statements, catechisms, doctrinal treatises, and certain types of sermons and homilies – concern themselves primarily with the clarification and defense of Christian beliefs. Of particular importance is a genre of literature devoted to the study of the Christian Bible, which includes biblical commentaries and sermons.

2   *A set of values.* Christianity is a strongly ethical faith. This does not, however, mean that Christianity is about a set of rules, in which Christians mechanically conform to a set of instructions. Rather, it is about a set of values which arises from being redeemed, such as loving other people and a willingness to deny oneself. These values are strongly linked with the character of Jesus of Nazareth, who is regarded by Christians as both the basis of the life of faith and the supreme example of a life lived in close fellowship with God. Certain types of Christian literature relate to the encouragement of these values. Biographies of those acknowledged to be outstanding examples of Christian living, or embodiments of Christian values, have always had a major role within the church. The "Lives of the Saints" – or "hagiographies," to use the preferred term – have been of fundamental importance in nurturing and inspiring certain ways of living within the Christian community.

3   *A way of life.* Being a Christian is not just about beliefs and values; it is about real life, in which those ideas and values are expressed and embodied in a definite way of living. The everyday life of believers is affected in certain ways by their faith. At its most obvious, this is reflected in going to a church or other form of Christian community which meets for prayer and worship. There are enormous variations in the ways in which Christianity expresses itself, reflecting differences of climate, geography, culture, tradition, and theology. Part of this way of life is the general area which has come to be known as "spirituality," and which covers a wide variety of literature – such as sermons, liturgies, hymns, homilies, devotional treatises, and formal prayers.

The nature of the Christian faith is thus such that both its propagation and consolidation involve the extensive use of literature. Yet this is not to suggest that Christianity is a purely textual phenomenon; it is simply to acknowledge the foundational role of literature in conveying, explaining, and defending Christian ideas to those outside the church; in educating and encouraging those within the church; in calling Christians, corporately and individually, to renew and reform their faith; and in providing norms to allow the "essence of the Christian faith" to be passed down from one generation to another.

But precisely what is to be understood by "Christian literature"? This is not an easy question to answer, and it must be appreciated from the outset that any reasonable response which might be offered will be contested. There is a significant debate within the scholarly world over precisely this issue which this volume cannot, and is certainly not intended to, settle. No definition of "Christian literature" has yet been offered which is immune from criticism or modification. Among the contested questions, the following may be noted. They are representative of the debate; many more can be added.

- Is the essentially "Christian" element in literature related to its content, its form, or the interpretation offered?
- Must a piece of writing be *exclusively* Christian to count as "Christian literature"?
- Can a minimalist definition be offered, by which "Christian" means "not offending Christian sensibilities," or "not contradicting Christian beliefs"?
- Is fiction disqualified from being a Christian literary form on account of its non-factuality?

Each of these questions illuminates an aspect of the debate. For the purposes of this work, a pragmatic definition has been used. "Christian literature" designates works which are the subject of study in college and university courses dealing with "Christian literature" or "religious literature" (where the emphasis is primarily upon Christianity). This work therefore aims to gather together extracts from works which would generally be agreed to be regarded as "Christian literature," without attempting to resolve the debates which rage around the issue. These writings fall into three broad categories:

1   Works of literature which are specifically written to serve the needs of Christians – such as prayers, devotional works, and sermons. The Christian faith has given rise to certain specific forms of writing, which Christians have sought to develop to the highest standards of cultural excellence. These works are a response to the nature of the Christian faith, and can be seen as both responding to the needs of that faith and expressing its nature.

2   Works of literature in general – such as stories and poems – which are not specific to the Christian faith, but which have been shaped or influenced by Christian ideas, values, images, and narratives. Christian poetry, in particular, reflects a quite distinct set of ideas and images, and it is important to appreciate the way in which these are reflected or assimilated in such writings. Although

most Christian literature is written by Christians, it is important to note that there are many examples of writings which have unquestionably been shaped by Christian influences, even though their writers would not necessarily regard themselves as Christians. The lyrical ballads of both William Wordsworth and Samuel Taylor Coleridge might be included within this category.

3   Works of literature which involve interaction with Christian ideas, individuals, schools of thought, or institutions, often written by those who would regard themselves as observers or critics of Christianity. One might include George Eliot or Thomas Hardy in this category. Here, the influence of Christianity is evident, at least through the subject matter of the writing. Yet even the mode of criticism itself often reflects a subtle appropriation, development, or modification of Christian assumptions – such as an assumption concerning what Christianity *ought* to be, which is then contrasted with what is observed through experience.

This anthology is primarily concerned with the Christian literature of the English language. Although a substantial amount of material relating to the patristic period – and hence written originally in Greek, Latin, or Syriac – has been included in Part I, this is primarily to illuminate the genres of Christian literature which emerged in the first formative phase of Christian history. The emergence of an English Christian literature can be dated fairly precisely, to some point around 680. Part II deals primarily with vernacular Christian writings from about 650 to 1050, exploring and illustrating how a sophisticated body of literature in Old English came to emerge at this time. Similarly, Part III, the "Middle Ages," includes a large amount of material written in Middle English. The chapters dealing with the early modern and modern periods are also devoted almost exclusively to English-language sources. This allows the continuities within the development of English-language Christian literature to be appreciated more easily than would otherwise be the case.

Some readers of a more explicitly theological inclination may feel aggrieved that there is relatively little of a specifically theological nature in this anthology. It must be stressed that emphasis has fallen on works of Christian *literature* rather than works of Christian *theology*. Many seminal works of modern Christian theology have not been included, due to the pervasive perception – which, though harsh, is not entirely unjustified – that, however worthy they might be as works of *theology*, they could not be seen as works of *literature*. The excessively technical nature of many of these writings does little to make their reading pleasurable, and it is clear that their authors' concerns, in any case, often lie elsewhere. Happily, there are many collections of readings from such works available to meet the needs of those who have a special interest in them.

Before moving on to present the readings contained in this work, it will be helpful to readers to set out the principles underlying their selection, and how to make best use of the additional material provided in this work.

How to Use This Work

This work aims to bring together two thousand years of Christian literature, from the patristic period to the end of the twentieth century. Yet it aims to be *comprehensible as well as comprehensive*. It has been written on the assumption that its readers need a lot of help to get the most out of interacting with texts taken from two thousand years of Christian literature. The object of the book is to help you enjoy and appreciate the considerable variety of material which it includes. To do this, you need to *engage actively with the texts*, rather than just read them passively. The book therefore provides you with the help that you need to do this, and offers a framework which will help you get the most out of your engagement with these fascinating writings.

Many anthologies seem to assume that all that they need to do is print out a collection of texts, and let their readers get on with reading them. My own experience is that this is hopelessly unrealistic. Really rewarding study demands and deserves a lot of help – and this anthology is designed to be as user-friendly as possible, by offering levels of explanation which go far beyond those traditionally found in works of this kind.

Each passage has been "framed" with introductory material, designed to enable you to get the most out of reading it. Each can be thought of as having three separate introductions.

1   An introduction to the general period in which it is set. Each of the five major sections (Parts I–V) of this work is provided with its own introduction, which identifies some of the major themes, issues, and personalities of importance at the time. This will help set the context for the specific text in which you are interested.

2   An introduction to the writer of the text. This introduction sets out some of the major features of the life and writings of the author, and allows you to establish both some biographical and some literary landmarks. In most cases, highly accessible "Study Panels" have been embedded in the text, providing you with a quick

and convenient summary of the key points you need to know about the writer under consideration.

3 An introduction to the specific text, which helps you identify the basic issues to look out for when you read it, and helps you to get the most out of studying it. In many cases, you will be given a substantial amount of help in understanding the text, particularly where you need additional knowledge or historical background to make sense of the passage.

Finally, each text is provided with a short series of "Questions for Discussion" or "Questions for Study." Use these to test your understanding of the texts. At times, they will invite you to find information within the text; at others, they will ask you to reflect on the use of a certain image, or a particular turn of phrase. In every case, the objective is to help you get further into the text, and thus to get more out of it. Try to use these questions to test yourself before moving on to the next text.

But enough has been said by way of introduction. Enjoy engaging with the texts!

The Structure of the Work

The present volume brings together a very substantial amount of material, drawn from two thousand years of Christian history, and it will be helpful to set out in a little detail the way in which it has been put together, particularly in regard to the arrangement of the material. Once the structure (which is actually quite simple) has been mastered, it will be found remarkably easy to use.

The Selection of Material

Christianity has been in business for two thousand years, and is the world's largest religious grouping. It is therefore to be expected that it should have generated and shaped the development of literature over the last two millennia. Given the vast amount of material which could reasonably be included in the category of "Christian literature," a degree of selectivity was essential if a manageable collection of material was to result. It was decided at a very early stage to ensure that this collection was as representative and useful as possible.

The process of selection was thus based on a process of consultation, in which a representative sample of university and college professionals who were actively engaged in research and teaching in the field of Christian literature, along with others who were known to have such an interest and expertise, were invited to compile "wish lists," identifying authors or specific works which they felt ought to be included in this collection.

The results of this consultation process were remarkably consistent. It became clear that there was a settled consensus over the identity of most landmark writers and writings up to the outbreak of the Second World War. After this point, the prevailing consensus began to fall apart. This reflects a number of issues, including the fact that sufficient time has not yet elapsed to allow us to gain a proper perspective on the literary achievements of the second half of the twentieth century. While the material included in this anthology which dates from after 1950 has been selected on the basis of wide consultation, it must be understood that this process showed significant disagreement on the part of those consulted over which writings ought to be included.

The decision was taken from the outset to include as substantial sections of writing as possible, to allow readers to really enter into the mind of the author, rather than providing brief snippets which allow readers only to nibble at works that cry out to be read in whole. However, it will be obvious that many important works have had to be excluded, due to lack of space. The editor and publisher regret this, but can see no alternative. When working within fixed limits, any decision to include one work is also a decision to exclude others. At times, decisions have been immensely painful. Why include C. S. Lewis, yet omit other "Inklings" such as J. R. R. Tolkein and Charles Williams? In an ideal world, when the cost of books is not an issue, all such worthies would be included. Sadly, the economic factors which govern the real world must be acknowledged, and have led to the limitations which have proved so frustrating to the editor, and are likely to frustrate others in turn. Yet if those frustrated readers should decide to move on, and seek out other works to read in detail . . . well, this selection will have served at least one useful purpose.

The Arrangement of the Material

The work is broken down into five broad sections, as follows:

1 The Patristic Period, ca. 100–600
2 English and Irish Sources, ca. 600–1050
3 The Middle Ages, 1050–1500
4 The Renaissance and Reformation, 1500–1700
5 The Modern Period, 1700–2000

Such a division is clearly open to criticism. For example, it might appear arbitrary at points: can the Middle Ages *really* be said to have ended at 1500? Such criticisms are entirely proper, and will be found to apply to any attempt to draw neat dividing lines within the continuum of human history. This division does, however, offer a convenient framework for organizing a vast body of material within a single volume, which is essential if a work of this size is to avoid lapsing into organizational chaos.

The divisions adopted can be justified on a number of grounds – historical, cultural, and theological. The divisions merge literary and theological considerations. For example, the division between the second and third parts can be seen as reflecting the change from Old English to Middle English, while the division between the third and fourth reflects the partly shared agenda of humanists and reformers, which would have such a significant influence on the reshaping of western Christianity. In adopting these divisions, however, I must confess that I have been influenced by their convenience as much as anything.

The periodization offered broadly parallels the four-fold division of Christian thought which I offer in my *Christian Theology: An Introduction*, which has established itself as the leading introduction to Christian theology. Yet an additional category proved necessary on account of the literary nature of this anthology. It is widely recognized that the conversion of England, Ireland, Scotland, and Wales led to a significant number of works of Christian literature in the second half of the first millennium, often involving an examination of the relationship of the original cultures of the region with the Christian faith. For example, one of the concerns of the *Beowulf* poet is to explore the way in which the Teutonic "culture of heroes" can be assimilated with his Christian faith. Equally, the substantial literature of Celtic Christianity shows a particular interest in the works of nature, often linked with invocations of the name of God as protection against its more hostile elements. After careful examination of the amount of material of this nature, along with its immense cultural significance, it was concluded that it was essential to have a separate section dealing with Old English and Celtic Christian writings.

Within each category, authors are arranged chronologically. Thus in Part IV, dealing with the Renaissance and Reformation periods, John Donne (1572–1631) is placed before George Herbert (1593–1633). Where there is some uncertainty as to a writer's precise date of birth or death, the best scholarly guess is accepted. In the case of anonymous works, the work is located at the most appropriate point in the text.

PART I

The Patristic Period, ca. 100–600

Introduction

The first major period for discussion is the patristic era. The term "patristic" comes from the Latin word *pater*, "father," and designates both the period of the Church Fathers, and the distinctive theological ideas and literary forms which came to develop within this period. The term "patristic period" is rather vaguely defined, but is often taken to refer to the period from the closing of the New Testament writings (ca. 100) to the definitive Council of Chalcedon (451). During this critically important phase of its history, Christianity established itself as a dominant religious force in the Mediterranean region.

The patristic period saw considerable thought being given to an issue of major importance to this anthology – the extent to which Christian writers could make use of existing secular approaches to rhetoric, literature, and poetry in developing a Christian literature. Initially, there was considerable hostility toward the use of such approaches. The secular establishment seemed dedicated to the eradication of Christianity; how, then, could Christian writers use its cultural norms with any degree of integrity? To employ the cultural values of an oppressor seemed to be tantamount to capitulation to those opposed to Christianity.

Yet with the conversion of Constantine, a distinct change of mood appears to have gained the ascendancy. No longer was classical Roman culture seen as embodying the values of an oppressor. At worst, the classical culture of the period was to be seen as neutral; increasingly, many came to see it as an ally. Augustine's famous image of Israel fleeing from Egypt with its treasures may be regarded as having given intellectual justification to the growing tendency to make extensive use of secular literary resources, and encourage a process of engagement and appropriation which can be seen as underlying the emergence of a significant Christian literature.

This period was also of major importance in crystallizing aspects of Christian thought, and can be seen as having achieved clarification of a number of major issues. A task of initial importance was sorting out the relationship between Christianity and Judaism. The letters of Paul in the New Testament bear witness to the importance of this issue in the first century of Christian history, as a series of doctrinal and practical issues came to the fore. Should Gentile (that is, non-Jewish) Christians be obliged to be circumcised? And how was the Old Testament to be correctly interpreted?

However, other issues soon came to the fore. One which was of especial importance in the second century is that of *apologetics* – the reasoned defense and justification of the Christian faith against its critics. During the first period of Christian history, the church was often persecuted by the state. Its agenda was that of survival; there was limited place for theological disputes when the very existence of the Christian church could not be taken for granted. This observation helps us understand why apologetics came to be of such importance to the early church, through writers such as Justin Martyr (ca. 100–ca. 165), concerned to explain and defend the beliefs and practices of Christianity to a hostile pagan public. Although this early period produced some outstanding theologians – such as Irenaeus of Lyons (ca. 130–ca. 200) in the west, and Origen (ca. 185–ca. 254) in the east – theological debate could only begin in earnest once the church had ceased to be persecuted.

With the conversion of the Roman Emperor Constantine, Christianity ceased to be persecuted throughout the Roman Empire. No longer was Christianity obliged to behave as an "underground" movement, holding its meetings in secret and concentrating on surviving from day to day. As a result, the later patristic period (from about 310 to 451) may be regarded as a high-water mark in the history of Christian theology. Theologians now enjoyed the freedom to work without the threat of persecution, and were able to address a series of issues of major importance to the consolidation of the emerging theological consensus within the churches. That consensus involved extensive debate and a painful learning process in which the church discovered that it had to come to terms with disagreements and continuing tensions. Nonetheless, a significant degree of consensus, eventually to be enshrined in the ecumenical creeds, can be discerned as emerging within this formative period.

As we noted earlier, it can be argued that a wide variety of literary forms are intrinsic to the self-expression of the Christian. Yet it is also important to appreciate that Christianity has gladly "borrowed" other types of literature. In view of the importance of the patristic period for laying the foundations of this development, we shall consider the point at issue in a little detail.

The Patristic Period and the Engagement with Secular Culture

One of the most important debates in the early church concerned the extent to which Christians could appropriate the immense cultural legacy of the classical world – poetry, philosophy, and literature. In what way can the *ars poetica* be adopted by Christian writers, anxious to use such classical modes of writing to expound and communicate their faith? Or was the very use of such a literary medium tantamount to compromising the essentials of the Christian faith? It was a debate of immense significance, as it raised the question of whether Christianity would turn its back on the classical heritage, or appropriate it, even if in a modified form. In view of its importance and interest, we shall cite extensively from some of the most important writings offered as contributions to this debate.

One early answer to this important question was given by Justin Martyr, a second-century writer with a particular concern to exploit the parallels between Christianity and Platonism as a means of communicating the gospel. For Justin, the seeds of divine wisdom had been sown throughout the world, which meant that Christians could and should expect to find aspects of the gospel reflected outside the church.

> We have been taught that Christ is the firstborn of God, and we have proclaimed that he is the Logos, in whom every race of people have shared. And those who live according to the Logos are Christians, even though they may have been counted as atheists – such as Socrates and Heraclitus, and others like them, among the Greeks. . . . Whatever either lawyers or philosophers have said well, was articulated by finding and reflecting upon some aspect of the Logos. However, since they did not know the Logos – which is Christ – in its entirety, they often contradicted themselves. . . . Whatever all people have said well belongs to us Christians. For we worship and love, next to God, the Logos, who comes from the unbegotten and ineffable God, since it was for our sake that he became a human being, in order that he might share in our sufferings and bring us healing. For all writers were able to see the truth darkly, on account of the implanted seed of the Logos which was grafted into them.

For Justin, Christians were therefore at liberty to draw upon classical culture, in the knowledge that whatever "has been said well" ultimately draws upon divine wisdom and insight.

Important though Justin's argument may have been, it received a somewhat frosty reception in most sections of the Christian church. The main difficulty was that it was seen to virtually equate Christianity with classical culture by failing to articulate adequate grounds for distinguishing them, apparently suggesting that Christian theology and Platonism were simply different ways of viewing the same divine realities. Justin's pupil Tatian (born ca. 120) was skeptical concerning the merits of classic rhetoric and poetry, both of which he regarded as encouraging deception and a disregard for matters of truth. The most severe criticism of this kind of approach was to be found in the writings of Tertullian, a third-century Roman lawyer who converted to Christianity. What, he asked, has Athens to do with Jerusalem? What relevance has the Platonic academy for the church? The manner in which the question is posed makes Tertullian's answer clear: Christianity must maintain its distinctive identity by avoiding such secular influences:

> Philosophy provides the material of worldly wisdom, in boldly asserting itself to be the interpreter of the divine nature and dispensation. The heresies themselves receive their weapons from philosophy. It was from this source that Valentinus, who was a disciple of Plato, got his ideas about the "aeons" and the "trinity of humanity." And it was from there that the god of Marcion (much to be preferred, on account of his tranquility) came; Marcion came from the Stoics. To say that the soul is subject to death is to go the way of Epicurus. And the denial of the resurrection of the body is found throughout the writings of all the philosophers. To say that matter is equal with God is to follow the doctrine of Zeno; to speak of a god of fire is to draw on Heracleitus. It is the same subjects which preoccupy both the heretics and the philosophers. Where does evil come from, and why? Where does human nature come from, and how? . . . What has Athens

to do with Jerusalem? What has the Academy to do with the church? Our system of beliefs comes from the Porch of Solomon, who himself taught that it was necessary to seek God in the simplicity of the heart. So much the worse for those who talk of a "stoic," "platonic" or "dialectic" Christianity!

This wholesale rejection of every aspect of pagan culture had the advantage of being simple to understand. Christianity, according to Tertullian, was basically a counter-cultural movement, which refused to allow itself to be contaminated in any way by the mental or moral environment in which it took root. Tertullian's basic question would find echoes throughout Christian history. For example, the English writer Alcuin rebuked the monks of Lindisfarne Abbey in 797 for reading too many Nordic sagas. "What has Ingeld to do with Christ?" he asked, and by doing so, posed exactly the same question raised by Tertullian centuries earlier. Alcuin's remedy for the situation was direct and to the point: "Let the words of God be read aloud at table in your refectory. It is the reader who should be heard there, not someone playing the flute. It is the fathers of the church, and not the songs of the heathen, who should be heard."

Yet there were difficulties with this consistently negative approach. It seemed to deny Christians access to or use of any of the intellectual and cultural heritage for a thoroughly laudable purpose – namely, the preaching of the gospel. Many early Christian writers studied classic rhetoric as a means to improve their preaching and writing, and thus facilitate the communication of the faith to those outside the church. Was Tertullian excluding this? Alongside this pragmatic approach could be found a more theological issue. Does not all true wisdom have its origins in God? And if so, should not Christians honor that truth where it is to be found? To his critics, Tertullian seemed to offer little in the way of response to these questions.

The matter became of greater significance with the conversion of the Roman Emperor Constantine. In view of the importance of this development, we need to explore the background to it in a little detail. Since it first established a significant presence at Rome in the 40s, Christianity had had a decidedly ambiguous legal status. On the one hand, it was not legally recognized, and so did not enjoy any special rights; on the other, it was not forbidden. However, its growing numerical strength led to periodic attempts to suppress it by force. Sometimes these persecutions were local, restricted to regions such as North Africa; sometimes, they were sanctioned throughout the Roman Empire as a whole.

A particularly significant period of persecution dates from the accession of the Emperor Decius in 249. His first major act of hostility toward Christianity was the execution of Fabian, Bishop of Rome, in January 250. The Decian persecution resulted from the Edict of Decius, issued in June 250, which commanded provincial governors and magistrates to ensure that there was universal observance of the requirement to offer sacrifices to the Roman gods, and to the emperor. A certificate (*libellus pacis*) was issued to those who offered such sacrifices. The edict seems to have been widely ignored, but was nevertheless enforced in some regions. Thousands of Christians were martyred during this difficult period. The Decian persecution ended in June 251, when Decius was killed on a military expedition. The persecution led to many Christians lapsing or abandoning their faith in the face of oppression. A further severe outburst of persecution came about in February 303, under the Emperor Diocletian. An edict was issued ordering the destruction of all Christian places of worship, the surrender and destruction of all their books, and the cessation of all acts of Christian worship. Christian civil servants were to lose all privileges of rank or status and were reduced to the status of slaves. Prominent Christians were forced to offer sacrifice according to traditional Roman practices. It is an indication of how influential Christianity had become that Diocletian forced both his wife and daughter, who were known to be Christians, to comply with this order. The persecution continued under successive emperors, including Galerius, who ruled the eastern region of the Empire.

Under these conditions, it is hardly surprising that many Christians felt negatively toward classic Roman culture. This was the culture of an oppressor, determined to eliminate Christianity. It was easy to see the force of Tertullian's arguments under these circumstances. To adopt Roman cultural norms was tantamount to betrayal of the Christian faith.

In 311, Galerius ordered the cessation of the persecution. It had been a failure, and had merely hardened Christians in their resolve to resist the reimposition of classical Roman pagan religion. Galerius issued an edict which permitted Christians to live normally again and "hold their religious assemblies, provided that they do nothing which would disturb public order." The edict explicitly identified Christianity as a religion, and offered it the full protection of the law. The legal status of Christianity, which had been ambiguous up to this point, was now resolved. The church no longer existed under a siege mentality.

Christianity was now a legal religion; it was, however, merely one among many such religions. The conversion of the Emperor Constantine changed this irreversibly, and brought about a complete change in the situation of Christianity throughout the Roman Empire. Constantine was born to pagan parents in 285. (His mother would eventually become a Christian, apparently through her son's influence.) Although he showed no particular attraction to Christianity in his early period, Constantine certainly seems to have regarded toleration as an essential virtue. Following Maxentius' seizure of power in Italy and North Africa, Constantine led a body of troops from western Europe in an attempt to gain authority in the region. The decisive battle took place on October 28, 312 at the Milvian Bridge, to the north of Rome. Constantine defeated Maxentius, and was proclaimed emperor. At some point shortly afterwards, he declared himself to be a Christian.

The issue of the interaction of Christianity and classical culture now assumed a new significance. Rome was now the servant of the gospel; might not the same be true of its culture? If the Roman state could be viewed positively by Christians, why not also its cultural heritage? It seemed as if a door had opened upon some very interesting possibilities. Prior to 313, this possibility could only have been dreamt of. After 313, its exploration became a matter of urgency for leading Christian thinkers – supreme among whom was Augustine of Hippo.

It is no surprise that the answer which would finally gain acceptance was set out by Augustine, and can perhaps be best described as the "critical appropriation of classical culture." For Augustine, the situation is comparable to Israel fleeing from captivity in Egypt at the time of the Exodus. Although they left the idols of Egypt behind them, they carried the gold and silver of Egypt with them, in order to make better and proper use of such riches, which were thus liberated in order to serve a higher purpose than before. In much the same way, the philosophy and culture of the ancient world could be appropriated by Christians, where this seemed right, and thus allowed to serve the cause of the Christian faith. Augustine clinched his argument by pointing out how several recent distinguished Christians had made use of classical wisdom in advancing the gospel:

> If those who are called philosophers, particularly the Platonists, have said anything which is true and consistent with our faith, we must not reject it, but claim it for our own use, in the knowledge that they possess it unlawfully. The Egyptians possessed idols and heavy burdens, which the children of Israel hated and from which they fled; however, they also possessed vessels of gold and silver and clothes which our forebears, in leaving Egypt, took for themselves in secret, intending to use them in a better manner (Exodus 3:21–22; 12:35–36) . . . In the same way, pagan learning is not entirely made up of false teachings and superstitions . . . It contains also some excellent teachings, well suited to be used by truth, and excellent moral values. Indeed, some truths are even found among them which relate to the worship of the one God. Now these are, so to speak, their gold and their silver, which they did not invent themselves, but which they dug out of the mines of the providence of God, which are scattered throughout the world, yet which are improperly and unlawfully prostituted to the worship of demons. The Christian, therefore, can separate these truths from their unfortunate associations, take them away, and put them to their proper use for the proclamation of the gospel. . . . What else have many good and faithful people from amongst us done. Look at the wealth of gold and silver and clothes which Cyprian – that eloquent teacher and blessed martyr – brought with him when he left Egypt! And think of all that Lactantius brought with him, not to mention Marius Victorinus, Optatus and Hilary of Poitiers, and others who are still living! And look at how much the Greeks have borrowed! And before all of these, we find that Moses, that most faithful servant of God, had done the same thing: after all, it is written of him that "he was learned in all the wisdom of the Egyptians" (Acts 7:22).

The fundamental theme is that of taking a way of thinking – or writing, or speaking – which had hitherto been put to pagan use, and liberating it so that it might be put to the service of the gospel. Augustine argues that what are essentially neutral yet valuable ways of thinking or self-expression have been quarried in "the mines of the providence of God"; the difficulty is the use to which they were put within pagan culture, in that they had been "improperly and unlawfully prostituted to the worship of demons."

Augustine's approach thus laid the foundation for the assertion that whatever was good, true, or beautiful could be used in the service of the gospel. It was this approach which would prove dominant in the western church, providing a theological foundation for the critical appropriation by Christian writers of literary genres whose origins lay outside the church. In addition to literary forms already known within the church, and widely recognized as entirely appropriate in Christian usage – such as the sermon and the biblical commentary – might be added others, whose cultural pedigree was thoroughly secular. Examples would include drama and – to anticipate a later development – the novel.

The scene was thus set for the creative interaction of Christian theology, liturgy and spirituality with the cultural tradition of the ancient world – unquestionably one of the most interesting and fertile examples of cultural cross-fertilization in human intellectual history.

Centers of Christian Thought during the Patristic Period

Christianity had its origins in Palestine – more specifically, the region of Judea, especially the city of Jerusalem. Christianity regarded itself as a continuation and development of Judaism, and initially flourished in regions with which Judaism was traditionally associated, supremely Palestine. However, it rapidly spread to neighboring regions, partially through the efforts of early Christian evangelists such as Paul of Tarsus. By the end of the first century, Christianity appears to have become established throughout the eastern Mediterranean world, and even to have gained a significant presence in the city of Rome, the capital of the Roman Empire. As the church at Rome became increasingly powerful, tensions began to develop between the Christian leadership at Rome and at Constantinople, foreshadowing the later schism between the western and eastern churches, centered on these respective centers of power.

In the course of this expansion, a number of regions emerged as significant centers of theological debate. Three may be singled out as having especial importance, the first two of which were Greek-speaking, and the third Latin-speaking.

1 The city of Alexandria, in modern-day Egypt, which emerged as a center of Christian theological education. A distinctive style of theology came to be associated with this city, reflecting its longstanding association with the Platonic tradition. "Alexandrian" approaches to a range of theological issues soon developed, reflecting both the importance and distinctiveness of the style of Christianity associated with the area.

2 The city of Antioch and the surrounding region of Cappadocia, in modern-day Turkey. A strong Christian presence came to be established in this northern region of the eastern Mediterranean at an early stage. Paul's missionary journeys, described in the Acts of the Apostles, often involved church-planting in this region, and Antioch features significantly at several points in the history of the very early church. Antioch itself soon became a leading center of Christian thought. Like Alexandria, it became associated with a distinct theological style. The "Cappadocian fathers" were also an important theological presence in this region in the fourth century, notable especially for their contribution to the doctrine of the Trinity.

3 Western North Africa, especially the area of modern-day Algeria. In the late classical period, this was the site of Carthage, a major Mediterranean city and at one time a political rival to Rome for dominance in the region. During the period when Christianity expanded in this region, it was a Roman colony. Major

writers of this region include Tertullian, Cyprian of Carthage, and Augustine of Hippo.

This is not to say that other cities around the Mediterranean were devoid of significance. Rome, Constantinople, Milan, and Jerusalem were also centers of Christian theological reflection, even if none was destined to achieve quite the significance of their rivals.

Theological Divisions of the Period

The patristic period saw a number of major disputes developing within the church. Three can be singled out as being of particular importance to the development of Christian theology.

1   *The Donatist controversy.* This debate centered on Roman North Africa, particularly the region around Carthage. Christians in this region suffered particularly during the Diocletian persecution. Such was the ferocity of the persecution that many Christians, including some senior church figures, collaborated with the Roman authorities, in the hope that the storm would pass and they could get back to a normal way of life. Others fiercely resisted the persecution. As a result, controversy developed within the church over the treatment of those who had compromised their principles during the persecution. One group, which centered on the figure of Donatus, took a hard line. No compromise could be permitted. Clergy who had collaborated in any way during the persecution could not be readmitted within the church. This controversy, which became particularly important during the fourth century, forced the western church to give careful thought to two areas of Christian doctrine – the doctrine of the church, and the doctrine of the sacraments.

2   *The Arian controversy.* This controversy broke out in the eastern section of the church during the fourth century. It focused on Arius, based in the Egyptian city of Alexandria. Arius argued that Jesus Christ could not be described as being fully divine. Rather, Jesus was to be thought of as supreme among God's creatures. Arius met stiff resistance from various opponents, especially Athanasius. The resulting dispute became so serious that the unity of the Roman Empire was threatened. As a result, the Emperor Constantine convened a council of 220 bishops at the city of Nicea in Asia Minor. He demanded that they settle the issue. The Council of Nicea decided against Arius, and affirmed that Jesus Christ was "of one substance" with God – in other words, that Jesus was both human and divine. This doctrine, which is generally referred to as "the doctrine of the two natures," is of particular importance to Christian thought, and features prominently in the Christian literature of the fourth century.

3   *The Pelagian controversy.* This debate broke out in the final years of the fourth century, and continues into the first two decades of the fifth century. The basic question under debate was the respective roles played by God and humanity in salvation. Who has the upper hand in salvation – God or ourselves? Is salvation something which is given to us by God? Or is it something which we earn or merit by our good

works? Such questions caused significant divisions within the church at the time, and would become controversial once more during the sixteenth century.

Institutional Developments: The Origins of Monasticism

One of the most important developments to take place during the patristic period was the development of monasticism. The origins of the movement are generally thought to lie in remote hilly areas of Egypt and parts of eastern Syria. Significant numbers of Christians began to make their homes in these regions, in order to get away from the population centers, with all the distractions that these offered. Anthony of Egypt, who left his parents' home in 273 to seek out a life of discipline and solitude in the desert, is an excellent representative of this movement.

The theme of withdrawal from a sinful and distracting world became of central importance to these communities. While some lone figures insisted on the need for individual isolation, the concept of a communal life in isolation from the world gained the ascendancy. One important early monastery was founded by Pachomius during the years 320–325. This monastery developed an ethos which would become normative in later monasticism. Members of the community agreed to submit themselves to a common life which was regulated by a Rule, under the direction of a superior. The physical structure of the monastery was significant: the complex was surrounded by a wall, highlighting the idea of separation and withdrawal from the world. The Greek word *koinonia* (often translated as "fellowship"), frequently used in the New Testament, now came to refer to the idea of a common corporate life, characterized by common clothing, meals, furnishing of cells (as the monks' rooms were known), and manual labor for the good of the community.

The monastic ideal proved to have a deep attraction for many. By the fourth century, monasteries had been established in many locations in the Christian east, especially in the regions of Syria and Asia Minor. It was not long before the movement was taken up in the western church. By the fifth century, monastic communities had come into existence in Italy (especially along the western coastline), Spain and Gaul. Augustine of Hippo, one of the leading figures of the western church at this time, established two monasteries in North Africa at some point during the period 400–425. For Augustine, the common life (now designated by the Latin phrase *vita communis*) was essential to the realization of the Christian ideal of love. He supplemented this emphasis on community life with an appreciation of the importance of intellectual activity and spiritual study.

During the sixth century, the number of monasteries in the region grew considerably. It was during this period that one of the most comprehensive monastic "Rules" – the "Rule of Benedict" – made its appearance. Benedict of Nursia (ca. 480–ca. 550) established his monastery at Monte Cassino at some point around 525. The Benedictine community followed a Rule which was dominated by the notion of the unconditional following of Christ, sustained by regular corporate and private prayer, and the reading of Scripture.

The monasteries would be major centers of literary activity for more than a thousand years. In addition to producing major works of devotion, theology and spirituality, the monasteries also established a reputation as centers of literacy in a generally illiterate culture. Works of history and poetry began to emerge. Perhaps one of the most interesting examples of this trend can be seen in late Anglo-Saxon England, and will be considered in Part II of this collection.

CHAPTER 1

Clement of Rome
(active around 96)

Clement was an early bishop of Rome. It is not clear whether he was the second or third bishop in succession to the apostle Peter in this position. Although a number of writings have been attributed to him, including a "Second Letter of Clement," their authenticity has not always been accepted. However, the first letter attributed to him is unquestionably genuine. The letter was written from Rome to the church in the city of Corinth, in order to urge reconciliation and understanding between opposing factions. Factionalism had been a problem in the Corinthian church from the earliest of times; the first letter of the apostle Paul to the church in the city, probably written around 52, makes explicit reference to the existence of personality-based factions, and the serious negative effect this was having on the life of the church.

Clement of Rome (active around 96)

Basic description
Early bishop of Rome; writer of letters.

Major work
First letter to the church at Corinth.

Major studies
Donald A. Hagner, *The Use of the Old and New Testaments in Clement of Rome*. Leiden: E. J. Brill, 1973.
Harry O. Meier, *The Social Setting of the Ministry as Reflected in the Writings of Hermas, Clement and Ignatius*. Waterloo, ON: Wilfred Laurier University Press, 1991.

Clement sought to bring peace to this troubled church, as Paul had before him. It is not entirely clear how the conflict within the church had arisen; but certain presbyters had been deposed, and feelings were running high on every side. Clement demanded humility from all involved, the reinstatement of those who had been deposed, and due respect for order within the church. An essential prerequisite for this is humility on the part of all concerned; the letter appeals to the example of Christ himself as a model for Christian humility.

Text: The First Letter to Corinth

The first letter of Clement, addressed to the church at Corinth, is important as a piece of literature, not simply on account of its antiquity – it is one of the earliest pieces of Christian literature outside the New Testament canon – but also on account of its style. It is a classic example of a pastoral letter, designed to bring peace and encourage mutual care. We know that the letter was still being read aloud in the churches of Corinth as late as 170, indicating how much it was valued by those to whom it was sent.

The opening section of the letter, which is reproduced below, deals with the importance of humility and repentance within the Christian church.

The Church of God which sojourns at Rome, to the Church of God sojourning at Corinth, to those that are called and sanctified by the will of God, through our Lord Jesus Christ: Grace and peace be to you from Almighty God through Jesus Christ.

1   Owing, my dear brethren, to the sudden and successive calamitous events which have happened to ourselves, we feel that we have been somewhat late in turning our attention to the points respecting which you consulted us; and especially to that shameful and detestable sedition, utterly abhorrent to the elect of God, which a few rash and self-confident persons have kindled to such a pitch of frenzy, that your venerable and illustrious name, worthy to be universally loved, has suffered grievous injury. For who ever dwelt even for a short time among you, and did not find your faith to be as fruitful of virtue as it was firmly established? Who did not admire the sobriety and moderation of your godliness in Christ? Who did not proclaim the magnificence of your habitual hospitality? And who did not rejoice over your perfect and well-grounded knowledge? For you did all things without respect of persons, and walked in the commandments of God, being obedient to those who had the rule over you, and giving all fitting honor to the presbyters among you. You urged young men to be of a sober and serious mind; you instructed your wives to do all things with a blameless and pure conscience, loving their husbands as in duty bound; and you taught them that, living in the rule of obedience, they should manage their household affairs appropriately, and be in every respect marked by discretion.

2   Moreover, you were all distinguished by humility, and were in no respect puffed up with pride, but yielded obedience rather than exhorted it, and were more willing to give than to receive. Content with the provision which God had made for you, and carefully attending to his words, you were inwardly filled with his doctrine, and his sufferings were before your eyes. Thus a profound and abundant peace was given to you all, and you had an insatiable desire for doing good, while a full outpouring of the Holy Spirit was upon you all. Full of holy designs, you stretched forth your hands toward God almighty with true earnestness of mind and with a godly confidence, asking him to be merciful unto you, if you had been guilty of any involuntary transgression. Day and night you were anxious for the whole brotherhood, that the number of God's elect might be saved with mercy and a good conscience. You were sincere and uncorrupted, and forgetful of injuries between one another.

Every kind of faction and schism was abominable in your sight. You mourned over the transgressions of your neighbors: their deficiencies you treated as if they were your own. You never grudged any act of kindness, being ready to do every good work. Adorned by a thoroughly virtuous and religious life, you did all things in the fear of God. The commandments and ordinances of the Lord were written upon the tablets of your hearts.

3   Every kind of honor and happiness was bestowed upon you, and so it was fulfilled that is written, "My beloved did eat and drink, and was enlarged and became fat, and kicked." Hence flowed emulation and envy, strife and sedition, persecution and disorder, war and captivity. So the worthless rose up against the honored; those of no reputation against such as were renowned; the foolish against the wise; the young against those advanced in years. For this reason righteousness and peace are now far departed from you, inasmuch as every one abandons the fear of God, and is become blind in His faith; he does not walk in the ways God desires, nor behave in a way appropriate for a Christian, but follows his own evil desires, resuming the practice of an unrighteous and ungodly envy, by which death itself entered into the world.

4   For it is written: "And it came to pass after certain days, that Cain brought of the fruits of the earth a sacrifice unto God; and Abel also brought of the firstlings of his sheep, and of the fat thereof. And God had respect to Abel and to his offerings, but Cain and his sacrifices He did not regard. And Cain was deeply grieved, and his countenance fell. And God said to Cain, Why art thou grieved, and why is thy countenance fallen? If thou offerest rightly, but dost not divide rightly, hast thou not sinned? Be at peace: thine offering returns to thyself, and thou shalt again possess it. And Cain said to Abel his brother, Let us go into the field. And it came to pass, while they were in the field, that Cain rose up against Abel his brother, and slew him." So you see, my brethren, how envy and jealousy led to the murder of a brother. Through envy, also, our father Jacob fled from the face of Esau his brother. Envy made Joseph be persecuted unto death, and to come into bondage. Envy compelled Moses to flee from the face of Pharaoh king of Egypt, when he heard these words from his fellow-countryman, "Who made you a judge or a ruler over us? Will you kill me, as you killed the Egyptian yesterday?" On account of envy, Aaron and Miriam had to live outside the camp. Envy brought down Dathan and Abiram alive to Hades, on account of the treachery against God's servant Moses. Through envy, David ont only underwent the hatred of foreigners, but was also persecuted by Saul king of Israel.

5   But not to dwell upon ancient examples, let us come to the most recent spiritual heroes. Let us take the noble examples furnished in our own generation. Through envy and jealousy, the greatest and most righteous pillars of the Church have been persecuted and put to death. Let us set before our eyes the illustrious apostles. Peter, through unrighteous envy, endured not one or two, but numerous labors and when he had at length suffered martyrdom, departed to the place of glory due to him. Owing to envy, Paul also obtained the reward of patient endurance, after being seven times thrown into captivity, compelled to flee, and stoned. After preaching both in the east and west, he gained the illustrious reputation due to his faith, having taught righteousness to the whole world, and come to the extreme limit of

the west, and suffered martyrdom under the Prefects. Thus was he removed from the world, and went into the holy place, having proved himself a striking example of patience.

6   To these men who spent their lives in the practice of holiness, there is to be added a great multitude of the elect, who, having through envy endured many indignities and tortures, furnished us with a most excellent example. Through envy, those women, the Danaids and Dircae, being persecuted, after they had suffered terrible and unspeakable torments, finished the course of their faith with steadfastness, and though weak in body, received a noble reward. Envy has alienated wives from their husbands, and changed that saying of our father Adam, "This is now bone of my bones, and flesh of my flesh." Envy and strife have overthrown great cities and rooted up mighty nations.

6   These things, beloved, we write to you, not simply to remind you of your obligations, but also to remind ourselves. For we are struggling in the same arena, and the same conflict is assigned to both of us. So let us give up vain and fruitless cares, and attend to the glorious and venerable rule of our holy calling. Let us attend to what is good, pleasing, and acceptable in the sight of Him who formed us. Let us look steadfastly to the blood of Christ, and see how precious that blood is to God, which, having been shed for our salvation, has set the grace of repentance before the whole world. Let us turn to every age that has passed, and learn that, from generation to generation, the Lord has granted a place of repentance to all such as would be converted unto Him. Noah preached repentance, and all those who listened to him were saved. Jonah proclaimed destruction to the Ninevites; but they, repenting of their sins, made peace with God through prayer, and obtained salvation, although they were strangers to God.

Questions for Discussion

1   Note the introduction to the letter. What does the image of "sojourning" suggest concerning early Christian understandings of the nature of the church? And how does this compare with the opening greetings of other Christian writings of the period. For example, compare it with the opening words of Paul's first letter to the church at Corinth: "Paul, called by the will of God to be an apostle of Christ Jesus, and our brother Sosthenes, to the church of God which is at Corinth, to those sanctified in Christ Jesus, called to be saints together with all those who in every place call on the name of our Lord Jesus Christ, both their Lord and ours: Grace to you and peace from God our Father and the Lord Jesus Christ."
2   Clement is concerned to heal the wounds within the Corinthian church by urging humility, reconciliation, and repentance within that church. How do these opening sections of the letter lay the foundation for such an appeal?
3   Why does Clement place such an emphasis upon the theme of repentance?

CHAPTER 2

Ignatius of Antioch (died ca. 107)

Ignatius, also called "Theophorus," was born in Syria, around the year 50, and died at Rome at some point around 107. Little is known for certain of his life, although internal evidence within his letters suggests that he may have been a pagan and a persecutor of the Christian church prior to his conversion. He was captured by the Romans during a period of persecution in the eastern Mediterranean region. Trajan, who was responsible for directing this in the region of Syria, ordered Ignatius to be taken from Antioch to Rome under a guard of ten soldiers. Part of this journey was by land; during the course of this section of the journey, Ignatius was received with honor by local Christian communities.

Ignatius of Antioch (died ca. 107)

Basic description
Early Christian bishop and martyr.

Major works
Seven letters to churches and individuals, written on his way to Rome.

Major studies
Cyril C. Richardson, *The Christianity of Ignatius of Antioch*. New York: AMS Press, 1967.
Christine Trevett, *A Study of Ignatius of Antioch in Syria and Asia*. Lewiston, NY: Edwin Mellen Press, 1992.

Text: The Letter to the Romans

Ignatius is known to have written seven letters as he traveled from Antioch to Rome. Six letters were written to Christian churches, five of which sought to encourage Christians during a period of uncertainty. The sixth of these letters was written to the church at Rome. In this letter, Ignatius urged Roman Christians not to intervene on his behalf. His death in the arena would be an act of witness to the Christian faith, and he did not want to be deprived of the honor and privilege of dying in such a magnificent manner. A seventh letter was written to Polycarp, who received Ignatius and treated him with great respect. Polycarp would eventually join the ranks of martyrs himself (see pp. 21–9).

The letter to the Roman Christians is of considerable historical and literary interest. It alludes to various New Testament passages, even though the letter was written at a very early stage in the development of Christianity, and the New Testament canon had yet to be finalized. It follows a classic epistolary form, particularly in its opening and closing sections.

Ignatius, who is also called Theophorus, to the Church which has obtained mercy, through the majesty of the Most High Father, and Jesus Christ, his only-begotten Son; to the Church which is beloved and enlightened by the will of him that wills all things which are according to the love of Jesus Christ our God, which also presides in the place of the report of the Romans, worthy of God, worthy of honor, worthy of the highest happiness, worthy of praise, worthy of obtaining her every desire, worthy of being deemed holy, and which presides over love, is named from Christ, and from the Father, which I also salute in the name of Jesus Christ, the Son of the Father: to those who are united, both according to the flesh and spirit, to every one of His commandments; who are filled inseparably with the grace of God, and are purified from every strange taint; may you have abundance of happiness without reproach, in Jesus Christ our God.

1   Through prayer to God I have obtained the privilege of seeing your most worthy faces, and have even been granted more than I requested; for I hope as a prisoner in Christ Jesus to greet you, if indeed it is the will of God that I should be thought worthy of attaining unto the end. For the beginning has been well ordered, if I may obtain grace to cling to my lot without hindrance unto the end. For I am afraid of your love, in case it should do me an injury. For it is easy for you to accomplish what you please; but it is difficult for me to attain to God, if you should spare me.

2   For it is not my desire to act toward you as someone who seeks to please other people, but as one who pleases God, just as you also please Him. For neither shall I ever have such opportunity of attaining to God; nor will you, if you shall now be silent, ever be entitled to the honor of a better work. For if you are silent concerning me, I shall become God's; but if you show your love to my flesh, I shall again have to run my race. So please do not seek to confer any greater favor upon me than that I be sacrificed to God while the altar is still prepared; that, being gathered together in love, you may sing praise to the Father, through Christ Jesus, that God has deemed me, the bishop of Syria, worthy to be sent for from the east to the west. It is good to set out from the world to God, so that I may rise again to him.

3   You have never envied any one; you have taught others. Now I desire that those things may be confirmed in you which you ask others to do in your instructions. Only request on my behalf both inward and outward strength, that I may speak fully and truly; and that I may not merely be called a Christian, but really be found to be one. For if I am truly found to be a Christian, I may also be called one, and therefore be thought of as being faithful, when I shall no longer appear to the world.

Nothing visible is eternal. "For the things which are seen are temporal, but the things which are not seen are eternal." For our God, Jesus Christ, now that He is with the Father is all the more revealed. Christianity is not only a thing of silence, but also of greatness.

4   I write to the Churches, and impress on them all, that I shall willingly die for God, unless you should prevent me. I beg you not to show an inappropriate affection for me. Allow me to become food for the wild beasts, through which I will be allowed to reach God. I am the wheat of God; let me be ground by the teeth of the wild beasts, so that I may be found to be the pure bread of Christ. Rather entice the wild beasts, that they may become my tomb, and may leave nothing of my body; so that when I have fallen asleep, I may be no trouble to any one. Then shall I truly be a disciple of Christ, when the world shall not see so much as my body. Pray to Christ for me, that I may be a sacrifice. I do not, as Peter and Paul, issue commands to you. They were apostles; I am nothing more than a condemned man. They were free; while I am, even until now, a slave. But when I suffer, I shall be the freed-man of Jesus, and shall rise again, set free in him. And now, being a prisoner, I learn not to desire anything worldly or vain.

5   From Syria even unto Rome I fight with beasts, both by land and sea, both by night and day, being bound to ten leopards, I mean a band of soldiers, who, even when they receive benefits, show themselves all the worse. But I am the more instructed by their injuries; yet am I not thereby justified. May I enjoy the wild beasts that are prepared for me; and I pray they may be found eager to rush upon me, which also I will entice to devour me quickly, and not deal with me as they have dealt with others who they have not touched, through being afraid of them. But if they be unwilling to attack me, I will force them to do so. Forgive me; I know what is for my benefit. Now I begin to be a disciple. And let no one, whether visible or invisible, envy me that I should attain to Jesus Christ. Let fire and the cross; let the crowds of wild beasts; let tearings, breakings, and dislocations of bones; let cutting off of members; let shatterings of the whole body; and let all the dreadful torments of the devil come upon me: only let me be with Jesus Christ.

6   All the pleasures of the world, and all the kingdoms of this earth, shall gain me nothing. It is better for me to die on behalf of Jesus Christ, than to reign over all the ends of the earth. "For what shall a man be profited, if he gain the whole world, but lose his own soul?" I seek the one who died for us: I desire the one who rose again for our sake. This is the gain which is laid up for me. Forgive me, my brethren; do not prevent me from living; do not wish to keep me in a state of death; and while I desire to belong to God, do not give me over to the world. Allow me to obtain pure light: when I have gone there, I shall indeed be a man of God. Permit me to be an imitator of the passion of my God. If any one has him within himself, let him consider what I desire, and let him have sympathy with me, as knowing how I am constrained.

7   The prince of this world wants to carry me away, and corrupt my attitude toward God. Let none of you, therefore, help him; rather be on my side, that is, on the side of God. Do not speak of Jesus Christ, and yet set your desires on the world. Do not allow envy to find a dwelling-place among you; nor even should I, when present with you, exhort you to it; be persuaded to listen to me, but rather give credit

to those things which I now write to you. For though I am alive while I write to you, yet I am eager to die. My love has been crucified, and there is no fire in me desiring to be fed; but there is within me a water that lives and speaks, saying to me inwardly, "Come to the Father." I have no delight in corruptible food, nor in the pleasures of this life. I desire the bread of God, the heavenly bread, the bread of life, which is the flesh of Jesus Christ, the Son of God, who became afterwards of the seed of David and Abraham; and I desire the drink of God, namely His blood, which is incorruptible love and eternal life.

8   I no longer wish to live according to human values, and my desire shall be fulfilled if you consent to this. Grant me this, then, so that you also may have your desires fulfilled. I beg you in this brief letter, to give credit to me. I speak truly; Christ will reveal these things to you. He is the mouth which is totally free from falsehood, by which the Father has truly spoken. Pray for me, that I may gain what I desire. I have not written to you according to the flesh, but according to the will of God. If I shall suffer, you will have wished well to me; but if I am rejected, you will have hated me.

9   Remember in your prayers the Church in Syria, which now has God for its shepherd, instead of me. Jesus Christ alone will oversee it. But as for me, I am ashamed to be counted one of them; for indeed I am not worthy, as being the very last of them, and one born out of due time. But I have obtained mercy to be somebody, if I shall attain to God. My spirit salutes you, and the love of the Churches that have received me – not merely as someone who passes by! – in the name of Jesus Christ. For even those Churches which were not near to me in the way (I mean according to the flesh) have gone before me, city by city.

10   Now I write these things to you from Smyrna by the Ephesians, who are deservedly most happy. There is also with me, along with many others, Crocus, one dearly beloved by me. As to those who have gone before me from Syria to Rome for the glory of God, I believe that you are acquainted with them; let them know that I am here. For they are all worthy, both of God and of you; and it is fitting that you should refresh them in all things. I have written these things to you on the day before the ninth of the Kalends of September (that is, on the twenty-third day of August). Fare well to the end, in the patience of Jesus Christ. Amen.

Questions for Study

1   Why does Ignatius not want the Roman church to plead for him? Why does he regard martyrdom as so important?
2   What do his references to wild animals tell us about Ignatius' expectations concerning the manner of his execution?
3   What anxieties does Ignatius express concerning the church in Antioch in his absence?
4   "It is better for me to die on behalf of Jesus Christ, than to reign over all the ends of the earth." Locate this citation within the text. What does Ignatius mean by this? And how do you think his readers would have responded to his words?

CHAPTER 3

The Martyrdom of Polycarp
(ca. 155)

Polycarp (ca. 69–ca. 155) was Bishop of Smyrna, in Roman Asia (modern-day Turkey). He appears to have been regarded as the leading Christian of the region, and was there-fore perhaps an inevitable target for hostility. The document known as the "Martyrdom of Polycarp" records the details of the events surrounding his arrest and death. The work is of literary importance, in that it is the oldest example reliably known to scholarship of the literary genre known as "Acts of the Martyrs." These were often read aloud within Christian communities to mark the anniversary of the martyr's death. In general, three distinct types of "Acts of the Martyrs" can be identified.

1   Documents relating to the trial and execution of martyrs which were placed in public archives, and hence were available for consultation. Such documents take the form of official court proceedings, including the questions posed to the martyr, the answers given, and the sentence imposed. Although these documents lack literary polish, they nevertheless represent primary documentation of immense importance to historians.

2   The reports of eyewitnesses and other contemporaries concerning the arrest, trial, and execution of the martyr. The "Martyrdom of Polycarp" belongs to this category. Although there is clearly some embellishment of the details, the account has the "feel" of raw history.

3   Legendary material composed some considerable time after the event, designed to encourage and uplift those who read the material.

The "Martyrdom of Polycarp" takes the form of a letter written from the church at Smyrna to the Christian community of Philomelium, in the region of Greater Phrygia. The date of the martyrdom and letter are slightly unclear; it is generally thought that Polycarp died on February 23, 155 or 156, and that the letter was written shortly after-wards. Despite the obvious interpolations in the text, which can probably be put down to the enthusiasm of later copyists, the document remains of historical and literary im-portance, and merits reproduction in full.

The Encyclical Epistle of the Church at Smyrna concerning the Martyrdom of the Holy Polycarp

The Church of God which sojourns at Smyrna, to the Church of God sojourning in Philomelium, and to all the congregations of the Holy and Catholic Church in every place: Mercy, peace, and love from God the Father, and our Lord Jesus Christ, be multiplied.

Chapter I – Subject of Which We Write

We have written to you, brethren, as to what relates to the martyrs, and especially to the blessed Polycarp, who put an end to the persecution, having, as it were, set a seal upon it by his martyrdom. For almost all the events that happened previously [to this one] took place that the Lord might show us from above a martyrdom becoming the Gospel. For he waited to be delivered up, even as the Lord had done, that we also might become his followers, while we look not merely at what concerns ourselves but have regard also to our neighbors. For it is the part of a true and well-founded love, not only to wish one's self to be saved, but also all the brethren.

Chapter II – The Wonderful Constancy of the Martyrs

All the martyrdoms, then, were blessed and noble which took place according to the will of God. For it becomes us who profess greater piety than others, to ascribe the authority over all things to God. And truly, who can fail to admire their nobleness of mind, and their patience, with that love toward their Lord which they displayed? – who, when they were so torn with scourges, that the frame of their bodies, even to the very inward veins and arteries, was laid open, still patiently endured, while even those that stood by pitied and bewailed them. But they reached such a pitch of magnanimity, that not one of them let a sigh or a groan escape them; thus proving to us all that those holy martyrs of Christ, at the very time when they suffered such torments, were absent from the body, or rather, that the Lord then stood by them, and communed with them. And, looking to the grace of Christ, they despised all the torments of this world, redeeming themselves from eternal punishment by [the suffering of] a single hour. For this reason the fire of their savage executioners appeared cool to them. For they kept before their view escape from that fire which is eternal and never shall be quenched, and looked forward with the eyes of their heart to those good things which are laid up for such as endure; things "which ear hath not heard, nor eye seen, neither have entered into the heart of man," but were revealed by the Lord to them, inasmuch as they were no longer men, but had already become angels. And, in like manner, those who were condemned to the wild beasts endured dreadful tortures, being stretched out upon beds full of spikes, and subjected to various other kinds of torments, in order that, if it were possible, the tyrant might, by their lingering tortures, lead them to a denial [of Christ].

Chapter III – The Constancy of Germanicus. The Death of Polycarp is Demanded

For the devil did indeed invent many things against them; but thanks be to God, he could not prevail over all. For the most noble Germanicus strengthened the timidity of others by his own patience, and fought heroically with the wild beasts. For, when the proconsul sought to persuade him, and urged him to take pity upon his age, he attracted the wild beast toward himself, and provoked it, being desirous to escape all the more quickly from an unrighteous and impious world. But upon this the whole multitude, marveling at the nobility of mind displayed by the devout and godly race of Christians, cried out, "Away with the Atheists; let Polycarp be sought out!"

Chapter IV – Quintus the Apostate

Now one named Quintus, a Phrygian, who was but lately come from Phrygia, when he saw the wild beasts, became afraid. This was the man who forced himself and some others to come forward voluntarily [for trial]. Him the proconsul, after many entreaties, persuaded to swear and to offer sacrifice. Wherefore, brethren, we do not commend those who give themselves up [to suffering], seeing the Gospel does not teach so to do.

Chapter V – The Departure and Vision of Polycarp

But the most admirable Polycarp, when he first heard [that he was sought for], was in no measure disturbed, but resolved to continue in the city. However, in deference to the wish of many, he was persuaded to leave it. He departed, therefore, to a country house not far distant from the city. There he stayed with a few [friends], engaged in nothing else night and day than praying for all men, and for the Churches throughout the world, according to his usual custom. And while he was praying, a vision presented itself to him three days before he was taken; and, behold, the pillow under his head seemed to him on fire. Upon this, turning to those that were with him, he said to them prophetically, "I must be burnt alive."

Chapter VI – Polycarp is Betrayed by a Servant

And when those who sought for him were at hand, he departed to another dwelling, whither his pursuers immediately came after him. And when they found him not, they seized upon two youths [that were there], one of whom, being subjected to torture, confessed. It was thus impossible that he should continue hid, since those that betrayed him were of his own household. The Irenarch then (whose office is the same as that of the Cleronomus), by name Herod, hastened to bring him into the stadium. [This all happened] that he might fulfill his special lot, being made a partaker of Christ, and that they who betrayed him might undergo the punishment of Judas himself.

Chapter VII – Polycarp is Found by His Pursuers

His pursuers then, along with horsemen, and taking the youth with them, went forth at supper-time on the day of the preparation with their usual weapons, as if going out against a robber. And being come about evening [to the place where he was], they found him lying down in the upper room of a certain little house, from which he might have escaped into another place; but he refused, saying, "The will of God be done." So when he heard that they were come, he went down and spake with them. And as those that were present marveled at his age and constancy, some of them said. "Was so much effort made to capture such a venerable man?" Immediately then, in that very hour, he ordered that something to eat and drink should be set before them, as much indeed as they cared for, while he besought them to allow him an hour to pray without disturbance. And on their giving him leave, he stood and prayed, being full of the grace of God, so that he could not cease for two full hours, to the astonishment of them that heard him, insomuch that many began to repent that they had come forth against so godly and venerable an old man.

Chapter VIII – Polycarp is Brought into the City

Now, as soon as he had ceased praying, having made mention of all that had at any time come in contact with him, both small and great, illustrious and obscure, as well as the whole Catholic Church throughout the world, the time of his departure having arrived, they set him upon an ass, and conducted him into the city, the day being that of the great Sabbath. And the Irenarch Herod, accompanied by his father Nicetes (both riding in a chariot), met him, and taking him up into the chariot, they seated themselves beside him, and endeavored to persuade him, saying, "What harm is there in saying, Lord Caesar, and in sacrificing, with the other ceremonies observed on such occasions, and so make sure of safety?" But he at first gave them no answer; and when they continued to urge him, he said, "I shall not do as you advise me." So they, having no hope of persuading him, began to speak bitter words unto him, and cast him with violence out of the chariot, insomuch that, in getting down from the carriage, he dislocated his leg [by the fall]. But without being disturbed, and as if suffering nothing, he went eagerly forward with all haste, and was conducted to the stadium, where the tumult was so great, that there was no possibility of being heard.

Chapter IX – Polycarp Refuses to Revile Christ

Now, as Polycarp was entering into the stadium, there came to him a voice from heaven, saying, "Be strong, and show thyself a man, O Polycarp!" No one saw who it was that spoke to him; but those of our brethren who were present heard the voice. And as he was brought forward, the tumult became great when they heard that Polycarp was taken. And when he came near, the proconsul asked him whether he was Polycarp. On his confessing that he was, [the proconsul] sought to persuade him to deny [Christ], saying, "Have respect to thy old age," and other similar things, according to their custom, [such as] "Swear by the fortune of Caesar; repent, and say, Away with the Atheists." But Polycarp, gazing with a stern countenance on all the multitude of the wicked heathen then in the stadium, and waving his hand toward them, while with groans he looked up to heaven, said, "Away with the Atheists." Then, the proconsul urging him, and saying, "Swear, and I will set thee at liberty, reproach Christ," Polycarp declared, "Eighty and six years have I served Him, and He never did me any injury: how then can I blaspheme my King and my Savior?"

Chapter X – Polycarp Confesses Himself a Christian

And when the proconsul yet again pressed him, and said, "Swear by the fortune of Caesar," he answered, "Since thou art vainly urgent that, as thou sayest, I should swear by the fortune of Caesar, and pretendest not to know who and what I am, hear me declare with boldness, I am a Christian. And if you wish to learn what the doctrines of Christianity are, appoint me a day, and thou shalt hear them." The proconsul replied, "Persuade the people." But Polycarp said, "To thee I have thought it right to offer an account [of my faith]; for we are taught to give all due honor (which entails no injury upon ourselves) to the powers and authorities which are ordained of God. But as for these, I do not deem them worthy of receiving any account from me."

Chapter XI – No Threats Have Any Effect on Polycarp

The proconsul then said to him, "I have wild beasts at hand; to these will I cast thee, except thou repent." But he answered, "Call them then, for we are not accustomed to repent of what is good in order to adopt that which is evil; and it is well for me to be changed from what is evil to what is righteous." But again the proconsul said to him, "I will cause thee to be consumed by fire, seeing thou despisest the wild beasts, if thou wilt not repent." But Polycarp said, "Thou threatenest me with fire which burneth for an hour, and after a little is extinguished, but art ignorant of the fire of the coming judgment and of eternal punishment, reserved for the ungodly. But why tarriest thou? Bring forth what thou wilt."

Chapter XII – Polycarp is Sentenced to Be Burned

While he spoke these and many other like things, he was filled with confidence and joy, and his countenance was full of grace, so that not merely did it not fall as if troubled by the things said to him, but, on the contrary, the proconsul was astonished, and sent his herald to proclaim in the midst of the stadium thrice, "Polycarp has confessed that he is a Christian." This proclamation having been made by the herald, the whole multitude both of the heathen and Jews, who dwelt at Smyrna, cried out with uncontrollable fury, and in a loud voice, "This is the teacher of Asia, the father of the Christians, and the overthrower of our gods, he who has been teaching many not to sacrifice, or to worship the gods." Speaking thus, they cried out, and besought Philip the Asiarch to let loose a lion upon Polycarp. But Philip answered that it was not lawful for him to do so, seeing the shows of wild beasts were already finished. Then it seemed good to them to cry out with one consent, that Polycarp should be burnt alive. For thus it behooved the vision which was revealed to him in regard to his pillow to be fulfilled, when, seeing it on fire as he was praying, he turned about and said prophetically to the faithful that were with him, "I must be burnt alive."

Chapter XIII – The Funeral Pile is Erected

This, then, was carried into effect with greater speed than it was spoken, the multitudes immediately gathering together wood and fagots out of the shops and baths; the Jews especially, according to custom, eagerly assisting them in it. And when the funeral pile was ready, Polycarp, laying aside all his garments, and loosing his girdle, sought also to take off his sandals – a thing he was not accustomed to do, inasmuch as every one of the faithful was always eager who should first touch his skin. For, on account of his holy life, he was, even before his martyrdom, adorned with every kind of good. Immediately then they surrounded him with those substances which had been prepared for the funeral pile. But when they were about also to fix him with nails, he said, "Leave me as I am; for He that giveth me strength to endure the fire, will also enable me, without your securing me by nails, to remain without moving in the pile."

Chapter XIV – The Prayer of Polycarp

They did not nail him then, but simply bound him. And he, placing his hands behind him, and being bound like a distinguished ram [taken] out of a great flock for sacrifice, and prepared to be an acceptable burnt-offering unto God, looked up to heaven, and said, "O Lord God Almighty, the Father of thy beloved and blessed Son Jesus Christ, by whom we have received the knowledge of Thee, the God of angels and powers, and of every creature, and of the whole race of the righteous who live before thee, I give Thee thanks that Thou hast counted me, worthy of this day and this hour, that I should have a part in the number of Thy martyrs, in the cup of thy Christ, to the resurrection of eternal life, both of soul and body, through the incorruption [imparted] by the Holy Ghost. Among whom may I be accepted this day before Thee as a fat and acceptable sacrifice, according as Thou, the ever-truthful God, hast fore-ordained, hast revealed beforehand to me, and now hast fulfilled. Wherefore also I praise Thee for all things, I bless Thee, I glorify Thee, along with the everlasting and heavenly Jesus Christ, Thy beloved Son, with whom, to Thee, and the Holy Ghost, be glory both now and to all coming ages. Amen."

Chapter XV – Polycarp is Not Injured by the Fire

When he had pronounced this amen, and so finished his prayer, those who were appointed for the purpose kindled the fire. And as the flame blazed forth in great fury, we, to whom it was given to witness it, beheld a great miracle, and have been preserved that we might report to others what then took place. For the fire, shaping itself into the form of an arch, like the sail of a ship when filled with the wind, encompassed as by a circle the body of the martyr. And he appeared within not like flesh which is burnt, but as bread that is baked, or as gold and silver glowing in a furnace. Moreover, we perceived such a sweet odour [coming from the pile], as if frankincense or some such precious spices had been smoking there.

Chapter XVI – Polycarp is Pierced by a Dagger

At length, when those wicked men perceived that his body could not be consumed by the fire, they commanded an executioner to go near and pierce him through with a dagger. And on his doing this, there came forth a dove, and a great quantity of blood, so that the fire was extinguished; and all the people wondered that there should be such a difference between the unbelievers and the elect, of whom this most admirable Polycarp was one, having in our own times been an apostolic and prophetic teacher, and bishop of the Catholic Church which is in Smyrna. For every word that went out of his mouth either has been or shall yet be accomplished.

Chapter XVII – The Christians are Refused Polycarp's Body

But when the adversary of the race of the righteous, the envious, malicious, and wicked one, perceived the impressive nature of his martyrdom, and [considered] the blameless life he had led from the beginning, and how he was now crowned with the wreath of immortality, having beyond dispute received his reward, he did his utmost that not the least memorial of him should be taken away by us, although many desired to do this, and to become possessors of his holy flesh. For this end he suggested it to Nicetes, the father of Herod and brother of Alce, to go and entreat the governor not to give up his body to be buried, "lest," said he, "forsaking Him that was crucified, they begin to worship this one." This he said at the suggestion and urgent persuasion of the Jews, who also watched us, as we sought to take him out of the fire, being ignorant of this, that it is neither possible for us ever to forsake Christ, who suffered for the salvation of such as shall be saved throughout the whole world (the blameless one for sinners), nor to worship any other. For Him indeed, as being the Son of God, we adore; but the martyrs, as disciples and followers of the Lord, we worthily love on account of their extraordinary affection toward their own King and Master, of whom may we also be made companions and fellow-disciples!

Chapter XVIII – The Body of Polycarp is Burned

The centurion then, seeing the strife excited by the Jews, placed the body in the midst of the fire, and consumed it. Accordingly, we afterwards took up his bones, as being more precious than the most exquisite jewels, and more purified than gold, and deposited them in a fitting place, whither, being gathered together, as opportunity is allowed us, with joy and rejoicing, the Lord shall grant us to celebrate the anniversary of his martyrdom, both in memory of those who have already finished their course, and for the exercising and preparation of those yet to walk in their steps.

Chapter XIX – Praise of the Martyr Polycarp

This, then, is the account of the blessed Polycarp, who, being the twelfth that was martyred in Smyrna (reckoning those also of Philadelphia), yet occupies a place of his own in the memory of all men, insomuch that he is everywhere spoken of by the heathen themselves. He was not merely an illustrious teacher, but also a pre-eminent martyr, whose martyrdom all desire to imitate, as having been altogether consistent with the Gospel of Christ. For, having through patience overcome the unjust governor, and thus acquired the crown of immortality, he now, with the apostles and all the righteous [in heaven], rejoicingly glorifies God, even the Father, and blesses our Lord Jesus Christ, the Savior of our souls, the Governor of our bodies, and the Shepherd of the Catholic Church throughout the world.

Chapter XX – This Epistle is to Be Transmitted to the Brethren

Since, then, ye requested that we would at large make you acquainted with what really took place, we have for the present sent you this summary account through our brother Marcus. When, therefore, ye have yourselves read this Epistle, be pleased to send it to the brethren at a greater distance, that they also may glorify the Lord, who makes such choice of His own servants. To Him who is able to bring us all by His grace and goodness into his everlasting kingdom, through His only-begotten Son Jesus Christ, to Him be glory, and honor, and power, and majesty, for ever. Amen. Salute all the saints. They that are with us salute you, and Evarestus, who wrote this Epistle, with all his house.

Chapter XXI – The Date of the Martyrdom

Now, the blessed Polycarp suffered martyrdom on the second day of the month Xanthicus just begun, the seventh day before the Kalends of May, on the great Sabbath, at the eighth hour. He was taken by Herod, Philip the Trallian being high priest, Statius Quadratus being proconsul, but Jesus Christ being King for ever, to whom be glory, honor, majesty, and an everlasting throne, from generation to generation. Amen.

Chapter XXII – Salutation

We wish you, brethren, all happiness, while you walk according to the doctrine of the Gospel of Jesus Christ; with whom be glory to God the Father and the Holy Spirit, for the salvation of His holy elect, after whose example the blessed Polycarp suffered, following in whose steins may we too be found in the kingdom of Jesus Christ!

These things Caius transcribed from the copy of Irenaeus (who was a disciple of Polycarp), having himself been intimate with Irenaeus. And I Socrates transcribed them at Corinth from the copy of Caius. Grace be with you all.

And I again, Pionius, wrote them from the previously written copy, having carefully searched into them, and the blessed Polycarp having manifested them to me through a revelation, even as I shall show in what follows. I have collected these things, when they had almost faded away through the lapse of time, that the Lord Jesus Christ may also gather me along with His elect into His heavenly kingdom, to whom, with the Father and the Holy Spirit, be glory for ever and ever. Amen.

Questions for Discussion

nomadic whole went people went compliant

1 The text opens with a reference to "the Church of God which sojourns at Smyrna." The word "sojourns" means something like "wanders" or "has temporary residence." It implies a lack of permanent fixture. What does this phrase tell us about early Christian understandings of the nature of the church?

2 The original text is thought to have been "improved" by later editors, who appeared to have inserted additional material at certain points. Can you identify points at which material seems to have been added? What kind of material does it seem to be?

3 Why do you think this document achieved such a wide circulation and readership in early Christian circles?

CHAPTER 4

Irenaeus of Lyons (ca. 130–ca. 200)

Relatively little is known of the life of Irenaeus. He was born in Asia Minor (now Turkey), and we find references within his writings to his memories as a boy, when he heard the sermons of the great bishop and martyr Polycarp of Smyrna, who many regarded as a disciple of the apostles themselves. It was from this source that he came to know what he called "the genuine unadulterated gospel," to which he would remain faithful throughout his long life and ministry.

There are suggestions that he may have accompanied Polycarp on his journey to Rome in connection with a controversy over the date of celebrating Easter, in 154. The churches of Irenaeus' native Asia Minor continued to celebrate Easter on the same date (the 14th of Nisan) as the Jews celebrated Passover. The church at Rome, however, insisted that Easter should always be celebrated on a Sunday (the day of the Resurrection). Irenaeus appears to have acted as a peacemaker in this controversy, and brokered some kind of deal between them. Irenaeus argued that differences in external factors, such as dates of festivals, need not be so serious as to destroy church unity.

What is known with greater certainty is that he later went as a missionary to southern Gaul, where he became a presbyter at the city of Lyons, although the date of his arrival in that city remains obscure. Irenaeus was absent from the city on ecclesiastical business when the persecution there reached its zenith. It seems that he had been sent to Rome by the Gallican churches in order to confer with Pope Eleutherus, perhaps as a mediator in the disputes over whether Montanism (a sect which would later number Tertullian as one of its more prominent converts) should be tolerated in Asia Minor. It seems that Irenaeus did not remain in Rome for long. By 178, he had been consecrated as bishop of Lyons as the successor to Pothinus. The date and circumstances of Irenaeus' death remain obscure. Jerome and other writers state that he died as a martyr in the persecution under the Emperor Septimus Severus (202).

Irenaeus of Lyons (ca. 130–ca. 200)

Basic description
Second-century bishop of Lyons, and defender of Christianity.

Major works
Against all Heresies; The Demonstration of the Apostolic Preaching.

Major studies
Robert M. Grant, *Irenaeus of Lyons*. London: Routledge, 1997.

Gustaf Wingren, *Man and the Incarnation: A Study in the Biblical Theology of Irenaeus*. Edinburgh: Oliver & Boyd, 1959.

Irenaeus can be seen as an important mediating link between eastern and western churches, at a time when they were beginning to go their separate ways. Irenaeus can be seen as the first great Catholic theologian, a champion of Christian orthodoxy against the forms of Gnosticism which were flourishing in the Roman Empire of his day. Irenaeus' most important work is considered to be his *Against all Heresies*, which specifically addresses Gnosticism as a major threat to the Christian faith. This work represents a highly significant literary genre, not by any means restricted to the early phase of Christianity – the polemical writing.

A polemical work aims to neutralize the threat posed by a rival approach to the Christian faith from within, or a threat from outside the church. *Against all Heresies* sets out to identify and refute the ideas of Gnosticism, and specifically the form of this movement which was associated with Valentinus. We shall explore this further in what follows.

Text: *Against all Heresies*

The work *Adversus Haereses*, more commonly known as *Against all heresies*, was written in the Greek language. Although some parts of the Greek text survive, the only full text of the work is found in Latin translation. The work consists of five major books, most of which are dedicated to identifying the precise nature of the Gnostic teachings, and indicating why they should be rejected by Christians. It is clear from the outset that Irenaeus has a particular concern for a form of Christian Gnosticism known as "Valentinianism," which was exercising considerable influence at the time.

So who was this Valentinus, against whom Irenaeus directed such severe criticisms? Valentinus was a second-century Christian mystic and poet, who is usually referred to as a "Gnostic" on account of the importance that he attaches to a mystical or secret knowledge (Greek: *gnosis*). Valentinus was born in Phrebonis in Upper Egypt about 100, and was educated in nearby Alexandria. There he became a disciple of the Christian teacher Theudas who had been a disciple of Saint Paul. He claimed that Theudas taught him a secret wisdom that Paul had taught privately to his inner circle.

Following what he described as a vision of the risen Christ, Valentinus began his career as a Christian teacher at Alexandria around 125. His esoteric theology quickly attracted a large following in Egypt and Syria. In 136, he went to Rome, where he quickly rose to prominence and attention. Nothing certain is known of his later career. Even his place and date of death are uncertain; he may have died at Rome around 155 AD. According to a late (and possibly unreliable) source, he left Rome and went to Cyprus. After Valentinus' death, his disciples developed his ideas further, and spread them throughout the Roman Empire.

The ideas against which Irenaeus campaigned so vigorously were thus relatively recent. Valentinianism was a recent arrival in the Latin-speaking world, and may well have attracted attention precisely on account of its novelty. Irenaeus clearly regarded it as a serious threat, and took it very seriously. Its appeal lay in its esoteric character; Valentinianism offered privileged access to spiritual secrets and mysteries, which were hidden from the masses, and made available to a select elite. According to Valentinus, his followers had access to certain secret esoteric teachings of Jesus that were passed on in secret. When Jesus spoke in public, he used metaphors that did not disclose his complete teachings. He only passed them on to his disciples in private. Valentinus claimed that he had learned these secret teachings from Theudas, who in turn learned them from Paul, who received them through a vision of the risen Christ.

According to Valentinus, this secret tradition provides the key that is essential for a complete understanding of Jesus' message. Irenaeus argued that all that Jesus said which was essential to salvation was publicly accessible through the preaching and teaching of the church. There were no spiritual "secrets," no hidden teachings.

To illustrate Irenaeus' approach we shall consider two sections of *Against all Heresies.* The first extract, taken from the preface and opening sections of Book 1, provides an introduction to the teachings of Valentinus; the second, taken from the opening sections of Book 2, offers a criticism of these teachings.

Book 1, Preface

1   Inasmuch as certain men have set the truth aside, and bring in lying words and vain genealogies, which, as the apostle says, "minister questions rather than godly edifying which is in faith," and by means of their craftily-constructed plausibilities draw away the minds of the inexperienced and take them captive, I have felt constrained, my dear friend, to compose the following treatise in order to expose and counteract their machinations. These men falsify the oracles of God, and prove themselves evil interpreters of the good word of revelation. They also overthrow the faith of many, by drawing them away, under a pretense of [superior] knowledge, from Him who rounded and adorned the universe; as if, forsooth, they had something more excellent and sublime to reveal, than that God who created the heaven and the earth, and all things that are therein. By means of specious and plausible words, they cunningly allure the simple-minded to inquire into their system; but they nevertheless clumsily destroy them, while they initiate them into their blasphemous and impious opinions respecting the Demiurge; and these simple ones are unable, even in such a matter, to distinguish falsehood from truth.

2   Error, indeed, is never set forth in its naked deformity, lest, being thus exposed, it should at once be detected. But it is craftily decked out in an attractive dress, so

as, by its outward form, to make it appear to the inexperienced (ridiculous as the expression may seem) more true than the truth itself. One far superior to me has well said, in reference to this point, "A clever imitation in glass casts contempt, as it were, on that precious jewel the emerald (which is most highly esteemed by some), unless it come under the eye of one able to test and expose the counterfeit. Or, again, what inexperienced person can with ease detect the presence of brass when it has been mixed up with silver?" Lest, therefore, through my neglect, some should be carried off, even as sheep are by wolves, while they perceive not the true character of these men – because they outwardly are covered with sheep's clothing (against whom the Lord has enjoined us to be on our guard), and because their language resembles ours, while their sentiments are very different – I have deemed it my duty (after reading some of the Commentaries, as they call them, of the disciples of Valentinus, and after making myself acquainted with their tenets through personal intercourse with some of them) to unfold to thee, my friend, these portentous and profound mysteries, which do not fall within the range of every intellect, because all have not sufficiently purged their brains. I do this, in order that thou, obtaining an acquaintance with these things, mayest in turn explain them to all those with whom thou art connected, and exhort them to avoid such an abyss of madness and of blasphemy against Christ. I intend, then, to the best of my ability, with brevity and clearness to set forth the opinions of those who are now promulgating heresy. I refer especially to the disciples of Ptolemaeus, whose school may be described as a bud from that of Valentinus. I shall also endeavor, according to my moderate ability, to furnish the means of overthrowing them, by showing how absurd and inconsistent with the truth are their statements. Not that I am practiced either in composition or eloquence; but my feeling of affection prompts me to make known to thee and all thy companions those doctrines which have been kept in concealment until now, but which are at last, through the goodness of God, brought to light. "For there is nothing hidden which shall not be revealed, nor secret that shall not be made known."

3 Thou wilt not expect from me, who am resident among the Keltae, and am accustomed for the most part to use a barbarous dialect, any display of rhetoric, which I have never learned, or any excellence of composition, which I have never practiced, or any beauty and persuasiveness of style, to which I make no pretensions. But thou wilt accept in a kindly spirit what I in a like spirit write to thee simply, truthfully, and in my own homely way; whilst thou thyself (as being more capable than I am) wilt expand those ideas of which I send thee, as it were, only the seminal principles; and in the comprehensiveness of thy understanding, wilt develop to their full extent the points on which I briefly touch, so as to set with power before thy companions those things which I have uttered in weakness. In fine, as I (to gratify thy long-cherished desire for information regarding the tenets of these persons) have spared no pains, not only to make these doctrines known to thee, but also to furnish the means of showing their falsity; so shalt thou, according to the grace given to thee by the Lord, prove an earnest and efficient minister to others, that men may no longer be drawn away by the plausible system of these heretics, which I now proceed to describe.

Chapter I – The Absurd Ideas Of The Disciples Of Valentinus As To The Origin, Name, Order, And Conjugal Productions Of Their Fancied Aeons, With The Passages Of Scripture Which They Adapt To Their Opinions

1   They maintain, then, that in the invisible and ineffable heights above there exists a certain perfect, pre-existent Æon, whom they call Proarche, Propator, and Bythus, and describe as being invisible and incomprehensible. Eternal and unbegotten, he remained throughout innumerable cycles of ages in profound serenity and quiescence. There existed along with him Ennoea, whom they also call Charis and Sige. At last this Bythus determined to send forth from himself the beginning of all things, and deposited this production (which he had resolved to bring forth) in his contemporary Sige, even as seed is deposited in the womb. She then, having received this seed, and becoming pregnant, gave birth to Nous, who was both similar and equal to him who had produced him, and was alone capable of comprehending his father's greatness. This Nous they call also Monogenes, and Father, and the Beginning of all Things. Along with him was also produced Aletheia; and these four constituted the first and first-begotten Pythagorean Tetrad, which they also denominate the root of all things. For there are first Bythus and Sige, and then Nous and Aletheia. And Monogenes, perceiving for what purpose he had been produced, also himself sent forth Logos and Zoe, being the father of all those who were to come after him, and the beginning and fashioning of the entire Pleroma. By the conjunction of Logos and Zoe were brought forth Anthropos and Ecclesia; and thus was formed the first-begotten Ogdoad, the root and substance of all things, called among them by four names, viz., Bythus, and Nous, and Logos, and Anthropos. For each of these is masculo-feminine, as follows: Propator was united by a conjunction with his Ennoea; then Monogenes, that is Nous, with Aletheia; Logos with Zoe, and Anthropos with Ecclesia.

2   These Æons having been produced for the glory of the Father, and wishing, by their own efforts, to effect this object, sent forth emanations by means of conjunction. Logos and Zoe, after producing Anthropos and Ecclesia, sent forth other ten Æons, whose names are the following: Bythius and Mixis, Ageratos and Henosis, Autophyes and Hedone, Acinetos and Syncrasis, Monogenes and Macaria. These are the ten Æons whom they declare to have been produced by Logos and Zoe. They then add that Anthropos himself, along with Ecclesia, produced twelve Æons, to whom they give the following names: Paracletus and Pistis, Patricos and Elpis, Metricos and Agape, Ainos and Synesis, Ecclesiasticus and Macariotes, Theletos and Sophia.

3   Such are the thirty Æons in the erroneous system of these men; and they are described as being wrapped up, so to speak, in silence, and known to none [except these professing teachers]. Moreover, they declare that this invisible and spiritual Pleroma of theirs is tripartite, being divided into an Ogdoad, a Decad, and a Duodecad. And for this reason they affirm it was that the "Saviour" – for they do not please to call Him "Lord" – did no work in public during the space of thirty years, thus setting forth the mystery of these Æons. They maintain also, that these thirty Æons are most plainly indicated in the parable of the laborers sent into the

vineyard. For some are sent about the first hour, others about the third hour, others about the sixth hour, others about the ninth hour, and others about the eleventh hour. Now, if we add up the numbers of the hours here mentioned, the sum total will be thirty: for one, three, six, nine, and eleven, when added together, form thirty. And by the hours, they hold that the Æons were pointed out; while they maintain that these are great, and wonderful, and hitherto unspeakable mysteries which it is their special function to develop; and so they proceed when they find anything in the multitude of things contained in the Scriptures which they can adopt and accommodate to their baseless speculations.

Chapter II – The Propator Was Known To Monogenes Alone. The Ambition, Disturbance, And Danger Into Which Sophia Fell; Her Shapeless Offspring: She Is Restored By Horos. The Production Of Christ And Of The Holy Spirit; The Completion Of The Æons. Manner Of The Production Of Jesus

1   They proceed to tell us that the Propator of their scheme was known only to Monogenes, who sprang from him; in other words, only to Nous, while to all the others he was invisible and incomprehensible. And, according to them, Nous alone took pleasure in contemplating the Father, and exulting in considering his immeasurable greatness; while he also meditated how he might communicate to the rest of the Æons the greatness of the Father, revealing to them how vast and mighty he was, and how he was without beginning – beyond comprehension, and altogether incapable of being seen. But, in accordance with the will of the Father, Sige restrained him, because it was his design to lead them all to an acquaintance with the aforesaid Propator, and to create within them a desire of investigating his nature. In like manner, the rest of the Æons also, in a kind of quiet way, had a wish to behold the Author of their being, and to contemplate that First Cause which had no beginning.

2   But there rushed forth in advance of the rest that Æon who was much the latest of them, and was the youngest of the Duodecad which sprang from Anthropos and Ecclesia, namely Sophia, and suffered passion apart from the embrace of her consort Theletos. This passion, indeed, first arose among those who were connected with Nous and Aletheia, but passed as by contagion to this degenerate Æon, who acted under a pretense of love, but was in reality influenced by temerity, because she had not, like Nous, enjoyed communion with the perfect Father. This passion, they say, consisted in a desire to search into the nature of the Father; for she wished, according to them, to comprehend his greatness. When she could not attain her end, inasmuch as she aimed at an impossibility, and thus became involved in an extreme agony of mind, while both on account of the vast profundity as well as the unsearchable nature of the Father, and on account of the love she bore him, she was ever stretching herself forward, there was danger lest she should at last have been absorbed by his sweetness, and resolved into his absolute essence, unless she had met with that Power which supports all things, and preserves them outside of the unspeakable greatness. This power they term Horos; by whom, they say, she was restrained and supported; and that then, having with difficulty been brought back to herself, she

was convinced that the Father is incomprehensible, and so laid aside her original design, along with that passion which had arisen within her from the overwhelming influence of her admiration.

3 But others of them fabulously describe the passion and restoration of Sophia as follows: They say that she, having engaged in an impossible and impracticable attempt, brought forth an amorphous substance, such as her female nature enabled her to produce. When she looked upon it, her first feeling was one of grief, on account of the imperfection of its generation, and then of fear lest this should end her own existence. Next she lost, as it were, all command of herself, and was in the greatest perplexity while endeavoring to discover the cause of all this, and in what way she might conceal what had happened. Being greatly harassed by these passions, she at last changed her mind, and endeavored to return anew to the Father. When, however, she in some measure made the attempt, strength failed her, and she became a sup-pliant of the Father. The other Æons, Nous in particular, presented their supplica-tions along with her. And hence they declare material substance had its beginning from ignorance and grief, and fear and bewilderment.

4 The Father afterwards produces, in his own image, by means of Monogenes, the above-mentioned Horos, without conjunction, masculo-feminine. For they maintain that sometimes the Father acts in conjunction with Sige, but that at other times he shows himself independent both of male and female. They term this Horos both Stauros and Lytrotes, and Carpistes, and Horothetes, and Metagoges. And by this Horos they declare that Sophia was purified and established, while she was also restored to her proper conjunction. For her enthymesis (or inborn idea) having been taken away from her, along with its supervening passion, she herself certainly remained within the Pleroma; but her enthymesis, with its passion, was separated from her by Horos, fenced off, and expelled from that circle. This enthymesis was, no doubt, a spiritual substance, possessing some of the natural tendencies of an Æon, but at the same time shapeless and without form, because it had received nothing. And on this account they say that it was an imbecile and feminine production.

5 After this substance had been placed outside of the Pleroma of the Æons, and its mother restored to her proper conjunction, they tell us that Monogenes, acting in accordance with the prudent forethought of the Father, gave origin to another conjugal pair, namely Christ and the Holy Spirit (lest any of the Æons should fall into a calamity similar to that of Sophia), for the purpose of fortifying and strength-ening the Pleroma, and who at the same time completed the number of the Æons. Christ then instructed them as to the nature of their conjunction, and taught them that those who possessed a comprehension of the Unbegotten were sufficient for themselves. He also announced among them what related to the knowledge of the Father – namely, that he cannot be understood or comprehended, nor so much as seen or heard, except in so far as he is known by Monogenes only. And the reason why the rest of the Æons possess perpetual existence is found in that part of the Father's nature which is incomprehensible; but the reason of their origin and for-mation was situated in that which may be comprehended regarding him, that is, in the Son. Christ, then, who had just been produced, effected these things among them.

6   But the Holy Spirit taught them to give thanks on being all rendered equal among themselves, and led them to a state of true repose. Thus, then, they tell us that the Æons were constituted equal to each other in form and sentiment, so that all became as Nous, and Logos, and Anthropos, and Christus. The female Æons, too, became all as Aletheia, and Zoe, and Spiritus, and Ecclesia. Everything, then, being thus established, and brought into a state of perfect rest, they next tell us that these beings sang praises with great joy to the Propator, who himself shared in the abounding exultation. Then, out of gratitude for the great benefit which had been conferred on them, the whole Pleroma of the Æons, with one design and desire, and with the concurrence of Christ and the Holy Spirit, their Father also setting the seal of His approval on their conduct, brought together whatever each one had in himself of the greatest beauty and preciousness; and uniting all these contributions so as skillfully to blend the whole, they produced, to the honor and glory of Bythus, a being of most perfect beauty, the very star of the Pleroma, and the perfect fruit [of it], namely Jesus. Him they also speak of under the name of Savior, and Christ, and patronymically, Logos, and Everything, because He was formed from the contributions of all. And then we are told that, by way of honor, angels of the same nature as Himself were simultaneously produced, to act as His body-guard.

Book 2, Preface

1   In the first book, which immediately precedes this, exposing "knowledge falsely so called," I showed thee, my very dear friend, that the whole system devised, in many and opposite ways, by those who are of the school of Valentinus, was false and baseless. I also set forth the tenets of their predecessors, proving that they not only differed among themselves, but had long previously swerved from the truth itself. I further explained, with all diligence, the doctrine as well as practice of Marcus the magician, since he, too, belongs to these persons; and I carefully noticed the passages which they garble from the Scriptures, with the view of adapting them to their own fictions. Moreover, I minutely narrated the manner in which, by means of numbers, and by the twenty-four letters of the alphabet, they boldly endeavor to establish [what they regard as] truth. I have also related how they think and teach that creation at large was formed after the image of their invisible Pleroma, and what they hold respecting the Demiurge, declaring at the same time the doctrine of Simon Magus of Samaria, their progenitor, and of all those who succeeded him. I mentioned, too, the multitude of those Gnostics who are sprung from him, and noticed the points of difference between them, their several doctrines, and the order of their succession, while I set forth all those heresies which have been originated by them. I showed, moreover, that all these heretics, taking their rise from Simon, have introduced impious and irreligious doctrines into this life; and I explained the nature of their "redemption," and their method of initiating those who are rendered "perfect," along with their invocations and their mysteries. I proved also that there is one God, the Creator, and that He is not the fruit of any defect, nor is there anything either above Him, or after Him.

2   In the present book, I shall establish those points which fit in with my design, so far as time permits, and overthrow, by means of lengthened treatment under distinct heads, their whole system; for which reason, since it is an exposure and subversion of their opinions, I have so entitled the composition of this work. For it is fitting, by a plain revelation and overthrow of their conjunctions, to put an end to these hidden alliances, and to Bythus himself, and thus to obtain a demonstration that he never existed at any previous time, nor now has any existence.

Chapter I – There Is But One God: The Impossibility Of Its Being Otherwise

1   It is proper, then, that I should begin with the first and most important head, that is, God the Creator, who made the heaven and the earth, and all things that are therein (whom these men blasphemously style the fruit of a defect), and to demonstrate that there is nothing either above Him or after Him; nor that, influenced by any one, but of His own free will, He created all things, since He is the only God, the only Lord, the only Creator, the only Father, alone containing all things, and Himself commanding all things into existence.

2   For how can there be any other Fulness, or Principle, or Power, or God, above Him, since it is a matter of necessity that God, the Pleroma (Fulness) of all these, should contain all things in His immensity, and should be contained by no one? But if there is anything beyond Him, He is not then the Pleroma of all, nor does He contain all. For that which they declare to be beyond Him will be wanting to the Pleroma, or, [in other words,] to that God who is above all things. But that which is wanting, and falls in any way short, is not the Pleroma of all things. In such a case, He would have both beginning, middle, and end, with respect to those who are beyond Him. And if He has an end in regard to those things which are below, He has also a beginning with respect to those things which are above. In like manner, there is an absolute necessity that He should experience the very same thing at all other points, and should be held in, bounded, and enclosed by those existences that are outside of Him. For that being who is the end downwards, necessarily circumscribes and surrounds him who finds his end in it. And thus, according to them, the Father of all (that is, He whom they call Proon and Proarche), with their Pleroma, and the good God of Marcion, is established and enclosed in some other, and is surrounded from without by another mighty Being, who must of necessity be greater, inasmuch as that which contains is greater than that which is contained. But then that which is greater is also stronger, and in a greater degree Lord; and that which is greater, and stronger, and in a greater degree Lord – must be God.

3   Now, since there exists, according to them, also something else which they declare to be outside of the Pleroma, into which they further hold there descended that higher power who went astray, it is in every way necessary that the Pleroma either contains that which is beyond, yet is contained (for otherwise, it will not be beyond the Pleroma; for if there is anything beyond the Pleroma, there will be a Pleroma within this very Pleroma which they declare to be outside of the Pleroma,

and the Pleroma will be contained by that which is beyond: and with the Pleroma is understood also the first God); or, again, they must be an infinite distance separated from each other – the Pleroma [I mean], and that which is beyond it. But if they maintain this, there will then be a third kind of existence, which separates by immensity the Pleroma and that which is beyond it. This third kind of existence will therefore bound and contain both the others, and will be greater both than the Pleroma, and than that which is beyond it, inasmuch as it contains both in its bosom. In this way, talk might go on for ever concerning those things which are contained, and those which contain. For if this third existence has its beginning above, and its end beneath, there is an absolute necessity that it be also bounded on the sides, either beginning or ceasing at certain other points [where new existences begin]. These, again, and others which are above and below, will have their beginnings at certain other points, and so on ad infinitum; so that their thoughts would never rest in one God, but, in consequence of seeking after more than exists, would wander away to that which has no existence, and depart from the true God.

4   These remarks are, in like manner, applicable against the followers of Marcion. For his two gods will also be contained and circumscribed by an immense interval which separates them from one another. But then there is a necessity to suppose a multitude of gods separated by an immense distance from each other on every side, beginning with one another, and ending in one another. Thus, by that very process of reasoning on which they depend for teaching that there is a certain Pleroma or God above the Creator of heaven and earth, any one who chooses to employ it may maintain that there is another Pleroma above the Pleroma, above that again another, and above Bythus another ocean of Deity, while in like manner the same successions hold with respect to the sides; and thus, their doctrine flowing out into immensity, there will always be a necessity to conceive of other Pleroma, and other Bythi, so as never at any time to stop, but always to continue seeking for others besides those already mentioned. Moreover, it will be uncertain whether these which we conceive of are below, or are, in fact, themselves the things which are above; and, [in like manner, will be doubtful] respecting those things which are said by them to be above, whether they are really above or below; and thus our opinions will have no fixed conclusion or certainty, but will of necessity wander forth after worlds without limits, and gods that cannot be numbered.

5   These things, then, being so, each deity will be contented with his own possessions, and will not be moved with any curiosity respecting the affairs of others; otherwise he would be unjust, and rapacious, and would cease to be what God is. Each creation, too, will glorify its own maker, and will be contented with him, not knowing any other; otherwise it would most justly be deemed an apostate by all the others, and would receive a richly-deserved punishment. For it must be either that there is one Being who contains all things, and formed in His own territory all those things which have been created, according to His own will; or, again, that there are numerous unlimited creators and gods, who begin from each other, and end in each other on every side; and it will then be necessary to allow that all the rest are contained from without by some one who is greater, and that they are each of them shut up within their own territory, and remain in it. No one of them all, therefore, is God.

For there will be [much] wanting to every one of them, possessing [as he will do] only a very small part when compared with all the rest. The name of the Omnipotent will thus be brought to an end, and such an opinion will of necessity fall to impiety.

Chapter II – The World Was Not Formed By Angels, Or By Any Other Being, Contrary To The Will Of The Most High God, But Was Made By The Father Through The Word

1 Those, moreover, who say that the world was formed by angels, or by any other maker of it, contrary to the will of Him who is the Supreme Father, err first of all in this very point, that they maintain that angels formed such and so mighty a creation, contrary to the will of the Most High God. This would imply that angels were more powerful than God; or if not so, that He was either careless, or inferior, or paid no regard to those things which took place among His own possessions, whether they turned out ill or well, so that He might drive away and prevent the one, while He praised and rejoiced over the other. But if one would not ascribe such conduct even to a man of any ability, how much less to God.

2 Next let them tell us whether these things have been formed within the limits which are contained by Him, and in His proper territory, or in regions belonging to others, and lying beyond Him? But if they say [that these things were done] beyond Him, then all the absurdities already mentioned will face them, and the Supreme God will be enclosed by that which is beyond Him, in which also it will be necessary that He should find His end. If, on the other hand, [these things were done] within His own proper territory, it will be very idle to say that the world was thus formed within His proper territory against His will by angels who are themselves under His power, or by any other being, as if either He Himself did not behold all things which take place among His own possessions, or He was not aware of the things to be done by angels.

3 If, however, [the things referred to were done] not against His will, but with His concurrence and knowledge, as some [of these men] think, the angels, or the Former of the world [whoever that may have been], will no longer be the causes of that formation, but the will of God. For if He is the Former of the world, He too made the angels, or at least was the cause of their creation; and He will be regarded as having made the world who prepared the causes of its formation. Although they maintain that the angels were made by a long succession downwards, or that the Former of the world [sprang] from the Supreme Father, as Basilides asserts; nevertheless that which is the cause of those things which have been made will still be traced to Him who was the Author of such a succession. [The case stands] just as regards success in war, which is ascribed to the king who prepared those things which are the cause of victory; and, in like manner, the creation of any state, or of any work, is referred to him who prepared materials for the accomplishment of those results which were afterwards brought about. Wherefore, we do not say that it was the axe which cut the wood, or the saw which divided it; but one would very properly say that the man cut and divided it who formed the axe and the saw for this purpose, and [who also formed] at a much earlier date all the tools by which the axe and the

saw themselves were formed. With justice, therefore, according to an analogous process of reasoning, the Father of all will be declared the Former of this world, and not the angels, nor any other [so-called] former of the world, other than He who was its Author, and had formerly been the cause of the preparation for a creation of this kind.

4   This manner of speech may perhaps be plausible or persuasive to those who know not God, and who liken Him to needy human beings, and to those who cannot immediately and without assistance form anything, but require many instrumentalities to produce what they intend. But it will not be regarded as at all probable by those who know that God stands in need of nothing, and that He created and made all things by His Word, while He neither required angels to assist Him in the production of those things which are made, nor of any power greatly inferior to Himself, and ignorant of the Father, nor of any defect or ignorance, in order that he who should know Him might become man. But He Himself in Himself, after a fashion which we can neither describe nor conceive, predestining all things, formed them as He pleased, bestowing harmony on all things, and assigning them their own place, and the beginning of their creation. In this way He conferred on spiritual things a spiritual and invisible nature, on super-celestial things a celestial, on angels an angelical, on animals an animal, on beings that swim a nature suited to the water, and on those that live on the land one fitted for the land – on all, in short, a nature suitable to the character of the life assigned them – while He formed all things that were made by His Word that never wearies.

5   For this is a peculiarity of the pre-eminence of God, not to stand in need of other instruments for the creation of those things which are summoned into existence. His own Word is both suitable and sufficient for the formation of all things, even as John, the disciple of the Lord, declares regarding Him: "All things were made by Him, and without Him was nothing made." Now, among the "all things" our world must be embraced. It too, therefore, was made by His Word, as Scripture tells us in the book of Genesis that He made all things connected with our world by His Word. David also expresses the same truth [when he says] "For He spake, and they were made; He commanded, and they were created." Whom, therefore, shall we believe as to the creation of the world – these heretics who have been mentioned that prate so foolishly and inconsistently on the subject, or the disciples of the Lord, and Moses, who was both a faithful servant of God and a prophet? He at first narrated the formation of the world in these words: "In the beginning God created the heaven and the earth," and all other things in succession; but neither gods nor angels [had any share in the work].

Now, that this God is the Father of our Lord Jesus Christ, Paul the apostle also has declared, [saying] "There is one God, the Father, who is above all, and through all things, and in us all." I have indeed proved already that there is only one God; but I shall further demonstrate this from the apostles themselves, and from the discourses of the Lord. For what sort of conduct would it be, were we to forsake the utterances of the prophets, of the Lord, and of the apostles, that we might give heed to these persons, who speak not a word of sense?

Questions for Study

1 On the basis of Irenaeus' opening statements, why do you think he regards Valentinianism as a serious threat to the Christian faith?
2 What point is Irenaeus trying to make through his references to exposing "knowledge falsely so called"?
3 What does Irenaeus identify as being some of the main features of Valentinianism?
4 What internal inconsistences does Irenaeus detect in Valentinus' ideas of God, especially the "Pleroma"?
5 Why does the doctrine of creation play such an important role in Irenaeus' thinking at this point?

CHAPTER 5

Quintus Septimius Florens Tertullian (ca. 160–ca. 225)

Tertullian was probably born about 160 in the North African city of Carthage, being the son of a Roman centurion in the proconsular service. He was an advocate in the secular law-courts, and frequently shows a close acquaintance with the procedure and terms of Roman law. A pagan until middle life, he initially shared many of the classic pagan prejudices against Christianity. His conversion is difficult to date with any precision, although it must have taken place by 197. His extant writings range in date from the *Apologeticus*, a major work of apologetics written in 197, to the attack on a bishop who is probably Pope Callistus (after 218).

Quintus Septimius Florens Tertullian (ca. 160–ca. 225)

Basic description
Early Roman Christian writer and apologist.

Major works
Apologeticus; *De Spectaculis*; *De corona militis*; *De paenitentia*.

Major studies
Timothy D. Barnes, *Tertullian: A Historical and Literary Culture*. Oxford: Clarendon Press, 1985.
David Rankin, *Tertullian and the Church*. Cambridge: Cambridge University Press, 1995.

A major development in Tertullian's career took place after the year 206. At this point, he joined the Montanist sect, and he seems to have definitively separated from the Church about 211. His writings against the church now become even more vigorous than those he had written earlier against his pagan critics and persecutors. Montanism was noted for its ethical rigorism and its emphasis upon the immediacy of the Christian experience of the Holy Spirit. Many commentators have suggested that there is some affinity between Montanism and modern forms of the charismatic movement, although such similarities must be regarded as speculative, in the lack of a full understanding of the origins and development of the Montanist movement.

Tertullian is important to the development of Christian thought and literature on account of his classic Roman heritage, which he puts to the service of the Christian faith. His legal background clearly persuaded him of the need to offer a defense of the Christian way of thinking, and especially living, to a secular Roman audience. It should therefore come as no surprise to learn that Tertullian is of particular importance as an apologist – a matter which we shall explore further in what follows.

Text: *The Apology*

One of the most interesting literary genres found in early Christianity is the "apology." This word is potentially misleading; in modern English, it bears the meaning of "saying sorry." In its classic sense, which derives from the Greek word *apologia* ("a defense"), the word refers to a defense of the Christian faith against its critics. This defense might take the form of a reasoned exposition of the main features of the Christian life, in order to guard against dangerous misunderstandings; for example, Christian references to "love-feasts" were misunderstood as orgies, and references to "eating the body of Christ" often raised the specter of cannibalism. Another form of apology involved the use of secular philosophy, especially Platonism, as a means of demonstrating the reasonableness of Christian doctrines. This approach is found in the writings of Justin Martyr (ca. 100–ca. 165), especially his two *Apologies* and his *Dialogue with Trypho*.

The year 197 saw the publication of a short address by Tertullian, "To the Martyrs," and of his two great apologetic works, the "Ad nationes" and the *Apologeticus* or *Apology*. The former has often been considered to be a preliminary sketch for the latter, but it is probably more accurate to suggest that the second work has a different purpose. Nevertheless, it is clear that the two works share much in common: a great deal of the same matter occurs in both, and the same arguments are often set out in the same manner, with the same examples offered as illustrations, and even the same phrases used in their justfication.

Tertullian also contributed to the development of this important literary genre. Whereas early Greek objections to Christianity tended to be theoretical, the criticisms leveled against the faith by early secular Roman commentators were chiefly practical and social in nature. The "Ad nationes" has as its object the refutation of certain severe criticisms directed against Christians. Tertullian offers the following defense of Christianity against his critics. In the first place, he argues that many of their criticisms rest on bias and dislike of Christians. The offense they have committed is nothing but bearing the name of Christian, which ought to be recognized as a title of honor. Furthermore, no proof is forthcoming of any crimes. In the second place, Tertullian offers rebuttals of the individual charges against Christianity – such as accusations of infanticide and incest. How, he asks, can Christians be thought of as the causes of earthquakes and floods and famine, when these happened long before Christianity arrived on the scene?

Out of this vigorous and occasionally crude response to pagan criticism, Tertullian went on to develop the more sophisticated *Apology*, addressed to the rulers of the empire and the administrators of justice. The former work simply attacked popular prejudices against Christianity, and rumors concerning believers. Tertullian's new work is apparently modeled on the apologies already developed by Greek-speaking Christian writers, and had a much more strategic goal – to secure better treatment of Christians by changing the law and its administration.

The section of the *Apologeticus* selected for study consists of the first four chapters.

Chapter I

Rulers of the Roman Empire, if, seated for the administration of justice on your lofty tribunal, under the gaze of every eye, and occupying there all but the highest position in the state, you may not openly inquire into and sift before the world the real truth in regard to the charges made against the Christians; if in this case alone you are afraid or ashamed to exercise your authority in making public inquiry with the carefulness which becomes justice; if, finally, the extreme severities inflicted on our people recently in private judgments, stand in the way of our being permitted to defend ourselves before you, you cannot surely forbid the Truth to reach your ears by the secret pathway of a noiseless book. She has no appeals to make to you in regard of her condition, for that does not excite her wonder. She knows that she is but a sojourner on the earth, and that among strangers she naturally finds foes; and more than this, that her origin, her dwelling-place, her hope, her recompense, her honors, are above. One thing, meanwhile, she anxiously desires of earthly rulers – not to be condemned unknown. What harm can it do to the laws, supreme in their domain, to give her a hearing? Nay, for that part of it, will not their absolute supremacy be more conspicuous in their condemning her, even after she has made her plea? But if, unheard, sentence is pronounced against her, besides the odium of an unjust deed, you will incur the merited suspicion of doing it with some idea that it is unjust, as not wishing to hear what you may not be able to hear and condemn. We lay this before you as the first ground on which we urge that your hatred to the name of Christian is unjust. And the very reason which seems to excuse this injustice (I mean ignorance) at once aggravates and convicts it. For what is there more unfair than to hate a thing of which you know nothing, even though it deserve to be hated? Hatred is only merited when it is known to be merited. But without that knowledge, whence is its justice to be vindicated? for that is to be proved, not from the mere fact that an aversion exists, but from acquaintance with the subject. When men, then, give way to a dislike simply because they are entirely ignorant of the nature of the thing disliked, why may it not be precisely the very sort of thing they should not dislike? So we maintain that they are both ignorant while they hate us, and hate us unrighteously while they continue in ignorance, the one thing being the result of the other either way of it. The proof of their ignorance, at once condemning and excusing their injustice, is this, that those who once hated Christianity because they knew nothing about it, no sooner come to know it than they all lay down at once their enmity. From being its haters they become its disciples. By simply getting acquainted with it, they begin now to hate what they had formerly been, and to profess what they had formerly hated; and their numbers are as great as are laid to our charge. The outcry is that the State is filled with Christians – that they are in the fields, in the citadels, in the islands: they make lamentation, as for some calamity, that both sexes, every age and condition, even high rank, are passing over to the profession of the Christian faith; and yet for all, their minds are not awakened to the thought of some good they have failed to notice in it. They must not allow any truer suspicions to cross their minds; they have no desire to make closer trial. Here alone the curiosity of human nature slumbers. They like to be ignorant, though to others the knowledge has been bliss. Anacharsis reproved the rude venturing to criticize the cultured; how much more this judging of those who know, by men who are entirely ignorant, might he have denounced! Because they already dislike, they want to know no more. Thus they prejudge that of which they are ignorant to be such, that, if they came to know it, it could no longer be the object of their aversion; since, if inquiry finds nothing worthy of dislike, it is certainly proper to cease from an unjust dislike, while if its bad character comes plainly out, instead of the detestation entertained for it being thus diminished, a stronger reason for perseverance in that detestation is obtained, even under the authority of justice itself. But, says one, a thing is not good merely because multitudes go over to it; for how many have the bent of their nature toward whatever is bad! how many go astray into ways of error! It is undoubted. Yet a thing that is thoroughly evil, not even those whom it carries away venture to defend as good. Nature throws a veil either of fear or shame over all evil. For instance, you find that criminals are eager to conceal themselves, avoid appearing in public, are in trepidation when they are caught, deny their guilt, when they are accused; even when they are put to the rack, they do not easily or always confess; when there is no doubt about their condemnation, they grieve for what they have done. In their self-communings they admit their being impelled by sinful dispositions, but they lay the blame either on fate or on the stars. They are unwilling to acknowledge that the thing is theirs, because they own that it is wicked. But what is there like this in the Christian's case? The only shame or regret he feels, is at not having been a Christian earlier. If he is pointed out, he glories in it; if he is accused, he offers no defense; interrogated, he makes voluntary confession; condemned he renders thanks. What sort of evil thing is this, which wants all the ordinary peculiarities of evil – fear, shame, subterfuge, penitence, lamenting? What! Is that a crime in which the criminal rejoices? To be accused of which is his ardent wish, to be punished for which is his felicity? You cannot call it madness, you who stand convicted of knowing nothing of the matter.

Chapter II

If, again, it is certain that we are the most wicked of men, why do you treat us so differently from our fellows, that is, from other criminals, it being only fair that the same crime should get the same treatment? When the charges made against us are made against others, they are permitted to make use both of their own lips and of hired pleaders to show their innocence. They have full opportunity of answer and debate; in fact, it is against the law to condemn anybody undefended and unheard. Christians alone are forbidden to say anything in exculpation of themselves, in defense of the truth, to help the judge to a righteous decision; all that is cared about is having what the public hatred demands – the confession of the name, not examination of the charge: while in your ordinary judicial investigations, on a man's confession of the crime of murder, or sacrilege, or incest, or treason, to take the points of which we are accused, you are not content to proceed at once to sentence – you do not take that step till you thoroughly examine the circumstances of the confession – what is the real character of the deed, how often, where, in what way, when he has done it, who were privy to it, and who actually took part with him in it. Nothing like this is done in our case, though the falsehoods disseminated about us ought to have the same sifting, that it might be found how many murdered children each of us had tasted; how many incests each of us had shrouded in darkness; what cooks, what dogs had been witness of our deeds. Oh, how great the glory of the ruler who should bring to light some Christian who had devoured a hundred infants! But, instead of that, we find that even inquiry in regard to our case is forbidden. For the younger Pliny, when he was ruler of a province, having condemned some Christians to death, and driven some from their steadfastness, being still annoyed by their great numbers, at last sought the advice of Trajan, the reigning emperor, as to what he was to do with the rest, explaining to his master that, except an obstinate disinclination to offer sacrifices, he found in the religious services nothing but meetings at early morning for singing hymns to Christ and God, and sealing home their way of life by a united pledge to be faithful to their religion, forbidding murder, adultery, dishonesty, and other crimes. Upon this Trajan wrote back that Christians were by no means to be sought after; but if they were brought before him, they should be punished. O miserable deliverance – under the necessities of the case, a self-contradiction! It forbids them to be sought after as innocent, and it commands them to be punished as guilty. It is at once merciful and cruel; it passes by, and it punishes. Why dost thou play a game of evasion upon thyself, O Judgment? If thou condemnest, why dost thou not also inquire. If thou dost not inquire, why dost thou not also absolve? Military stations are distributed through all the provinces for tracking robbers. Against traitors and public foes every man is a soldier; search is made even for their confederates and accessories. The Christian alone must not be sought, though he may be brought and accused before the judge; as if a search had any other end than that in view. And so you condemn the man for whom nobody wished a search to be made when he is presented to you, and who even now does not deserve punishment, I suppose, because of his guilt, but because, though forbidden to be sought, he was found. And then, too, you do not in that case deal with us in the ordinary way of judicial proceedings against offenders; for, in the case of others denying, you apply the torture to make them confess – Christians alone you torture, to make them deny; whereas, if we were guilty of any crime, we should be sure to deny it, and you with your tortures would force us to confession. Nor indeed should you hold that our crimes require no such investigation merely on the ground that you are convinced by our confession of the name that the deeds were done – you who are daily wont, though you know well enough what murder is, none the less to extract from the confessed murderer a full account of how the crime was perpetrated. So that with all the greater perversity you act, when, holding our crimes proved by our confession of the name of Christ, you drive us by torture to fall from our confession, that, repudiating the name, we may in like manner repudiate also the crimes with which, from that same confession, you had assumed that we were chargeable. I suppose, though you believe us to be the worst of mankind, you do not wish us to perish. For thus, no doubt, you are in the habit of bidding the murderer deny, and of ordering the man guilty of sacrilege to the rack if he persevere in his acknowledgment! Is that the way of it?

But if thus you do not deal with us as criminals, you declare us thereby innocent, when as innocent you are anxious that we do not persevere in a confession which you know will bring on us a condemnation of necessity, not of justice, at your hands. "I am a Christian," the man cries out. He tells you what he is; you wish to hear from him what he is not. Occupying your place of authority to extort the truth, you do your utmost to get lies from us. "I am," he says, "that which you ask me if I am. Why do you torture me to sin? I confess, and you put me to the rack. What would you do if I denied?" Certainly you give no ready credence to others when they deny. When we deny, you believe at once. Let this perversity of yours lead you to suspect that there is some hidden power in the case under whose influence you act against the forms, against the nature of public justice, even against the very laws themselves. For, unless I am greatly mistaken, the laws enjoin offenders to be searched out, and not to be hidden away. They lay it down that persons who own a crime are to be condemned, not acquitted. The decrees of the senate, the commands of your chiefs, lay this clearly down. The power of which you are servants is a civil, not a tyrannical domination. Among tyrants, indeed, torments used to be inflicted even as punishments: with you they are mitigated to a means of questioning alone. Keep to your law in these as necessary till confession is obtained; and if the torture is anticipated by confession, there will be no occasion for it: sentence should be passed; the criminal should be given over to the penalty which is his due, not released. Accordingly, no one is eager for the acquittal of the guilty; it is not right to desire that, and so no one is ever compelled to deny. Well, you think the Christian a man of every crime, an enemy of the gods, of the emperor, of the laws, of good morals, of all nature; yet you compel him to deny, that you may acquit him, which without his denial you could not do. You play fast and loose with the laws. You wish him to deny his guilt, that you may, even against his will, bring him out blameless and free from all guilt in reference to the past! Whence is this strange perversity on your part? How is it you do not reflect that a spontaneous confession is greatly more worthy of credit than a compelled denial; or consider whether, when compelled to deny, a man's denial may not be in good faith, and whether acquitted, he may not, then and there, as soon as the trial is over, laugh at your hostility, a Christian as much as ever? Seeing, then, that in everything you deal differently with us than with other criminals, bent upon the one object of taking from us our name (indeed, it is ours no more if we do what Christians never do), it is made perfectly clear that there is no crime of any kind in the case, but merely a name which a certain system, ever working against the truth, pursues with enmity, doing this chiefly with the object of securing that men may have no desire to know for certain what they are entirely ignorant of. Hence, too, it is that they believe about us things of which they have no proof, and they are disinclined to have them looked into, lest the charges, they would rather take on trust, are all proved to have no foundation, that the name so hostile to that rival power – its crimes presumed, not proved – may be condemned simply on its own confession. So we are put to the torture if we confess, and we are punished if we persevere, and if we deny we are acquitted, because all the contention is about a name. Finally, why do you read out of your tablet-lists that such a man is a Christian? Why not also that he is a murderer? And if a Christian is a murderer, why not guilty, too, of incest, or any other vile thing you believe of us? In our case alone you are either ashamed or unwilling to mention the very names of our crimes – If to be called a "Christian" does not imply any crime, the name is surely very hateful, when that of itself is made a crime.

Chapter III

What are we to think of it, that most people so blindly knock their heads against the hatred of the Christian name; that when they bear favorable testimony to any one, they mingle with it abuse of the name he bears? "A good man," says one, "is Gaius Seius, only that he is a Christian." So another, "I am astonished that a wise man like Lucius should have suddenly become a Christian." Nobody thinks it needful to consider whether Gaius is not good and Lucius wise, on this very account that he is a Christian; or a Christian, for the reason that he is wise and good. They praise what they know, they abuse what they are ignorant of, and they inspire their knowledge with their ignorance; though in fairness you should rather judge of what is unknown from what is known, than what is known from what is unknown. Others, in the case of persons whom, before they took the name of Christian, they had known as loose, and vile, and wicked, put on them a brand from the very thing which they praise. In the blindness of their hatred, they fall foul of their own approving judgment! "What a woman she was! how wanton! how gay! What a youth he was! how profligate! how libidinous! – they have become Christians!" So the hated name is given to a reformation of character. Some even barter away their comforts for that hatred, content to bear injury, if they are kept free at home from the object of their bitter enmity. The wife, now chaste, the husband, now no longer jealous, casts out of his house; the son, now obedient, the father, who used to be so patient, disinherits; the servant, now faithful, the master, once so mild, commands away from his presence; it is a high offense for any one to be reformed by the detested name. Goodness is of less value than hatred of Christians. Well now, if there is this dislike of the name, what blame can you attach to names? What accusation can you bring against mere designations, save that something in the word sounds either barbarous, or unlucky, or scurrilous, or unchaste? But Christian, so far as the meaning of the word is concerned, is derived from anointing. Yes, and even when it is wrongly pronounced by you "Chrestianus" (for you do not even know accurately the name you hate), it comes from sweetness and benignity. You hate, therefore, in the guiltless, even a guiltless name. But the special ground of dislike to the sect is, that it bears the name of its Founder. Is there anything new in a religious sect getting for its followers a designation from its master? Are not the philosophers called from the founders of their systems – Platonists, Epicureans, Pythagoreans? Are not the Stoics and Academics so called also from the places in which they assembled and stationed themselves? and are not physicians named from Erasistratus, grammarians from Aristarchus, cooks even from Apicius? And yet the bearing of the name, transmitted from the original institutor with whatever he has instituted, offends no one. No doubt, if it is proved that the sect is a bad one, and so its founder bad as well, that will prove that the name is bad and deserves our aversion, in respect of the character both of the sect and its author. Before, therefore, taking up a dislike to the name, it behoved you to consider the sect in the author, or the author in the sect. But now, without any sifting and knowledge of either, the mere name is made matter of accusation, the mere name is assailed, and a sound alone brings condemnation on a sect and its author both, while of both you are ignorant, because they have such and such a designation, not because they are convicted of anything wrong.

Chapter IV

And so, having made these remarks as it were by way of preface, that I might show in its true colors the injustice of the public hatred against us, I shall now take my stand on the plea of our blamelessness; and I shall not only refute the things which are objected to us, but I shall also retort them on the objectors, that in this way all may know that Christians are free from the very crimes they are so well aware prevail among themselves, that they may at the same time be put to the blush for their accusations against us – accusations I shall not say of the worst of men against the best, but now, as they will have it, against those who are only their fellows in sin. We shall reply to the accusation of all the various crimes we are said to be guilty of in secret, such as we find them committing in the light of day, and as being guilty of which we are held to be wicked, senseless, worthy of punishment, deserving of ridicule. But since, when our truth meets you successfully at all points, the authority of the laws as a last resort is set up against it, so that it is either said that their determinations are absolutely conclusive, or the necessity of obedience is, however unwillingly, preferred to the truth, I shall first, in this matter of the laws grapple with you as with their chosen protectors. Now first, when you sternly lay it down in your sentences, "It is not lawful for you to exist," and with unhesitating rigor you enjoin this to be carried out, you exhibit the violence and unjust domination of mere tyranny, if you deny the thing to be lawful, simply on the ground that you wish it to be unlawful, not because it ought to be. But if you would have it unlawful because it ought not to be lawful, without doubt that should have no permission of law which does harm; and on this ground, in fact, it is already determined that whatever is beneficial is legitimate. Well, if I have found what your law prohibits to be good, as one who has arrived at such a previous opinion, has it not lost its power to debar me from it, though that very thing, if it were evil, it would justly forbid to me? If your law has gone wrong, it is of human origin, I think; it has not fallen from heaven. Is it wonderful that man should err in making a law, or come to his senses in rejecting it? Did not the Lacedaemonians amend the laws of Lycurgus himself, thereby inflicting such pain on their author that he shut himself up, and doomed himself to death by starvation? Are you not yourselves every day, in your efforts to illumine the darkness of antiquity, cutting and hewing with the new axes of imperial rescripts and edicts, that whole ancient and rugged forest of your laws? Has not Severus, that most resolute of rulers, but yesterday repealed the ridiculous Papian laws which compelled people to have children before the Julian laws allow matrimony to be contracted, and that though they have the authority of age upon their side? There were laws, too, in old times, that parties against whom a decision had been given might be cut in pieces by their creditors; however, by common consent that cruelty was afterwards erased from the statutes, and the capital penalty turned into a brand of shame. By adopting the plan of confiscating a debtor's goods, it was sought rather to pour the blood in blushes over his face than to pour it out. How many laws lie hidden out of sight which still require to be reformed! For it is neither the number of their years nor the dignity of their maker that commends them, but simply that they are just; and therefore, when their injustice is recognized, they are deservedly condemned, even though they condemn. Why speak we of them as unjust? Nay, if they punish mere names, we may well call them irrational. But if they punish acts, why in our case do they punish acts solely on the ground of a name, while in others they must have them proved not from the name, but from the wrong done? I am a practicer of incest (so they say); why do they not inquire into it? I am an infant-killer; why do they not apply the torture to get from me the truth? I am guilty of crimes against the gods, against the Caesars; why am I, who am able to clear myself, not allowed to be heard on my own behalf? No law forbids the sifting of the crimes which it prohibits, for a judge never inflicts a righteous vengeance if he is not well assured that a crime has been committed; nor does a citizen render a true subjection to the law, if he does not know the nature of the thing on which the punishment is inflicted. It is not enough that a law is just, nor that the judge should be convinced of its justice; those from whom obedience is expected should have that conviction too. Nay, a law lies under strong suspicions which does not care to have itself tried and approved: it is a positively wicked law, if, unproved, it tyrannizes over men.

Questions for Discussion

1 Read the opening lines of the work carefully. What do these lines tell us about who Tertullian hoped to impress with his work? And what outcome was he hoping for?
2 What objections to Christianity does Tertullian identify?
3 How would you describe the strategies he uses to rebut these objections?

1. Roman Senet – The public.

CHAPTER 6

Eusebius of Caesarea
(ca. 260–ca. 340)

Eusebius was a student of Pamphilius (ca. 240–310), a native of what is now Beirut, and is sometimes referred to as "Eusebius Pamphilius" for this reason. After the death of Pamphilius, Eusebius found himself exiled to Egypt. For reasons that are not entirely clear, he was appointed Bishop of Caesarea shortly afterwards, and certainly by 315. During the Arian controversy* of this period, Eusebius sided with Arius, and as a result found himself under condemnation by the Council of Antioch (324/5). Although he was later restored to favor on the basis of his insistence upon his orthodoxy, he remained an opponent of Athanasius. Eusebius' reputation rests on his historical works, which may be regarded as establishing the basic pattern for subsequent works in this field.

Eusebius of Caesarea (ca. 260–ca. 340)

Basic description
Bishop and historian of early Christianity.

Major works
Ecclesiastical History; Life of Constantine.

Major studies
Robert M. Grant, *Eusebius as Church Historian.* Oxford: Clarendon Press, 1980.
Peter W. L. Walker, *Holy City, Holy Place: Christian Attitudes to Jerusalem and the Holy Land in the Fourth Century.* Oxford: Oxford University Press, 1990, 3–130.

Text: *Ecclesiastical History*

Eusebius is widely described as the "father of church history," and is remembered especially for his *Ecclesiastical History*. The work is important on account of the literary genre

---

* For a full discussion of the historical background to this controversy, and the issues which it raised, see Alister E. McGrath, *Christian Theology: An Introduction,* 2nd edn. Oxford: Blackwell, 1997, 330–7.

which it exemplifies and which, to some considerable extent, he may be said to have defined. The literary merits of the work are, however, not especially impressive. In addition to being poorly written, the work shows a lack of interest in the western church. Virtually the entire work considers the development of Christianity in the eastern Mediterranean region until his own day. The work consists of ten books. The first seven of these (which Eusebius completed before the Great Persecution of Diocletianic times) are largely devoted to doctrinal matters and heresy, and the successions of bishops. The last three books focus on events which took place in Eusebius' lifetime, and thus have especial importance on account of their contemporary accuracy. Some scholars suspect that the work originally consisted of the first seven books, with additional books being appended at various stages in Eusebius' later career, in response to events as they unfolded.

The extract for study is taken from Book 3, chapters I–XI, which describe the world into which Christianity initially expanded.

Chapter I – The Parts of the World in Which the Apostles Preached Christ

1   Such was the condition of the Jews. Meanwhile the holy apostles and disciples of our Savior were dispersed throughout the world. Parthia, according to tradition, was allotted to Thomas as his field of labor, Scythia to Andrew, and Asia to John, who, after he had lived some time there, died at Ephesus.

2   Peter appears to have preached in Pontus, Galatia, Bithynia, Cappadocia, and Asia to the Jews of the dispersion. And at last, having come to Rome, he was crucified head-downwards; for he had requested that he might suffer in this way. What do we need to say concerning Paul, who preached the Gospel of Christ from Jerusalem to Illyricum, and afterwards suffered martyrdom in Rome under Nero? These facts are related by Origen in the third volume of his Commentary on Genesis.

Chapter II – The First Ruler of the Church of Rome

1   After the martyrdom of Paul and of Peter, Linus was the first to obtain the episcopate of the church at Rome. Paul mentions him, when writing to Timothy from Rome, in the salutation at the end of the epistle.

Chapter III – The Epistles of the Apostles

1   One epistle of Peter, that called the first, is acknowledged as genuine. And this the ancient elders used freely in their own writings as an undisputed work. But we have learned that his extant second Epistle does not belong to the canon; yet, as it has appeared profitable to many, it has been used with the other Scriptures.

2   The so-called Acts of Peter, however, and the Gospel which bears his name, and the Preaching and the Apocalypse, as they are called, we know have not been universally accepted, because no ecclesiastical writer, ancient or modern, has made use of testimonies drawn from them.

3   But in the course of my history I shall be careful to show, in addition to the official succession, what ecclesiastical writers have from time to time made use of any of the disputed works, and what they have said in regard to the canonical and accepted writings, as well as in regard to those which are not of this class.

4   Such are the writings that bear the name of Peter, only one of which I know to be genuine and acknowledged by the ancient elders.

5   Paul's fourteen epistles are well known and undisputed. It is not indeed right to overlook the fact that some have rejected the Epistle to the Hebrews, saying that it is disputed by the church of Rome, on the ground that it was not written by Paul. But what has been said concerning this epistle by those who lived before our time I shall quote in the proper place. In regard to the so-called Acts of Paul, I have not found them among the undisputed writings.

6   But as the same apostle, in the salutations at the end of the Epistle to the Romans, has made mention among others of Hermas, to whom the book called The Shepherd is ascribed, it should be observed that this too has been disputed by some, and on their account cannot be placed among the acknowledged books; while by others it is considered quite indispensable, especially to those who need instruction in the elements of the faith. Hence, as we know, it has been publicly read in churches, and I have found that some of the most ancient writers used it.

7   This will serve to show the divine writings that are undisputed as well as those that are not universally acknowledged.

Chapter IV – The First Successors of the Apostles

1   That Paul preached to the Gentiles and laid the foundations of the churches "from Jerusalem round about even unto Illyricum," is evident both from his own words, and from the account which Luke has given in the Acts.

2   And in how many provinces Peter preached Christ and taught the doctrine of the new covenant to those of the circumcision is clear from his own words in his epistle already mentioned as undisputed, in which he writes to the Hebrews of the dispersion in Pontus, Galatia, Cappadocia, Asia, and Bithynia.

3   But the number and the names of those among them that became true and zealous followers of the apostles, and were judged worthy to tend the churches rounded by them, it is not easy to tell, except those mentioned in the writings of Paul.

4   For he had innumerable fellow-laborers, or "fellow-soldiers," as he called them, and most of them were honored by him with an imperishable memorial, for he gave enduring testimony concerning them in his own epistles.

5   Luke also in the Acts speaks of his friends, and mentions them by name.

6   Timothy, so it is recorded, was the first to receive the episcopate of the parish in Ephesus, Titus of the churches in Crete.

7   But Luke, who was of Antiochian parentage and a physician by profession, and who was especially intimate with Paul and well acquainted with the rest of the apostles, has left us, in two inspired books, proofs of that spiritual healing art which he learned from them. One of these books is the Gospel, which he testifies that he wrote as those who were from the beginning eyewitnesses and ministers of the word

delivered unto him, all of whom, as he says, he followed accurately from the first. The other book is the Acts of the Apostles which he composed not from the accounts of others, but from what he had seen himself.

8   And they say that Paul meant to refer to Luke's Gospel wherever, as if speaking of some gospel of his own, he used the words, "according to my Gospel."

9   As to the rest of his followers, Paul testifies that Crescens was sent to Gaul; but Linus, whom he mentions in the Second Epistle to Timothy as his companion at Rome, was Peter's successor in the episcopate of the church there, as has already been shown.

10   Clement also, who was appointed third bishop of the church at Rome, was, as Paul testifies, his co-laborer and fellow-soldier.

11   Besides these, that Areopagite, named Dionysius, who was the first to believe after Paul's address to the Athenians in the Areopagus (as recorded by Luke in the Acts) is mentioned by another Dionysius, an ancient writer and pastor of the parish in Corinth, as the first bishop of the church at Athens.

12   But the events connected with the apostolic succession we shall relate at the proper time. Meanwhile let us continue the course of our history.

Chapter V – The Last Siege of the Jews After Christ

1   After Nero had held the power thirteen years, and Galba and Otho had ruled a year and six months, Vespasian, who had become distinguished in the campaigns against the Jews, was proclaimed sovereign in Judea and received the title of Emperor from the armies there. Setting out immediately, therefore, for Rome, he entrusted the conduct of the war against the Jews to his son Titus.

2   For the Jews after the ascension of our Savior, in addition to their crime against him, had been devising as many plots as they could against his apostles. First Stephen was stoned to death by them, and after him James, the son of Zebedee and the brother of John, was beheaded, and finally James, the first that had obtained the episcopal seat in Jerusalem after the ascension of our Savior, died in the manner already described. But the rest of the apostles, who had been incessantly plotted against with a view to their destruction, and had been driven out of the land of Judea, went unto all nations to preach the Gospel, relying upon the power of Christ, who had said to them, "Go ye and make disciples of all the nations in my name."

3   But the people of the church in Jerusalem had been commanded by a revelation, vouchsafed to approved men there before the war, to leave the city and to dwell in a certain town of Perea called Pella. And when those that believed in Christ had come thither from Jerusalem, then, as if the royal city of the Jews and the whole land of Judea were entirely destitute of holy men, the judgment of God at length overtook those who had committed such outrages against Christ and his apostles, and totally destroyed that generation of impious men.

4   But the number of calamities which everywhere fell upon the nation at that time; the extreme misfortunes to which the inhabitants of Judea were especially subjected, the thousands of men, as well as women and children, that perished by the sword, by famine, and by other forms of death innumerable – all these things, as well as the many great sieges which were carried on against the cities of Judea,

and the excessive sufferings endured by those that fled to Jerusalem itself, as to a city of perfect safety, and finally the general course of the whole war, as well as its particular occurrences in detail, and how at last the abomination of desolation, proclaimed by the prophets, stood in the very temple of God, so celebrated of old, the temple which was now awaiting its total and final destruction by fire – all these things any one that wishes may find accurately described in the history written by Josephus.

5   But it is necessary to state that this writer records that the multitude of those who were assembled from all Judea at the time of the Passover, to the number of three million souls, were shut up in Jerusalem "as in a prison," to use his own words.

6   For it was right that in the very days in which they had inflicted suffering upon the Savior and the Benefactor of all, the Christ of God, that in those days, shut up "as in a prison," they should meet with destruction at the hands of divine justice.

7   But passing by the particular calamities which they suffered from the attempts made upon them by the sword and by other means, I think it necessary to relate only the misfortunes which the famine caused, that those who read this work may have some means of knowing that God was not long in executing vengeance upon them for their wickedness against the Christ of God.

Chapter VI – The Famine Which Oppressed Them

1   Taking the fifth book of the History of Josephus again in our hands, let us go through the tragedy of events which then occurred.

2   "For the wealthy," he says, "it was equally dangerous to remain. For under pretense that they were going to desert, men were put to death for their wealth. The madness of the seditions increased with the famine and both the miseries were inflamed more and more day by day.

3   "Nowhere was food to be seen; but, bursting into the houses men searched them thoroughly, and whenever they found anything to eat they tormented the owners on the ground that they had denied that they had anything; but if they found nothing, they tortured them on the ground that they had more carefully concealed it.

4   "The proof of their having or not having food was found in the bodies of the poor wretches. Those of them who were still in good condition they assumed were well supplied with food, while those who were already wasted away they passed by, for it seemed absurd to slay those who were on the point of perishing for want.

5   "Many, indeed, secretly sold their possessions for one measure of wheat, if they belonged to the wealthier class, of barley if they were poorer. Then shutting themselves up in the innermost parts of their houses, some ate the grain uncooked on account of their terrible want, while others baked it according as necessity and fear dictated.

6   "Nowhere were tables set, but, snatching the yet uncooked food from the fire, they tore it in pieces. Wretched was the fare, and a lamentable spectacle it was to see the more powerful secure an abundance while the weaker mourned.

7 "Of all evils, indeed, famine is the worst, and it destroys nothing so effectively as shame. For that which under other circumstances is worthy of respect, in the midst of famine is despised. Thus women snatched the food from the very mouths of their husbands and children, from their fathers, and what was most pitiable of all, mothers from their babes. And while their dearest ones were wasting away in their arms, they were not ashamed to take away froth them the last drops that supported life.

8 "And even while they were eating thus they did not remain undiscovered. But everywhere the rioters appeared, to rob them even of these portions of food. For whenever they saw a house shut up, they regarded it as a sign that those inside were taking food. And immediately bursting open the doors they rushed in and seized what they were eating, almost forcing it out of their very throats.

9 "Old men who clung to their food were beaten, and if the women concealed it in their hands, their hair was torn for so doing. There was pity neither for gray hairs nor for infants, but, taking up the babes that clung to their morsels of food, they dashed them to the ground. But to those that anticipated their entrance and swallowed what they were about to seize, they were still more cruel, just as if they had been wronged by them.

10 "And they devised the most terrible modes of torture to discover food, stopping up the privy passages of the poor wretches with bitter herbs, and piercing their seats with sharp rods. And men suffered things horrible even to hear of, for the sake of compelling them to confess to the possession of one loaf of bread, or in order that they might be made to disclose a single drachm of barley which they had concealed. But the tormentors themselves did not suffer hunger.

11 "Their conduct might indeed have seemed less barbarous if they had been driven to it by necessity; but they did it for the sake of exercising their madness and of providing sustenance for themselves for days to come.

12 "And when any one crept out of the city by night as far as the outposts of the Romans to collect wild herbs and grass, they went to meet him; and when he thought he had already escaped the enemy, they seized what he had brought with him, and even though oftentimes the man would entreat them, and, calling upon the most awful name of God, adjure them to give him a portion of what he had obtained at the risk of his life, they would give him nothing back. Indeed, it was fortunate if the one that was plundered was not also slain."

13 To this account Josephus, after relating other things, adds the following: "The possibility of going out of the city being brought to an end, all hope of safety for the Jews was cut off. And the famine increased and devoured the people by houses and families. And the rooms were filled with dead women and children, the lanes of the city with the corpses of old men.

14 "Children and youths, swollen with the famine, wandered about the marketplaces like shadows, and fell down wherever the death agony overtook them. The sick were not strong enough to bury even their own relatives, and those who had the strength hesitated because of the multitude of the dead and the uncertainty as to their own fate. Many, indeed, died while they were burying others, and many betook themselves to their graves before death came upon them.

15 "There was neither weeping nor lamentation under these misfortunes; but the famine stifled the natural affections. Those that were dying a lingering death

looked with dry eyes upon those that had gone to their rest before them. Deep silence and death-laden night encircled the city.

16   "But the robbers were more terrible than these miseries; for they broke open the houses, which were now mere sepulchres, robbed the dead and stripped the covering from their bodies, and went away with a laugh. They tried the points of their swords in the dead bodies, and some that were lying on the ground still alive they thrust through in order to test their weapons. But those that prayed that they would use their right hand and their sword upon them, they contemptuously left to be destroyed by the famine. Every one of these died with eyes fixed upon the temple; and they left the seditious alive.

17   "These at first gave orders that the dead should be buried out of the public treasury, for they could not endure the stench. But afterward, when they were not able to do this, they threw the bodies from the walls into the trenches.

18   "And as Titus went around and saw the trenches filled with the dead, and the thick blood oozing out of the putrid bodies, he groaned aloud, and, raising his hands, called God to witness that this was not his doing."

19   After speaking of some other things, Josephus proceeds as follows: "I cannot hesitate to declare what my feelings compel me to. I suppose, if the Romans had longer delayed in coming against these guilty wretches, the city would have been swallowed up by a chasm, or overwhelmed with a flood, or struck with such thunderbolts as destroyed Sodom. For it had brought forth a generation of men much more godless than were those that suffered such punishment. By their madness indeed was the whole people brought to destruction."

20   And in the sixth book he writes as follows: "Of those that perished by famine in the city the number was countless, and the miseries they underwent unspeakable. For if so much as the shadow of food appeared in any house, there was war, and the dearest friends engaged in hand-to-hand conflict with one another, and snatched from each other the most wretched supports of life.

21   "Nor would they believe that even the dying were without food; but the robbers would search them while they were expiring, lest any one should feign death while concealing food in his bosom. With mouths gaping for want of food, they stumbled and staggered along like mad dogs, and beat the doors as if they were drunk, and in their impotence they would rush into the same houses twice or thrice in one hour.

22   "Necessity compelled them to eat anything they could find, and they gathered and devoured things that were not fit even for the filthiest of irrational beasts. Finally they did not abstain even from their girdles and shoes, and they stripped the hides off their shields and devoured them. Some used even wisps of old hay for food, and others gathered stubble and sold the smallest weight of it for four Attic drachmae.

23   "But why should I speak of the shamelessness which was displayed during the famine toward inanimate things? For I am going to relate a fact such as is recorded neither by Greeks nor Barbarians; horrible to relate, incredible to hear. And indeed I should gladly have omitted this calamity, that I might not seem to posterity to be a teller of fabulous tales, if I had not innumerable witnesses to it in my own age. And besides, I should render my country poor service if I suppressed the account of the sufferings which she endured.

24   "There was a certain woman named Mary that dwelt beyond Jordan, whose father was Eleazer, of the village of Bathezor (which signifies the house of hyssop). She was distinguished for her family and her wealth, and had fled with the rest of the multitude to Jerusalem and was shut up there with them during the siege.

25   "The tyrants had robbed her of the rest of the property which she had brought with her into the city from Perea. And the remnants of her possessions and whatever food was to be seen the guards rushed in daily and snatched away from her. This made the woman terribly angry, and by her frequent reproaches and imprecations she aroused the anger of the rapacious villains against herself.

26   "But no one either through anger or pity would slay her; and she grew weary of finding food for others to eat. The search, too, was already become everywhere difficult, and the famine was piercing her bowels and marrow, and resentment was raging more violently than famine. Taking, therefore, anger and necessity as her counsellors, she proceeded to do a most unnatural thing.

27   "Seizing her child, a boy which was sucking at her breast, she said, Oh, wretched child, in war, in famine, in sedition, for what do I preserve thee? Slaves among the Romans we shall be even if we are allowed to live by them. But even slavery is anticipated by the famine, and the rioters are more cruel than both. Come, be food for me, a fury for these rioters, and a byword to the world, for this is all that is wanting to complete the calamities of the Jews.

28   "And when she had said this she slew her son; and having roasted him, she ate one half herself, and covering up the remainder, she kept it. Very soon the rioters appeared on the scene, and, smelling the nefarious odor, they threatened to slay her immediately unless she should show them what she had prepared. She replied that she had saved an excellent portion for them, and with that she uncovered the remains of the child.

29   "They were immediately seized with horror and amazement and stood transfixed at the sight. But she said This is my own son, and the deed is mine. Eat for I too have eaten. Be not more merciful than a woman, nor more compassionate than a mother. But if you are too pious and shrink from my sacrifice, I have already eaten of it; let the rest also remain for me.

30   "At these words the men went out trembling, in this one case being affrighted; yet with difficulty did they yield that food to the mother. Forthwith the whole city was filled with the awful crime, and as all pictured the terrible deed before their own eyes, they trembled as if they had done it themselves.

31   "Those that were suffering from the famine now longed for death; and blessed were they that had died before hearing and seeing miseries like these." '

32   Such was the reward which the Jews received for their wickedness and impiety, against the Christ of God.

Chapter VII – The Predictions of Christ

1   It is fitting to add to these accounts the true prediction of our Savior in which he foretold these very events.

2   His words are as follows: "Woe unto them that are with child, and to them that give suck in those days! But pray ye that your flight be not in the winter, neither

on the Sabbath day; For there shall be great tribulation, such as was not since the beginning of the world to this time, no, nor ever shall be."

3   The historian, reckoning the whole number of the slain, says that eleven hundred thousand persons perished by famine and sword, and that the rest of the rioters and robbers, being betrayed by each other after the taking of the city, were slain. But the tallest of the youths and those that were distinguished for beauty were preserved for the triumph. Of the rest of the multitude, those that were over seventeen years of age were sent as prisoners to labor in the works of Egypt, while still more were scattered through the provinces to meet their death in the theaters by the sword and by beasts. Those under seventeen years of age were carried away to be sold as slaves, and of these alone the number reached ninety thousand.

4   These things took place in this manner in the second year of the reign of Vespasian, in accordance with the prophecies of our Lord and Savior Jesus Christ, who by divine power saw them beforehand as if they were already present, and wept and mourned according to the statement of the holy evangelists, who give the very words which be uttered, when, as if addressing Jerusalem herself, he said:

5   "If thou hadst known, even thou, in this day, the things which belong unto thy peace! But now they are hid from thine eyes. For the days shall come upon thee, that thine enemies shall cast a rampart about thee, and compass thee round, and keep thee in on every side, and shall lay thee and thy children even with the ground."

6   And then, as if speaking concerning the people, he says, "For there shall be great distress in the land, and wrath upon this people. And they shall fall by the edge of the sword, and shall be led away captive into all nations. And Jerusalem shall be trodden down of the Gentiles, until the times of the Gentiles be fulfilled." And again: "When ye shall see Jerusalem compassed with armies, then know that the desolation thereof is nigh."

7   If any one compares the words of our Savior with the other accounts of the historian concerning the whole war, how can one fail to wonder, and to admit that the foreknowledge and the prophecy of our Savior were truly divine and marvelously strange.

8   Concerning those calamities, then, that befell the whole Jewish nation after the Savior's passion and after the words which the multitude of the Jews uttered, when they begged the release of the robber and murderer, but besought that the Prince of Life should be taken from their midst, it is not necessary to add anything to the account of the historian.

9   But it may be proper to mention also those events which exhibited the graciousness of that all-good Providence which held back their destruction full forty years after their crime against Christ – during which time many of the apostles and disciples, and James himself the first bishop there, the one who is called the brother of the Lord, were still alive, and dwelling in Jerusalem itself, remained the surest bulwark of the place. Divine Providence thus still proved itself long-suffering toward them in order to see whether by repentance for what they had done they might obtain pardon and salvation; and in addition to such long-suffering, Providence also furnished wonderful signs of the things which were about to happen to them if they did not repent.

10   Since these matters have been thought worthy of mention by the historian already cited, we cannot do better than to recount them for the benefit of the readers of this work.

Chapter VIII – The Signs Which Preceded the War

1   Taking, then, the work of this author, read what he records in the sixth book of his History. His words are as follows: 'Thus were the miserable people won over at this time by the impostors and false prophets; but they did not heed nor give credit to the visions and signs that foretold the approaching desolation. On the contrary, as if struck by lightning, and as if possessing neither eyes nor understanding, they slighted the proclamations of God.

2   At one time a star, in form like a sword, stood over the city, and a comet, which lasted for a whole year; and again before the revolt and before the disturbances that led to the war, when the people were gathered for the feast of unleavened bread, on the eighth of the month Xanthicus, at the ninth hour of the night, so great a light shone about the altar and the temple that it seemed to be bright day; and this continued for half an hour. This seemed to the unskillful a good sign, but was interpreted by the sacred scribes as portending those events which very soon took place.

3   And at the same feast a cow, led by the high priest to be sacrificed, brought forth a lamb in the midst of the temple.

4   And the eastern gate of the inner temple, which was of bronze and very massive, and which at evening was closed with difficulty by twenty men, and rested upon iron-bound beams, and had bars sunk deep in the ground, was seen at the sixth hour of the night to open of itself.

5   And not many days after the feast, on the twenty-first of the month Artemisium, a certain marvelous vision was seen which passes belief. The prodigy might seem fabulous were it not related by those who saw it, and were not the calamities which followed deserving of such signs. For before the setting of the sun chariots and armed troops were seen throughout the whole region in mid-air, wheeling through the clouds and encircling the cities.

6   And at the feast which is called Pentecost, when the priests entered the temple at night, as was their custom, to perform the services, they said that at first they perceived a movement and a noise, and afterward a voice as of a great multitude, saying, "Let us go hence."

7   But what follows is still more terrible; for a certain Jesus, the son of Ananias, a common countryman, four years before the war, when the city was particularly prosperous and peaceful, came to the feast, at which it was customary for all to make tents at the temple to the honor of God, and suddenly began to cry out: "A voice from the east, a voice from the west, a voice from the four winds, a voice against Jerusalem and the temple, a voice against bridegrooms and brides, a voice against all the people." Day and night he went through all the alleys crying thus.

8   But certain of the more distinguished citizens, vexed at the ominous cry, seized the man and beat him with many stripes. But without uttering a word in his own

behalf, or saying anything in particular to those that were present, he continued to cry out in the same words as before.

9   And the rulers, thinking, as was true, that the man was moved by a higher power, brought him before the Roman governor. And then, though he was scourged to the bone, he neither made supplication nor shed tears, but, changing his voice to the most lamentable tone possible, he answered each stroke with the words, "Woe, woe unto Jerusalem."

10   The same historian records another fact still more wonderful than this. He says that a certain oracle was found in their sacred writings which declared that at that time a certain person should go forth from their country to rule the world. He himself understood that this was fulfilled in Vespasian.

11   But Vespasian did not rule the whole world, but only that part of it which was subject to the Romans. With better right could it be applied to Christ; to whom it was said by the Father, "Ask of me, and I will give thee the heathen for thine inheritance, and the ends of the earth for thy possession." At that very time, indeed, the voice of his holy apostles "went throughout all the earth, and their words to the end of the world."

Questions for Discussion

1   What can we learn about Eusebius' agenda from reading this history?
2   Underlying Eusebius' narrative is a firm belief that the development of Christianity was favored by divine providence. At what points can this belief be seen in the narrative?
3   In this narrative, Eusebius deals with the relation of Christianity to two distinct groups in the region at this time: the imperial Roman authorities, and the Jews. How would you describe his attitude to each?

CHAPTER 7

Athanasius of Alexandria (ca. 296–373)

Athanasius is widely regarded as one of the most important Greek patristic writers, not least on account of his vigorous defense of the orthodox position on the identity of Jesus Christ in response to the Arian controversy. We know little about the early years of Athanasius, although it is known that he received an excellent classical education as a young man. He was appointed Bishop of Alexandria in 328. His strong stance against Arianism caused him to be intensely disliked by many in the political and ecclesiastical hierarchies of the day. He was deposed as bishop in 335; it was not until 346 that he was restored to the bishopric, which he held for a further ten years before political opposition again led to him being exiled intermittently until he finally was restored to his position in 366.

Athanasius of Alexandria (ca. 296–373)

Basic description
Major theologian and spiritual writer of the Alexandrian church.

Major works
De incarnatione (ca. 318?); *Epistles to Serapion*.

Major studies
Timothy D. Barnes, *Athanasius and Constantius: Theology and Politics in the Constantinian Empire.* Cambridge, MA: Harvard University Press, 1993.

David Brakke, *Athanasius and Asceticism.* Baltimore, MD: Johns Hopkins University Press, 1998.

Athanasius' literary works include substantial doctrinal treatises devoted to defending the full divinity of Christ against the Arians.* Of these, perhaps *de incarnatione* is the greatest; in this work, Athanasius sets out the grounds and consequences of affirming

---

* For a full discussion of the historical background to this controversy, and the issues which it raised, see Alister E. McGrath, *Christian Theology: An Introduction*, 2nd edn. Oxford: Blackwell, 1997, 330–7.

the divinity of Christ, and the threat which he perceived to be posed to the heart of the Christian faith by the Arian insistence that Christ was merely "first among the creatures." The work is distinguished by its clarity of argument, and it has remained widely used in discussions of the doctrine of the incarnation, even in modern theological debates.

Yet Athanasius was more than a "theologian," as we would understand this term today. Athanasius was a pastor and preacher, with a genuine concern for the care of souls. He was a close associate of St. Antony of Egypt (ca. 251–356), a hermit who sought to reform the church by withdrawing from the cities of Egypt, and settling in the desert. Athanasius admired him, and is traditionally regarded as the author of the "Vita Antonii" ("The Life of Antony"), a classic example of early Christian hagiography. Although some scholars regard this work as having its origins in the circle around Athanasius, rather than being the direct writing of Athanasius himself, there remains much support for the view that it can be attributed to him.

Text: *De Incarnatione*

The major treatise, known by its Latin title *de incarnatione* ("on the incarnation"), is thought by some to have been written as early as 318; others place it from at least fifteen years later. Its basic theme is that the doctrine that Christ is both truly divine and truly human is both the only adequate means of making sense of the biblical witness to the identity of Christ, and the only means by which the central themes of the Christian faith may be safeguarded. Athanasius makes the point that it is only God who can save. God, and God alone, can break the power of sin, and bring humanity to eternal life. No creature can save another creature. Only the creator can redeem the creation. Having emphasized that it is God alone who can save, Athanasius then makes the logical move which the Arians found difficult to counter. The New Testament and the Christian tradition both regard Jesus Christ as Savior. Yet, as Athanasius emphasized, only God can save. So how are we to make sense of this?

The only possible solution, Athanasius argues, is to accept that Jesus is God incarnate. His line of arguing goes like this:

1   No creature can redeem another creature.
2   According to Arius, Jesus Christ is a creature.
3   Therefore, according to Arius, Jesus Christ cannot redeem humanity.

At times, Athanasius uses a slightly different style of argument:

1   Only God can save.
2   Jesus Christ saves.
3   Therefore Jesus Christ is God.

Salvation, for Athanasius, involves divine intervention. God therefore entered into our human situation, in order to change it.

Our extract is taken from the fourth chapter of *de incarnatione*, in which Athanasius sets out some of the arguments for maintaining and defending the divinity of Christ.

All these things the Savior thought fit to do, so that, recognizing His bodily acts as works of God, men who were blind to His presence in creation might regain knowledge of the Father. For, as I said before, who that saw His authority over evil spirits and their response to it could doubt that He was, indeed, the Son, the Wisdom and the Power of God? Even the very creation broke silence at His behest and, marvelous to relate, confessed with one voice before the cross, that monument of victory, that He Who suffered thereon in the body was not man only, but Son of God and Savior of all. The sun veiled his face, the earth quaked, the mountains were rent asunder, all men were stricken with awe. These things showed that Christ on the cross was God, and that all creation was His slave and was bearing witness by its fear to the presence of its Master.

Thus, then, God the Word revealed Himself to men through His works. We must next consider the end of His earthly life and the nature of His bodily death. This is, indeed, the very center of our faith, and everywhere you hear men speak of it; by it, too, no less than by His other acts, Christ is revealed as God and Son of God.

(20) We have dealt as far as circumstances and our own understanding permit with the reason for His bodily manifestation. We have seen that to change the corruptible to incorruption was proper to none other than the Savior Himself, Who in the beginning made all things out of nothing; that only the Image of the Father could recreate the likeness of the Image in men, that none save our Lord Jesus Christ could give to mortals immortality, and that only the Word Who orders all things and is alone the Father's true and sole-begotten Son could teach men about Him and abolish the worship of idols But beyond all this, there was a debt owing which must needs be paid; for, as I said before, all men were due to die. Here, then, is the second reason why the Word dwelt among us, namely that having proved His Godhead by His works, He might offer the sacrifice on behalf of all, surrendering His own temple to death in place of all, to settle man's account with death and free him from the primal transgression. In the same act also He showed Himself mightier than death, displaying His own body incorruptible as the first-fruits of the resurrection.

You must not be surprised if we repeat ourselves in dealing with this subject. We are speaking of the good pleasure of God and of the things which He in His loving wisdom thought fit to do, and it is better to put the same thing in several ways than to run the risk of leaving something out. The body of the Word, then, being a real human body, in spite of its having been uniquely formed from a virgin, was of itself mortal and, like other bodies, liable to death. But the indwelling of the Word loosed it from this natural liability, so that corruption could not touch it. Thus it happened that two opposite marvels took place at once: the death of all was consummated in the Lord's body; yet, because the Word was in it, death and corruption were in the same act utterly abolished. Death there had to be, and death for all, so that the due of all might be paid. Wherefore, the Word, as I said, being Himself incapable of death, assumed a mortal body, that He might offer it as His own in place of all, and suffering for the sake of all through His union with it, "might bring to nought Him that had the power of death, that is, the devil, and might deliver them who all their lifetime were enslaved by the fear of death."

(21) Have no fears then. Now that the common Savior of all has died on our behalf, we who believe in Christ no longer die, as men died aforetime, in fulfillment

of the threat of the law. That condemnation has come to an end; and now that, by the grace of the resurrection, corruption has been banished and done away, we are loosed from our mortal bodies in God's good time for each, so that we may obtain thereby a better resurrection. Like seeds cast into the earth, we do not perish in our dissolution, but like them shall rise again, death having been brought to nought by the grace of the Savior. That is why blessed Paul, through whom we all have surety of the resurrection, says: "This corruptible must put on incorruption and this mortal must put on immortality; but when this corruptible shall have put on incorruption and this mortal shall have put on immortality, then shall be brought to pass the saying that is written, 'Death is swallowed up in victory. O Death, where is thy sting? O Grave, where is thy victory?'"

"Well then," some people may say, "if the essential thing was that He should surrender His body to death in place of all, why did He not do so as Man privately, without going to the length of public crucifixion? Surely it would have been more suitable for Him to have laid aside His body with honor than to endure so shameful a death." But look at this argument closely, and see how merely human it is, whereas what the Savior did was truly divine and worthy of His Godhead for several reasons. The first is this. The death of men under ordinary circumstances is the result of their natural weakness. They are essentially impermanent, so after a time they fall ill and when worn out they die. But the Lord is not like that. He is not weak, He is the Power of God and Word of God and Very Life Itself. If He had died quietly in His bed like other men it would have looked as if He did so in accordance with His nature, and as though He was indeed no more than other men. But because He was Himself Word and Life and Power His body was made strong, and because the death had to be accomplished, He took the occasion of perfecting His sacrifice not from Himself, but from others. How could He fall sick, Who had healed others? Or how could that body weaken and fail by means of which others are made strong? Here, again, you may say, "Why did He not prevent death, as He did sickness?" Because it was precisely in order to be able to die that He had taken a body, and to prevent the death would have been to impede the resurrection. And as to the unsuitability of sickness for His body, as arguing weakness, you may say, "Did He then not hunger?" Yes, He hungered, because that was the property of His body, but He did not die of hunger because He Whose body hungered was the Lord. Similarly, though He died to ransom all, He did not see corruption. His body rose in perfect soundness, for it was the body of none other than the Life Himself.

(22) Someone else might say, perhaps, that it would have been better for the Lord to have avoided the designs of the Jews against Him, and so to have guarded His body from death altogether. But see how unfitting this also would have been for Him. Just as it would not have been fitting for Him to give His body to death by His own hand, being Word and being Life, so also it was not consonant with Himself that He should avoid the death inflicted by others. Rather, He pursued it to the uttermost, and in pursuance of His nature neither laid aside His body of His own accord nor escaped the plotting Jews. And this action showed no limitation or weakness in the Word; for He both waited for death in order to make an end of it, and hastened to accomplish it as an offering on behalf of all. Moreover, as it was the death of all

mankind that the Savior came to accomplish, not His own, He did not lay aside His body by an individual act of dying, for to Him, as Life, this simply did not belong; but He accepted death at the hands of men, thereby completely to destroy it in His own body.

There are some further considerations which enable one to understand why the Lord's body had such an end. The supreme object of His coming was to bring about the resurrection of the body. This was to be the monument to His victory over death, the assurance to all that He had Himself conquered corruption and that their own bodies also would eventually be incorrupt; and it was in token of that and as a pledge of the future resurrection that He kept His body incorrupt. But there again, if His body had fallen sick and the Word had left it in that condition, how unfitting it would have been! Should He Who healed the bodies of others neglect to keep His own in health? How would His miracles of healing be believed, if this were so? Surely people would either laugh at Him as unable to dispel disease or else consider Him lacking in proper human feeling because He could do so, but did not.

(23) Then, again, suppose without any illness He had just concealed His body somewhere, and then suddenly reappeared and said that He had risen from the dead. He would have been regarded merely as a teller of tales, and because there was no witness of His death, nobody would believe His resurrection. Death had to precede resurrection, for there could be no resurrection without it. A secret and unwitnessed death would have left the resurrection without any proof or evidence to support it. Again, why should He die a secret death, when He proclaimed the fact of His rising openly? Why should He drive out evil spirits and heal the man blind from birth and change water into wine, all publicly, in order to convince men that He was the Word, and not also declare publicly that incorruptibility of His mortal body, so that He might Himself be believed to be the Life? And how could His disciples have had boldness in speaking of the resurrection unless they could state it as a fact that He had first died? Or how could their hearers be expected to believe their assertion, unless they themselves also had witnessed His death? For if the Pharisees at the time refused to believe and forced others to deny also, though the things had happened before their very eyes, how many excuses for unbelief would they have contrived, if it had taken place secretly? Or how could the end of death and the victory over it have been declared, had not the Lord thus challenged it before the sight of all, and by the incorruption of His body proved that henceforward it was annulled and void?

(24) There are some other possible objections that must be answered. Some might urge that, even granting the necessity of a public death for subsequent belief in the resurrection, it would surely have been better for Him to have arranged an honorable death for Himself, and so to have avoided the ignominy of the cross. But even this would have given ground for suspicion that His power over death was limited to the particular kind of death which He chose for Himself; and that again would furnish excuse for disbelieving the resurrection. Death came to His body, therefore, not from Himself but from enemy action, in order that the Savior might utterly abolish death in whatever form they offered it to Him. A generous wrestler, virile and strong, does not himself choose his antagonists, lest it should be thought that

of some of them he is afraid. Rather, he lets the spectators choose them, and that all the more if these are hostile, so that he may overthrow whomsoever they match against him and thus vindicate his superior strength.

Even so was it with Christ. He, the Life of all, our Lord and Savior, did not arrange the manner of his own death lest He should seem to be afraid of some other kind. No. He accepted and bore upon the cross a death inflicted by others, and those others His special enemies, a death which to them was supremely terrible and by no means to be faced; and He did this in order that, by destroying even this death, He might Himself be believed to be the Life, and the power of death be recognized as finally annulled. A marvelous and mighty paradox has thus occurred, for the death which they thought to inflict on Him as dishonor and disgrace has become the glorious monument to death's defeat. Therefore it is also, that He neither endured the death of John, who was beheaded, nor was He sawn asunder, like Isaiah: even in death He preserved His body whole and undivided, so that there should be no excuse hereafter for those who would divide the Church.

(25) So much for the objections of those outside the Church. But if any honest Christian wants to know why He suffered death on the cross and not in some other way, we answer thus: in no other way was it expedient for us, indeed the Lord offered for our sakes the one death that was supremely good. He had come to bear the curse that lay on us; and how could He "become a curse" otherwise than by accepting the accursed death? And that death is the cross, for it is written "Cursed is every one that hangeth on tree." Again, the death of the Lord is the ransom of all, and by it "the middle wall of partition" is broken down and the call of the Gentiles comes about. How could He have called us if He had not been crucified, for it is only on the cross that a man dies with arms outstretched? Here, again, we see the fitness of His death and of those outstretched arms: it was that He might draw His ancient people with the one and the Gentiles with the other, and join both together in Himself. Even so, He foretold the manner of His redeeming death, "I, if I be lifted up, will draw all men unto Myself."

Again, the air is the sphere of the devil, the enemy of our race who, having fallen from heaven, endeavors with the other evil spirits who shared in his disobedience both to keep souls from the truth and to hinder the progress of those who are trying to follow it. The apostle refers to this when he says, "According to the prince of the power of the air, of the spirit that now worketh in the sons of disobedience."

But the Lord came to overthrow the devil and to purify the air and to make "a way" for us up to heaven, as the apostle says, "through the veil, that is to say, His flesh." This had to be done through death, and by what other kind of death could it be done, save by a death in the air, that is, on the cross? Here, again, you see how right and natural it was that the Lord should suffer thus; for being thus "lifted up," He cleansed the air from all the evil influences of the enemy. "I beheld Satan as lightning falling," He says; and thus He re-opened the road to heaven, saying again, "Lift up your gates, O ye princes, and be ye lift up, ye everlasting doors."

For it was not the Word Himself Who needed an opening of the gates, He being Lord of all, nor was any of His works closed to their Maker. No, it was we who needed it, we whom He Himself upbore in His own body – that body which He first offered to death on behalf of all, and then made through it a path to heaven.

Questions for Study

1 This work takes the form both of a systematic exposition of the Christian understanding of the identity of Christ, and of a refutation of rival viewpoints. What rival viewpoints can be discerned in this extract, and how does Athanasius respond to them?
2 How would you describe the "tone" of this writing? What kind of audience do you think Athanasius has in mind?
3 What answer does Athanasius give to critics who argued that Christ ought to have avoided death on the cross?

4th Century

Text: *The Life of Antony*   *Father of all works.*

The "Life of Antony" is a classic example of early Christian hagiography. Although some have questioned whether the work was written by Athanasius, there are reasons for maintaining this attribution. If not written by Athanasius, however, it is certainly to be attributed to his circle. The work is widely regarded as an outstanding defense of the ideals of the monastic movement, as well as a significant contribution to the development of the literary genre of hagiography.

1 Antony, you must know, was by descent an Egyptian: his parents were of good family and possessed considerable wealth, and as they were Christians he also was reared in the same Faith. In infancy he was brought up with his parents, knowing nought else but them and his home. But when he was grown and arrived at boyhood, and was advancing in years, he could not endure to learn letters, not caring to associate with other boys; but all his desire was, as it is written of Jacob, to live a plain man at home. With his parents he used to attend the Lord's House, and neither as a child was he idle nor when older did he despise them; but was both obedient to his father and mother and attentive to what was read, keeping in his heart what was profitable in what he heard. And though as a child brought up in moderate affluence, he did not trouble his parents for varied or luxurious fare, nor was this a source of pleasure to him; but was content simply with what he found nor sought anything further.

2 After the death of his father and mother he was left alone with one little sister: his age was about eighteen or twenty, and on him the care both of home and sister rested. Now it was not six months after the death of his parents, and going according to custom into the Lord's House, he communed with himself and reflected as he walked how the Apostles left all and followed the Savior; and how they in the Acts sold their possessions and brought and laid them at the Apostles' feet for distribution to the needy, and what and how great a hope was laid up for them in heaven. Pondering over these things he entered the church, and it happened the Gospel was being read, and he heard the Lord saying to the rich man, "If thou wouldest be perfect, go and sell that thou hast and give to the poor; and come follow Me and thou shalt have treasure in heaven." Antony, as though God had put him in mind of

the Saints, and the passage had been read on his account, went out immediately from the church, and gave the possessions of his forefathers to the villagers – they were three hundred acres, productive and very fair – that they should be no more a clog upon himself and his sister. And all the rest that was movable he sold, and having got together much money he gave it to the poor, reserving a little however for his sister's sake.

3   And again as he went into the church, hearing the Lord say in the Gospel, "be not anxious for the morrow," he could stay no longer, but went out and gave those things also to the poor. Having committed his sister to known and faithful virgins, and put her into a convent to be brought up, he henceforth devoted himself outside his house to discipline, taking heed to himself and training himself with patience. For there were not yet so many monasteries in Egypt, and no monk at all knew of the distant desert; but all who wished to give heed to themselves practiced the discipline in solitude near their own village. Now there was then in the next village an old man who had lived the life of a hermit from his youth up. Antony, after he had seen this man, imitated him in piety. And at first he began to abide in places outside the village: then if he heard of a good man anywhere, like the prudent bee, he went forth and sought him, nor turned back to his own palace until he had seen him; and he returned, having got from the good man as it were supplies for his journey in the way of virtue. So dwelling there at first, he confirmed his purpose not to return to the abode of his fathers nor to the remembrance of his kinsfolk; but to keep all his desire and energy for perfecting his discipline. He worked, however, with his hands, having heard, "he who is idle let him not eat," and part he spent on bread and part he gave to the needy. And he was constant in prayer, knowing that a man ought to pray in secret unceasingly. For he had given such heed to what was read that none of the things that were written fell from him to the ground, but he remembered all, and afterwards his memory served him for books.

4   Thus conducting himself, Antony was beloved by all. He subjected himself in sincerity to the good men whom he visited, and learned thoroughly where each surpassed him in zeal and discipline. He observed the graciousness of one; the unceasing prayer of another; he took knowledge of another's freedom from anger and another's loving-kindness; he gave heed to one as he watched, to another as he studied; one he admired for his endurance, another for his fasting and sleeping on the ground; the meekness of one and the long-suffering of another he watched with care, while he took note of the piety toward Christ and the mutual love which animated all. Thus filled, he returned to his own place of discipline, and henceforth would strive to unite the qualities of each, and was eager to show in himself the virtues of all. With others of the same age he had no rivalry; save this only, that he should not be second to them in higher things. And this he did so as to hurt the feelings of nobody, but made them rejoice over him. So all they of that village and the good men in whose intimacy he was, when they saw that he was a man of this sort, used to call him God-beloved. And some welcomed him as a son, others as a brother.

5   But the devil, who hates and envies what is good, could not endure to see such a resolution in a youth, but endeavored to carry out against him what he had been wont to effect against others. First of all he tried to lead him away from

the discipline, whispering to him the remembrance of his wealth, care for his sister, claims of kindred, love of money, love of glory, the various pleasures of the table and the other relaxations of life, and at last the difficulty of virtue and the labor of it; he suggested also the infirmity of the body and the length of the time. In a word he raised in his mind a great dust of debate, wishing to debar him from his settled purpose. But when the enemy saw himself to be too weak for Antony's determination, and that he rather was conquered by the other's firmness, overthrown by his great faith and falling through his constant prayers, then at length putting his trust in the weapons which are "in the navel of his belly" and boasting in them – for they are his first snare for the young – he attacked the young man, disturbing him by night and harassing him by day, so that even the onlookers saw the struggle which was going on between them. The one would suggest foul thoughts and the other counter them with prayers: the one fire him with lust, the other, as one who seemed to blush, fortify his body with faith, prayers, and fasting. And the devil, unhappy wight, one night even took upon him the shape of a woman and imitated all her acts simply to beguile Antony. But he, his mind filled with Christ and the nobility inspired by Him, and considering the spirituality of the soul, quenched the coal of the other's deceit. Again the enemy suggested the ease of pleasure. But he like a man filled with rage and grief turned his thoughts to the threatened fire and the gnawing worm, and setting these in array against his adversary, passed through the temptation unscathed. All this was a source of shame to his foe. For he, deeming himself like God, was now mocked by a young man; and he who boasted himself against flesh and blood was being put to flight by a man in the flesh. For the Lord was working with Antony – the Lord who for our sake took flesh and gave the body victory over the devil, so that all who truly fight can say, "not I but the grace of God which was with me."

6 At last when the dragon could not even thus overthrow Antony, but saw himself thrust out of his heart, gnashing his teeth as it is written, and as it were beside himself, he appeared to Antony like a black boy, taking a visible shape in accordance with the color of his mind. And cringing to him, as it were, he plied him with thoughts no longer, for guileful as he was, he had been worsted, but at last spoke in human voice and said, "Many I deceived, many I cast down; but now attacking thee and thy labors as I had many others, I proved weak." When Antony asked, "Who art thou who speakest thus with me?" he answered with a lamentable voice, "I am the friend of whoredom, and have taken upon me incitements which lead to it against the young. I am called the spirit of lust. How many have I deceived who wished to live soberly, how many are the chaste whom by my incitements I have over-persuaded! I am he on account of whom also the prophet reproves those who have fallen, saying, 'Ye have been caused to err by the spirit of whoredom.' For by me they have been tripped up. I am he who have so often troubled thee and have so often been overthrown by thee." But Antony having given thanks to the Lord, with good courage said to him, "Thou art very despicable then, for thou art black-hearted and weak as a child. Henceforth I shall have no trouble from thee, 'for the Lord is my helper, and I shall look down on mine enemies.'" Having heard this, the black one straightway fled, shuddering at the words and dreading any longer even to come near the man.

7   This was Antony's first struggle against the devil, or rather this victory was the Savior's work in Antony, "Who condemned sin in the flesh that the ordinance of the law might be fulfilled in us who walk not after the flesh but after the spirit." But neither did Antony, although the evil one had fallen, henceforth relax his care and despise him; nor did the enemy as though conquered cease to lay snares for him. For again he went round as a lion seeking some occasion against him. But Antony having learned from the Scriptures that the devices of the devil are many, zealously continued the discipline, reckoning that though the devil had not been able to deceive his heart by bodily pleasure, he would endeavor to ensnare him by other means. For the demon loves sin. Wherefore more and more he repressed the body and kept it in subjection, lest haply having conquered on one side, he should be dragged down on the other. He therefore planned to accustom himself to a severer mode of life. And many marveled, but he himself used to bear the labor easily; for the eagerness of soul, through the length of time it had abode in him, had wrought a good habit in him, so that taking but little initiation from others he shewed great zeal in this matter. He kept vigil to such an extent that he often continued the whole night without sleep; and this not once but often, to the marvel of others. He ate once a day, after sunset, sometimes once in two days, and often even in four. His food was bread and salt, his drink, water only. Of flesh and wine it is superfluous even to speak, since no such thing was found with the other earnest men. A rush mat served him to sleep upon, but for the most part he lay upon the bare ground. He would not anoint himself with oil, saying it behooved young men to be earnest in training and not to seek what would enervate the body; but they must accustom it to labor, mindful of the Apostle's words, "when I am weak, then am I strong." "For," said he, "the fibre of the soul is then sound when the pleasures of the body are diminished." And he had come to this truly wonderful conclusion, "that progress in virtue, and retirement from the world for the sake of it, ought not to be measured by time, but by desire and fixity of purpose." He at last gave no thought to the past, but day by day, as if he were at the beginning of his discipline, applied greater pains for advancement, often repeating to himself the saying of Paul: "Forgetting the things which are behind and stretching forward to the things which are before." He was also mindful of the words spoken by the prophet Elijah, "the Lord liveth before whose presence I stand to-day." For he observed that in saying "to-day" the prophet did not compute the time that had gone by: but daily as though ever commencing he eagerly endeavored to make himself fit to appear before God, being pure in heart and ever ready to submit to His counsel, and to Him alone. And he used to say to himself that from the life of the great Elias the hermit ought to see his own as in a mirror.

8   Thus tightening his hold upon himself, Antony departed to the tombs, which happened to be at a distance from the village; and having bid one of his acquaintances to bring him bread at intervals of many days, he entered one of the tombs, and the other having shut the door on him, he remained within alone. And when the enemy could not endure it, but was even fearful that in a short time Antony would fill the desert with the discipline, coming one night with a multitude of demons, he so cut him with stripes that he lay on the ground speechless from the excessive pain. For he affirmed that the torture had been so excessive that no blows inflicted by man could ever have caused him such torment. But by the Providence

of God – for the Lord never overlooks them that hope in Him – the next day his acquaintance came bringing him the loaves. And having opened the door and seeing him lying on the ground as though dead, he lifted him up and carried him to the church in the village, and laid him upon the ground. And many of his kinsfolk and the villagers sat around Antony as round a corpse. But about midnight he came to himself and arose, and when be saw them all asleep and his comrade alone watching, he motioned with his head for him to approach, and asked him to carry him again to the tombs without waking anybody.

9   He was carried therefore by the man, and as he was wont, when the door was shut he was within alone. And he could not stand up on account of the blows, but he prayed as he lay. And after he had prayed, he said with a shout, Here am I, Antony; I flee not from your stripes, for even if you inflict more nothing shall separate rues from the love of Christ. And then he sang, "though a camp be set against me, my heart shall not be afraid." These were the thoughts and words of this ascetic. But the enemy, who hates good, marveling that after the blows he dared to return, called together his hounds and burst forth, "Ye see," said he, "that neither by the spirit of lust nor by blows did we stay the man, but that he braves us, let us attack him in another fashion." But changes of form for evil are easy for the devil, so in the night they made such a din that the whole of that place seemed to be shaken by an earthquake, and the demons as if breaking the four walls of the dwelling seemed to enter through them, coming in the likeness of beasts and creeping things. And the place was on a sudden filled with the forms of lions, bears, leopards, bulls, serpents, asps, scorpions, and wolves, and each of them was moving according to his nature. The lion was roaring, wishing to attack, the bull seeming to toss with its horns, the serpent writhing but unable to approach, and the wolf as it rushed on was restrained; altogether the noises of the apparitions, with their angry ragings, were dreadful. But Antony, stricken and goaded by them, felt bodily pains severer still. He lay watching, however, with unshaken soul, groaning from bodily anguish; but his mind was clear, and as in mockery he said, "If there had been any power in you, it would have sufficed had one of you come, but since the Lord hath made you weak you attempt to terrify me by numbers: and a proof of your weakness is that you take the shapes of brute beasts." And again with boldness he said, "If you are able, and have received power against me, delay not to attack; but if you are unable, why trouble me in vain? For faith in our Lord is a seal and a wall of safety to us." So after many attempts they gnashed their teeth upon him, because they were mocking themselves rather than him.

10   Nor was the Lord then forgetful of Antony's wrestling, but was at hand to help him. So looking up he saw the roof as it were opened, and a ray of light descending to him. The demons suddenly vanished, the pain of his body straightway ceased, and the building was again whole. But Antony feeling the help, and getting his breath again, and being freed from pain, besought the vision which had appeared to him, saying, "Where wert thou? Why didst thou not appear at the beginning to make my pains to cease?" And a voice came to him, "Antony, I was here, but I waited to see thy fight; wherefore since thou hast endured, and hast not been worsted, I will ever be a succor to thee, and will make thy name known everywhere." Having heard this, Antony arose and prayed, and received such strength that he perceived that he

had more power in his body than formerly. And he was then about thirty-five years old.

11   And on the day following he went forth still more eagerly bent on the service of God and having fallen in with the old man he had met previously, he asked him to dwell with him in the desert. But when the other declined on account of his great age, and because as yet there was no such custom, Antony himself set off forthwith to the mountain. And yet again the enemy seeing his zeal and wishing to hinder it, cast in his way what seemed to be a great silver dish. But Antony, seeing the guile of the Evil One, stood, and having looked on the dish, he put the devil in it to shame, saying, "Whence comes a dish in the desert? This road is not well-worn, nor is there here a trace of any wayfarer; it could not have fallen without being missed on account of its size; and he who had lost it having turned back, to seek it, would have found it, for it is a desert place. This is some wile of the devil. O thou Evil One, not with this shalt thou hinder my purpose; let it go with thee to destruction." And when Antony had said this it vanished like smoke from the face of fire.

Questions for Discussion

1   What attitude does Athanasius adopt to Anthony? Would you describe this as "neutral"? What factors do you think have led Athanasius to write in this way?
2   What is the likely readership of the work? And how does this affect our understanding both of the information Athanasius chooses to include, and the attitude he adopts toward Anthony?
3   What aspects of Anthony's life are of especial importance to Athanasius? What interpretation does he place upon them?
4   What light does this work cast on the motivations of those who pioneered the early monastic movement in Egypt?

CHAPTER 8

Ephraim the Syrian (303–373)

There is considerable uncertainty over the early life of Ephraim. He was born in the ancient city of Nisibis in Mesopotamia, on the eastern extremity of the Roman Empire. A number of references in his writings suggest that he was born in or before the earliest days of the reign of Constantine the Great (306–337). He served as a deacon and catechist under a number of leading Christians. The first of these was Jacob, Bishop of Nisibis, who died in 338. Jacob was one of those who attended the Council of Nicea in 325, and appointed Ephraim as catechist on his return. Ephraim continued to live in Nisibis after Jacob's death, serving under Babu (338–350), Vologeses (350–361), and Abraham (who was consecrated in 361).

Ephraim the Syrian (303–373)

Basic description
Leading Syrian Christian spiritual and theological writer.

Major works
The Hymns on Paradise; The Pearl.

Major studies
Sebastian Brock, *St Ephrem the Syrian: Hymns on Paradise*. Crestwood, NY: St Vladimir Seminary Press, 1990.
Tryggve Kronholm, *Motifs from Genesis 1–11 in the Genuine Hymns of Ephrem the Syrian with Particular Reference to the Influence of Jewish Exegetical Tradition*. Lund: Gleerup, 1978.

Throughout this period, Nisibis found itself to be vulnerable to Persian attack, on account of its exposed position on the easternmost flank of the Roman Empire. Ephraim remained in the city throughout three unsuccessful sieges laid by Sapor, King of Persia. However, in 363 the Emperor Julian was killed during the course of a Roman military expedition into Persian territory. Under the ensuing peace treaty concluded with Sapor by the Emperor Jovian after the defeat and death of his predecessor Julian, Nisibis became part of Persia. Its Christian population left the city, apparently as one of the conditions of the treaty. Ephraim finally settled at Edessa, about 150 kilometers west of Nisibis, and remained there until his death in 373. It was during this final phase of his life that he composed most of his works.

Text: The Pearl

The translation of this work into English was first undertaken in 1847 by John Brand Morris (1812–80), and published in the "Library of the Fathers," edited by E. B. Pusey. The translation attempts to capture the poetic style of the original. The central image which dominates the seven poems in this cycle is that of a pearl. The reference is to one of the "parables of the kingdom," told by Jesus during his ministry to explain the nature of the Kingdom of God: "The kingdom of heaven is like a merchant in search of fine pearls, who, on finding one pearl of great value, went and sold all that he had and bought it" (Matthew 13:45–46). The first two poems in the cycle are here reproduced in Morris's translation.

Hymn I

1

On a certain day a pearl did I take up, my brethren;
I saw in it mysteries pertaining to the Kingdom;
Semblances and types of the Majesty;
It became a fountain, and I drank out of it mysteries of the Son.

I put it, my brethren, upon the palm of my hand,
That I might examine it:
I went to look at it on one side,
And it proved faces on all sides.
I found out that the Son was incomprehensible,
Since He is wholly Light.

In its brightness I beheld the Bright One Who cannot be clouded,
And in its pureness a great mystery,
Even the Body of Our Lord which is well-refined:
In its undividedness I saw the Truth
Which is undivided.

It was so that I saw there its pure conception,
The Church, and the Son within her.
The cloud was the likeness of her that bare Him,
And her type the heaven,
Since there shone forth from her His gracious Shining.

I saw therein his Trophies, and His victories, and His crowns.
I saw His helpful and overflowing graces,
And His hidden things with His revealed things.

2

It was greater to me than the ark,
For I was astonished thereat:
I saw therein folds without shadow to them
Because it was a daughter of light,
Types vocal without tongues,
Utterances of mystery without lips,
A silent harp that without voice gave out melodies.

The trumpet falters and the thunder mutters;
Be not thou daring then;
Leave things hidden, take things revealed.
Thou hast seen in the clear sky a second shower;
The clefts of thine ears,
As from the clouds,
They are filled with interpretations.

And as that manna which alone filled the people,
In the place of pleasant meats,
With its pleasantnesses,
So does this pearl fill me in the place of books,
And the reading thereof,
And the explanations thereof.

And when I asked if there were yet other mysteries,
It had no mouth for me that I might hear from,
Neither any ears wherewith it might hear me.
O Thou thing without senses, whence I have gained new senses!

3

It answered me and said,   — pearl in the sea.
"The daughter of the sea am I, the illimitable sea!
And from that sea whence I came up it is
That there is a mighty treasury of mysteries in my bosom!
Search thou out the sea, but search not out the Lord of the sea!

"I have seen the divers who came down after me, when astonied,
So that from the midst of the sea they returned to the dry ground;
For a few moments they sustained it not.
Who would linger and be searching on into the depths of the Godhead?

"The waves of the Son are full of blessing,
And with mischiefs too.
Have ye not seen, then, the waves of the sea,
Which if a ship should struggle with them would break her to pieces,

And if she yield herself to them, and rebel not against them,
Then she is preserved?
In the sea all the Egyptians were choked, though they scrutinized it not,
And, without prying, the Hebrews too were overcome upon the dry land,
And how shall ye be kept alive?
And the men of Sodom were licked up by the fire,
And how shall ye prevail?

"At these uproars the fish in the sea were moved,
And Leviathan also.
Have ye then a heart of stone
That ye read these things and run into these errors?
O great fear that justice also should be so long silent!"

4

"Searching is mingled with thanksgiving,
And whether of the two will prevail?
From the tongue
The incense of praise riseth
Along with the fume of disputation
And unto which shall we hearken?
Prayer and prying from one mouth,
And which shall we listen to?

"For three days was Jonah a neighbour in the sea:
The living things that were in the sea were affrighted,
Saying, 'Who shall flee from God?'
Jonah fled,
And ye are obstinate at your scrutiny of Him!'"

Hymn 2

1

Whereunto art thou like?
Let thy stillness speak to one that hears;
With silent mouth speak with us:
For whoso hears the stammerings of thy silence,
to him thy type utters its silent cry concerning our Redeemer.   5

Thy mother is a virgin of the sea, though he took her not:
She fell into his bosom, though he knew her not;
She conceived thee near him, though he did not know her.

Do thou, that art a type, reproach the Jewish women
That have thee hung upon them.   10

Thou art the only progeny of all forms
Which art like to the Word on High,
Whom singly the Most High begot.
The engraven forms seem to be the type of created things above.
This visible offspring of the invisible womb   15
Is a type of great things.
Thy goodly conception was without seed,
And without wedlock was thy pure generation,
And without brethren was thy single birth.

Our Lord had brethren and yet not brethren,   20
Since He was an Only-Begotten.
O solitary one, thou type exact of the Only-Begotten!
There is a type of thine in the crown of kings,
Wherein thou hast brothers and sisters.
Goodly gems are thy brethren,   25
With beryls and unions as thy companions:
May gold be as it were thy kinsman,
May there be unto the King of kings
A crown from thy well-beloved ones!
When thou camest up from the sea, that living tomb,   30
Thou didst cry out,
Let me have a goodly assemblage of brethren, relatives and kinsmen.
As the wheat is in the stalk,
So thou art in the crown with princes:
And it is a just restoration to thee, as if of a pledge,   35
That from the depth thou shouldest be exalted to a goodly eminence.
Wheat the stalk bears in the field;
Thee the head of the king upon his chariot carries about.

O daughter of the water,
Who hast left the sea, wherein thou wert born,   40
And art gone up to the dry land, wherein thou art beloved:
For men have loved and seized and adorned themselves with thee,
Like as they did that Offspring Whom the Gentiles loved
And crowned themselves withal.   —> Sea monster

It is by the mystery of truth that Leviathan is trodden down of mortals: 45
The divers put him off, and put on Christ.
In the sacrament of oil did the Apostles steal Thee away, and came up.
They snatched their souls from his mouth, bitter as it was.
Thy Nature is like a silent lamb in its sweetness,
Of which if a man is to lay hold,   50

He lifts it in a crucial form by its ears, as it was on Golgotha.
He cast out abundantly all His gleams upon them that looked upon Him.

2

Shadowed forth in thy beauty is the beauty of the Son,
Who clothed Himself with suffering when the nails passed through Him.
The awl passed in thee since they handled thee roughly,
As they did His hands;
And because He suffered He reigned,
As by thy sufferings thy beauty increased.

And if they showed no pity upon thee,
Neither did they love thee:
Still suffer as thou mightest,
Thou hast come to reign! Simon Peter showed pity on the Rock;
Whoso hath smitten it, is himself thereby overcome;
It is by reason of Its suffering
That Its beauty hath adorned the height and the depth.

Questions for Study

1   In what way does Ephraim of Syria exploit the image of the pearl in this poem? You
will find it useful to note how the images of beauty dominate the early part of the
poem. Yet the image of recovery of a treasure from the sea begins to become more
important later. What use does Ephraim make of this theme?

2   What is the significance of the reference to "Jonah" and "Leviathan"? This term was
often used to refer to great sea creatures, and can be taken as a reference to the
whale in the story of Jonah. Yet Ephraim is approaching the account of Jonah from
a very specific perspective. The following words were spoken by Jesus to those who
demanded that he show them a sign to confirm his authority: "But he answered
them, 'An evil and adulterous generation seeks for a sign; but no sign shall be given
to it except the sign of the prophet Jonah. For as Jonah was three days and three
nights in the belly of the whale, so will the Son of man be three days and three nights
in the heart of the earth'" (Matthew 12:39–40). What light does this cast on
Ephraim's meaning here?

3   What is meant by the final few lines of the poem? Note how the theme of resurrection and crucifixion are interwoven at this point.

CHAPTER 9

Cyril of Jerusalem (ca. 315–387)

Cyril was appointed Bishop of Jerusalem around 349, and quickly established himself as a major presence in the intellectual and institutional life of the church in the eastern Mediterranean region. His ministry took place against a complex background of rivalry between various factions within the church, including disputes between the parties associated with the Arian controversy,* which was still a major issue throughout Cyril's lifetime. At one point in 357, Cyril was even exiled on the charge of selling church furniture during a famine.

Cyril of Jerusalem (ca. 315–387)

Basic description
Bishop of Jerusalem and catechetical writer.

Major work
Catechetical Lectures.

Major studies
Hugh M. Riley, *Christian Initiation: A Comparative Study of the Interpretation of the Baptismal Liturgy in the Mystagogical Writings of Cyril of Jerusalem, John Chrysostom, Theodore of Mopsuestia, and Ambrose of Milan*. Washington, D.C.: Catholic University of America, 1977.

Peter W. L. Walker, *Holy City, Holy Places? Christian Attitudes to Jerusalem and the Holy Land in the Fourth Century*. Oxford: Oxford University Press, 1996.

While Cyril's career reflects the complexities of Byzantine politics of the period, his major literary achievement is widely seen as the development of catechetical materials for the church. He delivered a series of catechetical lectures – that is, basic instruction in

---

* For a full discussion of the historical background to this controversy, and the issues which it raised, see Alister E. McGrath, *Christian Theology: An Introduction*, 2nd edn. Oxford: Blackwell, 1997, 330–7.

the Christian faith – during Lent, in preparation for the baptism of new believers on Easter eve. It may be noted at this point that the early church regarded the forty days of Lent as a time in which new believers could be instructed in the faith. Cyril's "Catechetical Lectures," which were delivered at some point around 350, are widely regarded as a classic example of this genre of Christian literature, and merit close study.

Text: *The Catechetical Lectures*

Cyril's catechetical lectures include an introductory address (the "Procatechesis"), eighteen lectures delivered in Lent to those who were preparing for baptism, and five "mystagogical" lectures given during Easter week to the same persons after their baptism. They contain many interesting local references, including several to the great basilica built by Constantine, in which these lectures were delivered. They seem to have been spoken extempore, and written down afterwards. The style is admirably clear, dignified, and well-ordered. The section of the lectures which is here reproduced is the opening "Procatechesis," which was delivered to the catechumenates (that is, those preparing for baptism) before the season of Lent actually began.

Procatechesis, or Prologue to the Catechetical Lectures of Our Holy Father, Cyril, Archbishop of Jerusalem

1   Already there is an odor of blessedness upon you, O you who are soon to be enlightened: already you are gathering the spiritual flowers, to weave heavenly crowns: already the fragrance of the Holy Spirit has breathed upon you: already you have gathered round the vestibule of the King's palace; may you be led in also by the King! For blossoms now have appeared upon the trees; may the fruit also be found perfect! Thus far there has been an inscription of your names, and a call to service, and torches of the bridal train, and a longing for heavenly citizenship, and a good purpose, and hope attendant thereon. For he lies not who said, that to them that love God all things work together for good. God is lavish in beneficence, yet He waits for each man's genuine will: therefore the Apostle added and said, to them that are called according to a purpose. The honesty of purpose makes you called: for if your body be here but not your mind, it profits you nothing.

2   Even Simon Magus once came to the Laver: he was baptized, but was not enlightened; and though he dipped his body in water, he did not enlighten his heart with the Spirit: his body went down and came up, but his soul was not buried with Christ, nor raised with Him. Now I mention the statements of (men's) falls, that you may not fall: for these things happened to them by way of example, and they are written for the admonition of those who to this day draw near. Let none of you be found tempting His grace, lest any root of bitterness spring up and trouble you. Let none of you enter saying, Let us see what the faithful are doing: let me go in and see, that I may learn what is being done. Do you expect to see, and not expect to be seen? And do you think, that while you art searching out what is going on, God is not searching your heart?

[handwritten margin note: like a story.]

3 A certain man in the Gospels once pried into the marriage feast, and took an unbecoming garment, and came in, sat down, and ate: for the bridegroom permitted it. But when he saw them all clad in white, he ought to have assumed a garment of the same kind himself: whereas he partook of the like food, but was unlike them in fashion and in purpose. The bridegroom, however, though bountiful, was not undiscerning: and in going round to each of the guests and observing them (for his care was not for their eating, but for their seemly behavior), he saw a stranger not having on a wedding garment, and said to him, Friend, how did you come in here? In what a color! With what a conscience! What though the door-keeper did not prevent you, because of the generosity of the entertainer? What though you were ignorant in what fashion you should come in to the banquet? – you did come in, and did see the glittering fashions of the guests: should you not have been taught even by what was before your eyes? Should you not have retired in good season, that you might enter in good season again? But now you have come in unseasonably, to be unseasonably cast out. So he commands the servants, Bind his feet, which daringly intruded: bind his hands, which knew not how to put a bright garment around him: and cast him into the outer darkness; for he is unworthy of the wedding torches. You see what happened to that man: make your own condition safe.

[handwritten margin note: Not comited to it. There but not for the right reasons.]

[handwritten margin note: Body their but Mind + Spirit Not.]

4 For we, the ministers of Christ, have admitted every one, and occupying, as it were, the place of door-keepers we left the door open: and possibly you did enter with your soul stained with sins, and with a will defiled. Enter you did, and were allowed: your name was inscribed. Tell me, do you behold this venerable constitution of the Church? Do you view her order and discipline, the reading of Scriptures, the presence of the ordained, the course of instruction? Be abashed at the place, and be taught by what you see. Go out opportunely now, and enter most opportunely tomorrow.

If the fashion of your soul is avarice, put on another fashion and come in. Put off your former fashion; do not cover it up. Put off, I ask you, fornication and unclean-ness, and put on the brightest robe of chastity. This charge I give you, before Jesus the Bridegroom of souls shall come in and see their fashions. A long notice is allowed you; you have forty days for repentance: you have full opportunity both to put off, and wash, and to put on and enter. But if you persist in an evil purpose, the speaker is blameless, but you must not look for the grace: for the water will receive, but the Spirit will not accept you. If any one is conscious of his wound, let him take the salve; if any has fallen, let him arise. Let there be no Simon among you, no hypocrisy, no idle curiosity about the matter.

[handwritten margin note: has 40 days to change mind and be there as a whole not part. All about Purity. Baptism Make a person Pure.]

5 Possibly too you have come on another pretext. It is possible that a man is wishing to pay court to a woman, and came hither on that account. The remark applies in like manner to women also in their turn. A slave also perhaps wishes to please his master, and a friend his friend. I accept this bait for the hook, and welcome you, though you came with an evil purpose, yet as one to be saved by a good hope. Perhaps you knew not whither you were coming, nor in what kind of net you are taken. You have come within the Church's nets: be taken alive, flee not: for Jesus is angling for you, not in order to kill, but by killing to make alive: for you must die and rise again. For you have heard the Apostle say, Dead indeed unto sin, but living

unto righteousness. Die to your sins, and live to righteousness, live from this very day.

6   See, I ask you, how great a dignity Jesus bestows on you. You were called a Catechumen, while the word echoed round you from without; hearing of hope, and knowing it not; hearing mysteries, and not understanding them; hearing Scriptures, and not knowing their depth. The echo is no longer around you, but within you; for the indwelling Spirit henceforth makes your mind a house of God. When you have heard what is written concerning the mysteries, then will you understand things which you did not know. And do think not that you receive a small thing: though a miserable man, you receive one of God's titles. Hear St. Paul saying, God is faithful. Hear another Scripture saying, God is faithful and just. Foreseeing this, the Psalmist, because men are to receive a title of God, spoke thus in the person of God: I said, you are Gods, and are all sons of the Most High. But beware lest you have the title of "faithful," but the will of the faithless. You have entered into a contest, toil on through the race: another such opportunity you cannot have. Were it your wedding-day before you, would you not have disregarded all else, and set about the preparation for the feast? And on the eve of consecrating your soul to the heavenly Bridegroom, will you not cease from carnal things, that you may win spiritual things?

7   We may not receive baptism twice or thrice; otherwise it might be said, Though I have failed once, I shall set it right a second time: whereas if you fail once, the thing cannot be set right; for there is one Lord, and one faith, and one baptism: for only the heretics are re-baptized, because the former was no baptism.

8   For God seeks nothing else from us, save a good purpose. Say not, How are my sins blotted out? I tell you, By willing, by believing. What can be shorter than this? But if, while your lips declare that you are willing, your heart is silent, He knows the heart, who judges you. Cease from this day from every evil deed. Let not your tongue speak unseemly words, let your eye abstain from sin, and from roving after things unprofitable.

9   Let your feet hasten to the catechizings; receive with earnestness the exorcisms: whether you be breathed upon or exorcized, the act is to your salvation. Suppose you have gold unwrought and alloyed, mixed with various substances, copper, and tin, and iron, and lead: we seek to have the gold alone. Can gold be purified from the foreign substances without fire? Even so, without exorcisms the soul cannot be purified; and these exorcisms are divine, having been collected out of the divine Scriptures. Your face has been veiled, that your mind may henceforward be free, lest the eye by roving make the heart rove also. But when your eyes are veiled, your ears are not hindered from receiving the means of salvation. For in like manner as those who are skilled in the goldsmith's craft throw in their breath upon the fire through certain delicate instruments, and blowing up the gold which is hidden in the crucible stir the flame which surrounds it, and so find what they are seeking; even so when the exorcists inspire terror by the Spirit of God, and set the soul, as it were, on fire in the crucible of the body, the hostile demon flees away, and there abide salvation and the hope of eternal life, and the soul henceforth is cleansed from its sins and hath salvation. Let us then, brethren, abide in hope, and surrender ourselves, and hope,

in order that the God of all may see our purpose, and cleanse us from our sins, and impart to us good hopes of our estate, and grant us repentance that brings salvation. God hath called, and His call is to you.

10   Attend closely to the catechizings, and though we should prolong our discourse, let not your mind be wearied out. For you are receiving armor against the adverse power, armor against heresies, against Jews, and Samaritans, and Gentiles. You have many enemies; take to you many darts, for you have many to hurl them at: and you need to learn how to strike down the Greek, how to contend against heretic, against Jew and Samaritan. And the armor is ready, and most ready the sword of the Spirit: but you also must stretch forth your right hand with good resolution, that you may war the Lord's warfare, and overcome adverse powers, and become invincible against every heretical attempt.

11   Let me give you this charge also. Study our teachings and keep them for ever. Do not think that they are the ordinary homilies; for though they also are good and trustworthy, yet if we should neglect them today we may study them tomorrow. But if the teaching concerning the layer of regeneration delivered in a consecutive course be neglected today, when shall it be made right? Suppose it is the season for planting trees: if we do not dig, and dig deep, when else can that be planted rightly which has once been planted badly? Suppose that the catechizing is a kind of building: if we do not bind the house together by regular bonds in the building, lest some gap be found, and the building become unsound, even our former labor is of no use. But stone must follow stone by course, and corner match with corner, and by our smoothing off inequalities the building must thus rise evenly. In a similar manner we are bringing to you stones, as it were, of knowledge. You must hear concerning the living God, you must hear of judgment, you must hear of Christ, and of the Resurrection. And many things there are to be discussed in succession, which though now dropped one by one are afterwards to be presented in harmonious connexion. But unless you fit them together in the one whole, and remember what is first, and what is second, the builder may build, but you will find the building unsound.

12   When, therefore, the Lecture is delivered, if a Catechumen ask you what the teachers have said, tell nothing to anyone from outside. For we deliver to you a mystery, and a hope of the life to come. Guard the mystery for Him who gives the reward. Let none ever say to you, What harm does it do you, if I also know it? So too the sick ask for wine; but if it is given at a wrong time it causes delirium, and two evils arise; the sick man dies, and the physician is blamed. Thus is it also with the Catechumen, if he hear anything from the believer: both the Catechumen becomes delirious (for he does not understand what he has heard, and finds fault with the thing, and scoffs at what is said), and the believer is condemned as a traitor. But you are now standing on the border: take heed, pray, to tell nothing out; not that the things spoken are not worthy to be told, but because his ear is unworthy to receive. You were once a Catechumen yourself, and I did not describe what lay before you. When by experience you have learned how high are the matters of our teaching, then you will know that the Catechumens are not worthy to hear them.

13   You who have been enrolled are become sons and daughters of one Mother. When you have come in before the hour of the exorcisms, let each one of you speak

things tending to godliness: and if any of your number be not present, seek for him. If you were called to a banquet, would you not wait for your fellow guest? If you had a brother, would you not seek your brother's good?

Afterwards do not busy yourself about unprofitable matters: neither, what the city has done, nor the village, nor the King, nor the Bishop, nor the Presbyter. Look upward; that is what your present hour needs. Be still, and know that I am God. If you see the believers ministering, and showing no care, they enjoy security, they know what they have received, they are in possession of grace. But you stand just now in the turn of the scale, to be received or not: copy not those who have freedom from anxiety, but cherish fear.

14   And when the Exorcism has been done, until the others who are being exorcised have come, let men be with men, and women with women. For now I need the example of Noah's ark: in which were Noah and his sons, and his wife and his sons' wives. For though the ark was one, and the door was shut, yet things had been suitably arranged. If the Church is shut, and you are all inside, yet let there be a separation, men with men, and women with women: lest the pretext of salvation become an occasion of destruction. Even if there be a fair pretext for sitting near each other, let passions be put away. Further, let the men when sitting have a useful book; and let one read, and another listen: and if there be no book, let one pray, and another speak something useful. And again let the party of young women sit together in like manner, either singing or reading quietly, so that their lips speak, but others' ears catch not the sound: for I do not allow a woman to speak in the Church. And let the married woman also follow the same example, and pray; and let her lips move, but her voice be unheard, that a Samuel may come, and your barren soul give birth to the salvation of "God who hath heard your prayer"; for this is the interpretation of the name Samuel.

15   I shall observe each man's earnestness, each woman's reverence. Let your mind be refined as by fire unto reverence; let your soul be forged as metal: let the stubbornness of unbelief be hammered out: let the superfluous scales of the iron drop off, and what is pure remain; let the rust of the iron be rubbed off, and the true metal remain. May God sometime show you that night, the darkness which shines like the day, concerning which it is said, The darkness shall not be hidden from you, and the night shall shine as the day. Then may the gate of Paradise be opened to every man and every woman among you. Then may you enjoy the Christ-bearing waters in their fragrance. Then may you receive the name of Christ, and the power of things divine. Even now, I beseech you, lift up the eye of the mind: even now imagine the choirs of angels, and God the Lord of all there sitting, and His Only-begotten Son sitting with Him on His right hand, and the Spirit present with them; and Thrones and Dominions doing service, and every man of you and every woman receiving salvation. Even now let your ears ring, as it were, with that glorious sound, when over your salvation the angels shall chant, Blessed are they whose iniquities are forgiven, and whose sins are covered: when like stars of the Church you shall enter in, bright in the body and radiant in the soul.

16   Great is the Baptism that lies before you: a ransom to captives; a remission of offences; a death of sin; a new birth of the soul; a garment of light; a holy indissoluble seal; a chariot to heaven; the delight of Paradise; a welcome into the kingdom;

the gift of adoption! But there is a serpent by the wayside watching those who pass by: beware lest he bite you with unbelief. He sees so many receiving salvation, and is seeking whom he may devour. You are coming in to the Father of Spirits, but you are going past that serpent. How then may you pass him? Have your feet shod with the preparation of the gospel of peace; that even if he should bite, he may not hurt you. Have faith indwelling, steadfast hope, a strong sandal, that you may pass the enemy, and enter the presence of your Lord. Prepare your own heart for reception of doctrine, for fellowship in holy mysteries. Pray more frequently, that God may make you worthy of the heavenly and immortal mysteries. Cease not day nor night: but when sleep is banished from your eyes, then let your mind be free for prayer. And if you find any shameful thought rise up in your mind, turn to meditation upon judgment to remind you of Salvation. Give your mind wholly to study, that it may forget base things. If you find any one saying to you, Are you then going in, to descend into the water? Has the city just now no baths? take notice that it is the dragon of the sea who is laying these plots against you. Attend not to the lips of the talker, but to God who works in you. Guard your own soul, that you be not ensnared, to the end that abiding in hope you may become an heir of everlasting salvation.

17   We for our part as men charge and teach you thus: but make not you our building hay and stubble and chaff, lest we suffer loss, from our work being burnt up: but make you our work gold, and silver, and precious stones! For it lies in me to speak, but in you to set your mind upon it, and in God to make perfect. Let us nerve our minds, and brace up our souls, and prepare our hearts. The race is for our soul: our hope is of things eternal: and God, who knows your hearts, and observes who is sincere, and who a hypocrite, is able both to guard the sincere, and to give faith to the hypocrite: for even to the unbeliever, if only he give his heart, God is able to give faith. So may He blot out the handwriting that is against you, and grant you forgiveness of your former trespasses; may He plant you into His Church, and enlist you in His own service, and put on you the armor of righteousness: may He fill you with the heavenly things of the New Covenant, and give you the seal of the Holy Spirit indelible throughout all ages, in Christ Jesus Our Lord: to whom be the glory for ever and ever! Amen.

Questions for Study

1   Cyril occasionally uses the image of refining gold in this lecture. What does he mean by this?
2   Why does Cyril not want his audience to discuss his teaching with those who are outside the church?
3   What is the point that Cyril is making through his illustration of the man who attends a marriage feast inappropriately dressed?

CHAPTER 10

Gregory of Nyssa (ca. 330–ca. 395)

Gregory was one of three notable Christian writers based in Cappadocia (a region of Asia Minor, now part of modern Turkey). Along with his colleagues Basil of Caesarea and Gregory of Nazianzus, Gregory of Nyssa is often referred to as a "Cappadocian father." Details of his early life are somewhat sketchy. Gregory's early years coincided with the last revival of pagan culture within the Roman Empire, culminating with the reign of Julian the Apostate (reigned 361–363). He was very positively impressed by the renewed classical learning of this period, and went on initially to become a teacher of rhetoric. Authors such as Plato (especially the *Phaedrus*, *Phaedo*, *Republic*), and representatives of Middle Platonism, such as Iamblicus (cosmology), Porphyry (logic), and Plotinus feature in his writings, in which he shows an awareness of the importance of the writers and the issues which they raised for Christian theology. Despite his obvious familiarity with classical philosophical ideas, however, he does not appear to have been educated at any of the important intellectual centers of the late Hellenistic world.

At a later stage, he traveled throughout Palestine and Egypt to visit monastic and hermetical communities, which stimulated him to take up this form of life at the family estate in Pontus along with Gregory of Nazianzus. Having been appointed by his brother Basil of Caesarea to the relatively minor bishopric of Nyssa at some point around 371, he was deposed five years later by the Arian faction on the pretense of mismanaging his jurisdiction. He was forced into exile until 378. The Roman Emperor Valens died in that same year, and was succeeded by Theodosius I. Theodosius was a strong supporter of Nicene orthodoxy, and was determined to combat the growth of Arianism.* In 381, the emperor charged Gregory with maintaining orthodoxy throughout the region of Pontus. Around this time, Gregory also played a significant role at the Council of Constantinople, and went on to provide a vigorous refutation of the ideas of the Arian theologian Eunomius who claimed that a person could attain direct knowledge of the divinity without the need for divine revelation.

---

* For a full discussion of the historical background to this controversy, and the issues which it raised, see Alister E. McGrath, *Christian Theology: An Introduction*, 2nd edn. Oxford: Blackwell, 1997, 330–7.

Gregory was a prolific writer, and his obvious competence in rhetoric makes his writings of unusually high literary quality and interest. His most important writings are those dealing with the exegesis of the Bible – particularly his homilies on Ecclesiastes, the Lord's Prayer, and the Beatitudes. He also wrote a number of major theological treatises, many of which took the form of polemical writings directed against individuals such as Apollinarius and Eunomius.

Gregory of Nyssa (ca. 330–ca. 395)

Basic description
Bishop of Nyssa; spiritual and theological writer.

Major works
"Life of Moses"; Homilies on the Lord's Prayer and the Beatitudes.

Major studies
Michael Azkoul, *St. Gregory of Nyssa and the Tradition of the Fathers.* Lampeter: Edwin Mellen Press, 1995.
Anthony Meredith, *Gregory of Nyssa.* London: Routledge, 1999.

Text: *Funeral Oration on Meletius*

Gregory is noted for his rhetorical skills, which are perhaps best seen deployed in his homilies and other orations, rather than in his more polemical works. One of Gregory's most polished pieces of rhetoric is the funeral oration for Meletius of Antioch, who died in 381, while presiding at the Council of Constantinople. Meletius was very highly regarded in Asia Minor, and his unexpected death was the occasion of much grief in the region. It also led to a split in the church at Antioch over which of two factions could be considered his true heirs. The oration provides little in the way of biographical information concerning Meletius, and is best read as an eulogy which is heavily studded with biblical imagery and allusions. It represents a classic example of an early Christian commemorative oration.

The number of the Apostles has been enlarged for us by this our late Apostle being reckoned among their company. These Holy ones have drawn to themselves one of like conversation; those athletes a fellow athlete; those crowned ones another crowned like them; the pure in heart one chaste in soul: those ministers of the Word another herald of that Word. Most blessed, indeed, is our Father for this his joining the Apostolic band and his departure to Christ. Most pitiable we! for the unseasonableness of our orphaned condition does not permit us to congratulate ourselves on our Father's happy lot. For him, indeed, better it was by his departure hence to be with Christ, but it was a grievous thing for us to be severed from his fatherly guidance.

Behold, it is a time of need for counsel; and our counselor is silent. War, the war of heresy, encompasses us, and our Leader is no more. The general body of the Church labors under disease, and we find not the physician. See in what a strait we are. Oh! that it were possible I could nerve my weakness, and rising to the full proportions of our loss, burst out with a voice of lamentation adequate to the greatness of the distress, as these excellent preachers of yours have done, who have bewailed with loud voice the misfortune that has befallen them in this loss of their father. But what can I do? How can I force my tongue to the service of the theme, thus heavily weighted, and shackled, as it were, by this calamity? How shall I open my mouth thus subdued to speechlessness? How shall I give free utterance to a voice now habitually sinking to the pathetic tone of lamentations? How can I lift up the eyes of my soul, veiled as I am with this darkness of misfortune? Who will pierce for me this deep dark cloud of grief, and light up again, as out of a clear sky, the bright ray of peace? From what quarter will that ray shine forth, now that our star has set? Oh! evil moonless night that gives no hope of any star!

With what an opposite meaning, as compared with those of late, are our words uttered in this place now! Then we rejoiced with the song of marriage, now we give way to piteous lamentation for the sorrow that has befallen us! Then we chanted an epithalamium, but now a funeral dirge! You remember the day when we entertained you at the feast of that spiritual marriage, and brought home the virgin bride to the house of her noble bridegroom; when to the best of our ability we proffered the wedding gifts of our praises, both giving and receiving joy in turn. But now our delight has been changed to lamentation, and our festal garb become sackcloth. It were better, maybe, to suppress our woe, and to hide our grief in silent seclusion, so as not to disturb the children of the bride-chamber, divested as we are of the bright marriage garment, and clothed instead with the black robe of the preacher.

For since that noble bridegroom has been taken from us, sorrow has all at once clothed us in the garb of black; nor is it possible for us to indulge in the usual cheerfulness of our conversation, since Envy has stripped us of our proper and becoming dress. Rich in blessings we came to you; now we leave you bare and poor. The lamp we held right above our head, shining with the rich fulness of light, we now carry away quenched, its bright flame all dissolved into smoke and dust. We held our great treasure in an earthen vessel. Vanished is the treasure, and the earthen vessel, emptied of its wealth, is restored to them who gave it. What shall we say to those who have consigned it? What answer will they make by whom it is demanded back?

Oh! miserable shipwreck! How, even with the harbor around us, have we gone to pieces with our hopes! How has the vessel, fraught with a thousand bales of goods, sunk with all its cargo, and left us destitute who were once so rich! Where is that bright sail which was ever filled by the Holy Ghost? Where is that safe helm of our souls which steered us while we sailed unhurt over the swelling waves of heresy? Where that immovable anchor of intelligence which held us in absolute security and repose after our toils? Where is that excellent pilot who steered our bark to its heavenly goal?

Is, then, what has happened of small moment, and is my passionate grief unreasoning? Is it not rather that I reach not the full extent of our loss, though I exceed it in the loudness of my expression of grief? Lend me, oh lend me, my brethren, the tear of sympathy. When you were glad we shared your gladness. Repay us, therefore, this sad recompense. "Rejoice with them that do rejoice." This we have done. It is for you to return it by "weeping with them that weep." It happened once that a strange people bewailed the loss of the patriarch Jacob, and made the misfortune of another people their own, when his united family transported their father out of Egypt, and lamented in another land the loss that had befallen them. They all prolonged their mourning over him for thirty days and as many nights. Ye, therefore, that are brethren, and of the same kindred, do as they who were of another kindred did. On that occasion the tear of strangers was shed in common with that of countrymen; be it shed in common now, for common is the grief.

Behold these your patriarchs. All these are children of our Jacob. All these are children of the free-woman. No one is base born, no one supposititious. Nor indeed would it have become that Saint to introduce into the nobility of the family of Faith a bond-woman's kindred. Therefore is he our father because he was the father of our father. Ye have just heard what and how great things an Ephraim and a Manasses related of their father, and how the wonders of the story surpassed description. Give me also leave to speak on them. For this beatification of him from henceforth incurs no risk.

Neither fear I envy; for what worse evil can it do me? Know, then, what the man was; one of the nobility of the East, blameless, just, genuine, devout, innocent of any evil deed. Indeed the great Job will not be jealous if he who imitated him be decked with the like testimonials of praise. But Envy, that has an eye for all things fair, cast a bitter glance upon our blessedness; and one who stalks up and down the world also stalked in our midst, and broadly stamped the foot-mark of affliction on our happy state. It is not herds of oxen or sheep that he has maltreated, unless in a mystical sense one transfers the idea of a flock to the Church. It is not in these that we have received injury from Envy; it is not in asses or camels that he has wrought us loss, neither has he excruciated our bodily feelings by a wound in the flesh; no, but he has robbed us of our very head. And with that head have gone away from us the precious organs of our senses. That eye which beheld the things of heaven is no longer ours, nor that ear which listened to the Divine voice, nor that tongue with its pure devotion to truth.

Where is that sweet serenity of his eyes? Where that bright smile upon his lips? Where that courteous right hand with fingers outstretched to accompany the benediction of the mouth. I feel an impulse, as if I were on the stage, to shout aloud for our calamity. Oh! Church, I pity you. To you, the city of Antioch, I address my words. I pity you for this sudden reversal. How has your beauty been despoiled! How have you been robbed of your ornaments! How suddenly has the flower faded! "Verily the grass withereth and the flower thereof falleth away." What evil eye, what witchery of drunken malice has intruded on that distant Church? What is there to compensate her loss? The fountain has failed. The stream has dried up. Again has water been turned into blood.

Oh! the sad tidings which tell the Church of her calamity! Who shall say to the children that they have no more a father? Who shall tell the Bride she is a widow? Alas for their woes! What did they send out? What do they receive back? They sent forth an ark, they receive back a coffin. The ark, my brethren, was that man of God; an ark containing in itself the Divine and mystic things. There was the golden vessel full of Divine manna, that celestial food. In it were the Tables of the Covenant written on the tablets of the heart, not with ink but by the Spirit of the living God. For on that pure heart no gloomy or inky thought was imprinted. In it, too, were the pillars, the steps, the chapters, the lamps, the mercy-seat, the baths, the veils of the entrances. In it was the rod of the priesthood, which budded in the hands of our Saint; and whatever else we have heard the Ark contained was all held in the soul of that man. But in their stead what is there now?

Let description cease. Cloths of pure white linen, scarves of silk, abundance of perfumes and spices; the loving munificence of a modest and beautiful lady. For it must be told, so as to be for a memorial of her, what she did for that Priest when, without stint, she poured the alabaster box of ointment on his head. But the treasure preserved within, what is it? Bones, now dead, and which even before dissolution had rehearsed their dying, the sad memorials of our affliction. Oh! what a cry like that of old will be heard in Ramah, Rachel weeping, not for her children but for a husband, and admitting not of consolation. Let alone, ye that would console; let alone; force not on us your consolation. Let the widow indulge the deepness of her grief. Let her feel the loss that has been inflicted on her. Yet she is not without previous practice in separation. In those contests in which our athlete was engaged she had before been trained to bear to be left.

Certainly you must remember how a previous sermon to ours related to you the contests of the man; how throughout, even in the very number of his contests, he had maintained the glory of the Holy Trinity, which he ever glorified; for there were three trying attacks that he had to repel. You have heard the whole series of his labors, what he was in the first, what in the middle, and what in the last. I deem it superfluous to repeat what has been so well described. Yet it may not be out of place to add just so much as this. When that Church, so sound in the faith, at the first beheld the man, she saw features truly formed after the image of God, she saw love welling forth, she saw grace poured around his lips, a consummate perfection of humility beyond which it is impossible to conceive anything further, a gentleness like that of David, the understanding of Solomon, a goodness like that of Moses, a strictness as of Samuel, a chastity as of Joseph, the skill of a Daniel, a zeal for the faith such as was in the great Elijah, a purity of body like that of the lofty-minded John, an unsurpassable love as of Paul. She saw the concurrence of so many excellences in one soul, and, thrilled with a blessed affection, she loved him, her own bridegroom, with a pure and virtuous passion. But ere she could accomplish her desire, ere she could satisfy her longing, while still in the fervor of her passion, she was left desolate, when those trying times called the athlete to his contests.

While, then, he was engaged in these toilsome struggles for religion, she remained chaste and kept the marriage vow. A long time intervened, during which one, with adulterous intent, made an attempt upon the immaculate bridal-chamber. But the Bride remained undefiled; and again there was a return, and again an exile. And thus it happened thrice, until the Lord dispelled the gloom of that heresy, and sending forth a ray of peace gave us the hope of some respite from these lengthened troubles. But when at length they had seen each other, when there was a renewal of those chaste joys and spiritual desires, when the flame of love had again been lit, all at once his last departure breaks off the enjoyment. He came to adorn you as his bride, he failed not in the eagerness of his zeal, he placed on this fair union the chaplets of blessing, in imitation of his Master.

As did the Lord at Cana of Galilee, so here did this imitator of Christ. The Jewish waterpots, which were filled with the water of heresy, he filled with genuine wine, changing its nature by the power of his faith. How often did he set before you a chalice, but not of wine, when with that sweet voice he poured out in rich abundance the wine of Grace, and presented to you the full and varied feast of reason! He went first with the blessing of his words, and then his illustrious disciples were employed in distributing his teaching to the multitude.

We, too, were glad, and made our own the glory of your nation. Up to this point how bright and happy is our narrative. What a blessed thing it were with this to bring our sermon to an end. But after these things what follows? "Call for the mourning women," as says the prophet Jeremiah. In no other way can the burning heart cool down, swelling as it is with its affliction, unless it relieves itself by sobs and tears. Formerly the hope of his return consoled us for the pang of separation, but now he has been torn from us by that final separation. A huge intervening chasm is fixed between the Church and him. He rests indeed in the bosom of Abraham, but there exists not one who might bring the drop of water to cool the tongue of the agonized. Gone is that beauty, silent is that voice, closed are those lips, fled that grace. Our happy state has become a tale that is told. Elijah of old time caused grief to the people of Israel when he soared from earth to God. But Elisha consoled them for the loss by being adorned with the mantle of his master. But now our wound is beyond healing; our Elijah has been caught up, and no Elisha left behind in his place.

You have heard certain mournful and lamenting words of Jeremiah, with which he bewailed Jerusalem as a deserted city, and how among other expressions of passionate grief he added this, "The ways of Zion do mourn." These words were uttered then, but now they have been realized. For when the news of our calamity shall have been spread abroad, then will the ways be full of mourning crowds, and the sheep of his flock will pour themselves forth, and like the Ninevites utter the voice of lamentation, or, rather, will lament more bitterly than they. For in their case their mourning released them from the cause of their fear, but with these no hope of release from their distress removes their need of mourning.

I know, too, of another utterance of Jeremiah, which is reckoned among the books of the Psalms; it is that which he made over the captivity of Israel. The words run thus: "We hung our harps upon the willows, and condemned ourselves as well as our harps to silence." I make this song my own. For when I see the confusion of heresy, this confusion is Babylon. And when I see the flood of trials that pours in upon us from this confusion, I say that these are "the waters of Babylon by which we sit down, and weep" because there is no one to guide us over them. Even if you mention the willows, and the harps that hung thereon, that part also of the figure shall be mine. For in truth our life is among willows, the willow being a fruitless tree, and the sweet fruit of our life having all withered away.

Therefore have we become fruitless willows, and the harps of love we hung upon those trees are idle and unvibrating. "If I forget thee, oh Jerusalem," he adds, "may my right hand be forgotten." Suffer me to make a slight alteration in that text. It is not we who have forgotten the right hand, but the right hand that has forgotten us: and the "tongue has cleaved to the roof of" his own "mouth," and barred the passage of his words, so that we can never again hear that sweet voice. But let me have all tears wiped away, for I feel that I am indulging more than is right in this womanish sorrow for our loss.

Our Bridegroom has not been taken from us. He stands in our midst, though we see him not. The Priest is within the holy place. He is entered into that within the veil, whither our forerunner Christ has entered for us. He has left behind him the curtain of the flesh. No longer does he pray to the type or shadow of the things in heaven, but he looks upon the very embodiment of these realities. No longer through a glass darkly does he intercede with God, but face to face he intercedes with Him: and he intercedes for us, and for the "negligences and ignorances" of the people. He has put away the coats of skin; no need is there now for the dwellers in paradise of such garments as these; but he wears the raiment which the purity of his life has woven into a glorious dress. "Precious in the sight of the Lord is the death" of such a man, or rather it is not death, but the breaking of bonds, as it is said, "Thou hast broken my bonds asunder."

Simeon has been let depart. He has been freed from the bondage of the body. The "snare is broken and the bird hath flown away." He has left Egypt behind, this material life. He has crossed, not this Red Sea of ours, but the black gloomy sea of life. He has entered upon the land of promise, and holds high converse with God upon the mount. He has loosed the sandal of his soul, that with the pure step of thought he may set foot upon that holy land where there is the Vision of God. Having therefore, brethren, this consolation, do ye, who are conveying the bones of our Joseph to the place of blessing, listen to the exhortation of Paul: "Sorrow not as others who have no hope." Speak to the people there; relate the glorious tale; speak of the incredible wonder, how the people in their myriads, so densely crowded together as to look like a sea of heads, became all one continuous body, and like some watery flood surged around the procession bearing his remains.

Tell them how the fair David distributed himself, in diverse ways and manners, among innumerable ranks of people, and danced before that ark in the midst of men of the same and of different language. Tell them how the streams of fire, from the succession of the lamps, flowed along in an unbroken track of light, and extended so far that the eye could not reach them. Tell them of the eager zeal of all the people, of his joining "the company of Apostles," and how the napkins that bound his face were plucked away to make amulets for the faithful. Let it be added to your narration how the Emperor showed in his countenance his sorrow for this misfortune, and rose from his throne, and how the whole city joined the funeral procession of the Saint.

Moreover console each other with the following words; it is a good medicine that Solomon has for sorrow; for he bids wine be given to the sorrowful; saying this to us, the laborers in the vineyard: "Give," therefore, "your wine to those that are in sorrow," not that wine which produces drunkenness, plots against the senses, and destroys the body, but such as gladdens the heart, the wine which the Prophet recommends when he says: "Wine maketh glad the heart of man." Pledge each other in that liquor undiluted and with the unstinted goblets of the word, that thus our grief may be turned to joy and gladness, by the grace of the Only-begotten Son of God, through Whom be glory to God, even the Father, for ever and ever. Amen.

Questions for Study

1 Suppose that you were dependent upon this oration for your knowledge of Meletius. What would you know about him as a result? What insights does this offer concerning Gregory's goals and interests?

2 How does Gregory use the following biblical images: (1) the mantle of Elijah passing to Elisha (1 Kings 19:19–20); (2) the marriage at Cana in Galilee (John 2:1–10)?

3 How is the imagery of Israel's exodus from Egypt worked into this oration? What points does Gregory make through using it in this way?

CHAPTER 11

The Peregrination of Egeria
(ca. 384)

One of the most remarkable documents to have come down to us from the early Christian era is an account of a journey of a woman to Egypt, Palestine, Asia Minor, and Constantinople. Although the date of the journey cannot be established with absolute certainty, it is generally agreed to date from 381 to 384. The text is found in an eleventh-century manuscript, which was discovered in the Italian city of Arezzo in 1884. The author of the piece is now widely agreed to be Egeria, a Spanish woman.

The work is one of the earliest known examples of the memoirs of a traveler. It offers an eye-witness account of the topography, culture and especially the church life of the regions through which Egeria wandered. The first part of the work deals with her reflections on various biblical sites in the eastern Mediterranean region; the second provides eye-witness accounts of the patterns of worship used in Jerusalem and its neighborhood. The section to be considered below deals with the services of the Jerusalem churches during Holy Week.

A number of technical terms used in the passage need comment. The "Anastasis" was a church at Jerusalem dedicated to the resurrection of Christ (Greek: *anastasis*). A "martyrium" is usually a church which has been built on the site of the tomb of a martyr, although in later times the term can be used to refer to a church which has been built in honor of such a martyr. In this case, the term is used to refer specifically to a church which is located at the site of the crucifixion. The "Lazarium" refers to a site associated with Lazarus, the brother of Mary and Martha, at the village of Bethany, near Jerusalem. The group of people referred to as "apotactitae" are those who are fasting as a form of spiritual discipline.

Holy Week and the Festivals at Easter

Saturday before Palm Sunday – Station at Bethany

2   Now when the seventh week has come, that is, when two weeks, including the seventh, are left before Easter, everything is done on each day as in the weeks that

are past, except that the vigils of the sixth weekday, which were kept in the Anastasis during the first six weeks, are, in the seventh week, kept in Sion, and with the same customs that obtained during the six weeks in the Anastasis. For throughout the whole vigil psalms and antiphons are said appropriate both to the place and to the day.

3   And when the morning of the Sabbath begins to dawn, the bishop offers the oblation. And at the dismissal the archdeacon lifts his voice and says: "Let us all be ready to-day at the seventh hour in the Lazarium." And so, as the seventh hour approaches, all go to the Lazarium, that is, Bethany, situated at about the second milestone from the city.

4   And as they go from Jerusalem to the Lazarium, there is, about five hundred paces from the latter place, a church in the street on that spot where Mary the sister of Lazarus met with the Lord. Here, when the bishop arrives, all the monks meet him, and the people enter the church, and one hymn and one antiphon are said, and that passage is read in the Gospel where the sister of Lazarus meets the Lord. Then, after prayer has been made, and when all have been blessed, they go thence with hymns to the Lazarium.

5   And on arriving at the Lazarium, so great a multitude assembles that not only the place itself, but also the fields around, are full of people. Hymns and antiphons suitable to the day and to the place are said, and likewise all the lessons are read. Then, before the dismissal, notice is given of Easter, that is, the priest ascends to a higher place and reads the passage that is written in the Gospel: When Jesus six days before the Passover had come to Bethany, and the rest. So, that passage having been read and notice given of Easter, the dismissal is made.

6   This is done on that day because, as it is written in the Gospel, these events took place in Bethany six days before the Passover; there being six days from the Sabbath to the fifth weekday on which, after supper, the Lord was taken by night. Then all return to the city direct to the Anastasis, and lucernare [ed.: a form of morning prayer] takes place according to custom.

Palm Sunday: Services in the Churches

1   On the next day, that is, the Lord's Day, which begins the Paschal week, and which they call here the Great Week, when all the customary services from cockcrow until morning have taken place in the Anastasis and at the Cross, they proceed on the morning of the Lord's Day according to custom to the greater church, which is called the Martyrium. It is called the Martyrium because it is in Golgotha behind the Cross, where the Lord suffered.

2   When all that is customary has been observed in the great church, and before the dismissal is made, the archdeacon lifts his voice and says first: "Throughout the whole week, beginning from tomorrow, let us all assemble in the Martyrium, that is, in the great church, at the ninth hour." Then he lifts his voice again, saying: "Let us all be ready to-day in Eleona at the seventh hour."

3   So when the dismissal has been made in the great church! that is, the martyrium, the bishop is escorted with hymns to the Anastasis, and after all things that are customary on the Lord's Day have been done there, after the dismissal from the

martyrium, every one hastens home to eat, that all may be ready at the beginning of the seventh hour in the church in Eleona, on the Mount of Olives, where is the cave in which the Lord was wont to teach.

Procession with Palms on the Mount of Olives

1   Accordingly at the seventh hour all the people go up to the Mount of Olives, that is, to Eleona, and the bishop with them, to the church, where hymns and antiphons suitable to the day and to the place are said, and lessons in like manner. And when the ninth hour approaches they go up with hymns to the Imbomon, that is, to the place whence the Lord ascended into heaven, and there they sit down, for all the people are always bidden to sit when the bishop is present; the deacons alone always stand. Hymns and antiphons suitable to the day and to the place are said, interspersed with lections and prayers.

2   And as the eleventh hour approaches, the passage from the Gospel is read, where the children, carrying branches and palms, met the Lord, saying; Blessed is He that cometh in the name of the Lord, and the bishop immediately rises, and all the people with him, and they all go on foot from the top of the Mount of Olives, all the people going before him with hymns and antiphons, answering one to another: Blessed is He that cometh in the name of the Lord.

3   And all the children in the neighborhood, even those who are too young to walk, are carried by their parents on their shoulders, all of them bearing branches, some of palms and some of olives, and thus the bishop is escorted in the same manner as the Lord was of old.

4   For all, even those of rank, both matrons and men, accompany the bishop all the way on foot in this manner, making these responses, from the top of the mount to the city, and thence through the whole city to the Anastasis, going very slowly lest the people should be wearied; and thus they arrive at the Anastasis at a late hour. And on arriving, although it is late, lucernare takes place, with prayer at the Cross; after which the people are dismissed.

Monday in Holy Week

1   On the next day, the second weekday, everything that is customary is done from the first cockcrow until morning in the Anastasis; also at the third and sixth hours everything is done that is customary throughout the whole of Quadragesima, but at the ninth hour all assemble in the great church, that is the martyrium, where hymns and antiphons are said continuously until the first hour of the night and lessons suitable to the day and the place are read, interspersed always with prayers.

2   Lucernare takes place when its hour approaches, that is, so that it is already night when the dismissal at the martyrium is made. When the dismissal has been made, the bishop is escorted thence with hymns to the Anastasis, where, when he has entered, one hymn is said, followed by a prayer; the catechumens and then the faithful are blessed, and the dismissal is made.

Tuesday in Holy Week

1   On the third weekday everything is done as on the second, with this one thing added – that late at night, after the dismissal of the Martyrium, and after the going to the Anastasis and after the dismissal there, all proceed at that hour by night to the church, which is on the mount Eleona.

2   And when they have arrived at that church, the bishop enters the cave where the Lord was wont to teach His disciples, and after receiving the book of the Gospel, he stands and himself reads the words of the Lord which are written in the Gospel according to Matthew, where He says: Take heed that no man deceive you. And the bishop reads through the whole of that discourse, and when he has read it, prayer is made, the catechumens and the faithful are blessed, the dismissal is made, and every one returns from the mount to his house, it being already very late at night.

Wednesday in Holy Week

1   On the fourth weekday everything is done as on the second and third weekdays throughout the whole day from the first cockcrow onwards, but after the dismissal has taken place at the Martyrium by night, and the bishop has been escorted with hymns to the Anastasis, he at once enters the cave which is in the Anastasis, and stands within the rails; but the priest stands before the rails and receives the Gospel, and reads the passage where Judas Iscariot went to the Jews and stated what they should give him that he should betray the Lord. And when the passage has been read, there is such a moaning and groaning of all the people that no one can help being moved to tears at that hour. Afterwards prayer follows, then the blessing, first of the catechumens, and then of the faithful, and the dismissal is made.

Maundy Thursday: Mass celebrated twice

1   On the fifth weekday everything that is customary is done from the first cock-crow until morning at the Anastasis, and also at the third and at the sixth hours. But at the eighth hour all the people gather together at the Martyrium according to custom, only earlier than on other days, because the dismissal must be made sooner. Then, when the people are gathered together, all that should be done is done, and the oblation is made on that day at the Martyrium, the dismissal taking place about the tenth hour. But before the dismissal is made there, the archdeacon raises his voice and says: "Let us all assemble at the first hour of the night in the church which is in Eleona, for great toil awaits us to-day, in this very night."

2   Then, after the dismissal at the Martyrium, they arrive behind the Cross, where only one hymn is said and prayer is made, and the bishop offers the oblation there, and all communicate. Nor is the oblation ever offered behind the Cross on any day throughout the year, except on this one day. And after the dismissal there they go to the Anastasis, where prayer is made, the catechumens and the faithful are blessed according to custom, and the dismissal is made.

Night Station on the Mount of Olives

And so every one hastens back to his house to eat, because immediately after they have eaten, all go to Eleona to the church wherein is the cave where the Lord was with His Apostles on this very day.

3   There then, until about the fifth hour of the night, hymns and antiphons suitable to the day and to the place are said, lessons, too, are read in like manner, with prayers interspersed, and the passages from the Gospel are read where the Lord addressed His disciples on that same day as He sat in the same cave which is in that church.

4   And they go thence at about the sixth hour of the night with hymns up to the Imbomon, the place whence the Lord ascended into heaven, where again lessons are read, hymns and antiphons suitable to the day are said, and all the prayers which are made by the bishop are also suitable both to the day and to the place.

Stations at Gethsemane

1   And at the first cockcrow they come down from the Imbomon with hymns, and arrive at the place where the Lord prayed, as it is written in the Gospel: and He was withdrawn (from them) about a stone's cast, and prayed, and the rest. There is in that place a graceful church. The bishop and all the people enter, a prayer suitable to the place and to the day is said, with one suitable hymn, and the passage from the Gospel is read where He said to His disciples: Watch, that ye enter not into temptation; the whole passage is read through and prayer is made.

2   And then all, even to the smallest child, go down with the bishop, on foot, with hymns to Gethsemane; where, on account of the great number of people in the crowd, who are wearied owing to the vigils and weak through the daily fasts, and because they have so great a hill to descend, they come very slowly with hymns to Gethsemane. And over two hundred church candles are made ready to give light to all the people.

3   On their arrival at Gethsemane, first a suitable prayer is made, then a hymn is said, then the passage of the Gospel is read where the Lord was taken. And when this passage has been read there is so great a moaning and groaning of all the people, together with weeping, that their lamentation may be heard perhaps as far as the city.

Return to Jerusalem

From that hour they go with hymns to the city on foot, reaching the gate about the time when one man begins to be able to recognize another, and thence right on through the midst of the city; all, to a man, both great and small, rich and poor, all are ready there, for on that special day not a soul withdraws from the vigils until morning. Thus the bishop is escorted from Gethsemane to the gate, and thence through the whole of the city to the Cross.

Good Friday: Service at daybreak

4 And when they arrive before the Cross the daylight is already growing bright. There the passage from the Gospel is read where the Lord is brought before Pilate, with everything that is written concerning that which Pilate spake to the Lord or to the Jews; the whole is read.

5 And afterwards the bishop addresses the people, comforting them for that they have toiled all night and are about to toil during that same day, (bidding) them not be weary, but to have hope in God, Who will for that toil give them a greater reward. And encouraging them as he is able, he addresses them thus: "Go now, each one of you, to your houses, and sit down awhile, and all of you be ready here just before the second hour of the day, that from that hour to the sixth you may be able to behold the holy wood of the Cross, each one of us believing that it will be profitable to his salvation; then from the sixth hour we must all assemble again in this place, that is, before the Cross, that we may apply ourselves to lections and to prayers until night."

The Column of the Flagellation

1 After this, when the dismissal at the Cross has been made, that is, before the sun rises, they all go at once with fervor to Sion, to pray at the column at which the Lord was scourged. And returning thence they sit for awhile in their houses, and presently all are ready.

Veneration of the Cross

1 Then a chair is placed for the bishop in Golgotha behind the Cross, which is now standing; the bishop duly takes his seat in the chair, and a table covered with a linen cloth is placed before him; the deacons stand round the table, and a silver-gilt casket is brought in which is the holy wood of the Cross. The casket is opened and (the wood) is taken out, and both the wood of the Cross and the title are placed upon the table.

2 Now, when it has been put upon the table, the bishop, as he sits, holds the extremities of the sacred wood firmly in his hands, while the deacons who stand around guard it. It is guarded thus because the custom is that the people, both faithful and catechumens, come one by one and, bowing down at the table, kiss the sacred wood and pass through. And because, I know not when, someone is said to have bitten off and stolen a portion of the sacred wood, it is thus guarded by the deacons who stand around, lest any one approaching should venture to do so again.

3 And as all the people pass by one by one, all bowing themselves, they touch the Cross and the title, first with their foreheads and then with their eyes; then they kiss the Cross and pass through, but none lays his hand upon it to touch it. When they have kissed the Cross and have passed through, a deacon stands holding the ring of Solomon and the horn from which the kings were anointed; they kiss the horn also and gaze at the ring . . . all the people are passing through up to the sixth hour, entering by one door and going out by another; for this is done in the same

place where, on the preceding day, that is, on the fifth weekday, the oblation was offered.

Station before the Cross. The Three Hours

4 And when the sixth hour has come, they go before the Cross, whether it be in rain or in heat, the place being open to the air, as it were, a court of great size and of some beauty between the Cross and the Anastasis; here all the people assemble in such great numbers that there is no thoroughfare.

5 The chair is placed for the bishop before the Cross, and from the sixth to the ninth hour nothing else is done, but the reading of lessons, which are read thus: first from the psalms wherever the Passion is spoken of, then from the Apostles, either from the epistles of the Apostles or from their Acts, wherever they have spoken of the Lord's Passion; then the passages from the Gospels, where He suffered, are read. Then the readings from the prophets where they foretold that the Lord should suffer, then from the Gospels where He mentions His Passion.

6 Thus from the sixth to the ninth hours the lessons are so read and the hymns said, that it may be shown to all the people that whatsoever the prophets foretold of the Lord's Passion is proved from the Gospels and from the writings of the Apostles to have been fulfilled. And so through all those three hours the people are taught that nothing was done which had not been foretold, and that nothing was foretold which was not wholly fulfilled. Prayers also suitable to the day are interspersed throughout.

7 The emotion shown and the mourning by all the people at every lesson and prayer is wonderful; for there is none, either great or small, who, on that day during those three hours, does not lament more than can be conceived, that the Lord had suffered those things for us. Afterwards, at the beginning of the ninth hour, there is read that passage from the Gospel according to John where He gave up the ghost. This read, prayer and the dismissal follow.

Evening Offices

8 And when the dismissal before the Cross has been made, all things are done in the greater church, at the Martyrium, which are customary during this week from the ninth hour – when the assembly takes place in the Martyrium – until late. And after the dismissal at the Martyrium, they go to the Anastasis, where, when they arrive, the passage from the Gospel is read where Joseph begged the Body of the Lord from Pilate and laid it in a new sepulcher. And this reading ended, a prayer is said, the catechumens are blessed, and the dismissal is made.

9 But on that day no announcement is made of a vigil at the Anastasis, because it is known that the people are tired; nevertheless, it is the custom to watch there. So all of the people who are willing, or rather, who are able, keep watch, and they who are unable do not watch there until the morning. Those of the clergy, however, who are strong or young keep vigil there, and hymns and antiphons are said throughout the whole night until morning; a very great crowd also keep night-long watch, some from the late hour and some from midnight.

Vigil of Easter

1   Now, on the next day, the Sabbath, everything that is customary is done at the third hour and also at the sixth; the service at the ninth hour, however, is not held on the Sabbath, but the Paschal vigils are prepared in the great church, the Martyrium. The Paschal vigils are kept as with us, with this one addition, that the children when they have been baptized and clothed, and when they issue from the font, are led with the bishop first to the Anastasis.

2   The bishop enters the rails of the Anastasis, and one hymn is said, then the bishop says a prayer for them, and then he goes with them to the greater church, where, according to custom, all the people are keeping watch. Everything is done there that is customary with us also, and after the oblation has been made, the dismissal takes place. After the dismissal of the vigils has been made in the greater church, they go at once with hymns to the Anastasis, where the passage from the Gospel about the Resurrection is read. Prayer is made, and the bishop again makes the oblation. But everything is done quickly on account of the people, that they should not be delayed any longer, and so the people are dismissed. The dismissal of the vigils takes place on that day at the same hour as with us.

Services in the Easter Octave

1   Moreover, the Paschal days are kept up to a late hour as with us, and the dismissals take place in their order throughout the eight Paschal days, as is the custom everywhere at Easter throughout the Octave. But the adornment (of the churches) and order (of the services) here are the same throughout the Octave of Easter as they are during Epiphany, in the greater church, in the Anastasis, at the Cross, in Eleona, in Bethlehem, as well as in the Lazarium, in fact, everywhere, because these are the Paschal days.

2   On the first Lord's Day they proceed to the great church, that is, the Martyrium, as well as on the second and third weekdays, but always so that after the dismissal has been made at the Martyrium, they go to the Anastasis with hymns. On the fourth weekday they proceed to Eleona, on the fifth to the Anastasis, on the sixth to Sion, on the Sabbath before the Cross, but on the Lord's Day, that is, on the Octave, [they proceed] to the great church again, that is, to the Martyrium.

3   Moreover, on the eight Paschal days the bishop goes every day after breakfast up to Eleona with all the clergy, and with all the children who have been baptized, and with all who are apotactitae, both men and women, and likewise with all the people who are willing. Hymns are said and prayers are made, both in the church which is on Eleona, wherein is the cave where Jesus was wont to teach His disciples, and also in the Imbomon, that is, in the place whence the Lord ascended into heaven.

4   And when the psalms have been said and prayer has been made, they come down thence with hymns to the Anastasis at the hour of lucernare. This is done throughout all the eight days.

Vesper Station at Sion on Easter Sunday

Now, on the Lord's Day at Easter, after the dismissal of lucernare, that is, at the Anastasis, all the people escort the bishop with hymns to Sion.

5   And, on arriving, hymns suitable to the day and place are said, prayer is made, and the passage from the Gospel is read where the Lord, on the same day, and in the same place where the church now stands in Sion, came in to His disciples when the doors were shut. That is, when one of His disciples, Thomas, was absent, and when he returned and the other Apostles told him that they had seen the Lord, he said: "Except I shall see, I will not believe." When this has been read, prayer is again made, the catechumens and the faithful are blessed, and every one returns to his house late, about the second hour of the night.

Questions for Study

1   This document is regarded as especially important by those interested in the history of Christian worship. Can you see why?
2   The descriptions of the liturgies are very exact. What might this say about the author of this work?
3   To what extent is the local geography of Jerusalem incorporated into the worship of the church, according to this text?

CHAPTER 12

Augustine of Hippo (354–430)

Augustine of Hippo is widely regarded as one of the most important writers of the Christian church. Augustine was born in the Roman province of Numidia (now in modern-day Algeria). His mother, Monica, was a devout Christian, and wished her son to share in her faith. Augustine showed no inclination to do so, and at the age of seventeen took a local girl as his mistress, and subsequently came under the influence of the Manichees, a religious group based on the gnostic philosophy of Mani. Augustine settled in Italy, and pursued a career within the Roman civil service. While staying at Milan, however, Augustine underwent a conversion experience in July 386. This conversion is described in the passage which has been selected for study.

Augustine of Hippo (354–430)

Basic description
Bishop of Hippo; leading early Christian theological writer.

Major works
Confessions; City of God; many anti-Pelagian and anti-Donatist works.

Major studies
Peter Brown, *Augustine of Hippo*. London: Faber, 1967.
John Burnaby, *Amor Dei: A Study of the Religion of St Augustine*. London: Hodder & Stoughton, 1938.
Henry Chadwick, *Augustine*. Oxford: Oxford University Press, 1986.

Augustine returned to his native North Africa in the late summer of 388. While visiting the coastal town of Hippo Regius in 391, he was ordained against his own wishes, and subsequently (probably in 395) became a bishop. Although the local affairs of the North African church figured prominently in his concerns, Augustine devoted himself particularly to the clarification, exposition, and defense of the Christian faith against its external opponents and internal dissidents. His writings deal with the major issues of Christian thought, including the doctrines of the Trinity, the church and grace (but significantly, not Christology).

We have already noted Augustine's considerable importance as a catalyst of constructive Christian engagement with the classical heritage, including its poetic and rhetorical traditions. Yet Augustine is of importance in other respects, not least of which is his interest in the introspective aspects of Christian existence. Augustine's development of the genre of autobiography as a means of simultaneously giving praise to God, encouraging others in their faith, and theological reflection must be seen as a landmark contribution to the development of Christian literature. Many Christian writings bear witness to the extent to which they have been shaped, whether consciously or unconsciously, by both the literary genre and theological assumptions of Augustine's *Confessions*.

Text: *Confessions*

The *Confessions*, written in Latin over the period 398–400, is widely recognized as one of the most significant works to be written in the west, whether sacred or secular. The *Confessions* take the form of an extended meditation on God, interspersed with prayer. Of its thirteen component sections (referred to as "books"), the first nine are essentially autobiographical, describing Augustine's youth and early loss of faith; his growing interest in and commitment to the Manichees; his subsequent alienation from the movement, and interest in Platonism; and his conversion in the summer of 386. A particularly moving section toward the end of this autobiographical portion of the work deals with the death of his mother, Monica. The four concluding sections deal with aspects of the relation of the universe to God, focusing on issues such as memory, time, and creation.

One of the dominant themes of the work is set out in its opening paragraph, in which Augustine – addressing God – declares that: "You have made us for yourself, and our hearts are restless until they find their rest in you." This theme of the human search for joy, which is reflected strongly in Augustine's personal history, permeates the *Confessions*, and is the subject of the extract which we shall consider in some detail. The extract is taken from the eighth book of the work, which deals with Augustine's conversion to Christianity.

14   On a certain day, when Nebridius was away – for some reason I cannot remember – there came to visit Alypius and me at our house one Ponticianus, a fellow countryman of ours from Africa, who held high office in the emperor's court. What he wanted with us I do not know; but we sat down to talk together, and it chanced that he noticed a book on a game table before us. He took it up, opened it, and, contrary to his expectation, found it to be the apostle Paul, for he imagined that it was one of my wearisome rhetoric textbooks. At this, he looked up at me with a smile and expressed his delight and wonder that he had so unexpectedly found this book and only this one, lying before my eyes; for he was indeed a Christian and a faithful one at that, and often he prostrated himself before thee, our God, in the church in constant daily prayer. When I had told him that I had given much attention to these writings, a conversation followed in which he spoke of Anthony, the Egyptian monk, whose name was in high repute among thy servants, although up to that time not familiar to me. When he learned this, he lingered on the topic, giving us an account

of this eminent man, and marveling at our ignorance. We in turn were amazed to hear of thy wonderful works so fully manifested in recent times – almost in our own – occurring in the true faith and the Catholic Church. We all wondered – we, that these things were so great, and he, that we had never heard of them.

15   From this, his conversation turned to the multitudes in the monasteries and their manners so fragrant to thee, and to the teeming solitudes of the wilderness, of which we knew nothing at all. There was even a monastery at Milan, outside the city's walls, full of good brothers under the fostering care of Ambrose – and we were ignorant of it. He went on with his story, and we listened intently and in silence. He then told us how, on a certain afternoon, at Trier, when the emperor was occupied watching the gladiatorial games, he and three comrades went out for a walk in the gardens close to the city walls. There, as they chanced to walk two by two, one strolled away with him, while the other two went on by themselves. As they rambled, these first two came upon a certain cottage where lived some of thy servants, some of the "poor in spirit" ("of such is the Kingdom of Heaven"), where they found the book in which was written the life of Anthony! One of them began to read it, to marvel and to be inflamed by it. While reading, he meditated on embracing just such a life, giving up his worldly employment to seek thee alone. These two belonged to the group of officials called "secret service agents." Then, suddenly being overwhelmed with a holy love and a sober shame and as if in anger with himself, he fixed his eyes on his friend, exclaiming: "Tell me, I beg you, what goal are we seeking in all these toils of ours? What is it that we desire? What is our motive in public service? Can our hopes in the court rise higher than to be 'friends of the emperor'? But how frail, how beset with peril, is that pride! Through what dangers must we climb to a greater danger? And when shall we succeed? But if I chose to become a friend of God, see, I can become one now." Thus he spoke, and in the pangs of the travail of the new life he turned his eyes again onto the page and continued reading; he was inwardly changed, as thou didst see, and the world dropped away from his mind, as soon became plain to others. For as he read with a heart like a stormy sea, more than once he groaned. Finally he saw the better course, and resolved on it. Then, having become thy servant, he said to his friend: "Now I have broken loose from those hopes we had, and I am determined to serve God; and I enter into that service from this hour in this place. If you are reluctant to imitate me, do not oppose me." The other replied that he would continue bound in his friendship, to share in so great a service for so great a prize. So both became thine, and began to "build a tower," counting the cost – namely, of forsaking all that they had and following thee. Shortly after, Ponticianus and his companion, who had walked with him in the other part of the garden, came in search of them to the same place, and having found them reminded them to return, as the day was declining. But the first two, making known to Ponticianus their resolution and purpose, and how a resolve had sprung up and become confirmed in them, entreated them not to take it ill if they refused to join themselves with them. But Ponticianus and his friend, although not changed from their former course, did nevertheless (as he told us) bewail themselves and congratulated their friends on their godliness, recommending themselves to their prayers. And with hearts inclining again toward earthly things, they returned to the palace. But the other two, setting their affections on heavenly things, remained in the cottage.

Both of them had affianced brides who, when they heard of this, likewise dedicated their virginity to thee.

[handwritten: fiancees.]

Chapter VII

[handwritten margin: Self-critical.]

16   Such was the story Ponticianus told. But while he was speaking, thou, O Lord, turned me toward myself, taking me from behind my back, where I had put myself while unwilling to exercise self-scrutiny. And now thou didst set me face to face with myself, that I might see how ugly I was, and how crooked and sordid, bespotted and ulcerous. And I looked and I loathed myself; but whither to fly from myself I could not discover. And if I sought to turn my gaze away from myself, he would continue his narrative, and thou wouldst oppose me to myself and thrust me before my own eyes that I might discover my iniquity and hate it. I had known it, but acted as though I knew it not – I winked at it and forgot it. *[handwritten: → Stops looking @ himself.]*

[handwritten margin: Augustine does not like what he sees.]

17   But now, the more ardently I loved those whose wholesome affections I heard reported – that they had given themselves up wholly to thee to be cured – the more did I abhor myself when compared with them. For many of my years – perhaps twelve – had passed away since my nineteenth, when, upon the reading of Cicero's *Hortensius*, I was roused to a desire for wisdom. And here I was, still postponing the abandonment of this world's happiness to devote myself to the search. For not just the finding alone, but also the bare search for it, ought to have been preferred above the treasures and kingdoms of this world; better than all bodily pleasures, though they were to be had for the taking. But, wretched youth that I was – supremely wretched even in the very outset of my youth – I had entreated chastity of thee and had prayed, "Grant me chastity and continence, but not yet." For I was afraid lest thou shouldst hear me too soon, and too soon cure me of my disease of lust which I desired to have satisfied rather than extinguished. And I had wandered through perverse ways of godless superstition – not really sure of it, either, but preferring it to the other, which I did not seek in piety, but opposed in malice.

[handwritten margin: Wisdom = God?]

[handwritten margin: Earthly pleasures]

*[handwritten margin: * rebuke / scold.]*

18   And I had thought that I delayed from day to day in rejecting those worldly hopes and following thee alone because there did not appear anything certain by which I could direct my course. And now the day had arrived in which I was laid bare to myself and my conscience was to chide me: "Where are you, O my tongue? You said indeed that you were not willing to cast off the baggage of vanity for uncertain truth. But behold now it is certain, and still that burden oppresses you. At the same time those who have not worn themselves out with searching for it as you have, nor spent ten years and more in thinking about it, have had their shoulders unburdened and have received wings to fly away." Thus was I inwardly confused, and mightily confounded with a horrible shame, while Ponticianus went ahead speaking such things. And when he had finished his story and the business he came for, he went his way. And then what did I not say to myself, within myself? With what scourges of rebuke did I not lash my soul to make it follow me, as I was struggling to go after thee? Yet it drew back. It refused. It would not make an effort. All its arguments were exhausted and confuted. Yet it resisted in sullen disquiet, fearing the

[handwritten margin: They are free of earthly needs]

[handwritten bottom: He wants to commit himself to the truth (God) but something is holding him back.]

cutting off of that habit by which it was being wasted to death, as if that were death itself.

[handwritten margin notes: "Habit = living of an unGodly life"]

[handwritten margin notes: "Death itself = one may as well already be dead when living this sort of 'life.'"]

[handwritten margin note: "No Spirit"]

Chapter VIII

[handwritten: "forceful."]

19   Then, as this *vehement* quarrel, which I waged with my soul in the chamber of my heart, was raging inside my inner dwelling, agitated both in mind and countenance, I seized upon Alypius and exclaimed: "What is the matter with us? What is this? What did you hear? The uninstructed start up and take heaven, and we – with all our learning but so little heart – see where we wallow in flesh and blood! Because others have gone before us, are we ashamed to follow, and not rather ashamed at our not following?" I scarcely knew what I said, and in my excitement I flung away from him, while he gazed at me in silent astonishment. For I did not sound like myself: my face, eyes, color, tone expressed my meaning more clearly than my words.

[handwritten margin note: "is he arguing that they too objected?"]

There was a little garden belonging to our lodging, of which we had the use – as of the whole house – for the master, our landlord, did not live there. The tempest in my breast hurried me out into this garden, where no one might interrupt the fiery struggle in which I was engaged with myself, until it came to the outcome that thou knewest though I did not. But I was mad for health, and dying for life; knowing what evil thing I was, but not knowing what good thing I was so shortly to become.

[handwritten margin note: "Needs 'some alone time.'"]

I fled into the garden, with Alypius following step by step; for I had no secret in which he did not share, and how could he leave me in such distress? We sat down, as far from the house as possible. I was greatly disturbed in spirit, angry at myself with a turbulent indignation because I had not entered thy will and covenant, O my God, while all my bones cried out to me to enter, extolling it to the skies. The way therein is not by ships or chariots or feet – indeed it was not as far as I had come from the house to the place where we were seated. For to go along that road and indeed to reach the goal is nothing else but the will to go. But it must be a strong and single will, not staggering and swaying about this way and that – a changeable, twisting, fluctuating will, wrestling with itself while one part falls as another rises.

20   Finally, in the very fever of my indecision, I made many motions with my body; like men do when they will to act but cannot, either because they do not have the limbs or because their limbs are bound or weakened by disease, or incapacitated in some other way. Thus if I tore my hair, struck my forehead, or, entwining my fingers, clasped my knee, these I did because I willed it. But I might have willed it and still not have done it, if the nerves had not obeyed my will. Many things then I did, in which the will and power to do were not the same. Yet I did not do that one thing which seemed to me infinitely more desirable, which before long I should have power to will because shortly when I willed, I would will with a single will. For in this, the power of willing is the power of doing; and as yet I could not do it. Thus my body more readily obeyed the slightest wish of the soul in moving its limbs at the order of my mind than my soul obeyed itself to accomplish in the will alone its great resolve.

[handwritten margin note: "He is annoyed that himself."]

Chapter IX

21   How can there be such a strange anomaly? And why is it? Let thy mercy shine on me, that I may inquire and find an answer, amid the dark labyrinth of human punishment and in the darkest contritions of the sons of Adam. Whence such an anomaly? And why should it be? The mind commands the body, and the body obeys. The mind commands itself and is resisted. The mind commands the hand to be moved and there is such readiness that the command is scarcely distinguished from the obedience in act. Yet the mind is mind, and the hand is body. The mind commands the mind to will, and yet though it be itself it does not obey itself. Whence this strange anomaly and why should it be? I repeat: The will commands itself to will, and could not give the command unless it wills; yet what is commanded is not done. But actually the will does not will entirely; therefore it does not command entirely. For as far as it wills, it commands. And as far as it does not will, the thing commanded is not done. For the will commands that there be an act of will – not another, but itself. But it does not command entirely. Therefore, what is commanded does not happen; for if the will were whole and entire, it would not even command it to be, because it would already be. It is, therefore, no strange anomaly partly to will and partly to be unwilling. This is actually an infirmity of mind, which cannot wholly rise, while pressed down by habit, even though it is supported by the truth. And so there are two wills, because one of them is not whole, and what is present in this one is lacking in the other.

Chapter X

22   Let them perish from thy presence, O God, as vain talkers, and deceivers of the soul perish, who, when they observe that there are two wills in the act of deliberation, go on to affirm that there are two kinds of minds in us: one good, the other evil. They are indeed themselves evil when they hold these evil opinions – and they shall become good only when they come to hold the truth and consent to the truth that thy apostle may say to them: "You were formerly in darkness, but now are you in the light in the Lord." But they desired to be light, not "in the Lord," but in themselves. They conceived the nature of the soul to be the same as what God is, and thus have become a thicker darkness than they were; for in their dread arrogance they have gone farther away from thee, from thee "the true Light, that lights every man that comes into the world." Mark what you say and blush for shame; draw near to him and be enlightened, and your faces shall not be ashamed.

While I was deliberating whether I would serve the Lord my God now, as I had long purposed to do, it was I who willed and it was also I who was unwilling. In either case, it was I. I neither willed with my whole will nor was I wholly unwilling. And so I was at war with myself and torn apart by myself. And this strife was against my will; yet it did not show the presence of another mind, but the punishment of my own. Thus it was no more I who did it, but the sin that dwelt in me – the punishment of a sin freely committed by Adam, and I was a son of Adam.

23   For if there are as many opposing natures as there are opposing wills, there will not be two but many more. If any man is trying to decide whether he should go to their conventicle or to the theater, the Manicheans at once cry out, "See, here are two natures – one good, drawing this way, another bad, drawing back that way; for how else can you explain this indecision between conflicting wills?" But I reply that both impulses are bad – that which draws to them and that which draws back to the theater. But they do not believe that the will which draws to them can be anything but good. Suppose, then, that one of us should try to decide, and through the conflict of his two wills should waver whether he should go to the theater or to our Church. Would not those also waver about the answer here? For either they must confess, which they are unwilling to do, that the will that leads to our church is as good as that which carries their own adherents and those captivated by their mysteries; or else they must imagine that there are two evil natures and two evil minds in one man, both at war with each other, and then it will not be true what they say, that there is one good and another bad. Else they must be converted to the truth, and no longer deny that when anyone deliberates there is one soul fluctuating between conflicting wills.

24   Let them no longer maintain that when they perceive two wills to be contending with each other in the same man the contest is between two opposing minds, of two opposing substances, from two opposing principles, the one good and the other bad. Thus, O true God, thou dost reprove and confute and convict them. For both wills may be bad: as when a man tries to decide whether he should kill a man by poison or by the sword; whether he should take possession of this field or that one belonging to someone else, when he cannot get both; whether he should squander his money to buy pleasure or hold onto his money through the motive of covetousness; whether he should go to the circus or to the theater, if both are open on the same day; or, whether he should take a third course, open at the same time, and rob another man's house; or, a fourth option, whether he should commit adultery, if he has the opportunity – all these things concurring in the same space of time and all being equally longed for, although impossible to do at one time. For the mind is pulled four ways by four antagonistic wills – or even more, in view of the vast range of human desires – but even the Manicheans do not affirm that there are these many different substances. The same principle applies as in the action of good wills. For I ask them, "Is it a good thing to have delight in reading the apostle, or is it a good thing to delight in a sober psalm, or is it a good thing to discourse on the gospel?" To each of these, they will answer, "It is good." But what, then, if all delight us equally and all at the same time? Do not different wills distract the mind when a man is trying to decide what he should choose? Yet they are all good, and are at variance with each other until one is chosen. When this is done the whole united will may go forward on a single track instead of remaining as it was before, divided in many ways. So also, when eternity attracts us from above, and the pleasure of earthly delight pulls us down from below, the soul does not will either the one or the other with all its force, but still it is the same soul that does not will this or that with a united will, and is therefore pulled apart with grievous perplexities, because for truth's sake it prefers this, but for custom's sake it does not lay that aside.

Chapter XI

25   Thus I was sick and tormented, reproaching myself more bitterly than ever, rolling and writhing in my chain till it should be utterly broken. By now I was held but slightly, but still was held. And thou, O Lord, didst press upon me in my inmost heart with a severe mercy, redoubling the lashes of fear and shame; lest I should again give way and that same slender remaining tie not be broken off, but recover strength and enchain me yet more securely.

I kept saying to myself, "See, let it be done now; let it be done now." And as I said this I all but came to a firm decision. I all but did it – yet I did not quite. Still I did not fall back to my old condition, but stood aside for a moment and drew breath. And I tried again, and lacked only a very little of reaching the resolve – and then somewhat less, and then all but touched and grasped it. Yet I still did not quite reach or touch or grasp the goal, because I hesitated to die to death and to live to life. And the worse way, to which I was habituated, was stronger in me than the better, which I had not tried. And up to the very moment in which I was to become another man, the nearer the moment approached, the greater horror did it strike in me. But it did not strike me back, nor turn me aside, but held me in suspense.

26   It was, in fact, my old mistresses, trifles of trifles and vanities of vanities, who still enthralled me. They tugged at my fleshly garments and softly whispered: "Are you going to part with us? And from that moment will we never be with you any more? And from that moment will not this and that be forbidden you forever?" What were they suggesting to me in those words "this or that"? What is it they suggested, O my God? Let thy mercy guard the soul of thy servant from the vileness and the shame they did suggest! And now I scarcely heard them, for they were not openly showing themselves and opposing me face to face; but muttering, as it were, behind my back; and furtively plucking at me as I was leaving, trying to make me look back at them. Still they delayed me, so that I hesitated to break loose and shake myself free of them and leap over to the place to which I was being called – for unruly habit kept saying to me, "Do you think you can live without them?"

27   But now it said this very faintly; for in the direction I had set my face, and yet toward which I still trembled to go, the chaste dignity of continence appeared to me – cheerful but not wanton, modestly alluring me to come and doubt nothing, extending her holy hands, full of a multitude of good examples – to receive and embrace me. There were there so many young men and maidens, a multitude of youth and every age, grave widows and ancient virgins; and continence herself in their midst: not barren, but a fruitful mother of children – her joys – by thee, O Lord, her husband. And she smiled on me with a challenging smile as if to say: "Can you not do what these young men and maidens can? Or can any of them do it of themselves, and not rather in the Lord their God? The Lord their God gave me to them. Why do you stand in your own strength, and so stand not? Cast yourself on him; fear not. He will not flinch and you will not fall. Cast yourself on him without fear, for he will receive and heal you." And I blushed violently, for I still heard the muttering of those "trifles" and hung suspended. Again she seemed to speak: "Stop your ears against those unclean members of yours, that they may be mortified. They

tell you of delights, but not according to the law of the Lord thy God." This struggle raging in my heart was nothing but the contest of self against self. And Alypius kept close beside me, and awaited in silence the outcome of my extraordinary agitation.

Chapter XII

28 Now when deep reflection had drawn up out of the secret depths of my soul all my misery and had heaped it up before the sight of my heart, there arose a mighty storm, accompanied by a mighty rain of tears. That I might give way fully to my tears and lamentations, I stole away from Alypius, for it seemed to me that solitude was more appropriate for the business of weeping. I went far enough away that I could feel that even his presence was no restraint upon me. This was the way I felt at the time, and he realized it. I suppose I had said something before I started up and he noticed that the sound of my voice was choked with weeping. And so he stayed alone, where we had been sitting together, greatly astonished. I flung myself down under a fig tree – how I know not – and gave free course to my tears. The streams of my eyes gushed out an acceptable sacrifice to thee. And, not indeed in these words, but to this effect, I cried to thee: "And thou, O Lord, how long? How long, O Lord? Wilt thou be angry forever? Oh, remember not against us our former iniquities." For I felt that I was still enthralled by them. I sent up these sorrowful cries: "How long, how long? Tomorrow and tomorrow? Why not now? Why not this very hour make an end to my uncleanness?"

29 I was saying these things and weeping in the most bitter contrition of my heart, when suddenly I heard the voice of a boy or a girl I know not which – coming from the neighboring house, chanting over and over again, "Pick it up, read it; pick it up, read it." Immediately I ceased weeping and began most earnestly to think whether it was usual for children in some kind of game to sing such a song, but I could not remember ever having heard the like. So, damming the torrent of my tears, I got to my feet, for I could not but think that this was a divine command to open the Bible and read the first passage I should light upon. For I had heard how Anthony, accidentally coming into church while the gospel was being read, received the admonition as if what was read had been addressed to him: "Go and sell what you have and give it to the poor, and you shall have treasure in heaven; and come and follow me." By such an oracle he was forthwith converted to thee.

So I quickly returned to the bench where Alypius was sitting, for there I had put down the apostle's book when I had left there. I snatched it up, opened it, and in silence read the paragraph on which my eyes first fell: "Not in rioting and drunkenness, not in chambering and wantonness, not in strife and envying, but put on the Lord Jesus Christ, and make no provision for the flesh to fulfill the lusts thereof." I wanted to read no further, nor did I need to. For instantly, as the sentence ended, there was infused in my heart something like the light of full certainty and all the gloom of doubt vanished away.

30 Closing the book, then, and putting my finger or something else for a mark I began – now with a tranquil countenance – to tell it all to Alypius. And he in turn

disclosed to me what had been going on in himself, of which I knew nothing. He asked to see what I had read. I showed him, and he looked on even further than I had read. I had not known what followed. But indeed it was this, "Him that is weak in the faith, receive." This he applied to himself, and told me so. By these words of warning he was strengthened, and by exercising his good resolution and purpose – all very much in keeping with his character, in which, in these respects, he was always far different from and better than I – he joined me in full commitment without any restless hesitation.

Then we went in to my mother, and told her what happened, to her great joy. We explained to her how it had occurred – and she leaped for joy triumphant; and she blessed thee, who art "able to do exceedingly abundantly above all that we ask or think." For she saw that thou hadst granted her far more than she had ever asked for in all her pitiful and doleful lamentations. For thou didst so convert me to thee that I sought neither a wife nor any other of this world's hopes, but set my feet on that rule of faith which so many years before thou hadst showed her in her dream about me. And so thou didst turn her grief into gladness more plentiful than she had ventured to desire, and dearer and purer than the desire she used to cherish of having grandchildren of my flesh.

Ephesians 3:20

Questions for Discussion

1   What light does this passage cast on Augustine's reasons for holding back from any form of Christian commitment, and especially any public declaration of faith?

2   "Grant me chastity and continence, but not yet." This famous quotation is found in this extract. What does it mean? And how does it cast light on the conflicting emotions which Augustine reports himself to have experienced at this time?

3   Why do you think Augustine pays so much attention to his inner mental states and feelings in this passage (and, indeed, throughout this work)?

4   The narrative includes an account of Augustine's conversion. Note the main features that Augustine highlights. How did the earlier conversion of Anthony influence this event, if at all?

CHAPTER 13

Venantius Honorius Clementianus Fortunatus (ca. 530–ca. 610)

Fortunatus was born in Ceneda, near Treviso, in northern Italy. He became a Christian at an early age and studied at Ravenna and Milan. He gained a reputation for excellence in poetry and rhetoric while studying at Ravenna, and while there nearly became blind. He recovered his sight, he believed, by anointing his eyes with oil sent to him from a friend, Gregory of Tours. Gregory had taken the oil from a lamp burned before the altar of St. Martin of Tours. This induced Fortunatus to make a pilgrimage to the tomb of Martin in Tours. During the course of his journey to Tours, he spent some time at the court of Sigebert of Austrasia, remaining there until 567. After this, he continued on his journey to Gaul. While there he formed a close relationship with Queen Rhadegunde (ca. 518–87), who had founded a community of nuns outside the city of Poitiers and who had convinced him to enter the service of the church. He was elected Bishop of Poitiers around 599.

Venantius Honorius Clementianus Fortunatus (ca. 530–ca. 610)

Basic description
Major sixth-century religious poet and bishop.

Major works
"Vexilla regis prodeunt"; "Pange lingua gloriosa."

Major studies
Peter Godman, *Poets and Emperors: Frankish Politics and Carolingian Poetry*. Oxford: Clarendon Press, 1987.
Raymond van Dam, *Saints and Their Miracles in Late Antique Gaul*. Princeton, NJ: Princeton University Press, 1993.

A substantial collection of writings has come down to us from Venantius Fortunatus, including a long metrical life of Martin of Tours and a prose life of Hilary of Poitiers. However, Venantius Fortunatus was also a poet, who wrote eleven books of verse, including elegies and hymns. While it is possible to see him as a late classical poet, many scholars see him as the first of the medieval religious poets. He is chiefly remembered for two poems, "Vexilla regis prodeunt" and "Pange lingua gloriosa." We shall consider the first of these.

Text: *Vexilla Regis Prodeunt*

According to a well-established tradition, in the year 569 St. Radegunde presented a large fragment of what was believed to be the True Cross to the town of Poitiers. Radegunde had obtained this fragment from the Emperor Justin II. Fortunatus was the one chosen to receive the relic on its arrival at Poitiers. When the bearers of the holy fragment were some two miles distant from the town, Fortunatus, with a great gathering of believers and enthusiasts – some of whom were carrying banners, crosses and other sacred emblems – went forth to meet them. As they marched, they sang this hymn, which Fortunatus had composed for the occasion. The hymn was soon incorporated within the Passiontide office of the western church, and is still widely used in marking Holy Week within western Christianity today. The English translation is taken from the *Mediaeval Hymns and Sequences* (1851) of the great Victorian hymnologist and medievalist John Mason Neale (1818–66).

> The royal banners forward go,
> The cross shines forth in mystic glow;
> Where he in flesh, our flesh Who made,
> Our sentence bore, our ransom paid.
>
> There whilst He hung, His sacred side
> By soldier's spear was opened wide,
> To cleanse us in the precious flood
> Of water mingled with His blood.
>
> Fulfilled is now what David told
> In true prophetic song of old,
> How God the heathen's King should be;
> For God is reigning from the tree.
>
> O tree of glory, tree most fair,
> Ordained those holy limbs to bear,
> How bright in purple robe it stood,
> The purple of a Saviour's blood!
>
> Upon its arms, like balance true,
> He weighed the price for sinners due,
> The price which none but He could pay,
> And spoiled the spoiler of his prey.
>
> To Thee, eternal Three in One,
> Let homage meet by all be done:

As by the cross Thou dost restore,
So rule and guide us evermore.

Questions for Study

1 To what extent do you think that Venantius Fortunatus used the model of a Roman triumphal procession for this hymn?
2 In the ancient world, purple dye was a precious commodity. It was made from a certain rare type of sea-shell, and the process of manufacture was difficult. As a result, purple became associated with wealth, prestige, and power. In what way does this poem develop this theme?
3 Read the following section from Mark's Gospel, in which Jesus speaks these words: "For the Son of man also came not to be served but to serve, and to give his life as a ransom for many" (Mark 10:45). In what way can this text be seen reflected in the poem under consideration?

PART II

English and Irish Sources, ca. 600–1050

Introduction

After the collapse of the western section of the Roman Empire in the later fifth century, Christianity was forced to go through a period of reconstruction. After, the conversion of Constantine, the church could more or less rely on the support of the emperor. With the destruction of the western Roman Empire, the church was suddenly exposed to uncertainty and instability. Christianity had become quite Roman in its culture and outlook; it now found itself having to adapt to a new environment in which Roman ideas and values carried little weight. Furthermore, Christianity had never really taken hold in the extreme regions of the empire. Its future in the regions seemed highly uncertain.

However, a program of consolidation and expansion began to get under way. Pope Gregory the Great encouraged missionary work in the outlying regions of the empire. The rise of Christianity in the Celtic regions of Europe – more specifically, Ireland, Scotland, Cornwall, Brittany, and Wales – is of considerable interest, not least in that this form of Christianity found itself in opposition to the more Romanized forms which rapidly gained the ascendancy in England, largely through the efforts of Gregory's missionaries, especially Augustine of Canterbury. Although the origins of Celtic Christianity are thought to lie in Wales, it was Ireland which established itself as a missionary center of distinction in the fifth and sixth centuries. Other centers of missionary activity in the Celtic sphere of influence are known from this period, most notably Candida Casa (modern-day Whithorn, in the Galloway region of Scotland), which was established by Bishop Ninian in the fifth century. The significance of this missionary station was that it lay outside the borders of Roman Britain, and was thus able to operate without the restrictions then associated with Roman forms of Christianity.

The person who is traditionally held to be responsible for the evangelization of Ireland was a Romanized Briton by the name of Magonus Sucatus Patricius, more usually known by his Celtic name "Patrick" (ca. 390–ca. 460). Born into a wealthy family, Patrick was taken captive by a raiding party at the age of sixteen, and sold into slavery in Ireland, probably in the region of Connaught. Here, he appears to have discovered the basics of the Christian faith, before escaping and making his way back to his family. He had been in captivity for six years. It is not clear precisely what happened between Patrick's escape from captivity and his subsequent return to Ireland as a missionary. A tradition, dating back to the seventh or eighth century, refers to Patrick spending time in Gaul before his return to Ireland. It is possible that some of Patrick's views on church organization and structures may reflect first-hand acquaintance with the monasticism of certain regions of southern France. There is excellent historical evidence for trading links between Ireland and the Loire Valley around this time.

At any rate, Patrick returned to Ireland, and established Christianity in the region. It is clear that some form of Christianity already existed; not only does Patrick's conversion account presuppose that others in the region knew about the gospel; contemporary records dating from as early as 429 speak of one Palladius as the bishop of Ireland, indicating that at least some form of rudimentary ecclesiastical structures existed in the region. Irish representatives are also known to have been present at the Synod of Arles (314). Patrick's achievement is perhaps best understood in terms of the consolidation and advancement of Christianity, rather than its establishment in the first place.

The monastic idea took hold very quickly in Ireland. Historical sources indicate that Ireland was largely a nomadic and tribal society at this time, without any permanent settlements of any importance. The monastic quest for solitude and isolation was ideally suited to the Irish way of life. Whereas in western Europe as a whole, monasticism was marginalized within the life of the church, in Ireland it rapidly became its dominant form. It is no exaggeration to say that the Irish church was monastic, with the abbot rather than the bishop being seen as pre-eminent.

The authority structures which emerged within Celtic Christianity were thus rather different from those which came to dominate the Roman–British church at this time. The Irish monastic model came to be seen as a threat to the Roman model of the episcopate, in which the government of the church resided firmly in the hands of the bishops. None of the abbots of Iona ever allowed bishops to formally ordain them, rejecting the need for any such "official" recognition. In Ireland, some of the older bishoprics (including Armagh) were reorganized on a monastic basis, while others were absorbed by monasteries. Abbeys were responsible for the pastoral care of the churches which grew up in their vicinity. The Roman episcopal system was thus marginalized. The Celtic church leaders were openly critical of worldly wealth and status, including the use of horses as a mode of transport, and any form of luxury.

Theologically, Celtic Christianity stressed the importance of the world of nature as a means of knowing God. This is especially clear from the ancient Irish hymn traditionally ascribed to Patrick, and known as "St Patrick's Breastplate." The theme of a "breastplate" was common in Celtic Christian spirituality. It is based upon Paul's references to the "armor of God" (Ephesians 6:10–18), and develops the theme of the believer being protected by the presence of God and a whole range of associated powers. Although strongly trinitarian in its structure, it shows a fascination with the natural world as a means of knowing God. The God who made the world is the same God who will protect Christians from all dangers. We shall consider this text presently.

The Irish monasteries acted as centers for missionary activity, often using sea lanes as channels for the transmission of Christianity. Brendan (died ca. 580) and Columba (died ca. 597) are excellent examples of this type of missionary. In a poem entitled "The Navigation of St Brendan" (ca. 1050), Brendan is praised for his journeys to the "northern and western isles" (usually assumed to be the Orkneys and Hebrides, off the coast of Scotland). Columba brought Christianity from the north of Ireland to the Western Isles of Scotland, and established the abbey of Iona as a missionary outpost. From there, Christianity spread southwards and eastwards. Aidan (died 651) is an excellent example of a monk from Iona who acted as a missionary in this way. At the invitation of the king of the region of Northumbria, he established a missionary monastery on the island of Lindisfarne, off the east coast of northern England.

Celtic Christianity began to penetrate into France, and become increasingly influential in the region. The tensions between Celtic Christianity and its Roman rivals could not be ignored. Celtic Christianity threatened to undermine the episcopate, reduce the power of Rome, make it more difficult for Christianity to become culturally acceptable, and to make monasticism the norm for Christian living. By 597, the year of Columba's death, the ascendancy of the Celtic vision seemed inevitable. However, the following century saw a series of developments which led to its gradual eclipse outside its heartlands of Ireland. By a coincidence of history, the event which led to its eclipse took place in the very year of Columba's death. In 597, Augustine was sent to England by Pope Gregory to evangelize the English, an event recorded in some detail in Bede's *History of the English Church and Nation*, completed in 731. As Roman forms of Christianity became established in England, tensions arose between northern and southern English Christians, the former remaining faithful to Celtic traditions, and the latter to Roman.

The Synod of Whitby (664) is widely seen as establishing the dominance of Roman Christianity in England. Although the Synod focused on the question of when Easter should be celebrated (Celtic and Roman traditions differing on the issue), the real issue concerned the growing influence of the see of Canterbury. The Saxon invasions of England in the previous century had resulted in major cultural changes in the region, making inevitable the gradual erosion of Celtic culture, including its distinctive approach to Christianity. Yet that same development may also be seen as marking a further major shift within Christianity in Britain – the growth of a vernacular Anglo-Saxon literature, particularly poetry, in the service of the Christian faith.

Why is this so important? It is essential to appreciate the importance of poetry to early Germanic culture. The Roman historian Tacitus implied that the considerable responsibility of chronicling the history of the Germanic peoples was entrusted to their poets. With the arrival of large numbers of Anglo-Saxon immigrants in England, the importance of poets appears to have increased. They became, in effect, the guardians of Anglo-Saxon culture, keeping the culture of their homelands alive in the strange land in which they had settled.

Yet the growth of Christian influence in the region would have a major effect on the role of the poet in the Anglo-Saxon world. In his *History of the English Church and Nation*, Bede attaches especial importance to the miracle of Caedmon. Caedmon was an elderly and virtually illiterate lay brother of the religious house of Whitby, in the northeast of England. According to Bede, Caedmon discovered that he had the gift of singing through a dream, in which he sang a hymn (now known as

"Caedmon's hymn"). This remarkable event, which took place at the monastery of Whitby, was seen as being of immense importance, as it led to the development of an explicitly Christian form of Anglo-Saxon poetry. On making known his gift, Caedmon was taken to Hilda, who was abbess of Whitby during the years 657–80, who promptly directed him to become a monk.

At first sight, this advice might seem strange. Yet, on reflection, its merits can be seen. During the Anglo-Saxon period, the monasteries were centers of literacy; indeed, one might say that they virtually enjoyed a monopoly in relation to this precious commodity. The monasteries rapidly became the centers of historical scholarship, and of the editing, production, and distribution of texts. It is clear that the texts which the monasteries thus edited and distributed included both Anglo-Saxon and Latin works, including both traditional vernacular poetry and the theological and liturgical works of the church. There is no doubt that tensions arose over the interaction of these two types of literature; in 797, Alcuin wrote to the monks of Lindisfarne, complaining that they seemed to be more interested in reading the fictional exploits of pagan heroes than the truths of the gospel.

Yet the monasteries also stimulated a complex process of dialogue and fusion, in which the tension between the hero-culture of the Anglo-Saxon peoples was creatively developed in the light of the new values and ideas of the Christian church. The poem *Beowulf*, for example, can be read as an attempt to explore and resolve the tensions between traditional Anglo-Saxon cultural values and those of the gospel. The heroic aspect of traditional pre-Christian Anglo-Saxon poetry is widely regarded as the most distinctive element of that poetry, owing its provenance to the mythical world of the Germanic tribes. Yet the heroic imagery and ideals were carried over, in a subtly changed manner, and put to the service of the gospel. The poem "The Dream of the Rood" can easily be read as "the saga of Christ the hero."

The result of this was that Anglo-Saxon poetry became a vehicle for the transmission and celebration of the Christian faith, rather than being viewed as the vestige of a pagan past, which should be abandoned for the sake of the gospel. Christian writers were encouraged to use the vernacular, rather than concentrate on the Latin, which had long been recognized as the *lingua franca* of the western church. Of the 30,000 lines of Anglo-Saxon poetry which have survived, the bulk deal with explicitly Christian themes. Old English Literature is defined as the literature of the period from AD 750 until the time of the invasion of the Normans in 1066, and a number of major works in this language are included in Part II.

It can therefore be seen why Bede attached such importance to Caedmon's mastery of the traditional *ars poetica*. Caedmon can be seen as a figure of transition, who adapted the traditional Anglo-Saxon poetic style to the service of the Christian faith. Hilda was abbess of Whitby during the period 657–80, allowing us to date Caedmon's activity to a relatively narrow time-span. His "Hymn" would therefore have the special significance of being the first piece of Christian writing in Anglo-Saxon. However, others might also lay claim to this fame; according to the twelfth-century writer William of Malmesbury, Aldhelm (ca. 640–709) was also "singing of Christ" in the Anglo-Saxon language, and winning converts in doing so.

The present section of the anthology brings together a wide range of Celtic and Anglo-Saxon literature from this important period in the history of the British Isles.

Although it is possible to argue that the long-term impact of this period on the development of English-language religious writing was less than might be expected, it remains a landmark period, in which the English language began to emerge and be adapted for specifically Christian purposes.

CHAPTER 14

Caedmon's Hymn (ca. 670)

We have already noted the importance of Caedmon to the development of the traditional Anglo-Saxon art of poetry as a means of communicating the Christian faith. Caedmon's success paved the way for several centuries of Anglo-Saxon religious poetry, in which the traditional structure and themes of this form of writing were used as a vehicle for the transmission and development of Christian ideas and values. Although Caedmon is known to have written extensively – for example, he composed poems on Genesis and Exodus, as well as the Gospels – only one work has come down to us which is generally accepted as authentic.

According to Bede, Caedmon spent most of his life as an illiterate cattle herder. After leaving a banquet because he could not join in the verse-making and singing, Caedmon slept in a cow barn. In his dreams an angel appeared and said, "Caedmon, sing something for me." Caedmon refused. "I can sing nothing. Because of that I left the banquet and came out here, for I do not know how to sing anything." "But you can sing for me," the angel replied. "Sing to me about the beginning of created things." Then Caedmon composed a hymn of nine lines in praise of the Creator.

Later Hilda, abbess of Whitby, heard about this and believed that he was divinely inspired. With her help he became a resident of a monastery. There he spent the rest of his life composing hymns and poems based on biblical stories. Scholars once attributed most of the Anglo-Saxon, or Old English, religious verse to Caedmon. But the only work definitely known to be his is the famous hymn.

Cædmon's "Hymn" is styled after the biblical version of creation. Since he could not read, Cædmon was obliged to paraphrase this narrative from biblical texts which he had heard, either read to him or transmitted by performance in his locality. The poem thus illustrates an oral, rather than a written, biblical culture, in which biblical imagery and narratives were transmitted indirectly through sermons, public readings and story-telling.

As this is the first piece of Anglo-Saxon Christian poetry to be considered, we shall print out the text in the Northumbrian version of that language, so that some of the characteristics of this type of poetry can be appreciated.

Nu scylun hergan   hefænricæs uard,
metudæs mæcti   end his modgidanc,
uerc uuldurfadur,   sue he uundra gihuæs,
eci dryctin,   or astelidæ.
He ærist scop   ælda barnum
heben til hrofe,   haleg scepen;
tha middungeard   moncynnæs uard,
eci dryctin,   æfter tiadæ
firum foldu,   frea allmectig.

Cædmon and his contemporaries used what is known as accentual-syllabic verse. Anglo-Saxon poetry utilized half lines known as "hemistichs," which are separated by a caesura or pause. There are one or two alliterating letters in the first half line preceding the medial caesura; these also alliterate with the first stressed syllable in the second half line. For example, in the ninth line of the hymn, a strong degree of alliteration is achieved through the repetitive use of the "f"s in *firum* and *foldu* in the first half line (hemistich), followed by *frea* in the second half line. Several variations on this style appear in the poem; for example, line five contains only one alliterative letter on each half line. Line nine may, however, be taken to be representative of the rhyming scheme of the work as a whole. This poetic device was effective, forcing the writer to maintain tight, well-scripted verse pleasing to the ear. In later centuries, the modern and more familiar rhyme scheme developed. This has made it much more difficult to translate Anglo-Saxon poetry into contemporary English, as the modern reader automatically expects to encounter rhyme rather than accentual-syllabic verse.

Now must we praise the Guardian of heaven,
The power and conception of the Lord,
And all His works, as He, eternal Lord,
Father of Glory, started every wonder.
First He created heaven as a roof.
The holy Maker, for the sons of men.
Then the eternal Keeper of mankind
Furnished the earth below, the land for men,
Almighty God and everlasting Lord.

Questions for Study

1 Identify the terms used for God in this poem. What do these titles suggest?
2 Why is there such an emphasis on the doctrine of creation in this poem?
3 You may find it interesting to compare this with the "Deer's Cry" (Text 16), in which some similar themes appear, including an emphasis on the importance of providence. At what points in this poem can we see reference to the idea of divine providence?

CHAPTER 15

Bede (ca. 673–735)

Bede was the most important historian, educationalist, and biblical commentator of the Anglo-Saxon period. He is best remembered for his *History of the English Church and Nation*, completed in 731, in which he set out details of the emergence and development of the Christian church in England. His *Life of St Cuthbert* (which exists in two versions, as prose and poetry) was widely read throughout Europe, and did much to establish the cult of St. Cuthbert in this region.

Bede (ca. 673–735)

Basic description
Leading Old English Christian monk, writer and historian.

Major works
History of the English Church and Nation; *Life of St Cuthbert*.

Major studies
Gerald Bonner (ed.), *Famulus Christi: Essays in Commemoration of the Thirteenth Centenary of the Birth of the Venerable Bede*. London: SPCK, 1976.
George H. Brown, *Bede, the Venerable*. Boston, MA: Twayne, 1987.

Relatively little is known of Bede's life, and virtually all of what is known derives from a brief autobiographical note contained in the final chapter of his *History of the English Church and Nation*. We are told that, at the age of seven, he went as an "oblate" (that is, a child dedicated to a monastery by his parents) to the monastery of Wearmouth. In 682 he transferred to the newly-founded abbey at Jarrow, where he would remain for the rest of his life, apart from occasional short visits to ecclesiastical centers at York and Lindisfarne. By the time of his death, his reputation for wisdom was immense, and his "Death Song" can be seen as a gentle mocking of this reputation.

Text: *History of the English Church and Nation*

Bede's *History of the English Church and Nation* is of major importance, both histori-
cally and theologically. The work shows a remarkable ability on the part of its author to
bring together a substantial number of fragments of information, apparently gleaned
form a variety of sources, and weave them into a continuous narrative. Where others
regarded history simply as the registration of facts, Bede sought to tell a story. Inevitably,
Bede's great account of early English church history can be criticized at many points. For
example, Bede clearly has some axes to grind; he relies on fewer sources than might be
wise for such a major undertaking; and he clearly regards certain episodes or individuals as having didactic value to the church, causing him to dwell upon them to a greater
extent than some of his modern readers would find appropriate. Theological interpretation is interwoven with the narrative, and Bede frequently interprets historical events in
explicitly theological ways – for example, he generally sees military defeat as a sign of
God's judgment on his people. This theme is developed further in the famous 1014
sermon of Wulfstan, entitled "Lupi Sermo ad Anglos."

To gain an appreciation of Bede's achievement, it is important to read him at
length. In common with many of the texts surveyed in this work, Bede's *History of
the English Church and Nation* must be drunk deeply. In what follows, we shall consider Bede's account of how Pope Gregory sent Augustine to convert the English,
and how he fared in this mammoth task. The account is found in Book I, chapters
23–27, of this substantial work, and deals with events which took place between
596 and 597.

Chapter XXIII

*How Pope Gregory Sent Augustine, With Other Monks, To Preach To The
English Nation, And Encouraged Them By A Letter Of Exhortation,
Not To Cease From Their Labor [AD 596]*

In the year of our Lord 582, Maurice, the fifty-fourth from Augustus, ascended the
throne, and reigned twenty-one years. In the tenth year of his reign, Gregory, a man
renowned for learning and behavior, was promoted to the apostolical see of Rome,
and presided over it thirteen years, six months and ten days. He, being moved by
Divine inspiration, in the fourteenth year of the same emperor, and about the one
hundred and fiftieth after the coming of the English into Britain, sent the servant of
God, Augustine, and with him several other monks, who feared the Lord, to preach
the word of God to the English nation. They having, in obedience to the pope's
commands, undertaken that work, were, on their journey, seized with a sudden fear,
and began to think of returning home, rather than proceed to a barbarous, fierce,
and unbelieving nation, to whose very language they were strangers; and this they
unanimously agreed was the safest course. In short, they sent back Augustine, who
had been appointed to be consecrated bishop in case they were received by the
English, that he might, by humble entreaty, obtain of the Holy Gregory, that they
should not be compelled to undertake so dangerous, toilsome, and uncertain a

journey. The pope, in reply, sent them a hortatory epistle, persuading them to proceed in the work of the Divine word, and rely on the assistance of the Almighty. The purport of which letter was as follows –

"*Gregory, the servant of the servants of God, to the servants of our Lord.* Forasmuch as it had been better not to begin a good work, than to think of desisting from that which has been begun, it behooves you, my beloved sons, to fulfill the good work, which, by the help of our Lord, you have undertaken. Let not, therefore, the toil of the journey, nor the tongues of evil-speaking men, after you; but with all possible earnestness and zeal perform that which, by God's direction, you have undertaken; being assured, that much labor is followed by an eternal reward. When Augustine, your chief, returns, whom we also constitute your abbot, humbly obey him in all things; knowing that whatsoever you shall do by his direction, will, in all respects, be available to your souls. Almighty God protect you with his grace, and grant that I may, in the heavenly country, see the fruits of your labor. Inasmuch as, though I cannot labor with you, I shall partake in the joy of the reward, because I am willing to labor. God keep you in safety, my most beloved sons. Dated the 23rd of July, in the fourteenth year of the reign of our pious and most august lord, Mauritius Tiberius, the thirteenth year after the consulship of our said lord. The fourteenth indiction."

Chapter XXIV

How He Wrote To The Bishop Of Arles To Entertain Them [AD 596]

The same venerable pope also sent a letter to Ætherius, bishop of Arles, exhorting him to give favorable entertainment to Augustine on his way to Britain; which letter was in these words –

"*To his most reverend and holy brother and fellow bishop Ætherius, Gregory, the servant of the servants of God.* Although religious men stand in need of no recommendation with priests who have the charity which is pleasing to God; yet as a proper opportunity is offered to write, we have thought fit to send you this our letter, to inform you that we have directed thither, for the good of souls, the bearer of these presents, Augustine, the servant of God, of whose industry we are assured, with other servants of God, whom it is requisite that your holiness assist with priestly affection, and afford him all the comfort in your power. And to the end that you may be the more ready in your assistance, we have enjoined him particularly to inform you of the occasion of his coming; knowing that when you are acquainted with it, you will as the matter requires, for the sake of God, zealously afford him your relief. We also in all things recommend to your charity, Candidus, the priest, our common son, whom we have transferred to the government of a small patrimony in our church. God keep you in safety, most reverend brother. Dated the 23rd day of July, in the fourteenth year of the reign of our most pious and august lord, Mauritius Tiberius, the thirteenth year after the consulship of our lord aforesaid. The fourteenth indiction."

Chapter XXV

Augustine, Coming Into Britain, First Preached In The Isle Of Thanet To King Ethelbert, And Having Obtained Licence, Entered The Kingdom Of Kent, In Order To Preach Therein [AD 597]

Augustine, thus strengthened by the confirmation of the blessed Father Gregory, returned to the work of the word of God, with the servants of Christ, and arrived in Britain. The powerful Ethelbert was at that time king of Kent; he had extended his dominions as far as the great river Humber, by which the Southern Saxons are divided from the Northern. On the east of Kent is the large Isle of Thanet containing according to the English way of reckoning, 600 families, divided from the other land by the river Wantsum, which is about three furlongs over, and fordable only in two places, for both ends of it run into the sea. In this island landed the servant of our Lord, Augustine, and his companions, being, as is reported, nearly forty men. They had, by order of the blessed Pope Gregory, taken interpreters of the nation of the Franks, and sending to Ethelbert, signified that they were come from Rome, and brought a joyful message, which most undoubtedly assured to all that took advantage of it everlasting joys in heaven and a kingdom that would never end with the living and true God. The king having heard this, ordered them to stay in that island where they had landed, and that they should be furnished with all necessaries, till he should consider what to do with them. For he had before heard of the Christian religion, having a Christian wife of the royal family of the Franks, called Bertha; whom he had received from her parents, upon condition that she should be permitted to practice her religion with the Bishop Luidhard, who was sent with her to preserve her faith. Some days after, the king came into the island, and sitting in the open air, ordered Augustine and his companions to be brought into his presence. For he had taken precaution that they should not come to him in any house, lest, according to an ancient superstition, if they practiced any magical arts, they might impose upon him, and so get the better of him. But they came furnished with Divine, not with magic virtue, bearing a silver cross for their banner, and the image of our Lord and Savior painted on a board; and singing the litany, they offered up their prayers to the Lord for the eternal salvation both of themselves and of those to whom they were come. When he had sat down, pursuant to the king's commands, and preached to him and his attendants there present, the word of life, the king answered thus:– "Your words and promises are very fair, but as they are new to us, and of uncertain import, I cannot approve of them so far as to forsake that which I have so long followed with the whole English nation. But because you are come from far into my kingdom, and, as I conceive, are desirous to impart to us those things which you believe to be true, and most beneficial, we will not molest you, but give you favorable entertainment, and take care to supply you with your necessary sustenance; nor do we forbid you to preach and gain as many as you can to your religion." Accordingly he permitted them to reside in the city of Canterbury, which was the metropolis of all his dominions, and, pursuant to his promise, besides allowing them sustenance, did not refuse them liberty to preach. It is reported that, as they drew near to the city, after their manner, with the holy cross, and the image of our sovereign Lord and King, Jesus Christ, they, in concert, sung this litany: "We beseech Thee, O Lord, in all Thy mercy, that thy anger and wrath be turned away from this city, and from the holy house, because we have sinned. Hallelujah."

Chapter XXVI

St. Augustine In Kent Followed The Doctrine And Manner
Of Living Of The Primitive Church, And Settled His Episcopal
See In The Royal City [AD 597]

As soon as they entered the dwelling-place assigned them they began to imitate the course of life practiced in the primitive church; applying themselves to frequent prayer, watching and fasting; preaching the word of life to as many as they could; despising all worldly things, as not belonging to them; receiving only their necessary food from those they taught; living themselves in all respects conformably to what they prescribed to others, and being always disposed to suffer any adversity, and even to die for that truth which they preached. In short, several believed and were baptized, admiring the simplicity of their innocent life, and the sweetness of their heavenly doctrine. There was on the east side of the city a church dedicated to the honor of St. Martin, built whilst the Romans were still in the island, wherein the queen, who, as has been said before, was a Christian, used to pray. In this they first began to meet, to sing, to pray, to say Mass, to preach, and to baptize, till the king, being converted to the faith, allowed them to preach openly, and build or repair churches in all places.

When he, among the rest, induced by the unspotted life of these holy men, and their delightful promises, which, by many miracles, they proved to be most certain, believed and was baptized, greater numbers began daily to flock together to hear the word, and, forsaking their heathen rites, to associate themselves, by believing, to the unity of the church of Christ. Their conversion the king so far encouraged, in that he compelled none to embrace Christianity, but only showed more affection to the believers, as to his fellow-citizens in the heavenly kingdom. For he had learned from his instructors and leaders to salvation, that the service of Christ ought to be voluntary, not by compulsion. Nor was it long before he gave his preachers a settled residence in his metropolis of Canterbury, with such possessions of different kinds as were necessary for their subsistence.

Questions for Study

1   What is Bede's intended audience for this work? How does this affect the way in which he presents his material?
2   How would you judge Bede's attitude to Augustine?
3   What points, if any, do you think Bede wishes to make through his important account of Augustine's work in England?

Text 2: Bede's Death Song

Bede wrote most of his major works in Latin, and even wrote books encouraging the study and correct writing of that language (such as *De Orthographia*, which consists of a list of Latin terms which are commonly misunderstood by those beginning the study of the language). Yet, just as Erasmus of Rotterdam lapsed into his native Flemish on his deathbed, after a lifetime of work promoting Latin as the scholarly language of Europe, so Bede penned a short poem in his native Anglo-Saxon during his final illness. Although Cuthbert, abbot of Wearmouth, provides a Latin paraphrase of this work in his *Epistola Cuthberti de obitu Bedae* ("Letter of Cuthbert on the Death of Bede"), the original Anglo-Saxon version is found in many early manuscripts, including one dating from the ninth century.

> Before the journey that awaits us all
> No man becomes so wise that he has not
> Need to think out, before his going hence,
> What judgment will be given to his soul,
> After his death, of evil or of good.

Questions for Study

1   Bede had a reputation for formidable wisdom. In what ways does this poem mock that reputation, however gently?
2   How does Bede's stress on future judgment relate to the heroic ideas of Saxon culture?

CHAPTER 16

The Deer's Cry (ca. 700)

This is perhaps the greatest of all Celtic hymns. Traditionally ascribed to St. Patrick – and often known as "St. Patrick's Breastplate" – this Gaelic work is generally agreed to date from the late seventh or early eighth century, while incorporating many themes which date from earlier Celtic traditions. While the characteristics of its language would assign it to the late seventh or early eighth century, there is little doubt that it reflects many of the themes found in Patrick's thought. Some Irish writers have argued that this work is to be seen as the earliest expression of European vernacular poetry; this is contestable, as there is far better reason to allow Caedmon's hymn this honor. Nevertheless, it represents a remarkably sophisticated vernacular poem, of immense importance both for the history of the Irish language and culture, and for the study of Celtic theology and spirituality.

The unusual name of the hymn derives from a legend, according to which Patrick and some of his followers were attempting to escape from Laeghaire of Tara on Holy Saturday 433. Their escape from the wrath of the king was ensured when the fugitives called upon the name of God, who transformed them into deer. The hymn is a celebration of the wisdom and power of God, as seen in his works of both creation and redemption. It is an excellent example of a *lorica* or "breastplate" – a prayer or statement of faith to be recited for protection, arming oneself for spiritual or physical battle.

Although there is a well-known translation of this by Mrs. Cecil F. Alexander, which can be found in the hymn books of many Christian denominations, the translation selected perhaps captures the spirit of the original somewhat better. The poem opens with an affirmation of the wisdom of God as redeemer, reciting the central events of the history of salvation. After calling upon the heavenly host, the poet moves on to depict the richness of God's creation. The final sections of the poem constitute the "breastplate" mentioned earlier – namely, an appeal to God to safeguard the believer against all the hostile forces which threaten to destroy life or faith. The poem concludes with the invocation of Christ, as protector in every situation.

> I arise today
> Through a mighty strength, the invocation of the Trinity,

Through the belief in the threeness,
Through confession of the oneness
Of the Creator of Creation.   5

I arise today
Through the strength of Christ's birth with his baptism,
Through the strength of his crucifixion with his burial,
Through the strength of his resurrection with his ascension,
Through the strength of his descent for the judgment of Doom.   10

I arise today
Through the strength of the love of Cherubim,
In obedience of angels,
In the service of archangels,
In hope of resurrection to meet with reward,   15
In prayers of patriarchs,
In predictions of prophets,
In preaching of apostles,
In faith of confessors,
In innocence of holy virgins,   20
In deeds of righteous men.

I arise today
Through the strength of heaven:
Light of sun,
Radiance of moon,   25
Splendor of fire,
Speed of lightning,
Swiftness of wind,
Depth of sea,
Stability of earth,   30
Firmness of rock.

I arise today
Through God's strength to pilot me:
God's might to uphold me,
God's wisdom to guide me,   35
God's eye to look before me,
God's ear to hear me,
God's word to speak for me,
God's hand to guard me,
God's way to lie before me,   40
God's shield to protect me,
God's host to save me
From snares of devils,
From temptations of vices,

From everyone who shall wish me ill,   45
Afar and anear,
Alone and in multitude.

I summon today all these powers between me and those evils,
Against every cruel merciless power that may oppose my body and soul,
Against incantations of false prophets,   50
Against black laws of pagandom
Against false laws of heretics,
Against craft of idolatry,
Against spells of witches and smiths and wizards,
Against every knowledge that corrupts man's body and soul.   55

Christ to shield me today
Against poison, against burning,
Against drowning, against wounding,
So that there may come to me abundance of reward.
Christ with me, Christ before me, Christ behind me,   60
Christ in me, Christ beneath me, Christ above me,
Christ on my right, Christ on my left,
Christ when I lie down, Christ when I sit down, Christ when I arise,
Christ in the heart of every man who thinks of me,
Christ in the mouth of everyone who speaks of me,   65
Christ in every eye that sees me,
Christ in every ear that hears me.

I arise today
Through a mighty strength, the invocation of the Trinity,
Through belief in the threeness,   70
Through confession of the oneness,
Of the Creator of Creation.

Questions for Study

1   The poem intermingles a number of major Christian themes, and it is important to disentangle them. Begin by identifying the sections of the poem which deal with the events of the life of Christ. What role are these understood to play?
2   The poem also includes some material which relates to the work of God in creation. Which sections are these? And what is their function within the overall structure of the poem?
3   The poem includes a section often referred to as a "Breastplate," which is basically an invocation of the name of God (or Christ) as a protection against evil and danger. Which section of the poem could be described as the "Breastplate"? And what does the poet want his readers to learn from this?

CHAPTER 17

The Dream of the Rood (ca. 750)

The most reliable text of this important work is found in the "Vercelli Book," a collection of Anglo-Saxon works which is dated to the second half of the tenth century. It bears some resemblance to the "Exeter Book," which is a similar collection of works dating from roughly the same period. It is far from clear how a collection of Old English texts came to end up in an Italian library. The most promising explanation lies in the observation that Vercelli was located on one of the main medieval pilgrim routes to Rome, and it is entirely possible that this work was brought there by an English cleric on his way to the city. Whether the work was accidentally left in Vercelli, or was a deliberate gift for hospitality received, remains a matter for speculation. Our concern is with one of the poems contained in this book – "The Dream of the Rood."

The Dream of the Rood (ca. 750)

Basic description
A major eighth-century Old English poem, dealing with the significance of the cross.

Major studies
Earl R. Anderson, "Liturgical Influence in The Dream of the Rood," *Neophilologus* 73 (1989), 293–304.

Anthony R. Grasso, "Theology and Structure in The Dream of the Rood," *Religion and Literature* 23 (1991), 23–38.

Sherman H. Kuhn, *Studies in the Language and Poetics of Anglo-Saxon England*. Ann Arbor, MI: Karoma, 1984.

"Rood" is the Old English word for "cross," and is still encountered as a living word in modern English, specifically in relation to church architecture. "The Dream of the Rood" is a remarkable work of the Christian imagination, which depicts the cross on which Christ died as telling its own story. The work is to be dated from before 750, in that sections of the poem can be discerned as engraved on the Ruthwell Cross, Dumfries, which is known to date from that era.

The work is written as a piece of Anglo-Saxon poetry, using half lines known as "hemistichs," which are separated by a caesura or pause, with alliterative repetition across each half line. For example, here are the first three lines of the poem:

> Hwæt! Ic swefna cyst   secgan wylle,
> hwæt me gemætte   to midre nihte,
> syðþan reordberend   reste wunedon!

We have already considered some of the features of this type of poetry when considering "Caedmon's Hymn" (see p. 127). The modern and more familiar rhyme scheme with which most of us are familiar has made it much more difficult to translate Anglo-Saxon poetry, as the modern reader automatically expects to encounter rhyme rather than accentual-syllabic verse. For this reason, we have used a translation which is easier to read as a piece of prose, thus avoiding some of the difficulties which readers might otherwise encounter.

The structure of the poem is complex and suggestive, and needs to be appreciated if the poem is to be fully understood. The poem opens with an address, in which the poet identifies himself, and relates how he dreamt a most wonderful dream in the middle of the night (lines 1–2; para 1). This is followed by a description of the cross (lines 4–12), in which the poet sees a richly jeweled and gilded cross, perhaps similar to those carried in church processions at this time. Yet as the poet gazes on the cross, it seems to change its appearance. Blood makes its appearance, as the dual aspects of the cross begin to impact upon the poet's imagination. At one time, it is studded with jewels; at another, it is drenched with blood (lines 9–17, para 3).

The poet then hears the cross tell its own story. There are three major elements to this: the crucifixion (lines 19–39; para 4), Christ's deposition and burial (lines 40–56, para 5), and the deposition and rediscovery of the cross (lines 57–66, para 5). Notice how Christ is depicted as a hero (see especially lines 27–30, para 4), who mounts the cross in order to achieve a magnificent victory. The poem then deals with the true meaning of the cross (lines 67–81, para 8) and the need to proclaim this message to the world (lines 82–84, para 9). The final section of the poem is devotional and meditative, focusing on the devotion of the poet to the cross, and his hopes for his personal future (lines 95–102, para 10).

Listen! I want to recount the most excellent of visions, and what I dreamed in the middle of the night when voiceful mortals lay abed.

It seemed to me that I saw a wondrous tree spreading aloft spun about with light, a most magnificent timber. The portent was all covered with gold; beautiful gems
5 appeared at the corners of the earth and there were also five upon the crossbeam. All the beautiful angels of the Lord throughout the universe gazed thereon; certainly it was not the gallows of a criminal there, but holy spirits gazed thereon, men across the earth and all this glorious creation.

Magnificent was the cross of victory and I was stained with sins, wounded by evil
10 deeds. I observed that the tree of glory, enriched by its coverings, decked with gold,

shone delightfully. Gems had becomingly covered the Ruler's tree. However, through the gold I could discern the earlier aggression of wretched men, in that it had once bled on the right side. I was altogether oppressed with anxieties; I was fearful in the presence of that beautiful sight. I observed the urgent portent shift its coverings and its hues; at times it was soaked with wetness, drenched by the coursing of blood, at 15 times adorned with treasure. Nevertheless, lying there a long while, I gazed, troubled, upon the Saviour's cross – until I heard that it was talking. Then that most noble tree spoke these words:

"Years ago it was – I still recall it – that I was cut down at the forest edge, removed from my root. Strong enemies seized me there, fashioned me as a spectacle for 20 themselves and required me to hoist up their felons. There men carried me upon their shoulders until they set me up on a hill. Abundant enemies secured me there.

"Then I saw the Lord of mankind hasten with much fortitude, for he meant to climb upon me. I did not dare then, against the word of the Lord, to give 25 way there or to break when I saw the earth's surfaces quake. All the enemies I could have felled; nonetheless I stood firm. The young man, who was almighty God, stripped himself, strong and unflinching. He climbed upon the despised gallows, courageous under the scrutiny of many, since he willed to redeem mankind. I quaked then, when the man embraced me; nonetheless I did not dare to collapse to the 30 ground and fall to the surfaces of the earth, but I had to stand fast. I was reared up as a cross; I raised up the powerful King, Lord of the heavens. I did not dare to topple over. They pierced me with dark nails: the wounds are visible upon me, gaping malicious gashes. I did not dare to harm any of them. They humiliated us both together. I was all soaked with blood issuing from the man's side after 35 he had sent forth his spirit. Many cruel happenings I have experienced on that hill. I saw the God of hosts violently racked. Darkness with its clouds had covered the corpse of the Ruler; a gloom, murky beneath the clouds, overwhelmed its pure splendour. All creation wept; they lamented the King's death: Christ was on the Cross.

"However, urgent people from afar came there to the Prince: all this I witnessed. 40 I was sorely oppressed with anxieties; nonetheless I bowed to the hands of those men, obedient with much fortitude. There they took hold of almighty God and lifted him out of that grievous torment. Me those valiant men left to stand covered with blood; I was thoroughly wounded by sharp points. There they laid down the man 45 weary of limb; they stood at his body's head. There they gazed upon the Lord of heaven and he rested himself there for a while, worn out after the great struggle. Then in the sight of the instrument of his death they made him a tomb; they carved it out of the gleaming rock and therein they placed the Lord of victories. Then, pitiful, they sang a song of mourning for him in the evening hour when they were 50 about to depart, worn out, from the glorious Prince. He remained there with little company. But we were standing in position, weeping, for a good while after the sound of the valiant men had ceased. The corpse, the beautiful lodging place of life, grew cold. Then we were all felled to the ground: that was a terrible experience. We were dug down into a deep pit. However, the Lord's servants, friends, found out I was 55 there and adorned me with gold and with silver.

"Now, my beloved man, you can hear that I have experienced the pain caused by men of evil, the grievous anxieties. Now a time has come when people far and wide throughout the earth, and all this glorious creation honour me and worship this sign.
60 On me the Son of God suffered for a time; for that cause I now tower up secure in majesty beneath the heavens and I am enabled to heal everyone who holds me in awe. Once I was made the cruellest of tortures, utterly loathsome to people – until I cleared for them, for mortals, the true path of life. You see! the Lord of glory, Guardian of heaven-kingdom, then honoured me above the trees of the forest, just
65 as he, the almighty God, in the sight of all men, also honoured his mother, Mary herself, above all womankind.

"Now, my beloved man, I enjoin you to declare this vision to people; make it plain by your words that it is the tree of glory on which almighty God suffered for the many sins of mankind and for the old deeds of Adam. There he tasted death, but
70 still the Lord rose again with his mighty power, to the benefit of men. He then ascended into the heavens. He will make the journey back here to earth, the Lord himself, the almighty God, and his angels with him, to seek out mankind on the day of judgment because he who has monopoly of judgment will at that time judge each one according as he previously merits here in this transitory life. No one there can
75 be unafraid in the face of the word which the Ruler will speak: he will ask in the presence of the many, where is that man who for the Lord's name would be willing to taste bitter death as he once did upon the tree. Rather, they will be fearful then, and will have little idea as to what they may begin to say to Christ. No one there at that time need be frightened who beforehand carries in his bosom the noblest of signs,
80 but through that Cross every soul which purposes to dwell with the Ruler shall find its way from the earthly path into the kingdom."

Then, in happy spirit and with much fortitude I worshipped that tree there where I was, alone with little company. My spirit was aroused to the onward way and experienced many longings. It is now my hope of life that I be allowed to approach
85 the tree of victory alone more often than all other people, and honour it abundantly. Determination for that is great in my mind and my support is directly in the Cross. I do not have many powerful friends on earth, but they have passed on from here out of the joys of the world, and found their way to the King of glory. Now they live in heaven with the high Father and dwell in glory – and I hope each day for the
90 time when the Cross of the Lord, which I once gazed upon here on earth, will fetch me from this transitory life and then bring me to where there is great happiness, joy in heaven, where the Lord's people are placed at the banquet, where there is unceasing happiness; and will then place me where I may afterwards dwell in glory and fully partake of joy with the saints.

95 May the Lord be a friend to me, who here on earth once suffered on the gallows-tree for the sins of men. He redeemed us and gave us life, and a heavenly home. Hope was renewed with dignity and with happiness for those who had once suffered burning. The Son was victorious in that undertaking, powerful and successful, when he came with a multitude, the company of souls, into God's kingdom, the one
100 almighty Ruler, to the delight of the angels and of all the saints who had previously dwelt in glory in the heavens, when their Ruler, almighty God, came where his home was.

Questions for Discussion

1 Why do you think the writer uses the framework of a dream to tell this story?
2 Why do you think the writer personifies the tree? What is gained by giving it human characteristics?
3 The story is set against the background of Nordic hero-culture, which placed great value on warriors and victories. In what way does the idea of "Christ as hero" emerge in this poem?

CHAPTER 18

The Junius Codex (ca. 870)

One of the most important pieces of Christian literature is usually known simply as the "Junius Codex" or the "Junius Manuscript," held in the Bodleian Library, Oxford. The text gained its name through having been owned by Francis Junius (1589–1677), an antiquarian who was a close personal acquaintance of John Milton. Indeed, some writers have suggested that similarities between Milton's *Paradise Lost* and parts of the "Genesis" material in this codex may rest on Milton having had access to this source through his friend. Though intriguing, this hypothesis cannot be proven. The work is also known as the "Caedmon Manuscript."

This manuscript consists of two books; the first of which consists of commentaries on Genesis, Exodus, and Daniel; the second of which consists of a complex work focusing on Christ and Satan. The Junius Codex appears to have been written in four different hands at some point in the late tenth or early eleventh century. However, it seems clear that the manuscript brings together older sources into a single compilation. It is possible that the works were brought together by a religious community, to meet their needs for an appropriate series of readings during the Lenten and Easter seasons.

The individual works which can be identified within the manuscript must therefore be dated earlier than the manuscript itself. How much earlier is, as might be expected, a matter of considerable debate. Some have suggested that at least parts of the codex ought to be ascribed to Caedmon himself; this has generally been rejected, not least because there is no direct evidence to link any part of the work with Caedmon. However, scholars have found it useful to speak of a "Caedmonian school of poetics," and it is entirely possible that sections of this work may be ascribed to such a school.

Strictly speaking, the biblical commentaries included in this work must be regarded as free reworkings of biblical themes, designed to engage their readers' attention. Dramatic license generally takes precedence over any scholarly concerns. The works are of considerable importance, not simply as witnesses to the continuing Anglo-Saxon tradition of religious literature, but as sources for our understanding of the popular theology of the early medieval church.

Text: Genesis B

Although the Junius Codex includes one single work on the book of Genesis, it is widely agreed that two distinct poems can be identified. These are usually referred to as "Genesis A" (lines 1–234 and 852–2935) and "Genesis B" (lines 235–851). The passage extracted for analysis is taken from "Genesis B," distinguished by its less rigid meter. It is possible that the freer structure of this poem may reflect the fact that it is actually a translation of an Old Saxon original. The work is generally dated to the middle of the ninth century, although it must be stressed that this is largely conjectural.

"Genesis B" is a self-contained account of the fall of the angels and of humanity. The portion selected for discussion is an imaginative and creative reworking of the narrative found in Genesis 3, and can be read without the need for comment as a powerful and dramatic presentation of the fall of humanity. As the fall of humanity can be regarded as the precondition for redemption through Christ, "Genesis B" can be said to set the scene for the drama of "Christ and Satan," which we shall explore later.

XI [*Genesis B*]

Then an adversary of God eager in his accoutrements got himself ready: he had an evil sense of purpose. He set on his head a concealing helm and fastened it very tightly and secured it with clasps. He had in him knowledge of plenty of speeches of perverse words. From there he wound his way upwards and passed through the gates of hell – he had a strong sense of purpose – and hovered aloft, malevolent-minded. He beat down the fire on both sides with his fiend's strength: he meant surreptitiously to seduce, to lead astray and to pervert with wicked deeds the followers of the Lord, men, so that they would become repugnant to God.

He journeyed on then with his fiend's strength until in the kingdom of earth he came upon the perfected Adam, God's wisely created handiwork, and his wife also, a most beautiful woman, so that they could accomplish much good whom mankind's ordaining Lord himself had appointed as his subordinates.

And near them stood two trees which were laden with a crop and covered with fruit according as God the Ruler, the high King of heaven, had planted them with his hands in order that thereby the children of men, each person, might choose between good and evil, well-being and woe. Their fruit was not alike. The one was so pleasant, beautiful and radiant, graceful and admirable – that was the tree of life. He would be allowed thereafter to live on and to exist in the world in eternity who ate of that fruit, so that age did not harm him after that nor severe sickness, but he would be allowed from then on always to live among pleasures and to have his existence and the heaven-King's favour here in the world and to have as his pledge assured honours in that high heaven when he should journey there. Then there was the other, entirely black, obscure and dark – that was the tree of death which brought forth much bitterness. Each man soever that tasted of what grew on that tree must needs become aware of the two things, the divergent ways of good and of evil in this world, and thereafter he would have to live by his sweat and in sorrows, forever under punishment. Old age must needs rob him of valorous deeds, of pleasures and of authority, and death be decreed him. For a little while he would enjoy his life and then go to the darkest of realms, into the fire, and would have to minister to fiends there where there will exist for an infinite duration the greatest of all perils for men. That the malignant creature, the devil's secret messenger who was contending against God, well knew.

He turned himself then into the form of a snake and then wound himself about the tree of death with the cunning of a devil; there he plucked a fruit and went thence back again to where he perceived the heaven-King's handiwork. Then in his first utterance the malignant creature began to question him with lies:

"Do you long for anything, Adam, from God above? I have journeyed here from far away on his business; it was not long since that I sat by his very self. He then commanded me to go on this mission. He commanded that you should eat of this fruit and he declared that your strength and skill and your mind would grow greater, and your body much more beautiful, your limbs more handsome, and he declared that to you there would prove no want of any wealth in the world. You have now done the will of the heaven-King and your loyal duty to him and served your Master to his satisfaction and you have made yourself precious to the Lord. I heard him in his splendour praise your deeds and your words and speak about your way of life. Accordingly, you are to carry out what his messengers bring word of here into this country. Broad are the green regions in the world and God, the Ruler of all, sits above in the most exalted realm of the heavens. The Lord of men is unwilling himself to have the hardships of travelling on this mission; rather he sends his subordinate to speak with you. Now he has commanded me to teach you by messages cunning skills. Carry out his bidding confidently. Take this fruit into your hand, bite it and taste it. Within your breast you will become untrammelled and your outward form will become the more beautiful. God the Ruler, your Lord, has sent you this help from the heaven-kingdom."

Adam, the self-determined man, standing there on the earth, spoke out:

"When I heard the triumphant Lord, mighty God, speak with stern voice, and when he commanded me to establish myself here and to keep his behests and gave me this wife, this lovely woman, and commanded me take heed that I should not be brought to ruin or utterly betrayed over that tree of death, he declared that he would have to inhabit black hell who of his own volition did anything evil. I do not know whether you come with lies from a hidden motive or whether you are the messenger of the Lord from heaven. You see, I cannot make any sense of your suggestions, of your words and reasons, your mission and declarations. I do know what he, our Saviour, himself enjoined upon me when I saw him last: he commanded me to honour and keep well his word and carry out his precepts. You are not like any of his angels whom I saw before, nor have you shown me any token that my Master has sent to me out of his favour and out of his grace. Therefore I cannot obey you, and you may go your way. I have a firm trust above in the almighty God who fashioned me here with his arms and with his hands. He is capable of endowing me with every advantage from his high kingdom, even if he did not send his subordinate."

XII [*Genesis B*]

He turned himself, the malevolent creature, to where in earth's domain he saw the woman Eve standing, beautifully formed; and he declared to her that it would prove the greatest harm in the world to all their children thereafter:

"I am certain that the Lord God will be incensed against the two of you when I return from this journey along the lengthy road if I personally tell him this message, that you two do not properly act upon whatever message he sends here from the east on this occasion. Now he himself will have to make the journey, according to your answer. His spokesman is not allowed to speak his business, therefore I am certain that in his heart he, the mighty God, is going to be incensed against you. But if you, a compliant woman, will listen to my words then you will be able to think circumspectly about a remedy for it. Consider in your heart that you can fend off punishment from the pair of you, as I shall show you.

"Eat of this fruit. Then your eyes will become so clear that you will afterwards be able to see as widely as beyond the whole world and the throne of your Master himself, and henceforth to enjoy his favour. You will be able moreover to manipulate Adam if you command his desire and he trusts in your words. If you tell him truly what an exemplary precept you yourself hold in your bosom, because you have carried out God's bidding and counsel, he will abandon in his heart this distasteful antagonism and his ill response, if we two both talk to him with effect. Coax him carefully so that he carries out your counsel, lest you should both be forced to prove abhorrent to God your Ruler.

"If you achieve that design, most excellent lady, I will conceal from your Master that Adam spoke so much insult and so many contemptible words to me. He accuses me of lies and says that I am a messenger intent upon malicious and hostile things, and not an angel of God. But I know the whole race of angels and the lofty roofs of the heavens so well, so long has been the time I have eagerly served God, my Master, the Lord himself, with loyal resolution. I am not like a devil."

So he led her on with lies and by cunning coaxed on the woman in that mischief until the snake's thinking began to seethe up inside her – the ordaining Lord had defined for her a frailer resolution – so that she began to let her mind go along with those counsels. Therefore she received from the abhorrent foe, against the word of the Lord, the tree of death's injurious fruit. A deed more evil was not defined for men. It is a great wonder that eternal God, the Prince, would ever tolerate it that so many a servant should be led astray by lies as happened because of those counsels.

She ate of the fruit then and violated the word and the will of the Ruler of all. Then through the gift of the abhorrent foe who betrayed her with lies and subtly defrauded her, which came to her because of his doings, she was enabled to see far afield so that heaven and earth seemed brighter to her and all this world more beautiful and God's work great and mighty – although she did not view it by means of a human perception, but the destroyer who had lent her the vision assiduously deluded her in her spirit so that she could gaze so widely over the heavenly domain.

Then the apostate spoke out of his malevolence; he did not teach her anything at all of profit:

"Now you can see for yourself, so I do not need to tell you it, virtuous Eve, that appearances and forms are different since you trusted in my words and carried out my counsels. Now light shines out before you and gracious radiance towards you which I have brought from God, gleaming from out of the heavens. Now you can lay hold on it. Tell Adam what powers of vision you possess through my coming. If even now he carries out my counsels in modest manner, then I shall give him abundance of this light with which, so virtuous, I have adorned you. I shall not reproach him for those blasphemies, even though he is not worthy of being excused for he expressed much that was abhorrent to me."

So must her children live in their turn: when they do something abhorrent they must achieve an amicable settlement, make good the blaspheming of their Master and enjoy his favour from then on.

To Adam then she went, the most lovely of women, the most beautiful of wives that might come into the world, because she was the work of the hand of the heaven-King, even though she had then been subtly corrupted and led astray by lies so that they were to prove abhorrent to God through the enemy's scheming and were to lose the esteem and favour of their Master through the devil's devices and to forfeit the kingdom of heaven for many a season. Misery replete will befall the man who does not keep on his guard while he enjoys self-determination.

One unblessed apple she carried in her hand, one lay at her heart, the fruit of the tree of death which the Lord of lords had previously forbidden her; and the Prince of glory had uttered this pronouncement, that men, his servants, lay under no necessity of suffering that great death, but he, the holy Lord, granted to each one of his people the kingdom of heaven and copious wealth if they would let be that one fruit which the abhorrent tree bore on its boughs, filled with bitterness: it was death's tree which the Lord forbade them. Her, then, and the mentality of Eve, the frail mind of woman, he seduced who was hostile to God and in hatred of the heaven-King, so that she believed in his words, carried out his counsels, and accepted in trust that he had brought those precepts from God which he so carefully communicated to her in his words and showed her a sign and gave assurance of his good faith and honest intent. Then she spoke to her master:

"Adam, my lord, this fruit is so sweet and delectable in my breast, and this handsome messenger is God's good angel: I see by his apparel that he is the envoy of our Master, the King of heaven. His favour is better for us to win than his enmity. If you spoke anything hurtful to him today he will nevertheless forgive it, if we two are willing to pay him deference. What will it avail you, such detestable quarrelling with your Master's messenger? We need his favour. He can intercede for us with the Ruler of all, the King of heaven. I can see from here where he himself is sitting – it is to the south-east – surrounded with wealth, who shaped the world. I see his angels moving about him on their wings, the hugest of all throngs, of multitudes the most joyous. Who could give me such discernment if God, the Ruler of heaven, had not sent it directly to me? I can hear amply and see so widely into all the world and beyond this spacious creation, I can hear the ethereal merriment in the heavens. My mind has become enlightened within and without since I ate the fruit. I have some of it here in my hands now, virtuous master. I give it to you gladly. I believe that it has come from God, brought by his command – so this messenger has told me with truthful words. It is like nothing else on earth except that, as this envoy says, it has come directly from God."

XIII [*Genesis B*]

She talked to him repeatedly and coaxed him the whole day towards the dismal act, that they should violate their Lord's will. The malignant messenger stayed; he foisted desires upon them, enticed them with cunning and audaciously dogged them. The fiend remained very close, who had travelled on the audacious journey along the lengthy road: he meant to make man fall into that great and mortal sin, to misguide people and lead them astray so that they should forgo God's benefaction, the Almighty's gift, possession of the kingdom of heaven. Indeed, the hellish mischief-maker well knew that they must be subject to God's wrath and imprisonment in hell and of necessity undergo that forcible oppression once they had broken God's command, when with lying words he misguided the lovely woman, the most beautiful of wives, into that indiscretion, so that she spoke under his will and became as an instrument to him in misguiding God's handiwork.

She talked quite often to Adam, then, this most lovely of women, until the man's mind was changed, so that he put his trust in the promise which the woman expressed to him in her words. Yet she did it out of loyal intent. She did not know that there were to follow so many hurts and terrible torments for humankind because she took to heart what she heard in the counsellings of that abhorrent messenger; but rather she thought that she was gaining the favour of the heavenly King with those words which she presented to the man as a sign, and gave assurance of her good faith until within his breast Adam's determination wavered and his heart began to incline towards her desire. From the woman he accepted hell and departure hence, though it was not so called, but had the name of fruit. Yet it was the sleep of death and the yoke of the devil, hell and death, and the perdition of men, the murder of mankind, that unholy fruit which they took as their food.

Questions for Study

1 What kind of document is this? Is it a biblical commentary, a drama, or what?
2 What does the author of this work identify as the cause of sin?
3 How would you describe the manner in which the author represents Adam and Eve? Does he appear to sympathize with one rather than the other? If so, what reasons could be offered for this?

Text: *Christ and Satan*

The second text deals with the final conflict between Christ and Satan. The work offers a highly dramatic understanding of the significance of Christ's death and resurrection, and reflects the importance attached to the theme of the "harrowing of hell" in popular Christian culture. The work can be read without the need for any comment.

VIII

That species of angel mentioned before, called Lucifer, the bearer of light, lived in days of old in the kingdom of God. Then he aroused strife in heaven, because he was willing to give way to pride. Then Satan darkly decided to fashion an exalted throne on high in the heavens, alongside the eternal God. He was their lord, the originator of evil. He afterwards rued it, when he was forced to sink down to hell, and his following with him, to slide into humiliation – the Saviour's hostility, and the fact that never to eternity would they be allowed to see the face of the eternal Lord after that time when a terrifying thing befell them, the din caused by the Judge when he broke asunder and crushed the gates in hell. Delight came upon the mortals when they saw the Redeemer's head – more than there was for the hideous being whom we previously named.

They were all at that time, abroad throughout that windswept habitation, panic-stricken with terror. They complained aloud:

"This is hard to withstand, now that this attack has come, a soldier with a battalion, the Prince of the angels. Ahead of him there goes a light more beautiful than we have ever before looked on with our eyes except when we were on high amidst the angels. Now by the strength of his glory he will utterly overthrow our tortures. Now that this terrifying thing is come, the din caused by the Lord, this horde of miserable beings must forthwith suffer horror now. It is the Son of the Ruler himself, the Lord of the angels. He means to lead the souls up and away from here, and we for ever afterwards shall suffer humiliation for that act of his wrath."

The ordaining Lord, then, by means of his might, went to hell to the sons of men; he meant to lead forth the full complement of mortals, many thousands, up to their fatherland. At that time there came the voice of angels, a thunderous sound in the dawning day: the Lord himself had outfought the fiend. His vengeance was made manifest even then in the early morning when that terrifying event took place. Then he let the blessed souls, Adam's kin, ascend – but Eve could not yet look upon heaven before she declared aloud:

"Once I provoked you, everlasting Lord, when we two, Adam and I, through the serpent's malice ate of an apple as we should never have done. The repulsive being – he who will now burn for ever in chains – persuaded us that we should have glory, the holy dwelling-place, heaven, at our command. Then we believed the words of the accursed creature: with our hands we took the bright fruit on that holy tree. We were bitterly repaid for this, when we were obliged to pass into this burning pit and afterwards remain in it the full complement of years, many thousands, cruelly scorched.

"Now I beseech you, Keeper of the heaven-kingdom, before the following you have led here, the battalions of angels, that I might be allowed and permitted to ascend from here with my family.

"Three days ago the Saviour's vassal came home to hell – he is now secure in shackles, cursed with punishments, according as the King of glory grew angry with him for his arrogance – and he told us as a sure fact that God himself would come down home to the tenants of hell. Then each one rose up and propped himself on his arm and leaned on his hands. Though the horror of hell seemed terrible, they all rejoiced at this among their sufferings, that their noble Lord meant to visit hell in their aid."

Then she reached out with her hands to the heaven-King and prayed the ordaining Lord for mercy through the person of Mary.

"Lo, Lord, you were born into the world by my daughter, as a succour to mortals. Now it is manifest that you are God himself and the everlasting Author of all created things."

IX

Then the everlasting Lord let them ascend. He had gloriously imposed the bonds of punishment upon the fiends and thrust them, forcibly crushed, deeper into that abysmal darkness where now Satan, wretched monster, and the hideous creatures with him, cursed with punishments, gloomily converse. They are allowed to possess not the light of heaven but the abyss of hell, and never hereafter may they look for change. The Lord God had grown angry with them and assigned to them, those hideous beings, the bond of punishment as their portion and the horror of that appalling thing, the dim and dark shadow of death – the burning abyss of hell and a horror of dying.

It was indeed a beautiful occasion when that throng came up into the homeland, and the eternal God, the ordaining Lord of mankind, with them, into the renowned citadel. The holy prophets, Abraham's kin, between them exalted him with their hands, up to the fatherland. The Lord himself had conquered death then and put the fiend to flight: in far-off days the prophets had said that he would do so. This all came about in the early morning before daybreak, that the thunderous noise occurred, loud from the heavens, when he broke down and crushed the gates of hell – their frames grew feeble when they saw that light so brilliant.

Then he sat, God's Son from the beginning, amidst the gathering, and with words of truth he said:

"Wise spirits, by my might I made you, first Adam and the noble woman. Then by God's will they begot forty children so that from then on multitudes were born on earth and were allowed to live, those people in their native home, for many years – until it eventually happened that the fiend in his wickedness later caused their exile: he is guilty in every way. In Paradise I had newly established a tree with boughs whose branches bore aloft apples; and then you ate those bright fruits just as the evil minion from hell urged you. Therefore you have tenanted the burning abyss, because you disregarded the Saviour's word and ate of those appalling things. That hideous being was at hand: he foisted evil ideas upon you both.

"Then I repented that the work of my hand suffered the bondage of this prison. There was then no human competence, no angelic strength, no achievement of wise men, no mortal wisdom that might help you – but only that God the Saviour, he who beforehand ordained that punishment in vengeance, came into the world from his fatherland above, through the person of a woman, and endured on earth many torments and much insult. Day and night many men conspired about me, as to how they, the pillars of the state, might inflict upon me the pain of death. Then the term of time was past, so that I had been in the world, by tally of winters, thirty years before I suffered.

"I kept in remembrance that the multitude in this evil dwelling-place was longing that I should lead them home out of their shackles up to their own land, so that they should enjoy the splendours of the Lord and the glory of the heavenly host. They shall dwell among joys. They shall have heaven's riches in their thousands. I atoned for you when men pierced me on the tree, with spears on the gallows: there the young man stabbed me, and I once more attained on high everlasting joys from the holy Lord."

Questions for Study

1 What reasons does the text offer to explain the descent of Christ to hell?
2 What interpretation of the story of the Fall (Genesis 3) is provided by the text? How does this relate to its account of redemption?
3 What sort of literature is this? Would you describe it as a theological treatise? If not, what is it? And what readership do you think that the author had in mind?

CHAPTER 19

The Exeter Book Riddles

The riddle was a major genre of Anglo-Saxon literature, and reached its greatest heights in the eighth century under Adhelm and Tatwine. The Exeter Book – a tenth-century collation of texts of varying ages, held in the library of Exeter Cathedral – was given by Leofric, then bishop of Exeter, to his cathedral library sometime before his death in 1072. It includes a collection of 95 riddles, of which only half have been satisfactorily solved. The "riddle" can be thought of as a verbal puzzle which invites its readers to identify an object which is being described in a number of different ways, each of which casts some light on the identity of the mysterious object. Some of the riddles are a mere four or five lines in length; others are as long as one hundred lines.

The Riddle

General description
A cryptic piece of verse which describes a common object, often in terms which are deliberately intended to mislead or confuse its reader.

Major studies
F. H. Witman, *Old English Riddles*. Port Credit, Ontario: Canadian Federation for the Humanities, 1982.

A. J. Wyatt, *Old English Riddles*. London: D.C. Heath, 1912.

Before going on to consider a specifically Christian riddle, we may examine the genre itself. Consider "Riddle 47," which is written in a standard indeterminate form of Saxon verse. This is printed out in the original Anglo-Saxon, for the benefit of those who can cope with this language, and is followed by my very literal modern English translation.

Text: Riddle 47

Moððe word fræt.   Me þæt þuhte
wrætlicu wyrd,   þa ic þæt wundor gefrægn,

þæt se wyrm forswealg   wera gied sumes,
þeof in þystro,   þrymfæstne cwide
ond þæs strangan staþol.   Stælgiest ne wæs
wihte þy gleawra,   þe he þam wordum swealg.

A moth ate words. To me that seemed
A puzzling fate, when I learned of that wonder,
That a worm would swallow the song of a man,
A thief in the darkness, a wonderful saying,
A support of the strong. The thieving stranger
Was not one bit the wiser when he swallowed the words.

The answer to this particular riddle is given at the end of this paragraph, and you are recommended not to read further until you have given some thought to what it might be. Having done this, we can move on to the specifically Christian riddle, also written in indeterminate Saxon verse, to be found in "Riddle 26," the Anglo-Saxon text of which is presented first, and the English translation following. And the answer to Riddle 47? A bookworm.

Text: Riddle 26

Mec feonda sum   feore besnyþede,
woruldstrenga binom,   wætte siþþan,
dyfde on wætre,   dyde eft þonan,
sette on sunnan,   þær ic swiþe beleas
herum þam þe ic hæfde.   Heard mec siþþan   5
snað seaxses ecg,   sindrum begrunden;
fingras feoldan,   ond mec fugles wyn
geond speddropum   spyrede geneahhe,
ofer brunne brerd,   beamtelge swealg,
streames dæle,   stop eft on mec,   10
siþade sweartlast.   Mec siþþan wrah
hæleð hleobordum,   hyde beþenede,
gierede mec mid golde;   forþon me gliwedon
wrætlic weorc smiþa,   wire bifongen.
Nu þa gereno   ond se reada telg   15
ond þa wuldorgesteald   wide mære
dryhtfolca helm,   nales dol wite.
Gif min bearn wera   brucan willað,
hy beoð þy gesundran   ond þy sigefæstran,
heortum þy hwætran   ond þy hygebliþran,   20
ferþe þy frodran,   habbaþ freonda þy ma,
swæsra ond gesibbra,   soþra ond godra,
tilra ond getreowra,   þa hyra tyr ond ead
estum ycað   ond hy arstafum

lissum bilecgað   ond hi lufan fæþmum   25
fæste clyppað.   Frige hwæt ic hatte,
niþum to nytte.   Nama min is mære,
hæleþum gifre   ond halig sylf.

An enemy ended my life, took away
my bodily strength; then he dipped me   30
in water and drew me out again,
and put me in the sun where I soon shed
all my hair. The knife's sharp edge
bit into me once my blemishes had been scraped away;
fingers folded me and the bird's feather   35
often moved across my brown surface,
sprinkling useful drops; it swallowed the wood-dye
(part of the stream) and again travelled over me,
leaving black tracks. Then a man bound me,
he stretched skin over me and adorned me   40
with gold; thus I am enriched by the wondrous work
of smiths, wound about with shining metal.
Now my clasp and my red dye
and these glorious adornments bring fame far and wide
to the Protector of Men, and not to the pains of hell.   45
If the sons of men would make use of me
they would be safer and more sure of victory,
their hearts would be bolder, their minds more at ease,
their thoughts wiser; they would have more friends,
companions and kinsmen (true and honourable,   50
brave and kind) who would gladly increase
their honour and prosperity, and heap
benefits upon them, holding them fast
in love's embraces. Ask that I am called,
of such use to men. My name is famous,   55
of service to men and sacred in itself.

The answer to this riddle will be provided at the end of the following analysis. However, you can solve it quite easily by following the argument through as follows:

1 Examine the first six lines. What process is being described in these lines? Note in particular the references to losing hair in the sun.
2 The next five lines describe a bird's feather leaving black tracks over the surface of the object. What process does this seem to describe?
3 By this stage, you will probably have realized that the riddle is referring to the production of a book, the leaves of which are made of vellum (derived from leather), on which words have been written with a quill. The next stage of the guessing game is to work out what kind of book. It is clear from the next few lines that the book in

question is important and valuable – note in particular the references to being adorned with gold.

4   The best clues to the identity of the book are the references to the "Protector of Men" and deliverance from hell.

5   The answer to the riddle is a gospel-book – that is, one of the beautifully produced editions of the four gospels, which were so important a feature of Anglo-Saxon and Celtic Christian life. Examples of this genre include the Book of Kells and the Lindisfarne Gospels.

CHAPTER 20

The Blickling Homilist (ca. 970)

Many authors of the past are destined to remain anonymous, or to be known by names which attempt to conceal how little we know about them. The medieval "Pearl Poet" is known only by the name of his chief work, even though many have attempted to identify him more precisely. The present text is taken from a collection of eighteen homilies which was assembled in the late tenth or early eleventh century. Internal evidence suggests that one of the sermons included in the collection was preached on Ascension Day 970 or 971, although this does not necessarily imply that the remaining seventeen were preached at the same time. Nevertheless, the collection of sermons covers a wide range of Sundays and saints' days, suggesting that it may indeed have been compiled over a short period of time. The author of these sermons – assuming that they all were indeed written by one individual – is unknown. Whoever he or she was, the author is known as the "Blickling homilist." The manuscript remained for many years at Blickling Hall, Norfolk, before being acquired by the John H. Scheide Library at Princeton in 1932.

Text: *Homily for Easter Day*

The text which we shall consider is the seventh of the set of eighteen, dealing with the meaning of Easter Day. This theme was of major importance in medieval vernacular works, such as Piers Plowman, and it is important to note its prominence in early English vernacular works. Its highly dramatic structure made it immensely popular with lay audiences, and it features prominently in the medieval "mystery plays." In addition, the strongly narrative nature of the concept – which is told as a story – contrasts sharply with the more abstract nature of some of the theological concepts linked with Christ's resurrection, such as "justification." Lay audiences found these ideas difficult; the theme of the harrowing of hell, in contrast, was both enjoyable and visualizible.

Dearly beloved, this Easter mystery presents to us a clear example of the life eternal, as we can now listen to it related and explained, so that none need doubt but that the event must come about in this present time, that the same Creator will sit on his judgement seat. There will be present before him all of the race of angels and of the race of men, and of the wicked spirits also. And there every man's actions will be investigated. And he who is now humble and with his whole heart mindful of the Lord's suffering and his resurrection, shall receive a heavenly reward; and he who now scorns to keep God's commandments, or to bear in mind the Lord's humility, shall there receive a stern judgement and afterwards dwell in eternal torments, which will never come to an end. Therefore this time is of all times the highest and holiest, and at this time we should have a divine joy – and a worldly also – because, as an example to mankind, the Lord rose up from death after his suffering, and after the bonds of his death and after the fetters of hell's darkness, and laid torment and eternal misery on the prince of devils, and delivered mankind; as the prophet David prophesied concerning this time, saying thus: "Our Lord delivered us" [Psalm cvii: 13ff.]. And he brought to pass what he had long threatened the accursed spirits. And he made known to men at this present time all those things which were ever before prophesied by the prophets about his suffering and about his resurrection and about his harrying in hell and about his many miracles which were foretold – all that he fulfilled. Let us now listen and consider what he did, and by what means he made us free.

He was not compelled by any necessity, but came down to earth by his own will, and here suffered many plots and snares by the Jews and by the miserable scribes; and then finally he allowed his body to be fastened to the cross with nails; and he endured death for us because he wanted to grant us eternal life. And then he sent his glorious spirit into the depths of hell, and there bound and humbled the prince of all darkness and of eternal death and greatly troubled all his gang. And he completely smashed the gates of hell and their bronze bolts; and all his chosen he led out from there; and he overcame the darkness of the devils with his shining light. Then, very fearful and terrified, they spoke thus: "Where does this come from, so strong and so bright and so terrible? The world was subjected to us for long, and death paid us great tribute before; it has never happened to us before that death has been put to an end thus, nor ever before has such terror been ordained for us in hell. Indeed, who is this who now enters our confines so unafraid? and not only does not fear our punishments, but wishes to deliver others from our bonds? We think this is he, through whose death we imagined all the world should be subjected to us. Do you hear, our prince? This is the same one for whose death you have long made a play; and in the event you promised us much plunder. But what will you do about him now? and what can you do to overthrow him? He has now put all your darkness to flight with his brightness, and he has broken up all your prison, and all of those whom you previously held captive he has released, and he has turned their life to joy; and those who formerly sighed in our bonds now mock at us. Why do you bring this man here, who in his coming has restored all his chosen to their former happiness? Though they formerly despaired of eternal life, they are now very glad. No weeping and no wailing is now heard here, as was formerly customary in this place of torment. Now alas, the wealth that in the beginning you our prince got from the boldness and disobedience of the first man, and from the loss of Paradise – all that he has now taken away from you. And through Christ's cross all your joy has turned to grief. When you longed to know that Christ hung on a cross, you did not know how many troubles should come upon us all by his death. You always wanted to corrupt him, in whom you knew no wrong at all. Why do you bring this noble and innocent one here? Now, in his coming here, he has condemned and humiliated all the guilty."

Then, immediately after the infamous speech of those who dwelt in hell, and their lamentation was heard, then it was that, because of the coming of the Kingdom of the Lord, all the iron bolts of hell's locks were broken without any delay. And at once, the countless host of holy souls who were previously held captive bowed down before the Saviour and prayed to him with weeping entreaties and spoke thus: "You came to us, Redeemer of the world; you came to us, the hope of those who dwell in heaven and earth, and our hope also, because of old the prophets told us of your coming, and we looked forward to and hoped for your coming here. On earth you granted forgiveness of men's sins. Now redeem us from the power of the devil and from the imprisonment of hell. Now that you have descended into the pit of hell for us, do not now leave us to live in torment, when you return to your kingdom on high. You set up the sign of your glory in the world; now set up the symbol of your glory in hell." This prayer was heard without delay, and immediately at the Lord's command the countless host of holy souls were lifted up from the burning sulphur, and he cast down the old Devil and threw him, bound, into the pit of hell. Then the holy souls cried to the Lord with indescribable joy, and spoke thus: "Now, Lord Saviour Christ, ascend, now that you have plundered hell and bound the prince of death in these torments. Now make known joy in the world, that all your chosen may rejoice and trust in your Ascension."

As yet Adam and Eve had not been set free, but were held in bonds. Then Adam with a weeping and wretched voice cried out to the Lord, and said: "Be merciful to me, Lord, be merciful to me in your great mercy and blot out my unrighteousness; for I have sinned against you alone and have done great wrong in your sight. I have erred, just like the sheep that perished. Seek out your servant now, Lord, for your hands created and shaped me; do not leave my soul with those who live in hell; but show me your mercy and lead me out of these bonds and out of this prison-house, and out of the shadow of death." Then the Lord Saviour was merciful to Adam, and quickly his bonds were released, and having clasped the Lord's knees, he said: "My soul shall bless the Lord, and all that is within me shall bless his holy name. You yourself have had mercy on all my unrighteousness; you yourself have healed my infirmities, and you released my life from eternal destruction, my longing you satisfied with good things." As yet, Eve remained in bonds and in woe. She said: "You are just, Lord, and your judgements are righteous; therefore I suffer this deservedly. I lived in honour in Paradise, and I did not realize it; I was perverse and became like the foolish animals. But you, Lord, shield of my youth, and mine, be not mindful of my lack of wisdom, nor turn away your face nor your mercy from me, nor depart in anger from your servant. Gracious God, listen to my voice with which I, wretched, cry to you; for my life any my years have been wasted in sorrow and in lamentation. If you consider my unrighteousness Lord, you will know my substance, that I am dust and ashes. I entreat you now, Lord, for the sake of your servant St Mary, whom you have honoured with heavenly glory. For nine months you filled her womb with the price of all the world; you know that you were born of my daughter, Lord, and that her flesh comes from my flesh and her bones from my bones. Forgive me now, my Lord, for the honour of her glory; forgive me, unhappiest of all women, and be merciful to me, my Maker, and save me from the bonds of this death." Then the Lord Saviour had mercy upon Eve, and immediately her bonds were loosed. Then she cried out, and spoke thus: "May your name be blessed in the world, Lord, because your mercy towards me is great; now you have saved my soul from lower hell." Then the patriarch Abraham, with all the holy souls that had been held captive from the beginning of the world, cried out with a joyful voice and said: "We give thanks to you, Lord, and praise you, for you redeemed us from the author of death and have enriched us in your coming."

With that, the Lord, with the plunder that he had taken in hell, quickly went out living from his grave, raised up by his own strength; and afterwards arrayed himself in his immaculate body and showed himself to his followers because he wanted to remove every doubt from their hearts. And he also showed the wounds and the scars of the nails to unbelieving men, because he did not want there to be any lack of faith concerning his resurrection. And then afterwards in the sight of many men he ascended into the heavens, and he sat on the right hand of God the Father, from whence, in his divinity, he was never absent, but was established there always. Now therefore let all faithful people rejoice and be glad, because God's blood was shed for us. Let us all be joyful in the Lord, we who celebrate his resurrection; for when he took on human body and redeemed us from the power of the devil, he diminished his divinity no whit. Now we hear, dearly beloved, how many things the Lord suffered for us when he bought us with his blood from the captivity of hell. Let us therefore consider what recompense we are able to offer him, when he recounts and tells all this, at this same time when he sits on his judgement seat; when with our souls alone we must repay and make amends for all those things which previously we have done against his commandment – or have neglected to do, which we ought.

Let us now consider how great a terror will come upon us created things, in this present time, when the Judgement draws near; and the revelation of that day will be very terrible to all created things. In that day heaven and earth and the sea, and all the things that are in them, will pass away; so also, because of the same happening, sun and moon will pass away, and so will all the light of the stars. And the cross of our Lord, which now puts wicked spirits to flight on earth, will be raised up into the concourse of the stars. And in that day heaven will be folded up like a book; and in that day the earth will be burned to ashes; and in that day the sea will dry up; and in that day all the power of the skies will be turned and stirred. And six days before this day, marvellous signs will occur every day. At noon on the first day, there will occur a great lamentation of all created things, and men will hear a great noise in the skies, as if an army were being assembled and set in order there; then a great bloody cloud will arise from out of the north and obscure the sky; and after the cloud will come lightning and thunder all day; and in the evening bloody rain will rain down. On the following day a great sound of the preparation of armies will be heard in the skies; and the earth will be moved out of her place, and the sky will be open at one end, in the east; and in the evening a great power will come forth through the open part, and obscure and cover up the sky; and a bloody and fiery rain will strive to devour and burn up this earth; and the sky will fall to the four ends of the earth, and all the earth will be covered up with darkness at the eleventh hour of the day. And then all people will say: "Now may the Lord have mercy and spare us, who when he was born in Bethlehem, was praised by ranks of angels when they cried out and spoke thus: 'Glory be to God on high, and in earth [peace] to men of goodwill'" [Luke ii: 14]. The third day the northern part and the eastern part of the earth will speak together; and the deeps will rage and want to devour the earth. Then all the power of the earth will be changed, and a great earthquake will occur on that day. After nine o'clock on the fourth day there shall be great thunderings in the skies; and then all idols will fall down; and then it will be sunset, and yet no light will show; and the moon will be quenched, and darkness will come to pass over all the earth, and the stars will run widdershins the whole day, and men will be able to see them as clearly as on a night when it freezes hard. And then in that day they will hate this world's wealth and the things that now they love. At nine o'clock on the fifth day the sky will be rent asunder from the eastern part to the western part; and then all the race of angels will gaze through the opening onto mankind. Then all men will see how it will be at this world's end. Then they will flee to the mountains and hide because of the sight of the angels; and then they will call to the earth and beg it to swallow and hide them, and will wish that they were never born of father or mother. So it was prophesied of old about this in Christ's books, saying thus: "Blessed are those who were barren, and blessed are the wombs that have never conceived, and the breasts which have never given suck." And then they shall say to the hills and to the mountains: "Fall on us, and cover and hide us so that we need no longer endure this terror from these angels. Now everything is visible which we formerly kept hidden" [Luke xxiii: 29–30 and cf. Revelation vi: 16–17]. Before nine o'clock on the sixth day all the world will be filled with accursed spirits from the four ends of the earth, who will strive to seize a great plunder of men's souls, as Antichrist did before; and when he comes, then he will threaten to send those souls who will not obey him into eternal punishments. And then at last he himself will be driven into everlasting woe. So then on that day St Michael will come with a heavenly host of holy spirits, and will then slay all those accursed ones and drive them into the pit of hell for their disobedience to God's commands, and for their wickednesses. Then all created things shall see the power of our Lord, although now human beings do not want to acknowledge or recognize it. Then after these things the seventh day will be near; and then the archangel St Michael will order the four trumpets to be blown at these four ends of the earth, and will rouse up all the bodies from death, though they had previously been covered with earth, or drowned in water, or eaten by wild animals, or carried off by birds, or torn by fishes, or departed from this world in any fashion. Then they will all have to arise and go forth to the Judgement in such fashion as they previously adorned themselves. Not with gold or with purple clothing, but with good and holy deeds must we be adorned if we want to be at the right hand of the Lord Saviour Christ then, with those righteous and chosen souls whom he will send into eternal light.

Therefore we should now consider the need of our souls while we may and are able, lest we put off this permitted time, and then wish to repent when we cannot.

Let us be humble and merciful and charitable, and remove and banish malice, lies and envy from our hearts, and have a righteous spirit towards other men; for God himself will not then heed any man's repentance; nor will there be any intercessions. But he will then be fiercer and more severe than any wild animal, or any anger might ever be. And to the extent that a man's power is the greater and he is the richer in this world, so much more will the Supreme Judge require from him, since he will earn for himself and receive a fierce and stern judgement; as it is written concerning such: the man who now judges the poor without mercy, shall afterwards be ordained a harsh judgement [cf. Matthew xviii: 35].

Now, dearly beloved, let us think about these things very prudently and wisely, so that through just works and acts of mercy we may find our Judge merciful, and through humility and through the true love of God and men we may merit eternal bliss with our Lord, where he lives and reigns in eternity for ever without end. Amen.

Questions for Study

1 Outline the main features of the "harrowing of hell," especially from the first half of this sermon.
2 Why do you think this theme was so important in vernacular sermons?
3 What does the author do with this theme? What impact does he expect it to have on his readers? What does he want them to think as a result? And what differences does he expect it to make to the way in which they live?

CHAPTER 21

Ælfric (ca. 955–ca. 1020)

Ælfric is noted as one of the most important Old English Christian writers. He initially trained at the Benedictine abbey at the cathedral city of Winchester, and moved in 987 to the newly-established abbey at Cerne Abbas in Dorset. This proved to be a remarkably productive period in his life, and resulted in two sets of homilies in Old English, dealing with various religious festivals, and doctrinal and historical themes. In 1005, he moved to become the first abbot of a newly-established religious house at Eynsham in Oxfordshire.

Ælfric (ca. 955–ca. 1020)

Basic description
Major monastic leader and writer.

Major works
Catholic homilies; *Lives of the Saints*.

Major studies
Milton McCormick Gatch, *Preaching and Theology in Anglo-Saxon England: Aelfric and Wulfstan*. Toronto: University of Toronto Press, 1977.
Peter Clemoes, *Interactions of Thought and Language in Old English Poetry*. Cambridge: Cambridge University Press, 1995.

Text: *The Passion of St Edmund*

Our text for study is taken from Ælfric's *Lives of the Saints*, a work which was compiled during the final decade of the tenth century. The work is clearly intended to form the basis of sermons, and could be used as the basis of a series of homilies for ecclesiastical use. The subject of this particular homily is Edmund, who came to the throne of East Anglia in 855, while still only in his teens. He was killed in 869, as a result of a major confrontation with Viking forces, led by Ivar and Ubbi, sons of the great Viking leader Ragnar Lothbrok, who were spending the winter in Norfolk. Edmund was captured alive during this battle, and was offered his life on condition that he would share his kingdom with the Vikings. Edmund refused, on the grounds that Christian kings should not associate with pagans in this way. The Vikings then used him for archery practice, and finally beheaded him – a tale which is told in much greater detail in this extract. Within years of his death, a cult had grown around Edmund, and his body was removed to the abbey of what is now known as "Bury St Edmunds," which rapidly became a place of pilgrimage.

The work is of importance as an example of hagiography with a specifically liturgical dimension – in other words, the work is written to be used as a homily in church, particularly on the occasion of the commemoration of his death. It should be noted that Ælfric uses an earlier work as his main historical source for this account of Edmund. Abbo of Fleury visited England at some point between 985 and 987 to teach at the newly-established monastery at Ramsey, Huntingdonshire. While there, Abbo composed the first life of Edmund, the *Passio Sancti Eadmundi*. Ælfric acknowledges use of this source in his opening paragraph.

In the time of King Æthelred a certain very learned monk came from the south over the sea from St Benoit sur Loire to Archbishop Dunstan, three years before he died; and the monk was called Abbo. Then they talked together until Dunstan told the story of St Edmund, just as Edmund's sword-bearer had told it to King Athelstan when Dunstan was a young man and the sword-bearer was a very old man. Then the monk set down all the information in a book; and afterwards, when the book came to us a few years later, then we translated it into English, just as it stands hereafter. Then within two years the monk Abbo returned home to his monastery and was straightway appointed abbot in that very monastery.

The blessed Edmund, King of East Anglia, was wise and honourable, and by his noble conduct ever glorified Almighty God. He was humble and virtuous, and continued resolutely thus so that he would not submit to shameful sins; nor did he alter his conduct in any way, but was always mindful of that true teaching: "You are appointed ruler? do not exalt yourself, but be amongst men as one of them" [Ecclesiasticus xxxii, 1]. He was as generous as a father to the poor and to widows, and with benevolence always guided his people towards righteousness, and restrained the violent, and lived happily in the true faith.

Then eventually it happened that the Danish people came with a pirate force, harrying and slaying widely throughout the land, as their custom is. In that fleet, united by the devil, were the very important leaders Ivar and Ubbi; and they landed with warships in Northumbria, and wasted the land and slew the people. Then Ivar turned eastwards with his ships and Ubbi remained behind in Northumbria, having won victory with savagery. Then Ivar came sailing to East Anglia in the year in which Prince Alfred (he who afterwards became the famous King of Wessex) was twenty-one years old; and the aforesaid Ivar abruptly stalked over the land like a wolf, and slew the people: men and women and the innocent children, and humiliated the honest Christians.

Then immediately afterwards he sent an arrogant message to the king that if he cared for his life, he should submit to do him homage. The messenger came to King

Edmund and quickly announced Ivar's message to him: "Ivar our king, brave and victorious by sea and by land, has subdued many nations and now suddenly landed here with an army, so that he might take winter quarters here with his host. Now he orders you to divide your secret treasures and the wealth of your forebears with him quickly, and if you want to live, you will be his under-king, because you haven't the power to be able to resist him."

Well, then King Edmund summoned a certain bishop who was very near at hand, and discussed with him how he should answer the savage Ivar. Then the bishop was afraid because of the unexpected disaster, and for the king's life, and said that he thought it advisable that he should submit to what Ivar commanded. Then the king was silent and looked at the ground, and then eventually said to him, regally: "Oh bishop! this wretched nation is humiliated, and I would rather fall in battle against him who might possess my people's land." And the bishop said: "Alas, dear king, your people lie slain, and you have not the forces to be able to fight; and these pirates will come and bind you alive, unless you save your life by flight, or save yourself by submitting to him thus." Then said King Edmund, very brave as he was: "Thus I desire and wish with my heart, that I alone should not be left, after my beloved thegns, who with wives and children were suddenly slain in their beds by these pirates. It was never my custom to take flight, but I would rather die for my own country if I must; and Almighty God knows that I would never turn away from his worship, nor from his true love, whether I die or live."

After these words he turned to the messenger that Ivar had sent to him and said to him, unafraid: "You would certainly deserve death now, but I would not dirty my clean hands in your filthy blood, for I follow Christ, who set us an example thus; and I will cheerfully be slain by you if God so ordains it. Go very quickly now and say to your savage lord: 'Edmund will never while living submit to the heathen war-leader, Ivar, unless he first submit in this land to Christ the Saviour in faith.'"

Then the messenger went away quickly and met the savage Ivar on the way hastening to Edmund with his entire army, and told the wicked man how he was answered. Then Ivar resolutely commanded the men of the warships that they should all seize only the king, who had scorned his behest, and immediately bind him. Well, then when Ivar came, King Edmund stood within his hall, mindful of the Saviour, and threw aside his weapons; he would imitate the example of Christ, who forbade Peter to fight against the savage Jews with weapons. So, then those wicked men bound Edmund and insulted him shamefully, and beat him with cudgels, and afterwards led the faithful king thus to a tree rooted in the ground, and tied him to it with tight bonds, and afterwards flogged him with whips for a long time; and amidst the floggings he unceasingly called on Christ the Saviour with true faith; and then, because of his faith, the heathen became insanely angry because he called on Christ to help him. Then, as if for sport, they shot at him with darts, until he was entirely covered with their missiles, like the bristles of a hedgehog, just as Sebastian was. When the wicked pirate Ivar saw that the noble king would not renounce Christ, but ever called on him with steadfast faith, he ordered him to be beheaded; and the heathens did so. While he still called on Christ the heathens dragged the saint away to slaughter and with one blow struck off his head, and his blessed soul went to Christ. There was at hand a certain man, hidden from the heathen by God, who heard all this and afterwards told it just as we tell it here.

Well, then the pirate force returned to ship, and hid the head of the holy Edmund in the dense brambles, so that it would not be buried. Then after a time, when they had gone away, the inhabitants who were left there came to where their lord's headless body lay, and were very sorrowful at heart because of his slaughter, and in particular because they did not have the head to the body. Then the observer who previously saw it, said that the pirates had taken the head with them, and he thought, as was perfectly true, that they had hidden the head somewhere in the wood. Then they all went in a body to the wood, searching everywhere through bushes and brambles, to see if they could find the head anywhere.

There was moreover a great miracle, in that a wolf was sent by God's guidance to protect the head against the other beasts by day and night. Then they went searching, and continually calling out, as is usual among those who frequent the woods, "Where are you now, comrade?" And the head answered them: "Here, here, here!", and called out frequently thus, answering them all, as often as any of them called out, until they all came to it by means of the calling. There lay the grey wolf who watched over the head, and had embraced the head with his two feet, ravenous and hungry, and because of God dare not eat the head, but kept it safe from the beasts. Then they were amazed at the wolf's care, and thanking the Almighty for all his miracles, carried the holy head home with them; but as if he were tame, the wolf followed the head along until they came to the town, and afterwards turned back to the wood again. Then afterwards the inhabitants laid the head with the holy body, and buried it as best they could in such haste, and erected a chapel over it forthwith.

Then in time, when after many years the raids stopped and peace was restored to the afflicted people, they joined together and built a church worthy of the saint, because miracles were frequently performed at his grave in the oratory where he was buried. They wished then to carry the holy body with universal veneration and lay it within the church. Then there was a great miracle, in that he was just as whole as if he were alive, with unblemished body; and his neck, which was previously cut through, was healed, and there was, as it were, a silken thread red about his neck as an indication to men of how he was slain. Likewise the wounds which the savage heathens had made in his body with repeated missiles, were healed by the heavenly God. And he lies uncorrupt thus to this present day, awaiting resurrection and the eternal glory. His body, which lies here undecayed, proclaims to us that he lived here in the world without fornication, and journeyed to Christ with a pure life. A certain widow called Oswyn lived in prayer and fasting at the saint's tomb for many years afterwards; each year she would cut the hair of the saint and cut his nails, circumspectly, with love, and keep them as relics in a shrine on the altar.

Then the inhabitants venerated the saint with faith, and Bishop Theodred richly endowed the monastery with gifts of gold and silver in honour of the saint. Then at one time there came wretched thieves, eight in a single night, to the venerable saint; they wanted to steal the treasures which men had brought there, and tried how they could get in by force. One struck at the bolt violently with a hammer; one of them filed around it with a file; one also dug under the door with a spade; one of them with a ladder wanted to unlock the window. But they laboured in vain and fared miserably, inasmuch as the holy man miraculously bound them, each as he stood, striving with his tool, so that none of them could commit that sinful deed nor move away from there, but they stood thus till morning. Then men marvelled at how the villains hung there, one up a ladder, one bent in digging, and each was bound fast in his labour. Then they were all brought to the bishop, and he ordered them all to be hung on a high gallows. But he was not mindful of how the merciful God spoke through his prophet the following words: *Eos qui ducuntur ad mortem eruere ne cesses* [Proverbs xxiv: 11], "Always redeem those whom they lead to death"; and also the holy canons forbid those in orders, both bishops and priests, to be concerned with thieves, for it is not proper that those who are chosen to serve God should be a party to any man's death, if they are the Lord's servants. Then after Bishop Theodred had examined his books, he repented, with lamentation, that he had appointed so cruel a judgement to those wretched thieves, and regretted it to the end of his life, and earnestly prayed the people to fast with him a whole three days, praying to the Almighty that he would have mercy on him.

There was in that land a certain man called Leofstan, powerful before the world and foolish before God, who rode to the saint with great arrogance, and insolently ordered them to show him whether the holy saint was uncorrupted; but as soon as he saw the saint's body, he immediately went insane and roared savagely and ended miserably by an evil death. This is like what the faithful Pope Gregory said in his treatise about the holy Lawrence who lies in Rome, that men, both good and evil, were forever wanting to see how he lay; but God stopped them, inasmuch as there once died seven men together in the looking; then the others left off looking at the martyr with human foolishness.

We have heard in common talk of many miracles concerning the holy Edmund, which we will not set down here in writing; but everyone knows of them. By this saint, and by others such, it is clear that Almighty God is able to raise man again at Judgement day, incorruptible from the earth, he who keeps Edmund whole in his body until the great day, although he came from the earth. The place was worthy of the venerable saint, in that men honoured it and supplied it well for Christ's service with pure servants of God, because the saint is more glorious than men might conceive.

The English nation is not deprived of the Lord's saints, since in England lie such saints as this saintly king, and the blessed Cuthbert, and in Ely Audrey, and her sister also, incorrupt in body, for the confirmation of the faith. There are also many other saints among the English who work many miracles – as is widely known – to the praise of the Almighty, in whom they believed. Through his glorious saints Christ makes clear to men that he who performs such miracles is Almighty God, even though the wretched Jews completely rejected him; wherefore they are damned, just as they wished for themselves [Matthew xxvii: 25]. There are no miracles performed at their graves, for they do not believe in the living Christ; but Christ makes clear to men where the true faith is, inasmuch as he performs such miracles through his saints widely throughout this earth. Wherefore to him, with his heavenly Father and the Holy Spirit, be glory for ever. Amen.

Questions for Study

1 Why does Ælfric consider Edmund to be such an important figure?
2 It is clear that Ælfric intends this piece to be used as a homily. How does this help us understand the way in which he presents and interprets the final hours of Edmund's life?
3 What does Ælfric want his readers (or perhaps his hearers) to learn and do as a result of hearing about the "passion of St Edmund"?

CHAPTER 22

Wulfstan (died 1023)

Relatively little is known of the life of Wulfstan before 996. He is occasionally confused with a later writer, Wulfstan, bishop of Worcester (ca. 1009–95). Wulfstan became bishop of London in 996, and archbishop of York in 1002. He was valued for his legal expertise, and drafted much of the legislation issued by Ethelred II and Canute. His reputation suffered through holding two sees in plurality; in addition to being archbishop of York from 1002, he was also bishop of Worcester. Some surprisingly negative comments in Worcester diocesan records from this period suggest that he incurred displeasure at Worcester on account of his absence from this southern diocese, due to his responsibilities further north. Wulfstan's appointment as archbishop of York and bishop of Worcester appears to have reflected a concern on the part of English kings concerning the stability of the northern regions, particularly Northumbria. An earlier archbishop of York (Wulfstan I, died 956) was thought to have encouraged secessionists in the region. By insisting that the Archbishop of York was also a bishop in the south of England, it was believed that greater political control over his activities might be exercised.

Wulfstan (died 1023)

Basic description
Ecclesiastical statesman and writer; Archbishop of York.

Major works
Institutes of Polity; *Lupi Sermo ad Anglos*; various homilies.

Major studies
Milton McCormick Gatch, *Preaching and Theology in Anglo-Saxon England: Aelfric and Wulfstan*. Toronto: University of Toronto Press, 1977.
Peter Clemoes, *Interactions of Thought and Language in Old English Poetry*. Cambridge: Cambridge University Press, 1995.

At this stage in its history, England was regularly subject to attack by Vikings. The raids from Denmark had begun in 980; by 991, following the famous "Battle of Maldon," the payment of "Danegeld" had begun. The Vikings were a serious menace to national stability and security by 996, when Wulftsan was appointed bishop of London. Major raids took place in Hampshire, Kent, and Sussex over the years 997–9. The archbishop of Canterbury was captured by Viking forces in 1011, and martyred in 1012. This sent shock waves throughout England and beyond. The military power of the Vikings was so great that sections of England found themselves with little option but to accept Swegn Forkbeard as king in 1013, forcing Ethelred into exile, initially on the Isle of Wight, and then in Normandy. Swegn's death in 1014 made it possible for Ethelred to return to England – but not as king.

It is against this background of national instability, uncertainty, and widespread suffering that Wulfstan's sermon is to be read.

Text: *Lupi Sermo ad Anglos*

The *Lupi Sermo ad Anglos* is so named from the opening Latin statement of the work: "Sermo Lupi ad Anglos quando Dani maxime persecuti sunt eos, quod fuit anno millesimo xiiii ab incarnatione Domini nostri Iesu Crist" – "The sermon of the Wolf to the English, when the Danes were greatly persecuting them, which was in the year 1014 after the Incarnation of our Lord Jesus Christ." The remainder of the sermon is in the form of Old English generally referred to as "West Saxon." It is generally accepted that the sermon dates from 1014, making this the last major work to be written in this language, soon to be superseded by "Middle English." Of particular interest is Wulfstan's apparent use of a significant number of words which owe their origins to Old Norse. This strongly suggests that the intended audience for the sermon was primarily based in the north of England, where Scandinavian idioms had begun to take root – a phenomenon which can be observed even in modern York, where many old street names are clearly based on Scandinavian words.

The opening words of the homily evoke the possibility of the end of the world being near, reflecting the millenarianism which appears in a number of works written around this time. Since a thousand years had passed since the coming of Christ, the expectation of an imminent "doomsday" was widespread, based on a literal reading of Revelation 20:2, 5.

Beloved men, recognize what the truth is: this world is in haste and it is drawing near the end, and therefore the longer it is the worse it will get in the world. And it needs must thus become very much worse as a result of the people's sins prior to the advent of Antichrist; and then, indeed, it will be terrible and cruel throughout the world. Understand properly also that for many years now the Devil has led this nation too far astray, and that there has been little loyalty among men although they spoke fair, and too many wrongs have prevailed in the land. And there were never many men who sought a remedy as diligently as they should; but daily they added one evil to another, and embarked on many wrongs and unlawful acts, all too commonly throughout this whole nation. And on that account, we have also suffered many injuries and insults. And if we are to expect any remedy then we must deserve better of God than we have done hitherto. Because we have earned the miseries which oppress us by great demerit, we must obtain the cure from God, if it is to improve henceforth by very great merit. Indeed, we know full well that a great breach requires a great repair and a great conflagration no little water if one is to quench the fire at all. And the necessity is great for every man henceforth to observe God's law diligently and pay God's dues properly. Among heathen peoples one dare not withhold little or much of what is appointed for the worship of false gods, and we everywhere withhold God's dues all too frequently. And among heathen peoples one dare not diminish, inside or out, any of the things which are brought to the false gods and are made over as gifts, and we have completely despoiled the houses of God inside and out. And God's servants are everywhere deprived of respect and protection; and with the heathen peoples one dare not in any way abuse the ministers of false gods, as one now does the servants of God, too commonly where Christians ought to keep God's law and protect God's servants. But it is true what I say; there is need of a remedy, because God's dues have for too long dwindled away in every region within this nation, and the laws of the people have deteriorated all too much, and sanctuaries are commonly violated, and the houses of God are completely despoiled of ancient rights, and stripped of everything decent inside. And widows are wrongfully forced to take a husband. And too many are harassed and greatly humiliated, and poor men are painfully deceived and cruelly enslaved and, completely innocent, commonly sold out of this country into the power of foreigners, and through cruel injustice children in the cradle are enslaved for petty theft commonly throughout this nation, and the rights of freemen are taken away and the rights of slaves restricted, and the right to alms diminished; and, to be brief, God's laws are hated and his teachings scorned. And therefore, through God's anger, we are all frequently put to shame; let him realize it who can. And although one might not imagine so, the harm will become common to this entire nation, unless God defend us.

For it is clear and evident in us all that we have hitherto more often transgressed than we have atoned, and therefore many things fall upon this nation. For long now, nothing has prospered here or elsewhere, but in every region there has been devastation and famine, burning and bloodshed over and again. And stealing and slaughter, plague and pestilence, murrain and disease, slander and hatred, and the plundering of robbers have damaged us very severely; and excessive taxes have greatly oppressed us, and bad weather has very often caused us crop-failures; wherefore for many years now, so it seems, there have been in this country many injustices and unsteady loyalties among men everywhere. Now very often kinsman will not protect a kinsman any more than a stranger, nor a father his son, nor sometimes a son his own father, nor one brother another. Nor has any of us regulated his life just as he ought, neither clerics according to rule, nor laymen according to the law. But all too frequently, we have made lust a law to us, and have kept neither the teachings nor the laws of God or man just as we ought; nor has anyone intended loyally towards another as justly as he ought, but almost all men have betrayed and injured others by word and deed; and in any case, almost all men wrongfully stab others in the back with shameful attack; let him do more if he can. For there are here in the land great disloyalties towards God and towards the state, and there are also many here in the country who are betrayers of their lords in various ways. And the greatest betrayal in the world of one's lord is that a man betray his lord's soul; and it is also a very great betrayal of one's lord in the world, that a man should plot against his lord's life or, living, drive him from the land; and both have happened in this country. They plotted against Edward and then killed, and afterwards burnt him. And they have destroyed too many godfathers and godchildren widely throughout this nation, as well as too many other innocent people who have been all too commonly slain. And all too many religious foundations have commonly been undone because previously certain men have been placed there, as they should not have been if one wished to show respect to God's sanctuary; and too many Christian people have been sold out of this country all the time now. And all that is hateful to God, let him believe it who will. And it is shameful to speak of what has too commonly happened, and it is dreadful to know what many too often do, who practise that wretchedness that they club together and buy one woman in common as a joint purchase, and with the one commit filth one after another and each after the other just like dogs who do not care about filth; and then sell for a price out of the land into the power of enemies the creature of God and his own purchase that he dearly bought.

Also we know well where the wretchedness has occurred that father has sold son for a price, and son his mother, and one brother has sold another into the power of foreigners; and all these are grave and dreadful deeds, let him understand who will. And yet what is injuring this nation is greater and also more multifarious. Many are forsworn and greatly perjured, and pledges are broken over and again; and it is evident in this nation that the wrath of God violently oppresses us, let him realize it who can.

And indeed, how can more shame befall men through the wrath of God than frequently does us on account of our own deeds? If any slave escape from his lord, and, leaving Christendom, becomes a Viking, and after that it happens that an armed encounter occurs between thegn and slave; if the slave should slay the thegn outright he will lie without payment to any of his family; and if the thegn should slay outright the slave whom he previously owned, he will pay the price of a thegn. Over-cowardly laws and shameful tributes are, through the wrath of God, common among us, understand it who can; and many misfortunes befall this nation over and again. For long now nothing has prospered, within or without, but there has been devastation and persecution in every part, over and again. And for long now the English have been entirely without victory and too much cowed because of the wrath of God, and the pirates so strong with God's consent, that in battle often one will put to flight ten, and sometimes less sometimes more, all because of our sins. And often ten or twelve, one after another, will disgracefully insult the thegn's wife, and sometimes his daughter or near kinswoman, while he who considered himself proud and powerful and brave enough before that happened, looks on. And often a slave will bind very fast the thegn who was previously his lord, and make him a slave through the wrath of God. Alas for the misery, and alas for the public disgrace which the English now bear, all because of the wrath of God! Often two pirates, or sometimes three, will drive herds of Christian men out through this people from sea to sea, huddled together as a public shame to us all, if we could in earnest properly feel any. But all the disgrace we often suffer we repay with honour to those who bring shame on us. We pay them continually, and they humiliate us daily. They ravage and they burn, plunder and rob, and carry away on board; and indeed, what else is there in all these events but the wrath of God clear and visible towards this nation?

And is it no wonder things go badly for us though. For we know full well that for many years now men have too often not cared what they did by word or deed; but this nation, so it seems, has become totally sinful through manifold sins and through many misdeeds: through deadly sins and through evil deeds, through avarice and through greed, through theft and through pillaging, through the selling of men and through heathen vices, through betrayals and through plots, through breaches of the law and through legal offences, through attacks on kinsmen and through manslaughters, through injury done to those in holy orders and through adulteries, through incest and through various fornications. And commonly also, as we said before, more than should be are ruined and perjured through the breaking of oaths and through the breaking of pledges and through various lies. And failure to observe festivals and the breaking of fasts occurs commonly over and again. And here in the land also there are all too many degenerate apostates and malignant enemies of the Church and cruel tyrants; and those who scorn the divine laws and Christian customs are widespread; and everywhere in the nation are those who foolishly mock, most often those things which the messengers of God command, and especially those things which always appertain to God's laws by right. And therefore it has now reached such an evil state of affairs far and wide, that men are now more ashamed of good deeds than of misdeeds; because too often they dismiss good deeds with derision, and God-fearing people are abused all too much, and especially reviled and treated with contempt are those who love justice and fear God in any action. And because they behave thus – that they blame all that they should praise, and hate too much what they should love – they bring all too many evil intentions and wicked deeds, so that they are not ashamed although they sin greatly and commit wrongs even against God himself. But because of idle calumny, they are ashamed to atone for their misdeeds as the books direct, like those fools who because of their pride will not guard against injury, until they cannot even though they wish to.

Here, so it seems, too many in the land are grievously hurt with the injuries of sin. Here are slayers of men and slayers of kinsmen and killers of priests and enemies of the monasteries; and here are perjurers and murderers; and here are whores and those who kill children and many foul fornicating adulterers; and here are wizards and witches; and here are plunderers and robbers and those who despoil; and, to be brief, countless numbers of all crimes and misdeeds. And we are not ashamed of it; but we are too ashamed to begin reparation as the books direct; and that is clear in this wretched nation, burdened with sin. Alas, many might easily recall much more in addition, which one man could not outline in a hurry, to indicate how wretchedly it has gone all the time now widely throughout this nation. And indeed, let each diligently examine himself, and not put it off all too long.

But look, in God's name, let us do as is necessary for us, defend ourselves as best we may, lest we all perish together. There was a historian in the time of the Britons called Gildas. He wrote about their misdeeds, how by their sins they angered God so very excessively that finally he allowed the host of the English to conquer their land and to destroy the nobility of the Britons altogether. And as he said, that came about through robbery by the powerful and through the coveting of ill-gotten gains, through the lawlessness of the nation and through unjust judgements, through the laziness of bishops and through the base cowardice of God's heralds, who all too frequently refrained from telling the truth and mumbled with their jaws where they ought to have cried out. Likewise, through the foul extravagance of the people and through gluttony and manifold sins, they destroyed their country and they themselves perished. But let us do as is necessary for us – warn ourselves by such things. And it is true what I say; we know of worse deeds among the English than we have anywhere heard of among the Britons. And therefore it is very necessary that we reflect about ourselves and earnestly plead with God himself. And let us do as is necessary for us – bow to justice and in some part to leave off injustice, and to compensate very carefully for what we previously broke. And let us love God and follow God's laws, and very diligently practise what we promised when we received baptism – or those who were our sponsors at baptism. And let us order words and works aright, and earnestly cleanse our conscience, and carefully keep oath and pledge, and have some loyalty between us without deceit. And let us frequently consider the great Judgement to which we must all come, and carefully defend ourselves against the surging flame of hell-torment, and earn for ourselves those glories and those joys which God has prepared for them that work his will in the world. May God help us. Amen.

Questions for Discussion

1 What kind of picture does Wulfstan offer us concerning the state of England at the time of this sermon?
2 What interpretation does Wulfstan place upon the various woes that the English people are suffering? How does he justify this?
3 The sermon makes a plea for self-examination and repentance. Analyze how Wulfstan is able to move from his opening statements concerning the plight of his nation to these concluding reflections.
4 What historical precedent does Wulfstan identify, as he seeks to interpret the events he sees around him?

PART III

The Middle Ages, 1050–1500

Introduction

The "Middle Ages" is one of the most fascinating periods in the history of Christian literature. A theological and spiritual renaissance got under way in western Europe, which led to the appearance of a substantial number of literary works, many of which have since come to be recognized as classics. In particular, the period saw the blossoming of "Middle English" literature, which flourished between the Norman conquest of 1066 and about 1485. Much of this literature was religious in its nature.

While the literature of this period can be read without the need for any detailed knowledge of the religious history of the period, a basic understanding of some of its major themes will be helpful. In what follows, we shall note some of the major developments of the period.

The patristic period centered on the Mediterranean world, and centers of power such as Rome and Constantinople. Instability was widespread throughout the region during this period. The following developments were of particular importance in relation to this unstable situation.

1   *The fall of Rome.* The northern frontier of the Roman Empire was more or less defined by the River Rhine. In 404, this frontier collapsed in the face of assault by "barbarians." Huge areas of the Roman Empire were now under the control of the Franks, Goths, and Vandals. Rome itself was sacked twice, most notably by the forces of Alaric the Goth in 410. By 476, the western regions of the Roman Empire were in ruins. The political stability of the region was eroded, with the result that Christianity found itself facing a period of considerable uncertainty.

2   *The Arab invasions.* Islam became a significant religious movement amongst the Arab people in the seventh century. A program of conquest was initiated, which eventually led to Arab forces taking control of the entire coastal region of North Africa by about 750. Islamic forces also moved north, posing a serious threat to Constantinople itself. Arab forces laid siege to the city during the period 711–778, eventually being forced to withdraw. The enforcement of Islam in the conquered

regions of the Holy Land led to intense concern in the western church, and was one of the factors which led to the Crusades during the period 1095–1204.

By the eleventh century, a degree of stability had settled upon the region, with three major power groupings having emerged to take the place of the former Roman Empire.

1 Byzantium, which focused especially on the city of Constantinople (now Istanbul, in modern-day Turkey). The form of Christianity which predominated in this region was based on the Greek language, and was deeply rooted in the writings of patristic writers of the eastern Mediterranean region, such as Athanasius, the Cappadocians, and John of Damascus.
2 Western Europe, particularly regions such as France, Germany, the Lowlands, and northern Italy. The form of Christianity which came to dominate this region was centered on the city of Rome, and its bishop, known as "the Pope." (However, for the period known as the "Great Schism," some confusion developed: there were two rival claimants for the papacy, one based at Rome, the other at the southern French city of Avignon.) Here, theology came to center on the great cathedral and university schools of Paris and elsewhere, based largely on the Latin writings of Augustine, Ambrose, and Hilary of Poitiers.
3 The Caliphate, an Islamic region embracing much of the extreme eastern and southern part of the Mediterranean. The expansion of Islam continued, with the fall of Constantinople (1453) sending shock waves throughout much of Europe. By the end of the fifteenth century, Islam had established a significant presence in several regions of the continent of Europe, including Spain, parts of southern Italy, and the Balkans. This advance was eventually halted by the defeat of the Moors in Spain in the final decade of the fifteenth century, and the defeat of Islamic armies outside Vienna in 1523.

The Schism between East and West

An event of fundamental importance to the history of the church took place during this period – the breakdown in relations between the western, Latin-speaking, and the eastern, Greek-speaking church. For a variety of reasons, relations between the eastern church, based at Constantinople, and the western, based at Rome, became increasingly strained during the ninth and tenth centuries. Growing disagreement over the wording of the Nicene creed was of no small importance to this increasingly sour atmosphere. However, other factors contributed, including the political rivalry between Latin-speaking Rome and Greek-speaking Constantinople, and the increasing claims to authority of the Roman Pope. The final break between the Catholic west and Orthodox east is usually dated to 1054; however, this date is slightly arbitrary.

The particular style of Christianity which flourished in the eastern region of the Roman Empire is generally referred to as "Byzantine," taking its name from the Greek city of Byzantium, which Constantine chose as the site of his new capital city in 330. At this point, it was renamed "Constantinople" ("city of Constantine"). However, the name of the older town remained, and gave its name to the distinctive type of Christianity which flourished in this region until the fall of Constantinople to invading Islamic armies in 1453. Constantinople was not the only center of Christian thought in the eastern Mediterranean. Egypt and Syria had been centers of theological reflection for some time. However, as political power increasingly came to be concentrated on the imperial city, so its status as a theological center advanced correspondingly.

Constantinople soon became a center of missionary activity. At some point around the year 860, the Moravian ruler Rastislav asked the Byzantine emperor to send missionaries to his people in central Europe. Two Greek brothers, Cyril and Methodius, were sent in response to this request. This development was of particular importance to the formation of eastern European culture. Not only did it eventually lead to the dominance of Orthodoxy in the region of eastern Europe; it also had a major impact on the alphabets used in the region. Cyril devised an alphabet suitable for writing down the Slavic languages. This became the basis for the modern Cyrillic alphabet, named after the younger of the two "apostles of the Slavs." The conversion of Moravia was followed by that of Bulgaria and Serbia later that century. This was followed by the conversion of the Russians, at some point around the year 988.

Any attempt to achieve a degree of rapprochement between east and west during the Middle Ages was complicated by a complex network of political, historical, and theological factors. By the time of the fall of Constantinople, the differences between east and west remained as wide as ever. With the fall of Byzantium, intellectual and political leadership within Orthodoxy tended to pass to Russia. The Russians, who had been converted through Byzantine missions in the tenth century, took the side of the Greeks in the schism of 1054. By the end of the fifteenth century, Moscow and Kiev were firmly established as patriarchates, each with its own distinctive style of Orthodox Christianity, which remains of major importance today. Other regions which converted to Orthodoxy during this period include Serbia and Bulgaria.

It is clear that the flourishing of the eastern Orthodox church in Russia during the Middle Ages was of major importance to the shaping of Moscovite Russia. It is estimated that during the fourteenth, fifteenth and sixteenth centuries, more than 250 monasteries and convents were established in the region. The monastic revival, under the guidance of leaders such as St. Sergius of Radonezh (died 1392), gave further impetus to the missionary efforts of the Russian church. During the thirteenth century, for example, the Finnish-speaking peoples of the Karelia region were converted to Orthodoxy.

The fall of Constantinople in 1453 caused a major development within Russian Orthodoxy. Traditionally, each new metropolitan of the Russian church was installed by the patriarch of Constantinople, and looked to the Byzantine emperor (based in Constantinople) for its political leadership. The Russian church was very much a daughter of the Byzantine church. But with the fall of Constantinople, this traditional approach became a thing of the past. What could replace it? In the event, the eastern Orthodox church in Moscow became autocephalous – that is, self-governing. As a result, the political and cultural links between the Russian church and state became deeper. By 1523, the relation between church and state was so close that some writers began to refer to Moscow as the "Third Rome," to be treated with a respect equal to Rome and Constantinople. Philotheus of Pskov proclaimed that, now that Rome and Byzantium had become corrupt, the leadership of the Christian world had passed to Moscow: "two Romes have fallen; the third stands; there will be no fourth."

Our concern in this chapter, however, is primarily with western Christianity, and we shall therefore sketch some of the more important developments within this movement during the Middle Ages.

The Development of Western Christianity to 1500

With the conversion of England, discussed in the introduction to the previous chapter, a base was established for the evangelization of other northern European nations. Missionaries from England became active in Germany. Under the rule of Charlemagne (ca. 742–814), Christianity was given new institutional and social stability. The importance of Charlemagne in the consolidation of Christianity in western Europe was given formal recognition by the Pope, who crowned him as the first "Holy Roman Emperor" on Christmas Day, 800. Although this coronation further strained relations between the eastern and western churches, it nevertheless gave Christianity a new authority in the western regions of Europe. By the end of the first millennium, Christianity was more or less established as the dominant religion of much of the region. The scene was set for further consolidation and renewal.

An important aspect of the Christian Renaissance of the period was a new flowering of interest in Christian theology, in terms of both its ideas and the literary forms in which those ideas might be expressed. The period 1050–1350 saw a remarkable consolidation of Christian thought at the intellectual level. When the Dark Ages finally lifted from over western Europe, giving birth to the Middle Ages, the scene was set for revival in every field of academic work. The restoration of some degree of political stability in France in the late eleventh century encouraged the re-emergence of the University of Paris, which rapidly became recognized as the intellectual center of Europe. A number of theological "schools" were established on the Left Bank of the Seine, and on the Île de la Cité, in the shadow of the newly-built cathedral of Notre Dame de Paris.

The University of Paris soon established itself as an outstanding center of theological speculation, producing such leading writers as Peter Abelard (1079–1142), Albert the Great (ca. 1200–80), Thomas Aquinas (ca. 1225–74), and Bonaventure (ca. 1217–74). The fourteenth and fifteenth centuries witnessed an expansion of the university sector in western Europe, with major new universities being founded in Germany and elsewhere. It was not long before these universities would begin to make their substantial contribution to the development of Christian literature. Yet it was not only the fledgling universities which were of importance to the development of Christian literature in the Middle Ages. Several monasteries produced outstanding Christian writers and thinkers. For example, the monastery at Bec, in Normandy, produced such outstanding writers as Lanfranc (ca. 1010–89) and Anselm (ca. 1033–1109).

It was not only the life of the mind, however, which underwent renewal during this period. The western church was subjected to a sustained program of reform under Gregory VII (ca. 1021–95), who was elected Pope in 1073. Although the "Gregorian Reform" was intensely controversial at the time, modern scholars are generally agreed that it led to the renewal of the church at this critical period in its history. In particular, Gregory managed to achieve an inversion of the existing understanding of the relation of church and state. Whereas it had been assumed that the church was subservient to the state, Gregory managed to establish the principle that, at least in some areas, the church has authority over the state.

The scene was set for further consolidation of papal authority during the later Middle Ages. One major development was the weakness of the empire following the death of Emperor Henry VI in 1197. Henry's predecessor as Emperor, Frederick I (also known as "Barbarossa"), ruled during the period 1152–90. He established his authority over much of northern Italy. Henry consolidated these gains. Yet in 1197, Henry died, leaving his empire to his three-year-old son. Chaos resulted, leaving the empire weak and divided. As it happened, a strong Pope was elected the following year, who seized the opportunity to re-establish the authority of the papacy. Under Innocent III (Pope from 1198 to 1216), the medieval papacy reached an unprecedented level of power throughout western Europe. Innocent adopted the title of "Vicar of Christ" (the term "vicar" here means "representative" or "substitute"). For Innocent, "no king can reign correctly unless he serves the Vicar of Christ."

Nevertheless, other developments undermined this process of consolidation. Of particular importance was the emergence of the Avignon papacy during the period 1378–1417. This development resulted from the temporary withdrawal of the papacy from Rome to Avignon for political reasons during the period 1309–77. On the return of the papacy to Rome in 1378, two pro-French antipopes ruled in Avignon. The resulting schism was finally settled through the Council of Pisa (1409) and the Council of Constance (1417).

The period was of enormous importance in other respects. Several major new religious orders were founded in the region. In 1097, the Cistercian order was founded at Cîteaux, in the middle of the wild countryside around the River Saône. This order placed an emphasis on the importance of manual labor, rather than of scholarship, and on private rather than corporate prayer. The Cistercian order was noted for its severe rule of life, which denied its members virtually all of the comforts of life. For example, fires were only permitted once a year, on Christmas Day. One of the most noted Cistercian leaders was the great spiritual writer and preacher Bernard of Clairvaux (1090–1153). By the dawn of the fourteenth century, it is estimated that some 600 Cistercian monasteries or convents had come into being.

Two other major orders were founded more than a century later – the Franciscans and Dominicans. The Franciscans were founded by Francis of Assisi (ca. 1181–1226), who renounced a life of wealth to live a life of prayer and poverty. The order was often referred to as "the Grey Friars," on account of the dark grey habits they wore. The order was distinguished by its emphasis on individual and corporate poverty. The order was often viewed as anti-intellectual; nevertheless, some of the greatest theologians of the period, such as Bonaventure, were members of the order.

The Dominicans (sometimes referred to as "Black Friars" on account of their black mantle worn over a white habit) were founded by the Spanish priest Dominic de Guzman (1170–1221), with a particular emphasis on education. By the end of the Middle Ages, the Dominicans had established houses in most major European cities, and made a significant contribution to the intellectual life of the church. Perhaps the greatest medieval theologian, Thomas Aquinas, was a member of this order.

The Middle Ages, then, can be seen as an immensely fertile and important period in the development of Christian literature. Let us, then, begin to interact with some of the classic texts to have been written during this era.

CHAPTER 23

Anselm of Canterbury (1033–1109)

Anselm was born at Aosta in northern Italy. At the age of twenty-three he appears to have quarreled with his father, and began a period of wandering through France in search of academic excellence. After short periods at the schools of Fleury-sur-Loire and Chartres, he arrived at the Benedictine abbey of Bec, in Normandy. At this point Lanfranc served as both prior and master of its school, and had managed to raise the profile of the abbey considerably. Anselm entered the abbey as a novice in 1060 and rapidly rose to eminence. When Lanfranc moved to a new monastery founded at Caen in 1063 by William, Duke of Normandy, Anselm was elected to succeed him as Prior at Bec, a position which he held until he became Abbot in 1078.

Anselm of Canterbury (1033–1109)

Basic description
Leading theological and spiritual writer of the eleventh century; sometime Archbishop of Canterbury.

Major works
De Libertate Arbitrii; *De Casu Diaboli*; *Proslogion*; *Monologion*; *Cur Deus Homo*; and many prayers and other devotional texts.

Major studies
G. R. Evans, *Anselm and Talking about God*. Oxford: Oxford University Press, 1978.
R. W. Southern, *St. Anselm and his Biographer*. Cambridge: Cambridge University Press, 1953.

In the meantime, events had moved on elsewhere. William had invaded England in 1066, and was now in the process of reorganizing England, and bringing it under Norman control. Part of that enterprise involved the "Normalization" of the English church, which William regarded as a matter of some import. He had brought Lanfranc over to England to serve as his Archbishop of Canterbury. When Lanfranc died, William Rufus – who had succeeded William the Conqueror as king of England – brought Anselm over to England to succeed him as Archbishop. Anselm finally arrived in 1093. He appears to have accepted the appointment with considerable reluctance. This concern appears to have been fully justified; virtually from the moment he touched English soil, Anselm found himself engaged in disputes with William over ecclesiastical freedom. By 1097 he was conducting the battle from exile, and was only able to return in 1100, when William Rufus was succeeded by Henry I. As events proved, Anselm's relations with Henry were at least as strained as those with his predecessor. By 1103, Anselm found himself once more in exile, returning only in 1107 when a compromise was arranged, which allowed a partial degree of independence of the church from the state. Anselm died in 1109.

Anselm is noted for his theological and philosophical works. In a series of short works such as *De Libertate Arbitrii* (On Free Will), *De Casu Diaboli* (The Fall of the Devil), and *Cur Deus Homo* (Why God became Man), Anselm propounded a theory of the atonement. He defended a notion of the relation between philosophy and theology that, like Augustine's, emphasized the methodological priority of faith over reason, since truth is to be achieved only through *fides quaerens intellectum* ("faith seeking understanding"). Anselm's combination of Christianity, neo-Platonic metaphysics, and Aristotelian logic in the form of dialectical question-and-answer was an important influence in the development of scholasticism during the next several centuries.

As a philosopher, Anselm is most often remembered for his attempts to prove the existence of God: In *De Veritate* ("On Truth") he argued that all creatures owe their being and value to God as the source of all truth, to whom a life lived well is the highest praise. In the *Monologion* he described God as the one most truly good thing, from which all real moral values derive and whose existence is required by the reality of those values.

Most famously, in the *Proslogion*, Anselm set out what has come to be known as the "ontological argument," according to which God is understood as *aliquid quod maius non cogitari potest* ("that than which nothing greater can be conceived"). The argument takes the form that the being so conceived must necessarily exist in reality as well as in thought, since otherwise it would in fact be possible to conceive something greater than the mere idea of God – that is, the reality of God.

Yet Anselm was also much in demand as a spiritual advisor, and many of his prayers and letters of spiritual guidance have survived. His prayers take the form of highly structured reflections on central Christian themes. They were widely circulated, and represent an important literary form. The passage selected for study is an extract from the work known as the "Prayer to Christ."

Text: A Prayer to Christ

The basic approach adopted by Anselm is that of stirring the conscience to a deeper love of God, involving the intellect, emotion, and will. As the title of the prayer suggests, there is a strong element of focusing on the passion and death of Christ as a means of deepening the love of the one who prays for the one who is prayed to. Anselm himself wrote that the prayer was intended to "stir up the mind of the reader to the love of God," and urged that it was "not to be read in a turmoil, but quietly; not skimmed or hurried through, but taken a little at a time, with deep and thoughtful meditation."

Hope of my heart, strength of my soul,
  help of my weakness,
  by your powerful kindness complete
  what in my powerless weakness I attempt.
My life, the end to which I strive,   5
  although I have not yet attained to love you as I ought,
  still let my desire for you
  be as great as my love ought to be.
My light, you see my conscience,
  because, "Lord, before you is all my desire,"   10
  and if my soul wills any good, you gave it me.
Lord, if what you inspire is good,
  or rather because it is good, that I should want to love you,
  give me what you have made me want:
  grant that I may attain to love you as much as you command.   15
I praise and thank you for the desire that you have inspired;
  and I offer you praise and thanks
  lest your gift to me be unfruitful,
  which you have given me of your own accord.
Perfect what you have begun,   20
  and grant me what you have made me long for,
  not according to my deserts but out of your kindness
  that came first to me.
Most merciful Lord,
  turn my lukewarmness into a fervent love of you.   25
Most gentle Lord,
  my prayer tends towards this –
  that by remembering and meditating
  on the good things you have done
  I may be enkindled with your love.   30
Your goodness, Lord, created me;
Your mercy cleansed what you had created from original sin;
  your patience has hitherto borne with me,
  fed me, waited for me,
  when after I had lost the grace of my baptism   35
  I wallowed in many sordid sins.
You wait, good Lord, for my amendment;
My soul waits for the inbreathing of your grace
  in order to be sufficiently penitent
  to lead a better life.   40
My Lord and my Creator,
  you bear with me and nourish me – be my helper.
I thirst for you, I hunger for you, I desire you,

I sigh for you, I covet you:
I am like an orphan deprived of the presence 45
   of a very kind father,
   who, weeping and wailing, does not cease to cling to
   the dear face with his whole heart.
So, as much as I can, though not as much as I ought,
   I am mindful of your passion, 50
   your buffeting, your scourging, your cross, your wounds,
   how you were slain for me,
   how prepared for burial and buried;
   and also I remember your glorious Resurrection,
   and wonderful Ascension. 55
All this I hold with unwavering faith,
   and weep over the hardship of exile,
   hoping in the sole consolation of your coming,
   ardently longing for the glorious contemplation of your face.

Read this passage through twice, noting Anselm's request to read slowly, before moving on to interact with the text.

1 Anselm begins by confessing the lukewarmness of his love for God. This is an allusion to the situation of the church in the Asian city of Laodicea, as described in Revelation 3:14–22 – the only point in the New Testament at which the word "lukewarm" is used. Read through this passage, and note the characteristics of this church: you might list these as including being "lukewarm," "self-satisfied," and "unwilling to acknowledge dependence on God." How does this passage cast light on Anselm's understanding of his own spiritual state, and the manner in which it might be changed?

2 Anselm asks that the lukewarmness of his love for God might be "enkindled" – that is, set alight. How does he expect this to happen?

3 Anselm's reference to "remembering and meditating on the good things [God] has done" picks up on a major theme from the Psalms: recalling the great acts of God in the past. To see what Anselm has in mind, read Psalm 136. Each verse of this Psalm includes the refrain: "[God's] love endures for ever." Note how the Psalm sets out the great acts of God in history – for example, the creation of the world (verses 5–9), the exodus from Egypt (verses 10–15), and the entry into the promised land (verses 16–22). Anselm's approach mirrors that of the Psalms at this point.

4 At several points, Anselm expresses a sense of longing for God, often using imagery which suggests human emptiness. Work through the text, and identify as many images or phrases of this type as you can. What is the cumulative effect of these images and phrases?

5 Identify two images of separation used in this passage by Anselm to indicate his sense of distance from God. We shall explore them presently; at this stage, read the text again, and see if you can identify the images in question.

6 The first of these images is that of an orphan who longs for a lost father. What emotions does Anselm arouse by his use of this image?

7   The second image is that of exile. What associations are linked with this image? And
     how does Anselm develop them?
8   Anselm expresses his longing for God, and his sense that he at present does not
     possess God fully. What does he expect to happen? At what point does he introduce
     the theme of the "beatific vision"? And what use does he make of it?

CHAPTER 24

Peter Abelard (1079–1142)

Peter Abelard is widely regarded as one of the great intellectuals of the twelfth century, of especial importance to the fields of theology and logic. He was born at Le Pallet, near Nantes, and studied under a series of masters, including William of Champeaux and Anselm of Laon. Theologically, Abelard was one of the earliest critics of Anselm of Canterbury, particularly in relation to the doctrine of redemption. In his "Commentary on Romans," dating from the early decades of the twelfth century, Abelard argued that one of the chief consequences of the death of Christ was its demonstration of the love of God for humanity. It is through our response of love to Christ that we are joined to him, and benefit from his passion. This contrasted sharply with the more objective and detached approach of Anselm. Abelard's apparent emphasis upon the subjective aspects of the Christian life made him many enemies at the time, but makes him particularly easy to read today, when such approaches to Christian theology and spirituality are much more acceptable than they were at this earlier stage.

Peter Abelard (1079–1142)

Basic description
Twelfth-century theologian, logician, and lover.

Major works
Commentary on Romans; *The History of Calamities*.

Major studies
D. E. Luscombe, "From Paris to the Paraclete: The Correspondence of Abelard and Heloise," *Proceedings of the British Academy* 74 (1988), 247–83.
Richard E. Weingart, *The Logic of Divine Love: A Critical Analysis of the Soteriology of Peter Abailard*. Oxford: Clarendon Press, 1970.

One of Abelard's more important contributions to the development of Christian literature is his book *Sic et Non* ("Yes and No"), which takes the form of a list of 158 philosophical and theological questions about which there were divided opinions. Abelard set himself the task of resolving these apparent contradictions by a form of reasoning which would grow in popularity, and can be seen reflected in what is often thought to be the greatest work of medieval theology – Thomas Aquinas' *Summa Theologiae*. The same method can also be seen in Gratian's approach to canon law, in which apparently contradictory authorities are reconciled by a synthesis of their opinions. This dialectical method of intellectual reflection would become an important feature of western education in general.

Abelard is probably best remembered today for his love affair with his mistress Heloise and its disastrous consequences, which resulted initially in her giving birth to a son; then to Abelard's castration by Heloise's angry relatives; and finally to both of them withdrawing from the world to seek safety and consolation in the monastic life. Heloise, who was the niece of Fulbert, Canon of the cathedral of Notre-Dame, was one of the most literate women of her time, and an able administrator. As far as can be judged, her monastic life was notably successful. Abelard was less fortunate; he incurred the displeasure and enmity of abbots, bishops, his fellow monks, a number of Church councils, and Bernard of Clairvaux. The last months of his life were spent under the protection of Peter the Venerable at the priory of Saint-Marcel, where he finally died. The tomb of Abelard and Heloise can be found in the Père Lachaise cemetery in Paris.

Text: *The History of Calamities*

The *Historia Calamitatum* ("History of Calamities") takes the form of a letter; in reality, it is to be regarded as an autobiography, showing clear similarities to Augustine's *Confessions*. It is easily one of the most readable documents to survive from the period. In addition to being a valuable account of intellectual life in Paris on the eve of the formal establishment of the University of Paris, the work can be seen as a remarkably frank self-portrait, along with the narration of a love story that remains part of the western literary canon. The text merits to be included in full in this anthology; considerations on space, sadly, made this impossible. The portion of the text which we shall set aside for study are the sixth and seventh chapters, which tell of his involvement with Heloise, and the results of this love affair for his career – perhaps the most familiar and best-loved section of the work.

Chapter VI – Of How, Brought Low By His Love For Heloise, He Was Wounded In Body And Soul

NOW there dwelt in that same city of Paris a certain young girl named Heloise, the niece of a canon who was called Fulbert. Her uncle's love for her was equalled only by his desire that she should have the best education which he could possibly procure for her. Of no mean beauty, she stood out above all by reason of her abundant knowledge of letters. Now this virtue is rare among women, and for that very reason it doubly graced the maiden, and made her the most worthy of renown in the entire kingdom. It was this young girl whom I, after carefully considering all those qualities which are wont to attract lovers, determined to unite with myself in the bonds of love, and indeed the thing seemed to me very easy to be done. So distinguished was my name, and I possessed such advantages of youth and comeliness, that no matter what woman I might favor with my love, I dreaded rejection of none. Then, too, I believed that I could win the maiden's consent all the more easily by reason of her knowledge of letters and her zeal therefore; so, even if we were parted, we might yet be together in thought with the aid of written messages. Perchance, too, we might be able to write more boldly than we could speak, and thus at all times could we live in joyous intimacy.

Thus, utterly aflame with my passion for this maiden, I sought to discover means whereby I might have daily and familiar speech with her, thereby the more easily to win her consent. For this purpose I persuaded the girl's uncle, with the aid of some of his friends, to take me into his household – for he dwelt hard by my school – in return for the payment of a small sum. My pretext for this was that the care of my own household was a serious handicap to my studies, and likewise burdened me with an expense far greater than I could afford. Now he was a man keen in avarice and likewise he was most desirous for his niece that her study of letters should ever go forward, so, for these two reasons I easily won his consent to the fulfillment of my wish, for he was fairly agape for my money, and at the same time believed that his niece would vastly benefit by my teaching. More even than this, by his own earnest entreaties he fell in with my desires beyond anything I had dared to hope, opening the way for my love; for he entrusted her wholly to my guidance, begging me to give her instruction whensoever I might be free from the duties of my school, no matter whether by day or by night, and to punish her sternly if ever I should find her negligent of her tasks. In all this the man's simplicity was nothing short of astounding to me; I should not have been more smitten with wonder if he had entrusted a tender lamb to the care of a ravenous wolf. When he had thus given her into my charge, not alone to be taught but even to be disciplined, what had he done save to give free scope to my desires, and to offer me every opportunity, even if I had not sought it, to bend her to my will with threats and blows if I failed to do so with caresses? There were, however, two things which particularly served to allay any foul suspicion: his own love for his niece, and my former reputation for continence.

Why should I say more? We were united first in the dwelling that sheltered our love, and then in the hearts that burned with it. Under the pretext of study we spent our hours in the happiness of love, and learning held out to us the secret opportunities that our passion craved. Our speech was more of love than of the books which lay open before us; our kisses far outnumbered our reasoned words. Our hands sought less the book than each other's bosoms – love drew our eyes together far more than the lesson drew them to the pages of our text. In order that there might be no suspicion, there were, indeed, sometimes blows, but love gave them, not anger; they were the marks, not of wrath, but of a tenderness surpassing the most fragrant balm in sweetness. What followed? No degree in love's progress was left untried by our passion, and if love itself could imagine any wonder as yet unknown, we discovered it. And our inexperience of such delights made us all the more ardent in our pursuit of them, so that our thirst for one another was still unquenched.

In measure as this passionate rapture absorbed me more and more, I devoted ever less time to philosophy and to the work of the school. Indeed it became loathsome to me to go to the school or to linger there; the labor, moreover, was very burdensome, since my nights were vigils of love and my days of study. My lecturing became utterly careless and lukewarm; I did nothing because of inspiration, but everything merely as a matter of habit. I had become nothing more than a reciter of my former discoveries, and though I still wrote poems, they dealt with love, not with the secrets of philosophy. Of these songs you yourself well know how some have become widely known and have been sung in many lands, chiefly, methinks, by those who delighted in the things of this world. As for the sorrow, the groans, the lamentations of my students when they perceived the preoccupation, nay, rather the chaos, of my mind, it is hard even to imagine them.

A thing so manifest could deceive only a few, no one, methinks, save him whose shame it chiefly bespoke, the girl's uncle, Fulbert. The truth was often enough hinted to him, and by many persons, but he could not believe it, partly, as I have said, by reason of his boundless love for his niece, and partly because of the well-known continence of my previous life. Indeed we do not easily suspect shame in those whom we most cherish, nor can there be the blot of foul suspicion on devoted love. Of this St. Jerome in his epistle to Sabinianus (Epist. 48) says: "We are wont to be the last to know the evils of our own households, and to be ignorant of the sins of our children and our wives, though our neighbors sing them aloud." But no matter how slow a matter may be in disclosing itself, it is sure to come forth at last, nor is it easy to hide from one what is known to all. So, after the lapse of several months, did it happen with us. Oh, how great was the uncle's grief when he learned the truth, and how bitter was the sorrow of the lovers when we were forced to part! With what shame was I overwhelmed, with what contrition smitten because of the blow which had fallen on her I loved, and what a tempest of misery burst over her by reason of my disgrace! Each grieved most, not for himself, but for the other. Each sought to allay, not his own sufferings, but those of the one he loved. The very sundering of our bodies served but to link our souls closer together; the plentitude of the love which was denied to us inflamed us more than ever. Once the first wildness of shame had passed, it left us more shameless than before, and as shame died within us the cause of it seemed to us ever more desirable. And so it chanced with us as, in the stories that the poets tell, it once happened with Mars and Venus when they were caught together.

It was not long after this that Heloise found that she was pregnant, and of this she wrote to me in the utmost exultation, at the same time asking me to consider what had best be done. Accordingly, on a night when her uncle was absent, we carried out the plan we had determined on, and I stole her secretly away from her uncle's house, sending her without delay to my own country. She remained there with my sister until she gave birth to a son, whom she named Astrolabe. Meanwhile her uncle, after his return, was almost mad with grief; only one who had then seen him could rightly guess the burning agony of his sorrow and the bitterness of his shame. What steps to take against me, or what snares to set for me, he did not know. If he should kill me or do me some bodily hurt, he feared greatly lest his dear-loved niece should be made to suffer for it among my kinsfolk. He had no power to seize me and imprison me somewhere against my will, though I make no doubt he would have done so quickly enough had he been able or dared, for I had taken measures to guard against any such attempt.

At length, however, in pity for his boundless grief, and bitterly blaming myself for the suffering which my love had brought upon him through the baseness of the deception I had practised, I went to him to entreat his forgiveness, promising to make any amends that he himself might decree. I pointed out that what had happened could not seem incredible to any one who had ever felt the power of love, or who remembered how, from the very beginning of the human race, women had cast down even the noblest men to utter ruin. And in order to make amends even beyond his extremest hope, I offered to marry her whom I had seduced, provided only the thing could be kept secret, so that I might suffer no loss of reputation thereby. To this he gladly assented, pledging his own faith and that of his kindred, and sealing with kisses the pact which I had sought of him – and all this that he might the more easily betray me.

Chapter VII – Of The Arguments Of Heloise Against Wedlock. Of How None The Less He Made Her His Wife

Forthwith I repaired to my own country, and brought back thence my mistress, that I might make her my wife. She, however, most violently disapproved of this, and for two chief reasons: the danger thereof, and the disgrace which it would bring upon me. She swore that her uncle would never be appeased by such satisfaction as this, as, indeed, afterwards proved only too true. She asked how she could ever glory in me if she should make me thus inglorious, and should shame herself along with me. What penalties, she said, would the world rightly demand of her if she should rob it of so shining a light! What curses would follow such a loss to the Church, what tears among the philosophers would result from such a marriage! How unfitting, how lamentable it would be for me, whom nature had made for the whole world, to devote myself to one woman solely, and to subject myself to such humiliation! She vehemently rejected this marriage, which she felt would be in every way ignominious and burdensome to me.

Besides dwelling thus on the disgrace to me, she reminded me of the hardships of married life, to the avoidance of which the Apostle exhorts us, saying: "Art thou loosed from a wife? seek not a wife. But and marry, thou hast not sinned; and if a virgin marry she hath not sinned. Nevertheless such shall have trouble in the flesh: but I spare you" (1 Cor. vii: 27). And again: "But I would have you to be free from cares" (1 Cor. vii: 32). But if I would heed neither the counsel of the Apostle nor the exhortations of the saints regarding this heavy yoke of matrimony, she bade me at least consider the advice of the philosophers, and weigh carefully what had been written on this subject either by them or concerning their lives. Even the saints themselves have often and earnestly spoken on this subject for the purpose of warning us. Thus St. Jerome, in his first book against Jovinianus, makes Theophrastus set forth in great detail the intolerable annoyances and the endless disturbances of married life, demonstrating with the most convincing arguments that no wise man should ever have a wife, and concluding his reasons for this philosophic exhortation with these words: "Who among Christians would not be overwhelmed by such arguments as these advanced by Theophrastus?"

Again, in the same work, St. Jerome tells how Cicero, asked by Hircius after his divorce of Terentia whether he would marry the sister of Hircius, replied that he would do no such thing, saying that he could not devote himself to a wife and to philosophy at the same time. Cicero does not, indeed, precisely speak of "devoting himself," but he does add that he did not wish to undertake anything which might rival his study of philosophy in its demands upon him.

Then, turning from the consideration of such hindrances to the study of philosophy, Heloise bade me observe what were the conditions of honorable wedlock. What possible concord could there be between scholars and domestics, between authors and cradles, between books or tablets and distaffs, between the stylus or the pen and the spindle? What man, intent on his religious or philosophical meditations, can possibly endure the whining of children, the lullabies of the nurse seeking to quiet them, or the noisy confusion of family life? Who can endure the continual untidiness of children? The rich, you may reply, can do this, because they have palaces or houses containing many rooms, and because their wealth takes no thought of expense and protects them from daily worries. But to this the answer is that the condition of philosophers is by no means that of the wealthy, nor can those whose minds are occupied with riches and worldly cares find time for religious or philosophical study. For this reason the renowned philosophers of old utterly despised the world, fleeing from its perils rather than reluctantly giving them up, and denied themselves all its delights in order that they might repose in the embraces of philosophy alone. One of them, and the greatest of all, Seneca, in his advice to Lucilius, says philosophy is "not a thing to be studied only in hours of leisure; we must give up everything else to devote ourselves to it, for no amount of time is really sufficient hereto" (Epist. 73).

It matters little, she pointed out, whether one abandons the study of philosophy completely or merely interrupts it, for it can never remain at the point where it was thus interrupted. All other occupations must be resisted; it is vain to seek to adjust life to include them, and they must simply be eliminated. This view is maintained, for example, in the love of God by those among us who are truly called monastics, and in the love of wisdom by all those who have stood out among men as sincere philosophers. For in every race, gentiles or Jews or Christians, there have always been a few who excelled their fellows in faith or in the purity of their lives, and who were set apart from the multitude by their continence or by their abstinence from worldly pleasures.

Among the Jews of old there were the Nazarites, who consecrated themselves to the Lord, some of them the sons of the prophet Elias and others the followers of Eliseus, the monks of whom, on the authority of St. Jerome (Epist. 4 and 13), we read in the Old Testament. More recently there were the three philosophical sects which Josephus defines in his Book of Antiquities (xviii: 2), calling them the Pharisees, the Sadducees, and the Essenes. In our times, furthermore, there are the monks who imitate either the communal life of the Apostles or the earlier and solitary life of John. Among the gentiles there are, as has been said, the philosophers. Did they not apply the name of wisdom or philosophy as much to the religion of life as to the pursuit of learning, as we find from the origin of the word itself, and likewise from the testimony of the saints?

There is a passage on this subject in the eighth book of St. Augustine's "City of God," wherein he distinguishes between the various schools of philosophy. "The Italian school," he says, "had as its founder Pythagoras of Samos, who, it is said, originated the very word 'philosophy'. Before his time those who were regarded as conspicuous for the praiseworthiness of their lives were called wise men, but he, on being asked of his profession, replied that he was a philosopher, that is to say a student or a lover of wisdom because it seemed to him unduly boastful to call himself a wise man." In this passage, therefore, when the phrase "conspicuous for the praise-worthiness of their lives" is used, it is evident that the wise, in other words the philosophers, were so called less because of their erudition than by reason of their virtuous lives. In what sobriety and continence these men lived it is not for me to prove by illustration, lest I should seem to instruct Minerva herself.

Now, she added, if laymen and gentiles, bound by no profession of religion, lived after this fashion, what ought you, a cleric and a canon, to do in order not to prefer base voluptuousness to your sacred duties, to prevent this Charybdis from sucking you down headlong, and to save yourself from being plunged shamelessly and irrevocably into such filth as this? If you care nothing for your privileges as a cleric, at least uphold your dignity as a philosopher. If you scorn the reverence due to God, let regard for your reputation temper your shamelessness. Remember that Socrates was chained to a wife, and by what a filthy accident he himself paid for this blot on philosophy, in order that others thereafter might be made more cautious by his example. Jerome thus mentions this affair, writing about Socrates in his first book against Jovinianus: "Once when he was withstanding a storm of reproaches which Xantippe was hurling at him from an upper story, he was suddenly drenched with foul slops; wiping his head, he said only, 'I knew there would be a shower after all that thunder.'"

Her final argument was that it would be dangerous for me to take her back to Paris, and that it would be far sweeter for her to be called my mistress than to be known as my wife; nay, too, that this would be more honorable for me as well. In such case, she said, love alone would hold me to her, and the strength of the marriage chain would not constrain us. Even if we should by chance be parted from time to time, the joy of our meetings would be all the sweeter by reason of its rarity. But when she found that she could not convince me or dissuade me from my folly by these and like arguments, and because she could not bear to offend me, with griev-ous sighs and tears she made an end of her resistance, saying: "Then there is no more left but this, that in our doom the sorrow yet to come shall be no less than the love we two have already known." Nor in this, as now the whole world knows, did she lack the spirit of prophecy.

So, after our little son was born, we left him in my sister's care, and secretly returned to Paris. A few days later, in the early morning, having kept our nocturnal vigil of prayer unknown to all in a certain church, we were united there in the bene-diction of wedlock her uncle and a few friends of his and mine being present. We departed forthwith stealthily and by separate ways, nor thereafter did we see each other save rarely and in private, thus striving our utmost to conceal what we had done. But her uncle and those of his household, seeking solace for their disgrace, began to divulge the story of our marriage, and thereby to violate the pledge they had given me on this point. Heloise, on the contrary, denounced her own kin and swore that they were speaking the most absolute lies. Her uncle, aroused to fury thereby, visited her repeatedly with punishments. No sooner had I learned this than I sent her to a convent of nuns at Argenteuil, not far from Paris, where she herself had been brought up and educated as a young girl. I had them make ready for her all the garments of a nun, suitable for the life of a convent, excepting only the veil, and these I bade her put on.

When her uncle and his kinsmen heard of this, they were convinced that now I had completely played them false and had rid myself forever of Heloise by forcing her to become a nun. Violently incensed, they laid a plot against me, and one night while I all unsuspecting was asleep in a secret room in my lodgings, they broke in with the help of one of my servants whom they had bribed. There they had vengeance on me with a most cruel and most shameful punishment, such as astounded the whole world; for they cut off those parts of my body with which I had done that which was the cause of their sorrow. This done, straightway they fled, but two of them were captured and suffered the loss of their eyes and their genital organs. One of these two was the aforesaid servant, who even while he was still in my service, had been led by his avarice to betray me.

Questions for Study

1   What light does this passage cast on Abelard's relationship with Heloise?
2   Why did Heloise refuse to marry Abelard?
3   In what ways can the passage be seen as showing an interest in the subjective experience of individuals? Note especially the way in which love is described.

CHAPTER 25

Bernard of Clairvaux (1090–1153)

Bernard was born the third son of seven children to a noble family at Fontaines-les-Dijon in Burgundy. He was sent to be educated at Chatillon, presumably with the intention of serving family interests. However, the death of his mother caused him to become interested in the religious life. This interest led to a radical change in his life around the age of 22. In 1112 Bernard convinced about 30 other young noblemen – including friends, relatives, and four of his brothers – to enter the monastery of Cîteaux, which had been founded in 1098 by some Benedictine monks in search of a more rigorous life. Their monastery attracted few converts until 1112. The arrival of Bernard and his entourage changed the profile of the order completely. Bernard would go on to become the greatest representative of this order, and lead it to new heights of prestige.

Bernard of Clairvaux (1090–1153)

Basic description
Leading twelfth-century spiritual writer and monastic reformer.

Major works
Sermons on the Song of Songs; *On Loving God*.

Major studies
Brian Patrick McGuire, *The Difficult Saint: Bernard of Clairvaux and His Tradition*. Kalamazoo, MI: Cistercian Publications, 1991.
John R. Sommerfeldt, *The Spiritual Teachings of Bernard of Clairvaux*. Kalamazoo, MI: Cistercian Publications, 1991.

In 1115, when Bernard was 25, the abbot of Cîteaux, Stephen Harding, invited Bernard to select a site for a new monastery, and supervise its construction. Bernard selected a site in what was then known as the Vallée d'Absinthe – a name which he immediately changed to Clairvaux. As the first abbot of Cîteaux, Bernard initially encountered problems on account of his expectation that the other monks would follow his stringent regime of prayer, silence, plainness, simple diet, self-denial, and manual labor. Yet many found this disciplined and spartan life attractive. The Cistercian ideal began to take hold, and daughter houses were founded. At least 68 more monasteries are known to have been established by monks from Clairvaux.

Bernard was deeply involved in the convoluted politics of the twelfth century. He acted as secretary to the Synod of Troyes (1128), and was instrumental in obtaining recognition for the rules of the new order of Knights Templar. He became embroiled in the dispute over the election of the successor to Pope Honorius II in 1130. Bernard backed Innocent II, who finally succeeded to the title; in consequence, the Cistercian Order found itself the recipient of many papal favors. He was critical of any form of luxury in the religious life, and was particularly critical of what he regarded as the extravagances of the monastery of Cluny, which constructed the largest church in Europe to serve its needs. Toward the end of his life, Bernard became involved in the organization of the Second Crusade, the failure of which he felt deeply in his final years.

Bernard is remembered particularly on account of his spiritual writings. Of these, perhaps the greatest is the incomplete cycle of sermons on the Song of Songs, widely known as the *Sermones super Cantica Canticorum*. The text selected for study is a shorter work, which is ideal for inclusion in this anthology – the treatise *On Loving God*.

Text: *On Loving God*

Bernard's treatise *de diligendo Deo* ("On Loving God") is regarded as one of his finest achievements. The dominant theme of the work is that God is to be loved simply and purely because God deserves such love; the benefits which such love brings to believers is of secondary importance. Our extract is taken from the fourth of its fifteen chapters.

Here we should note what class of people take comfort in the thought of God. Surely it is not that perverse and crooked generation to whom it was said, "Woe unto you that are rich; for you have already received your consolation" (Luke 6:24). Rather, it is those who can say with truth, "My soul refuses comfort" (Psalm 77:2). For it is appropriate that those who are not satisfied by the present should be sustained by the thought of the future; and that the contemplation of eternal happiness should console those who refuse to drink from the river of transitory joys. This is the generation of those who seek the Lord – those who seek the face of the God of Jacob, not their own. To those that long for the presence of the living God, the thought of Him is the sweetest of all things. Yet it does not satisfy; it merely increases our appetite for more, as the Scripture declares: "they that eat me shall still be hungry" (Ecclesiasticus 24:21); as one who was hungry put it: "When I awake up after your likeness, I shall be satisfied with it." Yes: blessed at this moment are those who hunger and thirst after righteousness, for they – and only they – shall be filled. Woe to you, wicked and perverse generation; woe to you, foolish and abandoned people, who hate Christ's memory, and dread his second coming! Your fear is well grounded, if you will not now seek deliverance from the snare of the hunter; because "they that will be rich will fall into temptation and a snare, and into many foolish and hurtful lusts" (1 Timothy 6:9). In that day we shall not escape the dreadful sentence of condemnation, "Depart from Me, you cursed ones, into the everlasting fire" (Matthew 25:41). This is indeed a dreadful sentence indeed, and a hard saying! How much harder to bear than that other saying which we repeat daily in church, in memory of the Passion: "Whoever eats my flesh and drinks my blood has eternal life" (John 6:54). This means that whoever honors my death and puts his physical body on earth to death after my example (Colossians 3:5) shall have eternal life, even as the apostle says, "If we suffer, we shall also reign with Him" (2 Timothy 2:12). And yet even today there are many who turn away from these words and go away, saying by their action if not with their lips, "This is a hard saying; who can hear it?" (John 6:60). "A generation that did not put their heart right, and whose spirit does not hold steadfastly to God" (Psalm 78:8), but chooses instead to trust in uncertain riches, is disturbed at the very name of the Cross, and counts the memory of the Passion intolerable. How can people like this bear the burden of that fearful sentence, "Depart from me, you that are cursed, into everlasting fire, prepared for the devil and his angels"? "The person on whom that stone shall fall will be ground to powder" (Luke 20:18). Yet "the generation of the faithful shall be blessed" (Psalm 112:2), since, like the apostle, they work so that, whether they are present or absent, they may be found acceptable to the Lord (2 Corinthians 5:9). At the last day they too shall hear the Judge pronounce their reward, "Come, you who have been blessed by my Father, inherit the kingdom which has been prepared for you from the foundation of the world" (Matthew 25:34).

In that day those who have not put their hearts right will realize, too late, how easy is Christ's yoke, to which they would not bend their necks and how light his burden, in comparison with the pains they must then endure. O wretched slaves of Mammon, you cannot glory in the Cross of our Lord Jesus Christ while you trust in treasures laid up on earth. You cannot taste and see how gracious the Lord is, while you are hungering for gold. If you have not rejoiced at the thought of his coming, that day will be indeed a day of wrath to you.

But the believing soul longs and faints for God; she rests sweetly in the contemplation of Him. She glories in the reproach of the Cross, until the glory of his face shall be revealed. Like the Bride, the dove of Christ, that is covered with silver wings (Psalm 68:13), white with innocence and purity, she takes her rest in the thought of your abundant kindness, Lord Jesus. Above all, she longs for that day when in the joyful splendor of your saints, gleaming with the radiance of the Beatific Vision, her feathers shall be like gold, resplendent with the joy of your face.

Rightly then may she exult: "His left hand is under my head and His right hand embraces me." The left hand signifies the memory of that matchless love, which moved him to lay down his life for His friends; and the right hand is the Beatific Vision which he has promised to his own, and the delight they have in His presence. The Psalmist sings rapturously, "At your right hand there is pleasure for evermore" (Psalm 16:11). For this reason, we have good reason to interpret "the right hand" as that divine and divinizing joy of His presence. Similarly, "his left hand" signifies that wondrous love, which is never to be forgotten. Here the Bride rests her head until iniquity has passed away, for he holds her mind firmly, so that it is not turned away to consider earthly or fleshly desires. For the flesh wars against the spirit: "The corruptible body presses down the soul, and the earthly tabernacle weighs down the mind that reflects on many things" (Wisdom 9:15). What could result from the contemplation of compassion so marvelous and so undeserved, favor so free and so well attested, kindness so unexpected, clemency so unconquerable, grace so amazing – except that the soul should withdraw from all sinful desires, and reject all that is inconsistent with the love of God, and yield herself totally to heavenly things? No wonder the Bride, moved by the fragrance of these unctions, runs ahead swiftly, inflamed with love, yet still reckons herself as loving all too little in return for the love of the Bridegroom. And rightly, since it is no great matter that someone who is of dust should be totally consumed with love for that Majesty, who loved her first and which revealed itself as totally committed to saving her. For "God so loved the world that he gave his only-begotten Son, that whoever believes in him should not perish but have everlasting life" (John 3:16). This sets forth the Father's love. But "He hath poured out His soul unto death," was written of the Son (Isaiah 53:12). And of the Holy Spirit it is said, "The Comforter which is the Holy Spirit who the Father will send in my name, he will teach you all things, and bring to mind all the things I have said unto you" (John 14:26). It is clear, therefore, that God loves us with all his heart; for the Holy Trinity altogether loves us, if we may dare to speak in this way of the infinite and incomprehensible Godhead, who is essentially one.

Questions for Study

1   What reasons does Bernard give for loving God above all other?
2   At some points in this section, Bernard suggests that nothing can satisfy human longing other than God; at others, he seems to imply that knowing God merely heightens our appetite to have more of God. Can these two strands of thought be reconciled?
3   Bernard refers to the Christian believer as "the Bride" and "a dove." Why does he use these images? And what do they imply?

CHAPTER 26

Francis of Assisi (1182–1226)

Francis of Assisi was the son of Pietro di Bernadone, a wealthy cloth merchant in the Italian city of Assisi. His father was absent at his birth; although his mother named him Giovanni, his father had this altered to Francesco on his return. As a young man, he opted for a military career. In 1202 he took part in a war between Assisi and Perugia, was held prisoner for almost a year, and on his release fell seriously ill. After his recovery, he attempted to join the papal forces under Count Gentile against Frederick II in Apulia in late 1205; at Spoleto, about 40 kilometers from Assisi, however, he had a vision or dream that he should return to Assisi and await a call to a new kind of knighthood. Soon afterwards, he received a vision of the crucified Christ, and felt that he was being called to some special mission.

Francis of Assisi (1182–1226)

Basic description
Founder of the Franciscan Order.

Major work
Canticle of the Creatures.

Further studies
John R. H. Moorman, *St Francis of Assisi: Writings and Early Biographies*. London: SPCK, 1979.
Brother Ramon, SSF, *Franciscan Spirituality: Following Francis Today*. London: SPCK, 1994.

Among the experiences which surround his conversion, we may note the following: a vision of Christ while Francis prayed in a grotto near Assisi; an experience of poverty during a pilgrimage to Rome, where he mingled with the beggars before St. Peter's Basilica and begged alms; an incident in which he not only gave alms to a leper but also kissed his hand. One day at the ruined chapel of S. Damiano outside the gate of Assisi, he heard the crucifix above the altar command him: "Go, Francis, and repair my house which, as you see, is virtually in ruins." Taking this literally, he went home, gathered much of the cloth in his father's shop, and rode off to the nearby town of Foligno, where he sold both cloth and horse, before offering the money he had raised to the priest at S. Damiano.

As a result of his conversion, he renounced the wealth of his father, and took upon himself a life of poverty. In 1224, the imprints of the wounds of the crucified Christ (usually referred to as "the stigmata") appeared on his body. Francis's life and ministry were marked by poverty and simplicity, and a particular closeness to the natural world.

The issue of poverty was of particular importance in marking Francis and his followers off from the contemporary ecclesiastical world. Yet it should be noted that it was not simply external poverty which Francis sought, but the total denial of the self, an ideal which he found in Philippians 2:7.

This close affinity with the natural order is particularly important in relation to Franciscan spirituality. Francis considered all nature to be the mirror of God and a means by which the individual could draw close to God. This can be seen stated with especial clarity in the famous *Canticle of the Creatures*, which we shall consider below.

Text: The *Canticle of the Creatures*

This canticle represents an important affirmation of a positive attitude toward the creation, which is typical of Franciscan spirituality. The canticle is noted for its theology of providence, in which the benefit of each aspect of creation for humanity is identified. The most famous feature of the canticle is its use of the terms "brother" and "sister" to refer to various aspects of the created order. Traditional English translations of this familiar poem have been heavily influenced by the need to ensure rhyming. My prose translation of the original Italian ignores such considerations in order to convey the sense of the poem, and has retained the lines of the original. Note that the first 22 lines, dealing with nature, date from an earlier point than the final 11, which extend the analysis to the world of human experience.

> Most high, all-powerful and good Lord!
> To you are due the praises, the glory,
> the honor and every blessing,
> To you only, O highest one, are they due
> and no human being is worthy to speak of you.   5
>
> Be praised, my Lord, with all your creatures
> especially by brother sun
> by whom we are lightened every day
> for he is fair and radiant with great splendor
> and bears your likeness, O highest one.   10
>
> Be praised, my Lord, for sister moon and the stars,
> you have set them in heaven, precious, fair and bright.

Be praised, my Lord, by brother wind
and by air and cloud and sky and every weather
through whom you give life to all your creatures.   15

Be praised, my Lord, by sister water
for she is useful and humble and precious and chaste.

By praised, my Lord, by brother fire,
by him we are lightened at night
and he is fair and cheerful and sturdy and strong.   20

Be praised, my Lord, by our sister, mother earth,
she sustains and governs us
and brings forth many fruits and colored flowers and plants.

Be praised, my Lord, by those who have been pardoned by your love
and who bear infirmity and tribulation;   25
blessed are those who suffer them in peace
for by you, O highest one, they shall be crowned.

Be praised, my Lord, by our sister, physical death
from whom no one who lives can escape;
woe to those who die in mortal sin   30
but blessed are those who are found in your most holy will
for the second death can do them no harm.

May I bless and praise you, my Lord, and give you thanks
and serve you with great humility.

Questions for Study

1   One of the most distinctive features of the canticle is its use of the language of broth-
    erhood and sisterhood to refer to aspects of the created order, such as the sun and
    moon. Begin by identifying as many of these personifications as you can.
2   What is the effect of referring to the moon as "sister," and so forth? In what ways
    does it change our attitude to the created order?
3   The text begins by praising God, before moving on to celebrate the created order.
    How are these connected? In what way does Francis relate the praise of God with a
    survey of the creation?
4   Work through the first 22 lines of the canticle, noting the way in which each element
    of the creation is assigned a useful function. Why do you think Francis identified the
    utility of the wind, fire, water and so forth?

CHAPTER 27

Ancrene Wisse (ca. 1230)

While scholars have constantly praised the literary merits of this work of spiritual guid-ance, the fact remains that relatively little is known about the circumstances of its com-position. The work was written for a small group of anchoresses. An "anchoress" is someone who has chosen to withdraw from the world into an essentially solitary life. This serves to distinguish an anchorite (the male form of the term) or anchoress (the female form) from monks and nuns; for the latter, withdrawal from the world entailed entering into a religious community. An anchorite withdrew from the world – and from others. This definition, of course, could also apply to a hermit. What distinguishes the hermit from the anchorite is that the former lived a solitary yet mobile life; the anchorite lived a solitary life attached to one specific physical location. Julian of Norwich will serve us very well as an example of an anchoress.

The author of the work remains elusive. An excellent case has recently been made for the author being Brian of Lingen, a canon of Wigmore Abbey, and that the work was written for anchoresses based at Limebrook in Herefordshire. This conclusion rests on a close reading of the various manuscript versions of the work, and an expert knowledge of the local history of Lingen, Wigmore, and Limebrook. In the end, of course, this con-clusion must remain a hypothesis. However, there are excellent reasons for supposing that the broad lines of identification are correct. The dialect found in the first copies of the work seems to originate from the northern region of Herefordshire and the south-ern part of Shropshire.

The work is remarkable for its direct manner of address, the extensive use of verbal illustrations, and its lightness of touch. The section to be considered is taken from the third section of the work, and makes use of a comparison between the anchoress and birds to make some significant spiritual points.

Part Three

Birds and Anchorites: the Inner Feelings

My dear sisters, just as you guard your senses well on the outside, so above all things see that you are on the inside soft and mild and humble, sweet and fragrant-hearted and patient in the face of injury caused by things that are said to you and of deeds that are wrongly done to you, lest you should lose all. Against bitter anchoresses David speaks this verse: *Similis factus sum pellicano solitudinis, et cetera*[1] – "I am," he says, "like a pelican that lives on its own." The pelican is a bird so passionate and so wrathful that it often kills its own chicks in anger, when they annoy it, and then soon afterwards it becomes very sorry and makes very great lamentation and strikes itself with its beak, with which it previously killed its chicks, and draws blood from its breast, and with the blood brings back to life its chicks which had been killed. This bird, the pelican, is the passionate anchoress. Her chicks are her good works, which she often kills with the beak of sharp wrath. But when she has done so, let her do as the pelican does: regret it very soon and with her own beak peck her breast – that is, with confession from her mouth, with which she sinned and killed her good works, draw the blood of sin out from her breast – that is, from the heart which the soul's life is in. And in this way will her chicks which had been killed come back to life – that is, her good works. Blood signifies sin. For just as a bloodstained man is fearful and horrible in men's eyes, so is the sinner before the eye of God. In addition, no one can examine blood well before it has cooled. So it is with sin. While the heart is boiling within with anger, there is no right judgement; or while desire is hot towards any sin, you cannot then judge well what it is or what will come of it. But let desire pass, and you will be pleased – let the heat cool, as someone who wants to examine blood does, and you will rightly judge the sin foul and loathsome which seemed attractive to you, and that so much evil would have come of it if you had done it while the heat lasted that you will judge yourself mad when you had thoughts of doing it. This is true of each sin (and is why blood signifies it), and especially of anger: *Impedit ira animum ne possit cernere uerum*[2] – "Anger," it says, "while it lasts, so blinds the heart that it is unable to recognize the truth." *Maga quedam est, transformans naturam humanam*[3] – anger is a shape-changer, like the ones in stories, since it takes from a man his reason and completely alters how he is and changes him from a man and gives him the nature of a beast. An angry woman is a she-wolf; a man a wolf, or a lion, or a unicorn. All the time anger is in a woman's heart, though she recite versicles, says her hours, *Aues, Pater nosters*, she is only howling. Like one who has been turned into a she-wolf in God's eyes, she only has a she-wolf's voice in his sensitive ears. *Ira furor breuis est.*[4] Wrath is a madness – isn't an angry man mad? How does he look, how does he speak, how is his heart going on inside? What's his behaviour all like outside? He doesn't recognize any man – how's he a man then?

[1]   [I am become like to a pelican of the wilderness, etc. (Psalm 101:7)].
[2]   [Anger impedes the spirit so that it is not able to discern the truth (*Distichs of Cato* 2.4)].
[3]   [It is a sort of sorceress, transforming human nature].
[4]   [Anger is a brief madness (Horace, *Epistles* 1.2, 62)].

Est enim homo animal mansuetum natura.[1] Man is naturally mild. As soon as he loses mild-heartedness, he loses man's nature, and anger, the shape-changer, changes him into a beast, as I said earlier. And what if any anchoress, Jesus Christ's wife, is changed into a she-wolf? Isn't that a great sorrow? The only thing is quickly to throw off that rough pelt around the heart and with soft reconciliation make herself smooth and soft, as a woman's skin naturally is, for with that she-wolf's skin nothing that she does is pleasing to God.

Look, here are many remedies against anger, a great crowd of comforts and various helps. If people speak ill of you, think that you are earth: isn't earth trampled, isn't earth spat on? Even if people treated you in this way, they would be treating the earth right. If you bark back, you are dog-natured; if you sting back, you are snake-natured and not Christ's bride. Think – did he act like this? *Qui tanquam ouis ad occisionem ductus est et non aperuit os suum.*[2] After all the shameful torments that he endured during the long night before the Friday, he was taken in the morning to be hanged on the gibbet and have iron nails driven through his four limbs. But no more than a sheep, as the Holy Writ says, did he ever stir or speak.

Think again, in addition, what is a word but wind? Too weakly is she fortified whom a puff of wind, a word, can fell and throw into sin. And who will not be amazed at an anchoress felled by the wind? Or again, once more, does she not show that she is dust and an unstable thing, who with the wind of a few words is immediately blown down? That same puff from his mouth, if you cast it beneath you, would bear you up towards the bliss of heaven; but, as it is, our great madness is a matter of great astonishment. Understand what I am saying: St Andrew was able to endure the hard cross lifting him towards heaven and lovingly embraced it. Lawrence likewise endured the gridiron lifting him upwards with burning coals, St Stephen the stones that were thrown at him; and he received them gladly, and prayed for those who threw them at him on bended knees – and we are unable to endure the wind of a word bearing us towards heaven, but are enraged at those whom we should thank as the very ones who are doing us a great service, though it be against their will. *Impius uiuit pio uelit nolit.*[3] All that the wicked and evil person does for the sake of evil is all for the good of the good man – all is his gain and a preparation for bliss. Let him – and do it gladly – plait your crown. Think how the holy man in *Vitas Patrum* kissed and blessed the hand of the other person who had harmed him and said so fervently, kissing it eagerly, "Blessed for ever be this hand, for it has prepared for me the blisses of heaven." And you should say likewise of the hand that does you ill, and of the mouth also that speaks any ill of you, "Blessed be your mouth," say, "for you make of it a tool for preparing my crown. I am pleased for my good, and unhappy, though, for your evil, for you are doing me a benefit and harming yourself." If any man or any woman has spoken ill of you or done you ill, you should speak like this. But, as it is, it is a matter of great astonishment, if we consider well how God's saints endured wounds in their bodies and we are enraged if a wind blows

---

[1]   [For man is an animal gentle by nature].

[2]   [Who was led as a sheep to the slaughter and did not open his mouth (see Isaiah 53:7)].

[3]   [The wicked person lives willy-nilly for the good person].

on us a bit – and the wind wounds nothing except only the air. For neither may the wind – that is, the words that are said – wound you in your flesh, or defile your soul, though it blows on you, unless you make it do so yourself. *Bernardus: Quid irritaris, quid inflammaris ad uerbi flatum, qui nec carnem uulnerat nec inquinat mentem.*[1] You may well gather that there was there little fire of charity, which all flames up from Our Lord's love, little fire was there, if a puff could put it out; for where there is much fire, it grows with the wind.

Against ill done or ill said look here, lastly, the best remedy. Listen to this illustration: a man who lay in prison and owed a great ransom and who was quite unable to get out, unless to be hanged, before he had paid the ransom in full – would he not be very grateful to a man who threw at him a purse of pennies with which to buy himself out and free himself from suffering? Even if he threw it very hard against his heart, all the hurt would be forgotten because of the gladness. In this same way we are all in prison here and owe God great debts for sin. Therefore we cry to him in the *Pater noster, Et dimitte nobis debita nostra*[2] – "Lord," we say, "forgive us our debts, just as we forgive our debtors injury that is done us, either of word or of deed." That is our ransom, with which we should redeem ourselves and clear our debts to Our Lord – that is, our sins – since without clearance no one is taken up out of this prison who is not immediately hanged, either in purgatory or in the torment of hell. And Our Lord himself says, *Dimittite et dimittetur uobis*[3] – "Forgive and I forgive you," as though he said, "You are greatly in debt to me because of your sins, but if you want a good agreement, all that any man says ill of you or does ill to you I will accept against the debt that you owe me." Now, then, though something said strike very hard on your breast and, as it seems to you at first, hurt your heart, think as the prisoner would whom the other hurt badly with the purse and accept it gladly to clear yourself with it and think that he who sends it at you, though God may never thank him for having sent it, harms himself and profits you, if you are able to endure it. For as David says very well indeed, "God puts in his treasury the wicked and the evil so as to hire with them, as one does with treasure, those who fight well." *Ponens in thesauris abyssos. Glosa: Crudeles quibus donat milites suos.*[4]

Again, in addition, this bird, the pelican, has a second characteristic – that it is always thin, and so, as I said, David likens himself to it, in the character of an anchorite, in an anchorite's voice: *Similis factus sum pellicano solitudinis*[5] – "I am like a pelican that lives on its own." And an anchoress ought to speak in this way and be like a pelican in so far as it is thin: *Judith, clausa in cubiculo, ieiunabat omnibus diebus uite sue, et cetera*[6] – Judith, shut in, as it tells in her book, led a very hard life, fasted and wore haircloth. Judith shut in signifies the anchoress shut in, who ought to lead a hard life, as did the lady Judith, according to her ability, not like a pig stalled in a sty to fatten and get large for the stroke of the axe.

[1] [Bernard: Why are you irritated, why are you inflamed at the breath of a word, which neither wounds the flesh nor defiles the mind? (*Declamations . . . from the Sermons of St Bernard* 36.43)].
[2] [And forgive us our debts].
[3] [Forgive and you shall be forgiven (Luke 6:37)].
[4] [Laying up the depths in storehouses (Psalm 32:7). Gloss: The cruel, whom he gives to his soldiers].
[5] [I am become like to a pelican of the wilderness (Psalm 101:7)].
[6] [Judith, shut up in her chamber, fasted all the days of her life, etc. (Judith 8:5–6)].

There are two kinds of anchoress of which Our Lord speaks in the Gospel, false and true: *Vulpes foueas habent et uolucres celi nidos*[1] – that is, "Foxes have their holes and birds of heaven their nests." The foxes are false anchorites, as the fox is the falsest of beasts. "These," he says, "have holes who dig holes into the earth with earthly vices and drag into their holes all that they can lay hold of and seize." Thus hoarding anchoresses are likened by God in the Gospel to foxes. The fox is a greedy beast and ravenous as well, and the false anchoress drags into her hole and eats, as the fox does, both geese and hens; she has, like the fox, an innocent look at times, but is nevertheless full of guile. They make themselves out to be other than they are, like the fox, which is a hypocrite. They think to beguile God as they dupe simple men – and beguile themselves most. They yelp as the fox does and boast of their goodness wherever they dare and are able. They chatter about trivial things and become so very worldly that in the end their name stinks like the fox as he goes about. For if they do evil, worse is said of them.

These went into the anchor-house as Saul did into the hole, not as the good David did. They both went into the hole, Saul and David, as it tells in *Regum*.[2] But Saul went into it to do his dirt in it, as is done by many. Some unfortunate anchoresses go into the hole of the anchor-house to befoul the place and do more secretly in it fleshly filthinesses than they might if they were out in the world. For who has more leisure to do her wickednesses than the false anchoress? Thus Saul went into the cave to defile the place; but David went into it only to hide himself from Saul, who hated him and was seeking him to slay him. The good anchoress does likewise, whom Saul – that is, the fiend – hates and hunts. She goes in to hide herself from his sharp claws: she hides herself in her hole both from worldly men and worldly sins, and therefore she is spiritually David, who is strong against the devil, and her face is lovely in Our Lord's eyes. For this is what this word 'David' means in the Hebrew language. The false anchoress is Saul, in accordance with what his name means. *Saul: Abutens, siue Abusio*[3] – for 'Saul' in Hebrew is 'misusing' in English, and the false anchoress misuses the name of an anchoress and all that an anchoress does. The good anchoress is Judith, as we said before, who is shut up, as she was, and just as she did fasts, keeps vigils, labours and wears harsh clothing. She is one of the birds of which Our Lord speaks after the foxes, which do not dig holes downwards with their desires, as do the foxes – that is, false anchoresses – but have, like birds of heaven, set their nests high up, that is, their rest. True anchoresses are called birds, for they leave the earth – that is, love of all worldly things – and through yearning in heart for heavenly things fly upwards towards heaven. And though they fly high in a high and holy life, they nevertheless hold their heads low in mild humility, as a flying bird bows its head, consider all that they do well worth nothing and say, as Our Lord taught all his own, *Cum omnia benefeceritis, dicite: Serui inutiles sumus*[4] – "When you have done everything well," says Our Lord, "say that you are useless servants." Fly high and always hold your head low, nevertheless. The wings which bear them upwards, they are virtues which they must stir into good deeds as a bird when it wants to fly stirs its

---

[1]   [The foxes have holes, and the birds of heaven nests (Matthew 8:20 and Luke 9:58)].
[2]   [Kings (1 Kings 24)].
[3]   [Saul: Abusing, or Abuse].
[4]   [When you shall have done all things well, say: We are unprofitable servants (Luke 17:10)].

wings. Again, the true anchoresses, whom we are likening to birds (not we, though, but God), spread their wings and make crosses of themselves as a bird does when it flies – that is, in the thought of the heart and in the bitterness of the flesh bear God's cross.

Questions for Discussion

1 How many verbal illustrations or analogies can you identify in this text? What does this suggest about its author, and his audience?
2 What points does the writer make with reference to the pelican? How valid do you regard the arguments leading up to these points?
3 How does the author's advice serve to encourage his readers? How would it help them live out their lives in isolation and confinement?

CHAPTER 28

Thomas Aquinas (1224–1274)

Thomas d'Aquino – better known to the English-speaking world as "Thomas Aquinas" – was born in the castle at Roccasecca, in central Italy, in 1224. At about the age of five, Thomas was placed by his parents in the Benedictine monastery at Monte Cassino in order to further his education and secure his future. His uncle had been abbot of the monastery, and his family had similar hopes for Thomas. Following the outbreak of serious conflict at Monte Cassino between papal and imperial troops, Thomas went to study at Naples, where he came into contact with Dominicans. Attracted by what he found, he made the decision, in the face of violent opposition by his family, to become a Dominican in 1244. He then went north to study (1245–52) at Paris and Cologne under the great Dominican teacher and theologian Albertus Magnus ("Albert the Great").

From 1252 to 1259, Thomas taught at the Dominican *studium generale* (house of studies) in Paris; he became a master of theology in 1256. From 1259 to 1269 he was in Italy, attached to the papal court. A second Parisian period followed, 1269–72, after which he was assigned to Naples to head the Dominican *studium generale* there. In 1274, going north again to attend the Council of Lyon, Thomas fell ill and died in the Cistercian abbey of Fossanova on March 7 of that year.

Aquinas left behind him a series of massive theological and philosophical works, of which the greatest are his *Summa contra Gentiles* (1258–60) and the *Summa Theologiae* (1267–73). In addition to these, he also wrote commentaries on Aristotle, various biblical works, and the *Sentences* of Peter Lombard. He was one of those who endorsed the adoption of Aristotelianism as a means of lending academic rigor to Christian theology. Thomas's synthesis of natural and revealed knowledge, using Aristotle as a catlyst, did not meet with wholehearted acceptance. In 1277 a number of ideas associated with him were condemned by the Bishop of Paris. Thomas met with a warmer reception in his own order, and in 1309 his doctrine was prescribed for the Dominicans. In 1323, Thomas was canonized, and since that time his thought has enjoyed special favor. He was declared a Doctor of the Church in 1567. The revival of interest in Aquinas continued in the nineteenth century, with Leo XIII singling him out for special praise.

Thomas Aquinas (1224–1274)

Basic description
Leading scholastic theologian.

Major work
Summa Theologiae.

Major studies
F. C. Copleston, *Aquinas*. Harmondsworth: Penguin, 1955.
Brian Davies, *The Thought of Thomas Aquinas.* Oxford: Oxford University Press, 1992.

[handwritten margin note: Evidentialist approach.]

Text: *Summa Theologiae*

Aquinas may be regarded as the supreme representative of scholastic theology, which has had a considerable influence – not entirely positive in character, it must be added – on western Christian literature. Aquinas never finished this work. On December 6, 1273, he declared that he could write no longer. "All that I have written seems like straw to me," he said. It is possible that he may have had some sort of breakdown, perhaps brought on by overwork. He died on March 7, 1274. Even in its unfinished form, the *Summa Theologiae* is massive: it has 512 questions, 2,669 articles, and more than 10,000 objections and replies. In view of his influence, it is clearly important to include a short extract from his most influential work, the *Summa Theologiae*, in order to allow readers to gain a "feel" for its tone and approach. The section chosen for discussion is from the First Part of the work, question 1, article 9, which poses the question: "Whether Holy Scripture should use metaphors?" Here is Aquinas' response.

[handwritten margin note: Socratic method.]

[handwritten margin note: Objection]

Objection 1. It seems that Holy Scripture should not use metaphors. For that which is proper to the lowest science seems not to be appropriate to this science, which holds the highest place of all. But to proceed by the aid of various similitudes and figures is proper to poetry, the least of all the sciences. Therefore it is not fitting that this science should make use of such similitudes.

Objection 2. Further, this doctrine seems to be intended to make truth clear. Hence a reward is held out to those who manifest it: "They that explain me shall have life everlasting" (Sirach 24:31). But truth is obscured by such similitudes. Therefore, to put forward divine truths by likening them to physical things is not appropriate to this science.

Objection 3. Further, the higher creatures are, the nearer they approach to the divine likeness. If therefore any creature be taken to represent God, this representation ought chiefly to be taken from the higher creatures, and not from the lower; yet this is often found in the Scriptures.

On the contrary, It is written (Hosea 12:10): "I have multiplied visions, and I have used similitudes by the ministry of the prophets." But to put forward anything by means of similitudes is to use metaphors. Therefore this sacred science may use metaphors.

I answer that, It is appropriate for Holy Scripture to put forward divine and spiritual truths by means of comparisons with material things. For God provides for everything according to the capacity of its nature. Now it is natural to humanity to attain to intellectual truths through sensible objects, because all our knowledge originates from sense. Hence in Holy Scripture, spiritual truths are appropriately taught under the likeness of material things. This is what Dionysius says (*Heavenly Hierarchy*, i): "We cannot be enlightened by the divine rays unless they are hidden within the covering of many sacred veils." It is also appropriate for Holy Scripture, which is set forth to all without distinction of persons – "To the wise and to the unwise I am a debtor" (Rom. 1:14) – that spiritual truths be expounded by means of figures taken from physical things, in order that thereby even the simple who are unable by themselves to grasp intellectual things may be able to understand it.

Reply to Objection 1. Poetry makes use of metaphors to produce a representation, for it is natural to humanity to be pleased with representations. But sacred doctrine makes use of metaphors as both necessary and useful.

Reply to Objection 2. The ray of divine revelation is not extinguished by the sensible imagery wherewith it is veiled, as Dionysius says (*Heavenly Hierarchy*, i); and its truth remains to the extent that it does not allow the minds of those to whom the revelation has been made to rest in the metaphors, but raises them to the knowledge of truths; and through those to whom the revelation has been made others also may receive instruction in these matters. Hence those things that are taught metaphorically in one part of Scripture, are taught more explicitly in other parts and taught more openly. The very hiding of truth in figures is useful for the exercise of thoughtful minds and as a defense against the ridicule of the impious, according to the words "Give not that which is holy to dogs" (Mt. 7:6).

Reply to Objection 3. As Dionysius says (*Heavenly Hierarchy*, i), it is more fitting that divine truths should be expounded under the figure of less noble than of nobler bodies, and this for three reasons. Firstly, because thereby men's minds are the better preserved from error. For then it is clear that these things are not literal descriptions of divine truths, which might have been open to doubt had they been expressed under the figure of nobler bodies, especially for those who could think of nothing nobler than bodies. Secondly, because this is more befitting the knowledge of God that we have in this life. For what He is not is clearer to us than what He is. Therefore similitudes drawn from things farthest away from God form within us a truer estimate that God is above whatsoever we may say or think of Him. Thirdly, because thereby divine truths are the better hidden from the unworthy.

Questions for Discussion

1 Examine the structure of this article. Note how he sets out various points which have to be considered, both positively and negatively. He then presents his own resolution of these points, and sorts out the objections in its light. Compare the three objections which he notes with the three responses which are made at the end of the article. Do you think he succeeds in resolving them?

2 What is the relevance of this question for Christian literature? Identify how the use of metaphors and analogies has literary implications, and how Thomas's response legitimates their use in both theology and literature.

3 What does Aquinas mean by this statement: "Poetry makes use of metaphors to produce a representation, for it is natural to humanity to be pleased with representations"?

CHAPTER 29

Hugh of Balma (ca. 1290)

Tantalizingly little is known of this thirteenth-century Carthusian writer. While we know he was active during the thirteenth century, nothing is known for certain concerning the dates of his birth or death. Like many other Carthusian spiritual writers, the writer who is now known as "Hugh of Balma" chose to remain anonymous. It is thought that the author of the work *Viae Sion lugent* ("The Roads to Zion mourn") was Prior of the Charterhouse (that is, the Carthusian house) at Meyriat, located roughly halfway between Lyons and Geneva. The work has been spuriously attributed to a number of leading medieval spiritual writers, including Jean Gerson and Bonaventure. The work is known to have been written before 1297 (in that Guigo de Ponte, who died in 1296, refers to it). It is also clearly of Carthusian origins, in that there are important references to the Carthusians at several points. This, incidentally, made the attribution to Bonaventure – who was a Franciscan – highly problematic, and even led some early editors to "modify" these passages to make it appear as if they did indeed refer to the Franciscan rather than the Carthusian order.

Text: *The Roads to Zion*

The Roads to Zion was widely translated in the centuries following its appearance, and translations are known in a number of western European languages, including English, French, German, and Portuguese. Its many attractions include a clear statement of the classic "threefold path" of spiritual advancement through the *via purgativa* (the "way of cleansing," in which the soul is cleansed of sin); the *via illuminativa* (the "way of illumination," in which the soul is enlightened by rays of divine wisdom through meditation on Scripture and prayer); and the *via unitiva* (the "way of union," in which the soul is united with God). Hugh argues that it is essential to begin by confessing one's sins and meditating on Scripture. However, these can be thought of as supports which eventually can be dispensed with, once a certain critical stage has been reached. He uses the analogy of the construction of a stone bridge to make this point, as can be seen from the passage which follows.

This way to God is threefold; that is, it consists of a way of cleansing (*via purgativa*), in which the human mind is disposed so that it may discern true wisdom; a way of illumination (*via illuminativa*), in which the mind is set on fire as it reflects with the fire of love; and the way of unity (*via unitiva*) in which the mind is carried upward by God alone, and is led beyond all reason, understanding and intelligence. Now when a bridge is being built, it should be noted that the builders first erect a wooden framework, over which the solid stonework is assembled. Then, when this has been completed, the wooden framework which had been supporting the stonework is completely removed. In the same way, the human mind (though initially imperfect in love) begins to rise to the perfection of love through meditation until, strengthened by practice in the love which leads to unity, it is raised far beyond itself... Thus any new disciple may rise by stages to the perfection of this knowledge by zealous application of the way of cleansing. This is the way of novices or children. It begins with these words: "Righteousness and judgment are the preparation for your throne" (Psalm 88:15). After a short time (perhaps a month or so, as appropriate), the disciple may rise to love by reflection, surrounded by the radiance of divine illumination. If anyone should think that it is presumptuous that such a sinful soul should dare to ask Christ for the union of love, they should recall that there is no difficulty provided that they first kiss his feet by recalling their sins; then kiss his hand by recognizing his goodness to them; and finally, go on to kiss him on the mouth, desiring Christ and clinging to him through love alone... [This leads to a knowledge in which] all reason, knowledge and understanding fall away, and the affection soars upwards, guided by love and passing all human understanding, directing the mind only by the guidance of the union of love toward the one who is the source of all goodness.

Questions for Discussion

1 What, according to Hugh, are the three stages in the spiritual life? How does he characterize them?

2 Pay careful attention to the bridge analogy. Try to visualize the process of constructing a stone bridge. The basic analogy presupposes that the bridge is an arch, held in place by a coping-stone. Until that stone is in place, the stonework cannot support itself – hence the need for the wooden framework to support it until this crucial stage is reached. Once you can visualize the analogy, identify what its component parts are meant to signify. According to Hugh, what does the wooden framework represent? And the stonework?

3 Hugh uses the analogy of three types of kiss to illustrate the "threefold path." Why does he use the analogy of a kiss in the first place? How do the types of kiss help illustrate the points in question?

CHAPTER 30

Dante Alighieri (1265–1321)

Dante was born into a well-established family in the city of Florence, which was at that time an independent city state, consciously modeling itself on the great city states of the classical period. We know virtually nothing concerning the first thirty years of his life; it is, however, clear that he established a reputation as a poet during this time. One of the most significant works of this early period in his life was *La Vita Nuova* ("The New Life"), which can be seen as a work in the tradition of "courtly love," focusing on the theme of unrequited love for a woman who lay beyond the reach of her admirers.

It is at this point that we need to introduce the figure of Beatrice Portinari (1266–90), a member of the Portinara family who went on to marry into the Bardi family. She died in 1290, at the age of 24. Dante tells his readers that he first saw her and fell in love with Beatrice when he was a mere nine years of age, but that this love came to dominate his thoughts and passions at the age of eighteen. His love for her could never be requited, in that the Dante family was considerably less important and wealthy than either the Portinara or Bardi dynasties. Beatrice features prominently in *La Vita Nuova*, and will later reappear in the *Divine Comedy*.

Beatrice's death in 1290 led Dante to turn his attention from romantic poetry to the world of philosophy and theology, and become embroiled in the Machiavellian world of Florentine politics. Florence had been severely shaken by a political crisis in 1293, which had seen the traditional power of the established families shaken by a rising mercantile class. Alongside this tension between established families and the rising middle classes there remained serious tensions between two such families – the Guelfs and Ghibellines – compounded by divisions within the Guelfs, which led to acrimonious infighting between sections of that family. In such a complex and politically unstable situation, it was easy to take a wrong step. To cut a long story short, Dante was unwise enough to ally himself with the wrong faction within the Guelf family. Realizing that his situation was untenable, he fled the city in October 1301. He was initially exiled and then condemned to death in his absence by the Florentine courts.

Exile was an established way of life in the world of the Italian city states, and Dante would hardly have been alone in his situation. Although it is virtually impossible to be sure what happened to Dante after his departure from Florence in 1301, it is entirely possible that he was able to secure some kind of patronage from the Ghibelline family in another part of Italy, away from his native Tuscany. What we do know is that his exile from Tuscany was of momentous importance to his understanding of his own destiny, and that he regarded it as a turning point in his life. It was at this stage in his life that he conceived and began to write the major work which we now know as the *Divine Comedy*. Dante died at Ravenna in 1321.

The *Divine Comedy*, a vernacular poem in 100 cantos (more than 14,000 lines), was composed in exile. It is the tale of the poet's journey through Hell and Purgatory (guided by Virgil) and through Heaven (guided by Beatrice, to whom the poem is a memorial). Written in a complex pentameter form known as *terza rima*, it is a magnificent synthesis of the medieval outlook, picturing a changeless universe ordered by God. Through it, Dante established his native Tuscan as the literary language of Italy. It must be noted that the title is misleading to English readers, in that the term "Comedy" implies something amusing or funny. The Italian term *Commedia* is better translated as "drama." The term "divine" appears to have been added by a Venetian publisher at a later stage.

Dante Alighieri (1265–1321)

Basic description
Italian poet and philosopher.

Major work
The Divine Comedy.

Editions of works
Dante's Lyric Poetry, ed. K. Foster and P. Boyde, 2 vols. Oxford: Clarendon Press, 1967.

Major studies
Edward Moore, *Studies in Dante*, 4 vols. Oxford: Clarendon Press, 1896–1917.
Jeremy Tambling, *Dante and Difference: Writing in the "Commedia."* Cambridge: Cambridge University Press, 1988.

The *Divine Comedy* takes the form of three major interconnected poems, respectively entitled *Inferno* ("Hell"), *Purgatorio* ("Purgatory"), and *Paradiso* ("Paradise"). The work makes substantial use of the leading themes of Christian theology and spirituality, while at the same time including comment on contemporary political and social events. The poem describes a journey which takes place in Holy Week 1300 – before Dante's exile from Florence. From the substantial number of clues in the text, it can be worked out that the journey begins at nightfall on Good Friday. After entering Hell, Dante journeys downwards for an entire day, before beginning his ascent toward Purgatory. After climbing Mount Purgatory, Dante rises further until he eventually enters into the presence of God.

Throughout the journey, Dante is accompanied by guides. The first guide is Virgil, the great Roman poet who wrote the *Aeneid*. It is widely thought that Dante uses Virgil as a symbol of classic learning and human reason. As they draw close to the peak of Mount Purgatory, Virgil falls behind, and Dante finds himself in the company of Beatrice, who leads him through the outer circles of heaven. Finally, he is joined by Bernard of Clairvaux, who leads Dante into the presence of God.

The structure of the poem is immensely intricate, and it can be read at a number of levels. It can, for example, be read as a commentary on medieval Italian politics, particularly the intricacies of Florentine politics over the period 1300–4; or it can be seen as a poetic guide to Christian beliefs concerning the afterlife. More fundamentally, it can be read as a journey of self-discovery and spiritual enlightenment, in which the poet finally discovers and encounters his heart's desire.

The *Divine Comedy* is notoriously difficult to translate into English, on account of its complex rhyme. *Terza rima* takes the form of a series of tercets in which the rhymes interlock (ABA; BCB; CDC; and so forth). To illustrate this, we shall consider the first four sets of three-line couplets (each of which is often referred to as a *Terzina*) in *Inferno*. Notice the rhyming pattern, which has been indicated with upper-case letters.

Nel mezzo del cammin di nostra vita	A
mi ritrovai per una selva oscura	B
ché la diritta via era smarrita.	A
Ah quanto a dir qual era è cosa dura	B
esta selva selvaggia e aspra e forte	C
che nel pensier rinova la paura!	B
Tant'è amara che poco è più morte;	C
ma per trattar del ben ch'io vi trovai,	D
dirò de l'altre cose ch'i' v'ho scorte.	C
Io non so ben ridir com'io v'intrai,	D
tant'era pieno di sonno a quel punto	E
che la verace via abbandonai.	D

It is exceptionally difficult to retain this pattern of rhyme in English translation, with the result that many translations make no attempt to retain it. The translation by Dorothy L. Sayers is widely regarded as among the best to retain the *terza rima*; the translation presented in what follows is by the nineteenth-century American scholar and poet Henry Wadsworth Longfellow (1807–82).

Text: *Inferno*

The Prologue to *Inferno* sets the scene for the entire drama. Dante finds himself lost in a dark wood at the foot of a hill, exhausted by his journey thus far. He is confronted by three wild animals, which terrify him:

1 a leopard (which Longfellow translates as "panther"), which is widely taken to be a symbol of lust;
2 a lion, which symbolizes pride;
3 a she-wolf, a symbol of greed and acquisitiveness.

These animals threaten to overwhelm him. However, he is rescued from his plight by Virgil. Virgil goes on to inform Dante that there is no way that he will be able to face up to the wolf until the savior comes; in the meantime, there is another possibility of salvation, which leads through Hell. Our extract, however, ends with the encounter with Virgil (note that Longfellow renders this as "Virgilius").

> Midway upon the journey of our life
>   I found myself within a forest dark,
> For the straightforward pathway had been lost.
>   Ah me! how hard a thing it is to say
>   What was this forest savage, rough, and stern, 5
> Which in the very thought renews the fear.
>   So bitter is it, death is little more;
>   But of the good to treat, which there I found,
> Speak will I of the other things I saw there.
>   I cannot well repeat how there I entered, 10
>   So full was I of slumber at the moment
> In which I had abandoned the true way.
>   But after I had reached a mountain's foot,
>   At that point where the valley terminated,
> Which had with consternation pierced my heart, 15
>   Upward I looked, and I beheld its shoulders,
>   Vested already with that planet's rays
> Which leadeth others right by every road.
>   Then was the fear a little quieted
>   That in my heart's lake had endured throughout 20
> The night, which I had passed so piteously.
>   And even as he, who, with distressful breath,
>   Forth issued from the sea upon the shore,
> Turns to the water perilous and gazes;
>   So did my soul, that still was fleeing onward, 25
>   Turn itself back to re-behold the pass
> Which never yet a living person left.
>   After my weary body I had rested,
>   The way resumed I on the desert slope,
> So that the firm foot ever was the lower. 30
>   And lo! almost where the ascent began,
>   A panther light and swift exceedingly,
> Which with a spotted skin was covered o'er!
>   And never moved she from before my face,
>   Nay, rather did impede so much my way, 35
> That many times I to return had turned.
>   The time was the beginning of the morning,
>   And up the sun was mounting with those stars
> That with him were, what time the Love Divine

At first in motion set those beauteous things;   40
   So were to me occasion of good hope,
The variegated skin of that wild beast,
   The hour of time, and the delicious season;
   But not so much, that did not give me fear
A lion's aspect which appeared to me.   45
   He seemed as if against me he were coming
   With head uplifted, and with ravenous hunger,
So that it seemed the air was afraid of him;
   And a she-wolf, that with all hungerings
   Seemed to be laden in her meagreness,   50
And many folk has caused to live forlorn!
   She brought upon me so much heaviness,
   With the affright that from her aspect came,
That I the hope relinquished of the height.
   And as he is who willingly acquires,   55
   And the time comes that causes him to lose,
Who weeps in all his thoughts and is despondent,
   E'en such made me that beast withouten peace,
   Which, coming on against me by degrees
Thrust me back thither where the sun is silent.   60
   While I was rushing downward to the lowland,
   Before mine eyes did one present himself,
Who seemed from long-continued silence hoarse.
   When I beheld him in the desert vast,
   'Have pity on me,' unto him I cried,   65
'Whiche'er thou art, or shade or real man!'
   He answered me: 'Not man; man once I was,
   And both my parents were of Lombardy,
And Mantuans by country both of them.
   "Sub Julio" was I born, though it was late,   70
   And lived at Rome under the good Augustus,
During the time of false and lying gods.
   A poet was I, and I sang that just
   Son of Anchises, who came forth from Troy,
After that Ilion the superb was burned.   75
   But thou, why goest thou back to such annoyance?
   Why climb'st thou not the Mount Delectable,
Which is the source and cause of every joy?'
   'Now, art thou that Virgilius and that fountain
   Which spreads abroad so wide a river of speech?'   80
I made response to him with bashful forehead.
   'O, of the other poets honour and light,
   Avail me the long study and great love
That have impelled me to explore thy volume!

Questions for Discussion

1   The first three lines are of immense importance. What does the poet mean when he writes of being "midway upon the journey of our life"? Is this a mid-life crisis? Or does it refer to the date of composition of the poem? Or some events in the poet's life? Or is there some mystical meaning?

2   The poet speaks of finding himself "within a forest dark." What does the forest represent? And how is this image developed by his following statement, in which he declares that he has lost "the straightforward pathway"?

3   How does the remainder of this part of the poem develop the ideas and imagery of its opening lines?

CHAPTER 31

Ludolf of Saxony (ca. 1300–1378)

The writer who goes by this, and other, names is a somewhat enigmatic figure, of whom relatively little is known. He is also referred to as "Ludolf the Carthusian," and the German name "Ludolf" is often spelled in its Latinized forms as "Ludolphus" or "Ludolph." Ludolf is known to have entered the Order of Preachers and gained a qualification in theology before joining the Carthusians at Strasbourg in 1340. In 1343, he moved to the Carthusian house at Coblenz, becoming its Prior. However, he does not appear to have been particularly enthusiastic for the responsibilities of this office, and in 1348 he resumed his life as an ordinary monk. The remainder of his life was spent in the cities of Mainz and Strasbourg.

Ludolf of Saxony (ca. 1300–1378)

Basic description
Fourteenth-century Carthusian spiritual writer.

Major work
Vita Jesu Christi redemptoris nostri ("The life of Jesus Christ our redeemer").

Further studies
M. I. Bodenstedt, The Vita Christi of Ludolphus the Carthusian. Washington, D.C.: Catholic University of America, 1955.
M. I. Bodenstedt, Praying the life of Christ. Salzburg: James Hogg, 1973.

Ludolf is noted for one work, which has had a substantial influence, both direct and indirect, on the way in which western Christians read the gospels as literature. While many scholars would argue that Ludolf's Vita Christi ("Life of Christ") is a work of literature in its own right, its importance can be more properly located in the manner in which it invites its readers to approach other pieces of Christian literature, supremely the gospels.

Text: *The Life of Christ*

Ludolf is remembered supremely for his *Vita Christi* ("The life of Christ"), which was first published at Cologne in 1474. The work is based largely on an earlier work by Michael de Massa (died 1337), which took the form of a life of Christ based on a number of highly-focused meditations. Ludolf's *Vita Christi* takes the form of an extended meditation on the life of Christ, interspersed with prayers and citations from earlier writers. Such compilations of earlier sayings or anecdotes were popular in the late Middle Ages, and were widely used both for personal devotion and as source-books for preaching. In this work, Ludolf sets out his intention to "recount things according to certain imaginative representations" so that his readers may "make themselves present for those things which Jesus did or said." The process involves the use of the imagination to construct a vivid and realistic mental image of the biblical scene. The important thing here is the *immediacy* with which the reader may represent the things that Jesus said or did.

Three key phrases may be noted in this passage: Ludolf asks his readers to enter into the gospel narrative "with the whole affective power of your mind, with loving care, with lingering delight." Each of these phrases is of considerable importance, as it encourages *a new way of reading the Bible*. One of Ludolf's concerns is to allow his readers to set distractions to one side, and focus on the reading of biblical passages relating to the life of Christ. He wants them to slow down and linger over the events described. His emphasis on "entering into" the scene, and using the "affective power" of the mind to allow his readers to experience the passages as immediate, direct and present (rather than distant and past). Notice also how this approach has another effect: *it slows down the reading process*. It takes much more time to enter into the passage in this way than it does simply to read it. The result – as Ludolf intends – is that readers of the gospels will "linger" over its passages, taking longer over it than they otherwise might, and thus gain more from it.

Draw close with a devout heart to the one who comes down from the bosom of the Father to the Virgin's womb. In pure faith be there with the angel, like another witness, at the moment of the holy conception, and rejoice with the Virgin Mother now with child for you. Be present at his birth and circumcision, like a faithful guardian, with St. Joseph. Go with the Wise Men to Bethlehem and adore the little king. Help his parents carry the child and present him in the Temple. Alongside the apostles, accompany the Good Shepherd as he performs his miracles. With his blessed mother and St. John, be there at his death, to have compassion on him and to grieve with him. Touch his body with a kind of devout curiosity, handling one by one the wounds of your Saviour who has died for you. With Mary Magdalene seek the risen Christ until you are found worthy to find him. Look with wonder at his ascent into heaven as though you were standing among his disciples on the Mount of Olives. Take your place with the apostles as they gather together; hide yourself away from other things so that you may be found worthy to be clothed from on high with the power of the Holy Spirit. If you want to draw fruit from these mysteries, you must offer yourself as present to what was said and done through our Lord Jesus Christ with the whole affective power of your mind, with loving care, with lingering delight, thus laying aside all other worries and care. Hear and see these things being narrated, as though you were hearing with your own ears and seeing with your own eyes, for these things are most sweet to him who thinks on them with desire, and even more so to him who tastes them. And although many of these are narrated as past events, you must meditate them all as though they were happening in the present moment, because in this way you will certainly taste a greater sweetness. Read then of what has been done as though they were happening now. Bring before your eyes past actions as though they were present. Then you will feel how full of wisdom and delight they are.

Questions for Study

1   Note the way in which Ludolf is concerned to draw his readers into the life of Christ. In what ways does he do this? How might this change the way in which his readers interact with the gospels?

2   Ludolf identifies a number of episodes in the life of Christ which he regards as being of particular importance, and links these specifically with certain individuals who were present on that occasion. Make out a list of the occasions and the witnesses: for example, the circumcision is witnessed by Joseph, and so forth. You will also find it helpful to identify the biblical passages to which he alludes.

3   Now note the way in which Ludolf draws us into the narrative. He does not simply recount what happened; he asks us to do things which draw us into the narrative. In each of the episodes which Ludolf describes, identify what it is he asks you to do. For example, he asks you to help Mary and Joseph carry the baby Jesus to the Temple. Notice how Ludolf portrays you, the reader, as an active participant in the events which are being described. You are to *project yourself* into the action.

4   Read the following sentence again, and try to summarize in your own words the approach that Ludolf wants you to adopt when reading the gospels. "If you want to draw fruit from these mysteries, you must offer yourself as present to what was said and done through our Lord Jesus Christ with the whole affective power of your mind, with loving care, with lingering delight, thus laying aside all other worries and care."

CHAPTER 32

The Cloud of Unknowing
(ca. 1350)

written by cloistered monk. (14)

The fourteenth century is rightly seen as representing a high point in English spiritual writing. One of the most remarkable spiritual works to have been written during this century is *The Cloud of Unknowing*. The work has often been ascribed to Walter Hilton, but is more likely to have been written by someone contemporary with Hilton. Unfortunately, nothing is reliably known of the author of this work, beyond the fact that he was a cloistered monk devoted to the contemplative life. The work can, however, be read with great profit without the need to know the identity of its author.

The major influence on the work is the anti-intellectualism of Dionysius the Pseudo-Areopagite, which stresses that God simply cannot be apprehended by the human intellect during the present life. For the medieval mystical traditions which converge in this important work, the Christian soul meets God in a "cloud of unknowing," a divine darkness of ignorance. This encounter with God is thus beyond all knowing and beyond all experiencing.

Although these ideas can be found in the works of Dionysius, there is a substantial body of evidence which suggests that they were mediated to an English readership through the writings of Thomas Gallus (died 1246), who published glosses on two major works of Dionysius – *The Celestial Hierarchy* and *On Mystical Theology*. These works offered more than an explanation of some of the more difficult ideas found in Dionysius' writings; they offered an interpretation of some of his leading themes, which occasionally represent significant new departures in thought. For example, Thomas links Dionysius' emphasis on mysticism with the notion that the deepest aspect of the human personality is a non-intellectual mystical faculty by which God may be apprehended in a non-rational manner. This idea was developed by the author of the *Cloud*, and may be regarded as one of the most important themes in the work.

The fundamental theme of the *Cloud* is that God cannot be grasped by the human intellect. There is always a "cloud of unknowing" between God and humanity. While this cloud cannot be pierced by human reason, there is – according to the *Cloud* – another way. The cloud of unknowing may be penetrated by arrows of love. There is no other way.

In addition to its obvious spiritual and theological importance, the work should be recognized as a significant piece of literature in its own right. The work offers sharp and perceptive observations of human foibles, which suggest that its author had access to ample sources of human company. He complains about "giggling girls and japing jugglers," and people who are so lacking in self-control that they "can neither sit still, stand still, nor lie still, unless they be either wagging with their feet or else somewhat doing with their hands." Part of the joy of reading this work is to note its juxtaposition of complex and sophisticated spiritual notions alongside shrewd observation of the quirks of everyday life.

The section chosen for inclusion here is chapters 17–24, which set out the importance of repose and love in the spiritual life. In many ways, they can be seen as setting the tone of this important work, and allow access to some of its leading ideas in a simple manner. Before beginning to engage with the text, read the following biblical narrative as a lead-in to the first of these chapters.

> Now as they went on their way, [Jesus] entered a village; and a woman named Martha received him into her house. And she had a sister called Mary, who sat at the Lord's feet and listened to his teaching. But Martha was distracted with much serving; and she went to him and said, "Lord, do you not care that my sister has left me to serve alone? Tell her then to help me." But the Lord answered her, "Martha, Martha, you are anxious and troubled about many things; one thing is needful. Mary has chosen the good portion, which shall not be taken away from her." (Luke 10:38–42) — *Sit and listen to Christ*

What does this mean? Well, read on, and find out what the *Cloud* author has to say on this matter.

Here Beginneth The Seventeenth Chapter

That a very contemplative list not meddle him with active life, nor of anything that is done or spoken about him, nor yet to answer to his blamers in excusing of himself.

IN the gospel of Saint Luke it is written, that when our Lord was in the house of Martha her sister, all the time that Martha made her busy about the dighting of His meat, Mary her sister sat at His feet. And in hearing of His word she beheld not to the business of her sister, although her business was full good and full holy, for truly it is the first part of active life; nor yet to the preciousness of His blessed body, nor to the sweet voice and the words of His manhood, although it is better and holier, for it is the second part of active life and the first of contemplative life.

But to the sovereignest wisdom of His Godhead lapped in the dark words of His manhood, thither beheld she with all the love of her heart. For from thence she would not remove, for nothing that she saw nor heard spoken nor done about her; but sat full still in her body, with many a sweet privy and a listy love pressed upon that high cloud of unknowing betwixt her and her God. For one thing I tell thee, that there was never yet pure creature in this life, nor never yet shall be, so high rav-

As Mary sits at Jesus' feet she presses upon the cloud of unknowing.

ished in contemplation and love of the Godhead, that there is not evermore a high
and a wonderful cloud of unknowing betwixt him and his God. In this cloud it was
that Mary was occupied with many a privy love pressed. And why? Because it was
the best and the holiest part of contemplation that may be in this life, and from this
part her list not remove for nothing. Insomuch, that when her sister Martha complained to our Lord of her, and bade Him bid her sister rise and help her and let her
not so work and travail by herself, she sat full still and answered not with one word,
nor shewed not as much as a grumbling gesture against her sister for any plaint that
she could make. And no wonder: for why, she had another work to do that Martha
wist not of. And therefore she had no leisure to listen to her, nor to answer her at
her plaint. _ *Mary not angry with Martha for complaining*

Lo! friend, all these works, these words, and these gestures, that were shewed
betwixt our Lord and these two sisters, be set in ensample of all actives [ed.: as an
example of the active Christian life] and all contemplatives that have been since in
Holy Church, and shall be to the day of doom. For by Mary is understood all contemplatives; for they should conform their living after hers. And by Martha, actives
on the same manner; and for the same reason in likeness.

Here Beginneth The Eighteenth Chapter

How that yet unto this day all actives complain of contemplatives as Martha did of Mary.
Of the which complaining ignorance is the cause.

AND right as Martha complained then on Mary her sister, right so yet unto this day
all actives complain of contemplatives. For an there be a man or a woman in any
company of this world, what company soever it be, religious or secular – I out-take
none – the which man or woman, whichever that it be, feeleth him stirred through
grace and by counsel to forsake all outward business, and for to set him fully for to
live contemplative life after their cunning and their conscience, their counsel according; as fast, their own brethren and their sisters, and all their next friends, with many
other that know not their stirrings nor that manner of living that they set them to,
with a great complaining spirit shall rise upon them, and say sharply unto them that
it is nought that they do. And as fast they will reckon up many false tales, and many
true also, of falling of men and women that have given them to such life before: and
never a good tale of them that stood.

I grant that many fall and have fallen of them that have in likeness forsaken the
world. And where they should have become God's servants and His contemplatives,
because that they would not rule them by true ghostly counsel they have become
the devil's servants and his contemplatives; and turned either to hypocrites or to
heretics, or fallen into frenzies and many other mischiefs, in slander of Holy Church.
Of the which I leave to speak at this time, for troubling of our matter. But nevertheless here after when God vouchsafeth and if need be, men may see some of the
conditions and the cause of their failings. And therefore no more of them at this
time; but forth of our matter.

Which is superior?

Here Beginneth The Nineteenth Chapter

A short excusation of him that made this book teaching how all contemplatives should have all actives fully excused of their complaining words and deeds.

SOME might think that I do little worship to Martha, that special saint, for I liken her words of complaining of her sister unto these worldly men's words, or theirs unto hers: and truly I mean no unworship to her nor to them. And God forbid that I should in this work say anything that might be taken in condemnation of any of the servants of God in any degree, and namely of His special saint. For me thinketh that she should be full well had excused of her plaint, taking regard to the time and the manner that she said it in. For that that she said, her unknowing was the cause. And no wonder though she knew not at that time how Mary was occupied; for I trow that before she had little heard of such perfection. And also that she said, it was but courteously and in few words: and therefore she should always be had excused.

And so me thinketh that these worldly living men and women of active life should also full well be had excused of their complaining words touched before, although they say rudely that they say; having beholding to their ignorance. For why? Right as Martha wist full little what Mary her sister did when she complained of her to our Lord; right so on the same manner these folk nowadays wot full little, or else nought, what these young disciples of God mean, when they set them from the business of this world, and draw them to be God's special servants in holiness and rightfulness of spirit. And if they wist truly, I daresay that they would neither do nor say as they say. And therefore me thinketh always that they should be had excused: for why, they know no better living than is that they live in themselves. And also when I think on mine innumerable defaults, the which I have made myself before this time in words and deeds for default of knowing, me thinketh then if I would be had excused of God for mine ignorant defaults, that I should charitably and piteously have other men's ignorant words and deeds always excused. And surely else, do I not to others as I would they did to me.

Here Beginneth The Twentieth Chapter

How Almighty God will goodly answer for all those that for the excusing of themselves list not leave their business about the love of Him.

AND therefore me thinketh, that they that set them to be contemplatives should not only have active men excused of their complaining words, but also me thinketh that they should be so occupied in spirit that they should take little heed or none what men did or said about them. Thus did Mary, our example of all, when Martha her sister complained to our Lord: and if we will truly do thus our Lord will do now for us as He did then for Mary.

And how was that? Surely thus. Our lovely Lord Jesus Christ, unto whom no privy thing is hid, although He was required of Martha as doomsman for to bid Mary rise and help her to serve Him; nevertheless yet, for He perceived that Mary was fervently occupied in spirit about the love of His Godhead, therefore courteously and as it was seemly for Him to do by the way of reason, He answered for her, that for the excusing of herself list not leave the love of Him. And how answered He? Surely not only as doomsman, as He was of Martha appealed: but as an advocate lawfully defended her that Him loved, and said, "Martha, Martha!" Twice for speed He named her name; for He would that she heard Him and took heed to His words. "Thou art full busy," He said, "and troubled about many things." For they that be actives behove always to be busied and travailed about many diverse things, the which them falleth, first for to have to their own use, and sithen in deeds of mercy to their even-Christian, as charity asketh. And this He said unto Martha, for He would let her wit that her business was good and profitable to the health of her soul. But for this, that she should not think that it were the best work of all that man might do, therefore He added and said: "But one thing is necessary."

And what is that one thing? Surely that God be loved and praised by Himself, above all other business bodily or ghostly that man may do. And for this, that Martha should not think that she might both love God and praise Him above all other business bodily or ghostly, and also thereto to be busy about the necessaries of this life: therefore to deliver her of doubt that she might not both serve God in bodily business and ghostly together perfectly – imperfectly she may, but not perfectly – He added and said, that Mary had chosen the best part; the which should never be taken from her. For why, that perfect stirring of love that beginneth here is even in number with that that shall last without end in the bliss of heaven, for all it is but one.

Here Beginneth The One And Twentieth Chapter

The true exposition of this gospel word, "Mary hath chosen the best part."

WHAT meaneth this; Mary hath chosen the best? Wheresoever the best is set or named, it asketh before it these two things – a good, and a better; so that it be the best, and the third in number. But which be these three good things, of the which Mary chose the best? Three lives be they not, for Holy Church maketh remembrance but of two, active life and contemplative life; the which two lives be privily understood in the story of this gospel by these two sisters Martha and Mary – by Martha active, by Mary contemplative. Without one of these two lives may no man be safe, and where no more be but two, may no man choose the best.

But although there be but two lives, nevertheless yet in these two lives be three parts, each one better than the other. The which three, each one by itself, be specially set in their places before in this writing. For as it is said before, the first part standeth in good and honest bodily works of mercy and of charity; and this is the first degree of active life, as it is said before. The second part of these two lives lieth in good ghostly meditations of a man's own wretchedness, the Passion of Christ, and of the joys of heaven. The first part is good, and this part is the better; for this is the second degree of active life and the first of contemplative life. In this part is contemplative life and active life coupled together in ghostly kinship, and made sisters at the ensample of Martha and Mary. Thus high may an active come to contemplation; and no higher, but if it be full seldom and by a special grace. Thus low may a contemplative come towards active life; and no lower, but if it be full seldom and in great need.

The third part of these two lives hangeth in this dark cloud of unknowing, with many a privy love pressed to God by Himself. The first part is good, the second is better, but the third is best of all. This is the "best part" of Mary. And therefore it is plainly to wit, that our Lord said not, Mary hath chosen the best *life*; for there be no more lives but two, and of two may no man choose the best. But of these two lives Mary hath chosen, He said, the best *part*; the which shall never be taken from her. The first part and the second, although they be both good and holy, yet they end with this life. For in the tother life shall be no need as now to use the works of mercy, nor to weep for our wretchedness, nor for the Passion of Christ. For then shall none be able to hunger nor thirst as now, nor die for cold, nor be sick, nor houseless, nor in prison; nor yet need burial, for then shall none be able to die. But the third part that Mary chose, choose who by grace is called to choose: or, if I soothlier shall say, whoso is chosen thereto of God. Let him lustily incline thereto, for that shall never be taken away: for if it begin here, it shall last without end.

And therefore let the voice of our Lord cry on these actives, as if He said thus now for us unto them, as He did then for Mary to Martha, "Martha, Martha!" – "Actives, actives! make you as busy as ye can in the first part and in the second, now in the one and now in the tother: and, if you list right well and feel you disposed, in both two bodily. And meddle you not of contemplatives. Ye wot not what them aileth: let them sit in their rest and in their play, with the third and the best part of Mary."

Here Beginneth The Two And Twentieth Chapter

Of the wonderful love that Christ had to man in person of all sinners truly turned and called to the grace of contemplation.

SWEET was that love betwixt our Lord and Mary. Much love had she to Him. Much more had He to her. For whoso would utterly behold all the behaviour that was betwixt Him and her, not as a trifler may tell, but as the story of the gospel will witness – the which on nowise may be false – he should find that she was so heartily set for to love Him, that nothing beneath Him might comfort her, nor yet hold her heart from Him. This is she, that same Mary, that when she sought Him at the sepulchre with weeping cheer would not be comforted of angels. For when they spake unto her so sweetly and so lovely and said, "Weep not, Mary; for why, our Lord whom thou seekest is risen, and thou shalt have Him, and see Him live full fair amongst His disciples in Galilee as He hight," she would not cease for them. For why? Her thought that whoso sought verily the King of Angels, them list not cease for angels.

And what more? Surely whoso will look verily in the story of the gospel, he shall find many wonderful points of perfect love written of her to our ensample, and as even according to the work of this writing, as if they had been set and written there-fore; and surely so were they, take whoso take may. And if a man list for to see in the gospel written the wonderful and the special love that our Lord had to her, in person of all accustomed sinners truly turned and called to the grace of contempla-tion, he shall find that our Lord might not suffer any man or woman – yea, not her own sister – speak a word against her, but if He answered for her Himself. Yea, and what more? He blamed Symon Leprous in his own house, for that he thought against her. This was great love: this was passing love.

Here Beginneth The Three And Twentieth Chapter

How God will answer and purvey for them in spirit, that for business about His love list not answer nor purvey for themselves.

AND truly we will lustily conform our love and our living, inasmuch as in us is, by grace and by counsel, unto the love and the living of Mary, no doubt but He shall answer on the same manner now for us ghostly each day, privily in the hearts of all those that either say or think against us. I say not but that evermore some men shall say or think somewhat against us, the whiles we live in the travail of this life, as they did against Mary. But I say, an we will give no more heed to their saying nor to their thinking, nor no more cease of our ghostly privy work for their words and their thoughts, than she did – I say, then, that our Lord shall answer them in spirit, if it shall be well with them that so say and so think, that they shall within few days have shame of their words and their thoughts.

And as He will answer for us thus in spirit, so will He stir other men in spirit to give us our needful things that belong to this life, as meat and clothes with all these other; if He see that we will not leave the work of His love for business about them. And this I say in confusion of their error, that say that it is not lawful for men to set them to serve God in contemplative life, but if they be secure before of their bodily necessaries. For they say, that God sendeth the cow, but not by the horn. And truly they say wrong of God, as they well know. For trust steadfastly, thou whatsoever that thou be, that truly turnest thee from the world unto God, that one of these two God shall send thee, without business of thyself: and that is either abundance of neces-saries, or strength in body and patience in spirit to bear need. What then recketh it, which man have? For all come to one in very contemplatives. And whoso is in doubt of this, either the devil is in his breast and reeveth him of belief, or else he is not yet truly turned to God as he should be; make he it never so quaint, nor never so holy reasons shew there again, whatnot ever that he be.

And therefore thou, that settest thee to be contemplative as Mary was, choose thee rather to be meeked under the wonderful height and the worthiness of God, the which is perfect, than under thine own wretchedness, the which is imperfect: that is to say, look that thy special beholding be more to the worthiness of God than to thy wretchedness. For to them that be perfectly meeked, no thing shall defail; neither bodily thing, nor ghostly. For why? They have God, in whom is all plenty; and whoso hath Him – yea, as this book telleth – him needeth nought else in this life.

Here Beginneth The Four And Twentieth Chapter

What charity is in itself, and how it is truly and perfectly contained in the work of this book.

AND as it is said of meekness, how that it is truly and perfectly comprehended in this little blind love pressed, when it is beating upon this dark cloud of unknowing, all other things put down and forgotten: so it is to be understood of all other virtues, and specially of charity.

For charity is nought else to bemean to thine understanding, but love of God for Himself above all creatures, and of man for God even as thyself. And that in this work God is loved for Himself, and above all creatures, it seemeth right well. For as it is said before, that the substance of this work is nought else but a naked intent directed unto God for Himself.

A naked intent I call it. For why, in this work a perfect Prentice asketh neither releasing of pain, nor increasing of meed, nor shortly to say, nought but Himself. Insomuch, that neither he recketh nor looketh after whether that he be in pain or in bliss, else that His will be fulfilled that he loveth. And thus it seemeth that in this work God is perfectly loved for Himself, and that above all creatures. For in this work, a perfect worker may not suffer the memory of the holiest creature that ever God made to commune with him.

And that in this work the second and the lower branch of charity unto thine even-Christian is verily and perfectly fulfilled, it seemeth by the proof. For why, in this work a perfect worker hath no special beholding unto any man by himself, whether that he be kin or stranger, friend or foe. For all men him thinks equally kin unto him, and no man stranger. All men him thinks be his friends, and none his foes. Insomuch, that him thinks all those that pain him and do him disease in this life, they be his full and his special friends: and him thinketh, that he is stirred to will them as much good, as he would to the homeliest friend that he hath.

[handwritten marginal note: Virtue to be charitable]

Questions for Study

1 How does the author interpret the story (Luke 10:38–42) of Mary and Martha? In what way did Mary choose the "good portion"?

2 What does the author mean by the following passage? "For by Mary is understood all contemplatives; for they should conform their living after hers. And by Martha, actives on the same manner; and for the same reason in likeness."

3 The author clearly places considerable emphasis on the importance of love. Identify two passages which discuss this matter, and analyze the argument. In particular, explain what is meant by this statement: charity is "love of God for Himself above all creatures, and of man for God even as thyself."

CHAPTER 33

William Langland
(ca. 1330–ca. 1400)

Little is known for certain of this remarkable poet, apart from some autobiographical references in his poems. It is thought that he was born around 1330 in the village of Cleobury Mortimer in Shropshire, as the illegitimate son of Eustace de Rokayle, who owned some land near Shipton-under-Wychwood in Oxfordshire. Although he trained for the priesthood of the church, it seems that he lost the support of some wealthy patrons, which prevented him from advancing within the hierarchy of the church. His writings show a good knowledge of the city of London, and indicate that he spent some time living with his wife Kit and daughter Colette in a cottage in Cornhill, eking out a meager living by saying Masses for the (wealthy) dead.

William Langland (ca. 1332–ca. 1400)

Basic description
Major English poet of the fourteenth century, writing in the dialect of the West Midlands.

Major work
Piers Plowman.

Editions of works
Piers Plowman, ed. W. W. Skeat, 2 vols. Oxford: Clarendon Press, 1886.

Major studies
David Aers, *Piers Plowman and Christian Allegory*. London: Edward Arnold, 1975.
Britton J. Harwood, *Piers Plowman and the Problem of Belief*. Toronto: University of Toronto Press, 1992.

It is not even certain that Langland wrote the work for which he is best known – *Piers Plowman* or *Piers the Ploughman*. After centuries of neglect, this long and complex work is now regarded as one of the most creative and brilliant pieces of religious writing of the Middle Ages. It exists in three forms, usually known as the "A," "B" and "C"- texts. Although it was once thought that these variations indicated multiple authorship of the work, more recent scholarship has suggested that they are best regarded as different versions of the same work. The B-text, which is the most widely cited (and has been chosen for the present anthology), was written in a dialect peculiar to the West Midlands, probably between the years 1377–9. Although the work was read widely during the fifteenth century, there are reasons for thinking that the dialect in which it was written became increasingly difficult to understand, with the result that the work fell into neglect.

It is therefore necessary to translate the text into modern English. The translation chosen for this anthology was produced by J. F. Goodridge in 1959, and allows the reader to gain a good sense of the highly vivid imagery and dramatic language used by Langland as he relates his tale.

Text: *Piers Plowman*

The tale of "Piers Plowman" begins with an account of how the poet set out on a warm May morning to wander in the Malvern Hills. Tired out by his traveling, he lay down to rest by the bank of a stream. The gentle noise of the stream caused him to drift off to sleep, during which he "dreamt a marvellous dream." The narrative of *Piers Plowman* relates the content of that dream.

Piers Plowman thus belongs to the same literary genre as Dante's *Divine Comedy*, Milton's *Paradise Lost*, and perhaps also Bunyan's *Pilgrim's Progress*. The entire drama of the poem is set in fourteenth-century England, and reflects the political events of that turbulent period in English history. Yet alongside the comedy and satire directed against his own age, we find an engagement with major theological themes, culminating in his dramatic depiction of the passion of Christ and the harrowing of Hell (Book XVIII). This is the climax of the poem, and offers a highly dramatic rendering of the Good Friday liturgy and Easter vigil, alongside a particularly striking portrayal of the "harrowing of Hell."

The narrative begins with Palm Sunday – that is, the Sunday immediately before Easter Day, which marks the beginning of Holy Week, and recalls Christ's triumphant entry into Jerusalem, in the course of which his path was strewn with palm leaves. A major feature of the Book is the dialogue between the four Virtues – Mercy, Truth, Righteousness and Peace – in which certain leading theological virtues are personified, and represented as debating with each other over, for example, how God's justice can be reconciled with God's mercy – a central theme of the Christian doctrine of redemption, which is here presented in a very dramatic and strikingly visual manner.

Much of the early part of this Book is based on the gospel accounts of the triumphant entry into Jerusalem. Langland also incorporates various apocryphal elements and popular embellishments into his narrative – for example, he includes "Longinus" as a witness to the crucifixion, a tradition which first appeared in the apocryphal Gospel of Nicodemus, and was developed further in *The Golden Legend*. Alongside this, we find Latin citations taken from the medieval liturgies, which would have been familiar to the work's readers. These have generally been translated within the text. However, the meaning of the text can generally be grasped without needing to know details of the liturgical background to the passage.

Book XVIII

The Passion and Harrowing of Hell

Once again I set out, with wet feet, and the rough wool chafing my skin. I wandered on heedlessly throughout my life, regardless of pain and misery, living as a beggar, till at last I grew tired of the world and longed to sleep. So I drowsed away till it was Lent, and slept for a long time, and lay there snoring heavily until Palm Sunday. I dreamt a long dream about children; – I could hear them chanting "Gloria, laus," and the old people singing "Hosanna in excelsis" to the sound of the organ; and then I dreamt of Christ's Passion, and of the penance which He suffered for all the people.

A man came riding along barefoot on an ass, unarmed and without spurs. He looked like the Good Samaritan – or was it Piers the Ploughman? He was young and lusty, like a squire coming to be dubbed knight and receive his golden spurs and cut-away shoes.

Then Faith, who was standing at a window, cried out, "See! The Son of David!" – like a herald proclaiming a knight who comes to the tournament. And the aged Jews of Jerusalem sang for joy, "Blessed is he that cometh in the name of the Lord."

So I asked Faith the meaning of all this stir – "Who was going to joust in Jerusalem?"

"Jesus," he said, "to win back Piers' fruit, which the Devil has claimed."

"Is Piers in this city?" I asked.

He looked at me keenly and answered, "Jesus, out of chivalry, will joust in Piers' coat-of-arms, and wear His helmet and mail, Human Nature; He will ride in Piers' doublet, that no one here may know Him as Almighty God. For whatever blows He receives, they cannot wound Him in His divine nature."

"Who will fight with Jesus?" I said. "The Jews and Scribes?"

"No," said Faith, "the Devil, False Judgement, and Death. For Death vows to destroy all living creatures, both on land and water; but Life has branded him a liar, and pledged His life that within three days He will fetch Piers' fruit from the fiend, carry it where He chooses, bind Lucifer and vanquish Sorrow and Death for ever. – 'O Death, I will be thy death; O grave, I will be thy destruction.'"

Then Pilate came with a great crowd, and sat down in the judgement seat to see how bravely Death would fight, and judge between the rival claims. The Judge himself and all the Jews were against Jesus, and the whole Court cried out against Him with shrill voices, saying, "Crucify Him!" Then a robber, pushing himself forward before Pilate, cried, "This Jesus mocked at and despised our Jewish Temple; He said He would destroy it in a day and rebuild it again in three – there He stands, the very man himself! And He boasted He would make it as wide and tall and spacious as it was before, every detail the same."

"Crucify Him!" cried an officer, "I'll swear He's a sorcerer."

"Off with him! Take Him away!" yelled another, and seizing some sharp thorns, he made a wreath and rammed it on His head, mocking Him with cries of, "Hail,

Rabbi!" and thrusting reeds at Him. Then they nailed Him, with three nails, naked, to the Cross, and putting poison to His lips on the end of a pole they told Him to drink His death-drink, for his days were over. "But if you're a magician," they said, "come down from the cross; then we'll believe that Life loves you so much, he won't let you die!"

Christ said, "It is finished," and began to grow fearfully pale, like a prisoner on the point of death. And so the Lord of Life and of Light closed His eyes. Then at once the daylight fled in fear and the sun became dark; the wall of the Temple shook and split, and the whole earth quaked.

On hearing this dreadful sound, the dead came forth from their deep graves and spoke to the living, to tell them why the storm raged for so long. "For in this darkness," said one of the dead, "Life and Death are waging a grievous battle; one is destroying the other, and no one will know who has won, until daybreak on Sunday" – and with those words he sank back into the earth.

When they saw how nobly He died, some said that Jesus was the Son of God – "Indeed, this was the Son of God" – but others still believed Him a sorcerer and added, "We'd better make sure He is really dead before He is taken down."

On either side of Christ two thieves had also been put to death on crosses (for this was the common practice of that time), and an officer came and broke their arms and legs. But not one of those wretches had the nerve to lay hands on the body of God; for since He was a true knight and the Son of a king, Nature, for once, saw to it that no common fellow should touch Him. Yet the Book tells of a knight with a sharp spear, whose name was Longinus, who had been blind a long time. And as he was standing near the crosses before Pilate and others, they forced him, in spite of his protests, to take his spear in hand and tilt against Christ. For all who stood about waiting on foot or on horseback were scared to handle Him and take Him down from the Cross. So this blind, young knight pierced Jesus through the heart; and as the Blood spurted down the steel, it unsealed his sight. Then he fell on his knees and cried for mercy, saying, "It was against my will, Lord, that I dealt you this grievous wound" – and he groaned and said, "I repent bitterly for what I have done, and cast myself on your mercy. O just Jesus, have pity on me," and with those words he wept.

Then Faith turned fiercely on the Jews and cursed them saying, "May God's vengeance fall on the lot of you, cowards that you are! For this vileness you shall be accursed for ever. What fouler trick than to force a blind knight to strike a man bound to the stake! Did you think it was chivalrous to maltreat a dead body, you damnable wretches?

"But Christ has won the day, in spite of this gaping wound. For at this very moment your chief knight and champion is yielding in the lists to Jesus' mercy. And as soon as this darkness is over, Christ's life shall be avenged, Life himself shall conquer, and you, my lords, will have lost your battle. Then all the liberties that God has given you shall turn to slavery; you shall become serfs, and all your children with you; never again shall you prosper, never have land or dominion or plough the soil again. But you shall lead barren lives, and make your money by usury, a livelihood condemned by God in all His commandments. For now, as Daniel prophesied, your good days have come to an end – 'When the Holy of Holies shall come, your anointing shall cease.'"

Appalled by this miracle and the treachery of the Jews, I drew back in the darkness and went down into the depths of the earth. And there, in accordance with Scripture, I dreamt that I saw a maiden come walking from the west, and looking towards hell. Mercy was her name, and she seemed a very gentle lady, courteous and kind in all that she said. And then I saw her sister come walking quietly out of the East, and gazing intently westwards. She was very fair, and her name was Truth; for she possessed a heavenly power that made her fearless.

When these ladies, Mercy and Truth, met together, they asked each other about the great wonder that had come to pass – the noise and darkness and then the sudden dawn. Why this light and radiance before the gates of hell? "The whole thing amazes me," said Truth; "I am now on my way to find out what it all means."

"Do not be surprised," said Mercy, "for these are signs of great joy. There is a maiden called Mary, who has conceived and grown big with child without any knowledge of a man, but through the word of the Holy Ghost alone; and she has brought Him into the world without sin, as God himself can vouch. It is thirty years now since the child was born, and at midday today he was put to death. That is why the sun is eclipsed – to show us that men are to be drawn out of darkness, while Lucifer is blinded by the dazzling light. The patriarchs and prophets have often preached about this – that mankind should be saved through the help of a virgin, that a tree should win back what was lost by a tree, and a death should raise up those whom Death has cast down."

"What a lot of clap-trap!" said Truth. "How could that light raise up Adam and Eve, Abraham and all the patriarchs and prophets who lie in pain? What power has it to draw them out of hell? Hold your tongue, Mercy, and stop talking nonsense! I am Truth, and I know the truth. Once in hell, no man ever comes out again; the patriarch Job condemns all these sayings of yours – 'He that goeth down to the grave shall come up no more.'"

Then Mercy answered mildly and said, "Yet from what I have seen, I have good reason to hope they will be saved. For poison is an antidote to poison – I can show you that by examples. A scorpion's sting is the most poisonous of all, and all remedies are useless against it. Yet if you apply the dead scorpion to the sore place, all the ill effects are cured, and the poison is dispelled by its own poison. So this death will destroy all that Death destroyed first, enticed by the Devil – I would stake my life on this. Just as man was deceived through the Devil's guile, so Grace, which was with man in the beginning, will beguile the Devil in turn – '*Ars ut artem falleret* – Art to deceive art.'"

"Now let's wait patiently a moment," said Truth, "for I think I can see Righteousness not far off, hurrying this way from the freezing North. Let us wait till she comes, for she knows more than we do; she was alive before we were born." "Yes," said Mercy, "I agree. And look, here comes Peace from the South, dancing gaily along in her garments of Patience. Love has set his heart on her for such a long time that I am sure he will have written to tell her what this light means that is hovering over hell. So she will be able to tell us."

When Peace, dressed in Patience, came up to the two maidens, Righteousness looked at her rich attire and greeted her politely, asking her where she was off to in these gay clothes.

"I am on my way to welcome all the lost souls," she said, "whom I have not seen for many a long day now, because of the darkness of sin. For Adam and Eve and Moses and many more of those in hell are to have a pardon. And oh, how I shall be dancing with joy when I see them – and you, dear sister, must come and dance too. Jesus has fought well, and joy is dawning at last – 'Weeping may endure for a night, but joy cometh in the morning.' For Charity, my lover, has sent me a letter to say that my sister Mercy and I are to save mankind – God has given us permission to stand bail for them for ever. See, here is the warrant, and these are the actual words – 'I will both lay me down in peace,' and, to make sure the deed is lasting, 'and rest secure.'"

"Have you gone off your head?" said Righteousness, "or had too much to drink! Do you really suppose that this light can unlock hell, and save the souls of men? Don't you believe it! God himself pronounced this Doom in the beginning, that Adam and Eve and all their seed should surely die, and after death live in torment, if ever they touched the fruit of a certain tree. In spite of this command Adam ate the fruit; so, in effect, he refused God's love as well as His law, and chose instead the word of the Devil and his wife's greed, out of all reason. I am Righteousness, and I tell you this for certain: that their suffering will never cease, and no prayer can ever help them. So leave them to the fate they chose and let us stop this argument, my sisters. The fruit which they ate was deadly poison and there's no remedy for it."

"But," said Peace, "I can prove that their pain must come to an end, and suffering is bound to turn to happiness in the end. For if they had never known any suffering, they could never know happiness. – No man can grasp what pleasure is who has never suffered, or understand hunger who has never been without food. I am sure that if there were no night, no one would know for certain the meaning of day! And a rich man living in ease and comfort couldn't have any notion of misery, if nature did not force him to die. That is why God, the creator of all things, of His goodness became a man and was born of a virgin to save mankind. He allowed himself to be sold so that He might feel the bitterness of death, which unravels all sorrow and is the beginning of rest.

"For until we meet with Scarcity no one knows what it is to have enough. And so God of His goodness placed the first man, Adam, in a state of contentment and perfect happiness, and then allowed him to sin and experience sorrow, so that he might learn for himself what real happiness was. And then God ventured himself and took Adam's nature to experience what he had suffered, not only on earth but in three different places, heaven, earth, and hell. For now He means to go into hell, so that, as He knows infinite bliss, He may also know infinite misery.

"And so it shall be with these folk: their folly and sin will show them what pain is, and then endless bliss. For no man living in times of peace can imagine war, nor can a man really know happiness till troubles come to teach him."

Then there appeared a man with two broad, open eyes – a Reverend Father by the name of Book, who was very outspoken. "By the Body of Christ, I bear witness," said this Book, "that when this Child was born a star blazed in the sky, and all the wise men in the world agreed what it meant – that a child was born in Bethlehem who would save man's soul and destroy sin. And all the four elements, air, water, fire, and earth bore witness to it. First the air and the sky proclaimed Him to be the God who created the world; for the spirits in heaven took a comet and kindled it for a torch to honour His birth; and the light followed its Lord down into the lowly earth.

"The water also witnessed that He was God, for He walked upon it; and Peter the Apostle, seeing Him coming, recognized Him as He walked on the water, and cried, 'Lord, bid me come to Thee upon the waters.'

"And now look how the sun itself, on seeing Him suffer who made the sun and the sea, has locked up her light within herself – while the earth, in anguish for His pain, quakes like a living thing and shatters the rocks. Behold, when God suffered, even Hell itself could no longer hold together, for when it saw Him hanging on the Cross it opened and let the sons of Simeon out. And now even Lucifer shall believe the truth of this, however he may hate it. For the Giant Jesus has forged a weapon with which to break and beat down all that stands in His way.

"And I, Book, will gladly be burnt if Jesus does not rise and live again with all the powers of a man, to bring back joy to his mother and comfort to all his kin, and to dash to pieces all the triumph of the Jews. For unless they adore His Cross and His Resurrection and believe in a New Law, they shall be lost both body and soul."

"Let us wait," said Truth, "for I can hear a spirit speaking to hell – Now I can see him. He is commanding them to unbar the gates: 'Lift up your heads, o ye gates; and be ye lift up, ye everlasting doors.'"

Then, from within the light, a loud voice cried out to Lucifer: "Princes of hell, unbar and unlock the gates, for there comes here a crowned monarch, the King of Glory."

Then Satan heaving a great sigh, spoke thus to all the fiends: "It was light like this which fetched Lazarus away without our leave, so we may as well be prepared for trouble. If this king comes in, He will seize mankind and carry them off where He likes, and it won't take Him long to bind me in chains. This has long been talked of by the patriarchs and prophets – that such a king and a light should lead them all away."

"Listen to me," said Lucifer, "I know this lord and this light – I met Him long ago. Death cannot hurt Him, nor any of your Devils' tricks: if He chooses to do a thing, He'll have His way. But he'd better consider the risks: for if He deprives me of my right, He is robbing me by force. The men who are here, both good and evil, are legally mine, body and soul of them. The ruler of Heaven said so himself – that if Adam ate the apple all men should die and live with us here. That was His threat, and He is the Truth that made it. I have been in possession now for seven hundred years, so I don't see how the Law can allow Him anything."

"That may be true enough," replied Satan, "but I still dread what will come of this; for you took them by guile, Lucifer – you broke into His garden disguised as a serpent, twined yourself round an apple-tree, and enticed Adam and Eve to eat the apple. And you went to Eve when she was alone, and told her a tale loaded with lies.

That was how you had them banished from the garden, and got them here at last. But nothing is won for sure if it is founded on guile."

"You can't catch God out that way. He won't be fooled," said an ugly demon. "We haven't a leg to stand on – they were damned through treachery."

"Exactly," said the Devil, "and I'm afraid Truth is going to carry them off. He has been going about on the earth and teaching men for a good thirty years now, I think. I have tried to tempt Him with sin, and I once asked Him if He was God or God's Son, but only got snubbed for my pains. So He has wandered at large these thirty-two years, which is why I went to Pilate's wife in her sleep, to warn her what make of man this Jesus was. For though the Jews hated Him and put Him to death, I would rather have prolonged His life – Why? Because I knew that, if He died, His soul would never endure the sight of sin like ours. For while He went about in a human body He was busy all the time absolving all who chose to be saved from their sins.

"And now I can see a soul sailing towards us, blazing with light and glory – I am certain it is God. Quickly, we must escape while we can; it would be more than our lives are worth to let Him find us here. It is you, Lucifer, with your lies, that have lost us all our prey. It was all your fault that we fell from the heights of heaven in the first place; not one of us would have leapt out after you, if we hadn't swallowed your talk. And now, thanks to your latest invention, we have lost Adam, and, more than likely, all our dominion over land and sea – 'Now shall the prince of this world be cast out.'"

Then again the light bade them unlock the gates, and Lucifer answered, saying, "What lord art thou? – 'Who is this King . . . ?'"

"The King of Glory," answered the Light at once; "the Lord of power and might, and king of every virtue. Unbar the gates quickly, you lords of this dreary place, so that Christ, the Son of the King of Heaven, may enter."

With that word, Hell itself, and all the bars of Belial, burst asunder, and the gates flew open in the face of the guards. And all the patriarchs and prophets, "the people that sat in darkness," sang aloud the hymn of St John the Baptist – "*Ecce agnus dei* – Behold the Lamb of God." But Lucifer could not look to see, for the Light had blinded his eyes. And then our Lord caught up into His Light all those that loved Him; and turning to Satan He said:

"Behold, here is my soul as a ransom for all these sinful souls, to redeem those that are worthy. They are mine; they came from me, and therefore I have the better claim on them. I do not deny that, in strict justice, they were condemned to die if they ate the apple. But I did not sentence them to stay in hell for ever. Your deceit was the cause of what they did; you won them by guile, without a semblance of justice. – You stole into my palace of Paradise in the form of an adder, and took away by treachery the thing that I loved; and disguised as a reptile with a woman's face, you crept in and robbed me like a common thief.

"The Old Law says that he who deceives shall be deceived, which is good reason – 'An eye for an eye, and a tooth for a tooth.' So I offer you soul for soul; sin shall counter sin, and I, as a man, will make amends for all that man has done wrong. Member for member, life for life – that was the old law of restitution. And it is by that law that I claim Adam and all his issue, to do what I wish to do with them from now onwards. What Death has destroyed in them, my death shall restore; it shall raise them to life, and pay for all whom sin has slain.

"Justice demands that grace should destroy guile. So do not think, Lucifer, that I take them away unlawfully. It is right and just that I should ransom my own subjects. 'I came not to destroy the Law but to fulfil.' You, by falsehood and crime and against all justice, took away what was mine, in my own domain; I, in fairness, recover them by paying the ransom, and by no other means. What you got by guile is won back by grace. You, Lucifer, like a slippery adder, got by guile those whom God loved; while I, that am Lord of Heaven, have come like a man, and graciously repaid your guile – guile against guile! And as a tree caused Adam and all mankind to die, so my gallows-tree shall bring them back to life.

"So Guile is beguiled, and fallen in his own guile – 'He made a pit, and digged it, and is fallen into the ditch he made.' At last your guile begins to turn against you, while my grace grows ever wider and greater. The bitterness that you have brewed, you shall drink yourself; you that are doctor of death, shall swallow your own medicine!

"For I, the Lord of Life, drink no drink but love, and for that drink I died today on earth. I have fought so hard for man's soul that I am still thirsty, and no drink can ever refresh me or quench my thirst, till the vintage fall in the valley of Jehoshaphat, so that I may drink the ripe new wine of the resurrection of the dead. Then I shall come as a king crowned with angels, and draw all men's souls out of hell. All the fiends, both great and small, shall stand before me, ready to do my bidding and go wherever I send them.

"And how can I, with my human nature, refuse men mercy on that day? For we are brothers of one blood, though we are not all of one baptism. And none who are wholly my brothers, in blood and in baptism, shall be condemned to eternal death; for it is written, 'Against thee only have I sinned.'

"When on earth a criminal is put to death, it is not the custom to hang the man again if the first hanging fails, even though he may be a traitor. And if the king of the country comes to the place of execution at the moment when the man is about to die, the law says that the king can grant him his life, if he but looks at the condemned man. So I, the King of kings, shall come at the moment when all the wicked are under sentence of death; and if the Law lets me look upon them, then it rests with my mercy whether they die or not, no matter what crimes they may have committed. And if their sin of pride against God has already been paid for, I can grant them mercy without offending justice, and all my words remain true.

"And though the words of Scripture require that I should take vengeance on the wicked, and say that 'No evil will go unpunished,' yet I have a prison called Purgatory, where they shall be thoroughly cleansed and washed from their sins, until I give the word of command to spare them. And then my mercy will be shown to many of my brethren. For a man may suffer his kind to go cold and hungry, but he cannot see them bleed without pitying them."

"And I heard secret words which it is not granted to man to utter."

"My righteousness and my justice shall rule over hell, and my mercy over all mankind before me in Heaven. I should be an inhuman king if I refused help to my own brethren, especially when they will need help so sorely. – 'Enter not into judgement with thy servant. O Lord.'

"Therefore, by lawful right," said our Lord, "I shall lead from this place the men who loved me and believed in my coming. And you, Lucifer, shall grievously pay for the lies you told to Eve" – and having said this He bound him in chains.

Then Ashtoreth and all the rout of devils scuttled away into the corners. Even the boldest dared not look upon our Lord, but left Him to do His will and lead away whom He chose.

Many hundreds of angels harped and sang –

> "*Culpat caro, purgat caro;*
> *Regnat deus dei caro.*"*

The Peace played on her pipe, singing this song –

> "*Clarior est solito post maxima nebula Phoebus,*
> *Post inimicitias clarior est et amor –*
> After the sharpest showers the sun shines brightest;
> No weather is warmer than after the blackest clouds,
> Nor any love fresher nor friendship fonder
> Than after strife and struggle, when Love and Peace have conquered.
> There was never a war in this world, nor wickedness so cruel,
> That Love, if he liked, might not turn to laughter,
> And Peace, through Patience, put an end to its perils."

"I give way," said Truth. "You are in the right, Mercy. Let us make our peace together, and seal it with a kiss."

"And nobody shall know that we ever quarrelled," said Peace, "for nothing is impossible with Almighty God."

"I agree," said Righteousness, and she solemnly kissed Peace, and Peace kissed her – world without end.

> "Mercy and Truth are met together:
> Righteousness and Peace have kissed each other."

Then Truth blew on a trumpet and sang the *Te Deum Laudamus*, and Love played on a lute, singing aloud –

> "Behold, how good and joyful a thing it is:
> brethren, to dwell together in unity!"

And so these maidens danced till daybreak, when the bells of Easter morning rang out for the Resurrection. And with that sound I awoke, and called out to my wife

---

*   "The flesh sins, the flesh atones for sin; the flesh of God reigns as God."

Kitty and my daughter Kate, "Get up, and come to honour God's Resurrection. Creep to the Cross on your knees and kiss it as a priceless jewel! For it bore God's blessed Body for our salvation, and such is its power that the Devil shrinks from it in terror, and evil spirits dare not glide beneath its shadow."

Questions for Study

1 The opening section of this Book represents a portrayal of the events of Holy Week. What purpose does this section play in the overall structure of this Book?

2 Langland provides us with an account of the "harrowing of Hell." Provide a summary of the main themes of this "harrowing."

3 Try to summarize the debate between the four Virtues. One of the main issues they discuss concerns the reconciliation of God's mercy with God's righteousness. What conclusions do they reach?

4 The poet is woken up from his dream by the sound of church bells on Easter Morning. How is the poet's everyday life affected by the dream which has just ended?

CHAPTER 34

Geoffrey Chaucer (ca. 1342–1400)

Chaucer is widely regarded as one of the most important English medieval writers, chiefly on account of his *Canterbury Tales*. Chaucer spent his early period in London, where he is thought to have received his education at St. Paul's Almonry. He then became a page in the household of the Countess of Ulster, which offered him contacts with some of the most important figures in England, including his future patron, John of Gaunt.

Geoffrey Chaucer (ca. 1342–1400)

Basic description
English courtier and author.

Major work
The Canterbury Tales.

Major studies
Harold Bloom, *Geoffrey Chaucer*. New York: Chelsea House, 1985.
J. Kerkhof, *Studies in the Language of Geoffrey Chaucer*, 2nd edn. Leiden: Brill, 1997.

The history of the fourteenth century was dominated by the apparently never-ending Hundred Years War between England and France. Chaucer found himself caught up in this affair. In 1359, he was sent to France on military business, and succeeded in getting himself captured near Rheims. He was sufficiently highly regarded to be judged worthy of ransoming, with Edward III himself contributing to the ransom. Yet his period in France was not without literary significance. There is ample evidence to suggest that he developed a competence in the French language, and a love for French literature – particularly the genre of "courtly love." One of his first major projects on his safe return to England was to begin an English translation of the thirteenth-century *Roman de la Rose*, widely regarded as the most elegant expression of *amour courtois*. This "courtly love" motif became of considerable importance at this stage in western European culture, and a substantial number of works are known to exist which dwell on the theme of the torments of unsatisfied love inspired by women who were beyond reach. By now, through the good offices of John of Gaunt, Chaucer was in the service of the king, and that service took him to Italy in 1372 (Genoa) and 1378 (Milan). Already well-versed in continental literature, Chaucer appears to have made use of this opportunity to discover Boccaccio and Dante.

Text: *The Canterbury Tales*

The origins of the writing of *The Canterbury Tales* can be dated to early 1387, when Chaucer suddenly found himself unemployed. John of Gaunt, Chaucer's patron, had left England on a military expedition to Spain. In his absence, the Duke of Gloucester became a major influence on William II, and proceeded to ensure that his own protégés were appointed to key positions. Chaucer was deprived of all his offices, in order that those favored by the Duke of Gloucester might take them. The situation was restored in 1389, when John of Gaunt returned and was able to secure Chaucer's reinstatement. Among his responsibilities was the maintenance of ditches, walls, and sewers between Greenwich and Woolwich. It was during his period of enforced leisure that Chaucer planned his best-known work, and began to compile it. It would remain unfinished at his death.

The context in which this great work is set is the medieval world of pilgrimages to sites of major importance. The cathedral city of Canterbury had become such a site, partly through its associations with the martyred Thomas à Becket. Large groups of pilgrims would make their way to the city throughout the Middle Ages. Chaucer's work takes the form of a series of tales told by pilgrims as they traveled. The *Prologue* suggests that the original idea was to have a group of thirty such pilgrims, each of whom would relate two stories on the way out, and two on the way back – making for a collection of 120 stories. The final version of the work is much smaller. The basic genius of the work lies in the development of a framework – the pilgrimage – within which stories of widely differing styles are told in ways that reflect the individuality of the pilgrims. The stories told are drawn from all over Europe, and reflect Chaucer's cosmopolitan interests. Only a few are thought to be Chaucer's own creation – such as that of the Canon's Yeoman.

The passage selected for discussion is the prologue to the Pardoner's Tale – a witty piece, in which the more venial aspects of contemporary clerical life are lampooned. The *Canterbury Tales* are written in Middle English; the much-admired modern translation of Nevill Coghill has been used, to allow the wit of this piece to be more effectively conveyed than would be possible through the original version.

The Pardoner's Tale

The Pardoner's Prologue

'My lords,' he said, 'in churches where I preach
I cultivate a haughty kind of speech
And ring it out as roundly as a bell;
I've got it all by heart, the tale I tell.
I have a text, it always is the same   5

And always has been, since I learnt the game,
Old as the hills and fresher than the grass,
Radix malorum est cupiditas.
   'But first I make pronouncement whence I come,
Show them my bulls in detail and in sum.   10
And flaunt the papal seal for their inspection
As warrant for my bodily protection,
That none may have the impudence to irk
Or hinder me in Christ's most holy work.
Then I tell stories, as occasion calls,   15
Showing forth bulls from popes and cardinals,
From patriarchs and bishops; as I do,
I speak some words in Latin – just a few –
To put a saffron tinge upon my preaching
And stir devotion with a spice of teaching.   20
Then I bring all my long glass bottles out
Cram-full of bones and ragged bits of clout,
Relics they are, at least for such are known.
Then, cased in metal, I've a shoulder-bone,
Belonging to a sheep, a holy Jew's.   25
"Good men," I say, "take heed, for here is news.
Take but this bone and dip it in a well;
If cow or calf, if sheep or ox should swell
From eating snakes or that a snake has stung,
Take water from that well and wash its tongue,   30
And it will then recover. Furthermore,
Where there is pox or scab or other sore,
All animals that water at that well
Are cured at once. Take note of what I tell.
If the good man – the owner of the stock –   35
Goes once a week, before the crow of cock,
Fasting, and takes a draught of water too,
Why then, according to that holy Jew,
He'll find his cattle multiply and sell.
   '"And it's a cure for jealousy as well;   40
For though a man be given to jealous wrath,
Use but this water when you make his broth,
And never again will he mistrust his wife,
Though he knew all about her sinful life,
Though two or three clergy had enjoyed her love.   45
   '"Now look; I have a mitten here, a glove.
Whoever wears this mitten on his hand
Will multiply his grain. He sows his land
And up will come abundant wheat or oats,
Providing that he offers pence or groats.   50
   '"Good men and women, here's a word of warning;

If there is anyone in church this morning
Guilty of sin, so far beyond expression
Horrible, that he dare not make confession,
Or any woman, whether young or old,   55
That's cuckolded her husband, be she told
That such as she shall have no power or grace
To offer to my relics in this place.
But those who can acquit themselves of blame
Can all come up and offer in God's name,   60
And I will shrive them by the authority
Committed in this papal bull to me."
    'That trick's been worth a hundred marks a year
Since I became a Pardoner, never fear.
Then, priestlike in my pulpit, with a frown,   65
I stand, and when the yokels have sat down,
I preach, as you have heard me say before,
And tell a hundred lying mockeries more.
I take great pains, and stretching out my neck
To east and west I crane about and peck   70
Just like a pigeon sitting on a barn.
My hands and tongue together spin the yarn
And all my antics are a joy to see.
The curse of avarice and cupidity
Is all my sermon, for it frees the pelf.   75
Out come the pence, and specially for myself,
For my exclusive purpose is to win
And not at all to castigate their sin.
Once dead what matter how their souls may fare?
They can go blackberrying, for all I care!   80
    'Believe me, many a sermon or devotive
Exordium issues from an evil motive.
Some to give pleasure by their flattery
And gain promotion through hypocrisy,
Some out of vanity, some out of hate;   85
Or when I dare not otherwise debate
I'll put my discourse into such a shape,
My tongue will be a dagger; no escape
For him from slandering falsehood shall there be.
If he has hurt my brethren or me.   90
For though I never mention him by name
The congregation guesses all the same
From certain hints that everybody knows,
And so I take revenge upon our foes
And spit my venom forth, while I profess   95
Holy and true – or seeming holiness.
    'But let me briefly make my purpose plain;

I preach for nothing but for greed of gain
And use the same old text, as bold as brass,
Radix malorum est cupiditas.   100
And thus I preach against the very vice
I make my living out of – avarice.
And yet however guilty of that sin
Myself, with others I have power to win
Them from it, I can bring them to repent;   105
But that is not my principal intent.
Covetousness is both the root and stuff
Of all I preach. That ought to be enough.
   'Well, then I give examples thick and fast
From bygone times, old stories from the past.   110
A yokel mind loves stories from of old,
Being the kind it can repeat and hold.
What! Do you think, as long as I can preach
And get their silver for the things I teach,
That I will live in poverty, from choice?   115
That's not the counsel of my inner voice!
No! Let me preach and beg from kirk to kirk
And never do an honest job of work,
No, nor make baskets, like St Paul, to gain
A livelihood. I do not preach in vain.   120
There's no apostle I would counterfeit;
I mean to have money, wool and cheese and wheat
Though it were given me by the poorest lad
Or poorest village widow, though she had
A string of starving children, all agape.   125
No, let me drink the liquor of the grape
And keep a jolly wench in every town!
   'But listen, gentlemen; to bring things down
To a conclusion, would you like a tale?
Now as I've drunk a draught of corn-ripe ale,   130
By God it stands to reason I can strike
On some good story that you all will like.
For though I am a wholly vicious man
Don't think I can't tell moral tales. I can!
Here's one I often preach when out for winning; 135
Now please be quiet. Here is the beginning.'

Questions for Discussion

1 What implicit criticism does Chaucer direct against the Pardoner? Note in particular the point that the Pardoner makes his living out of the same vice as that against which he preaches.
2 Chaucer portrays sections of the Christian population as being incredulous and superstitious. What examples does he give to illustrate this?
3 Why is the Pardoner well used to telling stories?

CHAPTER 35

Julian of Norwich (ca. 1342–after 1416)

Julian of Norwich is perhaps the best known of all the English female spiritual writers. Remarkably little is known about her. It is certain that "Julian" was not her real name; its origins are due to the fact that she established her "anchorage" (literally, a place of retreat or isolation) next to St. Julian's Church in the English cathedral city of Norwich. In some writings, she is referred to as "Juliana." According to her own account of her "shewings" (the Middle English term which is now usually translated as "revelations"), these were given to Julian at the age of thirty, in May 1373. All other dates in her life are the subject of conjecture, including both her birth and death. The date of her birth is usually established from her own assertion that she was thirty in 1373; the date of her death remains unknown, except that she is known to have received a bequest in 1412 (the last known date relating to her life).

Julian of Norwich (ca. 1342–after 1416)

Basic description
Fourteenth-century anchoress and mystic.

Major work
Revelations of Divine Love.

Major studies
Grace M. Jantzen, *Julian of Norwich: Mystic and Theologian*. London: SPCK, 1987.
Paul Molinari, *Julian of Norwich: The Teaching of a Fourteenth-Century Mystic*. New York: Arden Library, 1979.
Joan Nuth, *Wisdom's Daughter: The Theology of Julian of Norwich*. New York: Crossroad, 1991.

According to Julian, the revelations which she describes were "shewed" to her on 8 or 14 May (the readings differ), 1373, when she was thirty (and a half) years old. This would refer her birth to the end of 1342. Her statement that "for twenty years after the time of this shewing, save three months, I had teaching inwardly," suggests that the book was not written before 1393. Whatever their precise date, these "Revelations," or "Shewings," are widely accepted to be one of the most important works of later medieval mysticism in England. Julian described herself as a "simple creature unlettered" when she received them; but, in the years that intervened between the vision and the composition of the book, she evidently acquired some knowledge of theological terminology. Her work appears to show the influence of Walter Hilton, as well as some neo-Platonic analogies which could be argued to be derived from the anonymous author of *The Cloud of Unknowing*.

Text: *Revelations of Divine Love*

The text for study is taken from the opening part of the *Revelations of Divine Love*. The "Shewings" takes the form of a description of sixteen personal revelations, and subsequent reflection on their meanings, triggered off by Julian's serious illness in May 1373. While there are many themes that can be discerned within the text, two may be singled out for especial comment. The first is Julian's constant emphasis on the goodness and love of God for the world. Despite its weakness and frailty, it is the creation of God, and God loves and cares for it passionately. Despite all its trials and sorrows, in the end "all will be well." This note of reassurance is one of the most distinctive and admired features of the work. The second theme is the importance of prayer. For Julian, prayer is a thing of great delight to God, who rejoices when we pray. We should persevere in prayer, even when that prayer seems dry and useless. It is this theme which we shall explore further in the extract from the "Shewings."

The "Shewings" exists in two versions, which are generally referred to as the "short text" and "long text." The shorter version exists in one manuscript only, and may well represent an abbreviated version of the full text, suitable for the purposes of personal devotion. The extract for study consists of chapters 2–6, and is taken from the longer version of the text.

The time of the revelations, and Julian's three petitions

These revelations were shown to a simple and uneducated creature on the eighth of May 1373. Some time earlier she had asked three gifts from God: (i) to understand his passion; (ii) to suffer physically while still a young woman of thirty; and (iii) to have as God's gift three wounds.

With regard to the first I thought I had already had some experience of the passion of Christ, but by his grace I wanted still more. I wanted to be actually there with Mary Magdalene and the others who loved him, and with my own eyes to see and know more of the physical suffering of our Saviour, and the compassion of our Lady and of those who there and then were loving him truly and watching his pains. I would be one of them and suffer with him. I had no desire for any other vision of God until after such time as I had died. The reason for this prayer was that I might more truly understand the passion of Christ.

The second came to me with much greater urgency. I quite sincerely wanted to be ill to the point of dying, so that I might receive the last rites of Holy Church, in the belief – shared by my friends – that I was in fact dying. There was no earthly comfort I wanted to live for. In this illness I wanted to undergo all those spiritual and physical sufferings I should have were I really dying, and to know, moreover, the terror and assaults of the demons – everything, except death itself! My intention was that I should be wholly cleansed thereby through the mercy of God, and that thereafter, because of that illness, I might live more worthily of him. Perhaps too I might even die a better death, for I was longing to be with my God.

There was a condition with these two desires: "Lord, you know what I am wanting. If it is your will that I have it. . . . But if not, do not be cross, good Lord, for I want nothing but your will."

As for the third, through the grace of God and the teaching of Holy Church I developed a strong desire to receive three wounds, namely, the wound of true contrition, the wound of genuine compassion, and the wound of sincere longing for God. There was no proviso attached to any part of this third prayer.

I forgot all about the first two desires, but the third was with me continually.

The illness thus obtained from God

When I was half way through my thirty-first year God sent me an illness which prostrated me for three days and nights. On the fourth night I received the last rites of Holy Church as it was thought I could not survive till day. After this I lingered two more days and nights, and on the third night I was quite convinced that I was passing away – as indeed were those about me.

Since I was still young I thought it a great pity to die – not that there was anything on earth I wanted to live for, or on the other hand any pain that I was afraid of, for I trusted God and his mercy. But were I to live I might come to love God more and better, and so ultimately to know and love him more in the bliss of heaven. Yet compared with that eternal bliss the length of my earthly life was so insignificant and short that it seemed to me to be nothing. And so I thought, "Good Lord, let my ceasing to live be to your glory!" Reason and suffering alike told me I was going to die, so I surrendered my will wholeheartedly to the will of God.

Thus I endured till day. By then my body was dead from the waist downwards, so far as I could tell. I asked if I might be helped and supported to sit up, so that my heart could be more freely at God's disposal, and that I might think of him while my life lasted.

My parish priest was sent for to be at my end, and by the time he came my eyes were fixed, and I could no longer speak. He set the cross before my face and said, "I have brought you the image of your Maker and Saviour. Look at it, and be strengthened."

I thought indeed that what I was doing was good enough, for my eyes were fixed heavenwards where by the mercy of God I trusted to go. But I agreed none the less to fix my eyes on the face of the crucifix if I could. And this I was able to do. I thought that perhaps I could look straight ahead longer than I could look up.

Then my sight began to fail, and the room became dark about me, as if it were night, except for the image of the cross which somehow was lighted up; but how was beyond my comprehension. Apart from the cross everything else seemed horrible as if it were occupied by fiends.

Then the rest of my body began to die, and I could hardly feel a thing. As my breathing became shorter and shorter I knew for certain that I was passing away.

Suddenly all my pain was taken away, and I was as fit and well as I had ever been; and this was especially true of the lower part of my body. I was amazed at this sudden change, for I thought it must have been a special miracle of God, and not something natural. And though I felt so much more comfortable I still did not think I was going to survive. Not that this experience was any real comfort to me, for I was thinking I would much rather have been delivered from this world!

Then it came suddenly to mind that I should ask for the second wound of our Lord's gracious gift, that I might in my own body fully experience and understand his blessed passion. I wanted his pain to be my pain: a true compassion producing a longing for God. I was not wanting a physical vision or revelation of God, but such compassion as a soul would naturally have for our Lord Jesus, who for love became a mortal man. Therefore I desired to suffer with him.

The first revelation: the precious crowning of Christ; God fills the heart with the greatest joy; Christ's great humility; the sight of his passion is sufficient strength against all the temptations of the fiends; the glory and humility of the Blessed Virgin Mary

And at once I saw the red blood trickling down from under the garland,* hot, fresh, and plentiful, just as it did at the time of his passion when the crown of thorns was pressed on to the blessed head of God-and-Man, who suffered for me. And I had a strong, deep, conviction that it was he himself and none other that showed me this vision.

At the same moment the Trinity filled me full of heartfelt joy, and I knew that all eternity was like this for those who attain heaven. For the Trinity is God, and God the Trinity; the Trinity is our Maker and keeper, our eternal lover, joy and bliss – all through our Lord Jesus Christ. This was shown me in this first revelation, and, indeed, in them all; for where Jesus is spoken of, the blessed Trinity is always to be understood as I see it.

"*Benedicite Domine!*"** I said, and I meant it in all reverence even though I said it at the top of my voice. I was overwhelmed with wonder that he, so holy and aweful, could be so friendly to a creature at once sinful and carnal. I took it that all this was to prepare me for a time of temptation, for I thought that by God's leave I was bound to be tempted by fiends before I died. With this sight of the blessed passion, and with my mental vision of the Godhead, I knew that there was strength enough for me and, indeed, for every living creature against every fiend of hell, and all temptation.

And then he brought our blessed Lady to mind. In my spirit I saw her as though she were physically present, a simple humble girl, still in her youth, and little more than a child. God showed me something of her spiritual wisdom and honesty, and I understood her profound reverence when she saw her God and Maker;

---

* i.e. the crown of thorns.
** Literally: "Bless ye, O Lord" – "*Benedicite*" is the traditional greeting of religious to each other; almost, "Welcome!".

how reverently she marvelled that he should be born of his own creature, and of one so simple. This wisdom and honesty, which recognized the greatness of her Creator and the smallness of her created self, moved her to say to Gabriel in her utter humility, "Behold the handmaid of the Lord!" By this I knew for certain that in worth and grace she is above all that God made, save the blessed humanity of Christ.

God is all that is good, and gently enfolds us; in comparison with almighty God creation is nothing; man can have no rest until he totally denies himself and everything else for love of God

It was at this time that our Lord showed me spiritually how intimately he loves us. I saw that he is everything that we know to be good and helpful. In his love he clothes us, his goodness. Similarly the help that comes from particular saints and the blessed company of heaven, the delightful love and eternal fellowship we enjoy with them, are all due to his goodness. For through his goodness God has ordained the means to help us, both glorious and many. The chief of these is the blessed nature he took of the Maid Mary with all the resultant means of grace which concern our redemption and everlasting salvation. Therefore he is pleased that we should see him and worship him by these means, knowing and realizing that he is the goodness of it all.

To know the goodness of God is the highest prayer of all, and it is a prayer that accommodates itself to our most lowly needs. It quickens our soul, and vitalizes it, developing it in grace and virtue. Here is the grace most appropriate to our need, and most ready to help. Here is the grace which our soul is seeking now, and which it will ever seek until that day when we know for a fact that he has wholly united us to himself. He does not despise the work of his hands, nor does he disdain to serve us, however lowly our natural need may be. He loves the soul he has made in his own likeness.

For just as the body is clothed in its garments, and the flesh in its skin, and the bones in their flesh, and the heart in its body, so too are we, soul and body, clothed from head to foot in the goodness of God. Yes, and even more closely than that, for all these things will decay and wear out, whereas the goodness of God is unchanging, and incomparably more suited to us. Our lover desires indeed that our soul should cleave to him with all its might, and ever hold on to his goodness. Beyond our power to imagine does this most please God, and speed the soul on its course.

The love of God Most High for our soul is so wonderful that it surpasses all knowledge. No created being can know the greatness, the sweetness, the tenderness of the love that our Maker has for us. By his grace and help therefore let us in spirit stand and gaze, eternally marvelling at the supreme, surpassing, singleminded, incalculable love that God, who is goodness, has for us. Then we can ask reverently of our lover whatever we will. For by nature our will wants God, and the good will of God wants us. We shall never cease wanting and longing until we possess him in fulness and joy. Then we shall have no further wants. Meanwhile his will is that we go on knowing and loving until we are perfected in heaven.

It was for this reason that this lesson of love was shown, with all that follows from it, as you will see. For the strength and foundation of it all was revealed in the first vision. More than anything else, it is the loving contemplation of its Maker that causes the soul to realize its own insignificance, and fills it with holy fear and true humility, and with abundant love to our fellow Christians.

Questions for Study

1 Julian opens by stressing her own lowly condition. She is "simple and uneducated." What do you think lies behind these statements?
2 The passage deals with three "graces" which Julian hoped to obtain. Read the passage through, and ensure that you can identify all three. Which of them does Julian seem to regard as being the most significant?
3 Why does Julian want to see or experience the suffering of Christ on the cross? This is a recurrent theme in Christian spirituality, and Julian's interest in this theme is an excellent illustration of the way in which the passion of Christ relates to spirituality.
4 Julian's second desire is for physical illness. At first sight, this seems a rather morbid and curious request. What does she hope to gain from it? Note how her hope for a near-death experience is closely linked with her desire to be purified and to live a better life subsequently. You will find it helpful here to read 2 Corinthians 12:7–10. Here Paul writes of how God humbled him through a "thorn in the flesh" (generally thought to have been an illness, possibly malaria, contracted during his missionary journeys). What lessons does Paul indicate that he learned from this illness? Can you see any parallels between Paul and Julian in this matter?
5 How does Julian bring together the doctrines of creation, providence, and redemption in this section of her work?

CHAPTER 36

The York Mystery Plays (ca. 1415)

The York Cycle of Mystery Plays is one of the great literary achievements of the later Middle Ages. The "Mystery Play" was a well-established feature of late medieval English life, and a number of cycles have come down to us, most notably those associated with Chester and Wakefield. The York Cycle, however, is the most ambitious, in terms both of its literary and theatrical merits, and also of the number of people required to perform it. The text on which the present translation is based calls for more than 300 speaking parts.

The complexity of the play demanded that it be broken down into smaller parts; a different guild was given the responsibility for each. For example, the first eleven chapters of Genesis were enacted as follows:

Guild	*Drama*
The Barkers	The Fall of the Angels
The Plasterers	The Creation
The Cardmakers	The Creation of Adam and Eve
The Fullers	Adam and Eve in Eden
The Coopers	The Fall of Man
The Armorers	The Expulsion
The Glovers	Cain and Abel
The Shipwrights	The Building of the Ark
The Fishers and Mariners	The Flood

Sometimes a certain dry humor can be detected behind these allocations. For example, the death of Christ was assigned to the Butchers, and would probably have been enacted in the section of the city of York now known as "The Shambles," which was the site of a number of slaughter-houses in the Middle Ages.

The origins of the York Mystery Plays are to be found in the increasingly prosperous economic situation enjoyed by York after the outbreak of the Black Death in 1349. By the fifteenth century, the city was second only to London in terms of financial status. It seems that the text of the Mystery Plays reached its final form by 1415, and was per-

formed annually until it declined in the later sixteenth century, and was eventually abandoned. There are, of course, many who are working to re-establish the plays as an integ-
ral aspect of the life of the City of York, so that the theater which they provided in the
Middle Ages might become a living reality once more.

The York Cycle is basically a dramatic exposition and portrayal of the fall and redemption of humanity, mingling humor, drama, and pathos to yield a heady mixture, capable
of sustaining interest over many days. The section of the work which we shall be considering is the crucifixion of Christ, generally regarded as one of the finest sections of
the entire cycle. Many of the speeches incorporate liturgical elements, especially several
drawn from the Holy Week liturgy, which would have been recognized by the audience.
This section was assigned to the Guild of Pinners – that is, to those who made nails. The
dry humor of this would have been obvious to the crowd watching, as the dominant
theme of this section is the nailing of Christ to the cross. It is important to read this
section as theater, and try to imagine how it would have come across to its audience,
both visually and physically.

> 1 SOLDIER: Sir knights, take heed hither in hie,
> This deed on dreigh we may not draw.
> Ye wot yourselves as well as I
> How lords and leaders of our law
> Have given doom that this dote shall die.   5
> 2 SOLDIER: Sir, all their counsel well we know.
> Since we are come to Calvary
> Let ilk man help now as him owe.
> 3 SOLDIER: We are all ready, lo,
> That foreward to fulfil.   10
> 4 SOLDIER: Let hear how we shall do,
> And go we tite theretill.
>
> 1 SOLDIER: It may not help here for to hone
> If we shall any worship win.
> 2 SOLDIER: He must be dead needlings by noon.   15
> 3 SOLDIER: Then is good time that we begin.
> 4 SOLDIER: Let ding him down, then is he done –
> He shall not dere us with his din.
> 1 SOLDIER: He shall be set and learned soon,
> With care to him and all his kin.   20
> 2 SOLDIER: The foulest death of all
> Shall he die for his deeds.

---

1 *in hie* in haste   2 We may not draw this task out too long   3 *wot* know   4 *leaders*
upholders   5 *doom* judgement   *dote* fool   8 Let each man help now as he ought to
10 *foreward* undertaking   11 *Let hear* Let us see   12 *tite* quickly   *theretill* to it
13 *hone* tarry   14 *worship* esteem   15 *needlings* of necessity   17 Let him be struck
down, then [may he] be dealt with   18 *dere* harm   *din* clamour   19 *set* secured
learned taught (a lesson)   20 *care* woe

3 SOLDIER: That means cross him we shall.

4 SOLDIER: Behold, so right he redes.

1 SOLDIER: Then to this work us must take heed,   25
    So that our working be not wrong.

2 SOLDIER: None other note to neven is need,
    But let us haste him for to hang.

3 SOLDIER: And I have gone for gear good speed,
    Both hammers and nails large and long.   30

4 SOLDIER: Then may we boldly do this deed.
    Come on, let kill this traitor strong.

1 SOLDIER: Fair might ye fall in fere
    That has wrought on this wise.

2 SOLDIER: Us needs not for to lere   35
    Such faitours to chastise.

3 SOLDIER: Since ilka thing is right arrayed,
    The wiselier now work may we.

4 SOLDIER: The cross on ground is goodly graid
    And bored even as it ought to be.   40

1 SOLDIER: Look that the lad on length be laid
    And made me then unto this tree.

2 SOLDIER: For all his fare he shall be flayed,
    That on assay soon shall ye see.

3 SOLDIER: Come forth, thou cursed knave,   45
    Thy comfort soon shall keel.

4 SOLDIER: Thine hire here shall thou have.

1 SOLDIER: Walk on – now work we well.

JESUS: Almighty God, my Father free,
    Let these matters be made in mind: 50
    Thou bade that I should buxom be,
    For Adam's plight for to be pined.
    Here to death I oblige me,
    For that sin for to save mankind,
    And sovereignly beseech I thee   55

---

23 *cross* crucify   24 Indeed he advises us well   25 we must pay attention   27 There is no need to mention any other matter   29 *good speed* speedily   32 *let kill* let us kill *traitor strong* flagrant traitor   33–4 May you all have good luck who have acted in this way   35 We don't need to be taught   36 *faitours* deceivers   37 *ilka* every   *right arrayed* well prepared   39 *goodly graid* well prepared   40 *bored* bored with holes   41 *lad* wretch   42 And then fastened to this cross   43 *fare* practices   *flayed* punished   44 That [claim] you will soon see put to the test   46 *keel* cool (i.e. vanish)   47 *hire* reward   49 *free* gracious   50 *made in mind* particularly called to mind   51 *bade* commanded   *buxom* willing   52 *pined* tormented   53 *oblige me* pledge myself   55 *sovereignly* above all

That they for me may favour find.
And from the fiend them fend,
So that their souls be safe
In wealth without end –
I keep nought else to crave.   60

1 SOLDIER: We, hark sir knights, for Mahound's blood,
Of Adam's kind is all his thought.
2 SOLDIER: The warlock waxes war than wood;
This doleful death ne dreadeth he nought.
3 SOLDIER: Thou should have mind, with main and mood,   65
Of wicked works that thou hast wrought.
4 SOLDIER: I hope that he had been as good
Have ceased of saws that he upsought.
1 SOLDIER: Tho saws shall rue him sore,
For all his sauntering, soon.   70
2 SOLDIER: Ill speed them that him spare
Till he to death be done.

3 SOLDIER: Have done belive, boy, and make thee boun,
And bend thy back unto this tree.
4 SOLDIER: Behold, himself has laid him down   75
In length and breadth as he should be.
1 SOLDIER: This traitor here tainted of treason,
Go fast and fetter him then ye three;
And since he claimeth kingdom with crown,
Even as a king here hang shall he.   80
2 SOLDIER: Now, certes, I shall not fine
Ere his right hand be fast.
3 SOLDIER: The left hand then is mine –
Let see who bears him best.

4 SOLDIER: His limbs on length then shall I lead,   85
And even unto the bore them bring.
1 SOLDIER: Unto his head I shall take heed,
And with mine hand help him to hang.
2 SOLDIER: Now since we four shall do this deed

56 *for* because of   57 *fend* defend   59 *wealth* joy   60 I have no care to ask for anything else   61 *We* exclamation of contempt   *for Mahound's* by Muhammad's (diabolical oath)
62 *kind* offspring   63 The sorcerer grows worse than mad   64 He has no fear of this terrible death   65 You should try to think very hard   67–8 I believe he would have done well
to have stopped saying the things that he thought up   69 He will greatly regret those words
70 *sauntering* babbling   71 *Ill speed them* Bad luck to those   73 *belive* quickly   *boy*
wretch   *boun* ready   77 *tainted* convicted   81 *certes* indeed   *fine* stop   82 *Ere*
Before   84 *bears him* acquits himself   85 *on length* outstretched   *lead* hold

And meddle with this unthrifty thing,   90
Let no man spare for special speed
Till that we have made ending.
3 SOLDIER: This foreward may not fail;
    Now are we right arrayed.
4 SOLDIER: This boy here in our bail   95
    Shall bide full bitter braid.

1 SOLDIER: Sir knights, say, how work we now?
2 SOLDIER: Yes, certes, I hope I hold this hand,
    And to the bore I have it brought
    Full buxomly without band.   100
1 SOLDIER: Strike on then hard, for him thee bought.
2 SOLDIER: Yes, here is a stub will stiffly stand,
    Through bones and sinews it shall be sought –
    This work is well, I will warrand.
1 SOLDIER: Say sir, how do we there?   105
    This bargain may not blin.
3 SOLDIER: It fails a foot and more,
    The sinews are so gone in.

4 SOLDIER: I hope that mark amiss be bored.
2 SOLDIER: Then must he bide in bitter bale.   110
3 SOLDIER: In faith, it was over-scantily scored,
    That makes it foully for to fail.
1 SOLDIER: Why carp ye so? Fast on a cord
    And tug him to, by top and tail.
3 SOLDIER: Yah, thou commands lightly as a lord;   115
    Come help to haul, with ill hail.
1 SOLDIER: Now certes that shall I do –
    Full snelly as a snail.
3 SOLDIER: And I shall tache him to,
    Full nimbly with a nail.   120

This work will hold, that dare I hete,
For now are fest fast both his hend.

90 *unthrifty* unprofitable   91 *spare for* refrain from [using]   *special* the utmost   93 This deed must be assuredly done   95 *bail* custody   96 Shall undergo very dreadful torment 98 *hope* think   100 *buxomly* obediently   *without band* without using a rope   101 for he who redeemed you (usually refers to Christ)   102 *stub* short thick nail   *stiffly* stoutly   103 *sought* applied   104 *warrand* guarantee   106 This business is not at an end   107 It (the bore) is more than a foot out   108 *gone in* shrunken   109 I believe the spot which was marked has been bored in the wrong place (i.e. and not where it was marked)   110 *bide* endure *bale* pain   111 *over-scantily scored* inaccurately drilled   112 That is why it is such a bad piece of work   113 *carp* speak   *Fast* Fasten   114 And pull him [to the bores], by his head and feet   115 *lightly* effortlessly   116 *with ill hail* curse you   118 *snelly* swiftly (an aside) 119 *tache* fasten   *to* to [the cross]   121 *hete* promise   122 *hend* hands

4 SOLDIER: Go we all four then to his feet,
   So shall our space be speedily spend.

2 SOLDIER: Let see what bourd his bale might beet,   125
   Thereto my back now would I bend.

4 SOLDIER: Oh, this work is all unmeet –
   This boring must all be amend.

1 SOLDIER: Ah, peace man, for Mahound,
   Let no man wot that wonder,   130
   A rope shall rug him down
   If all his sinews go asunder.

2 SOLDIER: That cord full kindly can I knit,
   The comfort of this carl to keel.

1 SOLDIER: Fast on then fast, that all be fit,   135
   It is no force how fell he feel.

2 SOLDIER: Lug on ye both a little yet.

3 SOLDIER: I shall not cease, as I have sele.

4 SOLDIER: And I shall fond him for to hit.

2 SOLDIER: Oh, hale!

4 SOLDIER: Whoa, now, I hold it well.   140

1 SOLDIER: Have done, drive in that nail,
   So that no fault be found.

4 SOLDIER: This working would not fail
   If four bulls here were bound.

1 SOLDIER: These cords have evil increased his pains,   145
   Ere he were to the borings brought.

2 SOLDIER: Yea, asunder are both sinews and veins
   On ilka side, so have we sought.

3 SOLDIER: Now all his gauds nothing him gains,
   His sauntering shall with bale be bought.   150

4 SOLDIER: I will go say to our sovereigns
   Of all these works how we have wrought.

1 SOLDIER: Nay sirs, another thing
   Falls first to you and me,
   They bade we should him hang   155
   On high, that men might see.

---

124 So we shall usefully pass our time   125 *bourd* jest   *beet* lighten   127 *unmeet* out of place   128 *amend* altered   130 *wonder* strange thing (i.e. a piece of magic)   131 *rug* tug   132 *If* Even if   133 *kindly* fittingly   *knit* fasten   134 *carl* wretch   135 *Fast* Bind   *fit* ready   136 *no force* no matter   *fell* terrible (i.e. how much pain)   138 as I have joy   139 *fond* attempt   140 *hale* haul   141 *Have done* Stop   145 *evil* severely   148 *so . . . sought* as far as we can see   149–50 Now all his tricks are of no avail, he will pay for his babbling with pain   154 *Falls* Is allotted

2 SOLDIER: We wot well so their words were,
But sir, that deed will do us dere.
1 SOLDIER: It may not mend for to moot more,
This harlot must be hanged here.   160
2 SOLDIER: The mortice is made fit therefore.
3 SOLDIER: Fast on your fingers then, in fere.
4 SOLDIER: I ween it will never come there –
We four raise it not right to-year.
1 SOLDIER: Say man, why carps thou so?   165
Thy lifting was but light.
2 SOLDIER: He means there must be more
To heave him up on height.

3 SOLDIER: Now certes, I hope it shall not need
To call to us more company.   170
Methink we four should do this deed
And bear him to yon hill on high.
1 SOLDIER: It must be done, without dread.
No more, but look ye be ready,
And this part shall I lift and lead;   175
On length he shall no longer lie.
Therefore now make you boun,
Let bear him to yon hill.
4 SOLDIER: Then will I bear here down,
And tent his toes until.   180

2 SOLDIER: We two shall see to either side,
For else this work will wry all wrong.
3 SOLDIER: We are ready.
4 SOLDIER: Good sirs, abide,
And let me first his feet up fang.
2 SOLDIER: Why tent ye so to tales this tide?   185
1 SOLDIER: Lift up!
4 SOLDIER: Let see!
2 SOLDIER: Oh, lift along.
3 SOLDIER: From all this harm he should him hide
And he were God.
4 SOLDIER: The devil him hang!

---

157 *so* what   159 It won't do any good to argue any more   160 *harlot* scoundrel
162 *in fere* all together   163 *ween* believe   164 The four of us will not raise it upright this
year   166 *light* weak   173 *dread* doubt   174 Say no more, but make sure you're
ready   179 *here down* this end   180 And attend to his toes   182 *wry* go
183 *abide* wait   184 *up fang* catch up   185 Why are you paying such attention to talk just
now (i.e. instead of working)   186 *along* from end to end   187 *him hide* protect himself
188 *And* If

1 SOLDIER: For-great harm have I hent,
My shoulder is in sunder.   190

2 SOLDIER: And certes, I am near shent,
So long have I borne under.

3 SOLDIER: This cross and I in two must twin,
Else breaks my back in sunder soon.

4 SOLDIER: Lay down again and leave your din,   195
This deed for us will never be done.

1 SOLDIER: Assay, sirs, let see if any gin
May help him up without hone,
For here should wight men worship win,
And not with gauds all day to gone.   200

2 SOLDIER: More wighter men than we
Full few I hope ye find.

3 SOLDIER: This bargain will not be,
For certes, me wants wind.

4 SOLDIER: So will of work never we were –   205
I hope this carl some cautels cast.

2 SOLDIER: My burden sat me wonder sore,
Unto the hill I might not last.

1 SOLDIER: Lift up, and soon he shall be there,
Therefore fast on your fingers fast.   210

3 SOLDIER: Oh, lift!

1 SOLDIER: We, lo!

4 SOLDIER: A little more.

2 SOLDIER: Hold then!

1 SOLDIER: How now?

2 SOLDIER: The worst is past.

3 SOLDIER: He weighs a wicked weight.

2 SOLDIER: So may we all four say,
Ere he was heaved on height   215
And raised in this array.

4 SOLDIER: He made us stand as any stones,
So boistous was he for to bear.

1 SOLDIER: Now raise him nimbly for the nonce
And set him by this mortice here,   220

189 *For-great* Excessive   *hent* suffered   190 *in sunder* out of joint   191 *shent* exhausted   192 *borne under* held up from underneath   193 *twin* part   194 *sunder* half   196 *for* by   197 *gin* device   198 *hone* delay   199 *wight* robust   200 And not spend the whole day in jests   203 This job will never be done   204 *me wants wind* I am out of breath   205 *will of* at a loss in [our]   206 I believe this wretch has cast some spells   207 afflicted me most grievously   216 *array* fashion   217 He brought us to a standstill   218 *boistous* awkward   219 *for the nonce* (rhyming tag)

And let him fall in all at once,
For certes, that pain shall have no peer.
3 SOLDIER: Heave up!
4 SOLDIER: Let down, so all his bones
Are asunder now on sides sere.
1 SOLDIER: This falling was more fell   225
Than all the harms he had.
Now may a man well tell
The least lith of this lad.

3 SOLDIER: Methinketh this cross will not abide
Ne stand still in this mortice yet.   230
4 SOLDIER: At the first time was it made over-wide;
That makes it wave, thou may well wit.
1 SOLDIER: It shall be set on ilka side
So that it shall no further flit.
Good wedges shall we take this tide   235
And fast the foot, then is all fit.
2 SOLDIER: Here are wedges arrayed
For that, both great and small.
3 SOLDIER: Where are our hammers laid
That we should work withal?   240

4 SOLDIER: We have them even here at our hand.
2 SOLDIER: Give me this wedge, I shall it in drive.
4 SOLDIER: Here is another yet ordained.
3 SOLDIER: Do take it me hither belive.
1 SOLDIER: Lay on then fast.
2 SOLDIER: Yes, I warrand.   245
I thring them sam, so mote I thrive.
Now will this cross full stably stand,
All if he rave they will not rive.
1 SOLDIER: Say sir, how likes you now,
This work that we have wrought?   250
4 SOLDIER: We pray you say us how
Ye feel, or faint ye aught.

JESUS: All men that walk by way or street,
Take tent ye shall no travail tine.

---

222 *peer* equal   224 *on sides sere* in many places   225 *fell* terrible   227 *tell* count
228 *least lith* smallest part of the body   229 *abide* remain firm   230 *Ne* Nor
232 *wave* move about   *wit* understand   233 *set* fixed   *ilka* each   234 *flit* move
235 *this tide* at this time   236 *foot* base of cross   237 *arrayed* ready   240 *withal*
with   243 *ordained* ready   244 Bring it here to me quickly   246 I'll thrust them in
together, so may I prosper   247 *stably* firmly   248 *All if* Even if   *rive* split   252 or
whether you feel faint at all   254 Take heed that you miss none of my suffering

Behold mine head, mine hands, and my feet,   255
And fully feel now, ere ye fine,
If any mourning may be meet,
Or mischief measured unto mine.
My father, that all bales may beet,
Forgive these men that do me pine.   260
What they work, wot they not;
Therefore, my father, I crave,
Let never their sins be sought,
But see their souls to save.

1 SOLDIER: We, hark, he jangles like a jay.   265
2 SOLDIER: Methink he patters like a pie.
3 SOLDIER: He has been doing all this day,
    And made great moving of mercy.
4 SOLDIER: Is this the same that gan us say
    That he was God's son almighty?   270
1 SOLDIER: Therefore he feels full fell affray,
    And deemed this day for to die.
2 SOLDIER: *Vath, qui destruis templum!*
3 SOLDIER: His saws were so, certain.
4 SOLDIER: And sirs, he said to some   275
    He might raise it again.

1 SOLDIER: To muster that he had no might,
    For all the cautels that he could cast.
All if he were in word so wight,
    For all his force now is he fast.   280
As Pilate deemed is done and dight,
    Therefore I rede that we go rest.
2 SOLDIER: This race mun be rehearsed right,
    Through the world both east and west.
3 SOLDIER: Yea, let him hang there still   285
    And make mows on the moon.
4 SOLDIER: Then may we wend at will.
1 SOLDIER: Nay, good sirs, not so soon.

---

256 *fine* pass   257 *meet* equal   258 *mischief* misfortune   259 who may relieve all torments   260 *do...pine* torment me   261 They know not what they do 263 *sought* visited upon them   264 *see* see that   266 *pie* magpie   268 *moving of* reference to   269 *gan* did   271 Because of that he suffered this very cruel assault 272 *deemed* was judged   273 'Ah, thou who destroyest the temple' (Mark 14:58, John 2:19) 274 *saws* words   277 *muster* manifest   278 *cautels* spells   279 Even though his words were so bold   281 *dight* dealt with   282 *rede* advise   283 These events must be properly reported   286 *make mows on* pull faces at

For certes us needs another note:
This kirtle would I of you crave.   290
   2 SOLDIER: Nay, nay, sir, we will look by lot
Which of us four falls it to have.
   3 SOLDIER: I rede we draw cut for this coat –
Lo, see how soon – all sides to save.
   4 SOLDIER: The short cut shall win, that well ye wot,   295
Whether it fall to knight or knave.
   1 SOLDIER: Fellows, ye tharf not flite,
For this mantle is mine.
   2 SOLDIER: Go we then hence tite,
This travail here we tine.   300

Questions for Study

1 Throughout most of this scene, Christ would have been invisible to the audience. He is lying on the wagon, being nailed to the cross. How does the audience learn of what is going on?

2 Christ speaks only twice during this scene. Assess the significance of his words. In what way does his final speech from the cross implicate soldiers, pinners, and the audience in general in the act of crucifixion?

3 Try to assess the theological debate which is going on in the exchange of banter between the four soldiers.

289 we have other business   290 *kirtle* garment   291 *look ... lot* draw lots
292 *falls ... have* shall have it   293 *cut* straws   294 *all ... save* so everybody shall be content   297 *tharf not flite* need not wrangle   300 We are wasting effort here

CHAPTER 37

Thomas à Kempis (1379–1471)

Thomas Haemmerlein is more widely known as Thomas à Kempis (or "van Kempen"), taking this name from his native town of Kempen, near the Rhine, about forty miles north of Cologne. Haemmerlein was born in 1379 or 1380, and was known by the latinized form of his name ("Malleolus," literally "a little hammer") for much of his youth. At the age of 13, he entered the school of the Brethren of the Common Life at Deventer in the Lowlands. By this stage, the school had established a formidable reputation for educational excellence. It was also the center of the *Devotio Moderna*, a highly significant form of spirituality which sought to restore the enthusiasm typical of the early Christian church to its late medieval successor. The origins of this movement are usually traced to the ministry and writings of Gerard Groote, who established the basic principles which would govern its development.

Thomas à Kempis (1379–1471)

Basic description
Leading fifteenth-century Flemish spiritual writer.

Major work
The Imitation of Christ.

Major studies
Albert Hyma, *The Christian Renaissance: A History of the Devotio Moderna*, 2nd edn. New York: Archon Books, 1965.
Regnerus R. Post, *The Modern Devotion*. Leiden: Brill, 1968.

He remained at Deventer for seven years, after which he sought admission to the Canons Regular of Windesheim at Agnetenberg ("The Mount of St Agnes"), near Zwolle. The monastic house had only been established in 1388, so that Thomas arrived at a very early stage in its development. Buildings were still incomplete, and facilities rudimentary. It was not until 1406 that the cloister was completed, in which year Thomas was admitted to the novitiate. He was ordained priest in 1413, the year in which the monastic church was finally completed and consecrated. The relatively long probationary period which Thomas served appears to have reflected the practicalities of life within the

Windesheim congregation at this very early stage in its history, rather than any short-comings on Thomas's part.

A major disruption to the life of the monastic community took place in 1429, when a dispute over an appointment to the neighboring diocese of Utrecht resulted in the community being dispersed until a settlement could be reached. During this time, Thomas had to spend time with his dying brother at a convent near Arnheim. After his brother's death (November 1432), Thomas returned to the congregation, where he served as "sub-prior." As far as can be ascertained, this involved responsibility for the training of novices, and it is possible that the relatively large number of minor treatises which he wrote around this time reflect his teaching ministry in this capacity.

Text: *The Imitation of Christ*

The treatise "Of the Imitation of Christ" appears to have been originally written in Latin early in the fifteenth century. Its exact date and its authorship are still a matter of considerable debate. The book was first issued anonymously, probably in 1418, and was widely copied, generally with various hypothetical attributions – including St. Bernard of Clairvaux, Bonaventure, Innocent III, and Jean Gerson, the Chancellor of the University of Paris, who was a leading figure in the Church in the earlier part of the fifteenth century. Manuscripts of the Latin version survive in considerable numbers all over western Europe, and they, with the vast list of translations and of printed editions, testify to its almost unparalleled popularity. One scribe attributes it to St. Bernard of Clairvaux; but the fact that it contains a quotation from St. Francis of Assisi, who was born thirty years after the death of St. Bernard, disposes of this theory. In England there exist many manuscripts of the first three books, called "Musica Ecclesiastica," frequently ascribed to the English mystic Walter Hilton. But Hilton is generally thought to have died in or around 1395, and there is no evidence of the existence of the work before 1400. Internal evidence strongly points to Thomas as its author, including the use of Latinized forms of Dutch idioms and the use of the Latin word "devotus" in the sense of "an associate of the *Devotio Moderna*."

With the exception of the Bible, no Christian writing has had so wide a vogue or so sustained a popularity as this. And yet, in one sense, it is hardly an original work at all. It owes its structure largely to the writings of the medieval mystics, and its ideas and phrases are a mosaic from the Bible and the Fathers of the early Church. But these elements are interwoven with such delicate skill and a religious feeling at once so ardent and so simple that it promises to remain as popular in the future, as it has for the last five hundred years.

The first book of *The Imitation of Christ* takes the following form:

Thoughts Helpful In The Life Of The Soul

1 Imitating Christ and Despising All Vanities on Earth
2 Having A Humble Opinion of Self
3 The Doctrine of Truth
4 Prudence in Action

5 Reading the Holy Scripture
6 Unbridled Affections
7 Avoiding False Hope and Pride
8 Shunning Over-Familiarity
9 Obedience and Subjection
10 Avoiding Idle Talk
11 Acquiring Peace and Zeal for Perfection
12 The Value of Adversity
13 Resisting Temptation
14 Avoiding Rash Judgment
15 Works Done in Charity
16 Bearing With the Faults of Others
17 Monastic Life
18 The Example Set Us by the Holy Fathers
19 The Practices of a Good Religious
20 The Love of Solitude and Silence
21 Sorrow of Heart
22 Thoughts on the Misery of Man
23 Thoughts on Death
24 Judgment and the Punishment of Sin
25 Zeal in Amending Our Lives

Our text takes the form of the first three chapters of this first book, which can be thought of as setting the tone of this important work.

1 Imitating Christ and Despising All Vanities on Earth

"He who follows Me, walks not in darkness," says the Lord. By these words of Christ we are advised to imitate His life and habits, if we wish to be truly enlightened and free from all blindness of heart. Let our chief effort, therefore, be to study the life of Jesus Christ.

The teaching of Christ is more excellent than all the advice of the saints, and he who has His spirit will find in it a hidden manna. Now, there are many who hear the Gospel often but care little for it because they have not the spirit of Christ. Yet whoever wishes to understand fully the words of Christ must try to pattern his whole life on that of Christ.

What good does it do to speak learnedly about the Trinity if, lacking humility, you displease the Trinity? Indeed it is not learning that makes a man holy and just, but a virtuous life makes him pleasing to God. I would rather feel contrition than know how to define it. For what would it profit us to know the whole Bible by heart and the principles of all the philosophers if we live without grace and the love of God? Vanity of vanities and all is vanity, except to love God and serve Him alone.

This is the greatest wisdom – to seek the kingdom of heaven through contempt of the world. It is vanity, therefore, to seek and trust in riches that perish. It is vanity also to court honor and to be puffed up with pride. It is vanity to follow the lusts of the body and to desire things for which severe punishment later must come. It is vanity to wish for long life and to care little about a well-spent life. It is vanity to be concerned with the present only and not to make provision for things to come. It is vanity to love what passes quickly and not to look ahead where eternal joy abides.

Often recall the proverb: "The eye is not satisfied with seeing nor the ear filled with hearing." Try, moreover, to turn your heart from the love of things visible and bring yourself to things invisible. For they who follow their own evil passions stain their consciences and lose the grace of God.

2 Having A Humble Opinion of Self

Every man naturally desires knowledge; but what good is knowledge without fear of God? Indeed a humble rustic who serves God is better than a proud intellectual who neglects his soul to study the course of the stars. He who knows himself well becomes mean in his own eyes and is not happy when praised by men.

If I knew all things in the world and had not charity, what would it profit me before God Who will judge me by my deeds?

Shun too great a desire for knowledge, for in it there is much fretting and delusion. Intellectuals like to appear learned and to be called wise. Yet there are many things the knowledge of which does little or no good to the soul, and he who concerns himself about other things than those which lead to salvation is very unwise.

Many words do not satisfy the soul; but a good life eases the mind and a clean conscience inspires great trust in God.

The more you know and the better you understand, the more severely will you be judged, unless your life is also the more holy. Do not be proud, therefore, because of your learning or skill. Rather, fear because of the talent given you. If you think you know many things and understand them well enough, realize at the same time that there is much you do not know. Hence, do not affect wisdom, but admit your ignorance. Why prefer yourself to anyone else when many are more learned, more cultured than you?

If you wish to learn and appreciate something worthwhile, then love to be unknown and considered as nothing. Truly to know and despise self is the best and most perfect counsel. To think of oneself as nothing, and always to think well and highly of others is the best and most perfect wisdom. Wherefore, if you see another sin openly or commit a serious crime, do not consider yourself better, for you do not know how long you can remain in good estate. All men are frail, but you must admit that none is more frail than yourself.

3 The Doctrine of Truth

Happy is he to whom truth manifests itself, not in signs and words that fade, but as it actually is. Our opinions, our senses often deceive us and we discern very little.

What good is much discussion of involved and obscure matters when our ignorance of them will not be held against us on Judgment Day? Neglect of things which are profitable and necessary and undue concern with those which are irrelevant and harmful, are great folly.

We have eyes and do not see.

What, therefore, have we to do with questions of philosophy? He to whom the Eternal Word speaks is free from theorizing. For from this Word are all things and of Him all things speak – the Beginning Who also speaks to us. Without this Word no man understands or judges aright. He to whom it becomes everything, who traces all things to it and who sees all things in it, may ease his heart and remain at peace with God.

O God, You Who are the truth, make me one with You in love everlasting. I am often wearied by the many things I hear and read, but in You is all that I long for. Let the learned be still, let all creatures be silent before You; You alone speak to me.

The more recollected a man is, and the more simple of heart he becomes, the easier he understands sublime things, for he receives the light of knowledge from above. The pure, simple, and steadfast spirit is not distracted by many labors, for he does them all for the honor of God. And since he enjoys interior peace he seeks no selfish end in anything. What, indeed, gives more trouble and affliction than uncontrolled desires of the heart?

A good and devout man arranges in his mind the things he has to do, not according to the whims of evil inclination but according to the dictates of right reason. Who is forced to struggle more than he who tries to master himself? This ought to be our purpose, then: to conquer self, to become stronger each day, to advance in virtue.

Every perfection in this life has some imperfection mixed with it and no learning of ours is without some darkness. Humble knowledge of self is a surer path to God than the ardent pursuit of learning. Not that learning is to be considered evil, or knowledge, which is good in itself and so ordained by God; but a clean conscience and virtuous life ought always to be preferred. Many often err and accomplish little or nothing because they try to become learned rather than to live well.

If men used as much care in uprooting vices and implanting virtues as they do in discussing problems, there would not be so much evil and scandal in the world, or such laxity in religious organizations. On the day of judgment, surely, we shall not be asked what we have read but what we have done; not how well we have spoken but how well we have lived.

Tell me, where now are all the masters and teachers whom you knew so well in life and who were famous for their learning? Others have already taken their places and I know not whether they ever think of their predecessors. During life they seemed to be something; now they are seldom remembered. How quickly the glory of the world passes away! If only their lives had kept pace with their learning, then their study and reading would have been worth while.

How many there are who perish because of vain worldly knowledge and too little care for serving God. They became vain in their own conceits because they chose to be great rather than humble.

He is truly great who has great charity. He is truly great who is little in his own eyes and makes nothing of the highest honor. He is truly wise who looks upon all earthly things as folly that he may gain Christ. He who does God's will and renounces his own is truly very learned.

Questions for Study

1 Why does the author place such an emphasis on humility?
2 What impact does the author intend to have on his readers? The text inculcates certain virtues and attitudes, and condemns others. Try to list the virtues which are applauded (such as humility), and those other qualities which are condemned or criticized.
3 Why does Thomas dislike intellectuals? Do you agree with his criticisms? Can they be avoided?

CHAPTER 38

William Dunbar
(ca. 1460–ca. 1520)

Although the documentary evidence is lacking, William Dunbar was probably a member of the family of the earls of Dunbar and March and may have graduated from St. Andrews in 1479. It is believed that he was a Franciscan novice and traveled to England and France on royal business. In 1501 he was certainly in England, probably in connection with the arrangements for the marriage in 1503 of James IV of Scotland and Margaret Tudor. By 1504 he was in priest's orders, and in 1510 he received, as a mark of royal esteem, a pension of £80. After the death of the King at the Battle of Flodden (1513), his pension appears to have ceased, suggesting that he was finally given the benefice which he had so frequently requested.

William Dunbar (ca. 1460–ca. 1520)

Basic description
Scots poet and priest.

Major works
Secular and religious poems, including "The Goldyn Targe" and "Tretis of the tua mariit Wemen and the Wedo."

Major studies
Walter Scheps, *Middle Scots Poets: A Reference Guide to James I of Scotland, Robert Henryson, William Dunbar, and Gavin Douglas*. Boston, MA: G. K. Hall, 1986.
Tom Scott, *Dunbar: A Critical Exposition of the Poems*. Edinburgh: Oliver & Boyd, 1966.

More than 100 poems are attributed to Dunbar. These are generally short and occasional, written in response to personal moods or events at court. They range from the grossest satire to hymns of religious exaltation. Of his longer works, some are courtly Chaucerian pieces (in particular, the dream allegory "The Goldyn Targe"). Dunbar's most celebrated and shocking satire is the alliterative "Tretis of the tua mariit Wemen and the Wedo" ("Treatise of the Two Married Women and the Widow"). The contrast between these two styles is very marked, and helps us understand why he is ranked as Scotland's finest poet. He appears to have been equally at home in a variety of literary genres: religious verse and satire, morality and obscene comedy.

Dunbar is best viewed as one of the few fifteenth-century successors to the genius of Chaucer. There were many imitators of Chaucer's style; few, however, came even close to matching him. While there was no shortage of those who continued to treat the conventional range of courtly and moralizing topics, they rarely managed to approach the intelligence and stylistic accomplishment of their distinguished predecessor. To illustrate this point, we may consider the formidable body of work of John Lydgate, a monk at the abbey of Bury St. Edmunds. Lydgate wrote courtly verse in Chaucer's style ("The Complaint of the Black Knight" and "The Temple of Glas"), but it must be conceded that his imitation of this style was rarely successful. Lydgate may have admired above all Chaucer's "eloquence"; these poets' own polysyllabic style, however, fell short of Chaucer's achievement. Yet if the major English poets of the fifteenth century were generally undistinguished as successors of Chaucer, their contemporaries in Scotland fared substantially better. Chaucer's literary achievement was developed by the Scots *makaris* ("makers"), chief among whom were King James I of Scotland and Dunbar himself.

Text: *Rorate coeli desuper*

One of Dunbar's most famous religious poems is a celebration of Christmas. The opening text in Latin alludes to the liturgy for Christmas Eve. "Rorate, coeli, desuper, et nubes pluant Justum; aperiatur terra, et germinet Salvatorem." This is the Latin version of Isaiah 45:8, which reads as follows, in English translation: "Drop down dew, heavens, from above, and let the clouds rain down righteousness; let the earth be opened, and a saviour spring to life." The closing line to each verse is a variant on the Latin "Et nobis Puer natus est," which is a central feature of the liturgy for Christmas Day. In English translation, this reads: "A son is born to us."

> *Rorate coeli desuper!*
> Hevins, distil your balmy schouris!
> For now is risen the bricht day-ster,
> Fro the rose Mary, flour of flouris:
> The cleir Sone, quhom no cloud devouris,   5
> Surmounting Phebus in the Est,
> Is cumin of his hevinly touris:
> *Et nobis Puer natus est.*
>
> Archangellis, angellis, and dompnationis,
> Tronis, potestatis, and marteiris seir,   10
> And all ye hevinly operationis,
> Ster, planeit, firmament, and spheir,
> Fire, erd, air, and water cleir,
> To Him gife loving, most and lest,
> That come in to so meik maneir;   15
> *Et nobis Puer natus est.*

Synnaris be glad, and penance do,
And thank your Maker hairtfully;
For he that ye micht nocht come to
To you is cumin full humbly   20
Your soulis with his blood to buy
And loose you of the fiendis arrest –
And only of his own mercy;
Pro nobis Puer natus est.

All clergy do to him inclyne,   25
And bow unto that bairn benyng,
And do your observance divyne
To him that is of kingis King:
Encense his altar, read and sing
In holy kirk, with mind degest,   30
Him honouring attour all thing
Qui nobis Puer natus est.

Celestial foulis in the air,
Sing with your nottis upon hicht,
In firthis and in forrestis fair   35
Be myrthful now at all your mycht;
For passit is your dully nicht,
Aurora has the cloudis perst,
The Sone is risen with glaidsum licht,
Et nobis Puer natus est.   40

Now spring up flouris fra the rute,
Revert you upward naturaly,
In honour of the blissit frute
That raiss up fro the rose Mary;
Lay out your levis lustily,   45
Fro deid take life now at the lest
In wirschip of that Prince worthy
Qui nobis Puer natus est.

Sing, hevin imperial, most of hicht!
Regions of air mak armony!   50
All fish in flud and fowl of flicht
Be mirthful and mak melody!
All Gloria in excelsis cry!
Heaven, erd, se, man, bird, and best, –
He that is crownit abone the sky   55
Pro nobis Puer natus est!

Notes on Scots terms:

schouris   showers
cumin   come, entered
seir   various
erd   earth
lest   least
synnaris   sinners
benyng   benign
attour   over, above
perst   pierced
raiss   rose
best   beast

Questions for Discussion

1   In case of difficulty with the Scots, the following translation into modern English may be provided of the opening lines. What point does Dunbar make by opening the poem in this way?

> Rorate coeli desuper
> Heavens distill your balmy showers
> For now is risen the bright day star
> From the rose Mary, flower of flowers

2   The second verse makes specific reference to "fire, earth, air and water," which many pagan writers regarded as the four elements of the universe. What point does Dunbar make by including these elements?

3   Again, for those who find the Scots difficult, the opening lines of the third verse are here translated into modern English. What is the theological point, relating to the doctrine of the incarnation, that Dunbar wants to get across?

> Sinners, be glad and do penance
> And thank your maker heartily
> For he that you might not come to
> To you is come full humbly.

PART IV

The Renaissance and Reformation, 1500–1700

Introduction

The period 1500–1700 was of immense importance to the development of Christian literature, as it was to the shaping of the English language. As the general level of literacy rose, literature enjoyed a new role in an increasingly sophisticated society. Although many works were written in the vernacular during the Middle Ages, the English language itself became increasingly used as the medium of complex literary, philosophical, and religious argument. One of the leading themes of the English Reformation was that religious services and the public reading of the Bible should be in a language that could be understood by the people – in other words, in the vernacular.

The Reformation insistence on the public intelligibility of the liturgy thus led to the English language assuming a new role. No longer was it subordinated to Latin; it was a major language in its own right. As the great era of exploration and colonization began, English began to emerge as a global language. Along with French and Spanish, it was initially the language of conquerors and colonizers, just as it would later become the language of the international business community. The seeds for the future development of the English language and its literature were sown during the period we shall now be considering, which we have termed "Renaissance and Reformation."

Renaissance and Reformation: A Clarification of Terms

It is important to achieve at least some degree of clarification of what is meant by the terms "Renaissance" and "Reformation." We therefore begin by exploring these in some detail.

THE RENAISSANCE

Although the French term "Renaissance" is now universally used to designate the literary and artistic revival in fourteenth- and fifteenth-century Italy, contemporary writers tended to refer to the movement using other terms: "restoration," "revival," "awakening," and "reflowering." In 1546 Paolo Giovio referred to the fourteenth century as "that happy century in which Latin letters are conceived to have been reborn," anticipating this development. Certain historians, most notably Jacob Burckhardt, argued that the Renaissance gave birth to the modern era. It was in this era, Burckhardt argued, that human beings first began to think of themselves as individuals. The communal consciousness of the medieval period gave way to the individual consciousness of the Renaissance. Florence became the new Athens, the intellectual capital of a brave new world, with the river Arno separating the old and the new worlds.

In many ways, Burckhardt's definition of the Renaissance in purely individualist terms is highly questionable, in view of the powerful evidence for the strongly collective values of aspects of Italian Renaissance humanism – for example, a collective approach to city life (seen in Florentine civic humanism), to politics (for example, the parte Guelfa), to commerce (seen in the wool guild), and to family life. But in one sense, Buckhardt is unquestionably correct: something novel and exciting developed in Renaissance Italy, which proved capable of exercising a fascination over generations of thinkers.

The Italian origins of the Renaissance

It is not entirely clear why Italy in general, or Florence in particular, became the cradle of this brilliant new movement in the history of ideas. A number of factors have been identified as having some bearing on the question.

1 Italy was saturated with visible and tangible reminders of the greatness of antiquity. The ruins of ancient Roman buildings and monuments were scattered throughout the land. As Roberto Weiss points out in his *Renaissance Discovery of Classical Antiquity*, these ruins represented vital links with a great past. They appear to have kindled interest in the civilization of ancient Rome at the time of the Renaissance, and acted as a vital stimulus to its thinkers to recover the vitality of classical Roman culture at a time which they regarded as being culturally arid and barren.

2 Scholastic theology – the major intellectual force of the medieval period – was never particularly influential in Italy. Although many Italians achieved fame as theologians (such as Thomas Aquinas and Gregory of Rimini), they generally operated in northern Europe. There was thus an intellectual vacuum in Italy during the fourteenth century. Vacuums tend to be filled – and Renaissance humanism filled this particular gap.

3 The political stability of Florence depended upon the maintenance of her republican government. It was thus natural to turn to the study of the Roman Republic, including its literature and culture, as a model for Florence.

4 The economic prosperity of Florence created leisure, and hence a demand for literature and the arts. Patronage of culture and the arts was seen as a suitable use for surplus wealth.

5 As Byzantium began to crumble – Constantinople finally fell in 1454 – there was an exodus of Greek-speaking intellectuals westward. Italy happened to be con-

veniently close to Constantinople, with the result that many such émigrés settled in her cities. A revival of the Greek language was thus inevitable, and with it a revival of interest in the Greek classics.

The Renaissance and the rebirth of classical literary forms

One of the most important features of the Renaissance was the rise of classical scholarship, and the development of literary forms which reflected those found in the classical world. The Greek and Latin classics were widely studied in their original languages. This study was seen as a means to a literary end, rather than an end in itself. That end was the promotion of contemporary written and spoken eloquence. In other words, the humanists studied the substantial body of classical literature as models of written eloquence, in order to gain inspiration and instruction. Classical learning and philological competence were thus the tools used to exploit the resources of antiquity.

According to several recent interpreters of humanism, the movement embodied the new philosophy of the Renaissance, which arose as a reaction to scholasticism. Thus it was argued that the Renaissance was an age of Platonism, whereas scholasticism was a period of Aristotelianism. Others argued that the Renaissance was essentially an anti-religious phenomenon, foreshadowing the secularism of the eighteenth-century Enlightenment. Hans Baron argued that humanism was basically a republican movement, which studied Cicero in order to benefit from his political ideas.

Two major difficulties confronted this rather ambitious interpretation of humanism. First, as we have seen, humanists appear to have been primarily concerned with the promotion of eloquence. While it is not true to say that humanists made no significant contribution to philosophy, the fact remains that they were primarily interested in the world of letters. Thus in comparison with those devoted to the "pursuit of eloquence," there are remarkably few humanist writings devoted to philosophy – and these are generally somewhat amateurish. Baron's theory concerning the humanist use of Cicero was weakened through the observation that most humanists read Cicero to learn from his style of writing, rather than from his political ideas.

Second, intensive study of humanist writings uncovered the disquieting fact that "humanism" was remarkably heterogeneous. For example, many humanist writers did indeed favor Platonism – but others favored Aristotelianism. The stubborn persistence of Aristotelianism (for example, at the University of Padua) throughout the Renaissance is a serious obstacle to those who regard humanism as philosophically homogeneous. Some Italian humanists did indeed display what seem to be anti-religious attitudes – but other Italian humanists were profoundly pious. Some humanists were indeed republicans – but others adopted different political attitudes. Recent studies have also drawn attention to a less attractive side of humanism – the obsession of some humanists with magic and superstition – which is difficult to harmonize with the conventional view of the movement. In short, it became increasingly clear that "humanism" seemed to lack any coherent philosophy. No single philosophical or political idea dominated or characterized the movement. It seemed to many that the term "humanism" would have to be dropped from the vocabulary of historians, because it had no meaningful content. Designating a writer as a "humanist" conveys no essential information concerning his philosophical, political or religious views.

In fact, it is clear that the Italian Renaissance is so multifaceted that just about every generalization concerning its "characteristic ideas" tends to be a distortion. It is for this reason that the view of humanism developed by Paul Oskar Kristeller is of decisive importance. Kristeller's view of humanism has gained wide acceptance within North American and European scholarship, and has yet to be discredited. Kristeller envisages humanism as a cultural and educational movement, primarily concerned with the promotion of literary eloquence in its various forms. Its interests in morals, philosophy, and politics are of secondary importance. To be a humanist is to be concerned with eloquence first and foremost, and with other matters incidentally. Humanism was thus essentially a literary and cultural program, which appealed to classical antiquity as a model of eloquence. In art and architecture, as in the written and spoken word, antiquity was seen as a cultural resource, which could be appropriated by the Renaissance.

The transmission of the culture of the Italian Renaissance

At this point, we must pause to clarify one important point. The "humanism" in which we are interested is primarily northern European humanism, rather than Italian humanism. It is clear that northern European humanism was decisively influenced by Italian humanism at every stage of its development. If there were indigenous humanist movements in northern Europe which originated independently of their Italian counterpart (which is very doubtful), the evidence unambiguously points to those movements having subsequently been decisively influenced by Italian humanism. This does not mean that northern humanists simply took over Italian ideals in their totality; rather, these ideals were adopted and adapted, as they seemed to relate to the northern situation. Thus the civic humanism associated with, for example, the city of Florence, was not adopted extensively in northern Europe, except in a few German and Swiss cities.

So how did the culture of the Renaissance find its way north of the Alps? Three main channels for the diffusion of the methods and ideals of the Italian Renaissance into northern Europe have been identified.

1 Through northern European scholars moving south to Italy, perhaps to study at an Italian university or as part of a diplomatic mission. On returning to their homeland, they brought the spirit of the Renaissance back with them.
2 Through the foreign correspondence of the Italian humanists. Humanism was concerned with the promotion of written eloquence, and the writing of letters was seen as a means of embodying and spreading the ideals of the Renaissance. The foreign correspondence of Italian humanists was considerable, extending to most parts of northern Europe.
3 Through printed books, originating from sources such as the Aldine Press in Venice. These works were often reprinted by northern European presses, particularly those at Basle in Switzerland. Italian humanists often dedicated their works to northern European patrons, thus ensuring that they were taken notice of in potentially influential quarters.

The relation between Renaissance and Reformation

In what way are the Renaissance and Reformation related? Some scholars see the Reformation as the religious outworking of the Renaissance agenda; others argue that they are fundamentally different in orientation. Yet most of those who achieved prominence as Reformation thinkers – such as Philipp Melanchthon, John Calvin, and Huldrych Zwingli – were steeped in the learning of the Renaissance, suggesting that there is some positive link between the two movements. In fact, it can be shown that, despite real differences in emphasis between the movements, they share one important feature – the desire to return to their origins, in order to renew themselves.

The literary and cultural program of humanism can be summarized in the Latin slogan *ad fontes* – back to the original sources. Those who wanted to renew western culture argued that the squalor of the medieval period should be bypassed, in order to recover the intellectual and artistic glories of the classical period. The "filter" of medieval commentaries – whether on legal texts or on the Bible – is abandoned, in order to engage directly with the original texts. Applied to the Christian church, the slogan *ad fontes* meant a direct return to the title-deeds of Christianity – to the patristic writers, and supremely to the Bible.

The world of literature could thus be renewed and given a fresh vision by the study of classical literature; the Christian church could be renewed and given a fresh vision by the direct study of the New Testament. The parallelism is as obvious as it is important. With this point it mind, let us turn to consider the general characteristics of the Reformation, and its relevance to our subject.

THE REFORMATION

The term "Reformation" is used by historians and theologians to refer primarily to the western European movement, centering upon individuals such as Martin Luther, Huldrych Zwingli and John Calvin, concerned with the moral, theological and institutional reform of the Christian church in that region. Initially, up to about 1525, the Reformation may be regarded as centering upon Martin Luther and the University of Wittenberg, in modern-day northeastern Germany. However, the movement also gained strength, initially independently, in the Swiss city of Zurich in the early 1520s. Through a complex series of developments, the Zurich Reformation gradually underwent a series of political and theological developments, eventually coming to be associated primarily with the city of Geneva (now part of modern-day Switzerland, although then an independent city state) and John Calvin. Although initially focusing on regions such as Germany and Switzerland, the Reformation had a considerable impact on most of western Europe during the sixteenth century, provoking either a positive response to at least one aspect of the movement (as, for example, in England, Holland, and Scandinavia) or a reaction against the movement resulting in a consolidation of Catholicism (as, for example, in Spain and France).

The term "Reformation" is used in a number of senses, and it is helpful to distinguish them. Four elements may be involved in its definition, and each will be discussed briefly below: Lutheranism, the Reformed church (often referred to as

"Calvinism"), the "radical Reformation," often still referred to as "Anabaptism," and the "Counter Reformation" or "Catholic Reformation."

The Lutheran Reformation

The Lutheran Reformation is particularly associated with the German territories and the pervasive personal influence of one charismatic individual – Martin Luther. Luther was particularly concerned with the doctrine of justification, which formed the central point of his religious thought. The Lutheran Reformation was initially an academic movement, concerned primarily with reforming the teaching of theology at the University of Wittenberg. Wittenberg was an unimportant university, and the reforms introduced by Luther and his colleagues within the theology faculty attracted little attention. It was Luther's personal activities – such as his posting of the famous Ninety-Five Theses (October 31, 1517) – which attracted considerable interest, and brought the ideas in circulation at Wittenberg to the attention of a wider audience.

The Calvinist Reformation

The origins of Calvinist Reformation, which brought the Reformed churches (such as the Presbyterians) into being, lie with developments within the Swiss Confederation. Whereas the Lutheran Reformation had its origins in an academic context, the Reformed church owed its origins to a series of attempts to reform the morals and worship of the church (but not necessarily its doctrine) according to a more biblical pattern. It must be emphasized that although Calvin gave this style of Reformation its definitive form, its origins are to be traced back to earlier reformers, such as Huldrych Zwingli and Heinrich Bullinger, based at the leading Swiss city of Zurich.

Although most of the early Reformed theologians – such as Zwingli – had an academic background, their reforming programs were not academic in nature. They were directed toward the church, as they found it in the Swiss cities, such as Zurich, Berne, and Basle. Whereas Luther was convinced that the doctrine of justification was of central significance to his program of social and religious reform, the early Reformed thinkers had relatively little interest in doctrine, let alone one specific doctrine. Their reforming program was institutional, social and ethical, in many ways similar to the demands for reform emanating from the humanist movement.

The consolidation of the Reformed church is generally thought to begin with the stabilization of the Zurich reformation after Zwingli's death in battle (1531), under his successor Heinrich Bullinger, and to end with the emergence of Geneva as its power base, and John Calvin as its leading spokesman, in the 1550s. The gradual shift in power within the Reformed church (initially from Zurich to Berne, and subsequently from Berne to Geneva) took place over the period 1520–60, eventually establishing both the city of Geneva, its political system (republicanism) and its religious thinkers (initially Calvin, and after his death Theodore Beza) as predominant within the Reformed church. This development was consolidated through the establishment of the Genevan Academy (founded in 1559), at which Reformed pastors were trained.

The term "Calvinism" is often used to refer to the religious ideas of the Reformed church. Although still widespread in the literature relating to the Reformation, this practice is now generally discouraged. It is becoming increasingly clear that later sixteenth-century Reformed theology draws on sources other than the ideas of Calvin himself. To refer to later sixteenth- and seventeenth-century Reformed thought as "Calvinist" implies that it is essentially the thought of Calvin – and it is now generally agreed that Calvin's ideas were modified subtly by his successors. The term "Reformed" is generally preferred, whether to refer to those churches (mainly in Switzerland, the Lowlands, and Germany) or religious thinkers (such as Theodore Beza, William Perkins, or John Owen) which based themselves upon Calvin's celebrated religious textbook, *Institutes of the Christian Religion*, or church documents (such as the famous *Heidelberg Catechism*) based upon it.

Of the three constituents of the Protestant Reformation – Lutheran, Reformed or Calvinist, and Anabaptist – it is the Reformed wing which is of particular importance to the English-speaking world. Puritanism is a specific form of Reformed Christianity. To understand the religious and literary history of seventeenth-century England, it is necessary to come to grips with at least some of the theological insights and part of the religious outlook of Puritanism, which underlie their social and political attitudes.

The Radical Reformation (Anabaptism)

The term "Anabaptist" owes its origins to Zwingli (the word literally means "rebaptizers," and refers to what was perhaps the most distinctive aspect of Anabaptist practice – the insistence that only those who had made a personal public profession of faith should be baptized). Anabaptism seems to have first arisen around Zurich, in the aftermath of Zwingli's reforms within the city in the early 1520s. It centered on a group of individuals (among whom we may note Conrad Grebel) who argued that Zwingli was not being faithful to his own reforming principles. He preached one thing, and practiced another. Although Zwingli professed faithfulness to the *sola scriptura*, "by scripture alone," principle, Grebel argued that he retained a number of practices – including infant baptism, the close link between church and magistracy, and the participation of Christians in warfare – which were not sanctioned or ordained by Scripture. In the hands of such radical thinkers, the *sola scriptura* principle would be radicalized; reformed Christians would only believe and practice those things explicitly taught in Scripture. Zwingli was alarmed by this, seeing it as a destabilizing development which threatened to cut the Reformed church at Zurich off from its historical roots and its continuity with the Christian tradition of the past.

A number of common elements can be discerned within the various strands of the movement: a general distrust of external authority, the rejection of infant baptism in favor of the baptism of adult believers, the common ownership of property, and an emphasis upon pacifism and non-resistance. To take up one of these points: in 1527, the governments of Zurich, Berne, and St Gallen accused the Anabaptists of believing "that no true Christian can either give or receive interest or income on a sum of capital; that all temporal goods are free and common, and that all can have full property rights to them." It is for this reason that "Anabaptism" is often referred to as the "left wing of the Reformation" (Roland H. Bainton) or the "radical Reformation" (George Hunston Williams).

The Catholic Reformation

This term is often used to refer to the revival within Roman Catholicism in the period following the opening of the Council of Trent (1545). In older scholarly works, the movement is often designated the "Counter Reformation": as the term suggests, the Roman Catholic church developed means of combating the Protestant Reformation, in order to limit its influence. It is, however, becoming increasingly clear that the Roman Catholic church countered the Reformation partly by reforming itself from within, in order to remove the grounds of Protestant criticism. In this sense, the movement was a reformation of the Roman Catholic church, as much as it was a reaction against the Protestant Reformation.

The same concerns underlying the Protestant Reformation in northern Europe were channeled into the renewal of the Catholic church, particularly in Spain and Italy. The Council of Trent, the foremost component of the Catholic Reformation, clarified Catholic teaching on a number of confusing matters, and introduced much-needed reforms in relation to the conduct of the clergy, ecclesiastical discipline, religious education and missionary activity. The movement for reform within the church was greatly stimulated by the reformation of many of the older religious orders, and the establishment of new orders (such as the Jesuits). The more specifically theological aspects of the Catholic Reformation will be considered in relation to its teachings on Scripture and tradition, justification by faith, and the sacraments. As a result of the Catholic Reformation, many of the abuses which originally lay behind the demands for reform – whether these came from humanists or Protestants – were removed.

In its broadest sense, the term "Reformation" is used to refer to all four of the movements described above. The term is also used in a somewhat more restricted sense, meaning "the Protestant Reformation," excluding the Catholic Reformation. In this sense, it refers to the three Protestant movements noted above. In many scholarly works, however, the term "Reformation" is used to refer to what is sometimes known as the "magisterial Reformation," or the "mainstream Reformation" – in other words, that linked with the Lutheran and Reformed churches (including Anglicanism), and excluding the Anabaptists.

The Translation of the Bible into English

It will be clear that one of the most important events in the shaping of the modern English language was the translation of the Bible into the vernacular. When a medieval Christian writer refers to "Scripture," or cites from the Bible, the translation in question is almost invariably some version of the *textus vulgatus*, "common text," drawn up by the great patristic biblical scholar Jerome in the late fourth and early fifth centuries. Although the term "Vulgate" did not come into general use in the sixteenth century, it is perfectly acceptable to use the term to refer to the specific Latin translation of the Bible prepared by Jerome in the late fourth and early fifth centuries. This text was passed down to the Middle Ages in a number of forms, with considerable variations between them. For example, Theodulf and Alcuin, noted scholars of the Dark Ages, used quite different versions of the Vulgate text.

A new period of intellectual activity opened up in the eleventh century, as the Dark Ages lifted. It was clear that a standard version of this text was required to service the new interest in Christian theology and spirituality which developed as part of this intellectual renaissance. If theologians were to base their ideas upon different versions of the Vulgate, an equally great, if not greater, variation in their conclusions would seem to be inevitable. This need for standardization was met by what appears to have been a joint speculative venture by some Paris theologians and stationers in 1226, resulting in the "Paris version" of the Vulgate text. By then, Paris was recognized as the leading center of theology in Europe, with the inevitable result that – despite its many obvious imperfections – the "Paris version" of the Vulgate became established as normative. This version, it must be emphasized, was not commissioned or sponsored by any ecclesiastical figure: it appears to have been a purely commercial venture. History, however, concerns the fate of accidents, and it is necessary to note that medieval theologians, attempting to base their theology upon Scripture, were obliged to equate Scripture with a rather bad commercial edition of an already faulty Latin translation of the Bible. The rise of humanist textual and philological techniques would expose the distressing discrepancies between the Vulgate and the texts it purported to translate – and thus open the way to doctrinal reformation as a consequence.

During the Middle Ages, a number of vernacular versions of Scripture were produced. Although it was once thought that the medieval church condemned this process of translation, it is now known that neither the production of such translations, nor their use by clergy or laity, was ever explicitly forbidden. An important example of such translations is provided by the Wycliffe versions, produced by a group of scholars who gathered around John Wycliffe at Lutterworth. The motivation for the translation of the Bible into English was partly spiritual, partly political. It was spiritual in that the laity could now have access to "Goddis lawe," and political in that an implicit challenge was posed to the teaching authority of the church. The laity were enabled to detect the obvious differences between the scriptural vision of the church and its somewhat corrupt English successor, thus setting the agenda for a program of reform.

Important though such vernacular versions are, their importance must not be exaggerated. All these versions, it must be remembered, were simply translations of the Vulgate. They were not based upon the best manuscripts of Scripture, in their original languages, but upon the Vulgate version, with all its weaknesses and errors. The agenda for the Reformation would be set through the application of textual and philological techniques of a sophistication far beyond that of Wycliffe's circle at Lutterworth. It is to those methods, developed by humanist scholars such as Lorenzo Valla and Erasmus of Rotterdam, that we may now turn.

The great humanist emphasis upon the need to return *ad fontes* (literally, "to the fountainheads") established the priority of Scripture over its commentators, particularly those of the Middle Ages. It was necessary to go back to the fountainheads of Christian life and thought in the New Testament, rather than rest content with its rather dull medieval interpretations. The text of Scripture was therefore to be approached directly, rather than through a complicated system of glosses and commentaries, set out – with the best possible intentions – by medieval scholars.

But there was more to the humanist agenda than just returning directly to the Bible. Scripture was to be read directly in its original languages, rather than in Latin translation. Thus the Old Testament was to be studied in Hebrew (except for those few sections written in Aramaic), and the New Testament was to be read in Greek. The growing humanist interest in the Greek language (which many humanists held to be supreme in its capacity to mediate philosophical concepts) further consolidated the importance attached to the New Testament documents. The late Renaissance scholarly ideal was to be *trium linguarum gnarus,* "expert in three languages (Hebrew, Greek, and Latin)." Trilingual colleges were established at Alcalá in Spain, at Paris, and at Wittenberg. The new interest in, and availability of, Scripture in its original language soon brought to light a number of serious translation mistakes in the Vulgate, some of considerable importance.

Yet to translate the Bible accurately into the vernacular meant competence on the part of its translators in the classical languages. The humanist movement made available two essential tools required for the new method of study of the Bible. First, it made available the printed text of Scripture in its original languages. For example, Erasmus' *Novum Instrumentum omne* of 1516 allowed scholars direct access to the printed text of the Greek New Testament, and Jacques Lefèvre d'Etaples provided the Hebrew text of a group of important Psalms in 1509. Second, it made available manuals of classical languages, allowing scholars to learn languages which they otherwise could not have acquired. Reuchlin's Hebrew primer, *de rudimentis hebraicis* (1506), is an excellent example of this type of material. Greek primers were more common: the Aldine Press produced an edition of Lascaris' Greek grammar in 1495; Erasmus' translation of the famous Greek grammar of Theodore of Gaza appeared in 1516, and the leading German humanist and reformer Philipp Melanchthon produced a masterly Greek primer in 1518.

The humanist movement also developed textual techniques capable of establishing accurately the best text of Scripture. These techniques had been used, for example, by Lorenzo Valla to demonstrate the inauthenticity of the famous "Donation of Constantine." It was now possible to eliminate many of the textual errors which had crept into the Parisian edition of the Vulgate. Erasmus shocked his contemporaries by excluding a significant part of one verse of the Bible (1 John 5:7), which he could not find in any Greek manuscript. For Erasmus, this had to be regarded as a later addition. The Vulgate version reads as follows: "For there are three that testify [in heaven: the Father, the Word and the Holy Spirit, and these three are one. And there are three that testify on earth]: the Spirit, the water and the blood." The bracketed section of the verse, omitted by Erasmus, was certainly there in the Vulgate – but not in the Greek texts which it purported to translate. As this text had become an important proof-text for the doctrine of the Trinity, many were outraged at his action. Theological conservatism here often triumphed over scholarly progress: even the famous King James Version (also known as the Authorized Version) of 1611, for example, included the spurious verse, despite serious doubts over its authenticity.

These new scholarly developments meant that accurate translation of the text of the Bible into the living languages of Europe was a real possibility. In Germany, Luther provided translations of both Old and New Testaments into his native early modern high German, encountering considerable criticism in doing so. That criticism related partly to the very principle of translating the Bible into German, and partly to the specifics of Luther's translation. For example, Luther was widely accused of making the Bible say what Luther wanted it to say, through the translation process itself. Luther's "Letter on Biblical Translation" is a classic statement of the issues involved.

Yet our attention clearly must focus on the English language. The translation of the Bible into English can be argued to have been of momentous importance to the shaping of the modern English language. Although, as we have seen, vernacular versions of parts of the Bible were produced in medieval England, the real credit for modern English versions of the Bible must go to William Tyndale. Tyndale may be seen as having set in place developments which would eventually lead to that landmark of English Bibles – the King James Version of 1611. We shall be discussing the background to this translation at an appropriate point later in Part IV; it should be noted at this point, however, that the appearance of this translation can be seen as marking a defining moment in the emergence of modern English.

Yet the new importance attached to the Bible came to have an impact in other areas of literature. Although all Christians regard the Bible as having central importance to Christian thought and life, particular importance came to be attached to it as a result of the Reformation of the sixteenth century. "The Bible," wrote William Chillingworth, "I say, the Bible only, is the religion of Protestants." These famous words of this seventeenth-century English Protestant summarize the Reformation attitude to Scripture. It was inevitable that this new emphasis on the importance of the Bible would lead to the development of new literary genres, or the consolidation of existing forms of literature which were well suited to encouraging biblical literacy. These include the following:

1   The *biblical commentary*, which aimed to allow its readers to peruse and understand the word of God, explaining difficult phrases, identifying points of importance, and generally allowing its readers to become familiar with the thrust and concerns of the biblical passage. Writers such as John Calvin (1509–64), Martin Luther (1483–1546), and Huldrych Zwingli (1484–1531) produced commentaries aimed at a variety of readerships, both academic and lay.

2   The *expository sermon* aimed to fuse the horizons of the scriptural text and its hearers, applying the principles underlying the scriptural passage to the situation of the audience. Calvin's sermons at Geneva are a model of their kind. Calvin made extensive use in his preaching of the notion of *lectio continua* – the continuous preaching through a scriptural book, rather than on passages drawn from a lectionary or chosen by the preacher. For example, during the period between March 20, 1555 and July 15, 1556, Calvin is known to have preached some two hundred sermons on a single scriptural book – Deuteronomy.

3 Works of *biblical theology*, such as Calvin's *Institutes of the Christian Religion*, were intended to encourage their readers to gain an appreciation of the theological coherence of Scripture, by bringing together and synthesizing its statements on matters of theological importance. By doing this, it enabled its readers to establish a coherent and consistent worldview, which would undergird their everyday lives. For Calvin, as for the reformers in general, Scripture molded doctrine, which in turned shaped the realities of Christian life.

We shall be considering some of these types of literature in the rest of Part IV.

CHAPTER 39

Erasmus of Rotterdam (1469?–1536)

Erasmus of Rotterdam is widely acknowledged to be the leading representative of Renaissance humanism during the sixteenth century. Erasmus was the illegitimate son of Roger Gerard, a priest. After the death of his parents, his guardians sent him to a school in 's Hertogenbosch, run by the Brethren of the Common Life, a lay religious movement that fostered monastic vocations. Erasmus would remember this school only for a severe discipline intended, he said, to teach humility by breaking a boy's spirit. Erasmus then entered the Augustinian canons regular at Steyn, near Gouda, where he seems to have remained for about seven years (1485–92). During this period of his life, he paraphrased Lorenzo Valla's *Elegantiae*, which was both a compendium of pure classical usage and a manifesto against the scholastic "barbarians" who had allegedly corrupted it. After his ordination to the priesthood in April 1492, Erasmus accepted a post as Latin secretary to Henry of Bergen, Bishop of Cambrai.

This appointment rescued him from what he regarded as the barbarities of monastic life. However, as events turned out, Erasmus was not really suited to a courtier's life. He left to study theology at the University of Paris in 1495, but took an instant dislike to the Collège de Montaigu, and to the forms of theology he encountered there – which would be the subject of parody in his *Moriae Encomium*.

In 1499 one of his well-to-do Latin pupils invited Erasmus to England. There he met Sir Thomas More, who became a friend for life. An encounter with John Colet gave a new sense of direction and urgency to Erasmus' desire to expound Scripture in the manner of Jerome and the other Church Fathers, who lived in an age when men still understood and practiced the classical art of rhetoric – unlike the crude barbarisms which he found in the writings of scholastic theologians.

Erasmus of Rotterdam (1469?–1536)

Basic description
Leading Renaissance humanist.

Major works
Enchiridion Militis Christiani (1503); *Moriae Encomium* (1511); *Novum Instrumentum Omne* (1516).

Editions of works
The Complete Works of Erasmus, 86 vols. Toronto: University of Toronto Press, 1969–   .

Major studies
James K. McConica, *Erasmus*. Oxford: Oxford University Press, 1991.

Geraldine Thompson, *Under Pretext of Praise: Satiric Mode in Erasmus' Fiction*. Toronto: University of Toronto Press, 1977.

By 1502 Erasmus had settled down in the university town of Louvain, and was reading Origen and St. Paul in Greek. It was at this point that he wrote what some regard as his finest work – the *Enchiridion Militis Christiani* ("Handbook of the Christian Soldier"). Although the work was first published in 1503, and then reprinted in 1509, the real impact of the work dates from its third printing in 1515. From that moment onward, it became a cult work, apparently going through twenty-three editions in the next six years. Its appeal was to educated lay men and women, whom Erasmus regarded as the most important resource that the church possessed. Its amazing popularity in the years after 1515 may allow us to suggest that a radical alteration in lay self-perception took place as a result – and it can hardly be overlooked that the reforming rumbles at Zurich and Wittenberg date from soon after the *Enchiridion* became a bestseller. Erasmus' success also highlighted the importance of printing as a means of disseminating radical new ideas – a point which neither Zwingli nor Luther overlooked, when their turn came to propagate such ideas.

The *Enchiridion* developed the attractive thesis that the church of the day could be reformed by a collective return to the writings of the Fathers and Scripture. The regular reading of Scripture is put forward as the key to a new lay piety, on the basis of which the church may be renewed and reformed. Erasmus conceived of his work as a lay person's guide to Scripture, providing a simple yet learned exposition of the "philosophy of Christ." This "philosophy" is really a form of practical morality, rather than an academic philosophy: the New Testament concerns the knowledge of good and evil, in order that its readers may eschew the latter and love the former. The New Testament is the *lex Christi*, "the law of Christ," which Christians are called to obey. Christ is the example whom Christians are called to imitate. Yet Erasmus does not understand Christian faith to be a mere external observance of some kind of morality. His characteristically humanist emphasis upon inner religion leads him to suggest that the reading of Scripture transforms its readers, giving them a new motivation to love God and their neighbors.

A number of features of this book are of particular importance. First, Erasmus understands the future vitality of Christianity to lie with the laity, not the clergy. The clergy are seen as educators, whose function is to allow the laity to achieve the same level of understanding as themselves. There is no room for any superstitions which give the clergy a permanent status superior to their lay charges. Second, Erasmus' strong emphasis upon the "inner religion" results in an understanding of Christianity which makes no reference to the church – its rites, priests, or institutions. Why bother confessing sins to another human, asks Erasmus, just because he's a priest, when you can confess them directly to God himself? Religion is a matter of the individual's heart and mind: it is an inward state. Erasmus pointedly avoids any significant reference to the sacraments in his exposition of Christian living. Similarly, he discounts the view that the "religious life" (in other words, being a monk or a nun) is the highest form of the Christian life: the lay person who reads Scripture is just as faithful to his or her calling as any monk. The revolutionary character of Erasmus' *Enchiridion* lies in its daring new suggestion that the recognition of the Christian vocation of the lay person holds the key to the revival of the church. Clerical and ecclesiastical authority is discounted. Scripture should and must be made available to all, in order that all may return *ad fontes*, to drink of the fresh and living waters of the Christian faith, rather than the stagnant ponds of late medieval religion.

Erasmus, however, came to recognize that there were serious obstacles in the path of the course he proposed, and was responsible for a number of major developments to remove them. First, there was a need to be able to study the New Testament in its original language, rather than in the inaccurate Vulgate translation. This necessitated two tools, neither of which was then available: the necessary philological competence to handle the Greek text of the New Testament, and direct access to that text itself.

The first tool became available through Erasmus' discovery of Lorenzo Valla's fifteenth-century notes on the Greek text of the New Testament. These notes, which had languished in the archives of a local monastery, were discovered and published by Erasmus in 1505. The second was made available through the publication by Erasmus of the first printed Greek New Testament, the *Novum Instrumentum Omne*, which rolled off Froben's presses at Basle in 1516. Although a superior version of the same text had been set up in type at Alcalá in Spain two years earlier, publication of this version (the so-called Complutensian Polyglot) was delayed, probably for political reasons, until 1520. Erasmus' text was not as reliable as it ought to have been: Erasmus had access to a mere four manuscripts for most of the New Testament, and only one for its final part, the Book of Revelation. As it happened, that manuscript left out five verses, which Erasmus himself had to translate into Greek from the Latin of the Vulgate. Nevertheless, it proved to be a literary milestone. For the first time, theologians had the opportunity of comparing the original Greek text of the New Testament with the later Vulgate translation into Latin.

After this, Erasmus went on to spend some time in England (1509–14). Relatively little is known of this, except that he lectured at Cambridge and worked on scholarly projects, including the Greek text of the New Testament. It was during this period that he wrote the text which we shall be considering in detail – the "Praise of Folly" (*Moriae Encomium*).

Text: *Moriae Encomium*

Erasmus' *Moriae Encomium* ("Praise of Folly") was written in 1509 and first published in 1511. Erasmus states that he wrote the work in a week, while staying with Sir Thomas More in England. It is a complex and unusual text, which has proved notoriously resistant to interpretation. The title of the work is to be seen as a pun, reflecting Erasmus' high regard for Sir Thomas More, a humanist who had achieved high office in the court of Henry VIII – and who, incidentally, would later be executed for his loyalty to the Pope during the English Reformation. The title of the work could also be translated "Praise of More."

At one level, the work can be read as a criticism of the pointless theological debates of the late fifteenth and early sixteenth centuries, which Erasmus had known at first hand during his period at the University of Paris. There is ample documentary evidence that late medieval theologians saw the posing of apparently ridiculous questions as a legitimate way of opening up theological debates. For example, William of Ockham inquired whether God could have become incarnate as an ass, rather than as a human being; his later followers extended this mode of inquiry, speculating over whether God could have become incarnate as a cucumber. The point of the question was, in fact, serious; it allowed discussion of the essential features of the doctrine of the incarnation. Erasmus, however, had little difficulty in pointing out the more ridiculous aspects of this theological debate. (It is worth noting here that Martin Dorp [1485–1525], a conservative Louvain theologian, appears to have seen himself being paradied in the work, and took umbrage in consequence.) The work also includes a major critique of the behavior of senior figures within the church, and offers a highly satirical view of many widely observed religious practices of the late Middle Ages.

It is not clear why the work was so successful. In many ways, it can be seen to repeat the major themes of the *Enchiridion*, published several years earlier. However, there are good reasons for suggesting that its light, bantering style and charming irreverence made it a much easier and more enjoyable work to read. Certainly Leo X, a pope who must have recognized that the satirical barbs of the work were directed against his own church, is rumored to have enjoyed reading the work. The translation presented here was undertaken by John Wilson in 1688, and is itself a minor classic of the later English Renaissance. The work can be read without the need for commentary.

52   And next these come our philosophers, so much reverenced for their furred gowns and starched beards that they look upon themselves as the only wise men and all others as shadows. And yet how pleasantly do they dote while they frame in their heads innumerable worlds; measure out the sun, the moon, the stars, nay and heaven itself, as it were, with a pair of compasses; lay down the causes of lightning, winds, eclipses, and other the like inexplicable matters; and all this too without the least doubting, as if they were Nature's secretaries, or dropped down among us from the council of the gods; while in the meantime Nature laughs at them and all their blind conjectures. For that they know nothing, even this is a sufficient argument, that they don't agree among themselves and so are incomprehensible touching every particular. These, though they have not the least degree of knowledge, profess yet that they have mastered all; nay, though they neither know themselves, nor perceive a ditch or block that lies in their way, for that perhaps most of them are half blind, or their wits a wool-gathering, yet give out that they have discovered ideas, universalities, separated forms, first matters, quiddities, haecceities, formalities, and the like stuff; things so thin and bodiless that I believe even Lynceus himself was not able to perceive them. But then chiefly do they disdain the unhallowed crowd as often as with their triangles, quadrangles, circles, and the like mathematical devices, more confounded than a labyrinth, and letters disposed one against the other, as it were in battle array, they cast a mist before the eyes of the ignorant. Nor is there wanting of this kind

some that pretend to foretell things by the stars and make promises of miracles beyond all things of soothsaying, and are so fortunate as to meet with people that believe them.

53　But perhaps I had better pass over our divines in silence and not stir this pool or touch this fair but unsavory plant, as a kind of men that are supercilious beyond comparison, and to that too, implacable; lest setting them about my ears, they attack me by troops and force me to a recantation sermon, which if I refuse, they straight pronounce me a heretic. For this is the thunderbolt with which they fright those whom they are resolved not to favor. And truly, though there are few others that less willingly acknowledge the kindnesses I have done them, yet even these too stand fast bound to me upon no ordinary accounts; while being happy in their own opinion, and as if they dwelt in the third heaven, they look with haughtiness on all others as poor creeping things and could almost find in their hearts to pity them; while hedged in with so many magisterial definitions, conclusions, corollaries, propositions explicit and implicit, they abound with so many starting-holes that Vulcan's net cannot hold them so fast, but they'll slip through with their distinctions, with which they so easily cut all knots asunder that a hatchet could not have done it better, so plentiful are they in their new-found words and prodigious terms. Besides, while they explicate the most hidden mysteries according to their own fancy – as how the world was first made; how original sin is derived to posterity; in what manner, how much room, and how long time Christ lay in the Virgin's womb; how accidents subsist in the Eucharist without their subject.

But these are common and threadbare; these are worthy of our great and illuminated divines, as the world calls them! At these, if ever they fall athwart them, they prick up – as whether there was any instant of time in the generation of the Second Person; whether there be more than one filiation in Christ; whether it be a possible proposition that God the Father hates the Son; or whether it was possible that Christ could have taken upon Him the likeness of a woman, or of the devil, or of an ass, or of a stone, or of a gourd; and then how that gourd should have preached, wrought miracles, or been hung on the cross; and what Peter had consecrated if he had administered the Sacrament at what time the body of Christ hung upon the cross; or whether at the same time he might be said to be man; whether after the Resurrection there will be any eating and drinking, since we are so much afraid of hunger and thirst in this world. There are infinite of these subtle trifles, and others more subtle than these, of notions, relations, instants, formalities, quiddities, haecceities, which no one can perceive without a Lynceus whose eyes could look through a stone wall and discover those things through the thickest darkness that never were.

Add to this those their other determinations, and those too so contrary to common opinion that those oracles of the Stoics, which they call paradoxes, seem in comparison of these but blockish and idle – as 'tis a lesser crime to kill a thousand men than to set a stitch on a poor man's shoe on the Sabbath day; and that a man should rather choose that the whole world with all food and raiment, as they say, should perish, than tell a lie, though never so inconsiderable. And these most subtle subtleties are rendered yet more subtle by the several methods of so many Schoolmen, that one might sooner wind himself out of a labyrinth than the entanglements of the realists, nominalists, Thomists, Albertists, Occamists, Scotists. Nor have I named all the several sects, but only some of the chief; in all which there is so much doctrine and so much difficulty that I may well conceive the apostles, had they been to deal with these new kind of divines, had needed to have prayed in aid of some other spirit.

Paul knew what faith was, and yet when he said, "Faith is the substance of things hoped for, and the evidence of things not seen," he did not define it doctor-like. And as he understood charity well himself, so he did as illogically divide and define it to others in his first Epistle to the Corinthians, Chapter the thirteenth. And devoutly, no doubt, did the apostles consecrate the Eucharist; yet, had they been asked the question touching the "*terminus a quo*," and the "*terminus ad quem*" of transubstantiation; of the manner how the same body can be in several places at one and the same time; of the difference the body of Christ has in heaven from that of the cross, or this in the Sacrament; in what point of time transubstantiation is, whereas prayer, by means of which it is, as being a discrete quantity, is transient; they would not, I conceive, have answered with the same subtlety as the Scotists dispute and define it. They knew the mother of Jesus, but which of them has so philosophically demonstrated how she was preserved from original sin as have done our divines? Peter received the keys, and from Him too that would not have trusted them with a person unworthy; yet whether he had understanding or no, I know not, for certainly he never attained to that subtlety to determine how he could have the key of knowledge that had no knowledge himself. They baptized far and near, and yet taught nowhere what was the formal, material, efficient, and final cause of baptism, nor made the least mention of delible and indelible characters. They worshipped, 'tis true, but in spirit, following herein no other than that of the Gospel, "God is a Spirit, and they that worship, must worship him in spirit and truth"; yet it does not appear it was at that time revealed to them that an image sketched on the wall with a coal was to be worshipped with the same worship as Christ Himself, if at least the two forefingers be stretched out, the hair long and uncut, and have three rays about the crown of the head. For who can conceive these things, unless he has spent at least six and thirty years in the philosophical and supercelestial whims of Aristotle and the Schoolmen?

In like manner, the apostles press to us grace; but which of them distinguishes between free grace and grace that makes a man acceptable? They exhort us to good works, and yet determine not what is the work working, and what a resting in the work done. They incite us to charity, and yet make no difference between charity infused and charity wrought in us by our own endeavors. Nor do they declare whether it be an accident or a substance, a thing created or uncreated. They detest and abominate sin, but let me not live if they could define according to art what that is which we call sin, unless perhaps they were inspired by the spirit of the Scotists. Nor can I be brought to believe that Paul, by whose learning you may judge the rest, would have so often condemned questions, disputes, genealogies, and, as himself calls them, "strifes of words," if he had thoroughly understood those subtleties, especially when all the debates and controversies of those times were rude and blockish in comparison of the more than Chrysippean subtleties of our masters. Although yet the gentlemen are so modest that if they meet with anything written by the apostles not so smooth and even as might be expected from a master, they do not presently condemn it but handsomely bend it to their own purpose, so great respect and honor do they give, partly to antiquity and partly to the name of apostle. And truly 'twas a kind of injustice to require so great things of them that never heard the least word from their masters concerning it. And so if the like happen in Chrysostom, Basil, Jerome, they think it enough to say they are not obliged by it.

The apostles also confuted the heathen philosophers and Jews, a people than whom none more obstinate, but rather by their good lives and miracles than syllogisms: and yet there was scarce one among them that was capable of understanding the least "quodlibet" of the Scotists. But now, where is that heathen or heretic that must not presently stoop to such wire-drawn subtleties, unless he be so thickskulled that he can't apprehend them, or so impudent as to hiss them down, or, being furnished with the same tricks, be able to make his party good with them? As if a man should set a conjurer on work against a conjurer, or fight with one hallowed sword against another, which would prove no other than a work to no purpose. For my own part I conceive the Christians would do much better if instead of those dull troops and companies of soldiers with which they have managed their war with such doubtful success, they would send the bawling Scotists, the most obstinate Occamists, and invincible Albertists to war against the Turks and Saracens; and they would see, I guess, a most pleasant combat and such a victory as was never before. For who is so faint whom their devices will not enliven? who so stupid whom such spurs can't quicken? or who so quicksighted before whose eyes they can't cast a mist?

But you'll say, I jest. Nor are you without cause, since even among divines themselves there are some that have learned better and are ready to turn their stomachs at those foolish subtleties of the others. There are some that detest them as a kind of sacrilege and count it the height of impiety to speak so irreverently of such hidden things, rather to be adored than explicated; to dispute of them with such profane and heathenish niceties; to define them so arrogantly and pollute the majesty of divinity with such pithless and sordid terms and opinions. Meantime the others please, nay hug themselves in their happiness, and are so taken up with these pleasant trifles that they have not so much leisure as to cast the least eye on the Gospel or St. Paul's epistles. And while they play the fool at this rate in their schools, they make account the universal church would otherwise perish, unless, as the poets fancied of Atlas that he supported heaven with his shoulders, they underpropped the other with their syllogistical buttresses. And how great a happiness is this, think you? while, as if Holy Writ were a nose of wax, they fashion and refashion it according to their pleasure; while they require that their own conclusions, subscribed by two or three Schoolmen, be accounted greater than Solon's laws and preferred before the papal decretals; while, as censors of the world, they force everyone to a recantation that differs but a hair's breadth from the least of their explicit or implicit determinations. And those too they pronounce like oracles. This proposition is scandalous; this irreverent; this has a smack of heresy; this no very good sound: so that neither baptism, nor the Gospel, nor Paul, nor Peter, nor St. Jerome, nor St. Augustine, no nor most Aristotelian Thomas himself can make a man a Christian, without these bachelors too be pleased to give him his grace. And the like in their subtlety in judging; for who would think he were no Christian that should say these two speeches "*matula putes*" and "*matula putet*," or "*ollae fervere*" and "*ollam fervere*" were not both good

Latin, unless their wisdoms had taught us the contrary? who had delivered the church from such mists of error, which yet no one ever met with, had they not come out with some university seal for it? And are they not most happy while they do these things?

Then for what concerns hell, how exactly they describe everything, as if they had been conversant in that commonwealth most part of their time! Again, how do they frame in their fancy new orbs, adding to those we have already an eighth! a goodly one, no doubt, and spacious enough, lest perhaps their happy souls might lack room to walk in, entertain their friends, and now and then play at football. And with these and a thousand the like fopperies their heads are so full stuffed and stretched that I believe Jupiter's brain was not near so big when, being in labor with Pallas, he was beholding to the midwifery of Vulcan's ax. And therefore you must not wonder if in their public disputes they are so bound about the head, lest otherwise perhaps their brains might leap out. Nay, I have sometimes laughed myself to see them so tower in their own opinion when they speak most barbarously; and when they humh and hawh so pitifully that none but one of their own tribe can understand them, they call it heights which the vulgar can't reach; for they say 'tis beneath the dignity of divine mysteries to be cramped and tied up to the narrow rules of grammarians: from whence we may conjecture the great prerogative of divines, if they only have the privilege of speaking corruptly, in which yet every cobbler thinks himself concerned for his share. Lastly, they look upon themselves as somewhat more than men as often as they are devoutly saluted by the name of "Our Masters," in which they fancy there lies as much as in the Jews' "Jehovah"; and therefore they reckon it a crime if "Magister Noster" be written other than in capital letters; and if anyone should preposterously say "Noster Magister," he has at once overturned the whole body of divinity.

54   And next these come those that commonly call themselves the religious and monks, most false in both titles, when both a great part of them are farthest from religion, and no men swarm thicker in all places than themselves. Nor can I think of anything that could be more miserable did not I support them so many several ways. For whereas all men detest them to that height, that they take it for ill luck to meet one of them by chance, yet such is their happiness that they flatter themselves. For first, they reckon it one of the main points of piety if they are so illiterate that they can't so much as read. And then when they run over their offices, which they carry about them, rather by tale than understanding, they believe the gods more than ordinarily pleased with their braying. And some there are among them that put off their trumperies at vast rates, yet rove up and down for the bread they eat; nay, there is scarce an inn, wagon, or ship into which they intrude not, to the no small damage of the commonwealth of beggars. And yet, like pleasant fellows, with all this vileness, ignorance, rudeness, and impudence, they represent to us, for so they call it, the lives of the apostles. Yet what is more pleasant than that they do all things by rule and, as it were, a kind of mathematics, the least swerving from which were a crime beyond forgiveness – as how many knots their shoes must be tied with, of what color everything is, what distinction of habits, of what stuff made, how many straws broad their girdles and of what fashion, how many bushels wide their cowl, how many fingers long their hair, and how many hours sleep; which exact equality, how dispropor-

tionate it is, among such variety of bodies and tempers, who is there that does not perceive it? And yet by reason of these fooleries they not only set slight by others, but each different order, men otherwise professing apostolical charity, despise one another, and for the different wearing of a habit, or that 'tis of darker color, they put all things in combustion. And among these there are some so rigidly religious that their upper garment is haircloth, their inner of the finest linen; and, on the contrary, others wear linen without and hair next their skins. Others, again, are as afraid to touch money as poison, and yet neither forbear wine nor dallying with women. In a word, 'tis their only care that none of them come near one another in their manner of living, nor do they endeavor how they may be like Christ, but how they may differ among themselves.

And another great happiness they conceive in their names, while they call themselves Cordiliers, and among these too, some are Colletes, some Minors, some Minims, some Crossed; and again, these are Benedictines, those Bernardines; these Carmelites, those Augustines; these Williamites, and those Jacobines; as if it were not worth the while to be called Christians. And of these, a great part build so much on their ceremonies and petty traditions of men that they think one heaven is too poor a reward for so great merit, little dreaming that the time will come when Christ, not regarding any of these trifles, will call them to account for His precept of charity. One shall show you a large trough full of all kinds of fish; another tumble you out so many bushels of prayers; another reckon you so many myriads of fasts, and fetch them up again in one dinner by eating till he cracks again; another produces more bundles of ceremonies than seven of the stoutest ships would be able to carry; another brags he has not touched a penny these three score years without two pair of gloves at least upon his hands; another wears a cowl so lined with grease that the poorest tarpaulin would not stoop to take it up; another will tell you he has lived these fifty-five years like a sponge, continually fastened to the same place; another is grown hoarse with his daily chanting; another has contracted a lethargy by his solitary living; and another the palsy in his tongue for want of speaking. But Christ, interrupting them in their vanities, which otherwise were endless, will ask them, "Whence this new kind of Jews? I acknowledge one commandment, which is truly mine, of which alone I hear nothing. I promised, 'tis true, my Father's heritage, and that without parables, not to cowls, odd prayers, and fastings, but to the duties of faith and charity. Nor can I acknowledge them that least acknowledge their faults. They that would seem holier than myself, let them if they like possess to themselves those three hundred sixty-five heavens of Basilides the heretic's invention, or command them whose foolish traditions they have preferred before my precepts to erect them a new one." When they shall hear these things and see common ordinary persons preferred before them, with what countenance, think you, will they behold one another? In the meantime they are happy in their hopes, and for this also they are beholding to me.

And yet these kind of people, though they are as it were of another commonwealth, no man dares despise, especially those begging friars, because they are privy to all men's secrets by means of confessions, as they call them. Which yet were no less than treason to discover, unless, being got drunk, they have a mind to be pleasant, and then all comes out, that is to say by hints and conjectures but suppressing the names. But if anyone should anger these wasps, they'll sufficiently revenge themselves in their public sermons and so point out their enemy by circumlocutions that there's no one but understands whom 'tis they mean, unless he understand nothing at all; nor will they give over their barking till you throw the dogs a bone. And now tell me, what juggler or mountebank you had rather behold than hear them rhetorically play the fool in their preachments, and yet most sweetly imitating what rhetoricians have written touching the art of good speaking? Good God! what several postures they have! How they shift their voice, sing out their words, skip up and down, and are ever and anon making such new faces that they confound all things with noise! And yet this knack of theirs is no less a mystery that runs in succession from one brother to another; which though it be not lawful for me to know, however I'll venture at it by conjectures. And first they invoke whatever they have scraped from the poets; and in the next place, if they are to discourse of charity, they take their rise from the river Nilus; or to set out the mystery of the cross, from bell and the dragon; or to dispute of fasting, from the twelve signs of the zodiac; or, being to preach of faith, ground their matter on the square of a circle.

I have heard myself one, and he no small fool – I was mistaken, I would have said scholar – that being in a famous assembly explaining the mystery of the Trinity, that he might both let them see his learning was not ordinary and withal satisfy some theological ears, he took a new way, to wit from the letters, syllables, and the word itself; then from the coherence of the nominative case and the verb, and the adjective and substantive: and while most of the audience wondered, and some of them muttered that of Horace, "What does all this trumpery drive at?" at last he brought the matter to this head, that he would demonstrate that the mystery of the Trinity was so clearly expressed in the very rudiments of grammar that the best mathematician could not chalk it out more plainly. And in this discourse did this most superlative theologian beat his brains for eight whole months that at this hour he's as blind as a beetle, to wit, all the sight of his eyes being run into the sharpness of his wit. But for all that he thinks nothing of his blindness, rather taking the same for too cheap a price of such a glory as he won thereby.

And besides him I met with another, some eighty years of age, and such a divine that you'd have sworn Scotus himself was revived in him. He, being upon the point of unfolding the mystery of the name Jesus, did with wonderful subtlety demonstrate that there lay hidden in those letters whatever could be said of him; for that it was only declined with three cases, he said, it was a manifest token of the Divine Trinity; and then, that the first ended in S, the second in M, the third in U, there was in it an ineffable mystery, to wit, those three letters declaring to us that he was the beginning, middle, and end (*summum, medium, et ultimum*) of all. Nay, the mystery was yet more abstruse; for he so mathematically split the word Jesus into two equal parts that he left the middle letter by itself, and then told us that that letter in Hebrew was schin or sin, and that sin in the Scotch tongue, as he remembered, signified as much as sin; from whence he gathered that it was Jesus that took away the sins of the world. At which new exposition the audience were so wonderfully intent and struck with admiration, especially the theologians, that there wanted little but that Niobe-like they had been turned to stones; whereas the like had almost happened to me, as befell the Priapus in Horace. And not without cause, for when were the

Grecian Demosthenes or Roman Cicero ever guilty of the like? They thought that introduction faulty that was wide of the matter, as if it were not the way of carters and swineherds that have no more wit than God sent them. But these learned men think their preamble, for so they call it, then chiefly rhetorical when it has least coherence with the rest of the argument, that the admiring audience may in the meanwhile whisper to themselves, "What will he be at now?" In the third place, they bring in instead of narration some texts of Scripture, but handle them cursorily, and as it were by the bye, when yet it is the only thing they should have insisted on. And fourthly, as it were changing a part in the play, they bolt out with some question in divinity, and many times relating neither to earth nor heaven, and this they look upon as a piece of art. Here they erect their theological crests and beat into the people's ears those magnificent titles of illustrious doctors, subtle doctors, most subtle doctors, seraphic doctors, cherubic doctors, holy doctors, unquestionable doctors, and the like; and then throw abroad among the ignorant people syllogisms, majors, minors, conclusions, corollaries, suppositions, and those so weak and foolish that they are below pedantry. There remains yet the fifth act in which one would think they should show their mastery. And here they bring in some foolish insipid fable out of *Speculum Historiae* or *Gesta Romanorum* and expound it allegorically, tropologically, and anagogically. And after this manner do they and their chimera, and such as Horace despaired of compassing when he wrote "*Humano capiti,*" etc.

But they have heard from somebody, I know not whom, that the beginning of a speech should be sober and grave and least given to noise. And therefore they begin theirs at that rate they can scarce hear themselves, as if it were not matter whether anyone understood them. They have learned somewhere that to move the affections a louder voice is requisite. Whereupon they that otherwise would speak like a mouse in a cheese start out of a sudden into a downright fury, even there too, where there's the least need of it. A man would swear they were past the power of hellebore, so little do they consider where 'tis they run out. Again, because they have heard that as a speech comes up to something, a man should press it more earnestly, they, however they begin, use a strange contention of voice in every part, though the matter itself be never so flat, and end in that manner as if they'd run themselves out of breath. Lastly, they have learned that among rhetoricians there is some mention of laughter, and therefore they study to prick in a jest here and there; but, O Venus! so void of wit and so little to the purpose that it may be truly called an ass's playing on the harp. And sometimes also they use somewhat of a sting, but so nevertheless that they rather tickle than wound; nor do they ever more truly flatter than when they would seem to use the greatest freedom of speech. Lastly, such is their whole action that a man would swear they had learned it from our common tumblers, though yet they come short of them in every respect. However, they are both so like that no man will dispute but that either these learned their rhetoric from them, or they theirs from these. And yet they light on some that, when they hear them, conceive they hear very Demosthenes and Ciceroes: of which sort chiefly are our merchants and women, whose ears only they endeavor to please, because as to the first, if they stroke them handsomely, some part or other of their ill-gotten goods is wont to fall to their share. And the women, though for many other things they favor this order, this is not the least, that they commit to their breasts whatever discontents they have against their husbands. And now, I conceive me, you see how much this kind of people are beholding to me, that with their petty ceremonies, ridiculous trifles, and noise exercise a kind of tyranny among mankind, believing themselves very Pauls and Anthonies.

55   But I willingly give over these stage-players that are such ingrateful dissemblers of the courtesies I have done them and such impudent pretenders to religion which they haven't. And now I have a mind to give some small touches of princes and courts, of whom I am had in reverence, aboveboard and, as it becomes gentlemen, frankly. And truly, if they had the least proportion of sound judgment, what life were more unpleasant than theirs, or so much to be avoided? For whoever did but truly weigh with himself how great a burden lies upon his shoulders that would truly discharge the duty of a prince, he would not think it worth his while to make his way to a crown by perjury and parricide. He would consider that he that takes a scepter in his hand should manage the public, not his private, interest; study nothing but the common good; and not in the least go contrary to those laws whereof himself is both the author and exactor: that he is to take an account of the good or evil administration of all his magistrates and subordinate officers; that, though he is but one, all men's eyes are upon him, and in his power it is, either like a good planet to give life and safety to mankind by his harmless influence, or like a fatal comet to send mischief and destruction; that the vices of other men are not alike felt, nor so generally communicated; and that a prince stands in that place that his least deviation from the rule of honesty and honor reaches farther than himself and opens a gap to many men's ruin. Besides, that the fortune of princes has many things attending it that are but too apt to train them out of the way, as pleasure, liberty, flattery, excess; for which cause he should the more diligently endeavor and set a watch over himself, lest perhaps he be led aside and fail in his duty. Lastly, to say nothing of treasons, ill will, and such other mischiefs he's in jeopardy of, that that True King is over his head, who in a short time will call him to account for every the least trespass, and that so much the more severely by how much more mighty was the empire committed to his charge. These and the like if a prince should duly weigh, and weigh it he would if he were wise, he would neither be able to sleep nor take any hearty repast.

Questions for Discussion

1   How would you describe the general tone of this piece of writing? Does this help us understand why it was so popular?

2   What specific criticisms does Erasmus make of late medieval theology? For example, why is he so critical of theologians who write so extensively and eloquently on the nature of hell?

3   List the criticisms which Erasmus directs against the monks and clergy of his day. To what extent are these criticisms cultural, reflecting his belief that most clergy are illiterate, or at best, derive their learning second-hand? And what more specifically religious criticisms can be discerned?

CHAPTER 40

Martin Luther (1483–1546)

Martin Luther (1483–1546) is widely regarded as one of the most significant of the reformers. Luther was born on November 10, 1483 in the German town of Eisleben, and named after Martin of Tours, whose festival fell on 11 November, the day of Luther's baptism. Hans Luder (as the name was spelled at this stage) moved the following year to the neighboring town of Mansfeld, where he established a small copper-mining business. Luther's university education began at Erfurt in 1501. His father clearly intended him to become a lawyer, not unaware of the financial benefits which this would bring the family. In 1505, Luther completed the general arts course at Erfurt, and was in a position to move on to study law.

As events turned out, the study of law never got very far. At some point around June 30, 1505, Luther was returning to Erfurt from a visit to Mansfeld. As he neared the village of Storterheim, a severe thunderstorm gathered around him. Suddenly, a bolt of lightning struck the ground next to him, throwing him off his horse. Terrified, Luther cried out, "St. Anne, help me! I will become a monk!" (St. Anne was the patron saint of miners). On July 17, 1505, he entered the most rigorous of the seven major monasteries at Erfurt – the Augustinian priory. Luther's father was outraged at the decision, and remained alienated from his son for some considerable time.

The Erfurt Augustinian monastery had close links with the University of Erfurt, which allowed Luther to wrestle with the great names of late medieval religious thought – such as William of Ockham, Pierre d'Ailly, and Gabriel Biel – in the course of his preparation for ordination. He was ordained priest in 1507. By 1509, he had gained his first major theological qualification. Finally, on October 18, 1512, he was awarded the degree of Doctor of Divinity, the culmination of his academic studies. By then, however, he had moved from Erfurt, and established himself at the nearby town of Wittenberg, which was the home of one of the newer German universities.

Martin Luther (1483–1546)

Basic description

German reformer, hymn-writer, and Bible translator.

Major works

Appeal to the Christian Nobility of the German Nation (1520); *The Babylonian Captivity of the Church* (1520); *The Catechisms* (1529).

Editions of works

Luther's Works, 54 vols. Philadelphia: Fortress Press; and St Louis, MO: Augsburg Press, 1955–76.

Major studies

Roland H. Bainton, *Here I Stand: A Biography of Martin Luther*. New York: New American Library, 1950.

Alister E. McGrath, *Luther's Theology of the Cross: Martin Luther's Theological Breakthrough*. Oxford: Blackwell, 1985.

The University of Wittenberg was founded in 1502 by Frederick the Wise. His motives in establishing this seat of learning were not entirely educational: he probably wanted to overshadow the reputation of the neighboring university of Leipzig. Luther took up a chair of biblical studies at Wittenberg immediately after gaining his doctorate, and remained there (apart from occasional periods of absence) for the rest of his life. He owed this position to Johann von Staupitz, vicar general of the German Observant Augustinian friars, who had held the position before him.

Luther's lectures at Wittenberg are widely regarded as laying the foundations for his subsequent theological development. It is of considerable significance that Luther's emerging theology was forged against the backdrop of a sustained engagement with certain biblical texts. Over the critical period 1513–19, Luther lectured as follows:

1513–15	Psalms (first course of lectures)
1515–16	Romans
1516–17	Galatians
1517–18	Hebrews

At some point during this period, Luther radically changed his theological views. There is still intense scholarly debate over both the nature and the date of this breakthrough.

Luther was propelled to fame through a series of controversies. The first such controversy centered on the sale of indulgences. Archbishop Albert of Mainz had given permission for the sales of indulgences in his territories. Johann Tetzel, who was responsible for the sale of these indulgences in the Wittenberg region, irritated Luther considerably, and moved him to write to Archbishop Albert, protesting against the practice and offering Ninety-Five Latin Theses, which he proposed to dispute at the University of Wittenberg. Luther's colleague Philipp Melanchthon subsequently reported that these Ninety-Five Theses were also "posted" (that is, nailed for public display) on the door of the castle church at Wittenberg on October 31, 1517. This date has subsequently been observed by some as marking the beginning of the Reformation. In fact, the theses drew little attention until later, when Luther circulated them more widely and had them translated into German.

The archbishop regarded the theses as a direct challenge to his authority, and forwarded them with a letter of complaint to Rome. However, this had less impact than might have been expected. The papacy needed the support of Frederick the Wise to secure the election of its favored candidate to succeed the Holy Roman Emperor Maximillian. As a result, Luther was not summoned to Rome to answer the charges laid against him, but was examined locally in 1518 by the papal legate Cajetan. Luther refused to withdraw his criticisms of the practice of selling indulgences.

Luther's profile was raised considerably in 1519 at the Leipzig Disputation. This disputation pitted Luther and his Wittenberg colleague Andreas Bodenstein von Karlstadt against Johann Eck, a highly regarded theologian from Ingolstadt. During the course of a complicated debate over the nature of authority, Eck managed to get Luther to admit that, in his view, both popes and general councils could err. Even more, Luther indicated a degree of support for Jan Huss, the Bohemian reformer who had been condemned as a heretic some time previously. Eck clearly regarded himself to have won the debate, in that he had forced Luther to state views on papal authority which were unorthodox by the standards of the day.

Others, however, were delighted by Luther's criticisms. Of particular importance was the reaction of many humanists, who saw Luther's criticisms as indicating that he was one of their number. In fact, this was not the case. Nevertheless, this "constructive misunderstanding" led Luther to be lionized by humanists around this time, and given a high profile within humanist circles. Although Luther's controversy with Erasmus over the period 1524–5 finally ended any notion that Luther was sympathetic to a humanist agenda, he enjoyed at least the tacit support of many humanists (including Erasmus and Bucer) for several years after the Leipzig Disputation.

Luther's brief flirtation with humanism around 1519 can be illustrated from the way in which he styled himself. One of the conceits of the age was that humanist writers would insist on being known by the Latin or Greek versions of their personal names, perhaps in order to lend themselves a little more dignity. Thus Philip Schwarzerd became "Melanchthon" (literally, "black earth"); Johann Hauschein became "Oecolampadius" (literally, "house light"). At some point around 1519, Luther himself fell victim to this trend of the age. By then, Luther was gaining a reputation as a critic of the medieval church. His emphasis upon Christian freedom – evident in the 1520 writing *On the Freedom of a Christian* – led him to play around with the original spelling of his family name "Luder." He altered this to "Eleutherius" – literally, "liberator." Within what seems to have been a very short period of time, Martin tired of this pretension. But the new way of spelling his family name remained. Luder had become Luther.

In 1520, Luther published three major works which immediately established his reputation as a major popular reformer. Shrewdly, Luther wrote in German, making his ideas accessible to a wide public: where Latin was the language of the intellectual and ecclesiastical elite of Europe, German was the language of the common people. In the *Appeal to the Christian Nobility of the German Nation*, Luther argued passionately for the need for reform of the church. In both its doctrine and its practices, the church of the early sixteenth century had cast itself adrift from the New Testament. His pithy and witty German gave added popular appeal to some intensely serious theological ideas.

Encouraged by the remarkable success of this work, Luther followed it up with *The Babylonian Captivity of the Church*. In this powerful piece of writing, Luther argued that the gospel had become captive to the institutional church. The medieval church, he argued, had imprisoned the gospel in a complex system of priests and sacraments. The church had become the master of the gospel, where it should be its servant. This point was further developed in *The Liberty of a Christian*, in which Luther stressed both the freedom and obligations of the believer.

By now, Luther was at the center of both controversy and condemnation. On June 15, 1520, Luther was censured by a papal bull, and ordered to retract his views. He refused, adding insult to injury by publicly burning the bull. He was excommunicated in January of the following year, and summoned to appear before the Diet of Worms. Again, he refused to withdraw his views. Luther's position became increasingly serious. Realizing this, a friendly German prince arranged for him to be "kidnapped," and took him off to the safety of the Wartburg, a castle near Eisenach. During his eight months of isolation, Luther had time to think through the implications of many of his ideas, and to test the genuineness of his motives. By the time he returned to Wittenberg in 1522 to take charge of the Reformation in that town, his ideas were gaining considerable support throughout Europe. By this stage, the Reformation may be said to have begun. In its early phase, it was decisively shaped by Luther.

Luther's influence on the Reformation at this early stage was decisive. His period of isolation at the Wartburg allowed him to work on a number of major reforming projects, including liturgical revision, biblical translation, and other reforming treatises. The New Testament appeared in German in 1522, although it was not until 1534 that the entire Bible was translated and published. In 1524, Luther argued for the need to establish schools in German towns, and to extend education to women. The two Catechisms of 1529 broke new ground in religious education.

Serious controversy, however, was not slow to break out. In 1524, Erasmus published a work which was severely critical of his views on human free will. Luther's reply of 1525 was not the most diplomatic of documents, and led to a final break with Erasmus. More seriously, the Peasants' War of 1525 caused Luther's reputation to suffer severely. Luther argued that the feudal lords had every right to end the peasants' revolt, by force where necessary. Luther's writings on this matter – such as his *Against the Thieving and Murderous Hordes of Peasants* – had virtually no impact on the revolt itself, but tarnished his image severely.

Perhaps the most significant controversy erupted over the very different views on the nature of the real presence held by Luther and Huldrych Zwingli. Luther's strong commitment to the real presence of Christ in the eucharist contrasted sharply with Zwingli's metaphorical or symbolic approach. Although many sought to reconcile the two views, or at least to limit the damage caused by the differences – these eventually came to nothing. The Colloquy of Marburg (1529), arranged by Philip of Hesse, was of particular importance. Its failure can be argued to have led to the permanent alienation of the German and Swiss reforming factions at a time when increasingly adverse political and military considerations made collaboration imperative.

By 1527, it was clear that Luther was not a healthy man. What can now be recognized as Ménière's disease had established itself. Convinced that he had not long to live, Luther married a former nun, Katharina von Bora. Although Luther went on to produce a number of major theological works in his later period (most notably, a commentary on Galatians), his attention was increasingly taken up with his personal health, and the politics of the Reformation struggles. He died in 1546 while attempting to mediate in a somewhat minor quarrel which had broken out between some members of the German nobility in the city of Mansfeld.

Text: Letter on Translating the New Testament

Luther wrote a number of letters justifying his reforming program. One of the most important such letters was written in order to justify Luther's translation of certain passages in Paul's letters. Luther insisted that Paul taught justification by faith alone. A certain degree of difficulty was caused by the awkward fact that Paul himself did not state this explicitly, but preferred to talk in terms of "justification by faith" rather than "justification by faith alone." Luther solved this difficulty by adding the world "alone" to the text in his German translation, arguing that this accurately reflected the spirit and overall direction of Paul's thought, even if one did not find this precise verbal formulation in Paul's writings.

The letter is of considerable importance, in that one of Luther's major contributions to the development of the Reformation – and to German literature in general – was the translation of the Bible from the Latin of the Vulgate into the German of the masses. The principles underlying this are clearly of considerable importance. This letter also shows Luther's characteristically abrasive writing style, especially when dealing with people for whom he had little respect.

Grace and peace in Christ, honorable, worthy and dear Lord and friend. I received your writing with the two questions or queries requesting my response. In the first place, you ask why I, in the 3rd chapter of Romans, translated the words of St. Paul: "*Arbitramur hominem iustificari ex fide absque operibus*" as "We hold that the human will be justified without the works of the law but only by faith." You also tell me that the Papists are causing a great fuss because St. Paul's text does not contain the word *sola* (alone), and that my changing of the words of God is not to be tolerated. Secondly, you ask if the departed saints intercede for us. Regarding the first question, you can give the papists this answer from me – if you so desire.

On the first hand, if I, Dr. Luther, had thought that all the Papists together were capable of translating even one passage of Scripture correctly and well, I would have gathered up enough humility to ask for their aid and assistance in translating the New Testament into German. However, I spared them and myself the trouble, as I knew and still see with my own eyes that not one of them knows how to speak or translate German. It is obvious, however, that they are learning to speak and write German from my translations. Thus, they are stealing my language from me – a language they had little knowledge of before this. However, they do not thank me for this but instead use it against me. Yet I readily grant them this as it tickles me to know that I have taught my ungrateful students, even my enemies, to speak.

Secondly, you might say that I have conscientiously translated the New Testament into German to the best of my ability, and that I have not forced anyone to read it.

Rather I have left it open, only doing the translation as a service to those who could not do it as well. No one is forbidden to do it better. If someone does not wish to read it, he can let it lie, for I do not ask anyone to read it or praise anyone who does! It is my Testament and my translation – and it shall remain mine. If I have made errors within it (although I am not aware of any and would most certainly be unwilling to intentionally mistranslate a single letter) I will not allow the papists to judge for their ears continue to be too long and their hee-haws too weak for them to be critical of my translating. I know quite well how much skill, hard work, understanding and intelligence is needed for a good translation. They know it less than even the miller's donkey for they have never tried it.

It is said, "The one who builds along the pathway has many masters." It is like this with me. Those who have not ever been able to speak correctly (to say nothing of translating) have all at once become my masters and I their pupil. If I were to have asked them how to translate the first two words of Matthew "*Liber Generationis*" into German, not one of them would have been able to say "Quack!" And they judge all my works! Fine fellows! It was also like this for St. Jerome when he translated the Bible. Everyone was his master. He alone was entirely incompetent as people, who were not good enough to clean his boots, judged his works. This is why it takes a great deal of patience to do good things in public for the world believes itself to be the Master of Knowledge, always putting the bit under the horse's tail, and not judging itself for that is the world's nature. It can do nothing else.

I would gladly see a papist come forward and translate into German an epistle of St. Paul's or one of the prophets and, in doing so, not make use of Luther's German or translation. Then one might see a fine, beautiful and noteworthy translation into German.

We have seen that bungler from Dresden play master to my New Testament. (I will not mention his name in my books as he has his judge and is already well-known.) He does admit that my German is good and sweet and that he could not improve it. Yet, anxious to dishonor it, he took my New Testament word for word as it was written, and removed my prefaces and glosses, replacing them with his own. Then he published my New Testament under his name! Dear Children, how it pained me when his prince in a detestable preface condemned my work and forbid all from reading Luther's New Testament, while at the same time commending the Bungler's New Testament to be read – even though it was the very same one Luther had written!

So no one thinks I am lying, put Luther's and the Bungler's New Testaments side by side and compare them. You will see who did the translation for both. He has patched it in places and reordered it (and although it does not all please me) I can still leave it be for it does me no particular harm as far as the document is concerned. That is why I never intended to write in opposition to it. But I did have a laugh at the great wisdom that so terribly slandered, condemned and forbade my New Testament, when it was published under my name, but required its reading when published under an other's name! What type of virtue is this that slanders and heaps shame on someone else's work, and then steals it, and publishes it under one's own name, thereby seeking glory and esteem through the slandered work of someone else! I leave that for his judge to say. I am glad and satisfied that my work (as

St. Paul also boasts) is furthered by my enemies, and that Luther's work, without Luther's name but that of his enemy, is to be read. What better vengeance?!

Returning to the issue at hand, if your papist wishes to make a great fuss about the word "alone" (*sola*), say this to him: "Dr. Martin Luther will have it so and he says that a papist and an ass are the same thing." *Sic volo, sic iubeo, sit pro ratione voluntas* (I will it, I command it; my will is reason enough). For we are not going to become students and followers of the papists. Rather we will become their judge and master. We, too, are going to be proud and brag with these blockheads; and just as St. Paul brags against his madly raving saints, I will brag over these asses of mine! They are doctors? Me too. They are scholars? I am as well. They are philosophers? And I. They are dialecticians? I am too. They are lecturers? So am I. They write books? So do I.

I will go even further with my bragging: I can exegete the psalms and the prophets, and they cannot. I can translate, and they cannot. I can read Holy Scriptures, and they cannot. I can pray, they cannot. Coming down to their level, I can do their dialectics and philosophy better than all of them put together. Plus I know that not one of them understands Aristotle. If, in fact, any one of them can correctly understand one part or chapter of Aristotle, I will eat my hat! No, I am not overdoing it for I have been educated in and have practiced their science since my childhood. I recognize how broad and deep it is. They, too, know that everything they can do, I can do. Yet they handle me like a stranger in their discipline, these incurable fellows, as if I had just arrived this morning and had never seen or heard what they know and teach. How they do so brilliantly parade around with their science, teaching me what I grew beyond twenty years ago! To all their shouting and screaming I join the harlot in singing: "I have known for seven years that horseshoe nails are iron."

So this can be the answer to your first question. Please do not give these asses any other answer to their useless braying about that word "*sola*" than simply "Luther will have it so, and he says that he is a doctor above all the papal doctors." Let it remain at that. I will, from now on, hold them in contempt, and have already held them in contempt, as long as they are the kind of people that they are – asses, I should say. And there are brazen idiots among them who have never learned their own art of sophistry – like Dr. Schmidt and Snot-Nose, and such like them. They set themselves against me in this matter, which not only transcends sophistry, but as St. Paul writes, all the wisdom and understanding in the world as well. An ass truly does not have to sing much as he is already known for his ears.

For you and our people, however, I shall show why I used the word "*sola*" – even though in Romans 3 it wasn't "*sola*" I used but "*solum*" or "*tantum*." That is how closely those asses have looked at my text! However, I have used "*sola fides*" in other places, and I want to use both "*solum*" and "*sola*." I have continually tried translating in a pure and accurate German. It has happened that I have sometimes searched and inquired about a single word for three or four weeks. Sometimes I have not found it even then. I have worked Meister Philip and Aurogallus so hard in translating Job, sometimes barely translating 3 lines after four days. Now that it has been translated into German and completed, all can read and criticize it. One can now read three or four pages without stumbling one time – without realizing just what rocks and hindrances had once been where now one travels as if over a smoothly-cut plank. We had to sweat and toil there before we removed those rocks and hindrances, so one could go along nicely. The plowing goes nicely in a clear field. But nobody wants the task of digging out the rocks and hindrances. There is no such thing as earning the world's thanks. Even God cannot earn thanks, not with the sun, nor with heaven and earth, or even the death of his Son. It just is and remains as it is, in the devil's name, as it will not be anything else.

I also know that in Romans 3, the word "*solum*" is not present in either Greek or Latin text – the papists did not have to teach me that – it is fact! The letters s-o-l-a are not there. And these knotheads stare at them like cows at a new gate, while at the same time they do not recognize that it conveys the sense of the text – if the translation is to be clear and accurate, it belongs there. I wanted to speak German since it was German I had spoken in translation – not Latin or Greek. But it is the nature of our language that in speaking about two things, one which is affirmed, the other denied, we use the word "*solum*" only along with the word "not" (*nicht*) or "no" (*kein*). For example, we say "the farmer brings only (*allein*) grain and no money"; or "No, I really have no money, but only (*allein*) grain"; I have only eaten and not yet drunk"; "Did you write it only and not read it over?" There are a vast number of such everyday cases.

In all these phrases, this is a German usage, even though it is not the Latin or Greek usage. It is the nature of the German tongue to add "*allein*" in order that "*nicht*" or "*kein*" may be clearer and more complete. To be sure, I can also say "The farmer brings grain and no (*kein*) money," but the words "*kein* money" do not sound as full and clear as if I were to say, "the farmer brings *allein* grain and *kein* money." Here the word "*allein*" helps the word "*kein*" so much that it becomes a clear and complete German expression.

We do not have to ask about the literal Latin or how we are to speak German – as these asses do. Rather we must ask the mother in the home, the children on the street, the common person in the market about this. We must be guided by their tongue, the manner of their speech, and do our translating accordingly. Then they will understand it and recognize that we are speaking German to them.

For instance, Christ says: *Ex abundatia cordis os loquitur*. If I am to follow these asses, they will lay the original before me literally and translate it as: "Out of the abundance of the heart the mouth speaks." Is that speaking with a German tongue? What German could understand something like that? What is this "abundance of the heart"? No German can say that; unless, of course, he was trying to say that someone was altogether too magnanimous, or too courageous, though even that would not yet be correct, as "abundance of the heart" is not German, not any more than "abundance of the house," "abundance of the stove," or "abundance of the bench" is German. But the mother in the home and the common man say this: "What fills the heart overflows the mouth." That is speaking with the proper German tongue of the kind I have tried for, although unfortunately not always successfully. The literal Latin is a great barrier to speaking proper German.

So, as the traitor Judas says in Matthew 26: "*Ut quid perditio haec?*" and in Mark 14: "*Ut quid perditio iste unguenti facta est?*" Subsequently, for these literalist asses I would have to translate it: "Why has this loss of salve occurred?" But what kind of

German is this? What German says "loss of salve occurred"? And if he does understand it at all, he would think that the salve is lost and must be looked for and found again; even though that is still obscure and uncertain. Now if that is good German why do they not come out and make us a fine, new German testament and let Luther's testament be? I think that would really bring out their talents. But a German would say "*Ut quid*, etc." as "Why this waste?" or "Why this extravagance?" Even "it is a shame about the ointment" – these are good German, in which one can understand that Magdalene had wasted the salve she poured out and had done wrong. That was what Judas meant as he thought he could have used it better.

Now when the angel greets Mary, he says: "Greetings to you, Mary, full of grace, the Lord is with you." Well up to this point, this has simply been translated from the simple Latin, but tell me is that good German? Since when does a German speak like that – being "full of grace"? One would have to think about a keg "full of" beer or a purse "full of" money. So I translated it: "You gracious one." This way a German can at last think about what the angel meant by his greeting. Yet the papists rant about me corrupting the angelic greeting – and I still have not used the most satisfactory German translation. What if I had used the most satisfactory German and translated the salutation: "God says hello, Mary dear" (for that is what the angel was intending to say and what he would have said had he even been German!). If I had, I believe that they would have hanged themselves out of their great devotion to dear Mary and because I have destroyed the greeting.

Yet why should I be concerned about their ranting and raving? I will not stop them from translating as they want. But I too shall translate as I want and not to please them, and whoever does not like it can just ignore it and keep his criticism to himself, for I will neither look at nor listen to it. They do not have to answer for or bear responsibility for my translation. Listen up, I shall say "gracious Mary" and "dear Mary," and they can say "Mary full of grace." Anyone who knows German also knows what an expressive word "dear" (*liebe*) is: dear Mary, dear God, the dear emperor, the dear prince, the dear man, the dear child. I do not know if one can say this word "*liebe*" in Latin or in other languages with so much depth of emotion that it pierces the heart and echoes throughout as it does in our tongue.

I think that St. Luke, as a master of the Hebrew and Greek tongues, wanted to clarify and articulate the Greek word "*kecharitomene*" that the angel used. And I think that the angel Gabriel spoke with Mary just as he spoke with Daniel, when he called him "Chamudoth" and "*Ish chamudoth, vir desiriorum*," that is "Dear Daniel." That is the way Gabriel speaks, as we can see in Daniel. Now if I were to literally translate the words of the angel, and use the skills of these asses, I would have to translate it as "Daniel, you man of desires" or "Daniel, you man of lust." Oh, that would be beautiful German! A German would, of course, recognize "*Man*," "*Lueste*" and "*begirunge*" as being German words, although not altogether pure as "*lust*" and "*begir*" would be better. But when those words are put together you get "you man of desires" and no German is going to understand that. He might even think that Daniel is full of lustful desires. Now wouldn't that be a fine translation! So I have to let the literal words go, and try to discover how the German says what the Hebrew "*ish chamudoth*" expresses. I discover that the German says this, "You dear Daniel," "you dear Mary," or "you gracious maiden," "you lovely maiden," "you gentle girl" and so on. A translator must have a large vocabulary so he can have more words for when a particular one just does not fit in the context.

Why should I talk about translating so much? I would need an entire year were I to point out the reasons and concerns behind my words. I have learned what an art and job translating is by experience, so I will not tolerate some papal ass or mule as my critic, or judge. They have not tried the task. If anyone does not like my translation, they can ignore it; and may the devil repay the one who dislikes or criticizes my translation without my knowledge or permission. Should it be criticized, I will do it myself. If I do not do it, then they can leave my translations in peace. They can each do a translation that suits them – what do I care?

To this I can, with good conscience, give witness – that I gave my utmost effort and care and I had no ulterior motives. I have not taken or wanted even a small coin in return. Neither have I made any by it. God knows that I have not even sought honor by it, but I have done it as a service to the blessed Christians and to the honor of the One who sits above who blesses me every hour of my life that had I translated a thousand times more diligently, I should not have deserved to live or have a sound eye for even a single hour. All I am and have to offer is from his mercy and grace – indeed of his precious blood and bitter sweat. Therefore, God willing, all of it will also serve to his honor, joyfully and sincerely. I may be insulted by the scribblers and papists but true Christians, along with Christ, their Lord, bless me. Further, I am more than amply rewarded if just one Christian acknowledge me as a workman with integrity. I do not care about the papists, as they are not good enough to acknowledge my work and, if they were to bless me, it would break my heart. I may be insulted by their highest praise and honor, but I will still be a doctor, even a distinguished one. I am certain that they shall never take from me until the final day.

Yet I have not just gone ahead, ignoring the exact wording in the original. Instead, with great care, I have, along with my helpers, gone ahead and have kept literally to the original, without the slightest deviation, wherever it appeared that a passage was crucial. For instance, in John 6 Christ says: "Him has God the Father set his seal upon (*versiegelt*)." It would be more clear in German to say "Him has God the Father signified (*gezeiehent*)" or even "God the Father means him." But rather than doing violence to the original, I have done violence to the German tongue. Ah, translating is not every one's skill as some mad saints think. A right, devout, honest, sincere, God-fearing Christian, trained, educated, and experienced heart is required. So I hold that no false Christian or divisive spirit can be a good translator. That is obvious given the translation of the Prophets at Worms, which although carefully done and approximating my own German quite closely, does not show much reverence for Christ due to the Jews who shared in the translation. Aside from that it shows plenty of skill and craftsmanship there.

So much for translating and the nature of language. However, I was not depending upon or following the nature of language when I inserted the word "*solum*" (alone) in Romans 3 as the text itself, and St. Paul's meaning, urgently necessitated and demanded it. He is dealing with the main point of Christian doctrine in this passage – namely that we are justified by faith in Christ without any works of the Law. In fact, he rejects all works so completely as to say that the works of the Law, though it is God's law and word, do not aid us in justification. Using Abraham as an example, he argues that Abraham was so justified without works that even the highest work, which had been commanded by God, over and above all others, namely circumcision, did not aid him in justification. Instead, Abraham was justified without circumcision and without any works, but by faith, as he says in Chapter 4: "If Abraham is justified by works, he may boast, but not before God." However, when all works are so completely rejected – which must mean faith alone justifies – whoever would speak plainly and clearly about this rejection of works would have to say "Faith alone justifies and not works." The matter itself and the nature of language necessitates it.

"Yet," they say, "it has such an offensive tone that people infer from it that they need not do any good works." Dear, what are we to say? IS it not more offensive for St. Paul himself to not use the term "faith alone" but spell it even more clearly, putting the finishing touches on it by saying "Without the works of the Law?" Galatians 1 [2.16] says that "not by works of the law" (as well as in many other places) for the phrase "without the works of the law" is so ever offensive, and scandalous that no amount of revision can help it. How much more might people learn from "that they need not do any good works," when all they hear is preaching about the works themselves, stated in such a clear strong way: "No works," "without works," "not by works"! If it is not offensive to preach "without works," "not by works"! "no works," why is it offensive to preach "by faith alone"?

Still more offensive is that St. Paul does not reject just ordinary works, but works of the law! It follows that one could take offense at that all the more and say that the law is condemned and cursed before God and one ought only do what is contrary to the law as it is said in Romans 3: "Why not do evil so that there might be more good?" which is what that one divisive spirit of our time was doing. Should one reject St. Paul's word because of such "offense" or refrain from speaking freely about faith? Gracious, St. Paul and I want to offend like this for we preach so strongly against works, insisting on faith alone for no other reason than to offend people that they might stumble and fall and learn that they are not saved by good works but only by Christ's death and resurrection. Knowing that they cannot be saved by their good works of the law, how much more will they realize that they shall not be saved by bad works, or without the law! Therefore, it does not follow that because good works do not help, bad works will; just as it does not follow that because the sun cannot help a blind person see, the night and darkness must help him see.

It astounds me that one can be offended by something as obvious as this! Just tell me, is Christ's death and resurrection our work, what we do, or not? It is obviously not our work, nor is it the work of the law. Now it is Christ's death and resurrection alone which saves and frees us from sin, as Paul writes in Romans 4: "He died for our sin and arose for our righteousness." Tell me more! What is the work by which we take hold of Christ's death and resurrection? It must not be an external work but only the eternal faith in the heart that alone, indeed all alone, which takes hold of this death and resurrection when it is preached through the gospel. Then why all this ranting and raving, this making of heretics and burning of them, when it is clear at its very core, proving that faith alone takes hold of Christ's death and resurrection, without any works, and that his death and resurrection are our life and righteousness? As this fact is so obvious, that faith alone gives, brings, and takes a hold of this life and righteousness – why should we not say so? It is not heretical that faith alone holds on to Christ and gives life; and yet it seems to be heresy if someone mentions it. Are they not insane, foolish and ridiculous? They will say that one thing is right but brand the telling of this right thing as wrong – even though something cannot be simultaneously right and wrong.

Furthermore, I am not the only one, nor the first, to say that faith alone makes one righteous. There was Ambrose, Augustine and many others who said it before me. And if one is to read and understand St. Paul, the same thing must be said and not anything else. His words, as well, are blunt – "no works" – none at all! If it is not works, it must be faith alone. Oh what a marvelous, constructive and inoffensive teaching that would be, to be taught that one can be saved by works as well as by faith. That would be like saying that it is not Christ's death alone that takes away our sin but that our works have something to do with it. Now that would be a fine way of honoring Christ's death, saying that it is helped by our works, and that whatever it does our works can also do – that we are his equal in goodness and power. This is the devil itself for he cannot ever stop abusing the blood of Christ.

Therefore the matter itself, at its very core, necessitates that one say: "Faith alone makes one righteous." The nature of the German tongue teaches us to say it in the same way. In addition, I have the examples of the holy fathers. The dangers confronting the people also compel it so they do not continue to hang onto works and wander away from faith, losing Christ, especially at this time when they have been so accustomed to works they have to be pulled away from them by force. It is for these reasons that it is not only right but also necessary to say it as plainly and forcefully as possible: "Faith alone saves without works!" I am only sorry I did not add "*alle*" and "*aller*," and said "without any (*alle*) works or any (*aller*) laws." That would have stated it most effectively. Therefore, it will remain in the New Testament, and though all the papal asses rant and rave at me, they shall not take it away from me. Let this be enough for now. I will have to speak more about this in the treatise "On Justification" (if God grants me grace).

On the other question as to whether the departed saints intercede for us. For the present I am only going to give a brief answer as I am considering publishing a sermon on the beloved angels in which I will respond more fully on this matter (God willing).

First, you know that under the papacy it is not only taught that the saints in heaven intercede for us – even though we cannot know this as the Scripture does not tell us such – but the saints have been made into gods, and that they are to be our patrons to whom we should call. Some of them have never existed! To each of these saints a particular power and might has been given – one over fire, another over water, another over pestilence, fever and all sorts of plagues. Indeed, God must have been altogether idle to have let the saints work in his place. Of this atrocity the papists themselves are aware, as they quietly take up their pipes and preen and primp themselves over this doctrine of the intercession of the saints. I will leave this subject for now – but you can count on my not forgetting it and allowing this primping and preening to continue without cost.

And again, you know that there is not a single passage from God demanding us to call upon either saints or angels to intercede for us, and that there is no example of such in the Scriptures. One finds that the beloved angels spoke with the fathers and the prophets, but that none of them had ever been asked to intercede for them. Why even Jacob the patriarch did not ask the angel with whom he wrestled for any intercession. Instead, he only took from him a blessing. In fact, one finds the very opposite in Revelation as the angel will not allow itself to be worshipped by John [Rev. 22]. So the worship of saints shows itself as nothing but human nonsense, our own invention separated from the word of God and the Scriptures.

As it is not proper in the matter of divine worship for us to do anything that is not commanded by God (and that whoever does is putting God to the test), it is therefore also not advisable or tolerable for one to call upon the saints for intercession or to teach others to do so. In fact, it is to be condemned and people taught to avoid it. Therefore, I also will not advise it and burden my conscience with the iniquities of others. It was difficult for me to stop from worshipping the saints as I was so steeped in it to have nearly drowned. But the light of the gospel is now shining so brightly that from now on no one has an excuse for remaining in the darkness. We all very well know what we are to do.

This is itself a very risky and blasphemous way to worship for people are easily accustomed to turning away from Christ. They learn quickly to trust more in the saints than in Christ himself. When our nature is already all too prone to run from God and Christ, and trust in humanity, it is indeed difficult to learn to trust in God and Christ, even though we have vowed to do so and are therefore obligated to do so. Therefore, this offense is not to be tolerated whereby those who are weak and of the flesh participate in idolatry, against the first commandment and our baptism. Even if one tries nothing other than to switch their trust from the saints to Christ, through teaching and practice, it will be difficult to accomplish, that one should come to him and rightly take hold of him. One need not paint the Devil on the door – he will already be present.

We can finally be certain that God is not angry with us, and that even if we do not call on the saints for intercession, we are secure for God has never commanded it. God says that God is a jealous God granting their iniquities on those who do not keep his commandments [Ex. 20]; but there is no commandment here and, therefore, no anger to be feared. Since, then, there is on this side security and on the other side great risk and offense against the Word of God, why should we go from security into danger where we do not have the Word of God to sustain, comfort and save us in the times of trial? For it is written, "Whoever loves danger will perish by it" [Eccl. 3], and God's commandment says, "You shall not put the Lord your God to the test" [Matt. 4].

"But," they say, "this way you condemn all of Christendom which has always maintained this – until now." I answer: I know very well that the priests and monks seek this cloak for their blasphemies. They want to give to Christendom the damage caused by their own negligence. Then, when we say, "Christendom does not err," we shall also be saying that they do not err, since Christendom believes it to be so. So no pilgrimage can be wrong, no matter how obviously the devil is a participant in it. No indulgence can be wrong, regardless of how horrible the lies involved. In other words, there is nothing there but holiness! Therefore to this you reply, "It is not a question of who is and who is not condemned." They inject this irrelevant idea in order to divert us from the topic at hand. We are now discussing the Word of God. What Christendom is or does belongs somewhere else. The question here is: "What is or is not the Word of God?" What is not the Word of God does not make Christendom.

We read that in the days of Elijah the prophet there was apparently no word from God and no worship of God in Israel. For Elijah says, "Lord, they have killed your prophets and destroyed your altars, and I am left totally alone" [I Kings 19]. Here King Ahab and others could have said, "Elijah, with talk like that you are condemning all the people of God." However, God had at the same time kept seven thousand [I Kings 19]. How? Do you not also think that God could now, under the papacy, have preserved his own, even though the priests and monks of Christendom have been teachers of the devil and gone to hell? Many children and young people have died in Christ. For even under the Antichrist, Christ has strongly sustained baptism, the bare text of the gospel in the pulpit, the Lord's Prayer, and the Creed. By this means he sustained many of his Christians, and therefore also his Christendom, and said nothing about it to these devil's teachers.

Now even though Christians have done some parts of the papal blasphemy, the papal asses have not yet proved that they did it gladly. Still less does it prove that they even did the right thing. All Christians can err and sin, but God has taught them to pray in the Lord's Prayer for the forgiveness of sins. God could very well forgive the sins they had to unwillingly, unknowingly, and under the coercion of the Antichrist commit, without saying anything about it to the priests and monks! It can, however, be easily proven that there has always been a great deal of secret murmuring and complaining against the clergy throughout the world, and that they are not treating Christendom properly. And the papal asses have courageously withstood such complaining with fire and sword, even to the present day. This murmuring proves how happy Christians have been over these blasphemies, and how right they have been in doing them!

So out with it, you papal asses! Say that this is the teaching of Christendom: these stinking lies which you villains and traitors have forced upon Christendom and for the sake of which you murderers have killed many Christians. Why each letter of every papal law gives testimony to the fact that nothing has ever been taught by the counsel and the consent of Christendom. There is nothing there but *"districte precipiendo mandamus"* ["we teach and strictly command"]. That has been your Holy Spirit. Christendom has had to suffer this tyranny. This tyranny has robbed it of the sacrament and, not by its own fault, has been held in captivity. And still the asses would pawn off on us this intolerable tyranny of their own wickedness as a willing act and example of Christendom – and thereby acquit themselves!

But this is getting too long. Let this be enough of an answer to your questions for now. More another time. Excuse this long letter. Christ our Lord be with us all.

> Amen.
> Martin Luther,
> Your good friend.
> The Wilderness, September 8, 1530

Questions for Study

1 What is the criticism being directed against Luther's New Testament translations which he feels obliged to defend?
2 How successfully do you feel that Luther justifies his approach? In particular, how persuaded are you by his insistence that the addition of the word "alone" is entirely proper?
3 What general issues of translation arise from Luther's comments in this letter?

Text: The "Little Instruction Book" or "Lesser Catechism"

One of the most important types of literature to emerge from the Reformation was the catechism. This typically took the form of a question-and-answer format, in which some fundamental questions concerning the Christian faith were set out, and simple answers provided. Although what would now be agreed to be "catechisms" can be found in the medieval church, it is generally agreed that the extensive use of catechisms is especially associated with the Reformation. A visitation of Lutheran churches in Saxony over the period 1528–9 showed that most pastors and just about every lay person were ignorant of basic Christian teachings. Luther was shocked by his findings, and decided to put in place measures to increase public knowledge of basic Christian teachings.

The first result of Luther's new concern in this area made its appearance in April 1529. Although Luther himself termed it a "German Catechism," it is now more generally known as the "Greater Catechism." The work provides a detailed analysis of the Ten Commandments, the Apostles' Creed and the Lord's Prayer. These sections are followed by discussions of the two sacraments of the church – baptism and the "sacrament of the altar" (or Communion service). The work does not show Luther at his best. It draws upon earlier sermonical material, and was not written specifically for the purpose of catechizing. As a result, it failed to meet up to its goals.

This was followed in May 1529 by what is now known as the "Lesser Catechism" or as "The Little Instruction Book." The work was entirely original, written specifically for this purpose, and shows a lightness of touch, an ease of communication, and a general simplicity of expression which ensured that it was widely used and appreciated. The work was a remarkable success, and was widely adopted within Lutheran institutions. Its question-and-answer format was ideally suited to learning by rote, and the work was widely adopted within the schools of the region. It is important to note that both Luther's 1529 catechisms were written in German, the language of the people. Luther avoided the use of Latin for this purpose, recognizing the severe limitations which the use of this scholarly language would have on the appeal and readership of the works.

The entire work is here reprinted, to allow readers to appreciate the importance of the material and its potential impact on Protestant educational methods and literature. The translation used was undertaken by Robert E. Smith for "Project Gutenberg," and placed by him in the public domain.

Part One

The Ten Commandments: The Simple Way a Father Should Present Them to His Household

A. THE FIRST COMMANDMENT

You must not have other gods.

Q. What does this mean?

A. We must fear, love, and trust God more than anything else.

B. THE SECOND COMMANDMENT

You must not misuse your God's name.

Q. What does this mean?

A. We must fear and love God, so that we will not use His name to curse, swear, cast a spell, lie or deceive, but will use it to call upon Him, pray to Him, praise Him and thank Him in all times of trouble.

C. THE THIRD COMMANDMENT

You must keep the Sabbath holy.

Q. What does this mean?

A. We must fear and love God, so that we will not look down on preaching or God's Word, but consider it holy, listen to it willingly, and learn it.

D. THE FOURTH COMMANDMENT

You must honor your father and mother. [So that things will go well for you and you will live long on earth.]

Q. What does this mean?

A. We must fear and love God, so that we will neither look down on our parents or superiors nor irritate them, but will honor them, serve them, obey them, love them and value them.

E. THE FIFTH COMMANDMENT

You must not kill.

Q. What does this mean?

A. We must fear and love God, so that we will neither harm nor hurt our neighbor's body, but help him and care for him when he is ill.

F. THE SIXTH COMMANDMENT

You must not commit adultery.

Q. What does this mean?

A. We must fear and love God, so that our words and actions will be clean and decent and so that everyone will love and honor their spouses.

G. THE SEVENTH COMMANDMENT

You must not steal.

Q. What does this mean?

A. We must fear and love God, so that we will neither take our neighbor's money or property, nor acquire it by fraud or by selling him poorly made products, but will help him improve and protect his property and career.

H. THE EIGHTH COMMANDMENT

You must not tell lies about your neighbor.

Q. What does this mean?

A. We must fear and love God, so that we will not deceive by lying, betraying, slandering or ruining our neighbor's reputation, but will defend him, say good things about him, and see the best side of everything he does.

I. THE NINTH COMMANDMENT

You must not desire your neighbor's house.

Q. What does this mean?

A. We must fear and love God, so that we will not attempt to trick our neighbor out of his inheritance or house, take it by pretending to have a right to it, etc. but help him to keep & improve it.

J. THE TENTH COMMANDMENT

You must not desire your neighbor's wife, servant, maid, animals or anything that belongs to him.

Q. What does this mean?

A. We must fear and love God, so that we will not release his cattle, take his employees from him or seduce his wife, but urge them to stay and do what they ought to do.

K. THE CONCLUSION TO THE COMMANDMENTS

Q. What does God say to us about all these commandments?

A. This is what He says:

"I am the Lord Your God. I am a jealous God. I plague the grandchildren and great-grandchildren of those who hate me with their ancestor's sin. But I make whole those who love me for a thousand generations."

Q. What does it mean?

A. God threatens to punish everyone who breaks these commandments. We should be afraid of His anger because of this and not violate such commandments. But He promises grace and all good things to those who keep such commandments. Because of this, we, too, should love Him, trust Him, and willingly do what His commandments require.

Part Two

The Creed: The Simple Way a Father Should Present It to His Household

I. THE FIRST ARTICLE: ON CREATION

I believe in God the Almighty Father, Creator of Heaven and Earth.

Q. What does this mean?

A. I believe that God created me, along with all creatures. He gave to me: body and soul, eyes, ears and all the other parts of my body, my mind and all my senses and preserves them as well. He gives me clothing and shoes, food and drink, house and land, wife and children, fields, animals and all I own. Every day He abundantly provides everything I need to nourish this body and life. He protects me against all danger, shields and defends me from all evil. He does all this because of His pure, fatherly and divine goodness and His mercy, not because I've earned it or deserved it. For all of this, I must thank Him, praise Him, serve Him and obey Him. Yes, this is true!

II. THE SECOND ARTICLE: ON REDEMPTION

And in Jesus Christ, His only Son, our Lord, Who was conceived by the Holy Spirit, born of the Virgin Mary, suffered under Pontius Pilate, was crucified, died and was buried, descended to Hell, on the third day rose again from the dead, ascended to Heaven and sat down at the right hand of God the Almighty Father. From there He will come to judge the living and the dead.

Q. What does this mean?

A. I believe that Jesus Christ is truly God, born of the Father in eternity and also truly man, born of the Virgin Mary. He is my Lord! He redeemed me, a lost and condemned person, bought and won me from all sins, death and the authority of the Devil. It did not cost Him gold or silver, but His holy, precious blood, His innocent body – His death! Because of this, I am His very own, will live under Him in His kingdom and serve Him righteously, innocently and blessedly forever, just as He is risen from death, lives and reigns forever. Yes, this is true.

III. THE THIRD ARTICLE: ON BECOMING HOLY

I believe in the Holy Spirit, the holy Christian Church, the community of the saints, the forgiveness of sins, the resurrection of the body, and an everlasting life. Amen.

Q. What does this mean?

A. I believe that I cannot come to my Lord Jesus Christ by my own intelligence or power. But the Holy Spirit called me by the Gospel, enlightened me with His gifts, made me holy and kept me in the true faith, just as He calls, gathers together, enlightens and makes holy the whole Church on earth and keeps it with Jesus in the one, true faith. In this Church, He generously forgives each day every sin committed by me and by every believer. On the last day, He will raise me and all the dead from the grave. He will give eternal life to me and to all who believe in Christ. Yes, this is true!

Part Three

The Lord's Prayer

The Our Father: The Simple Way a Father Should Present It to His Household

I. INTRODUCTION

Our Father, Who is in Heaven.

Q. What does this mean?

A. In this introduction, God invites us to believe that He is our real Father and we are His real children, so that we will pray with trust and complete confidence, in the same way beloved children approach their beloved Father with their requests.

II. THE FIRST REQUEST

May Your name be holy.

Q. What does this mean?

A. Of course, God's name is holy in and of itself, but by this request, we pray that He will make it holy among us, too.

Q. How does this take place?

A. When God's Word is taught clearly and purely, and when we live holy lives as God's children based upon it. Help us, Heavenly Father, to do this! But anyone who teaches and lives by something other than God's Word defiles God's name among us. Protect us from this, Heavenly Father!

III. THE SECOND REQUEST

Your Kingdom come.

Q. What does this mean?

A. Truly God's Kingdom comes by itself, without our prayer. But we pray in this request that it come to us as well.

Q. How does this happen?

A. When the Heavenly Father gives us His Holy Spirit, so that we believe His holy Word by His grace and live godly lives here in this age and there in eternal life.

IV. THE THIRD REQUEST

May Your will be accomplished, as it is in Heaven, so may it be on Earth.

Q. What does this mean?

A. Truly, God's good and gracious will is accomplished without our prayer. But we pray in this request that it be accomplished among us as well.

Q. How does this happen?

A. When God destroys and interferes with every evil will and all evil advice, which will not allow God's Kingdom to come, such as the Devil's will, the world's will and will of our bodily desires. It also happens when God strengthens us by faith and by His Word and keeps us living by them faithfully until the end of our lives. This is His will, good and full of grace.

V. THE FOURTH REQUEST

Give us our daily bread today.

Q. What does this mean?

A. Truly, God gives daily bread to evil people, even without our prayer. But we pray in this request that He will help us realize this and receive our daily bread with thanksgiving.

Q. What does "Daily Bread" mean?

A. Everything that nourishes our body and meets its needs, such as: Food, drink, clothing, shoes, house, yard, fields, cattle, money, possessions, a devout spouse, devout children, devout employees, devout and faithful rulers, good government, good weather, peace, health, discipline, honor, good friends, faithful neighbors and other things like these.

VI. THE FIFTH REQUEST

And forgive our guilt, as we forgive those guilty of sinning against us.

Q. What does this mean?

A. We pray in this request that our Heavenly Father will neither pay attention to our sins nor refuse requests such as these because of our sins and because we are neither worthy nor deserve the things for which we pray. Yet He wants to give them all to us by His grace, because many times each day we sin and truly deserve only punishment. Because God does this, we will, of course, want to forgive from our hearts and willingly do good to those who sin against us.

VII. THE SIXTH REQUEST

And lead us not into temptation.

Q. What does this mean?

A. God tempts no one, of course, but we pray in this request that God will protect us and save us, so that the Devil, the world and our bodily desires will neither deceive us nor seduce us into heresy, despair or other serious shame or vice, and so that we will win and be victorious in the end, even if they attack us.

VIII. THE SEVENTH REQUEST

But set us free from the Evil One.

Q. What does this mean?

A. We pray in this request, as a summary, that our Father in Heaven will save us from every kind of evil that threatens body, soul, property and honor. We pray that when at last our final hour has come, He will grant us a blessed death, and, in His grace, bring us to Himself from this valley of tears.

IX. AMEN

Q. What does this mean?

A. That I should be certain that such prayers are acceptable to the Father in Heaven and will be granted, that He Himself has commanded us to pray in this way and that He promises to answer us. Amen. Amen. This means: Yes, yes it will happen this way.

Part Four

Holy Baptism

The Sacrament of Holy Baptism: The Simple Way a Father Should Present It to His Household

I. Q. WHAT IS BAPTISM?

A. Baptism is not just plain water, but it is water contained within God's command and united with God's Word.

Q. Which Word of God is this?

A. The one which our Lord Christ spoke in the last chapter of Matthew:

"Go into all the world, teaching all heathen nations, and baptizing them in the name of the Father, the Son and of the Holy Spirit."

II. Q. WHAT DOES BAPTISM GIVE? WHAT GOOD IS IT?

A. It gives the forgiveness of sins, redeems from death and the Devil, gives eternal salvation to all who believe this, just as God's words and promises declare.

Q. What are these words and promises of God?

A. Our Lord Christ spoke one of them in the last chapter of Mark:

"Whoever believes and is baptized will be saved; but whoever does not believe will be damned."

III. Q. HOW CAN WATER DO SUCH GREAT THINGS?

A. Water doesn't make these things happen, of course. It is God's Word, which is with and in the water. Because, without God's Word, the water is plain water and not baptism. But with God's Word it is a Baptism, a grace-filled water of life, a bath of new birth in the Holy Spirit, as St. Paul said to Titus in the third chapter:

"Through this bath of rebirth and renewal of the Holy Spirit, which He poured out on us abundantly through Jesus Christ, our Savior, that we, justified by the same grace are made heirs according to the hope of eternal life. This is a faithful saying."

IV. Q. WHAT IS THE MEANING OF SUCH A WATER BAPTISM?

A. It means that the old Adam in us should be drowned by daily sorrow and repentance, and die with all sins and evil lusts, and, in turn, a new person daily come forth and rise from death again. He will live forever before God in righteousness and purity.

Q. Where is this written?

A. St. Paul says to the Romans in chapter six:

"We are buried with Christ through Baptism into death, so that, in the same way Christ is risen from the dead by the glory of the Father, thus also must we walk in a new life."

Part Five

Confession

How One Should Teach the Uneducated to Confess

I. Q. WHAT IS CONFESSION?

A. Confession has two parts:
   First, a person admits his sin.

Second, a person receives absolution or forgiveness from the confessor, as if from God Himself, without doubting it, but believing firmly that his sins are forgiven by God in Heaven through it.

II. Q. WHICH SINS SHOULD PEOPLE CONFESS?
    A. When speaking to God, we should plead guilty to all sins, even those we don't know about, just as we do in the "Our Father," but when speaking to the confessor, only the sins we know about, which we know about and feel in our hearts.
    Q. Which are these?
    A. Consider here your place in life according to the Ten Commandments. Are you a father? A mother? A son? A daughter? A husband? A wife? A servant? Are you disobedient, unfaithful or lazy? Have you hurt anyone with your words or actions? Have you stolen, neglected your duty, let things go or injured someone?

Part Six

The Sacrament of the Altar

The Sacrament of the Altar: The Simple Way a Father Should Present It to His Household

I. Q. WHAT IS THE SACRAMENT OF THE ALTAR?
    A. It is the true body and blood of our Lord Jesus Christ under bread and wine for us Christians to eat and to drink, established by Christ Himself.

II. Q. WHERE IS THAT WRITTEN?
    A. The holy apostles Matthew, Mark and Luke and St. Paul write this:

"Our Lord Jesus Christ, in the night on which He was betrayed, took bread, gave thanks, broke it, gave it to His disciples and said: 'Take! Eat! This is My body, which is given for you. Do this to remember Me!' In the same way He also took the cup after supper, gave thanks, gave it to them, and said: 'Take and drink from it, all of you! This cup is the New Testament in my blood, which is shed for you to forgive sins. This do, as often as you drink it, to remember Me!'"

III. Q. WHAT GOOD DOES THIS EATING AND DRINKING DO?
    A. These words tell us: "Given for you" and "Shed for you to forgive sins." Namely, that the forgiveness of sins, life and salvation are given to us through these words in the sacrament. Because, where sins are forgiven, there is life and salvation as well.

IV. Q. HOW CAN PHYSICAL EATING AND DRINKING DO SUCH GREAT THINGS?
    A. Of course, eating and drinking do not do these things. These words, written here, do them: "Given for you" and "Shed for you to forgive sins." These

words, along with physical eating and drinking are the important part of the sacrament. Anyone who believes these words has what they say and what they record, namely, the forgiveness of sins.

V. Q. WHO, THEN, RECEIVES SUCH A SACRAMENT IN A WORTHY WAY?
A. Of course, fasting and other physical preparations are excellent disciplines for the body. But anyone who believes these words, "Given for you," and "Shed for you to forgive sins," is really worthy and well prepared. But whoever doubts or does not believe these words is not worthy and is unprepared, because the words, "for you" demand a heart that fully believes.

Morning Prayer

My Heavenly Father, I thank You, through Jesus Christ, Your beloved Son, that You kept me safe from all evil and danger last night. Save me, I pray, today as well, from every evil and sin, so that all I do and the way that I live will please you. I put myself in your care, body and soul and all that I have. Let Your holy Angels be with me, so that the evil enemy will not gain power over me. Amen.

Evening Prayer

My Heavenly Father, I thank You, through Jesus Christ, Your beloved Son, that You have protected me, by Your grace. Forgive, I pray, all my sins and the evil I have done. Protect me, by Your grace, tonight. I put myself in your care, body and soul and all that I have. Let Your holy angels be with me, so that the evil enemy will not gain power over me. Amen.

Questions for Study

1 This is a classic example of the "catechetical" form. How would you summarize its distinctive approach?
2 What audience do you think Luther has in mind for this work?
3 According to this catechism, why should Christians forgive those who sin against them?

CHAPTER 41

Ignatius Loyola (ca. 1491–1556)

It is widely agreed that Ignatius Loyola is one of the most important Spanish spiritual writers of the sixteenth century. Initially, Loyola's career was fairly typical of his age. After a period of service in the household of the Royal Treasurer of Castille, he joined the army of the Duke of Nájera. Any hopes he may have held for future advancement were called into question when he was wounded during the siege of Pamplona (May 1521). The leg wound which he received required a prolonged period of convalescence at the family home, the castle of Loyola. He had hoped to alleviate the boredom of this period of enforced rest by reading some novels; the family library, however, was not particularly well stocked. In the end, Loyola found himself reading Ludwig of Saxony's *Life of Christ*. As we noted earlier (p. 218), this work develops the idea of an imaginative projection of the reader into the biblical narrative. Although Loyola read other spiritual works (such as lives of the saints) at this time, there is little doubt that this work stimulated his thinking on the relation between the believer, God and the world.

Ignatius Loyola (ca. 1491–1556)

Basic description
Sixteenth-century Spanish spiritual writer; founder of the Society of Jesus.

Major work
The Spiritual Exercises.

Major studies
Philip Caraman, *Ignatius Loyola*. London: Collins, 1990.

Hugo Rahner, *Ignatius the Theologian*. London: Chapman, 1990.

The result of Loyola's immersion in this work was a decision to reform his life. His initial decision was to sell his possessions, and undertake a pilgrimage to Jerusalem. The latter task proved abortive. He was obliged to spend a period of ten months (March 1522–February 1523) at the town of Manresa waiting to be allowed to travel to Rome, prior to a further journey onward to Jerusalem. During that period, he developed the general approach to spirituality which is now embodied in the *Spiritual Exercises*. This book is primarily intended for those who conduct retreats, and is not really intended to be read by others. However, it has found a wide readership beyond its intended audience.

The most characteristic features of the *Spiritual Exercises* can be summarized as follows:

1 An imaginative approach to the reading of Scripture and prayer, in which those undertaking the exercises (often referred to as "exercitants") form mental images as aids to prayer and contemplation.
2 A structured and progressive program of reflection and meditation, which proceeds sequentially through the major themes of the Christian life. The four weeks specified for the *Exercises* focus on sin and its consequences; the life of Christ; the death of Christ; and the resurrection.
3 The use of a retreat director, who guides the exercitant through the exercises, allowing reflection on both God and self, leading to the taking of decisions for personal reform and renewal.

The "Ignatian retreat" has become a well established feature of modern Christian life, especially within Catholicism, just as Ignatian approaches to prayer have been welcomed by many who have found more cognitive or intellectual approaches to be spiritually dry and unhelpful.

Text: *The Spiritual Exercises*

The text chosen for study takes the form of extracts taken from the "Second Exercise" set for the first week of a retreat, focusing on the idea of sin and its consequences for the believer.

First Exercise

A Meditation With The Three Powers On The First, Second And Third Sin

It contains in it, after one Preparatory Prayer and two Preludes, three chief Points and one Colloquy.

Prayer. The Preparatory Prayer is to ask grace of God our Lord that all my intentions, actions and operations may be directed purely to the service and praise of His Divine Majesty.

First Prelude. The First Prelude is a composition, seeing the place.

Here it is to be noted that, in a visible contemplation or meditation – as, for instance, when one contemplates Christ our Lord, Who is visible – the composition will be to see with the sight of the imagination the corporeal place where the thing is found which I want to contemplate. I say the corporeal place, as for instance, a Temple or Mountain where Jesus Christ or Our Lady is found, according to what I want to contemplate. In an invisible contemplation or meditation – as here on the Sins – the composition will be to see with the sight of the imagination and consider that my soul is imprisoned in this corruptible body, and all the compound in this valley, as exiled among brute beasts: I say all the compound of soul and body.

Second Prelude. The second is to ask God our Lord for what I want and desire.

The petition has to be according to the subject matter; that is, if the contemplation is on the Resurrection, one is to ask for joy with Christ in joy; if it is on the Passion, one is to ask for pain, tears and torment with Christ in torment.

Here it will be to ask shame and confusion at myself, seeing how many have been damned for only one mortal sin, and how many times I deserved to be condemned forever for my so many sins.

Note. Before all Contemplations or Meditations, there ought always to be made the Preparatory Prayer, which is not changed, and the two Preludes already mentioned, which are sometimes changed, according to the subject matter.

First Point. The first Point will be to bring the memory on the First Sin, which was that of the Angels, and then to bring the intellect on the same, discussing it; then the will, wanting to recall and understand all this in order to make me more ashamed and confound me more, bringing into comparison with the one sin of the Angels my so many sins, and reflecting, while they for one sin were cast into Hell, how often I have deserved it for so many.

I say to bring to memory the sin of the Angels, how they, being created in grace, not wanting to help themselves with their liberty to reverence and obey their Creator and Lord, coming to pride, were changed from grace to malice, and hurled from Heaven to Hell; and so then to discuss more in detail with the intellect: and then to move the feelings more with the will.

Second Point. The second is to do the same – that is, to bring the Three Powers – on the sin of Adam and Eve, bringing to memory how on account of that sin they did penance for so long a time, and how much corruption came on the human race, so many people going the way to Hell.

I say to bring to memory the Second Sin, that of our First Parents; how after Adam was created in the field of Damascus and placed in the Terrestrial Paradise, and Eve was created from his rib, being forbidden to eat of the Tree of Knowledge, they ate and so sinned, and afterwards clothed in tunics of skins and cast from Paradise, they lived, all their life, without the original justice which they had lost, and in many labors and much penance. And then to discuss with the understanding more in detail; and to use the will as has been said.

Third Point. The third is likewise to do the same on the Third particular Sin of any one who for one mortal sin is gone to Hell – and many others without number, for fewer sins than I have committed.

I say to do the same on the Third particular Sin, bringing to memory the gravity and malice of the sin against one's Creator and Lord; to discuss with the understanding how in sinning and acting against the Infinite Goodness, he has been justly condemned forever; and to finish with the will as has been said.

Colloquy. Imagining Christ our Lord present and placed on the Cross, let me make a Colloquy, how from Creator He is come to making Himself man, and from life eternal is come to temporal death, and so to die for my sins.

Likewise, looking at myself, what I have done for Christ, what I am doing for Christ, what I ought to do for Christ.

And so, seeing Him such, and so nailed on the Cross, to go over that which will present itself.

The Colloquy is made, properly speaking, as one friend speaks to another, or as a servant to his master; now asking some grace, now blaming oneself for some misdeed, now communicating one's affairs, and asking advice on them.

And let me say an OUR FATHER.

Questions for Discussion

1 The passage is, in part, a meditation on sin, and is intended to deepen a sense of shame and sorrow for sin and its consequences. Notice particularly how Loyola regards sin not simply as something which is meant to be understood, but as something which generates an emotional reaction of sorrow. How effective is he in this matter?

2 Why does Loyola introduce a meditation on Christ on the cross? What purpose does this serve?

3 Loyola makes much use of what he terms the "three powers" – that is, memory, intellect and will. He asks his readers to remember, understand, and form an intention to improve. How is each of these three powers involved in the above reading?

CHAPTER 42

John Calvin (1509–1564)

For many, the name of John Calvin (1509–64) is virtually synonymous with that of Geneva. Although Geneva is now part of Switzerland, in the sixteenth century it was a small independent city state. Calvin, however, was a Frenchman. He was born on July 10, 1509 in the cathedral city of Noyon, about seventy miles northeast of Paris. His father was involved in the financial administration of the local diocese, and could rely on the patronage of the bishop to ensure support for his son. At some point in the early 1520s (probably 1523), the young Calvin was sent up to the University of Paris.

After a thorough grounding in Latin grammar at the hands of Mathurin Cordier, Calvin entered the Collège de Montaigu. After completing his rigorous education in the arts, Calvin moved to Orléans to study civil law, probably at some point in 1528. Although Calvin's father had originally intended that his son should study theology, he appears to have changed his mind. His father seems to have realized that the study of law, Calvin later remarked, generally makes people rich. It is also possible that Calvin's father may have lost the patronage of the local bishop on account of a financial wrangle back at Noyon.

It is generally thought that Calvin's detailed study of civil law gave him access to methods and ideas which he would later exploit in his career as a reformer. It was at Orléans that he learned Greek. At some point in 1529 Calvin moved to Bourges, attracted by the fame of the great Italian lawyer Andrea Alciati. Most Calvin scholars consider that Calvin's great clarity of expression is due to the influence of Alciati. Calvin's encounter with French legal humanism is generally thought to have been of fundamental importance in shaping his understanding of the way in which a classical text (such as the Bible or Roman legal texts) could be applied to modern situations.

By 1534 Calvin had become an enthusiastic supporter of the principles of the Reformation. During the following year, he settled down in the Swiss city of Basle, safe from any French threat. Making the best use of his enforced leisure, he published a book destined to exercise a decisive effect upon the Reformation: the *Institutes of the Christian Religion*. We shall consider this work further in the textual section below.

John Calvin (1509–1564)

Basic description
Leading Protestant reformer.

Major work
Institutes of the Christian Religion (1559).

Major studies
Alister E. McGrath, *A Life of John Calvin*. Oxford: Blackwell, 1990.

T. H. L. Parker, *John Calvin: A Biography*. London: Dent, 1975.

After winding up his affairs in Noyon early in 1536, Calvin decided to settle down to a life of private study in the city of Strasbourg. Unfortunately, the direct route from Noyon to Strasbourg was impassable, due to the outbreak of war between Francis I of France and the Emperor Charles V. Calvin had to make an extended detour, passing through the city of Geneva, which had recently gained its independence from the neighboring territory of Savoy. Geneva was then in a state of confusion, having just evicted its local bishop and begun a controversial program of reform under the Frenchmen Guillaume Farel and Pierre Viret. On hearing that Calvin was in the city, they demanded that he stay, and help the cause of the Reformation. Calvin reluctantly agreed; he remained there till Easter 1589, when he was expelled from the city as the result of an argument with the city council.

In September 1541, Calvin was asked to return to Geneva. In his absence, the religious and political situation had deteriorated. The city appealed to him to return, and restore order and confidence within the city. The Calvin who returned to Geneva was a wiser and more experienced young man, far better equipped for the massive tasks awaiting him than he had been three years earlier. Although Calvin would still find himself quarreling with the city authorities for more than a decade, it was from a position of strength. Finally, opposition to his program of reform died out. For the last decade of his life, he had virtually a free hand in the religious affairs of the city.

During this second period in Geneva, Calvin was able to develop both his own theology and the organization of the Genevan Reformed church. He established the Consistory as a means of enforcing church discipline, and founded the Genevan Academy to educate pastors in Reformed churches. The period was not without its controversies. Calvin found himself embroiled in serious theological debate with Sebastien Castellion over the correct interpretation of Christ's descent into hell, and whether the Song of Songs was canonical. A furious and very public debate broke out between himself and Jerome Bolsec over the doctrine of predestination. Both Castellion and Bolsec ended up having to leave Geneva. A more serious controversy concerned Michael Servetus, accused by Calvin of heresy, who was finally burned at the stake in 1553. Although Calvin's role in this matter was less significant than some of his critics have implied, the Servetus affair continues to stain Calvin's reputation as a Christian leader.

By the early spring of 1564, it was obvious that Calvin was seriously ill. He preached for the last time from the pulpit of Saint-Pierre on the morning of Sunday, February 6. By April, it was clear that Calvin had not much longer to live. He found breathing difficult, and was chronically short of breath. Calvin died at eight o'clock on the evening of May 27, 1564. At his own request, he was buried in a common grave, with no stone to mark his grave.

Although Calvin wrote many works, he is best known for one book – the *Institutes of the Christian Religion*, which is widely regarded as one of the most important religious works of the sixteenth century, and has had a significant impact on literature emanating from the Reformed constituency.

Text: *Institutes of the Christian Religion*

The first edition of the *Institutes of the Christian Religion* was published by the Basle printers Thomas Platter and Balthasar Lasius in March 1536. After being forced into exile in Strasbourg in 1538, Calvin found himself with time on his hands, alllowing him to produce a new edition of the *Institutes* (1539). The most obvious and important difference in the volume is that of size: the new work is about three times as long as the first edition of 1536, with seventeen chapters instead of six. A French edition was published in 1541, followed by a further Latin edition in 1543. The work had by now been expanded to 21 chapters. The Latin edition of 1550, and the subsequent French translation of 1551, attempted to make the work more readable by subdividing the 21 chapters into paragraphs. Nevertheless, it was not a particularly readable work.

Recognizing both the need for total revision and the limited time available in which to achieve this (illness was a recurring feature of Calvin's final years), the reformer decided to recast the entire work. The most obvious and positive change is the total reordering of the material, which virtually restores unity to what had almost degenerated into a series of unrelated fragments. The material is now distributed among four "books," arranged as follows:

1   the knowledge of God the creator;
2   the knowledge of God the redeemer;
3   the manner of participation in the grace of Jesus Christ;
4   the external means or aids which God uses to bring us to Jesus Christ.

The 21 chapters of 1551 are now expanded to 80 chapters, each carefully subdivided for ease of reading, distributed over these four books. This reworking ensured that the *Institutes* were now firmly established as the most influential theological work of the Protestant Reformation, eclipsing in importance the rival works of Luther, Melanchthon, and Zwingli.

The text selected for study is Book I, chapters 1 and 2, in which Calvin sets out one of the principles which is fundamental to his thought – namely, that knowledge of God is inextricably linked with knowledge of ourselves, and that it is by beginning to know God that we come to know ourselves.

Chapter 1

The Knowledge Of God And Of Ourselves Mutually Connected

1 OUR wisdom, in so far as it ought to be deemed true and solid Wisdom, consists almost entirely of two parts: the knowledge of God and of ourselves. But as these are connected together by many ties, it is not easy to determine which of the two precedes and gives birth to the other. For, in the first place, no man can survey himself without forthwith turning his thoughts toward the God in whom he lives and moves; because it is perfectly obvious that the endowments which we possess cannot possibly be from ourselves; nay, that our very being is nothing else than subsistence in God alone. In the second place, those blessings which unceasingly distil to us from heaven, are like streams conducting us to the fountain. Here, again, the infinitude of good which resides in God becomes more apparent from our poverty. In particular, the miserable ruin into which the revolt of the first man has plunged us, compels us to turn our eyes upwards; not only that while hungry and famishing we may thence ask what we want, but being aroused by fear may learn humility. For as there exists in man something like a world of misery, and ever since we were stript of the divine attire our naked shame discloses an immense series of disgraceful properties every man, being stung by the consciousness of his own unhappiness, in this way necessarily obtains at least some knowledge of God. Thus, our feeling of ignorance, vanity, want, weakness, in short, depravity and corruption, reminds us that in the Lord, and none but He, dwell the true light of wisdom, solid virtue, exuberant goodness. We are accordingly urged by our own evil things to consider the good things of God; and, indeed, we cannot aspire to Him in earnest until we have begun to be displeased with ourselves. For what man is not disposed to rest in himself? Who, in fact, does not thus rest, so long as he is unknown to himself; that is, so long as he is contented with his own endowments, and unconscious or unmindful of his misery? Every person, therefore, on coming to the knowledge of himself, is not only urged to seek God, but is also led as by the hand to find him.

2 On the other hand, it is evident that man never attains to a true self-knowledge until he have previously contemplated the face of God, and come down after such contemplation to look into himself. For (such is our innate pride) we always seem to ourselves just, and upright, and wise, and holy, until we are convinced, by clear evidence, of our injustice, vileness, folly, and impurity. Convinced, however, we are not, if we look to ourselves only, and not to the Lord also – He being the only standard by the application of which this conviction can be produced. For, since we are all naturally prone to hypocrisy, any empty semblance of righteousness is quite enough to satisfy us instead of righteousness itself. And since nothing appears within us or around us that is not tainted with very great impurity, so long as we keep our mind within the confines of human pollution, anything which is in some small degree less defiled delights us as if it were most pure just as an eye, to which nothing but black had been previously presented, deems an object

of a whitish, or even of a brownish hue, to be perfectly white. Nay, the bodily sense may furnish a still stronger illustration of the extent to which we are deluded in estimating the powers of the mind. If, at mid-day, we either look down to the ground, or on the surrounding objects which lie open to our view, we think ourselves endued with a very strong and piercing eyesight; but when we look up to the sun, and gaze at it unveiled, the sight which did excellently well for the earth is instantly so dazzled and confounded by the refulgence, as to oblige us to confess that our acuteness in discerning terrestrial objects is mere dimness when applied to the sun. Thus too, it happens in estimating our spiritual qualities. So long as we do not look beyond the earth, we are quite pleased with our own righteousness, wisdom, and virtue; we address ourselves in the most flattering terms, and seem only less than demigods. But should we once begin to raise our thoughts to God, and reflect what kind of Being he is, and how absolute the perfection of that righteousness, and wisdom, and virtue, to which, as a standard, we are bound to be conformed, what formerly delighted us by its false show of righteousness will become polluted with the greatest iniquity; what strangely imposed upon us under the name of wisdom will disgust by its extreme folly; and what presented the appearance of virtuous energy will be condemned as the most miserable impotence. So far are those qualities in us, which seem most perfect, from corresponding to the divine purity.

3   Hence that dread and amazement with which as Scripture uniformly relates, holy men were struck and overwhelmed whenever they beheld the presence of God. When we see those who previously stood firm and secure so quaking with terror, that the fear of death takes hold of them, nay, they are, in a manner, swallowed up and annihilated, the inference to be drawn is that men are never duly touched and impressed with a conviction of their insignificance, until they have contrasted themselves with the majesty of God. Frequent examples of this consternation occur both in the Book of Judges and the Prophetical Writings; so much so, that it was a common expression among the people of God, "We shall die, for we have seen the Lord." Hence the Book of Job, also, in humbling men under a conviction of their folly, feebleness, and pollution, always derives its chief argument from descriptions of the Divine wisdom, virtue, and purity. Nor without cause: for we see Abraham the readier to acknowledge himself but dust and ashes the nearer he approaches to behold the glory of the Lord, and Elijah unable to wait with unveiled face for His approach; so dreadful is the sight. And what can man do, man who is but rottenness and a worm, when even the Cherubim themselves must veil their faces in very terror? To this, undoubtedly, the Prophet Isaiah refers, when he says (Isaiah 24:23), "The moon shall be confounded, and the sun ashamed, when the Lord of Hosts shall reign"; i.e., when he shall exhibit his refulgence, and give a nearer view of it, the brightest objects will, in comparison, be covered with darkness.

But though the knowledge of God and the knowledge of ourselves are bound together by a mutual tie, due arrangement requires that we treat of the former in the first place, and then descend to the latter.

Chapter 2

What It Is To Know God

1   BY the knowledge of God, I understand that by which we not only conceive that there is some God, but also apprehend what it is for our interest, and conducive to his glory, what, in short, it is befitting to know concerning him. For, properly speaking, we cannot say that God is known where there is no religion or piety. I am not now referring to that species of knowledge by which men, in themselves lost and under curse, apprehend God as a Redeemer in Christ the Mediator. I speak only of that simple and primitive knowledge, to which the mere course of nature would have conducted us, had Adam stood upright. For although no man will now, in the present ruin of the human race, perceive God to be either a father, or the author of salvation, or propitious in any respect, until Christ interpose to make our peace; still it is one thing to perceive that God our Maker supports us by his power, rules us by his providence, fosters us by his goodness, and visits us with all kinds of blessings, and another thing to embrace the grace of reconciliation offered to us in Christ. Since, then, the Lord first appears, as well in the creation of the world as in the general doctrine of Scripture, simply as a Creator, and afterwards as a Redeemer in Christ – a twofold knowledge of him hence arises: of these the former is now to be considered, the latter will afterwards follow in its order. But although our mind cannot conceive of God without rendering some worship to him, it will not, however, be sufficient simply to hold that he is the only being whom all ought to worship and adore, unless we are also persuaded that he is the fountain of all goodness, and that we must seek everything in him, and in none but him. My meaning is: we must be persuaded not only that as he once formed the world, so he sustains it by his boundless power, governs it by his wisdom, preserves it by his goodness, in particular, rules the human race with justice and Judgment, bears with them in mercy, shields them by his protection; but also that not a particle of light, or wisdom, or justice, or power, or rectitude, or genuine truth, will anywhere be found, which does not flow from him, and of which he is not the cause; in this way we must learn to expect and ask all things from him, and thankfully ascribe to him whatever we receive. For this sense of the divine perfections is the proper master to teach us piety, out of which religion springs. By piety I mean that union of reverence and love to God which the knowledge of his benefits inspires. For, until men feel that they owe everything to God, that they are cherished by his paternal care, and that he is the author of all their blessings, so that nought is to be looked for away from him, they will never submit to him in voluntary obedience; nay, unless they place their entire happiness in him, they will never yield up their whole selves to him in truth and sincerity.

2   Those, therefore, who, in considering this question, propose to inquire what the essence of God is, only delude us with frigid speculations – it being much more our interest to know what kind of being God is, and what things are agreeable to his nature. For, of what use is it to join Epicurus in acknowledging some God who has cast off the care of the world, and only delights himself in ease? What avails

it, in short, to know a God with whom we have nothing to do? The effect of our knowledge rather ought to be, first, to teach us reverence and fear; and, secondly, to induce us, under its guidance and teaching, to ask every good thing from him, and, when it is received, ascribe it to him. For how can the idea of God enter your mind without instantly giving rise to the thought, that since you are his workmanship, you are bound, by the very law of creation, to submit to his authority? – that your life is due to him? – that whatever you do ought to have reference to him? If so, it undoubtedly follows that your life is sadly corrupted, if it is not framed in obedience to him, since his will ought to be the law of our lives. On the other hand, your idea of his nature is not clear unless you acknowledge him to be the origin and fountain of all goodness. Hence would arise both confidence in him, and a desire of cleaving to him, did not the depravity of the human mind lead it away from the proper course of investigation.

For, first of all, the pious mind does not devise for itself any kind of God, but looks alone to the one true God; nor does it feign for him any character it pleases, but is contented to have him in the character in which he manifests himself always guarding, with the utmost diligences against transgressing his will, and wandering, with daring presumptions from the right path. He by whom God is thus known perceiving how he governs all things, confides in him as his guardian and protector, and casts himself entirely upon his faithfulness, – perceiving him to be the source of every blessing, if he is in any strait or feels any want, he instantly recurs to his protection and trusts to his aid – persuaded that he is good and merciful, he reclines upon him with sure confidence, and doubts not that, in the divine clemency, a remedy will be provided for his every time of need – acknowledging him as his Father and his Lord he considers himself bound to have respect to his authority in all things, to reverence his majesty aim at the advancement of his glory, and obey his commands – regarding him as a just judge, armed with severity to punish crimes, he keeps the Judgment-seat always in his view. Standing in awe of it, he curbs himself, and fears to provoke his anger. Nevertheless, he is not so terrified by an apprehension of Judgment as to wish he could withdraw himself, even if the means of escape lay before him; nay, he embraces him not less as the avenger of wickedness than as the rewarder of the righteous; because he perceives that it equally appertains to his glory to store up punishment for the one, and eternal life for the other. Besides, it is not the mere fear of punishment that restrains him from sin. Loving and revering God as his father, honouring and obeying him as his master, although there were no hell, he would revolt at the very idea of offending him.

Such is pure and genuine religion, namely, confidence in God coupled with serious fear – fear, which both includes in it willing reverence, and brings along with it such legitimate worship as is prescribed by the law. And it ought to be more carefully considered that all men promiscuously do homage to God, but very few truly reverence him. On all hands there is abundance of ostentatious ceremonies, but sincerity of heart is rare.

Questions for Discussion

1 What, according to Calvin, is the source of true wisdom?
2 What does Calvin understand by the phrase "knowledge of God"? How does he illustrate what he has in mind?
3 Why, according to Calvin, are knowledge of God and self-knowledge so intimately connected? And how do we begin to acquire such knowledge?

CHAPTER 43

John Foxe (1516–1587)

John Foxe was one of the most influential writers of the English Reformation. He is known to have attended Brasenose College, Oxford, at an early age, although further details of his early life are not entirely reliable. In the forty years between 1547 and his death he produced some forty works, in both English and Latin. However, both in his own lifetime and since, he has been principally known for only one of them, *The Acts and Monuments*. The origins of this work are to be traced to the reign of Edward VI (1547–53), and can be seen as an attempt to write an historical justification of the Reformation as a whole, along the lines of an existing model – John Bale's *Image of Both Churches*. The idea was to portray human history as a cosmic struggle between the forces of Christ and Antichrist, in which the Protestants represented the latest incarnation of the true church. This task was interrupted when Foxe was forced into exile by the accession of the Catholic Mary Tudor as queen in 1553, after the early death of the pro-Protestant Edward VI.

John Foxe (1516–1587)

Basic description
English martyrologist.

Major work
The Acts and Monuments (1563).

Editions of works
Acts and Monuments, ed. G. Townsend. 8 vols, 1843–9.

Major studies
J. F. Mozley, *John Foxe and his Book*. London: SPCK, 1940.
V. Norskov Olsen, *John Foxe and the Elizabethan Church*. Berkeley, CA: University of California Press, 1973.

His exile allowed him to get to know other prominent Protestant refugees who had sought exile in the Protestant cities of Europe, including John Knox and Edmund Grindal. His experience of exile drove him to write the Latin work *Commentarii Rerum in*

Ecclesia Gestarum, which he published in Strasbourg in 1554. This work focused on the English Lollards; however, it is clear that Foxe had a much grander work in mind, which would take in a much wider range of historical events.

The stimulus which appears to have triggered his decision to write a much larger work in English was the onset of persecution of England's Protestants, which began in January 1555. This may be said to have changed Foxe's whole agenda. Prior to this he had written about the Lollards; the people he would now write about were people who he had known personally. However, his first attempt to put such a work in place came to little; in 1559 he produced what was not much more than an expanded version of his original work of 1554. This work, which was published in the Swiss city of Basle under the title *Rerum in Ecclesia Gestarum*, did little more than print a list of those who had suffered under Mary in England.

The accession of Elizabeth in 1558 changed the religious climate in England totally. It became clear from an early stage that Elizabeth was not unsympathetic toward Protestantism. Encouraged by this, Foxe returned to England in 1559, and began to plan and write a major new martyrology in English. Persuaded partly by his friend Edmund Grindal and partly by the publisher John Day, he turned his attention to the traumatic events of the last few years. He was now not only concerned to justify the Reformation as a major phase in English church history, but also to vindicate the memory of those who had suffered and died under Mary. The resulting work would also lend support to the new Protestant establishment which was emerging under Elizabeth, by stressing the sufferings of the Protestants and the cruelty of "bloody Mary." The resulting *Acts and Monuments of these Latter and Perilous Days*, published in London in 1563, was propaganda as much as history, in that it sought to defend the newly-founded Protestant establishment by an appeal to the bravery and sufferings of those who had made it possible.

Starting with the unbinding of Satan, which he dated to the late thirteenth century, he recounted the persecutions inflicted upon the godly, with particular reference to England, and particular attention to the reign of Mary Tudor. This very large book – it consists of more than 1,800 folio pages – complete with extensive documentation and charged with an impassioned polemic, made an immediate impact. Fox produced new editions in 1570, 1576 and 1583, each to a slightly different agenda. In 1563 he had been triumphalist. Elizabeth was the new Constantine who had defeated the forces of evil, and God was using England in a special way to prepare for his second coming. In 1570 he was apprehensive that the enemy was not finally defeated, and went back to his original intention by including much material on the early persecutions of the church. By 1583 he was reasonably sure that the Reformation had triumphed in England, but very uncertain that the new generation of Englishmen were worthy of their calling. They needed to be reminded of the sufferings of the recent past.

By the time of his death his book was a national institution. In 1570 the Privy Council had ordered it to be set up in cathedral churches alongside the English Bible, and many parishes followed suit, in spite of the expense of acquiring a work which by then ran to two folio volumes and over 2,000 pages. After the author's death, *The Acts and Monuments* was abridged in 1589, and issued in fresh full editions in 1596 and 1610.

In later generations, the work came to have a new significance. Although it was used to support the Protestant establishment under Elizabeth, the work developed strongly

Puritan associations following the publication of a new edition of the work in 1632, which included additional material on the imminence of a new persecution. This effectively converted it from a work supporting a Protestant establishment into a polemic for a godly opposition. It is known that this edition of the work had great influence on such Puritan leaders as John Bunyan and George Fox. Further editions appeared in the significant years 1641 and 1684, encouraging opposition to any form of rapprochement between the English church or state and Roman Catholicism. In the nineteenth century, *The Acts and Monuments* became the focus of a new controversy, arising out of conflict between the evangelical revival and the Oxford Movement. The ritualism of the Oxford Movement was seen as a challenge to the Protestantism of England, with the result that Foxe became a symbol and an expression of the integrity of the Protestant Church of England. The same factors which prompted the founders of the Parker Society to publish new editions of the writings of the English Reformers of the sixteenth century also prompted Stephen Cattley and George Townsend to issue a new edition of *The Acts and Monuments.*

Foxe's *Book of Martyrs* was second only to the English Bible as a formative influence on the language and culture of England, and it is therefore entirely appropriate to include it in this anthology. The text is here presented in a form edited by William Byron Forbush, which allows the text to be read easily, while retaining the distinctive "feel" of this major work of English literature.

Text: *The Acts and Monuments of Matters Happening in the Church* (1563)

Our extracts are taken from the sixteenth chapter of this work, entitled "Persecutions in England During the Reign of Queen Mary." This section of the work is of especial importance, as it is widely regarded as preserving Protestant oral history at a critical phase in the English Reformation. Despite Foxe's obvious Protestant bias, the accounts which he offers are of considerable historical importance. They are also of literary importance, in that they reflect important developments in the genre of biography. Our extract relates the events surrounding the execution of Archbishop Thomas Cranmer in 1556.

Dr. Thomas Cranmer was descended from an ancient family, and was born at the village of Aslocton, in the county of Northampton. After the usual school education he was sent to Cambridge, and was chosen a fellow of Jesus College. Here he married a gentleman's daughter, by which he forfeited his fellowship, and became a reader in Buckingham College, placing his wife at the Dolphin Inn, the landlady of which was a relation of hers, whence arose the idle report that he was an ostler. His lady shortly after dying in childbed; to his credit he was re-chosen a fellow of the college before mentioned. In a few years after, he was promoted to be Divinity Lecturer, and appointed one of the examiners over those who were ripe to become Bachelors or Doctors in Divinity. It was his principle to judge of their qualifications by the knowledge they possessed of the Scriptures, rather than of the ancient fathers, and hence many popish priests were rejected, and others rendered much improved.

He was strongly solicited by Dr. Capon to be one of the fellows on the foundation of Cardinal Wolsey's college, Oxford, of which he hazarded the refusal. While he continued in Cambridge, the question of Henry VIII's divorce with Catharine was agitated. At that time, on account of the plague, Dr. Cranmer removed to the house of a Mr. Cressy, at Waltham Abbey, whose two sons were then educating under him. The affair of divorce, contrary to the king's approbation, had remained undecided above two or three years, from the intrigues of the canonists and civilians, and though the cardinals Campeius and Wolsey were commissioned from Rome to decide the question, they purposely protracted the sentence.

It happened that Dr. Gardiner (secretary) and Dr. Fox, defenders of the king in the above suit, came to the house of Mr. Cressy to lodge, while the king removed to Greenwich. At supper, a conversation ensued with Dr. Cranmer, who suggested that the question whether a man may marry his brother's wife or not, could be easily and speedily decided by the Word of God, and this as well in the English courts as in those of any foreign nation. The king, uneasy at the delay, sent for Dr. Gardiner and Dr. Fox to consult them, regretting that a new commission must be sent to Rome, and the suit be endlessly protracted. Upon relating to the king the conversation which had passed on the previous evening with Dr. Cranmer, his majesty sent for him, and opened the tenderness of conscience upon the near affinity of the queen. Dr. Cranmer advised that the matter should be referred to the most learned divines of Cambridge and Oxford, as he was unwilling to meddle in an affair of such weight; but the king enjoined him to deliver his sentiments in writing, and to repair for that purpose to the earl of Wiltshire's, who would accommodate him with books, and everything requisite for the occasion.

This Dr. Cranmer immediately did, and in his declaration not only quoted the authority of the Scriptures, of general councils, and the ancient writers, but maintained that the bishop of Rome had no authority whatever to dispense with the Word of God. The king asked him if he would stand by this bold declaration, to which replying in the affirmative, he was deputed ambassador to Rome, in conjunction with the earl of Wiltshire, Dr. Stokesley, Dr. Carne, Dr. Bennet, and others, previous to which, the marriage was discussed in most of the universities of Christendom and at home.

When the pope presented his toe to be kissed, as customary, the earl of Wiltshire and his party refused. Indeed, it is affirmed that a spaniel of the earl's attracted by the littler of the pope's toes, made a snap at it, whence his holiness drew in his sacred foot, and kicked at the offender with the other.

Upon the pope demanding the cause of their embassy, the earl presented Dr. Cranmer's book, declaring that his learned friends had come to defend it. The pope treated the embassy honorably, and appointed a day for the discussion, which he delayed, as if afraid of the issue of the investigation. The earl returned, and Dr. Cranmer, by the king's desire, visited the emperor, and was successful in bringing him over to his opinion. Upon the doctor's return to England, Dr. Warham, archbishop of Canterbury, having quitted this transitory life, Dr. Cranmer was deservedly, and by Dr. Warham's desire, elevated to that eminent station.

In this function, it may be said that he followed closely the charge of St. Paul. Diligent in duty, he rose at five in the morning, and continued in study and prayer until nine: between then and dinner, he devoted to temporal affairs. After dinner, if any suitors wanted hearing, he would determine their business with such an affability that even the defaulters were scarcely displeased. Then he would play at chess for an hour, or see others play, and at five o'clock he heard the Common Prayer read, and from this until supper he took the recreation of walking. At supper his conversation was lively and entertaining; again he walked or amused himself until nine o'clock, and then entered his study.

He ranked high in favor with King Henry, and even had the purity and the interest of the English Church deeply at heart. His mild and forgiving disposition is recorded in the following instance. An ignorant priest, in the country, had called Cranmer an ostler, and spoken very derogatory of his learning. Lord Cromwell receiving information of it, the man was sent to the Fleet, and his case was told to the archbishop by a Mr. Chertsey, a grocer, and a relation of the priest's. His grace, having sent for the offender, reasoned with him, and solicited the priest to question him on any learned subject. This the man, overcome by the bishop's good nature, and knowing his own glaring incapacity, declined, and entreated his forgiveness, which was immediately granted, with a charge to employ his time better when he returned to his parish. Cromwell was much vexed at the lenity displayed, but the bishop was ever more ready to receive injury than to retaliate in any other manner than by good advice and good offices.

At the time that Cranmer was raised to be archbishop, he was king's chaplain, and archdeacon of Taunton; he was also constituted by the pope the penitentiary general of England. It was considered by the king that Cranmer would be obsequious; hence the latter married the king to Anne Boleyn, performed her coronation, stood godfather to Elizabeth, the first child, and divorced the king from Catharine. Though Cranmer received a confirmation of his dignity from the pope, he always protested against acknowledging any other authority than the king's, and he persisted in the same independent sentiments when before Mary's commissioners in 1555.

One of the first steps after the divorce was to prevent preaching throughout his diocese, but this narrow measure had rather a political view than a religious one, as there were many who inveighed against the king's conduct. In his new dignity Cranmer agitated the question of supremacy, and by his powerful and just arguments induced the parliament to "render to Caesar the things that are Caesar's." During Cranmer's residence in Germany, 1531, he became acquainted with Ossiander, at Nuremberg, and married his niece, but left her with him while on his return to England. After a season he sent for her privately, and she remained with him until the year 1539, when the Six Articles compelled him to return her to her friends for a time.

It should be remembered that Ossiander, having obtained the approbation of his friend Cranmer, published the laborious work of the *Harmony of the Gospels* in 1537. In 1534 the archbishop completed the dearest wish of his heart, the removal of every obstacle to the perfection of the Reformation, by the subscription of the nobles and bishops to the king's sole supremacy. Only Bishop Fisher and Sir Thomas More made objection; and their agreement not to oppose the succession Cranmer was willing to consider as sufficient, but the monarch would have no other than an entire concession.

Not long after, Gardiner, in a private interview with the king, spoke inimically of Cranmer, (whom he maliciously hated) for assuming the title of primate of all England, as derogatory to the supremacy of the king. This created much jealousy against Cranmer, and his translation of the Bible was strongly opposed by Stokesley, bishop of London. It is said, upon the demise of Queen Catharine, that her successor Anne Boleyn rejoiced – a lesson this to show how shallow is the human judgment! since her own execution took place in the spring of the following year, and the king, on the day following the beheading of this sacrificed lady, married the beautiful Jane Seymour, a maid of honor to the late queen. Cranmer was ever the friend of Anne Boleyn, but it was dangerous to oppose the will of the carnal tyrannical monarch.

In 1538, the Holy Scriptures were openly exposed to sale; and the places of worship overflowed everywhere to hear its holy doctrines expounded. Upon the king's passing into a law the famous Six Articles, which went nearly again to establish the essential tenets of the Romish creed, Cranmer shone forth with all the luster of a Christian patriot, in resisting the doctrines they contained, and in which he was supported by the bishops of Sarum, Worcester, Ely, and Rochester, the two former of whom resigned their bishoprics. The king, though now in opposition to Cranmer, still revered the sincerity that marked his conduct. The death of Lord Cromwell in the Tower, in 1540, the good friend of Cranmer, was a severe blow to the wavering Protestant cause, but even now Cranmer, when he saw the tide directly adverse to the truth, boldly waited on the king in person, and by his manly and heartfelt pleading, caused the Book of Articles to be passed on his side, to the great confusion of his enemies, who had contemplated his fall as inevitable.

Cranmer now lived in as secluded a manner as possible, until the rancor of Winchester preferred some articles against him, relative to the dangerous opinion he taught in his family, joined to other treasonable charges. These the king himself delivered to Cranmer, and believing firmly the fidelity and assertions of innocence of the accused prelate, he caused the matter to be deeply investigated, and Winchester and Dr. Lenden, with Thornton and Barber, of the bishop's household, were found by the papers to be the real conspirators. The mild, forgiving Cranmer would have interceded for all remission of punishment, had not Henry, pleased with the subsidy voted by parliament, let them be discharged. These nefarious men, however, again renewing their plots against Cranmer, fell victims to Henry's resentment, and Gardiner forever lost his confidence. Sir G. Gostwick soon after laid charges against the archbishop, which Henry quashed, and the primate was willing to forgive.

In 1544, the archbishop's palace at Canterbury was burnt, and his brother-in-law with others perished in it. These various afflictions may serve to reconcile us to a humble state; for of what happiness could this great and good man boast, since his life was constantly harassed either by political, religious, or natural crosses? Again the inveterate Gardiner laid high charges against the meek archbishop and would have sent him to the Tower; but the king was his friend, gave him his signet that he might defend him, and in the Council not only declared the bishop one of the best affected men in his realm, but sharply rebuked his accusers for their calumny.

A peace having been made, Henry, and the French king, Henry the Great, were unanimous to have the Mass abolished in their kingdom, and Cranmer set about this great work; but the death of the English monarch, in 1546, suspended the procedure, and King Edward his successor continued Cranmer in the same functions, upon whose coronation he delivered a charge that will ever honor his memory, for its purity, freedom, and truth. During this reign he prosecuted the glorious Reformation with unabated zeal, even in the year 1552, when he was seized with a severe ague, from which it pleased God to restore him that he might testify by his death the truth of that seed he had diligently sown.

The death of Edward, in 1553, exposed Cranmer to all the rage of his enemies. Though the archbishop was among those who supported Mary's accession, he was attainted at the meeting of parliament, and in November adjudged guilty of high treason at Guildhall, and degraded from his dignities. He sent a humble letter to Mary, explaining the cause of his signing the will in favor of Edward, and in 1554 he wrote to the Council, whom he pressed to obtain a pardon from the queen, by a letter delivered to Dr. Weston, but which the latter opened, and on seeing its contents, basely returned.

Treason was a charge quite inapplicable to Cranmer, who supported the queen's right; while others, who had favored Lady Jane, were dismissed upon paying a small fine. A calumny was now spread against Cranmer that he complied with some of the popish ceremonies to ingratiate himself with the queen, which he dared publicly to disavow, and justified his articles of faith. The active part which the prelate had taken in the divorce of Mary's mother had ever rankled deeply in the heart of the queen, and revenge formed a prominent feature in the death of Cranmer.

We have in this work noticed the public disputations at Oxford, in which the talents of Cranmer, Ridley, and Latimer shone so conspicuously, and tended to their condemnation. The first sentence was illegal, inasmuch as the usurped power of the pope had not yet been re-established by law.

Being kept in prison until this was effected, a commission was despatched from Rome, appointing Dr. Brooks to sit as the representative of his holiness, and Drs. Story and Martin as those of the queen. Cranmer was willing to bow to the authority of Drs. Story and Martin, but against that of Dr. Brooks he protested. Such were the remarks and replies of Cranmer, after a long examination, that Dr. Brooks observed, "We come to examine you, and methinks you examine us."

Being sent back to confinement, he received a citation to appear at Rome within eighteen days, but this was impracticable, as he was imprisoned in England; and as he stated, even had he been at liberty, he was too poor to employ an advocate. Absurd as it must appear, Cranmer was condemned at Rome, and on February 14, 1556, a new commission was appointed, by which, Thirlby, bishop of Ely, and Bonner, of London, were deputed to sit in judgment at Christ-Church, Oxford. By virtue of this instrument, Cranmer was gradually degraded, by putting mere rags on him to represent the dress of an archbishop; then stripping him of his attire, they took off his own gown, and put an old worn one upon him instead. This he bore unmoved, and his enemies, finding that severity only rendered him more determined, tried the opposite course, and placed him in the house of the dean of Christ-Church, where he was treated with every indulgence.

This presented such a contrast to the three years' hard imprisonment he had received, that it threw him off his guard. His open, generous nature was more easily to be seduced by a liberal conduct than by threats and fetters. When Satan finds the Christian proof against one mode of attack, he tries another; and what form is so seductive as smiles, rewards, and power, after a long, painful imprisonment? Thus it was with Cranmer: his enemies promised him his former greatness if he would but recant, as well as the queen's favor, and this at the very time they knew that his death was determined in council. To soften the path to apostasy, the first paper brought for his signature was conceived in general terms; this once signed, five others were obtained as explanatory of the first, until finally he put his hand to the following detestable instrument:

"I, Thomas Cranmer, late archbishop of Canterbury, do renounce, abhor, and detest all manner of heresies and errors of Luther and Zuinglius, and all other teachings which are contrary to sound and true doctrine. And I believe most constantly in my heart, and with my mouth I confess one holy and Catholic Church visible, without which there is no salvation; and therefore I acknowledge the Bishop of Rome to be supreme head on earth, whom I acknowledge to be the highest bishop and pope, and Christ's vicar, unto whom all Christian people ought to be subject.

"And as concerning the sacraments, I believe and worship in the sacrament of the altar the body and blood of Christ, being contained most truly under the forms of bread and wine; the bread, through the mighty power of God being turned into the body of our Savior Jesus Christ, and the wine into his blood.

"And in the other six sacraments, also, (alike as in this) I believe and hold as the universal Church holdeth, and the Church of Rome judgeth and determineth.

"Furthermore, I believe that there is a place of purgatory, where souls departed be punished for a time, for whom the Church doth godlily and wholesomely pray, like as it doth honor saints and make prayers to them.

"Finally, in all things I profess, that I do not otherwise believe than the Catholic Church and the Church of Rome holdeth and teacheth. I am sorry that I ever held or thought otherwise. And I beseech Almighty God, that of His mercy He will vouchsafe to forgive me whatsoever I have offended against God or His Church, and also I desire and beseech all Christian people to pray for me.

"And all such as have been deceived either by mine example or doctrine, I require them by the blood of Jesus Christ that they will return to the unity of the Church, that we may be all of one mind, without schism or division.

"And to conclude, as I submit myself to the Catholic Church of Christ, and to the supreme head thereof, so I submit myself unto the most excellent majesties of Philip and Mary, king and queen of this realm of England, etc., and to all other their laws and ordinances, being ready always as a faithful subject ever to obey them. And God is my witness, that I have not done this for favor or fear of any person, but willingly and of mine own conscience, as to the instruction of others."

"Let him that standeth take heed lest he fall!" said the apostle, and here was a falling off indeed! The papists now triumphed in their turn: they had acquired all they wanted short of his life. His recantation was immediately printed and dispersed, that it might have its due effect upon the astonished Protestants. But God counter worked all the designs of the Catholics by the extent to which they carried the implacable persecution of their prey. Doubtless, the love of life induced Cranmer to sign the above declaration: yet death may be said to have been preferable to life to him who lay under the stings of a goaded conscience and the contempt of every Gospel Christian; this principle he strongly felt in all its force and anguish.

The queen's revenge was only to be satiated by Cranmer's blood, and therefore she wrote an order to Dr. Pole, to prepare a sermon to be preached March 21, directly before his martyrdom, at St. Mary's, Oxford. Dr. Pole visited him the day previous, and was induced to believe that he would publicly deliver his sentiments in confirmation of the articles to which he had subscribed. About nine in the morning of the day of sacrifice, the queen's commissioners, attended by the magistrates, conducted the amiable unfortunate to St. Mary's Church. His torn, dirty garb, the same in which they habited him upon his degradation, excited the commiseration of the people. In the church he found a low mean stage, erected opposite to the pulpit, on which being placed, he turned his face, and fervently prayed to God.

The church was crowded with persons of both persuasions, expecting to hear the justification of the late apostasy: the Catholics rejoicing, and the Protestants deeply wounded in spirit at the deceit of the human heart. Dr. Pole, in his sermon, represented Cranmer as having been guilty of the most atrocious crimes; encouraged the deluded sufferer not to fear death, not to doubt the support of God in his torments, nor that Masses would be said in all the churches of Oxford for the repose of his soul. The doctor then noticed his conversion, and which he ascribed to the evident working of Almighty power and in order that the people might be convinced of its reality, asked the prisoner to give them a sign. This Cranmer did, and begged the congregation to pray for him, for he had committed many and grievous sins; but, of all, there was one which awfully lay upon his mind, of which he would speak shortly.

During the sermon Cranmer wept bitter tears: lifting up his hands and eyes to heaven, and letting them fall, as if unworthy to live: his grief now found vent in words: before his confession he fell upon his knees, and, in the following words unveiled the deep contrition and agitation which harrowed up his soul.

"O Father of heaven! O Son of God, Redeemer of the world! O Holy Ghost, three persons all one God! have mercy on me, most wretched caitiff and miserable sinner. I have offended both against heaven and earth, more than my tongue can express. Whither then may I go, or whither may I flee? To heaven I may be ashamed to lift up mine eyes and in earth I find no place of refuge or succor. To Thee, therefore, O Lord, do I run; to Thee do I humble myself, saying, O Lord, my God, my sins be great, but yet have mercy upon me for Thy great mercy. The great mystery that God became man, was not wrought for little or few offenses. Thou didst not give Thy Son, O Heavenly Father, unto death for small sins only, but for all the greatest sins of the world, so that the sinner return to Thee with his whole heart, as I do at present. Wherefore, have mercy on me, O God, whose property is always to have mercy, have mercy upon me, O Lord, for Thy great mercy. I crave nothing for my own merits, but for Thy name's sake, that it may be hallowed thereby, and for Thy dear Son, Jesus Christ's sake. And now therefore, O Father of Heaven, hallowed be Thy name," etc.

Then rising, he said he was desirous before his death to give them some pious exhortations by which God might be glorified and themselves edified. He then descanted upon the danger of a love for the world, the duty of obedience to their majesties, of love to one another and the necessity of the rich administering to the wants of the poor. He quoted the three verses of the fifth chapter of James, and then proceeded, "Let them that be rich ponder well these three sentences: for if they ever had occasion to show their charity, they have it now at this present, the poor people being so many, and victual so dear.

"And now forasmuch as I am come to the last end of my life, whereupon hangeth all my life past, and all my life to come, either to live with my master Christ for ever in joy, or else to be in pain for ever with the wicked in hell, and I see before mine eyes presently, either heaven ready to receive me, or else hell ready to swallow me up; I shall therefore declare unto you my very faith how I believe, without any color of dissimulation: for now is no time to dissemble, whatsoever I have said or written in times past.

"First, I believe in God the Father Almighty, Maker of heaven and earth, etc. And I believe every article of the Catholic faith, every word and sentence taught by our Savior Jesus Christ, His apostles and prophets, in the New and Old Testament.

"And now I come to the great thing which so much troubleth my conscience, more than any thing that ever I did or said in my whole life, and that is the setting abroad of a writing contrary to the truth, which now here I renounce and refuse, as things written with my hand contrary to the truth which I thought in my heart, and written for fear of death, and to save my life, if it might be; and that is, all such bills or papers which I have written or signed with my hand since my degradation, wherein I have written many things untrue. And forasmuch as my hand hath offended, writing contrary to my heart, therefore my hand shall first be punished; for when I come to the fire it shall first be burned.

"And as for the pope, I refuse him as Christ's enemy, and Antichrist, with all his false doctrine."

Upon the conclusion of this unexpected declaration, amazement and indignation were conspicuous in every part of the church. The Catholics were completely foiled, their object being frustrated, Cranmer, like Samson, having completed a greater ruin upon his enemies in the hour of death, than he did in his life.

Cranmer would have proceeded in the exposure of the popish doctrines, but the murmurs of the idolaters drowned his voice, and the preacher gave an order to "lead the heretic away!" The savage command was directly obeyed, and the lamb about to suffer was torn from his stand to the place of slaughter, insulted all the way by the revilings and taunts of the pestilent monks and friars.

With thoughts intent upon a far higher object than the empty threats of man, he reached the spot dyed with the blood of Ridley and Latimer. There he knelt for a short time in earnest devotion, and then arose, that he might undress and prepare for the fire. Two friars who had been parties in prevailing upon him to abjure, now endeavored to draw him off again from the truth, but he was steadfast and immovable in what he had just professed, and publicly taught. A chain was provided to bind him to the stake, and after it had tightly encircled him, fire was put to the fuel, and the flames began soon to ascend.

Then were the glorious sentiments of the martyr made manifest; then it was, that stretching out his right hand, he held it unshrinkingly in the fire until it was burnt to a cinder, even before his body was injured, frequently exclaiming, "This unworthy right hand."

His body did abide the burning with such steadfastness that he seemed to have no more than the stake to which he was bound; his eyes were lifted up to heaven, and he repeated "this unworthy right hand," as long as his voice would suffer him; and using often the words of Stephen, "Lord Jesus, receive my spirit," in the greatness of the flame, he gave up the ghost.

Questions for Study

1   Is Foxe a neutral historian? If not, what is his agenda? And how can this be seen in the accounts included in this section?
2   What particular factors does Foxe stress in the account of the execution of Cranmer? Why do you think that he draws our attention to these?
3   How do you think Protestant readers of Foxe's work would respond to his description of Cranmer's death?

CHAPTER 44

Edmund Spenser (1552–1599)

Born in 1552 as the son of a clothmaker, Edmund Spenser attended the Merchant Taylor's School under Richard Mulcaster, and went up to Cambridge University, at some point around 1569–76, as a sizar of Pembroke Hall. He graduated in 1573, and went on to serve as secretary to John Young, Bishop of Rochester. This appointment was of some considerable importance, as the Kentish landscape with which he became familiar is frequently mentioned in *The Shepheardes Calender*. In 1579, Spenser entered into employment with the Earl of Leicester. This allowed Spenser to establish contacts with leading figures in Renaissance English literature, such as Sir Philip Sidney, Edward Dyer, and Fulke Greville.

The Shepheardes Calender was published anonymously at the end of 1579. The work, which takes the form of a long allegorical poem about shepherds and shepherdesses, met with immediate success, partly on account of the popularity of such pastoral works at the time, and partly on account of its undoubted literary merits. During the following year, Spenser began work on *The Faerie Queene*, and entered the service of Lord Grey of Wilton, Lord Deputy of Ireland. This entailed moving to Ireland for ten years, which Spenser detested. Writing, it seems, was an effective way of distracting himself from the tedium of life in Ireland. In 1581 Spenser was appointed Clerk in Chancery for Faculties, and soon afterward befriended Sir Walter Ralegh, whose estate was not far from his own. The publication of the first section of *The Faerie Queene* (1589) seemed to open new possibilities for him. He was presented at the court of Elizabeth I by Ralegh. This, however, failed to lead to the anticipated royal appointment or favor. Spenser returned to Ireland to complete the work.

Two years after Spenser returned to Ireland he courted and married Elizabeth Boyle, and continued to produce a number of works, including the *Amoretti* and *Epithalamion*, *Colin Clouts Come Home Againe*, *Fowre Hymnes*, and *Prothalamion*. An edition of *The Faerie Queene*, Books I–VI, appeared in 1596. *The Stationers Register* carries an entry for *A Vewe of the present state of Irelande* in April 1598, but this did not appear until 1633. During the year before his abortive visit to the court of Queen Elizabeth, Spenser had acquired Kilcoman Castle as his home. This property had been seized by the English from its local Irish lord. This event, which must be seen against the general Elizabethan policy of establishing "Plantations" in Ireland, caused intense local resentment, and led to the castle being burned down in late 1598 during a local insurrection against the English presence in Ireland. Spenser and his family fled to London, where he died a few weeks later. He was buried in Westminster Abbey.

Edmund Spenser (1552–1599)

Basic description
Leading English Renaissance poet.

Major work
The Faerie Queene (1589–96).

Major studies
Helen Cooper, *Pastoral: Medieval into Renaissance*. Totowa, NJ: Rowman and Littlefield, 1977.
William A. Oram, *Edmund Spenser*. New York: Prentice-Hall International, 1997.

Spenser is widely regarded as a leading figure of early English poetry. He is often compared to Chaucer, although there are clear points of difference between them. The fine observation of character, so typical of Chaucer, is decidedly absent from most of Spenser's writings, which show a preference for what can reasonably be termed a more "escapist" approach to life. *The Shepheardes Calender* can be seen as a depiction of rural pastoral life as Spenser imagined it should be.

Text: The Hymn of Heavenly Beauty

Our text is taken from a work published by Spenser in 1596, entitled *Fowre Hymnes*. This work consists of four hymns, as follows:

1 An Hymne In Honour Of Love
2 An Hymne In Honour Of Beautie
3 An Hymne Of Heavenly Love
4 An Hymne of Heavenly Beautie

These four hymns are of considerable religious importance. For example, the "Hymne of Heavenly Love" contains one of the finest expositions of the idea of "kenosis" or "self-emptying," which is a major theme of Philippians 2:6–11.

> Out of the bosome of eternall blisse,
>   In which he reigned with his glorious fyre,
>   He downe descended, like a most demisse
>   And abject thrall, in fleshes fraile attyre,
>   That he for him might pay sinnes deadly hyre,
>   And him restore unto that happie state,
> In which he stood before his haplesse fate.

In flesh at first the guilt committed was,
  Therefore in flesh it must be satisfyde:
  Nor spirit, nor Angell, though they man surpas,
  Could make amends to God for mans misguyde,
  But onely man himselfe, who self did slyde.
  So taking flesh of sacred virgins wombe,
For mans deare sake he did a man become.

And that most blessed bodie, which was borne
  Without all blemish or reproachfull blame,
  He freely gaue to be both rent and torne
  Of cruell hands, who with despightfull shame
  Reuyling him, that them most vile became,
  At length him nayled on a gallow tree,
And slew the iust, by most vniust decree.

O huge and most vnspeakable impression
  Of loues deepe wound, the pierst the piteous hart
  Of that deare Lord with so entyre affection,
  And sharply launching euery inner part,
  Dolours of death into his soule did dart;
  Doing him die, that neuer it deserued,
To free his foes, that from his heast had swerued.

Our text for study is the fourth and final hymn in this collection, the "Hymn of Heavenly Beauty." In this remarkable piece of poetry, Spenser invites the human mind to disentangle itself from the contemplation of created and worldly matters, in order to discover the radiance of God, as the creator of that world. The poem is here printed out in full, and merits close and careful reading.

Rapt with the rage of mine own ravish'd thought,
  Through contemplation of those goodly sights,
  And glorious images in heaven wrought,
  Whose wondrous beauty, breathing sweet delights
  Do kindle love in high-conceited sprights;   5
  I fain to tell the things that I behold,
But feel my wits to fail, and tongue to fold.

Vouchsafe then, O thou most Almighty Spright,
  From whom all gifts of wit and knowledge flow,
  To shed into my breast some sparkling light   10
  Of thine eternal truth, that I may show
  Some little beams to mortal eyes below
  Of that immortal beauty, there with thee,
Which in my weak distraughted mind I see;

That with the glory of so goodly sight   15
   The hearts of men, which fondly here admire
   Fair seeming shews, and feed on vain delight,
   Transported with celestial desire
   Of those fair forms, may lift themselves up higher,
   And learn to love, with zealous humble duty,   20
Th' eternal fountain of that heavenly beauty.

Beginning then below, with th' easy view
   Of this base world, subject to fleshly eye,
   From thence to mount aloft, by order due,
   To contemplation of th' immortal sky;   25
   Of the soare falcon so I learn to fly,
   That flags awhile her fluttering wings beneath,
Till she herself for stronger flight can breathe.

Then look, who list thy gazeful eyes to feed
   With sight of that is fair, look on the frame   30
   Of this wide universe, and therein reed
   The endless kinds of creatures which by name
   Thou canst not count, much less their natures aim;
   All which are made with wondrous wise respect,
And all with admirable beauty deckt.   35

First th' earth, on adamantine pillars founded,
   Amid the sea engirt with brazen bands;
   Then th' air still flitting, but yet firmly bounded
   On every side, with piles of flaming brands,
   Never consum'd, nor quench'd with mortal hands;   40
   And last, that mighty shining crystal wall,
Wherewith he hath encompassed this All.

By view whereof it plainly may appear,
   That still as every thing doth upward tend,
   And further is from earth, so still more clear   45
   And fair it grows, till to his perfect end
   Of purest beauty it at last ascend;
   Air more than water, fire much more than air,
And heaven than fire, appears more pure and fair.

Look thou no further, but affix thine eye   50
   On that bright, shiny, round, still moving mass,
   The house of blessed gods, which men call sky,
   All sow'd with glist'ring stars more thick than grass,
   Whereof each other doth in brightness pass,

But those two most, which ruling night and day,   55
As king and queen, the heavens' empire sway;

And tell me then, what hast thou ever seen
     That to their beauty may compared be,
     Or can the sight that is most sharp and keen
     Endure their captain's flaming head to see?   60
     How much less those, much higher in degree,
     And so much fairer, and much more than these,
As these are fairer than the land and seas?

For far above these heavens, which here we see,
     Be others far exceeding these in light,   65
     Not bounded, not corrupt, as these same be,
     But infinite in largeness and in height,
     Unmoving, uncorrupt, and spotless bright,
     That need no sun t' illuminate their spheres,
But their own native light far passing theirs.   70

And as these heavens still by degrees arise,
     Until they come to their first Mover's bound,
     That in his mighty compass doth comprise,
     And carry all the rest with him around;
     So those likewise do by degrees redound,   75
     And rise more fair; till they at last arrive
To the most fair, whereto they all do strive.

Fair is the heaven where happy souls have place,
     In full enjoyment of felicity,
     Whence they do still behold the glorious face   80
     Of the divine eternal Majesty;
     More fair is that, where those Ideas on high
     Enranged be, which Plato so admired,
And pure Intelligences from God inspired.

Yet fairer is that heaven, in which do reign   85
     The sovereign Powers and mighty Potentates,
     Which in their high protections do contain
     All mortal princes and imperial states;
     And fairer yet, whereas the royal Seats
     And heavenly Dominations are set,   90
From whom all earthly governance is fet.

Yet far more fair be those bright Cherubins,
     Which all with golden wings are overdight,
     And those eternal burning Seraphins,

Which from their faces dart out fiery light;   95
   Yet fairer than they both, and much more bright,
   Be th' Angels and Archangels, which attend
On God's own person, without rest or end.

These thus in fair each other far excelling,
   As to the highest they approach more near,   100
   Yet is that highest far beyond all telling,
   Fairer than all the rest which there appear,
   Though all their beauties join'd together were;
   How then can mortal tongue hope to express
The image of such endless perfectness?   105

Cease then, my tongue, and lend unto my mind
   Leave to bethink how great that beauty is,
   Whose utmost parts so beautiful I find;
   How much more those essential parts of his,
   His truth, his love, his wisdom, and his bliss,   110
   His grace, his doom, his mercy, and his might,
By which he lends us of himself a sight.

Those unto all he daily doth display,
   And shew himself in th' image of his grace,
   As in a looking-glass, through which he may   115
   Be seen of all his creatures vile and base,
   That are unable else to see his face,
   His glorious face which glistereth else so bright,
That th' Angels selves cannot endure his sight.

But we, frail wights, whose sight cannot sustain   120
   The sun's bright beams when he on us doth shine,
   But that their points rebutted back again
   Are dull'd, how can we see with feeble eyne
   The glory of that Majesty Divine,
   In sight of whom both sun and moon are dark,   125
Compared to his least resplendent spark?

The means, therefore, which unto us is lent
   Him to behold, is on his works to look,
   Which he hath made in beauty excellent,
   And in the same, as in a brazen book,   130
   To read enregister'd in every nook
   His goodness, which his beauty doth declare;
For all that's good is beautiful and fair.

Thence gathering plumes of perfect speculation,
   To imp the wings of thy high-flying mind,   135

Mount up aloft through heavenly contemplation,
  From this dark world, whose damps the soul so blind,
  And, like the native brood of eagles' kind,
  On that bright Sun of Glory fix thine eyes,
Clear'd from gross mists of frail infirmities.   140

Humbled with fear and awful reverence,
  Before the footstool of his majesty
  Throw thyself down, with trembling innocence,
  Ne dare look up with corruptible eye
  On the dread face of that great Deity,   145
  For fear, lest if he chance to look on thee,
Thou turn to nought, and quite confounded be.

But lowly fall before his mercy seat,
  Close covered with the Lamb's integrity
  From the just wrath of his avengeful threat   150
  That sits upon the righteous throne on high;
  His throne is built upon eternity,
  More firm and durable than steel or brass,
Or the hard diamond, which them both doth pass.

His sceptre is the rod of righteousness,   155
  With which he bruiseth all his foes to dust,
  And the great Dragon strongly doth repress,
  Under the rigour of his judgement just;
  His seat is truth, to which the faithful trust,
  From whence proceed her beams so pure and bright   160
That all about him sheddeth glorious light:

Light far exceeding that bright blazing spark
  Which darted is from Titan's flaming head,
  That with his beams enlumineth the dark
  And dampish air, whereby all things are read;   165
  Whose nature yet so much is marvelled
  Of mortal wits, that it doth much amaze
The greatest wizards which thereon do gaze.

But that immortal light, which there doth shine,
  Is many thousand times more bright, more clear,   170
  More excellent, more glorious, more divine,
  Through which to God all mortal actions here,
  And even the thoughts of men, do plain appear;
  For from th' eternal truth it doth proceed,
Through heavenly virtue which her beams do breed.   175

With the great glory of that wondrous light
  His throne is all encompassed around,
  And hid in his own brightness from the sight
  Of all that look thereon with eyes unsound;
  And underneath his feet are to be found   180
  Thunder and lightning and tempestuous fire,
The instruments of his avenging ire.

There in his bosom Sapience doth sit,
  The sovereign darling of the Deity,
  Clad like a queen in royal robes, most fit   185
  For so great power and peerless majesty,
  And all with gems and jewels gorgeously
  Adorn'd, that brighter than the stars appear,
And make her native brightness seem more clear.

And on her head a crown of purest gold   190
  Is set, in sign of highest sovereignty;
  And in her hand a sceptre she doth hold,
  With which she rules the house of God on high,
  And manageth the ever-moving sky,
  And in the same these lower creatures all   195
Subjected to her power imperial.

Both heaven and earth obey unto her will,
  And all the creatures which they both contain;
  For of her fullness which the world doth fill
  They all partake, and do in state remain   200
  As their great Maker did at first ordain,
  Through observation of her high behest,
By which they first were made, and still increast.

The fairness of her face no tongue can tell;
  For she the daughters of all women's race,   205
  And angels eke, in beauty doth excel,
  Sparkled on her from God's own glorious face,
  And more increas'd by her own goodly grace,
  That it doth far exceed all human thought,
Ne can on earth compared be to aught.   210

Ne could that painter (had he lived yet)
  Which pictured Venus with so curious quill,
  That all posterity admired it,
  Have portray'd this, for all his mast'ring skill;
  Ne she herself, had she remained still,   215
  And were as fair as fabling wits do feign,
Could once come near this beauty sovereign.

But had those wits, the wonders of their days,
   Or that sweet Teian poet, which did spend
   His plenteous vein in setting forth her praise,   220
   Seen but a glimpse of this which I pretend,
   How wondrously would he her face commend,
   Above that idol of his feigning thought,
That all the world should with his rhymes be fraught.

How then dare I, the novice of his art,   225
   Presume to picture so divine a wight,
   Or hope t' express her least perfection's part,
   Whose beauty fills the heavens with her light,
   And darks the earth with shadow of her sight?
   Ah, gentle Muse, thou art too weak and faint   230
The portrait of so heavenly hue to paint.

Let angels, which her goodly face behold
   And see at will, her sovereign praises sing,
   And those most sacred mysteries unfold
   Of that fair love of mighty heaven's King;   235
   Enough is me t' admire so heavenly thing,
   And being thus with her huge love possest,
In th' only wonder of herself to rest.

But whoso may, thrice happy man him hold,
   Of all on earth whom God so much doth grace   240
   And lets his own beloved to behold;
   For in the view of her celestial face
   All joy, all bliss, all happiness, have place;
   Ne aught on earth can want unto the wight
Who of herself can win the wishful sight.   245

For she, out of her secret treasury,
   Plenty of riches forth on him will pour,
   Even heavenly riches, which there hidden lie
   Within the closet of her chastest bower,
   Th' eternal portion of her precious dower,   250
   Which mighty God hath given to her free,
And to all those which thereof worthy be.

None thereof worthy be, but those whom she
   Vouchsafeth to her presence to receive,
   And letteth them her lovely face to see,   255
   Whereof such wondrous pleasures they conceive,
   And sweet contentment, that it doth bereave

Their soul of sense, through infinite delight,
And them transport from flesh into the spright.

In which they see such admirable things,   260
   As carries them into an ecstasy,
   And hear such heavenly notes, and carollings
   Of God's high praise, that fills the brazen sky;
   And feel such joy and pleasure inwardly,
   That maketh them all worldly cares forget,   265
And only think on that before them set.

Ne from thenceforth doth any fleshly sense,
   Or idle thought of earthly things, remain;
   But all that erst seem'd sweet seems now offence,
   And all that pleased erst now seems to pain;   270
   Their joy, their comfort, their desire, their gain,
   Is fixed all on that which now they see;
All other sights but feigned shadows be.

And that fair lamp, which useth to inflame
   The hearts of men with self-consuming fire   275
   Thenceforth seems foul, and full of sinful blame;
   And all that pomp to which proud minds aspire
   By name of honour, and so much desire,
   Seems to them baseness, and all riches dross,
And all mirth sadness, and all lucre loss.   280

So full their eyes are of that glorious sight,
   And senses fraught with such satiety,
   That in nought else on earth they can delight,
   But in th' aspect of that felicity,
   Which they have written in their inward eye;   285
   On which they feed, and in their fastened mind
All happy joy and full contentment find.

Ah, then, my hungry soul, which long hast fed
   On idle fancies of thy foolish thought,
   And, with false beauty's flatt'ring bait misled,   290
   Hast after vain deceitful shadows sought,
   Which all are fled, and now have left thee nought
   But late repentance through thy follies prief;
Ah cease to gaze on matter of thy grief:

And look at last up to that sovereign light,   295
   From whose pure beams all perfect beauty springs,
   That kindleth love in every godly sprite,

Even the love of God, which loathing brings
Of this vile world and these gay-seeming things;
With whose sweet pleasures being so possest,   300
Thy straying thoughts henceforth for ever rest.

Questions for Study

1 In what way can this poem be seen as a criticism of introversion or narcissism?
2 How does Spenser encourage his readers to rise above worldly things and discover the God who created them?
3 Which section of the poem seems to you to best sum up the argument of the entire work?

CHAPTER 45

The King James Version of the Bible (1611)

One of the most important influences on the shaping of the modern English language was the publication of the King James Version of the Bible, also known as the Authorized Version. The need for an agreed English translation of the Bible had been known for some time. The origins of the move to have the Bible translated into English, directly from its original languages, is associated especially with William Tyndale, who was born about 1491 in Gloucestershire, in the west of England. At an early stage in his career, he translated Erasmus' *Enchiridion militis Christiani* (Handbook of the Christian Soldier, 1503). Having translated Erasmus, Tyndale declared his intention to undertake a more ambitious and radical work – the translation of the Bible into English.

Tyndale then traveled to London to seek the support of Bishop Cuthbert Tunstall. It soon became clear that this would not be forthcoming; indeed, more than this, Tyndale realized that he would not be able to undertake the task of translating the Bible into the English language on English soil.

Tyndale thus fled to Germany in 1524, supported by a well-intentioned patron, who supported his work in its early stages. As events turned out, Tyndale never returned to England, but lived a hand-to-mouth existence, managing to evade the Roman Catholic authorities on the one hand, while carrying out his translation work on the other. The first complete printed New Testament in English appeared in February 1526, and copies were exported – illegally, of course – to England about a month later. In October of that year, Bishop Tunstall ordered all the copies he could trace to be gathered and burned at St. Paul's Cross in London. When this proved ineffective in preventing the circulation of the work, Tunstall arranged to buy the books in bulk before they left the continent, so that they could be destroyed. Tyndale merely used the money this brought him for further translation work, including the translation of the first books of the Old Testament from Hebrew. He completed this work between Easter and December 1529, and arranged for it to be printed in Antwerp in early January 1530. Copies were in England by that summer.

The King James Version of the Bible

Basic description
The most influential English-language translation of the Bible.

Major studies
Charles Butterworth, *The Literary Lineage of the King James Bible, 1340–1611*. Philadelphia: University of Pennsylvania Press, 1941.

C. S. Lewis, "The Literary Impact of the Authorized Version," in *They Asked for a Paper*. London: Bless, 1962, 26–50.

David Norton, *A History of the Bible as Literature*, 2 vols. Cambridge: Cambridge University Press, 1993.

Tyndale's writings and especially his biblical translations gained considerable attention within England, to the irritation of many more conservative figures within the religious establishment. Inevitably, the success of these works led to pressure for an authorized English translation of the Bible to be made available within England. Henry VIII, fearing Tyndale's influence, sent an ambassador to persuade him to return to England. Tyndale agreed that he would return to England, providing that the king would agree to the publication of an English Bible. By the time Henry published this Bible, Tyndale was already dead, having been arrested and executed by the Flemish authorities on October 6, 1536. His last words reportedly were: "Oh Lord, open the King of England's eyes."

Tyndale's translation would prove to be of foundational importance to the shaping of later English translations. Many of the words and phrases used by Tyndale have found their way into the English language. Tyndale was a master of the pithy phrase, near to conversational English, but distinct enough to be used like a proverb. In his Bible translations, Tyndale coined such phrases as: "the powers that be" (Romans 13); "my brother's keeper" (Genesis 4); "the salt of the earth" (Matthew 5); "a law unto themselves" (Romans 2). These phrases continue to be used, even in modern English, precisely because they are so well formed in terms of alliteration, rhyme, and word repetitions. Tyndale also coined or revived many words that are still in use. He constructed the term "Jehovah" from the Hebrew construction known as the "tetragrammaton" in the Old Testament. He coined the English word "Passover" to represent the Jewish festival known as *Pesah*. Other neologisms developed by Tyndale to translate biblical words which had, up to that point, no real English equivalent include "scapegoat" and "atonement." This latter word was invented by Tyndale to convey the idea of "reconciliation." The word literally means "at-one-ment" – that is, a state of being "at one" with someone.

The English translation of the Bible which Tyndale had requested was issued in 1537. This took the form of a revision of Tyndale's translation, with supplementary material from Miles Coverdale. The work was printed at Antwerp in 1537. A new English version of the Bible appeared in the summer of 1539. It had been commissioned by Thomas Cromwell in September 1538, with the explicit instruction that it should be set up in every English parish church. The translation was undertaken by Miles Coverdale, and again drew heavily on Tyndale's work.

The need for a new translation of the Bible into English became a major issue after the death of Elizabeth I (1603). James I found himself facing pressure from the growing Puritan constituency within his kingdom. A petition, siged by a thousand ministers, was presented to him in April 1603, even as he traveled from Scotland to London, demanding that Puritans should be given greater religious freedom in England. James felt that he had little choice but to discuss the grievances noted in the petition, and arranged for a meeting to be held at Hampton Court Palace, near London, in January 1604. The conference was presided over by James I himself, and was attended both by the bishops of the Church of England and the leaders of the Puritan constituency. Among the reforms discussed were changes in church government, changes in The Book of Common Prayer, and a new translation of the Bible.

James firmly rejected most of the Puritans' demands and was equally firm in his rejection of any changes to the established episcopal form of church government. When confronted over this issue, he replied that he had learned the truth of a certain maxim in Scotland: "No bishop, no king." Having refused two of the Puritans' demands, James felt able to accede to the Puritans' third request, which was pressed with particular urgency by Dr. John Reynolds, for a new translation of the Bible. This can be seen as the one positive result of this conference – the preparation of the Authorized (King James) Version of the Bible, which was eventually published in 1611.

James subsequently ordered that a body of revisers should be assembled, consisting of 54 scholars, including the professors of Greek and Hebrew at both Oxford and Cambridge universities. Work began in 1607, and took nearly three years to prepare for publication. The revisors worked in six groups at three separate locations, taking into consideration both existing English translations and the biblical texts in the original languages.

The resulting translation had a marked influence on English style and was generally accepted as the standard English Bible for more than three centuries. The "Preface," written by Dr. Miles Smith, makes it clear that the resulting work is more to be considered a revision of existing translations, rather than a translation in its own right. There is no doubt that literary excellence was seen as a guiding consideration for the revisors, with the result that the "King James Version" must be seen as a work of English literature, as well as an important theological and religious document.

The work eventually achieved an influence which went far beyond anything that could realistically have been expected. Initially, it met with a lukewarm response, not least on account of its bulky size, its poor quality of printing, the absence of marginal notes on difficult points – matters on which its chief competitor, the Geneva Bible, scored highly. But gradually, it won acceptance. Not only did the work come to be widely accepted by both Anglicans and Puritans; it proved to be the basis of English language Christianity for more than three hundred years, and is still widely used as the translation of preference by many Christians. Its impact upon English literature is incalculable, making the inclusion of some material of relevance essential for the purposes of this anthology.

Text: The Translators' Preface

The translators' preface to the King James Version of the Bible is of considerable interest. Not only does it bear witness to the considerable uncertainty which descended on

England, politically and religiously, with the death of Elizabeth I in 1603; it also sets out some of the motivations lying behind the translation – if, indeed, it can be called a translation; the preface itself uses the language of comparison rather than translation.

The preface – which is properly titled "The Translators to the Reader" – was actually written by a single author, rather than being a work of corporate authorship, as the title might seem to imply. Miles Smith, Canon of Hereford (who would later go on to become Bishop of Gloucester), composed the preface, which sought to explain the reasons why a new translation was necessary, and how it was accomplished.

The preface goes out of its way to insist that the new translation should not be seen as implying any criticism of existing translations. The intention was not "to make a new translation" but "to make a good one better." The translators also acknowledged limitations in their own knowledge, especially of Hebrew vocabulary. Inevitably, this meant that many translations offered for the "rare names of certain birds, beasts and precious stones" were somewhat speculative. This limitation was an important consideration; one of the reasons why revision of the King James Version was urged in the late nineteenth century was that the growing body of scholarship relating to ancient Hebrew allowed much more definite identification of these unusual words.

The preface also helps us understand the theological pressures under which the translators worked. Some of the more radical English translators had abandoned traditional church terminology, and replaced "church" with "congregation," "baptism" with "washing," and so forth. The translators were under pressure to retain the traditional vocabulary – such as "church," "bishop" – while avoiding the excessively Latinized words often associated with Roman Catholic translations (such as "pasche" and "holocaust").

The Translators to the Reader

Zeal to promote the common good, whether it be by devising any thing ourselves, or revising that which hath been laboured by others, deserveth certainly much respect and esteem, but yet findeth but cold entertainment in the world. It is welcomed with suspicion instead of love, and with emulation instead of thanks: and if there be any hole left for cavil to enter, (and cavil, if it do not find a hole, will make one,) 5 it is sure to be misconstrued, and in danger to be condemned. This will easily be granted by as many as know story, or have any experience. For was there ever any thing projected, that savoured any way of newness or renewing, but the same endured many a storm of gainsaying or opposition? A man would think that civility, wholesome laws, learning and eloquence, synods, and Churchmaintenance, 10 (that we speak of no more things of this kind,) should be as safe as a sanctuary, and out of shot, as they say, that no man would lift up his heel, no, nor dog move his tongue against the motioners of them. For by the first we are distinguished from brute beasts led with sensuality: by the second we are bridled and restrained from outrageous behaviour, and from doing of injuries, whether by fraud or by violence: 15 by the third we are enabled to inform and reform others by the light and feeling that we have attained unto ourselves: briefly, by the fourth, being brought together to a parley face to face, we sooner compose our differences, than by writings, which are

endless: and lastly, that the Church be sufficiently provided for is so agreeable to
20 good reason and conscience, that those mothers are holden to be less cruel, that kill
their children as soon as they are born, than those nursing fathers and mothers
(wheresoever they be) that withdraw from them who hang upon their breasts (and
upon whose breasts again themselves do hang to receive the spiritual and sincere milk
of the word) livelihood and support fit for their estates. Thus it is apparent, that these
25 things which we speak of are of most necessary use, and therefore that none, either
without absurdity can speak against them, or without note of wickedness can spurn
against them.

Yet for all that, the learned know, that certain worthy men have been brought to
untimely death for none other fault, but for seeking to reduce their countrymen to
30 good order and discipline: and that in some Commonweals it was made a capital
crime, once to motion the making of a new law for the abrogating of an old, though
the same were most pernicious: and that certain, which would be counted pillars of
the State, and patterns of virtue and prudence, could not be brought for a long time
to give way to good letters and refined speech; but bare themselves as averse from
35 them, as from rocks or boxes of poison: and fourthly, that he was no babe, but a
great Clerk, that gave forth, (and in writing to remain to posterity,) in passion peradventure, but yet he gave forth, That he had not seen any profit to come by any
synod or meeting of the Clergy, but rather the contrary: and lastly, against Churchmaintenance and allowance, in such sort as the ambassadors and messengers of the
40 great King of kings should be furnished, it is not unknown what a fiction or fable
(so it is esteemed, and for no better by the reporter himself, though superstitious)
was devised: namely, That at such time as the professors and teachers of Christianity
in the Church of Rome, then a true Church, were liberally endowed, a voice forsooth was heard from heaven, saying, Now is poison poured down into the Church,
45 &c. Thus not only as oft as we speak, as one saith, but also as oft as we do any thing
of note or consequence, we subject ourselves to every one's censure, and happy is
he that is least tossed upon tongues; for utterly to escape the snatch of them it is
impossible. If any man conceit, that this is the lot and portion of the meaner sort
only, and that Princes are privileged by their high estate, he is deceived. As *the sword*
50 *devoureth as well one as an other*, as it is in *Samuel*; nay, as the great commander
charged his soldiers in a certain battle to strike at no part of the enemy, but at the
face; and as the king of *Syria* commanded his chief captains *to fight neither with small*
nor great, save only against the king of Israel: so it is too true, that envy striketh most
spitefully at the fairest, and the chiefest. *David* was a worthy prince, and no man to
55 be compared to him for his first deeds; and yet for as worthy an act as ever he did,
even for bringing back the ark of God in solemnity, he was scorned and scoffed at
by his own wife. *Solomon* was greater than *David*, though not in virtue, yet in power;
and by his power and wisdom he built a temple to the Lord, such an one as was the
glory of the land of Israel, and the wonder of the whole world. But was that his mag-
60 nificence liked of by all? We doubt of it. Otherwise why do they lay it in his son's
dish, and call unto him for easing of the burden? *Make*, say they, *the grievous servi-*
tude of thy father, and his sore yoke, lighter. Belike he had charged them with some
levies, and troubled them with some carriages; hereupon they raise up a tragedy, and
wish in their heart the temple had never been built. So hard a thing it is to please

all, even when we please God best, and do seek to approve ourselves to every one's conscience. 65

If we will descend to latter times, we shall find many the like examples of such kind, or rather unkind, acceptance. The first Roman Emperor did never do a more pleasing deed to the learned, nor more profitable to posterity, for conserving the record of times in true supputation, than when he corrected the Calendar, and 70 ordered the year according to the course of the sun: and yet this was imputed to him for novelty, and arrogancy, and procured to him great obloquy. So the first Christened Emperor (at the least wise, that openly professed the faith himself, and allowed others to do the like,) for strengthening the empire at his great charges, and providing for the Church, as he did, got for his labour the name *Pupillus*, as who would 75 say, a wasteful Prince, that had need of a guardian or overseer. So the best Christened Emperor, for the love that he bare unto peace, thereby to enrich both himself and his subjects, and because he did not seek war, but find it, was judged to be no man at arms, (though indeed he excelled in feats of chivalry, and shewed so much when he was provoked,) and condemned for giving himself to his ease, and to his 80 pleasure. To be short, the most learned Emperor of former times, (at the least, the greatest politician,) what thanks had he for cutting off the superfluities of the laws, and digesting them into some order and method? This, that he hath been blotted by some to be an Epitomist, that is, one that extinguished worthy whole volumes, to bring his abridgments into request. This is the measure that hath been rendered to 85 excellent Princes in former times, *cum bene facerent, male audire,* for their good deeds to be evil spoken of. Neither is there any likelihood that envy and malignity died and were buried with the ancient. No, no, the reproof of *Moses* taketh hold of most ages, *Ye are risen up in your fathers' stead, an increase of sinful men. What is that that hath been done? that which shall be done: and there is no new thing under the sun,* saith the 90 wise man. And St *Stephen, As your fathers did, so do ye.* This, and more to this purpose, his Majesty that now reigneth (and long, and long, may he reign, and his offspring for ever, *Himself, and children, and children's children always!*) knew full well, according to the singular wisdom given unto him by God, and the rare learning and experience that he hath attained unto; namely, That whosoever attempteth any thing for 95 the publick, (especially if it pertain to religion, and to the opening and clearing of the word of God,) the same setteth himself upon a stage to be glouted upon by every evil eye; yea, he casteth himself headlong upon pikes, to be gored by every sharp tongue. For he that meddleth with men's religion in any part meddleth with their custom, nay, with their freehold; and though they find no content in that which they 100 have, yet they cannot abide to hear of altering. Notwithstanding his royal heart was not daunted or discouraged for this or that colour, but stood resolute, *as a statue immoveable, and an anvil not easy to be beaten into plates,* as one saith; he knew who had chosen him to be a soldier, or rather a captain; and being assured that the course which he intended made much for the glory of God, and the building up of his 105 Church, he would not suffer it to be broken off for whatsoever speeches or practices. It doth certainly belong unto kings, yea, it doth specially belong unto them, to have care of religion, yea, to know it aright, yea, to profess it zealously, yea, to promote it to the uttermost of their power. This is their glory before all nations which mean well, and this will bring unto them a far most excellent weight of glory in the day of 110 the Lord Jesus. For the Scripture saith not in vain, *Them that honour me I will honour:* neither was it a vain word that *Eusebius* delivered long ago, That piety toward God was the weapon, and the only weapon, that both preserved *Constantine's* person, and avenged him of his enemies.

115   But now what piety without truth? What truth, what saving truth, without the word of God? What word of God whereof we may be sure, without the Scripture? The Scriptures we are commanded to search, *John* v. 39. *Isai.* viii. 20. They are commended that searched and studied them, *Acts* xvii. 11. and viii. 28, 29. They are reproved that were unskilful in them, or slow to believe them, *Matt.* xxii. 29. *Luke*

120   xxiv. 25. They can make us wise unto salvation, 2 *Tim.* iii. 15. If we be ignorant, they will instruct us; if out of the way, they will bring us home; if out of order, they will reform us; if in heaviness, comfort us; if dull, quicken us; if cold, inflame us. *Tolle, lege; tolle, lege;* Take up and read, take up and read the Scriptures, (for unto them was the direction,) it was said unto St *Augustine* by a supernatural voice. *Whatsoever*

125   *is in the Scriptures, believe me,* saith the same St *Augustine, is high and divine; there is verily truth, and a doctrine most fit for the refreshing and renewing of men's minds, and truly so tempered, that every one may draw from thence that which is sufficient for him, if he come to draw with a devout and pious mind, as true religion requireth.* Thus St *Augustine.* And St *Hierome, Ama Scripturas, et amabit te sapientia,* &c. Love the

130   Scriptures, and wisdom will love thee. And St *Cyrill* against *Julian, Even boys that are bred up in the Scriptures become most religious,* &c. But what mention we three or four uses of the Scripture, whereas whatsoever is to be believed, or practised, or hoped for, is contained in them? or three or four sentences of the Fathers, since whosoever is worthy the name of a Father, from Christ's time downward, hath like-

135   wise written not only of the riches, but also of the perfection of the Scripture? *I adore the fulness of the Scripture,* saith *Tertullian* against *Hermogenes.* And again, to *Apelles* an heretick of the like stamp he saith, *I do not admit that which thou bringest in* (or concludest) *of thine own* (head or store, *de tuo*) without Scripture. So St *Justin Martyr* before him; *We must know by all means* (saith he) *that it is not lawful* (or possible)

140   *to learn* (any thing) *of God or of right piety, save only out of the Prophets, who teach us by divine inspiration.* So St *Basil* after *Tertullian, It is a manifest falling away from the faith, and a fault of presumption, either to reject any of those things that are written, or to bring in* (upon the head of them, *ex eisagein*) *any of those things that are not written.* We omit to cite to the same effect St *Cyrill* Bishop of *Jerusalem* in his 4.

145   *Catech.* St *Hierome* against *Helvidius,* St *Augustine* in his third book against the letters of *Petilian,* and in very many other places of his works. Also we forbear to descend to later Fathers, because we will not weary the reader. The Scriptures then being acknowledged to be so full and so perfect, how can we excuse ourselves of negligence, if we do not study them? of curiosity, if we be not content with them?

150   Men talk much of *eiresione,* how many sweet and goodly things it had hanging on it; of the Philosopher's stone, that it turneth copper into gold; of *Cornu-copia,* that it had all things necessary for food in it; of *Panaces* the herb, that it was good for all diseases; of *Catholicon* the drug, that it is instead of all purges; of *Vulcan's* armour, that it was an armour of proof against all thrusts and all blows, &c. Well, that which

155   they falsely or vainly attributed to these things for bodily good, we may justly and with full measure ascribe unto the Scripture for spiritual. It is not only an armour,

but also a whole armoury of weapons, both offensive and defensive; whereby we may save ourselves, and put the enemy to flight. It is not an herb, but a tree, or rather a whole paradise of trees of life, which bring forth fruit every month, and the fruit thereof is for meat, and the leaves for medicine. It is not a pot of *Manna*, or a cruse 160 of oil, which were for memory only, or for a meal's meat or two; but, as it were, a shower of heavenly bread sufficient for a whole host, be it never so great, and, as it were, a whole cellar full of oil vessels; whereby all our necessities may be provided for, and our debts discharged. In a word, it is a panary of wholesome food against fenowed traditions; a physician's shop (as St *Basil* calls it) of preservatives against 165 poisoned heresies; a pandect of profitable laws against rebellious spirits; a treasury of most costly jewels against beggarly rudiments; finally, a fountain of most pure water springing up unto everlasting life. And what marvel? the original thereof being from heaven, not from earth; the author being God, not man; the inditer, the Holy Spirit, not the wit of the Apostles or Prophets; the penmen, such as were sanctified from 170 the womb, and endued with a principal portion of God's Spirit; the matter, verity, piety, purity, uprightness; the form, God's word, God's testimony. God's oracles, the word of truth, the word of salvation, &c., the effects, light of understanding, stableness of persuasion, repentance from dead works, newness of life, holiness, peace, joy in the Holy Ghost; lastly, the end and reward of the study thereof, fellowship 175 with the saints, participation of the heavenly nature, fruition of an inheritance immortal, undefiled, and that never shall fade away. Happy is the man that delighteth in the Scripture, and thrice happy that meditateth in it day and night.

But how shall men meditate in that which they cannot understand? How shall they understand that which is kept close in an unknown tongue? as it is written, 180 *Except I know the power of the voice, I shall be to him that speaketh a barbarian, and he that speaketh shall be a barbarian to me.* The Apostle excepteth no tongue; not *Hebrew* the ancientest, not *Greek* the most copious, not *Latin* the finest. Nature taught a natural man to confess, that all of us in those tongues which we do not understand are plainly deaf; we may turn the deaf ear unto them. The *Scythian* 185 counted the *Athenian*, whom he did not understand, barbarous: so the *Roman* did the *Syrian*, and the *Jew*: (even St *Hierome* himself calleth the *Hebrew* tongue barbarous; belike, because it was strange to so many:) so the Emperor of *Constantinople* calleth the *Latin* tongue barbarous, though Pope *Nicolas* do storm at it: so the *Jews* long before *Christ* called all other nations *Lognasim*, which is little better than 190 barbarous. Therefore as one complaineth that always in the Senate of *Rome* there was one or other that called for an interpreter; so lest the Church be driven to the like exigent, it is necessary to have translations in a readiness. Translation it is that openeth the window, to let in the light; that breaketh the shell, that we may eat the kernel; that putteth aside the curtain, that we may look into the most holy place; 195 that removeth the cover of the well, that we may come by the water; even as *Jacob* rolled away the stone from the mouth of the well, by which means the flocks of *Laban* were watered. Indeed without translation into the vulgar tongue, the unlearned are but like children at *Jacob's* well (which was deep) without a bucket or something to draw with: or as that person mentioned by *Esay*, to whom when a sealed 200 book was delivered with this motion, *Read this, I pray thee*, he was fain to make this answer, *I cannot, for it is sealed.*

While God would be known only in *Jacob*, and have his name great in *Israel*, and in none other place; while the dew lay on *Gideon's* fleece only, and all the earth besides
205 was dry; then for one and the same people, which spake all of them the language of *Canaan*, that is, *Hebrew*, one and the same original in *Hebrew* was sufficient. But when the fulness of time drew near, that the Sun of righteousness, the Son of God, should come into the world, whom God ordained to be a reconciliation through faith in his blood, not of the *Jew* only, but also of the *Greek*, yea, of all them that
210 were scattered abroad; then, lo, it pleased the Lord to stir up the spirit of a *Greek* prince, (*Greek* for descent and language,) even of *Ptolemy Philadelph* king of *Egypt*, to procure the translating of the book of God out of *Hebrew* into *Greek*. This is the translation of the *Seventy* interpreters, commonly so called, which prepared the way for our Saviour among the *Gentiles* by written preaching, as St *John Baptist* did among
215 the *Jews* by vocal. For the *Grecians*, being desirous of learning, were not wont to suffer books of worth to lie moulding in kings' libraries, but had many of their servants, ready scribes, to copy them out, and so they were dispersed and made common. Again the *Greek* tongue was well known and made familiar to most inhabitants in *Asia* by reason of the conquests that there the *Grecians* had made, as also by the
220 colonies which thither they had sent. For the same causes also it was well understood in many places of *Europe*, yea, and of *Africk* too. Therefore the word of God, being set forth in *Greek*, becometh hereby like a candle set upon a candlestick, which giveth light to all that are in the house; or like a proclamation sounded forth in the marketplace, which most men presently take knowledge of; and therefore that language was
225 fittest to contain the Scriptures, both for the first preachers of the Gospel to appeal unto for witness, and for the learners also of those times to make search and trial by. It is certain, that that translation was not so sound and so perfect, but that it needed in many places correction; and who had been so sufficient for this work as the Apostles or apostolick men? Yet it seemed good to the Holy Ghost and to them to take
230 that which they found, (the same being for the greatest part true and sufficient,) rather than by making a new, in that new world and green age of the Church, to expose themselves to many exceptions and cavillations, as though they made a translation to serve their own turn; and therefore bearing witness to themselves, their witness not to be regarded. This may be supposed to be some cause, why the trans-
235 lation of the *Seventy* was allowed to pass for current. Notwithstanding, though it was commended generally, yet it did not fully content the learned, no not of the *Jews*. For not long after *Christ*, *Aquila* fell in hand with a new translation, and after him *Theodotion*, and after him *Symmachus*: yea, there was a fifth, and a sixth edition, the authors whereof were not known. These with the *Seventy* made up the *Hexapla*,
240 and were worthily and to great purpose compiled together by *Origen*. Howbeit the edition of the *Seventy* went away with the credit, and therefore not only was placed in the midst by *Origen*, (for the worth and excellency thereof above the rest, as *Epiphanius* gathereth,) but also was used by the *Greek* Fathers for the ground and foundation of their commentaries. Yea, *Epiphanius* abovenamed doth attribute so
245 much unto it, that he holdeth the authors thereof not only for interpreters, but also for prophets in some respect: and *Justinian* the Emperor, injoining the *Jews* his subjects to use especially the translation of the *Seventy*, rendereth this reason thereof, Because they were, as it were, enlightened with prophetical grace. Yet for all that, as

the *Egyptians* are said of the Prophet to be men and not God, and their horses flesh and not spirit: so it is evident, (and St *Hierome* affirmeth as much,) that the *Seventy* 250 were interpreters, they were not prophets. They did many things well, as learned men; but yet as men they stumbled and fell, one while through oversight, another while through ignorance; yea, sometimes they may be noted to add to the original, and sometimes to take from it: which made the Apostles to leave them many times, when they left the *Hebrew*, and to deliver the sense thereof according to the truth 255 of the word, as the Spirit gave them utterance. This may suffice touching the *Greek* translations of the Old Testament.

There were also within a few hundred years after *Christ* translations many into the *Latin* tongue: for this tongue also was very fit to convey the Law and the Gospel by, because in those times very many countries of the West, yea of the South, East, and 260 North, spake or understood *Latin*, being made provinces to the *Romans*. But now the *Latin* translations were too many to be all good: for they were infinite; (*Latini interpretes nullo modo numerari possunt*, saith St *Augustine*.) Again, they were not out of the *Hebrew* fountain, (we speak of the *Latin* translations of the Old Testament,) but out of the *Greek* stream; therefore the *Greek* being not altogether clear, 265 the *Latin* derived from it must needs be muddy. This moved St *Hierome*, a most learned Father, and the best linguist without controversy of his age, or of any other that went before him, to undertake the translating of the Old Testament out of the very fountains themselves; which he performed with that evidence of great learning, judgment, industry, and faithfulness, that he hath for ever bound the Church unto 270 him in a debt of special remembrance and thankfulness.

Now though the Church were thus furnished with *Greek* and *Latin* translations, even before the faith of *Christ* was generally embraced in the Empire: (for the learned know, that even in St *Hierome's* time the Consul of *Rome* and his wife were both Ethnicks, and about the same time the greatest part of the Senate also:) yet for all 275 that the godly learned were not content to have the Scriptures in the language which themselves understood, *Greek* and *Latin*, (as the good lepers were not content to fare well themselves, but acquainted their neighbours with the store that God had sent, that they also might provide for themselves;) but also for the behoof and edifying of the unlearned, which hungered and thirsted after righteousness, and had 280 souls to be saved as well as they, they provided translations into the vulgar for their countrymen, insomuch that most nations under heaven did shortly after their conversion hear *Christ* speaking unto them in their mother tongue, not by the voice of their minister only, but also by the written word translated. If any doubt hereof, he may be satisfied by examples enough, if enough will serve the turn. First, St *Hierome* 285 saith, *Multarum gentium linguis Scriptura ante translata docet falsa esse quæ addita sunt*, &c. that is, *The Scripture being translated before in the languages of many nations doth shew that those things that were added* (by *Lucian* or *Hesychius*) *are false*. So St *Hierome* in that place. The same *Hierome* elsewhere affirmeth that he, the time was, had set forth the translation of the *Seventy, suæ linguæ hominibus*, that is, for his coun- 290 trymen of *Dalmatia*. Which words not only *Erasmus* doth understand to purport, that St *Hierome* translated the Scripture into the *Dalmatian* tongue; but also *Sixtus Senensis*, and *Alphonsus a Castro*, (that we speak of no more,) men not to be excepted against by them of *Rome*, do ingenuously confess as much. So St *Chrysostome*, that

295 lived in St *Hierome's* time, giveth evidence with him: *The doctrine of St John* (saith
he) *did not in such sort* (as the Philosophers' did) *vanish away: but the Syrians, Egyp-*
tians, Indians, Persians, Ethiopians, and infinite other nations, being barbarous people,
translated it into their (mother) tongue, and have learned to be (true) Philosophers, he
meaneth Christians. To this may be added *Theodoret,* as next unto him both for an-
300 tiquity, and for learning. His words be these, *Every country that is under the sun is*
full of these words, (of the Apostles and Prophets;) *and the Hebrew tongue* (he meaneth
the Scriptures in the *Hebrew* tongue) *is turned not only into the language of the Gre-*
cians, but also of the Romans, and Egyptians, and Persians, and Indians, and Arme-
nians, and Scythians, and Sauromatians, and, briefly, into all the languages that any
305 *nation useth.* So he. In like manner *Ulpilas* is reported by *Paulus Diaconus* and *Isidore,*
and before them by *Sozomen,* to have translated the Scriptures into the *Gothick*
tongue: *John* Bishop of *Sevil* by *Vasseus,* to have turned them into *Arabick* about the
Year of our Lord 717: *Beda* by *Cistertiensis,* to have turned a great part of them
into *Saxon: Efnard* by *Trithemius,* to have abridged the French Psalter (as *Beda*
310 had done the *Hebrew*) about the year 800: King *Alured* by the said *Cistertiensis,* to
have turned the Psalter into *Saxon: Methodius* by *Aventinus* (printed at *Ingolstad*) to
have turned the Scriptures into *Sclavonian: Valdo* Bishop of *Frising* by *Beatus*
Rhenanus, to have caused about that time the Gospels to be translated into *Dutch*
rhyme, yet extant in the library of *Corbinian: Valdus* by divers, to have turned them
315 himself, or to have gotten them turned, into *French,* about the Year 1160: *Charles*
the Fifth of that name, surnamed *The wise,* to have caused them to be turned into
French about 200 years after *Valdus'* time; of which translation there be many copies
yet extant, as witnesseth *Beroaldus.* Much about that time, even in our King *Richard*
the Second's days, *John Trevisa* translated them into *English,* and many *English* Bibles
320 in written hand are yet to be seen with divers; translated, as it is very probable, in
that age. So the *Syrian* translation of the New Testament is in most learned men's
libraries, of *Widminstadius'* setting forth; and the Psalter in *Arabick* is with many, of
Augustinus Nebiensis' setting forth. So *Postel* affirmeth, that in his travel he saw the
Gospels in the *Ethiopian* tongue: And *Ambrose Thesius* alledgeth the Psalter of the
325 *Indians,* which he testifieth to have been set forth by *Potken* in *Syrian* characters. So
that to have the Scriptures in the mother tongue is not a quaint conceit lately taken
up, either by the Lord *Cromwell* in *England,* or by the Lord *Radevile* in *Polony,* or
by the Lord *Ungnadius* in the Emperor's dominion, but hath been thought upon,
and put in practice of old, even from the first times of the conversion of any nation;
330 no doubt, because it was esteemed most profitable to cause faith to grow in men's
hearts the sooner, and to make them to be able to say with the words of the Psalm,
As we have heard, so we have seen.

Now the church of *Rome* would seem at the length to bear a motherly affection
toward her children, and to allow them the Scriptures in the mother tongue: but
335 indeed it is a gift, not deserving to be called a gift, an unprofitable gift: they must
first get a licence in writing before they may use them; and to get that, they must
approve themselves to their Confessor, that is, to be such as are, if not frozen in the
dregs, yet soured with the leaven of their superstition. Howbeit it seemed too much
to *Clement* the Eighth, that there should be any licence granted to have them in the
340 vulgar tongue, and therefore he overruleth and frustrateth the grant of *Pius* the

Fourth. So much are they afraid of the light of the Scripture, (*Lucifugæ Scripturarum,* as *Tertullian* speaketh,) that they will not trust the people with it, no not as it is set forth by their own sworn men, no not with the licence of their own Bishops and Inquisitors. Yea, so unwilling they are to communicate the Scriptures to the people's understanding in any sort, that they are not ashamed to confess, that we forced them 345 to translate it into *English* against their wills. This seemeth to argue a bad cause, or a bad conscience, or both. Sure we are, that it is not he that hath good gold, that is afraid to bring it to the touchstone, but he that hath the counterfeit; neither is it the true man that shunneth the light, but the malefactor, lest his deeds should be reproved; neither is it the plaindealing merchant that is unwilling to have the weights, 350 or the meteyard, brought in place, but he that useth deceit. But we will let them alone for this fault, and return to translation.

Many men's mouths have been opened a good while (and yet are not stopped) with speeches about the translation so long in hand, or rather perusals of translations made before: and ask what may be the reason, what the necessity, of the employ- 355 ment. Hath the Church been deceived, say they, all this while? Hath her sweet bread been mingled with leaven, her silver with dross, her wine with water, her milk with lime? (*lacte gypsum male miscetur,* saith St *Irenee.*) We hoped that we had been in the right way, that we had had the Oracles of God delivered unto us, and that though all the world had cause to be offended, and to complain, yet that we had none. Hath 360 the nurse holden out the breast, and nothing but wind in it? Hath the bread been delivered by the Fathers of the Church, and the same proved to be *lapidosus,* as *Seneca* speaketh? What is it to handle the word of God deceitfully, if this be not? Thus certain brethren. Also the adversaries of *Judah* and *Jerusalem,* like *Sanballat* in *Nehemiah,* mock, as we hear, both at the work and workmen, saying, *What do these weak Jews* 365 *&c. will they make the stones whole again out of the heaps of dust which are burnt? although they build, yet if a fox go up, he shall even break down their stony wall.* Was their translation good before? Why do they now mend it? Was it not good? Why then was it obtruded to the people? Yea, why did the Catholicks (meaning Popish *Roman- ists*) always go in jeopardy for refusing to go to hear it? Nay, if it must be translated 370 into *English,* Catholicks are fittest to do it. They have learning, and they know when a thing is well, they can *manum de tabula.* We will answer them both briefly: and the former, being brethren, thus, with St *Hierome, Damnamus veteres? Minime, sed post priorum studia in domo Domini quod possumus laboramus.* That is, *Do we condemn the ancient? In no case: but after the endeavours of them that were before us,* 375 *we take the best pains we can in the house of God.* As if he said, Being provoked by the example of the learned that lived before my time, I have thought it my duty to assay, whether my talent in the knowledge of the tongues may be profitable in any measure to God's Church, lest I should seem to have laboured in them in vain, and lest I should be thought to glory in men (although ancient) above that which was in them. 380 Thus St *Hierome* may be thought to speak.

And to the same effect say we, that we are so far off from condemning any of their labours that travelled before us in this kind, either in this land, or beyond sea, either in King *Henry's* time, or King *Edward's,* (if there were any translation, or correction of a translation, in his time,) or Queen *Elizabeth's* of ever renowned memory, 385 that we acknowledge them to have been raised up of God for the building and

furnishing of his Church, and that they deserve to be had of us and of posterity in everlasting remembrance. The judgment of *Aristotle* is worthy and well known: *If Timotheus had not been, we had not had much sweet musick: But if Phrynis (Timotheus'*
390   *master) had not been, we had not had Timotheus.* Therefore blessed be they, and most honoured be their name, that break the ice, and give the onset upon that which helpeth forward to the saving of souls. Now what can be more available thereto, than to deliver God's book unto God's people in a tongue which they understand? Since of an hidden treasure, and of a fountain that is sealed, there is no profit, as *Ptolemy*
395   *Philadelph* wrote to the Rabbins or masters of the *Jews,* as witnesseth *Epiphanius:* and as St *Augustine* saith, *A man had rather be with his dog than with a stranger* (whose tongue is strange unto him.) Yet for all that, as nothing is begun and perfected at the same time, and the latter thoughts are thought to be the wiser: so, if we building upon their foundation that went before us, and being holpen by their labours,
400   do endeavour to make that better which they left so good; no man, we are sure, hath cause to mislike us; they, we persuade ourselves, if they were alive, would thank us. The vintage of *Abiezer,* that strake the stroke: yet the gleaning of grapes of *Ephraim* was not to be despised. See *Judges* viii. 2. *Joash* the king of *Israel* did not satisfy himself till he had smitten the ground three times; and yet he offended the Prophet
405   for giving over then. *Aquila,* of whom we spake before, translated the Bible as carefully and as skilfully as he could; and yet he thought good to go over it again, and then it got the credit with the *Jews,* to be called *kat' akribeian,* that is, accurately done, as St *Hierome* witnesseth. How many books of profane learning have been gone over again and again, by the same translators, by others? Of one and the same
410   book of *Aristotle's* Ethicks there are extant not so few as six or seven several translations. Now if this cost may be bestowed upon the gourd, which affordeth us a little shade, and which to day flourisheth, but to morrow is cut down; what may we bestow, nay, what ought we not to bestow, upon the vine, the fruit whereof maketh glad the conscience of man, and the stem whereof abideth for ever? And this is the word of
415   God, which we translate. *What is the chaff to the wheat? saith the Lord. Tanti vitreum, quanti verum margaritum!* (saith *Tertullian.*) If a toy of glass be of that reckoning with us, how ought we to value the true pearl! Therefore let no man's eye be evil, because his Majesty's is good; neither let any be grieved, that we have a Prince that seeketh the increase of the spiritual wealth of *Israel;* (let *Sanballats* and *Tobiahs* do
420   so, which therefore do bear their just reproof;) but let us rather bless God from the ground of our heart for working this religious care in him to have the translations of the Bible maturely considered of and examined. For by this means it cometh to pass, that whatsoever is sound already, (and all is sound for substance in one or other of our editions, and the worst of ours far better than their authentick vulgar) the
425   same will shine as gold more brightly, being rubbed and polished; also, if any thing be halting, or superfluous, or not so agreeable to the original, the same may be corrected, and the truth set in place. And what can the King command to be done, that will bring him more true honour than this? And wherein could they that have been set a work approve their duty to the King, yea, their obedience to God, and love to
430   his Saints, more, than by yielding their service, and all that is within them, for the furnishing of the work? But besides all this, they were the principal motives of it, and therefore ought least to quarrel it. For the very historical truth is, that upon the

importunate petitions of the Puritanes at his Majesty's coming to this crown, the
conference at *Hampton-court* having been appointed for hearing their complaints,
when by force of reason they were put from all other grounds, they had recourse at   435
the last to this shift, that they could not with good conscience subscribe to the communion book, since it maintained the Bible as it was there translated, which was, as
they said, a most corrupted translation. And although this was judged to be but a
very poor and empty shift, yet even hereupon did his Majesty begin to bethink himself
of the good that might ensue by a new translation, and presently after gave order for   440
this translation which is now presented unto thee. Thus much to satisfy our scrupu-
lous brethren.

Now to the latter we answer, That we do not deny, nay, we affirm and avow, that
the very meanest translation of the Bible in *English*, set forth by men of our profession, (for we have seen none of their's of the whole Bible as yet) containeth the word   445
of God, nay, is the word of God: As the King's speech which he uttered in Parliament, being translated into *French, Dutch, Italian,* and *Latin,* is still the King's
speech, though it be not interpreted by every translator with the like grace, nor peradventure so fitly for phrase, nor so expressly for sense, every where. For it is confessed, that things are to take their denomination of the greater part; and a natural   450
man could say, *Verum ubi multa nitent in carmine, non ego paucis offendor maculis,*
&c. A man may be counted a virtuous man, though he have made many slips in his
life, (else there were none virtuous, for *in many things we offend all,*) also a comely
man and lovely, though he have some warts upon his hand; yea, not only freckles
upon his face, but also scars. No cause therefore why the word translated should be   455
denied to be the word, or forbidden to be current, notwithstanding that some imperfections and blemishes may be noted in the setting forth of it. For what ever was
perfect under the sun, where Apostles or apostolick men, that is, men endued with
an extraordinary measure of God's Spirit, and privileged with the privilege of infallibility, had not their hand? The Romanists therefore in refusing to hear, and daring   460
to burn the word translated, did no less than despite the Spirit of grace, from whom
originally it proceeded, and whose sense and meaning, as well as man's weakness
would enable, it did express. Judge by an example or two.

Plutarch writeth, that after that *Rome* had been burnt by the *Gauls,* they fell soon
to build it again: but doing it in haste, they did not cast the streets, nor proportion   465
the houses in such comely fashion, as had been most sightly and convenient. Was
Cataline therefore an honest man, or a good patriot, that sought to bring it to a
combustion? Or *Nero* a good Prince, that did indeed set it on fire? So by the story
of *Ezra* and the prophecy of *Haggai* it may be gathered, that the temple built by
Zerubbabel after the return from *Babylon* was by no means to be compared to the   470
former built by *Solomon*: for they that remembered the former wept when they considered the latter. Notwithstanding might this latter either have been abhorred and
forsaken by the *Jews,* or profaned by the *Greeks*? The like we are to think of translations. The translation of the *Seventy* dissenteth from the Original in many places,
neither doth it come near it for perspicuity, gravity, majesty. Yet which of the   475
Apostles did condemn it? Condemn it? Nay, they used it, (as it is apparent, and as
St *Hierome* and most learned men do confess;) which they would not have done, nor
by their example of using of it so grace and commend it to the Church, if it had

been unworthy the appellation and name of the word of God. And whereas they urge
480 for their second defence of their vilifying and abusing of the *English* Bibles, or some
pieces thereof, which they meet with, for that hereticks forsooth were the authors of
the translations: (hereticks they call us by the same right that they call themselves
catholicks, both being wrong:) we marvel what divinity taught them so. We are sure
Tertullian was of another mind: *Ex personis probamus fidem, an ex fide personas?* Do
485 we try men's faith by their persons? We should try their persons by their faith. Also
St *Augustine* was of another mind: for he, lighting upon certain rules made by *Tychonius* a *Donatist* for the better understanding of the word, was not ashamed to make
use of them, yea, to insert them into his own book, with giving commendation to
them so far forth as they were worthy to be commended, as is to be seen in St *Augus-
490 tine's* third book *De Doctr. Christ.* To be short, *Origen,* and the whole Church of
God for certain hundred years, were of another mind: for they were so far from tread-
ing under foot (much more from burning) the translation of *Aquila* a proselyte, that
is, one that had turned *Jew,* of *Symmachus,* and *Theodotion,* both *Ebionites,* that is,
most vile hereticks, that they joined them together with the *Hebrew* original, and the
495 translation of the *Seventy,* (as hath been before signified out of *Epiphanius,*) and
set them forth openly to be considered of and perused by all. But we weary the
unlearned, who need not know so much; and trouble the learned, who know it
already.

   Yet before we end, we must answer a third cavil and objection of their's against
500 us, for altering and amending our translations so oft; wherein truly they deal hardly
and strangely with us. For to whom ever was it imputed for a fault, (by such as were
wise,) to go over that which he had done, and to amend it where he saw cause? St
Augustine was not afraid to exhort St *Hierome* to a *Palinodia* or recantation. The
same St *Augustine* was not ashamed to retractate, we might say, revoke, many things
505 that had passed him, and doth even glory that he seeth his infirmities. If we will be
sons of the truth, we must consider what it speaketh, and trample upon our own
credit, yea, and upon other men's too, if either be any way an hinderance to it. This
to the cause. Then to the persons we say, that of all men they ought to be most silent
in this case. For what varieties have they, and what alterations have they made, not
510 only of their service books, portesses, and breviaries, but also of their *Latin* translation? The service book supposed to be made by St *Ambrose,* (*Officium Ambro-
sianum,*) was a great while in special use and request: but Pope *Adrian,* calling a
council with the aid of *Charles* the Emperor, abolished it, yea, burnt it, and commanded the service book of St *Gregory* universally to be used. Well, *Officium Gre-
515 gorianum* gets by this means to be in credit; but doth it continue without change or
altering? No, the very *Roman* service was of two fashions; the new fashion, and the
old, the one used in one Church, and the other in another; as is to be seen in *Pamelius*
a Romanist, his preface before *Micrologus.* The same *Pamelius* reporteth out of
Radulphus de Rivo, that about the year of our Lord 1277 Pope *Nicolas* the Third
520 removed out of the churches of *Rome* the more ancient books (of service,) and
brought into use the missals of the Friers Minorites, and commanded them to be
observed there; insomuch that about an hundred years after, when the above named
Radulphus happened to be at *Rome,* he found all the books to be new, of the new
stamp. Neither was there this chopping and changing in the more ancient times only,

but also of late. *Pius Quintus* himself confesseth, that every bishoprick almost had a 525
peculiar kind of service, most unlike to that which others had; which moved him to
abolish all other breviaries, though never so ancient, and privileged and published by
Bishops in their Dioceses, and to establish and ratify that only which was of his own
setting forth in the year 1568. Now when the Father of their Church, who gladly
would heal the sore of the daughter of his people softly and slightly, and make the 530
best of it, findeth so great fault with them for their odds and jarring; we hope the
children have no great cause to vaunt of their uniformity. But the difference that
appeareth between our translations, and our often correcting of them, is the thing
that we are specially charged with; let us see therefore whether they themselves be
without fault this way, (if it be to be counted a fault to correct,) and whether they 535
be fit men to throw stones at us: *O tandem major parcas insane minori*: They that
are less sound themselves ought not to object infirmities to others. If we should tell
them, that *Valla, Stapulensis, Erasmus,* and *Vives,* found fault with their vulgar translation, and consequently wished the same to be mended, or a new one to be made;
they would answer peradventure, that we produced their enemies for witnesses 540
against them; albeit they were in no other sort enemies, than as St *Paul* was to the
Galatians, for telling them the truth: and it were to be wished, that they had dared
to tell it them plainlier and oftener. But what will they say to this, That Pope *Leo* the
Tenth allowed *Erasmus'* translation of the New Testament, so much different from
the vulgar, by his apostolick letter and bull? That the same *Leo* exhorted *Pagnine* to 545
translate the whole Bible, and bare whatsoever charges was necessary for the work?
Surely, as the apostle reasoneth to the *Hebrews,* that *if the former Law and Testament
had been sufficient, there had been no need of the latter:* so we may say, that if the old
vulgar had been at all points allowable, to small purpose had labour and charges been
undergone about framing of a new. If they say, it was one Pope's private opinion, 550
and that he consulted only himself; then we are able to go further with them, and
to aver, that more of their chief men of all sorts, even their own *Trent* champions,
Paiva and *Vega,* and their own inquisitor *Hieronymus ab Oleastro,* and their own
Bishop *Isidorus Clarius,* and their own Cardinal *Thomas a vio Cajetan,* do either make
new translations themselves, or follow new ones of other men's making, or note the 555
vulgar interpreter for halting, none of them fear to dissent from him, nor yet to except
against him. And call they this an uniform tenor of text and judgment about the text,
so many of their worthies disclaiming the now received conceit? Nay, we will yet
come nearer the quick. Doth not their *Paris* edition differ from the *Lovain,* and *Hen-*
tenius's from them both, and yet all of them allowed by authority? Nay, doth not 560
Sixtus Quintus confess, that certain Catholicks (he meaneth certain of his own side)
were in such an humour of translating the Scriptures into *Latin,* that Satan taking
occasion by them, though they thought of no such matter, did strive what he could,
out of so uncertain and manifold a variety of translations, so to mingle all things,
that nothing might seem to be left certain and firm in them, &c.? Nay further, did 565
not the same *Sixtus* ordain by an inviolable decree, and that with the counsel and
consent of his Cardinals, that the *Latin* edition of the Old and New Testament, which
the council of *Trent* would have to be authentick, is the same without controversy
which he then set forth, being diligently corrected and printed in the printinghouse
of *Vatican?* Thus *Sixtus* in his preface before his Bible. And yet *Clement* the Eighth, 570

his immediate successor to account of, publisheth another edition of the Bible, containing in it infinite differences from that of *Sixtus*, and many of them weighty and material; and yet this must be authentick by all means. What is to have the faith of our glorious Lord *Jesus Christ* with yea and nay, if this be not? Again, what is sweet
575 harmony and consent, if this be? Therefore, as *Demaratus* of *Corinth* advised a great King, before he talked of the dissensions among the *Grecians*, to compose his domestick broils; (for at that time his queen and his son and heir were at deadly feud with him) so all the while that our adversaries do make so many and so various editions themselves, and do jar so much about the worth and authority of them, they
580 can with no shew of equity challenge us for changing and correcting.

But it is high time to leave them, and to shew in brief what we proposed to ourselves, and what course we held, in this our perusal and survey of the Bible. Truly, good Christian Reader, we never thought from the beginning that we should need to make a new translation, nor yet to make of a bad one a good one; (for then the
585 imputation of *Sixtus* had been true in some sort, that our people had been fed with gall of dragons instead of wine, with wheal instead of milk;) but to make a good one better, or out of many good ones one principal good one, not justly to be excepted against; that hath been our endeavour, that our mark. To that purpose there were many chosen, that were greater in other men's eyes than in their own, and that sought
590 the truth rather than their own praise. Again, they came, or were thought to come, to the work, not *exercendi causa*, (as one saith,) but *exercitati*, that is, learned, not to learn; for the chief overseer and ergodioktes under his Majesty, to whom not only we, but also our whole Church was much bound, knew by his wisdom, which thing also *Nazianzen* taught so long ago, that it is a preposterous order to teach first, and
595 to learn after; that *to en pitho keramian manthanein*, to learn and practise together, is neither commendable for the workman, nor safe for the work. Therefore such were thought upon, as could say modestly with St *Hierome*, *Et Hebræum sermonem ex parte didicimus, et in Latino pene ab ipsis incunabulis, &c. detriti sumus; Both we have learned the Hebrew tongue in part, and in the Latin we have been exercised almost from
600 our very cradle. St *Hierome* maketh no mention of the *Greek* tongue, wherein yet he did excel; because he translated not the Old Testament out of *Greek*, but out of *Hebrew*. And in what sort did these assemble? In the trust of their own knowledge, or of their sharpness of wit, or deepness of judgment, as it were in an arm of flesh? At no hand. They trusted in him that hath the key of *David*, opening, and no man
605 shutting; they prayed to the Lord, the Father of our Lord, to the effect that St *Augustine* did; *O let thy Scriptures be my pure delight; let me not be deceived in them, neither let me deceive by them.* In this confidence, and with this devotion, did they assemble together; not too many, lest one should trouble another; and yet many, lest many things haply might escape them. If you ask what they had before them; truly it was
610 the *Hebrew* text of the Old Testament, the *Greek* of the New. These are the two golden pipes, or rather conduits, wherethrough the olivebranches empty themselves into the gold. St *Augustine* calleth them precedent, or original, tongues; St *Hierome*, fountains. The same St *Hierome* affirmeth, and *Gratian* hath not spared to put it into his decree, That *as the credit of the old books* (he meaneth of the Old Testament)
615 *is to be tried by the Hebrew volumes; so of the New by the Greek tongue*, he meaneth by the original *Greek*. If truth be to be tried by these tongues, then whence should a

translation be made, but out of them? These tongues therefore (the Scriptures, we say, in those tongues) we set before us to translate, being the tongues wherein God was pleased to speak to his Church by his Prophets and Apostles. Neither did we run over the work with that posting haste that the *Septuagint* did, if that be true which 620 is reported of them, that they finished it in seventy two days; neither were we barred or hindered from going over it again, having once done it, like St *Hierome*, if that be true which himself reporteth, that he could no sooner write any thing, but presently it was caught from him, and published, and he could not have leave to mend it: neither, to be short, were we the first that fell in hand with translating the 625 Scripture into *English*, and consequently destitute of former helps, as it is written of *Origen*, that he was the first in a manner, that put his hand to write commentaries upon the Scriptures, and therefore no marvel if he overshot himself many times. None of these things: The work hath not been huddled up in seventy two days, but hath cost the workmen, as light as it seemeth, the pains of twice seven times seventy two 630 days, and more. Matters of such weight and consequence are to be speeded with maturity: for in a business of moment a man feareth not the blame of convenient slackness. Neither did we think much to consult the translators or commentators, *Chaldee, Hebrew, Syrian, Greek,* or *Latin*; no, nor the *Spanish, French, Italian,* or *Dutch*, neither did we disdain to revise that which we had done, and to bring back 635 to the anvil that which we had hammered: but having and using as great helps as were needful, and fearing no reproach for slowness, nor coveting praise for expedition, we have at length, through the good hand of the Lord upon us, brought the work to that pass that you see.

Some peradventure would have no variety of senses to be set in the margin, lest 640 the authority of the Scriptures for deciding of controversies by that shew of uncertainty should somewhat be shaken. But we hold their judgment not to be so sound in this point. For though *whatsoever things are necessary are manifest, as* St *Chrysostome* saith; and, as St *Augustine, in those things that are plainly set down in the Scriptures all such matters are found, that concern faith, hope, and charity.* Yet for all that 645 it cannot be dissembled, that partly to exercise and whet our wits, partly to wean the curious from lothing of them for their every where plainness, partly also to stir up our devotion to crave the assistance of God's Spirit by prayer, and lastly, that we might be forward to seek aid of our brethren by conference, and never scorn those that be not in all respects so complete as they should be, being to seek in many things 650 ourselves, it hath pleased God in his Divine Providence here and there to scatter words and sentences of that difficulty and doubtfulness, not in doctrinal points that concern salvation, (for in such it hath been vouched that the Scriptures are plain,) but in matters of less moment, that fearfulness would better beseem us than confidence, and if we will resolve, to resolve upon modesty with St *Augustine*, (though 655 not in this same case altogether, yet upon the same ground,) *Melius est dubitare de occultis, quam litigare de incertis:* It is better to make doubt of those things which are secret, than to strive about those things that are uncertain. There be many words in the Scriptures, which be never found there but once, (having neither brother nor neighbour, as the *Hebrews* speak,) so that we cannot be holpen by conference of 660 places. Again, there be many rare names of certain birds, beasts, and precious stones, &c. concerning which the *Hebrews* themselves are so divided among themselves for

judgment, that they may seem to have defined this or that, rather because they would say something, than because they were sure of that which they said, as St *Hierome*
665 somewhere saith of the *Septuagint*. Now in such a case doth not a margin do well to admonish the Reader to seek further, and not to conclude or dogmatize upon this or that peremptorily? For as it is a fault of incredulity, to doubt of those things that are evident; so to determine of such things as the Spirit of God hath left (even in the judgment of the judicious) questionable, can be no less than presumption. There-
670 fore as St *Augustine* saith, that variety of translations is profitable for the finding out of the sense of the Scriptures: so diversity of signification and sense in the margin, where the text is not so clear, must needs do good; yea, is necessary, as we are per-suaded. We know that *Sixtus Quintus* expressly forbiddeth that any variety of read-ings of their vulgar edition should be put in the margin; (which though it be not
675 altogether the same thing to that we have in hand, yet it looketh that way;) but we think he hath not all of his own side his favourers for this conceit. They that are wise had rather have their judgments at liberty in differences of readings, than to be cap-tivated to one, when it may be the other. If they were sure that their high priest had all laws shut up in his breast, as *Paul* the Second bragged, and that he were as free
680 from error by special privilege, as the dictators of *Rome* were made by law inviolable, it were another matter; then his word were an oracle, his opinion a decision. But the eyes of the world are now open, God be thanked, and have been a great while; they find that he is subject to the same affections and infirmities that others be, that his body is subject to wounds; and therefore so much as he proveth, not as much as he
685 claimeth, they grant and embrace.

Another thing we think good to admonish thee of, gentle Reader, that we have not tied ourselves to an uniformity of phrasing, or to an identity of words, as some peradventure would wish that we had done, because they observe, that some learned men somewhere have been as exact as they could that way. Truly, that we might not
690 vary from the sense of that which we had translated before, if the word signified the same thing in both places, (for there be some words that be not of the same sense every where,) we were especially careful, and made a conscience, according to our duty. But that we should express the same notion in the same particular word; as for example, if we translate the *Hebrew* or *Greek* word once by *purpose*, never to call it
695 *intent*; if one where *journeying*, never *travelling*; if one where *think*, never *suppose*; if one where *pain*, never *ache*; if one where *joy*, never *gladness*, &c. thus to mince the matter, we thought to savour more of curiosity than wisdom, and that rather it would breed scorn in the atheist, than bring profit to the godly reader. For is the kingdom of God become words or syllables? Why should we be in bondage to them,
700 if we may be free? use one precisely, when we may use another no less fit as com-modiously? A godly Father in the primitive time shewed himself greatly moved, that one of newfangledness called *krabbaton*, *skismos*, though the difference be little or none; and another reporteth, that he was much abused for turning *cucurbita* (to which reading the people had been used) into *hedera*. Now if this happen in better
705 times, and upon so small occasions, we might justly fear hard censure, if generally we should make verbal and unnecessary changings. We might also be charged (by scoffers) with some unequal dealing towards a great number of good *English* words. For as it is written of a certain great Philosopher, that he should say, that those logs

were happy that were made images to be worshipped; for their fellows, as good as they, lay for blocks behind the fire: so if we should say, as it were, unto certain words, Stand up higher, have a place in the Bible always; and to others of like quality, Get you hence, be banished for ever; we might be taxed peradventure with St *James's* words, namely, *To be partial in ourselves, and judges of evil thoughts.* Add hereunto, that niceness in words was always counted the next step to trifling; and so was to be curious about names too: also that we cannot follow a better pattern for elocution than God himself; therefore he using divers words in his holy writ, and indifferently for one thing in nature: we, if we will not be superstitious, may use the same liberty in our *English* versions out of *Hebrew* and *Greek*, for that copy or store that he hath given us. Lastly, we have on the one side avoided the scrupulosity of the Puritanes, who leave the old Ecclesiastical words, and betake them to other, as when they put *washing* for *baptism*, and *congregation* instead of *Church*: as also on the other side we have shunned the obscurity of the Papists, in their *azymes, tunike, rational, holocausts, prepuce, pasche*, and a number of such like, whereof their late translation is full, and that of purpose to darken the sense, that since they must needs translate the Bible, yet by the language thereof it may be kept from being understood. But we desire that the Scripture may speak like itself, as in the language of *Canaan*, that it may be understood even of the very vulgar.

Many other things we might give thee warning of, gentle Reader, if we had not exceeded the measure of a preface already. It remaineth that we commend thee to God, and to the Spirit of his grace, which is able to build further than we can ask or think. He removeth the scales from our eyes, the vail from our hearts, opening our wits that we may understand his word, enlarging our hearts, yea, correcting our affections, that we may love it above gold and silver, yea, that we may love it to the end. Ye are brought unto fountains of living water which ye digged not; do not cast earth into them, with the Philistines, neither prefer broken pits before them, with the wicked Jews. Others have laboured, and you may enter into their labours. O receive not so great things in vain: O despise not so great salvation. Be not like swine to tread under foot so precious things, neither yet like dogs to tear and abuse holy things. Say not to our Saviour with the *Gergesites*, Depart out of our coasts; neither yet with *Esau* sell your birthright for a mess of pottage. If light be come into the world, love not darkness more than light: if food, if clothing, be offered, go not naked, starve not yourselves. Remember the advice of *Nazianzene, It is a grievous thing* (or dangerous) *to neglect a great fair, and to seek to make markets afterwards*: also the encouragement of St *Chrysostome, It is altogether impossible, that he that is sober* (and watchful) *should at any time be neglected*: lastly, the admonition and menacing of St *Augustine, They that despise God's will inviting them shall feel God's will taking vengeance of them.* It is a fearful thing to fall into the hands of the living God; but a blessed thing it is, and will bring us to everlasting blessedness in the end, when God speaketh unto us, to hearken; when he setteth his word before us, to read it; when he stretcheth out his hand and calleth, to answer, Here am I, here we are to do thy will, O God. The Lord work a care and conscience in us to know him and serve him, that we may be acknowledged of him at the appearing of our Lord JESUS CHRIST, to whom with the Holy Ghost be all praise and thanksgiving. Amen.

Questions for Study

1 Does the preface specifically claim that the King James Version is a new translation?
2 The work is described as "authorized" to be read in churches. Does the preface give us any reasons why or how the need for such an "authorized" version came about?
3 What political factors may be said to have led to the production of this translation? Are those factors acknowledged in the preface?

Text: Selected Passages

The best way to appreciate any text is to read it. In what follows, we shall set out a number of sections of the King James Version, most of which are well known, particularly through works such as George Frederick Handel's *Messiah*, which is basically a compilation of texts dealing with the coming of Christ, taken from the King James Version. Note that modern English orthography has been used.

1   *The Creation Story: Genesis 1:1–23*

In the beginning God created the heaven and the earth. And the earth was without form, and void; and darkness was upon the face of the deep. And the Spirit of God moved upon the face of the waters. And God said, Let there be light: and there was light. And God saw the light, that it was good: and God divided the light from the darkness. And God called the light Day, and the darkness he called Night. And the evening and the morning were the first day. And God said, Let there be a firmament in the midst of the waters, and let it divide the waters from the waters. And God made the firmament, and divided the waters which were under the firmament from the waters which were above the firmament: and it was so. And God called the firmament Heaven. And the evening and the morning were the second day. And God said, Let the waters under the heaven be gathered together unto one place, and let the dry land appear: and it was so.

And God called the dry land Earth; and the gathering together of the waters called he Seas: and God saw that it was good. And God said, Let the earth bring forth grass, the herb yielding seed, and the fruit tree yielding fruit after his kind, whose seed is in itself, upon the earth: and it was so. And the earth brought forth grass, and herb yielding seed after his kind, and the tree yielding fruit, whose seed was in itself, after his kind: and God saw that it was good. And the evening and the morning were the third day. And God said, Let there be lights in the firmament of the heaven to divide the day from the night; and let them be for signs, and for seasons, and for days, and years: And let them be for lights in the firmament of the heaven to give light upon the earth: and it was so. And God made two great lights; the greater light to rule the day, and the lesser light to rule the night: he made the stars also. And God set them in the firmament of the heaven to give light upon the earth, And to rule over the day and over the night, and to divide the light from the darkness: and God saw that it was good. And the evening and the morning were the fourth day.

And God said, Let the waters bring forth abundantly the moving creature that hath life, and fowl that may fly above the earth in the open firmament of heaven. And God created great whales, and every living creature that moveth, which the waters brought forth abundantly, after their kind, and every winged fowl after his kind: and God saw that it was good. And God blessed them, saying, Be fruitful, and multiply, and fill the waters in the seas, and let fowl multiply in the earth. And the evening and the morning were the fifth day. And God said, Let the earth bring forth the living creature after his kind, cattle, and creeping thing, and beast of the earth after his kind: and it was so. And God made the beast of the earth after his kind, and cattle after their kind, and every thing that creepeth upon the earth after his kind: and God saw that it was good.

And God said, Let us make man in our image, after our likeness: and let them have dominion over the fish of the sea, and over the fowl of the air, and over the cattle, and over all the earth, and over every creeping thing that creepeth upon the earth. So God created man in his own image, in the image of God created he him; male and female created he them. And God blessed them, and God said unto them, Be fruitful, and multiply, and replenish the earth, and subdue it: and have dominion over the fish of the sea, and over the fowl of the air, and over every living thing that moveth upon the earth. And God said, Behold, I have given you every herb bearing seed, which is upon the face of all the earth, and every tree, in the which is the fruit of a tree yielding seed; to you it shall be for meat. And to every beast of the earth, and to every fowl of the air, and to every thing that creepeth upon the earth, wherein there is life, I have given every green herb for meat: and it was so. And God saw every thing that he had made, and, behold, it was very good. And the evening and the morning were the sixth day.

Thus the heavens and the earth were finished, and all the host of them. And on the seventh day God ended his work which he had made; and he rested on the seventh day from all his work which he had made. And God blessed the seventh day, and sanctified it: because that in it he had rested from all his work which God created and made.

2   Psalm 23

A Psalm of David

The LORD is my shepherd; I shall not want.
He maketh me to lie down in green pastures:
he leadeth me beside the still waters.
He restoreth my soul:
he leadeth me in the paths of righteousness for his name's sake.
Yea, though I walk through the valley of the shadow of death, I will fear no
    evil: for thou art with me; thy rod and thy staff they comfort me.
Thou preparest a table before me in the presence of mine enemies:
thou anointest my head with oil; my cup runneth over.
Surely goodness and mercy shall follow me all the days of my life:
and I will dwell in the house of the LORD for ever.

3   The Christmas Story: Matthew 1:18–25 to 2:1–12

Now the birth of Jesus Christ was on this wise: When as his mother Mary was espoused to Joseph, before they came together, she was found with child of the Holy Ghost. Then Joseph her husband, being a just man, and not willing to make her a publick example, was minded to put her away privily. But while he thought on these things, behold, the angel of the Lord appeared unto him in a dream, saying, Joseph, thou son of David, fear not to take unto thee Mary thy wife: for that which is conceived in her is of the Holy Ghost. And she shall bring forth a son, and thou shalt call his name JESUS: for he shall save his people from their sins. Now all this was done, that it might be fulfilled which was spoken of the Lord by the prophet, saying, Behold, a virgin shall be with child, and shall bring forth a son, and they shall call his name Emmanuel, which being interpreted is, God with us. Then Joseph being raised from sleep did as the angel of the Lord had bidden him, and took unto him his wife: And knew her not till she had brought forth her firstborn son: and he called his name JESUS.

Now when Jesus was born in Bethlehem of Judaea in the days of Herod the king, behold, there came wise men from the east to Jerusalem, Saying, where is he that is born King of the Jews? For we have seen his star in the east, and are come to worship him. When Herod the king had heard these things, he was troubled, and all Jerusalem with him. And when he had gathered all the chief priests and scribes of the people together, he demanded of them where Christ should be born. And they said unto him, In Bethlehem of Judaea: for thus it is written by the prophet, And thou Bethlehem, in the land of Juda, art not the least among the princes of Juda: for out of thee shall come a Governor, that shall rule my people Israel. Then Herod, when he had privily called the wise men, enquired of them diligently what time the star appeared. And he sent them to Bethlehem, and said, Go and search diligently for the young child; and when ye have found him, bring me word again, that I may come and worship him also. When they had heard the king, they departed; and, lo, the star, which they saw in the east, went before them, till it came and stood over where the young child was. When they saw the star, they rejoiced with exceeding great joy. And when they were come into the house, they saw the young child with Mary his mother, and fell down, and worshipped him: and when they had opened their treasures, they presented unto him gifts; gold, and frankincense, and myrrh. And being warned of God in a dream that they should not return to Herod, they departed into their own country another way.

4   The Christmas Story: Luke 2:1–20

And it came to pass in those days, that there went out a decree from Caesar Augustus, that all the world should be taxed. (And this taxing was first made when Cyrenius was governor of Syria.) And all went to be taxed, every one into his own city. And Joseph also went up from Galilee, out of the city of Nazareth, into Judaea, unto the city of David, which is called Bethlehem; (because he was of the house and lineage of David:) To be taxed with Mary his espoused wife, being great with child. And so it was, that, while they were there, the days were accomplished that she should be delivered. And she brought forth her firstborn son, and wrapped him in swaddling clothes, and laid him in a manger; because there was no room for them in the inn.

And there were in the same country shepherds abiding in the field, keeping watch over their flock by night. And, lo, the angel of the Lord came upon them, and the glory of the Lord shone round about them: and they were sore afraid. And the angel said unto them, Fear not: for, behold, I bring you good tidings of great joy, which shall be to all people. For unto you is born this day in the city of David a Saviour, which is Christ the Lord. And this shall be a sign unto you; Ye shall find the babe wrapped in swaddling clothes, lying in a manger. And suddenly there was with the angel a multitude of the heavenly host praising God, and saying, Glory to God in the highest, and on earth peace, good will toward men.

And it came to pass, as the angels were gone away from them into heaven, the shepherds said one to another, Let us now go even unto Bethlehem, and see this thing which is come to pass, which the Lord hath made known unto us. And they came with haste, and found Mary, and Joseph, and the babe lying in a manger. And when they had seen it, they made known abroad the saying which was told them concerning this child. And all they that heard it wondered at those things which were told them by the shepherds. But Mary kept all these things, and pondered them in her heart. And the shepherds returned, glorifying and praising God for all the things that they had heard and seen, as it was told unto them.

5 The Beatitudes: Matthew 5:1–16

[Note that the speaker in this section is Jesus himself.]

And seeing the multitudes, he went up into a mountain: and when he was set, his disciples came unto him: And he opened his mouth, and taught them, saying,

Blessed are the poor in spirit: for theirs is the kingdom of heaven.

Blessed are they that mourn: for they shall be comforted.

Blessed are the meek: for they shall inherit the earth.

Blessed are they which do hunger and thirst after righteousness: for they shall be filled.

Blessed are the merciful: for they shall obtain mercy.

Blessed are the pure in heart: for they shall see God.

Blessed are the peacemakers: for they shall be called the children of God.

Blessed are they which are persecuted for righteousness' sake: for theirs is the kingdom of heaven.

Blessed are ye, when men shall revile you, and persecute you, and shall say all manner of evil against you falsely, for my sake.

Rejoice, and be exceeding glad: for great is your reward in heaven: for so persecuted they the prophets which were before you.

Ye are the salt of the earth: but if the salt have lost his savour, wherewith shall it be salted? It is thenceforth good for nothing, but to be cast out, and to be trodden under foot of men.

Ye are the light of the world. A city that is set on an hill cannot be hid. Neither do men light a candle, and put it under a bushel, but on a candlestick; and it giveth light unto all that are in the house. Let your light so shine before men, that they may see your good works, and glorify your Father which is in heaven.

6   Paul on Charity: 1 Corinthians 13:1–13

Though I speak with the tongues of men and of angels, and have not charity, I am become as sounding brass, or a tinkling cymbal. And though I have the gift of prophecy, and understand all mysteries, and all knowledge; and though I have all faith, so that I could remove mountains, and have not charity, I am nothing. And though I bestow all my goods to feed the poor, and though I give my body to be burned, and have not charity, it profiteth me nothing. Charity suffereth long, and is kind; charity envieth not; charity vaunteth not itself, is not puffed up, Doth not behave itself unseemly, seeketh not her own, is not easily provoked, thinketh no evil; Rejoiceth not in iniquity, but rejoiceth in the truth; Beareth all things, believeth all things, hopeth all things, endureth all things. Charity never faileth: but whether there be prophecies, they shall fail; whether there be tongues, they shall cease; whether there be knowledge, it shall vanish away. For we know in part, and we prophesy in part. But when that which is perfect is come, then that which is in part shall be done away. When I was a child, I spake as a child, I understood as a child, I thought as a child: but when I became a man, I put away childish things. For now we see through a glass, darkly; but then face to face: now I know in part; but then shall I know even as also I am known. And now abideth faith, hope, charity, these three; but the greatest of these is charity.

7   The New Jerusalem: Revelation 21:1–7

And I saw a new heaven and a new earth: for the first heaven and the first earth were passed away; and there was no more sea. And I John saw the holy city, new Jerusalem, coming down from God out of heaven, prepared as a bride adorned for her husband. And I heard a great voice out of heaven saying, Behold, the tabernacle of God is with men, and he will dwell with them, and they shall be his people, and God himself shall be with them, and be their God. And God shall wipe away all tears from their eyes; and there shall be no more death, neither sorrow, nor crying, neither shall there be any more pain: for the former things are passed away. And he that sat upon the throne said, Behold, I make all things new. And he said unto me, Write: for these words are true and faithful. And he said unto me, It is done. I am Alpha and Omega, the beginning and the end. I will give unto him that is athirst of the fountain of the water of life freely. He that overcometh shall inherit all things; and I will be his God, and he shall be my son.

CHAPTER 46

Sir Walter Ralegh (ca. 1552–1618)

Walter Ralegh (the spelling "Raleigh" is incorrect) was born in 1552, and spent his early years in the area around East Budleigh and Budleigh Salterton in Devon. In common with many English people of the period, he was alienated from Roman Catholicism by the religious excesses which the nation experienced under the reign of Mary Tudor (1553–8). With the accession of the more Protestant Elizabeth I, a very different religious climate began to develop in England. Ralegh felt at home in this new religious environment, and had little hesitation in letting his Protestant sympathies be known, particularly within court circles. By 1581, he was a firm favorite of Elizabeth I.

Sir Walter Ralegh (ca. 1552–1618)

Basic description
English courtier, explorer and poet.

Major works
A History of the World (1604–16); various poems.

Major studies
Anna R. Beer, *Sir Walter Ralegh and his Readers in the Seventeenth Century*. London: Macmillan, 1997.
John Winton, *Sir Walter Ralegh*. London: Michael Joseph, 1975.

In 1585, Ralegh led an expedition to the Americas, which led to the annexation of Virginia as an English colony. His acheivements on this expedition led to his being knighted. However, the rapidly deteriorating relations between England and Spain brought Ralegh home again, and saw him in charge, with Sir Richard Grenville, of the defense of Devon and Cornwall against the expected Spanish invasion force. In fact, the main battles took place at sea, and Ralegh saw no action of any importance.

After the death of Elizabeth I in 1603, Ralegh found himself falling out of favor. He was accused of being involved in a plot to overthrow James I, and sentenced to death. He was released, but was arrested again, and finally executed in 1618.

Text: The Passionate Man's Pilgrimage

One of Ralegh's finest poems was written during the first year of the reign of James I, when Ralegh was under sentence of death (and may thus be dated to the period November 17–December 3, 1603). This is known as "The Passionate Man's Pilgrimage," which was first published in 1604. The poem has the subtitle: "Supposed to be written by one at the point of death." The text reproduced here includes the "Epitaph," which is traditionally understood to have been written by Ralegh the night before his execution.

> Give me my scallop shell of quiet,
> My staff of faith to walk upon,
> My scrip of joy, immortal diet,
> My bottle of salvation,
> My gown of glory, hope's true gage,   5
> And thus I'll take my pilgrimage.
>
> Blood must be my body's balmer,
> No other balm will there be given,
> Whilst my soul, like a white palmer,
> Travels to the land of heaven;   10
> Over the silver mountains,
> Where spring the nectar fountains;
> And there I'll kiss
> The bowl of bliss,
> And drink my eternal fill   15
> On every milken hill.
> My soul will be a-dry before,
> But after it will ne'er thirst more;
>
> And by the happy blissful way
> More peaceful pilgrims I shall see,   20
> That have shook off their gowns of clay,
> And go apparelled fresh like me.
> I'll bring them first
> To slake their thirst,
> And then to taste those nectar suckets,   25
> At the clear wells
> Where sweetness dwells,
> Drawn up by saints in crystal buckets.
>
> And when our bottles and all we
> Are fill'd with immortality,   30
> Then the holy paths we'll travel,
> Strew'd with rubies thick as gravel,
> Ceilings of diamonds, sapphire floors,
> High walls of coral, and pearl bowers.

From thence to heaven's bribeless hall   35
Where no corrupted voices brawl,
No conscience molten into gold,
Nor forg'd accusers bought and sold,
No cause deferr'd, nor vain-spent journey,
For there Christ is the king's attorney,   40
Who pleads for all without degrees,
And he hath angels, but no fees.

When the grand twelve million jury
Of our sins and sinful fury,
'Gainst our souls black verdicts give,   45
Christ pleads his death, and then we live.
Be thou my speaker, taintless pleader,
Unblotted lawyer, true proceeder,
Thou movest salvation even for alms,
Not with a bribed lawyer's palms.   50

And this is my eternal plea
To him that made heaven, earth, and sea,
Seeing my flesh must die so soon,
And want a head to dine next noon,
Just at the stroke when my veins start and spread,   55
Set on my soul an everlasting head.
Then am I ready, like a palmer fit,
To tread those blest paths which before I writ.

Epitaph

Even such is Time, which takes in trust
Our youth, our joys, and all we have,
And pays us but with age and dust;
Who in the dark and silent grave,
When we have wandered all our days:
And from which earth, and grave, and dust,
The Lord shall raise me up, I trust.

Questions for Discussion

1 Ralegh was noted as one of the great explorers of the Elizabethan age. In what ways
   does his interest in the exploration of exotic places figure in this poem? What purpose
   does it serve?
2 What criticism of English justice, presumably reflecting his own experience, can be
   detected in this poem?
3 The "Epitaph" is the most explicitly Christian part of the poem. In what way does
   the Christian doctrine of the resurrection inform this final section?

CHAPTER 47

Lancelot Andrewes (1555–1626)

Lancelot Andrewes was born in London, and attended school at Cooper's Free School, Radcliffe, and subsequently at the Merchant Taylors' School. His obvious scholarly abilities were noted at an early age, with the result that he went on to study at Pembroke Hall, Cambridge, which elected him to a fellowship in 1576. He won the favor of Sir Francis Walsingham, one of the ministers of Elizabeth I, with the result that he soon received preferment. In 1589 he became vicar of the parish of St. Giles, Cripplegate. This was supplemented shortly afterwards with a prebendship at St. Paul's Cathedral, London, which entitled him to a stall in the cathedral, and the right to preach there on a regular basis. His preaching soon attracted attention, and he was appointed as Chaplain-in-Ordinary to Elizabeth I. Elizabeth offered him two bishoprics, Ely and Salisbury; he rejected both, partly on financial grounds. In 1601, he accepted the position of Dean of Westminster.

With the accession of James I, Andrewes was offered the opportunity of rapid advancement within the Church of England. He was appointed Bishop of Chichester in 1605, translated (to use the technical term for moving from one bishopric to another) to Ely in 1609, and finally to Winchester in 1618. At this stage, he was also appointed Dean of the Royal Chapel, in public recognition of the high regard in which he was held within the court. His influence on the development of the distinctive ethos of the Church of England was considerable, and it can be argued that many of the developments introduced by Archbishop William Laud under Charles I were anticipated – although, it has to be said, in a rather more diplomatic manner – by Andrewes.

Andrewes' reputation was primarily grounded in his preaching. His "Ninety-Six Sermons" were brought together in 1627, at the express command of Charles I, in an edition by Bishops Laud and Buckeridge. The sermons are noted for their remarkably flamboyant style, which was greatly appreciated at the time, but often seems slightly excessive to modern readers. The sermons are heavily interspersed with Latin and Greek terms and quotations, often serving little purpose, and often seem excessively concerned with the minute detail of the text on which he was preaching. Nevertheless, his sermons are widely regarded as classics.

Lancelot Andrewes (1555–1626)

Basic description
Bishop and preacher.

Major works
"Ninety-Six Sermons" (1627); *Patterne of Catechisticall Doctrine* (1630).

Editions of works
Works, ed. J. P. Wilson and J. Bliss, 11 vols. Oxford: Library of Anglo-Catholic Theology, 1841–54.

Major studies
Nicolas Lossky, *Lancelot Andrewes the Preacher (1555–1626): The Origins of the Mystical Theology of the Church of England*. Oxford: Clarendon Press, 1991.
Paul A. Welsby, *Lancelot Andrewes, 1555–1626*. London: SPCK, 1964.

Text: Sermon XIV

Andrewes' style makes it impossible to do anything other than reproduce an entire sermon for the purposes of this anthology. To include only an extract would be to fail to allow readers to appreciate the complex structure of his sermons, and the intricate way in which he engaged with the biblical text. The sermon which has been chosen for study is one of a collection of seventeen sermons preached once each year before James I on Christmas Day, beginning in 1605 and ending in 1624. The sermon chosen was preached before James I at Whitehall on December 25, 1620, on Matthew 2:1–2, describing the visit of the Wise Men from the East to worship Christ. The work is not easy to follow, partly on account of its rhetorical embellishments and excessive use of foreign languages; nevertheless, it rewards patient study.

Sermon XIV

A SERMON PREACHED BEFORE THE KING'S MAJESTY, AT WHITEHALL, ON MONDAY, THE TWENTY-FIFTH OF DECEMBER, A.D. MDCXX., BEING CHRISTMAS-DAY

When Jesus then was born at Bethlehem in Judea, in the days of Herod the King, behold, there came wise men, from the East to Jerusalem, saying,
Where is the King of the Jews That is born? For we have seen His star in the East, and are come to worship Him. MATTHEW ii: 1, 2.

Cum ergo natus esset Jesus in Bethlehem Judæ, in diebus Herodis Regis, ecce magi ab Oriente venerunt Jerosolymam, dicentes.
Ubi est Qui natus est Rex Judæorum? Vidimus enim stellam Ejus in Oriente, et venimus adorare Eum.

We pass now this year from the shepherds and the Angels, to the wise men and their star. This star, and their coming, no less proper to this day than those other were.

For though they came not to Jerusalem this day, yet this day *venerunt ab Oriente*, "from the East they came." They set forth this very day. For they came when "Jesus
5 was born," and this day was He born. Howsoever the star brought them not to their journey's end till twelve days hence, yet this day it first shewed itself; how soon Jesus was born, *vidimus stellam*, it appeared straight. For which very appearing, you shall find the Fathers of the East Church do call this first day *ta ephiphaniea*, as well as the last. This first, wherein His star appeared and they began their journey. That last,
10 wherein He appeared Himself, and their journey was at an end. First and last, an appearing there was. One begins, the other ends the feast.

We pass from one of them to the other, but from the less to the greater; for of the twain this is the greater. Greater in itself, greater to us. Two ways greater in itself. The other of the shepherds, a poor one, poor and mean. This of the wise men, a
15 sign of some state, high and Heavenly.

God bade Ahaz ask a sign; "ask one from here below, or one from the height above" (Isa. vii: 11). He would ask neither, but God gave both. From below, *hoc erit Signum*, "you shall find the Babe in a manger" (Luke ii: 12) – low enough. That we have done withal. Now from above, *ecce vidimus Stellam*, the sign from Heaven
20 – His new star.

Besides, to speak uprightly, one might in some sort complain of the privateness of the Angels' appearing. Somewhat obscure it was, few privy to it; passed over in the night between the Angels and them. And upon it, three or four shepherds got them into the stable; and what there they did no man could take notice of.
25 More famous, and more manifestation-like was this here. A new light kindled in Heaven, a star never seen before. The world could not but look up at it, and ask what it meant. Nothing appeareth there, but "the sound of it goeth out into all lands, and the news of it to the utmost parts of the earth" (Ps. xix: 4).

This made another manner *venerunt*. Upon this came there to Jerusalem not a
30 rout of Shepherds, but a troop of great persons. And not from a heath or sheep-common hard by, but from afar, "from the East," twelve days' journey off. All Jerusalem rang of it. The King, Priests, and people busied with it. To this day remembered in all stories. It cannot be forgotten; "For this was not done in a corner" (Acts xxvi: 26), this was indeed a manifestation. Better in itself thus.
35 And for us better – for us all. For we all hold by this. It was a brack in the former; the sermon was made, and the anthem sung, and none at it but the shepherds. And what were they? Jews. What is that to us? This Scripture offereth "more grace" (James iv: 6). These here that "came from the East," first they were Gentiles. Gentiles – that concerns us, for so are we. We may then look out, if we can see this star. It is ours,
40 it is the Gentiles' star. We may set our course by it, to seek and find, and worship Him as well as they.

This is for us all. But there is yet more grace offered to some in particular. The shepherds were a sort of poor simple men altogether unlearned. But here come a troop of men of great place, high account in their country; and withal of great learned
45 men, their name gives them for no less. This lo, falls somewhat proper to this place and presence that will be glad to hear it. It is *faustum et salutare Sydus* to such; that wealth, worth, or wisdom shall hinder none, but they may have their parts in Christ's birth, as well as those of low degree. It is not only *Stella gentium*, but *Stella magorum*, "the great men's, the wise men's Star," this.

So *quoad nos*, "for us" it fitteth well. And *quoad se*, "of itself" it is fit every way. This 50
star leads us to another star; – even "the root and generation of David, the bright
morning Star" (Isa. xi: 1; 2 Pet. i: 19; Ps. cx: 3). He of whom Zachary saith in the Old
Testament, *Ecce Vir, Oriens nomen Ejus* (Zech. vi: 12); yea, *Oriens ab alto*, saith
Zachary in the New (Luke i: 78); visits those of the East whence the day springeth,
takes them that are nearest Him, and His rising works upon the place first that bears 55
His name. "The wisdom of God, the beginning of all His ways" (Prov. viii: 22), is
found by wise men of all other, because they be wise, most fit to find Him.

I. Two verses I have read. In the former after the matter of the feast first remembered, "When Jesus was born," accompanied with the two circumstances of place
and time, – the place where, "Bethlehem Judah;" the time when, "the days of Herod 60
the King" – there is a memorable accident that then happened set down; a *venerunt*,
"a coming or arrival" at Jerusalem. And they that so came were a company of *magi*
"from the East." And this lo, hath the *ecce* on the head of it, *Ecce, venerunt magi ab
Oriente*, "Behold, there came," &c. as the special point in the text; and so we to
make it. 65

II. In the latter is set down their errand. Both the 1. occasion, and the 2. end;
best expressed by themselves out of their own *dicentes*. 1. The occasion; *vidimus
stellam*, they had "seen His star." 2. The end; *venimus adorare*, they are "come to
worship Him." *Viderunt, venerunt, adorârunt*.

That they may come to their *finis ultimus* they must have a *medius finis*; that is, 70
to worship, they must find Him where he is.

So they ask *Ubi est?* Not whether He be born, but "where He is born." For born
He is they are sure, by the same token they have seen His star. His star is up, that is
risen, therefore he is risen too.

So the star in Heaven kindled another star in earth; St. Peter calls it the "Day-star 75
which riseth in the heart" (2 Peter i: 19), that is faith, which shined and manifested
itself by their labour in coming, diligence in enquiring, duty in worshipping.

Christ's birth made manifest to them by the star in Heaven. Their faith, "the star
in their hearts," made manifest to Christ and to all by the travel of it, which shewed
it manifestly. 80

That upon the matter there falls a threefold manifestation – you may call them
three stars if you please. 1. The star in Heaven. 2. The day-star in their hearts. 3.
And Christ Himself, "the bright morning Star," Whom both the other guide us to;
the Star of this morning which makes the day the greatest day in the year.

The sum of all riseth to this, that God hath "opened a door of faith to the 85
Gentiles" (Acts xiv: 27), and among them to wise men and great men, as well as to
the simpler sort. But with this condition, that they say with them, *venite adoremus*;
and so come, and seek, and find, and worship Him; that is, do as these did.

"When Jesus was born," That "when" is now. His birth is the ground of the feast
and the cause of our *venimus*, "our coming together." Where this we note first: it 90
is the very first time, the first "was born" in the Bible; "was born" never till now.
Here the tide turns, the sense changes from "shall be" to "was." A blessed change.
And the day is blessed on which it happened.

Before He was born, it was so sure He should be born as Esay said, *Puer natus
est nobis* (Isa. ix: 6). But for all that there is some odds between Esay's *natus est* and 95
St. Matthew's. That was but virtually as good as born, this actually born indeed.

"Jesus Christ yesterday, and to-day, and the same for ever" (Heb. xiii: 8). "The same," yet not altogether after the same manner. There is as much between Jesus Christ "yesterday," not come, and Jesus Christ "to-day" *cum natus esset*, as is between a state in reversion and one in being.

The Fathers aptly resemble their case, that were the *ante-nati* before Christ, and ours that came after, to the two men that "carried the great cluster of grapes upon a staff between them" (Num. xiii: 23). Both carried, but he that came behind saw that he carried; so did not he that went before. The *post-nati* sure are of the surer hand. And so for *cum natus esset*, the day and time, to hold a feast for "when Jesus was born."

Weighty circumstances are ever matter of moment, in a story specially. Three there are in the first verse. 1. The place. 2. The time. 3. The persons. 4. I add a fourth out of the second verse, the occasion. The place *ubi*, "Bethlehem Judah." The time *quando*, "the days of Herod the King." The persons *quibus*, "wise men from the East." The occasion whereupon, a new star appearing. Every one of the four having a several prophecy running of it, and every prophecy a filling of it in these words.

The place. He was born in Bethlehem Judah; "And thou Bethlehem Judah," saith the prophet Micah, "out of thee shall He come" (Micah v: 2). And now come He is.

The time. "The days of Herod the King." "The sceptre shall not quite depart from Judah till Shiloh come" (Gen. xlix: 10), said old Father Jacob in his prophecy. Shiloh then is now come. For the sceptre is in Herod's hand, his father an Edomite, his mother an Ishmaelite – Judah clean gone.

The persons. *Magi ab Oriente*, "Kings from the East." The Kings of Arabia and Saba shall come and bring gifts, saith David (Ps. lxxii: 10). And Esay specifies them, gold, myrrh, incense (Isa. lx: 6). These Kings are come – here they are; they and their gifts both.

The occasion whereupon. "A star risen." "A star shall rise of Jacob" (Num. xxiv: 17), saith Balaam – no very good man, yet a true prophet in this; and his prophecy true, and for such recorded in the Book of Moses. This "Star," is this morning up to be seen. Prophecies of all four, and all four accomplished.

Of the place, of Bethlehem, out of Micah, it hath formerly been treated. I but touch it and pass it now. It was the place where David himself was born. And what place more meet for the Son of David to be born in? It was the place where was heard the first news of the Temple. And where could the "Lord of the Temple" more fitly be heard of? It interpreted *domus panis*, "the house of bread." What place more proper for Him Who is "the living Bread that came down from Heaven" (John vi: 51), to give life to the world? It was the least and the lowest of all "the thousands of Judah" (Micah v: 2). What little and low is in things natural, that lowliness and humility is in spiritual. This natural birth-place of his showeth his spiritual. Humility is His place – humility, as I may call it, the Bethlehem of virtues: where you find it, "Lo, there is He born." So born in us, as born for us. Pass we Christ's *ubi*; and now to His *quando*.

Of the time. The days of Herod the King. And those were evil days – days of great affliction to that land. Judah's "sceptre" clean broken; not "a lawgiver left between his feet." Edom, that is Herod the Edomite, cried "Down with them, down to the ground" (Ps. cxxxvii: 7). Not so much as a sort of silly babes but barbarously slain in their mother's arms – enough to make Rachel mourn as she lay in her grave (Jer. xxxi: 15). Dismal days certainly. Why, then comes Shiloh; when man's help farthest 145 off, then God's nearest. When it is dark, then rises the star.

What one prophecy of Him but came even so, even at such a time when they were most out of heart, and needed comfort most? Jacob's (Gen. xlix: 10), when they were in Egypt, "the house of bondage." Balaam's (Num. xxiv: 17), when in the waste and barren wilderness, "among fiery serpents." Esay's, when they were ready to be 150 overrun with the two Kings of Syria and Israel. Daniel's (Dan. ix: 25), when in Babylon, the land of their captivity. Aggai's (Hag. ii: 7–9), when they built the wall with the trowel in one hand and the sword in the other. As His prophecies came still, so came He. His prophecies, saith Peter, as a candle; Himself as a star – in the dark both (2 Peter i: 19). For all the world like the time of the year His birth fell in; in 155 the sharpest season, in the deep of winter. As humility His place, so affliction His time. The time and place fit well. For the time of affliction makes the place – makes humility. Which place Christ is born in. I pass this also, and come to the third; of the persons.

For there stands the *ecce* upon it. Which *ecce* points us to it, as to the chief point 160 of all, as indeed it is. And our chief endeavour to include ourselves, to have our parts in this *venerunt*, in coming to Christ.

Here is a coming, *venerunt*. And they that come, *magi*. In which comers we consider four points; they sustain four persons. 1. Of Gentiles; 2. Gentiles from the East; 3. great persons, great princes – for so we may be bold to call them, as the prophecy 165 calls them, Kings; 4. of great learning and wisdom; so *magi* their name gives them.

"To Bethlehem came the shepherds." Nothing to us – they were Jews. But thither came these too, and they were Gentiles; and in this "Gentiles," we. So come we in. "Then hath God also to the Gentiles set open a door of faith" (Acts xiv: 27). At which door we enter, we with them and they with us, for they and we Gentiles both. 170 The star is *stella Gentium*, "the Gentiles' star," and so ours; and we to direct our course by it. All that ever write call them *Primitias Gentium*, "the first-fruits"; *Antesignanos*, the "standard-bearers" to all the Gentiles that came in after. Upon this I beg leave to stand a little, since it is our tenure we hold by.

And that God would thus do, call the Gentles in, there was some little *ecce* still, 175 some small star-light from the beginning.

By way of promise. So much promised by the Patriarchs. Noah; that "Japhet should at the last dwell in the tents of Shem" (Gen. ix: 27). Abraham; that "in his seed," not any one nation, but "all the nations of the earth be blessed" (Gen. xxii: 18). Jacob; that Shiloh's coming should be – *expectatio* say some, and some *aggre-* 180 *gatio gentium* (Gen. xlix: 10). All nations look for Him, all be gathered to Him.

By way of figure. As much was shadowed in the Law, the Tabernacle, and the Temple; all "figures of things to come" (Heb. x: 1). The Law: where was it given? Was it not in "Sinai, a mountain in Arabia" (Gal. iv: 25), saith the Apostle, and so upon heathen ground? I trust we may have leave to come upon our own ground. 185 And by whom? Was it not by Moses? And we claim to him by alliance. His wife was the daughter of the Priest of Midian (Exod. ii: 21) – so of a heathen woman; and his children, heathen of half blood.

190   The Tabernacle: was not the silk, and gold, and riches it was made of, the spoils
of Egypt, and so heathen stuff? (Exod. xii: 36, and xxv: 2, &c.).

The Temple: was it not founded upon the threshing-floor of Ornan the Jebusite,
a heathen man? (1 Chron. xxi: 18). So on heathen soil, and *ædificium cedit solo*. The
timber and materials of it, came they not from Hiram's country, a heathen king? (1
Kings v: 10, and vii: 13, &c.). And the chief workman in it, the son of a man of
195   Tyre, heathen also? So the heathen were never wholly out. *Venerunt*, "they came,"
they made their proffers. Some *ecce*, some little star still.

Now the Prophets, when they came, had we not hold there too? At the same time
that God gave Moses to the Jews who wrote of Christ, did He not likewise give
Balaam to the Gentiles who in the mountains of the East prophesied of Christ's star
200   (Num. xxiv: 17), here? Great odds, I know, between the men, none between their
prophecies; both alike true, both their places alike in the library of the Holy Ghost.
After that, Jonas. Howsoever his book stand in the volume of the Prophets, yet when
time was it was shewed, that in time he was the first of the sixteen Prophets – before,
and ancient to them all. And this was a fair star, that His first Prophet of all God sent
205   to Nineveh, the great city of the Gentiles then (Jonah i: 2); and sent him before He
sent any of the other fifteen to His own people then in shew, the people of the Jews.

But even of them He sent to the Jews, saith not Esay directly, "the root of Jesse
should be as a standard, all the nations gather unto Him"? (Isa. xi: 10). Saith not
God there, it was too poor a service for Christ to do to Him, to draw to Him a sort
210   of silly shepherds; He would give him, "as a light to lighten the Gentiles," to bring
them, even the very best of them, "from the ends of the earth"? (Isa. xliii: 6). That
"light to lighten the Gentiles" (Isa. xlii: 6), was this star, here; Simeon had it revealed
to him whereto this star referred, and what it meant (Luke ii: 32); for it lighted them
indeed. And this, standing the first Temple. And saith not Aggai, standing the second
215   Temple, "the desire of all nations should come" (Hag. ii: 8), meaning Christ; the
desire not of one nation alone, but even of all? So the Prophets will not be against
this *venerunt*, they are all for it.

And was not also this *venerunt* daily sung in their choir – the Psalm of the Nativity? "I will think upon Rahab (that is Egypt) and Babylon, among such as shall know
220   Me. Behold ye the Philistines also, and them of Tyre, with the Morians; lo, there
was He born" (Psa. lxxxvii: 4, 5). "Born," in all those places; that is, His birth
concerns them all – all their interest in it. In the Psalm of His Passion: "All the ends
of the earth shall remember themselves, and shall turn unto the Lord, and all the
kindreds of nations shall worship before Him" (Psa. xxii: 27). In the Psalm of the
225   Resurrection; that, He should then become "the Head-stone of the corner" (Psa.
cxviii: 22), and join both Jews and Gentiles in one coin or angle. And, in the Psalm
of His Ascension; that the "princes of the nations should be joined to the people of
the God of Abraham" (Psa. xlvii: 9). And in the Psalm of His Exaltation; "that all
Kings should kneel before Him, all nations do Him service" (Psa. lxxii: 11).

230   That which then was thus promised to, and by the Patriarchs, shadowed forth in
the figures of the Law, the Temple, and the Tabernacle; that which was foresaid by
the Prophets, and foresung of in the Psalms, that was this day fulfilled. *Venerunt*,
here "they are come"; and *venimus*, "we" in them and with them. Who not only in

their own names, but in ours make here their entry; came and sought after, and found and worshipped, their Saviour and ours, the Saviour of the whole world.   235

A little wicket there was left open before, whereat divers Gentiles did come in. Many a *venit* there was. *Venit* Job in the Patriarch's days (Job i: 1); *venit* Jethro in Moses' (Exod. xviii: 5), Rahab in Joshua's (Josh. ii: 1), Ruth in the Judges' time (Ruth i: 4); Ittai, the King of Gath's son (2 Sam. xviii: 2), in David's, the Queen of Sheba in Solomon's (1 Kings x: 1), the widow of Sarepta in Elias' (1 Kings xvii: 9), 240 Naaman the Syrian, in Elisha's time (2 Kings v: 15). Each of these in their times had the favour to be let in. This was but a *venit*, a little wicket for one or two. Now a *venerunt*, the great gate set wide open this day for all – for these here with their camels and dromedaries to enter, and all their carriage.

In the setting down His genealogy, the chapter before (Matt. i: 5), that Salmon 245 espoused Rahab the Canaanite, that Booz likewise Ruth the Moabite, it is plain that Christ descended according to the flesh of heathen. Descending of heathen, He will never disdain them of whom He is descended; never shut them out, but invite them to His child-house, as we see this day by His star he did.

And if you mark it of His first sermon, the widow of Sarepta and Naaman the 250 Syrian were the theme (Luke iv: 25, 27); which made, His sermon was not liked. Yet that theme He chose purposely. And the Queen of the South, and the men of Nineveh much in His mouth – He mentioned them willingly (Matt. xii: 42, 41). And to end this point, He That at His birth now received these of the East, a little before His death in like sort received Grecians from the West, to see and to salute Him 255 (John xii: 20). And straight upon it, upon the receiving them brake out and said, "The hour is come now that the Son of Man is glorified" (John xii: 23), when East and West are come in both.

I have a little stood on this, because it is the *ecce* point. I conclude: the place He was born in, an inn, which is for all passengers of what country soever (Luke ii: 7); 260 the time He was born in of the tax, when "all the world came up to be taxed" (Luke ii: 1); the very star which, as the nature of stars is, is common to all coasts and climates, peculiar to none; – all shew that from all coasts they may now come, that the Gentiles are now to be, as the Apostle in three pregnant terms delivers it, *sussōma*, *summetocha*, *sugklēronoma*, "fellow-members, fellow-partners, and fellow-heirs of 265 one body" (Ephes. iii: 6), co-partners and co-heirs of Christ and His birth. This for *stella gentium*, "the Gentiles' star," so both theirs and ours.

There came Gentiles, and they came from the East. This may seem to set us back again, for we are of the West, the contrary climate. That is no matter. For in that "they came from the East," there lieth yet farther hope for us, even from that point 270 of the compass. For that is not only Gentiles, but "sinners of the Gentiles" (Gal. ii: 15) – sinners, and that chief sinners. For so were they of the East; greater, far greater sinners than the rest. For tell me, what sin was there that came not from thence? There was the tower set in hand, that should have confronted God; and of it came Babel, and from it confusion (Gen. xi: 3). 2. Thence came all tyranny and oppres- 275 sion among men, from Nimrod that hunted and ranged over men as over beasts in a forest (Gen. x: 9). 3. Thence all idolatry and worship of false gods, both in earth from Belus' tomb first; and in Heaven, from "the star of their god Rempham" (Acts

vii: 43) which St. Stephen speaks of. 4. Thence, "from the mountains of the East"
280 (Num. xxiii: 7), the posterity of Baalam, false Prophets that love "the wages of
unrighteousness" (2 Pet. ii: 15), and from them all that naught is. And if in all these
it did, it cannot be denied but that the whole world received their infection that way
from the East.

And herein "appeared the grace of God which bringeth salvation to all men" (Tit.
285 ii: 11), and to all sinners, as fair and clear as the star itself; that thence out of the
mountains of the East God calleth these to seek, and guided them to find Christ;
that whence the poison first came, thence might come the triacle; and that as they
were the first that went out, so they should be the first that came in.

So the East sets us not farther back, but brings us nearer. For if the East may come
290 which are the greater, much more may the West which are the less (Matt. viii: 11);
if the seducers, the seduced. From the East to the West is *a majore ad minus*. That
if *venerunt ab Oriente, venient ab Occidente*; if the greater, much rather the lesser.
This for the star of the Gentiles first, and now the star of sinners, and chief sinners
of the Gentiles, even oriental sinners.

295   But they sustain yet a third person, these – to come nearer, and to make it come
nearer us, even to this place. For great men they were in their countries, of the highest
place and account there, as all stories testify. The Psalm calls them "Kings of Sheba
and Seba" (Ps. lxxii: 10), and so may we. It may appear by Herod's respect to them,
his calling a synod to resolve them, his privy conference with them (Matt. ii: 3, 8).
300 So may it by their treasures they opened, and by their presents they offered, presents
for a King, which give them for no less. So this is now thirdly, *stella magnatum*, "the
star of princes and nobles also." Yea, *stella regia*, "the star royal": Kings themselves
have their hold and claim by it.

Christ is not only for russet cloaks, shepherds and such; shews Himself to none
305 but such. But even the grandees, great states such as these, *venerunt*, "they came"
too; and when they came were welcome to Him. For they were sent for and invited
by this star, their star properly.

These at His birth, at His welcome into the world; and others such as these at
His death, at His going out of it. Then Joseph of Arimathea, an honourable coun-
310 sellor, bestowed on Him a fair new tomb (Matt. xxvii: 60); and others came with
their "hundred pound of sweet odours" (John xix: 39). So that coming and going
He was beholden to such. The tribe Christ came of was the royal tribe to whom the
sceptre belonged; and in the prophecy it follows, "a star shall rise out of Jacob, and
a sceptre out of Israel" (Num. xxiv: 17). To Kings, to sceptres, Christ cannot but be
315 well inclined.

Among His Prophets I find Amos, a herdsman (Amos i: 1). True; but I find Esay
and Daniel (Dan. i: 6), both nobly descended, and of the blood royal.

In His descent there are Booz and Jesse, plain countrymen; but there are David
and Solomon too (Matt. i: 6), and a list of Kings withal, that so there may be a
320 mixture of both. It is true St. Paul saith, "You see your calling; not many mighty,
not many noble after the flesh" (1 Cor. i: 26). "Not many" he saith; "not any" he
saith not, he should then have spoken contrary to his own knowledge. Some per-
tained to this star, went by it. The Lord Deputy of Cyprus (Acts xiii: 7), the great
Judge in Areopagus (Acts xvii: 34), divers of the nobler sort at Berea (Acts xvii: 11),

and divers of "Cæsar's household" (Phil. iv: 22), came in, and had all their calling 325
by, and from Him.

As likewise the great Lord Treasurer by St. Philip (Acts viii: 27); and "the elect
lady" (2 John i), by St. John. Those all were of this troop here; under this star all of
them, *stella magnatum*. To conclude from our Saviour Christ's own mouth: as there
is in Heaven room for poor Lazarus, so that room was in the bosom of one that was 330
rich, that is of Abraham, a great man, yea a great prince in his time.

1. *Stella gentium*; 2. *Stella peccatorum de gentibus*; 3. *Stella magnatum*. But yet
all this while we have not touched *Stella magorum*; not yet dealt with *magi*, the very
word of the text, and the chief person they represent. For beside that they were great
states, they were also great learned men; and being both, they are styled rather by 335
the name of their skill and learning than by that of their greatness, to point us to the
quality in them we are principally to regard.

You shall not need startle when you hear the word *magi*, as if they were such as
Simon Magus was. Of later times it sounds not well this name; of old it was a name
of great honour, as was the name of *Tyrannus* and *Sophistes*, all in the like case. Evil 340
and unworthy men took them up after, and so they lost their first reputation. But
originally *Magus* was a title of high knowledge.

I add of heathen knowledge, and comprehend in it this very knowledge, that they
were well seen in the course of Heaven, in the stars and bodies celestial. Their *vidimus
stellam* shews as much. "The stars God hath given for signs" (Gen. i: 14), saith the 345
Book of Genesis, even the ordinary. And if them, the extraordinary such as this much
more. For signs they are, open the signature who can.

This learning of theirs made them never the farther from Christ we see, it did
them no hurt in their coming to Christ. No more than it did Moses, that "he was
well learned in all the wisdom of the Egyptians" (Acts vii: 22), saith St. Stephen. Nor 350
no more than it did Solomon, that "he passed all the children of the East in their
own learning" (1 Kings iv: 30). No more than it did Daniel, that "he was brought
up and well seen in the cunning of the Chaldeans" (Dan. i: 4). No more these, than
the gold and spoils of Egypt did the Tabernacle hurt, that was hung all over with
them.   355

They that are seen in these learnings of Egypt, of Chaldea, of the East, are not
thereby barred at all. This is their star, their guide; a guide apt and proper for them
that knew the stars, for them that were learned. Christ applieth Himself to all, disposes all things; what every one is given to, even by that Christ calleth them. St.
Peter, Andrew, James, and John, fishermen, by a draught of fish. These that were 360
studious in the stars, by a star for the purpose.

And note that the apparition to the shepherds was no sooner over, but this star
appeared presently, if not the very same hour; that is, both at once. In like manner
Christ at first, to shew the glory of His greatness, took and employed fishermen, such
as had no bringing up in schools. But it was not long after but learned men came in 365
apace; learned men of all sorts; Zenas in law (Tit. iii: 13), Luke in physic (2 Tim. iv:
11), Apollos with his eloquence (Acts xviii: 24), Dionysius with his philosophy (Acts
xvii: 34), St. Paul with his *polla gramata*, "much learning," which he had at Tarsus,
as famous a University for Asia as Athens was for Greece. Which learning, for all
Festus' fancy, "turned not his brains" (Acts xxvi: 24), nor did them any hurt at all. 370

There is no star or beam of it; there is no truth at all in human learning or philosophy that thwarteth any truth in Divinity, but sorteth well with it and serveth it, and all to honour Him Who saith of Himself *Ego sum Veritas*, "I am the Truth" (John xiv: 6). None that will hinder this *venerunt*, keep back any wise man, or make
375   him less fit for coming to Christ.

So you see your calling, all four. 1. Gentiles may come; 2. Sinners of the Gentiles may come, yea though they be *peccatorum primi*, "of the primer sort"; 3. Men of place. 4. Men of gifts, learned and wise may come. *In magis insunt omnes hi*, all are in *venerunt magi*. The star goes before them, guides them all to Christ.
380   It remaineth that what we may do we will do; that is, "come." For farther than *venerunt* we are not like to come at this time. And though we go no farther it skills not, so we do but that – "come"; even that will serve. For it is all in all. We shall go in the company of wise men, that is once. And if the shepherds were too homely to sort with, these are company for the best; they were company for Cyrus and Darius,
385   and all the great Monarchs of Persia.

Ecce venerunt it is in the text; and indeed, not only the persons, *ecce magi*, but their very coming deserved an *ecce*. It is an *ecce venerunt*, theirs indeed, if we weigh it well whence they came, and whither. Whence? from the East, their own country. Whither? to Jerusalem, that was to them a strange land: that was somewhat. They
390   came a long journey, no less than twelve days together. They came an uneasy journey, for their way lay through Arabia Petræa, and the craggy rocks of it. And they came a dangerous journey, through Arabia Deserta too, and the black "tents of Kedar" (Ps. cxx: 5) there, then famous for their robberies, and even to this day. And they came now, at the worst season of the year. And all but to do worship at Christ's
395   birth. So great account they made; so highly did they esteem their being at it, as they took all this great travel, and came all this long journey, and came it at this time. Stayed not their coming till the opening of the year, till they might have better weather and way, and have longer days, and so more seasonable and fit to travel in. So desirous were they to come with the first, and to be there as soon as possibly they
400   might; broke through all these difficulties, *Et ecce venerunt*, "And behold, come they did."

And we, what excuse shall we have if we come not? If so short and so easy a way we come not, as from our chambers hither, not to be called away indeed? Shall not our *non venerunt* have an *ecce*, "Behold, it was stepping but over the threshold, and
405   yet they came not"?

And these were wise men, and never a whit the less wise for so coming; nay never so truly wise in any thing they did, as in so coming. The Holy Ghost recordeth them for wise, *in capite libri*, "even in the beginning of the New Testament." Of Christ, when He came into the world, that is, when He was born, the Psalm
410   saith, "In the beginning of the Book it was writ of Him, He said," *Ecce venio*, "Lo I come" (Ps. xl: 7): of these in the same words, when they came to meet Him so born, it is said here in the beginning of the Gospel, *Ecce venerunt*, "Behold they came."

And we, if we believe this, that this was their wisdom, if they and we be wise by
415   one Spirit, by the same principles, we will follow the same star, tread the same way, and so come at last whither they are happily gone before us.

Nay, not only that "come," but this withal; to think and set down with ourselves, that to come to Christ is one of the wisest parts that ever these wise men did, or we or any else can do in all our lives.

And how shall we that do? I know not any more proper way left us, than to come 420 to that which Himself by express order hath left us, as the most special remembrance of Himself to be come to. When He came into the world, saith the Psalm, that is at His birth now, He said, *Ecce venio*, "Lo, I come." What then? "Sacrifice and burnt-offerings Thou wouldst not have, but a body hast Thou ordained Me" (Ps. xl: 6). Mark, saith the Apostle, "He takes away the first to establish the second" (Heb. x: 425 9), that is, to establish His body, and the coming to it. By the "offering," breaking and partaking of which "body, we are all sanctified" (Heb. x: 10), so many as shall come to it. For "given it is, for the taking away of our sins" (Matt. xxvi: 28). Nothing is more fit than at the time His body was ordained Him, and that is to-day, to come to the body so ordained. 430

And in the old Ritual of the Church we find that on the cover of the canister, wherein was the sacrament of His body, there was a star engraven, to shew us that now the star leads us thither, to His body there.

And what shall I say now, but according as St. John saith, and the star, and the wise men say, "Come" (Rev. xxii: 17). And He, Whose the star is, and to Whom the 435 wise men came, saith "Come." And let them that are disposed, "Come." And let whosoever will, take of the "Bread of Life, which came down from Heaven" (John vi: 35, 41) this day into Bethlehem, the house of bread. Of which Bread the Church is this day the house, the true Bethlehem, and all the Bethlehem we have now left to come to for the Bread of life, – of that life which we hope for in Heaven. And 440 this our nearest coming that here we can come, till we shall by another *venite* come, unto Him in His Heavenly Kingdom. To which He grant we may come, that this day came to us in earth that we thereby might come to Him and remain with Him for ever, "Jesus Christ the Righteous."

Questions for Study

The sermon, though a little ponderous, is easy to understand, and you may find the following study questions help you interact with it.

1 Does the number of Greek and Latin words or phrases used in this sermon seem excessive to you? What purpose do you think they serve?

2 Note the way (p. 388) in which Andrewes interacts with the first of his two chosen verses, identifying the place, time, persons, and occasion of the event in question. Why does he do this? And what use does he make of this structure in the material which follows this section?

3 Look at the final paragraph of the sermon, which focuses on the single word "come." What point is Andrewes making in this final paragraph? And how does it relate to the sermon as a whole?

CHAPTER 48

William Shakespeare (1564–1616)

William Shakespeare was born in April 1564, the oldest son of John Shakespeare, who was a prominent trader and landowner in Stratford-upon-Avon. John Shakespeare had married Mary Arden, the daughter of an affluent landowner of Wilmcote. John Shakespeare filled many significant municipal offices in Stratford, including that of burgess, which gave him the privilege of educating his children without charge at the King's New School, Stratford. He was elected to the position of Alderman in 1565, and to that of Bailiff (equivalent to mayor) in 1568.

Although the documentary evidence is far from satisfactory, it is generally agreed that William Shakespeare married Ann Hathaway in November 1582, and that their daughter, Susanna, was born six months later. Two other children were born, the twins Hamnet and Judith, in February 1585. Sometime after this he joined a troupe of players and made his way to London. As a member of London's leading theater company, the Lord Chamberlain's Company, he wrote plays and eventually became a shareholder in the Globe theater. He was so successful that in 1596 he successfully renewed his father's application for a grant of arms, and the following year he bought and restored New Place, the second-largest house in Stratford. He also bought other real estate in Stratford and London.

Shakespeare appears to have retired from London life at some point around 1610. He died on April 23, 1616, disposing of his large estate in his will. Tradition has it that he died after an evening's drinking with some of his theater friends. He was buried in the Church of the Holy Trinity. His gravestone bears the words:

> Good frend for Jesus sake forebeare,
> to digg the dust encloased heare,
> Bleste be the man thatt spares thes stones,
> And curst be he that moves my bones.

There has been substantial discussion as to whether this William Shakespeare of Stratford-upon-Avon really was the author of the plays and poems that bear his name; other candidates have been suggested by revisionist historians. Nevertheless, the evidence for Shakespeare's authorship is generally agreed to be more than sufficient for most purposes. While it is true, for example, that no single document is known which states categorically that William Shakespeare of Stratford-upon-Avon wrote *Hamlet*, it must be pointed out that no such document exists for any other playwright of the time either. Plays were not considered "literature" until about 1600, and it was normal practice to omit the name of the author.

William Shakespeare (1564–1616)

Basic description
Leading English Renaissance playwright.

Major works
Dramatic histories, tragedies and comedies, including *Julius Caesar*, *King Lear*, *Twelfth Night*, *Macbeth*, and *The Winter's Tale*.

Major studies
E. Beatrice Batson (ed.), *Shakespeare and the Christian Tradition*. Lewiston, NY; Edwin Mellen Press, 1994.

Jonathan Dollimore, *Radical Tragedy: Religion, Ideology and Power in the Drama of Shakespeare and His Contemporaries*. Durham, NC: Duke University Press, 1993.

Robert W. Mendl, *Revelation in Shakespeare: A Study of the Supernatural, Religious and Spiritual Elements in His Art*. London: Calder, 1964.

For the purposes of this anthology, there is a much greater difficulty to be faced – namely, whether Shakespeare can be considered to have written anything that is specifically Christian. It should be no surprise that Shakespeare's plays show echoes of the biblical and liturgical language of his day; as we have already noted, the English language was deeply shaped by the insistence of English reformers such as Thomas Cranmer that both the public worship of the church and the public reading of the Bible should be in the English language, in order that the people should not be denied access to the spiritual riches which the reading of the Bible conveyed. Reflections of the public language of the Christian church within Shakespeare's texts is therefore to be expected as a matter of course, and cannot really be taken to imply any specific interest in matters of religion.

This is not, of course, to suggest that Shakespeare's plays lack religious significance. Many of his historical works offer comment on the public role of the church in English history. In *Richard II*, we find reflections on the divine rights of kings and the legitimacy of the Crusades; in *Henry V*, we encounter ecclesiastical anxiety over the threat posed to the temporal power and possessions of the church by recent political developments. Yet other works offer reflections on topics which are clearly "religious" in nature, even if Shakespeare's presentation of these matters does not appear to take a specifically Christian form. For example, in *Richard III*, we find reflections on how collective guilt may be expiated. *King Lear* offers an engagement with the issue of forgiveness, with portions of the text apparently rich in Christian allusion. For example, consider Cordelia's words to her father:

> And wast thou fain, poor father
> To hovel thee with swine and rogues forlorn
> In short and musty straw?

The allusions to the narrative of the Prodigal Son, who returned to his father after tending swine in a distant land, are unmistakable.

It is in Shakespeare's sonnets that we find what are perhaps the clearest religious statements of a recognizably Christian form. In what follows, we shall consider one such sonnet, and explore its structure and contents.

Text: Sonnet 146

It is not entirely clear over what period Shakespeare's "sonnets" were composed. What is certain is that the sonnets were published in a Quarto edition in 1609 by Thomas Thorpe; the period of their composition remains the subject of debate although there are reasons for supposing that they date from between 1592 and 1598.

With one exception, the 154 sonnets take the form of poems of 14 lines, virtually exclusively written in iambic pentameter. The sonnets use a highly distinctive rhyme scheme, which has come to be known as the "Shakespearean Sonnet": Abab; cdcd; efef; gg.

The sonnets are composed of an octet and sestet and typically – as in the text to be considered here – progress through three quatrains to a concluding couplet. The sonnet in question is one of those addressed to "the Dark Lady," whose identity has been the subject of intense speculation. Among those suggested as possibilities we may note Mary Fitton, Emilia Lanier, Lucy Morgan, and Penelope Rich.

> Poor soul, the centre of my sinful earth,
> Fooled by these rebel powers that thee array;
> Why dost thou pine within and suffer dearth,
> Painting thy outward walls so costly gay?
>
> Why so large cost, having so short a lease,
> Dost thou upon thy fading mansion spend?
> Shall worms, inheritors of this excess,
> Eat up thy charge? is this thy body's end?
>
> Then soul, live thou upon thy servant's loss,
> And let that pine to aggravate thy store;
> Buy terms divine in selling hours of dross;
> Within be fed, without be rich no more:
>
> So shalt thou feed on Death, that feeds on men,
> And Death once dead, there's no more dying then.

Questions for Study

1   What is the point being made in this sonnet concerning human mortality?
2   This sonnet is part of a group which are thought to be addressed to "the Dark Lady."
    Does this information have any bearing on the interpretation of the sonnet?
3   What is the meaning of the concluding couplet? How do the ideas expressed here
    compare, for example, with John Donne's sonnet "Death be not proud" (see
    pp. 416–17)?

CHAPTER 49

John Donne (1571/2–1631)

John Donne is widely regarded as one of the most important English poets and preachers of the early seventeenth century, and has established a reputation as the leading "metaphysical" poet. He was born in London into an old Roman Catholic family at a time when anti-Catholic feeling in England was near its height, and Catholics were subject to constant harassment. At the age of 11 he entered Hart Hall, Oxford University, where he studied for three years. It is thought that he may have spent the next three years at the University of Cambridge, although there is no documentary evidence of this. His initial inclination appears to have been toward a legal, or perhaps a diplomatic, career. He entered Thavies Inn in 1591, and Lincoln's Inn the following year.

Although he was a member of a distinguished Roman Catholic family (his maternal great-grandfather being Sir Thomas More), Donne appears to have gone through a period of uncertainty concerning his religious allegiance. There is little doubt that this was catalyzed by the death in prison of his younger brother Henry, after being arrested for harboring a priest. In 1596, Donne joined the naval expedition that Robert Devereux, Second Earl of Essex, was leading against the Spanish. On his return to England in 1598, Donne was appointed private secretary to Sir Thomas Egerton, Keeper of the Great Seal. He was a member of parliament in the final sessions under Queen Elizabeth, and cultivated those who wielded power and had patronage to dispense. But in 1601, he secretly married Lady Egerton's niece, seventeen-year-old Anne More, and thus caused some difficulty for himself and his hopes for advancement. Sir George More had Donne imprisoned and dismissed from his post, and for the next dozen years the poet had to take various temporary positions in order to support his growing family. The poet later summed up the experience more playfully than might be imagined possible: "John Donne, Anne Donne, Undone." Anne's cousin offered the couple refuge in Pyrford, Surrey.

During the next few years Donne made a somewhat erratic living as a lawyer, serving chiefly as counsel for Thomas Morton, an anti-Roman Catholic pamphleteer. It is possible that Donne may have collaborated with Morton in writing pamphlets that appeared under Morton's name between 1604 and 1607. Donne's principal literary accomplishments during this period were the *Divine Poems* (1607) and the prose work *Biathanatos*

(posthumously published 1644). In 1608 a reconciliation of sorts was effected between Donne and his father-in-law, and his wife received a much-needed dowry. This allowed Donne a degree of financial stability.

As Donne approached the age of forty, he published two anti-Catholic polemics which are widely seen as representing a public declaration of his earlier private renunciation of the Roman Catholic faith. Though Donne had once refused to take Anglican orders, James I declared that Donne could have no preferment or employment from him except in the church. Donne was accordingly ordained into the Church of England in 1615, and became Dean of St. Paul's Cathedral, London, in 1621. He would hold this position until his death.

Donne's first book of poems – Satires – was written during this period of residence in London, and is considered one of his most important literary efforts. Although not published for some time, the volume had a wide readership through private circulation of the manuscript. This was followed by other volumes of secular and religious verse, which attracted an increasingly positive response from their readers. Alongside his poetic works, Donne preached extensively, with more than 150 of his sermons surviving.

John Donne (1571/2–1631)

Basic description
Major English writer of both secular and religious prose and poetry.

Major works
An Anatomy of the World (1611); Of the Progress of the Soul (1612); Holy Sonnets (1618); Devotions upon Emergent Occasions (1624).

Editions of works
The Complete Poetry and Selected Prose of John Donne. New York: Random House, 1952.

Major studies
John Carey, John Donne: Life, Mind and Art, 2nd edn. London: Faber, 1990.

Winfried Schleiner, The Imagery of John Donne's Sermons. Providence, RI: Brown University Press, 1970.

Text: Sermon 1

The sermon selected for discussion was preached at St. Paul's Cathedral, London, on January 29, 1626. London had just suffered a ruinous epidemic of the plague, which had left countless of its leading citizens dead. Morale was low. Many of the preachers of the day declared that the plague was God's judgment against the sins of the city, and took great delight in pointing out what those sins were; they took a certain morbid delight in dwelling on the suffering of those who committed them. While Donne was by no means unsympathetic to the idea that the plague could be seen, in part, as God's judgment upon a wayward people, the sermon in question introduces many additional themes. Widely regarded as one of Donne's most important prose works, the sermon can be regarded as a celebration of the theme of victory over death, in which the theme of joy takes precedence over that of judgment.

The sermon has been printed in full, without any abbreviations or omissions, in order to help convey the impression of the sermon as a work of Jacobean pulpit theater, in which verbal imagery allows elements of the dramatic to be incorporated into the discourse. The very length of the sermon is itself of importance, as it indicates the extent to which such sermons were seen as major public statements and reference points by those attending divine service at the cathedral. Before engaging with the text, it is necessary to point out that the "St. Paul's Cathedral" in which this sermon was preached no longer exists. It was destroyed in the Great Fire of London (1666), having in any case fallen into ruin during the period of the Puritan Commonwealth, when it was used as a barracks for cavalry. The monument to Donne which can be seen in the present building, designed by Sir Christopher Wren, is original; it survived the Great Fire, and was incorporated into the new building.

In reading this sermon, it is essential that its context is taken into account. London was reeling from the latest outbreak of the plague, which had caused countless deaths. This helps us understand his reference to the mood of the moment, which he describes in terms of "an extraordinary sadnesse, a predominant melancholy, a faintnesse of heart, a chearlessnesse, a joylessnesse of spirit." The recent experience of London is compared to both the plagues of Egypt and the final judgments of the book of Revelation, in which the seven angels pour out their vials upon the earth.

Yet the dominant theme of the sermon is hope and joy. It is only in God that such joy and safety are to be found – yet they are there to be found in abundance. The text upon which Donne preached (Psalm 63:7) sets the tone for the entire discourse: there is safety only in the shadow of God. The sermon takes full account of the suffering of the world, yet offers hope in the face of its pain and bewilderment at the apparent inexplicability of that pain. The final long sentence of the sermon may be seen as a superb affirmation of the reality of the hope of the resurrection, paralleling in thought – though not style – the divine meditation "Death be not proud," to be discussed presently.

Number 1

The second of my Prebend Sermons upon my five Psalmes.
Preached at S. Pauls, Ianuary 29. 1625

PSAL. 63:7. *BECAUSE THOU HAST BEEN MY HELPE, THEREFORE IN THE SHADOW OF THY WINGS WILL I REJOYCE.*

The psalmes are the Manna of the Church. As Manna tasted to every man like that that he liked best, so doe the Psalmes minister Instruction, and satisfaction, to every man, in every emergency and occasion. *David* was not onely a cleare Prophet of Christ himselfe, but a Prophet of every particular Christian; He foretels what I, what 5 any shall doe, and suffer, and say. And as the whole booke of Psalmes is *Oleum effusum,* (as the Spouse speaks of the name of Christ) an Oyntment powred out upon all sorts of sores, A Searcloth that souples all bruises, A Balme that searches all wounds; so are there some certaine Psalmes, that are Imperiall Psalmes, that command over all affections, and spread themselves over all occasions, Catholique, universall Psalmes, that apply themselves to all necessities. This is one of those; for, 10 of those Constitutions which are called Apostolicall, one is, That the Church should meet every day, to sing this Psalme. And accordingly, S. *Chrysostome* testifies, That it was decreed, and ordained by the Primitive Fathers, that no day should passe without the publique singing of this Psalme. Under both these obligations, (those ancient Constitutions, called the Apostles, and those ancient Decrees made by the primitive 15 Fathers) belongs to me, who have my part in the service of Gods Church, the espe- ciall meditation, and recommendation of this Psalme. And under a third obligation too, That it is one of those five psalmes, the daily rehearsing whereof, is injoyned to me, by the Constitutions of this Church, as five other are to every other person of our body. As the whole booke is Manna, so these five Psalmes are my Gomer, which 20 I am to fill and empty every day of this Manna.

Now as the spirit and soule of the whole booke of Psalmes is contracted into this psalme, so is the spirit and soule of this whole psalme contracted into this verse. The key of the psalme, (as S. *Hierome* calls the Titles of the psalmes) tells us, that *David* uttered this psalme, *when he was in the wildernesse of Iudah*; There we see the present 25 occasion that moved him; And we see what was passed between God and him before, in the first clause of our Text; (*Because thou hast been my helpe*) And then we see what was to come, by the rest, (*Therefore in the shadow of thy wings will I rejoyce.*) So that we have here the whole compasse of Time, Past, Present, and Future; and these three parts of Time, shall be at this time, the three parts of this Exercise; first, what *Davids* 30 distresse put him upon for the present; and that lyes in the Context; secondly, how *David* built his assurance upon that which was past; (*Because thou hast been my help*) And thirdly, what he established to himselfe for the future, (*Therefore in the shadow of thy wings will I rejoyce.*) First, His distresse in the Wildernesse, his present estate carried him upon the memory of that which God had done for him before, And the 35 Remembrance of that carried him upon that, of which he assured himselfe after. Fixe upon God any where, and you shall finde him a Circle; He is with you now, when you fix upon him; He was with you before, for he brought you to this fixation; and he will be with you hereafter, for *He is yesterday, and to day, and the same for ever* [Heb. 13:8]. 40

For *Davids* present condition, who was now in a banishment, in a persecution in the Wildernesse of Judah, (which is our first part) we shall onely insist upon that, (which is indeed spread over all the psalme to the Text, and ratified in the Text) That in all those temporall calamities *David* was onely sensible of his spirituall losse; It grieved him not that he was kept from *Sauls* Court, but that he was kept from Gods 45 Church. For when he sayes, by way of lamentation, *That he was in a dry and thirsty land, where no water was*, he expresses what penury, what barrennesse, what drought and what thirst he meant; *To see thy power, and thy glory, so as I have seene thee in the Sanctuary.* For there, *my soule shall be satisfied as with marrow, and with fatnesse*, and there, *my mouth shall praise thee with joyfull lips.* And in some few considerations 50 conducing to this, That spirituall losses are incomparably heavier then temporall, and that therefore, The Restitution to our spirituall happinesse, or the continuation of it, is rather to be made the subject of our prayers to God, in all pressures and distresses, then of temporall, we shall determine that first part. And for the particular branches

55 of both the other parts, (The Remembring of Gods benefits past, And the building
of an assurance for the future, upon that Remembrance) it may be fitter to open
them to you, anon when we come to handle them, then now. Proceed we now to
our first part, The comparing of temporall and spirituall afflictions.

In the way of this Comparison, falls first the Consideration of the universality of
60 afflictions in generall, and the inevitablenesse thereof. It is a blessed Metaphore, that
the Holy Ghost hath put into the mouth of the Apostle, *Pondus Gloriæ*, That our
afflictions are but *light*, because there is an *exceeding*, and an *eternall waight of glory*
attending them [2 Cor. 4:17]. If it were not for that exceeding waight of glory, no
other waight in this world could turne the scale, or waigh downe those infinite
65 waights of afflictions that oppresse us here. There is not onely *Pestis valde gravis*, (*the
pestilence grows heavy upon the Land*) [Exod. 9:3] but there is *Musca valde gravis*,
God calls in but the fly, to vexe Egypt, and even the fly is a heavy burden unto them
[Exodus 8:24]. It is not onely *Iob* that complains [Job 7:20], *That he was a burden
to himselfe*, but even *Absaloms* haire was a burden to him [2 Sam. 14:26], till it was
70 polled. It is not onely *Ieremy* that complains, *Aggravavit compedes*, That God had
made their fetters and their chains heavy to them [Lament. 3:7], but the workmen
in harvest complaine, That God had made a faire day heavy unto them, (*We have
borne the heat, and the burden of the day* [Matt. 20:12]) *Sand is heavy*, sayes Solomon
[Prov. 27:3]; And how many suffer so? under a sand-hill of crosses, daily, hourely
75 afflictions, that are heavy by their number, if not by their single waight? And *a stone
is heavy*, (sayes he in the same place) And how many suffer so? How many, without
any former preparatory crosse, or comminatory, or commonitory crosse, even in the
midst of prosperity, and security, fall under some one stone, some grindstone, some
mil-stone, some one insupportable crosse that ruines them? But then, (sayes *Solomon*
80 there) *A fooles anger is heavier then both*; And how many children, and servants, and
wives suffer under the anger, and morosity, and peevishnesse, and jealousie of foolish
Masters, and Parents, and Husbands, though they must not say so? *David* and
Solomon have cryed out, That all this world is *vanity*, and *levity*; And (God knowes)
all is waight, and burden, and heavinesse, and oppression; And if there were not a
85 waight of future glory to counterpoyse it, we should all sinke into nothing.

I aske not *Mary Magdalen*, whether lightnesse were not a burden; (for sin is
certainly, sensibly a burden) But I aske *Susanna* whether even chast beauty were not
a burden to her; And I aske *Ioseph* whether personall comelinesse were not a burden
to him. I aske not *Dives*, who perished in the next world, the question; but I aske
90 them who are made examples of *Solomons* Rule, of that *sore evill*, (as he calls it) *Riches
kept to the owners thereof for their hurt* [Eccles. 5:13], whether Riches be not a burden.

All our life is a continuall burden, yet we must not groane; A continuall squeas-
ing, yet we must not pant; And as in the tendernesse of our childhood, we suffer,
and yet are whipt if we cry, so we are complained of, if we complaine, and made
95 delinquents if we call the times ill. And that which addes waight to waight, and mul-
tiplies the sadnesse of this consideration, is this, That still the best men have had most
laid upon them. As soone as I heare God say, that he hath found *an upright man,
that feares God, and eschews evill* [Job 1:1], in the next lines I finde a Commission to
Satan, to bring in Sabeans and Chaldeans upon his cattell, and servants, and fire and
100 tempest upon his children, and loathsome diseases upon himselfe. As soone as I heare

God say, That he hath found *a man according to his own heart* [1 Sam. 13:14], I see his sonnes ravish his daughters, and then murder one another, and then rebell against the Father, and put him into straites for his life. As soone as I heare God testifie of Christ at his Baptisme, *This is my beloved Sonne in whom I am well pleased* [Matt. 3:17], I finde that Sonne of his *led up by the Spirit, to be tempted of the Devill* [Matt. 105 4:1]. And after I heare God ratifie the same testimony againe, at his Transfiguration, (*This is my beloved Sonne, in whom I am well pleased* [Matt. 17:5]) I finde that beloved Sonne of his, deserted, abandoned, and given over to Scribes, and Pharisees, and Publicans, and Herodians, and Priests, and Souldiers, and people, and Judges, and witnesses, and executioners, and he that was called the beloved Sonne of God, 110 and made partaker of the glory of heaven, in this world, in his Transfiguration, is made now the Sewer of all the corruption, of all the sinnes of this world, as no Sonne of God, but a meere man, as no man, but a contemptible worme. As though the greatest weaknesse in this world, were man, and the greatest fault in man were to be good, man is more miserable then other creatures, and good men more miserable 115 then any other men.

But then there is *Pondus Gloriæ, An exceeding waight of eternall glory*, and that turnes the scale; for as it makes all worldly prosperity as dung, so it makes all worldly adversity as feathers. And so it had need; for in the scale against it, there are not onely put temporall afflictions, but spirituall too; And to these two kinds, we may 120 accommodate those words, *He that fals upon this stone*, (upon temporall afflictions) may be bruised, broken, *But he upon whom that stone falls*, (spirituall afflictions) *is in danger to be ground to powder* [Matt. 21:44]. And then, the great, and yet ordinary danger is, That these spirituall afflictions grow out of temporall; Murmuring, and diffidence in God, and obduration, out of worldly calamities; And so against nature, 125 the fruit is greater and heavier then the Tree, spirituall heavier then temporall afflictions.

They who write of Naturall story, propose that Plant for the greatest wonder in nature, which being no firmer then a bull-rush, or a reed, produces and beares for the fruit thereof no other but an intire, and very hard stone. That temporall afflic- 130 tion should produce spirituall stoninesse, and obduration, is unnaturall, yet ordinary. Therefore doth God propose it, as one of those greatest blessings, which he multi- plies upon his people, *I will take away your stony hearts, and give you hearts of flesh* [Ezek. 11:19; 36:26]; And, Lord let mee have a fleshly heart in any sense, rather then a stony heart. Wee finde mention amongst the observers of rarities in Nature, 135 of hairy hearts, hearts of men, that have beene overgrowne with haire; but of petri- fied hearts, hearts of men growne into stone, we read not; for this petrefaction of the heart, this stupefaction of a man, is the last blow of Gods hand upon the heart of man in this world. Those great afflictions [Rev. 16] which are powred out of the Vials of the seven Angels upon the world, are still accompanied with that heavy effect, 140 that that affliction hardned them. *They were scorched with heats and plagues*, by the fourth Angel, and it followes, *They blasphemed the name of God, and repented not, to give him glory* [Rev. 16:9]. Darknesse was induced upon them by the fift Angel, and it followes, *They blasphemed the God of heaven, and repented not of their deeds* [Rev. 16:11]. And from the seventh Angel there fell hailestones of the waight of talents, 145 (perchance foure pound waight) upon men; And yet these men had so much life left,

as to *blaspheme God*, out of that respect, which alone should have brought them to glorifie God, *Because the plague thereof was exceeding great* [Rev. 16:21]. And when a great plague brings them to blaspheme, how great shall that second plague be, that
150 comes upon them for blaspheming?

Let me wither and weare out mine age in a discomfortable, in an unwholesome, in a penurious prison, and so pay my debts with my bones, and recompence the wast-fulnesse of my youth, with the beggery of mine age; Let me wither in a spittle under sharpe, and foule, and infamous diseases, and so recompence the wantonnesse of my
155 youth, with that loathsomnesse in mine age; yet, if God with-draw not his spirituall blessings, his Grace, his Patience, If I can call my suffering his Doing, my passion his Action, All this that is temporall, is but a caterpiller got into one corner of my garden, but a mill-dew fallen upon one acre of my Corne; The body of all, the substance of all is safe, as long as the soule is safe. But when I shall trust to that, which wee call
160 a good spirit, and God shall deject, and empoverish, and evacuate that spirit, when I shall rely upon a morall constancy, and God shall shake, and enfeeble, and ener-vate, destroy and demolish that constancy; when I shall think to refresh my selfe in the serenity and sweet ayre of a good conscience, and God shall call up the damps and vapours of hell it selfe, and spread a cloud of diffidence, and an impenetrable
165 crust of desperation upon my conscience; when health shall flie from me, and I shall lay hold upon riches to succour me, and comfort me in my sicknesse, and riches shall flie from me, and I shall snatch after favour, and good opinion, to comfort me in my poverty; when even this good opinion shall leave me, and calumnies and misinfor-mations shall prevaile against me; when I shall need peace, because there is none but
170 thou, O Lord, that should stand for me, and then shall finde, that all the wounds that I have, come from thy hand, all the arrowes that stick in me, from thy quiver; when I shall see, that because I have given my selfe to my corrupt nature, thou hast changed thine; and because I am all evill towards thee, therefore thou hast given over being good towards me; When it comes to this height, that the fever is not in the
175 humors, but in the spirits, that mine enemy is not an imaginary enemy, fortune, nor a transitory enemy, malice in great persons, but a reall, and an irresistible, and an inexorable, and an everlasting enemy, The Lord of Hosts himselfe, The Almighty God himselfe, the Almighty God himselfe onely knowes the waight of this affliction, and except hee put in that *pondus gloriæ*, that exceeding waight of an eternall glory,
180 with his owne hand, into the other scale, we are waighed downe, we are swallowed up, irreparably, irrevocably, irrecoverably, irremediably.

This is the fearefull depth, this is spirituall misery, to be thus fallen from God. But was this *Davids* case? was he fallen thus farre, into a diffidence in God? No. But the danger, the precipice, the slippery sliding into that bottomlesse depth, is, to be
185 excluded from the meanes of comming to God, or staying with God; And this is that that *David* laments here, That by being banished, and driven into the wildernesse of Judah, hee had not accesse to the Sanctuary of the Lord, to sacrifice his part in the praise, and to receive his part in the prayers of the Congregation; for Angels passe not to ends, but by wayes and meanes, nor men to the glory of the triumphant
190 Church, but by participation of the Communion of the Militant. To this note *David* sets his Harpe, in many, many Psalms: Sometimes, that God had suffered his enemies to possesse his Tabernacle, (*Hee forsooke the Tabernacle of Shiloh, Hee delivered his*

strength into captivity, and his glory into the enemies hands [Ps. 78:60]) But most commonly he complaines, that God disabled him from comming to the Sanctuary. In which one thing he had summed up all his desires, all his prayers, (*One thing have I* 195 *desired of the Lord, that will I looke after; That I may dwell in the house of the Lord, all the dayes of my life, to behold the beauty of the Lord, and to enquire in his Temple* [Ps. 27:4]) His vehement desire of this, he expresses againe, (*My soule thirsteth for God, for the living God; when shall I come and appeare before God?* [Ps. 42:2]) He expresses a holy jealousie, a religious envy, even to the sparrows and swallows, (yea, 200 *the sparrow hath found a house, and the swallow a nest for her selfe, and where she may lay her yong, Even thine Altars, O Lord of Hosts, my King and my God* [Ps. 84:3].) Thou art my King, and my God, and yet excludest me from that, which thou affordest to sparrows, *And are not we of more value then many sparrows?* [Lk. 12:7].

And as though *David* felt some false ease, some half-tentation, some whispering 205 that way, That God is *in the wildernesse of Iudah*, in every place, as well as in his *Sanctuary*, there is in the Originall in that place, a patheticall, a vehement, a broken expressing expressed, *O thine Altars;* It is true, (sayes *David*) thou art here in the wildernesse, and I may see thee here, and serve thee here, but, *O thine Altars, O Lord of hosts, my King and my God* [Ps. 84:3]. When *David* could not come in person 210 to that place, yet he bent towards the Temple, (*In thy feare will I worship towards thy holy Temple* [Ps. 5:7].) Which was also *Daniels* devotion; when he prayed, *his Chamber windowes were open towards Ierusalem* [Dan. 6:10]; And so is *Hezekias* turning to the wall to weepe [Isa. 38:2], and to pray in his sick bed, understood to be to that purpose, to conforme, and compose himselfe towards the Temple. In the 215 place consecrated for that use, God by *Moses* fixes the service [Deut. 31:11], and fixes the Reward; And towards that place, (when they could not come to it) doth *Solomon* direct their devotion in the Consecration of the Temple, (*when they are in the warres, when they are in Captivity, and pray towards this house, doe thou heare them* [1 King. 8:44].) For, as in private prayer, when (according to Christs command) we are shut 220 in our chamber, there is exercised *Modestia fidei*, The modesty and bashfulnesse of our faith, not pressing upon God in his house: so in the publique prayers of the Congregation, there is exercised the fervor, and holy courage of our faith, for *Agmine facto obsidemus Deum*, It is a Mustering of our forces, and a besieging of God. Therefore does *David* so much magnifie their blessednesse, that are in this house of God; 225 (*Blessed are they that dwell in thy house, for they will be still praising thee* [Ps. 84:4]) Those that looke towards it, may praise thee sometimes, but those men who dwell in the Church, and whose whole service lyes in the Church, have certainly an advantage of all other men (who are necessarily withdrawne by worldly businesses) in making themselves acceptable to almighty God, if they doe their duties, and observe 230 their Church-services aright.

Man being therefore thus subject naturally to manifold calamities, and spirituall calamities being incomparably heavier then temporall, and the greatest danger of falling into such spirituall calamities being in our absence from Gods Church, where onely the outward meanes of happinesse are ministred unto us, certainly there is 235 much tendernesse and deliberation to be used, before the Church doores be shut against any man. If I would not direct a prayer to God, to excommunicate any man from the Triumphant Church, (which were to damne him) I would not oyle the key,

I would not make the way too slippery for excommunications in the Militant Church;
240 For, that is to endanger him. I know how distastfull a sin to God, contumacy, and
contempt, and disobedience to Order and Authority is; And I know, (and all men,
that choose not ignorance, may know) that our Excommunications (though calum-
niators impute them to small things, because, many times, the first complaint is of
some small matter) never issue but upon contumacies, contempts, disobediences to
245 the Church. But they are reall contumacies, not interpretative, apparant contumacies, not presumptive, that excommunicate a man in Heaven; And much circum-
spection is required, and (I am far from doubting it) exercised in those cases upon
earth; for, though every Excommunication upon earth be not sealed in Heaven,
though it damne not the man, yet it dammes up that mans way, by shutting him out
250 of that Church, through which he must goe to the other; which being so great a
danger, let every man take heed of Excommunicating himselfe. The imperswasible
Recusant does so; The negligent Libertin does so; The fantastique Separatist does
so; The halfe-present man, he, whose body is here, and minde away, does so; And
he, whose body is but halfe here, his limbes are here upon a cushion, but his eyes,
255 his eares are not here, does so: All these are selfe-Excommunicators, and keepe themselves from hence. Onely he enjoyes that blessing, the want whereof *David* deplores,
that is here intirely, and is glad he is here, and glad to finde this kinde of service here,
that he does, and wishes no other.

And so we have done with our first Part, *Davids* aspect, his present condition, and
260 his danger of falling into spirituall miseries, because his persecution, and banishment
amounted to an Excommunication, to an excluding of him from the service of God,
in the Church. And we passe, in our Order proposed at first, to the second, his retrospect, the Consideration, what God had done for him before, *Because thou hast
beene my helpe.*

265 Through this second part, we shall passe by these three steps. First, That it behoves
us, in all our purposes, and actions, to propose to our selves a copy to write by, a
patterne to worke by, a rule, or an example to proceed by, Because it hath beene thus
heretofore, sayes *David*, I will resolve upon this course for the future. And secondly,
That the copy, the patterne, the precedent which we are to propose to our selves, is,
270 The observation of Gods former wayes and proceedings upon us, Because God hath
already gone this way, this way I will awaite his going still. And then, thirdly and
lastly, in this second part, The way that God had formerly gone with *David*, which
was, That he had been his helpe, (*Because thou hast beene my helpe.*)

First then, from the meanest artificer, through the wisest Philosopher, to God him-
275 selfe, all that is well done, or wisely undertaken, is undertaken and done according
to pre-conceptions, fore-imaginations, designes, and patterns proposed to our selves
beforehand. A Carpenter builds not a house, but that he first sets up a frame in his
owne minde, what kinde of house he will build. The little great Philosopher *Epictetus*, would undertake no action, but he would first propose to himselfe, what *Socrates*,
280 or *Plato*, what a wise man would do in that case, and according to that, he would
proceed. Of God himselfe, it is safely resolved in the Schoole, that he never did
any thing in any part of time, of which he had not an eternall pre-conception, an
eternall Idea, in himselfe before. Of which Ideaes, that is, pre-conceptions, pre-
determinations in God, S. *Augustine* pronounces, *Tanta vis in Ideis constituitur,*

There is so much truth, and so much power in these Ideaes, as that without acknowl- 285
edging them, no man can acknowledge God, for he does not allow God Counsaile,
and Wisdome, and deliberation in his Actions, but sets God on worke, before he
have thought what he will doe. And therefore he, and others of the Fathers read that
place, (which we read otherwise) *Quod factum est, in ipso vita erat*; that is, in all their
Expositions, whatsoever is made, in time, was alive in God, before it was made, that 290
is, in that eternall Idea, and patterne which was in him. So also doe divers of those
Fathers read those words to the Hebrews, (which we read, *The things that are seene,
are not made of things that doe appeare* [Heb. 11:3]) *Ex invisibilibus visibilia facta
sunt, Things formerly invisible, were made visible*; that is, we see them not till now, till
they are made, but they had an invisible being, in that Idea, in that pre-notion, in 295
that purpose of God before, for ever before. Of all things in Heaven, and earth, but
of himselfe, God had an Idea, a patterne in himselfe, before he made it.

And therefore let him be our patterne for that, to worke after patternes; To
propose to our selves Rules and Examples for all our actions; and the more, the more
immediately, the more directly our actions concerne the service of God. If I aske 300
God, by what Idea he made me, God produces his *Faciamus hominem ad Imaginem
nostram* [Gen. 1:26], That there was a concurrence of the whole Trinity, to make
me in *Adam*, according to that Image which they were, and according to that Idea,
which they had pre-determined. If I pretend to serve God, and he aske me for my
Idea, How I meane to serve him, shall I bee able to produce none? If he aske me an 305
Idea of my Religion, and my opinions, shall I not be able to say, It is that which thy
word, and thy Catholique Church hath imprinted in me? If he aske me an Idea of
my prayers, shall I not be able to say, It is that which my particular necessities, that
which the forme prescribed by thy Son, that which the care, and piety of the Church,
in conceiving fit prayers, hath imprinted in me? If he aske me an Idea of my Sermons, 310
shall I not be able to say, It is that which the Analogy of Faith, the edification of the
Congregation, the zeale of thy worke, the meditations of my heart have imprinted
in me? But if I come to pray or to preach without this kind of Idea, if I come to
extemporall prayer, and extemporall preaching, I shall come to an extemporall faith,
and extemporall religion; and then I must looke for an extemporall Heaven, a Heaven 315
to be made for me; for to that Heaven which belongs to the Catholique Church, I
shall never come, except I go by the way of the Catholique Church, by former Idea's,
former examples, former patterns, To beleeve according to ancient beliefes, to pray
according to ancient formes, to preach according to former meditations. God does
nothing, man does nothing well, without these Idea's, these retrospects, this recourse 320
to pre-conceptions, pre-deliberations.

Something then I must propose to my selfe, to be the rule, and the reason of my
present and future actions; which was our first branch in this second Part; And then
the second is, That I can propose nothing more availably, then the contemplation of
the history of Gods former proceeding with me; which is *Davids* way here, Because 325
this was Gods way before, I will looke for God in this way still. That language in
which God spake to man, the Hebrew, hath no present tense; They forme not their
verbs as our Westerne Languages do, in the present, *I heare*, or *I see*, or *I reade*, But
they begin at that which is past, *I have seene* and *heard*, and *read*. God carries us in
his Language, in his speaking, upon that which is past, upon that which he hath done 330

already; I connot have better security for present, nor future, than Gods former mercies exhibited to me. *Quis non gaudeat*, sayes S. *Augustine*, Who does not triumph with joy, when hee considers what God hath done? *Quis non & ea, quæ nondum venerunt, ventura sperat, propter illa, quæ jam tanta impleta sunt?* Who can
335 doubt of the performance of all, that sees the greatest part of a Prophesie performed? If I have found that true that God hath said, of the person of Antichrist, why should I doubt of that which he sayes of the ruine of Antichrist? *Credamus modicum quod restat*, sayes the same Father, It is much that wee have seene done, and it is but little that God hath reserved to our faith, to beleeve that it shall be done.

340   There is no State, no Church, no Man, that hath not this tie upon God, that hath not God in these bands, That God by having done much for them already, hath bound himselfe to doe more. Men proceed in their former wayes, sometimes, lest they should confesse an error, and acknowledge that they had beene in a wrong way. God is obnoxious to no error, and therefore he does still, as he did before. Every
345 one of you can say now to God, Lord, Thou broughtest me hither, therefore enable me to heare; Lord, Thou doest that, therefore make me understand; And that, there-fore let me beleeve; And that too, therefore strengthen me to the practise; And all that, therefore continue me to a perseverance. Carry it up to the first sense and apprehension that ever thou hadst of Gods working upon thee, either in thy selfe,
350 when thou camest first to the use of reason, or in others in thy behalfe, in thy baptisme, yet when thou thinkest thou art at the first, God had done something for thee before all that; before that, hee had elected thee, in that election which S. *Augustine* speaks of, *Habet electos, quos creaturus est eligendos*, God hath elected certaine men, whom he intends to create, that he may elect them; that is, that
355 he may declare his Election upon them. God had thee, before he made thee; He loved thee first, and then created thee, that thou loving him, he might continue his love to thee. The surest way, and the nearest way to lay hold upon God, is the consideration of that which he had done already. So *David* does; And that which he takes knowledge of, in particular, in Gods former proceedings towards him, is,
360 Because God had been his helpe, which is our last branch in this part, *Because thou hast beene my helpe.*

    From this one word, That God hath been my *Helpe*, I make account that we have both these notions; first, That God hath not left me to my selfe, he hath come to my succour, He hath helped me; And then, That God hath not left out my selfe; He
365 hath been my Helpe, but he hath left some thing for me to doe with him, and by his helpe. My security for the future, in this consideration of that which is past, lyes not onely in this, That God hath delivered me, but in this also, that he hath deliv-ered me by way of a Helpe, and Helpe always presumes an endevour and co-operation in him that is helped. God did not elect me as a helper, nor create me, nor
370 redeeme me, nor convert me, by way of helping me; for he alone did all, and he had no use at all of me. God infuses his first grace, the first way, meerly as a Giver; intirely, all himselfe; but his subsequent graces, as a helper; therefore we call them Auxiliant graces, Helping graces; and we always receive them, when we endevour to make use of his former grace. *Lord, I beleeve* [Mark. 9:24], (sayes the Man in the Gospel to
375 Christ) *Helpe mine unbeliefe.* If there had not been unbeliefe, weaknesse, unperfect-nesse in that faith, there had needed no helpe; but if there had not been a Beliefe, a

faith, it had not been capable of helpe and assistance, but it must have been an intire act, without any concurrence on the mans part.

So that if I have truly the testimony of a rectified Conscience, That God hath helped me, it is in both respects; first, That he hath never forsaken me, and then, That he hath never suffered me to forsake my selfe; He hath blessed me with that grace, that I trust in no helpe but his, and with this grace too, That I cannot looke for his helpe, except I helpe my selfe also. God did not helpe heaven and earth to proceed out of nothing in the Creation, for they had no possibility of any disposition towards it; for they had no beeing: But God did helpe the earth to produce grasse, and herbes; for, for that, God had infused a seminall disposition into the earth, which, for all that, it could not have perfected without his farther helpe. As in the making of Woman, there is the very word of our Text, *Gnazar*, God made him a *Helper*, one that was to doe much for him, but not without him. So that then, if I will make Gods former working upon me, an argument of his future gracious purposes, as I must acknowledge that God hath done much for me, so I must finde, that I have done what I could, by the benefit of that grace with him; for God promises to be but a helper. *Lord open thou my lips*, says *David*; that is Gods worke intirely; And then, *My mouth, My mouth shall shew forth thy praise* [Ps. 51:15]; there enters *David* into the worke with God. And then, sayes God to him, *Dilata os tuum, Open thy mouth*, (It is now made *Thy mouth*, and therefore doe thou open it) *and I will fill it* [Ps. 81:10]; All inchoations and consummations, beginnings and perfectings are of God, of God alone; but in the way there is a concurrence on our part, (by a successive continuation of Gods grace) in which God proceeds as a Helper; and I put him to more then that, if I doe nothing. But if I pray for his helpe, and apprehend and husband his graces well, when they come, then he is truly, properly my helper; and upon that security, that testimony of a rectified Conscience, I can proceed to *Davids* confidence for the future, *Because thou hast been my Helpe, therefore in the shadow of thy wings will I rejoyce*; which is our third, and last generall part.

In this last part, which is, (after *Davids* aspect, and consideration of his present condition, which was, in the effect, an Exclusion from Gods Temple, And his retrospect, his consideration of Gods former mercies to him, That he had been his Helpe) his prospect, his confidence for the future, we shall stay a little upon these two steps; first, That that which he promises himselfe, is not an immunity from all powerfull enemies, nor a sword of revenge upon those enemies; It is not that he shall have no adversary, nor that that adversary shall be able to doe him no harme, but that he should have a refreshing, a respiration, *In velamento alarum*, under the shadow of Gods wings. And then, (in the second place) That this way which God shall be pleased to take, this manner, this measure of refreshing, which God shall vouchsafe to afford, (though it amount not to a full deliverance) must produce a joy, a rejoycing in us; we must not onely not decline to a murmuring, that we have no more, no nor rest upon a patience for that which remains, but we must ascend to a holy joy, as if all were done and accomplished, *In the shadow of thy wings will I rejoyce*.

First then, lest any man in his dejection of spirit, or of fortune, should stray into a jealousie or suspition of Gods power to deliver him, As God hath spangled the firmament with starres, so hath he his Scriptures with names, and Metaphors, and denotations of power. Sometimes he shines out in the name of a *Sword*, and of a *Target*,

and of a *Wall*, and of a *Tower*, and of a *Rocke*, and of a *Hill*; And sometimes in that glorious and manifold constellation of all together, *Dominus exercituum*, *The Lord*
425 *of Hosts*. God, as God, is never represented to us, with Defensive Armes; He needs them not. When the Poets present their great Heroes, and their Worthies, they alwayes insist upon their Armes, they spend much of their invention upon the description of their Armes; both because the greatest valour and strength needs Armes, (*Goliah* himselfe was armed) and because to expose ones selfe to danger unarmed, is
430 not valour, but rashnesse. But God is invulnerable in himselfe, and is never represented armed; you finde no shirts of mayle, no Helmets, no Cuirasses in Gods Armory. In that one place of *Esay*, where it may seeme to be otherwise, where God is said *to have put on righteousnesse as a breastplate, and a Helmet of Salvation upon his head* [Isa. 59:17]; in that prophecy God is Christ, and is therefore in that place,
435 called *the Redeemer*. Christ needed defensive armes, God does not. Gods word does; His Scriptures doe; And therefore S. *Hierome* hath armed them, and set before every booke his *Prologum galeatum*, that prologue that armes and defends every booke from calumny. But though God need not, nor receive not defensive armes for himselfe, yet God is to us a Helmet, a Breastplate, a strong tower, a rocke, every thing
440 that may give us assurance and defence; and as often as he will, he can refresh that Proclamation, *Nolite tangere Christos meos*, Our enemies shall not so much as touch us [Ps. 105:15].

But here, by occasion of his Metaphore in this Text, (*Sub umbra alarum, In the shadow of thy wings*) we doe not so much consider an absolute immunity, That we
445 shall not be touched, as a refreshing and consolation, when we are touched, though we be pinched and wounded. The Names of God, which are most frequent in the Scriptures, are these three, *Elohim*, and *Adonai*, and *Iehovah*; and to assure us of his Power to deliver us, two of these three are Names of Power. *Elohim* is *Deus fortis*, The mighty, The powerfull God: And (which deserves a particular consideration)
450 *Elohim* is a plurall Name; It is not *Deus fortis*, but *Dii fortes*, powerfull Gods. God is all kinde of Gods; All kinds, which either Idolaters and Gentils can imagine, (as Riches, or Justice, or Wisdome, or Valour, or such) and all kinds which God himself hath called gods, (as Princes, and Magistrates, and Prelates, and all that assist and helpe one another) God is *Elohim*, All these Gods, and all these in their height and
455 best of their power; for *Elohim*, is *Dii fortes*, Gods in the plurall, and those plurall gods in their exaltation.

The second Name of God, is a Name of power too, *Adonai*. For, *Adonai* is *Dominus*, The Lord, such a Lord, as is Lord and Proprietary of all his creatures, and all creatures are his creatures; And then, *Dominium est potestas tum utendi, tum abu-*
460 *tendi*, sayes the law; To be absolute Lord of any thing, gives that Lord a power to doe what he will with that thing. God, as he is *Adonai, The Lord*, may give and take, quicken and kill, build and throw downe, where and whom he will. So then two of Gods three Names are Names of absolute power, to imprint, and re-imprint an assurance in us, that hee can absolutely deliver us, and fully revenge us, if he will. But
465 then, his third Name, and that Name which hee chooses to himselfe, and in the signification of which Name, hee employes *Moses*, for the reliefe of his people under Pharaoh, that Name *Iehovah*, is not a Name of Power, but onely of Essence, of Being, of Subsistence, and yet in the vertue of that Name, God relieved his people. And if,

in my afflictions, God vouchsafe to visit mee in that Name, to preserve me in my
being, in my subsistence in him, that I be not shaked out of him, disinherited in him,   470
excommunicate from him, devested of him, annihilated towards him, let him, at his
good pleasure, reserve his *Elohim*, and his *Adonai*, the exercises and declarations of
his mighty Power, to those great publike causes, that more concerne his Glory, than
any thing that can befall me; But if he impart his *Iehovah*, enlarge himselfe so far
towards me, as that I may live, and move, and have my beeing in him, though I be   475
not instantly delivered, nor mine enemies absolutely destroyed, yet this is as much
as I should promise my selfe, this is as much as the Holy Ghost intends in this
Metaphor, *Sub umbra alarum, Vnder the shadow of thy wings*, that is a Refreshing,
a Respiration, a Conservation, a Consolation in all afflictions that are inflicted
upon me.   480

Yet, is not this Metaphor of *Wings* without a denotation of Power. As no Act
of Gods, though it seeme to imply but spirituall comfort, is without a denotation of
power, (for it is the power of God that comforts me; To overcome that sadnesse of
soule, and that dejection of spirit, which the Adversary by temporall afflictions would
induce upon me, is an act of his Power) So this Metaphor, *The shadow of his wings*,   485
(which in this place expresses no more, then consolation and refreshing in misery,
and not a powerfull deliverance out of it) is so often in the Scriptures made a denotation of Power too, as that we can doubt of no act of power, if we have this shadow
of his wings. For, in this Metaphor of *Wings*, doth the Holy Ghost expresse the
Maritime power, the power of some Nations at Sea, in Navies, (*Woe to the land shad-*   490
owing with wings [Isa. 18:1];) that is, that hovers over the world, and intimidates it
with her sailes and ships. In this Metaphor doth God remember his people, of his
powerfull deliverance of them, (*You have seene what I did unto the Egyptians, and*
how I bare you on Eagles wings, and brought you to my selfe [Ex. 19:4].) In this
Metaphor doth God threaten his and their enemies, what hee can doe, (*The noise of*   495
the wings of his Cherubims, are as the noise of great waters, and of an Army [Ezek.
1:24].) So also, what hee will doe, (*Hee shall spread his wings over Bozrah, and at*
that day shall the hearts of the mighty men of Edom, be as the heart of a woman in her
pangs [Jer. 49:22].) So that, if I have the shadow of his wings, I have the earnest of
the power of them too; If I have refreshing, and respiration from them, I am able to   500
say, (as those three Confessors did to *Nebuchadnezzar*) *My God is able to deliver me*,
I am sure he hath power; *And my God will deliver me*, when it conduces to his glory,
I know he will; *But, if he doe not, bee it knowne unto thee, O King, we will not serve*
thy Gods [Dan. 3:17–18]; Be it knowne unto thee, O Satan, how long soever God
deferre my deliverance, I will not seeke false comforts, the miserable comforts of this   505
world. I will not, for I need not; for I can subsist under this shadow of these Wings,
though I have no more.

The Mercy-seat it selfe was covered with the Cherubims Wings [Ex. 25:20]; and
who would have more then Mercy? and a Mercy-seat; that is, established, resident
Mercy, permanent and perpetuall Mercy; present and familiar Mercy; a Mercy-seat.   510
Our Saviour Christ intends as much as would have served their turne, if they had
laid hold upon it, when hee sayes, *That hee would have gathered Ierusalem, as a henne*
gathers her chickens under her wings [Matt. 23:37]. And though the other Prophets
doe (as ye have heard) mingle the signification of Power, and actuall deliverance, in

515 this Metaphor of Wings, yet our Prophet, whom wee have now in especiall consideration, *David*, never doth so; but in every place where hee uses this Metaphor of
Wings (which are in five or sixe severall Psalmes) still hee rests and determines in that
sense, which is his meaning here; That though God doe not actually deliver us, nor
actually destroy our enemies, yet if hee refresh us in the shadow of his Wings, if he
520 maintaine our subsistence (which is a religious Constancy) in him, this should not
onely establish our patience, (for that is but halfe the worke) but it should also
produce a joy, and rise to an exultation, which is our last circumstance, *Therefore in*
the shadow of thy wings, I will rejoice.

    I would always raise your hearts, and dilate your hearts, to a holy Joy, to a joy in
525 the Holy Ghost. There may be a just feare, that men doe not grieve enough for their
sinnes; but there may bee a just jealousie, and suspition too, that they may fall into
inordinate griefe, and diffidence of Gods mercy; And God hath reserved us to such
times, as being the later times, give us even the dregs and lees of misery to drinke.
For, God hath not onely let loose into the world a new spirituall disease; which is,
530 an equality, and an indifferency, which religion our children, or our servants, or our
companions professe; (I would not keepe company with a man that thought me a
knave, or a traitor; with him that thought I loved not my Prince, or were a faithlesse
man, not to be beleeved, I would not associate my selfe; And yet I will make him
my bosome companion, that thinks I doe not love God, that thinks I cannot be
535 saved) but God hath accompanied, and complicated almost all our bodily diseases of
these times, with an extraordinary sadnesse, a predominant melancholy, a faintnesse
of heart, a chearlesnesse, a joylesnesse of spirit, and therefore I returne often to this
endeavor of raising your hearts, dilating your hearts with a holy Joy, Joy in the holy
Ghost, for *Vnder the shadow of his wings*, you may, you should, *rejoyce*.
540   If you looke upon this world in a Map, you find two Hemisphears, two half worlds.
If you crush heaven into a Map, you may find two Hemisphears too, two half heavens;
Halfe will be Joy, and halfe will be Glory; for in these two, the joy of heaven, and
the glory of heaven, is all heaven often represented unto us. And as of those two
Hemisphears of the world, the first hath been knowne long before, but the other,
545 (that of America, which is the richer in treasure) God reserved for later Discoveries;
So though he reserve that Hemisphear of heaven, which is the Glory thereof, to the
Resurrection, yet the other Hemisphear, the Joy of heaven, God opens to our Discovery, and delivers for our habitation even whilst we dwell in this world. As God
hath cast upon the unrepentant sinner two deaths, a temporall, and a spirituall death,
550 so hath he breathed into us two lives; for so, as the word for death is doubled, *Morte*
morieris, Thou shalt die the death [Gen. 2:17], so is the word for life expressed in the
plurall, *Chaiim, vitarum, God breathed into his nostrils the breath of lives*, of divers
lives. Though our naturall life were no life, but rather a continuall dying, yet we have
two lives besides that, an eternall life reserved for heaven, but yet a heavenly life too,
555 a spirituall life, even in this world; And as God doth thus inflict two deaths, and infuse
two lives, so doth he also passe two Judgements upon man, or rather repeats the
same Judgement twice. For, that which Christ shall say to thy soule then at the last
Judgement, *Enter into thy Masters joy* [Matt. 25:23], Hee sayes to thy conscience
now, *Enter into thy Masters joy*. The everlastingnesse of the joy is the blessednesse of
560 the next life, but the entring, the inchoation is afforded here. For that which Christ

shall say then to us, *Venite benedicti, Come ye blessed* [Matt. 25:34], are words
intended to persons that are comming, that are upon the way, though not at home;
Here in this world he bids us *Come*, there in the next, he shall bid us *Welcome*. The
Angels of heaven have joy in thy conversion [Luke. 15:10], and canst thou bee
without that joy in thy selfe? If thou desire revenge upon thine enemies, as they are 565
Gods enemies, That God would bee pleased to remove, and root out all such as
oppose him, that Affection appertaines to Glory; Let that alone till thou come to the
Hemisphear of Glory; There joyne with those Martyrs under the Altar, *Vsquequo*
Domine, How long O Lord, dost thou deferre Judgement? [Revel. 6:10] and thou
shalt have thine answere there for that. Whilst thou art here, here joyne with *David*, 570
and the other Saints of God, in that holy increpation of a dangerous sadnesse, *Why*
art thou cast downe O my soule? why art thou disquieted in mee? [Ps. 42:5] That soule
that is dissected and anatomized to God, in a sincere confession, washed in the teares
of true contrition, embalmed in the blood of reconciliation, the blood of Christ Jesus,
can assigne no reason, can give no just answer to that Interrogatory, *Why art thou* 575
cast downe O my soule? why art thou disquieted in me? No man is so little, as that he
can be lost under these wings, no man so great, as that they cannot reach to him;
Semper ille major est, quantumcumque creverimus, To what temporall, to what spirituall greatnesse soever wee grow, still pray wee him to shadow us under his Wings;
for the poore need those wings against oppression, and the rich against envy. The 580
Holy Ghost, who is a Dove, shadowed the whole world under his wings [Gen. 1:2];
Incubabat aquis, He hovered over the waters, he sate upon the waters, and he hatched
all that was produced, and all that was produced so, was good. Be thou a Mother
where the Holy Ghost would be a father; Conceive by him; and be content that he
produce joy in thy heart here. First thinke, that as a man must have some land, or 585
els he cannot be in wardship, so a man must have some of the love of God, or els
he could not fall under Gods correction; God would not give him his physick, God
would not study his cure, if he cared not for him. And then thinke also, that if God
afford thee the shadow of his wings, that is, Consolation, respiration, refreshing,
though not a present, and plenary deliverance, in thy afflictions, not to thanke God, 590
is a murmuring, and not to rejoyce in Gods wayes, is an unthankfulnesse. Howling
is the noyse of hell, singing the voyce of heaven; Sadnesse the damp of Hell, Rejoycing the serenity of Heaven. And he that hath not this joy here, lacks one of the
best pieces of his evidence for the joyes of heaven; and hath neglected or refused that
Earnest, by which God uses to binde his bargaine, that true joy in this world shall 595
flow into the joy of Heaven, as a River flowes into the Sea; This joy shall not be put
out in death, and a new joy kindled in me in Heaven; But as my soule, as soone as
it is out of my body, is in Heaven, and does not stay for the possession of Heaven,
nor for the fruition of the sight of God, till it be ascended through ayre, and fire,
and Moone, and Sun, and Planets, and Firmament, to that place which we conceive 600
to be Heaven, but without the thousandth part of a minutes stop, as soone as it
issues, is in a glorious light, which is Heaven, (for all the way to Heaven is Heaven;
And as those Angels, which came from Heaven hither, bring Heaven with them, and
are in Heaven here, So that soule that goes to Heaven, meets Heaven here; and as
those Angels doe not devest Heaven by comming, so these soules invest Heaven, in 605
their going.) As my soule shall not goe towards Heaven, but goe by Heaven to

Heaven, to the Heaven of Heavens, So the true joy of a good soule in this world is
the very joy of Heaven; and we goe thither, not that being without joy, we might
have joy infused into us, but that as Christ sayes, *Our joy might be full* [John 16:24],
610 perfected, sealed with an everlastingnesse; for, as he promises, *That no man shall take
our joy from us* [John 16:22], so neither shall Death it selfe take it away, nor so much
as interrupt it, or discontinue it, But as in the face of Death, when he layes hold
upon me, and in the face of the Devill, when he attempts me, I shall see the face of
God, (for, every thing shall be a glasse, to reflect God upon me) so in the agonies
615 of Death, in the anguish of that dissolution, in the sorrowes of that valediction, in
the irreversiblenesse of that transmigration, I shall have a joy, which shall no more
evaporate, then my soule shall evaporate, A joy, that shall passe up, and put on a
more glorious garment above, and be joy super-invested in glory. *Amen.*

Questions for Study

1 What particular place does Donne ascribe to the Psalter in the Christian life?
2 How is the theme of Psalm 63:7 developed throughout the sermon?
3 What difference does the thought of "an exceeding weight of eternal glory" make
   to Donne's perception of the pain of the world?
4 Donne uses the analogy of a map with two hemispheres to illustrate the place of joy
   and glory in life. Find the section in question, and write down the way in which this
   analogy illuminates his point.
5 What is the dominant tone of the final paragraphs of the sermon? How does Donne
   link this with his opening statements?

Text: Divine Meditations

In 1633, a set of twelve meditations was published, to be followed by a further four in
1635. These sixteen "divine meditations" are widely acclaimed as among Donne's finest
religious poems. There is a debate within the scholarly literature concerning the correct
order of these sixteen meditations. The 1635 edition did not add the final four meditations after the first twelve; it dispersed them among the earlier ones. The three meditations here selected were all published in 1633, and are arranged in the order in which
they were then published. For the purposes of this anthology, they should be viewed as
independent poems, despite their obvious connections.

Death be not Proud

The first meditation takes as its major theme the hope of the resurrection. Death is personified as an enemy of humanity – yet an enemy which is not master of its own destiny.

> Death, be not proud, though some have called thee
> Mighty and dreadful, for thou art not so;
> For those whom thou think'st thou dost overthrow,

Die not, poor Death, nor yet canst thou kill me.
From rest and sleep, which but thy pictures be,
Much pleasure; then from thee much more must flow,
And soonest our best men with thee do go,
Rest of their bones, and soul's delivery.
Thou art slave to fate, chance, kings, and desperate men,
And dost with poison, war, and sickness dwell;
And poppy or charms can make us sleep as well
And better than thy stroke; why swell'st thou then?
One short sleep past, we wake eternally,
And death shall be no more; Death, thou shalt die.

Questions for Study

1   Read the following verse from the King James Version of the Bible. "The last enemy that shall be destroyed is death" (1 Corinthians 15:26). How is this theme of death as an enemy incorporated into the poem?
2   Now read the following verses from the King James Version of the Bible. "Then shall be brought to pass the saying that is written, Death is swallowed up in victory. O death, where is thy sting? O grave, where is thy victory? The sting of death is sin; and the strength of sin is the law. But thanks be to God, which giveth us the victory through our Lord Jesus Christ" (1 Corinthians 15:55–57). How is the theme of victory over death developed in the poem?
3   Both of these quotations are taken from 1 Corinthians 15, a chapter of the New Testament which deals with the theme of the resurrection, and which was – and is – widely used at Christian funeral services. Do you think this has influenced Donne at any point?

Batter my Heart

This poem deals with a central issue concerning the human free will. Western Christianity, following Augustine, argued that the human free will had been "taken captive" by sin – a notion expressed in the Latin slogan *liberum arbitrium captivatum*, "the captive free will." As a result, the human free will cannot freely respond to God, in that it is entrapped by sin. It is therefore necessary for God to break down a false human freedom – in that the free will is biased toward sin and a turning away from God – if true freedom is to be restored. In this meditation, Donne wrestles with this apparent paradox, using the image of a "usurped town" to make his point.

Batter my heart, three-person'd God, for you
As yet but knock, breathe, shine, and seek to mend;
That I may rise and stand, o'erthrow me, and bend
Your force to break, blow, burn, and make me new.
I, like an usurp'd town to another due,

Labor to admit you, but oh, to no end;
Reason, your viceroy in me, me should defend,
But is captiv'd, and proves weak or untrue.
Yet dearly I love you, and would be lov'd fain,
But am betroth'd unto your enemy;
Divorce me, untie or break that knot again,
Take me to you, imprison me, for I,
Except you enthrall me, never shall be free,
Nor ever chaste, except you ravish me.

Questions for Study

The following questions may help readers engage with the text.

1 Why is it necessary for God to "batter" the poet's heart? Why not just politely request admission?
2 What points does Donne make using the image of the "usurped town"?
3 Human reason is described as God's "viceroy" in humanity. A "viceroy" (literally, "in place of a king") refers to an individual to whom authority is entrusted by a monarch. So what point is Donne making here about the role of reason within the purposes of God?
4 In line 11, Donne uses three related images to refer to the breaking of the power of sin over fallen humanity. What are they? And who is doing the breaking?
5 Explain the paradox set out by Donne in his final assertion that he shall never be chaste, unless God shall ravish him.

Wilt thou love God?

This meditation takes as its subject the love of God for humanity. The argument of the poem is very simple, and can be followed without much difficulty. The opening lines invite the reader to reflect on the extent of the love of God for humanity. The poem sets out the extent of God's self-humility in choosing to enter into the human situation to redeem humanity.

Wilt thou love God, as he thee? then digest
My soul, this wholesome meditation,
How God the Spirit, by angels waited on
In heaven, doth make his temple in thy breast.
The Father having begot a Son most blessed,
And still begetting (for he ne'er begun)
Hath deigned to choose thee by adoption,
Coheir to his glory, and Sabbath's endless rest;
And as a robbed man, which by search doth find
His stol'n stuff sold, must lose or buy it again:
The Son of glory came down, and was slain,

Us whom he had made, and Satan stol'n, to unbind.
'Twas much, that man was made like God before,
But, that God should be made like man, much more.

Questions for Study

1 What affirmations of dignity are found in lines 3–5? And why does Donne stress these?

2 Read the following text from the King James Version. "Or else how can one enter into a strong man's house, and spoil his goods, except he first bind the strong man?" (Matthew 12:29). This is one of Christ's brief statements, traditionally interpreted as the need to bind Satan before making off with what Satan has stolen from others. How does Donne use this traditional image in this poem?

3 "Know ye not that ye are the temple of God, and that the Spirit of God dwelleth in you?" (1 Corinthians 3:16). This quotation, taken from the King James Version of the Bible, has shaped part of Donne's thinking in this poem. Which section of the poem seems to reflect this?

4 One of the great Christian themes is that humanity has been made in the image and likeness of God. Read the following text from the King James Version. "So God created man in his own image, in the image of God created he him; male and female created he them" (Genesis 1:27). At what stage in the poem does Donne develop this theme? And what point does he make in doing so?

CHAPTER 50

George Herbert (1593–1633)

George Herbert was born in Montgomery, Wales, on April 3, 1593, as the fifth son of Richard and Magdalen Newport Herbert. After his father's death in 1596, he and his six brothers and three sisters were raised by their mother, patron to John Donne who dedicated his "Holy Sonnets" to her. Herbert was educated at Westminster School and Trinity College, Cambridge. His first two sonnets, sent to his mother in 1610, maintained that the love of God is a worthier subject for verse than the love of woman. They foreshadowed his future religious and poetic inclinations. His first published verse (1612) took the form of two memorial poems in Latin on the death of Prince Henry, the heir apparent to the English throne.

Herbert went on to be elected as a Fellow of Trinity College in 1614, and was appointed Public Orator at Cambridge University six years later. This position required him to make public speeches on major university occasions, using the rather florid academic Latin of the period. While there is little doubt that Herbert could have used this prestigious position as a stepping-stone to high political office, he chose not to do so. It is possible that the death of James I in 1625 may have caused him to reconsider his future ambitions; it is also highly likely that the personal influence of Nicolas Ferrar led him to study divinity. He thus gave up his secular ambitions, took holy orders in the Church of England in 1630, and spent the rest of his life as rector of the parish of Fugglestone with Bemerton near Salisbury. At Bemerton, George Herbert conducted what is widely regarded as an exemplary parish ministry. He rebuilt the parish church at his own expense; he visited the poor, consoled the sick, and sat by the bed of the dying. "Holy Mr. Herbert" became the talk of the countryside in the three short years before he died of consumption on March 1, 1633.

George Herbert (1593–1633)

Basic description

Leading English devotional poet of the seventeenth century.

Major work

The Temple (1633).

Editions of works

The English Poems of George Herbert, ed. G. Patrides. London: Dent, 1974.

Major studies

Diana Benet, *Secretary of Praise: The Poetic Vocation of George Herbert*. Columbia, MO: University of Missouri Press, 1984.

Barbara Leah Harman, *Costly Monuments: Representations of the Self in George Herbert*. Cambridge, MA: Harvard University Press, 1982.

Richard Strier, *Love Known: Theology and Experience in George Herbert's Poetry*. Chicago: University of Chicago Press, 1983.

While on his deathbed, Herbert sent the manuscript of a collection of poems to his friend Nicholas Ferrar, and requested him to arrange for their publication. The resulting volume of poems, entitled *The Temple: Sacred Poems and Personal Ejaculations*, was published later in the year of Herbert's death. It met with popular acclaim, and had run to seven editions by 1640. Herbert's poems are characterized by a precision of language, a metrical versatility, and an ingenious use of imagery or "conceits" that was favored by the metaphysical school of poets. They include almost every known form of song and poem, but they also reflect Herbert's concern with speech – conversational, persuasive, proverbial. Carefully arranged in related sequences, the poems explore and celebrate the ways of God's love as Herbert discovered them within the fluctuations of his own personal experience. Yet Herbert must be seen as an "ecclesiastical" rather than just a "religious" poet. His writings concern the rhythms of the church year as much as his personal religious experiences. Although Herbert was strongly Anglican in his outlook, his religious poetry won admirers across the entire religious spectrum. For example, it was read and admired by Charles I before his execution, as it was by Oliver Cromwell's personal chaplain. Donne may be the greatest of the metaphysical poets; Herbert, however, is widely regarded as supreme among the English devotional poets.

Although Herbert is remembered primarily as a poet, his literary activities were by no means restricted to this genre. One of his most famous works of prose is *A Priest to the Temple; or the Country Parson* (1652). This is probably best seen as a Baconian manual of practical advice to country parsons, which bears witness to both the intelligence and devotion which he brought to his responsibilities as the rector of Fugglestone with Bemerton. Its elegance of style has been much admired, making its inclusion in this collection essential.

Text: *The Temple*

Four of Herbert's poems have been selected for discussion, all of which are taken from *The Temple*. In order to gain the most from engaging with these poems, the structure of this collection must be appreciated. Indeed, one of the major difficulties encountered in dealing with Herbert is that his poetry is often cited completely out of its original context, whereas Herbert intended his poems to be read as a whole. *The Temple* is divided into three sections: "The Church-Porch," "The Church," and "The Church Militant." The specific phrase "the temple" has complex associations, which pass into the structure of the collection of poems. It can be understood architecturally, to refer to the great building, constructed by Solomon for the praise of God in Israel (for example, see Herbert's comments on "Solomon's sea of brasse and world of stone"), or to the classical ideal of a temple, which was undergoing a new lease of life as a consequence of the agenda of the Renaissance. Yet it can also be understood to refer to the inner temple of the individual. A leading theme of the writings of Paul concerns the internalization of the Christian faith, with an emphasis on the human body as a temple within which the Holy Spirit dwells. "Know ye not that ye are the temple of God, and that the Spirit of God dwelleth in you?" (1 Corinthians 3:16, King James Version). The poems thus aim to celebrate and encourage the personal assimilation of faith. It is poems that focus on this aspect of the "temple" image which develop the themes of love and affliction for which Herbert is particularly remembered.

We shall consider the poems in the order in which they occur in *The Temple*.

1. Redemption

In this poem, the poet explores the associations of the term "redemption." Alluding to the Old Testament notion of "redeeming land," Herbert develops the idea of the death of Christ as the price by which God takes legitimate possession of a precious piece of land. While also exploring the idea of the shame and humility of the cross, Herbert is able to bring out the legal and financial dimensions of redemption.

> HAVING been tenant long to a rich Lord,
>   Not thriving, I resolved to be bold,
>   And make a suit unto Him, to afford
> A new small-rented lease, and cancell th' old.
> In heaven at His manour I Him sought:
>   They told me there, that He was lately gone
>   About some land, which he had dearly bought
> Long since on Earth, to take possession.
> I straight return'd, and knowing His great birth,
>   Sought Him accordingly in great resorts –
>   In cities, theatres, gardens, parks, and courts:
> At length I heard a ragged noise and mirth
>   Of theeves and murderers; there I Him espied,
>   Who straight, '*Your suit is granted*,' said, and died.

Questions for Study

1 In what way does the poem involve word-play with the term "redemption"?
2 What does Herbert want us to understand by the phrase "which he had dearly bought"?
3 What point does Herbert make by initially locating his search for the "rich Lord" (who, of course, is God) in "great resorts" or "cities . . . and courts"? How is this point developed by the contrast with "thieves and murderers."
4 Can you see any allusions to the gospel passion narratives in the final lines of the poem?
5 What is meant by the phrase "your suit is granted"? And what point does Herbert make by following this *immediately* with the brief statement "and died"?

2. Easter

This poem follows on almost immediately from "Redemption," being separated from it only by a brief poem entitled "Sepulchre," which takes the form of a meditation on Christ's final – or not-so-final, as events would prove – resting place. Easter is both a celebration of the feast of Easter in the church's liturgical year, and the spiritual realities which it embodies, particularly as these impact upon the individual believer. The poem has two parts, each consisting of three stanzas. The first part uses a complex mode of speaking, perhaps well known to Herbert from his time as Public Orator at Cambridge; the second is in a much simpler style, using common meter.

This particular poem is perhaps best appreciated by reading it aloud, and getting a grasp of Herbert's sense of rhythm and rhyme. Like all of Herbert's poems, "Easter" is studded with verbal richness, and clearly shows a Flaubertian concern for finding the right words to convey both the theological themes of Easter, and its impact upon the mood of the believer. Use the following study questions as a means of interacting with this poem.

> RISE, heart, thy Lord is risen. Sing his praise
> Without delays,
> Who takes thee by the hand, that thou likewise
> With him may'st rise:
> That, as his death calcined thee to dust,
> His life may make thee gold, and, much more, just.
>
> Awake, my lute, and struggle for thy part
> With all thy art,
> The cross taught all wood to resound his name
> Who bore the same.
> His stretched sinews taught all strings what key
> Is best to celebrate this most high day.
>
> Consort, both heart and lute, and twist a song
> Pleasant and long;

Or, since all music is but three parts vied
              And multiplied
Oh let thy blessèd Spirit bear a part,
And make up our defects with his sweet art.

I got me flowers to straw thy way;
I got me boughs off many a tree:
But thou wast up by break of day,
And brought'st thy sweets along with thee.

The Sunne arising in the East,
Though he give light, and th' East perfume;
If they should offer to contest
With thy arising, they presume.

Can there be any day but this,
Though many sunnes to shine endeavour?
We count three hundred, but we misse:
There is but one, and that one ever.

Questions for Study

1 The first stanza uses a variety of images to convey the central Easter theme that Christ's resurrection ensures the resurrection of believers. In what ways does Herbert allude to this theme in the first stanza of this poem?

2 Read the following verses from the King James Version of the Bible: "Therefore as by the offence of one judgment came upon all men to condemnation; even so by the righteousness of one the free gift came upon all men unto justification of life. For as by one man's disobedience many were made sinners, so by the obedience of one shall many be made righteous" (Romans 5:18–19). Paul here contrasts the effects of Adam and Christ upon humanity, and stresses what Christ has done for believers. In what way does Herbert echo such ideas in the first three stanzas of the poem?

3 The fourth stanza imagines the poet visiting Christ's tomb on Easter Morning, only to find that the tomb was empty. How does Herbert explore this theme?

4 The fifth stanza asserts that the once-for-all rising of Christ surpasses in glory and benefits the daily rising of the sun. The sixth follows through a related idea, in that the rising of the sun is a daily routine event, whereas Christ's resurrection is unique and once-for-all. Why do you think Herbert uses the analogy of the sun so extensively? (You might like to recall here that Easter Day invariably falls on a Sunday.)

5 What point do you think Herbert might be making through using "high" and "low" styles of writing in the two parts of this poem?

3. Prayer (I)

The Temple includes two poems with the title "Prayer," of which this is the first. It is one of the most remarkable and striking poems that Herbert ever wrote, in that it consists of nothing but ways of referring to or conceiving prayer. The poem does not make a statement. It is a collection of images or metaphors, designed to illuminate the nature of prayer.

> Prayer the Church's banquet, Angels' age,
>   God's breath in man returning to his birth,
>   The soul in paraphrase, heart in pilgrimage,
> The Christian plummet sounding heav'n and earth;
>
> Engine against th' Almighty, sinner's tow'r,
>   Reversed thunder, Christ-side-piercing spear,
>   The six-days world transposing in an hour,
> A kind of tune, which all things hear and fear;
>
> Softness, and peace, and joy, and love, and bliss,
>   Exalted manna, gladness of the best,
>   Heaven in ordinary, man well drest,
> The milky way, the bird of Paradise,
>   Church-bells beyond the stars heard, the soul's blood,
>   The land of spices; something understood.

The poem demands close study, in that each metaphor invites the reader to pause and "unpack" its content. What sort of points is Herbert making? The following reflections may help readers to appreciate the richness of the poem.

1 Prayer is corporate. Here we see Herbert's Anglican heritage expressing itself. Note in particular the metaphor of "the church's banquet," which conveys the notions both of "feasting" and of "corporate celebration."
2 Prayer is reciprocal, involving both God and the believer (for example, "Heaven in ordinary, man well drest").
3 Prayer is powerful (see, for example, "Engine against th' Almighty").
4 Prayer brings security (the "sinner's tow'r").
5 Prayer leads one into paradise – a restoration of Eden ("the bird of Paradise"; "The land of spices").

These represent very brief reflections on the poem, and the individual reader is strongly encouraged to interact with each image. Some of these images require additional comment:

1 "Angels' age": this probably contrasts the mortality of humanity, and the brevity of human life, with the eternal life of heaven, known by Angels.
2 "The bird of Paradise." It is possible that Herbert may have in mind the popular view that this newly-discovered bird never perches anywhere, but spends all its time in the air. If so, this would imply that prayer keeps the believer mindful of heaven, rather than constantly preoccupied with earthly matters.

4. Love (III)

This is the third poem entitled "Love" in *The Temple*, and it has particular significance in that it brings the entire work to an end. The poem is a meditation on the heavenly banquet. Three levels of imagery are woven into the text:

1   The Holy Communion service, which was a central feature of Herbert's ministry as a priest.
2   The gospel parables of the kingdom, particularly those which compare the kingdom of God to a feast or banquet, to which individuals are invited.
3   The "marriage supper of the lamb," which is mentioned in the book of Revelation as an element of the end of the age. "Blessed are they which are called unto the marriage supper of the Lamb" (Revelation 19:9, King James Version).

The poem describes the tension felt by the author as a result of this invitation. On the one hand, he is delighted to have been invited to this feast. On the other, his guilt and inadequacy make him feel that he should not be present. Note, for example, the way in which the poet "cannot look" at his host; the way in which he "drew back"; and offered to serve those already present, rather than partake in the banquet himself.

> Love bade me welcome, yet my soul drew back,
>   Guilty of dust and sin.
> But quick-ey'd Love, observing me grow slack
>   From my first entrance in,
> Drew nearer to me, sweetly questioning
>   If I lack'd anything.
>
> 'A guest,' I answer'd, 'worthy to be here';
>   Love said, 'You shall be he.'
> 'I, the unkind, the ungrateful? ah my dear,
>   I cannot look on thee.'
> Love took my hand and smiling did reply,
>   'Who made the eyes but I?'
>
> 'Truth, Lord, but I have marr'd them; let my shame
>   Go where it doth deserve.'
> 'And know you not,' says Love, 'who bore the blame?'
>   'My dear, then I will serve.'
> 'You must sit down,' says Love, 'and taste my meat.'
>   So I did sit and eat.

Questions for Study

1 Who is the "Love," personified in this poem?
2 The poet feels that he is "guilty of dust and sin." What does he mean by this? And what are the consequences of this recognition?
3 The poet wants to be designated "a guest." Why?
4 The poem suggests that Love "bore the blame." What blame? And in what way was this blame borne? And how does this relate to the three basic images which Herbert incorporates into this poem?
5 The poem achieves a subtle interplay of the doctrines of creation and redemption. Can you identify elements of each doctrine in this poem?
6 The invitation to "taste my meat" has several levels of meaning. What are they? (You need to read the poem in the specific light of its allusions to the Communion service at this point.)
7 Why do you think that Herbert chose this poem with which to end *The Temple*?

Text: *A Priest to the Temple*

The second text selected for inclusion is Herbert's major study of the life of a country parson, which clearly reflects his own experience and wisdom. *A Priest to the Temple* explores, in rich English prose, the many aspects of ministry and rural life, and offers insights into both church and secular life of the period. The section which is here reproduced needs no comment, other than noting how the pulpit is to be seen as the parson's "joy and throne" – but that the sermons delivered from its safety should not last more than an hour!

Chapter VII

The Parson preaching

The Countrey Parson preacheth constantly, the pulpit is his joy and his throne: if he at any time intermit, it is either for want of health, or against some great Festivall, that he may the better celebrate it, or for the variety of the hearers, that he may be heard at his returne more attentively. When he intermits, he is ever very well supplyed by some able man who treads in his steps, and will not throw down what he hath built; whom also he intreats to press some point, that he himself hath often urged with no great success, that so in the mouth of two or three witnesses the truth may be more established. When he preacheth, he procures attention by all possible art, both by earnestnesse of speech, it being naturall to men to think, that where is much earnestness, there is somewhat worth hearing; and by a diligent, and busy cast of his eye on his auditors, with letting them know, that he observes who marks, and who not; and with particularizing of his speech now to the younger sort, then to the elder, now to the poor, and now to the rich. This is for you, and This is for you; for particulars ever touch, and awake more then generalls. Herein also he serves himselfe of the judgements of God, as of those of antient times, so especially of the late ones; and those most, which are nearest to his Parish; for people are very attentive at such discourses, and think it behoves them to be so, when God is so neer them, and even over their heads. Sometimes he tells them stories, and sayings of others, according as his text invites him; for them also men heed, and remember better then exhortations; which though earnest, yet often dy with the Sermon, especially with Countrey people; which are thick, and heavy, and hard to raise to a poynt of Zeal, and fervency, and need a mountaine of fire to kindle them; but stories and sayings they will well remember. He often tels them, that Sermons are dangerous things, that none goes out of Church as he came in, but either better, or worse; that none is careless before his Judg, and that the word of God shal judge us. By these and other means the Parson procures attention; but the character of his Sermon is Holiness; he is not witty, or learned, or eloquent, but Holy. A Character, that *Hermogenes* never dream'd of, and therefore he could give no precepts thereof. But it is gained, first, by choosing texts of Devotion, not Controversie, moving and ravishing texts, whereof the Scriptures are full. Secondly, by dipping, and seasoning all our words and sentences in our hearts, before they come into our mouths, truly affecting, and cordially expressing all that we say; so that the auditors may plainly perceive that every word is hart-deep. Thirdly, by turning often, and making many Apostrophes to God, as, Oh Lord blesse my people, and teach them this point; or, Oh my Master, on whose errand I come, let me hold my peace, and doe thou speak thy selfe; for thou art Love, and when thou teachest, all are Scholers. Some such irradiations scatteringly in the Sermon, carry great holiness in them. The Prophets are admirable in this. So *Isa.* 64. *Oh that thou would'st rent the Heavens, that thou wouldst come down,* &c. And *Jeremy*, Chapt. 10. after he had complained of the desolation of *Israel*, turnes to God suddenly, *Oh Lord, I know that the way of man is not in himself,* &c. Fourthly, by frequent wishes of the peoples good, and joying therein, though he himself were with Saint *Paul* even sacrificed upon the service of their faith. For there is no greater sign of holinesse, then the procuring, and rejoycing in anothers good. And herein St *Paul* excelled in all his Epistles. How did he put the *Romans* in all his prayers? *Rom.* 1:9. And ceased not to give thanks for the *Ephesians, Eph.* 1:16. And for the *Corinthians, chap.* 1:4. And for the *Philippians* made request with joy, *ch.* 1:4. And is in contention for them whither to live, or dy; be with them, or Christ, *verse* 23. which, setting aside his care of his Flock, were a madnesse to doubt of. What an admirable Epistle is the second to the *Corinthians?* how full of affections? he joyes, and he is sorry, he grieves, and he gloryes, never was there such care of a flock expressed, save in the great shepherd of the fold, who first shed teares over *Jerusalem*, and afterwards blood. Therefore this care may be learn'd there, and then woven into Sermons, which will make them appear exceeding reverend, and holy. Lastly, by an often urging of the presence, and majesty of God, by these, or such like speeches. Oh let us all take heed what we do, God sees us, he sees whether I speak as I ought, or you hear as you ought, he sees hearts, as we see faces: he is among us; for if we be here, hee must be here, since we are here by him, and without him could not be here. Then turning the discourse to his Majesty, And he is a great God, and terrible, as great in mercy, so great in judgement: There are but two devouring elements, fire, and water, he hath both in him; *His voyce is as the sound of many waters, Revelations* 1. And he himselfe *is a consuming fire, Hebrews* 12. Such discourses shew very Holy. The Parsons Method in handling of a text consists of two parts; first, a plain and evident declaration of the meaning of the text; and secondly, some choyce Observations drawn out of the whole text, as it lyes entire, and unbroken in the Scripture it self. This he thinks naturall, and sweet, and grave. Whereas the other way of crumbling a text into small parts, as, the Person speaking, or spoken to, the subject, and object, and the like, hath neither in it sweetnesse, nor gravity, nor variety, since the words apart are not Scripture, but a dictionary, and may be considered alike in all the Scripture. The Parson exceeds not an hour in preaching, because all ages have thought that a competency, and he that profits not in that time, will lesse afterwards, the same affection which made him not profit before, making him then weary, and so he grows from not relishing, to loathing.

Questions for Study

1 What does this passage suggest about the importance of the sermon in the worship of the period?
2 Why do you think that Herbert attaches such importance to the sermon, when he himself is remembered as a poet, not a preacher?

CHAPTER 51

Sir Thomas Browne (1605–1682)

Sir Thomas Browne was born in London on October 19, 1605, educated at Winchester and Oxford, and trained for the practice of medicine. After traveling throughout continental Europe, he finally settled down as a physician in Norwich, and enjoyed a distinguished professional reputation. Later he became equally famous as a scholar and antiquary, and was knighted by Charles II on the occasion of the King's visit to Norwich in 1671. In 1641 he married, and he was survived by four of his ten children. He died on his seventy-seventh birthday.

Sir Thomas Browne (1605–1682)

Basic description
Natural historian, antiquary, and religious thinker.

Major works
Religio Medici (1642); *Pseudodoxia Epidemica* (1646).

Editions of works
Works, ed. Sir Geoffrey Keynes, 4 vols. London: Faber, 1964.

Major studies
Daniela Havenstein, *Democratizing Sir Thomas Browne: The Character and Style of Religio Medici and its Imitations*. Oxford: Clarendon Press, 1999.

Frank Livingstone Huntley, *Sir Thomas Browne: A Biographical and Critical Study*. Ann Arbor, MI: University of Michigan Press, 1962.

Browne's most important work is his *Religio Medici*, which seems to have been written about 1635, without actually being intended for publication. In 1642, however, two unauthorized editions appeared, and he was induced by the inaccuracies of these to issue an authorized edition in 1643. Since that time between thirty and forty editions have appeared, and the work has been translated into Latin, Dutch, French, German, and Italian. Of his other works the most famous are *Pseudodoxia Epidemica, or Enquiries into Vulgar Errors* (1646), a treatise of vast learning and wit; "Hydriotaphia, or Urn Burial," a discourse on burial customs, which closes with a chapter on death and immortality, the eloquence of which places Browne in the first rank of writers of English prose; and "The Garden of Cyrus," a fantastic account of horticulture from the Garden of Eden down to the time of Cyrus, King of Persia, with much discussion on the mystical significations of the number five. His miscellaneous writings cover a great variety of subjects, religious, scientific, and antiquarian.

Text: *Religio Medici* (1643)

The *Religio Medici*, from which the following extract is taken, offers an excellent example of the author's style and distinctive approach to religious issues. His highly individual and sometimes far-fetched vocabulary manage to obscure and illuminate matters in about equal proportions; nevertheless, it is impossible not to admire the richness of his prose. The section singled out for particular discussion is taken from Book II of the work, which deals with the question of whether the natural world can act as a window into the purposes and character of God. The work is of particular importance on account of its full statement of the "two books" of God – that is, the "book of nature" and the "book of Scripture."

XIV   There is but one first cause, and four second causes of all things. Some are without efficient [ed.: cause], as God; others without matter, as Angels; some without form, as the first matter: but every Essence, created or uncreated, hath its final cause, and some positive end both of its Essence and Operation. This is the cause I grope after in the works of Nature; on this hangs the Providence of God. To raise so beauteous a structure as the World and the Creatures thereof, was but His Art; but their sundry and divided operations, with their predestinated ends, are from the Treasure of His Wisdom. In the causes, nature, and affections of the Eclipses of the Sun and Moon, there is most excellent speculation; but to profound farther, and to contemplate a reason why His Providence hath so disposed and ordered their motions in that vast circle as to conjoyn and obscure each other, is a sweeter piece of Reason, and a diviner point of Philosophy. Therefore sometimes, and in some things, there appears to me as much Divinity in Galen his books *De Usu Partium*, as in Suarez Metaphysicks. Had Aristotle been as curious in the enquiry of this cause as he was of the other, he had not left behind him an imperfect piece of Philosophy, but an absolute tract of Divinity.

XV   *Natura nihil agit frustra*, [Nature does nothing in vain] is the only indisputed Axiome in Philosophy. There are no Grotesques in Nature; not anything framed to fill up empty Cantons, and unnecessary spaces. In the most imperfect Creatures, and such as were not preserved in the Ark, but, having their Seeds and Principles in the womb of Nature, are everywhere, where the power of the Sun is, in these is the Wisdom of His hand discovered. Out of this rank Solomon chose the object of his admiration. Indeed what Reason may not go to School to the Wisdom of Bees, Ants, and Spiders? What wise hand teacheth them to do what Reason cannot teach us? Ruder heads stand amazed at those prodigious pieces of Nature, Whales, Elephants, Dromidaries and Camels; these, I confess, are the Colossus and majestick pieces of her hand: but in these narrow Engines there is more curious

Mathematicks; and the civility of these little Citizens more neatly sets forth Wisdom of their Maker. Who admires not Regio-Montanus his Fly beyond his Eagle, or wonders not more at the operation of two Souls in those little Bodies, than but one in the Trunk of a Cedar? I could never content my contemplations with those general pieces of wonder, the Flux and Reflux of the Sea, the increase of Nile, the conversion of the Needle to the North; and have studied to match and parallel those in the more obvious and neglected pieces of Nature, which without further travel I can do in the Cosmography of myself. We carry with us the wonders we seek without us: there is all Africa and her prodigies in us; we are that bold and adventurous piece of Nature, which he that studies wisely learns in a compendium what others labour at in a divided piece and endless volume.

XVI   Thus there are two Books from whence I collect my Divinity; besides that written one of God, another of His servant Nature, that universal and publick Manuscript, that lies expans'd unto the Eyes of all: those that never saw Him in the one, have discovered Him in the other. This was the Scripture and Theology of the Heathens: the natural motion of the Sun made them more admire Him than its supernatural station did the Children of Israel; the ordinary effects of Nature wrought more admiration in them than in the other all His Miracles. Surely the Heathens knew better how to joyn and read these mystical Letters than we Christians, who cast a more careless Eye on these common Hieroglyphicks, and disdain to suck Divinity from the flowers of Nature. Nor do I so forget God as to adore the name of Nature; which I define not, with the Schools, to be the principle of motion and rest, but that straight and regular line, that settled and constant course the Wisdom of God hath ordained the actions of His creatures, according to their several kinds. To make a revolution every day is the Nature of the Sun, because of that necessary course which God hath ordained it, from which it cannot swerve but by a faculty from that voice which first did give it motion. Now this course of Nature God seldom alters or perverts, but, like an excellent Artist, hath so contrived His work, that with the self same instrument, without a new creation, He may effect His obscurest designs. Thus He sweetneth the Water with a Wood, preserveth the Creatures in the Ark, which the blast of His mouth might have as easily created; for God is like a skilful Geometrician, who, when more easily and with one stroak of his Compass he might describe or divide a right line, had yet rather do this in a circle or longer way, according to the constituted and forelaid principles of his Art. Yet this rule of His He doth sometimes pervert, to acquaint the World with His Prerogative, lest the arrogancy of our reason should question His power, and conclude He could not. And thus I call the effects of Nature the works of God, Whose hand and instrument she only is; and therefore to ascribe His actions unto her, is to devolve the honour of the principal agent upon the instrument; which if with reason we may do, then let our hammers rise up and boast they have built our houses, and our pens receive the honour of our writings. I hold there is a general beauty in the works of God, and therefore no deformity in any kind or species of creature whatsoever. I cannot tell by what Logick we call a Toad, a Bear, or an Elephant ugly; they being created in those outward shapes and figures which best express the actions of their inward forms, and having past that general Visitation of God, Who saw that all that He had made was good, that is, conformable to His Will, which abhors deformity, and is the rule of order and beauty. There is no deformity but in Monstrosity; wherein, notwithstanding, there is a kind of Beauty; Nature so ingeniously contriving the irregular parts, as they become sometimes more remarkable than the principal Fabrick. To speak yet more narrowly, there was never any thing ugly or mis-shapen, but the Chaos; wherein, notwithstanding, (to speak strictly,) there was no deformity, because no form; nor was it yet impregnant by the voice of God. Now Nature is not at variance with Art, nor Art with Nature, they being both servants of His Providence. Art is the perfection of Nature. Were the World now as it was the sixth day, there were yet a Chaos. Nature hath made one World, and Art another. In brief, all things are artificial; for Nature is the Art of God.

XVII This is the ordinary and open way of His Providence, which Art and Industry have in a good part discovered; whose effects we may foretell without an Oracle: to foreshew these, is not Prophesie, but Prognostication. There is another way, full of Meanders and Labyrinths, whereof the Devil and Spirits have no exact Ephemerides; and that is a more particular and obscure method of His Providence, directing the operations of individuals and single Essences: this we call Fortune, that serpentine and crooked line, whereby He draws those actions His Wisdom intends, in a more unknown and secret way. This cryptick and involved method of His Providence have I ever admired; nor can I relate the History of my life, the occurrences of my days, the escapes of dangers, and hits of chance, with a Bezo las Manos to Fortune, or a bare Gramercy to my good Stars. Abraham might have thought the Ram in the thicket came thither by accident; humane reason would have said that meer chance conveyed Moses in the Ark to the sight of Pharaoh's Daughter: what a Labyrinth is there in the story of Joseph, able to convert a Stoick! Surely there are in every man's Life certain rubs, doublings, and wrenches, which pass a while under the effects of chance, but at the last, well examined, prove the meer hand of God. 'Twas not dumb chance, that, to discover the Fougade or Powder-plot, contrived a miscarriage in the Letter. I like the Victory of '88 the better for that one occurrence, which our enemies imputed to our dishonour and the partiality of Fortune, to wit, the tempests and contrariety of Winds. King Philip did not detract from the Nation, when he said, he sent his Armado to fight with men, and not to combate with the Winds. Where there is a manifest disproportion between the powers and forces of two several agents, upon a Maxime of reason we may promise the Victory to the Superiour; but when unexpected accidents slip in, and unthought of occurrences intervene, these must proceed from a power that owes no obedience to those Axioms; where, as in the writing upon the wall, we may behold the hand, but see not the spring that moves it. The success of that petty Province of Holland (of which the Grand Seignour proudly said, if they should trouble him as they did the Spaniard, he would send his men with shovels and pick-axes, and throw it into the Sea,) I cannot altogether ascribe to the ingenuity and industry of the people, but the mercy of God, that hath disposed them to such a thriving Genius; and to the will of His Providence, that disposeth her favour to each Country in their pre-ordinate season. All cannot be happy at once; for, because the glory of one State depends upon the ruine of another, there is a revolution and vicissitude of their greatness, and must obey the swing of that wheel, not moved by Intelligences, but by the hand of God, whereby all Estates arise to their Zenith and Vertical points according to their predestinated periods. For the lives, not only of men, but of Commonwealths, and the whole World, run not upon an Helix, that still enlargeth, but on a Circle, where, arriving to their Meridian, they decline in obscurity, and fall under the Horizon again.

XVIII   These must not therefore be named the effects of Fortune, but in a relative way, and as we term the works of Nature. It was the ignorance of mans reason that begat this very name, and by a careless term miscalled the Providence of God; for there is no liberty for causes to operate in a loose and stragling way; nor any effect whatsoever, but hath its warrant from some universal or superiour Cause. 'Tis not a ridiculous devotion to say a prayer before a game at Tables; for even in sortilegies and matters of greatest uncertainty there is a settled and preordered course of effects. It is we that are blind, not Fortune: because our Eye is too dim to discover the mystery of her effects, we foolishly paint her blind, and hoodwink the Providence of the Almighty. I cannot justify that contemptible Proverb, That fools only are Fortunate, or that insolent Paradox, That a wise man is out of the reach of Fortune; much less those opprobrious epithets of Poets, Whore, Bawd, and Strumpet. 'Tis, I confess, the common fate of men of singular gifts of mind to be destitute of those of Fortune, which doth not any way deject the Spirit of wiser judgements, who thoroughly understand the justice of this proceeding; and being enriched with higher donatives, cast a more careless eye on these vulgar parts of felicity. It is a most unjust ambition to desire to engross the mercies of the Almighty, not to be content with the goods of mind, without a possession of those of body or Fortune; and it is an error worse than heresie, to adore these complemental and circumstantial pieces of felicity, and undervalue those perfections and essential points of happiness wherein we resemble our Maker. To wiser desires it is satisfaction enough to deserve, though not to enjoy, the favours of Fortune: let Providence provide for Fools. 'Tis not partiality, but equity in God, Who deals with us but as our natural Parents: those that are able of Body and Mind He leaves to their deserts; to those of weaker merits He imparts a larger portion, and pieces out the defect of one by the excess of the other. Thus have we no just quarrel with Nature for leaving us naked; or to envy the Horns, Hoofs, Skins, and Furs of other Creatures, being provided with Reason, that can supply them all. We need not labour with so many Arguments to confute Judicial Astrology; for, if there be a truth therein, it doth not injure Divinity. If to be born under Mercury disposeth us to be witty, under Jupiter to be wealthy; I do not owe a Knee unto these, but unto that merciful Hand that hath ordered my indifferent and uncertain nativity unto such benevolous Aspects. Those that hold that all things are governed by Fortune, had not erred, had they not persisted there. The Romans, that erected a Temple to Fortune, acknowledged therein, though in a blinder way, somewhat of Divinity; for, in a wise supputation, all things begin and end in the Almighty. There is a nearer way to Heaven than Homer's Chain; an easie Logic may conjoyn Heaven and Earth in one Argument, and with less than a Sorites, resolve all things into God. For though we christen effects by their most sensible and nearest Causes, yet is God the true and infallible Cause of all; whose concourse, though it be general, yet doth it subdivide it self into the particular Actions of every thing, and is that Spirit, by which each singular Essence not only subsists, but performs its operation.

The text is studded with allusions to classical literature and contemporary events, which make the text a little difficult for the modern reader. For example, "Regio-Montanus" is John Müller of Konigsberg (1636–75), who was rumored to have made an iron fly on a wooden eagle. The phrase "Bezo las Manos" is a Spanish term, which can be translated as "I kiss the hands," but has the deeper meaning of "acknowledge the importance of someone." The "Grand Seignour" is a reference to the Sultan of Turkey.

Questions for Study

1 What does Browne mean by "two books"? Do they share a common author?
2 Browne was both a natural historian and an antiquarian. In what ways can these two interests be seen in action in this text?
3 What role does Browne ascribe to divine providence?

CHAPTER 52

John Milton (1608–1674)

Milton is widely considered to be among the five greatest poets in the English language. John Milton was born and educated in London, the son of a musical composer. He was educated at St. Paul's School, London, before going up to Christ's College, Cambridge (1625–32). Even at this early stage, his literary talents were apparent; his *Ode on the Morning of Christ's Nativity* was written in 1629, and remains one of his most valued religious writings. On graduating, Milton returned to his father's estate at Horton in Buckinghamshire. His original intention was to become ordained in the Church of England; however, like many with Puritan sympathies at this time, he found himself alienated from that church by the repressive religious policies of Archbishop William Laud. Instead, he devoted himself to the study of literature and languages – including Greek, Latin, and Italian – and Christian theology, especially that of the early Church Fathers.

A number of significant literary works date from this period, including his poems *L'Allegro* and *Il Penseroso*, and his great pastoral elegy, *Lycidas*, held by most critics to be among the greatest examples of this literary form. In this elegy, Milton expresses his grief over the loss of a close college friend, Edward King. At this stage, Milton's interest in politics – both secular and ecclesiastical – began to develop. He became involved in what is known as the "Smectymnuus affair" of 1641. This centered on a defense of a presbyterian system of church government – as opposed to the episcopal system of the national church, and was penned by Stephen Marshall, Edmund Calamy, Thomas Young, Matthew Newcomen, and William Spurstow (whose initials gave rise to the curious title). Milton entered into this debate with treatises entitled *Of Reformation touching Church Discipline in England* and *The Reason of Church Government urged against Prelacy*.

As the Puritan constituency grew in influence, so Milton's status rose accordingly. Alongside this, a serious problem began to develop. During the mid-1640s, Milton began to suffer from deterioration of his eyesight, which eventually led to his becoming completely blind in 1651.

John Milton (1608–1674)

Basic description Puritan poet and ecclesiastical controversialist. **Major works** *Paradise Lost* (1667); *Paradise Regained* (1671).	**Major studies** C. S. Lewis, *A Preface to Paradise Lost*. Oxford: Oxford University Press, 1942. William Riley Parker, *Milton: A Biography*, 2nd edn. Oxford: Clarendon Press, 1996. Constantinos A. Patrides, *Milton and the Christian Tradition*. Oxford: Clarendon Press, 1966.

After the execution of Charles I, Milton became involved in the Commonwealth government of Oliver Cromwell, serving as Latin secretary to the Council of State. He served faithfully in these duties through the period, publishing a number of political works as circumstances demanded. Of particular note is his defense of the execution of Charles I, which is found in his *Tenure of Kings and Magistrates* (1649). Upon the restoration of the monarchy, Milton was arrested and fined, and eventually released.

After this fall from public power, John Milton found himself with time on his hands, and was thus free to make his most celebrated contribution to English literature. Although he is reputed to have penned parts of *Paradise Lost*, as early as 1642, the work was not completed until 1665, and was not published until 1667. The work consists of twelve books of blank verse, tracing the fall of humanity against the background of a cosmic drama which pitches Satan against God. This was followed by *Paradise Regained* (1671), a shorter work which focuses on Christ's temptation in the wilderness.

During the closing years of his life, Milton wrote miscellaneous prose works, including a history of Britain and a discussion of the logic of Peter Ramus, as well as a theological work, *De doctrina Christiana*, which was published posthumously (and, incidentally, shows Milton to have been of a decidedly independent cast of mind). He died of gout in 1674 and was buried next to his father in St. Giles Church, Cripplegate, London.

Text: *Paradise Lost*

The section of *Paradise Lost* which has been selected for study is the opening section of Book I, which sets the scene for the entire narrative of rebellion and fall of the angels and humanity. The difficulty which confronts readers of *Paradise Lost* – even this opening section – is that Milton seems to presuppose an almost encyclopedic knowledge on the part of his readers, especially in relation to the biblical material and the Christian theological tradition. The work can be read at many levels, including the following:

1 An epic poem, which stands in the tradition of *Beowulf* and Spenser's *Faerie Queene*. The opening lines of *Paradise Lost* suggest that Milton may have intended his epic to extend the biblical narrative of redemption – note, for example, the references to Horeb (= Sinai) in the opening section.

2 An example of theodicy – that is, a specific type of religious writing which aims to defend faith in God against criticisms regularly directed against it. *Paradise Lost* famously sets out to "justifie the wayes of God to men."

3 An *apologia* for human freedom. Milton was one of the most vigorous defenders of the freedom of speech, and published a number of political tracts to this end. Yet *Paradise Lost* can also be seen as a critical exploration of the limits of freedom, not least in regard to the consequences of the Fall.

4 A theological affirmation of divine providence. Milton develops a scenario in which every event is charged with meaning, and coinheres with other events to yield a complex yet ultimately unitary vision of the world.

The best approach to the work is probably just to start reading, and try to absorb the imagery and ideas as they develop. The original orthography has been used.

> Of Mans First Disobedience, and the Fruit
> Of that Forbidden Tree, whose mortal taste
> Brought Death into the World, and all our woe,
> With loss of *Eden*, till one greater Man
> Restore us, and regain the blissful Seat,   5
> Sing Heav'nly Muse, that on the secret top
> Of *Oreb*, or of *Sinai*, didst inspire
> That Shepherd, who first taught the chosen Seed,
> In the Beginning how the Heav'ns and Earth
> Rose out of *Chaos*: Or if *Sion* Hill   10
> Delight thee more, and *Siloa's* Brook that flowd
> Fast by the Oracle of God; I thence
> Invoke thy aid to my adventrous Song,
> That with no middle flight intends to soar
> Above th' *Aonian* Mount, while it persues   15
> Things unattempted yet in Prose or Rime.
> And chiefly Thou O Spirit, that dost preferr
> Before all Temples th' upright heart and pure,
> Instruct me, for Thou knowst; Thou from the first
> Wast present, and with mighty wings outspred   20
> Dove-like satst brooding on the vast Abyss
> And mad'st it pregnant: What in me is dark
> Illumin, what is low raise and support;
> That to the highth of this great Argument
> I may assert Eternal Providence,   25
> And justifie the wayes of God to men.
>   Say first, for Heav'n hides nothing from thy view
> Nor the deep Tract of Hell, say first what cause
> Mov'd our Grand Parents in that happy State,
> Favour'd of Heav'n so highly, to fall off   30
> From thir Creator, and transgress his Will
> For one restraint, Lords of the World besides?
> Who first seduc'd them to that foul revolt?
> Th' infernal Serpent; he it was, whose guile
> Stird up with Envy and Revenge, deceiv'd   35
> The Mother of Mankind, what time his Pride

Had cast him out from Heav'n, with all his Host
Of Rebel Angels, by whose aid aspiring
To set himself in Glory above his Peers,
He trusted to have equald the most High,   40
If he oppos'd; and with ambitious aim
Against the Throne and Monarchy of God
Rais'd impious War in Heav'n and Battel proud
With vain attempt. Him the Almighty Power
Hurld headlong flaming from th' Ethereal Skie   45
With hideous ruin and combustion down
To bottomless perdition, there to dwell
In Adamantine Chains and penal Fire,
Who durst defie th' Omnipotent to Arms.
Nine times the Space that measures Day and Night   50
To mortal men, hee with his horrid crew
Lay vanquisht, rouling in the fiery Gulf
Confounded though immortal: But his doom
Reserv'd him to more wrauth; for now the thought
Both of lost happiness and lasting pain   55
Torments him; round he throws his baleful eyes
That witnessd huge affliction and dismay
Mixt with obdurat pride and stedfast hate:
At once as far as Angels kenn he views
The dismal Situation waste and wild;   60
A Dungeon horrible, on all sides round
As one great Furnace flam'd, yet from those flames
No light, but rather darkness visible
Serv'd onely to discover sights of woe,
Regions of sorrow, doleful shades, where peace   65
And rest can never dwell, hope never comes
That comes to all; but torture without end
Still urges, and a fiery Deluge, fed
With ever-burning Sulphur unconsum'd:
Such place Eternal Justice had prepar'd   70
For those rebellious, here thir Pris'n ordaind
In utter darkness, and thir portion set
As far remov'd from God and light of Heav'n
As from the Center thrice to th' utmost Pole.
O how unlike the place from whence they fell!   75
There the companions of his fall, orewhelmd
With Floods and Whirlwinds of tempestuous fire,
He soon discerns, and weltring by his side
One next himself in power, and next in crime,
Long after known in *Palestine*, and nam'd   80
Beëlzebub. To whom th' Arch-Enemy,
And thence in Heav'n called *Satan*, with bold words
Breaking the horrid silence thus began.
    If thou beest he; But O how fall'n! how chang'd
From him, who in the happy Realms of Light   85
Cloth'd with transcendent brightness didst outshine
Myriads though bright: If he whom mutual league,

United thoughts and counsels, equal hope,
And hazard in the Glorious Enterprize,
Joind with me once, now misery hath joind   90
In equal ruin: into what Pit thou seest
From what highth fall'n, so much the stronger prov'd
Hee with his Thunder: and till then who knew
The force of those dire Arms? yet not for those
Nor what the Potent Victor in his rage   95
Can else inflict do I repent or change,
Though chang'd in outward lustre, that fixt mind
And high disdain, from sense of injurd merit,
That with the mightiest rais'd me to contend,
And to the fierce contention brought along   100
Innumerable force of Spirits armd
That durst dislike his reign, and mee preferring,
His utmost power with adverse power oppos'd
In dubious Battel on the Plains of Heav'n,
And shook his throne. What though the field be lost?   105
All is not lost; th'unconquerable Will,
And study of revenge, immortal hate,
And courage never to submit or yield:
And what is else not to be overcome?
That Glory never shall his wrauth or might   110
Extort from me. To bow and sue for grace
With suppliant knee, and deifie his power
Who from the terror of this Arm so late
Doubted his Empire, that were low indeed,
That were an ignominy and shame beneath   115
This downfall; since by Fate the strength of Gods
And this Empyreal substance cannot fail,
Since through experience of this great event
In Arms not worse, in foresight much advanc't,
We may with more successful hope resolve   120
To wage by force or guile eternal Warr
Irreconcileable, to our grand Foe,
Who now triumphs, and in th' excess of joy
Sole reigning holds the Tyranny of Heav'n.
    So spake th' Apostat Angel, though in pain,   125
Vaunting aloud, but rackt with deep despair:
And him thus answerd soon his bold Compeer.
    O Prince, O Chief of many Throned Powers,
That led th' imbatteld Seraphim to Warr
Under thy conduct, and in dreadful deeds   130
Fearless, endangerd Heav'ns perpetual King;
And put to proof his high Supremacy,
Whether upheld by strength, or Chance, or Fate;
Too well I see and rue the dire event,
That with sad overthrow and foul defeat   135
Hath lost us Heav'n, and all this mighty Host
In horrible destruction laid thus low,

As far as Gods and Heav'nly Essences
Can Perish: for the mind and spirit remains
Invincible, and vigor soon returns,   140
Though all our Glory extinct, and happy state
Here swallowd up in endless misery.
But what if hee our Conqueror (whom I now
Of force believe Almighty, since no less
Than such could have orepow'rd such force as ours)   145
Have left us this our spirit and strength entire
Strongly to suffer and support our pains,
That we may so suffice his vengeful ire
Or do him mightier service as his thralls
By right of Warr, what e're his buisness be   150
Here in the heart of Hell to work in Fire,
Or do his Errands in the gloomy Deep;
What can it then avail though yet we feel
Strength undiminisht, or eternal being
To undergo eternal punishment?   155
Whereto with speedy words th' Arch-fiend repli'd.
   Fall'n Cherube, to be weak is miserable
Doing or Suffering: but of this be sure,
To do aught good never will be our task,
But ever to do ill our sole delight,   160
As being the contrary to his high will
Whom we resist. If then his Providence
Out of our evil seek to bring forth good,
Our labour must be to pervert that end,
And out of good still to find means of evil;   165
Which oft times may succeed, so as perhaps
Shall grieve him, if I fail not, and disturb
His inmost counsels from thir destind aim.

Questions for Study

1 Read Genesis 1:1–2. In what way does Milton incorporate these opening verses of the Christian Bible into his epic? And what specific use does he make of them?
2 What initial reflections on the origins and consequences of the fall of humanity may be seen in this section? What is the "fruit of that forbidden tree" mentioned in lines 1–2? You may find it helpful to read Genesis 3 to make sense of this early part of the work.
3 Milton is particularly interested in the fall of the angels, and the role of Satan. What does this opening section of *Paradise Lost* tell us about the place and purpose of evil in the universe?
4 Milton speaks of asserting "the eternal providence" and of aiming to "justify the ways of God to men." How does this set the agenda for the work? And in what ways does this opening section begin this exploration?

CHAPTER 53

Jeremy Taylor (1613–1667)

Taylor was born in Cambridge as the son of a barber. After studying at the Perse School, he went on to become a sizar at Gonville and Caius College, paying his way through college by serving other wealthier students. He was ordained in 1634, after which he came to the attention of William Laud, who acted as his patron. He married Phoebe Langsdale in 1639. After serving as chaplain to William Laud, Taylor went on to serve as rector of Uppingham, Rutland.

Jeremy Taylor (1613–1667)

Basic description
Leading Caroline divine, preacher and moralist.

Major works
The Rules and Exercises of Holy Living (1650); *The Rules and Exercises of Holy Dying* (1651).

Editions of works
Holy Living and Holy Dying, ed. P. G. Stanwood, 2 vols. Oxford: Clarendon Press, 1989.

Major studies
Harry Boone Potter, *Christian Character: Jeremy Taylor, Liturgist*. London: SPCK, 1979.

C. J. Shanks, *The Life and Writings of Jeremy Taylor*. London: SPCK, 1952.

The outbreak of the English Civil War put an end to Taylor's hopes for preferment. Taylor supported the Royalist cause, and was thus out of favor during the period of the Puritan Commonwealth. He was imprisoned for part of the period of the Commonwealth; after his release, he spent the remaining years of the Protectorate living in Wales, serving as chaplain to Richard Vaughan. It was during this period that Taylor wrote the works for which he is best known, including *The Rules and Exercises of Holy Living* (1650) and *The Rules and Exercises of Holy Dying* (1651). This latter work was published in the year of his wife's death. These works are perhaps rather better known in their abbreviated forms of *Holy Living* and *Holy Dying*, and were often printed together in a single volume.

The works had a major influence on English piety; John Wesley founded the "Holy Club" in Oxford partly in response to the teachings of these works.

After the Restoration of Charles II (1660), he became bishop of the Irish diocese of Down and Connor. This was never an entirely happy time for Taylor. He faced considerable hostility from those who were opposed to the established church in Ireland, including both Roman Catholics and Presbyterians. Taylor felt that he was under siege from every corner of the theological spectrum. His repeated requests for a transfer to England were ignored, possibly on account of Taylor's slightly unorthodox views on original sin.

Called the "Shakespeare and the Spenser of the pulpit," Taylor was known for his mastery of fine metaphor and rhetorical flourishes in both his written and spoken prose. This can be seen particularly clearly from the opening section of *Holy Dying*, which we shall consider in what follows.

Text: *The Rules and Exercises of Holy Dying*

Holy Dying – to use the shorter version of the title of this work – is among Taylor's best-known works. Its full title is perhaps a little cumbersome, but has the immense advantage of allowing us to gain an immediate understanding of Taylor's objectives in writing the work: "The Rule And Exercises Of Holy Dying: In Which Are Described The Means And Instruments Of Preparing Ourselves And Others Respectively For A Blessed Death: And The Remedies Against The Evils And Temptations Proper To The State Of Sickness: Together With Prayers And Acts Of Virtue To Be Used By Sick And Dying Persons, Or By Others Standing In Their Attendance." The work includes a dedicatory preface to Richard Vaughan, Earl of Carberry, who had sheltered Taylor during his years of exile. "It is a great art to die well," commented Taylor; the work to which these words are prefaced aims to set out the means by which a Christian can die with dignity and peace.

While the work has a clear pastoral function, it is also possessed of considerable literary merit. Those merits can be seen from its opening section, in which Taylor deploys his considerable rhetorical skills to bring home to his readers that life is a precarious and transitory matter. If life is so short and uncertain, Taylor argues, it is natural to give thought as to how best to prepare for its ending.

A Consideration of the Vanity and Shortness of Man's Life

A man is a bubble, (said the Greek proverb) which Lucian represents with advantages and its proper circumstances, to this purpose; saying, that all the world is a storm, and men rise up in their several generations, like bubbles descending *a Jove pluvio*, from God and the dew of heaven, from a tear and drop of rain, from nature and Providence; and some of these instantly sink into the deluge of their first parent, and are hidden in a sheet of water, having had no other business in the world, but to be born, that they might be able to die: others float up and down two or three turns, and suddenly disappear, and give their place to others: and they that live longest upon the face of the waters are in perpetual motion, restless and uneasy; and, being crushed with a great drop of a cloud, sink into flatness and a froth; the change not being great, it being hardly possible it should be more a nothing than it was before. So is every man: he is born in vanity and sin; he comes into the world like morning mushrooms, soon thrusting up their heads into the air, and conversing with their kindred of the same production, and as soon they turn into dust and forgetfulness – some of them without any other interest in the affairs of the world, but that they made their parents a little glad and very sorrowful: others ride longer in the storm; it may be until seven years of vanity be expired, and then peradventure the sun shines hot upon their heads, and they fall into the shades below, into the cover of death and darkness of the grave to hide them. But if the bubble stands the shock of a bigger drop, and outlives the chances of a child, of a careless nurse, of drowning in a pail of water, of being overlaid by a sleepy servant, or such little accidents, then the young man dances like a bubble, empty and gay, and shines like a dove's neck, or the image of a rainbow, which hath no substance, and whose very imagery and colours are fantastical; and so he dances out the gaiety of his youth, and is all the while in a storm, and endures only because he is not knocked on the head by a drop of bigger rain, or crushed by the pressure of a load of indigested meat, or quenched by the disorder of an ill-placed humour: and to preserve a man alive in the midst of so many chances and hostilities is as great a miracle as to create him; to preserve him from rushing into nothing, and at first to draw him up from nothing were equally the issues of an almighty power. And therefore the wise men of the world have contended who shall best fit man's condition with words signifying his vanity and short abode. Honour calls a man "a leaf," the smallest, the weakest piece of a short-lived, unsteady plant. Pindar calls him "the dream of a shadow": another "the dream of the shadow of smoke." But St. James spake by a more excellent spirit, saying, "Our life is but a vapour," viz, drawn from the earth by a celestial influence; made of smoke, or the lighter parts of water tossed with every wind, moved by the motion of a superior body, without virtue in itself, lifted up on high, or left below, according as it pleased the sun, its foster-father. But it is lighter yet. It is but appearing; a fantastic vapour, an apparition, nothing real; it is not so much as a mist, not the matter of a shower, nor substantial enough to make a cloud; but it is like Cassiopeia's chair, or Pelop's shoulder, or the circles of heaven, for which you cannot have a word that can signify a verrier nothing. And yet the expression is one degree more made diminutive; a *vapour*, and *fantastical, or a mere appearance*, and this but for a little while neither, the very dream, the phantasm, disappears in a small time, "like the shadow that departed; or like a tale that is told, or as a dream when one waketh." A man is so vain, so unfixed, so perishing a creature, that he cannot long last in the scene of fancy: a man goes off, and is forgotten, like the dream of a distracted person. The sum of all is this: that thou art a man, than whom there is not in the world any greater instance of heights and declinations, of lights and shadows, of misery and folly, of laughter and tears, of groans and death.

And because this consideration is of great usefulness and great necessity to many purposes of wisdom and the spirit, all the succession of time, all the changes in nature, all the varieties of light and darkness, the thousand thousands of accidents in the world, and every contingency to every man and to every creature, doth preach our funeral sermon, and calls us to look and see how the old sexton, Time, throws up the earth, and digs a grave, where we must lay our sins or our sorrows, and sow our bodies, till they rise again in a fair or an intolerable eternity. Every revolution which the sun makes about the world divides between life and death; and death possesses both those portions by the next morrow; and we are dead to all those months of which we have already lived, and we shall never live them over again: and still God makes little periods of our age. First we change our world, when we come from the womb to feel the warmth of the sun. Then we sleep and enter into the image of death, in which state we are unconcerned in all the changes of the world: and if our mothers or our nurses die, or a wild boar destroy our vine-yards, or our king be sick, we regard it not, but, during that state, are as disinterested as if our eyes were closed with the clay that weeps in the bowels of the earth. At the end of seven years our teeth fall and die before us, representing a formal prologue to the tragedy; and still, every seven years it is odds [ed.: possible] but we shall finish the last scene: and when nature, or chance, or vice, takes our body in pieces, weakening some parts and loosing others, we taste the grave and the solemnities of our own funerals, first, in those parts that ministered to vice; and next, in them that served for ornament; and, in a short time, even they that served for necessity become useless and entangled like the wheels of a broken clock. Baldness is but a dressing to our funerals, the proper ornament of mourning, and of a person entered very far into the regions and possession of death; and we have many more of the same signification – gray hairs, rotten teeth, dim eyes, trembling joints, short breath, stiff limbs, wrinkled skin, short memory, decayed appetite. Every day's necessity calls for a reparation of that portion which death fed on all night, when we lay in his lap, and slept in his outer chambers. The very spirits of a man prey upon the daily portion of bread and flesh, and every meal is a rescue from one death, and lays up for another; and while we think a thought, we die; and the clock strikes, and reckons on our portion of eternity: we form our words with the breath of our nostrils – we have the less to live upon for every word we speak.

Thus nature calls us to meditate of death by those things which are the instruments of acting it; and God, by all the variety of his providence, makes us see death everywhere, in all variety of circumstances, and dressed up for all the fancies, and the expectation of every single person. Nature hath given us one harvest every year, but death hath two; and the spring and the autumn send throngs of men and women to charnel-houses; and the summer long men are recovering from their evils of the spring, till the dog-days come, and the Sirian star makes the summer deadly; and the fruits of autumn are laid up for all the year's provision, and the man that gathers them eats and surfeits, and dies and needs them not, and himself is laid up for eternity; and he that escapes till winter only stays for another opportunity, which the distempers of that quarter minister to him with great variety. Thus death reigns in all the portions of our time. The autumn with its fruit provides disorders for us, and the winter's cold turns them into sharp diseases, and the spring brings flowers to strew our hearse, and the summer gives green turf and brambles to bind upon our graves. Calentures and surfeit, cold and agues, are the four quarters of the year, and all minister to death; and you can no whither, but you tread upon a dead man's bones.

The wild fellow, in Petronius, that escaped upon a broken table from the furies of a shipwreck, as he was sunning himself upon the rocky shore, espied a man, rolled upon his floating bed of waves, ballasted with sand in the folds of his garment, and carried by his civil enemy, the sea, towards the shore to find a grave: and it cast him into some sad thoughts; that peradventure this man's wife, in some part of the continent, safe and warm, looks next month for the good man's return; or it may be, his son knows nothing of the tempest; or his father thinks of that affectionate kiss, which still is warm upon the good man's cheek, ever since he took a kind of farewell; and he weeps with joy to think how blessed he shall be when his beloved boy returns into the circle of his father's arms. These are the thoughts of mortals, this is the end and sum of all their designs: a dark night and an ill guide, a boisterous sea and a broken cable, a hard rock and a rough wind, dashed in pieces the fortune of a whole family; and they that shall weep loudest for the accident are not yet entered into the storm, and yet have suffered shipwreck. Then looking upon the carcass, he knew it, and found it to be the master of the ship, who, the day before, cast up the accounts of his patrimony and his trade, and named the day when he thought to be at home: see how the man swims who was so angry two days since; his passions are becalmed with the storm, his accounts cast up, his cares at an end, his voyage done, and his gains are the strange events of death, which, whether they be good or evil, the men that are alive seldom trouble themselves concerning the interest of the dead.

But seas alone do not break our vessel in pieces: everywhere we may be shipwrecked. A valiant general, when he is to reap the harvest of his crowns and triumphs, fights unprosperously, or falls into a fever with joy and wine, and changes his laurel into cypress, his triumphal chariot to a hearse; dying the night before he was appointed to perish in the drunkenness of his festival joys. It was a sad arrest of the loosenesses and wilder feasts of the French court, when their king [Henry II] was killed really by the sportive image of a fight. And many brides have died under the hands of paranymphs and maidens, dressing them for uneasy joy, the new and undiscerned chains of marriage, according to the saying of Bensirah, the wise Jew, "The bride went into her chamber, and knew not what should befall her there." Some have been paying their vows, and giving thanks for a prosperous return to their own house, and the roof hath descended upon their heads, and turned their loud religion into the deeper silence of a grave. And how many teeming mothers have rejoiced over their swelling wombs, and pleased themselves in becoming the channels of blessing to a family; and the midwife hath quickly bound their heads and feet, and carried them forth to burial! Or else the birth-day of an heir hath seen the coffin of the father brought into the house, and the divided mother hath been forced to travail twice, with a painful birth and a sudden death.

There is no state, no accident, no circumstance of our life, but it hath soured by some sad instance of a dying friend; a friendly meeting often ends in some mischance, and makes an eternal parting; and when the poet Eschylus was sitting under the walls of his house, an eagle hovering over his bald head mistook it for a stone, and let fall his oyster, hoping there to break the shell, but pierced the poor man's skull.

Death meets us everywhere, and is procured by every instrument, and in all chances and enters in at many doors; by violence and secret influence; by the aspect of a star and the stink of a mist; by the emissions of a cloud and the meeting of a vapour; by the fall of a chariot and the stumbling at a stone; by a full meal or an empty stomach; by watching at the wine or by watching at prayers; by the sun or the moon; by a heat or a cold; by sleepless nights or sleeping days; by water frozen into the hardness and sharpness of a dagger, or water thawed into the floods of a river; by a hair or a raisin; by violent motion or sitting still; by severity or dissolution; by God's mercy or God's anger; by everything in providence and everything in manners; by everything in nature and everything in chance. *Eripitur persona, manetres*, we take pains to heap up things useful to our life, and get our death in the purchase; and the person is snatched away, and the goods remain. And all this is the law and constitution of nature; it is a punishment to our sins, the unalterable event of Providence, and the decree of Heaven. The chains that confine us to this condition are strong as destiny, and immutable as the eternal laws of God.

I have conversed with some men who rejoiced in the death or calamity of others, and accounted it as a judgment upon them for being on the other side, and against them in the contention; but within the revolution of a few months the same man met with a more uneasy and unhandsome death; which when I saw, I wept, and was afraid; for I knew that it must be so with all men; for we also shall die, and end our quarrels and contentions by passing to a final sentence.

Questions for Study

1 Set out, in your own words, the chief arguments and images which Taylor uses to stress that life is short and unpredictable.
2 Human nature is like a bubble. How does Taylor develop and exploit this image?
3 How would you describe the tone of this work? "Gloomy," "realistic," "harsh," "depressing" – all these terms might be used. Why do you think that Taylor opens this work in this rather unpromising manner?

CHAPTER 54

Henry Vaughan (1622–1695)

Vaughan was born in the Brecon region of Wales, and went on to study at Jesus College, Oxford, where he became an ardent supporter of Charles I. He left Jesus College without taking a degree, and went on to study medicine in London. At some point around 1645, he returned to Brecon to practice medicine. A series of personal difficulties seem to have brought about some kind of spiritual conversion in his life. He would later comment that "certain divine rayes break out of the soul in adversity, like sparks out of the afflicted flint." In his own case, personal illness and the death of a brother combined with his distress at the total defeat of the Royalist cause in England under the Parliamentarian forces. His intense emotions can be seen expressed in his major work, *Silex Scintillans*, published in two parts in 1650 and 1655. Many have seen the influence of George Herbert in these poems. Discouraged by the lack of interest in his published works, Vaughan produced little after the second part of *Silex*.

Henry Vaughan (1622–1695)

Basic description
Welsh royalist poet.

Major work
Silex Scintillans (1650–5).

Editions of works
The Works of Henry Vaughan, ed. L. C. Martin, 2nd edn. Oxford: Clarendon Press, 1957.

Major studies
Thomas O. Calhoun, *Henry Vaughan: The Achievement of Henry Vaughan*. Newark, NJ: University of Delaware Press, 1981.
E. C. Pettet, *Of Paradise and Light: A Study of Vaughan's Silex Scintillans*. Cambridge: Cambridge University Press, 1960.

Text: The British Church

This major poem was included in the first part of *Silex Scintillans*, published in 1650. It reflects Vaughan's deep distress at the fate of the English national church under the Puritans. Vaughan was a passionate supporter of the royalist cause, and was shattered by the defeat of Charles I, and the devastating implications of this for the fate of the Church of England. The Puritan administration introduced radical church reforms, including the abolition of the episcopacy, and the replacement of traditional Prayer Books with new Puritan directories of public worship. It seemed to Vaughan that England's soul was being destroyed. "The British Church" conveys a deep sense of unease over the loss of the traditional ecclesiastical order. The radical changes are sweeping away the old order, and it is clear that Vaughan sees no hope of the restoration of traditional ecclesiastical structures and practices.

The British Church

Ah! he is fled!
And while these here their *mists*, and *shadowes* hatch,
My glorious head
Doth on those hills of Mirrhe, and Incense watch.
Haste, hast my dear,
The Souldiers here
Cast in their lots again,
That seamlesse coat
The Jews touch'd not,
These dare divide, and stain.

O get thee wings!
Or if as yet (until these clouds depart,
And the day springs,)
Thou think'st it good to tarry where thou art,
Write in thy bookes
My ravish'd looks
Slain flock, and pillag'd fleeces,
And hast thee so
As a young Roe
Upon the mounts of spices.

O Rosa Campi! O lilium Convallium! quomodo nunc facta es pabulum Aprorum!

The first stanza can be seen as a development of one of the themes of the passion narrative – the soldiers casting lots for the clothes of Christ. To understand the sources of Vaughan's imagery, we need to look at the relevant part of that narrative in the Jacobean English known to Vaughan:

Then the soldiers, when they had crucified Jesus, took his garments, and made four parts, to every soldier a part; and also his coat: now the coat was without seam, woven from the top throughout. They said therefore among themselves, Let us not rend it, but cast lots for it, whose it shall be: that the scripture might be fulfilled, which saith, They parted my raiment among them, and for my vesture they did cast lots. These things therefore the soldiers did. (John 19:23–24, King James Version)

There was a long tradition, stretching back to the third-century writer Cyprian of Carthage, which treated the "coat" as a metaphor or image of the church. Just as the soldiers did not rend the seamless robe of Christ, so no one was permitted to destroy the unity of the church.

Vaughan develops this image in a highly significant manner. The poem is written from the standpoint of the Bride of Christ – a traditional way of referring to the church, which is understood by Vaughan to refer specifically to the Church of England, as it had been under Charles I. This church is now being destroyed by the Puritans, and Vaughan protests against this in characteristically vigorous terms. The soldiers at the cross did not dare to divide the coat of Christ – yet the Puritans are tearing the Church of England apart. There is a sense of anger, even outrage, over what is happening.

This is developed further in the second stanza, which represents a direct appeal to the risen Christ to return and rescue his ravished and wounded bride. Three images are developed to bring home the idea that the church has been violated and pillaged. First, note the reference to "ravished looks"; the church has been violated by force. What was once a bride is now disfigured. Second, the reference to the "slain flock" is to be understood as a reference to the leading figures of the Church of England who have died defending its traditions during the English Civil War. Third, Vaughan's reference to "pillaged fleeces" is best understood as implying that the Parliamentarians have taken over the outward forms of the Church of England – for example, its buildings – while destroying its inner being.

The poem concludes with a remarkable appeal to the Song of Solomon, and it is perhaps best to cite the passages in question to grasp his meaning. "Make haste, my beloved, and be thou like to a roe or to a young hart upon the mountains of spices" (Song of Solomon 8:13, King James Version). Here, Vaughan appeals to Christ, as the lover of the church, to come to its aid in its darkest hour. The Latin tag with which the poem ends can be translated thus: "O rose of the field! O lily of the valley! How you have become the food of wild boars!" In this, we can see Vanghan's belief that the beauty of the church having been destroyed by the acts of vandalism and destruction perpetrated by the Puritans.

Text: Religion

The second poem is also taken from *Silex Scintillans*. "Religion" is perhaps the most familiar of Vaughan's poems, although it lacks the force of some of his more heartfelt writings. Its popularity reflects the ease with which it can be read and understood. The work is best seen as a lament for the loss of a sense of God. God, whose presence was known and acknowledged of old, seems to have become an absence, a memory rather than a living presence. Once more, Vaughan is pursuing an anti-Puritan agenda in this poem, taking the view that the recent religious changes involve dispossession and alienation. Vaughan's hope is that radical change may yet take place – but this time, undoing the damage of the Puritan era.

Religion

My God, when I walk in those groves
And leaves thy spirit still doth fan,
I see in each shade that there grows
An angel talking with a man.

Under a juniper some house,   5
Or the cool myrtle's canopy,
Others beneath an oak's green boughs,
Or at some fountain's bubbling eye;

Here Jacob dreams and wrestles; there
Elias by a raven is fed,   10
Another time by the angel, where
He brings him water with his bread;

In Abraham's tent the wingèd guests
(O how familiar then was heaven!)
Eat, drink, discourse, sit down, and rest   15
Until the cool and shady even;

Nay, thou thyself, my God, in fire,
Whirlwinds, and clouds, and the soft voice
Speak'st there so much, that I admire
We have no conference in these days.   20

Is the truce broke? or 'cause we have
A mediator now with thee,
Dost thou therefore old treaties waive
And by appeals from him decree?

Or is't so, as some green heads say,   25
That now all miracles muse cease,
Though thou hast promised they should stay
The tokens of the Church, and peace?

No, no; religion is a spring
That from some secret, golden mine   30
Derives her birth, and thence doth bring
Cordials in every drop, and wine;

But in her long and hidden course
Passing through the earth's dark veins,
Grows still from better unto worse,   35
And both her taste and colour stains,

Then drilling on, learns to increase
False echoes, and confusèd sounds,
And unawares doth often seize
On veins of sulphur underground;   40

So poisoned, breaks forth in some clime,
And at first sight doth many please,
But drunk, is puddle, or mere slime
And 'stead of physic, a disease.

Just such a tainted sink we have   45
Like that Samaritan's dead well,
Nor must we for the kernel crave
Because most voices like the shell.

Heal then these waters, Lord; or bring thy flock,
Since these are troubled, to the springing rock.   50
Look down, great Master of the Feast! O shine,
And turn once more our water into wine!

Questions for Study

1 The two opening verses depict what seems to be a paradise, in which God is seen
   and known everywhere. How many parallels can you see with Genesis 2, which
   depicts the state of humanity in the Garden of Eden?
2 The following pair of verses recall great moments in the Old Testament, when God
   was seen to be present and active. What are the incidents being related? Why do
   you think that Vaughan has chosen these?
3 The next two verses take on a darker tone. God may have been known in the past;
   but not now. The theme of "dispossession" makes its appearance. What does
   Vaughan mean when he writes: "We have no conference in these days"?
4 The verses which now follow mount an implicit criticism of Puritanism, even though
   it is never specifically mentioned. What might Vaughan mean when he writes that
   religion "grows still from better unto worse, and both her taste and colour stains"?
5 The final verse takes the form of a prayer, and is to be distinguished from the main
   body of the poem. What does the poem ask for? What does Vaughan mean when
   he asks God to "turn once more our water into wine"? (You will find it helpful to
   read John 2:1–11 first.)

CHAPTER 55

Andrew Marvell (1621–1678)

Marvell was born into a household with close connections with the Puritan movement in England. He was educated at Hull Grammar School in the north of England, and Trinity College, Cambridge. He appears to have spent the period 1642–6 outside England. According to a commendation from John Milton, he occupied himself with work in Holland, France, Italy, and Spain. Marvell's early writings suggest a sympathy for the Royalist cause during this turbulent period in English history.

Political discontent had been growing within England, and it was clear that a crisis was nearing. The English Civil War broke out in 1642, the year of Marvell's departure from England. By the time of Marvell's return to England, a Parliamentarian victory seemed assured. He secured appointments with leading figures in the new Parliamentarian establishment. In 1651, he accepted a position as tutor to the daughter of Lord Fairfax, who had defeated a Royalist army at Naseby in 1645. Some early poems reflect his debt to Fairfax, most notably his "Upon Appleton House, to my Lord Fairfax." Yet it was the rising figure of Oliver Cromwell who attracted Marvell's attention at this stage. Marvell's "Horatian Ode upon Cromwell's Return from Ireland" (1650) reflects the growing power of Cromwell within the Parliamentarian establishment. Marvell clearly regards Cromwell as constituting a force which would sweep away the remaining European monarchies, and usher in a new period of Protestant influence in Europe.

Marvell went on to serve as tutor to one of Oliver Cromwell's wards at Eton College in 1653, and became assistant to John Milton in 1657. The death of Oliver Cromwell in 1658 threw the Parliamentarian establishment into turmoil, something of which may be found in Marvell's "A Poem upon the Death of O.C."

Cromwell was succeeded by his son, Richard; this was a spectacular failure, and ended the following year. The restoration of Charles II seemed to put an end to Puritan hopes for a divine commonwealth in England. Marvell was elected Member of Parliament for Hull in 1659, and retained that position until his death. He continued to publish works of poetry anonymously, on account of the critical position they adopted toward the new establishment.

Andrew Marvell (1621–1678)

Basic description
English poet, with Puritan sympathies, whose most important writings date from the era of the Puritan commonwealth (1649–59).

Major works
"Horatian Ode upon Cromwell's Return from Ireland"; "Bermudas"; "The Coronet"; "The Mower against Gardens".

Editions of works
The Poems and Letters of Andrew Marvell, ed. H. M. Margoliouth, 2 vols, 3rd edn. Oxford: Clarendon Press, 1971.

Major studies
Rosalie Cole, *'My Echoing Song': Andrew Marvell's Poetry of Criticism*. Princeton, NJ: Princeton University Press, 1970.

John M. Wallace, *Destiny His Choice: The Loyalism of Andrew Marvell*. Cambridge: Cambridge University Press, 1968.

Text: Bermudas

Marvell's Puritan sympathies are perhaps best seen in a poem entitled "Bermudas," which was probably written around July 1653. At this point, Marvell was living in a house owned by John Oxenbridge, a Puritan divine who had been forced to flee to the Bermudas during the 1630s, during a particularly oppressive period in English religious history reflecting the intolerance of Archbishop William Laud for his Puritan rivals.

The Bermudas – a small group of uninhabited islands in the Atlantic, discovered in 1515 – come to play an almost mythical role in this poem. They are seen as a symbol of an unspoilt paradise, in which weary exiles from England can find peace and freedom. The poem reflects a general interest in the Americas, typical of much western European writing of the time. However, the New World had come to have new associations for Puritan writers, in that the first Puritan communities had been established in that region. The voyage of the *Mayflower* (1620) had become a major element in the Puritan self-consciousness. Marvell wrote this poem at a time in which there were heady expectations that the positive attitude toward Puritanism which an earlier generation could only dream of – or leave England to find – was about to emerge permanently within England itself, on account of the overthrow of the form of government which had persecuted the Puritans in the recent past.

The opening part of the poem (lines 1–4) sets the scene for the major section which follows. In this section (lines 5–36), Marvell depicts a small group of Puritan refugees arriving at the Bermudas, guided by a gracious providence (5–8). Note how the text implies that their arrival was unplanned; the refugees had set sail, and happened upon these islands "kinder than our own." Notice how the theme of divine providence dominates this section of the poem. It first emerges as Marvell depicts the refugees coming across the islands in the midst of a hostile sea; they have been guided there by the unseen hand of God. There are obvious parallels with the biblical account of Israel's exodus from Egypt and safe arrival in the Promised Land. The reference to being led through "the watry Maze" mingles both the theme of the crossing of the Red Sea and the wandering through the wilderness to the borders of Canaan.

The same theme then reappears as Marvell reflects on the exiles' newly-found safety from persecution. Note how Marvell comments on the refugees being delivered from both "Storms and Prelat's rage" – a reference to the persecutions instigated by Archbishop Laud in the 1630s. The extensive depiction of a paradise in which all manner of flora and fauna flourish is significant. The exiles will not be going hungry, just as the "eternal spring" will quench their thirst. Notice the constant reference to these resources being actively given by God. They are not just passively "there"; they have been actively provided by a kindly providence.

A final point of interest concerns the reference to the worship of the exiles.

> And in these Rocks for us did frame
> A Temple, where to sound his Name.

These lines should be seen as a criticism of one of the most distinctive features of Archbishop Laud's ecclesiastical policies – the building of architecturally elaborate church buildings, within which very grandiose forms of worship were performed. For Marvell, the Puritan exiles were content to worship God in the simplicity and purity of nature. The simplicity of that praise, for Marvell, would be enough to challenge the elaborate ceremonial of the Laudian English church – or, indeed, the Roman Catholic church (note the reference to "Mexique Bay," denoting the region of the Americas which had recently been colonized by Roman Catholics). The exiles may have failed to reform their own nation; God's providence had, however, placed them in a situation in which they might reform other regions of the world in its place.

> Where the remote *Bermudas* ride
> In th'Oceans bosome unespy'd,
> From a small Boat, that row'd along,
> The listning Winds receiv'd this Song.
>
> What should we do but sing his Praise   5
> That led us through the watry Maze,
> Unto an Isle so long unknown,
> And yet far kinder than our own?
> Where he the huge Sea-Monsters wracks,
> That lift the Deep upon their Backs.   10
> He lands us on a grassy Stage;
> Safe from the Storms, and Prelat's rage,
> He gave us this eternal Spring,
> Which here enamells every thing;
> And sends the Fowl's to us in care,   15
> On daily Visits through the Air.
> He hangs in shades the Orange bright,
> Like golden Lamps in a green Night.
> And does in the Pomgranates close,

Jewels more rich than *Ormus* show's.   20
He makes the Figs our mouths to meet;
And throws the Melons at our feet.
But Apples plants of such a price,
No Tree could ever bear them twice.
With Cedars, chosen by his hand,   25
From *Lebanon*, he stores the Land.
And makes the hollow Seas, that roar,
Proclaime the Ambergris on shoar.
He cast (of which we rather boast)
The Gospels Pearl upon our Coast.   30
And in these Rocks for us did frame
A Temple, where to sound his Name.
Oh let our Voice his Praise exalt,
Till it arrive at Heavens Vault:
Which thence (perhaps) rebounding, may   35
Eccho beyond the *Mexique Bay*.
Thus sung they, in the *English* boat,
An holy and a chearful Note,
And all the way, to guide their Chime,
With falling Oars they kept the time.   40

Questions for Study

1   Why do you think Marvell chose the Bermudas as the location for this poem?
2   What parallels do you think Marvell wants his readers to draw between the history
    of Israel from the exodus to the entry into the promised land and the fate of these
    refugees?
3   What do you think Marvell means by these lines?
       He cast (of which we rather boast)
       The Gospels Pearl upon our Coast.

Text: The Coronet

The second poem included in this collection is widely regarded as one of the finest pieces
of seventeenth-century devotional verse. The poem is unusual, in that Marvell chooses
to engage with the issue of poetry itself, rather than just the religious emotions and ideas
which poetry might convey. The poem is represented as coming from the mouth of a
repentant shepherd.

When for the Thorns with which I long, too long,
With many a piercing wound,
My Saviours head have crown'd,
I seek with Garlands to redress that Wrong:

Through every Garden, every Mead,
I gather flow'rs (my fruits are only flow'rs)
Dismantling all the fragrant Towers
That once adorn'd my Shepherdesses head.
And now when I have summ'd up all my store,
Thinking (so I my self deceive)
So rich a Chaplet thence to weave
As never yet the king of Glory wore:
Alas I find the Serpent old
That, twining in his speckled breast,
About the flow'rs disguis'd does fold,
With wreaths of Fame and Interest.
Ah, foolish Man, that would'st debase with them,
And mortal Glory, Heavens Diadem!
But thou who only could'st the Serpent tame,
Either his slipp'ry knots at once untie,
And disintangle all his winding Snare:
Or shatter too with him my curious frame:
And let these wither, so that he may die,
Though set with Skill and chosen out with Care.
That they, while Thou on both their Spoils dost tread,
May crown thy Feet, that could not crown thy Head.

The poem opens with an affirmation that devotional poetry has its origins in a sense of personal sin, which is brought home by contemplating the figure of Christ dying on the cross. The "fragrant towers" – that is, the elaborate and high head-dresses favored by women of this period – are dismantled, in order to refashion them into a "chaplet" fit for Christ. The basic idea is that the poet, deeply moved by Christ's suffering for his sins, chooses to redirect his skills from the praise of nature to that of the redeemer. The poet's skill, once deployed in the depiction and praise of the natural world, is now deployed in the service of religious devotion (lines 1–12). This is seen as an act of penance, by which the poet seeks to "redress that wrong" by which he has failed to honor the Savior.

Yet the garlands which the poet heaps upon his Savior prove to be hopelessly inadequate. Though "set with skill and chosen out with care" (line 24), the verbal garlands are just not good enough to do justice to Christ. They are perhaps worthy to adorn his feet – but certainly not his head. We can see here an important statement of the limitations of poetic language in relation to its devotional purpose.

However, Marvell detects a deeper concern. Calling to mind the Fall narrative of Genesis 3, he points out that sin is able to break into the very process of writing devotional poetry itself. His intention might have been

> So rich a chaplet thence to weave
> As never yet the King of Glory wore.

Yet the very act of wishing to outshine and outperform all tributes to date brings with it the sin of envy and rivalry. The "Serpent old" – which is here treated as a personification of sin, following Genesis 3 – makes its presence felt, as a poem which was intended to praise Christ becomes instead a means of raising its author's profile. Although the object was to praise Christ, the poem proves to be a subtle means of earning praise for its writer. The flowers that were meant to be a "chaplet" for Christ degenerate into "wreaths of fame and interest":

> Alas I find the Serpent old
> That, twining in its speckled breast,
> About the flow'rs disguis'd does fold,
> With wreaths of Fame and Interest.

So what is to be done? How is this intrusion of self-interest into the poetic process to be dealt with? "Slippery knots" entwine the honorable desire to praise God, and the sinful – yet largely unacknowledged – desire for fame as the creator of the work of art itself. The poet thus deceives himself, by failing to note this tension within the creative process. Marvell explores the possibility of destroying such a creation. Just as Christ, as redeemer, trod the serpent under his feet, so he must destroy this "curious frame" – that is, the elaborately-wrought structure of the poem itself. The poem thus stands out on account of its exploration of one of the most fundamental tensions of devotional poetry – namely, that the stated objective of such poetry (the praise of God) is all too subtly subverted into the praise of the poet.

Questions for Study

1 How many parallels can you see between this poem and the gospel passion narratives?
2 Notice that the "crown of thorns," which Christ was forced to wear at his crucifixion, is hinted at in the first line of the poem. How does this relate to the image of the "garland" in line 4?
3 Write down all the words or phrases in the poem which have to do with flowers. Why do you think Marvell makes such extensive use of this kind of imagery?
4 Why do you think the poem is titled "The Coronet"? (You may find it useful here to ask why Marvell did not use the more obvious title "The Crown").

Blaise Pascal (1623–1662)

Blaise Pascal was born in Clermont (now Clermont-Ferrand) in the Auvergne region of France, as the third of Etienne Pascal's children and his only son. The Pascal family was a conventional Catholic group, without any remarkable religious views or enthusiasm. Blaise's mother died when he was only three years old. In 1632 the Pascal family, Etienne and his four children, left Clermont and settled in Paris. Blaise Pascal's father was noted for his unorthodox educational views, which led him to teach his son himself rather than entrust him to anyone else. Etienne Pascal decided that Blaise was not to study mathematics before the age of fifteen and all mathematics texts were removed from their house. Blaise however, his curiosity raised by this, started to work on geometry himself at the age of twelve. He worked out for himself that the sum of the angles of a triangle are two right angles, and when his father found out he relented, and allowed Blaise a copy of Euclid.

Pascal showed precocious talent as a mathematician. At the age of fourteen Blaise Pascal started to accompany his father to Mersenne's meetings. Mersenne belonged to the religious order of the Minims, and his cell in Paris was a frequent meeting place for intellectuals such as Auzout, Carcavi, Desargues, Fermat, Gassendi, Mydorge, Mylonand, and Roberval. In June 1639, at the age of sixteen, Pascal presented a single piece of paper to one of Mersenne's meetings, on which were written down a number of projective geometry theorems relating to conic sections. This excited considerable interest and admiration on the part of other members of the group.

In December 1639 the Pascal family left Paris to live in Rouen where Etienne had been appointed as a tax collector for Upper Normandy. Shortly after settling in Rouen, Blaise had his first work, *An Essay on Conic Sections*, published in February 1640. His father's work as a tax collector led Pascal to invent what is now recognized as one of the world's earliest digital calculators. The process took three years (1642–5). The device, called the Pascaline, resembled a mechanical calculator of the 1940s. This, almost certainly, makes Pascal the second person to invent a mechanical calculator, in that Schickard had manufactured one in 1624.

Blaise Pascal (1623–1662)

Basic description
Mathematician, physicist and religious thinker.

Major works
Provincial Letters (1656–7); *Pensées* (1656–7).

Major studies
Thomas V, Morris, *Making Sense of it All: Pascal and the Meaning of Life*. Grand Rapids, MI: Eerdmans, 1992.

Marvin Richard O'Connell, *Blaise Pascal: Reasons of the Heart*. Grand Rapids, MI: Eerdmans, 1997.

The year 1646 was of particular significance for the young Pascal. In that year, his father injured his leg and had to recuperate in his house under the care of two young followers of Cornelius Jansen, who was based just outside Rouen. They had a profound effect on the young Pascal, who became deeply interested in religious matters as a result. In September 1651, Pascal's father died. This led the young man (then aged 29) to throw himself into the hectic and rather bucolic social life of his friends for about two years. His experiences of these hedonist days are generally thought to lie behind many of the more somber reflections on the shortcomings of the human condition which pervade his *Pensées*.

Pascal now began a series of experiments on atmospheric pressure. By 1647 he had proved to his satisfaction that a vacuum existed. In August of 1648 Pascal observed that the pressure of the atmosphere decreases with height and deduced that a vacuum existed above the atmosphere. From May 1653 Pascal worked on mathematics and physics, writing his *Treatise on the Equilibrium of Liquids* (1653), in which he explains Pascal's law of pressure. This treatise is basically a complete outline of a system of hydrostatics, the first in the history of science. It embodies his most distinctive and important contribution to physical theory. In addition, Pascal continued his work on conic sections and produced important theorems in projective geometry. In *The Generation of Conic Sections* (mostly completed by March 1648 but worked on again in 1653 and 1654) Pascal considered conics generated by central projection of a circle. This was meant to be the first part of a treatise on conics, which Pascal never completed. The work is now lost but Leibniz and Tschirnhaus both made notes from it and it is through these notes that a fairly complete picture of the work is now possible. Although Pascal was not the first to study what is now known as "Pascal's triangle," his work on the topic in *Treatise on the Arithmetical Triangle* was the most important on this topic and, through the work of Wallis, Pascal's work on the binomial coefficients was to lead Newton to his discovery of the general binomial theorem for fractional and negative powers. In correspondence with Fermat he laid the foundation for the theory of probability. Despite growing problems with his health, he worked intensely on scientific and mathematical questions until October 1654. Sometime around then he nearly lost his life in an accident. The horses pulling his carriage bolted and the carriage was left hanging over a bridge above the river Seine. Although he was rescued without any physical injury, it seems that he was much affected psychologically. Not long after, he underwent a further mystical religious experience, on November 23, 1654, and he pledged his life to Christianity. This experience is usually referred to as "the night of fire," on account of the prominence of the imagery of fire in his descriptions of what he underwent. A record of the event was sewn into the lining of his coat, and was only found after his death.

After this time Pascal made visits to the Jansenist monastery Port-Royal des Champs about 30 km southwest of Paris. He began to publish anonymous works on religious topics, eighteen *Provincial Letters* being published during 1656 and early 1657. These were written in defense of his friend Antoine Arnauld, an opponent of the Jesuits and a defender of Jansenism, who was on trial before the faculty of theology in Paris for his controversial religious works. Pascal's involvement with Jansenism – which orthodox Catholics regarded as heretical – is unquestionably one of the most important developments in his life, and it moved him to enter a longstanding and rather vicious dispute between the Jansenists and Jesuits. Pascal's *Provincial Letters*, written under the pseudonym of "Louis de Montalte," are widely regarded as setting new standards in French polemical prose style. Interestingly, it is far from clear how many distinctively Jansenist ideas Pascal actually adopted. What is much clearer is that Pascal developed an admiration for the writings of Augustine, which can be seen reflected in his later writings, especially his *Pensées*. Pascal's most famous theological and philosophical work is the *Pensées*, a collection of personal thoughts on human suffering and faith in God which he began in late 1656 and continued to work on during 1657 and 1658. This work contains a statement of what is known as "Pascal's wager," which claims to prove that belief in God is rational on account of the following consideration: If God does not exist, one will lose nothing by believing in him, while if he does exist, one will lose everything by not believing.

The text for study is taken from the *Pensées*, perhaps Pascal's best-known religious and philosophical work.

Text: *Pensées*

The *Pensées* take the form of a collection of thoughts (French: *pensées*), grouped loosely around certain major themes. The dating of the individual "thoughts" is often far from clear. In the section which we shall consider in this extract, Pascal wrestles with the limitations placed upon human nature, which he feels that philosophers are reluctant to accept, particularly in relation to the need for humanity to relate to God in order to achieve fulfillment. The themes developed in this extract are characteristic of the *Pensées* as a whole.

Section II: The Misery of Man Without God

60   First part: Misery of man without God.

Second part: Happiness of man with God.

Or, First part: That nature is corrupt. Proved by nature itself.

Second part: That there is a Redeemer. Proved by Scripture.

61   Order.   I might well have taken this discourse in an order like this: to show the vanity of all conditions of men, to show the vanity of ordinary lives, and then the vanity of philosophic lives, sceptics, stoics; but the order would not have been kept. I know a little what it is, and how few people understand it. No human science

can keep it. Saint Thomas did not keep it. Mathematics keep it, but they are useless on account of their depth.

62   Preface to the first part.   To speak of those who have treated of the knowledge of self; of the divisions of Charron, which sadden and weary us; of the confusion of Montaigne; that he was quite aware of his want of method and shunned it by jumping from subject to subject; that he sought to be fashionable. His foolish project of describing himself! And this not casually and against his maxims, since every one makes mistakes, but by his maxims themselves, and by first and chief design. For to say silly things by chance and weakness is a common misfortune, but to say them intentionally is intolerable, and to say such as that . . .

63   Montaigne.   Montaigne's faults are great. Lewd words; this is bad, notwithstanding Mademoiselle de Gournay. Credulous; people without eyes. Ignorant; squaring the circle, a greater world. His opinions on suicide, on death. He suggests an indifference about salvation, without fear and without repentance. As his book was not written with a religious purpose, he was not bound to mention religion; but it is always our duty not to turn men from it. One can excuse his rather free and licentious opinions on some relations of life; but one cannot excuse his thoroughly pagan views on death, for a man must renounce piety altogether, if he does not at least wish to die like a Christian. Now, through the whole of his book his only conception of death is a cowardly and effeminate one.

64   It is not in Montaigne, but in myself, that I find all that I see in him.

65   What good there is in Montaigne can only have been acquired with difficulty. The evil that is in him, I mean apart from his morality, could have been corrected in a moment, if he had been informed that he made too much of trifles and spoke too much of himself.

66   One must know oneself. If this does not serve to discover truth, it at least serves as a rule of life, and there is nothing better.

67   The vanity of the sciences.   Physical science will not console me for the ignorance of morality in the time of affliction. But the science of ethics will always console me for the ignorance of the physical sciences.

68   Men are never taught to be gentlemen and are taught everything else; and they never plume themselves so much on the rest of their knowledge as on knowing how to be gentlemen. They only plume themselves on knowing the one thing they do not know.

69   The infinites, the mean.   When we read too fast or too slowly, we understand nothing.

70   Nature . . .   Nature has set us so well in the centre, that if we change one side of the balance, we change the other also. This makes me believe that the springs in our brain are so adjusted that he who touches one touches also its contrary.

71   Too much and too little wine. Give him none, he cannot find truth; give him too much, the same.

72   Man's disproportion.   This is where our innate knowledge leads us. If it be not true, there is no truth in man; and if it be true, he finds therein great cause for humiliation, being compelled to abase himself in one way or another. And since he cannot exist without this knowledge, I wish that, before entering on deeper researches

into nature, he would consider her both seriously and at leisure, that he would reflect upon himself also, and knowing what proportion there is . . . Let man then contemplate the whole of nature in her full and grand majesty, and turn his vision from the low objects which surround him. Let him gaze on that brilliant light, set like an eternal lamp to illumine the universe; let the earth appear to him a point in comparison with the vast circle described by the sun; and let him wonder at the fact that this vast circle is itself but a very fine point in comparison with that described by the stars in their revolution round the firmament. But if our view be arrested there, let our imagination pass beyond; it will sooner exhaust the power of conception than nature that of supplying material for conception. The whole visible world is only an imperceptible atom in the ample bosom of nature. No idea approaches it. We may enlarge our conceptions beyond an imaginable space; we only produce atoms in comparison with the reality of things. It is an infinite sphere, the centre of which is everywhere, the circumference nowhere. In short, it is the greatest sensible mark of the almighty power of God that imagination loses itself in that thought.

Returning to himself, let man consider what he is in comparison with all existence; let him regard himself as lost in this remote corner of nature; and from the little cell in which he finds himself lodged, I mean the universe, let him estimate at their true value the earth, kingdoms, cities, and himself. What is a man in the Infinite?

But to show him another prodigy equally astonishing, let him examine the most delicate things he knows. Let a mite be given him, with its minute body and parts incomparably more minute, limbs with their joints, veins in the limbs, blood in the veins, humours in the blood, drops in the humours, vapours in the drops. Dividing these last things again, let him exhaust his powers of conception, and let the last object at which he can arrive be now that of our discourse. Perhaps he will think that here is the smallest point in nature. I will let him see therein a new abyss. I will paint for him not only the visible universe, but all that he can conceive of nature's immensity in the womb of this abridged atom. Let him see therein an infinity of universes, each of which has its firmament, its planets, its earth, in the same proportion as in the visible world; in each earth animals, and in the last mites, in which he will find again all that the first had, finding still in these others the same thing without end and without cessation. Let him lose himself in wonders as amazing in their littleness as the others in their vastness. For who will not be astounded at the fact that our body, which a little while ago was imperceptible in the universe, itself imperceptible in the bosom of the whole, is now a colossus, a world, or rather a whole, in respect of the nothingness which we cannot reach? He who regards himself in this light will be afraid of himself, and observing himself sustained in the body given him by nature between those two abysses of the Infinite and Nothing, will tremble at the sight of these marvels; and I think that, as his curiosity changes into admiration, he will be more disposed to contemplate them in silence than to examine them with presumption.

For, in fact, what is man in nature? A Nothing in comparison with the Infinite, an All in comparison with the Nothing, a mean between nothing and everything. Since he is infinitely removed from comprehending the extremes, the end of things and their beginning are hopelessly hidden from him in an impenetrable secret; he is equally incapable of seeing the Nothing from which he was made, and the Infinite in which he is swallowed up.

What will he do then, but perceive the appearance of the middle of things, in an eternal despair of knowing either their beginning or their end. All things proceed from the Nothing, and are borne towards the Infinite. Who will follow these marvellous processes? The Author of these wonders understands them. None other can do so.

Through failure to contemplate these Infinites, men have rashly rushed into the examination of nature, as though they bore some proportion to her. It is strange that they have wished to understand the beginnings of things, and thence to arrive at the knowledge of the whole, with a presumption as infinite as their object. For surely this design cannot be formed without presumption or without a capacity infinite like nature.

If we are well informed, we understand that, as nature has graven her image and that of her Author on all things, they almost all partake of her double infinity. Thus we see that all the sciences are infinite in the extent of their researches. For who doubts that geometry, for instance, has an infinite infinity of problems to solve? They are also infinite in the multitude and fineness of their premises; for it is clear that those which are put forward as ultimate are not self-supporting, but are based on others which, again having others for their support, do not permit of finality. But we represent some as ultimate for reason, in the same way as in regard to material objects we call that an indivisible point beyond which our senses can no longer perceive anything, although by its nature it is infinitely divisible.

Of these two Infinites of science, that of greatness is the most palpable, and hence a few persons have pretended to know all things. "I will speak of the whole," said Democritus.

But the infinitely little is the least obvious. Philosophers have much oftener claimed to have reached it, and it is here they have all stumbled. This has given rise to such common titles as First Principles, Principles of Philosophy, and the like, as ostentatious in fact, though not in appearance, as that one which blinds us, *De omni scibili*.

We naturally believe ourselves far more capable of reaching the centre of things than of embracing their circumference. The visible extent of the world visibly exceeds us; but as we exceed little things, we think ourselves more capable of knowing them. And yet we need no less capacity for attaining the Nothing than the All. Infinite capacity is required for both, and it seems to me that whoever shall have understood the ultimate principles of being might also attain to the knowledge of the Infinite. The one depends on the other, and one leads to the other. These extremes meet and reunite by force of distance and find each other in God, and in God alone.

Let us, then, take our compass; we are something, and we are not everything. The nature of our existence hides from us the knowledge of first beginnings which are born of the Nothing; and the littleness of our being conceals from us the sight of the Infinite.

Our intellect holds the same position in the world of thought as our body occupies in the expanse of nature.

Limited as we are in every way, this state which holds the mean between two extremes is present in all our impotence. Our senses perceive no extreme. Too much sound deafens us; too much light dazzles us; too great distance or proximity hinders our view. Too great length and too great brevity of discourse tend to obscurity; too much truth is paralysing (I know some who cannot understand that to take four from nothing leaves nothing). First principles are too self-evident for us; too much pleasure disagrees with us. Too many concords are annoying in music; too many benefits irritate us; we wish to have the wherewithal to overpay our debts. *Beneficia eo usque laeta sunt dum videntur exsolvi posse; ubi multum antevenere, pro gratia odium redditur.* We feel neither extreme heat nor extreme cold. Excessive qualities are prejudicial to us and not perceptible by the senses; we do not feel but suffer them. Extreme youth and extreme age hinder the mind, as also too much and too little education. In short, extremes are for us as though they were not, and we are not within their notice. They escape us, or we them.

This is our true state; this is what makes us incapable of certain knowledge and of absolute ignorance. We sail within a vast sphere, ever drifting in uncertainty, driven from end to end. When we think to attach ourselves to any point and to fasten to it, it wavers and leaves us; and if we follow it, it eludes our grasp, slips past us, and vanishes for ever. Nothing stays for us. This is our natural condition and yet most contrary to our inclination; we burn with desire to find solid ground and an ultimate sure foundation whereon to build a tower reaching to the Infinite. But our whole groundwork cracks, and the earth opens to abysses.

Let us, therefore, not look for certainty and stability. Our reason is always deceived by fickle shadows; nothing can fix the finite between the two Infinites, which both enclose and fly from it.

If this be well understood, I think that we shall remain at rest, each in the state wherein nature has placed him. As this sphere which has fallen to us as our lot is always distant from either extreme, what matters it that man should have a little more knowledge of the universe? If he has it, he but gets a little higher. Is he not always infinitely removed from the end, and is not the duration of our life equally removed from eternity, even if it lasts ten years longer?

In comparison with these Infinites, all finites are equal, and I see no reason for fixing our imagination on one more than on another. The only comparison which we make of ourselves to the finite is painful to us.

If man made himself the first object of study, he would see how incapable he is of going further. How can a part know the whole? But he may perhaps aspire to know at least the parts to which he bears some proportion. But the parts of the world are all so related and linked to one another that I believe it impossible to know one without the other and without the whole.

Man, for instance, is related to all he knows. He needs a place wherein to abide, time through which to live, motion in order to live, elements to compose him, warmth and food to nourish him, air to breathe. He sees light; he feels bodies; in short, he is in a dependent alliance with everything. To know man, then, it is necessary to know how it happens that he needs air to live, and, to know the air, we must know how it is thus related to the life of man, etc. Flame cannot exist without air; therefore, to understand the one, we must understand the other.

Since everything, then, is cause and effect, dependent and supporting, mediate and immediate, and all is held together by a natural though imperceptible chain which binds together things most distant and most different, I hold it equally impossible to know the parts without knowing the whole and to know the whole without knowing the parts in detail.

The eternity of things in itself or in God must also astonish our brief duration. The fixed and constant immobility of nature, in comparison with the continual change which goes on within us, must have the same effect.

And what completes our incapability of knowing things is the fact that they are simple and that we are composed of two opposite natures, different in kind, soul and body. For it is impossible that our rational part should be other than spiritual; and if any one maintain that we are simply corporeal, this would far more exclude us from the knowledge of things, there being nothing so inconceivable as to say that matter knows itself. It is impossible to imagine how it should know itself.

So, if we are simply material, we can know nothing at all; and if we are composed of mind and matter, we cannot know perfectly things which are simple, whether spiritual or corporeal. Hence it comes that almost all philosophers have confused ideas of things, and speak of material things in spiritual terms, and of spiritual things in material terms. For they say boldly that bodies have a tendency to fall, that they seek after their centre, that they fly from destruction, that they fear the void, that they have inclinations, sympathies, antipathies, all of which attributes pertain only to mind. And in speaking of minds, they consider them as in a place, and attribute to them movement from one place to another; and these are qualities which belong only to bodies. Instead of receiving the ideas of these things in their purity, we colour them with our own qualities, and stamp with our composite being all the simple things which we contemplate.

Who would not think, seeing us compose all things of mind and body, but that this mixture would be quite intelligible to us? Yet it is the very thing we least understand. Man is to himself the most wonderful object in nature; for he cannot conceive what the body is, still less what the mind is, and least of all how a body should be united to a mind. This is the consummation of his difficulties, and yet it is his very being. *Modus quo corporibus adhaerent spiritus comprehendi ab hominibus non potest, et hoc tamen homo est.*

Questions for Study

1   On the basis of this passage, what reasons does Pascal advance for human beings having a tendency toward dissatisfaction and "misery"?

2   The extract takes the form of a collection of individual passages or "thoughts." Sometimes these are quite short and succinct; at other times, they are more extended and developed. How does this literary form affect the reader of the text? Does it aid or inhibit comprehension?

3   "It is the greatest sensible mark of the almighty power of God that imagination loses itself in that thought." Locate this citation, and study it in its context. What does Pascal mean by it?

CHAPTER 57

John Bunyan (1626–1688)

Bunyan is perhaps one of the best-known Puritan writers of the seventeenth century. He was born in the English county of Bedfordshire, and became involved with the Puritan cause during the English Civil War. With the establishment of the Puritan commonwealth, Bunyan turned his attention to preaching, and became the minister of an independent congregation in Bedford. His Puritan sympathies caused him to be out of favor when the English monarchy was restored in 1660, with the result that he spent many years inside Bedford jail.

John Bunyan (1626–1688)

Basic description
English Puritan activist and writer.

Major works
Grace Abounding; The Pilgrim's Progress.

Major studies
Paula R. Backsheider, *A Being More Intense: A Study of the Prose Works of Bunyan, Swift, and Defoe.* New York: AMS Press, 1984.
E. Beatrice Batson, *John Bunyan: Allegory and Imagination.* London: Croom Helm, 1984.

Bunyan used his time in jail to write his autobiography, *Grace Abounding to the Chief of Sinners*, and begin work on his best-known work, *The Pilgrim's Progress*, the first part of which appeared in 1678, and the second in 1684. The book went on to become one of the best-loved works of English religious literature. It sets out to recount the journey of Christian from the "City of Destruction" to the "heavenly city," and offers a vivid account of the various spiritual trials and temptations faced by believers as they live out their faith in a frequently hostile world. Although the theme of the Christian life as a "pilgrimage" had been used by many writers before Bunyan, there are no reasons for suspecting that he was aware of these, or made any use of previous treatments in his own writing. *The Pilgrim's Progress* is best regarded as a brilliant and highly original narrative, incorporating biblical ideas and imagery without the mediating filter of previous writers.

The section of the text which has been included in this anthology is its first chapter, which sets the scene for the work. This is preceded by an opening "apology for the book" – which is set out in the form of a poem. We join the work as verse gives way to prose.

As I walked through the wilderness of this world, I lighted on a certain place where was a Den, and I laid me down in that place to sleep: and, as I slept, I dreamed a dream. I dreamed, and behold, I saw a man clothed with rags, standing in a certain place, with his face from his own house, a book in his hand, and a great burden upon his back. I looked, and saw him open the book, and read therein; and, as he read, he wept, and trembled; and, not being able longer to contain, he brake out with a lamentable cry, saying, What shall I do?

In this plight, therefore, he went home and refrained himself as long as he could, that his wife and children should not perceive his distress; but he could not be silent long, because that his trouble increased. Wherefore at length he brake his mind to his wife and children; and thus he began to talk to them: O my dear wife, said he, and you the children of my bowels, I, your dear friend, am in myself undone by reason of a burden that lieth hard upon me; moreover, I am for certain informed that this our city will be burned with fire from heaven; in which fearful overthrow, both myself, with thee my wife, and you my sweet babes, shall miserably come to ruin, except (the which yet I see not) some way of escape can be found, whereby we may be delivered. At this his relations were sore amazed; not for that they believed that what he had said to them was true, but because they thought that some frenzy distemper had got into his head; therefore, it drawing towards night, and they hoping that sleep might settle his brains, with all haste they got him to bed. But the night was as troublesome to him as the day; wherefore, instead of sleeping, he spent it in sighs and tears. So, when the morning was come, they would know how he did. He told them, Worse and worse: he also set to talking to them again; but they began to be hardened. They also thought to drive away his distemper by harsh and surly carriages to him; sometimes they would deride, sometimes they would chide, and sometimes they would quite neglect him. Wherefore he began to retire himself to his chamber, to pray for and pity them, and also to condole his own misery; he would also walk solitarily in the fields, sometimes reading, and sometimes praying: and thus for some days he spent his time.

Now, I saw, upon a time, when he was walking in the fields, that he was, as he was wont, reading in his book, and greatly distressed in his mind; and, as he read, he burst out, as he had done before, crying, What shall I do to be saved?

I saw also that he looked this way and that way, as if he would run; yet he stood still, because, as I perceived, he could not tell which way to go. I looked then, and saw a man named Evangelist coming to him, who asked, Wherefore dost thou cry? He answered, Sir, I perceive by the book in my hand, that I am condemned to die, and after that to come to judgment; and I find that I am not willing to do the first, nor able to do the second.

Christian no sooner leaves the World but meets Evangelist, who lovingly him greets with tidings of another: and doth shew Him how to mount to that from this below.

Then said Evangelist, Why not willing to die, since this life is attended with so many evils? The man answered, Because I fear that this burden that is upon my back will sink me lower than the grave, and I shall fall into Tophet. And, Sir, if I be not fit to go to prison, I am not fit, I am sure, to go to judgment, and from thence to execution; and the thoughts of these things make me cry.

Then said Evangelist, If this be thy condition, why standest thou still? He answered, Because I know not whither to go. Then he gave him a parchment roll, and there was written within, Flee from the wrath to come.

The man, therefore, read it, and looking upon Evangelist very carefully, said, Whither must I fly? Then said Evangelist, pointing with his finger over a very wide field, Do you see yonder wicket-gate? The man said, No. Then said the other, Do you see yonder shining light? He said, I think I do. Then said Evangelist, Keep that light in your eye, and go up directly thereto: so shalt thou see the gate; at which, when thou knockest, it shall be told thee what thou shalt do.

So I saw in my dream that the man began to run. Now, he had not run far from his own door, but his wife and children, perceiving it, began to cry after him to return; but the man put his fingers in his ears, and ran on, crying, Life! life! eternal life! So he looked not behind him, but fled towards the middle of the plain.

The neighbours also came out to see him run; and, as he ran, some mocked, others threatened, and some cried after him to return; and, among those that did so, there were two that resolved to fetch him back by force. The name of the one was Obstinate and the name of the other Pliable. Now, by this time, the man was got a good distance from them; but, however, they were resolved to pursue him, which they did, and in a little time they overtook him. Then said the man, Neighbours, wherefore are ye come? They said, To persuade you to go back with us. But he said, That can by no means be; you dwell, said he, in the City of Destruction, the place also where I was born: I see it to be so; and, dying there, sooner or later, you will sink lower than the grave, into a place that burns with fire and brimstone: be content, good neighbours, and go along with me.

Questions for Study

1 Identify the various images and analogies which you can discern within this opening section. Why does Bunyan make such extensive use of imagery in this writing?

2 The work is described as "The Pilgrim's Progress from This World to That Which is to Come, Delivered Under the Similitude of a Dream Wherein Is Discovered the Manner of His Setting Out, His Dangerous Journey, and Safe Arrival at the Desired Country." How many images of journeying may be discerned? And how does this relate to the biblical material, which Bunyan regarded with such great importance?

3 The passage makes reference to the "City of Destruction." What does Bunyan mean by this term? And why does he find the image of a city so useful for his narrative?

CHAPTER 58

The Book of Common Prayer (1662)

The Reformation in England is generally considered to have had its origins in the 1530s. Henry VIII, anxious to ensure the succession of the monarchy after his death, secured a divorce from his first wife, Catherine of Aragon, so that he could marry Anne Boleyn. The driving force behind the divorce was Henry's perception that only a male heir could ensure political stability after his death. However, it became clear that there were important religious aspects of this move, many of which may not have been appreciated at the time. Henry's growing alienation from the Pope developed alongside a new concern to establish an English national church, with Henry VIII as its "supreme head."

By this stage, the Reformation had become a significant movement on mainland Europe. Martin Luther and Huldrych Zwingli had developed ideas and institutions which were challenging the authority of the Pope, and creating new possibilities for Christian life and thought. It was inevitable that the new situation arising from Henry's growing alienation from Rome would lead to some kind of interaction between the continental Reformation and England. Although this process can be seen taking place to a limited extent under Henry VIII, it is generally agreed that the process reached its zenith under Henry's successor, Edward VI.

When Henry VIII died in 1537, Edward was still too young to assume the English throne in his own right. As a result, a "Lord Protector" was appointed to head the Privy Council, which was to govern England until such time as Edward reached the age of majority. Under Edward, the English church moved in an increasingly Protestant direction, due partly to the influence of the Archbishop of Canterbury, Thomas Cranmer. One of Cranmer's major reforms was the introduction of Prayer Books. Two such works were introduced, in 1549 and 1551. The basic principle underlying each of these books was to ensure that the English population worshipped in a fixed manner in the English language, thus minimizing the risk of any threat to the English Reformation.

The Book of Common Prayer (1662)

Basic description

The definitive seventeenth-century version of the fixed liturgy of the Church of England, which would have a major impact on the shaping of English-language Christianity until the First World War.

Major studies

G. W. Bromiley, "Prayer Book Development to 1662," *Churchman* 76 (1962), 7–15.

J. Gordon Davies "The Book of Common Prayer: Its Virtues and Vices," *Studia Liturgica* 1 (1962), 167–74.

C. P. M. Jones, G. Wainwright, and E. J. Yarnold (eds.), *The Study of Liturgy*. London: SPCK, 1978.

A. M. Ramsey, *The English Prayer Book, 1549–1662*. London: SPCK, 1963.

Edward VI died in 1553, and the throne passed to his half-sister Mary Tudor. Mary was a staunch defender of traditional Catholic ideas and values, and set in place measures designed to restore Catholicism to its former place of honor, including the execution of Thomas Cranmer. After her death in 1558, she was succeeded by her half-sister Elizabeth, who managed to secure a religious settlement in 1559, based on the use of a modified version of the 1559 Prayer Book. There was, however, considerable opposition to the Prayer Book, particularly from the Puritans, who disliked many of its features. The Hampton Court Conference (1604), early in the reign of James I, sought to resolve these differences, although without much tangible success – apart, of course, from agreement to produce a standard English translation of the Bible. This appeared in 1611, and is generally known as either the "King James Version" (after James I) or the "Authorized Version."

The outbreak of the English Civil War, culminating in a Puritan military victory, led to the Prayer Book being abolished, and replaced in 1645 by the "Directory of Public Worship." However, the Puritan commonwealth proved to be short-lived, and its collapse led to the restoration of Charles II in 1660. The Church of England was re-established, and in 1662 arrangements were made for the revision of the Prayer Book. In 1663, the "Book of Common Prayer" (BCP) was issued. It would prove to be the second most influential religious document in the English language – the most influential being, of course, the King James Version of the Bible.

Why was this book so important in shaping the English language? It needs to be recalled that the Book of Common Prayer was used in parish churches throughout England – and subsequently throughout the British Empire – on every occasion at which any form of public worship was demanded. For nearly three hundred years, the language of the English-speaking elite was subtly – and perhaps even unconsciously – shaped by the phrases used by the BCP. Many of its turns of phrase were simply absorbed into the English language, and are reflected in countless works of English literature written over this period. Although the BCP began to be replaced by more modern English-language liturgies from the 1960s, its cadences and turns of phrase can still be discerned in the writings of earlier periods. In what follows, we shall look at some of its more familiar and influential sections.

Text: The "General Confession"

The major text here is the "General Confession," which is a form of words used at Morning Prayer for the confession of sin. Although some Christian traditions insist upon the private confession of individual sins, the Church of England took the view that it was the general fact that members of its congregations had sinned – rather than the specific confession of those individual sins – which was of critical importance. The use of this prayer was mandatory; congregations were required to confess their sins before turning to the praise of God.

Almighty and most merciful Father; We have erred, and strayed from thy ways like lost sheep. We have followed too much the devices and desires of our own hearts. We have offended against thy holy laws. We have left undone those things which we ought to have done; And we have done those things which we ought not to have done; And there is no health in us. But thou, O Lord, have mercy upon us, miserable offenders. Spare thou them, O God, which confess their faults. Restore thou them that are penitent; According to thy promises declared unto mankind in Christ Jesu our Lord. And grant, O most merciful Father, for his sake; That we may hereafter live a godly, righteous, and sober life, To the glory of thy holy Name. Amen.

Questions for Study

1 The following text is taken from the King James Version of the Bible: "All we like sheep have gone astray; we have turned every one to his own way" (Isaiah 53:6). At what point does this image enter into the prayer?
2 Note the generality of the confession. List the specific ways in which sins are identified, and notice how individuals are not required to "own up" in public to specific named acts of wrongdoing.
3 These words are read out by the priest. What role – if any – does the prayer suggest the priest plays in forgiving those sins?
4 Notice how the prayer is broken down into short sections, separated by commas or semi-colons. Why? You may like to remember that most English people could not read; the priest would therefore read each section aloud, and get the congregation to repeat each section after him.

Text: The "General Thanksgiving"

The second text is taken from a collection of prayers which may be used – but are not required to be used – at Morning or Evening Prayer. This is the "General Thanksgiving." The text is very straightforward, and requires little in the way of comment, except to note that the archaic word "unfeignedly" means "sincerely" or "without pretense." The prayer sets out the grounds for thankfulness to God, which can be summed up under three categories:

1 What God is like – note the emphasis on God's "goodness and loving-kindness," directed toward humanity.
2 What God does for Christians in the present life – note the reference to God's "creation, preservation, and all the blessings of this life."
3 What God has done to secure future joy – note here the emphasis upon the grounds of salvation.

It also sets out what it regards as the proper human response to God's goodness, both through "lips" and "lives." The prayer leaves its users in no doubt that they are required to both praise God and obey God.

Almighty God, Father of all mercies, we thine unworthy servants do give thee most humble and hearty thanks for all thy goodness and loving-kindness to us, and to all men. We bless thee for our creation, preservation, and all the blessings of this life; but above all, for thine inestimable love in the redemption of the world by our Lord Jesus Christ; for the means of grace, and for the hope of glory. And, we beseech thee, give us that due sense of all thy mercies, that our hearts may be unfeignedly thankful, and that we shew forth thy praise, not only with our lips, but in our lives; by giving up ourselves to thy service, and by walking before thee in holiness and righteousness all our days; through Jesus Christ our Lord, to whom with thee and the Holy Ghost be all honor and glory, world without end. *Amen.*

Questions for Study

1 In what way does this set prayer encourage its readers to give thanks to God? Note in particular the way in which certain benefits are identified within the body of the prayer itself.
2 According to the prayer, what is the greatest thing that God has done for humanity?
3 What form of response does the prayer suggest would be appropriate to what God has done for humanity?

Text: The Solemnization of Matrimony

The words of the BCP marriage service have had an immense influence on the English language. Echoes, however distant, of this service can be found in virtually every English language form of marriage, whether religious or secular. The central part of the service has here been reprinted in its entirety, along with the directions (often known as "rubrics," here printed in italic text) to both the minister and the couple. Note that the identity of the couple is indicated by "N" – an abbreviation for "name."

At the day and time appointed for solemnization of Matrimony, the persons to be married shall come into the body of the Church with their friends and neighbors: and there standing together, the Man on the right hand, and the Woman on the left, the Priest shall say,

DEARLY beloved, we are gathered together here in the sight of God, and in the face of this congregation, to join together this Man and this Woman in holy Matrimony; which is an honorable estate, instituted of God in the time of man's innocency, signifying unto us the mystical union that is betwixt Christ and his Church; which holy estate Christ adorned and beautified with his presence, and first miracle that he wrought, in Cana of Galilee; and is commended of Saint Paul to be honorable among all men: and therefore is not by any to be enterprised, nor taken in hand, unadvisedly, lightly, or wantonly, to satisfy men's carnal lusts and appetites, like brute beasts that have no understanding; but reverently, discreetly, advisedly, soberly, and in the fear of God; duly considering the causes for which Matrimony was ordained.

First, It was ordained for the procreation of children, to be brought up in the fear and nurture of the Lord, and to the praise of his holy Name.

Secondly, It was ordained for a remedy against sin, and to avoid fornication; that such persons as have not the gift of continency might marry, and keep themselves undefiled members of Christ's body.

Thirdly, It was ordained for the mutual society, help, and comfort, that the one ought to have of the other, both in prosperity and adversity. Into which holy estate these two persons present come now to be joined. Therefore if any man can shew any just cause, why they may not lawfully be joined together, let him now speak, or else hereafter for ever hold his peace.

And also, speaking unto the persons that shall be married, he shall say,
I REQUIRE and charge you both, as ye will answer at the dreadful day of judgment when the secrets of all hearts shall be disclosed, that if either of you know any impediment, why ye may not be lawfully joined together in Matrimony, ye do now confess it. For be ye well assured, that so many as are coupled together otherwise than God's Word doth allow are not joined together by God; neither is their Matrimony lawful.

At which day of Marriage, if any man do allege and declare any impediment, why they may not be coupled together in Matrimony, by God's Law, or the Laws of this Realm; and will be bound, and sufficient sureties with him, to the parties; or else put in a Caution (to the full value of such charges as the persons to be married do thereby sustain) to prove his allegation: then the solemnization must be deferred, until such time as the truth be tried.

If no impediment be alleged, then shall the Curate say unto the Man,
N. WILT thou have this Woman to thy wedded wife, to live together after God's ordinance in the holy estate of Matrimony? Wilt thou love her, comfort her, honor, and keep her in sickness and in health; and, forsaking all other, keep thee only unto her, so long as ye both shall live?

The Man shall answer, I will.

Then shall the Priest say unto the Woman,

N. **WILT** thou have this Man to thy wedded husband, to live together after God's ordinance in the holy estate of Matrimony? Wilt thou obey him, and serve him, love, honor, and keep him in sickness and in health; and, forsaking all other, keep thee only unto him, so long as ye both shall live?

The Woman shall answer, I will.

Then shall the Minister say,
Who giveth this Woman to be married to this Man?

Then shall they give their troth to each other in this manner.

The Minister, receiving the Woman at her father's or friend's hands, shall cause the Man with his right hand to take the Woman by her right hand, and to say after him as followeth.
I *N.* take thee *N.* to my wedded wife, to have and to hold from this day forward, for better for worse, for richer for poorer, in sickness and in health, to love and to cherish, till death us do part, according to God's holy ordinance; and thereto I plight thee my troth.

Then shall they loose their hands; and the Woman, with her right hand taking the Man by his right hand, shall likewise say after the Minister,
I *N.* take thee *N.* to my wedded husband, to have and to hold from this day forward, for better for worse, for richer for poorer, in sickness and in health, to love, cherish, and to obey, till death us do part, according to God's holy ordinance; and thereto I give thee my troth.

Then shall they again loose their hands; and the Man shall give unto the Woman a Ring, laying the same upon the book with the accustomed duty to the Priest and Clerk. And the Priest, taking the Ring, shall deliver it unto the Man, to put it upon the fourth finger of the Woman's left hand. And the Man holding the Ring there, and taught by the Priest, shall say,
WITH this ring I thee wed, with my body I thee worship, and with all my worldly goods I thee endow: In the Name of the Father, and of the Son, and of the Holy Ghost. Amen.

Then the Man leaving the Ring upon the fourth finger of the Woman's left hand, they shall both kneel down; and the Minister shall say,

Let us pray.
O ETERNAL God, Creator and Preserver of all mankind, Giver of all spiritual grace, the Author of everlasting life: Send thy blessing upon these thy servants, this man and this woman, whom we bless in thy Name; that, as Isaac and Rebecca lived faithfully together, so these persons may surely perform and keep the vow and covenant betwixt them made, (whereof this Ring given and received is a token and pledge,) and may ever remain in perfect love and peace together, and live according to thy laws; through Jesus Christ our Lord. *Amen.*

Then shall the Priest join their right hands together, and say,
Those whom God hath joined together let no man put asunder.

Then shall the Minister speak unto the people.
FORASMUCH as *N.* and *N.* have consented together in holy wedlock, and have witnessed the same before God and this company, and thereto have given and pledged their troth either to other, and have declared the same by giving and receiving of a Ring, and by joining of hands; I pronounce that they be Man and Wife together, In the Name of the Father, and of the Son, and of the Holy Ghost. Amen.

The order of service begins by making the point that marriage has significance both in the "sight of God" and in the public arena. The term "congregation" is used in a technical sense; it does not mean simply "the group of people gathered together for the purposes of this service," but "the whole church." The reason for this is complicated, and reflects Martin Luther's preference for the German word *Gemeinde* ("congregation" or "community") to refer to the church. The English term "congregation" is here used to echo Luther's preference. Several points are then made concerning marriage, of which two need further discussion.

1   Marriage symbolizes the "mystical union that is betwixt Christ and his Church." (Note that "betwixt" is an archaic form of "between"). This theme is developed by St. Paul at several points in his letters, and is a leading theme of medieval Christian spirituality.
2   Jesus Christ graced a wedding with his presence at Cana in Galilee, at which the miracle of transforming water into wine took place (see John 2).

Three reasons are then given for marriage:

1   To bring children into the world
2   To limit the impact of sin
3   For company and comfort

Having set out this understanding of the place of marriage in God's purposes, the service now focuses on the couple who are to be married, who are now invited to "give their troth to each other." This unusual word requires comment. It derives from the Middle English term *trowthe*, which in turn comes from the Old English word for "truth," *treowth*. The best modern English equivalent is "loyalty." The couple – identified as "N. and N." (the abbreviation for "Name") – then "plight their troth" (in modern English, "swear their loyalty") to each other. Note that the man and woman use different forms of words, reflecting seventeenth-century understandings of the respective social roles of male and female.

Text: At the Burial of the Dead

The final section of the BCP that we shall consider is the form of words used at funerals. The words of commital of the corpse to the ground stress the frailty and mortality of human nature, and total dependence upon God for the hope of eternal life. The text incorporates a number of biblical passages, including the following, which is printed out in the King James Version:

> Man that is born of a woman is of few days, and full of trouble. He cometh forth like a flower, and is cut down: he fleeth also as a shadow, and continueth not. (Job 14:1–2)

The text is set out with the "rubrics" (that is, the directions that are given to the priest) printed in italic type.

When they come to the Grave, while the Corpse is made ready to be laid into the earth, the Priest shall say, or the Priest and Clerks shall sing:
MAN that is born of a woman hath but a short time to live, and is full of misery. He cometh up, and is cut down, like a flower; he fleeth as it were a shadow, and never continueth in one stay.

In the midst of life we are in death: of whom may we seek for succour, but of thee, O Lord, who for our sins art justly displeased?

Yet, O Lord God most holy, O Lord most mighty, O holy and most merciful Saviour, deliver us not into the bitter pains of eternal death.

Thou knowest, Lord, the secrets of our hearts; shut not thy merciful ears to our prayer; but spare us, Lord most holy, O God most mighty, O holy and merciful Saviour, thou most worthy Judge eternal, suffer us not, at our last hour, for any pains of death, to fall from thee.

Then, while the earth shall be cast upon the Body by some
standing by, the Priest shall say,
FORASMUCH as it hath pleased Almighty God of his great mercy to take unto himself the soul of our dear *brother* here departed, we therefore commit *his* body to the ground; earth to earth, ashes to ashes, dust to dust; in sure and certain hope of the Resurrection to eternal life, through our Lord Jesus Christ; who shall change our vile body, that it may be like unto his glorious body, according to the mighty working, whereby he is able to subdue all things to himself.

Questions for Study

1 Can you identify some biblical passages which are cited or alluded to in this text?
2 What understanding of death is implicit in the final prayer? And how is this shaped by the "sure and certain" hope of resurrection?

PART V

The Modern Period,
1700–2000

Introduction

The final period to be considered in this anthology covers one of the most creative and significant epochs in Christian literature. By the twentieth century, Christianity was firmly established as the dominant religion in the Americas, Australasia, southern Africa, and throughout many of the island nations of the South Pacific. Despite this dramatic expansion outside Europe, however, Christianity suffered a series of internal setbacks in Europe. Growing anxiety concerning the reliability of the Christian worldview found its literary expression at a number of levels, including the "literature of doubt," especially associated with the Victorian era. The growing importance of "apologetic" works (that is, works written by Christians with a view to defending the intellectual and moral plausibility of the Christian faith) since the nineteenth century also reflects this development.

The present introduction will introduce some of the developments which have contributed to the shaping of Christian literature over this period. Others will be discussed in the introductions to individual texts, as appropriate.

The Rise of Indifference to Religion in Europe

The first half of the eighteenth century witnessed major revivals of faith in both England and North America. The "evangelical revivals," linked with John and Charles Wesley, brought a new dynamism to the English church, particularly through their demands for an experience-based faith. The "Great Awakening" in America also witnessed an upsurge in popular religious commitment. Both these movements produced significant literatures, not least of which were their hymns and devotional works.

Yet alongside these revivals we can discern a general trend toward the rise of indifference to religion, which is often regarded as a leading theme of modern western European culture. The origins of this trend can be traced to the weariness with conflict which resulted with the ending of the European Wars of Religion. With this development, a degree of stability settled upon the continent. Although religious controversy continued intermittently, it became generally accepted that certain parts of Europe were Lutheran, Catholic, Orthodox, or Reformed. The sense of religious exhaustion which had been created by the Wars of Religion led to a new interest in religious toleration. The classic argument for toleration of diversity in matters of religion may be found in John Locke's *Letter Concerning Toleration*. Locke argues for religious toleration on the basis of three general considerations, as follows.

First, it is impossible for the state to adjudicate between competing religious truth-claims. Second, even if it could be established that one religion was superior to all others, the legal enforcement of this religion would not lead to the desired objective of that religion. Locke's argument here is based upon the notion that "true and saving religion consists in the inward persuasion of the mind, without which nothing is acceptable to God. And such is the nature of the understanding, that it cannot be compelled to the belief of any thing by outward force." Third, Locke argues, on pragmatic grounds, that the results of trying to impose religious uniformity are far worse than those which result from the continuing existence of diversity. Religious coercion leads to internal discord, or even civil war.

Locke's analysis can be seen as leading to the view that religion is a private matter of public indifference. What individuals believe should be regarded as private, with no relevance to the public field. This approach at one and the same time upheld religious toleration, while indicating that religion was a purely private matter. This perception was strengthened by the rise of the Enlightenment, which regarded the religions as different expressions of the same ultimate reality, which could be known through reason.

The Watershed in Europe: The French Revolution

The French Revolution is usually singled out as marking the high point of anti-religious feeling in Europe. In 1789, the established social structure in France was shaken to its foundations by a popular uprising, which eventually led to the ending of the monarchy and the setting up of a secular republic. The church and the monarchy were the two pillars of this established order (usually referred to as the *ancien régime*). What began as an attempt to reform both institutions ended up as a revolution, in which power was decisively transferred from the old feudal aristocracy to the rising middle classes.

There was little to indicate that such a radical shake-up was on the way. But there was a parallel to be drawn with the American Revolution of the previous decade, which had led to the consolidation of the influence of various forms of Protestant Christianity in the region. While the established religion of the area (the religion of the colonial power – the Church of England) suffered a serious setback, other forms of Christianity strengthened their position. The disestablishment of Christianity in the region is widely regarded as contributing to its future success. Yet the situation in France proved to be very different.

It was clear that both the pillars of traditional French society – the monarchy and the church – needed reform. Even late in the summer of the momentous year 1789, the general feeling was that the French monarch had allowed a series of measures which would abolish feudalism and remove some of the grievances felt by ordinary people against the power and privileges of the church. On November 2, it was agreed that all church lands should be nationalized, with a basic minimum wage for priests being set in place, guaranteed by the state. The Civil Constitution of the Clergy (July 1790) rejected the authority of the Pope, and reorganized and slimmed down the dioceses and the cathedral clergy. Although radical, the measures were not anti-Christian. The clergy split into a group which wished to remain loyal to Rome, and another wishing to comply with the new civil authority.

All changed soon afterwards. A more radical revolutionary faction, headed by Robespierre, gained power, and launched its celebrated "Reign of Terror." Louis XVI was publicly guillotined on January 21, 1793. A program of de-Christianization was put in place during the period 1793–4. The cult of the Goddess Reason was given official sanction. The old calendar was replaced by a republican calendar which eliminated Sundays and Christian festivals, replacing them with secular alternatives. Priests were placed under pressure to renounce their faith. A program of church closure was initiated. Although the impact of these measures seems to have been felt mostly in urban areas, they caused considerable disruption and hardship to the church throughout France.

The religious policies of the French Revolution were soon extended to neighboring regions. In November 1792, French revolutionary armies embarked on a campaign of conquest in the region. By 1799, six satellite republics had been established, embracing areas such as the Netherlands, Switzerland, parts of northern Italy, and areas of the Rhineland. In February 1798, the papal states were occupied, and the Pope was deported to France, where he died six months later. The French Revolution, it seemed to many, had destroyed not only the French church, but also the papacy.

On the eve of the nineteenth century, the future of Christianity in Europe thus seemed remarkably fragile. Many saw it as linked with the politics of a bygone era, an obstacle to progress and liberty. Its faith and its institutions seemed to be in irreversible decline. In fact, this would prove to be a false perception. The revolutionary experimentation with a secular state eventually fizzled out. Under Napoleon, relations with the Pope were re-established, although on very different terms from those in operation before the Revolution. The Bourbon monarchy was restored. In 1814, Louis XVIII returned to claim the throne of France, and re-established Catholicism. The situation was never easy, and real tensions between church and state continued unabated throughout most of the nineteenth century. Nevertheless, the church was able to regain at least some of its lost influence, prestige, and clergy. The period 1815–48 witnessed a series of popular revivals (usually referred to as "le Réveil") in French-speaking Europe.

It is clear that the French Revolution drew at least some of its strength from the rationalist worldview which pervaded the writings of leading French writers of the period – such as Denis Diderot (1713–84), Jean-Jacques Rousseau (1712–78), and Voltaire (1694–1778). This leads us to consider some of the worldviews which dominated western thinking in the modern period, and their impact on Christianity and its associated literature.

The Intellectual Context of Western Christianity

Western Christianity has been deeply influenced by its general cultural climate. For example, many writers of the patristic period were deeply influenced by Platonic ideas (whether they agreed with them or reacted against them). In much the same way, many medieval theologians were influenced by Aristotelianism, either by incorporating some of its ideas into their thinking, or by reacting against them. The same pattern can be seen in the way Christianity related to two major movements in modern western thought, which we shall consider in the present section: rationalism and Romanticism.

RATIONALISM

The movement which is now generally known as "the Enlightenment" ushered in a period of considerable uncertainty for Christianity in western Europe and North America. The trauma of the Reformation and the resulting Wars of Religion had barely subsided on the continent of Europe before a new and more radical challenge to Christianity arose. If the sixteenth-century Reformation challenged the church to rethink its external forms and the manner in which it expressed its beliefs, the Enlightenment saw the intellectual credentials of Christianity itself (rather than any one of its specific forms) facing a major threat on a number of fronts. The origins of this challenge may be traced back to the seventeenth century, with the rise of Cartesianism on the continent of Europe, and the growing influence of Deism in England. The growing emphasis upon the need to uncover the rational roots of religion had considerable negative implications for Christianity, as subsequent events were to prove.

The Enlightenment criticism of traditional Christianity was based upon the principle of the omnicompetence of human reason. A number of stages in the development of this belief may be discerned. First, it was argued that the beliefs of Christianity were rational, and thus capable of standing up to critical examination. This type of approach may be found in John Locke's *Reasonableness of Christianity* (1695), and within the early Wolffian school in Germany. Christianity was a reasonable supplement to natural religion. The notion of divine Revelation was thus maintained.

Second, it was argued that the basic ideas of Christianity, being rational, could be derived from reason itself. There was no need to invoke the idea of divine revelation. As this idea was developed by John Toland in his *Christianity not Mysterious* (1696) and by Matthew Tindal's *Christianity as Old as Creation* (1730), Christianity was essentially the re-publication of the religion of nature. It did not transcend natural religion, but was merely an example of it. All so-called "revealed religion" is actually nothing other than the reconfirmation of what can be known through rational reflection on nature. "Revelation" was simply a rational reaffirmation of moral truths already available to enlightened reason.

Third, the ability of reason to judge revelation was affirmed. As critical reason was omnicompetent, it was argued that it was supremely qualified to judge Christian beliefs and practices, with a view to eliminating any irrational or superstitious elements. This view placed reason firmly above revelation, and may be seen as symbolized in the enthronement of the Goddess of Reason in Notre-Dame de Paris in 1793, in the aftermath of the French Revolution.

The Enlightenment was primarily a European and American phenomenon, and thus took place in cultures in which the most numerically significant form of religion was Christianity. This historical observation is of importance: the Enlightenment critique of religion in general was often particularized as a criticism of Christianity in general. It was Christian doctrines which were subjected to a critical assessment of a vigor without any precedent. It was Christian sacred writings – rather than those of Islam or Hinduism – which were subjected to an unprecedented critical scrutiny, both literary and historical, with the Bible being treated "as if it were any other book" (Benjamin Jowett). It was the life of Jesus of Nazareth which was subjected to critical reconstruction, rather than that of Mohammed or Buddha.

The rise of "biblical criticism" must also be noted at this point. Jowett's approach to the Bible reflects the growing view that it is to be regarded as a human construction, rather than a work of divine inspiration, which can therefore be judged and evaluated as if it were any other piece of human literature. Debate over the authority, inspiration and reliability of the Bible would become an important part of the nineteenth-century literary scene.

The Enlightenment attitude to religion was subject to a considerable degree of regional variation, reflecting a number of local factors peculiar to different situations. One of the most important such factors is Pietism, perhaps best known in its English and American form of Methodism. As noted earlier, this movement placed considerable emphasis upon the experiential aspects of religion (for example, as with John Wesley's notion of "experimental religion"). This concern for religious experience served to make Christianity relevant and accessible to the experiential situation of the masses, contrasting sharply with the intellectualism of, for example, Lutheran Orthodoxy, which was perceived to be an irrelevance. Pietism forged a strong link between Christian faith and experience, thus making Christianity a matter of the heart, as well as of the mind.

Yet rationalism itself was soon realized to have its limits, as the rise of Romanticism was to prove. We may turn to consider this development in what follows.

ROMANTICISM

The period we are considering in this final section witnessed a number of important literary developments, such as the rise of the novel and the growth of the radical spirit of modernism. Yet perhaps the most important literary development over the period in question is the rise of Romanticism. In the closing decade of the eighteenth century, increasing misgivings came to be expressed concerning the arid quality of rationalism. Reason, once seen as a liberator, came increasingly to be regarded as spiritually enslaving. These anxieties were not expressed so much within university faculties of philosophy, as within literary and artistic circles, particularly in the Prussian capital, Berlin, where the Schlegel brothers became particularly influential.

"Romanticism" is notoriously difficult to define. The movement is perhaps best seen as a reaction against certain of the central themes of the Enlightenment, most notably the claim that reality can be known to the human reason. This reduction of reality to a series of rationalized simplicities seemed, to the Romantics, to be a culpable and crude misrepresentation. Where the Enlightenment appealed to the human reason, Romanticism made an appeal to the human imagination, which was capable of recognizing the profound sense of mystery which arises from realizing that the human mind cannot comprehend even the finite world, let alone the infinity beyond this. This ethos is expressed well by the English poet William Wordsworth, who spoke of the human imagination in terms of transcending the limitations of human reason, and reaching beyond its bounds to sample the infinite through the finite. Imagination, according to Wordsworth,

> Is but another name for absolute power
> And clearest insight, amplitude of mind,
> And Reason in her most exalted mood.

Romanticism thus found itself equally unhappy with both traditional Christian doctrines and the rationalist moral platitudes of the Enlightenment: both failed to do justice to the complexity of the world, in an attempt to reduce the "mystery of the universe" – to use a typically Romantic phrase found in the writings of August William Schlegel – to neat formulae.

A marked limitation of the competence of reason may be discerned in such sentiments. Reason threatens to limit the human mind to what may be deduced; the imagination is able to liberate the human spirit from this self-imposed bondage, and allow it to discover new depths of reality – a vague and tantalizing "something," which can be discerned in the world of everyday realities. The infinite is somehow present in the finite, and may be known through feeling and the imagination. As John Keats put it, "I am certain of nothing except the holiness of the heart's affections, and the truth of the imagination." William Blake contrasted those who were led by the imagination into the realms of spiritual truth with those who remained obstinately earth-bound through an excessive reliance on reason.

This introduction has aimed to identify some of the major themes and issues which are reflected in the Christian literature of the western world since 1700. We shall explore others in the introductions to individual items, which allow us the opportunity to explore specific themes in more detail than is possible in this brief opening section. We shall therefore move on immediately to engage with the vast literary heritage of this period, beginning with the work which is widely credited with being the first novel – Daniel Defoe's *Robinson Crusoe*.

CHAPTER 59

Daniel Defoe (1660–1731)

Defoe is generally regarded as the first novelist in the English language. The identity of that novel will come as no surprise; *Robinson Crusoe* remains one of the best-known works of English literature. Yet many fail to realize that this work is actually strongly religious in nature. Alongside the familiar narrative of the man shipwrecked on a desert island, there is another story – an account of personal rebirth and spiritual renewal. For both these reasons, it was essential to include *Robinson Crusoe* in this anthology.

Daniel Defoe (1660–1731)

Basic description
English novelist, pamphleteer, and journalist.

Major works
Robinson Crusoe (1719–22); *Moll Flanders* (1722).

Major studies
Paula R. Backscheider, *Daniel Defoe: His Life*. Baltimore, MD: Johns Hopkins University Press, 1992.
Roger D. Lund (ed.), *Critical Essays on Daniel Defoe*. New York: Prentice-Hall International, 1997.

Daniel Defoe was born as "Daniel Foe" in London in 1660, as the son of a tallow-chandler (that is, someone who made candles from animal fat). He changed his name at some point around 1695. Defoe's original intention seems to have been to become a Presbyterian minister. For this reason, he attended the "Academy for Dissenters" in Stoke Newington, now a suburb of London. Here, he was taught by Reverend Charles Morton, who later went on to become the first vice president of Harvard College. Many have argued that the clarity, simplicity, and ease of Morton's style of writing – together with the Bible, the works of John Bunyan, and the pulpit oratory of the day – may have helped to form Defoe's own literary style.

Although Defoe's intention was to become a non-conformist minister, this idea seems to have fallen into abeyance; instead, Defoe moved into hosiery manufacture, and appears to have established a successful business with numerous foreign contacts. He traveled widely in western Europe, and became fascinated with the concept of travel – a notion, of course, which is central to *Robinson Crusoe*. Things began to go seriously wrong in 1692, when Defoe was declared bankrupt, with debts of £17,000. Opinions differ as to the cause of this collapse. Defoe was apt to indulge in rash speculations and projects without due care, and it is possible that his difficulties reflect his own weaknesses. However, the main reason for his bankruptcy was the loss that he sustained in insuring ships during a war with France. He is known to have been one of nineteen such insurance brokers who were ruined in 1692. He suffered further severe losses in 1703, when his prosperous brick-and-tile works near Tilbury failed during his imprisonment for political offenses. He did not actively engage in trade after this time.

After this financial failure and the ensuing period of bankruptcy, Defoe managed to secure a position with Robert Harley, a senior goverment minister. During the eleven years of his appointment, Defoe seems to have acted as both political journalist and espionage agent for his employer. Although Defoe wrote at least five hundred known books, he is remembered today mainly for the work written in his sixtieth year, and published in 1719. *Robinson Crusoe* tells the story of a shipwrecked mariner, which is loosely yet recognizably based on the true story of Alexander Selkirk. The main action of the story takes place in 1659, when Crusoe is shipwrecked on an uninhabited island. With great skill, Defoe explores how Crusoe's intuition and skills allow him to survive in his new situation. Crusoe is portrayed as a man who had made his fortune as a trader, and who now finds himself in a situation in which goods and money are of no value to him. The novel's exploration of the consequences of this "inversion of values" is widely regarded as compelling.

Yet alongside this, we find an exploration of Crusoe's inner feelings, and especially his attitude toward God. Defoe tells a story of a personal and inward journey, leading to spiritual renewal, which parallels the account of self-sufficiency which allows Crusoe to survive at the physical level. Crusoe's journal entry for April 16, 1660 tells of how a wall which he had constructed fell down, and nearly killed him. The journal then relates how Crusoe felt about this:

> [I] sat still upon the ground, greatly cast down and disconsolate, not knowing what to do. All this while I had not the least serious religious thought, nothing but the common "Lord, have mercy on me!", and when it was over, that went away too.

Yet a spiritual rebirth lies not far away, as the journal entries for June 16–July 4, 1660 make clear. It is to this section of the work that we now turn. The original orthography has been used throughout this section.

June 16. Going down to the Sea-side, I found a large Tortoise or Turtle; this was the first I had seen, which it seems was only my Misfortune, not any Defect of the Place, or Scarcity; for had I happen'd to be on the other Side of the Island, I might have had Hundreds of them every Day, as I found afterwards; but perhaps had paid dear enough for them.

June 17. I spent in cooking the Turtle; I found in her threescore Eggs; and her Flesh was to me at that Time the most savoury and pleasant that ever I tasted in my Life, having had no Flesh, but of Goats and Fowls, since I landed in this horrid Place.

June 18. Rain'd all Day, and I stay'd within. I thought at this Time the Rain felt Cold, and I was something chilly, which I knew was not usual in that Latitude.

June 19. Very ill, and shivering, as if the Weather had been cold.

June 20. No Rest all Night, violent Pains in my Head, and feaverish.

June 21. Very ill, frighted almost to Death with the Apprehensions of my sad Condition, to be sick, and no Help: Pray'd to GOD for the first Time since the Storm off of Hull, but scarce knew what I said, or why; my Thoughts being all confused.

June 22. A little better, but under dreadful Apprehensions of Sickness.

June 23. Very bad again, cold and shivering, and then a violent Head-ach.

June 24. Much better.

June 25. An Ague very violent; the Fit held me seven Hours, cold Fit and hot, with faint Sweats after it.

June 26. Better; and having no Victuals to eat, took my Gun, but found my self very weak; however I kill'd a She-Goat, and with much Difficulty got it Home, and broil'd some of it, and eat; I wou'd fain have stew'd it, and made some Broath, but had no Pot.

June 27. The Ague again so violent, that I lay a-Bed all Day, and neither eat or drank. I was ready to perish for Thirst, but so weak, I had not Strength to stand up, or to get my self any Water to drink: Pray'd to God again, but was light-headed, and when I was not, I was so ignorant, that I knew not what to say; only I lay and cry'd, Lord look upon me, Lord pity me, Lord have Mercy upon me: I suppose I did nothing else for two or three Hours, till the Fit wearing off, I fell asleep, and did not wake till far in the Night; when I wak'd, I found my self much refresh'd, but weak, and exceeding thirsty: However, as I had no Water bin my whole Habitation, I was forc'd to lie till Morning, and went to sleep again: In this second Sleep, I had this terrible Dream.

I thought, that I was sitting on the Ground on the Outside of my Wall, where I sat when the Storm blew after the Earthquake, and that I saw a Man descend from a great black Cloud, in a bright Flame of Fire, and light upon the Ground: He was all over as bright as a Flame, so that I could but just bear to look towards him; his Countenance was most inexpressibly dreadful, impossible for Words to describe; when he stepp'd upon the Ground with his Feet, I thought the Earth trembl'd, just as it had done before in the Earthquake, and all the Air look'd, to my Apprehension, as if it had been fill'd with Flashes of Fire.

He was no sooner landed upon the Earth, but he moved forward towards me, with a long Spear or Weapon in his Hand, to kill me; and when he came to a rising Ground, at some Distance, he spoke to me, or I heard a Voice so terrible, that it is impossible to express the Terror of it; all that I can say, I understood, was this, Seeing all these Things have not brought thee to Repentance, now thou shalt die: At which Words, I thought he lifted up the Spear that was in his Hand, to kill me.

No one, that shall ever read this Account, will expect that I should be able to describe the Horrors of my Soul at this terrible Vision, I mean, that even while it was a Dream, I even dreamed of those Horrors; nor is it any more possible to describe the Impression that remain'd upon my Mind when I awak'd and found it was but a Dream.

I had alas! no divine Knowledge; what I had received by the good Instruction of my Father was then worn out by an uninterrupted Series, for 8 Years, of Seafaring Wickedness, and a constant Conversation with nothing but such as were like my self, wicked and prophane to the last Degree: I do not remember that I had in all that Time one Thought that so much as tended either to looking upwards toward God, or inwards towards a Reflection upon my own Ways: But a certain Stupidity of Soul, without Desire of Good, or Conscience of Evil, had entirely overwhelm'd me, and I was all that the most hardened, unthinking, wicked Creature among our common Sailors, can be supposed to be, not having the least Sense, either of the Fear of God in Danger, or of Thankfulness to God in Deliverances.

In the relating what is already past of my Story, this will be the more easily believ'd, when I shall add, that thro' all the Variety of Miseries that had to this Day befallen me, I never had so much as one Thought of it being the Hand of God, or that it was a just Punishment for my Sin; my rebellious Behaviour against my Father, or my present Sins which were great; or so much as a Punishment for the general Course of my wicked Life. When I was on the desperate Expedition on the desert Shores of Africa, I never had so much as one Thought of what would become of me; or one to direct me whither I should go, or to keep me from the Danger which apparently surrounded me, as well from voracious Creatures as cruel Savages: But I was meerly thoughtless of a God, or a Providence; acted like a meer Brute from the Principles of Nature, and by the Dictates of common Sense only, and indeed hardly that.

When I was deliver'd and taken up at Sea by the Portugal Captain, well us'd, and dealt justly and honourably with, as well as charitably, I had not the least Thankfulness on my Thoughts: When again I was shipwreck'd, ruin'd, and in Danger of drowning on this Island, I was as far from Remorse, or looking on it as a Judgment; I only said to my self often, that I was an unfortunate Dog, and born to be always miserable. It is true, when I got on Shore first here, and found all my Ship's Crew drown'd, and my self spar'd, I was surpriz'd with a Kind of Extasie, and some Transports of Soul, which, had the Grace of God assisted, might have come up to true Thankfulness; but it ended where it begun, in a meer common Flight of Joy, or as I may say, being glad I was alive, without the least Reflection upon the distinguishing Goodness of the Hand which had preserv'd me, and had singled me out to be preserv'd, when all the rest were destroy'd; or an Enquiry why Providence had been thus merciful to me; even just the same common Sort of Joy which Seamen generally have after they are got safe ashore from a Shipwreck, which they drown all in the next Bowl of Punch, and forget almost as soon as it is over, and all the rest of my Life was like it.

Even when I was afterwards, on due Consideration, made sensible of my Condition, how I was cast on this dreadful Place, out of the Reach of humane Kind, out of all Hope of Relief, or Prospect of Redemption, as soon as I saw but a Prospect of living, and that I should not starve and perish for Hunger, all the Sense of my Affliction wore off, and I begun to be very easy, apply'd my self to the Works proper for my Preservation and Supply, and was far enough from being afflicted at my Condition, as a Judgment from Heaven, or as the Hand of God against me; these were Thoughts which very seldom enter'd into my Head.

The growing up of the Corn, as is hinted in my Journal, had at first some little Influence upon me, and began to affect me with Seriousness, as long as I thought it had something miraculous in it; but as soon as ever that Part of the Thought was remov'd, all the Impression which was rais'd from it, wore off also, as I have noted already.

Even the Earthquake, tho' nothing could be more terrible in its Nature, or more immediately directing to the invisible Power which alone directs such Things, yet no sooner was the first Fright over, but the Impression it had made went off also. I had no more Sense of God or his Judgments, much less of the present Affliction of my Circumstances being from his Hand, than if I had been in the most prosperous Condition of Life.

But now when I began to be sick, and a leisurely View of the Miseries of Death came to place itself before me; when my Spirits began to sink under the Burthen of a strong Distemper, and Nature was exhausted with the Violence of the Feaver; Conscience that had slept so long, begun to awake, and I began to reproach my self with my past Life, in which I had so evidently, by uncommon Wickedness, provok'd the Justice of God to lay me under uncommon Strokes, and to deal with me in so vindictive a Manner.

These Reflections oppress'd me for the second or third Day of my Distemper, and in the Violence, as well of the Feaver, as of the dreadful Reproaches of my Conscience, extorted some Words from me, like praying to God, tho' I cannot say they were either a Prayer attended with Desires or with Hopes; it was rather the Voice of meer Fright and Distress; my Thoughts were confus'd, the Convictions great upon my Mind, and the Horror of dying in such a miserable Condition rais'd Vapours into my Head with the meer Apprehensions; and in these Hurries of my Soul, I know not what my Tongue might express: but it was rather Exclamation, such as, Lord! what a miserable Creature am I? If I should be sick, I shall certainly die for Want of Help, and what will become of me! Then the Tears burst out of my Eyes, and I could say no more for a good while.

In this Interval, the good Advice of my Father came to my Mind, and presently his Prediction which I mention'd at the Beginning of this Story, viz. That if I did take this foolish Step, God would not bless me, and I would have Leisure hereafter to reflect upon having neglected his Counsel, when there might be none to assist in my Recovery. Now, said I aloud, My dear Father's Words are come to pass: God's Justice has overtaken me, and I have none to help or hear me: I rejected the Voice of Providence, which had mercifully put me in a Posture or Station of Life, wherein I might have been happy and easy; but I would neither see it my self, or learn to know the Blessing of it from my Parents; I left them to mourn over my Folly, and now I am left to mourn under the Consequences of it: I refus'd their Help and Assistance who wou'd have lifted me into the World, and wou'd have made every Thing easy to me, and now I have Difficulties to struggle with, too great for even Nature itself to support, and no Assistance, no Help, no Comfort, no Advice; then I cry'd out, Lord be my Help, for I am in great Distress.

This was the first Prayer, if I may call it so, that I had made for many Years: But I return to my Journal.

June 28. Having been somewhat refresh'd with the Sleep I had had, and the Fit being entirely off, I got up; and tho' the Fright and Terror of my Dream was very great, yet I consider'd, that the Fit of the Ague wou'd return again the next Day, and now was my Time to get something to refresh and support my self when I should be ill; and the first Thing I did, I fill'd a large square Case Bottle with Water, and set it upon my Table, in Reach of my Bed; and to take off the chill or aguish Disposition of the Water, I put about a Quarter of a Pint of Rum into it, and mix'd them together; then I got me a Piece of the Goat's Flesh, and broil'd it on the Coals, but could eat very little; I walk'd about, but was very weak, and withal very sad and heavy-hearted in the Sense of my miserable Condition; dreading the Return of my Distemper the next Day; at Night I made my Supper of three of the Turtle's Eggs, which I roasted in the Ashes, and eat, as we call it, in the Shell; and this was the first Bit of Meat I had ever ask'd God's Blessing to, even as I cou'd remember, in my whole Life.

After I had eaten, I try'd to walk, but found my self so weak, that I cou'd hardly carry the Gun (for I never went out without that) so I went but a little Way, and sat down upon the Ground, looking out upon the Sea, which was just before me, and very calm and smooth: As I sat here, some such Thoughts as these occurred to me.

What is this Earth and Sea of which I have seen so much, whence is it produc'd, and what am I, and all the other Creatures, wild and tame, humane and brutal, whence are we?

Sure we are all made by some secret Power, who form'd the Earth and Sea, the Air and Sky; and who is that?

Then it follow'd most naturally, It is God that has made it all: Well, but then it came on strangely, if God has made all these Things, He guides and governs them all, and all Things that concern them; for the Power that could make all Things, must certainly have Power to guide and direct them.

If so, nothing can happen in the great Circuit of his Works, either without his Knowledge or Appointment.

And if nothing happens without his Knowledge, he knows that I am here, and am in this dreadful Condition; and if nothing happens without his Appointment, he has appointed all this to befal me.

Nothing occurr'd to my Thought to contradict any of these Conclusions; and therefore it rested upon me with the greater Force, that it must needs be, that God had appointed all this to befal me; that I was brought to this miserable Circumstance by his Direction, he having the sole Power, not of me only, but of every Thing that happen'd in the World. Immediately it follow'd,

Why has God done this to me? What have I done to be thus us'd?

My Conscience presently check'd me in that Enquiry, as if I had blasphem'd, and methought it spoke to me like a Voice; WRETCH! dost thou ask what thou hast done! look back upon a dreadful mis-spent Life, and ask thy self what thou hast not done? ask, Why is it that thou wert not long ago destroy'd? Why wert thou not drown'd in Yarmouth Roads? Kill'd in the Fight when the Ship was taken by the

Sallee Man of War? Devour'd by the wild Beasts on the Coast of Africa? Or, Drown'd HERE, when all the Crew perish'd but thy self? Dost thou ask, What have I done?

I was struck dumb with these Reflections, as one astonish'd, and had not a Word to say, no not to answer to my self, but rise up pensive and sad, walk'd back to my Retreat, and went up over my Wall, as if I had been going to Bed, but my Thoughts were sadly disturb'd, and I had no Inclination to Sleep; so I sat down in my Chair, and lighted my Lamp, for it began to be dark: Now as the Apprehension of the Return of my Distemper terrify'd me very much, it occurr'd to my Thought, that the Brasilians take no Physick but their Tobacco, for almost all Distempers; and I had a Piece of a Roll of Tobacco in one of the Chests, which was quite cur'd, and some also that was green and not quite cur'd.

I went, directed by Heaven no doubt; for in this Chest I found a Cure, both for Soul and Body, I open'd the Chest, and found what I look'd for, viz. the Tobacco; and as the few Books, I had sav'd, lay there too, I took out one of the Bibles which I mention'd before, and which to this Time I had not found Leisure, or so much as Inclination to look into; I say, I took it out, and brought both that and the Tobacco with me to the Table.

What Use to make of the Tobacco, I knew not, as to my Distemper, or whether it was good for it or no; but I try'd several Experiments with it, as if I was resolv'd it should hit one Way or other: I first took a Piece of a Leaf, and chew'd it in my Mouth, which indeed at first almost stupify'd my Brain, the Tobacco being green and strong, and that I had not been much us'd to it; then I took some and steeped it an Hour or two in some Rum, and resolv'd to take a Dose of it when I lay down; and lastly, I burnt some upon a Pan of Coals, and held my Nose close over the Smoke of it as long as I could bear it, as well for the Heat as almost for Suffocation.

In the Interval of this Operation, I took up the Bible and began to read, but my Head was too much disturb'd with the Tobacco to bear reading, at least that Time; only having open'd the Book casually, the first Words that occurr'd to me were these, Call on me in the Day of Trouble, and I will deliver, and thou shalt glorify me.

The Words were very apt to my Case, and made some Impression upon my Thoughts at the Time of reading them, tho' not so much as they did afterwards; for as for being deliver'd, the Word had no Sound, as I may say, to me; the Thing was so remote, so impossible in my Apprehension of Things, that I began to say as the Children of Israel did, when they were promis'd Flesh to eat, Can God spread a Table in the Wilderness? so I began to say, Can God himself deliver me from this Place? and as it was not for many Years that any Hope appear'd, this prevail'd very often upon my Thoughts: But however, the Words made a great Impression upon me, and I mused upon them very often. It grew now late, and the Tobacco had, as I said, doz'd my Head so much, that I inclin'd to sleep; so I left my Lamp burning in the Cave, least I should want any Thing in the Night, and went to Bed; but before I lay down, I did what I never had done in all my Life, I kneel'd down and pray'd to God to fulfil the Promise to me, that if I call'd upon him in the Day of Trouble, he would deliver me; after my broken and imperfect Prayer was over, I drunk the Rum in which I had steep'd the Tobacco, which was so strong and rank of the Tobacco, that indeed I could scarce get it down; immediately upon this I went to Bed, I found presently it flew up in my Head violently, but I fell into a sound Sleep, and wak'd no more 'till by the Sun it must necessarily be near Three a-Clock in the Afternoon the next Day; nay, to this Hour, I'm partly of the Opinion, that I slept all the next Day and Night, and 'till almost Three that Day after; for otherwise I knew not how I should lose a Day out of my Reckoning in the Days of the Week, as it appear'd some Years after I had done: for if I had lost it by crossing and re-crossing the Line, I should have lost more than one Day: But certainly I lost a Day in my Accompt, and never knew which Way.

Be that however one Way or th' other, when I awak'd I found my self exceedingly refresh'd, and my Spirits lively and chearful; when I got up, I was stronger than I was the Day before, and my Stomach better, for I was hungry; and in short, I had no Fit the next Day, but continu'd much alter'd for the better; this was the 29th.

The 30th was my well Day of Course, and I went abroad with my Gun, but did not care to travel too far, I kill'd a Sea Fowl or two, something like a brand Goose, and brought them Home, but was not very forward to eat them; so I ate some more of the Turtle's Eggs, which were very good: This Evening I renew'd the Medicine which I had suppos'd did me good the Day before, viz. the Tobacco steep'd in Rum, only I did not take so much as before, nor did I chew any of the Leaf, or hold my Head over the Smoke; however, I was not so well the next Day, which was the first of July, as I hop'd I shou'd have been; for I had a little Spice of the cold Fit, but it was not much.

July 2. I renew'd the Medicine all the three Ways, and doz'd my self with it as at first; and doubled the Quantity which I drank.

July 3. I miss'd the Fit for good and all, tho' I did not recover my full Strength for some Weeks after; while I was thus gathering Strength, my Thoughts run exceedingly upon this Scripture, I will deliver thee, and the Impossibility of my Deliverance lay much upon my Mind in Barr of my ever expecting it: But as I was discouraging my self with such Thoughts, it occurr'd to my Mind, that I pored so much upon my Deliverance from the main Affliction, that I disregarded the Deliverance I had receiv'd; and I was, as it were, made to ask my self such Questions as these, viz. Have I not been deliver'd, and wonderfully too, from Sickness? from the most distress'd Condition that could be, and that as so frightful to me, and what Notice I had taken of it?

Had I done my Part? God had deliver'd me, but I had not glorify'd him; that is to say, I had not own'd and been thankful for that as a Deliverance, and how cou'd I expect greater Deliverance?

This touch'd my Heart very much, and immediately I kneel'd down and gave God Thanks aloud, for my Recovery from my Sickness.

July 4. In the Morning I took the Bible, and beginning at the New Testament, I began seriously to read it, and impos'd upon my self to read a while every Morning and every Night, not tying my self to the Number of Chapters, but as long as my Thoughts shou'd engage me: It was not long after I set seriously to this Work, but I found my Heart more deeply and sincerely affected with the Wickedness of my past Life: The Impression of my Dream reviv'd, and the Words, All these Things have not brought thee to Repentance, ran seriously in my Thought: I was earnestly begging of God to give me Repentance, when it happen'd providentially the very Day that reading the Scripture, I came to these Words, He is exalted a Prince and a Saviour, to give Repentance, and to give Remission: I threw down the Book, and with my Heart as well as my Hands lifted up to Heaven, in a Kind of Extasy of Joy, I cry'd out aloud, Jesus, thou Son of David, Jesus, thou exalted Prince and Saviour, give me Repentance!

This was the first Time that I could say, in the true Sense of the Words, that I pray'd in all my Life; for now I pray'd with a Sense of my Condition, and with a true Scripture View of Hope founded on the Encouragement of the Word of God; and from this Time, I may say, I began to have Hope that God would hear me.

Now I began to construe the Words mentioned above, Call on me, and I will deliver you, in a different Sense from what I had ever done before; for then I had no Notion of any thing being call'd Deliverance, but my being deliver'd from the Captivity I was in; for tho' I was indeed at large in the Place, yet the Island was certainly a Prison to me, and that in the worst Sense in the World; but now I learn'd to take it in another Sense: Now I look'd back upon my past Life with such Horrour, and my Sins appear'd so dreadful, that my Soul sought nothing of God, but Deliverance from the Load of Guilt that bore down all my Comfort: As for my Solitary Life it was nothing; I did not SO much as pray to be deliver'd from it, or think of it; It was all of no Consideration in Comparison to this: And I add this Part here, to hint to whoever shall read it, that whenever they come to a true Sense of things, they will find Deliverance from Sin a much greater Blessing, than Deliverance from Affliction.

But leaving this Part, I return to my Journal.

Questions for Discussion

1 To what does Defoe's hero attribute his early loss of religious faith?
2 How does Crusoe's situation lead him to recover this faith?
3 Note the language with which Defoe depicts Crusoe's religious conversion. What are its major elements?

CHAPTER 60

Joseph Addison (1672–1719)

Joseph Addison was born in Milston, in Wiltshire, and was educated at Charterhouse. He went on to study at Queen's College, Oxford, and subsequently to become a fellow of Magdalen College. His intention was to become ordained into the Church of England; however, political patronage encouraged him to explore other possibilities. In 1708, he was elected to Parliament, but failed in his first attempt to make a speech. He therefore abandoned the political for the literary field. Addison founded *The Spectator*, a journal which was published daily between March 1711 and December 1712, to which he himself contributed at some length. He soon established a reputation as an essayist, humorist, and moralist. In particular, he showed a serious interest in religious poetry, and contributed a paraphrase of Psalm 23, an original hymn still widely used today ("When all thy mercies, O my God"), and an "Ode," appended to a major essay entitled "On the impressions of divine power and wisdom in the Universe."

Joseph Addison (1672–1719)

Basic description
Leading English essayist, humorist and moralist, with a particular interest in religious poetry.

Major works
Remarks on Several Parts of Italy (1705); *The Tatler* (1709–11); *The Spectator* (1711–14); *Cato: A Tragedy* (1713).

Editions of work
The Spectator, ed. D. F. Bond, 5 vols. Oxford: Clarendon Press, 1965.

Major studies
Edward A. Bloom and Lillian E. Bloom, *Joseph Addison and Richard Steele: The Critical Heritage*. London: Routledge, 1995.

Peter Smithers, *The Life of Joseph Addison*, 2nd edn. Oxford: Clarendon Press, 1968.

Text: Ode

In 1712, Addison published an essay in *The Spectator*, based upon Psalm 19. The essay concluded with the following "Ode," which is widely regarded as one of his finest works of religious poetry. It takes the form of an extended meditation on Psalm 19:1–4, which is here reprinted in the King James Version, familiar to Addison:

The heavens declare the glory of God; and the firmament sheweth his handywork.
Day unto day uttereth speech, and night unto night sheweth knowledge.
There is no speech nor language, where their voice is not heard.
Their line is gone out through all the earth, and their words to the end of the world.

In his "Ode," Addison develops the idea of the celestial bodies bearing witness to the power and providence of the one who created them:

> The spacious firmament on high,
> With all the blue ethereal sky,
> And spangled heavens, a shining frame,
> Their great Original proclaim.
> Th'unwearied Sun from day to day
> Does his Creator's power display;
> And publishes to every land
> The work of an Almighty hand.
>
> Soon as the evening shades prevail,
> The Moon takes up the wondrous tale;
> And nightly to the listening Earth
> Repeats the story of her birth:
> Whilst all the stars that round her burn,
> And all the planets in their turn,
> Confirm the tidings as they roll,
> And spread the truth from pole to pole.
>
> What though in solemn silence, all
> Move round the dark terrestrial ball?
> What though nor real voice nor sound
> Amidst their radiant orbs be found?
> In Reason's ear they all rejoice,
> And utter forth a glorious voice;
> For ever singing as they shine,
> 'The Hand that made us is divine'.

Questions for Discussion

1 Why does Addison pay such attention to the doctrine of creation in this poem?
2 The poem was written around the time of Newton's explanation of the basis of "celestial mechanics," which suggested that the entire universe obeyed certain fixed laws, established by God in creation. At what points does this interest in astronomy show itself in this poem?

Text: *Cato*

Addison wrote the tragedy *Cato* in 1713. One of the most remarkable sections of the fifth act of the drama takes the form of a speech reflecting on the notion of "eternity." Here, Addison draws on a great theme of both classical antiquity and Christian theology – that the desires and longings of human nature point beyond themselves, to their ultimate ground and fulfillment in God. The theme is found in the writings of Augustine, and was developed subsequently by writers as diverse as Blaise Pascal and C. S. Lewis. A sense of longing or awareness of emptiness is to be seen as a God-given indication of a world beyond that of the senses, to which we are finally called. As the passage is short, no study questions have been appended.

> It must be so – Plato, thou reasonst well! –
> Else whence this pleasing hope, this fond desire,
> This longing after immortality?
> Or whence this secret dread, and inward horror,
> Of falling into naught? Why shrinks the soul
> Back on herself, and startles at destruction?
> 'Tis the divinity that stirs within us;
> 'Tis heaven itself, that points out an hereafter,
> And intimates eternity to man.
> Eternity! thou pleasing, dreadful thought!

CHAPTER 61

Isaac Watts (1674–1748)

Isaac Watts was born in the southern English city of Southampton, and was educated at Stoke Newington, now a suburb of London. Watts was a man of deep faith, who realized that the singing of hymns could be a powerful aid to personal devotion. At the time, the use of music in worship was regarded with great suspicion within the rather strict form of Christianity to which Watts belonged. Watts' hymns did much to change those views, and pave the way for the widespread use of congregational hymn-singing in the English evangelical revival of the eighteenth century. His best-known hymns include many still sung today, including "When I survey the wondrous cross," "Jesus shall reign where'er the sun," and "O God, our help in ages past."

Watts was convinced that much of the Christianity of his day was superficial. He longed to go deeper, and learn more. His advice to his readers reflects this concern: "Do not hover always on the surface of things, nor take up suddenly, with mere appearances; but penetrate into the depth of matters, as far as your time and circumstances allow." We see this concern to "penetrate into the depth of matters" in his devotional hymns, which stimulate personal devotion through active engagement with their themes.

Isaac Watts (1674–1748)

Basic description
Leading non-conformist hymn writer.

Major works
"Jesus shall reign where'er the sun"; "When I survey the wondrous cross".

Major studies
A. P. Davis, *Isaac Watts: His Life and Works*. London: Independent Press, 1948.
Bernard L. Manning, *The Hymns of Wesley and Watts*. London: Epworth, 1942.

Text: "When I Survey the Wondrous Cross"

His best-loved hymn takes the form of a meditation on the cross, intended to evoke a sense of wonder and commitment on the part of its audience. In "When I survey the wondrous cross," Watts offers a reflection on the cross, designed to allow its audience to see the attractions of the world in their proper perspective. Through painting a vivid word-picture of the cross, Watts stresses that all else pales into insignificance in its light.

> When I survey the wondrous Cross
> On which the Prince of Glory died,
> My richest gain I count but loss,
> And pour contempt on all my pride.
>
> Forbid it, Lord, that I should boast
> Save in the Cross of Christ my Lord
> All the vain things that charm me most,
> I sacrifice them to his blood.
>
> See from his head, his hands, his feet
> Sorrow and love flow mingled down;
> Did e'er such love and sorrow meet?
> Or thorns compose so rich a crown?
>
> Were the whole realm of nature mine,
> That were an offering far too small;
> Love so amazing, so divine,
> Demands my soul, my life, my all.

Questions for Study

1 Is this hymn didactic or contemplative in its tone? In other words, does it aim to inculcate doctrines, or to enable its users to visualize the sufferings of Christ? Why do you
   think Watts took this approach?
2 Assess the technique used by Watts to build up his mental image of the crucified
   Christ. Which of his verbal brush-strokes do you consider to be the most effective?
3 What do you think Watts intends to achieve through this hymn? In particular, what
   does the final verse encourage its singers to *do* as a result of singing this hymn?

CHAPTER 62

Joseph Butler (1692–1752)

Joseph Butler is widely regarded as one of the most able Anglican apologists of the eighteenth century. His reasoned defense of the basic themes of the Christian faith in the face of rationalist criticism, especially when linked with his elegant literary style, has made his inclusion in this collection essential. Butler was born of Presbyterian parents, but embraced the faith of the Church of England in order to enter Oxford University. After studying at Oriel College, Oxford, he went on to be preacher at the Rolls Chapel (1718–26). This chapel, which has since been demolished, stood on the site of what is now the Public Record Office in London. Butler's sermons at this chapel – usually referred to as his "Rolls Sermons" – established his reputation as an able and gifted thinker and preacher.

Joseph Butler (1692–1752)

Basic description
Noted Anglican writer of the eighteenth century, whose writing ministry was chiefly concerned with the neutralization of the emerging deist arguments against traditional Christian beliefs.

Major works
Fifteen Sermons Preached at the Rolls Chapel (1726); *The Analogy of Religion* (1536).

Major studies
C. Cunliffe, *Joseph Butler's Moral and Religious Thought*. Oxford: Oxford University Press, 1992.

E. C. Mossner, *Bishop Butler and the Age of Reason*. New York: Macmillan, 1936.

In 1725, Butler accepted the wealthy living of Stanhope in County Durham, in the north of England. The relative leisure which this appointment allowed Butler was put to good literary use. The first product of this period in his career appeared in 1726. The *Fifteen Sermons Preached at the Rolls Chapel* made his Rolls Sermons available to a wider public. A second edition (1729) included a new preface, which made their general purpose clearer, and appears to have increased their influence. However, the most important work to have been composed during the Stanhope period is the *Analogy of Religion*, which was published in 1736. We shall return to this presently.

Butler was appointed Bishop of Bristol in 1738, and soon found himself engaged in controversy with John Wesley and George Whitefield, who found him unsympathetic to their ministry of evangelism and personal renewal. In 1750, he was translated to the diocese of Durham. He remained Bishop of Durham until his death two years later. His episcopal office led to him widely being referred to as "Bishop Butler," and it is possible that he remains better known by this title today.

The work which we shall be considering is the *Analogy of Religion* – or, to give it the full title which Butler bestowed upon it, *The Analogy of Religion, Natural and Revealed, to the Constitution and Course of Nature*. The work may be seen as a response to the general line of thinking which developed in the wake of the publication of John Locke's *Reasonableness of Christianity* (1695). The work was written when Deism was at its strongest, and shows Butler pitting his intellectual gifts against the deist critics of traditional Christianity, who argued, for example, that reason was to be preferred to revelation – even to the point of making the latter quite redundant and unnecessary.

Butler's response to this argument was partly based on a close reading of Samuel Clarke's Boyle Lectures, which argued that it was possible to demonstrate the being and nature of God from the natural order. While Butler clearly had considerable respect for aspects of Clarke's work, he nevertheless distanced himself from its basic method. Where Clarke argued on *a priori* grounds, Butler insisted that the proper way of proceeding was *a posteriori*. As a result it is not certainty but "probability [which] is the very guide of life." Butler argues that, while certain Christian beliefs are open to criticism on rational grounds, these criticisms are far from decisive. Non-religious beliefs can be criticized on exactly the same grounds. The best that can be hoped for is probability of belief, not certainty of conviction. As such, we must believe and act in accordance with the balance of probability, knowing that conclusive proof of any beliefs will always elude us.

The section singled out for special study is Butler's conclusion to the first part of *The Analogy of Religion*, in which he argues that the probability of evidence points to the existence of "an intelligent Author and Governor" of the world, and to a belief in everlasting life. The text is clearly written, and requires little comment. The important point to note is that Butler argues for the reasonableness of certain key Christian beliefs, without feeling the need to offer proofs for them. We can, he believes, live on the basis of probability, rather than certainty.

The observations of the last Chapter lead us to consider this little scene of human life in which we are so busily engaged, as having a reference of some sort or other to a much larger plan of things. Whether we are any way related to the more distant parts of the boundless universe into which we are brought, is altogether uncertain. But it is evident that the course of things which comes within our view is connected with somewhat past, present, and future, beyond it. So that we are placed, as one may speak, in the middle of a scheme, not a fixed but a progressive one, every way incomprehensible; incomprehensible in a manner equally with respect to what has been, what now is, and what shall be hereafter. And this scheme cannot but contain in it somewhat as wonderful, and as much beyond our thought and conception, as anything in that of Religion. For will any man in his senses say that it is less difficult to conceive how the world came to be and to continue as it is without than with an intelligent Author and Governor of it? or admitting an intelligent Governor of it, that there is some other rule of government more natural and of easier conception than that which we call moral? Indeed, without an intelligent Author and Governor of Nature, no account at all can be given how this universe or the part of it particularly in which we are concerned came to be, and the course of it to be carried on as it is; nor any of its general end and design, without a moral Governor of it. That there is an intelligent Author of Nature and natural Governor of the world is a principle gone upon in the foregoing treatise as proved, and generally known and confessed to be proved. And the very notion of an intelligent Author of Nature proved by particular final causes, implies a will and a character. Now as our whole nature, the nature which he has given us, leads us to conclude his will and character to be moral, just, and good; so we can scarce in imagination conceive what it can be otherwise. However, in consequence of this his will and character, whatever it be, he formed the universe as it is, and carries on the course of it as he does rather than in any other manner, and has assigned to us and to all living creatures a part and a lot in it. Irrational creatures act this their part, and enjoy and undergo the pleasures and the pains allotted them without any reflection. But one would think it impossible that creatures endued with reason could avoid reflecting sometimes upon all this, reflecting, if not from whence we came, yet at least, whither we are going, and what the mysterious scheme in the midst of which we find ourselves will at length come out and produce – a scheme in which it is certain we are highly interested, and in which we may be interested even beyond conception; for many things prove it palpably absurd to conclude that we shall cease to be at death. Particular analogies do most sensibly show us that there is nothing to be thought strange in our being to exist in another state of life. And that we are now living beings affords a strong probability that we shall *continue* so; unless there be some positive ground, and there is none from reason or analogy, to think death will destroy us. Were a persuasion of this kind ever so well grounded, there would surely be little reason to take pleasure in it. But indeed it can have no other ground than some such imagination as that of our gross bodies being ourselves, which is contrary to experience. Experience too most clearly shows us the folly of concluding from the body and the living agent affecting each other mutually, that the dissolution of the former is the destruction of the latter. And there are remarkable instances of their not affecting each other, which lead us to a contrary conclusion. The supposition, then, which in all reason we are to go upon, is that our living nature will *continue* after death. And it is infinitely unreasonable to form an institution of life, or to act upon any other supposition. Now all expectation of immortality, whether more or less certain, opens an unbounded prospect to our hopes and our fears; since we see the constitution of nature is such as to admit of misery as well as to be productive of happiness, and experience ourselves to partake of both in some degree, and since we cannot but know what higher degrees of both we are capable of. And there is no presumption against believing further that our future interest depends upon our present behaviour; for we see our present interest doth, and that the happiness and misery which are naturally annexed to our actions, very frequently do not follow till long after the actions are done, to which they are respectively annexed. So that were speculation to leave us uncertain, whether it were likely that the Author of Nature in giving happiness and misery to his creatures hath regard to their actions or not; yet, since we find by experience that he hath such regard, the whole sense of things which he has given us plainly leads us at once and without any elaborate inquiries to think that it may, indeed must be to good actions chiefly that he hath annexed happiness, and to bad actions misery, or that he will upon the whole reward those who do well, and punish those who do evil. To confirm this from the constitution of the world, it has been observed that some sort of moral government is necessarily implied in that natural government of God which we experience ourselves under; that good and bad actions at present are naturally rewarded and punished, not only as beneficial and mischievous to society, but also as virtuous and vicious; and that there is in the very nature of the thing, a tendency to their being rewarded and punished in a much higher degree than they are at present. And though this higher degree of distributive justice which nature thus points out and leads towards is prevented for a time from taking place, it is by obstacles which the state of this world unhappily throws in its way, and which therefore are in their nature temporary. Now, as these things in the natural conduct of Providence are observable on the side of virtue, so there is nothing to be set against them on the side of vice. A moral scheme of government, then, is visibly established, and in some degree carried into execution; and this, together with the essential tendencies of virtue and vice duly considered, naturally raise in us an apprehension that it will be carried on further towards perfection in a future state, and that every one shall there receive according to his deserts. And if this be so, then our future and general interest, under the moral government of God, is appointed to depend upon our behaviour, notwithstanding the difficulty which this may occasion of securing it, and the danger of losing it; just in the same manner as our temporal interest, under his natural government, is appointed to depend upon our behaviour, notwithstanding the like difficulty and danger. For, from our original constitution, and that of the world which we inhabit, we are naturally trusted with ourselves, with our own conduct and our own interest. And from the same constitution of nature, especially joined with that course of things which is owing to men, we have temptations to be unfaithful in this trust; to forfeit this interest, to neglect it, and run ourselves into misery and ruin. From these temptations arise the difficulties of behaving so as to secure our temporal interest, and the hazard of behaving so as to miscarry in it. There is therefore nothing incredible in supposing there may be the like difficulty and hazard with regard to that chief and final good which Religion lays before us. Indeed the whole account, how it came to pass that we were placed in such a condition as this, must be beyond our comprehension; but it is in part accounted for by what Religion teaches us, that the character of virtue and piety must be a necessary qualification for a future state of security and happiness under the moral government of God; in like manner, as some certain qualifications or other are necessary for every particular condition of life, under his natural government; and that the present state was intended to be a school of discipline for improving in ourselves that character. Now this intention of nature is rendered highly credible by observing that we are plainly made for improvement of all kinds; that it is a general appointment of Providence that we cultivate practical principles, and form within ourselves habits of action in order to become fit for what we were wholly unfit for before; that, in particular, childhood and youth is naturally appointed to be a state of discipline for mature age; and that the present world is peculiarly fitted for a state of moral discipline; and, whereas objections are urged against the whole notion of moral government and a probationary state from the opinion of Necessity, it has been shown that God has given us the evidence, as it were, of experience, that all objections against Religion on this head are vain and delusive. He has also, in his natural government, suggested an answer to all our short-sighted objections against the equity and goodness of his moral government, and in general he has exemplified to us the latter by the former.

These things, which, it is to be remembered, are matters of fact, ought in all common sense to awaken mankind, to induce them to consider in earnest their condition, and what they have to do. It is absurd, absurd to the degree of being ridiculous, if the subject were not of so serious a kind, for men to think themselves secure in a vicious life, or even in that immoral thoughtlessness, which far the greatest part of them are fallen into. And the credibility of Religion, arising from experience and facts here considered, is fully sufficient in reason to engage them to live in the general practice of all virtue and piety, under the serious apprehension, though it should be mixed with some doubt, of a righteous administration established in nature, and a future judgment in consequence of it; especially when we consider how very questionable it is whether anything at all can be gained by vice, how unquestionably little as well as precarious the pleasures and profits of it are at the best, and how soon they must be parted with at the longest. For in the deliberations of reason concerning what we are to pursue and what to avoid, as temptations to anything from mere passion are supposed out of the case, so inducements to vice from cool expectations of pleasure and interest so small and uncertain and short are really so insignificant, as in the view of reason to be almost nothing in themselves, and in comparison with the importance of Religion they quite disappear and are lost. Mere passion indeed may be alleged, though not as a reason, yet as an excuse for a vicious course of life. And how sorry an excuse it is will be manifest by observing that we are placed in a condition in which we are unavoidably inured to govern our passions by being necessitated to govern them; and to lay ourselves under the same kind of restraints, and as great ones too from temporal regards, as virtue and piety in the ordinary course of things require. The plea of ungovernable passion, then, on the side of vice is the poorest of all things; for it is no reason, and but a poor excuse. But the proper motives to religion are the proper proofs of it from our moral nature, from the presages of conscience, and our natural apprehension of God under the character of a righteous Governor and Judge; a nature and conscience and apprehension given us by him, and from the confirmation of the dictates of reason, by *life and immortality brought to light by the Gospel; and the wrath of God revealed from heaven against all ungodliness and unrighteousness of men.*

Questions for Study

1 What are the probable grounds for belief in God as the "Author and Governor" of the world? And what distinction is implied by the two terms here used for God?

2 What are the probable grounds for belief in everlasting life? And for final judgment?

3 What does Butler mean when he asserts that "the present state was intended to be a school of discipline for improving ourselves"?

4 Butler argues that certain arguments "ought in all common sense to awaken mankind, to induce them to consider in earnest their condition, and what they have to do." What are these arguments? And in what way do or could they "awaken" humanity?

CHAPTER 63

Jonathan Edwards (1703–1758)

Jonathan Edwards was born at East Windsor, Connecticut, on October 5, 1703. In September 1716 Edwards entered Yale College, New Haven (now Yale University) at the age of thirteen. Edwards graduated at the head of his class four years later and began a two-year course of theological study in New Haven. When he was around seventeen years of age, Edwards underwent a conversion experience. As he read 1 Timothy 1:17, he was overwhelmed by a sense of God's greatness and glory. "As I read the words," he wrote later in his personal journal, "there came into my soul, and it was, as it were, diffused through it, a sense of the glory of the divine Being; a new sense quite different from anything I ever experienced before."

Having completed his education in 1722, he took up a pastorate in a Presbyterian church in New York, but left there to take a position as tutor at Yale in 1724, a position that he held until 1726. From 1725 he served as an assistant to his maternal grandfather, Solomon Stoddard, who was the Congregationalist pastor of Northampton, Massachusetts. Upon Stoddard's death in 1729, Edwards succeeded him as pastor. Much of Edwards' most important literary and theological work comes from his Northampton period. These works include his *Treatise Concerning Religious Affections* (1746), and many of his more important sermons.

His preaching during his Northampton period was received with what can only be described as mixed reviews. On the one hand, his preaching is credited with bringing about the first "Great Awakening" in American history, beginning in 1734, when six sudden conversions in Edwards' parish cascaded into a flood of thirty or so every week, drawing people from up to a hundred miles away. His *Faithful Narrative of the Surprising Works of God* (1737) chronicles the early years of the Great Awakening, and brought him considerable fame. Despite this success, however, Edwards alienated many in his congregation by insisting on significantly more stringent membership requirements than were customary at the time. His first inclination was to insist on visible evidence of conversion and regeneration, but he eventually settled for a public profession of faith. His move to exclude those who did not meet these standards from attendance at the Lord's Supper led to a two-year battle within the congregation, and finally, in 1750, to Edwards being dismissed from his pastorate.

Jonathan Edwards (1703–1758)

Basic description

Leading American Puritan writer and preacher.

Major works

Treatise Concerning Religious Affections; Treatise on Grace; The Freedom of the Will.

Editions of works

The Works of Jonathan Edwards, 17 vols. New Haven, CT: Yale University Press, 1957–99.

Major studies

R. A. Delattre, *Beauty and Sensibility in the Thought of Jonathan Edwards.* New Haven, CT: Yale University Press, 1968.

Nathan O. Hatch and Harry S. Stout, *Jonathan Edwards and the American Experience.* New York: Oxford University Press, 1988.

The ensuing years were difficult for the family as they struggled with debt and loss of income. Edwards settled in Stockbridge, Massachusetts, then a frontier settlement, where he ministered to a small congregation and served as missionary to the Indians. It was here that he completed his major work, *The Freedom of the Will* (1754). After several years on the frontier, Edwards yielded to considerable pressure and assumed the presidency of Princeton in the fall of 1757. In the event, he held the position for less than a year, dying in March 1758 of a fever in reaction to a failed smallpox innoculation. He lies buried in the local cemetery.

Text: *Treatise Concerning Religious Affections*

The first text for consideration is one of Edwards' most widely-read treatises, dealing with the role of affections in religion. Against the Enlightenment idea that religion dealt simply with propositional beliefs, Edwards argued that there was an emotional or affective dimension to faith. There are important parallels here with the writings of John and Charles Wesley, who also stressed the experiential aspects of religion. The extract is taken from the second part of the first chapter of this important work.

The second thing proposed, which was to observe some things that render it evident, that true religion, in great part consists in the affections. And here:

What has been said of the nature of the affections makes this evident, and may be sufficient, without adding anything further, to put this matter out of doubt; for who will deny that true religion consists in a great measure, in vigorous and lively actings of the inclination and will of the soul, or the fervent exercises of the heart?

That religion which God requires, and will accept, does not consist in weak, dull, and lifeless wishes, raising us but a little above a state of indifference: God, in his word, greatly insists upon it, that we be good in earnest, "fervent in spirit," and our hearts vigorously engaged in religion: Rom. 12:11, "Be ye fervent in spirit, serving the Lord." Deut. 10:12, "And now, Israel, what doth the Lord thy God require of thee, but to fear the Lord thy God, to walk in all his ways, and to love him, and to serve the Lord thy God with all thy heart, and with all thy soul?" and chap. 6:4, 6, "Hear, O Israel, the Lord our God is one Lord: And thou shalt love the Lord thy God with all thy heart, and with all thy might." It is such a fervent vigorous engaged-ness of the heart in religion, that is the fruit of a real circumcision of the heart, or true regeneration, and that has the promises of life; Deut. 30:6, "And the Lord thy God will circumcise thine heart, and the heart of thy seed, to love the Lord thy God with all thy heart, and with all thy soul, that thou mayest live."

If we be not in good earnest in religion, and our wills and inclinations be not strongly exercised, we are nothing. The things of religion are so great, that there can be no suitableness in the exercises of our hearts, to their nature and importance, unless they be lively and powerful. In nothing is vigor in the actings of our inclina-tions so requisite, as in religion; and in nothing is lukewarmness so odious. True reli-gion is evermore a powerful thing; and the power of it appears, in the first place in the inward exercises of it in the heart, where is the principal and original seat of it. Hence true religion is called the power of godliness, in distinction from the external appearances of it, that are the form of it, 2 Tim. 3:5: "Having a form of godliness, but denying the power of it." The Spirit of God, in those that have sound and solid religion, is a spirit of powerful holy affection; and therefore, God is said "to have given the Spirit of power, and of love, and of a sound mind," 2 Tim. 1:7. And such, when they receive the Spirit of God, in his sanctifying and saving influences, are said to be "baptized with the Holy Ghost, and with fire"; by reason of the power and fervor of those exercises the Spirit of God excites in their hearts, whereby their hearts, when grace is in exercise, may be said to "burn within them"; as is said of the dis-ciples, Luke 24:32.

The business of religion is from time to time compared to those exercises, wherein men are wont to have their hearts and strength greatly exercised and engaged, such as running, wrestling or agonizing for a great prize or crown, and fighting with strong enemies that seek our lives, and warring as those, that by violence take a city or kingdom.

And though true grace has various degrees, and there are some that are but babes in Christ, in whom the exercise of the inclination and will, towards divine and heavenly things, is comparatively weak; yet everyone that has the power of godliness in his heart, has his inclinations and heart exercised towards God and divine things, with such strength and vigor that these holy exercises do prevail in him above all carnal or natural affections, and are effectual to overcome them: for every true disciple of Christ "loves him above father or mother, wife and children, brethren and sisters, houses and lands: yea, than his own life." From hence it follows, that wherever true religion is, there are vigorous exercises of the inclination and will towards divine objects: but by what was said before, the vigorous, lively, and sensible exercises of the will, are no other than the affections of the soul.

Questions for Study

1 What does Edwards understand by the term "affections"?
2 Edwards clearly regards religion as being closely linked with these affections. Why? Do you think he has established this point through the arguments which he sets forward?
3 Why does Edwards regard "lukewarmness" with such distaste?

Text: The Christian Pilgrim

One of Edwards' most compelling works is a sermon entitled "The Christian Pilgrim." In this sermon, Edwards is concerned to help Christians orientate themselves correctly as they travel along the road of faith. As we pass through the world, what should be our attitude toward it?

Edwards argues that, precisely because it is God's creation, it cannot be rejected as evil. Yet because it is not God, it falls short of the true glory of the ultimate goal of the Christian journey. Edwards reminds his hearers that their final goal is God, and that nothing else has the power to satisfy or right to be adored other than that same God. Edwards here declares that "God is the highest good of the reasonable creature; and the enjoyment of him is the only happiness with which our souls can be satisfied." Christians may therefore pass through the world and enjoy all that it has to offer, while realizing that the final delight of being with God will totally overwhelm whatever joy and delights this world may offer.

The Christian Pilgrim

Hebrews xi: 13, 14

And confessed that they were strangers and pilgrims on the earth. For they that say such things declare plainly that they seek a country.

The Apostle is here exhibiting the excellency of faith, by its glorious effects, and happy issue in the saints of the Old Testament. Having enumerated examples of Abel, Enoch and Noah, of Abraham and Sarah, of Isaac and Jacob, he relates that all "these died in faith, not having received the promises, but having seen them afar off, were persuaded of them and embraced them, and confessed that they were strangers and pilgrims on earth." In these words the apostle seems more immediately to refer to Abraham and Sarah, and their kindred who came with them from Haran, and from Ur of the Chaldees, as appears by the 15th verse, where he says, "and truly if they had been mindful of that country whence they came out, they might have had opportunity to have returned."

Two things may be here observed.

1   The confession which they made concerning themselves to it, that they were strangers and pilgrims on the earth; of this we have a particular account concerning Abraham, "I am a stranger and a sojourner with you." And it seems to have been a general sense of the patriarchs, by what Jacob says to Pharaoh. "And Jacob said to Pharaoh, the days of the years of my pilgrimage are an hundred and thirty years: few and evil have the days of the years of my life been, and have not attained to the days of the years of the life of my fathers in the days of their pilgrimage. I am a stranger and a sojourner with thee, as all my fathers were."

2   The inference that the apostle draws from hence, viz. *that they sought another country as their home.* "For they that say such things declare plainly that they seek a country." In confessing that they were strangers, they plainly declared that this is not their country, that this is not the place where they are at home. And in confessing themselves to be pilgrims, they declared plainly that this is not their settled abode; but that they have respect to some other country, which they seek and to which they are travelling.

Section I

That this life ought to be so spent by us, as to be only a journey, or pilgrimage, towards heaven.

HERE I would observe,

1   That we ought not to rest in the world and its enjoyments, but should desire heaven. We should *seek first the kingdom of God*. We ought above all things to desire a heavenly happiness; to be with God; and dwell with Jesus Christ. Though surrounded with outward enjoyments, and settled in families with desirable friends and relations; though we have companions whose society is delightful, and children in whom we see many promising qualifications; though we live by good neighbours, and are generally beloved where known; yet we ought not to take our rest in these things as our portion. We should be so far from resting in them, that we should desire to leave them all, in God's due time. We ought to possess, enjoy, and use them, with no other view but readily to quit them, whenever we are called to it, and to change them willingly and cheerfully for heaven.

A traveller is not wont to rest in what he meets with, however comfortable and pleasing on the road. If he passes through pleasant places, flowery meadows, or shady groves; he does not take up his content in these things, but only takes a transient view of them as he goes along. He is not enticed by fine appearances to put off the thought of proceeding. No, but his journey's end is in his mind. If he meets with comfortable accommodations at an inn; he entertains no thoughts of settling there. He considers that these things are not his own, that he is but a stranger, and when he has refreshed himself, or tarried for a night, he is for going forward. And it is pleasant to him to think that so much of the way is gone.

So should we desire heaven more than the comforts and enjoyments of this life. The apostle mentions it as an encouraging, comfortable consideration to Christians, that they draw nearer their happiness. "Now is our salvation nearer than when we believed." – Our hearts ought to be loose to these things, as that of a man on a journey; that we may as cheerfully part with them whenever God calls. "But this I say, brethren, the time is short: it remaineth, that both they that have wives, be as though they had none; and they that weep, as though they wept not; and they that rejoice, as though they rejoiced not; and they that buy, as though they possessed not; and they that use this world, as not abusing it; for the fashion of this world passeth away." – These things, as only lent to us for a little while, to serve a present turn; but we should set our *hearts* on heaven, as our inheritance for ever.

2   We ought to seek heaven, by travelling in the way that leads thither. This is a way of holiness. We should choose and desire to travel thither in this way and in no other; and part with all those carnal appetites, which as weights will tend to hinder us. "Let us lay aside every weight, and the sin which doth so easily beset us, and let us run with patience the race that is set before us." However pleasant the gratification of any appetite may be, we must lay it aside, if it be any hindrance, or a stumbling-block in the way to heaven.

We should travel on in the way of obedience to all God's commands, even the difficult as well as the easy; denying all our sinful inclinations and interests. The way to heaven is ascending; we must be content to travel up hill, though it be hard and tiresome, and contrary to the natural bias of our flesh. We should follow Christ; the path he travelled was the right way to heaven. We should take up our cross and follow him, in meekness and lowliness of heart, obedience and charity, diligence to do good, and patience under afflictions. The way to heaven is a heavenly life; an imitation of those who are in heaven, in their holy enjoyments, loving, adoring, serving, and praising God and the Lamb. Even if we *could* go to heaven with the gratification of our lusts, we should prefer a way of holiness and conformity to the spiritual self-denying rules of the gospel.

3   We should travel on in this way in a laborious manner. Long journeys are attended with toil and fatigue; especially if through a wilderness. Persons, in such a case, expect no other than to suffer hardships and weariness. So we should travel in this way of holiness, improving our time and strength, to surmount the difficulties and obstacles that are in the way. The land we have to travel through, is a wilderness; there are many mountains, rocks, and rough places that we must go over, and, therefore, there is a necessity that we should lay out our strength.

4   Our whole lives ought to be spent in travelling this road. We ought to begin *early*. This should be the *first* concern, when persons become capable of acting. When they first set out in the *world*, they should set out on *this* journey. And we ought to travel on with *assiduity*. It ought to be the work of every day. We should often think of our journey's end; and make it our daily work to travel on in the way that leads to it. He who is on a journey, is often thinking of the destined place; and it is his daily care and business to get along; and to improve his time to get towards his journey's end. Thus should heaven be continually in our thoughts; and the immediate entrance or passage to it, *viz.* death, should be present with us. We ought to *persevere* in this way as long as we live.

"Let us run with patience the race that is set before us." Though the road be difficult, and toilsome, we must hold out with patience, and be content to endure hardships. Though the journey be long, yet we must not stop short; but hold on till we arrive at the place we seek. Nor should we be discouraged with the length and difficulties of the way, as the children of Israel were, and be for turning back again. All our thought, and design, should be to press forward till we arrive.

5   We ought to be continually growing in holiness; and, in that respect, coming nearer and nearer to heaven. We should be endeavouring to come nearer to heaven, in being more heavenly; becoming more and more like the inhabitants of heaven, in respect of holiness, and conformity to God; the knowledge of God and Christ; in clear views of the glory of God, the beauty of Christ, and the excellency of divine things, as we come nearer to the beatific vision. We should labour to be continually growing in divine love – that this may be an increasing flame in our hearts, till they ascend wholly in this flame – in obedience and an heavenly conversation; that we may do the will of God on earth, as the angels do in heaven: in comfort and spiritual joy; in sensible communion with God and Jesus Christ. Our path should be as "the shining light, that shines more and more to the perfect day." We ought to be hungering and thirsting after righteousness; after an increase in righteousness. "As newborn babes desire the sincere milk of the word, that ye may grow thereby." The perfection of heaven should be our mark. "This one thing I do, forgetting those things which are behind, and reaching forth unto those things that are before, I press toward the mark, for the prize of the high calling of God in Christ Jesus."

6   All other concerns of life, ought to be entirely subordinate to this. When a man is on a journey, all the steps he takes are subordinated to the aim of getting to his journey's end. And, if he carries money or provisions with him, it is to supply him in his journey. So we ought wholly to subordinate all our other business, and all our temporal enjoyments, to this affair of travelling to heaven. When any thing we have, becomes a clog and hindrance to us, we should quit it immediately. The use of our worldly enjoyments and possessions, should be with such a view, and in such a manner, as to further us in our way heaven-ward. Thus we should eat, and drink, and clothe ourselves, and improve the conversation and enjoyment of friends. And, whatever business we are setting about, whatever design we are engaging in, we should inquire with ourselves, whether this business, or undertaking, will forward us in our way to heaven? And, if not, we should quit our design.

Section II

Why the Christian's life is a journey or pilgrimage?

1   THIS world is not our abiding place. Our continuance here is but very short. Man's days on the earth, are as a shadow. It was never designed by God that this world should be our home. Neither did God give us these temporal accommodations for that end. If God has given us ample estates, and children, or other pleasant friends, it is with no such design, that we should be furnished here, as for a settled abode; but with a design that we should use them for the present, and then leave them in a very little time. When we are called to any secular business, or charged with the care of a family, if we improve our lives to any other purpose, than as a journey toward heaven, all our labour will be lost. If we spend our lives in the pursuit of a temporal happiness; as riches, or sensual pleasures; credit and esteem from men;

delight in our children, and the prospect of seeing them well brought up, and well settled, &c. – All these things will be of little significancy to us. Death will blow up all our hopes, and will put an end to these enjoyments. "The places that have known us, will know us no more:" and "the eye that has seen us, shall see us no more." We must be taken away for ever from all these things; and it is uncertain when: it may be soon after we are put into the possession of them. And then, where will be all our worldly employments and enjoyments, when we are laid in the silent grave! "So man lieth down, and riseth not again, till the heavens be no more."

2   The future world was designed to be our settled and everlasting abode. There it was intended that we should be fixed; and there alone is a lasting habitation, and a lasting inheritance. The present state is short and transitory; but our state in the other world, is everlasting. And as we are there at first, so we must be without change. Our state in the future world, therefore, being eternal, is of so much greater importance than our state here, that all our concerns in this world should be wholly subordinated to it.

3   Heaven is that place alone where our highest end, and highest good is to be obtained. God hath made us for himself. "Of him, and through him, and to him are all things." Therefore, then do we attain to our highest end, when we are brought to God: but that is by being brought to heaven; for that is God's throne, the place of his special presence. There is but a very imperfect union with God to be had in this world, a very imperfect knowledge of him in the midst of much darkness: a very imperfect conformity to God, mingled with abundance of estrangement. Here we can serve and glorify God, but in a very imperfect manner; our service being mingled with sin, which dishonours God. – But when we get to heaven, (if ever that be,) we shall be brought to a perfect union with God, and have more clear views of him. There we shall be fully conformed to God, without any remaining sin: for "we shall see him as he is." There we shall serve God perfectly; and glorify him in an exalted manner, even to the utmost of the powers and capacity of our nature. Then we shall perfectly give up ourselves to God: our hearts will be pure and holy offerings, presented in a flame of divine love.

God is the highest good of the reasonable creature; and the enjoyment of him is the only happiness with which our souls can be satisfied. – To go to heaven fully to enjoy God, is *infinitely* better than the most pleasant accommodations here. Fathers and mothers, husbands, wives, or children, or the company of earthly friends, are but shadows; but the enjoyment of God is the substance. These are but scattered beams; but God is the sun. These are but streams; but God is the fountain. These are but drops; but God is the ocean. – Therefore it becomes us to spend this life only as a journey towards heaven, as it becomes us to make the seeking of our highest end and proper good, the whole work of our lives; to which we should subordinate all other concerns of life. Why should we labour for, or set our hearts on any thing else, but that which is our proper end, and true happiness?

4   Our present state, and all that belongs to it, is designed by him that made all things, to be wholly in order to another world. – This world was made for a place of preparation for another. Man's mortal life was given him, that he might be prepared for his fixed state. And all that God has here given us, is given to this purpose. The sun shines, and the rain falls upon us; and the earth yields her increase to us for

this end. Civil, ecclesiastical, and family affairs, and all our personal concerns, are designed and ordered in subordination to a future world, by the maker and disposer of all things. To this therefore they ought to be subordinated by us.

Questions for Study

1 What attitude toward the world does Edwards commend in his sermon. Where would you place it on the spectrum of possibilities ranging from total renunciation at one extreme, and uncritical affirmation on the other?
2 In what way does Edwards suggest that the model of "pilgrimage" illuminates the nature of the Christian life?
3 How does Edwards relate life on earth to the hope of heaven?

CHAPTER 64

John Wesley (1703–1791)

Along with his younger brother Charles, John Wesley is remembered primarily for his role in the evangelical revival in England during the eighteenth century. Wesley was born in 1703 in Epworth Rectory in Lincolnshire, son of Samuel and Susanna Wesley. Wesley was educated at Charterhouse, and then went on to study at Christ Church. He was elected to a fellowship at Lincoln College, Oxford, in 1726. After a brief absence (1727–9) to help his father in parish ministry at Epworth, during which he became ordained, John returned to Oxford to discover that his brother Charles had founded a "Holy Club" composed of young men interested in spiritual growth. John quickly became a leading participant of this group, which was dubbed "the Methodists" by its critics and disparagers. His Oxford days introduced him not only to the rich tradition of classical literature and philosophy but also to spiritual classics such as Thomas à Kempis' *Imitation of Christ*, Jeremy Taylor's *Holy Living* and *Holy Dying*, and William Law's *Serious Call*.

In 1735 Wesley accompanied his brother, Charles, and James Oglethorpe to the new American colony of Georgia, where his attempts to apply his then High Church views aroused hostility. Discouraged, he returned (1737) to England, where he found encouragement through the ministry of the Moravian preacher Peter Boehler. At a small religious meeting in Aldersgate Street, London, on May 24, 1738, Wesley had a conversion experience in which his heart was "strangely warmed." He would later identify this as the turning point in his life and ministry.

After this religious conversion, Wesley devoted his life to itinerant preaching and evangelism. Beginning in 1739, he established Methodist societies throughout the country. He traveled and preached constantly, especially in the London–Bristol–Newcastle triangle, with frequent forays into Wales, Ireland, and Scotland. He encountered much opposition and persecution, which only subsided once the scale of his success became apparent. Perhaps the most famous "exclusion order" issued against Wesley came from Joseph Butler, who was then (May 1739) Bishop of Bristol. Late in life Wesley married Mary Vazeille, a widow. He continued throughout his life a regimen of personal discipline and ordered living. He died at the age of 88, still preaching and traveling – and still, incidentally, an ordained clergyman of the Church of England, despite all his reservations concerning that church.

John Wesley (1703–1791)

Basic description

Leading preacher and hymn-writer of the evangelical revival in England; founder of Methodism.

Major works

Substantial numbers of sermons, hymns, and devotional treatises.

Major studies

Henry Abelowe, *The Evangelist of Desire: John Wesley and the Methodists*. Stanford, CA: Stanford University Press, 1990.

Gregory S. Clapper, *John Wesley on Religious Affections: His Views on Experience and Emotion and Their Role in Christian Life and Theology*. London: Scarecrow, 1989.

Wesley's ministry was built upon his preaching, which sought to relate faith and experience in everyday language. Wesley's sermons are characterized by a lack of the verbal sophistication of a Joseph Butler; they more than made up for this, however, by their determined attempt to engage with their hearers in plain English. Wesley's sermons set new standards in preaching, and were soon published. In view of their immense influence, and their undoubted literary importance, it is clearly appropriate to include some such material in this collection.

Text: "Preface" to *Sermons On Several Occasions*

Wesley's sermons were published in several series, making them available to a wide public during his lifetime. In what follows, we shall consider two sets of material. In his "Preface" to the First Series of sermons, published in 1771, Wesley set out clearly the general principles which he followed in writing his sermons. This "Preface" may thus be seen as offering the key to the fundamental themes and approaches of his preaching. This is followed by one of Wesley's most important early sermons, preached on Sunday, July 25, 1741. It is the second sermon in the collected edition, and is widely known by its intriguing title – "The Almost Christian." Taken together, these items offer invaluable insights into the development of the literary genre of the popular sermon in the mid-eighteenth century.

1   The following Sermons contain the substance of what I have been preaching for between eight and nine years last past. During that time I have frequently spoken in public, on every subject in the ensuing collection; and I am not conscious, that there is any one point of doctrine, on which I am accustomed to speak in public, which is not here, incidentally, if not professedly, laid before every Christian reader. Every serious man who peruses these, will therefore see, in the clearest manner, what these doctrines are which I embrace and teach as the essentials of true religion.

2   But I am thoroughly sensible, these are not proposed in such a manner as some may expect. Nothing here appears in an elaborate, elegant, or oratorical dress. If it had been my desire or design to write thus, my leisure would not permit. But, in truth, I, at present, designed nothing less; for I now write, as I generally speak, *ad*

populum – to the bulk of mankind, to those who neither relish nor understand the art of speaking; but who, notwithstanding, are competent judges of those truths which are necessary to present and future happiness. I mention this, that curious readers may spare themselves the labour of seeking for what they will not find.

3   I design plain truth for plain people: Therefore, of set purpose, I abstain from all nice and philosophical speculations; from all perplexed and intricate reasonings; and, as far as possible, from even the show of learning, unless in sometimes citing the original Scripture. I labour to avoid all words which are not easy to be understood, all which are not used in common life; and, in particular, those kinds of technical terms that so frequently occur in Bodies of Divinity; those modes of speaking which men of reading are intimately acquainted with, but which to common people are an unknown tongue. Yet I am not assured, that I do not sometimes slide into them unawares: It is so extremely natural to imagine, that a word which is familiar to ourselves is so to all the world.

4   Nay, my design is, in some sense, to forget all that ever I have read in my life. I mean to speak, in the general, as if I had never read one author, ancient or modern (always excepting the inspired). I am persuaded, that, on the one hand, this may be a means of enabling me more clearly to express the sentiments of my heart, while I simply follow the chain of my own thoughts, without entangling myself with those of other men; and that, on the other, I shall come with fewer weights upon my mind, with less of prejudice and prepossession, either to search for myself, or to deliver to others, the naked truths of the gospel.

5   To candid, reasonable men, I am not afraid to lay open what have been the inmost thoughts of my heart. I have thought, I am a creature of a day, passing through life as an arrow through the air. I am a spirit come from God, and returning to God: Just hovering over the great gulf; till, a few moments hence, I am no more seen; I drop into an unchangeable eternity! I want to know one thing, – the way to heaven; how to land safe on that happy shore. God himself has condescended to teach the way: For this very end he came from heaven. He hath written it down in a book. O give me that book! At any price, give me the book of God! I have it: Here is knowledge enough for me. Let me be *homo unius libri*. Here then I am, far from the busy ways of men. I sit down alone: Only God is here. In his presence I open, I read his book; for this end, to find the way to heaven. Is there a doubt concerning the meaning of what I read? Does anything appear dark or intricate? I lift up my heart to the Father of Lights: – "Lord, is it not thy word, 'If any man lack wisdom, let him ask of God?' Thou 'givest liberally, and upbraidest not.' Thou hast said, 'If any be willing to do thy will, he shall know.' I am willing to do, let me know, thy will." I then search after and consider parallel passages of Scripture, "comparing spiritual things with spiritual." I meditate thereon with all the attention and earnestness of which my mind is capable. If any doubt still remains, I consult those who are experienced in the things of God; and then the writings whereby, being dead, they yet speak. And what I thus learn, that I teach.

6   I have accordingly set down in the following sermons what I find in the Bible concerning the way to heaven; with a view to distinguish this way of God from all those which are the inventions of men. I have endeavoured to describe the true, the

scriptural, experimental religion, so as to omit nothing which is a real part thereof, and to add nothing thereto which is not. And herein it is more especially my desire, First, to guard those who are just setting their faces toward heaven, (and who, having little acquaintance with the things of God, are the more liable to be turned out of the way,) from formality, from mere outside religion, which has almost driven heart-religion out of the world; and, Secondly, to warn those who know the religion of the heart, the faith which worketh by love, lest at any time they make void the law through faith, and so fall back into the snare of the devil.

7   By the advice and at the request of some of my friends, I have prefixed to the other sermons contained in this volume, three sermons of my own, and one of my Brother's, preached before the University of Oxford. My design required some discourses on those heads; and I preferred these before any others, as being a stronger answer than any which can be drawn up now, to those who have frequently asserted that we have changed our doctrine of late, and do not preach now what we did some years ago. Any man of understanding may now judge for himself, when he has compared the latter with the former sermons.

8   But some may say, I have mistaken the way myself, although I take upon me to teach it to others. It is probable many will think this, and it is very possible that I have. But I trust, whereinsoever I have mistaken, my mind is open to conviction. I sincerely desire to be better informed. I say to God and man, "What I know not, teach thou me!"

9   Are you persuaded you see more clearly than me? It is not unlikely that you may. Then treat me as you would desire to be treated yourself upon a change of circumstances. Point me out a better way than I have yet known. Show me it is so, by plain proof of Scripture. And if I linger in the path I have been accustomed to tread, and am therefore unwilling to leave it, labour with me a little; take me by the hand, and lead me as I am able to bear. But be not displeased if I entreat you not to beat me down in order to quicken my pace: I can go but feebly and slowly at best; then, I should not be able to go at all. May I not request of you, further, not to give me hard names in order to bring me into the right way. Suppose I were ever so much in the wrong, I doubt this would not set me right. Rather, it would make me run so much the farther from you, and so get more and more out of the way.

10   Nay, perhaps, if you are angry, so shall I be too; and then there will be small hopes of finding the truth. If once anger arise, *Eute kapnos* (as Homer somewhere expresses it,) this smoke will so dim the eyes of my soul, that I shall be able to see nothing clearly. For God's sake, if it be possible to avoid it, let us not provoke one another to wrath. Let us not kindle in each other this fire of hell; much less blow it up into a flame. If we could discern truth by that dreadful light, would it not be loss, rather than gain? For, how far is love, even with many wrong opinions, to be preferred before truth itself without love! We may die without the knowledge of many truths, and yet be carried into Abraham's bosom. But, if we die without love, what will knowledge avail? Just as much as it avails the devil and his angels!

The God of love forbid we should ever make the trial! May he prepare us for the knowledge of all truth, by filling our hearts with his love, and with all joy and peace in believing!

Questions for Study

1   Why, according to this passage, does Wesley avoid complex English phrases and sophisticated analogies? How does his concern to "design plain truth for plain people" relate to this point?

2   What does Wesley mean when he declares that "mere outside religion . . . has almost driven heart-religion out of the world"? You will find it helpful to locate this citation, and study it in context.

3   Bishop Joseph Butler's sermons are characterized by their learnedness, and he is not afraid to display that learning prominently in the text. Wesley, on the other hand states: "my design is, in some sense, to forget all that ever I have read in my life." What does he mean by this? And why should he want to do this? Again, you will find it helpful to locate this quotation, and study it in its context.

Text: Sermon 2: The Almost Christian

This early sermon addresses the issue of "nominal" faith, and the need for personal conversion and renewal. The sermon raises many of the issues which were of central importance to the "experimental religion" (that is, experience-based religion) which John Wesley regarded as the only authentic form of the Christian faith. The sermon persistently attacks those who have the outward forms of religious faith, yet lack inner conviction and commitment.

Sermon II: The Almost Christian

preached at St. Mary's, Oxford, before the University, on July 25, 1741

Almost thou persuadest me to be a Christian. – Acts XXVI: 28

And many there are who go thus far: ever since the Christian religion was in the world, there have been many in every age and nation who were almost persuaded to be Christians. But seeing it avails nothing before God to go only thus far it highly imports us to consider, –

I. What Is Implied In Being Almost,

Ii. What In Being Altogether, A Christian.

I. (i.) 1.   Now, in the being almost a Christian is implied, first, heathen honesty. No one, I suppose, will make any question of this; especially, since by heathen honesty here, I mean, not that which is recommended in the writings of their philosophers only, but such as the common Heathens expected one of another, and many of them actually practised. By the rules of this they were taught that they ought not to be unjust; not to take away their neighbour's goods, either by robbery or theft; not to oppress the poor, neither to use extortion toward any; not to cheat or overreach either the poor or rich, in whatsoever commerce they had with them; to defraud no man of his right; and, if it were possible, to owe no man anything.

2.   Again: the common Heathens allowed, that some regard was to be paid to truth, as well as to justice. And, accordingly, they not only held him in abomination who was forsworn, who called God to witness to a lie; but him also who was known to be a slanderer of his neighbour, who falsely accused any man. And indeed, little better did they esteem wilful liars of any sort, accounting them the disgrace of human kind, and the pests of society.

3.   Yet again: there was a sort of love and assistance which they expected one from another. They expected whatever assistance any one could give another, without prejudice to himself. And this they extended not only to those little offices of humanity which are performed without any expense or labour, but likewise to the feeding the hungry, if they had food to spare; the clothing the naked with their own superfluous raiment; and, in general, the giving, to any that needed, such things as they needed not themselves. Thus far, in the lowest account of it, heathen honesty went; the first thing implied in the being almost a Christian.

(ii.) 4.   A second thing implied in the being almost a Christian is, the having a form of godliness; of that godliness which is prescribed in the gospel of Christ; the having the outside of a real Christian. Accordingly, the almost Christian does nothing which the gospel forbids. He taketh not the name of God in vain; he blesseth, and curseth not; he sweareth not at all, but his communication is, yea, yea; nay, nay. He profanes not the day of the Lord, nor suffers it to be profaned, even by the stranger that is within his gates. He not only avoids all actual adultery, fornication, and uncleanness, but every word or look that either directly or indirectly tends thereto; nay, and all idle words, abstaining both from detraction, backbiting, talebearing, evil speaking, and from "all foolish talking and Jesting" – *eutrapelia*, a kind of virtue in the heathen moralist's account – briefly, from all conversation that is not "good to the use of edifying," and that, consequently, "grieves the Holy Spirit of God, whereby we are sealed to the day of redemption."

5.   He abstains from "wine wherein is excess"; from revellings and gluttony. He avoids, as much as in him lies, all strife and contention, continually endeavouring to live peaceably with all men. And, if he suffer wrong, he avengeth not himself, neither returns evil for evil. He is no railer, no brawler, no scoffer, either at the faults or infirmities of his neighbour. He does not willingly wrong, hurt, or grieve any man; but in all things act and speaks by that plain rule, "Whatsoever thou wouldest not he should do unto thee, that do not thou to another."

6.   And in doing good, he does not confine himself to cheap and easy offices of kindness, but labours and suffers for the profit of many, that by all means he may help some. In spite of toil or pain, "whatsoever his hand findeth to do, he doeth it with his might"; whether it be for his friends, or for his enemies; for the evil, or for the good. For being "not slothful" in this, or in any "business," as he "hath opportunity" he doeth "good," all manner of good, "to all men"; and to their souls as well as their bodies. He reproves the wicked, instructs the ignorant, confirms the wavering, quickens the good, and comforts the afflicted. He labours to awaken those that sleep; to lead those whom God hath already awakened to the "Fountain opened

for sin and for uncleanness," that they may wash therein and be clean; and to stir up those who are saved through faith, to adorn the gospel of Christ in all things.

7.   He that hath the form of godliness uses also the means of grace; yea, all of them, and at all opportunities. He constantly frequents the house of God; and that, not as the manner of some is, who come into the presence of the Most High, either loaded with gold and costly apparel, or in all the gaudy vanity of dress, and either by their unseasonable civilities to each other, or the impertinent gaiety of their behaviour, disclaim all pretensions to the form as well as to the power of godliness. Would to God there were none even among ourselves who fall under the same condemnation! who come into this house, it may be, gazing about, or with all the signs of the most listless, careless indifference, though sometimes they may seem to use a prayer to God for His blessing on what they are entering upon; who, during that awful service, are either asleep, or reclined in the most convenient posture for it; or, as though they supposed God was asleep, talking with one another, or looking round, as utterly void of employment. Neither let these be accused of the form of godliness. No; he who has even this, behaves with seriousness and attention, in every part of that solemn service. More especially, when he approaches the table of the Lord, it is not with a light or careless behaviour, but with an air, gesture, and deportment which speaks nothing else but "God be merciful to me a sinner!"

8.   To this, if we add the constant use of family prayer, by those who are masters of families, and the setting times apart for private addresses to God, with a daily seriousness of behaviour; he who uniformly practises this outward religion, has the form of godliness. There needs but one thing more in order to his being almost a Christian, and that is, sincerity.

(iii.) 9.   By sincerity I mean, a real, inward principle of religion, from whence these outward actions flow. And, indeed if we have not this, we have not heathen honesty; no, not so much of it as will answer the demand of a heathen Epicurean poet. Even this poor wretch, in his sober intervals, is able to testify,

> Oderunt peccare boni, virtutis amore;
> Oderunt peccare mali, formidine poenae.
>
> Good men avoid sin from the love of virtue
> Wicked men avoid sin from a fear of punishment.

So that, if a man only abstains from doing evil in order to avoid punishment, *Non pasces in cruce corvos,* Thou shalt not be hanged, saith the Pagan; there, "thou hast thy reward." But even he will not allow such a harmless man as this to be so much as a good Heathen. If, then, any man, from the same motive, viz. to avoid punishment, to avoid the loss of his friends, or his gain, or his reputation, should not only abstain from doing evil, but also do ever so much good; yea, and use all the means of grace; yet we could not with any propriety say, this man is even *almost a Christian!* If he has no better principle in his heart, he is only a hypocrite altogether.

10.   Sincerity, therefore, is necessarily implied in the being almost a Christian; a real design to serve God, a hearty desire to do His will. It is necessarily implied, that

a man have a sincere view of pleasing God in all things; in all his conversation; in all his actions; in all he does or leaves undone. This design, if any man be almost a Christian, runs through the whole tenor of his life. This is the moving principle, both in his doing good, his abstaining from evil, and his using the ordinances of God.

11.   But here it will probably be inquired, "Is it possible that any man living should go so far as this, and, nevertheless, be only almost a Christian? What more than this, can be implied in the being a Christian altogether?" I answer, first, that it is possible to go thus far, and yet be but almost a Christian: I learn, not only from the oracles of God, but also from the sure testimony of experience.

12.   Brethren, great is "my boldness towards you in this behalf." And "forgive me this wrong," if I declare my own folly upon the house-top, for yours and the gospel's sake. – Suffer me, then, to speak freely of myself, even as of another man. I am content to be abased, so ye may be exalted, and to be yet more vile for the glory of my Lord.

13.   I did go thus far for many years, as many of this place can testify; using diligence to eschew all evil, and to have a conscience void of offence; redeeming the time; buying up every opportunity of doing all good to all men; constantly and carefully using all the public and all the private means of grace; endeavouring after a steady seriousness of behaviour, at all times, and in all places; and, God is my record, before whom I stand, doing all this in sincerity; having a real design to serve God; a hearty desire to do His will in all things; to please Him who had called me to "fight the good fight," and to "lay hold of eternal life." Yet my own conscience beareth me witness in the Holy Ghost, that all this time I was but almost a Christian.

II.   If it be inquired, "What more than this is implied in the being altogether a Christian?" I answer,

(i.) 1.   First, The love of God. For thus saith His word, "Thou shalt love the Lord thy God with all thy heart, and with all thy soul, and with all thy mind, and with all thy strength." Such a love is this, as engrosses the whole heart, as rakes up all the affections, as fills the entire capacity of the soul and employs the utmost extent of all its faculties. He that thus loves the Lord his God, his spirit continually "rejoiceth in God his Saviour." His delight is in the Lord, his Lord and his All, to whom "in everything he giveth thanks. All his desire is unto God, and to the remembrance of His name." His heart is ever crying out, "Whom have I in heaven but Thee? and there is none upon earth that I desire beside Thee." Indeed, what can he desire beside God? Not the world, or the things of the world: for he is "crucified to the world, and the world crucified to him." He is crucified to "the desire of the flesh, the desire of the eye, and the pride of life." Yea, he is dead to pride of every kind: for "love is not puffed up" but "he that dwelling in love, dwelleth in God, and God in him," is less than nothing in his own eyes.

(ii.) 2.   The second thing implied in the being altogether a Christian is, the love of our neighbour. For thus said our Lord in the following words, "Thou shalt love thy neighbour as thyself." If any man ask, "Who is my neighbour?" we reply, Every man in the world; every child of His who is the Father of the spirits of all flesh. Nor may we in any wise except our enemies or the enemies of God and their own souls. But every Christian loveth these also as himself, yea, "as Christ loved us." He that would more fully understand what manner of love this is, may consider St. Paul's description of it. It is "long-suffering and kind." It "envieth not." It is not rash or hasty in judging. It "is not puffed up"; but maketh him that loves, the least, the servant of all. Love "doth not behave itself unseemly," but becometh "all things to all men." She "seeketh not her own"; but only the good of others, that they may be saved. "Love is not provoked." It casteth out wrath, which he who hath is wanting in love. "It thinketh no evil. It rejoiceth not in iniquity, but rejoiceth in the truth. It covereth all things, believeth all things, hopeth all things, endureth all things."

(iii.) 3.   There is yet one thing more that may be separately considered; though it cannot actually be separate from the preceding, which is implied in the being altogether a Christian; and that is the ground of all, even faith. Very excellent things are spoken of this throughout the oracles of God. "Every one," saith the beloved disciple, "that believeth is born of God." "To as many as received Him, gave He power to become the sons of God, even to them that believe on His name." And "this is the victory that overcometh the world, even our faith." Yea, our Lord Himself declares, "He that believeth in the Son hath everlasting life; and cometh not into condemnation, but is passed from death unto life."

4.   But here let no man deceive his own soul. "It is diligently to be noted, the faith which bringeth not forth repentance, and love, and all good works, is not that right living faith, but a dead and devilish one. For, even the devils believe that Christ was born of a virgin: that He wrought all kinds of miracles, declaring Himself very God: that, for our sakes, He suffered a most painful death, to redeem us from death everlasting; that He rose again the third day: that He ascended into heaven, and sitteth at the right hand of the Father and at the end of the world shall come again to judge both the quick and dead. These articles of our faith the devils believe, and so they believe all that is written in the Old and New Testament. And yet for all this faith, they be but devils. They remain still in their damnable estate lacking the very true Christian faith."

5.   "The right and true Christian faith is" (to go on in the words of our own Church), "not only to believe that Holy Scripture and the Articles of our Faith are true, but also to have a sure trust and confidence to be saved from everlasting damnation by Christ. It is a sure trust and confidence which a man hath in God, that, by the merits of Christ, his sins are forgiven, and he reconciled to the favour of God; whereof doth follow a loving heart, to obey His commandments."

6.   Now, whosoever has this faith, which "purifies the heart" (by the power of God, who dwelleth therein) from "pride, anger, desire, from all unrighteousness" from "all filthiness of flesh and spirit"; which fills it with love stronger than death, both to God and to all mankind; love that doeth the works of God, glorying to spend and to be spent for all men, and that endureth with joy, not only the reproach of Christ, the being mocked, despised, and hated of all men, but whatsoever the wisdom of God permits the malice of men or devils to inflict, – whosoever has this faith thus working by love is not almost only, but altogether, a Christian.

7.   But who are the living witnesses of these things? I beseech you, brethren, as in the presence of that God before whom "hell and destruction are without a covering – how much more the hearts of the children of men?" – that each of you would ask his own heart, "Am I of that number? Do I so far practise justice, mercy,

and truth, as even the rules of heathen honesty require? If so, have I the very outside of a Christian? the form of godliness? Do I abstain from evil – from whatsoever is forbidden in the written Word of God? Do I, whatever good my hand findeth to do, do it with my might? Do I seriously use all the ordinances of God at all opportunities? And is all this done with a sincere design and desire to please God in all things?"

8.   Are not many of you conscious, that you never came thus far; that you have not been even almost a Christian; that you have not come up to the standard of heathen honesty; at least, not to the form of Christian godliness? – much less hath God seen sincerity in you, a real design of pleasing Him in all things. You never so much as intended to devote all your words and works, your business, studies, diversions, to His glory. You never even designed or desired, that whatsoever you did should be done "in the name of the Lord Jesus," and as such should be "a spiritual sacrifice, acceptable to God through Christ."

9.   But, supposing you had, do good designs and good desires make a Christian? By no means, unless they are brought to good effect. "Hell is paved," saith one, "with good intentions." The great question of all, then, still remains. Is the love of God shed abroad in your heart? Can you cry out, "My God, and my All"? Do you desire nothing but Him? Are you happy in God? Is He your glory, your delight, your crown of rejoicing? And is this commandment written in your heart, "That he who loveth God love his brother also"? Do you then love your neighbour as yourself? Do you love every man, even your enemies, even the enemies of God, as your own soul? as Christ loved you? Yea, dost thou believe that Christ loved thee, and gave Himself for thee? Hast thou faith in His blood? Believest thou the Lamb of God hath taken away thy sins, and cast them as a stone into the depth of the sea? that He hath blotted out the handwriting that was against thee, taking it out of the way, nailing it to His cross? Hast thou indeed redemption through His blood, even the remission of thy sins? And doth His Spirit bear witness with thy spirit, that thou art a child of God?

10.   The God and Father of our Lord Jesus Christ, who now standeth in the midst of us, knoweth, that if any man die without this faith and this love, good it were for him that he had never been born. Awake, then, thou that sleepest, and call upon thy God: call in the day when He may be found. Let Him not rest, till He make His "goodness to pass before thee"; till He proclaim unto thee the name of the Lord, "The Lord, the Lord God, merciful and gracious, long-suffering, and abundant in goodness and truth, keeping mercy for thousands, forgiving iniquity, and transgression, and sin." Let no man persuade thee, by vain words, to rest short of this prize of thy high calling. But cry unto Him day and night, who, "while we were without strength, died for the ungodly," until thou knowest in whom thou hast believed, and canst say, "My Lord, and my God!" Remember, "always to pray, and not to faint," till thou also canst lift up thy hand unto heaven, and declare to Him that liveth for ever and ever, "Lord, Thou knowest all things, Thou knowest that I love Thee."

11.   May we all thus experience what it is to be, not almost only; but altogether Christians; being justified freely by His grace, through the redemption that is in Jesus; knowing we have peace with God through Jesus Christ; rejoicing in hope of the glory

of God; and having the love of God shed abroad in our hearts, by the Holy Ghost given unto us!

Questions for Study

1 This sermon is a formidable assault on "formal" or "nominal" religion. Set out the main lines of criticism which Wesley develops.
2 What "voice" or "tone" does Wesley adopt in this sermon. Note how direct the language is, in contrast to the rather more indirect forms of address favored at the time.
3 How do you think his university audience would have responded to this demand for conversion and spiritual renewal?

CHAPTER 65

Charles Wesley (1707–1788)

Charles Wesley was born at Epworth in Lincolnshire, the youngest son of Samuel and Susanna Wesley. He was initially educated at Westminster School, and went on to study at Christ Church, Oxford, from 1726, where he was one of the founder members of the Holy Club or Oxford "Methodists," a small Christian group which included both Wesley brothers, George Whitefield, and Benjamin Ingham. Wesley was ordained in 1735, and spent a brief period as a missionary in the new American colony of Georgia. This was an unhappy experience, which brought home to him the inadequacies of the traditional Anglicanism which he had espoused to that point. Charles Wesley underwent a conversion experience in London in May 1738, a few days before John Wesley's famous Aldersgate experience. He wrote that he now found himself "at peace with God and rejoiced in hope of loving Christ."

Charles Wesley (1707–1788)

Basic description
Hymnodist and evangelist; early Methodist leader.

Major works
Some 9,000 hymns, many now forgotten.

Major studies
Frank Baker, *Representative Verse of Charles Wesley*. London: Epworth, 1962.
Bernard L. Manning, *The Hymns of Wesley and Watts*. London: Epworth, 1942.

Wesley went on to serve as curate at St. Mary's, Islington; however, he soon left this to pioneer, with his brother John, the art of field-preaching. For more than twenty years, Charles Wesley was one of the central figures in the great evangelical revival. He traveled constantly in England, Wales and Ireland, suffering frequent criticism and harassment, often at the hands of his fellow clergymen.

There is no doubt that Charles Wesley's greatest legacy to Christian literature is his hymns, which are regarded as among the finest ever written. Many of these were written on horse-back, as he traveled from one congregation to another. Most of the 9,000 hymns which he penned have been forgotten; others remain as classics, and are still sung to this day. Wesley can be seen as a pioneer of the literary genre of the popular English hymn. The genre often involved drawing on secular models. For example, one of Wesley's best-known hymns, which we shall consider below, has as its opening line:

Love divine, all loves excelling.

This bears a remarkable resemblance to an earlier writing of the English poet and play-wright John Dryden (1631–1700), known as the *Song of Venus*, which opens with the line:

Fairest Isle, all Isles excelling.

In view of the importance of hymnody as a literary genre, it is clearly important to include some of Charles Wesley's writings

Text: Love Divine

"Love Divine" was written in 1747, and soon established itself as a classic. It is here reproduced in modern English orthography, to allow easy interaction with the text.

1

Love divine, all loves excelling,
joy of heaven, to earth come down;
fix in us thy humble dwelling;
all thy faithful mercies crown!
Jesus thou art all compassion,
pure, unbounded love thou art;
visit us with thy salvation;
enter every trembling heart.

2

Breathe, O breathe thy loving Spirit
into every troubled breast!
Let us all in thee inherit;
let us find that second rest.
Take away our bent to sinning;
Alpha and Omega be;
end of faith, as its beginning,
set our hearts at liberty.

3

Come, Almighty to deliver,
let us all thy life receive;

suddenly return and never,
nevermore thy temples leave.
Thee we would be always blessing,
serve thee as thy hosts above,
pray and praise thee without ceasing,
glory in thy perfect love.

4

Finish, then, thy new creation;
pure and spotless let us be.
Let us see thy great salvation
perfectly restored in thee;
changed from glory into glory,
till in heaven we take our place,
till we cast our crowns before thee,
lost in wonder, love, and praise.

Questions for Discussion

1 What reasons does Wesley give for the love of God being unsurpassable? Does he justify what he asserts?
2 The theme of sanctification is of major importance to early Wesleyanism, which placed considerable emphasis upon personal renewal and transformation. At what points in this hymn can this interest be discerned?
3 The final verse of Wesley's hymn is a powerful statement of the Christian hope. Read the following biblical passage in the King James Version: "The four and twenty elders fall down before him that sat on the throne, and worship him that liveth for ever and ever, and cast their crowns before the throne, saying, Thou art worthy, O Lord, to receive glory and honour and power: for thou hast created all things, and for thy pleasure they are and were created" (Revelation 4:10–11). How is the imagery of this biblical passage incorporated into this verse?

Text: Free Grace

Wesley wrote this hymn shortly after his conversion experience of 1739. The hymn can be seen as a celebration of the saving love and power of God, and is rich in imagery. In an important study of Wesley's hymns, Bernard L. Manning comments that: "It is Wesley's glory that he united these three strains – dogma, experience, mysticism – in verse so simple that it could be understood, and so smooth that it could be used, by plain men." This text brings together these three elements in a remarkable way, making this theologically-rich hymn a classic example of the value of hymnody as a means of theological education and spiritual uplifting.

It is here reprinted in its original orthography, exactly as found in the first edition of the work in which it appeared, to allow readers to see how much the English language has changed since the work was published. The first edition of the work included a verse (here numbered 5) which was omitted from later editions; it is retained in this edition, as it brings out the strongly experiential dimension of Wesley's thought.

1

And can it be that I should gain
　　An int'rest in the Saviour's blood!
Dy'd he for me? – who caus'd his pain?
　　For me? – who Him to Death pursued?
Amazing love! How can it be
That Thou, my God, shouldst die for me?

2

'Tis mystery all! th'Immortal dies!
　　Who can explore his strange Design?
In vain the first-born Seraph tries
　　To sound the Depths of Love divine.
'Tis mercy all! Let earth adore;
Let Angel Minds inquire no more.

3

He left his Fathers throne above
　　(So free, so infinite his grace!)
Empty'd himself of All but Love,
　　And bled for *Adam's* helpless Race.
'Tis Mercy all, immense and free,
For, O my God! it found out Me!

4

Long my imprison'd Spirit lay,
　　Fast bound in Sin and Nature's Night
Thine Eye diffus'd a quickning Ray;
　　I woke; the Dungeon flam'd with Light.
My Chains fell off, my Heart was free,
I rose, went forth, and follow'd Thee.

5

Still the small inward Voice I hear,
　　That whispers all my Sins forgiv'n;
Still the atoning Blood is near,
　　That quench'd the Wrath of hostile Heav'n:

I feel the Life his Wounds impart;
  I feel my Saviour in my Heart.

6

No Condemnation now I dread,
  Jesus, and all in Him, is mine.
Alive in Him, my Living Head,
  And clothed in Righteousness Divine,
Bold I approach th'Eternal Throne,
And claim the Crown, thro' CHRIST my own.

Questions for Study

1 Read Manning's statement in the introduction to this text. Can you identify dogmatic, experiential, and mystical elements in this hymn?

2 How many images of sin and salvation can you identify in this hymn? Note especially the fourth verse, which is particularly rich in this imagery.

3 There is a progression of thought throughout this hymn. How would you describe it? How does the author's attitude to his subject-matter alter as the hymn progresses?

4 Wesley wrote these words in his journal after his conversion: "I now found myself at peace with God and rejoiced in hope of loving Christ." Might this be seen as autobiographical, given that it was written so soon after Wesley's conversion? Are the themes of this journal entry to be found in the hymn?

CHAPTER 66

John Newton (1725–1807)

John Newton was the primary author of the *Olney Hymns*, for which he is best remembered. From an early stage in life, he had associations with the sea. By the age of 11, his father had begun to inculcate into him some of the ways of a seafarer's life. Seven years later, John Newton was pressed into the service of the Royal Navy. Soon after, he deserted the Navy and ended up on a slave ship. Although there is ample evidence that Newton disliked the slave trade, and had considerable sympathy for those who he transported to the Americas, he still went on to become the captain of his own slave ship.

John Newton (1725–1807)

Basic description
Evangelical hymn-writer.

Major works
"Glorious Things of Thee are Spoken"; "How Sweet the Name of Jesus Sounds."

Major studies
Donald E. Demarey, *The Innovation of John Newton (1725–1807): Synergism of Word and Music in Eighteenth Century Evangelism.* Lewiston, NY: Edwin Mellen Press, 1988.
John Pollock, *Amazing Grace: John Newton's Story.* London: Hodder & Stoughton, 1981.

In 1748 he underwent a religious conversion, which led him to fully realize the inhumanity of his actions. He left his life as a slave ship captain, and settled down as a "surveyor of tides" at the port of Liverpool. He was ordained as a priest for the Church of England in 1764, and served in the village of Olney. That same year he published his "Authentic Narrative" which detailed his exploits commanding a slave vessel. In 1779, he published, in collaboration with William Cowper, the *Olney Hymns*, which retain their freshness and simplicity today. It is this work which we shall consider in more detail in what follows.

Text: The *Olney Hymns*

In his preface to his *Olney Hymns*, Newton made his objectives in writing hymns known to his readers:

> A desire of promoting the faith and comfort of sincere Christians, though the principal, was not the only motive to this undertaking. It was likewise intended as a monument, to perpetuate the remembrance of an intimate and endeared friendship.

The friendship to which he refers was that with William Cowper. Newton was never entirely happy with the quality of his writing, and we find him regularly complaining of his own incompetence with words. Nevertheless, it is clear that he hoped that his writing style would allow him to appeal to a wide variety of Christians, crossing over the increasingly acrimonious denominational divides as much as the more traditional barriers of class and education.

> If the Lord, whom I serve, has been pleased to favour me with that mediocrity of talent, which may qualify me for usefulness to the weak and the poor of his flock, without quite disguising persons of superior discernment, I have reason to be satisfied . . . I hope most of these hymns, being the fruit and expression of my own experiences, will coincide with the views of real Christians of all denominations.

It was clear to Newton that his task necessitated deliberately avoiding many of the literary themes and devices which would appeal to a more sophisticated audience. He was clear that his pieces of poetry

> should be Hymns, not Odes, if designed for public worship, and for the use of plain people. Perspicuity, simplicity and ease, should be chiefly attended to; and the imagery and colouring of poetry, if admitted at all, should be indulged very sparingly and with great judgement.

In one sense, then, Newton is almost inviting his readers *not* to see his writings as literature. Yet their literary and cultural impact has been so great that they could not conceivably be excluded from any anthology of Christian literature.

The *Olney Hymnal* is divided into three books, as follows:

1   On Select Passages of Scripture
2   On Occasional Subjects
3   On the Rise, Progress, Changes and Comforts of the Spiritual Life

We shall consider a representative selection of these hymns in what follows.

1   Walking with God – Genesis 5:24

Oh for a closer walk with God!
A calm and heavenly frame;

A light to shine upon the road
   That leads me to the Lamb!

Where is the blessedness I knew
   When first I saw the Lord?
Where is the soul-refreshing view
   Of Jesus and his word?

What peaceful hours I once enjoyed!
   How sweet their memory still!
But they have left an aching void
   The world can never fill.

Return, O holy Dove, return,
   Sweet messenger of rest!
I hate the sins that made thee mourn,
   And drove thee from my breast.

The dearest idol I have known,
   Whate'er that idol be,
Help me to tear it from thy throne
   And worship only thee.

So shall my walk be close with God,
   Calm and serene my frame;
So purer light shall mark the road
   That leads me to the Lamb.

2   *Praise For The Fountain Opened – Zechariah 13:1*

There is a fountain filled with blood
   Drawn from Emmanuel's veins;
And sinners, plunged beneath that flood,
   Lose all their guilty stains.

The dying thief rejoiced to see
   That fountain in his day;
And there have I, as vile as he,
   Washed all my sins away.

Dear dying Lamb, thy precious blood
   Shall never lose its power,
Till all the ransomed church of God
   Be saved, to sin no more.

E'er since, by faith, I saw the stream
    Thy flowing wounds supply,
Redeeming love has been my theme,
    And shall be till I die.

Then in a nobler, sweeter song
    I'll sing thy power to save;
When this poor lisping, stammering tongue
    Lies silent in the grave.

Lord, I believe thou hast prepared
    (Unworthy though I be)
For me a blood-bought free reward,
    A golden harp for me!

'Tis strung and tuned for endless years,
    And formed by power divine,
To sound in God the Father's ears
    No other name but thine.

3   *Light Shining Out Of Darkness*

GOD moves in a mysterious way
    His wonders to perform;
He plants his footsteps in the sea,
    And rides upon the storm.

Deep in unfathomable mines
    Of never-failing skill
He treasures up his bright designs,
    And works his sovereign will.

Ye fearful saints, fresh courage take,
    The clouds ye so much dread
Are big with mercy, and shall break
    In blessings on your head.

Judge not the Lord by feeble-sense,
    But trust him for his grace;
Behind a frowning providence
    He hides a smiling face.

His purposes will ripen fast,
    Unfolding every hour;

The bud may have a bitter taste,
 But sweet will be the flower.

Blind unbelief is sure to err,
 And scan his work in vain:
God is his own interpreter,
 And he will make it plain.

4   *The Negro's Complaint*

Forced from home and all its pleasures
 Afric's coast I left forlorn,
To increase a stranger's treasures
 O'er the raging billows borne.
Men from England bought and sold me,
 Paid my price in paltry gold;
But, though slave they have enrolled me,
 Minds are never to be sold.

Still in thought as free as ever,
 What are England's rights, I ask,
Me from my delights to sever,
 Me to torture, me to task?
Fleecy locks and black complexion
 Cannot forfeit nature's claim;
Skins may differ, but affection
 Dwells in white and black the same.

Why did all-creating nature
 Make the plant for which we toil?
Sighs must fan it, tears must water,
 Sweat of ours must dress the soil.
Think, ye masters iron-hearted,
 Lolling at your jovial boards,
Think how many backs have smarted
 For the sweets your cane affords.

Is there, as ye sometimes tell us,
 Is there One who reigns on high?
Has He bid you buy and sell us,
 Speaking from his throne, the sky?
Ask him, if your knotted scourges,
 Matches, blood-extorting screws,
Are the means that duty urges
 Agents of his will to use?

Hark! He answers! – Wild tornadoes
 Strewing yonder sea with wrecks,
Wasting towns, plantations, meadows,
 Are the voice with which he speaks.
He, foreseeing what vexations
 Afric's sons should undergo,
Fixed their tyrants' habitations
 Where his whirlwinds answer – "No."

By our blood in Afric wasted
 Ere our necks received the chain;
By the miseries that we tasted,
 Crossing in your barks the main;
By our sufferings, since ye brought us
 To the man-degrading mart,
All sustained by patience, taught us
 Only by a broken heart;

Deem our nation brutes no longer,
 Till some reason ye shall find
Worthier of regard and stronger
 Than the colour of our kind.
Slaves of gold, whose sordid dealings
 Tarnish all your boasted powers,
Prove that you have human feelings,
 Ere you proudly question ours!

Questions for Study

1 Each of these four hymns reveals a different aspect of Newton's concerns. Identify the main theme of each of the hymns.
2 The image of "the Lamb" is highly important to Newton, and is clearly developed in one of these hymns. Which one? And what is meant by this image? Read the following passage from the King James Version of the Bible, and write out in detail how this helps make sense of Newton's imagery.

And all the angels stood round about the throne, and about the elders and the four beasts, and fell before the throne on their faces, and worshipped God, Saying, Amen: Blessing, and glory, and wisdom, and thanksgiving, and honour, and power, and might, be unto our God for ever and ever. Amen. And one of the elders answered, saying unto me, What are these which are arrayed in white robes? and whence came they? And I said unto him, Sir, thou knowest. And he said to me, These are they which came out of great tribulation, and have washed their robes, and made them white in the blood of the Lamb. Therefore are they before the throne of God, and serve him day and night in his temple: and he that sitteth on the throne shall dwell among them. They shall hunger no more, neither thirst any more; neither shall the sun light on them, nor any heat. For the Lamb which is in the midst of the throne shall feed them, and shall lead them unto living fountains of waters: and God shall wipe away all tears from their eyes. (Revelation 7:11–17)

3   Consider the first verse of the hymn which begins with the line: "There is a fountain filled with blood." How does the imagery just considered help make sense of this? In what sense can blood be said to remove the stain of sin?

4   How does Newton's own past come into the fourth of these hymns? And what points does he make in response?

CHAPTER 67

William Paley (1743–1805)

William Paley is widely regarded as one of the most important influences on the "Christian evidence" movement, which had considerable influence on Victorian literature. Paley was educated at Christ's College, Cambridge, and went on to become a Fellow of the college. He left academic life to pursue a career in the Church of England. His two major appointments were in Cumbria, in the northwest of England, where he served initially as vicar of Musgrave (1776) and subsequently as Archdeacon of Carlisle (1782).

William Paley (1743–1805)

Basic description
Churchman and author.

Major works
A View of the Evidences of Christianity (1794);
Natural Theology (1802).

Editions of works
The Works of William Paley DD. London: John
Bumpus, 1827.

Major studies
M. L. Clarke, *Paley: Evidences for the Man.*
London: SPCK, 1974.
D. L. LeMahieu, *The Mind of William Paley: A
Philosopher and His Age.* Lincoln, NE:
University of Nebraska Press, 1976.

Paley wrote a number of very influential books on philosophy and Christianity. His 1794 book *A View of the Evidences of Christianity* was required reading at Cambridge University until the twentieth century. His most influential contribution to biological thought, however, was his book *Natural Theology: or, Evidences of the Existence and Attributes of the Deity, Collected from the Appearances of Nature*, first published in 1802. In this book, Paley set out a full exposition of natural theology, especially the belief that the nature of God could be understood by reference to His creation, the natural world. He developed one of the most famous metaphors in the philosophy of science – the image of the watchmaker, which has continued to be referred to, even by those who are most critical of his approach. For example, Richard Dawkin's well-known work *The*

Blind Watchmaker can be seen as an acknowledgment of the influence of Paley's image. For Paley, the natural world was like a watch – a construction which showed evidence of both design and purpose:

> When we come to inspect the watch, we perceive ... that its several parts are framed and put together for a purpose, e.g. that they are so formed and adjusted as to produce motion, and that motion so regulated as to point out the hour of the day; that if the different parts had been differently shaped from what they are, or placed after any other manner or in any other order than that in which they are placed, either no motion at all would have been carried on in the machine, or none which would have answered the use that is now served by it. ... the inference we think is inevitable, that the watch must have had a maker – that there must have existed, at some time and at some place or other, an artificer or artificers who formed it for the purpose which we find it actually to answer, who comprehended its construction and designed its use.

Living organisms, Paley argued, are even more complicated than watches, "in a degree which exceeds all computation." How else to account for the often amazing adaptations of aniamls and plants? Only an intelligent Designer could have created them, just as only an intelligent watchmaker can make a watch.

Charles Darwin was initially attracted to these ideas, as he comments in a passage in his *Autobiography*: "In order to pass the B.A. examination, it was, also, necessary to get up Paley's *Evidences of Christianity*, and his *Moral Philosophy* ... The logic of this book and as I may add of his *Natural Theology* gave me as much delight as did Euclid. The careful study of these works, without attempting to learn any part by rote, was the only part of the Academical Course which, as I then felt and as I still believe, was of the least use to me in the education of my mind. I did not at that time trouble myself about Paley's premises; and taking these on trust I was charmed and convinced of the long line of argumentation."

Paley's most famous works are his least original. Both his defenses of the evidential basis of the Christian faith are thoroughly derivative, drawing, for example, on earlier works such as John Ray's *The Wisdom of God Manifested in the Works of the Creation* (1691) and *Three Physico-Theological Discourses* (1692). Nevertheless, the lucidity of Paley's prose and the skill with which he assembled his arguments set him in a class of his own. Both as a prose writer, and as an influence on Victorian English literature, Paley deserves inclusion in this collection.

Text: *A View of the Evidences of Christianity*

The text chosen for inclusion is from Paley's first major defense of the evidential foundations of the Christian faith. *A View of the Evidences of Christianity* was published in 1794, while Paley was Archdeacon of Carlisle. The work can be regarded both as a positive affirmation of the intellectual credentials of Christianity, coupled with responses to various objections raised against it. In the passage chosen for discussion, Paley deals with one of the most significant popular objections to the Christian faith – namely, that the fact that so many people in human history have had no revelation of the Christian religion must call its universality and validity into question. The text is beautifully clear, and requires little in the way of comment.

Chapter VI

Want of Universality in the Knowledge and Reception of Christianity, and of Greater Clearness in the Evidence

Of a revelation which really came from God, the proof, it has been said, would in all ages be so public and manifest, that no part of the human species would remain ignorant of it, no understanding could fail of being convinced by it.

The advocates of Christianity do not pretend that the evidence of their religion possesses these qualities. They do not deny that we can conceive it to be within the compass of Divine power to have communicated to the world a higher degree of assurance, and to have given to His communication a stronger and more extensive influence. For anything we are able to discern, God *could* have so formed men, as to have perceived the truths of religion intuitively; or to have carried on a communication with the other world while they lived in this; or to have seen the individuals of the species, instead of dying, pass to Heaven by a sensible translation. He could have presented a separate miracle to each man's senses. He could have established a standing miracle. He could have caused miracles to be wrought in every different age and country. These, and many more methods, which we may imagine, if we once give loose to our imaginations, are, so far as we can judge, all practicable.

The question, therefore, is, not whether Christianity possesses the highest possible degree of evidence, but whether the not having more evidence be a sufficient reason for rejecting that which we have?

Now there appears to be no fairer method of judging concerning any dispensation which is alleged to come from God, when a question is made whether such a dispensation could come from God or not, than by comparing it with other things which are acknowledged to proceed from the same counsel, and to be produced by the same agency. If the dispensation in question labour under no defects but what apparently belong to other dispensations, these seeming defects do not justify us in setting aside the proofs which are offered of its authenticity, if they be otherwise entitled to credit.

Throughout that order then of nature, of which God is the Author, what we find is a system of *beneficence*: we are seldom or never able to make out a system of *optimism*. I mean, that there are few cases in which, if we permit ourselves to range in possibilities, we cannot suppose something more perfect, and more unobjectionable, than what we see. The rain which descends from heaven is confessedly among the contrivances of the Creator, for the sustentation of the animals and vegetables which subsist upon the surface of the earth; yet how partially and irregularly is it supplied! How much of it falls upon the sea, where it can be of no use! how often is it wanted, where it would be of the greatest! What tracts of continent are rendered deserts by the scarcity of it! Or, not to speak of extreme cases, how much, sometimes, do inhabited countries suffer by its deficiency or delay! – We could imagine, if to imagine were our business, the matter to be otherwise regulated. We could imagine showers to fall, just where and when they would do good; always seasonable, everywhere sufficient; so distributed as not to leave a field upon the face of the globe scorched by drought, or even a plant withering for the lack of moisture. Yet, does the difference between the real case and the imagined case, or the seeming inferiority of the one to the other, authorize us to say, that the present disposition of the atmosphere is not among the productions or the designs of the Deity? Does it check the inference which we draw from the confessed beneficence of the provision? or does it make us cease to admire the contrivance? The observation, which we have exemplified in the single instance of the rain of heaven, may be repeated concerning most of the phenomena of nature, and the true conclusion to which it leads is this: that to inquire what the Deity might have done, could have done, or, as we even sometimes presume to speak, ought to have done, or in hypothetical cases, would have done, and to build any propositions upon such inquiries against evidence of facts, is wholly unwarrantable. It is a mode of reasoning which will not do in natural history, which will not do in natural religion, which cannot therefore be applied with safety to revelation. It may have some foundation, in certain speculative *à priori* ideas of the Divine attributes; but it has none in experience, or in analogy. The general character of the works of nature is, on the one hand, goodness both in design and effect; and, on the other hand, a liability to difficulty, and to objections, if such objections be allowed, by reason of seeming incompleteness or uncertainty in attaining their end. Christianity participates of this character. The true similitude between nature and revelation consists in this; that they each bear strong marks of their original; that they each also bear appearances of irregularity and defect. A system of strict optimism may, nevertheless, be the real system in both cases. But what I contend is, that the proof is hidden from *us*; that we ought not to expect to perceive *that* in revelation which we hardly perceive in any thing; that beneficence, of which we *can* judge, ought to satisfy us; that optimism, of which we *cannot* judge, ought not to be sought after. We can judge of beneficence, because it depends upon effects which we experience, and upon the relation between the means which we see acting and the ends which we see produced. We cannot judge of optimism, because it necessarily implies a comparison of that which is tried, with that which is not tried; of consequences which we see, with others which we imagine, and concerning many of which it is more than probable we know nothing; concerning some, that we have no notion.

If Christianity be compared with the state and progress of natural religion, the argument of the objector will gain nothing by the comparison. I remember hearing an unbeliever say, that, if God had given a revelation, He would have written it in the skies. Are the truths of natural religion written in the skies, or in a language which every one reads? or is this the case with the most useful arts, or the most necessary sciences of human life? An Otaheitean or an Esquimaux knows nothing of Christianity; does he know more of the principles of deism or morality? which, notwithstanding his ignorance, are neither untrue, nor unimportant, nor uncertain. The existence of the Deity is left to be collected from observations, which every man does not make, which every man, perhaps, is not capable of making. Can it be argued, that God does not exist, because, if He did, He would let us see Him, or discover

Himself to mankind by proofs (such as, we may think, the nature of the subject merited), which no inadvertence could miss nor prejudice withstand?

If Christianity be regarded as a providential instrument for the melioration of mankind, its progress and diffusion resemble that of other causes by which human life is improved. The diversity is not greater, nor the advance more slow, in religion, than we find it to be in learning, liberty, government, laws. The Deity has not touched the order of nature in vain. The Jewish religion produced great and permanent effects; the Christian religion has done the same. It has disposed the world to amendment. It has put things in a train. It is by no means improbable, that it may become universal: and that the world may continue in that stage so long as that the duration of its reign may bear a vast proportion to the time of its partial influence.

When we argue concerning Christianity, that it must necessarily be true, because it is beneficial, we go, perhaps, too far on one side; and we certainly go too far on the other, when we conclude that it must be false because it is not so efficacious as we could have supposed. The question of its truth is to be tried upon its proper evidence, without deferring much to this sort of argument on either side. "The evidence," as Bishop Butler hath rightly observed, "depends upon the judgment we form of human conduct, under given circumstances, of which it may be presumed that we know something; the objection stands upon the supposed conduct of the Deity, under relations with which we are not acquainted."

What would be the real effect of that overpowering evidence which our adversaries require in a revelation, it is difficult to foretell: at least, we must speak of it as of a dispensation of which we have no experience. Some consequences however would, it is probable, attend this economy, which do not seem to befit a revelation that proceeded from God. One is, that irresistible proof would restrain the voluntary powers too much; would not answer the purpose of trial and probation; would call for no exercise of candour, seriousness, humility, inquiry; no submission of passion, interests, and prejudices, to moral evidence and to probable truth; no habits of reflection; none of that previous desire to learn and to obey the will of God, which forms perhaps the test of the virtuous principle, and which induces men to attend, with care and reverence, to every credible intimation of that will, and to resign present advantages and present pleasures to every reasonable expectation of propitiating His favour. "Men's moral probation may be, whether they will take due care to inform themselves by impartial consideration; and afterwards, whether they will act as the case requires, upon the evidence which they have. And this we find, by experience, is often our probation in our temporal capacity."

These modes of communication would leave no place for the admission of *internal evidence*; which ought, perhaps, to bear a considerable part in the proof of every revelation, because it is a species of evidence which applies itself to the knowledge, love, and practice of virtue, and which operates in proportion to the degree of those qualities which it finds in the person whom it addresses. Men of good dispositions among Christians are greatly affected by the impression which the Scriptures themselves make upon their minds. Their conviction is much strengthened by these impressions. And this perhaps was intended to be one effect to be produced by the religion. It is likewise true, to whatever cause we ascribe it (for I am not in this work at liberty to introduce the Christian doctrine of grace or assistance, or the Christian promise, that, "if any man will do His will, he shall know of the doctrine, whether it be of God,") – It is true, I say, that they who sincerely act, or sincerely endeavour to act, *according* to what they believe, that is, according to the just result of the probabilities, or, if you please, the possibilities, in natural and revealed religion, which they themselves perceive, and according to a rational estimate of consequences, and above all, according to the just effect of those principles of gratitude and devotion, which even the view of nature generates in a well-ordered mind, *seldom fail of proceeding farther.* This also may have been exactly what was designed.

Whereas, may it not be said that irresistible evidence would confound all characters and all dispositions? would subvert, rather than promote, the true purpose of the Divine counsels; which is, not to produce *obedience* by a force little short of mechanical constraint (which obedience would be regularity, not virtue, and would hardly perhaps differ from that which inanimate bodies pay to the laws impressed upon their nature), but to treat moral agents agreeably to what they are; which is done, when light and motives are of such kinds, and are imparted in such measures, that the influence of them depends upon the recipients themselves? "It is not meet to govern rational free agents *in viâ* by sight and sense. It would be no trial or thanks to the most sensual wretch to forbear sinning, if Heaven and hell were open to his sight. That spiritual vision and fruition is our state *in patriâ.*" There may be truth in this thought, though roughly expressed. Few things are more improbable than that we (the human species) should be the highest order of beings in the universe; that animated nature should ascend from the lowest reptile to us, and all at once stop there. If there be classes above us of rational intelligences, clearer manifestations may belong to them. This may be one of the distinctions; and it may be one to which we ourselves hereafter shall attain.

But may it not be also asked, whether the perfect display of a future state of existence would be compatible with the activity of civil life, and with the success of human affairs? I can easily conceive that this impression may be overdone; that it may so seize and fill the thoughts, as to leave no place for the cares and offices of men's several stations, no anxiety for worldly prosperity, or even for a worldly provision, and, by consequence, no sufficient stimulus to secular industry. Of the first Christians we read, "that all that believed were together, and had all things common; and sold their possessions and goods, and parted them to all men, as every man had need; and, continuing daily with one accord in the temple, and breaking bread from house to house, did eat their meat with gladness and singleness of heart." This was extremely natural, and just what might be expected from miraculous evidence coming with full force upon the senses of mankind: but I much doubt whether, if this state of mind had been universal, or long continued, the business of the world could have gone on. The necessary arts of social life would have been little cultivated. The plough and the loom would have stood still. Agriculture, manufactures, trade, and navigation, would not, I think, have flourished, if they could have been exercised at all. Men would have addicted themselves to contemplative and ascetic lives, instead of lives of business and of useful industry. We observe that Saint Paul found it necessary frequently to recall his converts to the ordinary labours and domestic duties of their condition; and to give them, in his own example, a lesson of contented application to their worldly employments.

By the manner in which the religion is now proposed, a great portion of the human species is enabled, and of these multitudes of every generation are induced, to seek and to effectuate their salvation, through the medium of Christianity, without interruption of the prosperity, or of the regular course of human affairs.

Questions for Study

1 Set out, in your own words, the precise difficulty which Paley feels he should meet in this passage.
2 Why does Paley consider that what he calls "natural religion" has no significant advantages over Christianity?
3 What is the significance of Paley's discussion of what he terms "rational free agents"?
4 Read the concluding sentence of Paley's argument. Is this a fair summary of what he has argued throughout the chapter? What impression might this final sentence leave upon his readers?
5 How convincing do you think a critical reader would find the general lines of argument used by Paley in this chapter?

CHAPTER 68

William Blake (1757–1827)

William Blake was born in London in 1757 as one of the seven children of James Blake and Catherine Hermitage. At the age of ten, Blake began to attend Henry Par's Drawing School, which was located on The Strand, in central London. Having gained the skills necessary to become a professional engraver, Blake began to work in 1771 for James Basire, the engraver to the Society of Antiquaries, and found himself occupied with drawing some of the monuments in Westminster Abbey. Blake married Catherine Boucher in 1782, and set up in business as an engraver. Most of his work from 1788 was for the Unitarian publisher Joseph Johnson, who numbered William Wordsworth and Tom Paine among his authors.

William Blake (1757–1827)

Basic description
English Romantic artist and poet.

Major works
Book of Thel (1789); *Milton* (1804–?), *Jerusalem* (1804–?20).

Major studies
Peter Ackroyd, *Blake*. London: Minerva, 1996.
Northrop Frye, *Fearful Symmetry: A Study of William Blake*. Princeton, NJ: Princeton University Press, 1947.

Throughout the 1780s, Blake experimented with various forms of verse, and means of producing them in visually stimulating ways. Blake's artistic genius found its expression both visually and verbally. The *Book of Thel* (1789) used what would be known as Blake's "infernal" method of printing. The work brought together illustration and text in a unitary conception of the nature of poetry. Blake is at least as well known for his illustrations – especially the "Ancient of Days" – as he is for his poetry. Both can be regarded as pointing to his highly imaginative approach to art. Blake found the writings of Milton especially stimulating, and produced watercolours of both *Paradise Lost* and *Paradise Regained*. At the time of his death in August 1827, Blake was at work on a series of illustrations for an edition of Dante's *Divine Comedy*.

From an early stage in his life, Blake experienced "visions," which many of his family and friends regarded as symptoms of an incipient insanity. Blake was beaten by his father at an early age for claiming that he saw angels in the treetops at Peckham Rye; while engraving some monuments at Westminster Abbey, Blake had a vision of monks and choirs marching in procession. These visions, which often seemed bizarre to his colleagues, would serve as the inspiration for one of his best-known religious poems, which is found embedded in the complex text of a work entitled *Milton*, probably written between 1803 and 1808. We shall consider this in what follows.

Text: "And Did those Feet?" from *Milton*

Blake's work *Milton* does not, as might at first sight seem probable, take the form of a work of homage to the great Puritan poet John Milton, for whose poetry Blake had an especially high regard. In fact, the work is a response to a vision. Blake and his wife had accepted the invitation of his new patron, the philanthropist William Hayley, to move from the London slums to Hayley's magnificent estate at the seaside town of Felpham. Blake was to earn his living painting and engraving commissions for Hayley's wealthy friends. Blake felt at home in his new situation, but sensed – and resented – Hayley's hostility toward his esoteric "visionary" works. Hayley, for his part, was of the view that Blake suffered from some form of mental illness. Perhaps it was inevitable that the arrangement would not work out for long. After three years at Felpham, the Blakes chose to return to London. Blake published his visionary poem *Milton* soon afterwards, engraving every letter and design onto copper sheets and coloring each printed page by hand.

The poem opens with a vision, in which Blake is united with the spirit of Milton:

> Then first I saw him in the Zenith as a falling star,
> Descending perpendicular, swift as the swallow or swift;
> And on my left foot falling on the tarsus, entering there;
> But from my left foot a black cloud redounding spread over Europe.

To abbreviate what is actually a rather long account of matters, Blake declares that Milton returned from heaven in the form of a meteor, tearing a great hole in the sky, and entered Blake's foot. Milton only emerged from Blake's foot when a twelve-year-old girl flew down to Blake, and visited him in his cottage. The emergence of Milton transformed the ordinary world:

> But Milton entering my Foot; I saw in the nether
> Regions of the Imagination; also all men on Earth,
> And all in Heaven, saw in the nether regions of the Imagination
> In Ulro beneath Beulah, the vast breach of Milton's descent.
> But I knew not that it was Milton, for man cannot know
> What passes in his members till periods of Space and Time
> Reveal the secrets of Eternity; for more extensive
> Than any other earthly things, are Mans earthly lineaments.
> And all this Vegetable World appeard on my left Foot,

> As a bright sandal formd immortal of precious stones & gold:
> I stooped down & bound it on to walk forward thro' Eternity.

Blake's poem can be seen as an attempt both to heighten its readers' sense of artistic beauty, and to open up the world of transcendent visionary experience. The poem can easily be mis-read as a critique of the Industrial Revolution's impact on rural England. In fact, it is a rather different kind of critique which Blake mounts – a major onslaught against ordinariness. Blake regards Satan as the god of the mundane and pragmatic; the one who is in charge of the practical things that are needed simply to enable things to exist. Blake calls these tedious necessities "dark Satanic mills," and is especially critical of the way in which art is put to commercial use, as portrait painting. Within the allegory, Blake's Satan is to be identified with anyone who "thinks himself righteous in his vegetated spectre," by which Blake apparently means resting in the physical security which destroys artistic creativity. Blake suggests that Satan is opposed to creative self-giving, and tries to promote the physical security and well-being of people who lack "vision" (in Blake's rather arcane sense of the word), imagination and creativity.

By the later phase of his life, from which this poem dates, Blake had come to view the great struggle in life as being between the "visionaries," concerned with the artistic enhancement of the human race, and the rationalizing masses, concerned only with their own personal comforts and security. Satan thus keeps the ordinary and everyday world from collapsing, by ensuring that the necessities of life – however dull and un-visionary – are provided for. "The mills of Satan" are thus, for Blake, not buildings in which inhuman social conditions exist – though that meaning has been read into such phrases by later interpreters – but the humdrum necessities of life which dull most into the evasion of creativity – yet which paradoxically are also, in a sense, necessary if the artistic vision is to be encouraged.

The poem opens with an allusion to the feet of Joseph of Arimathea, one of the disciples of Christ, who, according to a long-established legend, brought Christianity to England, and lies buried somewhere in Glastonbury.

> AND did those feet in ancient time
> Walk upon England's mountains green?
> And was the holy Lamb of God
> On England's pleasant pastures seen?
>
> And did the Countenance Divine
> Shine forth upon our clouded hills?
> And was Jerusalem builded here
> Among these dark Satanic mills?
>
> Bring me my bow of burning gold:
> Bring me my arrows of desire:
> Bring me my spear: O clouds unfold!
> Bring me my chariot of fire.

I will not cease from mental fight,
Nor shall my sword sleep in my hand
Till we have built Jerusalem
In England's green and pleasant land.

Questions for Study

1 Read the following verse in the King James Version: "And it came to pass, as they still went on, and talked, that, behold, there appeared a chariot of fire, and horses of fire, and parted them both asunder; and Elijah went up by a whirlwind into heaven" (2 Kings 2:11). At what point in the poem does Blake use this imagery? And what point does he make in doing so?

2 What does "Jerusalem" represent in this poem? And how is it related to "England's green and pleasant land"?

3 There are four images in the third stanza, all concerned with breaking through into the heavens. What does Blake wish us to understand by this section of the poem? And how is this related to the agenda set out in the final section?

CHAPTER 69

William Wordsworth (1770–1850)

William Wordsworth was born on April 7, 1770, in the northern English town of Cockermouth in Cumberland, to John and Anne Wordsworth. William was the second of their five children. His father was a legal agent and rent collector for Lord Lonsdale, a local dignitary, and the family was reasonably comfortable as a result of this employment. After his mother's death in 1778, Wordsworth was sent to Hawkshead Grammar School, near Windermere, in England's magnificent Lake District. He went on from there in 1787 to St. John's College, Cambridge. During the summer vacation of 1790, he toured France on foot with a friend, Robert Jones, and saw the effects of the Revolution at first hand.

In common with many young men of the time, he found himself infatuated with the French Revolution of 1789. The Revolution would feature prominently in some of his later writings. As he would later write in his "French Revolution, as it appeared to enthusiasts at its commencement":

> Bliss was it in that dawn to be alive
> But to be young was very heaven!

His interest in this topic took him to France again in 1791, this time to Blois, a town on the River Loire. Here he met Michel Beaupuy, who would serve as a kind of mentor to him over several years. He also had an affair with Annette Vallon, who gave birth to his illegitimate daughter, Caroline, in December of the following year. Wordsworth was unable to return to France to visit his daughter, partly due to financial difficulties, and also on account of the outbreak of war between France and England in the aftermath of the Reign of Terror in Paris.

In 1795, Wordsworth met Samuel Taylor Coleridge. It was to prove an immensely important friendship. The two men met daily throughout 1797–8 to discuss poetry and to plan the seminal volume *Lyrical Ballads*, which was published in 1798. Wordsworth settled in the Lake District shortly afterwards, near Grasmere, with his sister Dorothy. They were joined in 1800 by Coleridge and his family, who moved into a house near Keswick. Coleridge's growing opium addiction made this a difficult time for all concerned, and may be argued to have been a factor in the later alienation between the two men.

William Wordsworth (1770–1850)

Basic description
Romantic poet.

Major works
Lyrical Ballads (1798, with Samuel Taylor Coleridge); Poems in Two Volumes (1807).

Major studies
Arthur Beatty, William Wordsworth: His Doctrine and Art in their Historical Relations. Madison, WI: University of Wisconsin Press, 1960.
Jonathan Wordsworth, William Wordsworth and the Age of English Romanticism. New Brunswick, NJ: Rutgers University Press, 1987.

Wordsworth was never especially well off. Although he was due to receive an inheritance from his father, following his death in 1783, this failed to materialize, largely due to the blocking tactics of Lord Lonsdale. In 1802, Lonsdale changed his mind, and allowed Wordsworth to receive the money due to him. This allowed William to marry Mary Hutchinson. By 1810 – the year in which the alienation between Coleridge and Wordsworth developed – they had five children, two of whom died in 1812. In 1813 Wordsworth was appointed Distributor of Stamps for Westmorland, and the £400 salary attached to this post made him financially secure. The whole family, including Dorothy, moved to Rydal Mount, between Grasmere and Rydal Water.

Wordsworth's literary career began with Descriptive Sketches (1793) and reached new heights with Lyrical Ballads, on which he collaborated with Coleridge. His powers are widely agreed to have peaked with Poems in Two Volumes (1807). His greatest work, however, is The Prelude, which was published posthumously in 1850. Yet recognition came also during his lifetime. Durham University granted him an honorary Doctor of Civil Law degree in 1838, and Oxford conferred the same honor the next year. When Robert Southey died in 1843, Wordsworth was named Poet Laureate. He died in 1850, and his wife published the much-revised Prelude that summer.

Two of Wordsworth's best-known poems have religious themes, and will be considered in this volume. They are "Lines Written A Few Miles Above Tintern Abbey, on Revisiting the Banks of the Wye during a Tour. July 13, 1798" – usually known by the more convenient title "Tintern Abbey" – and "Intimations of Immortality."

Text: Tintern Abbey

This important poem takes the form of 159 blank verse lines in five verse paragraphs. The place and date of composition are given very precisely, as the subtitle indicates. The main title of the work is the one-word "Lines" – what follows is an extended subtitle, in which place and date are given high prominence. Tintern Abbey is set against the green wooded valley of the River Wye. The abbey was founded in 1131 for Cistercian monks by the order of the Norman Lord of Chepstow, Walter de Clare. The great abbey church seen today was rebuilt in the late thirteenth century. At the time of the dissolution of the monasteries under Henry VIII in 1536, Tintern was the richest abbey in Wales and this is reflected in its majestic archways and elegant windows. Wordsworth later wrote that "no poem of mine was composed under circumstances more pleasant for me to remember than this: I began it upon leaving Tintern, after crossing the Wye, and concluded it just as I was entering Bristol in the evening, after a ramble of four or five days, with my sister. Not a line of it was altered."

The poem is immensely complex and nuanced, and needs careful comment. Read it through, and then engage with it, using the detailed study questions provided later.

Lines
Written A Few Miles Above Tintern Abbey, on
Revisiting the Banks of the Wye during
a Tour.
July 13, 1798

FIVE years have passed; five summers, with the length
Of five long winters! and again I hear
These waters, rolling from their mountain-springs
With a sweet inland murmur. – Once again
Do I behold these steep and lofty cliffs,   5
Which on a wild secluded scene impress
Thoughts of more deep seclusion; and connect
The landscape with the quiet of the sky.
The day is come when I again repose
Here, under this dark sycamore, and view   10
These plots of cottage-ground, these orchard-tufts,
Which, at this season, with their unripe fruits,
Among the woods and copses lose themselves,
Nor, with their green and simple hue, disturb
The wild green landscape. Once again I see   15
These hedge-rows, hardly hedge-rows, little lines
Of sportive wood run wild; these pastoral farms
Green to the very door; and wreathes of smoke
Sent up, in silence, from among the trees,
With some uncertain notice, as might seem,   20
Of vagrant dwellers in the houseless woods,
Or of some hermit's cave, where by his fire
The hermit sits alone.

               Though absent long,
These forms of beauty have not been to me,
As is a landscape to a blind man's eye: 25
But oft, in lonely rooms, and mid the din
Of towns and cities, I have owed to them,
In hours of weariness, sensations sweet,
Felt in the blood, and felt along the heart,

And passing even into my purer mind 30
With tranquil restoration:– feelings too
Of unremembered pleasure; such, perhaps,
As may have had no trivial influence
On that best portion of a good man's life;
His little, nameless, unremembered acts 35
Of kindness and of love. Nor less, I trust,
To them I may have owed another gift,
Of aspect more sublime; that blessed mood,
In which the burthen of the mystery,
In which the heavy and the weary weight 40
Of all this unintelligible world
Is lighten'd – that serene and blessed mood,
In which the affections gently lead us on,
Until, the breath of this corporeal frame,
And even the motion of our human blood 45
Almost suspended, we are laid asleep
In body, and become a living soul:
While with an eye made quiet by the power
Of harmony, and the deep power of joy,
We see into the life of things. 50

                If this
Be but a vain belief, yet, oh! how oft,
In darkness, and amid the many shapes
Of joyless day-light; when the fretful stir
Unprofitable, and the fever of the world,
Have hung upon the beatings of my heart, 55
How oft, in spirit, have I turned to thee
O sylvan Wye! Thou wanderer through the wood
How often has my spirit turned to thee!

And now, with gleams of half-extinguished thought,
With many recognitions dim and faint, 60
And somewhat of a sad perplexity,
The picture of the mind revives again:
While here I stand, not only with the sense
Of present pleasure, but with pleasing thoughts
That in this moment there is life and food 65
For future years. And so I dare to hope
Though changed, no doubt, from what I was, when first
I came among these hills; when like a roe
I bounded o'er the mountains, by the sides
Of the deep rivers, and the lonely streams, 70
Wherever nature led; more like a man
Flying from something that he dreads, than one

Who sought the thing he loved. For nature then
(The coarser pleasures of my boyish days,
And their glad animal movements all gone by,)   75
To me was all in all. – I cannot paint
What then I was. The sounding cataract
Haunted me like a passion: the tall rock,
The mountain, and the deep and gloomy wood,
Their colours and their forms, were then to me   80
An appetite: a feeling and a love,
That had no need of a remoter charm,
By thought supplied, or any interest
Unborrowed from the eye. – That time is past,
And all its aching joys are now no more,   85
And all its dizzy raptures. Not for this
Faint I, nor mourn nor murmur: other gifts
Have followed, for such loss, I would believe,
Abundant recompence. For I have learned
To look on nature, not as in the hour   90
Of thoughtless youth, but hearing oftentimes
The still, sad music of humanity,
Not harsh or grating, though of ample power
To chasten and subdue. And I have felt
A presence that disturbs me with the joy   95
Of elevated thoughts; a sense sublime
Of something far more deeply interfused,
Whose dwelling is the light of setting suns,
And the round ocean, and the living air,
And the blue sky, and in the mind of man,   100
A motion and a spirit, that impels
All thinking things, all objects of all thought,
And rolls through all things. Therefore am I still
A lover of the meadows and the woods,
And mountains; and of all that we behold   105
From this green earth; of all the mighty world
Of eye and ear, both what they half-create,
And what perceive; well pleased to recognize
In nature and the language of the sense,
The anchor of my purest thoughts, the nurse,   110
The guide, the guardian of my heart, and soul
Of all my moral being.

            Nor, perchance,
If I were not thus taught, should I the more
Suffer my genial spirits to decay:
For thou art with me, here, upon the banks   115
Of this fair river; thou, my dearest Friend,

My dear, dear Friend, and in thy voice I catch
The language of my former heart, and read
My former pleasures in the shooting lights
Of thy wild eyes. Oh! yet a little while   120
May I behold in thee what I was once,
My dear, dear Sister! And this prayer I make,
Knowing that Nature never did betray
The heart that loved her; 'tis her privilege,
Through all the years of this our life, to lead   125
From joy to joy: for she can so inform
The mind that is within us, so impress
With quietness and beauty, and so feed
With lofty thoughts, that neither evil tongues,
Rash judgments, nor the sneers of selfish men,   130
Nor greetings where no kindness is, nor all
The dreary intercourse of daily life,
Shall e'er prevail against us, or disturb
Our chearful faith that all which we behold
Is full of blessings. Therefore let the moon   135
Shine on thee in thy solitary walk;
And let the misty mountain winds be free
To blow against thee: and in after years,
When these wild ecstasies shall be matured
Into a sober pleasure, when thy mind   140
Shall be a mansion for all lovely forms,
Thy memory be as a dwelling-place
For all sweet sounds and harmonies; Oh! then,
If solitude, or fear, or pain, or grief,
Should be thy portion, with what healing thoughts   145
Of tender joy wilt thou remember me,
And these my exhortations! Nor, perchance,
If I should be, where I no more can hear
Thy voice, nor catch from thy wild eyes these gleams
Of past existence, wilt thou then forget   150
That on the banks of this delightful stream
We stood together; And that I, so long
A worshipper of Nature, hither came,
Unwearied in that service: rather say
With warmer love, oh! with far deeper zeal   155
Of holier love. Now wilt thou then forget,
That after many wanderings, many years
Of absence, these steep woods and lofty cliffs,
And this green pastoral landscape, were to me
More dear, both for themselves, and for thy sake.   160

END.

Questions for Discussion

This is a complex poem, and it requires detailed comment, far beyond any that could be provided in this volume. To indicate the complexity of the poem, we shall consider two questions, and offer the beginnings of an answer to them, in order to encourage readers to develop these matters further. A few additional questions will also be provided, without any assistance provided.

1   In what ways does Wordsworth allude to Psalm 23 – "The Lord is my Shepherd" – in this poem? And what use does he make of this image?

You may find the following musings helpful in exploring this question. The Psalm is alluded to in Wordsworth's words, addressed to his sister, Dorothy, which imply that he may trust in her religious faith, regardless of the condition of his own. This is clear at lines 115–16, where he writes: "For thou art with me, here, upon the banks / Of this fair river." Yet it is clear that Wordsworth is also addressing God in this poem. He believes that God has led him beside the still waters of the river – the Wye in this case – and that God will care for him even when he faces the shadow of death. This seems to be what Wordsworth has in mind when he imagines a time when he can no more hear Dorothy's voice.

2   What role does Dorothy play in this poem, particularly in relation to Wordsworth's faith? This question has already been touched upon in the previous question; it now merits much closer attention.

It is clear that Wordsworth sees himself as needing the support of a faith more stead-fast than his own. In "Tintern Abbey" – as, it may be added, in real life – it was to his sister, Dorothy, that the poet turned. Yet the biblical image of a sister is developed in some unexpected ways. For example, consider the poem's final words: "for thy sake." These have both biblical and liturgical associations. In Genesis 12 we are told the story of Abraham who, though a nomad, was given by God the gift of land, a gift that requires that he and his descendants settle down. During their journey to this land, Abraham fears that the Egyptians will kill him in order to have his beautiful wife. "For thy sake" (v. 11), he says to Sarah, "say thou art my sister, that it may be well with me" (v. 13). Sarah is thus welcomed into Pharaoh's house as his sister, and both she and Abraham are thus treated well.

3   Consider the following section of the poem, which muses over the joy of revisiting a site which has past memories.

> While here I stand, not only with the sense
> Of present pleasure, but with pleasing thoughts
> That in this moment there is life and food
> For future years. And so I dare to hope

Is this simply about recharging his spiritual batteries through revisiting a place he likes? Or is there something deeper involved? What has changed over the years?

4   What does Wordsworth mean by the "still sad music of humanity"? You will need to locate this citation, and study its context carefully.

Text: *Ode* : Intimations of Immortality from Recollections of Early Childhood

This is widely regarded as one of Wordsworth's masterpieces, and merits detailed study. Wordsworth himself provided an introduction to the work in *The Fenwick Notes* (dictated 1843), as follows:

Nothing was more difficult for me in childhood than to admit the notion of death as a state applicable to my own being. I have said elsewhere:

> A simple child . . . that lightly draws its breath
> And feels its life in every limb –
> What should it know of death?

But it was not so much from excess of animal vivacity that *my* difficulty came, as from a sense of the indominitableness of the spirit within me. I used to brood over the stories of Enoch and Elijah, and almost to persuade myself that, whatever might become of others, I should be translated in the same way to heaven. . . .

Archimedes said that he could move the world if he had a point whereon to rest his machine. Who has not felt the same aspirations as regards the world of his own mind? Having to wield some of its elements when I was impelled to write this poem on the immortality of the soul, I took hold of the notion of pre-existence as having sufficient foundation in humanity for authorizing me to make for my purpose the best use of it I could as a poet.

The *Ode* was composed between March 27, 1802 and March 6, 1804.

> There was a time when meadow, grove, and stream,
> The earth, and every common sight,
>   To me did seem
>   Apparelled in celestial light,
> The glory and the freshness of a dream.   5
> It is not now as it hath been of yore;–
>   Turn wheresoe'er I may,
>   By night or day.
> The things which I have seen I now can see no more.
>
>   The Rainbow comes and goes,   10
>   And lovely is the Rose,
>   The Moon doth with delight
> Look round her when the heavens are bare,
>   Waters on a starry night
>   Are beautiful and fair;   15
>   The sunshine is a glorious birth;
>   But yet I know, where'er I go,
> That there hath past away a glory from the earth.

Now, while the birds thus sing a joyous song,
   And while the young lambs bound   20
     As to the tabor's sound,
To me alone there came a thought of grief:
A timely utterance gave that thought relief,
    And I again am strong:
The cataracts blow their trumpets from the steep;   25
No more shall grief of mine the season wrong;
I hear the Echoes through the mountains throng,
The Winds come to me from the fields of sleep,
    And all the earth is gay;
      Land and sea   30
   Give themselves up to jollity,
    And with the heart of May
   Doth every Beast keep holiday;–
    Thou Child of Joy,
Shout round me, let me hear thy shouts, thou happy Shepherd-boy.   35

   Ye blessèd creatures, I have heard the call
Ye to each other make; I see
The heavens laugh with you in your jubilee;
    My heart is at your festival,
     My head hath its coronal,   40
The fulness of your bliss, I feel – I feel it all.
    Oh evil day! if I were sullen
    While Earth herself is adorning,
     This sweet May-morning,
    And the Children are culling   45
     On every side,
   In a thousand valleys far and wide,
   Fresh flowers; while the sun shines warm,
And the Babe leaps up on his Mother's arm:–
    I hear, I hear, with joy I hear!   50
    – But there's a Tree, of many, one,
A single field which I have looked upon,
Both of them speak of something that is gone;
    The Pansy at my feet
    Doth the same tale repeat: 55
Whither is fled the visionary gleam?
Where is it now, the glory and the dream?

Our birth is but a sleep and a forgetting:
The Soul that rises with us, our life's Star,
    Hath had elsewhere its setting,   60
    And cometh from afar:

Not in entire forgetfulness,
  And not in utter nakedness,
But trailing clouds of glory do we come
    From God, who is our home: 65
Heaven lies about us in our infancy!
Shades of the prison-house begin to close
    Upon the growing Boy,
But he beholds the light, and whence it flows,
    He sees it in his joy; 70
The Youth, who daily farther from the east
  Must travel, still is Nature's Priest,
    And by the vision splendid
    Is on his way attended;
At length the Man perceives it die away, 75
And fade into the light of common day.

Earth fills her lap with pleasures of her own;
Yearnings she hath in her own natural kind,
And, even with something of a Mother's mind,
    And no unworthy aim, 80
  The homely Nurse doth all she can
To make her Foster-child, her Inmate Man,
  Forget the glories he hath known,
And that imperial palace whence he came.

Behold the Child among his new-born blisses, 85
A six years' Darling of a pigmy size!
See, where 'mid work of his own hand he lies,
Fretted by sallies of his mother's kisses,
With light upon him from his father's eyes!
See, at his feet, some little plan or chart, 90
Some fragment from his dream of human life,
Shaped by himself with newly-learnèd art
    A wedding or a festival,
    A mourning or a funeral;
    And this hath now his heart, 95
    And unto this he frames his song:
    Then will he fit his tongue
To dialogues of business, love, or strife;
    But it will not be long
    Ere this be thrown aside, 100
    And with new joy and pride
The little Actor cons another part;
Filling from time to time his 'humorous stage'
With all the Persons, down to palsied Age,
That Life brings with her in her equipage; 105

As if his whole vocation
    Were endless imitation.

Thou, whose exterior semblance doth belie
        Thy Soul's immensity;
Thou best Philosopher, who yet dost keep   110
Thy heritage, thou Eye among the blind,
That, deaf and silent, read'st the eternal deep,
Haunted for ever by the eternal mind,–
        Mighty Prophet! Seer blest!
            On whom those truths do rest,   115
Which we are toiling all our lives to find,
Thou, over whom thy Immortality
Broods like the Day, a Master o'er a Slave,
A Presence which is not to be put by;
            To whom the grave   120
Is but a lonely bed without the sense or sight
        Of day or the warm light,
A place of thought where we in waiting lie
Thou little Child, yet glorious in the might
Of untamed pleasures on thy being's height,   125
Why with such earnest pains dost thou provoke
The years to bring the inevitable yoke,
Thus blindly with thy blessedness at strife?
Full soon thy Soul shall have her earthly freight,
And custom lie upon thee with a weight,   130
Heavy as frost, and deep almost as life!

        O joy! that in our embers
        Is something that doth live,
        That Nature yet remembers
        What was so fugitive!   135
The thought of our past years in me doth breed
Perpetual benediction: not indeed
For that which is most worthy to be blest;
Delight and liberty, the simple creed
Of Childhood, whether busy or at rest,   140
With new-fledged hope still fluttering in his breast:–
        Not for these I raise
        The song of thanks and praise
    But for those obstinate questionings
    Of sense and outward things,   145
    Fallings from us, vanishings;
    Blank misgivings of a Creature
Moving about in worlds not realised,
High instincts before which our mortal Nature

Did tremble like a guilty thing surprised: 150
   But for those first affections,
   Those shadowy recollections,
   Which, be they what they may
Are yet the fountain-light of all our day,
Are yet a master-light of all our seeing;   155
    Uphold us, cherish, and have power to make
Our noisy years seem moments in the being
Of the eternal Silence: truths that wake,
   To perish never;
Which neither listlessness, nor mad endeavour,   160
   Nor Man nor Boy,
Nor all that is at enmity with joy,
Can utterly abolish or destroy!
  Hence in a season of calm weather
   Though inland far we be,   165
Our Souls have sight of that immortal sea
   Which brought us hither,
   Can in a moment travel thither,
And see the Children sport upon the shore,
And hear the mighty waters rolling evermore.   170

Then sing, ye Birds, sing, sing a joyous song!
   And let the young Lambs bound
   As to the tabor's sound!
  We in thought will join your throng,
   Ye that pipe and ye that play,   175
   Ye that through your hearts to-day
   Feel the gladness of the May!
What though the radiance which was once so bright
Be now for ever taken from my sight,
  Though nothing can bring back the hour   180
Of splendour in the grass, of glory in the flower;
   We will grieve not, rather find
   Strength in what remains behind;
   In the primal sympathy
   Which having been must ever be;   185
   In the soothing thoughts that spring
   Out of human suffering;
   In the faith that looks through death,
In years that bring the philosophic mind.

And O, ye Fountains, Meadows, Hills, and Groves,   190
Forebode not any severing of our loves!
Yet in my heart of hearts I feel your might;
I only have relinquished one delight

To live beneath your more habitual sway.
I love the Brooks which down their channels fret,   195
Even more than when I tripped lightly as they;
The innocent brightness of a new-born Day
    Is lovely yet;
The Clouds that gather round the setting sun
Do take a sober colouring from an eye   200
That hath kept watch o'er man's mortality;
Another race hath been, and other palms are won.
Thanks to the human heart by which we live,
Thanks to its tenderness, its joys, and fears,
To me the meanest flower that blows can give   205
Thoughts that do often lie too deep for tears.

Questions for Study

This is an immensely rich and complex poem, and the following questions can only begin to encourage engagement with it.

1 In his 1843 *Fenwick Notes*, Wordsworth comments: "To that dreamlike vividness and splendour which invest objects of sight in childhood, everyone (I believe, if he would look back) could bear testimony." What does he mean by these words? And how are they reflected in the opening eight lines of the poem?
2 The fourth stanza ends with these words: "Whither is fled the visionary gleam? / Where is it now, the glory and the dream?" Locate these lines, and consider their context. Does the remainder of the poem answer this question?
3 What are the last four lines of the poem all about?

CHAPTER 70

Samuel Taylor Coleridge (1791–1834)

Coleridge was the son of an Anglican parson in the Devonshire village of Ottery St. Mary. After attending school at Christ's Hospital, he went on to study at Jesus College, Cambridge, in 1791. Despite an auspicious beginning, however, Cambridge was far from a happy experience for Coleridge. He found himself distracted from his academic studies by mounting debts, academic disappointments, and especially a growing fascination with radical politics and Unitarian religious ideas. In December 1793 he enlisted in the 15th Light Dragoons at Reading under the name of Silas Tomkyn Comberbache. After a good deal of time and trouble, his release from the Dragoons was secured by his brothers, and Coleridge, temporarily chastened and filled with new resolution, was permitted to return to Cambridge in April 1794. But the mood did not last, and he eventually left the university in December 1794 without obtaining a degree.

In 1795, Coleridge met and began a long association with Wordsworth, which led to the publication of their *Lyrical Ballads* (1798). In October of that same year he married Sara Fricher. This collection included what is often regarded as Coleridge's masterpiece, "The Rime of the Ancient Mariner." Virtually all of the poetic works for which Coleridge is best known were either written or planned during his year of residence in a cottage in the village of Nether Stowey (1797–8). In 1800, Coleridge and his family moved to the town of Keswick in the Lake District, in the north-west of England, to join the Wordsworth family, who had already settled in that region. However, this move was not entirely successful, and Coleridge complained that the climate was affecting his health. The situation was compounded by his use of laudanum to control his pain. As his health declined over the next three years, he took increasingly large doses of this opium derivative; but, completely unaware of the addictive properties of opium, he unwittingly made his cure a major cause of his suffering. Laudanum did not bring relief but produced hallucinations and nightmares. His marriage also came under pressure, partly from his illness, but also through Coleridge's continued interest in Sara Hutchinson.

Samuel Taylor Coleridge (1772–1834)

Basic description
Poet and essayist.

Major works
Lyrical Ballads (with William Wordsworth, 1798);
"Kubla Khan" (1816); Aids to Reflection (1825);
Confessions of an Enquiring Spirit (1840).

Editions of works
Complete Works, ed. W. G. T. Shedd, 7 vols. New
York: Harper & Brothers, 1853.

Major studies
J. Robert Barth, Coleridge and Christian Doctrine.
Cambridge, MA: Harvard University Press,
1969.
Stephen Prickett, Romanticism and Religion: The
Tradition of Coleridge and Wordsworth in the
Victorian Church. Cambridge: Cambridge
University Press, 1976.

In the end, Coleridge decided to flee from his troubles. In 1804, he took up an appointment as secretary to the governor of the Mediterranean island of Malta, and spent the next two years in Malta and Italy. He subsequently returned to England, although he never fully recovered his health. After staying in London for two months, he returned to the north of England in October 1806. By the end of the year he had separated from his wife, and was living with the Wordsworths at Colerton in Leicestershire in a farmhouse lent to them by Sir George Beaumont. His sense of frustration and failure was enhanced when, in January 1807, Wordsworth read The Prelude to him – a poem whose grandeur and brilliance brought home to him his own inadequacies. In October 1810, Coleridge set off in the company of Basil Montagu for London, intending to seek medical help for his opium habit. During a particularly difficult argument, Montagu told Coleridge that Wordsworth regarded Coleridge as a "rotten drunkard" who had been an "absolute nuisance." As a result, a coolness descended upon the relationship between Coleridge and Wordsworth. The relationship never recovered its earlier warmth and intimacy.

Coleridge continued to struggle with his addiction to opium. On April 15, 1816, after a nearly fatal collapse, Coleridge turned up, in utter desperation, at the front door of Moreton House on Highgate Hill, the home of Dr. James Gillman and his wife Anne. Gillman soon ascertained that Coleridge's case was not hopeless but that, if he were to survive, he would require retirement and strict medical supervision. Gillman, whose practice was in Highgate, agreed to take him in as a house-patient for a month. In the event, Coleridge remained with the Gillman household for the remainder of his life. Although Coleridge managed to get some opium smuggled into the house within a week or two of his arrival, Gillman managed to regulate his habit sufficiently to enable him to produce a substantial body of work in the following years. Shortly after his arrival at Highgate, "Christabel" and "Kubla Khan" were published. These were followed by some of his best-known religious works, including Lay Sermons (1816), Aids to Reflection (1825) and The Constitution of Church and State (1830). By the time of his death, Coleridge had regained much of his earlier prestige, and was being fêted as the "Sage of Highgate" by English literary society.

Despite his early flirtations with Unitarianism, Coleridge remained an Anglican, and many of his poems and prose works have strongly religious themes and overtones. The texts which we shall consider illustrate some aspects of his wide-ranging interests, and show both his literary ability and his personal theological convictions. We begin with an early poem, which shows his youthful flirtation with Unitarian ideas, encouraged by the new intellectual climate ushered in by the French Revolution.

Text: Religious Musings

In 1797, Coleridge published a short collection of poems, which included some "religious musings," composed over the period 1794–6. At this stage in his career, Coleridge showed a strong interest in the concept of the "millennium" – that is, a period of one thousand years, during which Christ would rule on earth, before the final judgment (see Revelation 20:1–7). Coleridge appears to have seen the French Revolution as presaging this cosmic event, which would lead to a new world order, in which the reign of God would be established. The poem offers a vision of this new era in world history, and allows us to understand something of Coleridge's poetic vision at this stage. The poem is dense and often obscure; the extract chosen illustrates some of the religious themes which underlie his worldview around this period in his thinking.

> THERE is one Mind, one omnipresent Mind
> Omnific. His most holy name is LOVE –
> Truth of subliming import! with the which
> Who feeds and saturates his constant soul,
> He from his small particular orbit flies
> With blessed outstarting! From himself he flies,
> Stands in the sun, and with no partial gaze
> Views all creation, and he loves it all
> And blesses it, and calls it very good!
> This is indeed to dwell with the most high –
> Cherubs and rapture-trembling seraphim
> Can press no nearer to th' Almighty's throne.
> But that we roam unconscious, or with hearts
> Unfeeling of our universal Sire,
> And that in his vast family no Cain
> Injures uninjured (in her best-aimed blow
> Victorious murder a blind suicide),
> Haply for this some younger angel now
> Looks down on human nature – and behold!
> A sea of blood bestrewed with wrecks where mad
> Embattling interests on each other rush
> With unhelmed rage!
>   'Tis the sublime of man,
> Our noontide majesty, to know ourselves
> Parts and proportions of one wondrous whole;
> This fraternizes man, this constitutes
> Our charities and bearings – but 'tis God

Diffused through all that doth make all one whole.
This the worst superstition: Him except,
Aught to desire, supreme reality,
The plenitude and permanence of bliss!
Oh fiends of superstition! – not that oft
Your pitiless rites have floated with man's blood
The skull-piled temple, not for this shall wrath
Thunder against you from the Holy One!
But (whether ye, th' unclimbing bigot, mock
With secondary gods, or if more pleased
Ye petrify th' imbrothelled atheist's heart –
The atheist your worst slave) I o'er some plain
Peopled with death, and to the silent sun
Steaming with tyrant-murdered multitudes,
Or where mid groans and shrieks loud-laughing trade
More hideous packs his bales of living anguish –
I will raise up a mourning, oh ye fiends,
And curse your spells that film the eye of faith,
Hiding the present God, whose presence lost,
The moral world's cohesion, we become
An anarchy of spirits! Toy-bewitched,
Made blind by lusts, disherited of soul,
No common centre man, no common sire
Knoweth! A sordid solitary thing,
Mid countless brethren with a lonely heart,
Through courts and cities the smooth savage roams
Feeling himself, his own low self the whole,
When he by sacred sympathy might make
The whole one self! Self, that no alien knows!
Self, far diffused as fancy's wing can travel!
Self, spreading still, oblivious of its own,
Yet all of all possessing! This is faith!
This the Messiah's destined victory!

The poem is best read line by line, pausing where necessary. The following notes may be useful.

1   The poem opens with a strong affirmation of the absolute unity and simplicity of God, who is "omnific" – a term used earlier by John Milton, meaning "creating all things."

2   Coleridge introduces the reality of sin. You will find it helpful to list the various images and phrases that he uses to convey the fallenness of the creation, and its departure from the goals which God set for it in creation.

3   Read Genesis 1:31 in the King James Version, as follows: "And God saw every thing that he had made, and, behold, it was very good." At what points does this text seem to enter into Coleridge's reflections?

4 The references to a "sea of blood" is taken from Revelation 16:3. However, it also clearly hints at the "Reign of Terror" which was unleashed in the aftermath of the French Revolution. This finally came to an end with the execution of Robespierre; however, it had been replaced by war, as republican armies sought to spread the ideas of the French Revolution by force to other parts of Europe from 1793.

Questions for Discussion

1 This poem was written during the period 1794–6. How does this development figure in the poem?
2 The second part of the poem reflects on the paradoxes of human nature, and the relevance of religion to humanity. Identify Coleridge's specific criticisms of superstition on the one hand, and atheism on the other.
3 What does the final section of the poem suggest about Coleridge's early views concerning the ultimate goal of human nature?

Text: *Confessions of an Enquiring spirit*

This work appeared posthumously in 1840. It was written during Coleridge's stay at the London home of James Gillman. The context to the section for study is the debate over the authority of the Bible, which was followed with considerable interest in educated English religious circles at this time. Coleridge makes an essentially literary point of importance in this extract – namely, that the interpretation of a text lies with its readers, who are not free from the general human propensity to make mistakes, or get things wrong. Given that this is so, how can one speak of an "infallible" Scripture, when the process of interpretation introduces the possibility of error?

III   *The Authority of Scripture*

The Bible is the appointed conservatory, an indispensable criterion, and a continual source and support of true Belief. But that the Bible is the sole source; that it not only contains, but constitutes, the Christian Religion; that it is, in short, a Creed, consisting wholly of articles of Faith; that consequently we need no rule, help, or guide, spiritual or historical, to teach us what parts are and what are not articles of Faith – all being such – and the difference between the Bible and the Creed being this, that the clauses of the latter are all unconditionally necessary to salvation, but those of the former conditionally so, that is, as soon as the words are known to exist in any one of the canonical Books; and that, under this limitation, the belief is of the same necessity in both, and not at all affected by the greater or lesser importance of the matter to be believed – this scheme differs widely from the preceding, though its adherents often make use of the same words in expressing their belief. And this latter scheme, I assert, was brought into currency by and in favour of those by whom the operation of grace, the aids of the Spirit, the necessity of regeneration, the corruption of our nature, in short, all the peculiar and spiritual mysteries of the Gospel were explained and diluted away.

And how have these men treated this very Bible? I, who indeed prize and reverence this sacred library, as of all outward means and conservatives of Christian faith and practice the surest and the most reflective of the inward Word; I, who hold that the Bible contains the religion of Christians, but who dare not say that whatever is contained in the Bible is the Christian religion, and who shrink from all question respecting the comparative worth and efficacy of the written Word as weighed against the preaching of the Gospel, the discipline of the Churches, the continued succession of the Ministry, and the communion of Saints, lest by comparing I should seem to detach them; I tremble at the processes, which the Grotian divines without scruple carry on in their treatment of the sacred Writers, as soon as any texts declaring the peculiar tenets of our Faith are cited against them, even tenets and mysteries which the believer at his baptism receives as the title-writ and bosom-roll of his adoption; and which, according to my scheme, every Christian born in Church-membership ought to bring with him to the study of the sacred Scriptures as the master-key of interpretation. Whatever the doctrine of infallible dictation may be in itself, in *their* hands it is to the last degree nugatory, and to be paralleled only by the Romish tenet of Infallibility – in the existence of which all agree, but where, and in whom, it exists *stat adhuc sub lite*. Every sentence found in a canonical Book, rightly interpreted, contains the *dictum* of an infallible Mind; but what the right interpretation is – or whether the very words now extant are corrupt or genuine – must be determined by the industry and understanding of fallible, and alas! more or less prejudiced theologians . . .

'Friend! The truth revealed through Christ has its evidence in itself, and the proof of its divine authority in its fitness to our nature and needs – the clearness and cogency of this proof being proportionate to the degree of self-knowledge in each individual hearer. Christianity has likewise its historical evidences, and these as strong as is compatible with the nature of history, and with the aims and objects of a religious dispensation. And to all these Christianity itself, as an existing Power in the world, and Christendom as an existing Fact, with the no less evident fact of a progressive expansion, give a force of moral demonstration that almost supersedes particular testimony. These proofs and evidences would remain unshaken, even though the sum of our religion were to be drawn from the theologians of each successive century, on the principle of receiving that only as divine which should be found in all – *quod semper, quod ubique, quod ab omnibus*. Be only, my Friend! as orthodox a believer as you would have abundant reason to be, though from some accident of birth, country, or education, the precious boon of the Bible, with its additional evidence, had up to this moment been concealed from you – and then read its contents with only the same piety which you freely accord on other occasions to the writings of men, considered the best and wisest of their several ages! What you find therein coincident with your pre-established convictions, you will of course recognize as the Revealed Word, while, as you read the recorded workings of the Word and the Spirit in the minds, lives, and hearts of spiritual men, the influence of the same Spirit on your own being, and the conflicts of grace and infirmity in your own soul, will enable you to discern and to know in and by what spirit they spake and acted – as far at least as shall be needful for you, and in the times of your need.

"Thenceforward, therefore, your doubts will be confined to such parts or passages of the received Canon, as seem to you irreconcilable with known truths, and at variance with the tests given in the Scriptures themselves, and as shall continue so to appear after you have examined each in reference to the circumstances of the Writer or Speaker, the dispensation under which he lived, the purpose of the particular passage, and the intent and object of the Scriptures at large. Respecting these, decide for yourself: and fear not for the result. I venture to tell it you beforehand. The result will be, a confidence in the judgment and fidelity of the compilers of the Canon increased by the apparent exceptions. For they will be found neither more nor greater than may well be supposed requisite, on the one hand, to prevent us from sinking into a habit of slothful, undiscriminating acquiescence, and on the other to provide a check against those presumptuous fanatics, who would rend the *Urim and Thummim from the breastplate of judgement*, and frame oracles by private divination from each letter of each disjointed gem, uninterpreted by the Priest, and deserted by the Spirit, which shines in the parts only as it pervades and irradiates the whole."

Such is the language in which I have addressed a halting friend – halting, yet with his face toward the right path. If I have erred, enable me to see my error. Correct me, or confirm me. Farewell.

Questions for Study

1 Set out in your own words the way in which Coleridge regards Scripture. Why does Coleridge insist that the Bible, while *containing* the Christian faith, does not *constitute* that same faith?
2 What is the precise point that Coleridge is making concerning the role of the interpreter of a text?
3 The Latin phrase *'quod semper, quod ubique, quod ab omnibus'* is due to Vincent of Lérins, who insisted that the authenticity or "catholicity" of a belief was to be determined according to whether it had been believed "always, everywhere, and by all." Why does he regard this issue as being of importance?

CHAPTER 71

John Keble (1792–1866)

John Keble's reputation rests largely on his major collection of poems entitled *The Christian Year*, which can be thought of as a devotional aid to the celebration of the feasts of the Christian year. Keble became a Fellow of Oriel College, Oxford, in 1817, and became a close personal acquaintance of John Henry Newman. Keble's skills as a poet were widely acknowleged; the publication of *The Christian Year* (1827) drew him to public attention. In 1831, Keble was elected as professor of poetry at Oxford University. Many of the poems in *The Christian Year* retain their popularity, such as the poem entitled "Morning":

> New every morning is the love
> Our wakening and uprising prove;
> Through sleep and darkness safely brought,
> Restored to life, and power, and thought.

Although he had secured academic recognition at an early stage in his career, Keble never felt entirely at home in an academic context. In 1836, he became vicar of Hursley in Hampshire, and remained there until his death.

Along with John Henry Newman and Edward Bouverie Pusey, Keble was instrumental in the development of the "Oxford Movement" – the High Church revival, which gathered momentum during the 1830s. For Newman, the origin of the movement was to be traced back to a sermon preached by Keble in the University Church of St. Mary the Virgin, Oxford, on Sunday, July 14, 1833. This must be regarded as a personal judgment, in that there are no reasons for thinking that the sermon in question attracted any great attention at the time, let alone that it was seen as the spearhead of a new movement within the Church of England.

The background to the sermon was the pending decision by the British government to suppress several Irish bishoprics, on the grounds that they could no longer be sustained. There were ten bishoprics too many, and it seemed to the eminently pragmatic House of Commons that the easiest way of resolving this anomaly was to reform the system to make it more manageable.

John Keble (1792–1866)

Basic description
Anglo-Catholic churchman and poet.

Major work
The Christian Year (1827).

Major studies
Willem J. A. M. Beek, *John Keble's Literary and Religious Contributions to the Oxford Movement*. Ph.D. Thesis: University of Nijmegen, 1959.
Brian Martin, *John Keble: Priest, Professor and Poet*. London: Croom Helm, 1976.

Keble was shocked by this development, which confirmed his fears of Erastianism within the English church. It seemed to imply that it was the British Parliament, rather than Christ, who was the true founder and governor of the church. How could the Church of England avoid the stigma of being dubbed a "Parliamentarian Church" in the light of this development? Keble sought to highlight such issues in his 1833 sermon, which was provocatively entitled "National Apostasy."

Text: "National Apostasy"

The sermon in question illustrates well the importance of the sermon as a piece of Christian literature. Although Keble understates virtually all of his points, and makes some of them in a manner which makes them decidedly less than memorable, the work fully merits inclusion in this anthology on account of its historical interest and literary style. Once the historical background has been grasped, the sermon requires no additional comment, other than to note that the parliamentary decision which Keble feared so much was enacted within a week of the sermon.

'National Apostasy'

> *"As for me, God forbid that I should sin against the Lord in ceasing to pray for you: but I will teach you the good and the right way." – 1 Samuel xii: 23*

On public occasions, such as the present, the minds of Christians naturally revert to that portion of Holy Scripture, which exhibits to us the will of the Sovereign of the world in more immediate relation to the civil and national conduct of mankind. We naturally turn to the Old Testament, when public duties, public errors, and public dangers, are in question. And what in such cases is natural and obvious, is sure to be more or less right and reasonable. Unquestionably it is mistaken theology, which would debar Christian nations and statesmen from the instruction afforded by the Jewish Scriptures, under a notion, that the circumstances of that people were altogether peculiar and unique, and therefore irrelevant to every other case. True, there is hazard of misapplication, as there is whenever men teach by example. There is peculiar hazard, from the sacredness and delicacy of the subject; since dealing with things supernatural and miraculous as if they were ordinary human precedents, would be not only unwise, but profane. But these hazards are more than counterbalanced by the absolute certainty, peculiar to this history, that what is there commended was right, and what is there blamed, wrong. And they would be effectually obviated, if men would be careful to keep in view this caution: – suggested everywhere, if I mistake not, by the manner in which the Old Testament is quoted in the New: – that, as regards reward and punishment, God dealt formerly with the Jewish people in a manner analogous to that in which He deals now, not so much with Christian nations, as with the souls of individual Christians.

Let us only make due allowances for this cardinal point of difference, and we need not surely hesitate to avail ourselves, as the time may require, of those national warnings, which fill the records of the elder Church: the less so, as the discrepancy lies rather in what is revealed of God's providence, than in what is required in the way of human duty. Rewards and punishments may be dispensed, visibly at least, with a less even hand; but what tempers, and what conduct, God will ultimately reward and punish, – this is a point which cannot be changed: for it depends not on our circumstances, but on His essential, unvarying Attributes.

I have ventured on these few general observations, because the impatience with which the world endures any remonstrance on religious grounds, is apt to show itself most daringly, when the Law and the Prophets are appealed to. Without any scruple or ceremony, men give us to understand that they regard the whole as obsolete: thus taking the very opposite ground to that which was preferred by the same class of persons two hundred years ago; but, it may be feared, with much the same purpose and result. Then, the Old Testament was quoted at random for every excess of fanatical pride and cruelty: now, its authority goes for nothing, however clear and striking the analogies may be, which appear to warrant us in referring to it. The two extremes, as usual, meet; and in this very remarkable point: that they both avail themselves of the supernatural parts of the Jewish revelation to turn away attention from that, which they, of course, most dread and dislike in it: its authoritative confirmation of the plain dictates of conscience in matters of civil wisdom and duty.

That portion, in particular, of the history of the chosen people, which drew from Samuel, the truest of patriots, the wise and noble sentiment in the text, must ever be an unpleasing and perplexing page of Scripture, to those, who would fain persuade themselves, that a nation, even a Christian nation, may do well enough, as such, without God, and without His Church. For what if the Jews were bound to the Almighty by ties common to no other people? What if He had condescended to know them in a way in which He was as yet unrevealed to all families of the earth besides? What if, as their relation to Him was nearer, and their ingratitude more surpassing, so they might expect more exemplary punishment? Still, after all has been said, to exaggerate their guilt, in degree, beyond what is supposed possible in any nation whatever now, what can it come to, in kind and in substance, but only this; – that they rejected God? that they wished themselves rid of the moral restraint implied in His peculiar presence and covenant? They said, what the prophet Ezekial, long after, represents their worthy posterity as saying, "We will be as the heathen, the families of the countries" (Ezek. xx: 32). "Once for all, we will get rid of these disagreeable, unfashionable scruples, which throw us behind, as we think, in the race of worldly honour and profit." Is this indeed a tone of thought, which Christian nations cannot fall into? Or, if they should, has it ceased to be displeasing to God? In other words, has He forgotten to be angry with impiety and practical atheism? Either this must be affirmed, or men must own, (what is clear at once to plain unsophisticated readers,) that this first overt act, which began the downfall of the Jewish nation, stands on record, with its fatal consequences, for a perpetual warning to all nations, as well as to all individual Christians, who, having accepted God for their King, allow themselves to be weary of subjection to Him, and think they should be happier if they were freer, and more like the rest of the world.

I do not enter into the question, whether visible temporal judgements are to be looked for by Christian nations, transgressing as those Jews did. Surely common sense and piety unite, in representing this inquiry as, practically, one of no great importance. When it is once known for certain that such and such conduct is displeasing to the King of kings, surely common sense and piety concur in setting their mark of reprobation on such conduct, whether the punishment, sure to overtake it, come tomorrow, or a year hence, or wait till we are in another world.

Waiving this question, therefore, I proceed to others, which appear to me, I own, at the present moment especially, of the very gravest practical import.

What are the symptoms, by which one may judge most fairly, whether or no a nation, as such, is becoming alienated from God and Christ?

And what are the particular duties of sincere Christians, whose lot is cast by Divine Providence in a time of such dire calamity?

The conduct of the Jews, in asking for a king, may furnish an ample illustration of the first point: the behaviour of Samuel, then and afterwards, supplies as perfect a pattern of the second, as can well be expected from human nature.

I. The case is at least possible, of a nation, having for centuries acknowledged, as an essential part of its theory of government, that, as a Christian nation, she is also a part of Christ's Church, and bound, in all her legislation and policy, by the fundamental rules of that Church – the case is, I say, conceivable, of a government and people, so constituted, deliberately throwing off the restraint, which in many respects such a principle would impose on them, nay, disavowing the principle itself; and that, on the plea, that other states, as flourishing or more so in regard of wealth and dominion, do well enough without it. Is not this desiring, like the Jews, to have an earthly king over them, when the Lord their God is their King? Is it not saying in other words, "We will be as the heathen, the families of the countries," the aliens to the Church of our Redeemer?

To such a change, whenever it takes place, the immediate impulse will probably be given by some pretence of danger from without, – such as, at the time now spoken of, was furnished to the Israelites by an incursion of the children of Ammon; or by some wrong or grievance in the executive government, such as the malversation of Samuel's sons, to whom he had deputed his judicial functions. Pretences will never be hard to find; but, in reality, the movement will always be traceable to the same decay or want of faith, the same deficiency in Christian resignation and thankfulness, which leads so many, as individuals, to disdain and forfeit the blessings of the Gospel. Men not impressed with religious principle attribute their ill success in life, – the hard times they have to struggle with, – to anything rather than their own ill-desert: and the institutions of the country, ecclesiastical and civil, are always at hand to bear the blame of whatever seems to be going amiss. Thus, the discontent in Samuel's time, which led the Israelites to demand a change of constitution, was discerned by the Unerring Eye, though perhaps little suspected by themselves, to be no better than a fresh development of the same restless, godless spirit, which had led them so often into idolatry. "They have not rejected thee, but they have rejected Me, that I should not reign over them. According to all the works, which they have done since the day that I brought them up out of Egypt even unto this day, wherewith they have forsaken Me, and served other gods, so do they also unto thee" (I Sam. viii: 7, 8).

The charge might perhaps surprise many of them, just as, in other times and countries, the impatient patrons of innovation are surprised, at finding themselves rebuked on religious grounds. Perhaps the Jews pleaded the express countenance, which the words of their Law, in one place (Deut. xvii: 14–20), seemed, by anticipation, to lend to the measure they were urging. And so, in modern times, when liberties are to be taken, and the intrusive passions of men to be indulged, precedent and permission, or what sounds like them, may be easily found and quoted for everything. But Samuel, in God's Name, silenced all this, giving them to understand, that in His sight the whole was a question of motive and purpose, not of ostensible and colourable argument; – in His sight, I say, to Whom we, as well as they, are nationally responsible for much more than the soundness of our deductions as matter of disputation, or of law; we are responsible for the meaning and temper in which we deal with His Holy Church, established among us for the salvation of our souls.

These, which have been hitherto mentioned as omens and tokens of an Apostate Mind in a nation, have been suggested by the portion itself of sacred history, to which I have ventured to direct your attention. There are one or two more, which the nature of the subject, and the palpable tendency of things around us, will not allow to be passed over.

One of the most alarming, as a symptom, is the growing indifference, in which men indulge themselves, to other men's religious sentiments. Under the guise of charity and toleration we are come almost to this pass; that no difference, in matters of faith, is to disqualify for our approbation and confidence, whether in public or domestic life. Can we conceal it from ourselves, that every year the practice is becoming more common, of trusting men unreservedly in the most delicate and important matters, without one serious inquiry, whether they do not hold principles which make it impossible for them to be loyal to their Creator, Redeemer, and Sanctifier? Are not offices conferred, partnerships formed, intimacies courted, – nay, (what is almost too painful to think of,) do not parents commit their children to be educated, do they not encourage them to intermarry, in houses, on which Apostolical Authority would rather teach them to set a mark, as unfit to be entered by a faithful servant of Christ?

I do not now speak of public measures only or chiefly; many things of that kind may be thought, whether wisely or no, to become from time to time necessary, which are in reality as little desired by those who lend them a seeming concurrence, as they are, in themselves, undesirable. But I speak of the spirit which leads men to exult in every step of that kind; to congratulate one another on the supposed decay of what they call an exclusive system.

Very different are the feelings with which it seems natural for a true Churchman to regard such a state of things, from those which would arise in his mind on witnessing the mere triumph of any given set of adverse opinions, exaggerated or even heretical as he might deem them. He might feel as melancholy, – he could hardly feel so indignant.

But this is not a becoming place, nor are these safe topics, for the indulgence of mere feeling. The point really to be considered is, whether, according to the coolest estimate, the fashionable liberality of this generation be not ascribable, in a great measure, to the same temper which led the Jews voluntarily to set about degrading themselves to a level with the idolatrous Gentiles? And, if it be true anywhere, that such enactments are forced on the Legislature by public opinion, is APOSTASY too hard a word to describe the temper of that nation?

The same tendency is still more apparent, because the fair gloss of candour and forbearance is wanting, in the surly or scornful impatience often exhibited, by persons who would regret passing for unbelievers, when Christian motives are suggested, and checks from Christian principles attempted to be enforced on their public conduct. I say, "their public conduct," more especially; because in that, I know not how, persons are apt to be more shameless, and readier to avow the irreligion that is in them; – amongst other reasons, probably, from each feeling that he is one of a multitude, and fancying, therefore, that his responsibility is divided.

For example: – whatever be the cause, in this country of late years, (though we are lavish in professions of piety,) there has been observable a growing disinclination, on the part of those bound by VOLUNTARY OATHS, to whatever reminds them of their obligation; a growing disposition to explain it all away. We know what, some years ago, would have been thought of such uneasiness, if betrayed by persons officially sworn, in private, legal, or commercial life. If there be any subjects or occasions, now, on which men are inclined to judge of it more lightly, it concerns them deeply to be quite sure, that they are not indulging or encouraging a profane dislike of God's awful Presence; a general tendency, as a people, to leave Him out of all their thoughts.

They will have the more reason to suspect themselves, in proportion as they see and feel more of that impatience under pastoral authority, which our Savior Himself has taught us to consider as a never-failing symptom of an unchristian temper. "He that heareth you, heareth Me; and he that despiseth you, despiseth Me" (S. Luke x: 16). Those words of divine truth put beyond all sophistical exception, what common sense would lead us to infer, and what daily experiences teaches; – that disrespect to the Successors of the Apostles, as such, is an unquestionable symptom of enmity to Him, Who gave them their commission at first, and has pledged Himself to be with them for ever. Suppose such disrespect general and national, suppose it also avowedly grounded not on any fancied tenet of religion, but on mere human reasons of popularity and expediency, either there is no meaning at all in these emphatic declarations of our Lord, or that nation, how highly soever she may think of her religion and morality, stands convicted in His sight of a direct disavowal of His Sovereignty.

To this purpose it may be worth noticing, that the ill-fated chief, whom God gave to the Jews, as the prophet tells us, in His anger (Hosea xiii: 11), and whose disobedience and misery were referred by himself to his 'fearing the people, and obeying their voice' (I Sam. xv: 24), whose conduct, therefore, may be fairly taken as a sample of what public opinion was at that time supposed to require, – his first step in apostasy was, perhaps, an intrusion on the sacrificial office (I Sam. xiii: 8–14), certainly an impatient breach of his engagement with Samuel, as the last and great-est of his crimes was persecuting David, whom he well knew to bear God's special commission. God forbid, that any Christian land should ever, by her prevailing temper and policy, revive the memory and likeness of Saul, or incur a sentence of reprobation like his. But if such a thing should be, the crimes of that nation will probably begin in infringement on Apostolical Rights; she will end in persecuting the true Church; and in the several stages of her melancholy career, she will continually be led on from bad to worse by vain endeavours at accommodation and compromise with evil. Sometimes toleration may be the word, as with Saul when he spared the Amalekites; sometimes state security, as when he sought the life of David; sometimes sympathy with popular feeling, as appears to have been the case, when violating solemn treaties, he attempted to exterminate the remnant of the Gibeonites, in his zeal for the children of Israel and Judah (2 Sam. xxi: 2). Such are the sad but obvious results of separating religious resignation altogether from men's notions of civil duty.

II. But here arises the other question, on which it was proposed to say a few words; and with a view to which, indeed, the whole subject must be considered, if it is to lead to any practical improvement. What should be the tenor of their conduct, who find themselves cast on such times of decay and danger? How may a man best recon-cile his allegiance to God and his Church with his duty to his country, that country, which now, by the supposition, is fast becoming hostile to the Church, and cannot therefore long be the friend of God?

Now in proportion as any one sees reason to fear that such is, or soon may be, the case in his own land, just so far may he see reason to be thankful, especially if he be called to any national trust, for such a complete pattern of his duty, as he may find in the conduct of Samuel. That combination of sweetness with firmness, of con-sideration with energy, which constitutes the temper of a perfect public man, was never perhaps so beautifully exemplified. He makes no secret of the bitter grief and dismay, with which the resolution of his countrymen had filled him. He was prepared to resist it at all hazards, had he not received from God Himself directions to give them their own way; protesting, however, in the most distinct and solemn tone, so as to throw the whole blame of what might ensue on their wilfulness. Having so protested, and found them obstinate, he does not therefore at once forsake their service, he continues discharging all the functions they had left him, with a true and loyal, though most heavy, heart. "God forbid that I should sin against the Lord in ceasing to pray for you: but I will teach you the good and the right way."

Should it ever happen (which God avert, but we cannot shut our eyes to the danger) that the Apostolical Church should be forsaken, degraded, nay trampled on and despoiled by the State and people of England, I cannot conceive a kinder wish for her, on the part of her most affectionate and dutiful children, than that she may, consistently, act in the spirit of this most noble sentence; nor a course of conduct more likely to be blessed by a restoration to more than her former efficiency. In speak-ing of the Church, I mean, of course, the laity, as well as the clergy in their three orders, – the whole body of Christians united, according to the will of Jesus Christ, under the Successors of the Apostles. It may, by God's blessing, be of some use, to show how, in the case supposed, the example of Samuel might guide her collectively, and each of her children individually, down even to minute details of duty.

The Church would, first of all, have to be constant, as before, in INTERCES-SION. No despiteful usage, no persecution, could warrant her in ceasing to pray, as did her first fathers and patterns, for the State, and all who are in authority. That duty once well and cordially performed, all other duties, so to speak, are secured. Candour, respectfulness, guarded language, – all that the Apostle meant, in warning men not to "speak evil of dignities," may then, and then only, be practised, without compromise of truth and fortitude, when the habit is attained of praying as we ought for the very enemies of our precious and holy cause.

The constant sense of God's presence and consequent certainty of final success, which can be kept up no other way, would also prove an effectual bar against the more silent but hardly less malevolent feeling, of disgust, almost amounting to mis-anthropy, which is apt to lay hold on sensitive minds, when they see oppression and wrong triumphant on a large scale. The custom of interceding, even for the wicked, will keep the Psalmist's reasoning habitually present to their thoughts: "Fret not thyself because of the ungodly, neither be thou envious against the evil doers: for they shall soon be cut down like the grass, and be withered even as the green herb. . . . Leave off from wrath, and let go displeasure: fret not thyself, else shalt thou be moved to do evil" (Ps. xxxvii: 1, 2, 8).

Thus not only by supernatural aid, which we have warrant of God's word for expecting, but even in the way of natural consequence, the first duty of the Church and of Churchmen, INTERCESSION, sincerely practised, would prepare them for the second; – which, following the words of Samuel as our clue, we may confidently pronounce to be REMONSTRANCE. "I will teach you the good and the right way." REMONSTRANCE, calm, distinct, and persevering, in public and in private, direct and indirect, by word, look, and demeanour, is the unequivocal duty of every Chris-tian, according to his opportunities, when the Church landmarks are being broken down.

Among laymen, a deep responsibility would appear to rest on those particularly, whose profession leads them most directly to consider the boundaries of the various rights and duties, which fill the space of civilized Society. The immediate machinery of change must always pass through their hands: and they have also very great power in forming and modifying public opinion. The very solemnity of this day may remind them, even more than others, of the close amity which must ever subsist between equal justice and pure religion; Apostolical religion, more especially, in proportion to her superior truth and exactness. It is an amity, made still more sacred, if pos-sible, in the case of the Church and Law of England, by historical recollections, associations, and precedents, of the most engaging and ennobling cast.

But I return to the practical admonition afforded her, in critical periods, by Samuel's example.

After the accomplishment of the change which he deprecated, his whole behavi-our, to Saul especially, is a sort of expansion of the sentiment in the text. It is all earn-est INTERCESSION with God, grave, respectful, affectionate REMONSTRANCE with the misguided man himself. Saul is boldly rebuked, and that publicly, for his impious liberality in sparing the Amalekites, yet so as not to dishonour him in the presence of the people. Even when it became necessary for God's prophet to show that he was in earnest, and give the most effectual of warnings, by separating himself from so unworthy a person, – when "Samuel came no more to see Saul" (I Sam. xv: 35) – even then, we are told, he still "mourned for him."

On the same principle, come what may, we have ill learned the lessons of our Church, if we permit our patriotism to decay, together with the protecting care of the State. "The powers that be are ordained of God," whether they foster the true church or no. Submission and order are still duties. They were so in the days of pagan persecution; and the more of loyal and affectionate feeling we endeavour to mingle with our obedience, the better.

After all, the surest way to uphold or restore our endangered Church, will be for each of her anxious children, in his own place and station, to resign himself more thoroughly to his God and Saviour in those duties, public and private, which are not immediately affected by the emergencies of the moment: the daily and hourly duties, I mean, of piety, purity, charity, justice. It will be a consolation understood by every thoughtful Churchman, that let his occupation be, apparently, never so remote from such great interests, it is in his power, by doing all as a Christian, to credit and advance the cause he has most at heart; and what is more, to draw down God's blessing upon it. This ought to be felt, for example, as one motive more to exact punctuality in those duties, personal and official, which the return of an Assize week offers to our practice; one reason more for veracity in witnesses, fairness in pleaders, strict impartiality, self-command, and patience, in those on whom decisions depend; and for an awful sense of God's presence in all. An Apostle once did not disdain to urge good conduct upon his proselytes of lowest condition, upon the ground, that, so doing, they would adorn and recommend the doctrine of God our Savior (Titus ii: 10). Surely, then, it will be no unworthy principle, if any man be more circumspect in his behaviour, more watchful and fearful of himself, more earnest in his petitions for spiritual aid, from a dread of disparaging the holy name of the English Church, in her hour of peril, by his own personal fault or negligence.

As to those who, either by station or temper, feel themselves most deeply interested, they cannot be too careful in reminding themselves, that one chief danger, in times of change and excitement, arises from their tendency to engross the whole mind. Public concerns, ecclesiastical or civil, will prove indeed ruinous to those, who permit them to occupy all their care and thoughts, neglecting or undervaluing ordinary duties, more especially those of a devotional kind.

These cautions being duly observed, I do not see how any person can devote himself too entirely to the cause of the Apostolical Church in these realms. There may be, as far as he knows, but a very few to sympathize with him. He may have to wait long, and very likely pass out of this world before he see any abatement in the triumph of disorder and irreligion. But, if he be consistent, he possesses, to the utmost, the personal consolations of a good Christian: and as a true Churchman, he has that encouragement, which no other cause in the world can impart in the same degree: – he is calmly, soberly, demonstrably, SURE, that, sooner or later, HIS WILL BE THE WINNING SIDE, and that the victory will be complete, universal, eternal.

He need not fear to look upon the efforts of anti-Christian powers, as did the holy Apostles themselves, who welcomed the first persecution in the words of the Psalmist:

"Why do the heathen rage, and the people imagine a vain thing?

"The kings of the earth stand up, and the rulers take counsel together, against the Lord, and against His Anointed.

"For of a truth against Thy Holy Child Jesus, Whom Thou hast anointed, both Herod and Pontius Pilate, with the Gentiles, and the people of Israel, were gathered together,

"FOR TO DO WHATSOEVER THY HAND AND THY COUNSEL DETERMINED BEFORE TO BE DONE" (Acts iv: 25–28).

Questions for Study

1 Would the audience for this sermon have seen it as the envisaged manifesto for a major reforming religious movement?
2 What specific references does Keble make in this sermon to the religious and political events of his own day?
3 What does Keble expect his audience to do as a result of listening to this sermon?

CHAPTER 72

John Henry Newman (1801–1890)

John Henry Newman was born in London on February 21, 1801. He was the son of a banker, John Newman, and Jemima (Fourdrinier) Newman. He entered a private school at Ealing in 1808, at the age of seven. Following the failure of his father's bank in 1816, Newman, who was then in his final year at Ealing, underwent what he would later refer to as a "conversion." His early phase was thus dominated by the influence of evangelicalism, which shaped his early religious views decisively. At the age of sixteen, he went up to Trinity College, Oxford, beginning an association with the University of Oxford that would last for nearly thirty years. After graduating with third-class honors in 1921, Newman went on to become a Fellow of Oriel College in 1822, and a tutor in 1826.

John Henry Newman (1801–1890)

Basic description
Initially Anglican, then Roman Catholic theologian, preacher and poet.

Major works
Parochial and Plain Sermons (1833–41); Apologia Pro Vita Sua (1864); The Dream of Gerontius (1866).

Major studies
Sheridan Gilley, Newman and His Age. London: DLT, 1990.

Ian Ker, Healing the Wound of Humanity: The Spirituality of John Henry Newman. London: DLT, 1993.

Geoffrey Warnsley, "Newman's Dream of Gerontius," Downside Review 91 (1973), 167–85.

In 1828, Newman was appointed vicar of the University Church of St. Mary, of which Oriel College was the patron. That same year, Edward Hawkins became the new Provost of Oriel. Newman supported Hawkins in his candidacy for this position. It soon became clear, however, that the two held quite incompatible views concerning the responsibilities of a college tutor. Newman believed that the tutors had pastoral responsibilities toward their students, whereas Hawkins insisted that the relationship between tutor and student was purely academic in nature. When Newman objected to this view, Hawkins cut off his supply of new students, leaving him little choice but to resign his post in 1832, and concentrate on his duties as vicar of the University Church. He remained in this position until 1843, attracting hundreds of students, university officials, and townspeople to St. Mary's with his scholarly yet earnest preaching.

Newman's preaching achieved legendary status at Oxford. In 1884, looking back over forty years, Matthew Arnold recalled the enchanting voices of his youth at Oxford, supreme among which was that of Newman every Sunday at the University Church, St. Mary's.

> Who could resist the charm of that spiritual apparition, gliding in the dim afternoon light through the aisles of St. Mary's, rising into the pulpit, and then, in the most entrancing of voices, breaking the silence with words and thoughts which were a religious music – subtle, sweet, mournful? I seem to hear him still, saying: "After the fever of life, after weariness and sicknesses, fightings and despondings, languor and fretfulness, struggling and succeeding; after all the changes and chances of this troubled, unhealthy state – at length comes death, at length the white throne of God, at length the beatific vision."

The high point of Newman's Anglican career was his influential role in the Oxford Movement, a High Church effort to return to the foundations of the faith – the sacraments, episcopal governance, and apostolic succession – and to affirm the Church's status as the *via media*, the middle ground between Roman Catholicism's unfounded claims to authority and infallibility and the Dissenters' equally unfounded emphasis upon spiritual liberty and private judgment. According to Newman, the Oxford Movement began on July 14, 1833, when John Keble delivered his sermon "National Apostasy" from the pulpit of St. Mary's. Newman became involved a few months later and soon came to be seen as the Movement's primary spokesman, promoting its doctrinal and moral concerns through his editorship of the *British Critic*, his contributions to *The Tracts for the Times*, and his weekly sermons at the University Church.

Yet all was not well. By 1839, Newman had begun to lose confidence in the cause. He gradually became convinced that Rome, not Canterbury, was the home of the true Church. He expressed his new views in February 1841 in the infamous "Tract Ninety," which brought *The Tracts for the Times* to an ignominious and abrupt end. In this work, Newman argued that the Thirty-Nine Articles – which set out the doctrinal position of the Church of England – could be interpreted in a manner supportive of Roman Catholic doctrine. The tract met with a hostile reaction throughout Oxford University and beyond. In consequence, Newman began to withdraw from the public life of the Church of England. Over the next eighteen months, he resigned his position at the *British Critic*, moved from Oxford to a semi-monastic community at Littlemore, retracted the anti-Catholic statements he had published in his youth, and resigned his position at the University Church. His final sermon as an Anglican priest – "The Parting of Friends" – was preached at Littlemore in September 1843, a few days after he had resigned as vicar of St. Mary's. He was officially received into the Roman Catholic church on October 9, 1845 and was ordained to the priesthood the next year.

Newman's work with the Roman Catholic church was extensive. He was instrumental in establishing the Oratory of St. Philip Neri near Birmingham in 1848, and was a leading force in the movement to create the Catholic University of Ireland, of which he served as Rector from 1854 to 1858. Major works from this period include *The Idea of a University* (1852), *An Essay in Aid of a Grammar of Assent* (1870), and his autobiography, *Apologia Pro Vita Sua* (1864). In 1879, Pope Leo XIII created him a cardinal. He died on August 11, 1890, and was buried in Warwickshire. His epitaph reads, "Ex umbris et imaginibus in veritatem" – "out of shadows and pictures into truth."

Text: *The Dream of Gerontius*

In 1865, Newman wrote a short piece entitled "The Dream of Gerontius." (The word literally means "an old man.") The work was initially published in two consecutive editions of *The Month* in April and May 1865, and then in book form the following year. The work takes the form of the vision of a dying man, as he leaves the body at death and encounters the angelic realm. It includes two poems which have become firmly established as classics in the tradition of Christian hymnody, which we shall consider in what follows.

Yet *Gerontius* is also important as a landmark in Newman's literary development. Most of Newman's poetry had been written during the 1830s. These poems were predominantly devotional or meditative, and reflect the somewhat moralistic understanding of poetry found in Newman's essay "Poetry with Reference to Aristotle's Poetics." These poems are essentially sermons in verse, with the sermonical tone dominating the mode of presentation. Newman's poetic abilities at this stage were summarized in a less than flattering manner by one of his admirers, C. F. Harrold: "in Newman, the moralist was fiercely at war with the poet. And the moralist won." All this changed with *Gerontius*.

Gerontius is basically a theological poem which dramatizes a recurrent theme of Newman's sermons in particular, and the Christian spiritual tradition in general: that in this world there is no lasting city. This theme can be found in many of his parochial sermons – such as "On the Greatness and Littleness of Human Life," which includes the following passage which can be seen to contain in a nutshell much of the theological substance of *Gerontius*:

> We should remember that [this life] is scarcely more than an accident of our being – that it is no part of ourselves, who are immortal spirits, independent of time and space, and that this life is but a sort of outward stage, on which we act for a time. . . . We should consider ourselves to be in this world in no fuller sense than players in any game are in the game; and life to be a sort of dream, as detached and as different from our real external existence, as a dream differs from waking; a serious dream, indeed, as affording a means of judging us, yet in itself a kind of shadow without substance.

Perhaps this theme can be found in other religious poems of the Victorian era. Yet it must be stressed that *Gerontius* differs from much of the religious poetry of the nineteenth century with respect to the sheer artistry with which a subject of the highest didactic nature is handled without lapsing into rather wooden didacticism. In *Gerontius*, Newman does not preach; he contemplates – and draws his readers into his contemplation as he does so. *The Dream of Gerontius* dramatizes the passage of the central character – a dying old Christian man – from mortality to immortality. It can be seen as a compendium of Newman's basic beliefs concerning human nature, the purpose of humanity upon earth, and the higher reality of the unseen spiritual world. Yet this is not set out as a credal statement; rather, it is what Helen G. Hole has called a "poetry of dogma which conceives of dogma as a mystery appealing to the imagination as well as the reason."

We shall consider two poems taken from this work. The first is a credal poem, setting out the basic ideas of the Christian faith. It is recited by Gerontius himself, and sets out the doctrinal truths on which his salvation is grounded. This is followed by an angelic hymn of adoration and praise, which sets out the praise of heaven in response to the saving work of God. It is instructive to set these side by side, in that both refer to the same set of realities – the redemption of humanity by God in Christ. Yet the first is didactive, the second contemplative. The first deals with ideas, the second with imagery and narrative. It is as if Newman wishes to suggest that dogma has its place – but that it must give way to adoration. In this, he echoes a theme of Thomas Aquinas – that the true task of theology is to lead to adoration.

> 1. *Firmly I believe*
> Firmly I believe and truly
> God is Three, and God is One;
> And I next acknowledge duly
> Manhood taken by the Son.
>
> And I trust and hope most fully
> In that Manhood crucified;
> And each thought and deed unruly
> Do to death, as He has died.
>
> Simply to His grace and wholly
> Light and life and strength belong,
> And I love supremely, solely,
> Him the holy, Him the strong.
>
> And I hold in veneration,
> For the love of Him alone,
> Holy Church as His creation,
> And her teachings are His own.
>
> Adoration aye be given,
> With and through the angelic host,
> To the God of earth and heaven,
> Father, Son and Holy Ghost.
>
> 2. *Praise to the holiest in the height*
> Praise to the Holiest in the height,
> And in the depth be praise;
> In all His words most wonderful,
> Most sure in all His ways.

O loving wisdom of our God!
When all was sin and shame,
A second Adam to the fight
And to the rescue came.

O wisest love! that flesh and blood,
Which did in Adam fall,
Should strive afresh against the foe,
Should strive and should prevail.

And that a higher gift than grace
Should flesh and blood refine,
God's Presence and His very Self,
And Essence all divine.

O generous love! that He, Who smote,
In Man for man the foe,
The double agony in Man
For man should undergo.

And in the garden secretly,
And on the Cross on high,
Should teach His brethren, and inspire
To suffer and to die.

Praise to the Holiest in the height,
And in the depth be praise;
In all His words most wonderful,
Most sure in all His ways.

Questions for Discussion

1   Compare the style of these two hymns. What are their chief points of difference? And how might these be explained?
2   The first hymn takes the form of a credal statement in verse. What does the hymn tell us about Newman's main theological concerns? Which statements of faith does he give greatest place to? Are there any obvious omissions?
3   The second hymn takes the form of a contemplation on the death of Christ. What is Newman's purpose in writing in this manner?
4   On the basis of this hymn, what would you judge Newman's particular theological emphases to be? Does this agree with what you answered earlier, in relation to the first poem?
5   What is the "higher gift than grace"? And what point is Newman making in using this phrase?

CHAPTER 73

Ralph Waldo Emerson (1803–1882)

Emerson was born in Boston, Massachusetts, in 1803, the son of a Unitarian minister. He studied at Harvard College, before going on to train for the Unitarian ministry at Harvard Divinity School, then widely regarded as a stronghold of Unitarianism. His ministry in that church began in 1826, and ended in 1829 following a rather tetchy dispute over sacramental theology with the senior members of the church. While Emerson would not be entirely happy to be included in an anthology of Christian literature – see, for example, the criticisms of traditional Christian life and thought set out in his 1835 lecture "Defects of Historical Christianity" – the ideas to be found in his earliest published work, *Nature* (1836), can be argued to reflect certain fundamental aspects of the Christian doctrine of creation, despite obvious influences from Eastern religions.

Ralph Waldo Emerson (1803–1862)

Basic description
Leading American philosophical, religious and ethical writer, with a strong sense of "the mystical unity of nature," set out in his transcendentalist worldview.

Major works
Nature (1836); *Conduct of Life* (1860); *Letters and Social Aims* (1876).

Editions of works
Complete Prose Works. London: Ward & Lock, 1889.

Major studies
A. D. Hodder, *Emerson's Rhetoric of Revelation: Nature, the Reader and the Revelation Within.* University Park, PA: Pennsylvania State University Press, 1989.

B. L. Packer, *Emerson's Fall: A New Interpretation of the Major Essays.* New York: Continuum, 1982.

Emerson is widely regarded as one of America's most influential authors, philosophers and thinkers. Although he produced a large number of poems – such as "Threnody,"

"Brahma," and "The Problem," Emerson is best remembered for his prose, which shows both a highly developed literary style and a remarkable ability to set out difficult ideas. He is also noted for his call for American intellectual independence from Europe in his 1837 Phi Beta Kappa address at Harvard, entitled "The American Scholar."

> The scholar is that man who must take up into himself all the ability of the time, all the contributions of the past, all the hopes of the future. He must be an university of knowledges. If there be one lesson more than another, which should pierce his ear, it is, The world is nothing, the man is all; in yourself is the law of all nature, and you know not yet how a globule of sap ascends; in yourself slumbers the whole of Reason; it is for you to know all, it is for you to dare all. Mr. President and Gentlemen, this confidence in the unsearched might of man belongs, by all motives, by all prophecy, by all preparation, to the American Scholar. We have listened too long to the courtly muses of Europe.

Text: *Nature*

The passage selected for discussion is taken from the 1836 essay *Nature*. This small book took the form of a ninety-page essay. Sales were not good; it would take twelve years to sell the first five hundred copies. In contrast, his address of July 15, 1838 to the graduating class of the Harvard Divinity School sold three hundred copies within weeks of its printing. *Nature* is an immensely important and creative work of religious literature, not least on account of its fourth chapter, which is here reproduced. Emerson here deals with the role of language, and especially the relation between words and the reality which they seek to depict. The theme of the "mystical unity of all nature" is clearly affirmed within this section, allowing Emerson to posit that "every natural fact is a state of some spiritual fact."

A third use which nature subserves to man is that of Language. Nature is the vehicle of thought, and in a simple, double, and threefold degree.

1   Words are signs of natural facts.
2   Particular natural facts are symbols of particular facts.
3   Nature is the symbol of spirits.

    1   Words are signs of natural facts. The use of natural history is to give us aid in supernatural history. The use of the outer creation is to give us language for the beings and changes of the inward creation. Every word which is used to express a moral or intellectual fact, if traced to its root, is found to be borrowed from some material appearance. *Right* originally means *straight*; *wrong* means *twisted*. *Spirit* primarily means *wind*; *transgression*, the crossing of a *line*; *supercilious*, the *raising of the eye-brow*. We say the *heart* to express emotion, the *head* to denote thought; and *thought* and *emotion* are, in their turn, words borrowed from sensible things, and now appropriated to spiritual nature. Most of the process by which this transformation is made, is hidden from us in the remote time when language was framed; but the same tendency may be daily observed in children. Children and savages use only

nouns or names of things, which they continually convert into verbs, and apply to analogous mental acts.

2   But this origin of all words that convey a spiritual import – so conspicuous a fact in the history of language – is our least debt to nature. It is not words only that are emblematic; it is things which are emblematic. Every natural fact is a symbol of some spiritual fact. Every appearance in nature corresponds to some state of the mind, and that state of the mind can only be described by presenting that natural appearance as its picture. An enraged man is a lion, a cunning man is a fox, a firm man is a rock, a learned man is a torch. A lamb is innocence; a snake is subtle spite; flowers express to us the delicate affections. Light and darkness are our familiar expression for knowledge and ignorance; and heat for love. Visible distance behind and before us, is respectively our image of memory and hope.

Who looks upon a river in a meditative hour, and is not reminded of the flux of all things? Throw a stone into the stream, and the circles that propagate themselves are the beautiful type of all influence. Man is conscious of a universal soul within or behind his individual life, wherein, as in a firmament, the natures of Justice, Truth, Love, Freedom, arise and shine. This universal soul, he calls Reason: it is not mine or thine or his, but we are its; we are its property and men. And the blue sky in which the private earth is buried, the sky with its eternal calm, and full of everlasting orbs, is the type of Reason. That which, intellectually considered, we call Reason, considered in relation to nature, we call Spirit. Spirit is the Creator. Spirit hath life in itself. And man in all ages and countries, embodies it in his language, as the FATHER.

It is easily seen that there is nothing lucky or capricious in these analogies, but that they are constant, and pervade nature. These are not the dreams of a few poets, here and there, but man is an analogist, and studies relations in all objects. He is placed in the center of beings, and a ray of relation passes from every other being to him. And neither can man be understood without these objects, nor these objects without man. All the facts in natural history taken by themselves, have no value, but are barren like a single sex. But marry it to human history, and it is full of life. Whole Floras, all Linnæus' and Buffon's volumes, are but dry catalogs of facts; but the most trivial of these facts, the habit of a plant, the organs, or work, or noise of an insect, applied to the illustration of a fact in intellectual philosophy, or, in any way associated to human nature, affects us in the most lively and agreeable manner. The seed of a plant – to what affecting analogies in the nature of man, is that little fruit made use of, in all discourse, up to the voice of Paul, who calls the human corpse a seed – "It is sown a natural body; it is raised a spiritual body." The motion of the earth round its axis, and round the sun, makes the day, and the year. These are certain amounts of brute light and heat. But is there no intent of an analogy between man's life and the seasons? And do the seasons gain no grandeur or pathos from that analogy? The instincts of the ant are very unimportant considered as the ant's; but the moment a ray of relation is seen to extend from it to man, and the little drudge is seen to be a monitor, a little body with a mighty heart, then all its habits, even that said to be recently observed, that it never sleeps, become sublime.

Because of this radical correspondence between visible things and human thoughts, savages, who have only what is necessary, converse in figures. As we go back in history, language becomes more picturesque, until its infancy, when it is all poetry; or, all spiritual facts are represented by natural symbols. The same symbols are found to make the original elements of all languages. It has moreover been observed, that the idioms of all languages approach each other in passages of the greatest eloquence and power. And as this is the first language, so is it the last. This immediate dependence of language upon nature, this conversion of an outward phenomenon into a type of somewhat in human life, never loses its power to affect us. It is this which gives that piquancy to the conversation of a strong-natured farmer or back-woodsman, which all men relish.

Thus is nature an interpreter, by whose means man converses with his fellow men. A man's power to connect his thought with its proper symbol, and so utter it, depends on the simplicity of this character, that is, upon his love of truth and his desire to communicate it without loss. The corruption of man is followed by the corruption of language. When simplicity of character and the sovereignty of ideas is broken up by the prevalence of secondary desires, the desire of riches, the desire of pleasure, the desire of power, the desire of praise – and duplicity and falsehood take place of simplicity and truth, the power over nature as an interpreter of the will, is in a degree lost; new imagery ceases to be created, and old words are perverted to stand for things which are not; a paper currency is employed when there is no bullion in the vaults. In due time, the fraud is manifest, and words lose all power to stimulate the understanding or the affections. Hundreds of writers may be found in every long-civilized nation, who for a short time believe, and make others believe, that they see and utter truths, who do not of themselves clothe one thought in its natural garment, but who feed unconsciously upon the language created by the primary writers of the country, those, namely, who hold primarily on nature.

But wise men pierce this rotten diction and fasten words again to visible things; so that picturesque language is at once a commanding certificate that he who employs it, is a man in alliance with truth and God. The moment our discourse rises above the ground line of familiar facts, and is inflamed with passion or exalted by thought, it clothes itself in images. A man conversing in earnest, if he watches his intellectual processes, will find that always a material image, more or less luminous, arises in his mind, contemporaneous with every thought, which furnishes the vestment of the thought. Hence, good writing and brilliant discourse are perpetual allegories. This imagery is spontaneous. It is the blending of experience with the present action of the mind. It is proper creation. It is the working of the Original Cause through the instruments he has already made.

These facts may suggest the advantage which the country-life possesses for a powerful mind, over the artificial and curtailed life of cities. We know more from nature than we can at will communicate. Its light flows into the mind evermore, and we forget its presence. The poet, the orator, bred in the woods, whose senses have been nourished by their fair and appeasing changes, year after year, without design and without heed – shall not lose their lesson altogether, in the roar of cities or the broil of politics. Long hereafter, amidst agitation and terror in national councils – in the hour of revolution – these solemn images shall reappear in their morning lustre, as fit symbols and words of the thoughts which the passing events shall awaken. At the call of a noble sentiment, again the woods wave, the pines murmur, the river rolls and shines, and the cattle low upon the mountains, as he saw and heard them in his infancy. And with these forms, the spells of persuasion, the keys of power are put into his hands.

3   We are thus assisted by natural objects in the expression of particular meanings. But how great a language to convey such peppercorn informations! Did it need such noble races of creatures, this profusion of forms, this host of orbs in heaven, to furnish man with the dictionary and grammar of his municipal speech? Whilst we use this grand cipher to expedite the affairs of our pot and kettle, we feel that we have not yet put it to its use, neither are able. We are like travelers using the cinders of a volcano to roast their eggs. Whilst we see that it always stands ready to clothe what we would say, we cannot avoid the question, whether the characters are not significant of themselves. Have mountains, and waves, and skies, no significance but what we consciously give them, when we employ them as emblems of our thoughts? The world is emblematic. Parts of speech are metaphors because the whole of nature is a metaphor of the human mind. The laws of moral nature answer to those of matter as face to face in a glass. "The visible world and the relation of its parts, is the dial plate of the invisible." The axioms of physics translate the laws of ethics. Thus, "the whole is greater than its part"; "reaction is equal to action"; "the smallest weight may be made to lift the greatest, the difference of weight being compensated by time"; and many the like propositions, which have an ethical as well as physical sense. These propositions have a much more extensive and universal sense when applied to human life, than when confined to technical use.

In like manner, the memorable words of history, and the proverbs of nations, consist usually of a natural fact, selected as a picture or parable of a moral truth. Thus: A rolling stone gathers no moss; A bird in the hand is worth two in the bush; A cripple in the right way, will beat a racer in the wrong; Make hay whilst the sun shines; 'Tis hard to carry a full cup even; Vinegar is the son of wine; The last ounce broke the camel's back; Long-lived trees make roots first – and the like. In their primary sense these are trivial facts, but we repeat them for the value of their analogical import. What is true of proverbs, is true of all fables, parables, and allegories.

This relation between the mind and matter is not fancied by some poet, but stands in the will of God, and so is free to be known by all men. It appears to men, or it does not appear. When in fortunate hours we ponder this miracle, the wise man doubts, if, at all other times, he is not blind and deaf;

> ———— "Can these things be,
> And overcome us like a summer's cloud,
> Without our special wonder?"

for the universe becomes transparent, and the light of higher laws than its own, shines through it. It is the standing problem which has exercised the wonder and the study of every fine genius since the world began; from the era of the Egyptians and the Brahmins, to that of Pythagoras, of Plato, of Bacon, of Leibnitz, of Swedenborg. There sits the Sphinx at the roadside, and from age to age, as each prophet comes by, he tries his fortune at reading her riddle. There seems to be a necessity in spirit to manifest itself in material forms; and day and night, river and storm, beast and bird, acid and alkali, preexist in necessary Ideas in the mind of God, and are what they are by virtue of preceding affections, in the world of spirit. A Fact is the end or last issue of spirit. The visible creation is the terminus or the circumference of the invisible world. "Material objects," said a French philosopher, "are necessarily kinds of *scoriæ* of the substantial thoughts of the Creator, which must always preserve an exact relation to their first origin; in other words, visible nature must have a spiritual and moral side."

This doctrine is abstruse, and though the images of "garment," "scoriæ," "mirror," etc., may stimulate the fancy, we must summon the aid of subtler and more vital expositors to make it plain. "Every Scripture is to be interpreted by the same spirit which gave it forth" – is the fundamental law of criticism. A life in harmony with nature, the love of truth and of virtue, will purge the eyes to understand her text. By degrees we may come to know the primitive sense of the permanent objects of nature, so that the world shall be to us an open book, and every form significant of its hidden life and final cause.

A new interest surprises us, whilst, under the view now suggested, we contemplate the fearful extent and multitude of objects; since "every object rightly seen, unlocks a new faculty of the soul." That which was unconscious truth, becomes, when interpreted and defined in an object, a part of the domain of knowledge – a new amount to the magazine of power.

Questions for Study

1   At what points does Emerson argue for a direct relation between the natural and spiritual worlds? What does he consider to be the basis of this relation?
2   "There is nothing lucky or capricious in these analogies . . . they are constants, and pervade nature." What does Emerson mean by this? Identify the analogies which underlie these comments. How does he develop them?
3   "The world is emblematic." What does Emerson mean by this? And how does he illustrate this point?
4   In what ways can the Christian doctrine of creation be seen as undergirding Emerson's approach to language and nature? Emerson cites no biblical passages directly, yet it is clear that several are alluded to. What might they be?
5   Emerson notes a number of writers to whom he acknowledges a debt. Identify them; if you have access to an encyclopedia, look up two of them in particular – Francis Bacon and Emanuel Swedenborg. What sort of influence might they have had on Emerson?

CHAPTER 74

Anthony Trollope (1815–1882)

Anthony Trollope was born on April 24, 1815 in London, the fourth of six surviving children of Thomas Anthony Trollope, a barrister. As Trollope relates in his *Autobiography* (1883), poverty and debt made his childhood acutely unhappy and disrupted his education. An expected inheritance failed to materialize, and the family's fortunes went from bad to worse. His school fees at Harrow and Winchester were frequently unpaid, and his attempts to gain scholarships met with complete failure. His family attempted to restore their fortunes by going to America, leaving the young Anthony alone in England but it was not until his mother, Frances, began to write that there was any improvement in their financial situation. Her first work, *Domestic Manners of the Americans*, was published in 1832. In any case, her success came too late for her husband, who died in exile in the Belgian city of Bruges in 1835.

As a result of the family situation, Trollope was unable to afford a university education and in 1834 he became a junior clerk in the General Post Office in London. After seven years of relentless poverty, he was appointed Surveyor's Clerk in Banagher, Ireland in 1841. Here he worked hard, traveled widely, took up hunting and still found time for his literary career. He married Rose Heseltine, the daughter of a Rotherham bank manager, in 1844; they had two sons, one of whom emigrated to Australia. Trollope frequently went abroad on Post Office business, and did not make his home in England again until 1859. Perhaps his greatest achievement during his time with the General Post Office was the invention of the letter-box, still widely used today.

Trollope's literary career began in 1847, with the publication of *The Macdermots of Ballycloran*. This novel and its successor, *The Kellys and the O'Kellys* (1848), drew on his experience of Ireland, and sought to explore the grounds of Irish discontent over British rule. A period spent working in the west of England on Post Office business (1851–3) allowed him to gain the experience of everyday life in mid-Victorian country towns, which is so essential a feature of many of his novels. In 1867 he resigned from the Post Office and became the editor of *St Paul's Magazine* for the next three years. His attempt to enter Parliament as a Liberal in 1868 came to nothing. Instead, Trollope took his place among London literary society and counted Thackeray, George Eliot, and G. H. Lewes among his friends. He died on December 6, 1882 as the result of a stroke.

Antony Trollope (1815–1882)

Basic description
English novelist and chronicler of mid-Victorian clerical life.

Major work
The Chronicles of Barsetshire (1855–67).

Editions of works
The Chronicles of Barsetshire, 6 vols. London: Folio Society, 1976.

Major studies
Victoria Glendinning, Trollope. London: Hutchinson, 1992.
Richard Mullen, The Penguin Guide to Trollope. London: Penguin Books, 1996.

Anthony Trollope wrote forty-seven novels and five volumes of short stories as well as travel books, biographies, and collections of sketches. The Chronicles of Barsetshire and the six Palliser novels were the first novel-sequences to be written in English. His works offer an unsurpassed portrait of the professional and landed classes of Victorian England. In his Autobiography (published posthumously in 1883) Trollope describes the self-discipline that enabled his prolific output: he would produce a given number of words per hour in the early morning, before work; he always wrote while traveling by rail or sea and as soon as he finished one novel, he began another. His efforts resulted in him becoming one of England's most successful and popular writers. Yet after his death, Trollope's literary reputation sank substantially, not least on account of precisely the revelation in his Autobiography that we have just noted. He was seen to have treated literature as a trade – the ultimate sin in a highly class-conscious age – and wrote "by the clock."

Yet with the passing of time, Trollope's reputation has regained its former glory. He is widely admired as the chronicler of the ordinary life of upper middle-class England (and especially clerical England) of his time. Though there is a good deal of implied satire concerning the worldliness of the clergy of the Church of England, the burning social indignation of someone such as Charles Dickens is conspicuously absent. He has been described as the "chronicler of storms in teacups," and perhaps he is at his shrewdest in his minute observation of the social aspects of preferment within the Church of England in the mid-Victorian era. The set of works which shows him at his best in this respect is the six-volume Chronicles of Barsetshire, as follows:

The Warden (1855)
Barchester Towers (1857)
Dr. Thorne (1858)
Framley Parsonage (1861)
The Small House at Allington (1864)
The Last Chronicle of Barset (1867)

Some small controversy has raged over the identity of the cathedral city upon which Barchester is based; while Salisbury has its defenders, it seems that Trollope based his town and diocese on Winchester, while the details of the countryside appear to correspond to the English county of Somerset, which Trollope came to know during his 1851 postal business.

Text: *Barchester Towers*

Our extract is taken from *Barchester Towers* (1857), the second of Trollope's *Chronicles of Barsetshire*. Trollope wrote enthusiastically of this novel in his *Autobiography*: "In the writing of *Barchester Towers* I took great delight. The Bishop and Mrs Proudie were very real to me, as were also the troubles of the archdeacon and the loves of Mr Slope . . . it was one of the novels which novel readers were called upon to read." Others shared that enthusiasm. One contemporary review wrote: "*The Warden* was a remarkable book; *Barchester Towers* is still more remarkable" while another saw it as "the cleverest novel of the season."

The extract concerns Mr Slope, the personal chaplain of the newly-appointed Bishop of Barchester, who cannot help but feel that his patron's new appointment might not be without consequence for his own preferment within the church. So this most odious clerical literary creation begins to plot his ascent within the hierarchy, into which he slowly draws both Bishop and Mrs Proudie – the latter, by the way, being one of Trollope's most brilliant of creations.

Chapter 4

The Bishop's Chaplain

Of the Rev. Mr Slope's parentage I am not able to say much. I have heard it asserted that he is lineally descended from that eminent physician who assisted at the birth of Mr T. Shandy, and that in early years he added an 'e' to his name, for the sake of euphony, as other great men have done before him. If this be so, I presume he was christened Obadiah, for that is his name, in commemoration of the conflict in which his ancestor so distinguished himself. All my researches on the subject have, however, failed in enabling me to fix the date on which the family changed its religion.

He had been a sizar at Cambridge, and had there conducted himself at any rate successfully, for in due process of time he was an M.A., having university pupils under his care. From thence he was transferred to London, and became preacher at a new district church built on the confines of Baker Street. He was in this position when congenial ideas on religious subjects recommended him to Mrs Proudie, and the intercourse had become close and confidential.

Having been thus familiarly thrown among the Misses Proudie, it was no more than natural that some softer feeling than friendship should be engendered. There have been some passages of love between him and the eldest hope, Olivia; but they have hitherto resulted in no favourable arrangement. In truth, Mr Slope, having made a declaration of affection, afterwards withdrew it on finding that the doctor had no immediate worldly funds with which to endow his child; and it may easily be conceived that Miss Proudie, after such an announcement on his part, was not readily disposed to receive any further show of affection. On the appointment of Dr Proudie to the bishopric of Barchester, Mr Slope's views were in truth somewhat altered. Bishops, even though they be poor, can provide for clerical children, and Mr Slope began to regret that he had not been more disinterested. He no sooner heard the tidings of the doctor's elevation, than he recommenced his siege, not violently, indeed, but respectfully, and at a distance. Olivia Proudie, however, was a girl of spirit: she had the blood of two peers in her veins, and, better still, she had another lover on her books; so Mr Slope sighed in vain; and the pair soon found it convenient to establish a mutual bond of inveterate hatred.

It may be thought singular that Mrs Proudie's friendship for the young clergyman should remain firm after such an affair; but, to tell the truth, she had known nothing of it. Though very fond of Mr Slope herself, she had never conceived the idea that either of her daughters would become so, and remembering their high birth and social advantages, expected for them matches of a different sort. Neither the gentleman nor the lady found it necessary to enlighten her. Olivia's two sisters had each known of the affair, so had all the servants, so had all the people living in the adjoining houses on either side; but Mrs Proudie had been kept in the dark.

Mr Slope soon comforted himself with the reflection that, as he had been selected as chaplain to the bishop, it would probably be in his power to get the good things in the bishop's gift, without troubling himself with the bishop's daughter; and he found himself able to endure the pangs of rejected love. As he sat himself down in the railway carriage, confronting the bishop and Mrs Proudie as they started on their first journey to Barchester, he began to form in his own mind a plan of his future life. He knew well his patron's strong points, but he knew the weak ones as well. He understood correctly enough to what attempts the new bishop's high spirit would soar, and he rightly guessed that public life would better suit the great man's taste, than the small details of diocesan duty.

He, therefore, he, Mr Slope, would in effect be Bishop of Barchester. Such was his resolve; and, to give Mr Slope his due, he had both courage and spirit to bear him out in his resolution. He knew that he should have a hard battle to fight, for the power and patronage of the see would be equally coveted by another great mind – Mrs Proudie would also choose to be Bishop of Barchester. Mr Slope, however, flattered himself that he could out-manoeuvre the lady. She must live much in London, while he would always be on the spot. She would necessarily remain ignorant of much, while he would know everything belonging to the diocese. At first, doubtless, he must flatter and cajole, perhaps yield, in some things; but he did not doubt of ultimate triumph. If all other means failed, he could join the bishop against his wife; inspire courage into the unhappy man, lay an axe at the root of the woman's power, and emancipate the husband.

Such were his thoughts as he sat looking at the sleeping pair in the railway carriage, and Mr Slope is not the man to trouble himself with such thoughts for nothing. He is possessed of more than average abilities, and is of good courage. Though he can stoop to fawn, and stoop low indeed, if need be, he has still within him the power to assume the tyrant; and with the power he has certainly the wish. His acquirements are not of the highest order, but such as they are they are completely under control, and he knows the use of them. He is gifted with a certain kind of pulpit eloquence, not likely indeed to be persuasive with men, but powerful with the softer sex. In his sermons he deals greatly in denunciations, excites the minds of his weaker hearers with a not unpleasant terror, and leaves an impression on their minds that all mankind are in a perilous state, and all womankind too, except those who attend regularly to the evening lectures in Baker Street. His looks and tones are extremely severe, so much so that one cannot but fancy that he regards the greater part of the world as being infinitely too bad for his care. As he walks through the streets, his very face denotes his horror of the world's wickedness; and there is always an anathema lurking in the corner of his eye.

In doctrine, he, like his patron, is tolerant of dissent, if so strict a mind can be called tolerant of anything. With Wesleyan-Methodists he has something in common, but his soul trembles in agony at the iniquities of the Puseyites. His aversion is carried to things outward as well as inward. His gall rises at a new church with a high-pitched roof; a full-breasted black silk waistcoat is with him a symbol of Satan; and a profane jest-book would not, in his view, more foully desecrate the church seat of a Christian, than a book of prayer printed with red letters and ornamented with a cross on the back. Most active clergymen have their hobby, and Sunday observances are his. Sunday, however, is a word which never pollutes his mouth – it is always 'the Sabbath'. The 'desecration of the Sabbath', as he delights to call it, is to him meat and drink: he thrives upon that as policemen do on the general evil habits of the community. It is the loved subject of all his evening discourses, the source of all his eloquence, the secret of all his power over the female heart. To him the revelation of God appears only in that one law given for Jewish observance. To him the mercies of our Saviour speak in vain, to him in vain has been preached that sermon which fell from divine lips on the mountain – 'Blessed are the meek, for they shall inherit the earth' – 'Blessed are the merciful, for they shall obtain mercy'. To him the New Testament is comparatively of little moment, for from it can he draw no fresh authority for that dominion which he loves to exercise over at least a seventh part of man's allotted time here below.

Mr Slope is tall, and not ill-made. His feet and hands are large, as has ever been the case with all his family, but he has a broad chest and wide shoulders to carry off these excrescences, and on the whole his figure is good. His countenance, however, is not specially prepossessing. His hair is lank, and of a dull, pale, reddish hue. It is always formed into three straight lumpy masses, each brushed with admirable precision, and cemented with much grease; two of them adhere closely to the sides of his face, and the other lies at right angles above them. He wears no whiskers, and is always punctiliously shaven. His face is nearly of the same colour as his hair, though perhaps a little redder: it is not unlike beef – beef, however, one would say, of a bad quality. His forehead is capacious and high, but square and heavy, and unpleasantly shining. His mouth is large, though his lips are thin and bloodless; and his big, prominent, pale brown eyes inspire anything but confidence. His nose, however, is his redeeming feature: it is pronounced straight and well-formed; though I myself should have liked it better did it not possess a somewhat spongy, porous appearance, as though it had been cleverly formed out of a red-coloured cork.

I never could endure to shake hands with Mr Slope. A cold, clammy perspiration always exudes from him, the small drops are ever to be seen standing on his brow, and his friendly grasp is unpleasant.

Such is Mr Slope – such is the man who has suddenly fallen into the midst of Barchester Close, and is destined there to assume the station which has heretofore been filled by the son of the late bishop. Think, oh, my meditative reader, what an associate we have here for those comfortable prebendaries, those gentlemanlike clerical doctors, those happy, well-used, well-fed minor canons, who have grown into existence at Barchester under the kindly wings of Bishop Grantly!

But not as a mere associate for these does Mr Slope travel down to Barchester with the bishop and his wife. He intends to be, if not their master, at least the chief among them. He intends to lead, and to have followers; he intends to hold the purse strings of the diocese, and draw round him an obedient herd of his poor and hungry brethren.

And here we can hardly fail to draw a comparison between the archdeacon and our new private chaplain; and despite the manifold faults of the former, one can hardly fail to make it much to his advantage.

Both men are eager, much too eager, to support and increase the power of their order. Both are anxious that the world should be priest-governed, though they have probably never confessed so much, even to themselves. Both begrudge any other kind of dominion held by man over man. Dr Grantly, if he admits the Queen's supremacy in things spiritual, only admits it as being due to the quasi-priesthood conveyed in the consecrating qualities of her coronation; and he regards things temporal as being by their nature subject to those which are spiritual. Mr Slope's ideas of sacerdotal rule are of quite a different class. He cares nothing, one way or the other, for the Queen's supremacy; these to his ears are empty words, meaning nothing. Forms he regards but little, and such titular expressions as supremacy, consecration, ordination, and the like, convey of themselves no significance to him. Let him be supreme who can. The temporal king, judge, or gaoler, can work but on the body. The spiritual master, if he have the necessary gifts and can duly use them, has a wider field of empire. He works upon the soul. If he can make himself be believed, he can be all-powerful over those who listen. If he be careful to meddle with none who are too strong in intellect, or too weak in flesh, he may indeed be supreme. And such was the ambition of Mr Slope.

Dr Grantly interfered very little with the worldly doings of those who were in any way subject to him. I do not mean to say that he omitted to notice misconduct among his clergy, immorality in his parish, or omissions in his family; but he was not anxious to do so where the necessity could be avoided. He was not troubled with a propensity to be curious, and as long as those around him were tainted with no heretical leaning towards dissent, as long as they fully and freely admitted the efficacy of Mother Church, he was willing that that mother should be merciful and affectionate, prone to indulgence, and unwilling to chastise. He himself enjoyed the good things of this world, and liked to let it be known that he did so. He cordially despised any brother rector who thought harm of dinner-parties, or dreaded the dangers of a moderate claret-jug; consequently dinner-parties and claret-jugs were common in the diocese. He liked to give laws and to be obeyed in them implicitly, but he endeavoured that his ordinances should be within the compass of the man, and not unpalatable to the gentleman. He had ruled among his clerical neighbours now for sundry years, and as he had maintained his power without becoming unpopular, it may be presumed that he had exercised some wisdom.

Of Mr Slope's conduct much cannot be said, as his grand career is yet to commence; but it may be premised that his tastes will be very different from those of the archdeacon. He conceives it to be his duty to know all the private doings and desires of the flock entrusted to his care. From the poorer classes he exacts an unconditional obedience to set rules of conduct, and if disobeyed he has recourse, like his great ancestor, to the fulminations of an Ernulfus: 'Thou shalt be damned in thy going in and in thy coming out – in thy eating and thy drinking,' etc. etc. etc. With the rich, experience has already taught him that a different line of action is necessary. Men in the upper walks of life do not mind being cursed, and the women, presuming that it be done in delicate phrase, rather like it. But he has not, therefore, given up so important a portion of believing Christians. With the men, indeed, he is generally at variance; they are hardened sinners, on whom the voice of the priestly charmer too often falls in vain; but with the ladies, old and young, firm and frail, devout and dissipated, he is, as he conceives, all-powerful. He can reprove faults with so much flattery, and utter censure in so caressing a manner, that the female heart, if it glow with a spark of low church susceptibility, cannot withstand him. In many houses he is thus an admired guest: the husbands, for their wives' sake, are fain to admit him; and when once admitted it is not easy to shake him off. He has, however, a pawing, greasy way with him, which does not endear him to those who do not value him for their souls' sake, and he is not a man to make himself at once popular in a large circle such as is now likely to surround him at Barchester.

Questions for Discussion

1 What would you judge Trollope's attitude to Slope to be? Does he approve of his creation? If not, what verbal clues are we offered to allow us to infer that he dislikes Slope?

2 Are there any clues in the passage concerning the theological or ecclesiastical views for which either Mr Slope or Bishop Proudie are noted?

3 Trollope compares the regime at Barchester under Bishop Proudie somewhat unfavourably with that which preceded it, under Bishop Grantly. What changes does he particularly dislike?

CHAPTER 75

Benjamin Jowett (1817–1893)

Jowett was one of the most important figures in the history of the University of Oxford during the nineteenth century. He became Master of Balliol College in 1870, and famously set out to "innoculate England with Balliol." Under his Mastership, Balliol secured a position of pre-eminence within the University of Oxford, and exercised an influence over English cultural life out of all proportion to its size. Jowett was originally elected a Fellow of Balliol while still an undergraduate. He went on to take first-class honors in *Literae Humaniores*, winning the Chancellor's Prize for a Latin Essay. He became involved in the movement for university reform, but he remained a dedicated tutor, a stimulating lecturer, and conscientious student of Philosophy and Theology. In 1854 he was a candidate for the mastership of Balliol in succession to Richard Jenkyns, but Robert Scott (1811–87), the lexicographer, was chosen instead.

Benjamin Jowett (1817–1893)

Basic description
English Classics scholar and educationalist, of major importance to the history of Oxford University in the nineteenth century.

Major works
Commentaries on the Epistles of St Paul (1855); "The Interpretation of Scripture" (1860).

Editions of works
Evelyn Abbott and Lewis Campbell, *The Life and Letters of Benjamin Jowett*, 2 vols. London: John Murray, 1897.

Major studies
Ieuan Ellis, *Seven against Christ: A Study of "Essays and Reviews."* Leiden: Brill, 1980.
Peter Hinchliff, *Benjamin Jowett and the Christian Religion*. Oxford: Clarendon Press, 1987.

In 1855, Jowett found himself embroiled in controversy over his religious views, as set out in his *Commentaries on the Epistles of St Paul*. The two volumes of these commentaries, which focused on the letters to the Thessalonians, Galatians and Romans, attracted critical attention on account of Jowett's views on the significance of the death of Christ. For Jowett, Christ's relevance to the individual was personal and subjective. This went counter to the predominantly objective approaches to the doctrine of the Atonement of the period. Although Jowett reworked this material for the second edition of the work (1859), he did not materially alter his views on this matter. Despite vigorous opposition to his candidacy, he was appointed Regius Professor of Greek at Oxford University in succession to Thomas Gaisford. Finally, in 1870, he was elected Master of Balliol. Having published his *Dialogues of Plato* in four volumes in 1871, he was elected Vice-Chancellor of Oxford University in 1882.

Text: The Interpretation of Scripture

Jowett was of major importance to the shifting religious situation in Victorian England on account of a substantial essay which he contributed on the subject of "The Interpretation of Scripture" to a collection entitled *Essays and Reviews* (1860). The seven contributors to this collection were all committed to the idea of freedom of inquiry in matters of religion, and adopted generally critical ideas to the religious orthodoxy of the mid-Victorian period. The work initially attracted little attention until it was vigorously criticized by Bishop Samuel Wilberforce. Thereafter, it was vigorously condemned by senior church figures and leading ecclesiastical authorities. In effect, the work became a symbol of a growing climate of revolt against traditional Christian ways of thinking, reflected, for example, in Matthew Arnold's poem "Dover Beach."

Jowett's essay was the final item in the collection, and the most substantial. Although it could be argued that the essay does little more than develop the ideas already set out in his Pauline commentaries of a few years earlier, the essay was written in a particularly lucid and persuasive manner. The essay merits inclusion in this collection as a piece of literature, and for its subsequent major influence on English religious writing. Its fundamental theme can be summarized in its assertion that "[Scripture] is to be interpreted like other books, with attention to the character of its authors, and the prevailing state of civilization and knowledge." It remains a landmark in English religious thought and writing, and can be read today without the need for detailed comment.

As the time has come when it is no longer possible to ignore the results of criticism, it is of importance that Christianity should be seen to be in harmony with them. That objections to some received views should be valid, and yet that they should be always held up as the objections of infidels, is a mischief to the Christian cause. It is a mischief that critical observations which any intelligent man can make for himself, should be ascribed to atheism or unbelief. It would be a strange and almost incredible thing that the Gospel, which at first made war only on the vices of mankind, should now be opposed to one of the highest and rarest of human virtues – the love of truth. And that in the present day the great object of Christianity should be, not to change the lives of men, but to prevent them from changing their opinions; that would be a singular inversion of the purposes for which Christ came into the world. The

Christian religion is in a false position when all the tendencies of knowledge are opposed to it. Such a position cannot be long maintained, or can only end in the withdrawal of the educated classes from the influences of religion. It is a grave consideration whether we ourselves may not be in an earlier stage of the same religious dissolution, which seems to have gone further in Italy and France. The reason for thinking so is not to be sought in the external circumstances of our own or any other religious communion, but in the progress of ideas with which Christian teachers seem to be ill at ease. Time was when the Gospel was before the age; when it breathed a new life into a decaying world – when the difficulties of Christianity were difficulties of the heart only, and the highest minds found in its truths not only the rule of their lives, but a well-spring of intellectual delight. Is it to be held a thing impossible that the Christian religion, instead of shrinking into itself, may again embrace the thoughts of men upon the earth? Or is it true that since the Reformation 'all intellect has gone the other way?' and that in Protestant countries reconciliation is as hopeless as Protestants commonly believe to be the case in Catholic.

Those who hold the possibility of such a reconcilement or restoration of belief, are anxious to disengage Christianity from all suspicion of disguise or unfairness. They wish to preserve the historical use of Scripture as the continuous witness in all ages of the higher things in the heart of man, as the inspired source of truth and the way to the better life. They are willing to take away some of the external supports, because they are not needed and do harm; also, because they interfere with the meaning. They have a faith, not that after a period of transition all things will remain just as they were before, but that they will all come round again to the use of man and to the glory of God. When interpreted like any other book, by the same rules of evidence and the same canons of criticism, the Bible will still remain unlike any other book; its beauty will be freshly seen, as of a picture which is restored after many ages to its original state; it will create a new interest and make for itself a new kind of authority by the life which is in it. It will be a spirit and not a letter; as it was in the beginning, having an influence like that of the spoken word, or the book newly found. The purer the light in the human heart, the more it will have an expression of itself in the mind of Christ; the greater the knowledge of the development of man, the truer will be the insight gained into the 'increasing purpose' of revelation. In which also the individual soul has a practical part, finding a sympathy with its own imperfect feelings, in the broken utterance of the Psalmist or the Prophet as well as in the fullness of Christ. The harmony between Scripture and the life of man, in all its stages, may be far greater than appears at present. No one can form any notion from what we see around us, of the power which Christianity might have if it were at one with the conscience of man, and not at variance with his intellectual convictions. There, a world weary of the heat and dust of controversy – of speculations about God and man – weary too of the rapidity of its own motion, would return home and find rest.

But for the faith that the Gospel might win again the minds of intellectual men, it would be better to leave religion to itself, instead of attempting to draw them together. Other walks in literature have peace and pleasure and profit; the path of the critical Interpreter of Scripture is almost always a thorny one in England. It is not worth while for any one to enter upon it who is not supported by a sense that he has a Christian and moral object. For although an Interpreter of Scripture in modern times will hardly say with the emphasis of the Apostle, 'Woe is me, if I speak not the truth without regard to consequences', yet he too may feel it a matter of duty not to conceal the things which he knows. He does not hide the discrepancies of Scripture, because the acknowledgement of them is the first step towards agreement among interpreters. He would restore the original meaning, because 'seven other' meanings take the place of it; the book is made the sport of opinion and the instrument of perversion of life. He would take the excuses of the head out of the way of the heart; their is hope too that by drawing Christians together on the ground of Scripture, he may also draw them nearer to one another. He is not afraid that inquiries, which have for their object the truth, can ever be displeasing to the God of truth; or that the Word of God is in any such sense a word as to be hurt by investigations into its human origin and conception.

It may be thought another ungracious aspect of the preceding remarks, that they cast a slight upon the interpreters of Scripture in former ages. The early Fathers, the Roman Catholic mystical writers, the Swiss and German Reformers, the Nonconformist divines, have qualities for which we look in vain among ourselves; they throw an intensity of light upon the page of Scripture which we nowhere find in modern commentaries. But it is not the light of interpretation. They have a faith which seems indeed to have grown dim nowadays, but that faith is not drawn from the study of Scripture; it is the element in which their own mind moves which overflows on the meaning of the text. The words of Scripture suggest to them their own thoughts or feelings. They are preachers, or in the New Testament sense of the word, prophets rather than interpreters. There is nothing in such a view derogatory to the saints and doctors of former ages. That Aquinas or Bernard did not shake themselves free from the mystical method of the Patristic times, or the Scholastic one which was more peculiarly their own; that Luther and Calvin read the Scriptures in connexion with the ideas which were kindling in the mind of their age, and the events which were passing before their eyes, these and similar remarks are not to be construed as depreciatory of the genius or learning of famous men of old; they relate only to their interpretation of Scripture, in which it is no slight upon them to maintain that they were not before their day.

What remains may be comprised in a few precepts, or rather is the expansion of a single one. *Interpret the Scripture like any other book.* There are many respects in which Scripture is unlike any other book; these will appear in the results of such an interpretation. The first step is to know the meaning, and this can only be done in the same careful and impartial way that we ascertain the meaning of Sophocles or of Plato. The subordinate principles which flow out of this general one will also be gathered from the observation of Scripture. No other science of Hermeneutics is possible but an inductive one, that is to say, one based on the language and thoughts and narrations of the sacred writers. And it would be well to carry the theory of interpretation no further than in the case of other works. Excessive system tends to create an impression that the meaning of Scripture is out of our reach, or is to be attained in some other way than by the exercise of manly sense and industry. Who would write a bulky treatise about the method to be pursued in interpreting Plato or Sophocles? Let us not set out on our journey so heavily equipped that there is little chance of our arriving at the end of it. The method creates itself as we go on, beginning only with a few reflexions directed against plain errors. Such reflexions are the rules of common sense, which we acknowledge with respect to other works written in dead languages: without pretending to novelty they may help us to 'return to nature' in the study of the sacred writings.

First, it may be laid down that Scripture has one meaning – the meaning which it had to the mind of the prophet or evangelist who first uttered or wrote, to the hearers or readers who first received it. Another view may be easier or more familiar to us, seeming to receive a light and interest from the circumstances of our own age. But such accommodation of the text must be laid aside by the interpreter, whose business is to place himself as nearly as possible in the position of the sacred writer. That is no easy task – to call up the inner and outer life of the contemporaries of our Saviour; to follow the abrupt and involved utterance of St Paul or one of the old Prophets; to trace the meaning of words when language first became Christian. He will often have to choose the more difficult interpretation (Gal. ii: 20; Rom. iii: 15, etc.), and to refuse one more in agreement with received opinions, because the latter is less true to the style and time of the author. He may incur the charge of singularity, or confusion of ideas, or ignorance of Greek, from a misunderstanding of the peculiarity of the subject in the person who makes the charge. For if it be said that the translation of some Greek words is contrary to the usages of grammar (Gal. iv: 13), that is not in every instance to be denied; the point is whether the usages of grammar are always observed. Or if it be objected to some interpretation of Scripture that it is difficult and perplexing, the answer is – 'that may very well be – it is the fact', arising out of differences in the modes of thought of other times, or irregularities in the use of language which no art of the interpreter can evade. One consideration should be borne in mind, that the Bible is the only book in the world written in different styles and at many different times, which is in the hands of persons of all degrees of knowledge and education. The benefit of this outweighs the evil, yet the evil should be admitted – namely, that it leads to a hasty and partial interpretation of Scripture, which often obscures the true one. A sort of conflict arises between scientific criticism and popular opinion. The indiscriminate use of Scripture has a further tendency to maintain erroneous readings or translations; some which are allowed to be such by scholars have been stereotyped in the mind of the English reader; and it becomes almost a political question how far we can venture to disturb them.

There are difficulties of another kind in many parts of Scripture, the depth and inwardness of which require a measure of the same qualities in the interpreter himself. There are notes struck in places, which like some discoveries of science have sounded before their time; and only after many days have been caught up and found a response on the earth. There are germs of truth which after thousands of years have never yet taken root in the world. There are lessons in the Prophets which, however simple, mankind have not yet learned even in theory; and which the complexity of society rather tends to hide; aspects of human life in Job and Ecclesiastes which have a truth of desolation about them which we faintly realize in ordinary circumstances. It is, perhaps, the greatest difficulty of all to enter into the meaning of the words of Christ – so gentle, so human, so divine, neither adding to them nor marring their simplicity. The attempt to illustrate or draw them out in detail, even to guard against their abuse, is apt to disturb the balance of truth. The interpreter needs nothing short of 'fashioning' in himself the image of the mind of Christ. He has to be born again into a new spiritual or intellectual world, from which the thoughts of this world are shut out. It is one of the highest tasks on which the labour of a life can be spent, to bring the words of Christ a little nearer the heart of man.

But while acknowledging this inexhaustible or infinite character of the sacred writings, it does not, therefore, follow that we are willing to admit of hidden or mysterious meanings in them (in the same way we recognize the wonders and complexity of the laws of nature to be far beyond what eye has seen or knowledge reached, yet it is not therefore to be supposed that we acknowledge the existence of some other laws different in kind from those we know which are incapable of philosophical analysis). In like manner we have no reason to attribute to the Prophet or Evangelist any second or hidden sense different from that which appears on the surface. All that the Prophet meant may not have been consciously present to his mind; there were depths which to himself also were but half revealed. He beheld the fortunes of Israel passing into the heavens; the temporal kingdom was fading into an eternal one. It is not to be supposed that what he saw at a distance only was clearly defined to him; or that the universal truth which was appearing and reappearing in the history of the surrounding world took a purely spiritual or abstract form in his mind. There is a sense in which we may still say with Lord Bacon, that the words of prophecy are to be interpreted as the words of one 'with whom a thousand years are as one day, and one day as a thousand years'. But that is no reason for turning days into years, or for interpreting the things 'that must shortly come to pass' in the book of Revelation, as the events of modern history, or for separating the day of judgement from the destruction of Jerusalem in the Gospels. The double meaning which is given to our Saviour's discourse respecting the last things is not that 'form of eternity' of which Lord Bacon speaks; it resembles rather the doubling of an object when seen through glasses placed at different angles. It is true also that there are types in Scripture which were regarded as such by the Jews themselves, as for example, the scapegoat, or the paschal lamb. But that is no proof of all outward ceremonies being types when Scripture is silent (if we assume the New Testament as a tradition running parallel with the Old, may not the Roman Catholic assume with equal reason a tradition running parallel with the New?). Prophetic symbols, again, have often the same meaning in different places (e.g. the four beasts or living creatures, the colours white or red); the reason is that this meaning is derived from some natural association (as of fruitfulness, purity, or the like); or again, they are borrowed in some of the later prophecies from earlier ones; we are not, therefore, justified in supposing any hidden connexion in the prophecies where they occur. Neither is there any ground for assuming design of any other kind in Scripture any more than in Plato or Homer. Wherever there is beauty and order, there is design; but there is no proof of any artificial design, such as is often traced by the Fathers, in the relation of the several parts of a book, or of the several books to each other. That is one of those mischievous notions which enables us, under the disguise of reverence, to make Scripture mean what we please. Nothing that can be said of the greatness or sublimity, or truth, or depth, or tenderness, of many passages, is too much. But that greatness is of a simple kind; it is not increased by double senses, or systems of types, or elaborate structure, or design. If every sentence was a mystery, every word a riddle, every letter a symbol, that would not make the Scriptures more worthy of a Divine author; it is a heathenish or Rabbinical fancy which reads them in this way. Such complexity would not place them above but below human compositions in general; for it would deprive them of the ordinary intelligibleness of human language. It is not for a Christian theologian to say that words were given to mankind to conceal their thoughts, neither was revelation given them to conceal the Divine.

The second rule is an application of the general principle; 'interpret Scripture from itself' as in other respects, like any other book written in an age and country of which little or no other literature survives, and about which we know almost nothing except what is derived from its pages. Not that all the parts of Scripture are to be regarded as an indistinguishable mass. The Old Testament is not to be identified with the New, nor the Law with the Prophets, nor the Gospels with the Epistles, nor the Epistles of St Paul to be violently harmonized with the Epistle of St James. Each writer, each successive age, has characteristics of its own, as strongly marked, or more strongly, than those which are found in the authors or periods of classical literature. These differences are not to be lost in the idea of a Spirit from whom they proceed or by which they were overruled. And therefore, illustration of one part of Scripture by another should be confined to writings of the same age and the same authors, except where the writings of different ages or persons offer obvious similarities. It may be said further that illustration should be chiefly derived, not only from the same author, but from the same writing, or from one of the same period of his life. For example, the comparison of St John and the 'synoptic' Gospels, or of the Gospel of St John with the Revelation of St John, will tend rather to confuse than to elucidate the meaning of either; while, on the other hand, the comparison of the Prophets with one another, and with the Psalms, offers many valuable helps and lights to the interpreter. Again, the connexion between the Epistles written by the Apostle St Paul about the same time (e.g. Romans, 1 and 2 Corinthians, Galatians – Colossians, Philippians, Ephesians – compared with Romans, Colossians – Ephesians, Galatians, etc.) is far closer than of Epistles which are separated by an interval of only a few years.

But supposing all this to be understood, and that by the interpretation of Scripture from itself is meant a real interpretation of like by like, it may be asked, what is it that we gain from a minute comparison of a particular author or writing? The indiscriminate use of parallel passages taken from one end of Scripture and applied to the other (except so far as earlier compositions may have afforded the material or the form of later ones) is useless and uncritical. The uneducated, or imperfectly educated person who looks out the marginal references of the English Bible, imagining himself in this way to gain a clearer insight into the Divine meaning, is really following the religious associations of his own mind. Even the critical use of parallel passages is not without danger. For are we to conclude that an author meant in one place what he says in another? Shall we venture to mend a corrupt phrase on the model of some other phrase, which memory, prevailing over judgement, calls up and thrusts into the text? It is this fallacy which has filled the pages of classical writers with useless and unfounded emendations.

The meaning of the Canon '*Non nisi ex Scriptura Scripturam potes interpretari*', is only this, 'That we cannot understand Scripture without becoming familiar with it.' Scripture is a world by itself, from which we must exclude foreign influences, whether theological or classical. To get inside that world is an effort of thought and imagination, requiring the sense of a poet as well as a critic – demanding much more than learning a degree of original power and intensity of mind. Any one who, instead of burying himself in the pages of the commentators, would learn the sacred writings by heart, and paraphrase them in English, will probably make a nearer approach to their true meaning than he would gather from any commentary. The intelligent mind will ask its own questions, and find for the most part its own answers. The true use of interpretation is to get rid of interpretation, and leave us alone in company with the author. When the meaning of Greek words is once known, the young student has almost all the real materials which are possessed by the greatest Biblical scholar, in the book itself. For almost our whole knowledge of the history of the Jews is derived from the Old Testament and the Apocryphal books, and almost our whole knowledge of the life of Christ and of the Apostolical age is derived from the New; whatever is added to them is either conjecture, or very slight topographical or chronological illustration. For this reason the rule given above, which is applicable to all books, is applicable to the New Testament more than any other.

Yet in this consideration of the separate books of Scripture it is not to be forgotten that they have also a sort of continuity. We make a separate study of the subject, the mode of thought, in some degree also of the language of each book. And at length the idea arises in our minds of a common literature, a pervading life, an overruling law. It may be compared to the effect of some natural scene in which we suddenly perceive a harmony or picture, or to the imperfect appearance of design which suggests itself in looking at the surface of the globe. That is to say, there is nothing miraculous or artificial in the arrangement of the books of Scripture; it is the result, not the design, which appears in them when bound in the same volume. Or if we like so to say, there *is* design, but a natural design which is revealed to after ages. Such continuity or design is best expressed under some notion of progress or growth, not regular, however, but with broken and imperfect stages, which the want of knowledge prevents our minutely defining. The great truth of the unity of God was there from the first; slowly as the morning broke in the heavens, like some central light, it filled and afterwards dispersed the mists of human passion in which it was itself enveloped. A change passes over the Jewish religion from fear to love, from power to wisdom, from the justice of God to the mercy of God, from the nation to the individual, from this world to another; from the visitation of the sins of the fathers upon the children, to 'every soul shall bear its own iniquity'; from the fire, the earthquake, and the storm, to the still small voice. There never was a time after the deliverance from Egypt, in which the Jewish people did not bear a kind of witness against the cruelty and licentiousness of the surrounding tribes. In the decline of the monarchy, as the kingdom itself was sinking under foreign conquerors, whether springing from contact with the outer world, or from some reaction within, the undergrowth of morality gathers strength; first, in the anticipation of prophecy, secondly, like a green plant in the hollow rind of Pharisaism – and individuals pray and commune with God each one for himself. At length the tree of life blossoms; the faith in immortality which had hitherto slumbered in the heart of man, intimated only in doubtful words (2 Sam. xii: 23; Ps. xvii. 15), or beaming for an instant in dark places (Job xix: 25), has become the prevailing belief.

There is an interval in the Jewish annals which we often exclude from our thoughts, because it has no record in the canonical writings – extending over about four hundred years, from the last of the prophets of the Old Testament to the forerunner of Christ in the New. This interval, about which we know so little, which is regarded by many as a portion of secular rather than of sacred history, was nevertheless as fruitful in religious changes as any similar period which preceded. The establishment of the Jewish sects, and the wars of the Maccabees, probably exercised as great an influence on Judaism as the captivity itself. A third influence was that of the Alexandrian literature, which was attracting the Jewish intellect, at the same time that the Galilean zealot was tearing the nation in pieces with the doctrine that it was lawful to call 'no man master but God'. In contrast with that wild fanaticism as well as with the proud Pharisee, came One most unlike all that had been before, as the kings or rulers of mankind. In an age which was the victim of its own passions, the creature of its own circumstances, the slave of its own degenerate religion, our Saviour taught a lesson absolutely free from all the influences of a surrounding world. He made the last perfect revelation of God to man; a revelation not indeed immediately applicable to the state of society or the world, but in its truth and purity inexhaustible by the after generations of men. And of the first application of the truth which he taught as a counsel of perfection to the actual circumstances of mankind, we have the example in the Epistles.

Such a general conception of growth or development in Scripture, beginning with the truth of the Unity of God in the earliest books and ending with the perfection of Christ, naturally springs up in our minds in the perusal of the sacred writings. It is a notion of value to the interpreter, for it enables him at the same time to grasp the whole and distinguish the parts. It saves him from the necessity of maintaining that the Old Testament is one and the same everywhere; that the books of Moses contain truths or precepts, such as the duty of prayer or the faith in immortality, or the spiritual interpretation of sacrifice, which no one has ever seen there. It leaves him room enough to admit all the facts of the case. No longer is he required to defend or to explain away David's imprecations against his enemies, or his injunctions to Solomon, any more than his sin in the matter of Uriah. Nor is he hampered with a theory of accommodation. Still the sense of 'the increasing purpose which through the ages ran' is present to him, nowhere else continuously discernible or ending in a divine perfection. Nowhere else is there found the same interpenetration of the political and religious element – a whole nation, 'though never good for much at any time,' possessed with the conviction that it was living in the face of God – in whom the Sun of righteousness shone upon the corruption of an Eastern nature – the 'fewest of all people', yet bearing the greatest part in the education of the world.

Nowhere else among the teachers and benefactors of mankind is there any form like His, in whom the desire of the nation is fulfilled, and 'not of that nation only', but of all mankind, whom He restores to His Father and their Father, to His God and their God.

Such a growth or development may be regarded as a kind of progress from childhood to manhood. In the child there is an anticipation of truth; his reason is latent in the form of feeling; many words are used by him which he imperfectly understands; he is led by temporal promises, believing that to be good is to be happy always; he is pleased by marvels and has vague terrors. He is confined to a spot of earth, and lives in a sort of prison of sense, yet is bursting also with a fullness of childish life: he imagines God to be like a human father, only greater and more awful; he is easily impressed with solemn thoughts, but soon 'rises up to play' with other children. It is observable that his ideas of right and wrong are very simple, hardly extending to another life; they consist chiefly in obedience to his parents, whose word is his law. As he grows older he mixes more and more with others; first with one or two who have a great influence in the direction of his mind. At length the world opens upon him; another work of education begins; and he learns to discern more truly the meaning of things and his relation to men in general. (You may complete the image, by supposing that there was a time in his early days when he was a helpless outcast 'in the land of Egypt and the house of bondage'.) And as he arrives at manhood he reflects on his former years, the progress of his education, the hardships of his infancy, the home of his youth (the thought of which is ineffaceable in after life), and he now understands that all this was but a preparation for another state of being, in which he is to play a part for himself. And once more in age you may imagine him like the patriarch looking back on the entire past, which he reads anew, perceiving that the events of life had a purpose or result which was not seen at the time; they seem to him bound 'each to each by natural piety'.

'Which things are an allegory', the particulars of which any one may interpret for himself. For the child born after the flesh is the symbol of the child born after the Spirit. 'The law was a schoolmaster to bring men to Christ', and now 'we are under a schoolmaster' no longer. The anticipation of truth which came from without to the childhood or youth of the human race is witnessed to within; the revelation of God is not lost but renewed in the heart and understanding of the man. Experience has taught us the application of the lesson in a wider sphere. And many influences have combined to form the 'after life' of the world. When at the close (shall we say) of a great period in the history of man, we cast our eyes back on the course of events, from the 'angel of his presence in the wilderness' to the multitude of peoples, nations, languages, who are being drawn together by His Providence – from the simplicity of the pastoral state in the dawn of the world's day, to all the elements of civilization and knowledge which are beginning to meet and mingle in a common life, we also understand that we are no longer in our early home, to which, nevertheless, we fondly look; and that the end is yet unseen, and the purposes of God towards the human race only half revealed. And to turn once more to the Interpreter of Scripture, he too feels that the continuous growth of revelation which he traces in the Old and New Testament is a part of a larger whole extending over the earth and reaching to another world.

Questions for Discussion

1. What are the implications of Jowett's assertion that the Bible is to be approached like any other book?
2. What aspects of this essay might have proved especially shocking to Victorian religious sensibilities?
3. Jowett asserts that "Scripture has one meaning – the meaning which it had to the mind of the prophet or evangelist who first uttered or wrote, to the hearers or readers who first received it." Find this quotation, and explore what Jowett takes to be its importance and implications.

CHAPTER 76

George Eliot (1819–1880)

Mary Ann Evans was born on South Farm, part of the estate of Arbury Hall, Nuneaton, Warwickshire, on November 22, 1819. She was the daughter of a farmer, Robert Evans, who was also land agent at Arbury. When she was four months old, the family moved to Griff House on the edge of the estate. Mary Ann attended church with her family at Chilvers Coton and she attended two boarding schools in Nuneaton and then went to school in Coventry between the ages of 13 and 16. After her mother's death in 1836 she came home to Griff to help run the household but continued to educate herself; she was also allowed free use of the library at Arbury Hall.

George Eliot [= Mary Ann Evans] (1819–1880)

Basic description
Victorian novelist and critic of the Christian faith.

Major works
Scenes of Clerical Life; Adam Bede; The Mill on the Floss; Middlemarch; Daniel Deronda.

Major studies
Gordon S. Haight, *George Eliot's Originals and Contemporaries: Essays in Victorian Literary History and Biography*. Basingstoke: Macmillan, 1991.
Frederick Robert Karl, *George Eliot: A Biography*. London: Flamingo, 1996.

During the course of this early period in her life, she came to know several evangelical clergy, whose influence can be discerned in *Scenes of Clerical Life*. George Eliot grew up at a time when the pastoral life she knew as a child was being destroyed by the rapid rise of industrialism. She moved to Coventry in November 1841, and hence came to meet Charles and Caroline Bray, who had established a certain local reputation as progressive intellectuals. Her striking intelligence brought her to the attention of the radical publisher John Chapman, who enlisted her to work on the intellectual *Westminster Review* in London.

By now, she had lost her Christian faith, partly through reading Charles Hennell's *Inquiry into the Origins of Christianity*. She moved to London, adopted the pen-name of "George Eliot," and became part of a circle of radical thinkers which included Herbert Spencer and George Henry Lewes. Although Lewes was married, and had no intention of divorcing his wife, he set up house with George Eliot, and lived with her until his death in 1878. Lewes encouraged Eliot to write, and a stream of books appeared from her pen, including *Scenes of Clerical Life, Adam Bede, The Mill on the Floss, Middlemarch*, and *Daniel Deronda*.

Eliot's novels are important on account of their exploration of the Christian faith from a critical perspective. However, Eliot did not adopt an antagonistic attitude to Christianity, as might be expected. Some early works in the 1840s pointed to a markedly hostile attitude to her old faith. Yet in the 1850s, a much more generous attitude developed, which is reflected in many of her novels, including both *Scenes of Clerical Life* and *Adam Bede*. The scorn and derision which might have been anticipated simply did not make their appearance. For Eliot, Christianity was not something to be *rejected*, but to be *transformed* into something more noble and universal. We therefore find a considerably more subtle criticism of the Christian faith in her novels than might be anticipated.

This is particularly evident in the work which we shall consider for study – *Scenes of Clerical Life*.

Text: *Scenes of Clerical Life*

This novel was first published in serial form in *Blackwood's Magazine*, beginning with the January 1857 number. The novel takes the form of three vignettes, entitled "The Sad Fortunes of the Rev. Amos Barton," "Mr Gilfil's Love Story," and "Janet's Repentance." Our extract is taken from the third of these. Eliot makes frequent reference to "evangelicalism," and especially to Henry Venn (1796–1873), a leading representative of this movement. Evangelicalism can be thought of as a form of Protestant Christianity which placed enormous emphasis on the importance of the Bible, the atoning death of Christ on the cross, the need for personal conversion, and the importance of mission and evangelism. Evangelicalism played a major role in early Victorian religious culture, although its influence began to wane in the second half of the nineteenth century.

Chapter 10

HISTORY, we know, is apt to repeat herself, and to foist very old incidents upon us with only a slight change of costume. From the time of Xerxes downwards, we have seen generals playing the braggadocio at the outset of their campaigns, and conquering the enemy with the greatest ease in after-dinner speeches. But events are apt to be in disgusting discrepancy with the anticipations of the most ingenious tacticians; the difficulties of the expedition are ridiculously at variance with able calculations; the enemy has the impudence not to fall into confusion as had been reasonably expected of him; the mind of the gallant general begins to be distracted by news of intrigues against him at home, and, notwithstanding the handsome compliments he paid to Providence as his undoubted patron before setting out, there seems every probability that the Te Deums will be all on the other side.

So it fell out with Mr Dempster in his memorable campaign against the Tryanites. After all the premature triumph of the return from Elmstoke, the battle of the Evening Lecture had been lost; the enemy was in possession of the field; and the utmost hope remaining was, that by a harassing guerilla warfare he might be driven to evacuate the country.

For some time this sort of warfare was kept up with considerable spirit. The shafts of Milby ridicule were made more formidable by being poisoned with calumny; and very ugly stories, narrated with circumstantial minuteness, were soon in circulation concerning Mr Tryan and his hearers, from which stories it was plainly deducible that Evangelicalism led by a necessary consequence to hypocritical indulgence in vice. Some old friendships were broken asunder, and there were near relations who felt that religious differences, unmitigated by any prospect of a legacy, were a sufficient ground for exhibiting their family antipathy. Mr Budd harangued his workmen, and threatened them with dismissal if they or their families were known to attend the evening lecture; and Mr Tomlinson, on discovering that his foreman was a rank Tryanite, blustered to a great extent, and would have cashiered that valuable functionary on the spot, if such a retributive procedure had not been inconvenient.

On the whole, however, at the end of a few months, the balance of substantial loss was on the side of the Anti-Tryanites. Mr Pratt, indeed, had lost a patient or two besides Mr Dempster's family; but as it was evident that Evangelicalism had not dried up the stream of his anecdote, or in the least altered his view of any lady's constitution, it is probable that a change accompanied by so few outward and visible signs, was rather the pretext than the ground of his dismissal in those additional cases. Mr Dunn was threatened with the loss of several good customers, Mrs Phipps and Mrs Lowme having set the example of ordering him to send in his bill; and the draper began to look forward to his next stock-taking with an anxiety which was but slightly mitigated by the parallel his wife suggested between his own case and that of Shadrach, Meshech, and Abednego, who were thrust into a burning fiery furnace. For, as he observed to her the next morning, with that perspicacity which belongs to the period of shaving, whereas their deliverance consisted in the fact that their linen and woollen goods were not consumed, his own deliverance lay in precisely the opposite result. But convenience, that admirable branch system from the main line of self-interest, makes us all fellow-helpers in spite of adverse resolutions. It is probable that no speculative or theological hatred would be ultimately strong enough to resist the persuasive power of convenience: that a latitudinarian baker, whose bread was honourably free from alum, would command the custom of any dyspeptic Puseyite; that an Arminian with the toothache would prefer a skilful Calvinistic dentist to a bungler stanch against the doctrines of Election and Final Perseverance, who would be likely to break the tooth in his head; and that a Plymouth Brother, who had a well furnished grocery shop in a favourable vicinage, would occasionally have the pleasure of furnishing sugar or vinegar to orthodox families that found themselves unexpectedly 'out of those indispensable commodities.' In this persuasive power of convenience lay Mr Dunn's ultimate security from martyrdom.

His drapery was the best in Milby; the comfortable use and wont of procuring satisfactory articles at a moment's notice proved too strong for Anti-Tryanite zeal; and the draper could soon look forward to his next stock-taking without the support of a Scriptural parallel.

On the other hand, Mr Dempster had lost his excellent client, Mr Jerome – a loss which galled him out of proportion to the mere monetary deficit it represented. The attorney loved money, but he loved power still better. He had always been proud of having early won the confidence of a conventicle-goer, and of being able to 'turn the prop of Salem round his thumb.' Like most other men, too, he had a certain kindness towards those who had employed him when he was only starting in life; and just as we do not like to part with an old weather-glass from our study, or a two-feet ruler that we have carried in our pocket ever since we began business, so Mr Dempster did not like having to erase his old client's name from the accustomed drawer in the bureau. Our habitual life is like a wall hung with pictures, which has been shone on by the suns of many years: take one of the pictures away, and it leaves a definite blank space, to which our eyes can never turn without a sensation of discomfort. Nay, the involuntary loss of any familiar object almost always brings a chill as from an evil omen; it seems to be the first finger-shadow of advancing death.

From all these causes combined, Mr Dempster could never think of his lost client without strong irritation, and the very sight of Mr Jerome passing in the street was wormwood to him.

One day, when the old gentleman was coming up Orchard Street on his roan mare, shaking the bridle, and tickling her flank with the whip as usual, though there was a perfect mutual understanding that she was not to quicken her pace, Janet happened to be on her own door-step, and he could not resist the temptation of stopping to speak to that 'nice little woman,' as he always called her, though she was taller than all the rest of his feminine acquaintances. Janet, in spite of her disposition to take her husband's part in all public matters, could bear no malice against her old friend; so they shook hands.

'Well, Mrs Dempster, I'm sorry to my heart not to see you sometimes, that I am,' said Mr Jerome, in a plaintive tone. 'But if you've got any poor people as wants help, and you know's deservin', send 'em to me, send 'em to me, just the same.'

'Thank you, Mr Jerome, that I will. Good-bye.'

Janet made the interview as short as she could, but it was not short enough to escape the observation of her husband, who, as she feared, was on his mid-day return from his office at the other end of the street, and this offence of hers, in speaking to Mr Jerome, was the frequently recurring theme of Mr Dempster's objurgatory domestic eloquence.

Associating the loss of his old client with Mr Tryan's influence, Dempster began to know more distinctly why he hated the obnoxious curate. But a passionate hate, as well as a passionate love, demands some leisure and mental freedom. Persecution and revenge, like courtship and toadyism, will not prosper without a considerable expenditure of time and ingenuity, and these are not to spare with a man whose law-business and liver are both beginning to show unpleasant symptoms. Such was the disagreeable turn affairs were taking with Mr Dempster, and, like the general distracted by home intrigues, he was too much harassed himself to lay ingenious plans for harassing the enemy.

Meanwhile, the evening lecture drew larger and larger congregations; not perhaps attracting many from that select aristocratic circle in which the Lowmes and Pittmans were predominant, but winning the larger proportion of Mr Crewe's morning and afternoon hearers, and thinning Mr Stickney's evening audiences at Salem. Evangelicalism was making its way in Milby, and gradually diffusing its subtle odour into chambers that were bolted and barred against it. The movement, like all other religious 'revivals,' had a mixed effect. Religious ideas have the fate of melodies, which, once set afloat in the world, are taken up by all sorts of instruments, some of them woefully coarse, feeble, or out of tune, until people are in danger of crying out that the melody itself is detestable. It may be that some of Mr Tryan's hearers had gained a religious vocabulary rather than religious experience; that here and there a weaver's wife, who, a few months before, had been simply a silly slattern, was converted into that more complex nuisance, a silly and sanctimonious slattern; that the old Adam, with the pertinacity of middle age, continued to tell fibs behind the counter, notwithstanding the new Adam's addiction to Bible-reading and family prayer: that the children in the Paddiford Sunday-school had their memories crammed with phrases about the blood of cleansing, imputed righteousness, and justification by faith alone, which an experience lying principally in chuckfarthing, hop-scotch, parental slappings, and longings after unattainable lollypop, served rather to darken than to illustrate; and that at Milby, in those distant days, as in all other times and places where the mental atmosphere is changing, and men are inhaling the stimulus of new ideas, folly often mistook itself for wisdom, ignorance gave itself airs of knowledge, and selfishness, turning its eyes upward, called itself religion.

Nevertheless, Evangelicalism had brought into palpable existence and operation in Milby society that idea of duty, that recognition of something to be lived for beyond the mere satisfaction of self, which is to the moral life what the addition of a great central ganglion is to animal life. No man can begin to mould himself on a faith or an idea without rising to a higher order of experience: a principle of subordination, of self-mastery, has been introduced into his nature; he is no longer a mere bundle of impressions, desires, and impulses. Whatever might be the weaknesses of the ladies who pruned the luxuriance of their lace and ribbons, cut out garments for the poor, distributed tracts, quoted Scripture, and defined the true Gospel, they had learned this – that there was a divine work to be done in life, a rule of goodness higher than the opinion of their neighbours; and if the notion of a heaven in reserve for themselves was a little too prominent, yet the theory of fitness for that heaven consisted in purity of heart, in Christ-like compassion, in the subduing of selfish desires. They might give the name of piety to much that was only puritanic egoism; they might call many things sin that were not sin; but they had at least the feeling that sin was to be avoided and resisted, and colour-blindness, which may mistake drab for scarlet, is better than total blindness, which sees no distinction of colour at all. Miss Rebecca Linnet, in quiet attire, with a somewhat excessive solemnity of countenance, teaching at the Sunday-school, visiting the poor, and striving after a standard of purity and goodness, had surely more moral loveliness than in those flaunting peony-days, when she had no other model than the costumes of the heroines in the circulating library. Miss Eliza Pratt, listening in rapt attention to Mr Tryan's evening lecture, no doubt found evangelical channels for vanity and egoism; but she was clearly in moral advance of Miss Phipps giggling under her feathers at old Mr Crewe's peculiarities of enunciation. And even elderly fathers and mothers, with minds, like Mrs Linnet's, too tough to imbibe much doctrine, were the better for having their hearts inclined towards the new preacher as a messenger from God. They became ashamed, perhaps, of their evil tempers, ashamed of their worldliness, ashamed of their trivial, futile past. The first condition of human goodness is something to love; the second, something to reverence. And this latter precious gift was brought to Milby by Mr Tryan and Evangelicalism.

Yes, the movement was good, though it had that mixture of folly and evil which often makes what is good an offence to feeble and fastidious minds, who want human actions and characters riddled through the sieve of their own ideas, before they can accord their sympathy or admiration. Such minds, I daresay, would have found Mr Tryan's character very much in need of that riddling process. The blessed work of helping the world forward, happily does not wait to be done by perfect men; and I should imagine that neither Luther nor John Bunyan, for example, would have satisfied the modern demand for an ideal hero, who believes nothing but what is true, feels nothing but what is exalted, and does nothing but what is graceful. The real heroes, of God's making, are quite different: they have their natural heritage of love and conscience which they drew in with their mother's milk; they know one or two of those deep spiritual truths which are only to be won by long wrestling with their own sins and their own sorrows; they have earned faith and strength so far as they have done genuine work; but the rest is dry barren theory, blank prejudice, vague hearsay. Their insight is blended with mere opinion; their sympathy is perhaps confined in narrow conduits of doctrine, instead of flowing forth with the freedom of a stream that blesses every weed in its course; obstinacy or self-assertion will often interfuse itself with their grandest impulses; and their very deeds of self-sacrifice are sometimes only the rebound of a passionate egoism. So it was with Mr Tryan: and any one looking at him with the bird's-eye glance of a critic might perhaps say that he made the mistake of identifying Christianity with a too narrow doctrinal system; that he saw God's work too exclusively in antagonism to the world, the flesh, and the devil; that his intellectual culture was too limited – and so on; making Mr Tryan the text for a wise discourse on the characteristics of the Evangelical school in his day.

But I am not poised at that lofty height. I am on the level and in the press with him, as he struggles his way along the stony road, through the crowd of unloving fellow-men. He is stumbling, perhaps; his heart now beats fast with dread, now heavily with anguish; his eyes are sometimes dim with tears, which he makes haste to dash away; he pushes manfully on, with fluctuating faith and courage, with a sensitive failing body; at last he falls, the struggle is ended, and the crowd closes over the space he has left.

'One of the Evangelical clergy, a disciple of Venn,' says the critic from his bird's-eye station. 'Not a remarkable specimen; the anatomy and habits of his species have been determined long ago.'

Yet surely, surely the only true knowledge of our fellow-man is that which enables us to feel with him – which gives us a fine ear for the heart-pulses that are beating under the mere clothes of circumstance and opinion. Our subtlest analysis of schools and sects must miss the essential truth, unless it be lit up by the love that sees in all forms of human thought and work, the life and death struggles of separate human beings.

Chapter 11

MR TRYAN'S most unfriendly observers were obliged to admit that he gave himself no rest. Three sermons on Sunday, a night-school for young men on Tuesday, a cottage-lecture on Thursday, addresses to school-teachers, and catechizing of school-children, with pastoral visits, multiplying as his influence extended beyond his own district of Paddiford Common, would have been enough to tax severely the powers of a much stronger man. Mr Pratt remonstrated with him on his imprudence, but could not prevail on him so far to economize time and strength as to keep a horse. On some ground or other, which his friends found difficult to explain to themselves, Mr Tryan seemed bent on wearing himself out. His enemies were at no loss to account for such a course. The Evangelical curate's selfishness was clearly of too bad a kind to exhibit itself after the ordinary manner of a sound, respectable selfishness. 'He wants to get the reputation of a saint,' said one; 'He's eaten up with spiritual pride,' said another; 'He's got his eye on some fine living, and wants to creep up the Bishop's sleeve,' said a third.

Mr Stickney, of Salem, who considered all voluntary discomfort as a remnant of the legal spirit, pronounced a severe condemnation on this self-neglect, and expressed his fear that Mr Tryan was still far from having attained true Christian liberty. Good Mr Jerome eagerly seized this doctrinal view of the subject as a means of enforcing the suggestions of his own benevolence; and one cloudy afternoon, in the end of November, he mounted his roan mare with the determination of riding to Paddiford and 'arguying' the point with Mr Tryan.

The old gentleman's face looked very mournful as he rode along the dismal Paddiford lanes, between rows of grimy houses, darkened with hand-looms, while the black dust was whirled about him by the cold November wind. He was thinking of the object which had brought him on this afternoon ride, and his thoughts, according to his habit when alone, found vent every now and then in audible speech. It seemed to him, as his eyes rested on this scene of Mr Tryan's labours, that he could understand the clergyman's self-privation without resorting to Mr Stickney's theory of defective spiritual enlightenment. Do not philosophic doctors tell us that we are unable to discern so much as a tree, except by an unconscious cunning which combines many past and separate sensations; that no one sense is independent of another, so that in the dark we can hardly taste a fricassee, or tell whether our pipe is alight or not, and the most intelligent boy, if accommodated with claws or hoofs instead of fingers, would be likely to remain on the lowest form? If so, it is easy to understand that our discernment of men's motives must depend on the completeness of the elements we can bring from our own susceptibility and our own experience. See to it, friend, before you pronounce a too hasty judgement, that your own moral sensibilities are not of a hoofed or clawed character. The keenest eye will not serve, unless you have the delicate fingers, with their subtle nerve filaments, which elude scientific lenses, and lose themselves in the invisible world of human sensations.

As for Mr Jerome, he drew the elements of his moral vision from the depths of his veneration and pity. If he himself felt so much for these poor things to whom life was so dim and meagre, what must the clergyman feel who had undertaken before God to be their shepherd?

'Ah!' he whispered, interruptedly, 'it's too big a load for his conscience. Poor man! He wants to mek himself their brother, like; can't abide to preach to the fastin' on a full stomach. Ah! he's better nor we are, that's it – he's a deal better nor we are.'

Here Mr Jerome shook his bridle violently, and looked up with an air of moral courage, as if Mr Stickney had been present, and liable to take offence at this conclusion. A few minutes more brought him in front of Mrs Wagstaff's, where Mr Tryan lodged. He had often been here before, so that the contrast between this ugly square brick house, with its shabby bit of grass-plot, stared at all round by cottage windows, and his own pretty white home, set in a paradise of orchard and garden and pasture was not new to him; but he felt it with fresh force today, as he slowly fastened his roan by the bridle to the wooden paling, and knocked at the door. Mr Tryan was at home, and sent to request that Mr Jerome would walk up into his study, as the fire was out in the parlour below.

At the mention of a clergyman's study, perhaps, your too active imagination conjures up a perfect snuggery, where the general air of comfort is rescued from a secular character by strong ecclesiastical suggestions in the shape of the furniture, the pattern of the carpet, and the prints on the wall; where, if a nap is taken, it is in an easy-chair with a Gothic back, and the very feet rest on a warm and velvety simulation of church windows; where the pure art of rigorous English Protestantism smiles above the mantelpiece in the portrait of an eminent bishop, or a refined Anglican taste is indicated by a German print from Overbeck; where the walls are lined with choice divinity in sombre binding, and the light is softened by a screen of boughs with a grey church in the background.

But I must beg you to dismiss all such scenic prettiness, suitable as they may be to a clergyman's character and complexion; for I have to confess that Mr Tryan's study was a very ugly little room indeed, with an ugly slapdash pattern on the walls, an ugly carpet on the floor, and an ugly view of cottage roofs and cabbage-gardens from the window. His own person, his writing-table, and his book-case, were the only objects in the room that had the slightest air of refinement; and the sole provision for comfort was a clumsy straight-backed arm-chair covered with faded chintz. The man who could live in such a room, unconstrained by poverty, must either have his vision fed from within by an intense passion, or he must have chosen that least attractive form of self-mortification which wears no haircloth and has no meagre days, but accepts the vulgar, the commonplace, and the ugly, whenever the highest duty seems to lie among them.

'Mr Tryan, I hope you'll excuse me disturbin' on you,' said Mr Jerome. 'But I'd summat partickler to say.'

'You don't disturb me at all, Mr Jerome; I'm very glad to have a visit from you,' said Mr Tryan, shaking him heartily by the hand, and offering him the chintz-covered 'easy' chair; 'it is some time since I've had an opportunity of seeing you, except on a Sunday.'

'Ah, sir! your time's so taken up, I'm well aware o' that; it's not only what you hev to do, but it's goin' about from place to place; an' you don't keep a hoss, Mr Tryan. You don't take care enough o' yourself – you don't indeed, an' that's what I come to talk to y' about.'

'That's very good of you, Mr Jerome; but I assure you I think walking does me no harm. It is rather a relief to me after speaking or writing. You know I have no great circuit to make. The farthest distance I have to walk is to Milby Church, and if ever I want a horse on a Sunday, I hire Radley's, who lives not many hundred yards from me.'

'Well, but now! the winter's comin' on, an' you'll get wet i' your feet, an' Pratt tells me as your constitution's dillicate, as anybody may see, for the matter o' that, wi'out bein' a doctor. An' this is the light I look at it in, Mr Tryan: who's to fill up your place, if you was to be disabled, as I may say? Consider what a valyable life yours is. You've begun a great work i' Milby, and so you might carry it on, if you'd your health and strength. The more care you take o' yourself, the longer you'll live, belike, God willing, to do good to your fellow-creaturs.'

'Why, my dear Mr Jerome, I think I should not be a long-lived man in any case; and if I were to take care of myself under the pretext of doing more good, I should very likely die and leave nothing done after all.'

'Well! but keepin' a hoss wouldn't hinder you from workin'. It 'ud help you to do more, though Pratt says as it's usin' your voice so constant as does you the most harm. Now, isn't it – I'm no scholard, Mr Tryan, an' I'm not a-goin' to dictate to you – but isn't it a'most a-killin' o' yourself, to go on a' that way beyond your strength? We mustn't fling our lives away.'

'No, not fling them away lightly, but we are permitted to lay down our lives in a right cause. There are many duties, as you know, Mr Jerome, which stand before taking care of our own lives.'

'Ah! I can't arguy wi' you, Mr Tryan; but what I wanted to say 's this – There's my little chacenut hoss; I should take it quite a kindness if you'd hev him through the winter an' ride him. I've thought o' sellin' him a many times, for Mrs Jerome can't abide him; and what do I want wi' two nags? But I'm fond o' the little cha-cenut, an' I shouldn't like to sell him. So if you'll only ride him for me, you'll do me a kindness – you will, indeed, Mr Tryan.'

'Thank you, Mr Jerome. I promise you to ask for him, when I feel that I want a nag. There is no man I would more gladly be indebted to than you; but at present I would rather not have a horse. I should ride him very little, and it would be an inconvenience to me to keep him rather than otherwise.'

Mr Jerome looked troubled and hesitating, as if he had something on his mind that would not readily shape itself into words. At last he said, 'You'll excuse me, Mr Tryan, I wouldn't be takin' a liberty, but I know what great claims you hev on you as a clergyman. Is it the expense, Mr Tryan? Is it the money?'

'No, my dear sir. I have much more than a single man needs. My way of living is quite of my own choosing, and I am doing nothing but what I feel bound to do, quite apart from money considerations. We cannot judge for one another, you know; we have each our peculiar weaknesses and temptations. I quite admit that it might be right for another man to allow himself more luxuries, and I assure you I think it no superiority in myself to do without them. On the contrary, if my heart were less rebellious, and if I were less liable to temptation, I should not need that sort of self-denial. But,' added Mr Tryan, holding out his hand to Mr Jerome, 'I understand your kindness, and bless you for it. If I want a horse, I shall ask for the chestnut.'

Mr Jerome was obliged to rest contented with this promise, and rode home sorrowfully, reproaching himself with not having said one thing he meant to say when setting out, and with having 'clean forgot' the arguments he had intended to quote from Mr Stickney.

Mr Jerome's was not the only mind that was seriously disturbed by the idea that the curate was over-working himself. There were tender women's hearts in which anxiety about the state of his affections was beginning to be merged in anxiety about the state of his health. Miss Eliza Pratt had at one time passed through much sleepless cogitation on the possibility of Mr Tryan's being attached to some lady at a distance – at Laxeter, perhaps, where he had formerly held a curacy; and her fine eyes kept close watch lest any symptom of engaged affections on his part should escape her. It seemed an alarming fact that his handkerchiefs were beautifully marked with hair, until she reflected that he had an unmarried sister of whom he spoke with much affection as his father's companion and comforter. Besides, Mr Tryan had never paid any distant visit, except one for a few days to his father, and no hint escaped him of his intending to take a house, or change his mode of living. No! he could not be engaged, though he might have been disappointed. But this latter misfortune is one from which a devoted clergyman has been known to recover, by the aid of a fine pair of grey eyes that beam on him with affectionate reverence. Before Christmas, however, her cogitations began to take another turn. She heard her father say very confidently that 'Tryan was consumptive, and if he didn't take more care of himself, his life would not be worth a year's purchase'; and shame at having speculated on suppositions that were likely to prove so false, sent poor Miss Eliza's feelings with all the stronger impetus into the one channel of sorrowful alarm at the prospect of losing the pastor who had opened to her a new life of piety and self-subjection. It is a sad weakness in us, after all, that the thought of a man's death hallows him anew to us; as if life were not sacred too – as if it were comparatively a light thing to fail in love and reverence to the brother who has to climb the whole toilsome steep with us, and all our tears and tenderness were due to the one who is spared that hard journey.

The Miss Linnets, too, were beginning to take a new view of the future, entirely uncoloured by jealousy of Miss Eliza Pratt.

'Did you notice,' said Mary, one afternoon when Mrs Pettifer was taking tea with them – 'did you notice that short dry cough of Mr Tryan's yesterday? I think he looks worse and worse every week, and I only wish I knew his sister; I would write to her about him. I'm sure something should be done to make him give up part of his work, and he will listen to no one here.'

'Ah,' said Mrs Pettifer, 'it's a thousand pities his father and sister can't come and live with him, if he isn't to marry. But I wish with all my heart he could have taken to some nice woman as would have made a comfortable home for him. I used to think he might take to Eliza Pratt; she's a good girl, and very pretty; but I see no likelihood of it now.'

'No, indeed,' said Rebecca, with some emphasis: 'Mr Tryan's heart is not for any woman to win; it is all given to his work; and I could never wish to see him with a young inexperienced wife who would be a drag on him instead of a help-mate.'

'He'd need have somebody, young or old,' observed Mrs Linnet, 'to see as he wears a flannel wescoat, an' changes his stockins when he comes in. It's my opinion he's got that cough wi' sittin i' wet shoes and stockins; an' that Mrs Wagstaff's a poor addle-headed thing; she doesn't half tek care on him.'

'O mother!' said Rebecca, 'she's a very pious woman. And I'm sure she thinks it too great a privilege to have Mr Tryan with her, not to do the best she can to make him comfortable. She can't help her rooms being shabby.'

'I've nothing to say again' her piety, my dear; but I know very well I shouldn't like her to cook my victual. When a man comes in hungry an' tired, piety won't feed him, I reckon. Hard carrots 'ull lie heavy on his stomach, piety or no piety. I called in one day when she was dishin' up Mr Tryan's dinner, an' I could see the potatoes was as watery as watery. It's right enough to be speritial – I'm no enemy to that; but I like my potatoes mealy. I don't see as anybody 'ull go to heaven the sooner for not digestin' their dinner – providin' they don't die sooner, as mayhap Mr Tryan will, poor dear man!'

'It will be a heavy day for us all when that comes to pass,' said Mrs Pettifer. 'We shall never get anybody to fill up that gap. There's the new clergyman that's just come to Shepperton – Mr Parry; I saw him the other day at Mrs Bond's. He may be a very good man, and a fine preacher; they say he is; but I thought to myself, What a difference between him and Mr Tryan! He's a sharp-sort-of-looking man, and hasn't that feeling way with him that Mr Tryan has. What is so wonderful to me in Mr Tryan is the way he puts himself on a level with one, and talks to one like a brother. I'm never afraid of telling him anything. He never seems to look down on anybody. He knows how to lift up those that are cast down, if ever man did.'

'Yes,' said Mary. 'And when I see all the faces turned up to him in Paddiford Church. I often think how hard it would be for any clergyman who had to come after him; he has made the people love him so.'

Questions for Discussion

1 Eliot is critical of evangelicalism in this passage. What specific criticisms of this religious movement, which Eliot knew well from her youth, can be discerned?

2 What criticisms are implicit of Christianity in this section? And how forcefully are these stated?

3 At several points, Eliot makes comments which indicate how she would like to see Christianity improved or modified. What are these?

CHAPTER 77

Fyodor Mikhailovich Dostoevsky
(1821–1881)

Dostoevsky was the son of a Russian army surgeon, who initially followed his father into a career in the army. He spent the years 1838 to 1843 in the Military Engineering College at St. Petersburg, and went on to become an officer in the Russian Army. After three years he resigned his commission and began to engage in political activity against the political establishment. This led to imprisonment, and he was at one point condemned to death for his revolutionary activities. Although he was reprieved, there is little doubt that this experience made a deep impact upon him. His best-known works are all novels, including *Crime and Punishment* (1865–6), *The Idiot* (1869), and *The Brothers Karamazov* (1880). Religious themes abound in these novels, and they have had a significant influence on subsequent Christian literature, particularly in relation to the issue of the purpose and place of suffering in the world.

Fyodor Mikhailovich Dostoevsky (1821–1881)

Basic description
Leading nineteenth-century Russian novelist.

Major works
Crime and Punishment (1865–6); *The Idiot* (1869); *The Brothers Karamazov* (1880).

Editions of works
The Novels of Fyodor Dostoevsky, translated by Constance Black Garnett, 12 vols. London: Heinemann, 1912–20.

Major studies
A. Boyce Gibson, *The Religion of Dostoevsky*. London: SCM Press, 1973.

Text: *The Brothers Karamazov*

In order to allow readers significant exposure to Dostoevsky's writings, a substantial section of *The Brothers Karamazov* has been reprinted here. The section included follows the famous section in which Alyosha threatens to give God his ticket back, on account of the existence of suffering and evil in the world. The discussion of the place of God in the suffering of the world is then explored in the famous "Grand Inquisitor" story. This short story is widely regarded as one of the most important sections of this work from a religious point of view, and needs some comment. The story invites its readers to imagine the reappearance of Christ during the Spanish Inquisition of the sixteenth century. Christ is labeled a heretic, and is finally brought to judgment before the old, haughty, cynical Grand Inquisitor. During the compelling and highly dramatic dialogue between the two men, the Inquisitor gradually realizes he is not dealing with an imposter.

The Inquisitor then launches on a major diatribe against Christ, for having committed the unthinkable and unforgivable sin of having given humanity freedom of choice. This, he declares, is an intolerable burden, which humanity simply cannot carry. The Inquisitor, out of a deeper concern for humanity, wishes to *deny* them freedom, and replaces the curse of freedom with the intellectual and spiritual opiates of miracle, mystery, and authority. By revering the mystery, believing and accepting the miracles, and following the dictates and directives of the church, people can live their lives without the heavy load of accepting responsibility for their own actions. The wrathful Inquisitor asks Christ how he dare appear again on earth to repeat his errors. In the end, knowing full well what he is doing, the Inquisitor finds Christ guilty of blasphemy and condemns him to death. Then he returns to his lifelong work of correcting Christ's mistakes.

The majority of people, according to the Grand Inquisitor, are weak and are to be compared to sheep. He accuses Jesus of valuing freedom above all else. The Inquisitor, in contrast, is – at least, in his own eyes – a philanthropist, and therefore aims for the happiness of humanity – a happiness which can only be achieved by the surrender of human freedom, so that only a select few are burdened by its weight and responsibility. The Grand Inquisitor and the Catholic church, as represented by the Inquisitor, therefore reject Jesus, and demand his crucifixion. Only the strong who, like the Inquisitor, can "go the forty days and nights in the desert," are capable of attaining the reward of Heaven, while the weak millions, "who are weak but still love Thee . . . must exist for the sake of the strong." The Inquisitor declares that the reason the weak cannot take the narrow road to Heaven is that they are actually afraid of freedom, so that, in fact, "they can never be free." People may cry out for freedom – but in fact, they prefer slavery.

The most important section of the narrative of the Grand Inquisitor centers on the gospel accounts of the temptation of Jesus by the Devil in the desert, and it is important to read this section carefully. The Inquisitor claims that even if people were to have "earthly bread" in abundance, without a "stable conception of the object of life," they would not continue to live in any meaningful sense of the word. It therefore must follow that anyone who would lead people must first captivate their consciences. So how can this be done? According to the Grand Inquisitor, there are only three powers that can do this: miracle, mystery, and authority. Christ rejects all three; the Inquisitor knows better. The Inquisitor and the church thus "pick up the Sword of Caesar," symbolic of earthly power, and use it to captivate and rule the entire world.

The Grand Inquisitor declares that he can allow the many a much happier life, by offering them "earthly bread," symbolizing the necessities and pleasures of life. He will do this by captivating their consciences, and by gaining authority and power over the entire world. The Inquisitor tells Christ, "Thou art proud of Thine elect, while we give rest to all." Because the masses will not have freedom, that most terrible of gifts and curses, they will be like happy, innocent, sinless children, and will live "like a child's game, with children's songs and innocent dance." Only the strong, those few at the top of the power structure, will have to bear the weight and responsibility of freedom. There are significant similarities between the argument of the Inquisitor and the thoughts found in Nietzsche's *The AntiChrist*.

To allow the story to be seen in its context, a few paragraphs from the previous chapter are included. The context is the debate between Alyosha and his brother over God's ability to forgive, and the place of freedom and suffering in the world.

'No, I can't admit it. Brother,' said Alyosha suddenly, with flashing eyes, 'you said just now, is there a being in the whole world who would have the right to forgive and could forgive? But there is a Being and He can forgive everything, all and for all, because He gave His innocent blood for all and everything. You have forgotten Him, and on Him is built the edifice, and it is to Him they cry aloud, "Thou art just, O Lord, for Thy ways are revealed!"'

'Ah! the One without sin and His blood! No, I have not forgotten Him; on the contrary I've been wondering all the time how it was you did not bring Him in before, for usually all arguments on your side put Him in the foreground. Do you know, Alyosha – don't laugh I made a poem about a year ago. If you can waste another ten minutes on me, I'll tell it to you.'

'You wrote a poem?'

'Oh, no, I didn't write it,' laughed Ivan, and I've never written two lines of poetry in my life. But I made up this poem in prose and I remembered it. I was carried away when I made it up. You will be my first reader – that is listener. Why should an author forgo even one listener?' smiled Ivan. 'Shall I tell it to you?'

'I am all attention.' said Alyosha.

'My poem is called The Grand Inquisitor; it's a ridiculous thing, but I want to tell it to you.

Chapter 5

The Grand Inquisitor

'EVEN this must have a preface – that is, a literary preface,' laughed Ivan, 'and I am a poor hand at making one. You see, my action takes place in the sixteenth century, and at that time, as you probably learnt at school, it was customary in poetry to bring down heavenly powers on earth. Not to speak of Dante, in France, clerks, as well as the monks in the monasteries, used to give regular performances in which the Madonna, the saints, the angels, Christ, and God Himself were brought on the stage. In those days it was done in all simplicity. In Victor Hugo's Notre Dame de Paris an edifying and gratuitous spectacle was provided for the people in the Hotel de Ville of Paris in the reign of Louis XI in honour of the birth of the dauphin. It was called *Le bon jugement de la très sainte et gracieuse Vierge Marie*, and she appears herself on the stage and pronounces her *bon jugement*. Similar plays, chiefly from the Old Testament, were occasionally performed in Moscow too, up to the times of Peter the Great. But besides plays there were all sorts of legends and ballads scattered about the world, in which the saints and angels and all the powers of Heaven took part when required. In our monasteries the monks busied themselves in translating, copying, and even composing such poems – and even under the Tatars. There is, for instance, one such poem (of course, from the Greek), The Wanderings of Our Lady through Hell, with descriptions as bold as Dante's. Our Lady visits hell, and the Archangel Michael leads her through the torments. She sees the sinners and their punishment. There she sees among others one noteworthy set of sinners in a burning lake; some of them sink to the bottom of the lake so that they can't swim out, and "these God forgets" – an expression of extraordinary depth and force. And so Our Lady, shocked and weeping, falls before the throne of God and begs for mercy for all in hell – for all she has seen there, indiscriminately. Her conversation with God is immensely interesting. She beseeches Him, she will not desist, and when God points to the hands and feet of her Son, nailed to the Cross, and asks, "How can I forgive His tormentors?" she bids all the saints, all the martyrs, all the angels and archangels to fall down with her and pray for mercy on all without distinction. It ends by her winning from God a respite of suffering every year from Good Friday till Trinity Day, and the sinners at once raise a cry of thankfulness from hell, chanting, "Thou art just, O Lord, in this judgment." Well, my poem would have been of that kind if it had appeared at that time. He comes on the scene in my poem, but He says nothing, only appears and passes on. Fifteen centuries have passed since He promised to come in His glory, fifteen centuries since His prophet wrote, "Behold, I come quickly"; "Of that day and that hour knoweth no man, neither the Son, but the Father," as He Himself predicted on earth. But humanity awaits him with the same faith and with the same love. Oh, with greater faith, for it is fifteen centuries since man has ceased to see signs from heaven.

> No signs from heaven come to-day
> To add to what the heart doth say.

'There was nothing left but faith in what the heart doth say. It is true there were many miracles in those days. There were saints who performed miraculous cures; some holy people, according to their biographies, were visited by the Queen of Heaven herself. But the devil did not slumber, and doubts were already arising among men of the truth of these miracles. And just then there appeared in the north of Germany a terrible new heresy. "A huge star like to a torch" (that is, to a church) "fell on the sources of the waters and they became bitter." These heretics began blasphemously denying miracles. But those who remained faithful were all the more ardent in their faith. The tears of humanity rose up to Him as before, awaited His coming, loved Him, hoped for Him, yearned to suffer and die for Him as before. And so many ages mankind had prayed with faith and fervour, "O Lord our God, hasten Thy coming"; so many ages called upon Him, that in His infinite mercy He deigned to come down to His servants. Before that day He had come down, He had visited some holy men, martyrs, and hermits, as is written in their lives. Among us, Tyutchev, with absolute faith in the truth of his words, bore witness that

> Bearing the Cross, in slavish dress,
> Weary and worn, the Heavenly King
> Our mother, Russia, came to bless,
> And through our land went wandering.

And that certainly was so, I assure you.

'And behold, He deigned to appear for a moment to the people, to the tortured, suffering people, sunk in iniquity, but loving Him like children. My story is laid in Spain, in Seville, in the most terrible time of the Inquisition, when fires were lighted every day to the glory of God, and "in the splendid auto da fe the wicked heretics were burnt." Oh, of course, this was not the coming in which He will appear, according to His promise, at the end of time in all His heavenly glory, and which will be sudden "as lightning flashing from east to west." No, He visited His children only for a moment, and there where the flames were crackling round the heretics. In His infinite mercy He came once more among men in that human shape in which He walked among men for thirty-three years fifteen centuries ago. He came down to the "hot pavements" of the southern town in which on the day before almost a hundred heretics had, *ad majorem Dei gloriam*, been burnt by the cardinal, the Grand Inquisitor, in a magnificent *auto da fe*, in the presence of the king, the court, the knights, the cardinals, the most charming ladies of the court, and the whole population of Seville.

'He came softly, unobserved, and yet, strange to say, everyone recognised Him. That might be one of the best passages in the poem. I mean, why they recognised Him. The people are irresistibly drawn to Him, they surround Him, they flock about Him, follow Him. He moves silently in their midst with a gentle smile of infinite compassion. The sun of love burns in His heart, and power shines from His eyes, and their radiance, shed on the people, stirs their hearts with responsive love. He holds out His hands to them, blesses them, and a healing virtue comes from contact with Him, even with His garments. An old man in the crowd, blind from childhood, cries out, "O Lord, heal me and I shall see Thee!" and, as it were, scales fall from his eyes and the blind man sees Him. The crowd weeps and kisses the earth under His feet. Children throw flowers before Him, sing, and cry hosannah. "It is He – it is He!" repeat. "It must be He, it can be no one but Him!" He stops at the steps of the Seville cathedral at the moment when the weeping mourners are bringing in a little open white coffin. In it lies a child of seven, the only daughter of a prominent citizen. The dead child lies hidden in flowers. "He will raise your child," the crowd shouts to the weeping mother. The priest, coming to meet the coffin, looks perplexed, and frowns, but the mother of the dead child throws herself at His feet with a wail. "If it is Thou, raise my child!" she cries, holding out her hands to Him. The procession halts, the coffin is laid on the steps at His feet. He looks with compassion, and His lips once more softly pronounce, "Maiden, arise!" and the maiden arises. The little girl sits up in the coffin and looks round, smiling with wide-open wondering eyes, holding a bunch of white roses they had put in her hand.

'There are cries, sobs, confusion among the people, and at that moment the cardinal himself, the Grand Inquisitor, passes by the cathedral. He is an old man, almost ninety, tall and erect, with a withered face and sunken eyes, in which there is still a gleam of light. He is not dressed in his gorgeous cardinal's robes, as he was the day before, when he was burning the enemies of the Roman Church – at this moment he is wearing his coarse, old, monk's cassock. At a distance behind him come his gloomy assistants and slaves and the "holy guard." He stops at the sight of the crowd and watches it from a distance. He sees everything; he sees them set the coffin down at His feet, sees the child rise up, and his face darkens. He knits his thick grey brows and his eyes gleam with a sinister fire. He holds out his finger and bids the guards take Him. And such is his power, so completely are the people cowed into submission and trembling obedience to him, that the crowd immediately makes way for the guards, and in the midst of deathlike silence they lay hands on Him and lead him away. The crowd instantly bows down to the earth, like one man, before the old Inquisitor. He blesses the people in silence and passes on. The guards lead their prisoner to the close, gloomy vaulted prison – in the ancient palace of the Holy Inquisition and shut him in it. The day passes and is followed by the dark, burning, "breathless" night of Seville. The air is "fragrant with laurel and lemon." In the pitch darkness the iron door of the prison is suddenly opened and the Grand Inquisitor himself comes in with a light in his hand. He is alone; the door is closed at once behind him. He stands in the doorway and for a minute or two gazes into His face. At last he goes up slowly, sets the light on the table and speaks.

'"Is it Thou?" but receiving no answer, he adds at once. "Don't answer, be silent. What canst Thou say, indeed? I know too well what Thou wouldst say. And Thou hast no right to add anything to what Thou hadst said of old. Why, then, art Thou come to hinder us? For Thou hast come to hinder us, and Thou knowest that. But dost thou know what will be to-morrow? I know not who Thou art and care not to know whether it is Thou or only a semblance of Him, but to-morrow I shall condemn Thee and burn Thee at the stake as the worst of heretics. And the very people who have to-day kissed Thy feet, to-morrow at the faintest sign from me will rush to heap up the embers of Thy fire. Knowest Thou that? Yes, maybe Thou knowest it," he added with thoughtful penetration, never for a moment taking his eyes off the Prisoner.'

'I don't quite understand, Ivan. What does it mean?' Alyosha, who had been listening in silence, said with a smile. 'Is it simply a wild fantasy, or a mistake on the part of the old man – some impossible quid pro quo?'

'Take it as the last,' said Ivan, laughing, 'if you are so corrupted by modern realism and can't stand anything fantastic. If you like it to be a case of mistaken identity, let it be so. It is true,' he went on, laughing, 'the old man was ninety, and he might well be crazy over his set idea. He might have been struck by the appearance of the Prisoner. It might, in fact, be simply his ravings, the delusion of an old man of ninety, over-excited by the auto da fe of a hundred heretics the day before. But does it matter to us after all whether it was a mistake of identity or a wild fantasy? All that matters is that the old man should speak out, that he should speak openly of what he has thought in silence for ninety years.'

'And the Prisoner too is silent? Does He look at him and not say a word?'

'That's inevitable in any case,' Ivan laughed again. 'The old man has told Him He hasn't the right to add anything to what He has said of old. One may say it is the most fundamental feature of Roman Catholicism, in my opinion at least. "All has been given by Thee to the Pope," they say, "and all, therefore, is still in the Pope's hands, and there is no need for Thee to come now at all. Thou must not meddle for the time, at least." That's how they speak and write too – the Jesuits, at any rate. I have read it myself in the works of their theologians. "Hast Thou the right to reveal to us one of the mysteries of that world from which Thou hast come?" my old man asks Him, and answers the question for Him. "No, Thou hast not; that Thou mayest not add to what has been said of old, and mayest not take from men the freedom which Thou didst exalt when Thou wast on earth. Whatsoever Thou revealest anew will encroach on men's freedom of faith; for it will be manifest as a miracle, and the freedom of their faith was dearer to Thee than anything in those days fifteen hundred years ago. Didst Thou not often say then, 'I will make you free'? But now Thou hast seen these 'free' men," the old man adds suddenly, with a pensive smile. "Yes, we've paid dearly for it," he goes on, looking sternly at Him, "but at last we have completed that work in Thy name. For fifteen centuries we have been wrestling with Thy freedom, but now it is ended and over for good. Dost Thou not believe that it's over for good? Thou lookest meekly at me and deignest not even to be wroth with me. But let me tell Thee that now, to-day, people are more persuaded than ever that they have perfect freedom, yet they have brought their freedom to us and laid it humbly at our feet. But that has been our doing. Was this what Thou didst? Was this Thy freedom?"'

'I don't understand again.' Alyosha broke in. 'Is he ironical; is he jesting?'

'Not a bit of it! He claims it as a merit for himself and his Church that at last they have vanquished freedom and have done so to make men happy. "For now" (he is speaking of the Inquisition, of course) "for the first time it has become possible to think of the happiness of men. Man was created a rebel; and how can rebels be happy? Thou wast warned," he says to Him. "Thou hast had no lack of admonitions and warnings, but Thou didst not listen to those warnings; Thou didst reject the only way by which men might be made happy. But, fortunately, departing Thou didst hand on the work to us. Thou hast promised, Thou hast established by Thy word, Thou hast given to us the right to bind and to unbind, and now, of course, Thou canst not think of taking it away. Why, then, hast Thou come to hinder us?"'

'And what's the meaning of "no lack of admonitions and warnings"?' asked Alyosha.

'Why, that's the chief part of what the old man must say.

' "The wise and dread spirit, the spirit of self-destruction and non-existence," the old man goes on, "great spirit talked with Thee in the wilderness, and we are told in the books that he 'tempted' Thee. Is that so? And could anything truer be said than what he revealed to Thee in three questions and what Thou didst reject, and what in the books is called 'the temptation'? And yet if there has ever been on earth a real stupendous miracle, it took place on that day, on the day of the three temptations. The statement of those three questions was itself the miracle. If it were possible to imagine simply for the sake of argument that those three questions of the dread spirit had perished utterly from the books, and that we had to restore them and to invent them anew, and to do so had gathered together all the wise men of the earth – rulers, chief priests, learned men, philosophers, poets – and had set them the task to invent three questions, such as would not only fit the occasion, but express in three words, three human phrases, the whole future history of the world and of humanity – dost Thou believe that all the wisdom of the earth united could have invented anything in depth and force equal to the three questions which were actually put to Thee then by the wise and mighty spirit in the wilderness? From those questions alone, from the miracle of their statement, we can see that we have here to do not with the fleeting human intelligence, but with the absolute and eternal. For in those three questions the whole subsequent history of mankind is, as it were, brought together into one whole, and foretold, and in them are united all the unsolved historical contradictions of human nature. At the time it could not be so clear, since the future was unknown; but now that fifteen hundred years have passed, we see that everything in those three questions was so justly divined and foretold, and has been so truly fulfilled, that nothing can be added to them or taken from them.

' "Judge Thyself who was right – Thou or he who questioned Thee then? Remember the first question; its meaning, in other words, was this: 'Thou wouldst go into the world, and art going with empty hands, with some promise of freedom which men in their simplicity and their natural unruliness cannot even understand, which they fear and dread – for nothing has ever been more insupportable for a man and a human society than freedom. But seest Thou these stones in this parched and barren wilderness? Turn them into bread, and mankind will run after Thee like a flock of sheep, grateful and obedient, though for ever trembling, lest Thou withdraw Thy hand and deny them Thy bread.' But Thou wouldst not deprive man of freedom and didst reject the offer, thinking, what is that freedom worth if obedience is bought with bread? Thou didst reply that man lives not by bread alone. But dost Thou know that for the sake of that earthly bread the spirit of the earth will rise up against Thee and will strive with Thee and overcome Thee, and all will follow him, crying, 'Who can compare with this beast? He has given us fire from heaven!' Dost Thou know that the ages will pass, and humanity will proclaim by the lips of their sages that there is no crime, and therefore no sin; there is only hunger? 'Feed men, and then ask of them virtue!' that's what they'll write on the banner, which they will raise against Thee, and with which they will destroy Thy temple. Where Thy temple stood will rise a new building; the terrible tower of Babel will be built again, and though, like the one of old, it will not be finished, yet Thou mightest have prevented that new tower and have cut short the sufferings of men for a thousand years; for they will come back to us after a thousand years of agony with their tower. They will seek us again, hidden underground in the catacombs, for we shall be again persecuted and tortured. They will find us and cry to us, 'Feed us, for those who have promised us fire from heaven haven't given it!' And then we shall finish building their tower, for he finishes the building who feeds them. And we alone shall feed them in Thy name, declaring falsely that it is in Thy name. Oh, never, never can they feed themselves without us! No science will give them bread so long as they remain free. In the end they will lay their freedom at our feet, and say to us, 'Make us your slaves, but feed us.' They will understand themselves, at last, that freedom and bread enough for all are inconceivable together, for never, never will they be able to share between them! They will be convinced, too, that they can never be free, for they are weak, vicious, worthless, and rebellious. Thou didst promise them the bread of Heaven, but, I repeat again, can it compare with earthly bread in the eyes of the weak, ever sinful and ignoble race of man? And if for the sake of the bread of Heaven thousands shall follow Thee, what is to become of the millions and tens of thousands of millions of creatures who will not have the strength to forgo the earthly bread for the sake of the heavenly? Or dost Thou care only for the tens of thousands of the great and strong, while the millions, numerous as the sands of the sea, who are weak but love Thee, must exist only for the sake of the great and strong? No, we care for the weak too. They are sinful and rebellious, but in the end they too will become obedient. They will marvel at us and look on us as gods, because we are ready to endure the freedom which they have found so dreadful and to rule over them – so awful it will seem to them to be free. But we shall tell them that we are Thy servants and rule them in Thy name. We shall deceive them again, for we will not let Thee come to us again. That deception will be our suffering, for we shall be forced to lie.

' "This is the significance of the first question in the wilderness, and this is what Thou hast rejected for the sake of that freedom which Thou hast exalted above everything. Yet in this question lies hid the great secret of this world. Choosing 'bread,' Thou wouldst have satisfied the universal and everlasting craving of humanity – to find someone to worship. So long as man remains free he strives for nothing so incessantly and so painfully as to find someone to worship. But man seeks to worship what is established beyond dispute, so that all men would agree at once to worship it. For these pitiful creatures are concerned not only to find what one or the other can worship, but to find community of worship is the chief misery of every man individually and of all humanity from the beginning of time. For the sake of common worship they've slain each other with the sword. They have set up gods and challenged one another, 'Put away your gods and come and worship ours, or we will kill you and your gods!' And so it will be to the end of the world, even when gods disappear from the earth; they will fall down before idols just the same. Thou didst know, Thou couldst not but have known, this fundamental secret of human nature, but Thou didst reject the one infallible banner which was offered Thee to make all men bow down to Thee alone – the banner of earthly bread; and Thou hast rejected it for the sake of freedom and the bread of Heaven. Behold what Thou didst further. And all again in the name of freedom! I tell Thee that man is tormented by no greater anxiety than to find someone quickly to whom he can hand over that gift of freedom with which the ill-fated creature is born. But only one who can appease their conscience can take over their freedom. In bread there was offered Thee an invincible banner; give bread, and man will worship thee, for nothing is more certain than bread. But if someone else gains possession of his conscience – Oh! then he will cast away Thy bread and follow after him who has ensnared his conscience. In that Thou wast right. For the secret of man's being is not only to live but to have something to live for. Without a stable conception of the object of life, man would not consent to go on living, and would rather destroy himself than remain on earth, though he had bread in abundance. That is true. But what happened? Instead of taking men's freedom from them, Thou didst make it greater than ever! Didst Thou forget that man prefers peace, and even death, to freedom of choice in the knowledge of good and evil? Nothing is more seductive for man than his freedom of conscience, but nothing is a greater cause of suffering. And behold, instead of giving a firm foundation for setting the conscience of man at rest for ever, Thou didst choose all that is exceptional, vague and enigmatic; Thou didst choose what was utterly beyond the strength of men, acting as though Thou didst not love them at all – Thou who didst come to give Thy life for them! Instead of taking possession of men's freedom, Thou didst increase it, and burdened the spiritual kingdom of mankind with its sufferings for ever. Thou didst desire man's free love, that he should follow Thee freely, enticed and taken captive by Thee. In place of the rigid ancient law, man must hereafter with free heart decide for himself what is good and what is evil, having only Thy image before him as his guide. But didst Thou not know that he would at last reject even Thy image and Thy truth, if he is weighed down with the fearful burden of free choice? They will cry aloud at last that the truth is not in Thee, for they could not have been left in greater confusion and suffering than Thou hast caused, laying upon them so many cares and unanswerable problems.

' "So that, in truth, Thou didst Thyself lay the foundation for the destruction of Thy kingdom, and no one is more to blame for it. Yet what was offered Thee? There are three powers, three powers alone, able to conquer and to hold captive for ever the conscience of these impotent rebels for their happiness: those forces are miracle, mystery and authority. Thou hast rejected all three and hast set the example for doing so, when the wise and dread spirit set Thee on the pinnacle of the temple and said to Thee, 'If Thou wouldst know whether Thou art the Son of God then cast Thyself down, for it is written: the angels shall hold him up lest he fall and bruise himself, and Thou shalt know then whether Thou art the Son of God and shalt prove then how great is Thy faith in Thy Father.' But Thou didst refuse and wouldst not cast Thyself down. Oh, of course, Thou didst proudly and well, like God; but the weak, unruly race of men, are they gods? Oh, Thou didst know then that in taking one step, in making one movement to cast Thyself down, Thou wouldst be tempting God and have lost all Thy faith in Him, and wouldst have been dashed to pieces against that earth which Thou didst come to save. And the wise spirit that tempted Thee would have rejoiced. But I ask again, are there many like Thee? And couldst Thou believe for one moment that men, too, could face such a temptation? Is the nature of men such, that they can reject miracle, and at the great moments of their life, the moments of their deepest, most agonising spiritual difficulties, cling only to the free verdict of the heart? Oh, Thou didst know that Thy deed would be recorded in books, would be handed down to remote times and the utmost ends of the earth, and Thou didst hope that man, following Thee, would cling to God and not ask for a miracle. But Thou didst not know that when man rejects miracle he rejects God too; for man seeks not so much God as the miraculous. And as man cannot bear to be without the miraculous, he will create new miracles of his own for himself, and will worship deeds of sorcery and witchcraft, though he might be a hundred times over a rebel, heretic and infidel. Thou didst not come down from the Cross when they shouted to Thee, mocking and reviling Thee, 'Come down from the cross and we will believe that Thou art He.' Thou didst not come down, for again Thou wouldst not enslave man by a miracle, and didst crave faith given freely, not based on miracle. Thou didst crave for free love and not the base raptures of the slave before the might that has overawed him for ever. But Thou didst think too highly of men therein, for they are slaves, of course, though rebellious by nature. Look round and judge; fifteen centuries have passed, look upon them. Whom hast Thou raised up to Thyself? I swear, man is weaker and baser by nature than Thou hast believed him! Can he, can he do what Thou didst? By showing him so much respect, Thou didst, as it were, cease to feel for him, for Thou didst ask far too much from him – Thou who hast loved him more than Thyself! Respecting him less, Thou wouldst have asked less of him. That would have been more like love, for his burden would have been lighter. He is weak and vile. What though he is everywhere now rebelling against our power, and proud of his rebellion? It is the pride of a child and a schoolboy. They are little children rioting and barring out the teacher at school. But their child-ish delight will end; it will cost them dear. Mankind as a whole has always striven to organise a universal state. There have been many great nations with great histories, but the more highly they were developed the more unhappy they were, for they felt more acutely than other people the craving for world-wide union. The great con-querors, Timours and Ghenghis-Khans, whirled like hurricanes over the face of the earth striving to subdue its people, and they too were but the unconscious expres-sion of the same craving for universal unity. Hadst Thou taken the world and Caesar's purple, Thou wouldst have founded the universal state and have given universal peace. For who can rule men if not he who holds their conscience and their bread in his hands? We have taken the sword of Caesar, and in taking it, of course, have rejected Thee and followed him. Oh, ages are yet to come of the confusion of free thought, of their science and cannibalism. For having begun to build their tower of Babel without us, they will end, of course, with cannibalism. But then the beast will crawl to us and lick our feet and spatter them with tears of blood. And we shall sit upon the beast and raise the cup, and on it will be written, 'Mystery.' But then, and only then, the reign of peace and happiness will come for men. Thou art proud of Thine elect, but Thou hast only the elect, while we give rest to all. And besides, how many of those elect, those mighty ones who could become elect, have grown weary waiting for Thee, and have transferred and will transfer the powers of their spirit and the warmth of their heart to the other camp, and end by raising their free banner against Thee. Thou didst Thyself lift up that banner. But with us, all will be happy and will no more rebel nor destroy one another as under Thy freedom. Oh, we shall persuade them that they will only become free when they renounce their freedom to us and submit to us. And shall we be right or shall we be lying? They will be convinced that we are right, for they will remember the horrors of slavery and confusion to which Thy freedom brought them. Freedom, free thought, and science will lead them into such straits and will bring them face to face with such marvels and insoluble mys-teries, that some of them, the fierce and rebellious, will destroy themselves, others, rebellious but weak, will destroy one another, while the rest, weak and unhappy, will crawl fawning to our feet and whine to us: 'Yes, you were right, you alone possess His mystery, and we come back to you, save us from ourselves!'

' "Receiving bread from us, they will see clearly that we take the bread made by their hands from them, to give it to them, without any miracle. They will see that we do not change the stones to bread, but in truth they will be more thankful for taking it from our hands than for the bread itself! For they will remember only too well that in old days, without our help, even the bread they made turned to stones in their hands, while since they have come back to us, the very stones have turned to bread in their hands. Too, too well will they know the value of complete submission! And until men know that, they will be unhappy. Who is most to blame for their not knowing it? – Speak! Who scattered the flock and sent it astray on unknown paths? But the flock will come together again and will submit once more, and then it will be once for all. Then we shall give them the quiet humble happiness of weak creatures such as they are by nature. Oh, we shall persuade them at last not to be proud, for Thou didst lift them up and thereby taught them to be proud. We shall show them that they are weak, that they are only pitiful children, but that childlike happiness is the sweetest of all. They will become timid and will look to us and huddle close to us in fear, as chicks to the hen. They will marvel at us and will be awe-stricken before us, and will be proud at our being so powerful and clever that we have been able to subdue such a turbulent flock of thousands of millions. They will tremble impotently before our wrath, their minds will grow fearful, they will be quick to shed tears like women and children, but they will be just as ready at a sign from us to pass to laughter and rejoicing, to happy mirth and childish song. Yes, we shall set them to work, but in their leisure hours we shall make their life like a child's game, with children's songs and innocent dance. Oh, we shall allow them even sin, they are weak and helpless, and they will love us like children because we allow them to sin. We shall tell them that every sin will be expiated, if it is done with our permission, that we allow them to sin because we love them, and the punishment for these sins we take upon ourselves. And we shall take it upon ourselves, and they will adore us as their saviours who have taken on themselves their sins before God. And they will have no secrets from us. We shall allow or forbid them to live with their wives and mistresses, to have or not to have children according to whether they have been obedient or disobedient – and they will submit to us gladly and cheerfully. The most painful secrets of their conscience, all, all they will bring to us, and we shall have an answer for all. And they will be glad to believe our answer, for it will save them from the great anxiety and terrible agony they endure at present in making a free decision for themselves. And all will be happy, all the millions of creatures except the hundred thousand who rule over them. For only we, we who guard the mystery, shall be unhappy. There will be thousands of millions of happy babes, and a hundred thousand sufferers who have taken upon themselves the curse of the knowledge of good and evil. Peacefully they will die, peacefully they will expire in Thy name, and beyond the grave they will find nothing but death. But we shall keep the secret, and for their happiness we shall allure them with the reward of heaven and eternity. Though if there were anything in the other world, it certainly would not be for such as they. It is prophesied that Thou wilt come again in victory, Thou wilt come with Thy chosen, the proud and strong, but we will say that they have only saved themselves, but we have saved all. We are told that the harlot who sits upon the beast, and holds in her hands the mystery, shall be put to shame, that the weak will rise up again, and will rend her royal purple and will strip naked her loathsome body. But then I will stand up and point out to Thee the thousand millions of happy children who have known no sin. And we who have taken their sins upon us for their happiness will stand up before Thee and say: 'Judge us if Thou canst and darest.' Know that I fear Thee not. Know that I too have been in the wilderness, I too have lived on roots and locusts, I too prized the freedom with which Thou hast blessed men, and I too was striving to stand among Thy elect, among the strong and powerful, thirsting 'to make up the number.' But I awakened and would not serve madness. I turned back and joined the ranks of those who have corrected Thy work. I left the proud and went back to the humble, for the happiness of the humble. What I say to Thee will come to pass, and our dominion will be built up. I repeat, to-morrow Thou shalt see that obedient flock who at a sign from me will hasten to heap up the hot cinders about the pile on which I shall burn Thee for coming to hinder us. For if anyone has ever deserved our fires, it is Thou. To-morrow I shall burn Thee. Dixi."'*

Ivan stopped. He was carried away as he talked, and spoke with excitement; when he had finished, he suddenly smiled.

Alyosha had listened in silence; towards the end he was greatly moved and seemed several times on the point of interrupting, but restrained himself. Now his words came with a rush.

'But . . . that's absurd!' he cried, flushing. 'Your poem is in praise of Jesus, not in blame of Him – as you meant it to be. And who will believe you about freedom? Is that the way to understand it? That's not the idea of it in the Orthodox Church. . . . That's Rome, and not even the whole of Rome, it's false – those are the worst of the Catholics the Inquisitors, the Jesuits! . . . And there could not be such a fantastic creature as your Inquisitor. What are these sins of mankind they take on themselves? Who are these keepers of the mystery who have taken some curse upon themselves for the happiness of mankind? When have they been seen? We know the Jesuits, they are spoken ill of, but surely they are not what you describe? They are not that at all, not at all. . . . They are simply the Romish army for the earthly sovereignty of the world in the future, with the Pontiff of Rome for Emperor . . . that's their ideal, but there's no sort of mystery or lofty melancholy about it. . . . It's simple lust of power, of filthy earthly gain, of domination – something like a universal serfdom with them as masters – that's all they stand for. They don't even believe in God perhaps. Your suffering Inquisitor is a mere fantasy.'

'Stay, stay,' laughed Ivan. 'How hot you are! A fantasy you say, let it be so! Of course it's a fantasy. But allow me to say: do you really think that the Roman Catholic movement of the last centuries is actually nothing but the lust of power, of filthy earthly gain? Is that Father Paissy's teaching?'

'No, no, on the contrary, Father Paissy did once say something rather the same as you . . . but of course it's not the same, not a bit the same,' Alyosha hastily corrected himself.

'A precious admission, in spite of your "not a bit the same." I ask you why your Jesuits and Inquisitors have united simply for vile material gain? Why can there not

---

*   I have spoken.

be among them one martyr oppressed by great sorrow and loving humanity? You see, only suppose that there was one such man among all those who desire nothing but filthy material gain – if there's only one like my old Inquisitor, who had himself eaten roots in the desert and made frenzied efforts to subdue his flesh to make himself free and perfect. But yet all his life he loved humanity, and suddenly his eyes were opened, and he saw that it is no great moral blessedness to attain perfection and freedom, if at the same time one gains the conviction that millions of God's creatures have been created as a mockery, that they will never be capable of using their freedom, that these poor rebels can never turn into giants to complete the tower, that it was not for such geese that the great idealist dreamt his dream of harmony. Seeing all that he turned back and joined – the clever people. Surely that could have happened?'

'Joined whom, what clever people?' cried Alyosha, completely carried away. 'They have no such great cleverness and no mysteries and secrets. . . . Perhaps nothing but Atheism, that's all their secret. Your Inquisitor does not believe in God, that's his secret!'

'What if it is so! At last you have guessed it. It's perfectly true, it's true that that's the whole secret, but isn't that suffering, at least for a man like that, who has wasted his whole life in the desert and yet could not shake off his incurable love of humanity? In his old age he reached the clear conviction that nothing but the advice of the great dread spirit could build up any tolerable sort of life for the feeble, unruly, "incomplete, empirical creatures created in jest." And so, convinced of this, he sees that he must follow the counsel of the wise spirit, the dread spirit of death and destruction, and therefore accept lying and deception, and lead men consciously to death and destruction, and yet deceive them all the way so that they may not notice where they are being led, that the poor blind creatures may at least on the way think themselves happy. And note, the deception is in the name of Him in Whose ideal the old man had so fervently believed all his life long. Is not that tragic? And if only one such stood at the head of the whole army "filled with the lust of power only for the sake of filthy gain" – would not one such be enough to make a tragedy? More than that, one such standing at the head is enough to create the actual leading idea of the Roman Church with all its armies and Jesuits, its highest idea. I tell you frankly that I firmly believe that there has always been such a man among those who stood at the head of the movement. Who knows? there may have been some such even among the Roman Popes. Who knows? perhaps the spirit of that accursed old man who loves mankind so obstinately in his own way, is to be found even now in a whole multitude of such old men, existing not by chance but by agreement, as a secret league formed long ago for the guarding of the mystery, to guard it from the weak and the unhappy, so as to make them happy. No doubt it is so, and so it must be indeed. I fancy that even among the Masons there's something of the same mystery at the bottom, and that that's why the Catholics so detest the Masons as their rivals breaking up the unity of the idea, while it is so essential that there should be one flock and one shepherd. . . . But from the way I defend my idea I might be an author impatient of your criticism. Enough of it.'

'You are perhaps a Mason yourself!' broke suddenly from Alyosha. 'You don't believe in God,' he added, speaking this time very sorrowfully. He fancied besides that his brother was looking at him ironically. 'How does your poem end?' he asked, suddenly looking down. 'Or was it the end?'

'I meant to end it like this. When the Inquisitor ceased speaking he waited some time for his Prisoner to answer him. His silence weighed down upon him. He saw that the Prisoner had listened intently all the time, looking gently in his face and evidently not wishing to reply. The old man longed for him to say something, however bitter and terrible. But He suddenly approached the old man in silence and softly kissed him on his bloodless aged lips. That was all his answer. The old man shuddered. His lips moved. He went to the door, opened it, and said to Him: "Go, and come no more . . . come not at all, never, never!" And he let Him out into the dark alleys of the town. The Prisoner went away.'

'And the old man?'

'The kiss glows in his heart, but the old man adheres to his idea.'

'And you with him, you too?' cried Alyosha, mournfully. Ivan laughed.

'Why, it's all nonsense, Alyosha. It's only a senseless poem of a senseless student, who could never write two lines of verse. Why do you take it so seriously? Surely you don't suppose I am going straight off to the Jesuits, to join the men who are correcting His work? Good Lord, it's no business of mine. I told you, all I want is to live on to thirty, and then . . . dash the cup to the ground!'

'But the little sticky leaves, and the precious tombs, and the blue sky, and the woman you love! How will you live, how will you love them?' Alyosha cried sorrowfully. 'With such a hell in your heart and your head, how can you? No, that's just what you are going away for, to join them . . . if not, you will kill yourself, you can't endure it!'

'There is a strength to endure everything,' Ivan said with a cold smile.

'The strength of the Karamazovs – the strength of the Karamazov baseness. To sink into debauchery, to stifle your soul with corruption, yes?'

'Possibly even that . . . only perhaps till I am thirty I shall escape it, and then –'

'How will you escape it? By what will you escape it? That's impossible with your ideas.'

'In the Karamazov way, again.'

' "Everything is lawful," you mean? Everything is lawful, is that it?'

Ivan scowled, and all at once turned strangely pale.

'Ah, you've caught up yesterday's phrase, which so offended Muisov – and which Dmitri pounced upon so naively and paraphrased!' he smiled queerly. 'Yes, if you like, "everything is lawful" since the word has been said, I won't deny it. And Mitya's version isn't bad.'

Alyosha looked at him in silence.

'I thought that going away from here I have you at least,' Ivan said suddenly, with unexpected feeling; 'but now I see that there is no place for me even in your heart, my dear hermit. The formula, "all is lawful," I won't renounce – will you renounce me for that, yes?'

Alyosha got up, went to him and softly kissed him on the lips.

'That's plagiarism,' cried Ivan, highly delighted. 'You stole that from my poem. Thank you though. Get up, Alyosha, it's time we were going, both of us.'

They went out, but stopped when they reached the entrance of the restaurant.

'Listen, Alyosha,' Ivan began in a resolute voice, 'if I am really able to care for the sticky little leaves I shall only love them, remembering you. It's enough for me that you are somewhere here, and I shan't lose my desire for life yet. Is that enough for you? Take it as a declaration of love if you like. And now you go to the right and I to the left. And it's enough, do you hear, enough. I mean even if I don't go away to-morrow (I think I certainly shall go) and we meet again, don't say a word more on these subjects. I beg that particularly. And about Dmitri too, I ask you specially, never speak to me again,' he added, with sudden irritation; 'it's all exhausted, it has all been said over and over again, hasn't it? And I'll make you one promise in return for it. When at thirty, I want to "dash the cup to the ground," wherever I may be I'll come to have one more talk with you, even though it were from America, you may be sure of that. I'll come on purpose. It will be very interesting to have a look at you, to see what you'll be by that time. It's rather a solemn promise, you see. And we really may be parting for seven years or ten. Come, go now to your Pater Seraphicus, he is dying. If he dies without you, you will be angry with me for having kept you. Good-bye, kiss me once more; that's right, now go.'

Ivan turned suddenly and went his way without looking back. It was just as Dmitri had left Alyosha the day before, though the parting had been very different. The strange resemblance flashed like an arrow through Alyosha's mind in the distress and dejection of that moment. He waited a little, looking after his brother. He suddenly noticed that Ivan swayed as he walked and that his right shoulder looked lower than his left. He had never noticed it before. But all at once he turned too, and almost ran to the monastery. It was nearly dark, and he felt almost frightened; something new was growing up in him for which he could not account. The wind had risen again as on the previous evening, and the ancient pines murmured gloomily about him when he entered the hermitage copse. He almost ran. 'Pater Seraphicus – he got that name from somewhere – where from?' Alyosha wondered. 'Ivan, poor Ivan, and when shall I see you again? . . . Here is the hermitage. Yes, yes, that he is, Pater Seraphicus, he will save me – from him and for ever!'

Several times afterwards he wondered how he could, on leaving Ivan, so completely forget his brother Dmitri, though he had that morning, only a few hours before, so firmly resolved to find him and not to give up doing so, even should he be unable to return to the monastery that night.

Questions for Study

1 What is the Grand Inquisitor's view of human nature? What does he feel that people *need* if they are to prosper?
2 What role does the temptation of Christ play in his analysis of the situation? Identify each of the elements which the Grand Inquisitor notes, and establish how he develops them in support of his basic theme.
3 How important is power to the Grand Inquisitor? Does he feel that Christianity has made the best use of the power at its disposal? In what way is the Inquisitor to be seen as a critic of traditional Christian values?

CHAPTER 78

Matthew Arnold (1822–1888)

Arnold was the son of one of England's most celebrated educationalists – Thomas Arnold, Master of Rugby School. He was educated at Winchester College and Rugby School, before going on to study at Balliol College, Oxford. Here he was awarded the Newdigate Prize for his poem *Cromwell* (1843). He gained second-class honors, and went on to become a fellow of Oriel College in 1845. He traveled in Europe and indulged in what many of his friends regarded as an essentially frivolous interest in literature.

His professional interests, like those of his father, lay in the field of education, and in 1851 he was appointed one of "Her Majesty's Inspectors of Schools." He never received further advancement within the English establishment, which appears to have caused only minimal resentment on his part. Several of his publications – most notably, *Schools and Universities on the Continent* (1868) – show his professional interest in issues of education. However, his reputation soon came to rest on a quite different style of literature.

The publication of his earliest volume of verse – *The Strayed Reveller* – in 1849 caused initial surprise to his circle of friends, followed by growing admiration. This was followed, in 1852, by *Empedocles on Etna*, and, in the following year, by *Poems*, a collection that established Arnold as a leading poet of the day. This work also included a "Preface" that was his first important publication in prose. He was elected professor of poetry at Oxford University for the decade 1857–67.

Arnold held religious matters to be of high importance, and frequently addressed religious issues in his later publications. It seems that the religious aspects of life came to occupy his attention increasingly as his career developed. Among his writings which specifically address religious issues, the following may be noted as having particular importance: *St Paul and Protestantism* (1870); *Literature and Dogma* (1873); *God and the Bible* (1875); and *Last Essays on Church and Religion* (1877).

Matthew Arnold (1822–1888)

Basic description

English poet, essayist and cultural critic.

Major works

St Paul and Protestantism (1870); Literature and Dogma (1873): God and the Bible (1875); Last Essays on Church and Religion (1877).

Editions of works

The Complete Prose Works of Matthew Arnold, ed. Robert H. Super, 11 vols. Ann Arbor, MI: University of Michigan Press, 1960–77.

Major studies

James C. Livingstone, Matthew Arnold and Christianity: His Religious Prose Writings. Columbia, SC: University of South Carolina Press, 1986.

William Robbins, The Ethical Idealism of Matthew Arnold: A Study of the Nature and Sources of his Moral and Religious Ideas. Toronto, ON: University of Toronto Press, 1959.

These works were met with opposition, from both High Church and Low Church critics. Perhaps the most strident criticism came from a former colleague at Oriel College, Oxford. It could be argued that the reputation of Arnold has to some extent been established largely by the testimony of his most influential critic – John Henry Newman. Newman had first known Arnold as one of the "noetics" at Oriel College whom he had been tempted to follow into some form of liberalism. In his Apologia Pro Vita Sua, Newman repeatedly declared that the great enemy he was fighting was liberalism, and that Arnold was a prime exemplar of that pernicious ideology. At one point, he asked rhetorically whether Arnold could even be considered a Christian. But others were more charitable, seeing Arnold as offering interpretations and criticisms which were necessary to Christianity in the light of developments in the High Victorian era.

For Arnold, religion was an essential element of British culture. He had little time for those who advocated, on the one hand, a rigid and unthinking orthodoxy, and on the other, a free-floating skepticism. "At the present moment," he wrote, "two things about the Christian religion must surely be clear to anybody with eyes in his head. One is, that men cannot do without it; the other, that they cannot do with it as it is." These words may be seen as setting out a religious manifesto, addressing an agenda which may be seen under consideration in a number of his later writings, particularly his Religion and Dogma (1870).

Text: Dover Beach

In his collection of poetry entitled New Poems (1867), Arnold included a short work entitled "Dover Beach." The poem is best read as a lament over the decline of religious faith in Victorian England, with the haunting image of the receding tide on Dover Beach seen as a metaphor of the seemingly inexorable erosion of religion.

> The sea is calm to-night.
> The tide is full, the moon lies fair
> Upon the straits; – on the French coast the light

Gleams and is gone; the cliffs of England stand,
Glimmering and vast, out in the tranquil bay.   5
Come to the window, sweet is the night-air!
Only, from the long line of spray
Where the sea meets the moon-blanch'd land,
Listen! you hear the grating roar
Of pebbles which the waves draw back, and fling,   10
At their return, up the high strand,
Begin, and cease, and then again begin,
With tremulous cadence slow, and bring
The eternal note of sadness in.

Sophocles long ago   15
Heard it on the Ægean, and it brought
Into his mind the turbid ebb and flow
Of human misery; we
Find also in the sound a thought,
Hearing it by this distant northern sea.   20

The Sea of Faith
Was once, too, at the full, and round earth's shore
Lay like the folds of a bright girdle furl'd.
But now I only hear
Its melancholy, long, withdrawing roar,   25
Retreating, to the breath
Of the night-wind, down the vast edges drear
And naked shingles of the world.

Ah, love, let us be true
To one another! for the world, which seems   30
To lie before us like a land of dreams,
So various, so beautiful, so new,
Hath really neither joy, nor love, nor light,
Nor certitude, nor peace, nor help for pain;
And we are here as on a darkling plain   35
Swept with confused alarms of struggle and flight,
Where ignorant armies clash by night.

Questions for Discussion

The poem opens by painting a verbal picture of Dover Beach, facing the distant French coastline. The following questions will help you interact with this text.

1   In the opening sections of the poem, we find Arnold depicting the scene on Dover Beach. Notice how he evokes the waves breaking against the shoreline. Why should this be associated in any way with an "eternal note of sadness"?
2   In the second stanza, Arnold explores the way in which the ancient Greek writer Sophocles developed the image of the tide. According to Arnold, what did Sophocles see it as indicating?
3   Arnold then makes the point that the same ebb and flow of the tide can bear meaning to those in northern Europe. What is the central point made in the third stanza concerning the "Sea of Faith." What does Arnold gain through using this image?
4   The final verse is openly pessimistic in its outlook. How does it relate to his earlier musings concerning an "eternal note of sadness"? Is there any hint that the receding tide of faith might turn?

CHAPTER 79

George MacDonald (1824–1905)

George MacDonald was born at Huntley in west Aberdeenshire in 1824. After attending local schools, he went up to Aberdeen University in 1840–1 and again in 1844–5, taking prizes in chemistry and natural philosophy. At some point between these courses of study at Aberdeen, MacDonald appears to have catalogued the library of an estate in northern Scotland, possibly Thurso Castle.

After completing his studies at Aberdeen, MacDonald traveled south to London, where he tutored for three years. Yet MacDonald had long cherished the idea of entering into Christian ministry; at some point around 1848, he began to study for the Congregationalist ministry at the Independent College, Highbury. He was made pastor at Trinity Congregational Church, Arundel, in 1850, and married Louisa Powell two years later. By this stage, however, it was clear that his ministry was running into difficulty. His Arundel congregation expressed irritation at what they saw as the unbiblical ideas contained in his sermons. The deacons of the church managed to force his resignation in 1853.

George MacDonald (1824–1905)

Basic description
Leading nineteenth-century Scottish novelist, poet, clergyman, and author of children's stories.

Major works
Within and Without (1855); *Poems* (1857); *Phantastes* (1858); *David Elginbrod* (1862); *Alec Forbes* (1865); *Robert Falconer* (1868).

Major studies
Joseph Johnson, *George MacDonald: A Biographical and Critical Appreciation*. London: Pitman, 1906.

Cynthia Marshall, *Essays on C. S. Lewis and George MacDonald: Truth, Fiction and the Power of Imagination*. Lewiston, NY: Mellen, 1991.

William Raeper, *The Gold Thread: Essays on George MacDonald*. Edinburgh: Edinburgh University Press, 1990.

Disillusioned with the ministry of his church, MacDonald settled briefly in Manchester. He went to Algiers for a short time for the sake of his health, and then returned to England. He was now convinced that his calling was to be a professional writer. He abandoned his Congregationalist denomination, and became instead a lay member of the Church of England in 1860.

In 1855, his first work – a poem entitled "Within and Without" – was published. This was followed by a series of works, which gradually established his reputation as a professional writer. The first major success was *David Elginbrod* (1862), a novel which reflected the Scottish country life MacDonald had known as a young man. Two more successful novels followed in the same vein – *Alec Forbes* (1865) and *Robert Falconer* (1868). Yet MacDonald is perhaps best remembered for his children's stories, such as *The Princess and the Goblin* (1872), and *The Princess and Curdie* (1882). MacDonald's *Phantastes* is recognized as a classic of adult fantasy writing, and had a considerable impact on later writers, particularly J. R. R. Tolkien and C. S. Lewis.

Yet despite his considerable literary success, MacDonald's financial returns from his works was very modest. He proved unable to provide for the needs of his wife and family. In 1877 he was pensioned at the request of Queen Victoria. An additional complication was that he was in poor health. In 1877, he traveled to Italy in an attempt to find a more congenial climate for his daughter Mary Josephine, who was seriously ill. She died the following year; yet MacDonald found the Italian climate so beneficial to himself that he resolved to spend the greater part of each year at Bordighera, in a house that he had built with the aid of friends. Both MacDonald and his wife are buried in the grounds of the house (Casa Coraggio).

Text: *Lilith: A Romance*

Lilith is widely regarded as MacDonald's masterpiece. Yet it is also a dark and brooding work, which caused considerable distress to Louisa. It seemed to her that MacDonald was losing his mind as he wrote the work. On reading *Lilith* for the first time, it is not difficult to understand her fears. The work appears to have gone through as many as eight drafts before MacDonald was prepared to allow it to be published. MacDonald's eldest son Greville preferred the first draft, as he argued that it was in this version that the work's complex spiritual structure was most clearly seen.

To understand the work, we need to consider its title. "Lilith" is a mythological female figure encountered in the Jewish *Cabbala*. In one version of the medieval cabbalistic tradition, Lilith was the original woman, created directly by God along with Adam. Yet Lilith refused to accept any position of inferiority to Adam, and rebelled against him, leaving Eden, to embark on an eternal vendetta against infants and young men. She figures in Milton's *Paradise Lost* and Goethe's *Faust*. Yet it seems that MacDonald first became familiar with the "Lilith" tradition through one of the most striking works of Dante Gabriel Rossetti. Rossetti's 1864 painting *Lady Lileth* depicts her as a surreal figure with long golden hair, surrounded by roses and poppies. MacDonald made use of this figure for the first time in *Adela Cathcart* (1864), in which Lilith appears as the daughter of an artist who enjoys depicting scenes of torture. The importance of the Lilith-figure for MacDonald appears to have been enhanced through the publication of Algernon Charles Swinburne's poem "Dolores" (1866).

The book opens by narrating how its central character – we cannot call him a "hero" – visits a library, and steps through a mirror into a dream-world. There are obvious parallels here with Lewis Carroll's *Alice Through the Looking Glass*, and it should be recalled that Carroll (Charles Dodgson) and MacDonald were close friends during the 1860s. The dream-world that Mr Vane enters, however, is very different from the slightly comical world encountered by Alice; it is sinister, even occult. Vane has to learn that he is spiritually empty before he can achieve self-knowledge and fulfillment. In one sense, Vane can be seen as representing the spiritual condition of humanity in general. Yet *Lilith* cannot really be thought of as an allegory. Although biblical allusions can easily be discerned, it is often far from clear what they are intended to mean.

Mr Vane proves totally unable to comprehend the world he has entered – a difficulty, incidentally, which will not be unfamiliar to most readers of the work. Early reviewers of the work found it to be nothing less than baffling. While there are clear parallels between MacDonald and both Dante and Blake, it is far from clear how much light this observation casts on things. It is probably most helpful to think of the book as an exploration of the human fears of sexuality and death, with the figure of Lilith embodying both. Lilith is both a sexual temptress and the one who brings death. Yet this fails to do justice to the immense complexity of the work, which deals with such subjects as the inalienable subjectivity of the author.

Our extract consists of the second and third chapters, which relate Mr Vane's passage into the mysterious dream-world.

Chapter 2: The Mirror

NOTHING more happened for some days. I think it was about a week after, when what I have now to tell took place.

I had often thought of the manuscript fragment, and repeatedly tried to discover some way of releasing it, but in vain: I could not find out what held it fast.

But I had for some time intended a thorough overhauling of the books in the closet, its atmosphere causing me uneasiness as to their condition. One day the intention suddenly became a resolve, and I was in the act of rising from my chair to make a beginning, when I saw the old librarian moving from the door of the closet toward the farther end of the room. I ought rather to say only that I caught sight of something shadowy from which I received the impression of a slight, stooping man, in a shabby dress-coat reaching almost to his heels, the tails of which, disparting a little as he walked, revealed thin legs in black stockings, and large feet in wide, slipper-like shoes.

At once I followed him: I might be following a shadow, but I never doubted I was following something. He went out of the library into the hall, and across to the foot of the great staircase, then up the stairs to the first floor, where lay the chief rooms. Past these rooms, I following close, he continued his way, through a wide corridor, to the foot of a narrower stair leading to the second floor. Up that he went also, and when I reached the top, strange as it may seem, I found myself in a region almost unknown to me. I never had brother or sister to incite to such romps as make children familiar with nook and cranny; I was a mere child when my guardian took me away; and I had never seen the house again until, about a month before, I returned to take possession.

Through passage after passage we came to a door at the bottom of a winding wooden stair, which we ascended. Every step creaked under my foot, but I heard no sound from that of my guide. Somewhere in the middle of the stair I lost sight of him, and from the top of it the shadowy shape was nowhere visible. I could not even imagine I saw him. The place was full of shadows, but he was not one of them.

I was in the main garret, with huge beams and rafters over my head, great spaces around me, a door here and there in sight, and long vistas whose gloom was thinned by a few lurking cobwebbed windows and small dusky skylights. I gazed with a strange mingling of awe and pleasure: the wide expanse of garret was my own, and unexplored!

In the middle of it stood an unpainted inclosure of rough planks, the door of which was ajar. Thinking Mr. Raven might be there, I pushed the door, and entered.

The small chamber was full of light, but such as dwells in places deserted: it had a dull, disconsolate look, as if it found itself of no use, and regretted having come. A few rather dim sunrays, marking their track through the cloud of motes that had just been stirred up, fell upon a tall mirror with a dusty face, old-fashioned and rather narrow – in appearance an ordinary glass. It had an ebony frame, on the top of which stood a black eagle, with outstretched wings, in his beak a golden chain, from whose end hung a black ball.

I had been looking at rather than into the mirror, when suddenly I became aware that it reflected neither the chamber nor my own person. I have an impression of having seen the wall melt away, but what followed is enough to account for any uncertainty: – could I have mistaken for a mirror the glass that protected a wonderful picture?

I saw before me a wild country, broken and heathy. Desolate hills of no great height, but somehow of strange appearance, occupied the middle distance; along the horizon stretched the tops of a far-off mountain range; nearest me lay a tract of moorland, flat and melancholy.

Being short-sighted, I stepped closer to examine the texture of a stone in the immediate foreground, and in the act espied, hopping toward me with solemnity, a large and ancient raven, whose purply black was here and there softened with gray. He seemed looking for worms as he came. Nowise astonished at the appearance of a live creature in a picture, I took another step forward to see him better, stumbled over something – doubtless the frame of the mirror – and stood nose to beak with the bird: I was in the open air, on a houseless heath!

Chapter 3: The Raven

I TURNED and looked behind me: all was vague and uncertain, as when one cannot distinguish between fog and field, between cloud and mountain-side. One fact only was plain – that I saw nothing I knew. Imagining myself involved in a visual illusion, and that touch would correct sight, I stretched my arms and felt about me, walking in this direction and that, if haply, where I could see nothing, I might yet come in contact with something; but my search was vain. Instinctively then, as to the only living thing near me, I turned to the raven, which stood a little way off, regarding me with an expression at once respectful and quizzical. Then the absurdity of seeking counsel from such a one struck me, and I turned again, overwhelmed with bewilderment, not unmingled with fear. Had I wandered into a region where both the material and psychical relations of our world had ceased to hold? Might a man at any moment step beyond the realm of order, and become the sport of the lawless? Yet I saw the raven, felt the ground under my feet, and heard a sound as of wind in the lowly plants around me!

'How *did* I get here?' I said – apparently aloud, for the question was immediately answered.

'You came through the door,' replied an odd, rather harsh voice.

I looked behind, then all about me, but saw no human shape. The terror that madness might be at hand laid hold upon me: must I henceforth place no confidence either in my senses or my consciousness? The same instant I knew it was the raven that had spoken, for he stood looking up at me with an air of waiting. The sun was not shining, yet the bird seemed to cast a shadow, and the shadow seemed part of himself.

I beg my reader to aid me in the endeavour to make myself intelligible – if here understanding be indeed possible between us. I was in a world, or call it a state of things, an economy of conditions, an idea of existence, so little correspondent with the ways and modes of this world – which we are apt to think the only world, that the best choice I can make of word or phrase is but an adumbration of what I would convey. I begin indeed to fear that I have undertaken an impossibility, undertaken to tell what I cannot tell because no speech at my command will fit the forms in my mind. Already I have set down statements I would gladly change did I know how to substitute a truer utterance; but as often as I try to fit the reality with nearer words, I find myself in danger of losing the things themselves, and feel like one in process of awaking from a dream, with the thing that seemed familiar gradually yet swiftly changing through a succession of forms until its very nature is no longer recognisable.

I bethought me that a bird capable of addressing a man must have the right of a man to a civil answer; perhaps, as a bird, even a greater claim.

A tendency to croak caused a certain roughness in his speech, but his voice was not disagreeable, and what he said, although conveying little enlightenment, did not sound rude.

'I did not come through any door,' I rejoined.

'I saw you come through it! – saw you with my own ancient eyes!' asserted the raven, positively but not disrespectfully.

'I never saw any door!' I persisted.

'Of course not!' he returned; 'all the doors you had yet seen – and you haven't seen many – were doors in; here you came upon a door out! The strange thing to you,' he went on thoughtfully, 'will be, that the more doors you go out of, the farther you get in!'

'Oblige me by telling me where I am.'

'That is impossible. You know nothing about whereness. The only way to come to know where you are is to begin to make yourself at home.'

'How am I to begin that where everything is so strange?'

'By doing something.'

'What?'

'Anything; and the sooner you begin the better! For until you are at home, you will find it as difficult to get out as it is to get in.'

'I have, unfortunately, found it too easy to get in; once out I shall not try again!'

'You have stumbled in, and may, possibly, stumble out again. Whether you have got in *unfortunately* remains to be seen.'

'Do you never go out, sir?'

'When I please I do, but not often, or for long. Your world is such a half-baked sort of place, it is at once so childish and so self-satisfied – in fact, it is not sufficiently developed for an old raven – at your service!'

'Am I wrong, then, in presuming that a man is superior to a bird?'

'That is as it may be. We do not waste our intellects in generalising, but take man or bird as we find him – I think it is now my turn to ask you a question!'

'You have the best of rights,' I replied, 'in the fact that you *can* do so!'

'Well answered!' he rejoined. 'Tell me, then, who you are – if you happen to know.'

'How should I help knowing? I am myself, and must know!'

'If you know you are yourself, you know that you are not somebody else; but do you know that you are yourself? Are you sure you are not your own father? – or, excuse me, your own fool? – Who are you, pray?'

I became at once aware that I could give him no notion of who I was. Indeed, who was I? It would be no answer to say I was who! Then I understood that I did not know myself, did not know what I was, had no grounds on which to determine that I was one and not another. As for the name I went by in my own world, I had forgotten it, and did not care to recall it, for it meant nothing, and what it might be was plainly of no consequence here. I had indeed almost forgotten that there it was a custom for everybody to have a name! So I held my peace, and it was my wisdom; for what should I say to a creature such as this raven, who saw through accident into entity?

'Look at me,' he said, 'and tell me who I am.'

As he spoke, he turned his back, and instantly I knew him. He was no longer a raven, but a man above the middle height with a stoop, very thin, and wearing a long black tail-coat. Again he turned, and I saw him a raven.

'I have seen you before, sir,' I said, feeling foolish rather than surprised.

'How can you say so from seeing me behind?' he rejoined. 'Did you ever see yourself behind? You have never seen yourself at all! – Tell me now, then, who I am.'

'I humbly beg your pardon,' I answered: 'I believe you were once the librarian of our house, but more *who* I do not know.'

'Why do you beg my pardon?'

'Because I took you for a raven,' I said – seeing him before me as plainly a raven as bird or man could look.

'You did me no wrong,' he returned. 'Calling me a raven, or thinking me one, you allowed me existence, which is the sum of what one can demand of his fellow-beings. Therefore, in return, I will give you a lesson: – No one can say he is himself, until first he knows that he *is*, and then what *himself* is. In fact, nobody is himself, and himself is nobody. There is more in it than you can see now, but not more than you need to see. You have, I fear, got into this region too soon, but none the less you must get to be at home in it; for home, as you may or may not know, is the only place where you can go out and in. There are places you can go into, and places you can go out of; but the one place, if you do but find it, where you may go out and in both, is home.'

He turned to walk away, and again I saw the librarian. He did not appear to have changed, only to have taken up his shadow. I know this seems nonsense, but I cannot help it.

I gazed after him until I saw him no more; but whether distance hid him, or he disappeared among the heather, I cannot tell.

Could it be that I was dead, I thought, and did not know it? Was I in what we used to call the world beyond the grave? And must I wander about seeking my place in it? How was I to find myself at home? The raven said I must do something: what could I do here? – And would that make me somebody? For now, alas, I was nobody!

I took the way Mr. Raven had gone, and went slowly after him. Presently I saw a wood of tall slender pine-trees, and turned toward it. The odour of it met me on my way, and I made haste to bury myself in it.

Plunged at length in its twilight glooms, I spied before me something with a shine, standing between two of the stems. It had no colour, but was like the translucent trembling of the hot air that rises, in a radiant summer noon, from the sun-baked ground, vibrant like the smitten chords of a musical instrument. What it was grew no plainer as I went nearer, and when I came close up, I ceased to see it, only the form and colour of the trees beyond seemed strangely uncertain. I would have passed between the stems, but received a slight shock, stumbled, and fell. When I rose, I saw before me the wooden wall of the garret chamber. I turned, and there was the mirror, on whose top the black eagle seemed but that moment to have perched.

Terror seized me, and I fled. Outside the chamber the wide garret spaces had an *uncanny* look. They seemed to have long been waiting for something; it had come, and they were waiting again! A shudder went through me on the winding stair: the house had grown strange to me! Something was about to leap upon me from behind! I darted down the spiral, struck against the wall and fell, rose and ran. On the next floor I lost my way, and had gone through several passages a second time ere I found the head of the stair. At the top of the great stair I had come to myself a little, and in a few moments I sat recovering my breath in the library.

Nothing should ever again make me go up that last terrible stair! The garret at the top of it pervaded the whole house! It sat upon it, threatening to crush me out of it! The brooding brain of the building, it was full of mysterious dwellers, one or other of whom might any moment appear in the library where I sat! I was nowhere safe! I would let, I would sell the dreadful place, in which an aërial portal stood ever open to creatures whose life was other than human! I would purchase a crag in Switzerland, and thereon build a wooden nest of one story with never a garret above it, guarded by some grand old peak that would send down nothing worse than a few tons of whelming rock!

I knew all the time that my thinking was foolish, and was even aware of a certain undertone of contemptuous humour in it; but suddenly it was checked, and I seemed again to hear the croak of the raven.

'If I know nothing of my own garret,' I thought, 'what is there to secure me against my own brain? Can I tell what it is even now generating? – what thought it may present me the next moment, the next month, or a year away? What is at the heart of my brain? What is behind my *think*? Am I there at all? – Who, what am I?'

I could no more answer the question now than when the raven put it to me in – at – 'Where in? – where at?' I said, and gave myself up as knowing anything of myself or the universe.

I started to my feet, hurried across the room to the masked door, where the mutilated volume, sticking out from the flat of soulless, bodiless, non-existent books, appeared to beckon me, went down on my knees, and opened it as far as its position would permit, but could see nothing. I got up again, lighted a taper, and peeping as into a pair of reluctant jaws, perceived that the manuscript was verse. Further I could not carry discovery. Beginnings of lines were visible on the left-hand page, and ends of lines on the other; but I could not, of course, get at the beginning and end of a single line, and was unable, in what I could read, to make any guess at the sense. The mere words, however, woke in me feelings which to describe was, from their strangeness, impossible. Some dreams, some poems, some musical phrases, some pictures, wake feelings such as one never had before, new in colour and form – spiritual sensations, as it were, hitherto unproved: here, some of the phrases, some of the senseless half-lines, some even of the individual words affected me in similar fashion – as with the aroma of an idea, rousing in me a great longing to know what the poem or poems might, even yet in their mutilation, hold or suggest.

I copied out a few of the larger shreds attainable, and tried hard to complete some of the lines, but without the least success. The only thing I gained in the effort was so much weariness that, when I went to bed, I fell asleep at once and slept soundly.

In the morning all that horror of the empty garret spaces had left me.

Questions for Study

1 Compare the above reading with Lewis Carroll's *Alice in Wonderland*. What similarities can you discern? And what differences?
2 C. S. Lewis's *The Lion, the Witch and the Wardrobe* includes a similar motif. What parallels can you discern? What is the equivalent to the mirror in Lewis's novel?
3 The motif of shadows occurs at several points in this extract. What role do shadows play for MacDonald?
4 The dream-world entered by Mr Vane can be thought of as the occult and irrational, which stands in contrast to the sensible and rational world of everyday life. What points do you think MacDonald is making here?

CHAPTER 80

Thomas Hardy (1840–1928)

Thomas Hardy was born in a cottage in Higher Bockhampton, near Dorchester, on June 2, 1840 as the eldest child of Thomas Hardy and Jemima Hand. He was educated locally, initially in the village school at Stinsford, and then at Dorchester, under Isaac Last. At the age of sixteen, Hardy was articled to a Dorchester architect, John Hicks. His intellectual development was stimulated by his friendship with Horace Moule, the son of Henry Moule, a local cleric. Moule encouraged Hardy to begin studying Latin and Greek.

In 1862, Hardy moved to London to begin with another architect, Arthur Blomfield. At this stage, he began his long relationship with Eliza Nicholls. He purchased copies of Nuttall's *Standard Pronouncing Dictionary* and Walker's *Rhyming Dictionary*, so that he could begin to write poetry. Although his writings from this period are for the most part poetry, his first publication took the form of an essay – "How I Built Myself a House," which appeared in *Chambers's Journal* in March 1865.

By 1867 he had returned to Dorset to work as Hicks's assistant, specializing in church restoration. He began work on his first (unpublished) novel, *The Poor Man and the Lady*, which he submitted for publication to Alexander Macmillan. Macmillan rejected the work, but recommended submission of the text to Chapman and Hall. Hardy proved unable to secure publication of his novel with this company, or any other he approached.

His professional and personal life took a new turn in 1869, when he accepted a position with the Weymouth architect G. R. Crickmay, who specialized in church restoration. While working on the restoration of the local parish church of St. Juliot in Cornwall in 1870, Hardy met his first wife, Emma Lavinia Gifford, the daughter of the rector of the church which was being restored. They were married in 1874, by which stage he had published four novels and was earning his living as a writer.

Thomas Hardy (1840–1928)

Basic description

English novelist and poet.

Major works

The Mayor of Casterbridge (1886); *The Woodlanders* (1887); *Tess of the D'Urbervilles* (1891); *The Pursuit of the Well-Beloved* (1892); *Jude the Obscure* (1895).

Major studies

Robert Gittings, *Young Thomas Hardy*. London: Heinemann, 1975.

Martin Seymour-Smith, *Hardy*. London: Bloomsbury, 1994.

More novels followed. In 1878 the Hardys moved from Dorset to Tooting in London, so that Hardy could be involved in the capital's literary scene. But in 1885, after building Max Gate, on the outskirts of Dorchester, Hardy again returned to his native Dorset. He then produced most of his major novels: *The Mayor of Casterbridge* (1886), *The Woodlanders* (1887), *Tess of the D'Urbervilles* (1891), *The Pursuit of the Well-Beloved* (1892), and *Jude the Obscure* (1895). This final work caused some considerable controversy, and led Hardy to turn his attention from prose to poetry. During the next thirty years he published over nine hundred poems and an epic drama in verse, *The Dynasts*.

Hardy's personal life was turbulent, to say the least. The controversy which was generated by the publication of *Jude the Obscure* did much to exacerbate the worsening relationship between Hardy and his wife. After a long and bitter estrangement, Emma Gifford died suddenly at Max Gate in 1912. Paradoxically, the event triggered some of Hardy's finest love poetry. After her death, Hardy kept his desk calendar permanently fixed on the date of their first meeting – March, 7 [1870]. In 1914, however, he married Florence Dugdale, to whom he had been close for several years. By then, he had been awarded the Order of Merit and was widely acknowledged as the major literary figure of the time. He died on January 11, 1928. His ashes were buried in Westminster Abbey, and his heart at Stinsford Churchyard in Dorset, next to the body of his first wife, Emma.

Text: *Jude the Obscure*

The text chosen for inclusion is taken from Hardy's last novel, *Jude the Obscure*. This is a complex novel, which draws heavily on Hardy's experience as a restorer of churches. One of the most helpful ways of reading the novel is to see it as a critical commentary on the modern period, and especially its relation to the past. The work has many religious facets, making its inclusion in this anthology essential. The book focuses on Jude Fawley and his cousin and lover, Sue Bridehead, each of whom is deeply wedded to Romantic ideals – ideals which are deeply embedded in their personalities, and yet are almost completely antithetical to the society in which they live. Hardy had touched on a similar theme in *The Woodlanders*, where we find a tone of sad, quiet, lament for the passing of the traditional rural ways of the past. The tone of *Jude* is much darker, more bitter and cynical, and expresses a far more tragic vision – namely, that Romantic ideals simply could not exist in a universe which was so strongly Darwinian in its outlook. There is thus a tension between the Romantic and the realist element in *Jude*: the reader wants Jude to succeed, yet realizes that he cannot. The resulting novel could thus be described as a tragedy, not only because of its plot, but also because of Hardy's obvious pity for Jude's suffering. This sympathy is perhaps more obvious and natural than it might have otherwise been, in that Hardy's decision to cast Jude as a stonemason and church restorer aspiring to academia bears a remarkable parallel to Hardy's own career and aspirations.

Hardy creates Jude as a Romantic idealist, who is disappointed by both the objects of his idealization – Christminster (a very thinly disguised Oxford), and his cousin and lover, Sue Bridehead. Sue has no time for a romanticized past. Where Jude would find solace in a cathedral, Sue would prefer to find it in a railway station. Jude's religion is strongly idealist, inspired by medieval visions of what Christianity ought to be. He is considering taking Holy Orders, which Sue regards as hopelessly outmoded, and showing an unhealthy attachment to an outdated past.

The town of Christminster itself is of critical importance to the novel, in that it embodies all that religion and culture ought to be. Christminster and the other towns through which Jude passes in his travels allow Hardy to show off his knowledge of stonemasonry – and hence develop this image of Gothic restoration as an allegory of the false repristination of the past. These towns also function as symbols of what Victorian modernity regarded as the useless romanticized past. The first old town that fails to meet Jude's aspirations is Marygreen. Though rural and backward, the town had been "restored." It was now artificially gothic. Marygreen thus clashes with Jude's sincerely medieval temperament. Disappointed, he attaches his longings to the city "veiled in mist" – Christminster. Every decision that Jude consciously makes from the moment he first sees the town is calculated to ensure that he finds a place inside the city gates. He learns Latin and Greek; he becomes an apprentice stonemason so that he can be near the colleges.

It is important to note that Hardy deliberately uses Jude's expertise in every kind of masonry to bring out his character's complete blindness to the reality of Christminster. Christminster is presented as a Romantic ideal; it is the glorious spirit of medievalism embodied in stone. Yet Jude sees only the superficial. Even though he ought to have been able to see the inconsistencies and tensions, he ignores the signs of falsehood, signs that go deeper than the false faces of buildings. Describing Jude's approach to the first "mediaeval pile," Hardy comments that when Jude "passed objects out of harmony with its general expression he allowed his eyes to slip over them as if he did not see them." Jude appreciates that "copying, patching, and imitating went on," but naively chooses to believe that this is due to a "temporary and local cause." Jude completely fails to see that "mediaevalism was as dead as a fernleaf in a lump of coal; that other developments were shaping in the world around him, in which Gothic architecture and its associations had no place." Jude represents an earlier period in history – one which is incompatible with Victorian modernity. So why is Jude blind to Christminster's defects? Perhaps the simplest answer is the right answer – because he *wants* to believe in its ideals.

Jude can be seen as a critique of those who wished to restore the cultural, moral, and religious outlook of earlier periods in Victorian England. These ideals are lost and illusory, and will only disappoint those who look to them for salvation. The restoration of the religious past is as artificial as Gothic restoration. Hardy's criticism of the medievalism of the Oxford Movement was no accident.

The section of *Jude* selected for consideration describes Jude's arrival in Christminster, and his initial reaction to what he observes.

'Save his own soul he hath no star.' – SWINBURNE

'Notitiam primosque gradus vicinia fecit; Tempore crevit amor.' – OVID

THE next noteworthy move in Jude's life was that in which he appeared gliding steadily onward through a dusky landscape of some three years' later leafage than had graced his courtship of Arabella, and the disruption of his coarse conjugal life with her. He was walking towards Christminster City, at a point a mile or two to the south-west of it.

He had at last found himself clear of Marygreen and Alfredston: he was out of his apprenticeship, and with his tools at his back seemed to be in the way of making a new start – the start to which, barring the interruption involved in his intimacy and married experience with Arabella, he had been looking forward for about ten years.

Jude would now have been described as a young man with a forcible, meditative, and earnest rather than handsome cast of countenance. He was of dark complexion, with dark harmonizing eyes, and he wore a closely trimmed black beard of more advanced growth than is usual at his age; this, with his great mass of black curly hair, was some trouble to him in combing and washing out the stone-dust that settled on it in the pursuit of his trade. His capabilities in the latter, having been acquired in the country, were of an all-round sort, including monumental stone-cutting, gothic free-stone work for the restoration of churches, and carving of a general kind. In London he would probably have become specialized and have made himself a 'moulding mason', a 'foliage sculptor' – perhaps a 'statuary'.

He had that afternoon driven in a cart from Alfredston to the village nearest the city in this direction, and was now walking the remaining four miles rather from choice than from necessity, having always fancied himself arriving thus.

The ultimate impulse to come had had a curious origin – one more nearly related to the emotional side of him than to the intellectual, as is often the case with young men. One day while in lodgings at Alfredston he had gone to Marygreen to see his old aunt, and had observed between the brass candlesticks on her mantelpiece the photograph of a pretty girlish face, in a broad hat with radiating folds under the brim like the rays of a halo. He had asked who she was. His grand-aunt had gruffly replied that she was his cousin Sue Bridehead, of the inimical branch of the family; and on further questioning the old woman had replied that the girl lived in Christminster, though she did not know where, or what she was doing.

His aunt would not give him the photograph. But it haunted him; and ultimately formed a quickening ingredient in his latent intent of following his friend the school-master thither.

He now paused at the top of a crooked and gentle declivity, and obtained his first near view of the city. Grey stoned and dun-roofed, it stood within hail of the Wessex border, and almost with the tip of one small toe within it, at the northernmost point of the crinkled line along which the leisurely Thames strokes the fields of that ancient kingdom. The buildings now lay quiet in the sunset, a vane here and there on their many spires and domes giving sparkle to a picture of sober secondary and tertiary hues.

Reaching the bottom he moved along the level way between pollard willows growing indistinct in the twilight, and soon confronted the outmost lamps of the town – some of those lamps which had sent into the sky the gleam and glory that caught his strained gaze in his days of dreaming, so many years ago. They winked their yellow eyes at him dubiously, and as if, though they had been awaiting him all these years in disappointment at his tarrying, they did not much want him now.

He was a species of Dick Whittington whose spirit was touched to finer issues than a mere material gain. He went along the outlying streets with the cautious tread of an explorer. He saw nothing of the real city in the suburbs on this side. His first want being a lodging he scrutinized carefully such localities as seemed to offer on inexpensive terms the modest type of accommodation he demanded; and after inquiry took a room in a suburb nick-named 'Beersheba', though he did not know this at the time. Here he installed himself, and having had some tea sallied forth.

It was a windy, whispering, moonless night. To guide himself he opened under a lamp a map he had brought. The breeze ruffled and fluttered it, but he could see enough to decide on the direction he should take to reach the heart of the place.

After many turnings he came up to the first ancient mediæval pile that he had encountered. It was a college, as he could see by the gateway. He entered it, walked round, and penetrated to dark corners which no lamplight reached. Close to this college was another; and a little further on another; and then he began to be encircled as it were with the breath and sentiment of the venerable city. When he passed objects out of harmony with its general expression he allowed his eyes to slip over them as if he did not see them.

A bell began clanging, and he listened till a hundred-and-one strokes had sounded. He must have made a mistake, he thought: it was meant for a hundred.

When the gates were shut, and he could no longer get into the quadrangles, he rambled under the walls and doorways, feeling with his fingers the contours of their mouldings and carving. The minutes passed, fewer and fewer people were visible, and still he serpentined among the shadows, for had he not imagined these scenes through ten bygone years, and what mattered a night's rest for once? High against the black sky the flash of a lamp would show crocketed pinnacles and indented battlements. Down obscure alleys, apparently never trodden now by the foot of man, and whose very existence seemed to be forgotten, there would jut into the path porticoes, oriels, doorways of enriched and florid middle-age design, their extinct air being accentuated by the rottenness of the stones. It seemed impossible that modern thought could house itself in such decrepit and superseded chambers.

Knowing not a human being here, Jude began to be impressed with the isolation of his own personality, as with a self-spectre, the sensation being that of one who walked but could not make himself seen or heard. He drew his breath pensively, and, seeming thus almost his own ghost, gave his thoughts to the other ghostly presences with which the nooks were haunted.

During the interval of preparation for this venture, since his wife and furniture's uncompromising disappearance into space, he had read and learnt almost all that could be read and learnt by one in his position, of the worthies who had spent their youth within these reverend walls, and whose souls had haunted them in their maturer age. Some of them, by the accidents of his reading, loomed out in his fancy disproportionately large by comparison with the rest. The brushings of the wind against the angles, buttresses, and door-jambs were as the passing of these only other inhabitants, the tappings of each ivy leaf on its neighbour were as the mutterings of their mournful souls, the shadows as their thin shapes in nervous movement, making him comrades in his solitude. In the gloom it was as if he ran against them without feeling their bodily frames.

The streets were now deserted, but on account of these things he could not go in. There were poets abroad, of early date and of late, from the friend and eulogist of Shakespeare down to him who has recently passed into silence, and that musical one of the tribe who is still among us. Speculative philosophers drew along, not always with wrinkled foreheads and hoary hair as in framed portraits, but pink-faced, slim, and active as in youth; modern divines sheeted in their surplices, among whom the most real to Jude Fawley were the founders of the religious school called Tractarian; the well-known three, the enthusiast, the poet, and the formularist, the echoes of whose teachings had influenced him even in his obscure home. A start of aversion appeared in his fancy to move them at sight of those other sons of the place, the form in the full-bottomed wig, statesman, rake, reasoner, and sceptic; the smoothly shaven historian so ironically civil to Christianity; with others of the same incredulous temper, who knew each quad as well as the faithful, and took equal freedom in haunting its cloisters.

He regarded the statesmen in their various types, men of firmer movement and less dreamy air; the scholar, the speaker, the plodder; the man whose mind grew with his growth in years, and the man whose mind contracted with the same.

The scientists and philologists followed on in his mind-sight in an odd impossible combination, men of meditative faces, strained foreheads, and weak-eyed as bats with constant research; then official characters – such men as Governor-Generals and Lord-Lieutenants, in whom he took little interest; Chief-Justices and Lord Chancellors, silent thin-lipped figures of whom he knew barely the names. A keener regard attached to the prelates, by reason of his own former hopes. Of them he had an ample band – some men of heart, others rather men of head; he who apologized for the Church in Latin; the saintly author of the Evening Hymn; and near them the great itinerant preacher, hymn-writer, and zealot, shadowed like Jude by his matrimonial difficulties.

Jude found himself speaking out loud, holding conversations with them as it were, like an actor in a melodrama who apostrophizes the audience on the other side of the footlights; till he suddenly ceased with a start at his absurdity. Perhaps those incoherent words of the wanderer were heard within the walls by some student or thinker over his lamp; and he may have raised his head, and wondered what voice it was, and what it betokened. Jude now perceived that, so far as solid flesh went, he had the whole aged city to himself with the exception of a belated townsman here and there, and that he seemed to be catching a cold.

A voice reached him out of the shade; a real and local voice:

'You've been a-settin' a long time on that plinth-stone, young man. What med you be up to?'

It came from a policeman who had been observing Jude without the latter observing him.

Jude went home and to bed, after reading up a little about these men and their several messages to the world from a book or two that he had brought with him concerning the sons of the University. As he drew towards sleep various memorable words of theirs that he had just been conning seemed spoken by them in muttering utterances; some audible, some unintelligible to him. One of the spectres (who afterwards mourned Christminster as 'the home of lost causes', though Jude did not remember this) was now apostrophizing her thus:

'Beautiful city! so venerable, so lovely, so unravaged by the fierce intellectual life of our century, so serene! . . . Her ineffable charm keeps ever calling us to the true goal of all of us, to the ideal, to perfection.'

Another voice was that of the Corn Law convert, whose phantom he had just seen in the quadrangle with a great bell. Jude thought his soul might have been shaping the historic words of his master-speech:

'Sir, I may be wrong, but my impression is that my duty towards a country threatened with famine requires that that which has been the ordinary remedy under all similar circumstances should be resorted to now, namely, that there should be free access to the food of man from whatever quarter it may come. . . . Deprive me of office to-morrow, you can never deprive me of the consciousness that I have exercised the powers committed to me from no corrupt or interested motives, from no desire to gratify ambition, for no personal gain.'

Then the sly author of the immortal Chapter on Christianity: 'How shall we excuse the supine inattention of the Pagan and philosophic world, to those evidences [miracles] which were presented by Omnipotence? . . . The sages of Greece and Rome turned aside from the awful spectacle, and appeared unconscious of any alterations in the moral or physical government of the world.'

Then the shade of the poet, the last of the optimists:

'How the world is made for each of us!

. . .

And each of the Many helps to recruit
The life of the race by a general plan.'

Then one of the three enthusiasts he had seen just now, the author of the *Apologia*:

'My argument was . . . that absolute certitude as to the truths of natural theology was the result of an assemblage of concurring and converging probabilities . . . that probabilities which did not reach to logical certainty might create a mental certitude.'

The second of them, no polemic, murmured quieter things:

> 'Why should we faint, and fear to live alone,
> Since all alone, so Heaven has will'd, we die?'

He likewise heard some phrases spoken by the phantom with the short face, the genial Spectator:

> 'When I look upon the tombs of the great, every motion of envy dies in me; when I read the epitaphs of the beautiful, every inordinate desire goes out; when I meet with the grief of parents upon a tombstone, my heart melts with compassion; when I see the tombs of the parents themselves, I consider the vanity of grieving for those whom we must quickly follow.'

And lastly a gentle-voiced prelate spoke, during whose meek, familiar rhyme, endeared to him from earliest childhood, Jude fell asleep:

> 'Teach me to live, that I may dread
> The grave as little as my bed.
> Teach me to die. . . .'

He did not wake till morning. The ghostly past seemed to have gone, and everything spoke of to-day. He started up in bed, thinking he had overslept himself, and then said:

'By Jove – I had quite forgotten my sweet-faced cousin, and that she's here all the time! . . . and my old schoolmaster, too.' His words about his school-master had, perhaps, less zest in them than his words concerning his cousin.

Questions for Study

1 In what ways can this chapter be seen as introducing criticism of the medievalism of Hardy's time?
2 Why do you think Hardy depicts Jude as being easily taken in by appearances?
3 Hardy clearly regards Christminster as a pretentious and somewhat superficial place. What parts of the text make this particularly clear?

CHAPTER 81

Gerard Manley Hopkins
(1844–1889)

Gerard Hopkins was born July 28, 1844, to Manley and Catherine (Smith) Hopkins, the first of their nine children. The household was well used to the mingling of religion and poetry. His parents were both active Anglo-Catholics; his father – a marine insurance adjuster – had published a volume of poetry the year before Gerald's birth. At grammar school in Highgate (1854–63), he won the poetry prize for "The Escorial" and a scholarship to Balliol College, Oxford (1863–7), where his tutors included Benjamin Jowett. At one time he wanted to be a painter-poet like D. G. Rossetti (two of his brothers became professional painters); this, however, came to nothing. He was nevertheless strongly influenced by the aesthetic theory of John Ruskin, and by the poetry of Anglicans such as George Herbert and Christina Rossetti.

Gerard Manley Hopkins (1844–1889)

Basic description
Roman Catholic poet.

Major work
"The Wreck of the Deutschland."

Major studies
W. H. Gardner, *Gerard Manley Hopkins: A Study of Poetic Idiosyncrasy in Relation to Poetic Tradition*, 2nd edn. Oxford: Oxford University Press, 1962.

Margaret R. Ellsberg, *Created to Praise: The Language of Gerard Manley Hopkins*. Oxford: Oxford University Press, 1987.

Hopkins' religious views underwent significant development during his time at Oxford, when he came under the influence of John Henry Newman. Newman had converted from Anglicanism to Roman Catholicism in 1845; this clearly provided Hopkins with a convenient role model. In 1866, he followed Newman into the Catholic Church. During the following year, Hopkins was awarded first-class honors at Oxford, and was considered by Jowett to be the star of Balliol. He entered the Society of Jesus in 1868.

At this point, it seemed that his poetic gifts would not be put to any use. The practice of poetry, he felt, was too individualistic and self-indulgent for a Jesuit priest committed to the deliberate sacrifice of personal ambition. He therefore burned his early poems. However, a period spent studying the writings of Duns Scotus in 1872 led him to revise this opinion. In 1874, while studying theology at a Jesuit house in North Wales, he learned Welsh. He would later adapt the rhythms of Welsh poetry to his own verse, inventing what he called "sprung rhythm."

The event that prompted him to begin writing again was the sinking of a ship, the *Deutschland*, whose passengers included five Catholic nuns exiled from Germany. The resulting "Wreck of the *Deutschland*" is widely regarded as a *tour de force* containing most of the devices he had been working out in theory for the past few years. However, it must be appreciated that Hopkins regarded his vocation as a priest to be of greater importance than his poetic writing, and thus wrote substantially less than might be expected. Virtually none of his poety was published in his own lifetime. His friend Robert Bridges (1844–1930), whom he met at Oxford and who became Poet Laureate in 1913, agreed to serve as his literary executor. Hopkins sent him copies of his poems as they were written, and Bridges arranged for their publication. Eleven were published in 1893, and six in 1915. The first edition of his collected works appeared in 1918. The 750 printed copies took more than ten years to sell. The recognition of Hopkins' greatness came late in the day, and it was not until the 1930s that he came to be appreciated as one of the greatest Victorian poets.

Text: God's Grandeur

Although many consider Hopkins' greatest poem to be "The Wreck of the *Deutschland*," others have argued that his genius is best to be seen in his shorter poems, especially those which reflect the themes of natural theology. Perhaps the finest of his poems to address the reflection of God in the creation is "God's Grandeur":

> The world is charged with the grandeur of God.
>   It will flame out, like shining from shook foil;
>   It gathers to a greatness, like the ooze of oil
> Crushed. Why do men then now not reck his rod?
> Generations have trod, have trod, have trod;
>   And all is seared with trade; Bleared, smeared with toil;
>   And wears man's smudge and shares man's smell: the soil
> Is bare now, nor can foot feel, being shod.
>
> And for all this, nature is never spent;
>   There lives the dearest freshness deep down things;
> And though the last lights off the black West went
>   Oh, morning, at the brown brink eastward, springs –
> Because the Holy Ghost over the bent
>   World broods with warm breast and with ah! bright wings.

Questions for Study

1 What is the fundamental concern that Hopkins expresses in the first stanza? Is this a response to the Industrial Revolution's impact on the British landscape? Or is there something deeper at stake?

2 The second verse develops the theme of the renewal of the creation by its creator. What points does Hopkins make in this section of the poem?

3 You should study the distinctive use of words and imagery in the poem, particularly the first stanza. Notice especially the cumulative use of terms, as in "seared with trade; bleared, smeared with toil." What is the impact of this usage on the reading of the poem?

CHAPTER 82

Oscar Wilde (1854–1900)

Oscar Fingal O'Flahertie Wills Wilde was born on October 10, 1854, the son of Sir William Wilde, an eminent eye specialist who went on to be appointed Surgeon Oculist to Queen Victoria. Wilde attended Portora Royal School in Enniskillen until he was seventeen, after which he won a scholarship to Trinity College, Dublin. In 1874 he was awarded a scholarship at Magdalen College, Oxford, and went on to take First Class in Classical Moderations in 1876; two years later he took a First Class in *Literae Humaniores*. He won the Newdigate Prize for English verse for his poem *Ravenna* which he recited in the Sheldonian Theatre, Oxford, on June 26, 1878.

It was during his years at Oxford that Wilde began to gain a reputation for both his artistic abilities and inclinations. He found himself increasingly drawn to the philosophy of Walter Pater (1839–94), who propounded the notion of art for art's sake. His eccentric manner of dressing and acting was the subject of much comment, and would be heavily satirized in Gilbert and Sullivan's comic opera "Patience" (1881). After leaving Oxford in 1879, Wilde moved to London and started to write for his living. He styled himself the "Apostle of Aestheticism," again drawing attention to himself by the eccentricity of his dress. In an era noted for conventionality amongst the middle classes, Wilde caused amazement and occasionally outrage by dressing in a velvet coat, black silk stockings, lavender gloves, and a large flowing tie. He married Constance Lloyd, the daughter of a rich Dublin barrister, in 1884, and settled down at 34 Tite Street, Chelsea, where he lived from 1884 to 1895.

During this period, Wilde's artistic reputation grew. He published an essay on Shakespeare's sonnets in 1889, arguing that many of the sonnets were addressed to a man. His 1891 novel *The Picture of Dorian Gray* met with wide acclaim. Yet Wilde's greatest successes were theatrical. *Lady Windermere's Fan* (1892) enjoyed a huge success at St James' Theatre; it was eclipsed, however, by *The Importance of Being Earnest* (1895).

Yet Wilde's homosexuality was something that late Victorian England found immensely distasteful. It needs to be noted that Wilde's much publicized affection for younger male Oxford students must be seen as more than purely sexual; it can be seen as reflecting what Wilde regarded as a realization of some of the themes found in classic

Greek culture, particularly in Epicureanism and Plato's *Symposium*. Thus it has been suggested that the garden of Basil Hallward's house in *The Picture of Dorian Gray* is to be seen as an idealized recollection of Oxford college gardens – such as that of Magdalen College – in which attractive young men are affectionately mentored by older students. Perhaps some such ideal lay behind the friendship which Wilde began in 1891 with Lord Alfred Douglas, with disastrous results.

Oscar Wilde (1854–1900)

Basic description
Leading late Victorian playwright, aesthete and cultural figure, whose homosexuality led to imprisonment and disgrace.

Major works
The Picture of Dorian Gray (1891); *Lady Windermere's Fan* (1892); *A Woman of No Importance* (1893); *The Importance of Being Earnest* (1895); *De profundis* (1897); "The Ballad of Reading Gaol" (1898).

Major studies
Richard Ellmann, *Oscar Wilde*. New York: Vintage Books, 1988.
Peter Raby (ed.), *The Cambridge Companion to Oscar Wilde*. Cambridge: Cambridge University Press, 1997.

On February 18, 1895 – a mere four days after the highly successful first night of *The Importance of Being Earnest* – Alfred Douglas's father (the Marquess of Queensberry) accused Wilde of "posing as a sodomite." Wilde launched a libel suit against the Marquess, which failed. Some of the criminal evidence concerning Wilde's homosexual activity presented by the Marquess of Queensbury at the libel trial led to Wilde being charged with homosexual offences, and brought to trial. He was eventually found guilty, and sentenced to two years in prison. He served the first six months of his sentence at Wandsworth Prison (London), and then was moved to Reading Gaol for the remainder of the sentence. While in prison Wilde wrote *De Profundis*, a work which mingles description of his spiritual growth with accusations against Douglas.

Wilde was released from prison on May 19, 1897, and settled (under the alias "Sebastian Lemoth") in the French town of Berneval with Douglas. During this period he composed his best-known poem "The Ballad of Reading Gaol." Wilde died in Paris from cerebral meningitis on November 30, 1900. Earlier that year, he had been baptized into the Roman Catholic church. He was buried in the French National Cemetery of Père Lachaise, Paris.

Wilde's religious poetry has been given less than full attention, not least on account of his importance as a writer of plays and the interest in his homosexuality. Yet his religious poems merit close study. Several echo a sense of tension between the splendor of the church and the humility of Christ – such as "Holy Week at Genoa," "Easter Day," and especially "On Hearing the *Dies Irae* Sung in the Sistine Chapel," in which the lush and ornate ritual of the Sistine Chapel is compared with the simplicity of nature and the lonely figure of Christ:

Nay, Lord, not thus! white lilies in the spring,
Sad olive-groves, or silver-breasted dove,
Teach me more clearly of Thy life and love
Than terrors of red flame and thundering.
The empurpled vines dear memories of Thee bring:
A bird at evening flying to its nest,
Tells me of One who had no place of rest:
I think it is of Thee the sparrows sing.
Come rather on some autumn afternoon,
When red and brown are burnished on the leaves,
And the fields echo to the gleaner's song,
Come when the splendid fulness of the moon
Looks down upon the rows of golden sheaves,
And reap Thy harvest: we have waited long.

Yet the most famous of Wilde's religious poems is unquestionably "The Ballad of Reading Gaol," to which we now turn. The poem exists in a full and a shorter form; the full version is printed here.

Text: The Ballad of Reading Gaol

The Ballad of Reading Gaol
by
Oscar Wilde
In Memoriam
C.T.W.
Sometime Trooper of
The Royal Horse Guards.
Obiit H.M. Prison, Reading, Berkshire,
July 7th, 1896

1

He did not wear his scarlet coat,
  For blood and wine are red,
And blood and wine were on his hands
  When they found him with the dead,
The poor dead woman whom he loved,   5
  and murdered in her bed.

He walked amongst the Trial Men
  In a suit of shabby grey;
A cricket cap was on his head,
  And his step seemed light and gay;   10
But I never saw a man who looked
  So wistfully at the day.

I never saw a man who looked
  With such a wistful eye
Upon that little tent of blue   15
  Which prisoners call the sky,
And at every drifting cloud that went
  With sails of silver by.

I walked, with other souls in pain,
  Within another ring,   20
And was wondering if the man had done
  A great or little thing,
When a voice behind me whispered low,
  'That fellow's got to swing.'

Dear Christ! the very prison walls   25
  Suddenly seemed to reel,
And the sky above my head became
  Like a casque of scorching steel;
And, though I was a soul in pain,
  My pain I could not feel.   30

I only knew what hunted thought
  Quickened his step, and why
He looked upon the garish day
  With such a wistful eye;
The man had killed the thing he loved,   35
  And so he had to die.
*
Yet each man kills the thing he loves,
  By each let this be heard,
Some do it with a bitter look,
  Some with a flattering word.   40
The coward does it with a kiss,
  The brave man with a sword!

Some kill their love when they are young,
  And some when they are old;
Some strangle with the hands of Lust,   45
  Some with the hands of Gold:
The kindest use a knife, because
  The dead so soon grow cold.

Some love too little, some too long,
  Some sell, and others buy;   50
Some do the deed with many tears,

And some without a sigh:
For each man kills the thing he loves,
Yet each man does not die.

He does not die a death of shame   55
On a day of dark disgrace,
Nor have a noose about his neck,
Nor a cloth upon his face,
Nor drop feet foremost through the floor
Into an empty space.   60

He does not sit with silent men
Who watch him night and day;
Who watch him when he tries to weep,
And when he tries to pray;
Who watch him lest himself should rob   65
The prison of its prey.

He does not wake at dawn to see
Dread figures throng his room,
The shivering Chaplain robed in white,
The Sheriff stern with gloom,   70
And the Governor all in shiny black,
With the yellow face of Doom.

He does not rise in piteous haste
To put on convict-clothes,
While some coarse-mouthed Doctor gloats, and notes   75
Each new and nerve-twitched pose,
Fingering a watch whose little ticks
Are like horrible hammer-blows.

He does not feel that sickening thirst
That sands one's throat, before   80
The hangman with his gardener's gloves
Comes through the padded door,
And binds one with three leathern thongs,
That the throat may thirst no more.

He does not bend his head to hear   85
The Burial Office read,
Nor, while the anguish of his soul
Tells him he is not dead,
Cross his own coffin, as he moves
Into the hideous shed.   90

He does not stare upon the air
  Through a little roof of glass:
He does not pray with lips of clay
  For his agony to pass;
Nor feel upon his shuddering cheek   95
  The kiss of Caiaphas.

2

Six weeks the guardsman walked the yard,
  In the suit of shabby grey:
His cricket cap was on his head,
  And his step seemed light and gay,
But I never saw a man who looked   5
  So wistfully at the day.

I never saw a man who looked
  With such a wistful eye
Upon that little tent of blue
  Which prisoners call the sky,   10
And at every wandering cloud that trailed
  Its ravelled fleeces by.

He did not wring his hands, as do
  Those witless men who dare
To try to rear the changeling Hope   15
  In the cave of black Despair:
He only looked upon the sun,
  And drank the morning air.

He did not wring his hands nor weep,
  Nor did he peek or pine,
But he drank the air as though it held   20
  Some healthful anodyne;
With open mouth he drank the sun
  As though it had been wine!

And I and all the souls in pain,   25
  Who tramped the other ring,
Forgot if we ourselves had done
  A great or little thing,
And watched with gaze of dull amaze
  The man who had to swing.   30

For strange it was to see him pass
  With a step so light and gay,
And strange it was to see him look

So wistfully at the day,
And strange it was to think that he   35
    Had such a debt to pay.
                *

For oak and elm have pleasant leaves
    That in the spring-time shoot;
But grim to see is the gallows-tree,
    With its adder-bitten root,   40
And, green or dry, a man must die
    Before it bears its fruit!

The loftiest place is that seat of grace
    For which all worldlings try:
But who would stand in hempen band   45
    Upon a scaffold high,
And through a murderer's collar take
    His last look at the sky?

It is sweet to dance to violins
    When Love and Life are fair: 50
To dance to flutes, to dance to lutes
    Is delicate and rare;
But it is not sweet with nimble feet
    To dance upon the air!

So with curious eyes and sick surmise   55
    We watched him day by day,
And wondered if each one of us
    Would end the self-same way,
For none can tell to what red Hell
    His sightless soul may stray.   60

At last the dead man walked no more
    Amongst the Trial Men,
And I knew that he was standing up
    In the black dock's dreadful pen,
And that never would I see his face   65
    For weal or woe again.

Like two doomed ships that pass in storm
    We had crossed each other's way:
But we made no sign, we said no word,
    We had no word to say;   70
For we did not meet in the holy night,
    But in the shameful day.

A prison wall was round us both,
   Two outcast men we were:
The world had thrust us from its heart,   75
   And God from out His care:
And the iron gin that waits for Sin
   Had caught us in its snare.

3

In Debtor's Yard the stones are hard,
   And the dripping wall is high,
So it was there he took the air
   Beneath the leaden sky,
And by each side a Warder walked   5
   For fear the man might die.

Or else he sat with those who watched
   His anguish night and day;
Who watched him when he rose to weep,
   And when he crouched to pray;   10
Who watched him lest himself should rob
   Their scaffold of its prey.

The Governor was strong upon
   The Regulations Act:
The Doctor said that Death was but   15
   A scientific fact:
And twice a day the Chaplain called,
   And left a little tract.

And twice a day he smoked his pipe,
   And drank his quart of beer: 20
His soul was resolute, and held
   No hiding-place for fear;
He often said that he was glad
   The hangman's day was near.

But why he said so strange a thing   25
   No warder dared to ask:
For he to whom a watcher's doom
   Is given as his task,
Must set a lock upon his lips
   And make his face a mask.   30

Or else he might be moved, and try
   To comfort or console:
And what should Human Pity do

Pent up in Murderer's Hole?
What word of grace in such a place   35
    Could help a brother's soul?

With slouch and swing around the ring
    We trod the Fools' parade!
We did not care: we knew we were
    The Devil's Own Brigade: 40
And shaven head and feet of lead
    Make a merry masquerade.

We tore the tarry rope to shreds
    With blunt and bleeding nails;
We rubbed the doors, and scrubbed the floors,   45
    And cleaned the shining rails:
And, rank by rank, we soaped the plank,
    And clattered with the pails.

We sewed the sacks, we broke the stones,
    We turned the dusty drill;   50
We banged the tins, and bawled the hymns,
    And sweated on the mill;
But in the heart of every man
    Terror was lying still.

So still it lay that every day   55
    Crawled like a weed-clogged wave:
And we forgot the bitter lot
    That waits for fool and knave,
Till once, as we tramped in from work,
    We passed an open grave.   60

With yawning mouth the yellow hole
    Gaped for a living thing;
The very mud cried out for blood
    To the thirsty asphalte ring:
And we knew that ere one dawn grew fair   65
    Some prisoner had to swing.

Right in we went, with soul intent
    On Death and Dread and Doom:
The hangman, with his little bag,
    Went shuffling through the gloom: 70
And I trembled as I groped my way
    Into my numbered tomb.

                    *

That night the empty corridors
    Were full of forms of Fear,
And up and down the iron town   75
    Stole feet we could not hear,
And through the bars that hide the stars
    White faces seemed to peer.

He lay as one who lies and dreams
    In a pleasant meadow-land,   80
The watchers watched him as he slept,
    And could not understand
How one could sleep so sweet a sleep
    With a hangman close at hand.

But there is no sleep when men must weep   85
    Who never yet have wept:
So we – the fool, the fraud, the knave –
    That endless vigil kept,
And through each brain on hands of pain
    Another's terror crept.   90

Alas! it is a fearful thing
    To feel another's guilt!
For, right within, the Sword of Sin
    Pierced to its poisoned hilt,
And as molten lead were the tears we shed   95
    For the blood we had not spilt.

The warders with their shoes of felt
    Crept by each padlocked door,
And peeped and saw, with eyes of awe,
    Grey figures on the floor,   100
And wondered why men knelt to pray
    Who never prayed before.

All through the night we knelt and prayed,
    Mad mourners of a corse!
The troubled plumes of midnight shook   105
    The plumes upon a hearse:
And bitter wine upon a sponge
    Was the savour of Remorse.

                        *

The grey cock crew, the red cock crew,
    But never came the day: 110
And crooked shapes of Terror crouched,

In the corners where we lay:
And each evil sprite that walks by night
Before us seemed to play.

They glided past, they glided fast, 115
Like travellers through a mist:
They mocked the moon in a rigadoon
Of delicate turn and twist,
And with formal pace and loathsome grace
The phantoms kept their tryst. 120

With mop and mow, we saw them go,
Slim shadows hand in hand:
About, about, in ghostly rout
They trod a saraband:
And the damned grotesques made arabesques, 125
Like the wind upon the sand!

With the pirouettes of marionettes,
They tripped on pointed tread:
But with flutes of Fear they filled the ear,
As their grisly masque they led, 130
And loud they sang, and loud they sang,
For they sang to wake the dead.

'Oho!' they cried, 'The world is wide,
But fettered limbs go lame!
And once, or twice, to throw the dice 135
Is a gentlemanly game,
But he does not win who plays with Sin
In the secret House of Shame.'

No things of air these antics were,
That frolicked with such glee: 140
To men whose lives were held in gyves,
And whose feet might not go free,
Ah! wounds of Christ! they were living things
Most terrible to see.

Around, around, they waltzed and wound; 145
Some wheeled in smirking pairs;
With the mincing step of demirep
Some sidled up the stairs:
And with subtle sneer, and fawning leer,
Each helped us at our prayers. 150

The morning wind began to moan,
  But still the night went on:
Through its giant loom the web of gloom
  Crept till each thread was spun:
And, as we prayed, we grew afraid   155
  Of the Justice of the Sun.

The moaning wind went wandering round
  The weeping prison-wall:
Till like a wheel of turning steel
  We felt the minutes crawl: 160
O moaning wind! what had we done
  To have such a seneschal?

At last I saw the shadowed bars,
  Like a lattice wrought in lead,
Move right across the whitewashed wall   165
  That faced my three-plank bed,
And I knew that somewhere in the world
  God's dreadful dawn was red.

At six o'clock we cleaned our cells,
  At seven all was still,   170
But the sough and swing of a mighty wing
  The prison seemed to fill,
For the Lord of Death with icy breath
  Had entered in to kill.

He did not pass in purple pomp,   175
  Nor ride a moon-white steed.
Three yards of cord and a sliding board
  Are all the gallows' need:
So with rope of shame the Herald came
  To do the secret deed.   180

We were as men who through a fen
  Of filthy darkness grope:
We did not dare to breathe a prayer,
  Or to give our anguish scope:
Something was dead in each of us,   185
  And what was dead was Hope.

For Man's grim Justice goes its way,
  And will not swerve aside:
It slays the weak, it slays the strong,
  It has a deadly stride: 190

With iron heel it slays the strong,
  The monstrous parricide!

We waited for the stroke of eight:
  Each tongue was thick with thirst:
For the stroke of eight is the stroke of Fate   195
  That makes a man accursed,
And Fate will use a running noose,
  For the best man and the worst.

We had no other thing to do,
  Save to wait for the sign to come: 200
So, like things of stone in a valley lone,
  Quiet we sat and dumb:
But each man's heart beat thick and quick,
  Like a madman on a drum!

With sudden shock the prison-clock   205
  Smote on the shivering air,
And from all the gaol rose up a wail
  Of impotent despair,
Like the sound that frightened marches hear
  From some leper in his lair.   210

And as one sees most fearful things
  In the crystal of a dream,
We saw the greasy hempen rope
  Hooked to the blackened beam,
And heard the prayer the hangman's snare   215
  Strangled into a scream.

And all the woe that moved him so
  That he gave that bitter cry,
And the wild regrets, and the bloody sweats,
  Nobody knew so well as I: 220
For he who lives more lives than one
  More deaths than one must die.

4

There is no chapel on the day
  On which they hang a man:
The Chaplain's heart is far too sick,
  Or his face is far too wan,
Or there is that written in his eyes   5
  Which none should look upon.

So they kept us close till nigh on noon,
  And then they rang the bell,
And the warders with their jingling keys
  Opened each listening cell,
And down the iron stair we tramped,   10
  Each from his separate Hell.

Out into God's sweet air we went,
  But not in wonted way,
For this man's face was white with fear,   15
  And that man's face was grey,
And I never saw sad men who looked
  So wistfully at the day.

I never saw sad men who looked
  With such a wistful eye   20
Upon that little tent of blue
  We prisoners called the sky,
And at every happy cloud that passed
  In such strange freedom by.

But their were those amongst us all   25
  Who walked with downcast head,
And knew that, had each got his due,
  They should have died instead:
He had but killed a thing that lived,
  Whilst they had killed the dead.   30

For he who sins a second time
  Wakes a dead soul to pain,
And draws it from its spotted shroud,
  And makes it bleed again,
And makes it bleed great gouts of blood,   35
  And makes it bleed in vain!
              *
Like ape or clown, in monstrous garb
  With crooked arrows starred,
Silently we went round and round
  The slippery asphalte yard;   40
Silently we went round and round,
  And no man spoke a word.

Silently we went round and round,
  And through each hollow mind
The Memory of dreadful things   45
  Rushed like a dreadful wind,

And Horror stalked before each man,
    And Terror crept behind.
             *

The warders strutted up and down,
    And watched their herd of brutes,   50
Their uniforms were spick and span,
    And they wore their Sunday suits,
But we knew the work they had been at,
    By the quicklime on their boots.

For where a grave had opened wide,   55
    There was no grave at all:
Only a stretch of mud and sand
    By the hideous prison-wall,
And a little heap of burning lime,
    That the man should have his pall.   60

For he has a pall, this wretched man,
    Such as few men can claim:
Deep down below a prison-yard,
    Naked for greater shame,
He lies, with fetters on each foot,   65
    Wrapt in a sheet of flame!

And all the while the burning lime
    Eats flesh and bone away,
It eats the brittle bone by night,
    And the soft flesh by day,   70
It eats the flesh and bone by turns,
    But it eats the heart alway.
             *

For three long years they will not sow
    Or root or seedling there:
For three long years the unblessed spot   75
    Will sterile be and bare,
And look upon the wondering sky
    With unreproachful stare.

They think a murderer's heart would taint
    Each simple seed they sow.   80
It is not true! God's kindly earth
    Is kindlier than men know,
And the red rose would but blow more red,
    The white rose whiter blow.

Out of his mouth a red, red rose!   85
  Out of his heart a white!
For who can say by what strange way,
  Christ brings His will to light,
Since the barren staff the pilgrim bore
  Bloomed in the great Pope's sight?   90

But neither milk-white rose nor red
  May bloom in prison-air;
The shard, the pebble, and the flint,
  Are what they give us there:
For flowers have been known to heal   95
  A common man's despair.

So never will wine-red rose or white,
  Petal by petal, fall
On that stretch of mud and sand that lies
  By the hideous prison-wall,   100
To tell the men who tramp the yard
  That God's Son died for all.

Yet though the hideous prison-wall
  Still hems him round and round,
And a spirit may not walk by night   105
  That is with fetters bound,
And a spirit may but weep that lies
  In such unholy ground,

He is at peace – this wretched man –
  At peace, or will be soon: 110
There is no thing to make him mad,
  Nor does Terror walk at noon,
For the lampless Earth in which he lies
  Has neither Sun nor Moon.

They hanged him as a beast is hanged!   115
  They did not even toll
A requiem that might have brought
  Rest to his startled soul,
But hurriedly they took him out,
  And hid him in a hole.   120

The warders stripped him of his clothes,
  And gave him to the flies:
They mocked the swollen purple throat,
  And the stark and staring eyes:

And with laughter loud they heaped the shroud   125
   In which the convict lies.

The Chaplain would not kneel to pray
   By his dishonoured grave:
Nor mark it with that blessed Cross
   That Christ for sinners gave,   130
Because the man was one of those
   Whom Christ came down to save.

Yet all is well; he has but passed
   To Life's appointed bourne:
And alien tears will fill for him   135
   Pity's long-broken urn,
For his mourners will be outcast men,
   And outcasts always mourn.

5

I know not whether Laws be right,
   Or whether Laws be wrong:
All that we know who lie in gaol
   Is that the wall is strong;
And that each day is like a year,   5
   A year whose days are long.

But this I know, that every Law
   That men hath made for Man,
Since first Man took his brother's life,
   And the sad world began,   10
But straws the wheat and saves the chaff
   With a most evil fan.

This too I know – and wise it were
   If each could know the same –
That every prison that men build   15
   Is built with bricks of shame,
And bound with bars lest Christ should see
   How men their brothers maim.

With bars they blur the gracious moon,
   And blind the goodly sun;   20
And they do well to hide their Hell,
   For in it things are done
That Son of God nor son of Man
   Ever should look upon!

*

The vilest deeds like poison weeds,   25
   Bloom well in prison-air;
It is only what is good in Man
   That wastes and withers there:
Pale Anguish keeps the heavy gate,
   And the Warder is Despair.   30

For they starve the little frightened child
   Till it weeps both night and day:
And they scourge the weak, and flog the fool,
   And gibe the old and grey,
And some grow mad, and all grow bad,   35
   And none a word may say.

Each narrow cell in which we dwell
   Is a foul and dark latrine,
And the fetid breath of living Death
   Chokes up each grated screen,   40
And all, but Lust, is turned to dust
   In Humanity's machine.

The brackish water that we drink
   Creeps with loathsome slime,
And the bitter bread they weigh in scales   45
   Is full of chalk and lime,
And Sleep will not lie down, but walks
   Wild-eyed, and cries to Time.

         *

But though lean Hunger and green Thirst
   Like asp with adder fight,   50
We have little care of prison fare,
   For what chills and kills outright
Is that every stone one lifts by day
   Becomes one's heart by night.

With midnight always in one's heart,   55
   And twilight in one's cell,
We turn the crank, or tear the rope
   Each in his separate Hell,
And the silence is more awful far
   Than the sound of a brazen bell.   60

And never a human voice comes near
   To speak a gentle word:
And the eye that watches through the door

Is pitiless and hard:
And by all forgot, we rot and rot   65
    With soul and body marred.

And thus we rust Life's iron chain
    Degraded and alone:
And some men curse, and some men weep,
    And some men make no moan: 70
But God's eternal Laws are kind
    And break the heart of stone.

And every human heart that breaks,
    In prison-cell or yard,
Is as that broken box that gave   75
    Its treasure to the Lord,
And filled the unclean leper's house
    With the scent of costliest nard.

Ah! happy they whose hearts can break
    And peace of pardon win!   80
How else may man make straight his plan
    And cleanse his soul from Sin?
How else but through a broken heart
    May Lord Christ enter in?

*

And he of the swollen purple throat,   85
    And the stark and staring eyes,
Waits for the holy hands that took
    The Thief to Paradise;
And a broken and a contrite heart
    The Lord will not despise.   90

The man in red who reads the Law
    Gave him three weeks of life,
Three little weeks in which to heal
    His soul of his soul's strife,
And cleanse from every blot of blood   95
    The hand that held the knife.

And with tears of blood he cleansed the hand,
    The hand that held the steel:
For only blood can wipe out blood,
    And only tears can heal: 100
And the crimson stain that was of Cain
    Became Christ's snow-white seal.

6

In Reading gaol by Reading town
    There is a pit of shame,
And in it lies a wretched man
    Eaten by teeth of flame,
In a burning winding-sheet he lies,   5
    And his grave has got no name.

And there, till Christ call forth the dead,
    In silence let him lie:
No need to waste the foolish tear,
    Or heave the windy sigh: 10
The man had killed the thing he loved,
    And so he had to die.

And all men kill the thing they love,
    By all let this be heard,
Some do it with a bitter look,   15
    Some with a flattering word,
The coward does it with a kiss,
    The brave man with a sword!

Questions for Discussion

1   What specifically *religious* issues does the poem raise?
2   Wilde published two letters on prison reform in 1898, the year of publication of this poem. In what way does the poem reflect such a reforming agenda?
3   In what ways does Wilde incorporate imagery drawn from the gospel narratives of the trial and crucifixion of Christ into this poem? How effective do you consider this to be? And what points do you think Wilde is trying to make in this way?
4   Locate the following lines within the poem:

    And the crimson stain that was of Cain
    Became Christ's snow-white seal.

What does Wilde mean by them? What specifically religious point is being made here? You may find it useful to see if there are any other allusions to Cain in the poem, and work out what Wilde does with them. For example, does he see there to be any parallelism between Christ and Cain?

CHAPTER 83

Gilbert Keith Chesterton (1874–1936)

Chesterton was born in the London Borough of Kensington on May 29, 1874. Although he initially began to train as an artist in 1891, he subsequently abandoned this for journalism, and became a frequent contributor to the *Illustrated London News*. Although Chesteron considered himself to be little more than a "rollicking journalist," this fails to do justice to his immense range of writings, which extended to virtually every area of literature. His biographies of authors and historical figures such as Charles Dickens and St. Francis of Assisi, though not written for a scholarly audience, often contain genuinely important insights into their subjects. His "Father Brown" detective novels, written between 1911 and 1936, are still widely read, and reflect his warm admiration for the Roman Catholic church, which he joined in 1922. Chesterton died on June 14, 1936 in Beaconsfield, Buckinghamshire.

G. K. Chesterton (1874–1936)

Basic description
English journalist, with a strong interest in religious and moral issues, who wrote some of the twentieth century's most admired works in defense of Christian orthodoxy.

Major works
Heretics (1905); *Orthodoxy* (1908); *The Everlasting Man* (1927); the "Father Brown" detective novels.

Major studies
Quentin Lauer, *G. K. Chesterton: Philosopher without Portfolio*. New York: Fordham University Press, 1988.
J. C. Pearce, *Wisdom and Innocence: The Life of G. K. Chesterton*. London: Hodder & Stoughton, 1997.

Chesterton's immense literary output included a significant number of works concerned with defending and articulating the Christian faith. For Chesterton, life was full of puzzles and enigmas, which only the Christian faith could resolve to his satisfaction. His two most important early works to deal with these themes are *Heretics* (1905) and

Orthodoxy (1908). However, it is generally considered that his finest work of Christian literature is *The Everlasting Man* (1927), which C. S. Lewis regarded as one of the most important works which he had ever read. In 1922, Chesterton left the Church of England for the Roman Catholic church. Although it is clear that he regarded this as a major step in his own personal development, it does not appear to have had a major impact on his writing style or the approach he adopted to most issues.

In this chapter, we shall consider extracts from two of his most widely-acclaimed works of Christian apologetics.

Text: *Orthodoxy*

Orthodoxy is widely regarded as one of Chesterton's finest works. In it, he took issue with many of the prevailing ideas of his time, including the generally "liberal" outlook of writers such as George Bernard Shaw. Such ideas had gained considerable acceptance in the late Victorian period, and Chesterton here sets out what he regards as the intellectual weaknesses and internal inconsistencies of this approach. Although the text focuses especially on the question of miracles, it is clear that Chesterton's real target is the general intellectual and cultural outlook which gave rise to skepticism about such miracles. The title of the chapter from which this extract is taken is "The Romance of Orthodoxy." The very title indicates Chesterton's determination to counter the widespread allegation that orthodox Christianity was dogmatic and anything but romantic!

Chesterton's argument is very clear, and requires little in the way of comment. The important thing is to identify the criticisms which he anticipates, and the refutations which he offers.

It is customary to complain of the bustle and strenuousness of our epoch. But in truth the chief mark of our epoch is a profound laziness and fatigue; and the fact is that the real laziness is the cause of the apparent bustle. Take one quite external case; the streets are noisy with taxicabs and motorcars; but this is not due to human activity but to human repose. There would be less bustle if there were more activity, if people were simply walking about. Our world would be more silent if it were more strenuous. And this which is true of the apparent physical bustle is true also of the apparent bustle of the intellect. Most of the machinery of modern language is labour-saving machinery; and it saves mental labour very much more than it ought. Scientific phrases are used like scientific wheels and piston-rods to make swifter and smoother yet the path of the comfortable. Long words go rattling by us like long railway trains. We know they are carrying thousands who are too tired or too indolent to walk and think for themselves. It is a good exercise to try for once in a way to express any opinion one holds in words of one syllable. If you say 'The social utility of the indeterminate sentence is recognized by all criminologists as a part of our sociological evolution towards a more humane and scientific view of punishment,' you can go on talking like that for hours with hardly a movement of the gray matter inside your skull. But if you begin 'I wish Jones to go to gaol and Brown to say when Jones shall come out,' you will discover, with a thrill of horror, that you are obliged to think. The long words are not the hard words, it is the short words that are hard. There is much more metaphysical subtlety in the word 'damn' than in the word 'degeneration'.

But these long comfortable words that save modern people the toil of reasoning have one particular aspect in which they are especially ruinous and confusing. This difficulty occurs when the same long word is used in different connections to mean quite different things. Thus, to take a well-known instance, the word 'idealist' has one meaning as a piece of philosophy and quite another as a piece of moral rhetoric. In the same way the scientific materialists have had just reason to complain of people mixing up 'materialist' as a term of cosmology with 'materialist' as a moral taunt. So, to take a cheaper instance, the man who hates 'progressives' in London always calls himself a 'progressive' in South Africa.

A confusion quite as unmeaning as this has arisen in connection with the word 'liberal' as applied to religion and as applied to politics and society. It is often suggested that all Liberals ought to be freethinkers, because they ought to love everything that is free. You might just as well say that all idealists ought to be High Churchmen, because they ought to love everything that is high. You might as well say that Low Churchmen ought to like Low Mass, or that Broad Churchmen ought to like broad jokes. The thing is a mere accident of words. In actual modern Europe a freethinker does not mean a man who thinks for himself. It means a man who, having thought for himself, has come to one particular class of conclusions, the material origin of phenomena, the impossibility of miracles, the improbability of personal immortality and so on. And none of these ideas are particularly liberal. Nay, indeed almost all these ideas are definitely illiberal, as it is the purpose of this chapter to show.

In the few following pages I propose to point out as rapidly as possible that on every single one of the matters most strongly insisted on by liberalisers of theology their effect upon social practice would be definitely illiberal. Almost every contemporary proposal to bring freedom into the church is simply a proposal to bring tyranny into the world. For freeing the church now does not even mean freeing it in all directions. It means freeing that peculiar set of dogmas loosely called scientific, dogmas of monism, of pantheism, or of Arianism, or of necessity. And every one of these (and we will take them one by one) can be shown to be the natural ally of oppression. In fact, it is a remarkable circumstance (indeed not so very remarkable when one comes to think of it) that most things are the allies of oppression. There is only one thing that can never go past a certain point in its alliance with oppression – and that is orthodoxy. I may, it is true, twist orthodoxy so as partly to justify a tyrant. But I can easily make up a German philosophy to justify him entirely.

Now let us take in order the innovations that are the notes of the new theology or the modernist church. We concluded the last chapter with the discovery of one of them. The very doctrine which is called the most old-fashioned was found to be the only safeguard of the new democracies of the earth. The doctrine seemingly most unpopular was found to be the only strength of the people. In short, we found that the only logical negation of oligarchy was in the affirmation of original sin. So it is, I maintain, in all the other cases.

I take the most obvious instance first, the case of miracles. For some extraordinary reason, there is a fixed notion that it is more liberal to disbelieve in miracles than to believe in them. Why, I cannot imagine, nor can anybody tell me. For some inconceivable cause a 'broad' or 'liberal' clergyman always means a man who wishes at least to diminish the number of miracles; it never means a man who wishes to increase that number. It always means a man who is free to disbelieve that Christ came out of His grave; it never means a man who is free to believe that his own aunt came out of her grave. It is common to find trouble in a parish because the parish priest cannot admit that St. Peter walked on water; yet how rarely do we find trouble in a parish because the clergyman says that his father walked on the Serpentine? And this is not because (as the swift secularist debater would immediately retort) miracles cannot be believed in our experience. It is not because 'miracles do not happen,' as in the dogma which Matthew Arnold recited with simple faith. More supernatural things are alleged to have happened in our time than would have been possible eighty years ago. Men of science believe in such marvels much more than they did: the most perplexing, and even horrible, prodigies of mind and spirit are always being unveiled in modern psychology. Things that the old science at least would frankly have rejected as miracles are hourly being asserted by the new science. The only thing which is still old-fashioned enough to reject miracles is the New Theology. But in truth this notion that it is 'free' to deny miracles has nothing to do with the evidence for or against them. It is a lifeless verbal prejudice of which the original life and beginning was not in the freedom of thought, but simply in the dogma, of materialism. The man of the nineteenth century did not disbelieve in the Resurrection because his liberal Christianity allowed him to doubt it. He disbelieved in it because his very strict materialism did not allow him to believe it. Tennyson, a very typical nineteenth century man, uttered one of the instinctive truisms of his contemporaries when he said that there was faith in their honest doubt. There was indeed. Those words have a profound and even a horrible truth. In their doubt of miracles there was a faith in a fixed and godless fate; a deep and sincere faith in the incurable routine of the cosmos. The doubts of the agnostic were only the dogmas of the monist.

Of the fact and evidence of the supernatural I will speak afterwards. Here we are only concerned with this clear point; that in so far as the liberal idea of freedom can be said to be on either side in the discussion about miracles, it is obviously on the side of miracles. Reform or (in the only tolerable sense) progress means simply the gradual control of matter by mind. A miracle simply means the swift control of matter by mind. If you wish to feed the people, you may think that feeding them miraculously in the wilderness is impossible – but you cannot think it illiberal. If you really want poor children to go to the seaside, you cannot think it illiberal that they should go there on flying dragons; you can only think it unlikely. A holiday, like Liberalism, only means the liberty of man. A miracle only means the liberty of God. You may conscientiously deny either of them, but you cannot call your denial a triumph of the liberal idea. The Catholic Church believed that man and God both had a sort of spiritual freedom. Calvinism took away the freedom from man, but left it to God. Scientific materialism binds the Creator Himself; it chains up God as the Apocalypse chained the devil. It leaves nothing free in the universe. And those who assist this process are called the 'liberal theologians.'

This, as I say, is the lightest and most evident case. The assumption that there is something in the doubt of miracles akin to liberality or reform is literally the opposite of the truth. If a man cannot believe in miracles there is an end of the matter; he is not particularly liberal, but he is perfectly honourable and logical, which are much better things. But if he can believe in miracles, he is certainly the more liberal for doing so; because they mean first, the freedom of the soul, and secondly, its control over the tyranny of circumstance. Sometimes this truth is ignored in a singularly naïve way, even by the ablest men. For instance, Mr. Bernard Shaw speaks with hearty old-fashioned contempt for the idea of miracles, as if they were a sort of breach of faith on the part of nature: he seems strangely unconscious that miracles are only the final flowers of his own favourite tree, the doctrine of the omnipotence of will. Just in the same way he calls the desire for immortality a paltry selfishness, forgetting that he has just called the desire for life a healthy and heroic selfishness. How can it be noble to wish to make one's life infinite and yet mean to wish to make it immortal? No, if it is desirable that man should triumph over the cruelty of nature or custom, then miracles are certainly desirable; we will discuss afterwards whether they are possible.

But I must pass on to the larger cases of this curious error; the notion that the 'liberalising' of religion in some way helps the liberation of the world. The second example of it can be found in the question of pantheism – or rather of a certain modern attitude which is often called immanentism, and which often is Buddhism. But this is so much more difficult a matter that I must approach it with rather more preparation.

The things said most confidently by advanced persons to crowded audiences are generally those quite opposite to the fact; it is actually our truisms that are untrue. Here is a case. There is a phrase of facile liberality uttered again and again at ethical societies and parliaments of religion: 'the religions of the earth differ in rites and forms, but they are the same in what they teach.' It is false; it is the opposite of the fact. The religions of the earth do not greatly differ in rites and forms; they do greatly differ in what they teach. It is as if a man were to say, 'Do not be misled by the fact that the Church Times and the Freethinker look utterly different, that one is painted on vellum and the other carved on marble, that one is triangular and the other hectagonal; read them and you will see that they say the same thing.' The truth is, of course, that they are alike in everything except in the fact that they don't say the same thing. An atheist stockbroker in Surbiton looks exactly like a Swedenborgian stockbroker in Wimbledon. You may walk round and round them and subject them to the most personal and offensive study without seeing anything Swedenborgian in the hat or anything particularly godless in the umbrella. It is exactly in their souls that they are divided. So the truth is that the difficulty of all the creeds of the earth is not as alleged in this cheap maxim: that they agree in meaning, but differ in machinery. It is exactly the opposite. They agree in machinery; almost every great religion on earth works with the same external methods, with priests, scriptures, altars, sworn brotherhoods, special feasts. They agree in the mode of teaching; what they differ about is the thing to be taught. Pagan optimists and Eastern pessimists would both have temples, just as Liberals and Tories would both have newspapers. Creeds that exist to destroy each other both have scriptures, just as armies that exist to destroy each other both have guns.

Questions for Study

1 What are the objections to the Christian faith that Chesterton seeks to neutralize in this passage? You will find it useful to state them in your own words, rather than simply recycling Chesterton's.
2 What are the responses that Chesterton offers to these? How persuasive do you find them?
3 Find the following citation in the text: "the religions of the earth differ in rites and forms, but they are the same in what they teach." How does Chesterton evaluate this thesis? In what way does he see it as reflecting a broader agenda? And how does Chesterton begin to set out a rival approach?

Text: *The Everlasting Man*

In his major work of Christian apologetics *The Everlasting Man* (1927), Chesterton provides a response to the intellectual rivals of Christianity. This entire chapter can be seen as a vigorous defense of the incarnational principle – that God entered into human history in Christ. The sentence which seems to sum up Chesterton's argument is this: "The place that the shepherds found was not an academy or an abstract republic; it was not a place of myths allegorised or dissected or explained or explained away. It was a place of dreams come true."

Traditions in art and literature and popular fable have quite sufficiently attested, as has been said, this particular paradox of the divine being in the cradle. Perhaps they have not so clearly emphasised the significance of the divine being in the cave. Curiously enough, indeed, tradition has not very clearly emphasised the cave. It is a familiar fact that the Bethlehem scene has been represented in every possible setting of time and country of landscape and architecture; and it is a wholly happy and admirable fact that men have conceived it as quite different according to their different individual traditions and tastes. But while all have realised that it was a stable, not so many have realised that it was a cave. Some critics have even been so silly as to suppose that there was some contradiction between the stable and the cave; in which case they cannot know much about caves or stables in Palestine. As they see differences that are not there it is needless to add that they do not see differences that are there. When a well-known critic says, for instance, that Christ being born in a rocky cavern is like Mithras having sprung alive out of a rock, it sounds like a parody upon comparative religion. There is such a thing as the point of a story, even if it is a story in the sense of a lie. And the notion of a hero appearing, like Pallas from the brain of Zeus, mature and without a mother, is obviously the very opposite of the idea of a god being born like an ordinary baby and entirely dependent on a mother. Whichever ideal we might prefer, we should surely see that they are contrary ideals. It is as stupid to connect them because they both contain a substance called stone as to identify the punishment of the Deluge with the baptism in the Jordan because they both contain a substance called water. Whether as a myth or a mystery, Christ was obviously conceived as born in a hole in the rocks primarily because it marked the position of one outcast and homeless. . . .

It would be vain to attempt to say anything adequate, or anything new, about the change which this conception of a deity born like an outcast or even an outlaw had upon the whole conception of law and its duties to the poor and outcast. It is profoundly true to say that after that moment there could be no slaves. There could be and were people bearing that legal title, until the Church was strong enough to weed them out, but there could be no more of the pagan repose in the mere advantage to the state of keeping it a servile state. Individuals became important, in a sense in which no instruments can be important. A man could not be a means to an end, at any rate to any other man's end. All this popular and fraternal element in the story has been rightly attached by tradition to the episode of the Shepherds; the hinds who found themselves talking face to face with the princes of heaven. But there is another aspect of the popular element as represented by the shepherds which has not perhaps been so fully developed; and which is more directly relevant here.

Men of the people, like the shepherds, men of the popular tradition, had everywhere been the makers of the mythologies. It was they who had felt most directly, with least check or chill from philosophy or the corrupt cults of civilisation, the need we have already considered; the images that were adventures of the imagination; the mythology that was a sort of search; the tempting and tantalising hints of something half-human in nature; the dumb significance of seasons and special places. They had best understood that the soul of a landscape is a story, and the soul of a story is a personality. But rationalism had already begun to rot away these really irrational though imaginative treasures of the peasant; even as a systematic slavery had eaten the peasant out of house and home. Upon all such peasantries everywhere there was descending a dusk and twilight of disappointment, in the hour when these few men discovered what they sought. Everywhere else Arcadia was fading from the forest. Pan was dead and the shepherds were scattered like sheep. And though no man knew it, the hour was near which was to end and to fulfil all things; and, though no man heard it, there was one far-off cry in an unknown tongue upon the heaving wilderness of the mountains. The shepherds had found their Shepherd.

And the thing they found was of a kind with the things they sought. The populace had been wrong in many things; but they had not been wrong in believing that holy things could have a habitation and that divinity need not disdain the limits of time and space. And the barbarian who conceived the crudest fancy about the sun being stolen and hidden in a box, or the wildest myth about the god being rescued and his enemy deceived with a stone, was nearer to the secret of the cave and knew more about the crisis of the world, than all those in the circle of cities round the Mediterranean who had become content with cold abstractions or cosmopolitan generalisations; than all those who were spinning thinner and thinner threads of thought out of the transcendentalism of Plato or the orientalism of Pythagoras. The place that the shepherds found was not an academy or an abstract republic; it was not a place of myths allegorised or dissected or explained or explained away. It was a place of dreams come true. . . .

The philosophers had also heard. It is still a strange story, though an old one, how they came out of orient lands, crowned with the majesty of kings and clothed with something of the mystery of magicians. That truth that is tradition has wisely remembered them almost as unknown quantities, as mysterious as their mysterious and melodious names; Melchior, Caspar, Balthazar. But there came with them all that world of wisdom that had watched the stars in Chaldea and the sun in Persia; and we shall not be wrong if we see in them the same curiosity that moves all the sages. They would stand for the same human ideal if their names had really been Confucius or Pythagoras or Plato. They were those who sought not tales but the truth of things; and since their thirst for truth was itself a thirst for God, they also have had their reward. But even in order to understand that reward, we must understand that for philosophy as much as mythology, that reward was the completion of the incomplete. . . .

The Magi, who stand for mysticism and philosophy, are truly conceived as seeking something new and even as finding something unexpected. That sense of crisis which still tingles in the Christmas story and even in every Christmas celebration, accentuates the idea of a search and a discovery. For the other mystical figures in the miracle play, for the angel and the mother, the shepherds and the soldiers of Herod, there may be aspects both simpler and more supernatural, more elemental or more emotional. But the Wise Men must be seeking wisdom; and for them there must be a light also in the intellect. And this is the light; that the Catholic creed is catholic and that nothing else is catholic. The philosophy of the Church is universal. The philosophy of the philosophers was not universal. Had Plato and Pythagoras and Aristotle stood for an instant in the light that came out of that little cave, they would have known that their own light was not universal. It is far from certain, indeed, that they did not know it already. Philosophy also, like mythology, had very much the air of a search. It is the realisation of this truth that gives its traditional majesty and mystery to the figures of the Three Kings; the discovery that religion is broader than philosophy and that this is the broadest of religions, contained within this narrow space. . . .

We might well be content to say that mythology had come with the shepherds and philosophy with the philosophers; and that it only remained for them to combine in the recognisation of religion. But there was a third element that must not be ignored and one which that religion for ever refuses to ignore, in any revel or reconciliation. There was present in the primary scenes of the drama that Enemy that had rotted the legends with lust and frozen the theories into atheism, but which answered the direct challenge with something of that more direct method which we have seen in the conscious cult of the demons. In the description of that demon-worship, of the devouring detestation of innocence shown in the works of its witchcraft and the most inhuman of its human sacrifice, I have said less of its indirect and secret penetration of the saner paganism; the soaking of mythological imagination with sex; the rise of imperial pride into insanity. But both the indirect and the direct influence make themselves felt in the drama of Bethlehem. A ruler under the Roman suzerainty, probably equipped and surrounded with the Roman ornament and order though himself of eastern blood, seems in that hour to have felt stirring within him the spirit of strange things. We all know the story of how Herod, alarmed at some rumour of a mysterious rival, remembered the wild gesture of the capricious despots of Asia and ordered a massacre of suspects of the new generation of the populace. Everyone knows the story; but not everyone has perhaps noted its place in the story of the strange religions of men. Not everybody has seen the significance even of its very contrast with the Corinthian columns and Roman pavement of that conquered and superficially civilised world. Only, as the purpose in this dark spirit began to show and shine in the eyes of the Idumean, a seer might perhaps have seen something like a great grey ghost that looked over his shoulder; have seen behind him filling the dome of night and hovering for the last time over history, that vast and fearful fact that was Moloch of the Carthaginians; awaiting his last tribute from a ruler of the races of Shem. The demons in that first festival of Christmas, feasted also in their own fashion.

Questions for Study

1   What is the main point that Chesterton makes in this passage? Can you restate the argument in your own words?

2   Note Chesterton's reference to "Melchior, Caspar, Balthazar." Find this in the text. These are the traditional names of the Magi, or three wise men, who came to adore the new-born Christ. What role do Melchior, Caspar, and Balthazar play in Chesterton's argument?

3   What is the difference between a "myth" and a "mystery"? Why do you think Chesterton regards this point as being important?

CHAPTER 84

T. S. Eliot (1888–1965)

Thomas Stearns Eliot was born in St. Louis, Missouri, on September 26, 1888, as the seventh and youngest child of Henry Ware Eliot and Charlotte Champe Stearns. He entered Harvard University in 1906, and would remain there until 1914. His chosen field of specialization was philosophy. During this period, Eliot published some poetry in *The Harvard Advocate*, a student literary journal which Eliot edited. Initially, it seemed to those who knew him that Eliot was destined for a career as a philosopher at Harvard. Yet this proved not to be the case.

The Eliot family had its roots in England; Andrew Eliot had left the Somerset village of East Coker in 1670, and settled in Boston, Massachusetts. His descendant may thus be thought of as picking up his family's roots once more when he chose to set aside the philosophical career which beckoned him at Harvard, and moved to England. He initially began his studies at the University of Marburg in June 1914. The outbreak of the First World War threw his original plans into disarray, and led to his returning to England in August. In October of that year, he resumed his studies at Oxford University, completing his studies of the noted idealist philosopher F. H. Bradley. While in England, he met his first wife, Vivien Haigh-Wood, who he married in 1915. It proved to be a spectacular failure. Vivien became ill towards the end of the year; they would eventually separate in 1933.

Eliot found himself drifting from one job to another. He taught for four terms in the Junior Department of Highgate School, before taking up a position in the Colonial and Foreign Department of Lloyds Bank, in the City of London. He would remain in this position for eight years. During this time, he brought out *Prufrock and Other Observations*, his first volume of poetry. Five years later, after a nervous breakdown and a stay in a Swiss sanatorium in Lausanne, he published *The Waste Land*. It proved to be a landmark in modern poetry, and established Eliot as a major voice in English literature. Although Eliot would later establish a reputation as a literary critic as much as a poet, this early work was widely seen as a manifesto of "modernism" in English literature, making a deliberate and conscious break with the past.

T. S. Eliot (1888–1965)

Basic description

Leading English-language poet of the twentieth century.

Major works

The Waste Land (1922); The Four Quartets (1943).

Major studies

Peter Ackroyd, T. S. Eliot: A Life. London: Penguin, 1994.

Helen Gardner, The Composition of the Four Quartets. London: Faber, 1978.

Grover Smith, T. S. Eliot's Poetry and Plays: A Study in Sources and Meaning, 2nd edn. Chicago: University of Chicago Press, 1974.

That Eliot had developed a religious agenda became clear when he was baptized into the Church of England on June 29, 1927. In the early years of his first marriage, Eliot would visit churches to admire their beauty; in later years, he visited them for the sake of peace, contemplation, and spiritual refreshment. In 1926, while visiting Rome with his brother and sister-in-law, Eliot caused considerable surprise by kneeling before Michelangelo's *Pietà*. His biographers have suggested that Eliot had a sense of tradition and an instinct for order within himself and found the church and faith gave him this security within a life of frustrations and struggles. Perhaps Eliot's awareness of what he came to term "the void" in all human affairs led him to look for a framework of meaning which allowed him both to understand and endure the disorder, meaninglessness, and futility which he found in his own experience.

His poems now began to include explicitly religious themes, even in their titles – such as "Ash-Wednesday" (1930), "A Song for Simeon" (1928), and "The Visit of the Magi" (1927). Eliot's Christian concerns are perhaps best seen in *The Four Quartets* (1943). However, it could be argued that anticipations of the spiritual quest, to which these later works bear witness, can be seen in *The Waste Land*, which we shall consider in this section.

Eliot was awarded the Nobel Prize for Literature in 1948, and died in London in 1965.

Text: *The Waste Land*

Eliot's masterly poem must be set against the background of the First World War, and its aftermath. It seemed to many that an old order had passed away, and that something new was about to be born. The Russian Revolution sent political as much as cultural shock waves throughout Europe. On June 23, 1919, Marcel Proust (1871–1922) published *A l'ombre des jeunes filles*, a radical literary experiment with subliminal sexual emotions and disjointed time. J. B. Bury (1861–1927) poured scorn upon the idea of continuous development of human culture, civilization and ideas in his *Idea of Progress*, published in 1920. In that same year, the ideas of Sigmund Freud suddenly broke free of their captivity within specialized medical and psychiatric circles with the founding of the first psychiatric polyclinic at Berlin, and the launching of the *International Journal of Psycho-Analysis*. James Joyce's (1882–1941) *Ulysses* appeared in 1922, shocking the literary world, and causing Eliot to remark that it "destroyed the whole world of the nineteenth century." For Eliot and for others, the immediate postwar years were seen as witnessing the final collapse of the cultural heritage of the nineteenth century.

So what lay ahead? *The Waste Land* is an immensely difficult poem, which makes severe demands of its readers, particularly with its at times ostentatious parade of classical learning. Dorothy Wellesley, writing to W. B. Yeats, suggested that Eliot "wrings the past dry and pours the juice down the throats of those who are either too busy, or too creative to read as much as he does." The phrase "the juice of the past" serves well as description of the leading themes of *The Waste Land*; nevertheless, it must be said that it is a past which is presented in a highly fragmented and apparently disordered manner – the Buddha is placed next to St. Augustine, and Ovid next to Wagner. Its frequent use of foreign languages, culminating in its cascade of lines in English, Italian, Latin, French and Sanskrit, was puzzling to many. Nevertheless, many of its readers sensed the spirit of dissatisfaction with modernity, and the earnest spiritual quest which lay behind the poem.

We shall consider the first of the five components of this work, entitled "The Burial of the Dead." This section was probably completed as early as October 1919, and probably takes its title from the familiar service of the Book of Common Prayer (1662), entitled "At the Burial of the Dead."

Taken as a whole, *The Waste Land* is a deeply pessimistic poem, which draws heavily, and perhaps rather uncritically, in its later sections on the theosophist theories of symbolism found in Jessie Weston's *From Ritual to Romance* (1920). Yet an embryonic Christian influence can also be discerned; in his notes to lines 307–9 of the poem, Eliot draws attention to the words of Augustine of Hippo, which conclude the second chapter of *The Confessions*: "I wandered, O my God, too much astray from Thee my stay, in these days of my youth, and I became to myself a waste land."

I. The Burial of the Dead

    April is the cruellest month, breeding
Lilacs out of the dead land, mixing
Memory and desire, stirring
Dull roots with spring rain.
Winter kept us warm, covering   5
Earth in forgetful snow, feeding
A little life with dried tubers.
Summer surprised us, coming over the Starnbergersee
With a shower of rain; we stopped in the colonnade
And went on in sunlight, into the Hofgarten,   10
And drank coffee, and talked for an hour.
Bin gar keine Russin, stamm' aus Litauen, echt deutsch.
And when we were children, staying at the arch-duke's,
My cousin's, he took me out on a sled,
And I was frightened. He said, Marie,   15
Marie, hold on tight. And down we went.
In the mountains, there you feel free.
I read, much of the night, and go south in winter.

    What are the roots that clutch, what branches grow
Out of this stony rubbish? Son of man,   20

You cannot say, or guess, for you know only
A heap of broken images, where the sun beats,
And the dead tree gives no shelter, the cricket no relief,
And the dry stone no sound of water. Only
There is shadow under this red rock   25
(Come in under the shadow of this red rock),
And I will show you something different from either
Your shadow at morning striding behind you
Or your shadow at evening rising to meet you;
I will show you fear in a handful of dust.   30

> *Frisch weht der Wind*
> *Der heimat zu*
> *Mein Irisch kind,*
> *Wo weilest du?*

'You gave me hyacinths first a year ago;   35
'They called me the hyacinth girl.'
—Yet when we came back, late, from the hyacinth garden,
Your arms full, and your hair wet, I could not
Speak, and my eyes failed, I was neither
Living nor dead, and I knew nothing,   40
Looking into the heart of light, the silence.
Oed' und leer das Meer.

Madame Sosostris, famous clairvoyante,
Has a bad cold, nevertheless
Is known to be the wisest woman in Europe,   45
With a wicked pack of cards. Here, said she,
Is your card, the drowned Phoenician Sailor.
(Those are pearls that were his eyes. Look!)
Here is Belladonna, the Lady of the Rocks,
The lady of situations.   50
Here is the man with three staves, and here the Wheel,
And here is the one-eyed merchant, and this card,
Which is blank, is something he carries on his back,
Which I am forbidden to see. I do not find
The Hanged Man. Fear death by water.   55
I see crowds of people, walking round in a ring.
Thank you. If you see dear Mrs. Equitone,
Tell her I bring the horoscope myself;
One must be so careful these days.

Unreal City   60
Under the brown fog of a winter dawn,
A crowd flowed over London Bridge, so many,
I had not thought death had undone so many.

Sighs, short and infrequent, were exhaled,
And each man fixed his eyes before his feet,   65
Flowed up the hill and down King William Street
To where Saint Mary Woolnoth kept the hours
With a dead sound on the final stroke of nine.
There I saw one I knew, and stopped him, crying, 'Stetson!
'You who were with me in the ships at Mylae!   70
'That corpse you planted last year in your garden,
'Has it begun to sprout? Will it bloom this year?
'Or has the sudden frost disturbed its bed?
'Oh keep the Dog far hence, that's friend to men,
'Or with his nails he'll dig it up again!   75
'You! hypocrite lecteur! – mon semblable! – mon frère!'

Questions for Study

1   The opening lines referring to April as the "cruellest month" contrast sharply with
    the poem "The Old Vicarage, Grantchester," by Rupert Brooke (1887–1915). For
    Brooke, the spring is a time of lilac blossom and promise. What does it mean for
    Eliot? And how might this attitude be accounted for?
2   As the poem progresses, a series of *tableaux* unfolds. We read of the "Starnberger-
    see," a fashionable lake resort just south of Munich, which Eliot visited in August
    1911; the "Hofgarten," a public park in Munich; "Madame Sosostris" – a charlatan
    fortune teller who appears in Aldous Huxley's 1921 novel *Chrome Yellow*; and
    various tarot cards. What point is Eliot making as he leads us through these? In what
    sense is the land "waste" on account of the absence of God or meaning?
3   In a later essay entitled "*Ulysses*, Order and Myth," Eliot writes of "the immense
    panorama of futility and anarchy which is contemporary history." How is this theme
    reflected in "The Burial of the Dead"? And just what is being buried in this opening
    section?

Text: "The Journey of the Magi"

"The Journey of the Magi" was the first in a series of poems Eliot later grouped together
as "the Ariel Poems." It was published in August of 1927, shortly after his baptism. There
are excellent reasons for suggesting that the poem can be seen as reflecting Eliot's state
of mind in transition between his old and new faiths. The work opens with a slightly
modified citation from a nativity sermon, preached by Lancelot Andrewes in 1622, in
which the Magi (that is, the "wise men from the east," who came to worship the
newborn Christ) reflect on their journey.

'A cold coming we had of it,
Just the worst time of the year
For a journey, and such a long journey:
The ways deep and the weather sharp,
The very dead of winter.'   5
And the camels galled, sore-footed, refractory,
Lying down in the melting snow.
There were times we regretted
The summer palaces on slopes, the terraces,
And the silken girls bringing sherbet.   10
Then the camel men cursing and grumbling
And running away, and wanting their liquor and women,
And the night-fires going out, and the lack of shelters,
And the cities hostile and the towns unfriendly
And the villages dirty and charging high prices: 15
A hard time we had of it.
At the end we preferred to travel all night,
Sleeping in snatches,
With the voices singing in our ears, saying
That this was all folly.   20

   Then at dawn we came down to a temperate valley,
Wet, below the snow line, smelling of vegetation;
With a running stream and a water-mill beating the darkness,
And three trees on the low sky,
And an old white horse galloped away in the meadow.   25
Then we came to a tavern with vine-leaves over the lintel,
Six hands at an open door dicing for pieces of silver,
And feet kicking the empty wine-skins.
But there was no information, so we continued
And arrived at evening, not a moment too soon   30
Finding the place; it was (you may say) satisfactory.

   All this was a long time ago, I remember,
And I would do it again, but set down
This set down
This: were we led all that way for   35
Birth or Death? There was a Birth, certainly,
We had evidence and no doubt. I had seen birth and death,
But had thought they were different; this Birth was
Hard and bitter agony for us, like Death, our death.
We returned to our places, these Kingdoms,   40
But no longer at ease here, in the old dispensation,
With an alien people clutching their gods.
I should be glad of another death.

Questions for Study

1 Why does Eliot begin this poem with a (modified) quotation from one of Lancelot Andrewes' nativity sermons?

2 What is meant by the reference to "beating the darkness"? Are we to see this as a reference to Christ's resurrection, in which he defeated the forces of darkness and evil?

3 The reference to "beating the darkness" is followed by the image of "three trees on the low sky." What might this mean? Some scholars feel that this is a clear reference to the three crosses erected at Golgotha; Christ, it will be recalled, was placed on the central cross, while two convicted men were then placed, one on either side of him. How convincing do you find this? And if this interpretation is correct, what are we to make of the allusion to the "low sky"?

4 Why were the Magi "no longer at ease . . . in the old dispensation"? What is meant by this? And do we have any reasons for supposing that Eliot may intend this as a reference to his own newly-developed faith?

CHAPTER 85

Dorothy L. Sayers (1893–1957)

Dorothy Leigh Sayers was born at Oxford on June 13, 1893, the only child of Rev. Henry Sayers, headmaster of Christ Church Cathedral School. She attended the Godolphin School, Salisbury, from which she won a scholarship to Somerville College, Oxford. In 1915 she graduated with first-class honors in modern languages. Despite her obvious academic ability, she had no interest in academic life, and went on to join the Oxford publishing company Basil Blackwell. In 1916, this company published her first work – entitled *Op. I* – which was basically a collection of short poems. From 1922 until 1931 she served as a copywriter at the London advertising firm of Bensons – experience which she would put to good use in her later detective novel *Murder Must Advertise*.

Dorothy L. Sayers (1893–1957)

Basic description
One of England's best-known writers of detective fiction, with a deep personal interest in religious questions.

Major works
The Mind of the Maker; *The Man Born to be King*; *Creed or Chaos?*; fourteen detective novels featuring Lord Peter Wimsey.

Major studies
James Brabazon, *Dorothy L. Sayers: A Biography*. London: Gollancz, 1988.

Ralph E. Hone, *Dorothy L. Sayers: A Literary Biography*. Kent, OH: Kent State University Press, 1979.

Barbara Reynolds, *Dorothy L. Sayers: Her Life and Soul*. London: Sceptre, 1994.

Her first novel was published in 1923. *Whose Body?* introduced Lord Peter Wimsey, an aristocratic sleuth whose adventures occupied some fourteen volumes of novels and short stories. *Gaudy Night* was originally intended to be the culmination of the Wimsey novels, but Sayer's friend Muriel St Clare Byrne persuaded her to collaborate in putting Lord Peter on the stage in *Busman's Honeymoon*. The play was successfully launched in December 1936, and she gave up crime writing except for the book of the play and three short stories. It is interesting to note how religious and ecclesiastical themes feature prominently in many of the later Wimsey novels, especially *The Nine Tailors*.

She now turned her attention to more literary projects, making particular use of her knowledge of European languages. She translated *Tristan* and the *Song of Roland* from medieval French, and made a translation in *terza rima* of Dante's *Divine Comedy* which remains unmatched for its popularity. Her death from heart failure on December 17, 1957 prevented her from completing the third volume of the *Divine Comedy*, which was eventually seen through to publication by her friend Dr. Barbara Reynolds.

Her works dealing with aspects of Christian theology remain highly esteemed. Two such works have stood the test of time: *The Mind of the Maker* (1941) and *Creed or Chaos?* (1947; based on lectures given during the Second World War). Yet it was her interest in the stage which gave rise to one her most notable works. She wrote a play entitled *The Zeal of Thy House* for the Canterbury Festival in 1937, and produced a highly-acclaimed nativity play *He That Should Come* for the British Broadcasting Corporation in 1938. The high point of her work in this field is universally agreed to be her radio drama *The Man Born to be King*, in which Christ is represented as speaking modern English, which raised a storm of protest and can be said to have revolutionized religious play-writing.

Text: The Man Born to be King

In February 1940, Dr. J. W. Welch, director of religious broadcasting at the British Broadcasting Corporation (BBC), wrote to Sayers, inviting her to write a series of plays on the life of Christ. Sayers agreed to do this, but attached some conditions to her acceptance. Of these, the most significant were that Christ himself should be featured in the plays, rather than just being a "presence" who was referred to obliquely, and that modern English speech should be used, rather than the kind of English found in the King James Version.

By December 1941, five of the series of six plays had been completed. A news conference was held at the BBC, at which Sayers explained some of the difficulties that she had encountered in writing the plays. To illustrate some of the issues, she read aloud from some sample passages. An outcry resulted. Two main themes emerge from the torrent of criticism directed against the BBC in general, and Sayers in particular. First, that it was outrageous to put into the mouth of Christ words which he is not recorded as having spoken. This was seen by many as being blasphemous. Second, there was considerable unease at the total avoidance of the distinctive style of English associated with the King James Version of the Bible. In the end, the BBC was forced to delay broadcasting some episodes while the criticisms were evaluated.

Sayers responded vigorously to the criticisms, particularly the use of modern English. The seventeenth-century English of the King James Version merely obscured the fact that the New Testament was written in the popular language of its day – and therefore any translation had to be into a contemporary, not classical, form of English. "Tear off the disguise of the Jacobean idiom, go back to the homely and vigorous Greek of Mark or John, translate it into its current English counterpart, and there every man may see his own face." The issues faced by Sayers are, in effect, those faced by anyone who has to translate the Bible – namely, how to achieve "dynamic equivalence" between the text itself and the receptor language of its reader. It is a classic problem, to which Sayers offered her own solution. The play *The Man Born to be King* has become a classic, in terms of its own intrinsic merits and of the issues which it so forcefully raised.

The extract is taken from the second of the cycle of six dramas, broadcast on January 25, 1942, having been delayed due to the protests of the previous month. The play was entitled "The King's Herald," and dealt with the role of John the Baptist. The play opens with the reading of what might be assumed to be a gospel text, but is actually a composite, bringing together material from John 1:28 and Matthew 4:1. Notice how the language is modern, at least by the standards of 1942. In particular, note the complete absence of "King James Version" language.

The initial sequence focuses on John the Baptist, who is portrayed as discussing matters of theology with Judas. In her "Notes" for the play, Sayers describes John as "about 31" with "a harsh, strong and not very flexible" voice. Judas is "infinitely the most intelligent of all the disciples, and has the boldness and drive that belong to a really imaginative brain." The dialog is intended to evoke the sense of "realism" which Sayers regarded as essential to her task. In the second sequence, we encounter Jesus, who is referred to as "Jesus bar-Joseph" ("bar" is the Aramaic term for "son of"). Sayers places ordinary yet dignified language on his lips; in her "Notes," she allows him a sense of humor.

Scene II (Bethabara)

Sequence 1 (The Tent of John the Baptist)

THE EVANGELIST: Then was Jesus led up by the Spirit into the wilderness to be tempted of the devil. And when he had fasted forty days and forty nights, he came into Bethabara beyond Jordan, where John was baptising.

ANDREW: I say, Judas?

JUDAS: Well, Andrew?

ANDREW: How many did we baptise yesterday?

JUDAS: Twenty-three men, fourteen women and ten children. Forty-seven in all.

JOHN EVANGELIST: I call that very encouraging. Especially the women and children.

ANDREW: My dear John bar-Zebedee! you can't run a campaign on women and children.

JUDAS: You're wrong, Andrew. The women and children are very important. Women talk, and bring other women. Then their husbands come to see that they don't get into mischief.

(*Laughter*)

Besides, when the wife's converted too, the man doesn't have to face continual rows and nagging at home. If it wasn't for his wife, your brother Simon would be with us now.

ANDREW: That's true enough.

JUDAS: You can't expect a man to take risks for a cause if his wife's always at him to put the interests of the family first.

JAMES: There speaks the practical Judas.

JUDAS: Well, somebody must be practical.

JOHN EVANGELIST: Besides, if once a woman makes up her mind to a thing –

JUDAS: Nothing will stop her. True.

ANDREW: In fact, she behaves just like John bar-Zebedee. If *he* sees a thing he wants he makes a bee-line for it, charges up to it like a bull at a gate –

JUDAS: And then comes over all bashful and tongue-tied and leaves somebody else to do the work.

JOHN EVANGELIST: I d-d-don't.

JUDAS: D-d-d-don't you?

JOHN EVANGELIST: I know I get excited. But you don't understand. If a thing means a tremendous lot to one and one goes after it – and then, suddenly, unbelievably, it's *there*, within reach – one's almost afraid to touch it, for fear it shouldn't be there after all. It isn't that I want somebody else to do the work. It's just that – (*He gives it up*) I can't explain.

JAMES: Never mind them, John. You have the rare gift of humility – and that's more than can be said of you, Judas, or of most of us.

ANDREW: That's right, James bar-Zebedee. Stick up for your brother.

JAMES: What's more, if it comes to taking risks, you'll find my brother in the front line.

ANDREW: It may very well come to that. Just between ourselves I wish John Baptist would be a bit more cautious. . . . Where is he, by the way?

JUDAS: He went out alone about the sixth hour.

ANDREW: Oh, I see. Well, his attacks on Herod are attracting attention.

JAMES: Herod! it's time somebody did speak plainly about Herod. A fine ruler he makes for the Jewish nation! Weak, cruel, self-indulgent – and letting that gang of women lead him by the nose –

JUDAS: Herod's easily influenced. But that's rather to our advantage. If Herod himself could be brought to repentance and baptism –

ANDREW: Now is that likely?

JUDAS: He respects John Baptist and listens to him. He knows he's an honest man and a true prophet.

ANDREW: Yes, Judas, I dare say. But it's his wife you've got to reckon with. Herodias will never forgive John Baptist for the things he's said about her, and she's out for his blood.

JUDAS: Herod wouldn't let it go as far as that. And his conversion would make a tremendous impression.

JOHN EVANGELIST: John Baptist doesn't think twice about making an impression. He's out to rebuke sin, and he wouldn't care who it was.

JUDAS: I know. That's why he's such a grand leader. And that's why I say, Take the risk: it's worth it.

ANDREW: He intends to take it. He never seemed to value his own life. But just lately he has grown more reckless than ever – almost as though –

JOHN EVANGELIST: As though he saw the end of his mission in sight. I know. I have seen the change in him, these forty days; and so has James.

JAMES: His flesh is wasted – the fire of God consumes his very soul. Something happened that week we were away. What was it, Judas?

JUDAS: I don't know. He had been superb that day, and we had made a great many converts. When he had almost finished baptising there was a thunder-clap. He looked up – and something came into his face as though he had felt the hand of God laid on his shoulder. That look has been there ever since.

JOHN EVANGELIST: Yes. James and I noticed it the minute we got back. I tried to ask him about it . . . but when it came to the point I c-c-couldn't find the words.

JUDAS: So you just st-st-stood and st-st-stuttered at him.

JOHN EVANGELIST: I was afraid. He looked at me as though he didn't see me.

JAMES: Shut up. He's just coming in. . . . Ah! welcome back, John Baptist! . . . Why – what has happened?

JOHN EVANGELIST: You have brought good news?

JOHN BAPTIST: Jesus has returned. He is here.

ANDREW: Jesus? What Jesus?

JUDAS: Jesus bar-Joseph your cousin?

JOHN BAPTIST: My cousin after the flesh; my Lord after the Spirit.

JUDAS: Whom you baptised in Jordan forty days since?

JAMES: Forty days since!

JOHN BAPTIST: All these forty days he has been in the wilderness. And I waited and wondered and taught the people. To-day, while I was preaching, he came walking by the river, and I saw the Spirit of God shine through the tabernacle of his flesh like the Shekinah of glory that rested upon the tabernacle of the Ark. And I cried to the people saying, "This, this is he of whom I spoke – the greater one than I, that should come after me". And they stared at me and him, but they could not see what I saw. And how could I blame them? For I have known him all these years and still I did not know him. . . . So I hurried back here, thinking that you my disciples would see and understand. . . . And as I went, I felt his presence close behind me – following hard upon me, and yet leading me on. For wherever I go he is behind me and before me, as he was before me from the beginning.

ANDREW: I don't understand you, John Baptist.

JOHN BAPTIST: Bring out the roll of the Scriptures. . . . Read what Isaiah says about the redeemer of Israel.

ANDREW: You are the best scholar, John bar-Zebedee.

JOHN EVANGELIST: Where shall I begin?

JOHN BAPTIST: "He is despised and rejected of men; a man of sorrows and acquainted with grief" – begin from there.

JOHN EVANGELIST (*a little surprised*): Oh! . . . "Surely he hath borne our griefs, and carried our sorrows: yet we did esteem him stricken, smitten of God and afflicted." . . . John, is this a prophecy of the Messiah? I always thought it spoke of the sufferings of our nation.

JOHN BAPTIST: All Israel is in Israel's Messiah. Read on.

JOHN EVANGELIST: "He was wounded for our transgressions, he was bruised for our iniquities; the chastisement of our peace was upon him; and with his stripes we are healed."

JUDAS: John Baptist, I begin to see.

JOHN BAPTIST: To see what, Judas?

JUDAS: Why your call is to baptism and repentance. Why the false peace of heart must be broken and its complacency chastised. . . . I had imagined something different . . . but now – but now – Yes; it is bigger and stranger than that. . . . I am sorry I interrupted.

JOHN EVANGELIST: "He is brought as a lamb to the slaughter, and as a sheep before her shearers is dumb" –

JOHN BAPTIST (*suddenly*): Look!

ALL: What? – Where? –

JOHN BAPTIST: There walks the Lamb of God, carrying away the sins of the world.

JAMES: Who is it?

ANDREW: The sun is in my eyes.

JUDAS: I recognise him. It is Jesus bar-Joseph.

JAMES: He is coming to us.

ANDREW: No, he is passing on.

JAMES: He looked this way, but he didn't see us.

JUDAS: John bar-Zebedee, what are you trembling for?

JOHN EVANGELIST: He looked at me.

JUDAS: If this is the Messiah of Israel –

ANDREW: What do you want us to do, John Baptist?

JAMES: Are we to follow him or stay with you?

JOHN EVANGELIST: *I* have no choice. I don't know what you have seen, John Baptist, and I can't understand half you say. But he looked at me. I must see and speak to him. I must follow and find him, or never know peace again. . . . Don't think I'm ungrateful. I don't want to desert you. But I must go. I must. It's something I can't explain. You do understand, don't you? Let me go, John Baptist! Let me go.

JOHN BAPTIST: Go quickly, John bar-Zebedee. Never mind me.

JAMES: He's off. . . . Run after him, Andrew. He'll stammer and get mixed up and not be able to explain himself.

ANDREW: Won't you – ?

JAMES: A friend is less embarrassing than a brother. I'll stay. . . . Come back and report.

ANDREW: All right. . . . (*He hurries off, calling*) John! John! Wait a moment. . . .

JOHN BAPTIST (*his voice fading into the background*): "He shall see of the travail of his soul and shall be satisfied . . . he shall be satisfied. . . ."

Sequence 2 (On the Road)

ANDREW (*running*): Hi, John!

JOHN EVANGELIST: Come on, quick.

ANDREW (*panting*): Where's the hurry? . . . Here, let me get my breath. . . .

JOHN EVANGELIST: The world might come to an end before we found him.

ANDREW (*good-humouredly*): Well, it might: but it's not very likely. He can't have got far.

JOHN EVANGELIST: He disappeared behind the olive-trees.

ANDREW: Yes. Well, take it easy. You'll kill yourself, running like that in all this heat.

JOHN EVANGELIST: Suppose, when we turned the corner, he wasn't there.

ANDREW (*placidly*): I shan't suppose anything of the sort. . . . There! what did I tell you? Here we are at the corner, and there is Jesus bar-Joseph.

JOHN EVANGELIST: Yes. Yes. It's all right.

ANDREW: What are you stopping for?

JOHN EVANGELIST: Nothing. I mean, he's there and it's all right.

ANDREW: What's come over you?

JOHN EVANGELIST: Let's follow and keep him in sight.

ANDREW: You are the most extraordinary person – up in the air one minute and down the next. . . . I don't know what to make of you. Why can't you – ?

JOHN EVANGELIST: He's heard us.

ANDREW: He's waiting for us. . . . *Go* on, John.

JOHN EVANGELIST: *You* speak to him.

JESUS: What are you looking for? Do you want me?

ANDREW: Rabbi, we are disciples of John the Baptist. You passed our tent just now and he told us – Well, anyway, we wanted very much to speak to you. So we ran after you. My name's Andrew, by the way, Andrew bar-Jonah.

JESUS: You are very welcome, Andrew.

ANDREW: And this is John bar-Zebedee. He was the one who was so terribly keen to come, and I came with him. . . . Say something, John. . . . (*apologetically*) He ran very fast and he's out of breath.

JESUS: What do you want of me, John bar-Zebedee?

JOHN EVANGELIST: You called me, and I came.

ANDREW: We don't want to bother you now, if it isn't convenient, but if you would tell us where you live –

JESUS: Quite near here. Come and see.

ANDREW: Now?

JESUS: Yes. We will all go together.

ANDREW: Wake up, John.

JOHN EVANGELIST: I feel as though I were dreaming.

JESUS: Follow me.

Questions for Study

1 The following passage (John 1:37–39) lies behind the second sequence of Sayers' text. Read it in the King James Version, and then compare it with Sayers' narrative. What differences do you notice?

And the two disciples heard him speak, and they followed Jesus. Then Jesus turned, and saw them following, and saith unto them, What seek ye? They said unto him, Rabbi, (which is to say, being interpreted, Master,) where dwellest thou? He saith unto them, Come and see.

2   Why do you think many who heard the plays found them difficult to cope with?
3   Read the discussion between John the Baptist and his colleagues concerning the identity of Jesus, particularly the sections dealing with Old Testament prophecies. What are the issues that Sayers wants her audience to think about?

Text: *The Mind of the Maker*

It was during the Second World War that Sayers began to write works of substance dealing with the major themes of the Christian faith, with a view to making them more accessible and intelligible to a lay readership. Having firmly established herself as a major writer through her detective novels, Sayers now put her ability to communicate through words to the service of Christian theology. In doing so, she joined a relatively small group of English writers – including G. K. Chesterton and C. S. Lewis – who managed to make theology accessible to a wider readership.

It is widely agreed that *The Mind of the Maker* is the best of these works of Christian theology. Sayers made it clear from the outset that the work should not be seen as an apology for Christianity, but as "a commentary, in the light of specialized knowledge, on a particular set of statements made in the Christian creeds and their claim to be statements of fact." The statements which Sayers focused on are those "which aim at defining the nature of God, conceived in his capacity as Creator," which she sought to interpret and explain in the light of her professional literary capacity. The passage which has been selected for comment is of particular interest, in that it offers the analogy of a book as a means of understanding the various aspects of the work of God in creation.

In this section, Sayers begins to explore the trinitarian aspects of creation, considering particularly the question of how the nature and purposes of God can be expressed in the creation. It is at this point that she deploys the analogy of a book. The analogy has already been used in the work; for example, Shakespeare writing *Hamlet* is affirmed to be an "act of creation." Yet what does this mean? At first sight, it might appear that it is simply the expression of some ideas that were present in the writer's mind. Yet Sayers argues that this is not enough to allow us to understand the complex relationship between the author, the book and the reader. She therefore explores the way in which the nature and purposes of God can be revealed to humanity, on the basis of her explicitly-stated assumption that this is analogous to the way in which an author sets out to communicate to her readers.

The critically important stage of the argument is the three-fold aspect of the book: the book as *thought*, as *written*, and as *read*. There is a clear trinitarian trajectory of thought here, which can be argued to correspond to the classic Christian understanding of Father, Son, and Spirit. For example, note the judicious use of the notion of "incarnation" in Sayers' discussion of "the book as written." One of the key theological questions being debated here is whether God can really be said to be "revealed" unless that revelation is recognized as revelation. Sayers points out that "a book has no influence till somebody can read it." In making this observation, she is reinforcing the parallel between the ideas of an author, mediated to readers through a book, and the nature and purposes of God, mediated to humanity through God's revelation in Christ.

VIII

Pentecost

WHEN THE writer's Idea is revealed or incarnate by his Energy, then, and only then, can his Power work on the world. More briefly and obviously, a book has no influence till somebody can read it.

Before the Energy was revealed or incarnate it was, as we have seen, already present in Power within the creator's mind, but now that Power is released for communication to other men, and returns from their minds to his with a new response. It dwells in them and works upon them with creative energy, producing in them fresh manifestations of Power.

This is the Power of the Word, and it is dangerous. Every word – even every idle word – will be accounted for at the day of judgment, because the word itself has power to bring to judgment. It is of the nature of the word to reveal itself and to incarnate itself – to assume material form. Its judgment is therefore an intellectual, but also a material judgment. The habit, very prevalent to-day, of dismissing words as "just words" takes no account of their power. But once the Idea has entered into other minds, it will tend to reincarnate itself there with ever-increasing Energy and ever-increasing Power. It may for some time only incarnate itself in more words, more books, more speeches; but the day comes when it incarnates itself in actions, and this is its day of judgment. At the time when these words are being written, we are witnessing a fearful judgment of blood, resulting from the incarnation in deeds of an Idea to which, when it was content with a verbal revelation, we paid singularly little heed. Which Ideas are (morally) Good and which are anti-Good it is not the purpose of this book to discuss; what is now abundantly manifest is the Power. Any Idea whose Energy manifests itself in a Pentecost of Power is good from its own point of view. It shows itself to be a true act of creation, although, if it is an evil Idea, it will create to a large extent by active negation – that is to say, by destruction. The fact, however, that "all activity is of God" means that no creative Idea can be wholly destructive: some creation will be produced together with the destruction; and it is the work of the creative mind to see that the destruction is redeemed by its creative elements.

It is the business of education to wait upon Pentecost. Unhappily, there is something about educational syllabuses, and especially about examination papers, which seems to be rather out of harmony with Pentecostal manifestations. The Energy of Ideas does not seem to descend into the receptive mind with quite that rush of cloven fire which we ought to expect. Possibly there is something lacking in our Idea of education; possibly something inhibiting has happened to the Energy. But Pentecost will happen, whether within or without official education. From some quarter or other, the Power will descend, to flame or to smoulder until it is ready to issue in a new revelation. We need not suppose that, because the mind of the reader is inert to Plato, it will therefore be inert to Nietzsche or Karl Marx; failing those, it may respond to Wilhelmina Stitch or to Hollywood. No incarnate Idea is altogether devoid of Power; if the Idea is feeble, the Energy dispersed, and the Power dim, the indwelling spirit will be dim, dispersed and feeble – but such as it is, so its response will be and such will be its manifestation in the world.

It is through the Power that we get a reflection in the mind of the world of the original Trinity in the mind of the writer. For the reader, that is, the book itself is presented as a threefold being.

First: the Book as Thought – the Idea of the book existing in the writer's mind. Of this, the reader can be aware only by faith. He knows that it does exist, but it is unknowable to him except in its manifestations. He can, of course, suppose if he likes that the book corresponds to nothing at all in the writer's mind; he can, if he likes, think that it got into its visible form by accident and that there is not and never was any such person as the writer. He is perfectly free to think these things, though in practice he seldom avails himself of this freedom. Where a book is concerned, the average man is a confirmed theist. There was, certainly, a little time ago, a faint tendency to polytheism among the learned. In particular cases, that is, where there was no exterior evidence about the writer, the theory was put forward that the *Iliad*, for example, and the *Song of Roland* were written by "the folk"; some extremists actually suggested that they "just happened" – though even such people were forced to allow the mediation of a little democracy of godlets to account for the material form in which these manifestations presented themselves. To-day, the polytheistic doctrine is rather at a discount; at any rate it is generally conceded that the Energy exhibited in written works must have emanated from some kind of Idea in a personal mind.

Secondly: the Book as Written – the Energy or Word incarnate, the express image of the Idea. This is the book that stands upon our shelves, and everything within and about it: characters, episodes, the succession of words and phrases, style, grammar, paper and ink, and, of course, the story itself. The incarnation of the Energy stands wholly within the space-time frame: it is written by a material pen and printed by a material machine upon material paper; the words were produced as a succession of events succeeding one another in time. Any timelessness, illimitability or uncreatedness which may characterise the book belongs not here but in the mind; the *body* of the Energy is a created thing, strictly limited by time and space, and subject to any accident that may befall matter. If we do not like it, we are at liberty to burn it in the market-place, or subject it to any other indignity, such as neglecting it, denying it, spitting upon it, or writing hostile reviews about it. We must, however, be careful to see that nobody reads it before we take steps to eliminate it; otherwise, it may disconcert us by rising again – either as a new Idea in somebody's mind, or even (if somebody has a good memory) in a resurrected body, substantially the same though made of new materials. In this respect, Herod showed himself much more competent and realistic than Pilate or Caiaphas. He grasped the principle that if you are to destroy the Word, you must do so before it has time to communicate itself. Crucifixion gets there too late.

Thirdly: the Book as Read – the Power of its effect upon and in the responsive mind. This is a very difficult thing to examine and analyse, because our own perception of the thing is precisely what we are trying to perceive. We can, as it were, note various detached aspects of it: what we cannot pin down and look at is the movement of our own mind. In the same way, we cannot follow the movement of our own eyes in a mirror. We can, by turning our head, observe them in this position and in that position with respect to our body, but never in the act of moving themselves from one position to the other, and never in the act of gazing at anything but the mirror. Thus our idea of ourself is bound to be falsified, since what to others appears the most lively and mobile part of ourself, appears to us unnaturally fixed. The eye is the instrument by which we see everything, and for that reason it is the one thing we cannot see with truth. The same thing is true of our Power of response to a book, or to anything else; incidentally, this is why books about the Holy Ghost are apt to be curiously difficult and unsatisfactory – we cannot really look at the movement of the Spirit, just because It is the Power by which we do the looking.

We may, however, note one or two things – fixed aspects of the Power. Like the Idea itself, it is immaterial and timeless. When we say we "know *Hamlet*", we do not mean merely that we can memorise the whole succession of words and events in *Hamlet*. We mean that we have in our minds an awareness of *Hamlet* as a complete whole – "the end in the beginning". We can prove this by observing how differently we feel when seeing a performance of *Hamlet* on the one hand and an entirely new play on the other. While watching the new play we are in contact with the Energy, which we experience as a sequence in time; we wonder "how it is going to work out". If, during the interval, we are asked what we think of it, we can only give a very incomplete answer. Everything depends, we feel, on the last act. But when the final curtain has come down, we feel quite differently towards the play – we can think of it as a whole, and see how all the episodes are related to one another to produce something inside our mind which is *more* than the sum-total of the emotions we experienced while sitting in the stalls. It is in this timeless and complete form that it remains in our recollection: the Energy is now related to the Idea more or less as it was in the mind of the playwright: the Word has returned to the Father.

When we see *Hamlet* (or any other play that we already "know") we start already in this frame of mind. We are able, as the performance proceeds, to relate the part to the whole and the time-sequence to eternity at every point. Just as the writer realised while writing that there was a complete Idea in his mind, because, step by step, he found himself relating the progress of his work *to* that Idea, so also we realise while watching the play that there is a "whole *Hamlet*" in our own minds to which we are busily referring every word and action as it passes before us. Our knowledge of how the whole thing "hangs together" gives us a deeper understanding and a better judgment of each part, because we can now refer it, not only to the past but also to the future; and, more than that, to a unity of the work which exists for us right outside the sequence of time. It is as though the writer's Idea had passed from eternity into time and then back into eternity again – still the same Idea, but charged with a different emphasis of Power derived from our own response. Not only that: if it is a play like *Hamlet*, which has already stimulated powerful responses in the minds of other men, our personal response will be related to a greater unity which includes all those other foci of Power. Every scholar and critic who has written about *Hamlet*, every great actor who has ever played the part, every painter or musician who has found a source of power in *Hamlet*, retransmits that power to the spectator, in accordance with the capacity for response that is in each.

Questions for Study

1 How effective is Sayers' analogy of a book as a way of understanding revelation?
2 Trace her line of thought from the original ideas of the author to their effective communication through the written word. What does she identify as the key stages in this trajectory? And how does this help her with her trinitarian agenda?

CHAPTER 86

C. S. Lewis (1898–1963)

Clive Staples Lewis – "Jack" to his friends – was born in Belfast, Northern Ireland on November 29, 1898. His father was a successful solicitor, who was doing well enough to allow the family to move to a large house ("Little Lea") on the outskirts of Belfast in 1905. Shortly afterwards, Lewis's mother died, leaving his father to look after Lewis and his elder brother Warren. The two brothers spent hours alone in the vast attic of the old house, inhabiting imaginary worlds of their own making.

If Lewis ever had any Christian faith to begin with, he soon lost it. After a period serving in the British Army during the First World War, Lewis went up to Oxford. He was a student at University College in the period 1919–23, taking first-class honors in Greats (Classics and Philosophy) in 1922, and first-class honors in English the following year. After a period during which his future seemed uncertain, he was elected a fellow of Magdalen College in the spring of 1925. He would remain at the college until 1954, when he was invited to take up the newly-created chair of Medieval and Renaissance English at Cambridge. The chair was linked with a fellowship at Magdalene College, Cambridge. (As his extensive correspondence indicates, Lewis took some pleasure in pointing out the verbal link between his old and new colleges.) Lewis died at his Oxford home at 5.30 p.m. on November 22, 1963, a few hours before the world was shocked by the news of the assassination of President John F. Kennedy at Dallas, Texas.

During the 1920s, Lewis had time to reconsider his attitude to Christianity. The story of his return to the faith he abandoned as a boy is described in great detail in his autobiography, *Surprised by Joy*. After wrestling with the clues concerning God he found in human reason and experience, he eventually decided that intellectual honesty compelled him to believe and trust in God. He did not want to; he felt, however, that he had no choice. The passage in *Surprised by Joy* describing this great moment of decision merits study:

> You must picture me alone in that room at Magdalen, night after night, feeling, whenever my mind lifted even for a second from my work, the steady unrelenting approach of Him whom I so earnestly desired not to meet. That which I greatly feared had at last come upon me. In the Trinity Term of 1929 I gave in, and admitted that God was God, and knelt and

prayed: perhaps, that night, the most dejected and reluctant convert in all England. I did not then see what is now the most shining and obvious thing; the divine humility which will accept a convert even on such terms. The Prodigal Son at least walked home on his own feet. But who can duly adore that Love which will open the high gates to a prodigal who is brought in kicking, struggling, resentful, and darting his eyes in every direction for a chance of escape?

After his conversion, Lewis began to establish his reputation as a leading authority on medieval and Renaissance English literature. *The Allegory of Love*, published in 1936, is still regarded as a masterpiece, as is his *Preface to Paradise Lost*. Alongside his scholarly writings, however, Lewis wrote books of a very different nature. Aiming at clarity and conviction, Lewis produced a series of works aimed at communicating the reasonableness of Christianity to his own generation. The works brought him popular acclaim, but seemed to some to destroy his scholarly reputation. This was especially the case with *The Screwtape Letters*, which alienated many of his academic colleagues on account of their "populist" or "vulgar" tone. In 1946, he was passed over for the Merton professorship of English Literature at Oxford.

The first popular book was *The Pilgrim's Regress*, based loosely on John Bunyan's *Pilgrim's Progress*. It was not a great publishing success. Nevertheless, Lewis continued writing at this popular level. *The Problem of Pain*, which appeared in 1940, was well received, and on the basis of its clarity and intelligence of argument, Lewis was invited to give a series of radio talks by the British Broadcasting Corporation. In 1942, these were published as *The Case for Christianity*. Such was their success that Lewis combined them with two other short works – *Christian Behaviour* (1943) and *Beyond Personality* (1944) – to yield the composite work *Mere Christianity*. The year 1942 also saw the publication of *The Screwtape Letters*, whose wit and insight firmly established Lewis's reputation as a leading defender of the Christian faith, at the cost of estranging many of his academic colleagues in Oxford.

C. S. Lewis (1898–1963)

Basic description
Oxford literary critic and popular religious writer.

Major works
Mere Christianity (1943); The Screwtape Letters (1942); The Chronicles of Narnia (1950–6); Surprised by Joy (1955).

Major studies
Corbin Scott Carnell, *Bright Shadow of Reality: Spiritual Longing in C. S. Lewis*. Grand Rapids, MI: Eerdmans, 1999.

R. L. Green and W. Hooper, *C. S. Lewis: A Biography*. London: Collins, 1974.

Richard L. Purtill, *C. S. Lewis' Case for the Christian Faith*. San Francisco: Harper & Row, 1985.

That reputation was consolidated by further works, including *Miracles* (1947) and *The Four Loves* (1960). His seven-volumed *Chronicles of Narnia* brought his ideas about

Christianity to a wide audience, and opened his writings up to a new generation of readers. Outspokenly critical of "Christianity-and-water" (as he dubbed liberal versions of Christianity), he struck a deep chord of sympathy with his readers. Professional theologians were irritated at Lewis's success, and accused him of simplifying things; Lewis responded by suggesting that, if professional theologians had done their job properly, there would be no need for lay theologians such as himself. His death in 1963 did nothing to stem the growing tide of interest in his writings. In April 1980, *Time* magazine reported that Lewis was unquestionably "this century's most-read apologist for God." Even after his death, his influence lives on; thousands who never knew Lewis in the flesh attribute their discovery of, or return to, Christianity to the influence of his writings.

What is it about those writings which possesses such an appeal to so many? Unquestionably, it is Lewis's intelligent and persuasive approach to Christianity. For Lewis, Christianity makes sense. It commends itself by its reasonableness. Believing in God makes more sense, Lewis argued, than not believing in him. *Mere Christianity* is perhaps as outstanding an example of a lucid and intelligent presentation of the rational and moral case for Christian belief as we are ever likely to see.

Yet there is more to Lewis than this. Alongside Lewis the cool-headed thinker we find a very different style of thinker – a man who is aware of the power of the human imagination, and the implications of this power for our understanding of reality. Perhaps one of the most original aspects of Lewis's writing is his persistent and powerful appeal to the religious imagination.

The passages for study are taken from *The Screwtape Letters*, one of Lewis's most controversial pieces of writing, which is widely regarded as his most original contribution to Christian literature, and from *Till We Have Faces*, which Lewis regarded as the most successful of his novels.

Text: *The Screwtape Letters*

This work, published in 1942, purports to be the correspondence sent by Screwtape, a senior devil, to his nephew Wormwood, concerning the proper methods for leading a newly-converted Christian soul astray. Its originality lies partly in its perspective; it is written from the point of view of two devils, differing considerably in their experience of misleading their unfortunate victims. When the book first appeared, it surprised and delighted its readers, and since then its popularity has never waned. The work is clever, inventive, and humorous; it exposes human weaknesses and foibles with a gentle sense of humor. Screwtape's advice to the young tempter Wormword, who prefers "spectacular wickedness," is to make evil subtle, even banal; the safest road to hell is, as he puts it, "the gradual one."

The extract consists of Lewis's brief preface to the work, followed by the first two letters of Screwtape to his nephew, Wormwood.

Preface

I have no intention of explaining how the correspondence which I now offer to the public fell into my hands.

There are two equal and opposite errors into which our race can fall about the devils. One is to disbelieve in their existence. The other is to believe, and to feel an excessive and unhealthy interest in them. They themselves are equally pleased by both errors and hail a materialist or a magician with the same delight. The sort of script which is used in this book can be very easily obtained by anyone who has once learned the knack; but ill-disposed or excitable people who might make a bad use of it shall not learn it from me.

Readers are advised to remember that the devil is a liar. Not everything that Screwtape says should be assumed to be true even from his own angle. I have made no attempt to identify any of the human beings mentioned in the letters; but I think it very unlikely that the portraits, say, of Fr. Spike or the patient's mother, are wholly just. There is wishful thinking in Hell as well as on Earth.

In conclusion, I ought to add that no effort has been made to clear up the chronology of the letters. Number XVII appears to have been composed before rationing became serious; but in general the diabolical method of dating seems to bear no relation to terrestrial time and I have not attempted to reproduce it. The history of the European War, except in so far as it happens now and then to impinge upon the spiritual condition of one human being, was obviously of no interest to Screwtape.

C. S. LEWIS

MAGDALEN COLLEGE
July 5, 1941

I

My dear Wormwood,

I note what you say about guiding your patient's reading and taking care that he sees a good deal of his materialist friend. But are you not being a trifle *naïf*? It sounds as if you supposed that *argument* was the way to keep him out of the Enemy's clutches. That might have been so if he had lived a few centuries earlier. At that time the humans still knew pretty well when a thing was proved and when it was not; and if it was proved they really believed it. They still connected thinking with doing and were prepared to alter their way of life as the result of a chain of reasoning. But what with the weekly press and other such weapons we have largely altered that. Your man has been accustomed, ever since he was a boy, to have a dozen incompatible philosophies dancing about together inside his head. He doesn't think of doctrines as primarily "true" or "false", but as "academic" or "practical", "outworn" or "contemporary", "conventional" or "ruthless". Jargon, not argument, is your best ally in keeping him from the Church. Don't waste time trying to make him think that materialism is *true*! Make him think it is strong, or stark, or courageous – that it is the philosophy of the future. That's the sort of thing he cares about.

The trouble about argument is that it moves the whole struggle onto the Enemy's own ground. He can argue too; whereas in really practical propaganda of the kind

I am suggesting He has been shown for centuries to be greatly the inferior of Our Father Below. By the very act of arguing, you awake the patient's reason; and once it is awake, who can foresee the result? Even if a particular train of thought can be twisted so as to end in our favour, you will find that you have been strengthening in your patient the fatal habit of attending to universal issues and withdrawing his attention from the stream of immediate sense experiences. Your business is to fix his attention on the stream. Teach him to call it "real life" and don't let him ask what he means by "real".

Remember, he is not, like you, a pure spirit. Never having been a human (Oh that abominable advantage of the Enemy's!) you don't realise how enslaved they are to the pressure of the ordinary. I once had a patient, a sound atheist, who used to read in the British Museum. One day, as he sat reading, I saw a train of thought in his mind beginning to go the wrong way. The Enemy, of course, was at his elbow in a moment. Before I knew where I was I saw my twenty years' work beginning to totter. If I had lost my head and begun to attempt a defence by argument I should have been undone. But I was not such a fool. I struck instantly at the part of the man which I had best under my control and suggested that it was just about time he had some lunch. The Enemy presumably made the counter-suggestion (you know how one can never *quite* overhear what He says to them?) that this was more important than lunch. At least I think that must have been His line for when I said "Quite. In fact much *too* important to tackle at the end of a morning", the patient brightened up considerably; and by the time I had added "Much better come back after lunch and go into it with a fresh mind", he was already half way to the door. Once he was in the street the battle was won. I showed him a newsboy shouting the midday paper, and a No. 73 bus going past, and before he reached the bottom of the steps I had got into him an unalterable conviction that, whatever odd ideas might come into a man's head when he was shut up alone with his books, a healthy dose of "real life" (by which he meant the bus and the newsboy) was enough to show him that all "that sort of thing" just couldn't be true. He knew he'd had a narrow escape and in later years was fond of talking about "that inarticulate sense for actuality which is our ultimate safeguard against the aberrations of mere logic". He is now safe in Our Father's house.

You begin to see the point? Thanks to processes which we set at work in them centuries ago, they find it all but impossible to believe in the unfamiliar while the familiar is before their eyes. Keep pressing home on him the *ordinariness* of things. Above all, do not attempt to use science (I mean, the real sciences) as a defence against Christianity. They will positively encourage him to think about realities he can't touch and see. There have been sad cases among the modern physicists. If he must dabble in science, keep him on economics and sociology; don't let him get away from that invaluable "real life". But the best of all is to let him read no science but to give him a grand general idea that he knows it all and that everything he happens to have picked up in casual talk and reading is "the results of modern investigation". Do remember you are there to fuddle him. From the way some of you young fiends talk, anyone would suppose it was our job to *teach*!

Your affectionate uncle

SCREWTAPE

II

My dear Wormwood,

I note with grave displeasure that your patient has become a Christian. Do not indulge the hope that you will escape the usual penalties; indeed, in your better moments, I trust you would hardly even wish to do so. In the meantime we must make the best of the situation. There is no need to despair; hundreds of these adult converts have been reclaimed after a brief sojourn in the Enemy's camp and are now with us. All the *habits* of the patient, both mental and bodily, are still in our favour.

One of our great allies at present is the Church itself. Do not misunderstand me. I do not mean the Church as we see her spread out through all time and space and rooted in eternity, terrible as an army with banners. That, I confess, is a spectacle which makes our boldest tempters uneasy. But fortunately it is quite invisible to these humans. All your patient sees is the half-finished, sham Gothic erection on the new building estate. When he goes inside, he sees the local grocer with rather an oily expression on his face bustling up to offer him one shiny little book containing a liturgy which neither of them understands, and one shabby little book containing corrupt texts of a number of religious lyrics, mostly bad, and in very small print. When he gets to his pew and looks round him he sees just that selection of his neighbours whom he has hitherto avoided. You want to lean pretty heavily on those neighbours. Make his mind flit to and fro between an expression like "the body of Christ" and the actual faces in the next pew. It matters very little, of course, what kind of people that next pew really contains. You may know one of them to be a great warrior on the Enemy's side. No matter. Your patient, thanks to Our Father below, is a fool. Provided that any of those neighbours sing out of tune, or have boots that squeak, or double chins, or odd clothes, the patient will quite easily believe that their religion must therefore be somehow ridiculous. At his present stage, you see, he has an idea of "Christians" in his mind which he supposes to be spiritual but which, in fact, is largely pictorial. His mind is full of togas and sandals and armour and bare legs and the mere fact that the other people in church wear modern clothes is a real – though of course an unconscious – difficulty to him. Never let it come to the surface; never let him ask what he expected them to look like. Keep everything hazy in his mind now, and you will have all eternity wherein to amuse yourself by producing in him the peculiar kind of clarity which Hell affords.

Work hard, then, on the disappointment or anticlimax which is certainly coming to the patient during his first few weeks as a churchman. The Enemy allows this disappointment to occur on the threshold of every human endeavour. It occurs when the boy who has been enchanted in the nursery by *Stories from the Odyssey* buckles down to really learning Greek. It occurs when lovers have got married and begin the real task of learning to live together. In every department of life it marks the transition from dreaming aspiration to laborious doing. The Enemy takes this risk because He has a curious fantasy of making all these disgusting little human vermin into what He calls His "free" lovers and servants – "sons" is the word He uses, with His inveterate love of degrading the whole spiritual world by unnatural liaisons with the two-legged animals. Desiring their freedom, He therefore refuses to carry them, by their mere affections and habits, to any of the goals which He sets before them: He leaves them to "do it on their own". And there lies our opportunity. But also, remember, there lies our danger. If once they get through this initial dryness successfully, they become much less dependent on emotion and therefore much harder to tempt.

I have been writing hitherto on the assumption that the people in the next pew afford no *rational* ground for disappointment. Of course if they do – if the patient knows that the woman with the absurd hat is a fanatical bridgeplayer or the man with squeaky boots a miser and an extortioner – then your task is so much the easier. All you then have to do is to keep out of his mind the question "If I, being what I am, can consider that I am in some sense a Christian, why should the different vices of those people in the next pew prove that their religion is mere hypocrisy and convention?" You may ask whether it is possible to keep such an obvious thought from occurring even to a human mind. It is, Wormwood, it is! Handle him properly and it simply won't come into his head. He has not been anything like long enough with the Enemy to have any real humility yet. What he says, even on his knees, about his own sinfulness is all parrot talk. At bottom, he still believes he has run up a very favourable credit-balance in the Enemy's ledger by allowing himself to be converted, and thinks that he is showing great humility and condescension in going to church with these "smug", commonplace neighbours at all. Keep him in that state of mind as long as you can.

Your affectionate uncle

SCREWTAPE

Questions for Study

1 What advantages does Lewis gain by treating his topic from the perspective of the devil?
2 Lewis clearly felt that the literary device of a collection of letters would serve his purposes well. What are those purposes? And in what way does Lewis's chosen approach help him achieve them?
3 The theme of "ordinariness" is of especial importance in these early letters. What role does a "No. 73 bus" serve in Lewis's argument? And what is the deeper issue which Lewis attempts to explore in this way?

Text: *Till We Have Faces*

Lewis's late novel *Till We Have Faces* (1956) is a creative reworking of Apuleius' tale of Cupid and Pysche. The work deals with the issue of spiritual longing in a slightly oblique and subtle manner. The two central characters of the story are Orual – the eldest daughter of the king of Glome – and Psyche (or Istra). Orual's mother having died, her father determines to marry again in order that he may have a male heir. His second wife dies while giving birth to a daughter, Istra. Orual undertakes to care for Istra, and raises her half-sister as if she were her own daughter.

A series of calamities befalls the kingdom of Glome, leading the priest of the House of Ungit to declare that Istra must be sacrificed to the god of the mountain. Psyche – as the narrative now styles her – faces her death without fear, seeing it as a return to a mystical home. In the section of the work which has been selected for comment, Psyche speaks of her longing for death.

The theme of "longing" has considerable importance for Lewis. Lewis was aware of certain deep human emotions which, he argued, pointed to a dimension of our existence beyond time and space. There is, Lewis suggested, a deep and intense feeling of longing within human beings, which no earthly object or experience can satisfy. Lewis often terms this sense "joy," and argues that it points to God as its source and goal (hence the title of his autobiography, *Surprised by Joy*).

To understand Lewis at this point, the idea of "joy" needs to be explained a little. From the windows of his childhood home in Belfast, the young Lewis could see the distant Castlereagh Hills. These far off hills seemed to symbolize something which lay beyond his reach. A sense of intense longing arose as he contemplated them. He could not say exactly what it was that he longed for; merely that there was a sense of emptiness within him, which the mysterious hills seemed to heighten, without satisfying. In his early work *The Pilgrim's Regress*, these hills appear as a symbol of the heart's unknown desire. In *Till We Have Faces*, the motif of "the Mountain" is encountered again as a symbol of longing.

'Orual,' she [Psyche] said, very softly, 'we are the blood of the gods. We must not shame our lineage. Maia, it was you who taught me not to cry when I fell.'

'I believe you are not afraid at all,' said I; almost, though I had not meant it to sound so, as if I were rebuking her for it.

'Only of one thing,' she said. 'There is a cold doubt, a horrid shadow, in some corner of my soul. Supposing – supposing – how if there were no god of the Mountain and even no holy Shadowbrute, and those who are tied to the tree only die, day by day, from thirst and hunger and wind and sun, or are eaten piecemeal by the crows and catamountains? And it is this – oh, Maia, Maia . . .'

And now she did weep and now she was a child again. What could I do but fondle and weep with her? But this is a great shame to write; there was now (for me) a kind of sweetness in our misery for the first time. This was what I had come to her in her prison to do.

She recovered before I did. She raised her head, queenlike again, and said, 'But I'll not believe it. The Priest has been with me. I never knew him before. He is not what the Fox thinks. Do you know, Sister, I have come to feel more and more that the Fox hasn't the whole truth. Oh, he has much of it. It'd be dark as a dungeon within me but for his teaching. And yet . . . I can't say it properly. He calls the whole world a city. But what's a city built on? There's earth beneath. And outside the wall? Doesn't all the food come from there as well as all the dangers? . . . things growing and rotting, strengthening and poisoning, things shining wet . . . in one way (I don't know which way) more like, yes, even more like the House of——'

'Yes, of Ungit,' said I. 'Doesn't the whole land smell of her? Do you and I need to flatter gods any more? They're tearing us apart . . . oh, how shall I bear it? . . . and what worse can they do? Of course the Fox is wrong. He knows nothing about her. He thought too well of the world. He thought there were no gods, or else (the fool!) that they were better than men. It never entered his mind – he was too good – to believe that the gods are real, and viler than the vilest man.'

'Or else,' said Psyche, 'they are real gods but don't really do these things. Or even – mightn't it be – they do these things and the things are not what they seem to be? How if I am indeed to wed a god?'

She made me, in a way, angry. I would have died for her (this, at least, I know is true) and yet, the night before her death, I could feel anger. She spoke so steadily and thoughtfully; as if we had been disputing with the Fox, up behind the pear trees, with hours and days still before us. The parting between her and me seemed to cost her so little.

'Oh, Psyche,' I said, almost in a shriek, 'what can these things be except the cowardly murder they seem? To take you – you whom they have worshipped and who never hurt so much as a toad – to make you food for a monster . . .'

You will say – I have said it many thousand times to myself – that, if I saw in her any readiness to dwell on the better part of the Priest's talk and to think she would be a god's bride more than a Brute's prey, I ought to have fallen in with her and encouraged it. Had I not come to her to give comfort, if I could? Surely not to take it away. But I could not rule myself. Perhaps it was a sort of pride in me, a little like her own; not to blind our eyes, not to hide terrible things; or a bitter impulse in anguish itself to say, and to keep on saying, the worst.

'I see,' said Psyche in a low voice. 'You think it devours the offering. I mostly think so myself. Anyway, it means death. Orual, you didn't think I was such a child as not to know that? How can I be the ransom for all Glome unless I die? And if I am to go to the god, of course it must be through death. That way, even what is strangest in the holy sayings might be true. To be eaten and to be married to the god might not be so different. We don't understand. There must be so much that neither the Priest nor the Fox knows.'

This time I bit my lip and said nothing. Unspeakable foulness seethed in my mind; did she think the Brute's lust better than its hunger? To be mated with a worm, or a giant eft, or a spectre?

'And as for death,' she said, 'why, Bardia there (I love Bardia) will look on it six times a day and whistle a tune as he goes to find it. We have made little use of the Fox's teaching if we're to be scared by death. And you know, Sister, he has sometimes let out that there were other Greek masters than those he follows himself; masters who have taught that death opens a door out of a little, dark room (that's all the life we have known before it) into a great, real place where the true sun shines and we shall meet——'

'Oh, cruel, cruel!' I wailed. 'Is it nothing to you that you leave me here alone? Psyche; did you love me at all?'

'Love you? Why, Maia, what have I ever had to love save you and our grandfather the Fox?' (But I did not want her to bring even the Fox in now.) 'But, Sister, you will follow me soon. You don't think any mortal life seems a long thing to me tonight? And how would it be better if I had lived? I suppose I should have been given to some king in the end; perhaps such another as our father. And there you can see again how little difference there is between dying and being married. To leave your home – to lose you, Maia, and the Fox – to lose one's maidenhead – to bear a child – they are all deaths. Indeed, indeed, Orual, I am not sure that this which I go to is not the best.'

'This!'

'Yes. What had I to look for if I lived? Is the world – this palace, this father – so much to lose? We have already had what would have been the best of our time. I must tell you something, Orual, which I never told to anyone, not even you.'

I know now that this must be so even between the lovingest hearts. But her saying it that night was like stabbing me.

'What is it?' said I, looking down at her lap where our four hands were joined.

'This,' she said, 'I have always – at least, ever since I can remember – had a kind of longing for death.'

'Ah, Psyche,' I said, 'have I made you so little happy as that?'

'No, no, no,' she said. 'You don't understand. Not that kind of longing. It was when I was happiest that I longed most. It was on happy days when we were up there on the hills, the three of us, with the wind and the sunshine . . . where you couldn't see Glome or the palace. Do you remember? The colour and the smell, and looking across at the Grey Mountain in the distance? And because it was so beautiful, it set me longing, always longing. Somewhere else there must be more of it. Everything seemed to be saying, Psyche come! But I couldn't (not yet) come and I didn't know where I was to come to. It almost hurt me. I felt like a bird in a cage when the other birds of its kind are flying home.'

She kissed both my hands, flung them free, and stood up. She had her father's trick of walking to and fro when she talked of something that moved her. And from now till the end I felt (and this horribly) that I was losing her already, that the sacrifice tomorrow would only finish something that had already begun. She was (how long had she been, and I not to know?) out of my reach; in some place of her own.

Since I write this book against the gods, it is just that I should put into it whatever can be said against myself. So let me set this down; as she spoke I felt, amid all my love, a bitterness. Though the things she was saying gave her (that was plain enough) courage and comfort, I grudged her that courage and comfort. It was as if someone or something else had come in between us. If this grudging is the sin for which the gods hate me, it is one I have committed.

'Orual,' she said, her eyes shining. 'I am going, you see, to the Mountain. You remember how we used to look and long? And all the stories of my gold and amber house, up there against the sky, where we thought we should never really go? The greatest King of all was going to build it for me. If only you could believe it, Sister! No, listen. Do not let grief shut up your ears and harden your heart——'

'Is it *my* heart that is hardened?'

'Never to me; nor mine to you at all. But listen. Are these things so evil as they seemed? The gods will have mortal blood. But they say whose. If they had chosen any other in the land, that would have been only terror and cruel misery. But they chose me. And I am the one who has been made ready for it ever since I was a little child in your arms, Maia. The sweetest thing in all my life has been the longing – to reach the Mountain, to find the place where all the beauty came from——'

'And that was the sweetest? Oh, cruel, cruel. Your heart is not of iron; stone, rather,' I sobbed. I don't think she even heard me.

'—— my country, the place where I ought to have been born. Do you think it all meant nothing, all the longing? The longing for home? For indeed it now feels not like going, but like going back. All my life the god of the Mountain has been wooing me. Oh, look up once at least before the end and wish me joy. I am going to my lover. Do you not see now——?'

'I only see that you have never loved me,' said I. 'It may well be you are going to the gods. You are becoming cruel like them.'

'Oh, Maia!' cried Psyche, tears at last coming into her eyes again. 'Maia, I——'

Bardia knocked on the door. No time for better words, no time to unsay anything. Bardia knocked again, and louder. My oath on his sword, itself like a sword, was upon us.

So, the last, spoiled embrace. Those are happy who have no such in their memory. For those who have – would they endure that I should write of it?

Questions for Study

1 Why is Orual so distressed when Psyche tells her of her longing for death?
2 Identify sections of this passage which develop the theme of "returning home." Why does Psyche relate this to the Mountain?
3 "The sweetest thing in all my life has been the longing – to reach the Mountain, to find the place where all the beauty came from." How could this passage be interpreted in a Christian manner?

CHAPTER 87

Graham Greene (1904–1991)

Graham Greene is widely regarded as one of the most important literary writers of the twentieth century. Henry Graham Greene was born on October 2, 1904 in Berkhamsted, in the English county of Hertfordshire, as the fourth of six children. From the beginning Greene was a shy and sensitive youth, who disliked sports and often stayed away from school in order to read adventure stories by authors such as Rider Haggard and R. M. Ballantyne. These novels had a deep influence on him and helped shape his writing style. A further factor in shaping his attitude toward school was the fact that he was bullied and teased for being the son of the school's headmaster. It is thought that the recurring themes of treachery and betrayal, which are so characteristic features of Greene's writing, stem from these troubled school years, during which he was moved to attempt suicide on several occasions. Matters reached a climax when Greene left school, and wrote to his parents that he did not wish to return. This resulted in his being sent to a therapist in London at age fifteen. His analyst, Kenneth Richmond, encouraged him to write and introduced him to his circle of literary friends, which included the poet Walter de la Mare.

After leaving school, Greene went up to Balliol College, Oxford, from which he graduated in 1925. Initially, he found employment as a subeditor at the *Nottingham Journal*. He met his future wife Vivien Dayrell-Browning as a result of corresponding with her; she had written to him to point out some errors concerning Roman Catholicism in his writings. Upon her urging, Greene took instructions in the faith and was formally received into the Roman Catholic church in 1926. They were married the following year. By then, Greene had moved on to London, to take up a position as subeditor at *The Times*. He left this position after the success of his early writings. In addition to serious literary works, he also wrote adaptations for the cinema as well as original screenplays, the most famous of which is *The Third Man*.

Greene felt that he needed more experience of the world in order to stimulate and inform his writing. In 1938, he traveled to Mexico to witness the religious purges, in which Roman Catholics were subjected to considerable intimidation and harassment; these experiences were described in *The Lawless Roads*. During the Second World War, he worked for the British Secret Intelligence Service in Sierra Leone; his experiences at this time were incorporated into *The Heart of the Matter*. Greene's experience of the Catholic persecution in Mexico also led him to write *The Power and the Glory*, arguably the best novel of his career. The novel received considerable critical acclaim, and was awarded the Hawthornden Prize in 1941. It also later attracted criticism from the Vatican, which was disturbed by the portrayals of "the Whisky priest."

Graham Greene (1904–1991)

Basic description
Leading twentieth-century writer.

Major works
Brighton Rock (1938); *The Power and the Glory* (1940); *The Heart of the Matter* (1948); *The End of the Affair* (1951).

Major studies
A. F. Cassis and Peter Wolfe, *Graham Greene; Man of Paradox*. Chicago: Loyola University Press, 1994.

Norman Sherry, *A Life of Graham Greene*. London: Jonathan Cape, 1999.

Greene's later life was the subject of considerable criticism. His substantial royalty income allowed him to live in style in London, Antibes, and Capri. After the publication of *The Quiet American*, Greene was accused of being anti-American and consequently developed a strong dislike of Americans, particularly Ronald Reagan. He began to become involved in the complex and rather seedy politics of Central America, cultivating friendships with individuals such as Fidel Castro, Manuel Noriega, and Omar Torrijos. He separated from his wife in 1948 but they never divorced. Toward the end of his life, Greene lived in Vevey, Switzerland, with his companion Yvonne Cloetta. He died there peacefully on April 3, 1991.

The text selected for study is widely regarded as Greene's masterpiece – *The Power and the Glory*. In many ways, this is Greene's most ambitious piece of writing, incorporating many Christian themes – such as the relationship of sin and grace, and the issue of how personal weaknesses may be transcended by the unseen grace of God.

Text: *The Power and the Glory*

This novel, published in 1940, is set in Mexico during a period of state-sponsored persecution of Roman Catholicism The central character of the novel is the priest, who is being hunted by the authorities. The village people, who shelter him, call him "the Whisky priest," on account of his alcoholism. The priest is portrayed as weak and sinful, struggling within himself to cope with his personal failings. Against him, Greene pits the Lieutenant, a man with no doubts about himself or his cause: the important thing is to close the churches and eliminate the clergy.

In his later work *Ways Of Escape*, Greene commented as follows on the two central characters in this work:

> I had always, even when I was a schoolboy, listened with impatience to the scandalous stories
> of tourists concerning the priests they had encountered in remote Latin villages (this priest

had a mistress, another was constantly drunk), for I had been adequately taught in my Protestant history books what Catholics believed; I could distinguish even then between the man and his office. Now, many years later, as a Catholic in Mexico, I read and listened to stories of corruption which were said to have justified the persecution of the Church under Calles and under his successor and rival Cardenas, but I had also observed for myself how courage and the sense of responsibility had revived with persecution – I had seen the devotion of peasants praying in the priestless churches and I had attended Masses in upper rooms where the sanctus bell could not sound for fear of the police. I had not found the idealism or integrity of the lieutenant of *The Power and the Glory* among the police and *pistoleros* I had actually encountered – I had to invent him as a counter to the failed priest: the idealistic police officer who stifled life from the best possible motives: the drunken priest who continued to pass life on.

We join the narrative as the priest begins his journey to the city of Carmen, in the company of a half-caste (*mestizo*). Eventually, this person will betray the priest. In the course of the journey, the priest finds himself reflecting on his vocation, weaknesses and hopes.

It had been a dinner given at Concepción in honour of the tenth anniversary of his ordination. He sat in the middle of the table with – who was it on his right hand? There were twelve dishes – he had said something about the Apostles, too, which was not thought to be in the best of taste. He was quite young and he had been moved by a gentle devilry, surrounded by all the pious and middle-aged and respectable people of Concepción, wearing their guild ribbons and badges. He had drunk just a little too much; in those days he wasn't used to liquor. It came back to him now suddenly who was on his right hand – it was Montez, the father of the man they had shot.

Montez had talked at some length. He had reported the progress of the Altar Society in the last year – they had a balance in hand of twenty-two pesos. He had noted it down for comment – there it was, A.S. 22. Montez had been very anxious to start a branch of the Society of St Vincent de Paul, and some woman had complained that bad books were being sold in Concepción, fetched in from the capital by mule: her child had got hold of one called *A Husband for a Night*. In his speech he said he would write to the Governor on the subject.

The moment he had said that the local photographer had set off his flare, and so he could remember himself at that instant, just as if he had been a stranger looking in from the outside – attracted by the noise – on some happy and festal and strange occasion: noticing with envy, and perhaps a little amusement, the fat youngish priest who stood with one plump hand splayed authoritatively out while the tongue played pleasantly with the word 'Governor.' Mouths were open all round fishily, and the faces glowed magnesium-white, with the lines and individuality wiped out.

That moment of authority had jerked him back to seriousness – he had ceased to unbend and everybody was happier. He said, 'The balance of twenty-two pesos in the accounts of the Altar Society – though quite revolutionary for Concepción – is not the only cause for congratulation in the last year. The Children of Mary have increased their membership by nine – and the Guild of the Blessed Sacrament last autumn made our annual retreat more than usually successful. But we mustn't rest on our laurels, and I confess I have got plans you may find a little startling. You already think me a man, I know, of inordinate ambitions – well, I want Concepción to have a better school – and that means a better presbytery too, of course. We are a big parish and the priest has a position to keep up. I'm not thinking of myself but of the Church. And we shall not stop there – though it will take a good many years, I'm afraid, even in a place the size of Concepción, to raise the money for that.' As he talked a whole serene life lay ahead – he *had* ambition: he saw no reason why one day he might not find himself in the state capital, attached to the cathedral, leaving another man to pay off the debts in Concepción. An energetic priest was always known by his debts. He went on, waving a plump and eloquent hand, 'Of course, many dangers here in Mexico threaten our dear Church. In this state we are unusually lucky – men have lost their lives in the north and we must be prepared' – he refreshed his dry mouth with a draught of wine – 'for the worst. Watch and pray,' he went vaguely on, 'watch and pray. The devil like a raging lion –' The Children of Mary stared up at him with their mouths a little open, the pale blue ribbons slanting across their dark best blouses.

He talked for a long while, enjoying the sound of his own voice: he had discouraged Montez on the subject of the St Vincent de Paul Society, because you had to be careful not to encourage a layman too far, and he had told a charming story about a child's deathbed – she was dying of consumption very firm in her faith at the age of eleven. She asked who it was standing at the end of her bed, and they had said, 'That's Father So-and-so,' and she had said, 'No, no. I know Father So-and-so. I mean the one with the golden crown.' One of the Guild of the Blessed Sacrament had wept. Everybody was very happy. It was a true story too, though he couldn't quite remember where he had heard it. Perhaps he had read it in a book once. Somebody refilled his glass. He took a long breath and said, 'My children . . .'

. . . and as the mestizo stirred and grunted by the door he opened his eyes and the old life peeled away like a label: he was lying in torn peon trousers in a dark unventilated hut with a price upon his head. The whole world had changed – no church anywhere: no brother priest, except Padre José, the outcast, in the capital. He lay listening to the heavy breathing of the half-caste and wondered why he had not gone the same road as Padre José and conformed to the laws. I was too ambitious, he thought, that was it. Perhaps Padre José was the better man – he was so humble that he was ready to accept any amount of mockery; at the best of times he had never considered himself worthy of the priesthood. There had been a conference once of the parochial clergy in the capital, in the happy days of the old governor, and he could remember Padre José slinking in at the tail of every meeting, curled up half out of sight in a back row, never opening his mouth. It was not, like some more intellectual priests, that he was overscrupulous: he had been simply filled with an overwhelming sense of God. At the Elevation of the Host you could see his hands trembling – he was not like St Thomas who needed to put his hands into the wounds in order to believe: the wounds bled anew for him over every altar. Once Padre José had said to him in a burst of confidence, 'Every time . . . I have such fear.' His father had been a peon.

But it was different in his case – he had ambition. He was no more an intellectual than Padre José, but his father was a storekeeper, and he knew the value of a balance of twenty-two pesos and how to manage mortgages. He wasn't content to remain all his life the priest of a not very large parish. His ambitions came back to him now as something faintly comic, and he gave a little gulp of astonished laughter in the candlelight. The half-caste opened his eyes and said, 'Are you still not asleep?'

'Sleep yourself,' the priest said, wiping a little sweat off his face with his sleeve.

'I am so cold.'

'Just a fever. Would you like this shirt? It isn't much, but it might help.'

'No, no. I don't want anything of yours. You don't trust me.'

No, if he had been humble like Padre José, he might be living in the capital now with Maria on a pension. This was pride, devilish pride, lying here offering his shirt to the man who wanted to betray him. Even his attempts at escape had been half-hearted because of his pride – the sin by which the angels fell. When he was the only priest left in the state his pride had been all the greater; he thought himself the devil of a fellow carrying God around at the risk of his life; one day there would be a reward. . . . He prayed in the half-light: 'O God, forgive me – I am a proud, lustful, greedy man. I have loved authority too much. These people are martyrs – protecting me with their own lives. They deserve a martyr to care for them – not a man like me, who loves all the wrong things. Perhaps I had better escape – if I tell people how it is over here, perhaps they will send a good man with a fire of love . . .' As usual his self-confession dwindled away into the practical problem – what am I to do?

Over by the door the mestizo was uneasily asleep.

How little his pride had to feed on – he had celebrated only four Masses this year, and he had heard perhaps a hundred confessions. It seemed to him that the dunce of any seminary could have done as well . . . or better. He raised himself very carefully and began to move on his naked toes across the floor. He must get to Carmen and away again quickly before this man . . . the mouth was open, showing the pale hard toothless gums. In his sleep he was grunting and struggling; then he collapsed upon the floor and lay still.

There was a sense of abandonment, as if he had given up every struggle from now on and lay there a victim of some power. . . . The priest had only to step over his legs and push the door – it opened outwards.

He put one leg over the body and a hand gripped his ankle. The mestizo stared up at him. 'Where are you going?'

'I want to relieve myself,' the priest said.

The hand still held his ankle. 'Why can't you do it here?' the man whined at him. 'What's preventing you, father? You are a father, aren't you?'

'I have a child,' the priest said, 'if that's what you mean.'

'You know what I mean. You understand about God, don't you?' The hot hand clung. 'Perhaps you've got him there – in a pocket. You carry him around, don't you, in case there's anybody sick. . . . Well, I'm sick. Why don't you give him to me? or do you think he wouldn't have anything to do with me . . . if he knew?'

'You're feverish.'

But the man wouldn't stop. The priest was reminded of an oil-gusher which some prospectors had once struck near Concepción – it wasn't a good enough field apparently to justify further operations, but there it had stood for forty-eight hours against the sky, a black fountain spouting out of the marshy useless soil and flowing away to waste – fifty thousand gallons an hour. It was like the religious sense in man, cracking suddenly upwards, a black pillar of fumes and impurity, running to waste. 'Shall I tell you what I've done? – It's your business to listen. I've taken money from women to do you know what, and I've given money to boys . . .'

'I don't want to hear.'

'It's your business.'

'You're mistaken.'

'Oh no, I'm not. You can't deceive me. Listen. I've given money to boys – you know what I mean. And I've eaten meat on Fridays.' The awful jumble of the gross, the trivial, and the grotesque shot up between the two yellow fangs, and the hand on the priest's ankle shook and shook with the fever. 'I've told lies, I haven't fasted in Lent for I don't know how many years. Once I had two women – I'll tell you what I did . . .' He had an immense self-importance; he was unable to picture a world of which he was only a typical part – a world of treachery, violence, and lust in which his shame was altogether insignificant. How often the priest had heard the same confession – Man was so limited he hadn't even the ingenuity to invent a new vice: the animals knew as much. It was for this world that Christ had died; the more evil you saw and heard about you, the greater glory lay around the death. It was too easy to die for what was good or beautiful, for home or children or a civilization – it needed a God to die for the half-hearted and the corrupt. He said, 'Why do you tell me all this?'

The man lay exhausted, saying nothing; he was beginning to sweat, his hand loosed its hold on the priest's ankle. He pushed the door open and went outside – the darkness was complete. How to find the mule? He stood listening – something howled not very far away. He was frightened. Back in the hut the candle burned – there was an odd bubbling sound: the man was weeping. Again he was reminded of oil land, the little black pools and the bubbles blowing slowly up and breaking and beginning again.

The priest struck a match and walked straight forward – one, two, three paces into a tree. A match in that immense darkness was of no more value than a firefly. He whispered, '*Mula, mula,*' afraid to call out in case the half-caste heard him; besides, it was unlikely that the stupid beast would make any reply. He hated it – the lurching mandarin head, the munching greedy mouth, the smell of blood and ordure. He struck another match and set off again, and again after a few paces he met a tree. Inside the hut the gaseous sound of grief went on. He had got to get to Carmen and away before that man found a means of communicating with the police. He began again, quartering the clearing – one, two, three, four – and then a tree. Something moved under his foot, and he thought of scorpions. One, two, three, and suddenly the grotesque cry of the mule came out of the dark; it was hungry, or perhaps it smelt some animal.

It was tethered a few yards behind the hut – the candleflame swerved out of sight. His matches were running low, but after two more attempts he found the mule. The half-caste had stripped it and hidden the saddle. He couldn't waste time looking any more. He mounted, and only then realized how impossible it was to make it move without even a piece of rope round the neck; he tried twisting its ears, but they had no more sensitivity than door-handles: it stood planted there like an equestrian statue. He struck a match and held the flame against its side – it struck up suddenly with its back hooves and he dropped the match; then it was still again, with drooping sullen head and great antediluvian haunches. A voice said accusingly, 'You are leaving me here to die.'

'Nonsense,' the priest said. 'I am in a hurry. You will be all right in the morning, but I can't wait.'

There was a scuffle in the darkness and then a hand gripped his naked foot. 'Don't leave me alone,' the voice said. 'I appeal to you – as a Christian.'

'You won't come to any harm here.'

'How do you know with the gringo somewhere about?'

'I don't know anything about the gringo. I've met nobody who has seen him. Besides, he's only a man – like one of us.'

'I won't be left alone. I have an instinct . . .'

'Very well,' the priest said wearily, 'find the saddle.'

When they had saddled the mule they set off again, the mestizo holding the stirrup. They were silent – sometimes the half-caste stumbled, and the grey false dawn began; a small coal of cruel satisfaction glowed at the back of the priest's mind – this was Judas sick and unsteady and scared in the dark. He had only to beat the mule on to leave him stranded in the forest once he dug in the point of his stick and forced it forward at a weary trot, and he could feel the pull, pull of the half-caste's arm on the stirrup holding him back. There was a groan – it sounded like 'Mother of God,' and he let the mule slacken its pace. He prayed silently, 'God forgive me.' Christ had died for this man too: how could he pretend with his pride and lust and cowardice to be any more worthy of that death than the half-caste? This man intended to betray him for money which he needed, and he had betrayed God for what? Not even for real lust. He said, 'Are you sick?' and there was no reply. He dismounted and said, 'Get up. I'll walk for a while.'

'I'm all right,' the man said in a tone of hatred.

'Better get up.'

'You think you're very fine,' the man said. 'Helping your enemies. That's Christian, isn't it?'

'Are you my enemy?'

'That's what you think. You think I want seven hundred pesos – that's the reward. You think a poor man like me can't afford not to tell the police . . .'

'You're feverish.'

The man said in a sick voice of cunning, 'You're right, of course.'

'Better mount.' The man nearly fell: he had to shoulder him up. He leant hopelessly down from the mule with his mouth almost on a level with the priest's, breathing bad air into the other's face. He said, 'A poor man has no choice, father. Now if I was a rich man – only a little rich – I should be good.'

The priest suddenly – for no reason – thought of the Children of Mary eating pastries. He giggled and said, 'I doubt it.' If that were goodness . . .

'What was that you said, father? You don't trust me,' he went ambling on, 'because I'm poor, and because you don't trust me –' he collapsed over the pommel of the saddle, breathing heavily and shivering. The priest held him on with one hand and they proceeded slowly towards Carmen. It was no good; he couldn't stay there now. It would be unwise even to enter the village, for if it became known, somebody would lose his life – they would take a hostage. Somewhere a long way off a cock crew. The mist came up knee-high out of a spongy ground, and he thought of the flashlight going off in the bare church hall among the trestle tables. What hour did the cocks crow? One of the oddest things about the world these days was that there were no clocks – you could go a year without hearing one strike. They went with the churches, and you were left with the grey slow dawns and the precipitate nights as the only measurements of time.

Slowly, slumped over the pommel, the half-caste became visible, the yellow canines jutting out of the open mouth; really, the priest thought, he deserved his reward – seven hundred pesos wasn't so much, but he could probably live on it – in that dusty hopeless village – for a whole year. He giggled again; he could never take the complications of destiny quite seriously, and it was just possible, he thought, that a year without anxiety might save this man's soul. You only had to turn up the underside of any situation and out came scuttling these small absurd contradictory situations. He had given way to despair – and out of that had emerged a human soul and love – not the best love, but love all the same. The mestizo said suddenly, 'It's fate. I was told once by a fortuneteller . . . a reward . . .'

He held the half-caste firmly in the saddle and walked on. His feet were bleeding, but they would soon harden. An odd stillness dropped over the forest, and welled up in the mist from the ground. The night had been noisy, but now all was quiet. It was like an armistice with the guns silent on either side: you could imagine the whole world listening to what they had never heard before – peace.

A voice said 'You *are* the priest, aren't you?'

'Yes.' It was as if they had climbed out of their opposing trenches and met to fraternize among the wires in No Man's Land. He remembered stories of the European war – how during the last years men had sometimes met on an impulse between the lines.

'Yes,' he said again, and the mule plodded on. Sometimes, instructing children in the old days, he had been asked by some black lozenge-eyed Indian child, 'What is God like?' and he would answer facilely with references to the father and the mother, or perhaps more ambitiously he would include brother and sister and try to give some idea of all loves and relationships combined in an immense and yet personal passion. . . . But at the centre of his own faith there always stood the convincing mystery – that we were made in God's image. God was the parent, but He was also the policeman, the criminal, the priest, the maniac, and the judge. Something resembling God dangled from the gibbet or went into odd attitudes before the bullets in a prison yard or contorted itself like a camel in the attitude of sex. He would sit in the confessional and hear the complicated dirty ingenuities which God's image had thought out, and God's image shook now, up and down on the mule's back, with the yellow teeth sticking out over the lower lip, and God's image did its despairing act of rebellion with Maria in the hut among the rats. He said, 'Do you feel better now? Not so cold, eh? Or so hot?' and pressed his hand with a kind of driven tenderness upon the shoulders of God's image.

The man didn't answer, as the mule's backbone slid him first to one side, then the other.

'It isn't more than two leagues now,' the priest said encouragingly – he had to make up his mind. He carried around with him a clearer picture of Carmen than any other village or town in the state: the long slope of grass which led up from the river to the cemetery on a tiny hill where his parents were buried. The wall of the burial-ground had fallen in: one or two crosses had been smashed by enthusiasts: an angel had lost one of its stone wings, and what gravestones were left undamaged leant at an acute angle in the long marshy grass. One image of the Mother of God had lost ears and arms and stood like a pagan Venus over the grave of some rich forgotten timber merchant. It was odd – this fury to deface, because, of course, you could never deface enough. If God had been like a toad, you could have rid the globe of toads, but when God was like yourself, it was no good being content with stone figures – you had to kill yourself among the graves.

He said, 'Are you strong enough now to hold on?' He took away his hand. The path divided – one way led to Carmen, the other west. He pushed the mule on, down the Carmen path, flogging at its haunches. He said, 'You'll be there in two hours,' and stood watching the mule go on towards his home with the informer humped over the pommel.

The half-caste tried to sit upright. 'Where are you going?'

'You'll be my witness,' the priest said. 'I haven't been in Carmen. But if you mention me, they'll give you food.'

'Why . . . why . . .' The half-caste tried to wrench round the mule's head, but he hadn't enough strength: it just went on. The priest called out, 'Remember. I haven't been in Carmen.' But where else now could he go? The conviction came to him that there was only one place in the whole state where there was no danger of an innocent man being taken as a hostage – but he couldn't go there in these clothes. . . . The half-caste held hard on to the pommel and swivelled his yellow eyes beseechingly, 'You wouldn't leave me here – alone.' But it was more than the half-caste he was leaving behind on the forest track: the mule stood sideways like a barrier, nodding a stupid head, between him and the place where he had been born. He felt like a man without a passport who is turned away from every harbour.

The half-caste was calling after him, 'Call yourself a Christian.' He had somehow managed to get himself upright. He began to shout abuse – a meaningless series of indecent words which petered out in the forest like the weak blows of a hammer. He whispered, 'If I see you again, you can't blame *me* . . .' Of course, he had every reason to be angry: he had lost seven hundred pesos. He shrieked hopelessly, 'I don't forget a face.'

Questions for Study

1 From the passage which you have just read, how would you judge the character of the priest? What weaknesses does Graham Greene bring out?

2 What role does the half-caste play in this section of the narrative?
3 What are the religious issues, especially relating to sin and grace, which are illuminated by this passage?
4 In what way does Greene's Catholic faith find expression in this section of the novel?

CHAPTER 88

R. S. Thomas (1913–)

Ronald Stuart Thomas was born in Cardiff, the capital city of Wales, in 1913, and studied Classics at the University College of North Wales in Bangor. He then studied for ordination in the Church of Wales at St. Michael's College, Llandaff, being ordained deacon in 1936, and priest in 1937. His first senior appointment was as rector of the country parish of Manafon in Montgomeryshire, which he held for twelve years (1942–54). During this period, two major collections of poetry and one single poem made their appearance: *The Stones of the Field* (1946), *An Acre of Land* (1952), and *The Minister* (1953). The fertile and gentle countryside of this part of rural Wales is subtly incorporated into these early poems.

In 1954, Thomas moved to become vicar of St. Michael's, Eglwys Fach in north Dyfed. He would remain in this parish until 1967, when he moved to become vicar of Eglwys Hywyn Sant at Aberdaron, on the very tip of the Llyn Pensinsula. His period at Eglwys Fach would be one of the most productive of his career, and saw his writing gain increasing recognition. His *Song at the Year's Turning* (1955) brought together the major poems of earlier collections, and added nineteen new ones. Four major collections appeared around this time: *Poetry for Supper* (1958), *Tares* (1961), *The Bread of Truth* (1963), and *Pietà* (1966). He received the Heinemann Award of the Royal Society of Literature in 1959, and the Queen's Gold Medal for Poetry in 1964. He retired from parish ministry in 1978.

Thomas was quite clear that the two things which appealed most to his imagination were Wales and nature – and by "Wales," we are to understand a green and unspoiled land before the Industrial Revolution destroyed the innocence of its valleys, and towns eroded the countryside. Although Welsh, Thomas chose to express his ideas in the English language. Perhaps we can gain some understanding for his motives in choosing this language from his comments in a 1946 article published in the journal *Wales*, entitled "Some Contemporary Scottish Writing":

> We have to face the possibility not, I think, of the disappearance of Welsh, but of its inadequacy as a medium for expressing the complex phantasmagoria of modern life. But if we choose English as that medium, have we the singleness of mind, the strength of will to remain

primarily Welshmen? Ireland has done it, Scotland is striving after it, and we should do the same.

For the purposes of this anthology, Thomas's decision places us in the most happy position of being able to cite his poetry directly, without having to entrust ourselves to the foibles and hidden agendas of (occasionally) well-meaning translators.

R. S. Thomas (1913–)

Basic description
Welsh priest and poet.

Major works
Song at the Year's Turning (1955); Poetry for Supper (1958); Tares (1961); The Bread of Truth (1963); Pietà (1966).

Editions of works
R. S. Thomas, Collected Poems 1945–1990. London: Dent, 1992.

Major studies
D. Z. Phillips, R. S. Thomas: Poet of the Hidden God: Meaning and Mediation in the Poetry of R. S. Thomas. Basingstoke: Macmillan, 1986.
Elaine Shepherd, R. S. Thomas: Conceding an Absence: Images of God Explored. London: Macmillan, 1996.

Although Wales and nature may have been of primary importance as stimuli to Thomas's writing, the significance of the Christian faith in this respect must not be overlooked. His earlier poems tended to be somewhat ambivalent in relation to both Christianity and the Christian church. For example, the hill farmer is portrayed as someone whose view of the world is not limited by buildings or by institutionalized religion. The farmer glories in a solitary faith, directly informed by the natural world rather than mediated through any institution. Thomas also shows himself a willing and acute critic of Protestantism, particularly those Reformed theologies which discourage any engagement with nature or affirmation of the importance of human culture. Several lines in The Minister confirm this point: for example, his comments concerning

> Protestantism – the adroit castrator
> Of art; the bitter negation
> Of song and dance and the heart's innocent joy.

In what follows, we shall consider some of Thomas's later poems, in which specifically Christian issues are addressed.

Text: Pietà

The poem "Pietà" occurs in the collection of the same name, published in 1966. The Italian term pietà is often used to refer particularly to a picture or sculpture of the Virgin Mary holding the dead body of Christ on her lap, or in her arms. Thomas here meditates on such a scene, as follows, bringing together the classic themes of "crucifixion"

(Christ being executed on a cross) and "deposition" (Christ's dead body being removed from the cross).

Pietà

Always the same hills
Crowd the horizon,
Remote witnesses
Of the still scene.

And in the foreground
The tall Cross,
Sombre, untenanted,
Aches for the Body
That is back in the cradle
Of a maid's arms.

The poem opens with a disconcerting vagueness. What hills? What horizon? Are we talking about hills in Wales – or near Jerusalem? The poem is best read as a verbal embellishment of traditional depictions of the crucifixion and deposition – for example, Bellini's *Virgin and Child* and *Pietà*, both of which depict Mary and Christ against virtually identical backgrounds. In the former, Christ is a child; in the latter, a corpse. Thomas paints a verbal picture with the empty cross in the foreground, and the hills in the background, framing the image of the dead Christ.

Questions for Study

1 Thomas clearly enjoys using the word "untenanted" to refer to the cross. For example, consider his poem "In Church," contained as the final poem in the collection *Pietà*:

> Testing his faith
> On emptiness, nailing his questions
> One by one to an untenanted cross.

What does Thomas mean by this curious turn of phrase? What are the overtones of "an untenanted cross"?

2 Thomas suggests that the empty cross "aches for the body that is back in the cradle of a maid's arms." What does he mean by this?

Text: *Via Negativa*

In 1972, Thomas published a collection of poems entitled *H'm*. This collection was dominated by dark themes. It was as if the elements of anger and despair – which can readily be discerned in earlier poems, even if they are not dominant – had come to the fore, resulting in a collection which exuded sadness, even pain. Many of the poems portray

God as remote, cruel and hostile, with human beings powerless in comparison. The opening lines of *Postscript*, contained in this collection, are perhaps suggestive here:

> As life improved, their poems
> Grew sadder and sadder.

The poem from this somewhat sombre collection which we shall consider is entitled *"Via Negativa."* This Latin phrase is to be translated as "the negative way," and refers to a particular way of approaching the question of human knowledge of God, especially associated with the eastern Christian tradition, which stresses the severe limits placed upon such knowledge. The main themes of this approach, which is also known as "apophatic" theology (from the Greek term for "negation" or "denial"), can be seen in the treatise *On the Incomprehensibility of God* by John Chrysostom (347–407). Chrysostom stresses the limits to human knowledge and comprehension of God:

> Let us invoke God as inexpressible, incomprehensible, invisible and unknowable. Let us affirm that God surpasses all power of human speech; that he eludes the grasp of every mortal intelligence; that the angels cannot penetrate him; that the seraphim cannot see him clearly; that the cherubim cannot fully understand him. For he is invisible to the principalities and powers, the virtues and all creatures, without exception. Only the Son and the Holy Spirit know him.

Chrystostom's point is that only God truly knows God. Any creature – whether human or angelic – must accept the serious limitations which creatureliness imposes upon their grasp and vision of God.

The term "apophatic" is also used by the sixth-century writer Dionysius the Pseudo-Areopagite to refer to an approach to theology which rejects all positive ideas or images of God, and stresses instead the unknowability of God. The soul is understood to enter into a "darkness that is beyond understanding," in which it finds itself quite at a loss to use words or images to describe what it encounters. Apophatic theology identifies and stresses the limitations of human knowledge of God, and especially the ability of human ideas and images to convey the full reality of God.

It must be noted, however, that Dionysius also allows positive statements concerning God; his concern is to stress their limitations, and avoid falling into the fallacy of assuming that we know all that there is to be known about God. However, some of Dionysius' later interpreters chose to stress the more negative aspects of his thought. This particular approach is found in the fourteenth-century work of English mysticism, *The Cloud of Unknowing*, which picks up and develops the negative elements of Dionysius' thought.

Thomas's poem *"Via Negativa"* picks up and develops this important strand of theology.

Via Negativa

Why no! I never thought other than
That God is that great absence
In our lives, the empty silence

Within, the place where we go
Seeking, not in hope to
Arrive or find. He keeps the interstices
In our knowledge, the darkness
Between stars. His are the echoes
We follow, the footprints he has just
Left. We put our hands in
His side hoping to find
It warm. We look at people
And places as though he had looked
At them, too; but miss the reflection.

Questions for Study

1 How many of the traditional themes of "apophatic" theology can you discern within this poem?
2 Examine each of the following words: "interstices" (a rather grand word for "gaps"); "darkness"; "echoes"; "footprints." What do these words have in common? How do they illuminate Thomas's understanding of the absence of God?
3 What does Thomas mean when he suggests that we "miss the reflection"?

CHAPTER 89

Martin Luther King, Jr.
(1929–1968)

Martin Luther King is widely regarded as one of the most important voices in the Black Civil Rights movement in the United States during the 1960s. Born in Atlanta on January 15, 1929, King's roots were firmly grounded in the African-American Baptist church. His grandfather (A. D. Williams) had been pastor of Ebenezer Baptist Church and a founder of Atlanta's National Association for the Advancement of Colored People chapter; his father (Martin Luther King, Sr.) had succeeded Williams as the pastor of Ebenezer Church, and had also been deeply involved in civil rights issues. King began his education at Morehouse College, where he formed a vision for Christian social activism. This influenced King's decision, taken after his junior year at Morehouse, to become a minister and thereby serve society. He went on to undertake theological studies at Crozer Theological Seminary (Chester, Pennsylvania), and at Boston University, where he received a doctorate in systematic theology in 1955. Rejecting offers for academic positions, King decided while completing his Ph.D. requirements to return to the South, and accepted the pastorate of Dexter Avenue Baptist Church in Montgomery, Alabama.

He found himself in a tense racial situation, with the issue of segregation causing serious social division. On December 5, 1955, five days after Montgomery civil rights activist Rosa Parks refused to obey the city's rules mandating segregation on buses, black residents launched a bus boycott and elected King as president of the newly-formed Montgomery Improvement Association. As the boycott continued throughout 1956, King gained national prominence as a result of his oratorical skills and courage. The Montgomery buses were finally desegregated in December 1956, after the United States Supreme Court declared that Alabama's segregation laws were unconstitutional.

The success of this boycott led to new plans to advance the social status of black people. King and other Southern black ministers founded the Southern Christian Leadership Conference in 1957. As the president of this movement, King set out their goal of full black voting rights when he spoke at the Lincoln Memorial during the 1957 Prayer Pilgrimage for Freedom. During 1958, he published his first book, *Stride Toward Freedom: The Montgomery Story*. At the end of 1959, he resigned from Dexter and returned to Atlanta.

Martin Luther King, Jr. (1929–1968)

Basic description
Leading Black American civil rights activist and religious leader.

Major works
Stride Toward Freedom (1958); *Why We Can't Wait* (1964).

Major studies
Adam Fairclough, *To Redeem the Soul of America: The Southern Christian Leadership Conference and Martin Luther King, Jr.* Atlanta, GA: University of Georgia Press, 1987.

David J. Gorrow, *Bearing the Cross: Martin Luther King, Jr. and the Southern Christian Leadership Conference.* New York: William Morrow & Company, 1999.

Meanwhile, division was developing within the black civil rights movement. King was seen as being docile and failing to act decisively by a growing body of young black students, especially members of the Student Nonviolent Coordinating Committee, founded in April 1960. Conflicts between King and younger militants became increasingly common and bitter. In the end, King decided to free himself of the encumbrance of student militants, and concentrated his attention on mass demonstrations in Birmingham, Alabama, in the spring of 1963. Clashes between black demonstrators and police using police dogs and fire hoses generated newspaper headlines throughout the world. In June, President Kennedy reacted to the Birmingham protests and the obstinacy of segregationist Alabama Governor George Wallace by agreeing to submit broad civil rights legislation to Congress (which eventually passed the Civil Rights Act of 1964). Subsequent mass demonstrations in many communities culminated in a march on August 28, 1963, that attracted more than 250,000 protesters to Washington, D.C. Addressing the marchers from the steps of the Lincoln Memorial, King delivered his famous oration now known by its leading theme: "I have a dream."

During the year following this march, King's reputation developed still further. *Time* magazine declared him to be their "Man of the Year" and he was awarded the Nobel Peace Prize. Yet he was seen as a moderate in a struggle in which militancy often seemed to gain the upper hand. Malcolm X (1927–65) preached a very different message of self-defense and black nationalism, which seemed to express the discontent and anger of northern, urban blacks more effectively than did King's moderation. King lost the support of many white liberals when he criticized American intervention in the Vietnam war; this also poisoned his relations with the Lyndon Johnson administration. On April 4, 1968, while seeking to assist a garbage workers' strike in Memphis, he was assassinated. The motives for this have never been satisfactorily explained. After his death, King remained a somewhat controversial symbol of the African-American civil rights struggle, admired by some for his commitment to non-violence, and condemned by others for his militancy.

Text: I Have a Dream

The text chosen for study is the address given by Martin Luther King at the "March on Washington for Jobs and Freedom," on August 28, 1963. This is an excellent example of a political speech which almost takes a sermonical form, making extensive use of biblical imagery, particularly the entry into the promised land. It also incorporates the language and imagery of the traditional "negro spiritual." The speech has become widely admired as a piece of literature, even though, strictly speaking, it was intended to be a spoken, rather than a written, piece. The text has been transcribed from a recording of the speech, made from the Lincoln Memorial – a fact alluded to in its opening lines.

I am happy to join with you today in what will go down in history as the greatest demonstration for freedom in the history of our nation.

Five score years ago, a great American, in whose symbolic shadow we stand today, signed the Emancipation Proclamation. This momentous decree came as a great beacon light of hope to millions of Negro slaves, who had been seared in the flames of withering injustice. It came as a joyous daybreak to end the long night of their captivity. But one hundred years later, the Negro still is not free. One hundred years later, the life of the Negro is still sadly crippled by the manacle of segregation and the chains of discrimination.

One hundred years later, the Negro lives on a lonely island of poverty in the midst of a vast ocean of material prosperity. One hundred years later, the Negro is still languished in the corners of American society and finds himself an exile in his own land. So we've come here today to dramatize a shameful condition.

In a sense we have come to our nation's capital to cash a check. When the architects of our republic wrote the magnificent words of the Constitution and the Declaration of Independence, they were signing a promissory note to which every American was to fall heir.

This note was a promise that all men, yes, black men as well as white men, would be guaranteed the inalienable rights of life, liberty and the pursuit of happiness.

It is obvious today that America has defaulted on this promissory note insofar as her citizens of color are concerned. Instead of honoring this sacred obligation, America has given the Negro people a bad check, a check which has come back marked "insufficient funds."

But we refuse to believe that the bank of justice is bankrupt. We refuse to believe that there are insufficient funds in the great vaults of opportunity of this nation. So we have come to cash this check, a check that will give us upon demand the riches of freedom and the security of justice.

We have also come to this hallowed spot to remind America of the fierce urgency of Now. This is no time to engage in the luxury of cooling off or to take the tranquilizing drug of gradualism. Now is the time to make real the promises of democracy. Now is the time to rise from the dark and desolate valley of segregation to the sunlit path of racial justice. Now is the time to lift our nation from the quicksands of racial injustice to the solid rock of brotherhood. Now is the time to make justice a reality for all of God's children.

It would be fatal for the nation to overlook the urgency of the moment. This sweltering summer of the Negro's legitimate discontent will not pass until there is an invigorating autumn of freedom and equality. Nineteen sixty-three is not an end but a beginning. Those who hope that the Negro needed to blow off steam and will now be content will have a rude awakening if the nation returns to business as usual.

There will be neither rest nor tranquility in America until the Negro is granted his citizenship rights. The whirlwinds of revolt will continue to shake the foundations of our nation until the bright day of justice emerges.

But there is something that I must say to my people who stand on the warm threshold which leads into the palace of justice. In the process of gaining our rightful place we must not be guilty of wrongful deeds.

Let us not seek to satisfy our thirst for freedom by drinking from the cup of bitterness and hatred. We must ever conduct our struggle on the high plane of dignity and discipline. We must not allow our creative protest to degenerate into physical violence. Again and again we must rise to the majestic heights of meeting physical force with soul force.

The marvelous new militancy which has engulfed the Negro community must not lead us to a distrust of all white people, for many of our white brothers, as evidenced by their presence here today, have come to realize that their destiny is tied up with our destiny. They have come to realize that their freedom is inextricably bound to our freedom. We cannot walk alone.

And as we walk, we must make the pledge that we shall always march ahead. We cannot turn back. There are those who are asking the devotees of civil rights, "When will you be satisfied?" We can never be satisfied as long as the Negro is the victim of the unspeakable horrors of police brutality.

We can never be satisfied as long as our bodies, heavy with the fatigue of travel, cannot gain lodging in the motels of the highways and the hotels of the cities. We cannot be satisfied as long as a Negro in Mississippi cannot vote and a Negro in New York believes he has nothing for which to vote.

No, no, we are not satisfied and we will not be satisfied until justice rolls down like waters and righteousness like a mighty stream.

I am not unmindful that some of you have come here out of great trials and tribulations. Some of you have come fresh from narrow jail cells. Some of you have come from areas where your quest for freedom left you battered by the storms of persecutions and staggered by the winds of police brutality. You have been the veterans of creative suffering. Continue to work with the faith that unearned suffering is redemptive.

Go back to Mississippi, go back to Alabama, go back to South Carolina, go back to Georgia, go back to Louisiana, go back to the slums and ghettos of our northern cities, knowing that somehow this situation can and will be changed.

Let us not wallow in the valley of despair. I say to you today, my friends, that even though we face the difficulties of today and tomorrow. I still have a dream. It is a dream deeply rooted in the American dream.

I have a dream that one day this nation will rise up and live out the true meaning of its creed – we hold these truths to be self-evident that all men are created equal.

I have a dream that one day on the red hills of Georgia the sons of former slaves and the sons of former slave owners will be able to sit down together at the table of brotherhood.

I have a dream that one day even the state of Mississippi, a state sweltering with the heat of injustice, sweltering with the heat of oppression, will be transformed into an oasis of freedom and justice.

I have a dream that my four little children will one day live in a nation where they will not be judged by the color of their skin but by the content of their character.

I have a dream today!

I have a dream that one day, down in Alabama, with its vicious racists, with its governor having his lips dripping with the words of interposition and nullification; one day right down in Alabama little black boys and black girls will be able to join hands with little white boys and white girls as sisters and brothers.

I have a dream today!

I have a dream that one day every valley shall be exalted, and every hill and mountain shall be made low, the rough places will be made plain and the crooked places will be made straight and the glory of the Lord shall be revealed and all flesh shall see it together.

This is our hope. This is the faith that I will go back to the South with. With this faith we will be able to hew out of the mountain of despair a stone of hope. With this faith we will be able to transform the jangling discords of our nation into a beautiful symphony of brotherhood. With this faith we will be able to work together, to pray together, to struggle together, to go to jail together, to stand up for freedom together, knowing that we will be free one day. This will be the day, this will be the day when all of God's children will be able to sing with new meaning "My country 'tis of thee, sweet land of liberty, of thee I sing. Land where my fathers died, land of the Pilgrim's pride, from every mountainside, let freedom ring!" And if America is to be a great nation, this must become true.

And so let freedom ring from the prodigious hilltops of New Hampshire.

Let freedom ring from the mighty mountains of New York.

Let freedom ring from the heightening Alleghenies of Pennsylvania.

Let freedom ring from the snow-capped Rockies of Colorado.

Let freedom ring from the curvaceous slopes of California.

But not only that.

Let freedom ring from Stone Mountain of Georgia.

Let freedom ring from Lookout Mountain of Tennessee.

Let freedom ring from every hill and molehill of Mississippi, from every mountainside, let freedom ring!

And when this happens, when we allow freedom to ring, when we let it ring from every tenement and every hamlet, from every state and every city, we will be able to speed up that day when all of God's children, black men and white men, Jews and Gentiles, Protestants and Catholics, will be able to join hands and sing in the words of the old Negro spiritual, "Free at last, free at last. Thank God Almighty, we are free at last."

Questions for Discussion

1 What biblical imagery can be discerned within this speech?
2 How is the central theme of "I have a dream" developed and consolidated?
3 Why do you think King concludes with the citation from the negro spiritual, "Free at last, free at last. Thank God Almighty, we are free at last"?

CHAPTER 90

David Lodge (1935–)

David Lodge is currently Honorary Professor of Modern English Literature at the University of Birmingham, England, where he taught from 1960 until 1987. He then retired from academic life in order to concentrate on his writing. Lodge was born in London in 1935, and was educated at University College, London. After graduating, he did National Service in the British Army (an experience which can be seen reflected in his *Ginger, You're Barmy* (1962)). He then returned to University College, where he took an MA in 1959, before beginning his career at Birmingham.

He has written extensively in the area of literary criticism; his most noted works include *Language of Fiction, The Modes of Modern Writing*, and *The Art of Fiction*. He is also an accomplished author in his own right. His most widely-read novels deal with aspects of modern academic culture, particularly the personalities and politics of modern literary studies. His first book in this field, *Changing Places* (1975), was awarded the *Yorkshire Post* Fiction Prize.

Yet Lodge also has an interest in religious matters. Adopting what might best be termed a liberal Catholic perspective, Lodge offers a critical yet warm portrayal of developments within Roman Catholicism during his lifetime. His most important novel to deal with Christianity is *How Far Can You Go?*, which won the Whitbread Book of the Year award in 1980. It is this work which we shall consider in the present section.

Text: *How Far Can You Go?*

The background to this novel needs to be grasped to appreciate its subtlety. The work reflects the rapid pace of change within English Roman Catholicism in the late 1960s as a result of the decisions of the Second Vatican Council. John XXIII (pope, 1958–63) summoned the Second Vatican Council to deal with the issue of "updating" the agenda of the church. The Council began its meetings in October 1962. In four sessions, spread over the fall of each year during the period 1962–5, more than 2,450 bishops from all over the world met at Rome to discuss the future direction of the Catholic church. The death of John XXIII on June 3, 1963 did not interrupt the work of the Council, which was continued by his successor Paul VI (pope, 1963–78).

The agenda set before the Council was enormous. In general terms, the Council considered the place of the Christian faith in the modern world, particularly the relation between Christians and non-Christians, and between Catholics and other Christians. The importance of evangelism was affirmed, within a context of respecting the identities and integrities of non-Christians. Particular attention was paid to the nature of the church itself, and the relation of the bishops and pope. Yet the main impact of the Council can be argued to lie in the new atmosphere which it created, rather than the individual elements of its reforming program. A breath of fresh air swept through the church. Not all found it welcome – especially more conservative Catholics.

Lodge considers the impact of the Second Vatican Council on English Roman Catholicism, particularly as seen through the eyes of a small group of Catholic students at London University. While some of the changes debated were doctrinal, the main issues to affect students concerned the legitimacy of contraception – an issue that is explored in some depth in the novel. Yet other issues are given an airing, including the virtual elimination of the notion of hell from popular religious culture – perhaps one of the most striking features of the 1960s. Where earlier generations of Christian leaders could assume that their audiences had a residual belief in hell (and were generally interested in avoiding the place), the erosion of this belief would have major implications for Christian apologetics and preaching.

We join Lodge's narrative as he describes these developments in his distinctive style.

4

How They Lost the Fear of Hell

AT some point in the nineteen-sixties, Hell disappeared. No one could say for certain when this happened. First it was there, then it wasn't. Different people became aware of the disappearance of Hell at different times. Some realized that they had been living for years as though Hell did not exist, without having consciously registered its disappearance. Others realized that they had been behaving, out of habit, as though Hell were still there, though in fact they had ceased to believe in its existence long ago. By Hell we mean, of course, the traditional Hell of Roman Catholics, a place where you would burn for all eternity if you were unlucky enough to die in a state of mortal sin.

On the whole, the disappearance of Hell was a great relief, though it brought new problems.

In 1968, the campuses of the world rose in chain-reaction revolt, Russia invaded Czechoslovakia, Robert Kennedy was assassinated, and the civil rights movement started campaigning in Ulster. For Roman Catholics, however, even in Ulster, the event of the year was undoubtedly the publication, on 29 July, of the Pope's long-awaited encyclical letter on birth control, *Humanae Vitae*. Its message was: no change.

The omniscience of novelists has its limits, and we shall not attempt to trace here the process of cogitation, debate, intrigue, fear, anxious prayer and unconscious motivation which finally produced that document. It is as difficult to enter into the mind of a Pope as it must be for a Pope to enter into the mind of, say, a young mother of three, in a double bed, who feels her husband's caressing touch and is divided between the desire to turn to him and the fear of an unwanted pregnancy. It is said that Pope Paul was astonished and dismayed by the storm of criticism and dissent which his encyclical aroused within the Church. It was certainly not the sort of reception Popes had come to expect for their pronouncements. But in the democratic atmosphere recently created by Vatican II, Catholics convinced of the morality of contraception were no longer disposed to swallow meekly a rehash of discredited doctrine just because the Pope was wielding the spoon. Of course, if the Pope had come down on the other side of the argument, there would no doubt have been an equally loud chorus of protest and complaint from the millions of Catholics who had loyally followed the traditional teaching at the cost of having many more children and much less sex than they would have liked, and were now too old, or too worn-out by parenthood, to benefit from a change in the rules – not to mention the priests who had sternly kept them toeing the line by threats of eternal punishment if they didn't. The Pope, in short, was in a no-win situation. With hindsight, it is clear that his best course would have been to procrastinate and equivocate indefinitely so that the ban on contraception was never explicitly disowned, but quietly allowed to lapse, like earlier papal anathemas against co-education, gaslighting and railways. However, by setting up in the glare of modern publicity a commission to investigate and report on the matter, first Pope John and then Pope Paul had manoeuvred the Papacy into a dogmatic cul-de-sac from which there was no escape. The only saving grace in the situation (suggesting that the Holy Spirit might, after all, have been playing some part in the proceedings) was that it was made clear on its publication that the encyclical was not an "infallible" pronouncement. This left open the theoretical possibility, however narrowly defined, of conscientious dissent from its conclusions, and of some future reconsideration of the issue.

Thus it came about that the first important test of the unity of the Catholic Church after Vatican II, of the relative power and influence of conservatives and progressives, laity and clergy, priests and bishops, national Churches and the Holy See, was a great debate about – not, say, the nature of Christ and the meaning of his teaching in the light of modern knowledge – but about the precise conditions under which a man was permitted to introduce his penis and ejaculate his semen into the vagina of his lawfully wedded wife, a question on which Jesus Christ himself had left no recorded opinion.

This was not, however, quite such a daft development as it seems on first consideration, for the issue of contraception was in fact one which drew in its train a host of more profound questions and implications, especially about the pleasure principle and its place in the Christian scheme of salvation. It may seem bizarre that Catholics should have been solemnly debating whether it was right for married couples to use reliable methods of contraception at a time when society at large was calling into question the value of monogamy itself – when schoolgirls still in gym-slips were being put on the Pill by their mothers, when young couples were living together in what used to be called sin as a matter of course, adultery was being institutionalized as a party game, and the arts and mass media were abandoning all restraints in the depiction and celebration of sexuality. But in fact there was a more than merely ironic connection between these developments inside and outside the Church. The availability of effective contraception was the thin end of a wedge of modern hedonism that had already turned Protestantism into a parody of itself and was now challenging the Roman Catholic ethos. Conservatives in the Church who predicted that approval of contraception for married couples would inevitably lead sooner or later to a general relaxation of traditional moral standards and indirectly encourage promiscuity, marital infidelity, sexual experiment and deviation of every kind, were essentially correct, and it was disingenuous of liberal Catholics to deny it. On the other hand, the conservatives had unknowingly conceded defeat long before by approving, however grudgingly, the use of the Rhythm or Safe Method. Let me explain. (Patience, the story will resume shortly.)

It has always been recognized that the sexual act has two aspects or functions: I, procreation and II, the reciprocal giving and receiving of sensual pleasure. In traditional Catholic theology, Sex II was only legitimate as an incentive to, or spin-off from, Sex I – which of course was restricted to married couples; and some of the early Fathers thought that even for married couples, Sex II was probably a venial sin. With the development of a more humane theology of marriage, Sex II was dignified as the expression of mutual love between spouses, but it was still forbidden to separate this from Sex I, until the twentieth century, when, at first cautiously, and then more and more explicitly, the Church began to teach that married couples might deliberately confine their sexual intercourse to the infertile period of the woman's monthly cycle in order to regulate their families. This permission was still hedged about with qualifications – the method was only to be used with "serious reasons" – but the vital principle had been conceded: Sex II was a Good Thing In Itself. Catholic pastoral and theological literature on the subject of marriage took up the topic with enthusiasm; the bad old days of repression, of shame and fear about human sexuality, were denounced – it was all the fault of St Paul, or Augustine, or Plato – anyway, it was all a regrettable mistake; and married couples were joyfully urged to make love with, metaphorically speaking (and literally too if they liked), the lights on.

This was all very well, but certain consequences followed. If Sex II is recognized as a Good Thing In Itself, it is difficult to set limits, other than the general humanistic rule that nobody should be hurt, on how it may be enjoyed. For example, the traditional Christian disapproval of extramarital sex had an obvious social justification as a means of ensuring responsible parenthood and avoiding inbreeding, but with the development of efficient contraception these arguments lost most of their force, as secular society had already discovered by the mid-twentieth century. Why, therefore, should responsible adults have to be married to share with each other something Good In Itself? Or to take a more extreme example, anal intercourse, whether homosexual or heterosexual, had always been condemned in terms of the deepest loathing by traditional Christian moralists, sodomy being listed in the Penny Catechism as one of the Four Sins Crying to Heaven for Vengeance (the others, you may be curious to know, being Wilful Murder, Oppression of the Poor, and Defrauding Labourers of Their Wages). But if the sharing of sexual pleasure is a Good Thing In Itself, irrespective of the procreative function, it is difficult to see any objections, other than hygienic and aesthetic ones, to anal intercourse between consenting adults, for who is harmed by it? The same applies to masturbation, whether solitary or mutual, and oral-genital sex. As long as non-procreative orgasms are permitted, what does it matter how they are achieved?

Thus it can be seen that the ban on artificial birth control, the insistence that every sexual act must remain, at least theoretically, open to the possibility of conception, was the last fragile barrier holding back the Catholic community from joining the great collective pursuit of erotic fulfilment increasingly obsessing the rest of Western society in the sixth decade of the twentieth century; but the case for the ban had been fatally weakened by the admission that marital sex might be confined to the "safe period" with the deliberate intention of avoiding conception. In practice, the Safe Method was so unreliable that many couples wondered if it hadn't been approved only because it wasn't safe, thus ensuring that Catholics were restrained by the consciousness that they might after all have to pay the traditional price for their pleasure. Clerical and medical apologists for the method, however, never admitted as much; on the contrary, they encouraged the faithful with assurances that Science would soon make the Safe Method as reliable as artificial contraception. (Father Brierley's Parish Priest, in the course of a heated argument, assured him that "the Yanks were working on a little gadget like a wristwatch that would make it as simple as telling the time.") But the greater the efforts made to achieve this goal, the more difficult it became to distinguish between the permitted and forbidden methods. There was nothing, for instance, noticeably "natural" about sticking a thermometer up your rectum every morning compared to slipping a diaphragm into your vagina at night. And if the happy day *did* ever dawn when the Safe Method was pronounced as reliable as the Pill, what possible reason, apart from medical or economic considerations, could there be for choosing one method rather than the other? And in that case, why wait till then to make up your mind?

Following such a train of thought to its logical conclusion, millions of married Catholics had, like Michael and Miriam, come to a decision to use artificial contraception without dropping out of the Church. Some couples needed the impetus of a special hardship or particular crisis to take this step (Angela went on the Pill immediately after the birth of her mentally handicapped child; and Tessa, though happily her new baby was born sound and healthy, followed suit, with Edward's full support, neither of them being inclined to take any further risks) but once they had done so it seemed such an obviously sensible step to take that they could hardly understand why they had hesitated so long. It helped, of course – indeed, it was absolutely vital – that, as explained above, they had lost the fear of Hell, since the whole system of religious authority and obedience in which they had been brought up, binding the Church together in a pyramid of which the base was the laity and the apex the Pope, depended on the fear of Hell as its ultimate sanction. If a Catholic couple decided, privately and with a clear conscience, to use contraceptives, there was

nothing that priest, bishop or Pope could do to stop them (except, in some countries, making the wherewithal difficult to obtain). Thus contraception was the issue
on which many lay Catholics first attained moral autonomy, rid themselves of superstition, and ceased to regard their religion as, in the moral sphere, an encyclopaedic
rule-book in which a clear answer was to be found to every possible question of
conduct. They were not likely to be persuaded to reverse their decision by the tired
arguments of *Humanae Vitae*, and some previously loyal souls were actually provoked by it into joining the rebels (Adrian, who had been teetering on the con-
traceptive brink for years, was so exasperated by the first reports of the encyclical
that he rushed out of the house and startled the local chemist's shop by strident
demands for "a gross of sheaths prophylactic" – a phrase he dimly remembered
from Army invoices, but which smote strangely on the ears of the girl behind the
counter). Of course, there were many Catholics who with more or less resignation
continued to believe that the Pope's word was law, and many who disobeyed it with
a residual sense of guilt that they were never able to lose completely, and yet others
who finally left the Church in despair or disgust; but on the whole the most remarkable aspect of the whole affair was the new-found moral independence of the laity
which it gradually revealed. Indeed, it could be said that those who suffered most
from *Humanae Vitae* were not married layfolk at all, but the liberal and progressive
clergy.

Conservative bishops and priests had the satisfaction of seeing their beliefs and
pastoral practice endorsed by the Pope, but those who had, in the period of uncertainty immediately preceding the publication of *HV*, interpreted the rules flexibly,
or actually argued the case for their revision, were now awkwardly placed. What was
for the laity a question of conduct which they might settle privately according to their
own consciences, was for the clergy a question of doctrine and obedience that was
necessarily public. The Holy Father had spoken, and bishops and priests, whatever
their own opinions about the matter, were required to promulgate and enforce his
message from the pulpit and in the confessional. Some were only too pleased to do
so; but many were not, and feared massive disillusionment and disaffection among
the laity if the Church simply reverted to the old hard-line teaching. Bishops were
in a particularly difficult position, because they could not reject *Humanae Vitae*
without the risk of provoking schism. What the more liberal hierarchies did was to
make a minimalist interpretation of the encyclical – to say that, while contraception
was, as the Pope affirmed, objectively wrong, there might be subjective circumstances
which made it so venial a sin as scarcely to be worth worrying about, and certainly
not a reason for ceasing to go to mass and Holy Communion. By this casuistry they
accepted *HV* in principle while encouraging a tolerant and flexible approach to its
enforcement in pastoral practice. Most of the priests who had been dismayed by the
encyclical accepted this compromise, but some were unwilling or unable to do so,
and if their bishop or religious superior happened to be conservative and authori-
tarian, the consequences could be serious.

Such priests were apt to become acutely conscious of internal contradictions in
their own vocations. For the more deeply they were driven, by the pressure of debate
and the threats of ecclesiastical discipline, to analyse the grounds of their dissent from

HV, the further they were carried towards an endorsement of sexual pleasure as a Good Thing In Itself. And the further they were carried in *that* direction, the more problematical their own vows of celibacy appeared. As long as sexual pleasure had been viewed with suspicion by Christian divines, as something hostile to spirituality, lawful only as part of man's procreative function in God's scheme, the vow of celibacy had obvious point. Unmarried and chaste, the priest was materially free to serve his flock, and spiritually free from the distractions of fleshly indulgence. But when the new theology of marriage began to emerge, in which sexual love was redeemed from the repression and reticence of the past, and celebrated as (in the words of the Catholic Theological Society of America) "self-liberating, other-enriching, honest, faithful, socially responsible, life-giving and joyous," the value of celibacy no longer seemed self-evident, and a progressive priest might find himself in the paradoxical position of defending the right of the laity to enjoy pleasures he himself had renounced long ago, on grounds he no longer believed in. A similar collapse of confidence in the value of vowed virginity affected nuns.

Of course, it could still be argued that, without families of their own to care for, priests and nuns were free to dedicate themselves to the service of others; but this argument, too, only holds good as long as reliable contraception is forbidden. Otherwise, why should not priests and nuns marry each other, and take vows of sterility rather than chastity, forgoing the satisfactions of having offspring in order to serve the community at large, but still enjoying the consolations of that interpersonal genital communion which, the orthodox wisdom of the modern age insists, is essential to mental and physical health? For that matter, why, given new control over their own biology, should not women themselves be priests? For the prejudice against the ordination of women is demonstrably rooted in traditional sexual attitudes rather than in theology or logic.

The crisis in the Church over birth control was not, therefore, the absurd diversion from more important matters that it first appeared to many observers, for it compelled thoughtful Catholics to re-examine and redefine their views on fundamental issues: the relationship between authority and conscience, between the religious and lay vocations, between flesh and spirit. The process of questioning and revision it triggered off continues, although *Humanae Vitae* itself is a dead letter to most of the laity and merely an embarrassing nuisance to most of the clergy. It is clear that the liberal, hedonistic spirit has achieved irresistible momentum within the Church as without, that young Catholics now reaching adulthood have much the same views about the importance of sexual fulfilment and the control of fertility as their non-Catholic peers, and that it is only a matter of time before priests are allowed to marry and women are ordained. There is, however, no cause for progressives to gloat or for conservatives to sulk. Let copulation thrive, by all means; but man cannot live by orgasms alone, and he certainly cannot die by them, except, very occasionally, in the clinical sense. The good news about sexual satisfaction has little to offer those who are crippled, chronically sick, mad, ugly, impotent – or old, which all of us will be in due course, unless we are dead already. Death, after all, is the overwhelming question to which sex provides no answer, only an occasional brief respite from thinking about it. But enough of this philosophizing.

Questions for Study

1 According to Lodge's narrative, what was the background to the Second Vatican Council? How much did it reflect the rapidly changing cultural mood of the period?
2 What was the impact of the Second Vatican Council on traditional English Roman Catholicism, as portrayed in this section of Lodge's narrative?
3 Why does Lodge pay such attention to the issue of contraception, which had been prohibited for Roman Catholics by the papal encyclical *Humanae Vitae*?

CHAPTER 91

Garrison Keillor (1942–)

Garrison Edward Keillor was born in Anoka, Minnesota, in 1942, and was educated at Anoka High School. He went on from there to study English at the University of Minnesota, graduating in 1966. It was while he was a freshman at the University that he started working in radio, initially on the closed-circuit station, WMMR. After graduating from the University of Minnesota in 1966, he took a bus to New York to try and find employment at magazines (such as *The Atlantic Monthly*) and various publishing houses. The trip lasted for about a month, and failed to deliver what he had hoped. Keillor returned to work in Minnesota at KUOM, and was finally hired by Minnesota Public Radio in 1969. He has remained with this company ever since.

Garrison Keillor (1942–)

Basic description
Public radio show writer and presenter; author.

Major works
Lake Wobegon Days (1985); *Wobegon Boy* (1997)

Major studies
Judith Yaross Lee, *Garrison Keillor: A Voice of America*. Minneapolis, MN: University of Minnesota Press, 1991.
Peter A. Scholl, *Garrison Keillor*. Dubuque, IA: University of Iowa Press, 1994.

Keillor is especially associated with the fictional town of Lake Wobegon, Minnesota. On July 6, 1974, Keillor hosted the first broadcast of "A Prairie Home Companion," before an audience of twenty persons in a theater in St. Paul, Minnesota. He intended it to be a live musical-variety show. "Lake Wobegon" was brought in as the location of a weekly monologue, designed to give continuity to the program. In the event, it became its most celebrated feature, and led to Keillor becoming something of a national institution. The show ended in its original format in 1987; it was later relaunched. By 1999, the program was heard every week on more than 410 public radio stations by approximately 2.2 million listeners. *Lake Wobegon Days* (1985), which became one of the most widely discussed works in America, prompted intense discussion of regionalism on the part of its largely urban readership.

The work can be seen as a humorous yet affectionate commentary on the "small town America" which Keillor knew so well. It is a world in which religion plays a major part, as can be seen from Keillor's description of Lake Wobegon:

> LAKE WOBEGON (1418 alt., 942 pop.), named for the body of water that it borders. Bleakly typical of the prairie, Lake Wobegon has its origins in the utopian vision of nineteenth-century New England Transcendentalists but now is populated mainly by Norwegians and Germans who attend LAKE WOBEGON LUTHERAN CHURCH (left at BANK .1 m.), and OUR LADY OF PERPETUAL RESPONSIBILITY CHURCH (right at CHURCH, .08 m.), neither of which are remarkable.

Inevitably, religious squabbles and tensions were part of the everyday life of the town. Our extract from *Lake Wobegon Days* offers a wry evaluation of the origins and importance of these tensions.

Keillor's attention focuses especially on what he refers to as "the Brethren." By this, he means the "Christian Brethren," a group of Christians who traced their origins back to 1825, and a group of young men associated with Trinity College, Dublin. The movement soon spread, and became known as the "Plymouth Brethren" in England, on account of the establishment of a Brethren assembly in that town in 1831. John Nelson Darby, a former clergyman in the Church of Ireland, soon became the dominant personality in the movement. He founded groups of Brethren in many parts of the British Isles and in continental Europe, especially in French Switzerland, where he spent the greater part of the period 1838–45.

After Darby returned to England in 1845, disputes over doctrine and church government split the Brethren. Darby's followers formed a closely knit federation of churches and soon became known as the "Exclusive Brethren"; the others, who came to be known as the "Open Brethren," maintained a congregational form of church government and adopted significantly less rigorous membership requirements. The tension between the two groups was considerable, and was reflected in Brethren communities in North America, which were founded from the early 1860s onwards.

Text: *Lake Wobegon Days*

Our family was dirt poor, which I figured out as a child from the fact we had such a bad vacuum. When you vacuumed the living room, it would groan and stop and you had to sit and wait for it to groan and start up, then vacuum like mad before it quit again, but it didn't have good suction either. You had to stuff the hairballs into it. I also knew it because Donald Hoglund told me. He asked me how much my dad earned, and I said a thousand dollars, the most money I could imagine, and he shrieked, "You're poor! You're poor!" So we were. And, in a town where everyone was either Lutheran or Catholic, we were neither one. We were Sanctified Brethren, a sect so tiny that nobody but us and God knew about it, so when kids asked what I was, I just said Protestant. It was too much to explain, like having six toes. You would rather keep your shoes on.

Grandpa Cotten was once tempted toward Lutheranism by a preacher who gave a rousing sermon on grace that Grandpa heard as a young man while taking Aunt Esther's dog home who had chased a Model T across town. He sat down on the church steps and listened to the voice boom out the open windows until he made up his mind to go in and unite with the truth, but he took one look from the vestibule and left. "He was dressed up like the pope of Rome," said Grandpa, "and the altar and the paintings and the gold candlesticks – my gosh, it was just a big show. And he was reading the whole darn thing off a page, like an actor."

Jesus said, "Where two or three are gathered together in my name, there am I in the midst of them," and the Brethren believed that was enough. We met in Uncle Al's and Aunt Flo's bare living room with plain folding chairs arranged facing in toward the middle. No clergyman in a black smock. No organ or piano, for that would make one person too prominent. No upholstery, it would lead to complacency. No picture of Jesus, He was in our hearts. The faithful sat down at the appointed hour and waited for the Spirit to move one of them to speak or to pray or to give out a hymn from out Little Flock hymnal. No musical notation, for music must come from the heart and not off a page. We sang the texts to a tune that fit the meter, of the many tunes we all knew. The idea of reading a prayer was sacrilege to us – "if a man can't remember what he wants to say to God, let him sit down and think a little harder," Grandpa said.

"There's the Lord's Prayer," said Aunt Esther meekly. We were sitting on the porch after Sunday dinner. Esther and Harvey were visiting from Minneapolis and had attended Lake Wobegon Lutheran, she having turned Lutheran when she married him, a subject that was never brought up in our family.

"You call that prayer? Sitting and reciting like a bunch of schoolchildren?"

Harvey cleared his throat and turned to me with a weak smile. "Speaking of school, how are you doing?" he asked.

There was a lovely silence in the Brethren assembled on Sunday morning as we waited for the Spirit. Either the Spirit was moving someone to speak who was taking his sweet time or else the Spirit was playing a wonderful joke on us and letting us sit, or perhaps silence was the point of it. We sat listening to rain on the roof, distant traffic, a radio playing from across the street, kids whizzing by on bikes, dogs barking, as we waited for the Spirit to inspire us. It was like sitting on the porch with your family, when nobody feels that they have to make talk. So quiet in church. Minutes drifted by in silence that was sweet to us. The old Regulator clock ticked, the rain stopped and the room changed light as the sun broke through – shafts of brilliant sun through the windows and motes of dust falling through it – the smell of clean clothes and floor wax and wine and the fresh bread of Aunt Flo which was Christ's body given for us. Jesus in our midst, who loved us. So peaceful, and we loved each other too. I thought perhaps the Spirit was leading me to say that, but I was just a boy, and children were supposed to keep still. And my affections were not pure. They were tainted with a sneaking admiration of Catholics – Catholic Christmas, Easter, the Living Rosary, and the Blessing of the Animals, all magnificent. Everything we did was plain, but they were regal and gorgeous – especially the Feast Day of St. Francis, which they did right out in the open, a feast for the eyes. Cows, horses, some pigs, right on the church lawn. The turmoil, animals bellowing and barking and clucking and cats scheming how to escape and suddenly leaping out of the girl's arms who was holding on tight, the cat dashing through the crowd, dogs straining at the leash, and the ocarina band of third-graders playing Catholic dirges, and the great calm of the sisters, and the flags, and the Knights of Columbus decked out in their handsome black suits – I stared at it until my eyes almost fell out, and then I wished it would go on much longer.

"Christians," my uncle Al used to say, "do not go in for show," referring to the Catholics. We were sanctified by the blood of the Lord, therefore we were saints, like St. Francis, but we didn't go in for feasts or ceremonies, involving animals or not. We went in for sitting, all nineteen of us, in Uncle Al's and Aunt Flo's living room on Sunday morning and having a plain meeting and singing hymns in our poor thin voices while not far away the Catholics were whooping it up. I wasn't allowed inside Our Lady, of course, but if the Blessing of the Animals on the Feast Day of St. Francis was any indication, Lord, I didn't know but what they had elephants in there and acrobats. I sat in our little group and envied them for the splendor and gorgeousness, as we tried to sing without even a harmonica to give us the pitch. Hymns, Uncle Al said, didn't have to be sung perfect, because God looks on the heart, and if you are In The Spirit, then all praise is good.

The Brethren, also known as the Saints Gathered in the Name of Christ Jesus, who met in the living room were all related to each other and raised in the Faith from infancy except Brother Mel who was rescued from a life of drunkenness, saved as a brand from the burning, a drowning sailor, a sheep on the hillside, whose immense red nose testified to his previous condition. I envied his amazing story of how he came to be with us. Born to godly parents, Mel left home at fifteen and joined the Navy. He sailed to distant lands in a submarine and had exciting experiences while traveling the downward path, which led him finally to the Union Gospel Mission in Minneapolis where he heard God's voice "as clear as my voice speaking to you." He was twenty-six, he slept under bridges and in abandoned buildings, he drank two quarts of white muscatel every day, and then God told him that he must be born again, and so he was, and became the new Mel, except for his nose.

Except for his nose, Mel Burgess looked like any forty-year-old Brethren man: sober, preferring dark suits, soft-spoken, tending toward girth. His nose was what made you look twice: battered, swollen, very red with tiny purplish lines, it looked ancient and very dead on his otherwise fairly handsome face, the souvenir of what he had been saved from, the "Before" of his "Before . . . and After" advertisement for being born again.

For me, there was nothing before. I was born among the born-again. This living room so hushed, the Brethren in their customary places on folding chairs (the comfortable ones were put away on Sunday morning) around the end-table draped with a white cloth and the glass of wine and loaf of bread (unsliced) was as familiar to me as my mother and father, the founders of my life. I had always been here.

Our family sat in one row against the picture window. Al and Florence and their three, Janet and Paul and Johnny, sat opposite us, I saw the sky and the maple tree reflected in my uncle's glasses. To our left, Great-Aunt Mary sat next to Aunt Becky and Uncle Louie, and to our right were Grandma and Grandpa and Aunt Faith, and behind them was Mel, sitting on the piano bench. His wife, Rita, was a Lutheran.

She only came occasionally and when she did, she stood out like a brass band. She used lipstick and had plucked eyebrows and wore bright hats. Brethren women showed only a faint smudge of powder on their cheeks and their hats were small and either black or navy blue. Once Rita spoke up in the meeting – Al had stood up to read from the Lord's Word, and she said, "Pardon me, which chapter did you say?" – and we all shuddered as if she had dropped a plate on the floor: *women did not speak in meeting.* Another time, Sunday morning, she made as if to partake of the bread as it was passed, and Grandpa snatched it away from her. It had to be explained to Rita later that she could not join in the Lord's Supper with us because she was not in fellowship.

We were "exclusive" Brethren, a branch that believed in keeping itself pure of false doctrine by avoiding association with the impure. Some Brethren assemblies, mostly in larger cities, were not so strict and broke bread with strangers – we referred to them as "the so-called Open Brethren," the "so-called" implying the shakiness of their position – whereas we made sure that any who fellowshiped with us were straight on all the details of the Faith, as set forth by the first Brethren who left the Anglican Church in 1865 to worship on the basis of correct principles. In the same year, they posed for a photograph: twenty-one bearded gentlemen in black frock coats, twelve sitting on a stone wall, nine standing behind, gazing solemnly into a sunny day in Plymouth, England, united in their opposition to the pomp and corruption of the Christian aristocracy.

Unfortunately, once free of the worldly Anglicans, these firebrands were not content to worship in peace but turned their guns on each other. Scholarly to the core and perfect literalists every one, they set to arguing over points that, to any outsider, would have seemed very minor indeed but which to them were crucial to the Faith, including the question: if Believer *A* is associated with Believer *B* who has somehow associated himself with *C* who holds a False Doctrine, must *D* break off association with *A*, even though *A* does not hold the Doctrine, to avoid the taint?

The correct answer is: Yes. Some Brethren, however, felt that *D* should only speak with *A* and urge him to break off with *B*. The Brethren who felt otherwise promptly broke off with them. This was the Bedford Question, one of several controversies that, inside of two years, split the Brethren into three branches.

Once having tasted the pleasure of being Correct and defending True Doctrine, they kept right on and broke up at every opportunity, until, by the time I came along, there were dozens of tiny Brethren groups, none of which were speaking to any of the others.

Our Lake Wobegon bunch was part of a Sanctified Brethren branch known as the Cox Brethren, which was one of a number of "exclusive" Brethren branches – that is to *non*-Coxians, we were known as "Cox Brethren"; to ourselves, we were simply *The* Brethren, the last remnant of the true Church. Our name came from Brother Cox in South Dakota who was kicked out of the Johnson Brethren in 1932 – for preaching the truth! So naturally my Grandpa and most of our family went with Mr. Cox and formed the new fellowship.

The split with the Johnsons was triggered by Mr. Johnson's belief that what was abominable to God in the Old Testament must be abominable still, which he put forward at the Grace & Truth Bible Conference in Rapid City in 1932. Mr. Cox stood up and walked out, followed by others. The abomination doctrine not only went against the New Covenant of Grace principle, it opened up rich new areas of controversy in the vast annals of Jewish law. Should Brethren then refrain from pork, meat that God had labeled "Unclean"? Were we to be thrown into the maze of commandments laid out in Leviticus and Deuteronomy, where we are told to smite our enemies with the sword and stone to death rebellious children?

Mr. Johnson's sermon was against women's slacks, and he had quoted Deuteronomy 22.5, "The woman shall not wear that which pertaineth unto a man, neither shall a man put on a woman's garment: for all that do so are abomination unto the Lord thy God," but Mr. Cox, though he was hardy pro-slacks, felt Mr. Johnson failed to emphasize grace as having superseded the law, and when Mr. Johnson said, "An abomination to God under the law is still an abomination to God under grace," Mr. Cox smelled the burning rubber of Error and stood up and marched. He and the other walkouts proceeded to a grove of trees and prayed for Mr. Johnson's soul, and Mr. Johnson and those seated inside did the same for them. The split was never repaired, though as a result of being thought in favor of slacks, the Cox Brethren became death on the subject. My mother never wore slacks, though she did dress my sister in winter leggings, which troubled Grandpa. "It's not the leggings so much as what they represent and what they could lead to," he told her. He thought that baby boys should not wear sleepers unless they were the kind with snaps up the legs. Mother pointed out that the infant Jesus was wrapped in swaddling clothes. "That doesn't mean he wore a dress," Grandpa said. "They probably wrapped his legs separately."

Questions for Study

1   What religious tensions does Keillor describe in this passage? To what extent are these the result of small-town concerns?

2   How would you evaluate Keillor's attitude to the Brethren, and especially the two different sections of the movement which he notes?

3   Why do you think Keillor tells us so much about Mr Johnson's sermon against women's slacks? What issues are opened up by this? Do you think Keillor took this seriously – or was he writing tongue in cheek here?

A Glossary of Terms

What follows is a brief discussion of a series of technical terms that the reader is likely to encounter in the course of reading works relating to Christianity in general, or Christian literature in particular. Many of the terms are considered in greater detail within the text of this work.

Abandonment This term, which is often used to translate the French word "abandon," refers to a trusting acceptance in divine providence, and a willingness to live out the Christian life on the basis of that trust. It is particularly associated with writers such as Jean-Pierre de Caussade, but can be found in other writers of the period, such as St. Francis de Sales and Jacques Benigne Bossuet.

Adoptionism The heretical view that Jesus was "adopted" as the Son of God at some point during his ministry (usually his baptism), as opposed to the orthodox teaching that Jesus was Son of God by nature from the moment of his conception.

aggiornamento The process of renewing the church, which was particularly associated with Pope John XXIII. The Second Vatican Council (1962–5). The Italian word can be translated as "a bringing up to date" or "renewal," and refers to the process of theological, spiritual, and institutional renewal and updating which resulted from the work of this council.

Alexandrian School A patristic school of thought, especially associated with the city of Alexandria in Egypt, noted for its Christology (which placed emphasis upon the divinity of Christ) and its method of biblical interpretation (which employed allegorical methods of exegesis). A rival approach in both areas was associated with Antioch.

Anabaptism A term derived from the Greek word for "re-baptizer," and used to refer to the radical wing of the sixteenth-century Reformation, based on thinkers such as Menno Simons or Balthasar Hubmaier.

Analogy of being (*analogia entis*) The theory, especially associated with Thomas Aquinas, that there exists a correspondence or analogy between the created order and God, as a result of the divine creatorship. The idea gives theoretical justification to the practice of drawing conclusions from the known objects and relationships of the natural order concerning God.

Analogy of faith (*analogia fidei*) The theory, especially associated with Karl Barth, which holds that any correspondence between the created order and God is only established on the basis of the self-revelation of God.

Anthropomorphism The tendency to ascribe human features (such as hands or arms) or other human characteristics to God.

Antiochene School A patristic school of thought, especially associated with the city of Antioch in modern-day Turkey, noted for its Christology (which placed emphasis upon the humanity of Christ) and its method of biblical interpretation (which employed literal methods of exegesis). A rival approach in both areas was associated with Alexandria.

anti-Pelagian writings The writings of Augustine relating to the Pelagian controversy, in which he defended his views on grace and justification. *See* "Pelagianism."

Apocalyptic A type of writing or religious outlook in general which focuses on the last things and the end of the world, often taking the form of visions with complex symbolism. The book of Daniel (Old Testament) and Revelation (New Testament) are examples of this type of writing.

Apologetics The area of Christian theology which focuses on the defense of the Christian faith, particularly through the rational justification of Christian belief and doctrines.

Apophatic A term used to refer to a particular style of theology which stressed that God cannot be known in terms of human categories. "Apophatic" (which derives from the Greek *apophasis*, "negation" or "denial") approaches to theology are especially associated with the monastic tradition of the Eastern Orthodox church.

Apophthegmata The term used to refer to the collections of monastic writings often known as the "Sayings of the Desert Fathers." The writings often take the form of brief and pointed sayings, reflecting the concise and practical guidance typical of these writers.

Apostolic era The period of the Christian church, regarded as definitive by many, bounded by the resurrection of Jesus Christ (ca. 35) and the death of the last apostle (ca. 90?). The ideas and practices of this period were widely regarded as normative, at least in some sense or to some degree, in many church circles.

Appopriation A term relating to the doctrine of the Trinity, which affirms that while all three persons of the Trinity are active in all the outward actions of the Trinity, it is appropriate to think of those actions as being the particular work of one of the persons. Thus it is appropriate to think of creation as the work of the Father, or redemption as the work of the Son, despite the fact that all three persons are present and active in both these works.

Arianism A major early Christological heresy, which treated Jesus Christ as the supreme of God's creatures, and denied his divine status. The Arian controversy was of major importance in the development of Christology during the fourth century.

Asceticism A term used to refer to the wide variety of forms of self-discipline used by Christians to deepen their knowledge of and commitment to God. The term derives from the Greek term *askesis* ("discipline").

Atonement An English term originally coined by William Tyndale to translate the Latin term *reconciliatio*, which has since come to have the developed meaning of "the work of Christ" or "the benefits of Christ gained for believers by his death and resurrection."

Barthian An adjective used to describe the theological outlook of the Swiss theologian Karl Barth (1886–1968), and noted chiefly for its emphasis upon the priority of revelation and its focus upon Jesus Christ. The terms "neo-Orthodoxy" and "dialectical theology" are also used in this connection.

Beatific Vision A term used, especially in Roman Catholic theology, to refer to the full vision of God, which is allowed only to the elect after death. However, some writers, including Thomas Aquinas, taught that certain favored individuals – such as Moses and Paul – were allowed this vision in the present life.

Beatitudes, The A term used to describe the eight promises of blessing found in the opening section of the Sermon on the Mount (Matthew 5:3–11). Examples include "Blessed are the pure in heart, for they shall see God" and "Blessed are the peacemakers, for they shall be called children of God."

Calvinism An ambiguous term, used with two quite distinct meanings. First, it refers to the religious ideas of religious bodies (such as the Reformed church) and individuals (such as Theodore Beza) who were profoundly influenced by John Calvin, or by documents written by him. Second, it refers to the religious ideas of John Calvin himself. Although the first sense is by far the more common, there is a growing recognition that the term is misleading.

Cappadocian Fathers A term used to refer collectively to three major Greek-speaking writers of the patristic period: Basil of Caesarea, Gregory of

Nazianzen and Gregory of Nyssa, all of whom date from the late fourth century. "Cappadocia" designates an area in Asia Minor (modern-day Turkey), in which these writers were based.

Cartesianism The philosophical outlook especially associated with René Descartes (1596–1650), particularly in relation to its emphasis on the separation of the knower from the known, and its insistence that the existence of the individual thinking self is the proper starting point for philosophical reflection.

Catechism A popular manual of Christian doctrine, usually in the form of question and answer, intended for religious instruction.

Catharsis The process of cleansing or purification by which the individual is freed from obstacles to spiritual growth and development.

Catholic An adjective which is used to refer both to the universality of the church in space and time, and also to a particular church body (sometimes also known as the Roman Catholic church) which lays emphasis upon this point.

Chalcedonian definition The formal declaration at the Council of Chalcedon that Jesus Christ was to be regarded as having two natures, one human and one divine.

Charisma, charismatic A set of terms especially associated with the gifts of the Holy Spirit. In medieval theology, the term "charisma" is used to designate a spiritual gift, conferred upon individuals by the grace of God. Since the early twentieth century, the term "charismatic" has come to refer to styles of theology and worship which place particular emphasis upon the immediate presence and experience of the Holy Spirit.

Charismatic Movement A form of Christianity which places particular emphasis upon the personal experience of the Holy Spirit in the life of the individual and community, often associated with various "charismatic" phenomena, such as speaking in tongues.

Christology The section of Christian theology dealing with the identity of Jesus Christ, particularly the question of the relation of his human and divine natures.

Circumincession *See "Perichoresis."*

Conciliarism An understanding of ecclesiastical or theological authority which places an emphasis on the role of ecumenical councils.

Confession Although the term refers primarily to the admitting of sin, it acquired a rather different technical sense in the sixteenth century – that of a document which embodies the principles of faith of a Protestant church, such as the Lutheran Augsburg Confession (1530) embodying the ideas of early Lutheranism, and the Reformed First Helvetic Confession (1536).

Consubstantial A Latin term, deriving from the Greek term *homoousios*, literally meaning "of the same substance." The term is used to affirm the full divinity of Jesus Christ, particularly in opposition to Arianism.

Consubstantiation A term used to refer to the theory of the real presence, especially associated with Martin Luther, which holds that the substance of the eucharistic bread and wine are given together with the substance of the body and blood of Christ.

Contemplation A form of prayer, distinguished from meditation, in which the individual avoids or minimizes the use of words or images in order to experience the presence of God directly.

Creed A formal definition or summary of the Christian faith, held in common by all Christians. The most important are those generally known as the "Apostles' Creed" and the "Nicene Creed."

Dark Night of the Soul A phrase especially associated with John of the Cross, referring to the manner in which the soul is drawn closer to God. John distinguishes an "active" night (in which the believer actively works to draw nearer to God) and a "passive" night, in which God is active and the believer passive.

Deism A term used to refer to the views of a group of English writers, especially during the seventeenth century, the rationalism of which anticipated many of the ideas of the Enlightenment. The term is often used to refer to a view of God which recognizes the divine creatorship, yet which rejects the notion of a continuing divine involvement with the world.

Detachment The cultivation of a habit of mind in which the individual aims to abandon dependence upon worldly objects, passions, or concerns. This is not intended to imply that these worldly things are evil; rather, the point being made is that they have the ability to enslave individuals if they are not approached with the right attitude. Detachment is about fostering a sense of independence from the world, so that it may be enjoyed without becoming a barrier between the individual and God.

Devotio Moderna	A school of thought which developed in the Netherlands in the fourteenth century, and is especially associated with Geert Groote (1340–84) and Thomas à Kempis (1380–1471), which placed an emphasis on the imitation of the humanity of Christ. The *Imitation of Christ* is the best-known work emanating from this school.

Dialectical Theology	A term used to refer to the early views of the Swiss theologian Karl Barth (1886–1968), which emphasized the "dialectic" between God and humanity.

Docetism	An early Christological heresy, which treated Jesus Christ as a purely divine being who only had the "appearance" of being human.

Donatism	A movement, centering upon Roman North Africa in the fourth century, which developed a rigorist view of the church and sacraments.

Doxology	A form of praise, usually especially associated with formal Christian worship. A "doxological" approach to theology stresses the importance of praise and worship in theological reflection.

Ebionitism	An early Christological heresy, which treated Jesus Christ as a purely human figure, although recognizing that he was endowed with particular charismatic gifts which distinguished him from other humans.

Ecclesiology	The section of Christian theology dealing with the theory of the church.

Enlightenment, The	A term used since the nineteenth century to refer to the emphasis upon human reason and autonomy, characteristic of much of western European and North American thought during the eighteenth century.

Eschatology	The section of Christian theology dealing with the "end things," especially the ideas of resurrection, hell, and eternal life.

Eucharist	The term used in the present volume to refer to the sacrament variously known as "the Mass," "the Lord's Supper," and "holy communion." Also refers to the bread and wine used during the ceremony.

Evangelical	A term initially used to refer to reforming movements, especially in Germany and Switzerland, in the 1510s and 1520s, but now used of the movement, especially in English-language theology, which places especial emphasis upon the supreme authority of Scripture and the atoning death of Christ.

Exegesis	The science of textual interpretation, usually referring specifically to the Bible. The term "biblical exegesis" basically means "the process of interpreting the Bible." The specific techniques employed in the exegesis of Scripture are usually referred to as "hermeneutics."

Exemplarism	A particular approach to the atonement, which stresses the moral or religious example set to believers by Jesus Christ.

Fathers	An alternative term for "patristic writers."

Fideism	An understanding of Christian theology which refuses to accept the need for (or sometimes the possibility of) criticism or evaluation from sources outside the Christian faith itself.

Five Ways, The	A standard term for the five "arguments for the existence of God" associated with Thomas Aquinas.

Fourth Gospel	A term used to refer to the Gospel according to John. The term highlights the distinctive literary and theological character of this gospel, which sets it apart from the common structures of the first three gospels, usually known as the "Synoptic Gospels."

Fundamentalism	A form of American Protestant Christianity, which lays especial emphasis upon the authority of an inerrant Bible.

Hermeneutics	The principles underlying the interpretation, or exegesis, of a text, particularly of Scripture, particularly in relation to its present-day application.

Hesychasm	A tradition, especially associated with the eastern church, which places considerable emphasis upon the idea of "inner quietness" (Greek: *hesychia*) as a means of achieving a vision of God. It is particularly associated with writers such as Simeon the New Theologian and Gregory Palamas.

Historical Jesus	A term used, especially during the nineteenth century, to refer to the historical person of Jesus of Nazareth, as opposed to the Christian interpretation of that person, especially as presented in the New Testament and the creeds.

Historico-critical method An approach to historical texts, including the Bible, which argues that only proper meaning must be determined on the basis of the specific historical conditions under which it was written.

History of Religions School The approach to religious history, and Christian origins in particular, which treats Old and New Testament developments as responses to encounters with other religions, such as Gnosticism.

Homoousion A Greek term, literally meaning "of the same substance," which came to be used extensively during the fourth century to designate the mainline Christological belief that Jesus Christ was "of the same substance as God." The term was polemical, being directed against the Arian view that Christ was "of similar substance (*homoiousios*)" as God. See also "Consubstantial."

Humanism In the strict sense of the word, an intellectual movement linked with the European Renaissance. At the heart of the movement lay, not (as the modern sense of the word might suggest) a set of secular or secularizing ideas, but a new interest in the cultural achievements of antiquity. These were seen as a major resource for the renewal of European culture and Christianity during the period of the Renaissance.

Hypostatic union The doctrine of the union of divine and human natures in Jesus Christ, without confusion of their respective substances.

Icons Sacred pictures, particularly of Jesus, which play a significant role in Orthodox spirituality as "windows for the divine."

Ideology A group of beliefs and values, usually secular, which govern the actions and outlooks of a society or group of people.

Ignatian spirituality A loose term used to refer to the approach to spirituality associated with Ignatius Loyola (1491–1556), based on his *Spiritual Exercises.*

Incarnation A term used to refer to the assumption of human nature by God, in the person of Jesus Christ. The term "incarnationalism" is often used to refer to theological approaches which lay especial emphasis upon God's becoming human.

Jesus Prayer A prayer which has the basic form "Lord Jesus Christ, Son of God, have mercy on me." This can be seen as an adaptation of the words spoken to Jesus by the blind man outside Jericho (Luke 18:38). The prayer is widely used in Orthodox spirituality, often accompanied by certain physical postures, such as specific patterns of breathing.

Justification by faith, doctrine of The section of Christian theology dealing with how the individual sinner is able to enter into fellowship with God. The doctrine was to prove to be of major significance at the time of the Reformation.

Kenoticism A form of Christology which lays emphasis upon Christ's "laying aside" of certain divine attributes in the incarnation, or his "emptying himself" of at least some divine attributes, especially omniscience or omnipotence.

Kerygma A term used, especially by Rudolf Bultmann (1884–1976) and his followers, to refer to the essential message or proclamation of the New Testament concerning the significance of Jesus Christ.

Liberal Protestantism A movement, especially associated with nineteenth-century Germany, which stressed the continuity between religion and culture, flourishing between the time of F. D. E. Schleiermacher and that of Paul Tillich.

Liberation theology Although this term designates any theological movement laying emphasis upon the liberating impact of the gospel, the term has come to refer to a movement which developed in Latin America in the late 1960s, which stressed the role of political action and orientated itself toward the goal of political liberation from poverty and oppression.

Liturgy The written text and set forms of public services, especially of the Eucharist. In the Greek Orthodox church, the word "Liturgy" often means "the [liturgy of] the Eucharist."

Logos A Greek term meaning "word," which played a crucial role in the development of patristic Christology. Jesus Christ was recognized as the "word of God"; the question concerned the implications of this recognition, and especially the way in which the divine "logos" in Jesus Christ related to his human nature.

Lutheranism The religious ideas associated with Martin Luther, particularly as expressed in the Lesser Catechism (1529) and the Augsburg Confession (1530).

Manicheism A strongly fatalist position associated with the Manichees, to which Augustine of Hippo attached himself during his early period. A distinction is drawn between two different divinities, one of which is regarded as evil, and the other good. Evil is thus seen as the direct result of the influence of the evil god.

Meditation A form of prayer, distinguished from contemplation, in which the mind uses images (such as those provided by Scripture) as a means for focusing on God.

Middle English literature Literature produced in the English language from the Norman invasion of 1066 to ca. 1485.

Modalism A trinitarian heresy, which treats the three persons of the Trinity as different "modes" of the Godhead. A typical modalist approach is to regard God as active as Father in creation, as Son in redemption, and as Spirit in sanctification.

Monophysitism The doctrine that there is only one nature in Christ, which is divine (from the Greek words *monos*, "only one," and *physis*, "nature"). This view differed from the orthodox view, upheld by the Council of Chalcedon (451), that Christ had two natures, one divine and one human.

Mysticism A multifaceted term, which can bear a variety of meanings. In its most important sense, the term refers to the union with God, which is seen as the ultimate goal of the Christian life. This union is not to be thought of in rational or intellectual terms, but more in terms of a direct consciousness or experience of God.

Neo-Orthodoxy A term used to designate the general position of Karl Barth (1886–1968), especially the manner in which he drew upon the theological concerns of the period of Reformed Orthodoxy.

Old English literature The English literature of the period from 750 until the time of the invasion of the Normans in 1066.

Ontological argument A term used to refer to the type of argument for the existence of God especially associated with the scholastic theologian Anselm of Canterbury.

Orthodoxy A term used in a number of senses, of which the following are the most important: Orthodoxy in the sense of "right belief," as opposed to heresy; Orthodoxy in the sense of the forms of Christianity which are dominant in Russia and Greece; Orthodoxy in the sense of a movement within Protestantism, especially in the late sixteenth and early seventeenth century, which laid emphasis upon need for doctrinal definition.

Parousia A Greek term which literally means "coming" or "arrival," used to refer to the second coming of Christ. The notion of the *parousia* is an important aspect of Christian understandings of the "last things."

Patripassianism A theological heresy which arose during the third century, associated with writers such as Noetus, Praxeas and Sabellius, focusing on the belief that the Father suffered as the Son. In other words, the suffering of Christ on the cross is to be regarded as the suffering of the Father. According to these writers, the only distinction within the Godhead was a succession of modes or operations, so that Father, Son, and Spirit were just different modes of being, or expressions, of the same basic divine entity.

Patristic An adjective used to refer to the first centuries in the history of the church, following the writing of the New Testament (the "patristic period"), or thinkers writing during this period (the "patristic writers"). For many writers, the period thus designated seems to be ca. 100–451 (in other words, the period between the completion of the last of the New Testament writings and the landmark Council of Chalcedon).

Pelagianism An understanding of how humans are able to merit their salvation which is diametrically opposed to that of Augustine of Hippo, placing considerable emphasis upon the role of human works and playing down the idea of divine grace.

Perichoresis A term relating to the doctrine of the Trinity, often also referred to by the Latin term *circumincessio*. The basic notion is that all three persons of the Trinity mutually share in the life of the others, so that none is isolated or detached from the actions of the others.

Philokalia A Greek term (literally meaning "a love of that which is beautiful"), which is generally used to refer to two anthologies of Greek spiritual works: extracts from the works of Origen, or the collection of writings assembled by

Macarius of Corinth and Nicodemus of the Holy Mountain in the eighteenth century.

Pietism   An approach to Christianity, especially associated with German writers in the seventeenth century, which places an emphasis upon the personal appropriation of faith, and the need for holiness in Christian living. The movement is perhaps best known within the English-language world in the form of Methodism.

Postliberalism   A theological movement, especially associated with Duke University and Yale Divinity School in the 1980s, which criticized the liberal reliance upon human experience, and reclaimed the notion of community tradition as a controlling influence in theology.

Postmodernism   A general cultural development, especially in North America, which resulted from the collapse in confidence of the universal rational principles of the Enlightenment.

Praxis   A Greek term, literally meaning "action," adopted by Karl Marx to emphasize the importance of action in relation to thinking. This emphasis on "praxis" has had considerable impact within Latin American liberation theology.

Protestantism   A term used in the aftermath of the Diet of Speyer (1529) to designate those who "protested" against the practices and beliefs of the Roman Catholic church. Prior to 1529, such individuals and groups had referred to themselves as "evangelicals."

Quadriga   The Latin term used to refer to the "four-fold" interpretation of Scripture according to its literal, allegorical, tropological moral, and analogical senses.

Radical Reformation   A term used with increasing frequency to refer to the Anabaptist movement – in other words, the wing of the Reformation which went beyond what Luther and Zwingli envisaged, particularly in relation to the doctrine of the church.

Reformed   A term used to refer to a tradition of theology which draws inspiration from the writings of John Calvin (1510–64) and his successors. The term is now generally used in preference to "Calvinist."

Sabellianism   An early trinitarian heresy, which treated the three persons of the Trinity as different historical manifestations of the one God. It is generally regarded as a form of modalism.

Sacrament   A church service or rite which was held to have been instituted by Jesus Christ himself. Although Roman Catholic theology and church practice recognize seven such sacraments (baptism, confirmation, eucharist, marriage, ordination, penance, and unction), Protestant theologians generally argue that only two (baptism and eucharist) are to be found in the New Testament itself.

Salesian   Relating to Francis de Sales (1567–1622), or organizations which aim to base themselves on his ideas and values. The most important Salesian group is the Society of St. Francis de Sales, founded in 1859.

Schism   A deliberate break with the unity of the church, condemned vigorously by influential writers of the early church, such as Cyprian and Augustine.

Scholasticism   A particular approach to Christian theology, associated especially with the Middle Ages, which lays emphasis upon the rational justification and systematic presentation of Christian theology.

Scripture Principle   The theory, especially associated with Reformed theologians, that the practices and beliefs of the church should be grounded in Scripture. Nothing that could not be demonstrated to be grounded in Scripture could be regarded as binding upon the believer. The phrase *sola scriptura*, "by Scripture alone," summarizes this principle.

Soteriology   The section of Christian theology dealing with the doctrine of salvation (Greek: *soteria*).

Synoptic Gospels   A term used to refer to the first three gospels (Matthew, Mark and Luke). The term (derived from the Greek word *synopsis*, "summary") refers to the way in which the three gospels can be seen as providing similar "summaries" of the life, death and resurrection of Jesus Christ.

Synoptic Problem   The scholarly question of how the three Synoptic Gospels relate to each other. Perhaps the most common approach to the relation of the three Synoptic Gospels is the "Two Source" theory, which claims that Matthew and Luke used Mark as a source, while also drawing upon a second source (usually known as "Q").

Other possibilities exist: for example, the Grise-bach hypothesis, which treats Matthew as having been written first, followed by Luke and then Mark.

Theodicy A term coined by Leibnitz to refer to a theoretical justification of the goodness of God in the face of the presence of evil in the world.

Theopaschitism A disputed teaching, regarded by some as a heresy, which arose during the sixth century, associated with writers such as John Maxentius and the slogan "one of the Trinity was crucified." The formula can be interpreted in a perfectly orthodox sense and was defended as such by Leontius of Byzantium. However, it was regarded as potentially misleading and confusing by more cautious writers, including Pope Hormisdas (died 523), and the formula gradually fell into disuse.

Theotokos Literally, "the bearer of God." A Greek term that is used to refer to Mary, the mother of Jesus Christ, with the intention of reinforcing the central insight of the doctrine of the incarnation – that is, that Jesus Christ is none other than God. The term was extensively used by writers of the eastern church, especially around the time of the Nestorian controversy, to articu-late both the divinity of Christ and the reality of the incarnation.

Transubstantiation The doctrine according to which the bread and the wine are transformed into the body and blood of Christ in the eucharist, while retaining their outward appearance.

Trinity The distinctively Christian doctrine of God which reflects the complexity of the Christian experience of God. The doctrine is usually summarized in maxims such as "three persons, one God."

Two Natures, doctrine of A term generally used to refer to the doctrine of the two natures, human and divine, of Jesus Christ. Related terms include "Chalcedonian definition" and "hypostatic union."

Vulgate The Latin translation of the Bible, largely deriving from Jerome, upon which medieval theology was largely based.

Zwinglianism The term is used generally to refer to the thought of Huldrych Zwingli, but is often used to refer specifically to his views on the sacraments, especially on the "real presence" (which for Zwingli was more of a "real absence").

Sources of Extracts

p. 5
Justin Martyr, *Apologia* I.xlvi.2–3; II.x.2–3; II.xiii.4–6.
p. 5
Tertullian, *de praescriptione haereticorum*, 7
p. 8
Augustine, *de doctrina Christiana*, II.xl.60–61.

1   p. 14
Clement of Rome, *First Letter to the Corinthians*, 1–6.

2   p. 18
Ignatius of Antioch, *Letter to the Romans*, 1–10.

3   p. 22
The Martyrdom of Polycarp, 1–22.

4   p. 32
Irenaeus of Lyons, *Adversus omnes Haereses*, I.1.1–I.2.6; II.1.1–II.2.5; translation from *Ante-Nicene Fathers to A.D. 325*, edited Alexander Roberts and James Donaldson, 10 volumes. Grand Rapids: Eerdmans, 1985–7, vol. 4.

5   p. 45
Tertullian, "Apologeticus," 1–4; translation from *Ante-Nicene Fathers to A.D. 325*, edited Alexander Roberts and James Donaldson, 10 volumes. Grand Rapids: Eerdmans, 1985–7, vol. 3.

6   p. 53
Eusebius of Caesarea, *Ecclesiastical History*, III.1–11; translation from *A Select Library of Nicene and Post-Nicene Fathers of the Christian Church. Second series*, edited Philip Schaff, 14 volumes. Grand Rapids: Eerdmans, 1988–91, vol. 1.

7   p. 65
Athanasius, *de incarnatione* IV.19–25; translation from *A Select Library of Nicene and Post-Nicene Fathers of the Christian Church. Second series*, edited Philip Schaff, 14 volumes. Grand Rapids: Eerdmans, 1988–91, vol. 4.

p. 69

Athanasius, *de vita Antonii*, 1–11; translation from *A Select Library of Nicene and Post-Nicene Fathers of the Christian Church. Second series*, edited Philip Schaff, 14 volumes. Grand Rapids: Eerdmans, 1988–91, vol. 4.

8   p. 76

Ephraim of Syria, "The Pearl"; translation from *Select Works of Ephrem the Syrian*, translated by J. B. Morris. Oxford: Parker, 1847.

9   p. 82

Cyril of Jerusalem, *Catechetical Lectures* Prochesis 1–17; translation from *A Select Library of Nicene and Post-Nicene Fathers of the Christian Church. Second series*, edited Philip Schaff, 14 volumes. Grand Rapids: Eerdmans, 1988–91, vol. 7.

10   p. 89

Gregory of Nyssa, "Funeral Oration on Meletius"; translation from *A Select Library of Nicene and Post-Nicene Fathers of the Christian Church. Second series*, edited Philip Schaff, 14 volumes. Grand Rapids: Eerdmans, 1988–91, vol. 5.

11   p. 96

"The Peregrination of Egeria"; translation from Louis Duchesne, *Christian Worship: Its Origin and Evolution. A Study of the Latin Liturgy up to the Time of Charlemagne*. London: SPCK, 1903.

12   p. 106

Augustine of Hippo, *Confessions* VIII.vi.14–xii.30; translation by Albert C. Outler, Ph.D., D.D., Professor of Theology, Perkins School of Theology, Southern Methodist University, Dallas, Texas; published 1955, and placed by him in the public domain.

13   p. 116

Venantius Honorius Clementianus Fortunatus, "Vexilla Regis prodeunt"; translation by John Mason Neale. Text in *Hymns Ancient and Modern Revised*. London: William Clowes, 1926, p. 73.

14   p. 127

Caedmon's Hymn; in Richard Hamer, *A Choice of Anglo-Saxon Verse*. London: Faber & Faber, 1970, p. 123.

15   p. 129

Bede, *History of the English Church and Nation*, I.23–27; translation in The Venerable Bede, *The Ecclesiastical History of the English Nation*. London: J. M. Dent, 1910.

p. 133

Bede's Death Song; in Richard Hamer, *A Choice of Anglo-Saxon Verse*. London: Faber & Faber, 1970, p. 127.

16   p. 134

"The Deer's Cry"; in *Selections from Ancient Irish Poetry*. London: Constable, 1911, pp. 25–7.

17   p. 138

"The Dream of the Rood"; in S. A. J. Bradley, *Anglo-Saxon Poetry*. Everyman Library. London: J. M. Dent, 1982, pp. 160–3.

18   p. 143
"Genesis B XI–XIII"; in S. A. J. Bradley, *Anglo-Saxon Poetry*. Everyman Library. London: J. M. Dent, 1982, pp. 25–32.
p. 148
"Christ and Satan VIII–IX"; in S. A. J. Bradley, *Anglo-Saxon Poetry*. Everyman Library. London: J. M. Dent, 1982, pp. 95–9.

19   p. 151
Kevin Crossley-Holland, *The Exeter Book Riddles*. London: Penguin, 1993, No. 26, p. 29.

20   p. 155
The Blickling Homilist, "An Easter Day Sermon," in *Anglo-Saxon Prose*, translated by Michael Swanson. London: Dent, 1993, pp. 122–9.

21   p. 162
Aelfric, "The Passion of St Edmund," in *Anglo-Saxon Prose*, translated by Michael Swanson. London: Dent, 1993, pp. 158–64.

22   p. 168
Wulfstan, "Sermo Lupi ad Anglos," in *Anglo-Saxon Prose*, translated by Michael Swanson. London: Dent, 1993, pp. 178–84.

23   p. 183
Anselm of Canterbury, "Prayer to Christ"; translation in *The Prayers and Meditations of St. Anselm*, translated by Benedicta Ward. Harmondsworth: Penguin Books, 1973, pp. 94–5.

24   p. 187
Peter Abelard, *Historia Calamitatum*, 6–7; translation in Peter Abelard, *Historia Calamitatum: The Story of My Misfortunes*. New York: Macmillan, 1922.

25   p. 195
Bernard of Clairvaux, *de diligendo Deo*, 4.

26   p. 199
Francis of Assisi, "*Canticle of the Creatures*"; original Italian in H. Goad, *Greyfriars: The Story of St Francis and His Followers*. London: John Westhouse, 1947, pp. 137–8.

27   p. 202
Ancrene Wisse, Part 3; translation in *Ancrene Wisse: Guide for an Anchoress*. London: Penguin Books, 1993, pp. 60–6.

28   p. 208
Thomas Aquinas, *Summa Theologiae* Prima Pars quaest. 1, art. 9.

29   p. 211
Hugh of Balma, *The Roads to Zion*, prologue, 5–7; Latin text in Francis Ruello and Jeanne Barbet, *Theologia Mystica*, 2 vols. Paris: Editions du Cerf, 1995, vol. 1, 130–2.

30   p. 215
Dante Alighieri, *Inferno*, canto 1; translation in Henry Wadsworth Longfellow, *The Divine Comedy of Dante Alighieri*. London: Routledge, 1867.

31   p. 219
Ludolf of Saxony, *Vita Jesu Christi Domini ac salvatoris nostri*. Paris: U. Gering

& B. Rembolt, 1502, praefatio. Note that this edition uses a variant title: the more common title is *Vita Jesu Christi redemptoris nostri*.

32   p. 222
The Cloud of Unknowing, 17–24; translation in *A Book Of Contemplation The Which Is Called The Cloud Of Unknowing*, edited Evelyn Underhill, 2nd edn. London: Watkins, 1922.

33   p. 231
William Langland, *Piers the Ploughman*, XVII; translated by J. F. Goodridge. Harmondsworth: Penguin Books, 1959, pp. 217–30.

34   p. 241
Geoffrey Chaucer, "The Pardoner's Prologue"; translation in Chaucer, *The Canterbury Tales*, translated by Nevill Coghill. Harmondsworth: Penguin Books, 1951, pp. 259–62.

35   p. 247
Julian of Norwich, *Revelations of Divine Love, 6–7*; translated by Clifton Wolters. Harmondsworth: Penguin, 1966, pp. 63–71.

36   p. 253
York Mystery Plays: A Selection in Modern Spelling, edited by Richard Beadle and Pamela M. King. Oxford: Oxford University Press, 1984, pp. 212–21.

37   p. 265
Thomas à Kempis, *The Imitation of Christ* I.1–3; translation by Aloysius Croft and Harold Bolton. London: J. M. Dent, 1910.

38   p. 270
William Dunbar, "*Rorate coeli desuper.*" Full bibliographical references to poems are not given, in that these are easily accessed through collections of the poets' writings, or appropriate anthologies.

39   p. 290
Erasmus of Rotterdam, *Moriae Encomium*, 52–5; translation by John Wilson. Erasmus, *The Praise of Folly*. Oxford: Clarendon Press, 1913.

40   p. 313
"Letter on Translating the New Testament". Translated from: "Sendbrief von Dolmetschen"; in *Dr. Martin Luthers Werke* (Weimar: Hermann Boehlaus Nachfolger, 1909), Band 30, Teil II, pp. 632–46 by Gary Mann, Ph.D. Assistant Professor of Religion/Theology, Augustana College, Rock Island, Illinois. This text was translated by Dr. Gary Mann in 1995 and was placed by him in the public domain.

   "Luther's Little Instruction Book"; (The Small Catechism of Martin Luther). This text was translated in 1994 for Project Wittenberg by Robert E. Smith and has been placed in the public domain by him.

41   p. 323
Ignatius Loyola, *Spiritual Exercises*, second exercise; translation by Father Elder Mullan, S.J. New York: P. J. Kenedy & Sons, 1914.

42   p. 329
John Calvin, *Institutes of the Christian Religion*, I.1–2; translation by Henry Beveridge. Grand Rapids, MI: Eerdmans, 1867.

43 p. 336
John Foxe, *Acts and Monuments*, 8. Text from *Acts and Monuments of John Foxe*, 4th edn. London: Religious Tract Society, 1877.

44 p. 347
Edmund Spenser, "Hymne of Heavenly Beauty."

45 p. 359
"Preface," *The Holy Bible, containing the Old and New Testaments, translated out of the original tongues and with the former translations diligently compared and revised by His Majesty's Special Command. Appointed to be read in churches.* London, 1611.

46 p. 382
Sir Walter Ralegh, "The Passionate Man's Pilgrimage."

47 p. 385
Lancelot Andrewes, "Sermon XIV on the Nativity"; in *Seventeen Sermons on the Nativity*. London: Griffith, Farran, Okeden and Welsh, 1903, pp. 229–44.

48 p. 398
William Shakespeare, "Sonnet 146."

49 p. 402
John Donne, "Sermon No. 1," in *The Sermons of John Donne*, edited E. M. Simpson and G. R. Potter, 10 vols. Berkeley/Los Angeles: University of California Press, 1954, vol. 7, pp. 51–71.
pp. 416–19
John Donne, "Divine Meditations."

50 pp. 422
George Herbert, *The Temple*.
p. 427
George Herbert, "The Parson Preaching," from *A Priest to the Temple*; in *The Works of George Herbert*, ed. F. E. Hutchinson. Oxford: Clarendon Press, 1941, pp. 232–5.

51 p. 431
Sir Thomas Browne, *Religio Medici* II.xiv–xviii. Text in Sir Thomas Browne, *Religio Medici*. Harvard Classics. Cambridge, MA: Harvard University Press, 1913.

52 p. 438
John Milton, "Paradise Lost."

53 p. 443
Jeremy Taylor, *Holy Dying*, chapter 1, section 1. Text in Jeremy Taylor, *The Rules and Exercises of Holy Dying*. Oxford: Clarendon Press, 1989.

54 p. 449
Henry Vaughan, "The British Church."
p. 451
Henry Vaughan, "Religion."

55 p. 455
Andrew Marvell, "Bermudas."
p. 456
Andrew Marvell, "The Coronet."

56   p. 461
Blaise Pascal, *Pensées* 60–72; translation by W. F. Trotter, Pascal's *Pensées*. London: Dent, 1932.

57   p. 468
John Bunyan, *The Pilgrim's Progress*, chapter 1. Text in *Grace Abounding To The Chief Of Sinners: And, The Pilgrim's Progress From This World To That Which Is To Come*. London: Oxford University Press, 1966.

59   p. 488
Daniel Defoe, *Robinson Crusoe*. London: Penguin Books, 1994, pp. 88–98.

60   p. 497
Joseph Addison, "Ode."
p. 498
Joseph Addison, "Cato," act 5, scene 1, lines 1–10.

61   p. 500
Isaac Watts, "When I survey the wondrous cross."

62   p. 502
Joseph Butler, *The Analogy of Religion, Natural and Revealed*. London: Dent, 1906, pp. 110–15.

63   p. 508
Jonathan Edwards, *Treatise on the Religious Affections*, chapter 1.
p. 510
Jonathan Edwards, "The Christian Pilgrim"; in Jonathan Edwards, *Basic Writings*. New York: New American Library, 1966, pp. 135–42.

64   p. 517
John Wesley, "Preface," *Sermons On Several Occasions*, 4 vols. London, 1771, vol. 1.
p. 520
John Wesley, "Sermon 2," *Sermons On Several Occasions*, 4 vols. London, 1771, vol. 1.

65   p. 528
Charles Wesley, "Love Divine."
p. 530
Charles Wesley, "Free Grace."

66   pp. 533
John Newton, *Olney Hymns*.

67   p. 541
William Paley, *A View of the Evidences of Christianity*. London: Christian Evidence Committee of the Society for Promoting Christian Knowledge, 1872, pp. 601–12.

68   p. 548
William Blake, "And did those feet?", from *Milton*.

69   p. 552
William Wordsworth, "Tintern Abbey."
p. 557
William Wordsworth, "Intimations of Immortality from Recollections of Early Childhood."

70   p. 565
Samuel Taylor Coleridge, "Religious Musings."
p. 567
Samuel Taylor Coleridge, *Confessions of an Inquiring Spirit*. London: George Bell, 1893.
71   p. 571
John Keble, *National Apostasy*. Abingdon: Rocket Press, 1983.
72   pp. 583
John Henry Newman, "The Dream of Gerontius."
73   p. 586
Ralph Waldo Emerson, *Nature*. Boston: Beacon Press, 1985.
74   p. 593
Anthony Trollope, *Barchester Towers*. London: Penguin Books, 1982, pp. 22–8.
75   p. 599
Benjamin Jowett, "On the Interpretation of Scripture," in *Essays and Reviews*. London: John W. Parker, 1860.
76   p. 610
George Eliot, *Scenes of Clerical Life*. London: Penguin, 1973, pp. 316–29.
77   p. 622
Fyodor Mikhailovich Dostoevsky, *The Brothers Karamazov*. Text from *The Novels of Fyodor Dostoevsky*, translated by Constance Black Garnett, 12 vols. London: Heinemann, 1912–20.
78   p. 637
Matthew Arnold, "Dover Beach."
79   p. 642
George MacDonald, *Lilith: A Romance*. London: Allen & Unwin, 1924.
80   p. 651
Thomas Hardy, *Jude the Obscure*. London: Macmillan, 1974, pp. 82–8.
81   p. 657
Gerard Manley Hopkins, "God's Grandeur."
82   p. 661
Oscar Wilde, "The Ballad of Reading Gaol."
83   p. 680
G. K. Chesteron, *Orthodoxy*. London: John Lane, 1909.
p. 684
G. K. Chesterton, *The Everlasting Man*. London: Hodder & Stoughton, 1925.
84   p. 690
T. S. Eliot, *The Waste Land*: "The Burial of the Dead"; in *T. S. Eliot: Selected Poems*. London: Faber & Faber, 1963, 51–3.
p. 693
T. S. Eliot, "The Journey of the Magi"; in *T. S. Eliot: Selected Poems*. London: Faber & Faber, 1963, 597–8.
85   p. 697
Dorothy L. Sayers, *The Man Born to be King*. London: Victor Gollancz, 1943, pp. 79–83.

p. 703
Dorothy L. Sayers, *The Mind of the Maker*. London: Methuen, 1941, pp. 88–93.

86 p. 710
C. S. Lewis, *The Screwtape Letters*. London: Fontana, 1955, pp. 9–19.
p. 714
C. S. Lewis, *Till We Have Faces*. London: Fount Paperbacks, 1998, pp. 52–6.

87 p. 720
Graham Greene, *The Power and the Glory*. London: Penguin, 1962, pp. 92–102.

88 p. 730
R. S. Thomas, "Pietà"; in *Collected Poems 1945–1990*. London: Dent, 1993, p. 159.
p. 731
R. S. Thomas, "*Via Negativa*"; in *Collected Poems 1945–1990*. London: Dent, 1993, p. 220.

89 p. 735
Martin Luther King, Jr., "I have a Dream"; Transcription of Address at March on Washington for Jobs and Freedom, August 28, 1963, Washington, D. C.

90 p. 740
David Lodge, *How Far Can You Go?* London: Penguin Books, 1981, pp. 113–21.

91 p. 748
Garrison Keillor, *Lake Wobegon Days*. New York: Viking Penguin, 1985, pp. 149–58.

For Further Reading

Each reading selected for discussion has its own individual bibliography, included within the "Study Panel." What follows are some works which address more general issues relating to Christian literature.

David Anderson, *The Tragic Protest: A Christian Study of Some Modern Literature*. Richmond, VA: John Knox Press, 1969.

Stuart Barton Babbage, *The Mark Of Cain: Studies in Literature and Theology*. Exeter: Paternoster Press, 1967.

David Barrett, Leland Ryken and Roger Pooley (eds), *Discerning Reader: Essays on Christian Literary Criticism*. Grand Rapids, MI: Baker Book House, 1995.

E. Beatrice Batson, *A Reader's Guide to Religious Literature*. Chicago: Moody Press, 1968.

Lee Archer Belford, *Religious Dimensions in Literature*. New York: Seabury Press, 1982.

Harold Bloom, *Ruin the Sacred Truths: Poetry and Belief from the Bible to the Present*. Cambridge, MA: Harvard University Press, 1987.

Norman Reed Cary, *Christian Criticism in the Twentieth Century: Theological Approaches to Literature*. Port Washington, NY: Kennikat Press, 1975.

David Duiches, *God and the Poets*. Oxford: Oxford University Press, 1984.

Northrope Frye, *The Great Code: The Bible and Literature*. London: Routledge & Kegan Paul, 1982.

John Spencer Hill, *Infinity, Faith and Time: Christian Humanism and Renaissance Literature*. Montreal: McGill–Queen's University Press, 1997.

David Jasper, *The Study of Literature and Theology: An Introduction*. London: Macmillan, 1989.

David Lyle Jeffrey, *People of the Book: Christian Identity and Literary Culture*. Grand Rapids, MI: Eerdmans, 1996.

George Kane, *Middle English Literature: A Critical Study of the Romances, The Religious Lyrics, Piers Plowman*. Westport, CT: Greenwood Press, 1979.

Gisbert Kranz, *Three Centuries of Christian Literature*. London: Burns & Oates, 1961.

Neal E. Lambert, *Literature of Belief: Sacred Scripture and Religious Experience*. Provo, UT: Religious Studies Center, Brigham Young University, 1981.

David L. Larsen, *The Company of the Creative: A Christian Reader's Guide to Great Literature and its Themes*. Grand Rapids, MI: Kregel, 1999.

C. S. Lewis, *The Literary Impact of the Authorized Version*. Philadelphia: Fortress Press, 1967.

Rose Macaulay, *Some Religious Elements in English Literature*. St. Clair Shores, MI: Scholarly Press, 1972.

Frank Northen Magill, *Masterpieces of Christian Literature in Summary Form*. New York: Harper & Row, 1963.

John L. Mahoney, *Seeing into the Life of Things: Essays on Literature and Religious Experience*. Fordham, NY: Fordham University Press, 1998.

Walter Arthur Mccray, *A Rationale for Black Christian Literature: An Essay*, 2nd edn. Chicago, IL: Black Light Fellowship, 1992.

Sallie McFague, *Literature and the Christian Life*. New Haven, CT: Yale University Press, 1966.

Peter Milward, *Christian Themes in English Literature*. Tokyo: Kenkyusha, 1967.

C. A. Patrides, *The Grand Design of God: The Literary Form of the Christian View of History*. London: Routledge & Kegan Paul, 1972.

Lynn M. Poland, *Literary Criticism and Biblical Hermeneutics: A Critique of Formalist Approaches*. Chico, CA: Scholars Press, 1985.

Stephen Prickett, *Words and the Word: Language, Poetics and Biblical Interpretation*. Cambridge: Cambridge University Press, 1986.

David S. Reynolds, *Faith in Fiction: The Emergence of Religious Literature in America*. Cambridge, MA: Harvard University Press, 1981.

Isabel Rivers, *Classical and Christian Ideas in English Renaissance Poetry: A Students' Guide*. London and Boston: G. Allen & Unwin, 1979.

Leland Ryken, *Triumphs of the Imagination: Literature in Christian Perspective*. Downers Grove, IL: InterVarsity Press, 1979.

Nathan A. Scott, *The Poetics of Belief*. Chapel Hill, NC: University of North Carolina Press, 1985.

Gene Edward Veith, *Reading Between the Lines: A Christian Approach to Literature*. Wheaton, IL: Crossway Books, 1990.

John Raymond Whitney and Susan W. Howe, *Religious Literature of the West*. Minneapolis, MN: Augsburg, 1971.

T. R. Wright, *Theology and Literature*. Oxford: Blackwell, 1988.

Acknowledgments

I am indebted for many discussions with colleagues in Europe and North America which led to the selection of the passages included in the present work. In particular, I would like to thank Dr. Santha Bhattacharji (St. Hilda's College, Oxford), Dr. Samuel Fanous, Revd. Malcolm Guite, and Dr. Hugh White (St. Catherine's College, Oxford) for their meticulous assessment of potential sources. Without their help, this work could not have been assembled. I also wish to acknowledge the kind assistance of student readers of the text, who offered invaluable guidance concerning the levels of introduction and explanation which were appropriate to the individual texts. Inevitably, a much longer book would have resulted if their requests had been fully heeded; it is hoped that the levels of introduction and explanation offered in this volume will go at least part of the way toward meeting student needs.

In addition, Blackwell Publishers would like to thank the following individuals for invaluable advice and suggestions regarding the selection and inclusion of material at the planning stage of this volume: David Aers, James Barr, Rachel Boulding, Peter Brown, Robert P. Carroll, Michael Clanchy, Gavin D'Costa, David A. S. Fergusson, David Jasper, Fergus Kerr, OP, Ann K. S. Lambton, Margaret R. Miles, Jolyon Mitchell, Mike Payne, Martyn Percy, Stephen Prickett, Peter Sedgwick, Naomi Starkey, and Vernon White.

Special thanks must be accorded to David Jasper and Peter McCulloch for their invaluable engagement with the penultimate version of this volume, and to Rachel Boulding and Naomi Starkey for generously taking time off from their own editorial duties to assist with the undertaking of another publisher.

The authors and publishers gratefully acknowledge the following for permission to reproduce copyright material:

"The Dream of the Rood" from S. A. J. Bradley, *Anglo-Saxon Poetry* (Everyman Library, J. M. Dent & Sons, London, 1982);
The Blickling Homilist, "An Easter Day Sermon" from *Anglo-Saxon Prose* (trans. Michael Swanson) (J. M. Dent & Sons, London, 1993);

"Genesis B XI–XIII" from S. A. J. Bradley, *Anglo-Saxon Poetry* (Everyman Library, J. M. Dent & Sons, London, 1982);

"Christ and Satan VIII–IX" from S. A. J. Bradley, *Anglo-Saxon Poetry* (Everyman Library, J. M. Dent & Sons, London, 1982);

R. S. Thomas, *Collected Poems 1945–1990* (J. M. Dent & Sons, London, 1993);

"Bede's Death Song" from Richard Hamer, *A Choice of Anglo-Saxon Verse* (Faber & Faber Ltd, London, 1970);

"Caedmon's Hymn" from Richard Hamer, *A Choice of Anglo-Saxon Verse* (Faber & Faber Ltd, London, 1970);

Kevin Crossley-Holland, *The Exeter Book of Riddles*. Copyright © Kevin Crossley-Holland, 1993. Reproduced by permission of the author c/o Rogers, Coleridge & White Ltd., 29 Powis Mews, London, W11 1JN;

Aelfric, "The Passion of St Edmund" from *Anglo-Saxon Prose* (trans. Michael Swanson) (J. M. Dent & Sons, London, 1993);

Wulfstan, "Sermo Lupi ad Anglos" from *Anglo-Saxon Prose* (trans. Michael Swanson) (J. M. Dent & Sons, London, 1993);

T. S. Eliot, *The Waste Land*: "The Burial of the Dead" from *T. S. Eliot Selected Poems 1909–1962* (Faber & Faber Ltd., London, 1963);

T. S. Eliot, "Journey of the Magi" from *T. S. Eliot Selected Poems 1909–1962* (Faber & Faber Ltd., London, 1963);

York Mystery Plays: A Selection in Modern Spelling © Richard Beadle and Pamela M. King, 1984. Reprinted from *York Mystery Plays: A Selection in Modern Spelling*, edited by Richard Beadle and Pamela M. King (1983) by permission of Oxford University Press;

The Prayers and Meditations of St. Anselm (trans. by Benedicta Ward) (Penguin Classics, 1973) copyright © Benedicta Ward, 1973. Reproduced by permission of Penguin Books Ltd;

Ancrene Wisse: Guide for Anchoresses (trans. Hugh White) (Penguin Classics, 1993), translation copyright © Hugh White, 1993. Reproduced by permission of Penguin Books Ltd;

Piers the Ploughman by William Langland (trans. J. F. Goodridge) (Penguin Classics, 1959, revised 1966) copyright © J. F. Goodridge, 1959. Reproduced by permission of Penguin Books Ltd;

Revelations of Divine Love by Julian of Norwich (trans. Clifton Wolters) (Penguin Classics, 1966) copyright © Clifton Wolters, 1966. Reproduced by permission of Penguin Books Ltd;

Graham Greene, *The Power and the Glory* (Heinemann Publishers, 1940, reproduced by permission of David Higham Associates, London);

David Lodge, *How Far Can You Go?* (Secker & Warburg, London, 1962);

Garrison Keillor, *Lake Wobegon Days* (Viking Penguin, New York, 1985);

C. S. Lewis, *The Screwtape Letters* (Fontana, London, 1955, copyright © C. S. Lewis Pte. Ltd, 1942. Extract reprinted by permission);

Dorothy L. Sayers, *The Man Born to be King* (Hodder & Stoughton, 1943, reproduced by permission of David Higham Associates, London);

Dorothy L. Sayers, *The Mind of the Maker* (Methuen, London, 1941, reproduced by permission of David Higham Associates, London);

Martin Luther King, Jr., "A Testament of Hope" from *The Essential Writings and Speeches of Martin Luther King Jr.* (ed. James M. Washington) (Harper, San Francisco, 1991, copyright © 1986 by Coretta Scott King, Executrix of the Estate of Martin Luther King Jr.);

C. S. Lewis, *Till We Have Faces* (Fount Paperbacks, London, 1998, copyright © C. S. Lewis Pte. Ltd, 1942. Extract reprinted by permission).

The publishers apologize for any errors or omissions in the above list and would be grateful to be notified of any corrections that should be incorporated in the next edition or reprint of this book.

Index

Aaron, 15
abbeys, 122
Abbo of Fleury, 162
Abel, 15, 510
Abelard, Peter, 178, 186–93
Abiezer, 368
Abiram, 15
Abraham
  biblical image of Sarah as
    sister, 556
  "Blickling Homilist," 158
  Ignatius of Antioch's "Letter
    to the Romans," 20
  John Calvin's *Institutes of the
    Christian Religion*, 330
  Jonathan Edwards' "Christian
    Pilgrim," 510, 511
  Lancelot Andrewes' sermons,
    389, 393
  Martin Luther's "Letter on
    Translating the New
    Testament," 309
  Paul, 309
  as pilgrim, 510, 511
  Sir Thomas Browne's *Religio
    Medici*, 433
  William Langland's *Piers
    Plowman*, 233
Abraham, Bishop of Nisibis,
  75
Academics, 49
Academy for Dissenters, 487

accentual-syllabic verse, 127,
  138
Acinetos, 34
An Acre of Land, 728
actives, 222–8
Acts of the Apostles, xi, 9
  Athanasius of Alexandra's
    Life of Antony, 69
  Augustine of Hippo, 8
  Eusebius of Caesarea's
    Ecclesiastical History, 54,
    55
  John Keble's sermon, 579
  John Wesley's sermon, 520
  King James Version of the
    Bible, 362
  Lancelot Andrewes' sermons,
    386, 387, 389, 391–2, 393
  The Peregrination of Egeria,
    102
"Acts of the Martyrs," 21
The Acts and Monuments, 334,
  335–44
"Ad nationes," 44
Adam
  Augustine of Hippo's
    Confessions, 110
  "Blickling Homilist," 157
  Clement of Rome's "First
    Letter to Corinth," 16
  "The Dream of the Rood,"
    140

effects on humanity as
  described by Paul, 424
George MacDonald's *Lilith*,
  641
Ignatius Loyola's *Spiritual
  Exercises*, 324
John Calvin's *Institutes of the
  Christian Religion*, 331
John Donne's sermon, 409
"Junius Codex," 143, 144,
  145, 146–7, 148
William Langland's *Piers
  Plowman*, 233, 234, 235,
  236, 237
Adam Bede, 610
Addison, Joseph, 496–8
Adela Cathcart, 641
Adhelm, 151
Adonai, 412, 413
Adrian, Pope, 370
Adversus Haereses, 31–42
Aelfric, 161–6
Aeneid, 213
aeons, 5, 34–7
Aethelred, King, 162
Aetherius, Bishop of Arles, 130
affections, 508–10
Against all Heresies, 31–42
*Against the Thieving and
  Murderous Hordes of
  Peasants*, 302
Agape, 34

Ageratos, 34
Aggai, 389, 390
Ahab, King, 312
Ahaz, 386
Aidan, 123
Aids to Reflection, 564
d'Ailly, Pierre, 299
Ainos, 34
Alaric the Goth, 175
Albert the Great, 178, 207
Albert of Mainz, Archbishop, 300–1
Albertists, 291, 293
Alciati, Andrea, 326
Alcuin, 6, 124, 283
Aldhelm, 124
Aldine Press, 278, 284
Alec Forbes, 641
Aletheia, 34, 35, 37
Alexander, Mrs. Cecil F., 134
Alexandria, 9, 10
Alfred, King of Wessex, 162
Alice Through the Looking Glass, 642, 647
The Allegory of Love, 708
L'Allegro, 436
"The Almost Christian," 517, 520–6
Alphonsus a castro, 365
Alured, King, 366
Alypius, 106, 109, 113–14
Amalekites, 576, 578
Ambrose, 107, 176, 310, 370
Ambrose Thesius, 366
American Revolution, 482
"The American Scholar," 586
Amoretti, 345
Amos, Book of, 392
Anabaptism, 281
Anacharsis, 46
analogies, 208–9
Analogy of Religion, 502–6
Anastasis, 96, 97, 98, 99, 102, 103, 104
anchoresses/anchorites, 201–6, 246
ancien régime, 482
"Ancient of Days," 546
Ancrene Wisse, 201–6
"And Did those Feet?," 547–9

Andrew, Saint, 53, 203, 393, 697–701
Andrewes, Lancelot, 384–95, 692
angels, 40–1
anger, 202–3
Anglicans, 358
Anselm of Canterbury, 179, 181–5
Anselm of Laon, 186
Anthropos, 34, 35, 37
anti-intellectualism, 221
The AntiChrist, 622
Antioch, 9
Antioch, Council of, 52
antiphons, 97, 98, 100, 102
Antony of Egypt, Saint, 11, 64, 69–74, 106–7, 113
Apelles, 362
Apicius, 49
Apollinarius, 89
Apollos, 393
apologetics, xii, 4, 44, 438, 481
Apologia Pro Vita Sua, 582, 637
Apologies (Justin Martyr), 44
Apology (Tertullian), 43, 44–51
apophatic theology, 731–2
apotactitae, 96, 103
Appeal to the Christian Nobility of the German Nation, 301
Apuleius, 713
Aquila, Ponticus, 364, 368, 370
Arab invasions, 175–6
Aratus, xi
Archimedes, 557
Arden, Mary, 396
Arezzo, 96
Arian controversy, 10, 52, 63, 64, 81, 88
Aristarchus, 49
Aristotelianism, 207, 277, 484
Aristotle
  Erasmus of Rotterdam's Moriae Encomium, 292
  G. K. Chesterton's The Everlasting Man, 686
  King James Version of the Bible, 368

Martin Luther's "Letter on Translating the New Testament," 305
rhetorical skills, xi
Sir Thomas Browne's Religio Medici, 431
Thomas Aquinas, 207
Arius, 10, 52
Arles, Synod of, 122
Armagh, 122
Arnauld, Antoine, 461
Arnold, Matthew, 581, 599, 636–9, 682
Arnold, Thomas, 636
The Art of Fiction, 739
"Ash-Wednesday," 689
Ashtoreth, 238
Astrolabe, 189
"At the Burial of the Dead," 476–7, 690
Athanasius of Alexandria, 10, 52, 63–74, 176
Athelstan, King, 162
The Atlantic Monthly, 747
Atlas, 293
atonement, 182, 357
Audrey, 165
Augustine of Canterbury, 121, 123, 129–32
Augustine of Hippo, 10, 11, 105–14, 176, 182
  City of God, 192
  classical literature, xii, 3, 7–8
  Confessions, 106–14, 187
  David Lodge's How Far Can You Go?, 742
  desires and longings of human nature, 498
  Erasmus of Rotterdam's Moriae Encomium, 293
  free will, 417
  human sexuality, 742
  John Donne's sermon, 408, 410
  King James Version of the Bible, 362, 365, 368, 370, 372, 373, 374, 375
  Martin Luther's "Letter on Translating the New Testament," 310

Pascal's admiration of, 461
Peter Abelard's *History of Calamities*, 192
poets, xi
T. S. Eliot's "The Waste Land," 690
Augustines, 295, 299
Authentic Narrative, 532
authority, 621, 622, 629
autobiography
  Augustine of Hippo's *Confessions*, 106–14, 187
  Peter Abelard's *History of Calamities*, 187–93
Autophyes, 34
Auzout, Adrien, 459
Aventinus, 366
Avignon papacy, 176, 179

Babu, 75
The Babylonian Captivity of the Christian Church, 302
Bacon, Francis, 589, 590, 603
Bainton, Roland H., 281
Balaam, 388, 389, 390, 392
Bale, John, 334
"The Ballad of Reading Gaol," 660, 661–78
Ballantyne, R. M., 718
baptism
  Cyril of Jerusalem's *Catechetical Lectures*, 82–7
  Martin Luther's "Lesser Catechism," 318–19
Barbarossa, 179
Barber, John, 339
Barchester Towers, 592, 593–7
Bardi family, 212
Baron, Hans, 277
Basil, Saint, 88, 293, 362, 363
Basilides, 40
Basire, James, 546
"Batter my heart," 417–18
Baxter, Richard, xii
Beatus Rhenanus, 366
Beaumont, Sir George, 564
Beaupuy, Michel, 550
Bec Abbey, 179, 181

Becket, Thomas à, 241
Bede, 123, 124, 126, 128–33, 366
Bedford Question, 751
beliefs, xiii
Bellini, Giovanni, 730
Belus, 391
Benedict of Nursia, 11
Benedictine community, 11, 181, 194, 207, 295
Bennet, Dr., 337
Bensirah, 446
Beowulf, xx, 124, 437
"Bermudas," 454–6
Bernard of Clairvaux, 179, 187, 194–7, 213, 264, 601
Bernardines, 295
Berne, 280, 281
Beroaldus, 366
Bertha, 131
Bethany, 96–7
Bethlehem, 103
Beyond Personality, 708
Beza, Theodore, 280, 281
Biathanatos, 400–1
Bible, 279
  Benjamin Jowett's "Interpretation of Scripture," 599–608
  Coleridge's *Confession of an Enquiring Spirit*, 567–9
  Geneva Bible, 358
  in German, 302
  King James Version, 284, 356–80, 471, 497
  literary character, xii
  translation into English, 282–5
  Vulgate, 282–4, 289
  see also New Testament
biblical commentaries, xiii, 8
  "Junius Codex," 142–7
biblical criticism, 485
biblical sermons *see* sermons
biblical theology, 286
Biel, Gabriel, 299
biographies, xiii
  see also autobiography; hagiographies

birth control, 740–6
Black Civil Rights movement, 733–4
Blackwood's Magazine, 610
Blake, James, 546
Blake, William, 486, 546–9, 642
blessings, 97, 98, 99
"Blickling Homilist," 155–60
The Blind Watchmaker, 539–40
Blomfield, Arthur, 648
blood, 202
Boccaccio, Giovanni, 241
Bodenstein von Karlstadt, Andreas, 301
Bodleian Library, 142
Boehler, Peter, 516
Boleyn, Anne, 338, 339, 470
Bolsec, Jerome, 327
Bonaventure, 178, 180, 210, 264
Bonner, Bishop of London, 340
Book of Antiquities, 191
"Book of Common Prayer" (BCP), 358, 470–7, 690
Book of Thel, 546
Booz, 391, 392
Bora, Katharina von, 302
Boucher, Catherine, 546
Bradley, F. H., 688
"Brahma," 586
Bray, Caroline, 609
Bray, Charles, 609
The Bread of Truth, 728
breastplate, 122, 134
Brendan, 122–3
Brethren of the Common Life, 287
Brian of Lingen, 201
Bridges, Robert, 657
"The British Church," 448–50
British Critic, 581
Brittany, 121
Brooke, Rupert, 692
Brooks, Dr., 340
The Brothers Karamazov, 620, 621–35
Browne, Sir Thomas, 430–5
Bucer, Martin, 301
Buckeridge, Bishop, 384

Buddha, 690
Buddhism, 683
Buffon, Georges Louis Leclerc, 587
Bulgaria, 177
Bullinger, Heinrich, 280
Bunyan, John, 230, 336, 467–9, 487, 614, 708
Burckhardt, Jacob, 276
"The Burial of the Dead," 690
Bury, J. B., 689
Bury St Edmunds, 162
Busman's Honeymoon, 695
Butler, Joseph, 501–6, 516, 517, 520, 543
Byrne, Muriel St Clare, 695
Bythius, 34
Bythus, 34, 37, 38
Byzantium, 176–7, 178, 276

Cabbala, 641
Caedmon, 123–4, 126–7, 142
"Caedmon manuscript," 142
"Caedmon's hymn," 123–4, 126–7, 134, 138
Caiaphas, 704
Cain, 15
Caius, 28
Cajetan, Gaetano (Thomas de Vio), 301, 371
Calamy, Edmund, 436
Caliphate, 176
Calles, Plutarco Elias, 720
Callistus, Pope, 43
Calvin, John, 279, 280, 281, 286, 326–33, 601
Calvinist Reformation, 280–1
Campeius, Cardinal, 337
Candida Casa, 121
Candidus, 130
canon law, 187
Canterbury, 123, 131–2
Canterbury Tales, xii, 240–5
"Canticle of the Creatures," 199–200
Canute, King of England, 167
Capon, Dr., 337
Cappadocians, 9, 88, 176
Carcavi, Pierre de, 459
Cardenas, Lazaro, 720

Carmelites, 295
Carne, Dr., 337
Carpistes, 36
Carroll, Lewis, 642, 647
Cartesianism, 484
Carthage, 9, 10
Carthusians, 210, 218
The Case for Christianity, 708
Cassiopeia, 444
Castellion, Sebastien, 327
Castro, Fidel, 719
Cataline, 369
Catechetical Lectures, 81–7
catechisms, xiii, 313–21
catechumenates, 82–7
Catherine of Aragon, 337, 338, 339, 470
Catholic Reformation, 282
Catholicism, 279, 739–46
Cato, 498
Cattley, Stephen, 336
The Celestial Hierarchy, 221
celibacy, 745
Celtic Christianity, xx, 121–3
"St Patrick's Breastplate" hymn, 122, 134–6
certainty, 502
Chalcedon, Council of, 3
Chamber's Journal, 648
Changing Places, 739
Chapman, John, 609
Charis, 34
charismatic movement, 43
charity, 228, 380
Charlemagne, 178
Charles I, King of England, 384, 421, 437, 448, 449
Charles II, King of England, 430, 443, 453, 471
Charles V, Holy Roman Emperor, 327, 370
Charles V, King of France, 366
Charterhouse, 210
Chaucer, Geoffrey, xii, 240–5, 270, 346
Chertsey, Mr., 338
Chester, 252
Chesterton, Gilbert Keith, 679–87, 702

"Christabel," 564
Christian Behaviour, 708
Christian Brethren, 748–52
Christian evidence movement, 539, 540–5
Christian literature, definition, xiv
"The Christian Pilgrim," 510–15
Christian Theology: An Introduction, xix
The Christian Year, 570
Christianity not Mysterious, 484
Christianity as Old as Creation, 484
Christmas, 270–2, 378–9
Christus, 37
Chrome Yellow, 692
The Chronicles of Barsetshire, 592
Chronicles, Books of, 390
Chronicles of Narnia, 708–9
Chrysostom, Saint John
  classical literature, xi–xii
  Erasmus of Rotterdam's *Moriae Encomium*, 293
  John Donne's sermon, 403
  King James Version of the Bible, 365–6, 373, 375
  On the Incomprehensibility of God, 731
church
  doctrine of, 10
  history in England, 128, 129–33
Church of England, 448–50, 471, 482
Cicero, 108, 191, 277, 297
Cistercians, 179, 194–5
Cistertiensis, 366
Cîteaux monastery, 179, 194
City of God, 192
civil rights movements, 733–4, 740
Clairvaux, 194–5
Clarke, Samuel, 502
classical culture, xi–xii, 3–9, 106, 277–8
cleansing, way of, 210, 211
Cleanthes, xi

Clement VIII, Pope, 366, 371–2
Clement of Rome, 13–16, 55
clergy, 288–9
Cloetta, Yvonne, 719
The Cloud of Unknowing, 221–8, 247, 731
Cluny monastery, 195
Coghill, Nevill, 241
Coleridge, Samuel Taylor, 550–1, 563–9
Colet, John, 287
Colin Clouts Come Home Againe, 345
Colletes, 295
Colossians, Epistle to the, 196
Columba, 122–3
commandments, 314–15
Commentaries on the Epistles of St Paul, 598–9
Commentarii Rerum in Ecclesia Gestarum, 334–5
"Commentary on Romans," 186
Communion service, 320–1
"The Complaint of the Black Knight," 270
Complutensian Polyglot, 289
confession
  "Book of Common Prayer" (BCP), 472
  Martin Luther's "Lesser Catechism," 319–20
  Tertullian's *Apology*, 46–8
Confessions, 106–14, 187
Confessions of an Enquiring Spirit, 567–9
Constance, Council of, 179
Constantine, 75, 176
  conversion of, 3, 4, 6, 7, 121
  Council of Nicea, 10
  Cyril of Jerusalem's *Catechetical Lectures*, 82
  King James Version of the Bible, 362
Constantinople, 9, 10, 175, 176, 177, 276–7
The Constitution of Church and State, 564

contemplation, 323–5
contemplatives, 222–8
contraception, 740–6
Corbinian, 366
Cordelia, 397–8
Cordier, Mathurin, 326
Cordiliers, 295
Corinthian church, 13–16
Corinthians, Epistles to the, xi
  Bernard of Clairvaux's *On Loving God*, 195
  death, 417
  Erasmus of Rotterdam's *Moriae Encomium*, 292
  George Herbert's sermon, 428
  human body as a temple, 422
  illness of Paul, 251
  John Donne's "Death be not Proud," 417
  John Donne's sermon, 404
  John Donne's "Wilt thou love God?," 419
  King James Version of the Bible, 380
  Lancelot Andrewes' sermons, 392
  Peter Abelard's *History of Calamities*, 190
Cornwall, 121
"The Coronet," 456–8
courtly love genre, 240
Coverdale, Miles, 357
Cowper, William, 532, 533
Cox Brethren, 751–2
Cranmer, Thomas, Archbishop, 336–44, 397, 470, 471
creation
  Addison's Ode on Psalm 19, 497–8
  Caedmon's hymn, 126
  Dorothy L. Sayers' *Mind of the Maker*, 702, 703
  Francis of Assisi's "Canticle of the Creatures," 199–200
  Irenaeus of Lyons' *Against all Heresies*, 37, 38, 40–1
  King James Version of the Bible, 376–7

Martin Luther's "Lesser Catechism," 315
Samuel Taylor Coleridge's "Religious Musings," 566
credal statements, xiii
Creed or Chaos?, 696
Creeds of Christianity, xiii
Crescens, 55
Cressy, Mr., 337
Crickmay, G. R., 648
Crime and Punishment, 620
criminals, 46–9
Crocus, 20
Cromwell, 636
Cromwell, Oliver, 437, 453
Cromwell, Richard, 453
Cromwell, Thomas, 338, 339, 357, 366
Cross
  "The Dream of the Rood," 137–41
  The Peregrination of Egeria, 97, 98, 99, 101–2, 103
  "When I survey the wondrous cross," 499–500
Crossed, 295
crucifixion, 138–9, 729–30
crusades, 176
Cupid, 713
Cur Deus Homo, 182
Cursor Mundi, xii
Cuthbert, Abbot of Wearmouth, 133
Cuthbert, Saint, 128, 165
Cyprian of Carthage, 8, 10, 450
Cyril of Jerusalem, 81–7, 362
Cyril (missionary), 177
Cyrus, King of Persia, 394, 431

Danaids, 16
Danegeld, 167
Daniel, 307, 392, 393, 407
Daniel, Book of John Donne's sermon, 407, 413
"Junius Codex," 142
Lancelot Andrewes' sermons, 389, 392, 393
William Langland's *Piers Plowman*, 232–3
Daniel Deronda, 610

Dante Aligheri, 212–17, 230, 241, 546, 642, 696
Darby, John Nelson, 748
Darius, 394
Darwin, Charles, 540
Datham, 15
David
   Ancrene Wisse, 202, 204, 205
   Benjamin Jowett's "Interpretation of Scripture," 606
   "Blickling Homilist," 156
   Clement of Rome's "First Letter to Corinth," 15
   Gregory of Nyssa's "Funeral Oration on Meletius," 94
   Ignatius of Antioch's "Letter to the Romans," 20
   Irenaeus of Lyons' *Against all Heresies*, 41
   John Donne's sermon, 402, 403, 404, 406–7, 408, 410, 411, 414, 415
   John Keble's sermon, 576
   King James Version of the Bible, 360
   Lancelot Andrewes' sermons, 388, 392
   Psalm 23, 377
David Elginbrod, 641
Dawkins, Richard, 539–40
Day, John, 335
Dayrell-Browning, Vivien, 718
De Casu Diaboli, 182
De doctrina Christiana, 437
De incarnatione, 63–8
de la Mare, Walter, 718
De Libertate Arbitrii, 182
De Orthographia, 133
De Profundis, 660
de rudimentis hebraicis, 284
De Veritate, 182
death
   Athanasius of Alexandria's *de incarnatione*, 65–8
   "Book of Common Prayer" (BCP), 476–7
   John Donne's "Death be not Proud," 416–17
   Taylor's *Holy Dying*, 442–7

"Death be not Proud," 416–17
"Death Song," 128, 133
Decad, 34
Decius, 6
"Deer's Cry," 134–6
"Defects of Historical Christianity," 585
Defoe, Daniel, 486, 487–95
Deism, 484
Demaratus of Corinth, 372
Democritus, 464
Demosthenes, 297
deposition, 730
Desargues, Gerard, 459
Descriptive Sketches, 551
Deuteronomy, 407, 509, 574, 752
Devereux, Robert, 400
devil
   Athanasius of Alexandra's *Life of Antony*, 70–4
   C. S. Lewis' *Screwtape Letters*, 709–13
Devotio Moderna, 263, 264
devotional works, xiii, xiv
Dialogue with Trypho, 44
Dialogues of Plato, 599
Dickens, Charles, 592, 679
Diderot, Denis, 483
Diocletian, 7, 10
Dionysius the Areopagite/ Pseudo-Areopagite, 55, 209, 221, 393, 731
Dionysius of Corinth, 55
Dircae, 16
"Directory of Public Worship," 471
Divine Comedy, 212, 213–17, 230, 546, 696
Divine Meditations, 416–19
Divine Poems, 400
doctrinal treatises, xiii
Dodgson, Charles, 642
"Dolores," 642
Domestic Manners of the Americans, 591
Dominic de Guzman, 180
Dominicans, 179, 180, 207
"Donation of Constantine," 284

Donatist controversy, 10
Donatus, 10
Donne, Henry, 400
Donne, John, xx, 400–19, 420
Dorp, Martin, 290
Dostoevsky, Fyodor Mikhailovich, 620–35
Douglas, Lord Alfred, 660
"Dover Beach," 599, 637–9
Dr. Thorne, 592
"The Dream of Gerontius," 582–4
"The Dream of the Rood," 124, 137–41
Dryden, John, 528
Dudley, Robert, Earl of Leicester, 345
Dugdale, Florence, 649
Dunbar, William, 269–72
Duns Scotus, John, 296, 657
Dunstan, Archbishop, 162
Duodecad, 34, 35
Dyer, Edward, 345
The Dynasts, 649

"Easter," 423–4
"Easter Day," 660
Easter festivals, 30, 96–104, 155–60
Ecclesia, 34, 35, 37
Ecclesiastes, Book of, 311, 404, 602
Ecclesiastical History, 52–62
Ecclesiasticus, 34
Ecclesiasticus, Book of, 162, 195
Eck, Johann, 301
Edessa, 75
Edmund, King of East Anglia, 161–6
Edward, St (ca. 962–978), 170
Edward III, King of England, 240
Edward VI, King of England, 334, 340, 367, 470, 471
Edwards, Jonathan, 507–15
Efnard, 366
Egeria, 96–104
Egerton, Sir Thomas, 400
Egypt, 177

Eleazer, 59
Elegantiae, 287
Eleona, 97–8, 99, 100, 103
Eleutherius, 301
Eleutherus, Pope, 30
Elias the hermit, 72
Elias the prophet, 191
Elijah, 72, 93, 312, 330, 549, 557
Eliot, Andrew, 688
Eliot, George, xv, 591, 609–19
Eliot, Henry Ware, 688
Eliot, T. S., 688–94
Eliseus, 191
Elisha, 93
Elizabeth I, Queen of England, 335, 345, 358, 359, 367, 381, 384
Elohim, 412, 413
Elpis, 34
Emerson, Ralph Waldo, 585–90
Empedocles on Etna, 636
Enchiridion Militis Christiani, 288–9, 290, 356
England, 123, 167–72, 178
    Church of England, 448–50, 471, 482
    church history, 128, 129–33
    Normanization, 181
    Reformation, 275, 279, 334–44, 470
    see also Puritanism
English language, 275
Enlightenment, 482, 484–5, 486
Ennoea, 34
Enoch, 510, 557
envy, 15–16
Ephesians, 20
Ephesians, Epistle to the, 122, 391, 428
Ephraim, 368
Ephraim the Syrian, 75–80
Epiatola Cuthberti de obitu Bedae, 133
Epictetus, 408
Epicureanism, 49, 660
Epicurus, 5, 331
Epimenides, xi
Epiphanius, 364, 368, 370

episcopal system, 122, 123
Epithalamion, 345
Erasistratus, 49
Erasmus of Rotterdam, 133, 283, 287–98, 356
    Greek grammar translation, 284
    King James Version of the Bible, 365, 371
    and Luther, 301, 302
    monasticism, 287
    and Paul, 288, 292, 293
Erastianism, 571
Erfurt, 299
Esau, 15, 375
Esay *see* Isaiah
Eschylus, 446
"The Escorial," 656
An Essay in Aid of a Grammar of Assent, 582
An Essay on Conic Sections, 459
Essays and Reviews, 599
Essenes, 191
eternity, 498
Ethelbert, King of Kent, 131–2
Ethelred II, King, 167, 168
Euclid, 459, 540
Eunomius, 88, 89
Eusebius of Caesarea, 52–62, 362
Eustace de Rokayle, 229
evangelical revivals, 481, 499, 516, 527, 610, 611, 613–14
Evans, Mary Ann, 609
Evans, Robert, 609
Evarestus, 28
Eve
    "Blickling Homilist," 157–8
    Ignatius Loyola's *Spiritual Exercises*, 324
    "Junius Codex," 145–7, 148–9
    William Langland's *Piers Plowman*, 233, 234, 235, 238
The Everlasting Man, 680, 684–7
evil, 46
Exclusive Brethren, 748

exercitants, 323
"Exeter Book," 137, 151–4
Exodus, Book of
    Augustine of Hippo, 8
    Caedmon, 126
    John Donne's sermon, 404, 413
    "Junius Codex," 142
    Lancelot Andrewes' sermons, 389, 390, 391
    Martin Luther's "Letter on Translating the New Testament," 311
exorcisms, 84
experiential religion, 485
Ezekiel, Book of, 405, 413, 572
Ezra, 369

Fabian, bishop of Rome, 6
factionalism, 13
The Faerie Queene, 345, 437
Fairfax, Lord Thomas, 453
faith
    Anselm of Canterbury, 182
    Martin Luther, 303, 308–10
Faithful Narrative of the Surprising Works of God, 507
famine, 56–9
Farel, Guillaume, 327
fasting, 96
Faust, 641
The Fenwick Notes, 557, 562
Fermat, Pierre de, 459, 460
Ferrar, Nicolas, 420, 421
Fifteen Sermons Preached at the Rolls Chapel, 501
"First Letter to the Corinthians," 14–16
Fisher, Bishop, 338
Fitton, Mary, 398
Florence, 276
Forbush, William Byron, 336
Fortunatus, Venantius Honorius Clementianus, 115–17
The Four Loves, 708
The Four Quartets, 689
Fowre Hymnes, 345, 346–55
Fox, Dr., 337

Foxe, George, 336
Foxe, John, 334–44
Framley Parsonage, 592
France, 123, 178, 279
  see also French Revolution
Francis I, King of France, 327
Francis of Assisi, 179, 198–200,
  264, 679
Franciscans, 179–80, 199
Franks, 131, 175
Frederick I, Holy Roman
  Emperor, 179
Frederick II, Holy Roman
  Emperor, 198
Frederick the Wise, 300, 301
"Free Grace," 529–31
free will, 417–18
The Freedom of the Will, 508
French Revolution, 482–3, 550,
  565, 567
Freud, Sigmund, 689
Froben, Johannes, 289
From Ritual to Romance, 690
Fulbert, 187, 189–90, 192–3
"Funeral Oration on Meletius,"
  89–95
funerals, 476–7

Gabriel, 307
Gaisford, Thomas, 599
Galatians, Epistle to the
  Benjamin Jowett's
    "Interpretation of
    Scripture," 599, 602
  King James Version of the
    Bible, 371
  Lancelot Andrewes' sermons,
    389, 391
  Martin Luther, 300, 303,
    309
Galba, 55
Galen, 431
Galerius, 7
Gallus, Thomas, 221
"The Garden of Cyrus," 431
Gardiner, Dr., 337, 339
Gassendi, Pierre, 459
Gaudy Night, 695
"The General Confession,"
  472

"The General Thanksgiving,"
  472–3
*The Generation of Conic
  Sections*, 460
Genesis, Book of
  biblical image of a sister, 556
  Caedmon, 126
  humanity in image of God,
    419
  Irenaeus of Lyons' *Against
    all Heresies*, 41
  John Donne's sermon, 409,
    414, 415
  "Junius Codex," 142, 143–7
  King James Version of the
    Bible, 376–7
  Lancelot Andrewes' sermons,
    388, 389, 391, 393
  Milton's *Paradise Lost*, 441
  Newton's "Walking with
    God," 533–4
  Samuel Taylor Coleridge's
    "Religious Musings," 567
  Tyndale's translation, 357
  Vaughan's "Religion," 452
  Wordsworth's "Tintern
    Abbey," 556
Geneva, 280, 326, 327
Geneva Bible, 358
Genevan Academy, 280, 327
Gentile, Count, 198
Gerard, Roger, 287
"German Catechism," 313
Germanicus, 23
Germany, 178, 279, 280
  see also Luther, Martin
Gerson, Jean, 210, 264
Gesta Romanorum, 297
Gethsemane, 100
Ghibelline family, 212, 213
Gifford, Emma Lavinia, 648,
  649
Gildas, 171
Gillman, Anne, 564
Gillman, Dr. James, 564, 567
Ginger, You're Barmy, 739
Giovio, Paolo, 276
Gloucester, Duke of, 241
gnosis, 31
Gnosticism, 31, 37, 105

God, xii–xiii
  Aelfric's "Passion of St
    Edmund," 165
  Anselm of Canterbury's
    "Prayer to Christ," 182–5
  Athanasius of Alexandra's *de
    incarnatione*, 64–8
  Augustine of Hippo's
    Confessions, 106
  Bernard of Clairvaux's *On
    Loving God*, 195–7
  Caedmon, 127
  Celtic Christianity, 122
  Clement of Rome's "First
    Letter to Corinth," 14–15,
    16
  The Cloud of Unknowing,
    221, 224–5, 227–8
  C. S. Lewis' *Surprised by Joy*,
    707–8
  Cyril of Jerusalem's
    Catechetical Lectures, 82,
    84, 87
  "Deer's Cry," 134–6
  Defoe's *Robinson Crusoe*,
    489–95
  Dionysius the Pseudo-
    Areopagite, 731
  Dorothy L. Sayers' *Mind of
    the Maker*, 702–3
  Francis of Assisi's "Canticle
    of the Creatures," 199–200
  Fyodor Dostoevsky's *Brothers
    Karamazov*, 623–4
  "The General Thanksgiving,"
    472–3
  Henry Vaughan's "Religion,"
    450–2
  Ignatius of Antioch's "Letter
    to the Romans," 18–20
  Irenaeus of Lyons' *Against
    all Heresies*, 32, 37–41
  John Calvin's *Institutes of the
    Christian Religion*, 328–
    33
  John Chrysostom's *On the
    Incomprehensibility of God*,
    731
  John Donne's sermon,
    404–16

John Donne's "Wilt thou love God?," 418–19

John Keble's "National Apostasy," 571–9

John Newton's "Walking with God," 533–4

John Wesley's sermons, 518–19, 521–6

Jonathan Edwards' "Christian Pilgrim," 510, 511–15

Jonathan Edwards' *Treatise on Religious Affections*, 508–9

Julian of Norwich's *Revelations of Divine Love*, 247–50

"Junius Codex," 148–50

Justin Martyr, 5

King James Version of the Bible, 376–7

Martin Luther's "Letter on Translating the New Testament," 311–12

Martyrdom of Polycarp, 22

Pascal's *Pensées*, 461, 463, 464

Pelagian controversy, 10–11

R. S. Thomas' "Via Negativa," 731–2

Samuel Taylor Coleridge's "Religious Musings," 566

Sir Thomas Browne's *Religio Medici*, 431–5

Thomas à Kempis' *Imitation of Christ*, 265–7

William Langland's *Piers Plowman*, 230, 234

William Paley's *View of the Evidences of Christianity*, 541–3

Wulfstan's *Lupi Sermo ad Anglos*, 168–72

God and the Bible, 636

"God's Grandeur," 657–8

Goethe, Johann Wolfgang von, 641

gold, refining of, 84

The Golden Legend, 230

"The Goldyn Targe," 269

Golgotha, 97, 101

Good Friday, 101

Goodridge, J. F., 230

Gospel readings, *The Peregrination of Egeria*, 87, 97, 98, 99, 100, 101, 102, 103, 104

Gostwick, Sir G., 339

Goths, 175

Gournay, Marie de, 462

Grace Abounding to the Chief of Sinners, 467

Grand Inquisitor story, 621–32, 634

Gratian, 187, 372

Great Awakening, 481, 507

Great Schism, 176

"Greater Catechism," 313

Grebel, Conrad, 281

Greek culture, xi–xii, 5–6

Greene, Graham, 718–27

Gregorian Reform, 179

Gregory I, Pope, 121, 123, 129–30, 131, 165, 370

Gregory VII, Pope, 179

Gregory of Nazienzus, 88

Gregory of Nyssa, 88–95

Gregory of Rimini, 276

Gregory of Tours, 115

Grenville, Sir Richard, 381

Greville, Fulke, 345

Grey of Wilton, Lord, 345

Grindal, Edmund, 334, 335

Groote, Gerard, 263

Guelf family, 212

Guigo de Ponte, 210

H'm, 730

Haemmerlein, Thomas, 263

Haggai, Book of, 369, 389, 390

Haggard, Rider, 718

hagiographies, xiii

    The Life of Antony, 64, 69–74

    "The Passion of St Edmund," 161–6

Haigh-Wood, Vivien, 688

Hallward, Basil, 660

Hamlet, 397, 702, 705–6

Hampton Court Conference (1604), 358, 471

Hand, Jemima, 648

Handbook of the Christian Soldier (*Enchiridion*), 288–9, 290, 356

Handel, George Frederick, 376

Harding, Stephen, 194

Hardy, Thomas, xv, 648–55

Harley, Robert, 488

Harmony of the Gospels, 338

Harrold, C. F., 582

The Harvard Advocate, 688

Hathaway, Ann, 396

hatred, 45

Hauschein, Johann, 301

Hawkins, Edward, 580–1

Hayley, William, 547

He That Should Come, 696

The Heart of the Matter, 718

heaven, 511–15

Heavenly Hierarchy, 209

Hebrews, Epistle to

    Eusebius of Caesarea's *Ecclesiastical History*, 54

    George Herbert's sermon, 428

    John Donne's sermon, 403, 409

    Jonathan Edwards' sermon, 510

    Lancelot Andrewes' sermons, 388, 389, 395

    Martin Luther, 300

Hedone, 34

Heidelberg Catechism, 281

hell

    "Blickling Homilist," 156–8

    David Lodge's *How Far Can You Go?*, 740, 742

    Erasmus of Rotterdam's *Moriae Encomium*, 294

    "Junius Codex," 148–9

    William Langland's *Piers Plowman*, 233–4, 235–8

Heloise, 187–93

Helvidius, 362

hemistichs, 127, 138

Hennell, Charles, 609

Henosis, 34

Henry I, King of England, 182

Henry II, King of France, 446

Henry V, 397

Henry VI, Holy Roman Emperor, 179
Henry VII, King of England, 289
Henry VIII, King of England, 337, 338–40, 357, 367, 470, 552
Henry of Bergen, 287
Henry the Great, King of France, 339
Hentenius, 371
Heraclitus, 5
Herbert, George, xx, 420–9, 448, 656
Herbert, Magdalen Newport, 420
Herbert, Richard, 420
Heretics, 679
Hermas, 54
Hermitage, Catherine, 546
hermits, 201
Hermogenes, 362, 427
Herod
    Dorothy L. Sayers' *Mind of the Maker*, 704–5
    Dorothy L. Sayers' "The Man Born to be King," 698
    G. K. Chesterton's *The Everlasting Man*, 687
    King James Version of the Bible, 378
    Lancelot Andrewes' sermons, 388–9, 392
    Martyrdom of Polycarp, 23, 24, 28
Heseltine, Rose, 591
Hesychius, 365
Hezekias, 407
Hicks, John, 648
Hierome, Saint
    John Donne's sermon, 403, 412
    King James Version of the Bible, 362, 363, 365, 367, 368, 369, 370, 372, 373, 374
Hieronymous ab Oleastro, 371
Hilary of Poitiers, 8, 115, 176
Hilda, Abbess of Whitby, 124, 126

Hilton, Walter, 221, 247, 264
Hircius, 191
Historia Calamitatum, 187–93
The History of Calamities, 187–93
History of the English Church and Nation, 123, 128, 129–33
Hole, Helen G., 583
holiness (Martin Luther, *On Becoming Holy*), 316
Holland, 279
Holy Club, 443, 516, 527
Holy Dying, 442–7, 516
Holy Living, 442–3, 516
"Holy Sonnets," 420
Holy Spirit, 36, 37, 197
Holy Week, 96–104
"Holy Week at Genoa," 660
Homer, xi, 434, 519
homilies, xiii
    "Blickling Homilist," 155–60
    Lupi Sermo ad Anglos, 168–72
    "The Passion of St Edmund," 161–6
Honorius II, Pope, 195
Hopkins, Catherine, 656
Hopkins, Gerald Manley, 656–8
Hopkins, Manley, 656
Horace, 296, 297
"Horatian Ode upon Cromwell's Return from Ireland," 453
Horos, 35, 36
Horothetes, 36
Hortensius, 108
Hosea, Book of, 208, 575
"How I Built Myself a House," 648
How Far Can You Go?, 739–46
Hugh of Balma, 210–11
Hugo, Victor, 623
Humanae Vitae, 741, 744–5
humanism, 276, 277–8, 283–4, 301
    see also Erasmus of Rotterdam
humanity
    effects of Adam and Christ upon, 424

    fall of, 143
    as image of God, 419
    Pelagian controversy, 10–11
humility
    Clement of Rome's "First Letter to Corinth," 13, 14–16
    Thomas à Kempis' *Imitation of Christ*, 266, 267
Huss, Jan, 301
Hutchinson, Mary, 551
Hutchinson, Sara, 563
Huxley, Aldous, 692
"Hydriotaphia, or Urn Burial," 430
"Hymne of Heavenly Beautie," 347–55
"Hymne of Heavenly Love," 346–7
hymns, xiii
    "Caedmon's hymn," 123–4, 126–7, 134, 138
    Charles Wesley, 527–31
    "Deer's Cry," 134–6
    "The Dream of Gerontius," 582–4
    Fowre Hymnes, 345, 346–55
    "Free Grace," 529–31
    Isaac Watts, 499–50
    John Henry Newman, 582–4
    John Newton, 532–8
    Joseph Addison, 496
    "Light Shining out of Darkness," 535–6
    "Love Divine," 528–9
    "The Negro's Complaint," 536–7
    Olney Hymns, 532–8
    The Peregrination of Egeria, 97, 98, 99, 100, 102, 103, 104
    "Praise for the Fountain Opened," 534–5
    "St Patrick's Breastplate," 122, 134–6
    Venantius Honorius Clementianus Fortunatus, 115–17
    "Vextilla regis prodeunt," 116–17

"Walking with God," 533–4
"When all thy mercies, O my God," 496
"When I survey the wondrous cross," 499–500

"I Have a Dream," 734, 735–8
Iamblicus, 88
Idea of Progress, 689
The Idea of a University, 582
The Idiot, 620
Ignatius of Antioch, 17–20
ignorance, 45–6
Iliad, 704
illumination, way of, 210, 211
Illustrated London News, 679
Images of Both Churches, 334
imagination, 486
Imbomon, 98, 100, 103
Imitation of Christ, 264–8, 516
immanentism, 683
The Importance of Being Earnest, 659
"In Church," 730
incarnation, 64–8, 290, 684–7
incest, 44
indulgences, 300
infanticide, 44
Inferno, 213, 214–16
Ingham, Benjamin, 527
Innocent II, Pope, 195
Innocent III, Pope, 179, 264
Inquiry into the Origins of Christianity, 609
Institutes of the Christian Religion, 281, 286, 326, 328–33
intellect, 324
intellectuals, 266
International Journal of Psycho-Analysis, 689
"The Interpretation of Scripture," 599–608
"Intimations of Immortality," 551, 557–62
Iona, 122, 123
Ireland, 121–3
Irenaeus of Lyons, 4, 28, 30–42

Irenee, Saint, 367
Isaac, 475, 510
Isaiah, 68, 363, 387, 388, 389, 390, 392, 412
Isaiah, Book of
    Bernard of Clairvaux's *On Loving God*, 197
    "Book of Common Prayer" (BCP), 472
    Dorothy L. Sayers' "The Man Born to be King," 699–700
    George Herbert's sermon, 428
    John Calvin's *Institutes of the Christian Religion*, 330
    John Donne's sermon, 407, 412, 413
    Lancelot Andrewes' sermons, 386, 387, 388, 390
    William Dunbar's "Rorate coeli desuper," 270
Isidore, 366
Isidorus Clarius, 371
Islam, 175–6
Italy, Renaissance, 275–9
Ittai, 391
Ivar, 161, 162–3

Jacob
    Clement of Rome's "First Letter to Corinth," 15
    Gregory of Nyssa's "Funeral Oration on Meletius," 90–1
    Jonathan Edwards' "Christian Pilgrim," 510, 511
    King James Version of the Bible, 363, 364
    Lancelot Andrewes' sermons, 389
    Martin Luther's "Letter on Translating the New Testament," 311
Jacob, Bishop of Nisibis, 75
Jacobines, 295
James I, King of England, 358, 381, 384, 385, 401, 420, 471
James I, King of Scotland, 270

James IV, King of Scotland, 269
James, Epistle of, 343, 386
James, Saint, 55, 60, 375
James, son of Zebedee, 55, 393, 698–700
Jansen, Cornelius, 460
Jansenism, 461
Jarrow, 128
jealousy, 15
Jehovah, 357, 412–13
Jenkyns, Richard, 598
Jeremiah, 93
Jeremiah, Book of, 389, 413, 428
Jeremy, 404
Jerome, Saint
    classical literature, xii
    death of Irenaeus of Lyons, 30
    Erasmus of Rotterdam, 287, 293
    Peter Abelard's *History of Calamities*, 189, 190–1, 192
    translation of Bible, 282, 304
Jerusalem, 9, 10
Jerusalem churches, 96–104
Jesse, 392
Jesuits, 282, 461, 626, 632
Jesus Christ, xiii
    Aelfric's "Passion of St Edmund," 165
    Andrew Marvell's "The Coronet," 456–8
    Anselm of Canterbury's "Prayer to Christ," 182–5
    Arian controversy, 10
    Athanasius of Alexandria's *de incarnatione*, 63–8
    beatitudes, 379–80
    Benjamin Jowett's *Commentaries on the Epistles of St Paul*, 599
    Benjamin Jowett's "Interpretation of Scripture," 603, 606
    "Blickling Homilist," 156–8
    The Cloud of Unknowing, 222–8

"Deer's Cry," 135, 136
Dorothy L. Sayers' "The Man Born to be King," 696, 701
"The Dream of the Rood," 138–40
Eusebius of Caesarea's *Ecclesiastical History,* 59–61
Fyodor Dostoevsky's *Brothers Karamazov,* 621–32, 634
George Herbert's "Easter," 423–4
George Herbert's "Redemption," 422–3
Ignatius of Antioch's "Letter to the Romans," 19–20
Ignatius Loyola's *Spiritual Exercises,* 324
Irenaeus of Lyons' *Against all Heresies,* 32, 36, 37
John Wesley's sermons, 524
"Junius Codex," 142, 147–50
Justin Martyr, 5
King James Version of the Bible, 378–80
Lancelot Andrewes' sermons, 385–95
Ludolf of Saxony's *Life of Christ,* 218–20
Martyrdom of Polycarp, 22, 24–5, 27, 28
parables of the kingdom, 76
Peter Abelard, 186
soldier's casting of lots for the clothes of, 449–50
Thomas à Kempis' *Imitation of Christ,* 265–6
Valentinianism, 32, 37
water into wine miracle, 452, 476
William Langland's *Piers Plowman,* 231–2, 235–8
York Mystery Plays, 253–62
"Jesus shall reign wher'er the sun," 499
Jesus, son of Ananias, 61–2
Jethro, 391
Joash, 368

Job, 91, 233, 404
Job, Book of, 305, 330, 391, 404, 477, 602
John XXIII, Pope, 739–40, 741
John the Baptist, 68, 364, 697, 698–700
John, Bishop of Sevil, 366
John of Damascus, 176
John, First Letter of, 284
John of Gaunt, 240, 241
John, Gospel of
    Bernard of Clairvaux's *On Loving God,* 196, 197
    Dorothy L. Sayers' "The Man Born to be King," 697, 701–2
    John Donne's sermon, 416
    King James Version of the Bible, 362
    Lancelot Andrewes' sermons, 388, 391, 392, 394, 395
    Martin Luther's "Letter on Translating the New Testament," 308
    The Peregrination of Egeria, 102
    soldier's casting of lots for the clothes of Jesus Christ, 449–50
    Vaughan's "Religion," 452
    water into wine miracle, 452, 476
John, Saint, 41, 53, 191, 219, 393, 395, 697–701
John, Second Letter of, 393
John Trevisa, 366
Johnson Brethren, 751–2
Johnson, Joseph, 546
Jonah, 16, 80
Jonah, Book of, 390
Jonas, 390
Jones, Robert, 550
Joseph of Arimathea, 102, 392, 548
Joseph (husband of Mary), 219, 378–9
Joseph (son of Jacob), 15, 404, 433
Josephus, 56, 57, 58, 191
Joshua, Book of, 391

"The Journey of the Magi," 689, 692–4
Jovian, Emperor, 75
Jovinianus, 190, 192
Jowett, Benjamin, 485, 598–608, 656
Joyce, James, 689
Judaism, 3, 9
Judas Iscariot, 99, 306–7, 697–700
Jude the Obscure, 649–55
Judea, 9
Judges, Book of, 330, 368
Judith, 204, 205
Julian, Emperor (Flavius Claudius Julianus), 75, 88, 362
Julian laws, 50
Julian of Norwich, 201, 246–51
"Junius Codex," 142–50
Junius, Francis, 142
Jupiter, 294
justification, 280, 303, 308–10
Justin II, Emperor, 116
Justin Martyr, 4, 5, 44, 362
Justinian, 364

Karelia region, 177
Keats, John, 486
Keble, John, 570–9, 581
Keillor, Garrison, 747–52
The Kellys and the O'Kellys, 591
Kennedy, John F., 734
Kennedy, Robert, 740
Kiev, 177
King, Edward, 436
King Lear, 397–8
King, Martin Luther, Jr., 733–8
King, Martin Luther Sr., 733
Kings, Books of, 312, 390, 391, 407, 549
"The King's Herald," 697
Knights Templar, 195
Knox, John, 334
koinonia, 11
Kristeller, Paul Oskar, 278
"Kubla Khan," 564

Lacedaemonians, 50
Lactantius, 8

Lady Lilith, 641
Lady Windermere's Fan, 659
laity, 288–9
Lake Wobegon Days, 747–52
Lamentations, Book of, 404
Lanfranc, 179, 181
Langland, Colette, 229, 239
Langland, Kit, 229, 239
Langland, William, 229–39
Langsdale, Phoebe, 442
language, 586–90
Language of Fiction, 739
Lanier, Emilia, 398
Laodicea, 184
Lascaris, Constantine, 284
Lasius, Balthasar, 328
The Last Chronicle of Barset, 592
Last Essays on Church and Religion, 636
Last, Isaac, 648
Latimer, Hugh, 340, 343
Laud, Archbishop William, 384, 436, 442, 454, 455
Law, William, 516
The Lawless Roads, 718
Lawrence, 165, 203
Lay Sermons, 564
Lazarium, 96, 97, 103
Lazarus, 96, 235, 393
Lefèvre d'Etaples, Jacques, 284
Leibniz, Gottfried Wilhelm von, 460, 589
Leicester, Earl of, 345
Leipzig Disputation, 301
Lenden, Dr., 339
Lent, 82
Leo X, Pope, 290, 371
Leo XIII, Pope, 207, 582
Leofric, 151
Leofstan, 165
"Lesser Catechism," 313–21
lesson reading, 97, 98, 100, 102
Letter Concerning Toleration, 482
Letter of Cuthbert on the Death of Bede, 133
"Letter to the Romans," 17–20
"Letter on Translating the New Testament," 303–12

letter writing, 278
Lewes, George Henry, 591, 610
Lewis, C. S., xix, 498, 641, 647, 680, 702, 707–17
Lewis, Warren, 707
liberalism, 680–4
The Liberty of a Christian, 302
Library of the Fathers, 76
The Life of Antony, 64, 69–74
The Life of Christ, 218–20, 322
Life of St Cuthbert, 128
"Light Shining out of Darkness," 535–6
Lilith, 641–7
Lindisfarne Abbey, 6, 123, 124
Linnaeus, 587
Linus, 53, 55
The Lion, the Witch and the Wardrobe, 647
literacy, 124
Literature and Dogma, 636
"The Little Instruction Book," 313–21
liturgies, xiii, 96–104, 162
Lives of the Saints, 161
Lloyd, Constance, 659
Locke, John, 482, 484, 502
Lodge, David, 739–46
Logos, 5
Logos (Aeon), 34, 37
Lollards, 335
Longfellow, Henry Wadsworth, 214
Longinus, 230, 232
Lonsdale, Lord, 550, 551
Lord's Prayer, 316–18
lorica, 134
Louis XVI, King of France, 483
Louis XVIII, King of France, 483
love, 226–8
"Love," 425–6
"Love Divine," 528–9
love-feasts, 44
Loyola, Ignatius, 322–5
lucernare, 97, 98
Lucian, 365, 443
Lucifer, 148, 235–8
Lucilius, 191

Luder, Hans, 299
Ludolf of Saxony, 218–20, 322
Luidhard, Bishop, 131
Luke, 54–5, 307, 393
Luke, Gospel of
    Bernard of Clairvaux's *On Loving God*, 195, 196
    "Blickling Homilist," 159
    Christmas story, 378–9
    The Cloud of Unknowing, 222
    Eusebius of Caesarea's *Ecclesiastical History*, 54–5
    John Donne's sermon, 407, 415
    John Keble's sermon, 575
    Jonathan Edwards' *Treatise on Religious Affections*, 509
    King James Version of the Bible, 362, 378–9
    Lancelot Andrewes' sermons, 386, 387, 390, 391
    Martin Luther's "Lesser Catechism," 320
    Sacrament of the altar, 320
Lupi Sermo ad Anglos, 129, 168–72
Luther, Martin, 279, 280, 285, 299–321, 328, 470
    Benjamin Jowett's "Interpretation of Scripture," 601
    church as *Gemeinde*, 476
    faith, 303, 308–10
    George Eliot's *Scenes of Clerical Life*, 614
    importance of printing, 288
    John Foxe's *Acts and Monuments*, 341
Lutheran Reformation, 279–80
Lycidas, 436
Lycurgus, 50
Lydgate, John, 270
Lynceus, 291
lyrical ballads, xv
Lyrical Ballads, xii, 550, 551, 563
Lytrotes, 36

Macaria, 34
Macariotes, 34

The Macdermots of Ballycloran, 591

MacDonald, George, 640–7

MacDonald, Greville, 641

MacDonald, Mary Josephine, 641

Macmillan, Alexander, 648

magic, 277

Malcolm X, 734

Maldon, Battle of, 167

Malleolus, 263

The Man Born to be King, 696–702

Mani, 105

Manicheans, 105, 111

Manning, Bernard L., 529

Marburg, Colloquy of, 302

Marcion, 5, 38

Marcus, 28

Marcus the magician, 37

Marius Victorinus, 8

Mark, Gospel of, 117, 306–7, 319, 320, 410

marriage
  "Book of Common Prayer" (BCP), 473–6
  David Lodge's *How Far Can You Go?*, 741–5

marriage feast, 83

Marshall, Stephen, 436

Martha, 222–6

Martin, Dr., 340

Martin of Tours, Saint, 115, 132, 299

martyrdom
  Ignatius of Antioch, 17–20
  Polycarp, 21–9

Martyrdom of Polycarp, 21–9

martyrium, 96, 97–8, 99, 102, 103

Marvell, Andrew, 453–8

Marx, Karl, 704

Mary I, Queen of England, 334, 335, 340, 341, 342, 381, 471

Mary, daughter of Eleazer, 59

Mary Magdalene, 219, 247, 307, 404

Mary (Martha's sister), 222–7

Mary, mother of Jesus, 140, 157–8, 219, 233, 307, 378–9

Mary, sister of Lazarus, 97

matter, 5

Matthew, Gospel of
  Aelfric's "Passion of St Edmund," 165
  baptism, 319
  beatitudes, 379–80
  Bernard of Clairvaux's *On Loving God*, 195, 196
  binding of Satan, 419
  "Blickling Homilist," 160
  Christmas story, 378
  Dorothy L. Sayers' "The Man Born to be King," 697
  Ephraim the Syrian's "Pearl," 76, 80
  John Donne's sermon, 404, 405, 413, 414, 415
  Jonah, 80
  King James Version of the Bible, 362, 378, 379–80, 419
  kingdom of heaven, 76
  Lancelot Andrewes' sermons, 385, 391, 392, 395
  Martin Luther's "Lesser Catechism," 319, 320
  Martin Luther's "Letter on Translating the New Testament," 304, 306–7, 311

The Peregrination of Egeria, 99

sacrament of the altar, 320

Thomas Aquinas' *Summa Theologiae*, 209

Tyndale's translation, 357

Maurice, 129

Maxentius, 7

Mayflower, 454

The Mayor of Casterbridge, 649

Mediaeval Hymns and Sequences, 116

meditation
  Ignatius Loyola's *Spiritual Exercises*, 323–5

John Donne's *Divine Meditations*, 416–19

Melanchthon, Philipp, 279, 284, 300, 301, 305, 328

Meletius of Antioch, 89–95

memory, 324

Menander, xi

Mercy, 230, 233

Mere Christianity, 708, 709

Mersenne, Marin, 459

Messiah, 376

Metagoges, 36

metaphors, 208–9

Methodism, 485, 516, 527

Methodius, 177, 366

Metricos, 34, 319

Micah, Book of, 388

Michael de Massa, 219

Michael, Saint, 159

Michelangelo, 689

Micrologus, 370

Middlemarch, 610

Milan, 10

The Mill on the Floss, 610

millenarianism, 168, 565

Milton, 547–9

Milton, John, xii, 230, 436–41
  and Andrew Marvell, 453
  "Junius Codex," 142
  Lilith, 641
  omnific quality of God, 566
  and William Blake, 546, 547

Milvian Bridge, 7

The Mind of the Maker, 696, 702–6

Minerva, 192

Minims, 295, 459

The Minister, 728, 729

Minors, 295

miracles, 621, 622, 629–30, 680, 683–4

Miracles, 708

Miriam, 15

missionaries, 122–3, 177, 178

Mixis, 34

The Modes of Modern Writing, 739

monasticism, 11–12, 122–3, 124, 177, 178–9
  Athanasius of Alexandra's *Life of Antony*, 69–74
  Augustine of Hippo's *Confessions*, 107
  Bernard of Clairvaux, 194–5
  Erasmus of Rotterdam, 287
  Heloise, 187
  Martin Luther, 299
  Peter Abelard, 187
  Thomas à Kempis, 263–4
  see also Benedictine community; Cistercians
Monica, 104, 106, 114
Monogenes, 34, 35, 36
Monologian, 182
Montagu, Basil, 564
Montaigne, Michel Eyquem de, 462
Montanism, 30, 43
Monte Cassino, 11, 207
The Month, 582
Moral Philosophy, 540
morality, 288
Moravia, 177
More, Anne, 400
More, Sir George, 400
More, Sir Thomas, 287, 289–90, 338, 400
Morgan, Lucy, 398
Moriae Encomium, 289–98
"Morning," 570
Morris, John Brand, 76
Morton, Reverend Charles, 487
Morton, Thomas, 400
Moscow, 177–8
Moses
  Augustine of Hippo, 8
  Benjamin Jowett's "Interpretation of Scripture," 606
  Clement of Rome's "First Letter to Corinth," 15
  Irenaeus of Lyons' *Against all Heresies*, 41
  John Donne's sermon, 407
  King James Version of the Bible, 361

Lancelot Andrewes' sermons, 389, 390, 393
  Sir Thomas Browne's *Religio Medici*, 433
  William Langland's *Piers Plowman*, 234
Moule, Henry, 648
Moule, Horace, 648
Mount of Olives, 98, 100
Mulcaster, Richard, 345
Müller, John, of Konigsberg, 435
Murder Must Advertise, 695
"Musica Ecclesiastica," 264
Mydorge, Claude, 459
Mylonand, 459
mystery, 621, 622, 629, 630–1
mystery plays, 155, 252–62
mysticism, 221

Naaman the Syrian, 391
Napoleon, 483
"National Apostasy," 571–9, 581
National Association for the Advancement of Colored People, 733
Natural Theology, 539, 540
Nature, 585, 586–90
nature
  Celtic Christianity, xx, 122
  Sir Thomas Browne's *Religio Medici*, 431–5
  William Paley, 539–40, 541–2
"The Navigation of St. Brendan," 123
Nazarites, 191
Nazianzen, 372, 375
Neale, John Mason, 116
Nebridius, 106
Nebuchadnezzar, 413
"The Negro's Complaint," 536–7
Nehemiah, 367
Nero, 55, 369
The New Life, 212
New Poems (Matthew Arnold), 637

New Testament, 279, 284, 288, 289
  in English, 356
  in German, 302, 303–12
Newcomen, Matthew, 436
Newman, Jemima, 580
Newman, John, 580
Newman, John Henry, 570, 580–4, 637, 656
Newton, John, 532–8
Newton, Sir Isaac, 460, 498
Nicea, Council of, 10, 75, 176
Nicetes, 24, 27
Nicholls, Eliza, 648
Nicodemus, Gospel of, 230
Nicolas I, Pope, 363
Nicolas III, Pope, 370
Nietzsche, Friedrich, 622, 704
Nimrod, 391
The Nine Tailors, 696
Ninety-Five Theses, 280, 300–1
"Ninety-Six Sermons," 384–95
Ninevites, 16
Ninian, 121
Nisibis, 75
Noah, 16, 86, 389, 510
nominalists, 291
Nordic sagas, 6
Noriega, Manuel, 719
Normanization, 181
North Africa, 9, 10
Nottingham Journal, 718
Nous, 34, 35, 36, 37
novels, 9
Novum Instrumentum omne, 284, 289
Numbers, Book of, 388, 389, 390, 392
Nuttall, P. Austin, 648

"O God, our help in ages past," 499
obedience, Clement of Rome, 14
oblation, 97, 99, 103
Occamists, 291, 293
Ode on the Morning of Christ's Nativity, 436
Oecolampadius, 301

Of Reformation touching Church Discipline in England, 436
Ogdoad, 34
Oglethorpe, James, 516
"The Old Vicarage, Grantchester," 692
Olney Hymns, 532–8
A l'ombre des jeunes filles, 689
On the Freedom of a Christian, 301
"On the Greatness and Littleness of Human Life," 582
"On Hearing the *Dies Irae* Sung In The Sistine Chapel," 660
"On the impressions of divine power and wisdom in the Universe," 496
On the Incomprehensibility of God, 731
On Loving God, 195–7
On Mystical Theology, 221
ontological argument, 182
Op. 1, 695
Open Brethren, 748, 751
Optatus, 8
orgies, 44
Origen, 4, 53, 288, 364, 370, 373
Ornan the Jebusite, 390
Orthodox Christianity, 177
Orthodoxy, 680–4
Ossiander, Andreas, 338
Oswyn, 164
Otho, 55
Ovid, 651, 690
Owen, John, 281
Oxenbridge, John, 454
Oxford Movement, 336, 570, 581, 651

Pachomius, 11
Pagnine, 371
Paine, Tom, 546
Paiva, 371
Palestine, 9
Paley, William, 539–45

Palladius, 122
Pallas, 294
Palm Sunday, 97–8, 230, 231
Pamelius, 370
Pamphilius, 52
pantheism, 683
papacy, 176, 179, 483
Papian laws, 50
Paracletus, 34
Paradise Lost, 142, 230, 437–41, 546, 641
Paradise Regained, 437, 546
Paris, 283
Paris University, 178
Parker Society, 336
Parks, Rosa, 733
"The Parting of Friends," 581
Pascal, Blaise, 459–66, 498
Pascal, Etienne, 459
Pascaline, 459
Paschal vigils, 103
Passio Sancti Eadmundi, 162
"The Passion of St Edmund," 161–6
"The Passionate Man's Pilgrimage," 382–3
Passover, 357
pastoral letters, 14
Pater, Walter, 659
"Patience," 659
Patrick, Saint, 121–2, 134
Paul II, Pope, 374
Paul VI, Pope, 740, 741
Paul, Saint, xi, 9
  armor of God, 122
  Athanasius of Alexandra's *Life of Antony*, 72
  Athanasius of Alexandria's *de incarnatione*, 66
  Augustine of Hippo's *Confessions*, 106
  charity, 380
  Christianity and Judaism, 3
  Clement of Rome's "First Letter to Corinth," 15–16
  Cyril of Jerusalem's *Catechetical Lectures*, 84
  David Lodge's *How Far Can You Go?*, 742

  effects of Adam and Christ on humanity, 424
  Erasmus of Rotterdam, 288, 292, 293
  Eusebius of Caesarea's *Ecclesiastical History*, 53, 54, 55
  factionalism, 13
  George Herbert's sermon, 428
  God, 41
  Gospel of Luke, 55
  Gregory of Nyssa's "Funeral Oration on Meletius," 94
  human body as a temple, 422
  human corpse as seed, 587
  human sexuality, 742
  Ignatius of Antioch's "Letter to the Romans," 19
  illness, 251
  Irenaeus of Lyons' *Against all Heresies*, 31, 32, 41
  John Foxe's *Acts and Monuments*, 337
  John Wesley's sermons, 523–4
  King James Version of the Bible, 371, 380
  Lancelot Andrewes' sermons, 392, 393
  love of neighbours, 523–4
  Martin Luther's "Lesser Catechism," 319, 320
  Martin Luther's "Letter on Translating the New Testament," 303, 305, 308–9, 310
  Ralph Waldo Emerson's *Nature*, 587
  recall of converts, 544–5
  sacrament of the altar, 320
  symbolization of marriage, 476
  teaching of secret wisdom, 31, 32
  William Paley's *View of the Evidences of Christianity*, 544–5
Paulus Diaconus, 366

Peace, 230, 233–4, 238
The Pearl, 76–80
Peasants' War, 302
Pelagian controversy, 10–11
Pella, 55
Pelop, 444
Pensées, 460, 461–6
Il Penseroso, 436
Perea, 55
The Peregrination of Egeria,
  96–104
Perkins, William, 281
persecution, 4, 6–7, 10
Pesah, 357
Peter, Epistles of, 53–4, 387,
  389, 392
Peter Lombard, 207
Peter, Saint, 13
  Clement of Rome's "First
    Letter to Corinth," 15
  Erasmus of Rotterdam's
    Moriae Encomium, 291,
    292, 293
  Eusebius of Caesarea's
    Ecclesiastical History, 53, 54
  G. K. Chesterton's *The*
    Everlasting Man, 682
  Ignatius of Antioch's "Letter
    to the Romans," 19
  Lancelot Andrewes' sermons,
    393
  "The Passion of St Edmund,"
    163
  William Langland's *Piers*
    Plowman, 235
Peter the Venerable, 187
Petilian, 362
Petronius, 446
Phadeo, 88
Phaedrus, 88
Phantastes, 641
Pharaoh, 511
Pharisees, 67, 191
Philip II, King of Spain, 433
Philip the Asiarch, 25
Philip of Hesse, 302
Philip the Trallian, 28
Philippians, Epistle to, 199,
  346, 393, 428
Philomelium, 21–9

philosophy, 5, 44, 191–2, 277
Philotheus of Pskov, 178
Phrynis, 368
The Picture of Dorian Gray,
  659, 660
Piers Plowman, 155, 229–39
Pietà (collection of poetry),
  728
Pietà (Michelangelo), 689
"Pietà" (poem), 729–30
Pietism, 485
Pietro de Bernadone, 198
Pilate, Pontius, 101, 102, 231,
  704
pilgrimages, 241, 467–9,
  510–15
The Pilgrim's Progress, 230,
  467–9, 708
The Pilgrim's Regress, 708, 714
Pindar, 444
Pionius, 28–9
Pisa, Council of, 179
Pistis, 34
Pius IV, Pope, 366–7
Pius V, Pope, 371
Plato, xi, 660
  David Lodge's *How Far Can*
    You Go?, 742
  Dorothy L. Sayers' *Mind of*
    the Maker, 704
  G. K. Chesterton's *The*
    Everlasting Man, 686
  Gregory of Nyssa, 88
  John Donne's sermon, 408
  Ralph Waldo Emerson's
    Nature, 589
  Tertullian, 5
Platonism, 5, 8, 9, 44, 49, 277,
  484
Platter, Thomas, 328
Pleroma, 34, 36, 37, 38–9
Pliny, 47
Plotinus, 88
Plutarch, 369
Plymouth Brethren, 747
"A Poem upon the Death of
  O. C.," 453
Poems (Matthew Arnold), 636
Poems in Two Volumes
  (Wordsworth), 551

poetry, xi, xiv
  accentual-syllabic verse, 127,
    138
  Addison's "Ode," 497–8
  "And Did those Feet?,"
    547–9
  Andrew Marvell, 453–8
  Anglo-Saxon, 123–4, 126–7,
    133, 137–41
  "The Ballad of Reading
    Gaol," 660, 661–78
  "Batter my heart," 417–18
  Bede, 133
  Beowulf, xx, 124, 437
  "Bermudas," 454–6
  "The British Church,"
    448–50
  "Caedmon's hymn," 123–4,
    126–7, 134, 138
  "Canticle of the Creatures,"
    199–200
  "The Coronet," 456–8
  Dante Aligheri, 212–17, 230,
    696
  "Death be not Proud,"
    416–17
  "Death Song," 128, 133
  "Deer's Cry," 134–6
  Divine Comedy, 212, 213–17,
    230, 546, 696
  Divine Meditations, 416–19
  "Dover Beach," 599, 637–
    9
  "The Dream of Gerontius,"
    582–4
  "The Dream of the Rood,"
    124, 137–41
  "Easter," 423–4
  Edmund Spenser, 346–55
  Ephraim the Syrian, 76–80
  Francis of Assisi, 199–200
  George Herbert, 420–6
  Gerald Manley Hopkins,
    656–8
  "God's Grandeur," 657–8
  Henry Vaughan, 448–52
  "Hymne of Heavenly
    Beautie," 347–55
  "Hymne of Heavenly Love,"
    346–7

"Intimations of Immortality,"
551, 557–62
John Donne, 416–19
John Henry Newman, 582–4
John Keble, 570
John Milton, 436–41
Joseph Addison, 497–8
"The Journey of the Magi,"
689, 692–4
"Junius Codex," 143–7
"Love," 425–6
Matthew Arnold, 599, 636–9
metaphors, 208, 209
"The Navigation of St.
Brendan," 123
Oscar Wilde, 660–78
Paradise Lost, 142, 230,
437–41, 546, 641
"The Passionate Man's
Pilgrimage," 382–3
"The Pearl," 76–80
"Pietà," 729–30
"Prayer," 424–5
Ralph Waldo Emerson,
585–6
"Redemption," 422
"Religion," 450–2
"Religious Musings," 565–7
"Rorate coeli desuper,"
270–2
R. S. Thomas, 728–32
"St Patrick's Breastplate,"
122, 134–6
Samuel Taylor Coleridge,
563, 565–7
Sir Walter Ralegh, 382–3
"Sonnet 146," 398
terza rima, 213, 214
*The Temple: Sacred Poems and
Personal Ejaculations*,
421–6
"Tintern Abbey," 551–6
T. S. Eliot, 688–94
Venantius Honorius
Clementianus Fortunatus,
115–17
"Vextilla regis prodeunt,"
116–17
"Via Negativa," 730–2

The Waste Land, 688,
689–92
William Blake, 546–9
William Dunbar, 269, 270–2
William Shakespeare, 398
William Wordsworth, 550–62
"Wilt thou love God?,"
418–19
"Poetry with Reference to
Aristotle's Poetics," 582
Poetry for Supper, 728
Poitiers, 115, 116
Pole, Dr., 342
polemical writing, 31
Polycarp, 17–18, 21–9, 30
Ponticianus, 106–8
The Poor Man and the Lady,
648
Porphyry, 88
Portinari, Beatrice, 212, 213
Postel, 366
"Postscript," 731
Pothinus, 30
Potken, 366
poverty, 198, 199
Powell, Louisa, 640, 641
The Power and the Glory, 718,
719–27
"A Prairie Come Home," 747
Praise of Folly, 289–98
"Praise for the Fountain
Opened," 534–5
"Prayer," 424–5
Prayer Books, 470–1
"A Prayer to Christ," 182–5
prayers, xiii, xiv
Anselm of Canterbury's
"Prayer to Christ," 182–5
"Book of Common Prayer"
(BCP), 358, 470–7, 690
Cyril of Jerusalem's
Catechetical Lectures, 87
Holy Week, 97, 98, 99, 100,
102, 103, 104
Julian of Norwich, 247, 250
Lord's Prayer, 316–18
Martin Luther's "Lesser
Catechism," 321

The Peregrination of Egeria,
97, 98, 99, 100, 102, 103,
104
Preface to Paradise Lost, 708
The Prelude, 551, 564
Presbyterians, 280
*A Priest to the Temple: or the
Country Parson*, 421,
427–9
The Princess and Curdie, 641
The Princess and the Goblin, 641
printed books, 278, 288
Proarche, 34, 38
probability, 502
"The Problem," 586
The Problem of Pain, 708
Procatechesis, 82–7
Proon, 38
Propator, 34, 35, 37
Prophetical Writings, 102, 330
Proslogion, 182
Protestant Reformation, 282
Calvinist, 280–1
England, 275, 279, 334–44,
470
Lutheran, 279–80
Radical, 281
Prothalamion, 345
Proust, Marcel, 689
Proverbs, Book of, 165, 387,
404
Provincial Letters, 461
*Prufrock and Other
Observations*, 688
psalms, 97, 102, 103
Psalms, Book of, 284
Addison's Ode on Psalm 19,
497–8
Addison's paraphrase of
Psalm 23, 496
Anselm of Canterbury's
"Prayer to Christ," 184
Benjamin Jowett's
"Interpretation of
Scripture," 606
Bernard of Clairvaux's *On
Loving God*, 195, 196
"Blickling Homilist," 156
Hugh of Balma's *Roads to
Zion*, 211

John Donne's sermon,
    402–16
John Keble's sermon, 577
King James Version of the
    Bible, 377, 497
Lancelot Andrewes' sermons,
    386, 387, 388, 389, 390,
    392, 394, 395
Martin Luther, 300
Wordsworth's "Tintern
    Abbey," 556
"Pseudodoxia Epidemica, or
    Enquiries into Vulgar
    Errors," 430
Ptolemaeus, 33
Ptolemy Philadelph, 364, 368
Pupillus, 361
Puritanism, 281
    Andrew Marvell, 453
    Henry Vaughan's "British
        Church," 448–50
    John Bunyan, 467
    John Foxe's *Acts and
        Monuments*, 336
    John Milton, 436
    King James Version of the
        Bible, 358, 369, 375
    Marvell's "Bermudas," 454–6
    Prayer Book, 471
The Pursuit of the Well-Beloved,
    649
Pusey, Edward Bouverie, 570
Pysche, 713
Pythagoras, 192, 589, 686
Pythagorean Tetrad, 34
Pythagoreans, 49

Quadragesima, 98
Queensbury, Marquess of, 660
The Quiet American, 719
Quintus the Apostate, 23

Rachel, 389
racial segregation, 733–4
Radegunde, Saint, 116
Radevile, Lord, 366
Radical Reformation, 281
Radulphus de Rivo, 370
Ragnar Lothbrok, 161
Rahab the Canaanite, 391

Ralegh, Sir Walter, 345, 381–3
Ramus, Peter, 437
Rastislav, 177
rationalism, 484–5
Ravenna, 659
Ray, John, 540
Reagan, Ronald, 719
realists, 291
reality, 486
reason, 182, 486, 502, 587
*The Reason of Church
    Government urged against
    Prelacy*, 436
Reasonableness of Christianity,
    484, 502
Rebecca, 475
reconciliation, Clement of
    Rome's "First Letter to
    Corinth," 14–16
"Redemption," 422
redemption
    George Herbert's
        "Redemption," 422–3
    Irenaeus of Lyons' *Against
        all Heresies*, 37
    Martin Luther's "Lesser
        Catechism," 316
    Peter Abelard, 186
    William Langland's *Piers
        Plowman*, 230
Reformation, 279–82
    England, 275, 279, 334–44,
        470
Reformed Christianity, 280–1
Reign of Terror, 483, 567
Religio Medici, 430, 431–5
"Religion," 450–2
Religion and Dogma, 637
"Religious Musings," 565–7
religious toleration, 482
Rempham, 391–2
Renaissance, 275–9
*Renaissance Discovery of
    Classical Antiquity*, 276
repentance
    Clement of Rome's "First
        Letter to Corinth," 14–16
    Cyril of Jerusalem's
        Catechetical Lectures, 83
Republic, 88

Rerum in Ecclesia Gestarum,
    335
resurrection
    Athanasius of Alexandra's *de
        incarnatione*, 66, 67
    "Blickling Homilist," 156,
        158
    John Donne's "Death be not
        Proud," 416–17
    Tertullian, 5
retreats, 323
Reuchlin, Johann, 284
revelation, 484–5, 502
Revelation, Book of
    Anselm of Canterbury's
        "Prayer to Christ," 184
    Benjamin Jowett's
        "Interpretation of
        Scripture," 603
    "Blickling Homilist," 159
    Charles Wesley's "Love
        Divine," 529
    Coleridge's "Religious
        Musings," 567
    George Herbert's sermon,
        428
    image of lamb, 537–8
    John Donne's sermon, 405,
        406, 415
    King James Version of the
        Bible, 380, 529, 537–8
    Lancelot Andrewes' sermons,
        395
    marriage supper of the lamb,
        425
    Martin Luther's "Letter on
        Translating the New
        Testament," 311
    millenarianism, 168, 565
    Wulfstan's *Lupi Sermo ad
        Anglos*, 168
Revelations of Divine Love,
    246–51
Reynolds, Dr. Barbara, 696
Reynolds, Dr. John, 358
Rhadegunde, Queen, 115
rhyme scheme, 127, 138
Rhyming Dictionary, 648
Rich, Penelope, 398
Richard II, 397

Richard II, King of England, 366
Richard III, 397
Richmond, Kenneth, 718
riddles, 151–4
Ridley, Nicholas, 340, 343
Righteousness, 230, 233–4, 238
"The Rime of the Ancient Mariner," 563
The Roads to Zion, 210–11
Robert Falconer, 641
Roberval, Gilles Personne de, 459
Robespierre, 483
Robinson Crusoe, 486, 487, 488–95
Roman culture, 3–4, 6–7, 276
Roman de la Rose, 240
Romans, Epistle to the, 300
    baptism, 319
    Benjamin Jowett's "Interpretation of Scripture," 599, 602
    effects of Adam and Christ on humanity, 424
    Eusebius of Caesarea's *Ecclesiastical History*, 54
    George Herbert's sermon, 428
    Jonathan Edwards' *Treatise on Religious Affections*, 509
    Martin Luther's "Lesser Catechism," 319
    Martin Luther's "Letter on Translating the New Testament," 303, 305, 306, 308–9
    Thomas Aquinas' *Summa Theologiae*, 209
    Tyndale's translation, 357
Romanticism, 485–6
Rome, 9, 10, 175, 176, 178
"Rorate coeli desuper," 270–2
Rossetti, Christina, 656
Rossetti, Dante Gabriel, 641, 656
Rousseau, Jean-Jacques, 483
The Rules and Exercises of Holy Dying, 442–7, 516

The Rules and Exercises of Holy Living, 442–3, 516
Ruskin, John, 656
Russia, 177–8
Ruth, 391
Ruthwell Cross, 138

Sabinianus, 189
sacrament of the altar, 320–1
sacraments, doctrine of, 10
Sadducees, 191
St Gallen, 281
"St Patrick's Breastplate," 122, 134–6
St Paul and Protestantism, 636
St Paul's Magazine, 591
saints, intercession of, 310–11
Salmon, 391
salvation
    Athanasius of Alexandra's *de incarnatione*, 64
    Cyril of Jerusalem's *Catechetical Lectures*, 84–5, 86
    Pelagian controversy, 10–11
Samuel, 86, 360, 572, 573, 574, 576, 577
Samuel, Books of
    Benjamin Jowett's "Interpretation of Scripture," 606
    John Donne's sermon, 404, 405
    John Keble's "National Apostasy," 571, 574, 576, 578
    Lancelot Andrewes' sermons, 391
Sanballat, 367, 368
Sapor, King of Persia, 75
Sarah, 510, 556
Sarepta, widow of, 391
Satan
    binding of, 419
    "Junius Codex," 142, 147–50
    William Blake's "And Did those Feet?," 548
    William Langland's *Piers Plowman*, 235–7

Satires, 401
Saul, 15, 205, 576, 577–8
Sayers, Dorothy L., xi, 214, 695–706
Sayers, Rev. Henry, 695
Scandinavia, 279
Scenes of Clerical Life, 609, 610–19
Schickard, Wilhelm, 459
Schlegel, August Wilhelm, 485, 486
Schlegel, Friedrich, 485
scholasticism, 208, 276, 277, 287
Schools and Universities on the Continent, 636
Schwarzerd, Philip, 301
Scotists, 291, 292, 293
Scotland, 121, 123
Scott, Robert, 598
The Screwtape Letters, 708, 709–13
Sebastian, 163
"Second Letter of Clement," 13
Second Vatican Council, 739–40
secular culture, patristic period, 3–9
segregation, 733–4
Selkirk, Alexander, 488
Seneca, 191, 367
Septimus Severus, Emperor, 30, 50
"Sepulchre," 423
Serbia, 177
Sergius of Radonezh, Saint, 177
Serious Call, 516
Sermones super Cantica Canticorum, 195
sermons, xiii, xiv, 8
    Aelfric, 161–6
    Bernard of Clairvaux, 195
    "Blickling Homilist," 155–60
    "The Christian Pilgrim," 510–15
    George Herbert, 427–9
    John Donne, 401–16
    John Henry Newman, 582
    John Keble, 571–9
    John Wesley, 517–26

Jonathan Edwards, 510–15
Lancelot Andrewes, 384–95
Lupi Sermo ad Anglos,
  168–72
"Ninety-Six Sermons,"
  384–95
"The Passion of St Edmund,"
  161–6
*A Priest to the Temple: or the
  Country Parson*, 427–9
Wulfstan, 168–72
Servetus, Michael, 327
sexuality, 741–6
Seymour, Jane, 339, 340
Shakespeare, Hamnet, 396
Shakespeare, John, 396
Shakespeare, Judith, 396
Shakespeare, Susanna, 396
Shakespeare, William, xii,
  396–9, 702
Shaw, George Bernard, 680,
  683
Sheba, Queen of, 391
Shelley, Percy Bysshe, xii
The Shepheardes Calendar, 345,
  346
Shiloh, 388, 389
Sic et Non, 186–7
Sidney, Sir Philip, 345
Sige, 34, 35, 36
Sigebert of Austrasia, 115
Silex Scintillans, 448–52
Simeon, 390
Simon Magus of Samaria, 37,
  82, 393
sin
  Ancrene Wisse, 202
  Andrew Marvell's "The
    Coronet," 457–8
  "Book of Common Prayer"
    (BCP), 472
  John Donne's "Batter my
    heart," 417–18
  Samuel Taylor Coleridge's
    "Religious Musings," 566
Sion, 97, 101, 103, 104
Sirach, 208
Six Articles, 338, 339
Sixtus V, Pope, 371, 372, 374
Sixtus Senensis, 365

The Small House at Allington,
  592
Smectymnuus Affair, 436
Smith, Dr. Miles, 358, 359
Smith, Robert E., 313
Smyrna church, 21–9
Socrates, 5, 192, 408
sola scriptura principle, 281
"The Solemnization of
  Matrimony," 473–6
Solomon
  Benjamin Jowett's
    "Interpretation of
    Scripture," 606
  George Herbert, 422
  Gregory of Nyssa's "Funeral
    Oration on Meletius," 94
  John Donne's sermon, 404,
    407
  King James Version of the
    Bible, 360, 369
  Lancelot Andrewes' sermons,
    392, 393
  Sir Thomas Browne's *Religio
    Medici*, 431
"Some Contemporary Scottish
  Writing," 728–9
Song at the Year's Turning, 728
Song of Roland, 696, 704
"A Song for Simeon," 689
Song of Songs, 195, 327, 450
Song of Venus, 528
"Sonnet 146," 398
Sophia, 34, 35–6
Sophistes, 393
Sophocles, 639
Southern Christian Leadership
  Conference, 733
Southey, Robert, 551
Sozomen, 366
Spain, 176, 279
The Spectator, 496, 497
Speculum Historiae, 297
Spencer, Herbert, 610
Spenser, Edmund, 345–55,
  437
Spiritual Exercises, 323–5
spirituality, xiii
Spiritus, 37
Spurstow, William, 436

*Standard Pronouncing
  Dictionary*, 648
Stapulensis, 371
The Stationers Register, 345
Statius Quadratus, 28
Staupitz, Johann von, 300
Stauros, 36
Stearns, Charlotte Champe, 688
Stephen, Saint, 55, 203, 361,
  392, 393
Stitch, Wilhelmina, 704
Stoddard, Solomon, 507
Stoics, 5, 49, 291
Stokesley, Dr., 337, 339
The Stones of the Field, 728
Story, Dr., 340
The Strayed Reveller, 636
*Stride Toward Freedom: The
  Montgomery Story*, 733
Student Nonviolent
  Coordinating Committee,
  734
Summa contra Gentiles, 207
Summa Theologiae, 187, 207,
  208–9
superstition, 277
Surprised by Joy, 707–8, 714
Susanna, 404
Swedenborg, Emanuel, 589,
  590
Swegn Forkbeard, 168
Swinburne, Algernon Charles,
  642, 651
Switzerland, 279, 280
  see also Calvin, John
Symmachus, 364, 370
Symon Leprous, 227
Symposium, 660
Syncrasis, 34
Synesis, 34
Syria, 177

Tacitus, 123
Tares, 728
Tatian, 5
Tatwine, 151
Taylor, Jeremy, 442–7, 516
*The Temple: Sacred Poems and
  Personal Ejaculations*,
  421–6

"The Temple of Glas," 270
Ten Commandments, 314–15
Tennyson, Lord Alfred, 682
Tenure of Kings and Magistrates, 437
Terentia, 191
Tertullian, 10, 43–51
   classical literature, xi–xii, 5–6, 7
   King James Version of the Bible, 362, 367, 368, 370
   Montanism, 30, 43
terza rima, 213, 214
Tess of the D'Urbervilles, 649
Tetzel, Johann, 300
Thackeray, William Makepeace, 591
Theletos, 34, 35
theodicy, 438
Theodore of Gaza, 284
Theodoret, 366
Theodosius, 88
Theodotion, 364, 370
Theodred, Bishop, 164, 165
Theodulf, 283
theology, xv, xix, 4, 9
Theophorus, 17
Theophrastus, 190
Thessalonians, Epistle to, 599
Theudas, 31, 32
"The Third Man," 718
Thirlby, Bishop of Ely, 340
Thomas à Kempis, 263–8, 516
Thomas Aquinas, 178, 180, 187, 207–9, 276, 583, 601
Thomas, R. S., 728–32
Thomas, Saint, 53, 104, 462
Thomists, 291
Thornton (Thornden), Richard, 339
Thorpe, Thomas, 398
Three Physico-Theological Discourses, 540
"Threnody," 585
Till We Have Faces, 709, 713–17
Time, 709, 734
The Times, 718
Timotheus, 368
Timothy, 53, 54

Timothy, First Epistle to, 195, 507
Timothy, Second Epistle to, 55, 196, 362, 393, 509
Tindal, Matthew, 484
"Tintern Abbey," 551–6
Titus, 54
Titus, Emperor, 55, 58
Titus, Epistle to, xi, 319, 392, 393, 578
"To the Martyrs," 44
Tobiahs, 368
Toland, John, 484
toleration, 482
Tolkien, J. R. R., xix, 641
Torrijos, Omar, 719
Townsend, George, 336
The Tracts for the Times, 581
Trajan, 17, 47
travel memoirs, 96–104
Treatise on the Arithmetical Triangle, 460
Treatise Concerning Religious Affections, 507
Treatise on the Equilibrium of Liquids, 460
Treatise on Religious Affections, 508–10
"Treatise of the Two Married Women and the Widow," 269
Trent, Council of, 282, 371
trinity of humanity, 5
Tristan, 696
Trithemius, 366
Trollope, Anthony, 591–7
Trollope, Frances, 591
Trollope, Thomas Anthony, 591
Troyes, Synod of, 195
Truth, 230, 233, 235, 238
truth, doctrine of, 266–8
Tschirnhaus, Ehrenfried Walter von, 460
Tudor, Margaret, 269
Tunstall, Bishop Cuthbert, 356
Tychonius, 370
Tyndale, William, 356–7
Tyrannus, 393
Tyutchev, Fyodor Ivanovich, 624

Ubba, 161, 162
Ulpilas, 366
Ulysees, 689
"*Ulysees*, Order and Myth," 692
Ungnadius, Lord, 366
union, way of, 210, 211
Unitarianism, 563, 564–5, 585
universities, 178
"Upon Appleton House, to my Lord Fairfax," 453
Uriah, 606

Valdo, Bishop of Frising, 366
Valdus, 366
Valens, 88
Valentinianism, 31, 32, 34–7
Valentinus, 5, 31–2, 33
Valla, Lorenzo, 283, 284, 287, 289, 371
Vallon, Annette, 550
Vallon, Caroline, 550
values, xiii
Vandals, 175
vanity, 265–6
Vasseus, 366
Vaughan, Henry, 448–52
Vaughan, Richard, Earl of Carberry, 442, 443
Vazeille, Mary, 516
Vega, 371
Venn, Henry, 610
"Vercelli Book," 137
Vespasian, 55, 60, 62
A Vewe of the present state of Irelande, 345
"Via Negativa," 730–2
Viae Sion lugent, 210–11
A View of the Evidences of Christianity, 539, 540–5
Vikings, 161–2, 167–8
Vincent of Lérins, 569
Viret, Pierre, 327
Virgil, 213, 215
Virgin and Child, 730
Virtues, 230
Vita Antonii, 64, 69–74
Vita Christi, 218–20
La Vita Nuova, 212
Vives, 371
Vologeses, 75

Voltaire, 483
Vulcan, 294
Vulgate, 282–4, 289

Wagner, Richard, 690
Wakefield, 252
Wales, 121
Wales, 728–9
Walker, John, 648
"Walking with God," 533–4
Wallace, George, 734
Wallis, John, 460
Walsingham, Sir Francis, 384
Walter de Clare, 551
The Warden, 592
Warham, Dr., 337
The Waste Land, 688, 689–92
watchmaker image, 539–40
Watts, Isaac, 499–500
way of life, xiii
Ways of Escape, 719–20
Wearmouth, 128
Weiss, Roberto, 276
Welch, Dr. J. W., 696
Wellesley, Dorothy, 690
Wesley, Charles, 481, 508, 516, 527–31
Wesley, John, 443, 481, 485, 502, 508, 516–26, 527
Wesley, Samuel, 516, 527
Wesley, Susanna, 516, 527
Westminster Review, 609
Weston, Dr., 340
Weston, Jessie, 690
"When all thy mercies, O my God," 496
"When I survey the wondrous cross," 499–500

Whitby, Synod of, 123
Whitefield, George, 502, 527
Whithorn, 121
Whose Body?, 695
Widminstadius, 366
Wilberforce, Bishop Samuel, 599
Wilde, Oscar, 659–78
Wilde, Sir William, 659
will, 110–11, 324
William II, King of England, 241
William of Champeaux, 186
William the Conqueror, 181
William of Malmesbury, 124
William of Ockham, 290, 299
William Rufus, 181–2
Williamites, 295
Williams, A. D., 733
Williams, Charles, xix
Williams, George Hunston, 281
Wilson, John, 290
"Wilt thou love God?," 418–19
Wiltshire, Earl of, 337
Windesheim, 263–4
wisdom, 329–30
The Wisdom of God Manifested in the Works of the Creation, 540
Wisdom of Solomon, 196
"Within and Without," 641
Wittenberg, 279, 280, 288, 299–300, 302
Wolffian school, 484
Wolsey, Cardinal, 337
The Woodlanders, 649
Wordsworth, Anne, 550

Wordsworth, Dorothy, 550, 556
Wordsworth, John, 550
Wordsworth, William, xii, xv, 486, 546, 550–62, 563, 564
worship patterns, 96–104
"Wreck of the Deutschland," 657
Wren, Sir Christopher, 402
Wulfstan, 129, 167–72
Wulfstan, Archbishop of York, 167
Wulfstan, Bishop of Worcester, 167
Wycliffe, John, 283

Xantippe, 192

Yeats, W. B., 690
York Mystery Plays, 252–62
Yorkshire Post Fiction Prize, 739
Young, John, Bishop of Rochester, 345
Young, Thomas, 436

Zachary, 387
The Zeal of Thy House, 696
Zechariah, Book of, 387, 534–5
Zenas, 393
Zeno, 5
Zerubbabel, 369
Zoe, 34, 37
Zurich, 279, 280, 281, 288
Zwingli, Huldrych, 279, 280, 281, 288, 302, 328, 341, 470